"Exhaustively complemented (fully rigged, one might say) by indexes, notes, and maps, *The Command of the Ocean* is destined to remain the reference on the subject for the coming generations."
—Erik Svane, *Naval History*

"The second installment of Rodger's projected three-part naval history of Britain is one of very few books that actually warrant the adjective 'majisterial'. In this 900-plus-page volume . . . Rodger elucidates the Royal Navy's rise to global preponderance and its consolidation as the single most influential institution in the nation's life."
—Benjamin Schwartz, *Atlantic Monthly*

"Exhaustively complemented. . . . *The Command of the Ocean* is destined to remain the reference on the subject for the coming generations."
—U.S. Naval Institute

"I have been reviewing books for more than 20 years, but I have never reviewed one that has given me more pleasure than this . . . a masterpiece."
—Kevin Myers, *Mail on Sunday*

"Nothing written during the past century, perhaps ever, approaches N.A.M. Rodger's ambitious and masterly three-volume naval History of Britain . . . a truly satisfying book that one puts down with regret, yet also with a sense that one has encountered a great work of history. . . . This is, surely, an award-winning book."
—Paul Kennedy, *Sunday Times*

"A stunning book—stunning in its scope, its scholarship, its erudition and its wit."
—Simon Heffer, *Saul David Literary Review*

"The series is fast becoming a classic."
—*Daily Telegraph*

THE COMMAND
OF THE OCEAN

A Naval History of Britain
1649–1815

N.A.M. RODGER

W. W. Norton & Company
New York   London

The publishers and author gratefully acknowledge the
Society for Nautical Research and the Navy Records Society
for their help and assistance with the publication of this volume.

For information about permission to reproduce selections from this book,
write to Permissions, W. W. Norton & Company, Inc.,
500 Fifth Avenue, New York, NY 10110

Manufacturing by R. R. Donnelley, Harrisonburg, VA

Library of Congress Cataloging-in-Publication Data

Rodger, N. A. M., 1949–
The command of the ocean : a naval history of Britain, 1649–1815 / N. A. M. Rodger.
    p. cm.
Includes bibliographical references and index.
ISBN 0-393-06050-0
1. Great Britain—History, Naval—18th century. 2. Great Britain—History, Naval—Stuarts,
    1603–1714. 3. Great Britain—History, Naval—19th century. I. Title.

DA87.R65 2005
359'.00941'0903—dc22

2004061665

ISBN-10: 0-393-32847-3 pbk.
ISBN-13: 978-0-393-32847-9 pbk.

W. W. Norton & Company, Inc., 500 Fifth Avenue, New York, N.Y. 10110
www.wwnorton.com

W. W. Norton & Company Ltd., Castle House, 75/76 Wells Street, London W1T 3QT

1 2 3 4 5 6 7 8 9 0

For M. F., who made it possible

'To pretend to Universal Monarchy without Fleets was long since looked upon, as a politick chimaera ... whoever commands the ocean, commands the trade of the world, and whoever commands the trade of the world, commands the riches of the world, and whoever is master of that, commands the world itself.'

John Evelyn, *Navigation and Commerce,*
their Origin and Progress (London, 1674), pp. 15–17 and 32–3.

CONTENTS

LIST OF ILLUSTRATIONS

All illustrations are reproduced by courtesy of the National Maritime Museum. The relevant NMM reference number appears in square brackets.

FOREWORD

'The ultimate view of an indigent historian is profit,' declared a candid writer who preferred to remain anonymous. 'It is not expected that he will consume his years in laborious researches after truth. His subsistence depends on the immediate sale of his labours. Hence he compiles in haste the errors and contradictions of former historians, and perpetuates error from want of time to investigate truth.'[1] Anyone who sets out to write a history largely based on the work of others must be conscious that there is something in this warning. If I have in any measure succeeded in investigating truth, it is thanks to the generous financial support which I have received during the years of writing this book from the Oxford Maritime Trust, the National Maritime Museum, the Society for Nautical Research and the Navy Records Society. I am profoundly grateful to them all.

I have received a great deal of practical help from my former colleagues in the National Maritime Museum and the Public Record Office, and from my present colleagues in the University of Exeter. In addition I thank Professor Daniel Baugh, Dr Michael Duffy, Professor Roger Knight, Miss Sarah Lenton, Mr Richard Ollard and my parents, who read part or all of the manuscript and corrected some of its errors. I am grateful to Miss Moira Bracknall, Dr Randolph Cock and Dr Oliver Walton, who at various times acted as my research assistant. Dr Jonathan Dull generously allowed me to read his book *The French Navy and the Loss of Canada* in manuscript, and Dr Ann Coats, Dr Philip MacDougall and Dr Roger Morriss allowed me to use unpublished notes and papers of theirs. For references, advice, copies of articles and other offices of scholarly friendship I am indebted to Mr and Mrs Derek Ayshford, Dr Alan Booth, Dr Philip Carter, Captain Peter Hore, Dr C. S. Knighton, Dr Robert Smith, Dr David Starkey, M. Etienne Taillemite, Dr Roger Tomlin and Dr C. O. van der Meij. I am especially grateful to the authors and custodians of the many unpublished university theses and dissertations referred to in the notes and bibliography: much of the originality of this book derives from their work. Most of all I owe to my wife and children, who supported a distracted and querulous author through long years of research and writing.

N.A.M.R.

Feast of St Felix of Dunwich, 2004

Note

1. *Proposals for a Temple of Fame containing the History and Portraits of Celebrated Men from the Age of Richard the Third to the Conclusion of the Present Century* (London, 1789), p. vi.

A NOTE ON CONVENTIONS

DATES

During the period covered by this book, the majority of European countries followed the Gregorian Calendar, first promulgated by Pope Gregory XIII in 1582, which restored and maintained a close connection with astronomical reality. England, Wales and Ireland, however, retained the older Julian Calendar, which was ten days behind until 1700, and thereafter eleven. They also continued to date the New Year officially from the Lady Day (25 March) after 1 January. English Old Style dates were therefore ten or eleven days behind Continental New Style, while the year between 1 January and 24 March was one year behind. Scotland retained the Julian Calendar, but from 1600 until the Union of 1707 dated the new year from 1 January. The whole of the British Isles adopted the Gregorian Calendar in 1752, by omitting the dates from 3 to 13 September (adjusting all civil and financial obligations accordingly),[1] and from 1753 dating the New Year from 1 January.

Calendars are a notorious trap for the unwary. In documents it is often uncertain which calendar a writer is using, while modern authors or editors sometimes spread confusion by being unaware of the problem, or by silently adjusting dates without warning their readers. In this book, following the usual convention among modern British historians, all dates up to 1752 are Old Style unless otherwise indicated, but the year is taken to begin on 1 January throughout.

BATTLE NAMES

Conventions on the naming of battles have varied a good deal. In English various actions are or have been named from the date ('the First of June'),[2] the commander-in-chief ('Calder's action') or the nearest point of land. It is most common now to take a point of land, but there is no agreement between writers of different nationality on which to take, so that the unwary reader of naval history may not realize, for example, that the English battle of Scheveningen and the Dutch battle of Ter Heide are the same. The following table is offered as a modest contribution to the reduction of confusion. In each case the phrase 'battle of' or its equivalent is to be understood, and C. stands for Cape, Cabo, Cap, etc. according to the language.

Date	British Admiral	English Name	French Name	Spanish Name	Dutch/Danish Name
19/29 May 1652	Blake	Dover			Dover
16/26 Aug 1652	Ayscue	Plymouth			Plymouth
28 Aug/6 Sep 1652	Baddiley	Monte Christi			Elba
28–29 Sep/ 8–9 Oct 1652	Blake	Kentish Knock			Duins
30 Nov/ 10 Dec 1652	Blake	Dungeness			Dungeness, Singels
18/28 Feb– 20 Feb/2 Mar 1653	Blake	Portland			Driedaagse
4/14 Mar 1653	Baddiley	Leghorn			Livorno
2/12–3/13 Jun 1653	Monck and Deane	Gabbard			Nieuwpoort
31 Jul/10 Aug 1653	Monck	Scheveningen, Texel			Ter Heide
3/13 Jun 1665	York	Lowestoft			Lowestoft
2/12 Aug 1665	Teddiman	Bergen			Bergen
1/11–4/14 Jun 1666	Albemarle	Four Days			Vierdaagse
25–26 Jul/ 4–5 Aug 1666	Albemarle	St James's Day			Tweedaagse
9/19–14/24 Jun 1667		Medway Raid			Tocht naar Chatham
25 Jun/5 Jul 1667	Harman	Fort St Pierre	Fort Saint Pierre		
28 May/7 Jun 1672	York	Solebay	Solebay		Solebay
28 May/7 Jun 1673	Rupert	1st Schooneveld	Schooneveldt		1e Schooneveld

Date	British Admiral	English Name	French Name	Spanish Name	Dutch/Danish Name
4/14 Jun 1673	Rupert	2nd Schooneveld	Walcheren		2e Schooneveld
11/21 Aug 1673	Rupert	Texel	Texel		Kijkduin
1/11 May 1689	Herbert	Bantry Bay	Bantry		
30 Jun/10 Jul 1690	Torrington	Beachy Head	Béveziers		Bevesier
19/29 May 1692	Russell	Barfleur	Barfleur		Barfleur
22–24 May/ 1–3 Jun 1692	Russell	La Hogue	La Hougue		La Hogue
17/27 Jun 1693	Rooke	Smyrna Convoy	Lagos		Lagos
18/29 Aug–25 Aug/4 Sep 1702	Benbow	Last Fight	Santa Marta		
12/23 Oct 1702	Rooke	Vigo	Vigo	Vigo	Vigo
13/24 Aug 1704	Rooke	Malaga	Velez Malaga		Malaga
31 Jul/11 Aug 1718	Byng	C. Passaro		C. Passaro	
11/22 Feb 1744	Mathews	Toulon	Toulon, C. Sicié	C. Sicié, Tolón	
25 Jun/6 Jul 1746	Peyton	Negapatam	Négapatam		
3/14 May 1747	Anson	1st Finisterre	C. Ortégal		
14/25 Oct 1747	Hawke	2nd Finisterre	C. Finisterre		
20 May 1756	Byng	Minorca	Port Mahón		
28 Feb 1758	Osborn	Moonlight	C. Palos		
29 Apr 1758	Pocock	Cuddalore	Gondelour		
3 Aug 1758	Pocock	Negapatam	Karikal		
18–19 Aug 1759	Boscawen	Lagos	Lagos, C. Sta. Maria		
10 Sep 1759	Pocock	Pondicherry	Porto Novo		
20 Nov 1759	Hawke	Quiberon Bay	Cardinaux		
27 Jul 1778	Keppel	Ushant	Ouessant		
10 Aug 1778	Vernon	Pondicherry	Pondicherry		
15 Dec 1778	Barrington	St Lucia	Saint Lucie		
6 Jul 1779	Byron	Grenada	Grenade		

Date	British Admiral	English Name	French Name	Spanish Name	Dutch/Danish Name
16 Jan 1780	Rodney	Moonlight		C. Sta. Maria	
17 Apr 1780	Rodney	Martinique	Martinique		
16 Mar 1781	Arbuthnot	C. Henry	Chesapeake		
16 Apr 1781	Johnstone	Porto Praya	La Praya		
29 Apr 1781	Hood	Martinique	Fort Royal		
5 Aug 1781	Parker	Dogger Bank			Doggersbank
5 Sep 1781	Graves	Chesapeake	Chesapeake		
25–26 Jan 1782	Hood	St Kitts	Saint Christophe		
17 Feb 1782	Hughes	Sadras	Sadras		
12 Apr 1782	Rodney	Saintes	Saintes		
12 Apr 1782	Hughes	Provedien	Provedien		
6 Jul 1782	Hughes	Negapatam	Negapatam		
3 Sep 1782	Hughes	Trincomalee	Trincomali		
20 Oct 1782	Howe	C. Spartel	C. Spartel	Espartel	
20 Jun 1783	Hughes	Cuddalore	Gondelour		
1 Jun 1794	Howe	First of June	Prairial		
13–14 Mar 1795	Hotham	C. Noli	C. Noli		
23 Jun 1795	Bridport	Ile de Groix	Groix		
13 Jul 1795	Hotham	Hyères	Fréjus		
14 Feb 1797	Jervis	C. St Vincent		C. San Vicente	
11 Oct 1797	Duncan	Camperdown			Kamperduin
1 Aug 1798	Nelson	Nile	Aboukir		
2 Apr 1801	Nelson	Copenhagen			Reden
6 Jul 1801	Saumarez	Algeçiras	Algésiras	Algeçiras	
12 Jul 1801	Saumarez	Straits	Cadiz	Estrecho	
14 Feb 1804	Dance	Pulo Aor			
22 Jul 1805	Calder		Quinze-Vingt		
21 Oct 1805	Nelson	Trafalgar	Trafalgar	Trafalgar	
4 Nov 1805	Strachan		C. Ortegal		
6 Feb 1806	Duckworth	San Domingo	Santo Domingo		
11 Apr 1809	Gambier	Basque Roads	Ile d'Aix		

EXCHANGE RATES

In the later seventeenth century the rate of the French *livre* against sterling varied from 1s 5¾d to 1s 7¾d (i.e. 12.6–13.75 *livres* to the pound). From 1697 its sterling value declined, and at the worst point of the Law crisis in 1720 it was only 5½d (43.7 to the pound), but by 1727 its value had been stablized at 11d, and it remained in the range 10d–11d (21.8–23.8 to the pound) until the runaway inflation of the 1790s.

The Spanish silver dollar, the *pieza de ocho reales* or 'piece of eight', first minted in 1497, was worth one *peso* or *piastre* of eight *reales*. Its silver content and intrinsic value (4s 2d sterling) remained almost unvaried in 400 years of issue. The *real* coin, however, was progressively debased, which led to the invention of a notional *peso de cambio* worth eight debased *reales*. This *peso de cambio* steadily declined in value against sterling, though the original *peso de plata antigua*, corresponding to the dollar, did not. It is therefore essential to know which of the two Spanish units of account is meant in order to calculate exchange rates.

The Dutch guilder remained steady throughout this period at approximately 1s 9½d, or just over 11 to the pound sterling.[3]

FOREIGN RANKS AND TITLES

I have left all foreign ranks and titles in their original languages (and explained them in the foreign glossary) unless there were more or less exact English equivalents. I have not translated titles of nobility, even though many of them have notional equivalents, considering, for example, that a French comte or a Dutch Graaf were so unlike an English earl in social and political standing that to translate their titles would be thoroughly misleading. The obvious case where foreign titles can in many cases be translated more or less exactly is naval commissioned officers' ranks, which can be set out in a table as they stood in the eighteenth century. Note that this expresses equivalent ranks, not literal meanings, so 'Lieutenant-Général des Armées Navales' and 'Schout-bij-Nacht' are translated Vice-Admiral and Rear-Admiral respectively, not 'Lieutenant-General of Naval Forces' and 'Night Watchman'. Each of these navies also had other ranks, not directly translatable.

English	French	French (from 1791)	Dutch	Spanish
Lieutenant	Lieutenant de Vaisseau	[same]	Luitenant ter Zee	Teniente de Navío
Commander	Capitaine de Frégate[4]	[same]	Kapitein-Luitenant	Capitán de Fragata
Post-Captain	Capitaine de Vaisseau	[same]	Kapitein	Capitán de Navío
Commodore	[none]	Chef de Division[5]	Kommandeur	Brigadier[6]
Rear-Admiral	Chef d'Escadre	Contre-Amiral	Schout-bij-Nacht	Jefe de Escuadra
Vice-Admiral	Lieutenant-Général des Armées Navales	Vice-Amiral	Vice-Admiraal	Teniente General
Admiral	Vice-Amiral	[none]	Luitenant-Admiraal	Almirante

MONEY VALUES

Readers often ask for historical money values to be translated into modern values. This is a difficult, indeed impossible, task, because of what economists call the 'index number problem', the fact that both the prices and the economic significance of different things change at different rates, and in different directions, so that all attempts to relate prices over long periods are intrinsically misleading. In the sixty years from 1770, for example, the price of cotton fell by one-third, and that of iron by more than two-thirds, but the price of beer increased by 156 per cent.[7] Which, if any, of these commodities is more meaningful as the basis of a price index, and by what criteria could they be 'weighted' against one another? In practice even to attempt to answer such questions is frequently impossible, for few items have been traded continuously over long periods of history, and fewer still have left evidence allowing price series to be compiled. Most of those used by economic historians are based on the price of grain or the wages of artisans, neither perfectly relevant to naval history. But a naval shipbuilding price index running just from the eighteenth century to the twentieth would have to face the fact that the principal material of shipbuilding has changed in that time from oak to wrought iron and then mild steel, and that none of the three has been continuously traded in large volumes throughout the period, so that it is impossible to compare their prices.[8]

The only component of naval power which has not essentially changed over time is people, and this indicates a crude solution to the problem. Certain officers' ranks already existed in 1649, with established rates of pay, and still exist today. On the heroic assumption that a post-captain's pay has retained broadly the same real value over 350 years, we may construct a simple naval price index:[9]

1649	=	100
1694		200
1700		133
1713[10]		100
1807		200
1815		261
1817		321
1844		366
1856		412
1862[11]		418
1864		450
1870		459
1918		475
1919		1,086
1955		1,336
2003		58,254

This suggests that for most of the seventeenth and eighteenth centuries the ratio of contemporary to current money values was about 600:1. It is obvious, however, that captains' pay, like seamen's, had declined in real value by the end of the eighteenth century, and then caught up after the Napoleonic War (which was in addition a period of falling retail prices). Taking the 1817 pay scale reduces the ratio to about 180:1. In any case the calculation is very crude, and greatly affected by underlying assumptions. Adding servants' pay, which was arguably a normal part of a captain's income, at least in wartime, and became an automatic addition in 1794, would reduce the ratio in 1817 to 145:1.

NOTES AND REFERENCES

Every direct quotation has its own reference, but with that exception, in most of this book I have thought it sufficient to support passages of general description or argument, drawing on secondary sources and dealing with matters known to history, with a single composite note for each paragraph. Wherever I felt that the argument was too complex or too novel, however, I have provided references more densely.

QUOTATIONS

English quotations in the text are given in modern English spelling, capitalization and, if necessary, punctuation, except for verse, and a few other cases where it seemed valuable to give a sense of the degree of literacy of the original writer. Unambiguous abbreviations and contractions have been silently expanded. Editorial omissions are indicated thus . . ., additions [thus] and the original wording [*thus*]; other words in italics are emphasized in the original. Quotations from other languages are translated in the text (by the author unless otherwise indicated), with the original wording given in the note. Where no original wording is given, the quotation has been taken already translated from the source cited.

RATES OF SHIPS

English warships had been classified into five or six 'Rates' since the late sixteenth century.[12] A scheme of six Rates defined by the size of their crews was adopted in 1653.[13] There followed a number of different schemes, mostly based on numbers of guns. As overhauled and standardized by Pepys in 1677 and 1685 the classification stood thus:

First Rates	90–100 guns[14]
Second Rates	64–90 guns
Third Rates	56–70 guns
Fourth Rates	38–62 guns
Fifth Rates	28–38 guns
Sixth Rates	4–18 guns.

First and Second Rates had three gun decks, Third and Fourth Rates two, and these four Rates were reckoned fit to fight in the line of battle. They were therefore 'ships of the line' or 'line of battleships', in the terminology which became standard.[15]

The scheme of Rates remained in force until 1817, with continual minor adjustments as warship design developed.[16]

Rate	1697	1714	1721	1760	1782	1801
First	94–100	100	100	100	100	100–120
Second	90–96	90	90	90	90 and 98	90 and 98
Third	64–80	70 and 80	70 and 80	64–80	64–80	64–84
Fourth	44–64	50 and 60	50 and 60	50–60	50–62	50–60
Fifth	26–44	30 and 40	30 and 40	30–44	30–44	30–44
Sixth	10–24	10 and 20	20 and 24	20–30	20–28	20–28

From 1756 Fourth Rates with fewer than sixty guns were not regarded as fit to lie in the line of battle. When carronades were adopted they were not treated as proper guns nor included in ships' official armament, with the result that by the time of the Great Wars British ships, especially frigates, tended to be more heavily armed than their official rating and number of guns would indicate.

TONNAGE

There are many methods of calculating ships' tonnage. Most of them were in the period covered by this book, and still are, measures of the internal capacity or volume of the ship, or the weight of the cargo. The only system of ship tonnage which directly expresses the weight of the ship is displacement, which was not widely used in Britain before the nineteenth century. It calculates the weight of water displaced by the underwater body of the ship, and hence (by Archimedes' rule) the weight of the ship herself. It is only useful for warships (with no weight of cargo to distort the calculation), and only then if their state of loading is exactly defined, but it is the most precise measure for technical purposes, and it was, and is, sometimes calculated for eighteenth-century warships. The formulae used for calculating the 'burthen' or tonnage of ships in this period varied in different countries and contexts, but for a fully stored warship, they would yield figures very roughly half the displacement. In this book ships' tonnage is given in tons burthen unless otherwise indicated, and the spelling 'tun' is used for the cask.

WEIGHTS AND MEASURES

Unless otherwise indicated, the weights, measures and currencies in this book are the current or recent British standards, the 'Imperial' system of the 1820 Weights and Measures Act. The following may be unfamiliar:

barrel (bb.): A cask, of varying capacity according to commodity. The barrel of beer contained 36 gallons to 1688 and thereafter 34; the barrel of wine contained 31½ gallons.

bushel (bus.): The Winchester bushel of 8 gallons was the standard English dry measure, though there were very many local variations.

butt: A cask, equivalent to the pipe, of half a tun or 2 hogsheads.

cable: A length of 120 fathoms or 240 yards.

fathom: A length of 6 feet.

gallon (gal.): The standard English capacity measure, equivalent to 4 quarts or 8 pints. The beer gallon contained 282 cubic inches, the grain gallon 268.8 cubic inches, the wine gallon, 231 cubic inches. In the Imperial system of 1820 the gallon was fixed at 277.42 cubic inches for all commodities.

guinea: An English gold coin, whose sterling value varied with the state of the silver coinage, but was fixed at 21s in 1717.

hogshead (hhd.): A cask, containing half a pipe, 1½ barrels (beer), or 2 barrels (wine).

hundredweight (cwt.): An English standard weight, normally of 4 quarters, 8 stone or 112 lbs, but varying extensively for different commodities and in different places.

knot: A measure of speed, one nautical mile an hour.

last: A capacity measure for various commodities, normally equivalent to 12 barrels. The last of pitch and tar was 12 barrels each of 32 gallons wine measure.

league: A distance, 3 miles. The mile itself varied from country to country; the nautical mile is properly one minute of arc of latitude or 6,080 feet, but in the seventeenth and eighteenth centuries most navigators preferred to take an average or conventional figure for a minute of longitude, often 5,000 feet.

livre [*tournois*]: The principal money of account in France. Like the pound sterling it was divided into twenty shillings (*sous*) each of twelve pence (*deniers*). In 1795 it was renamed the *franc*, and divided into 100 *centîmes*.

tun: A cask containing two butts or pipes or four hogsheads.[17]

Note that these definitions apply to the contexts occurring in this book; most of these have many other possible values for other commodities in other circumstances or periods.

Notes

1. This is why the British Treasury, no enthusiast for wanton innovation, still dates the tax year from Old Lady Day, 6 April.

2. Not generally 'Glorious' until much later.

3. John J. McCusker, *Money and Exchange in Europe and America, 1600–1775: A Handbook* (Chapel Hill, N.C., 1978).

4. Suppressed 1772–7, renamed Major de Vaisseau 1786–95.

5. Rank established 1786.

6. Rank established 1773.

7. Crafts, *British Economic Growth*, pp. 24–5.

8. Cf. Philip Pugh, *The Cost of Seapower: The Influence of Money on Naval Affairs from 1815 to the Present Day* (London, 1986).

9. This is based on the gross pay of the most junior post-captain; i.e. of a Fifth Rate until 1713, thereafter of a Sixth Rate, or from first promotion.

10. In this year captains of Sixth Rates were made post, but the pay for the Rate remained unchanged, so the lowest rate of captain's pay fell.

11. From this year 'command pay' was payable to virtually all captains in employment. I have included the minimum rate, 5s a day, up to 1919, by which time a significant proportion of captains were employed other than in command of ships or shore establishments.

12. Glete, *Navies and Nations*, I, 80–81. Rodger, *Safeguard*, pp. 500–503.

13. *FDW* III, 396.

14. These are war establishments; the number of guns was reduced for peacetime and overseas commissions.

15. *CPM* I, 234–42; IV, cv–cvii, 425–6 and 527. Fox, *Great Ships*, p. 20.

16. Derrick, *Memoirs*, pp. 111–112, 124–5, 128, 146–7, 166–7 and 209–10.

17. Ronald E. Zupko, *A Dictionary of Weights and Measures for the British Isles: The Middle Ages to the Twentieth Century* (American Philosophical Society, Philadelphia, 1985).

MAPS

The British Isles and
Northern Europe

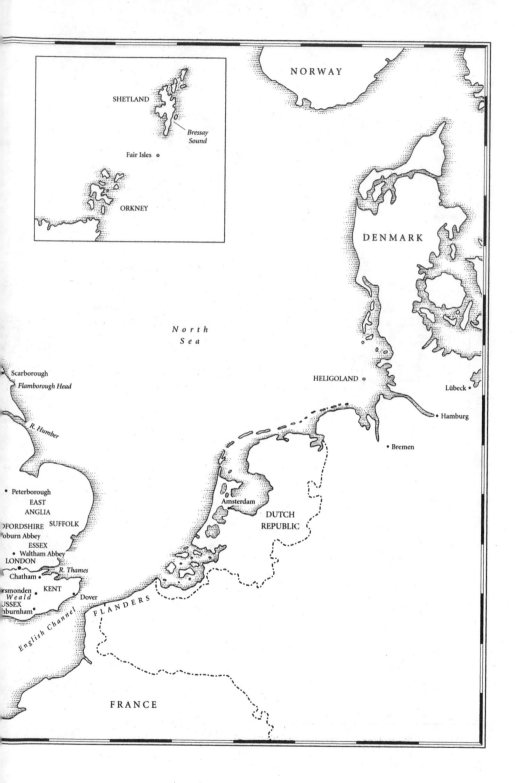

NORWAY

SHETLAND

Bressay
Sound

Fair Isles

ORKNEY

DENMARK

North
Sea

Scarborough
Flamborough Head

HELIGOLAND

Lübeck

Hamburg

R. Humber

Bremen

Peterborough
EAST
ANGLIA
DFORDSHIRE SUFFOLK
oburn Abbey
ESSEX
Waltham Abbey
LONDON
Chatham
R. Thames

Amsterdam

DUTCH
REPUBLIC

rsmonden KENT
Weald
USSEX Dover
burnham

FLANDERS

English Channel

FRANCE

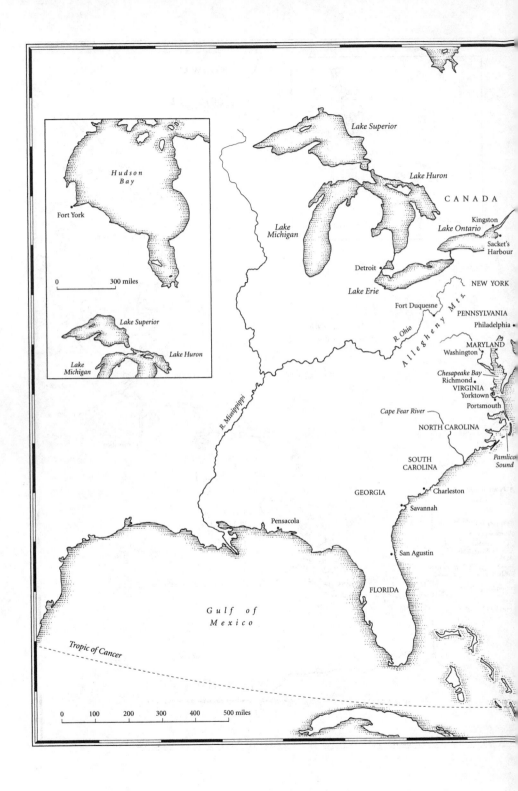

Lake Superior

Lake Huron

C A N A D A

Kingston
Lake Ontario
Sacket's
Harbour

Lake
Michigan

NEW YORK

Detroit

Fort Duquesne

Lake Erie

PENNSYLVANIA
Philadelphia

R. Ohio

MARYLAND
Washington

Chesapeake Bay
Richmond
VIRGINIA
Yorktown
Portsmouth

Cape Fear River

NORTH CAROLINA

Pamlico
Sound

SOUTH
CAROLINA

GEORGIA   Charleston

Savannah

Pensacola

San Agustin

FLORIDA

Gulf of
Mexico

Tropic of Cancer

0   100   200   300   400   500 miles

Inset map (top left):

Hudson
Bay

Fort York

0   300 miles

Lake Superior

Lake Huron

Lake
Michigan

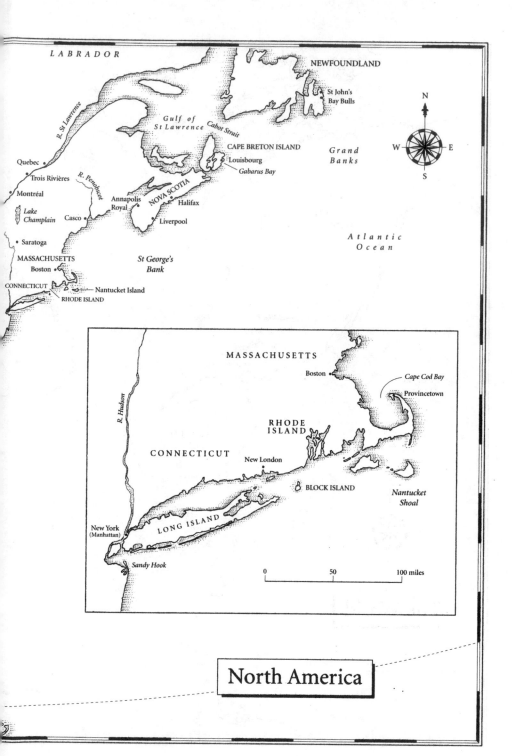

LABRADOR

NEWFOUNDLAND

St John's
Bay Bulls

R. St Lawrence

Gulf of
St Lawrence

Cabot Strait

N

W — E

S

Quebec

Trois Rivières

R. Penobscot

CAPE BRETON ISLAND

Louisbourg

Gabarus Bay

*Grand
Banks*

Montréal

Lake
Champlain

Casco

Annapolis
Royal

NOVA SCOTIA

Halifax

Saratoga

Liverpool

*Atlantic
Ocean*

MASSACHUSETTS

Boston

St George's
Bank

CONNECTICUT

Nantucket Island

RHODE ISLAND

MASSACHUSETTS

Boston

Cape Cod Bay

Provincetown

R. Hudson

RHODE
ISLAND

CONNECTICUT

New London

*Nantucket
Shoal*

BLOCK ISLAND

New York
(Manhattan)

LONG ISLAND

Sandy Hook

0   50   100 miles

North America

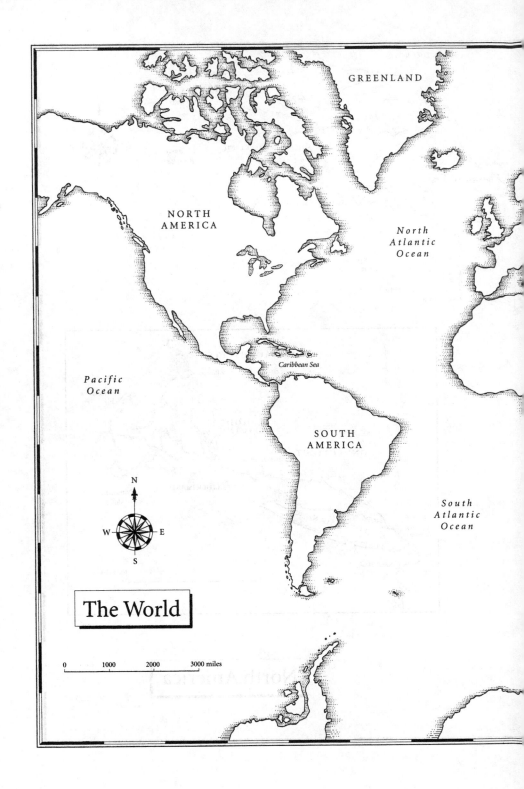

GREENLAND

NORTH
AMERICA

*North
Atlantic
Ocean*

Caribbean Sea

*Pacific
Ocean*

SOUTH
AMERICA

*South
Atlantic
Ocean*

N

W — E

S

The World

0   1000   2000   3000 miles

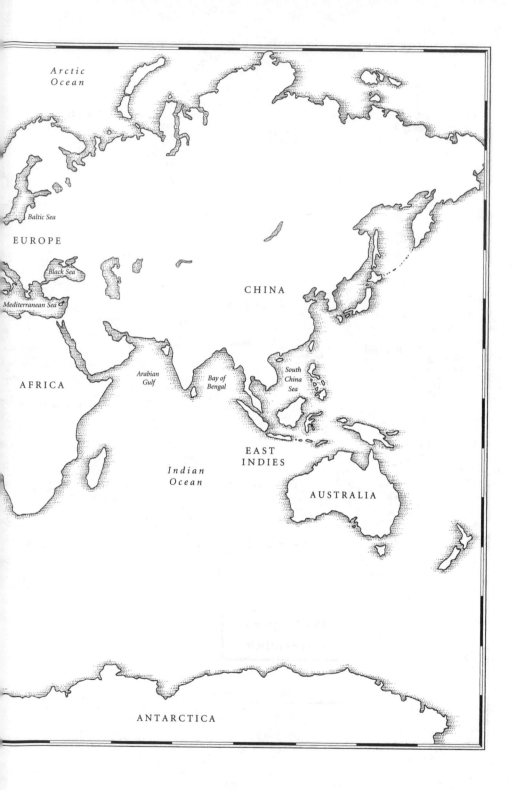

Arctic
Ocean

Baltic Sea

EUROPE

Black Sea

CHINA

Mediterranean Sea

AFRICA

Arabian
Gulf

Bay of
Bengal

South
China
Sea

EAST
INDIES

Indian
Ocean

AUSTRALIA

ANTARCTICA

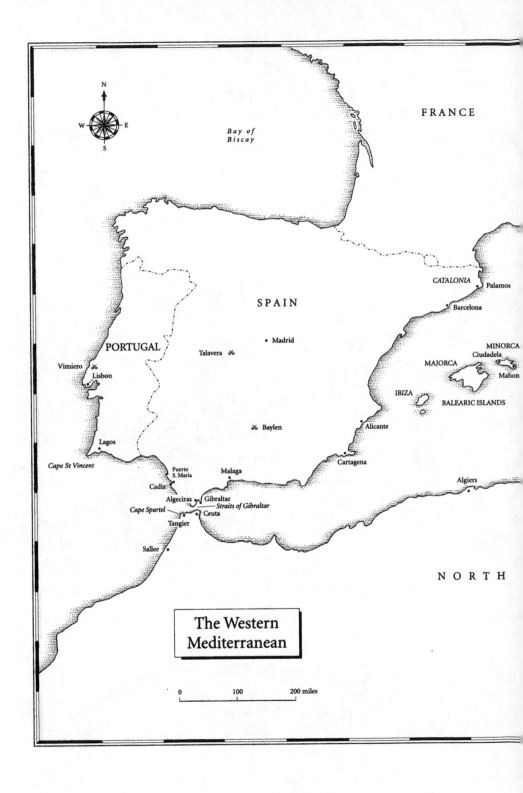

FRANCE

*Bay of
Biscay*

CATALONIA • Palamos

• Barcelona

SPAIN

PORTUGAL   Talavera ⚔   • Madrid

MINORCA
Ciudadela
MAJORCA   Mahon

Vimiero ⚔
Lisbon   IBIZA   BALEARIC ISLANDS

⚔ Baylen   • Alicante

Lagos

Cape St Vincent   • Cartagena

Puerto   Malaga
S. Maria   Algiers

Cadiz

Algeciras ⚓ Gibraltar
Cape Spartel ⚓ ⟶ Straits of Gibraltar
• Ceuta
Tangier

Sallee •

NORTH

The Western
Mediterranean

0   100   200 miles

Alps

Milan

Venice • _ISTRIA_

Trieste

SAVOY   _LOMBARDY_

DALMATIA

LIGURIA

Savona • • Genoa

San Remo   _Cape_
Ventimiglia   _Noli_

Leghorn

LISSA

Antibes

PROVENCE   • _LÉRINS_
Toulon   _ISLANDS_

ITALY

_Adriatic
Sea_

_HYÈRES
ISLANDS_

Bastia

ELBA

• Rome

CORSICA

Calvi

MADDALENA ISLANDS

Naples

KINGDOM OF THE TWO SICILIES

CORFU

_Tyrrhenian
Sea_

SARDINIA

CALABRIA

_IONIAN
ISLANDS_

Cagliari

Maida

Messina

_M e d i t e r r a n e a n_

Palermo

Messina Straits

_Ionian
Sea_

_Bugia
Bay_

Porto Farina

SICILY

Syracuse

Tabarka   Tunis

_S e a_

Cape Passaro

MALTA

AFRICA

Tripoli

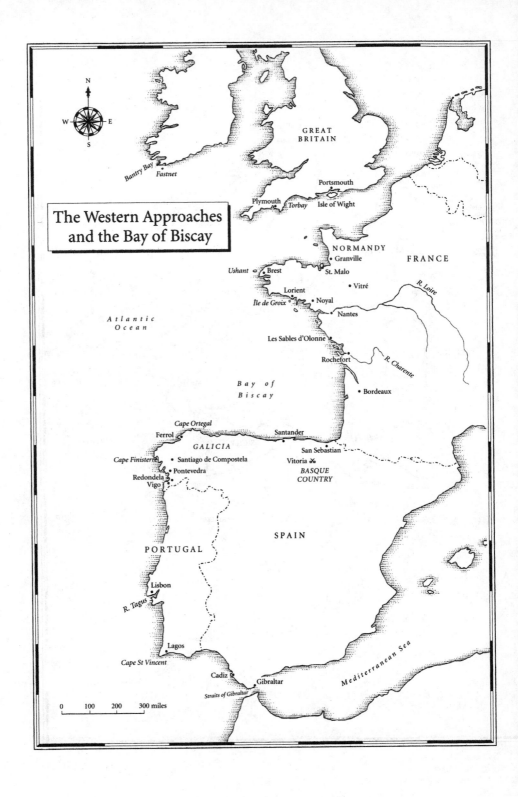

The Western Approaches
and the Bay of Biscay

N
W E
S

GREAT
BRITAIN

Bantry Bay
Fastnet

Portsmouth

Plymouth Torbay Isle of Wight

NORMANDY
Granville

Ushant Brest St. Malo

FRANCE

Vitré

R. Loire

Lorient

Île de Groix Noyal

Nantes

Atlantic
Ocean

Les Sables d'Olonne

Rochefort

R. Charente

Bay of
Biscay

Bordeaux

Cape Ortegal

Ferrol Santander

GALICIA

Cape Finisterre Santiago de Compostela San Sebastian

Vitoria

Redondela Pontevedra
Vigo

BASQUE
COUNTRY

SPAIN

PORTUGAL

Lisbon

R. Tagus

Lagos

Cape St Vincent

Mediterranean Sea

Cadiz Gibraltar

Straits of Gibraltar

0   100   200   300 miles

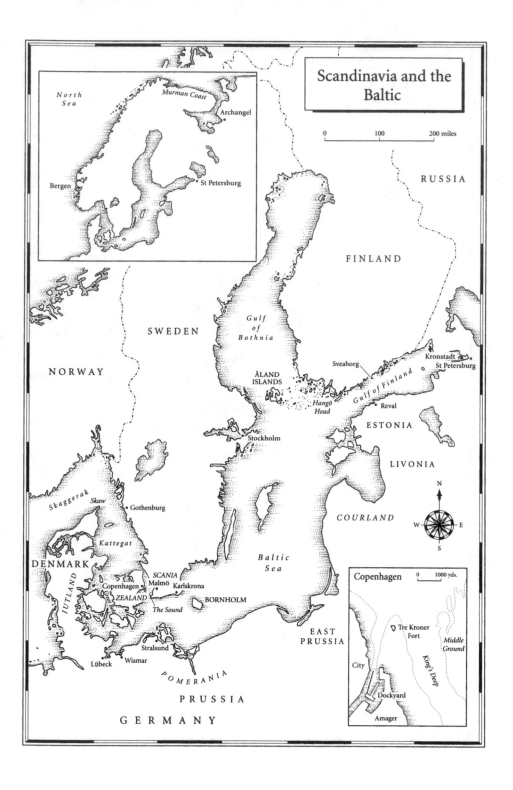

Scandinavia and the Baltic

Europe
Frontiers at 1721

IRELAND

GREAT
BRITAIN

*North
Sea*

*Atlantic
Ocean*

Klosterzeven
PRUSSIA

Berlin

DUTCH REP.
Minden

HANOVER
GERMANY
Leipzig

FLANDERS
Liége

Rhine

SAXONY

RHINE-
LAND
PALATINATE
Luxemburg

HOLY
ROMAN
EMPIRE

Paris

Seine

Danube

*Black
Forest*
Ulm

BAVARIA

Loire
Nantes

*Bay of
Biscay*

VENDEE
Le Creusot

Berne
SWITZ.

FRANCE

SAVOY

Piacenza
Parma

PORTUGAL

SPAIN

ITALY

Mediterranean Sea

0   100   200   300 miles

RUSSIA

Borodino ⚔   • Moscow

• Tilsit

⚔ Friedland

LITHUANIA

• Warsaw

SILESIA

POLAND

⚔ Austerlitz

⚔ Wagram

Vienna

HUNGARY

Ochakov

Black Sea

OTTOMAN   EMPIRE

GREECE

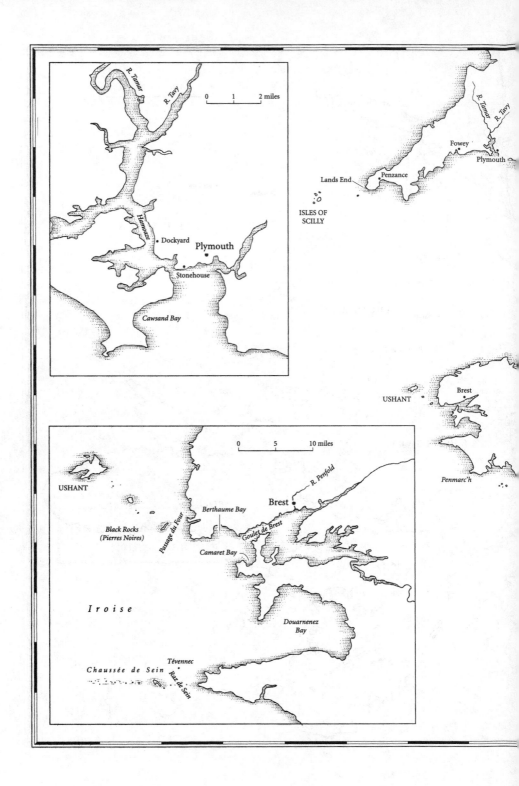

R. Tamar
R. Tavy
0 1 2 miles

Hamoaze
Dockyard
Plymouth
Stonehouse
Cawsand Bay

R. Tamar
R. Tavy
Fowey
Plymouth
Lands End
Penzance
ISLES OF
SCILLY

USHANT
Brest
Penmarc'h

0 5 10 miles

USHANT
R. Penfeld
Brest
Berthaume Bay
Passage du Four
Goulet de Brest
Black Rocks
(Pierres Noires)
Camaret Bay

Iroise

Douarnenez
Bay

Tévennec
Chaussée de Sein
Raz de Sein

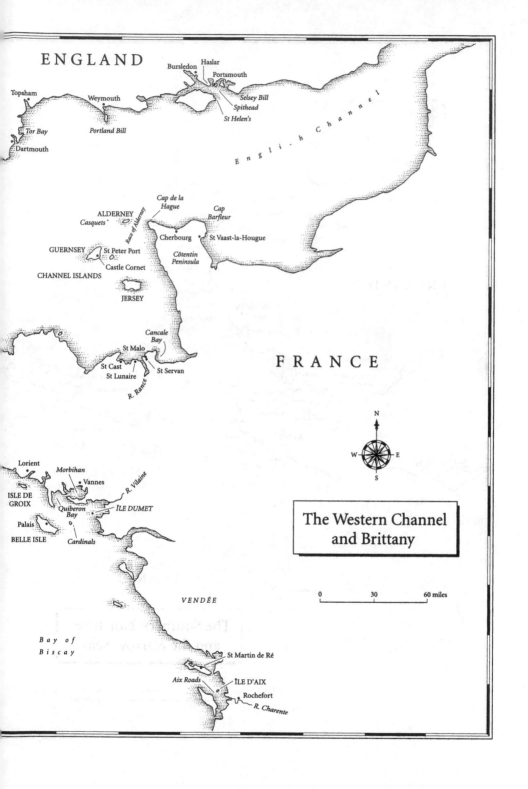

ENGLAND

Topsham
Weymouth
Tor Bay
Dartmouth
Portland Bill

Bursledon   Haslar
Portsmouth
Selsey Bill
Spithead
St Helen's

English Channel

Cap de la Hague
Cap Barfleur

ALDERNEY
Casquets
Race of Alderney
Cherbourg   St Vaast-la-Hougue

GUERNSEY   St Peter Port
Castle Cornet
Côtentin Peninsula

CHANNEL ISLANDS

JERSEY

Cancale Bay
St Malo
St Cast   St Servan
St Lunaire
R. Rance

FRANCE

N
W   E
S

Lorient
Morbihan
Vannes
R. Vilaine
ISLE DE GROIX
Quiberon Bay   ÎLE DUMET
Palais
BELLE ISLE   Cardinals

The Western Channel
and Brittany

VENDÉE

0   30   60 miles

Bay of Biscay

St Martin de Ré
Aix Roads   ÎLE D'AIX
Rochefort
R. Charente

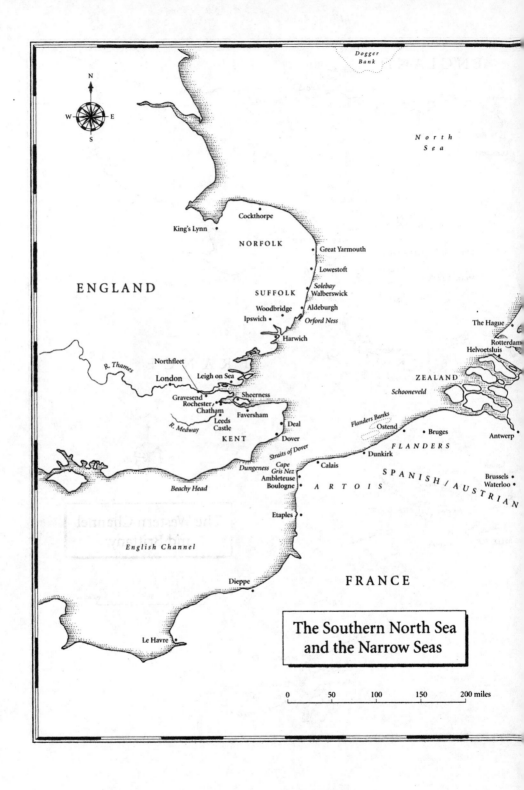

The Southern North Sea
and the Narrow Seas

HELIGOLAND ○

Lübeck •

• Hamburg

TERSCHELLING

VLIE

TEXEL • Harlingen
Marsdiep FRIESLAND
Den Helder
Zuider Zee
• Enkhuizen
• Hoorn
HOLLAND
R.IJ
Pampus
Amsterdam

Bremen •

Verden •

R. Waal
R. Maas

R. Rhine

NETHERLANDS

Helvoetsluis • • Rotterdam

GOEREE

Steendiep

ZEALAND

Deurloo

Spleet

WALCHEREN
Middleburg •
Flushing •

Western Scheldt

R. Scheldt

• Antwerp

0   10   20 miles

Orford Ness
Woodbridge •
Ipswich •

Harwich •

Gunfleet

King's Channel

Long Sand
Head

Galloper

Gabbard

Swin

Barrow Deep

Black Deep

Kentish Knock

Isle of Grain
Leigh on Sea

• Nore

Sheerness

Chatham

• Faversham

Kentish Flats

North Foreland

Gull Stream

Goodwin Sands

Deal •

The Downs

Dover •

South Foreland

0   10   20 miles

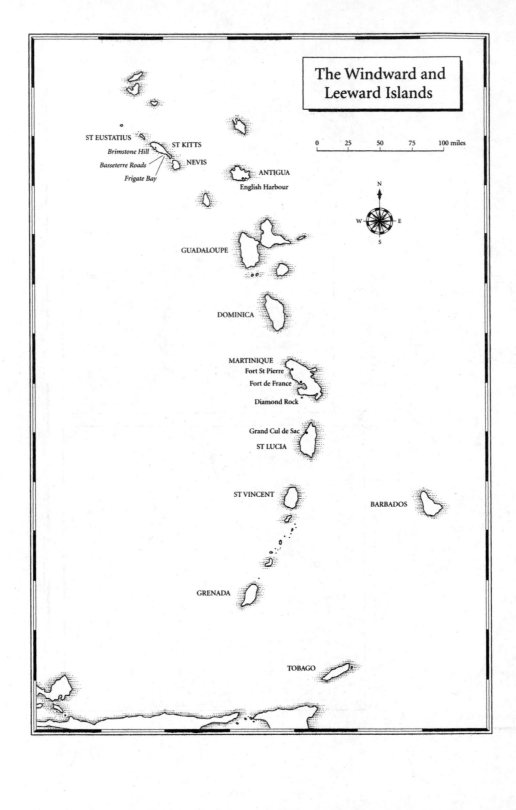

The Windward and
Leeward Islands

0   25   50   75   100 miles

N
W — E
S

ST EUSTATIUS
Brimstone Hill
Basseterre Roads   ST KITTS
Frigate Bay   NEVIS

ANTIGUA
English Harbour

GUADALOUPE

DOMINICA

MARTINIQUE
Fort St Pierre
Fort de France
Diamond Rock

Grand Cul de Sac
ST LUCIA

ST VINCENT

BARBADOS

GRENADA

TOBAGO

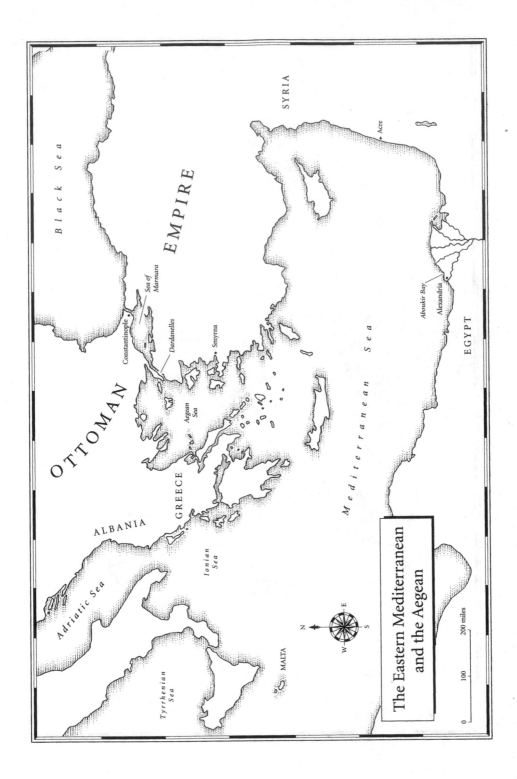

The Eastern Mediterranean
and the Aegean

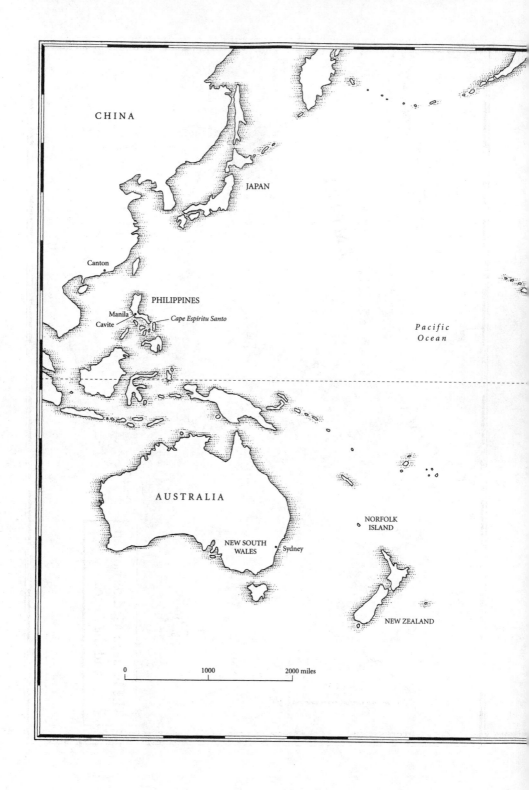

CHINA

JAPAN

Canton

PHILIPPINES

Manila
Cavite

Cape Espíritu Santo

*Pacific
Ocean*

AUSTRALIA

NORFOLK
ISLAND

NEW SOUTH
WALES

Sydney

NEW ZEALAND

0   1000   2000 miles

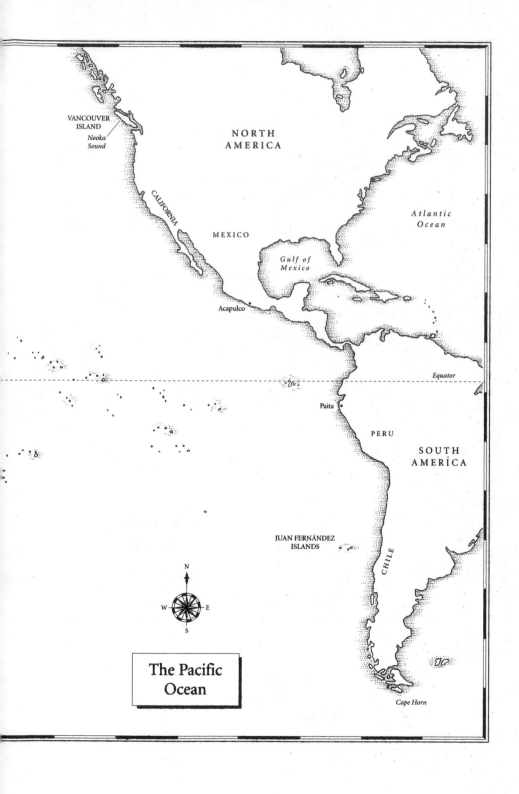

VANCOUVER
ISLAND
*Nooka
Sound*

NORTH
AMERICA

CALIFORNIA

MEXICO

*Atlantic
Ocean*

*Gulf of
Mexico*

Acapulco

Equator

Paita

PERU

SOUTH
AMERICA

JUAN FERNÁNDEZ
ISLANDS

CHILE

N

W   E

S

Cape Horn

The Pacific
Ocean

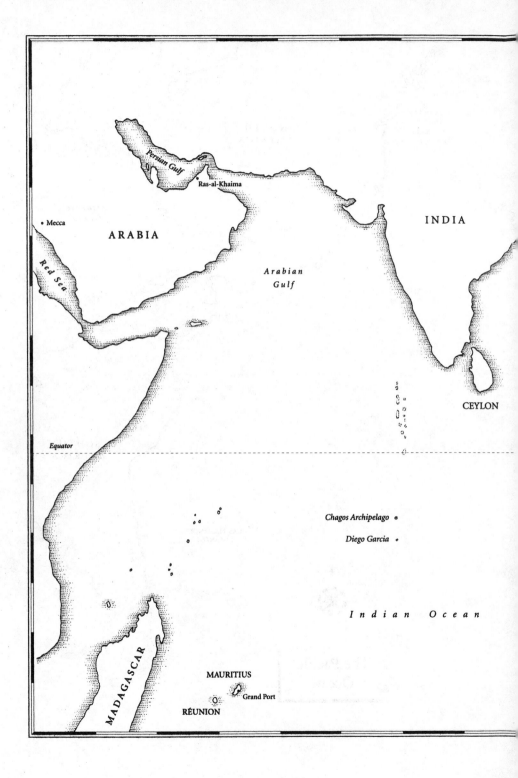

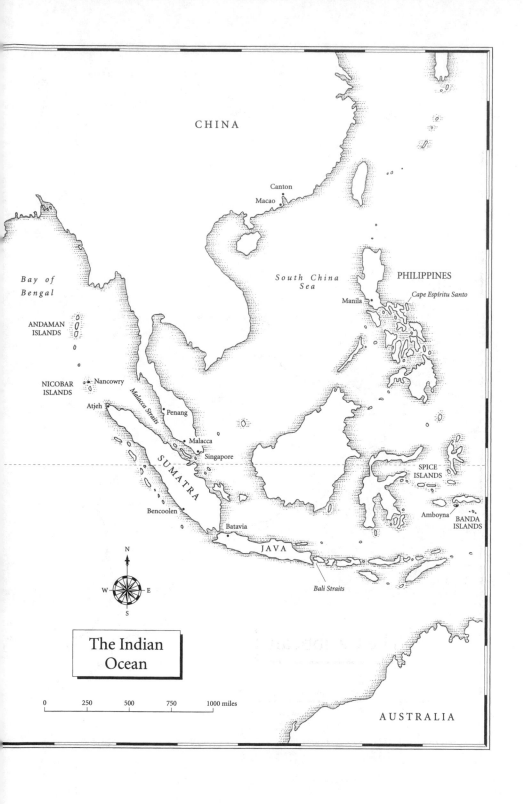

CHINA

Canton
Macao

*Bay of
Bengal*

*South China
Sea*

PHILIPPINES

ANDAMAN
ISLANDS

Manila

Cape Espíritu Santo

NICOBAR
ISLANDS

Nancowry

Atjeh

Malacca Straits

Penang

S U M A T R A

Malacca

Singapore

SPICE
ISLANDS

Bencoolen

Amboyna

BANDA
ISLANDS

Batavia

J A V A

Bali Straits

N

W   E

S

The Indian
Ocean

0   250   500   750   1000 miles

AUSTRALIA

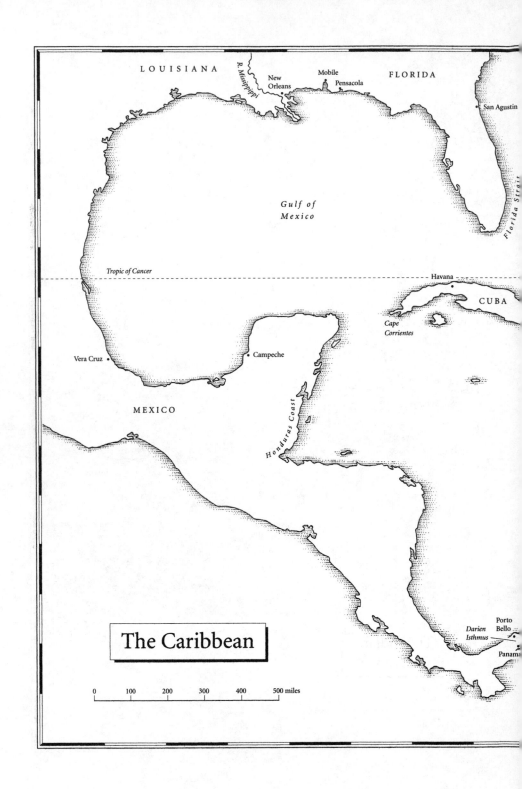

LOUISIANA

R. Missippippi

New Orleans

Mobile

Pensacola

FLORIDA

San Agustin

Gulf of Mexico

Tropic of Cancer

Florida Strait

Havana

CUBA

Cape Corrientes

Vera Cruz

Campeche

MEXICO

Honduras Coast

Darien Isthmus

Porto Bello

Panama

The Caribbean

0   100   200   300   400   500 miles

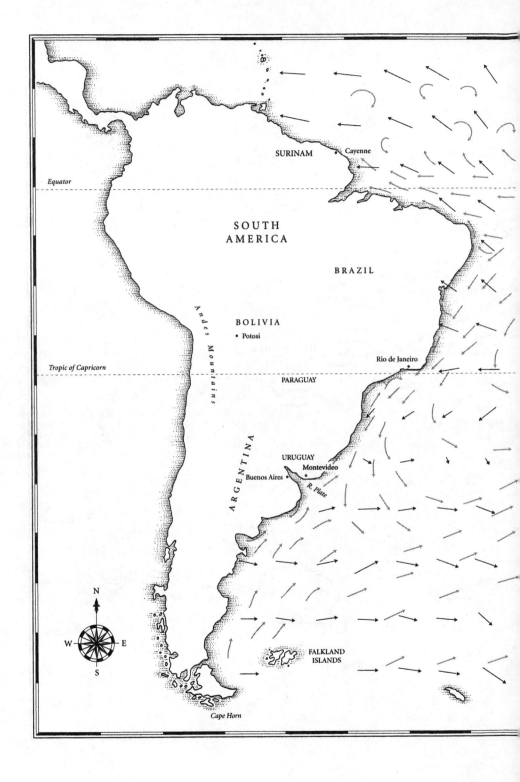

Equator

SOUTH
AMERICA

BRAZIL

SURINAM   • Cayenne

BOLIVIA
• Potosi

Tropic of Capricorn

Rio de Janeiro
•

PARAGUAY

Andes Mountains

ARGENTINA

URUGUAY
Montevideo
Buenos Aires •
R. Plate

N

W   E

S

FALKLAND
ISLANDS

Cape Horn

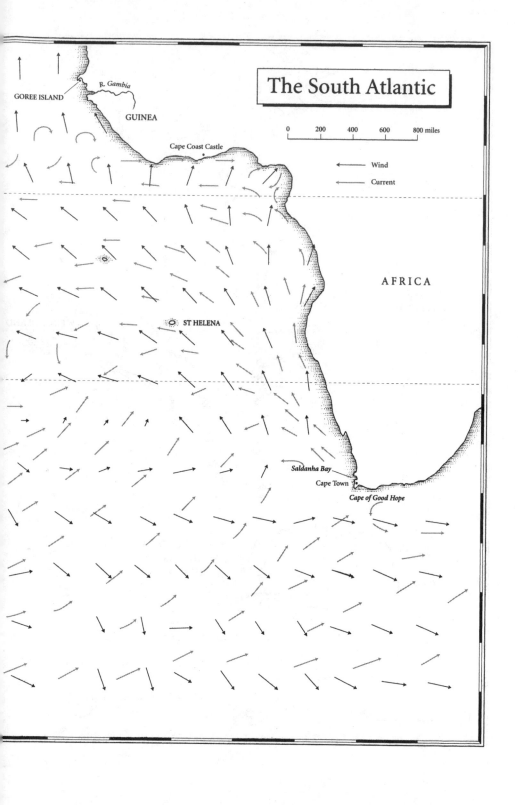

The South Atlantic

GOREE ISLAND

R. Gambia

GUINEA

Cape Coast Castle

0   200   400   600   800 miles

Wind

Current

AFRICA

ST HELENA

Saldanha Bay

Cape Town

Cape of Good Hope

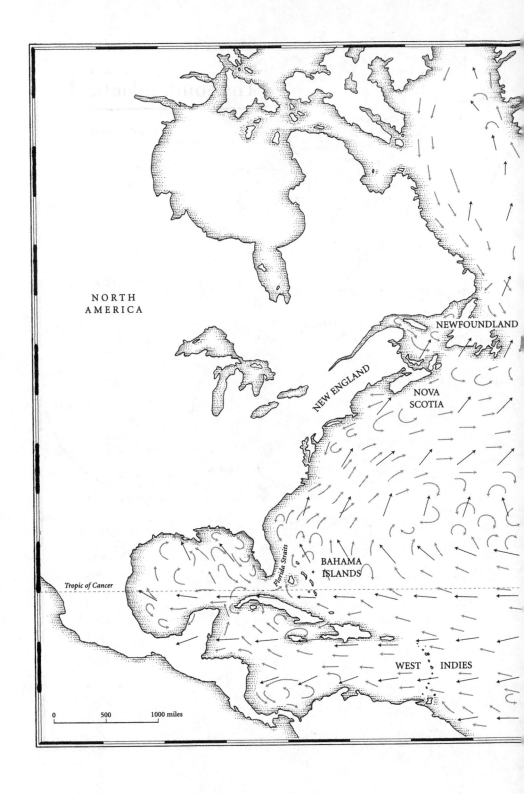

NORTH
AMERICA

NEWFOUNDLAND

NEW ENGLAND

NOVA
SCOTIA

Florida Straits

BAHAMA
ISLANDS

Tropic of Cancer

WEST   INDIES

0   500   1000 miles

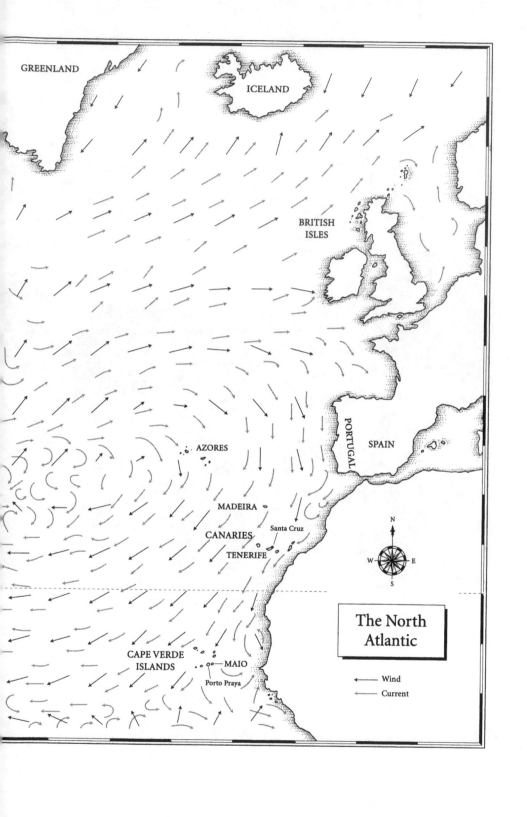

GREENLAND

ICELAND

BRITISH
ISLES

PORTUGAL SPAIN

AZORES

MADEIRA

CANARIES   Santa Cruz

TENERIFE

N

W   E

S

The North
Atlantic

CAPE VERDE
ISLANDS   MAIO

Porto Praya

⟵ Wind
⟵ Current

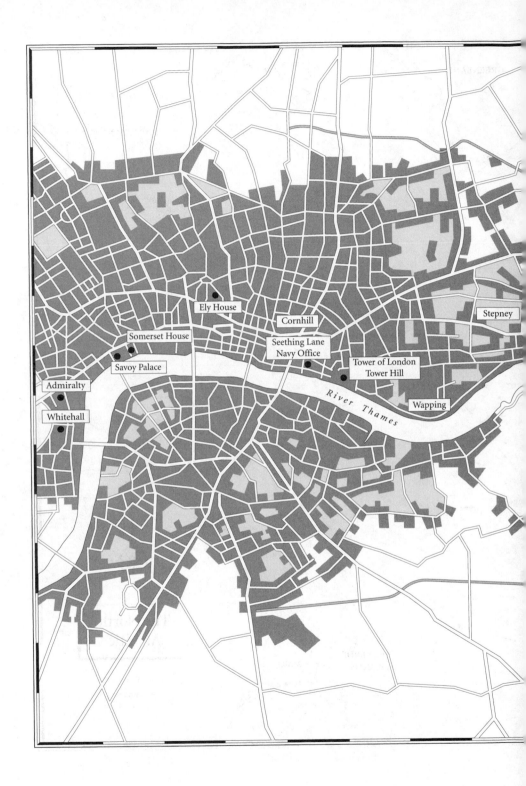

Ely House

Cornhill

Stepney

Somerset House

Seething Lane
Navy Office

Savoy Palace

Tower of London
Tower Hill

Admiralty

Wapping

Whitehall

River Thames

London in the
18th Century

0   1 mile

Blackwall
Yard

Dockyard

Woolwich

Dockyard

Deptford

Greenwich

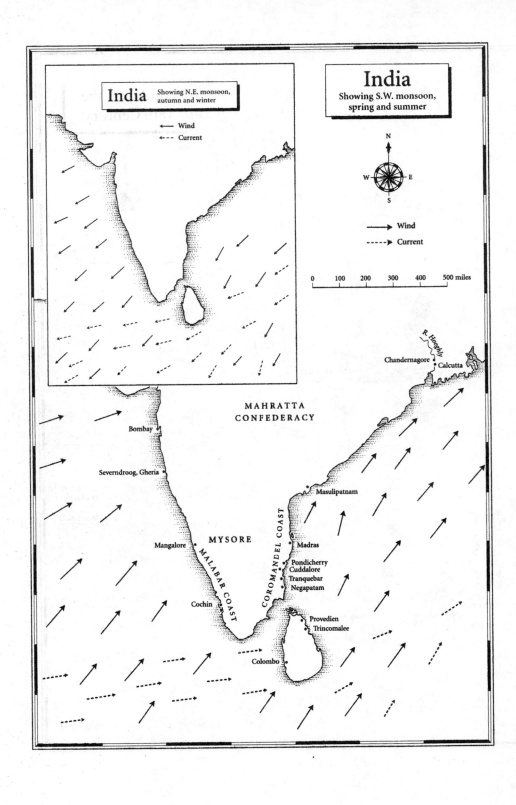

India
Showing N.E. monsoon,
autumn and winter

←— Wind
←-- Current

India
Showing S.W. monsoon,
spring and summer

N
W — E
S

—→ Wind
---→ Current

0   100   200   300   400   500 miles

Chandernagore • Calcutta
R. Hooghly

MAHRATTA
CONFEDERACY

Bombay

Severndroog, Gheria

Masulipatnam

MYSORE

Mangalore

Madras

COROMANDEL COAST

Pondicherry
Cuddalore
Tranquebar
Negapatam

MALABAR COAST

Cochin

Provedien
Trincomalee

Colombo

INTRODUCTION

Writing in the Preface to his *Naval History of England* in 1735, Thomas Lediard lamented the unaccountable neglect of his subject.

> I know not by what fatal mistake, or blind neglect, no part of English history has been so little the care of our ablest writers, of ancient as well as modern times; though materials need not have been wanting to those who had the capacity, and would have been at the pains of enquiring after them.[1]

It is not necessary today to deplore the total neglect of naval history, but there is still some work to be done to install it in its proper place. In a recent work comparing the development of government in eighteenth-century Germany and Britain, for example, Britain is treated as a military power directly comparable to Prussia.[2] None of the distinguished contributors to the book seem to be aware that Britain's contribution to warfare, and warfare's contribution to British history, were rather unlike those of Prussia. To describe the eighteenth-century British state, in war or peace, without mentioning the Royal Navy is quite a feat of intellectual virtuosity; it must have been as difficult as writing a history of Switzerland without mentioning mountains, or writing a novel without using the letter 'e'.

The purpose of this, the second of three volumes of a *Naval History of Britain*, is to put naval affairs back into the history of Britain. It is not to write a self-contained 'company history' of the Royal Navy, but to describe the contribution which naval warfare, with all its associated activities, has made to national history. That certainly includes the history of the Royal Navy as an institution, but it is broader; the intention is to link naval warfare to the many other aspects of history in which it was involved. As far as the limitations of a single work and a single author will allow, this is meant as a contribution to political, social, economic, diplomatic, administrative, agricultural, medical, religious and other histories which will never be complete until the naval component of them is recognized and understood. By the same token it is an attempt to spread the meaning of naval history well beyond the conduct of war at sea and the internal history of the Royal Navy, and to treat it instead as a national endeavour, involving many, and in some ways all, aspects of government and society.

It follows that this is a book which tries to make connections, some of which have not been explored or even noticed, and about which we know too little as yet to reach definite conclusions. Specialists in the many areas of national history on which this book trespasses will doubtless deplore the author's ignorance of them: his hope is that they will be stimulated to do better what he has done first. Readers whose primary interest is in war at sea may be disappointed that almost half the book is devoted to the background rather than the foreground of naval history, but this is quite deliberate, for there is no understanding battles and campaigns otherwise. In practice the book is arranged in four parallel 'streams': policy, strategy and naval operations; finance, administration and logistics, including all sorts of technical and industrial support; social history; and the material elements of sea power, ships and weapons. Chapters are devoted to each in turn, but they are not meant to be read in isolation. The author's intention is to unite rather than to divide.

The same observation applies to the national scope of the work. 'Britain' in the title is shorthand for the whole British Isles, but it is not intended to ignore or submerge the national histories of England, Scotland, Wales and Ireland. In the period covered by this volume, however, unlike the first, naval warfare became a semi-professional business, dominated by the English and later British Royal Navy. Scottish warships make only a brief appearance, and there was no Irish naval establishment. The three kingdoms therefore figure distinctly mainly in the chapters on social history. This is a 'national' history, therefore, in reference to the British state rather than its component nations. It is also an international history, as all maritime history must necessarily be, for the sea links nations in peace or war. There can be no naval history of Britain which is not also a naval history of her neighbours and enemies. I have therefore tried to deal as fully as space would permit with the relevant parts of the naval histories of France, Spain, the Netherlands, Denmark, the United States and other naval powers of whom the British were friends or foes.

All this is largely based on printed sources, as it must be in a work on this scale, very much enriched by unpublished theses and dissertations, and garnished in places with my own researches. Most of the facts and many of the ideas will be known to specialists. Nevertheless it is over a century since the publication of Sir William Laird Clowes's *History of the Royal Navy*, the last work to tackle the subject on a comparable scale, and it does not seem too soon to stand back from the subject and take a fresh look at it. The first volume of this work, *The Safeguard of the Sea*, dealt with the naval history of the British Isles from 660 to 1649. Much of it was a history of failure – failure to understand and exploit the facts of geography. It is still easy to find deterministic histories which assume that being an island somehow made Britain 'invasion-proof', and removed the necessity to go to any trouble or expense to defend against foreign enemies. Readers of *The Safeguard of the Sea* will know that England was successfully invaded by sea eight times, and Scotland once, between 1066 and 1485, while on numerous other occasions enemy forces large and small were put ashore in various parts of the three kingdoms. The sea is a broad highway, easier and faster than most of those available ashore until modern times, and provides no safeguard whatever to those who have not learned how to use it. In spite of several promising starts, notably under Richard I, Henry V and Elizabeth I of England, and James IV of Scots, it cannot be said that people had really mastered the use of the sea for national defence before 1649. It is in the 166 years covered by this volume that state and nation finally gained the real sovereignty of the seas around the British Isles. To do so they had to overcome numerous strictly professional challenges of seamanship and sea warfare, but it was even more essential to construct administrative systems capable of keeping fleets at sea for long periods, and equally they had to confront questions of ideology, policy and politics without which it would have been impossible to maintain public support. Success in this great national undertaking was not simply important for its obvious fruits, security at home and wealth abroad. Naval dominance of European waters was the largest, longest, most complex and expensive project ever undertaken by the British state and society. Few aspects of national life were unaffected by it, and no history of Britain can be complete which ignores it.

ONE

A Mountain of Iron

Operations 1649–1654

The English Commonwealth which executed its former king Charles I on 30 January 1649 was in principle a republic governed by a sovereign Parliament, but the Parliament was the 'Rump' remaining of the Long Parliament (originally elected in 1640) after Colonel Thomas Pride's troops had purged it of all remaining opponents of military rule in December. Supreme power was held by the Council of State, made up of the senior officers of the New Model Army, and senior Parliamentarians of their mind. In all essentials, England was a military dictatorship, which ruled by force without law, executing troublesome opponents by the use of tribunals without juries. Crudely summarizing a complex and fluid political situation, we may say that this government, like the army officers who stood behind it, was radical in politics and Independent in religion – meaning that its members belonged to 'gathered congregations' outside the now-Presbyterian Church of England. Not only Royalists but the vast majority of those who had supported Parliament during the first Civil War were excluded from political life. Nevertheless the Rump represented a faction within the pre-war governing classes, men of property and education, and it feared the yet more radical voices among the common people and the common soldiers of the army; groups like the Levellers, who wished to replace the existing social order with utopian communism, and the Fifth Monarchists, who looked forward to sweeping away all ecclesiastical order in preparation for the Second Coming of Christ.[1]

The Rump government did not pretend to have, or to desire, the support of the people at large. On the contrary, it gloried in being a godly remnant which had crushed all its enemies with the help of God alone. The new regime was presently to build a formidable fleet of warships named after English victories: the victories the New Model Army had won over its domestic enemies. The new flagship the *Naseby* (unofficially nicknamed the 'Great Oliver') bore a figurehead of the army's commander-in-chief General

Cromwell on horseback, trampling six nations underfoot: England, Scotland, Ireland, France, Spain and the Netherlands.[2] This was not a government of national unity. Nor was it building warships because the military regime was warmly disposed towards the English Navy. On the contrary, the Navy had long been more moderate in politics than the army, and it had played a leading part in the 1648 rebellion which had helped to provoke the army's coup d'état. In the aftermath of that a large part of the fleet had deserted to the Royalists in Holland, and the loyalty of the remainder was doubtful.[3]

The soldiers did not like or trust the Navy, but in their situation they could not do without it. In the spring of 1649 the English Commonwealth was completely isolated. Scotland and Ireland, the Channel Isles, the Scillies, the Isle of Man and the colonies were all in Royalist hands. All Europe stood aghast at the murder of an anointed king, and the Peace of Westphalia had freed the powerful armies and fleets hitherto engaged in the Thirty Years' War for operations against England. A Swedish expedition was known to be preparing to support the Stuarts in Scotland, and others were feared.[4] Private men-of-war with commissions from the exiled Prince of Wales, now proclaimed by his friends as King Charles II, sailed from ports in Ireland, Scotland, the Channel Isles, France and Flanders to capture English merchant ships, financing the Royalist cause, cutting sharply into the Customs revenue which formed a major prop of the Commonwealth's shaky finances, and undermining its claims to be an effective government.[5] There was nothing the army by itself could do to deal with any of these threats; a powerful fleet was essential to the survival of the military regime.

In this crisis the Commonwealth's first priority was to correct 'the manifold distempers of the Navy, and the great decay of Customs, occasioned by evil, malignant, unfaithful and supernumerary officers, employed both by sea and land, to the great prejudice of the Commonwealth'[6] – that is, to eject all those not certainly loyal to the new regime, which meant the great majority. Of those who had managed and commanded the Parliamentary naval cause during the first Civil War, only those were left whose Independent credentials were impeccable.[7] Even so, the army trusted no one connected with the Navy, and ensured that the command of the fleet was put in safe hands. An Act of February 1649 established the new office of General at Sea, having the powers of seagoing command formerly held by the Lord High Admiral without his administrative and legal responsibilities. It is a common misunderstanding to speak of three Generals at Sea: there was but one single General (in the old sense of 'commander-in-chief'), but the office was put in commission among three colonels, Edward Popham, Richard Deane and Robert Blake, 'to hold, and execute by yourselves, or any two of you, the place of Admiral and General of the said fleet'. All three were reliable regimental officers, but they were unequivocally junior in rank to the senior officers of the army, and two signatures were required for their orders; none of them was trusted to act alone. Though all three had some relevant experience, and Popham had been a pre-war officer in the Royal Navy, they were chosen entirely for political reasons, to rivet the army's control on the Navy.[8]

The State's Navy, as it was now formally known, flying the new 'cross and harp' jack in place of 'the disunion flag or late king's colours',[9] had thirty-nine ships, four more than Charles I had had in 1642, but its situation was in every other respect much worse: its experienced officers and administrators mostly removed, its morale shaky, its finances disastrous, and its enemies very numerous.[10] The Council of State encouraged the three colonels with the thought that 'our own forces are such at sea as our enemies looked not for, and ourselves could scarce have hoped, consisting of so many good ships and faithful and able commanders as have not formerly been set out in any one year. But', they continued, 'that it was difficult to have so many set out and furnished you very well know, and how this Commonwealth will be able to continue the same in successive years is not easy to evidence.'[11] In short there was possibly one season only in which to defeat the Royalists at sea.

The main Royalist naval force was the squadron which had mutinied in 1648 and taken refuge in the port of Helvoetsluis in Holland. They were now commanded by Charles I's German nephew Prince Rupert, who made up for his lack of seagoing experience with an unequalled energy and determination. Selling an old ship's guns and pawning his mother's jewels, Rupert raised enough money to fit the squadron for sea, and on 20 January 1649[12] he sailed for Kinsale, in southern Ireland, far from the Commonwealth's naval bases in the Thames, and perfectly placed to prey on English shipping to the westward. With the Royalist privateers already there he claimed a force of twenty-eight ships, greatly exceeding the Commonwealth's small Irish Sea squadron.[13] English merchantmen in the Channel and North Sea now had to be convoyed to protect them from Royalist privateers. It was not until May that the main English fleet commanded by Blake and Deane arrived in Irish waters to blockade Kinsale and cover the passage of Cromwell's army across the Irish Sea. Only the support of the Navy allowed Cromwell to campaign in an impoverished country without decent roads. It transported his supplies, sustained his siege of Drogheda and then carried the siege train south to attack Wexford. Prince Rupert soon realized that Cromwell's rapid advance would force him to seek a new base. Early in October the State's fleet was driven off station by a gale, and on the 17th Rupert sailed again, this time for Lisbon, with a squadron of seven ships, including three powerful vessels inherited from Charles I's fleet: the *Constant Reformation* of 52 guns, the *Convertine* of 46, and the *Swallow* of 40. At the end of the year he had a squadron as large as before (prizes having made up for losses), and a much safer base. The State's Navy had played an essential part in the still incomplete conquest of Ireland, but it was a long way from controlling the sea.[14]

King John IV of Portugal was friendly to the Stuart cause, but the presence of Rupert's squadron, preying on English ships and all those who traded with the English Republic, soon became embarrassing. It became more embarrassing when the main English fleet, now commanded by Robert Blake,[15] arrived off the Tagus on 10 March 1650. The Portuguese refused to allow Republicans to attack Royalists within the port, but they could not stop Blake blockading the mouth of the river, and taking an increasingly hostile line towards Portuguese ships. They must have assumed that it would be impossible for the State's ships to remain for long on a station so far from their bases, and indeed it was acutely difficult, but all summer Blake maintained his exposed situation. While part of Blake's fleet was away watering at Cadiz on 16 July, and again on 7 September in fog, Rupert attempted to break out, but each time he was frustrated. On 14 September Blake seized part of a rich Portuguese convoy coming from Brazil; virtually an act of war, which placed the Portuguese government under intense pressure. Finally in October Blake withdrew his remaining ships to refit at Cadiz, allowing Rupert to escape from Lisbon, 'poverty and despair being companions and revenge a guide'.[16]

Rupert's squadron entered the Mediterranean, pursued by Blake, who met it on the coast of Spain early in November and captured or drove ashore most of the Royalist ships near Cartagena. Only Rupert himself, in the *Constant Reformation*, and his brother Prince Maurice in the *Swallow* were elsewhere, and were able to take refuge in Toulon. Soon afterwards Blake was recalled to England (where he arrived in February 1651), to be relieved in the Mediterranean by a small squadron under Captain William Penn. Blake had shown great determination and powers of leadership in maintaining two long, exhausting and dangerous blockades with inadequate supplies, far from home, achieving both the elimination of much of the Royalist naval force, and a demonstration of English naval power to coerce unfriendly neutrals which was noted elsewhere; particularly in Madrid, where the Spanish government recognized the English Republic in December 1650.[17]

Throughout 1649 and 1650 the State's Navy was further stretched by an undeclared war with France, provoked by Royalist privateers operating out of

French ports and sustained by French hostility to the English Republic. The Levant Company, which traded to Turkish ports in the eastern Mediterranean, claimed that in two years French privateers had captured ships worth £600,000, carrying 480 valuable guns. On 31 October 1650 an Act of Parliament imposed a surcharge of 15 per cent on all Customs duties to pay for convoys; the first explicit acknowledgement by any English government of a duty to protect merchantmen outside home waters. The first Mediterranean convoy sailed in February 1651.[18]

In May of that year Prince Rupert left Toulon, heading now for the West Indies. On 30 September he barely escaped when his flagship the *Constant Reformation* foundered in a gale off the Azores. When he reached the West Indies in May 1652 there was no island left in Royalist hands to welcome him, and in September he lost his brother in a hurricane in the Windward Passage. Finally in March 1653, with his one remaining ship, the *Swallow*, Prince Rupert entered the Loire and ended an epic of improvisation and endurance in which he had sustained a naval campaign over four years and many thousands of miles, without any permanent base or institutional support. But the Royalist cause was ruined ashore and afloat long before Prince Rupert finally returned from the sea.[19]

In June 1650 Charles II was proclaimed King of Scots. Scotland was, of course, an independent country and a recent ally of the English Parliamentarians, but the Rump government had no love for Presbyterians or Royalists, and easily persuaded itself that it was justified in invading Scotland. As ever, the roads between the two kingdoms were too few and poor to sustain an invasion without ample seaborne support. The Scottish army was formidable, commanded by officers with long experience in the German wars, and Cromwell was lucky to win a victory at Dunbar on 3 September which allowed the English to take the port of Leith, and thus sustain themselves over the winter. In July 1651 the English outflanked the main Scottish position with a major amphibious operation across the Firth of Forth, using a force of flatboats specially constructed for the purpose. At this the Scottish army boldly invaded England down the west coast. Its defeat at Worcester on 3 September 1651 marked the end of Royalist military operations on the mainland of Britain. Charles II escaped to France, but his cause was in ruins.[20]

Meanwhile Blake had been appointed to command the main English fleet for the summer of 1651 in the Irish Sea, covering the armies in Ireland and Scotland. On his way down the Channel he learned that a Dutch squadron under the famous admiral Maarten Harpertszoon Tromp was preparing to attack the Royalist-held Scilly Isles, from which privateers had been preying impartially on Dutch as well as English shipping. Jealous of this interference, and fearful of a Dutch base at the mouth of the Channel, the English government ordered Blake to forestall Tromp. The two admirals were off the Scillies together on 15 April, but Tromp was content to leave the English to undertake a very perilous and costly series of landings, which led finally to the surrender of the Isles on 1 June.[21]

The alarm of the Scottish invasion stopped major naval operations over the summer, and it was not until the end of September that Blake was sent with a landing force to attack Jersey, still held for Charles II and sheltering active and dangerous privateers; and Guernsey, where only Castle Cornet remained in Royalist hands. These operations, including a night landing on a dangerous coast at the beginning of winter, were successfully completed by the end of the year. With the capture of Waterford in March 1651, Dundee in September, the Isle of Man in October, and Galway in April 1652, the last Royalist privateer bases in the British Isles had fallen to the English Republic.[22] After the surrender of Barbados to a squadron commanded by Sir George Ayscue in January 1652, there was no significant Royalist foothold on English territory anywhere in the world.[23]

The Commonwealth had now crushed all its domestic enemies, and sufficiently impressed foreign powers to deter any thoughts of intervention. It might have felt secure – but security and contentment are not in the nature of military dictatorships. All the internal divisions now revived which had been suppressed while the regime fought for survival. The government feared Leveller influence in the army and doubted the loyalty of the Navy. It knew that it was disliked or hated by the majority of the people of the three kingdoms, and that even by force it was unlikely to be able to raise enough taxes to pay for its forces, but the more unpopular it became, and the more widely it spread its conquests, the more force it needed to remain in power: an army of 47,000 in March 1649 had swollen to 70,000 by 1652. Everywhere it looked, at home and abroad, the Commonwealth saw or suspected the friends of Charles Stuart, and the enemies of God.[24]

A foreign war has always been the natural way for a military regime to employ its forces and justify its existence, and England already had a low-level, undeclared war with France, but in 1652 circumstances were pushing it towards a different opponent, the Dutch Republic. Throughout the short life of the Rump government, England had been in deep economic difficulty, with poor harvests, famine and plague. English shipowners, who had prospered during the troubled times of the Thirty Years' War as neutral shippers with well-armed ships, were half-ruined by the civil wars, and altogether ruined by the return of general peace in 1648. Dutch shipowners were now free again to deploy their formidable advantages: unarmed, cheaply built ships with small, ill-paid and ill-fed crews which translated into low freight costs, backed by the most sophisticated economy in Europe, with developed banks, insurance and stock markets. Immediately they resumed their former dominance of the European carrying trades. A 1649 treaty gave Dutch ships a discount on the 'Sound tolls', which all shipping entering and leaving the Baltic paid to Denmark. In 1650 there had been thirteen Dutch merchantmen in the Baltic for every one English; by the next year the ratio was fifty to one. A treaty with Spain in 1650 gave the Dutch further advantages, and English ships were rapidly driven out of the Spanish and Mediterranean trades.[25]

All this was serious for English shipowners, but it did not necessarily trouble English merchants, who were as happy as anyone else to cut their costs by shipping in Dutch bottoms. Direct economic competition with the more advanced Dutch economy was limited to narrow sectors. In particular the group known as the 'New Merchants', mostly Independent in religion and many of them serving in the Commonwealth's naval administration, had been heavily involved in pre-war shipping to the colonies, and resented the Dutch breaking into their trade. They had much to do with the Act of 1650 which forbade foreign shipping to trade with English colonies – particularly meaning those still at that date under Royalist control – under the terms of which Ayscue seized a large number of Dutch ships at Barbados. These merchants had also been responsible for breaking up the monopoly of the English East India Company, and had hopes of making inroads into the trade of its Dutch rival the VOC. They were the principal sponsors of the Navigation Ordinance (later Act) of 1651, which required goods to be shipped to and from English colonies only under the English flag, and imports from elsewhere to come either in English ships or ships of the producing country. This, of course, was aimed at promoting English shipowning at Dutch expense – and at the expense of English merchants, who were forced to abandon cheap Dutch carriers for high-cost English ones. The Ordinance, however, represented more of an aspiration than a policy, for the English merchant fleet to carry it out did not exist; and the direct trade of an economically underdeveloped country like England was anyway of relatively little importance to the Dutch. These measures were irritants to Anglo-Dutch relations, but they would never have led to war by themselves. More serious was Dutch resentment at the repeated searches and seizures of their ships in the course of the naval wars against the Royalists and the French, both by English warships, and even more by English privateers which frequently used torture.[26]

Historians used to regard economic factors alone as sufficient to explain the Anglo-Dutch wars, but it is now recognized that religion and politics were essential considerations.[27] The leaders of the Commonwealth government, even the small proportion of them who were connected with overseas trade, were profoundly religious men for whom the will of God was the fundamental determinant of policy and the only guarantee of success. Though Cromwell and his colleagues were not immune to the temptations of human nature, and the promptings of the Holy Ghost did mysteriously tend to align with their political objectives, they were not chiefly motivated by worldly rationality. Believing that they were God's instruments, that His favour was proved by their repeated victories, they were apt to interpret opposition, not simply as misguided, but wicked, predestined to failure in this life and damnation in the next. They punished the ungodly and solved one political problem by conquering Scotland and absorbing it into England. At the same time and in the same spirit they offered to the Dutch a federation of the two republics, to form the core of the Protestant league which would go on to overthrow the Anti-Christ (meaning the Papacy and all Catholic countries). When the Dutch declined to give up their hard-won independence, they were written off as bad Protestants, Presbyterians and therefore (from the Independent point of view) little better than Papists, obsessed with laying up wealth in this world rather than the next. It became a pious duty to punish them in order to bring them back to the truth. It was this attitude as much as economic calculation which lay behind the Navigation Act, and distracted the subsequent negotiations between the two countries.[28]

One further factor must be explained, because it had a crucial influence not only on these negotiations but on the whole course of Anglo-Dutch relations in the seventeenth century: the Dutch constitution.[29] The Republic of the Seven United Provinces was a loose federation of semi-independent states. There was no permanent central government, but sovereign authority resided in the States-General, which in turn was made up of delegates (not representatives) of the provincial assemblies. Voting power in the States-General was in proportion to tax revenue, which gave the single province of Holland nearly 60 per cent of the votes, and Holland in turn was dominated (though not controlled) by the rival cities of Amsterdam and Rotterdam. The closed oligarchies of wealthy merchants who made up the regents, or aldermen, of the cities of Holland, though only a few thousands strong, were able in many circumstances to control the policy of the whole Republic. Their policies favoured their interests: the shipping, trade and industry on which Holland's wealth was built, in particular the carrying trade, the Baltic and Mediterranean trades, and the East India Company (the VOC). Zealand, equally a maritime province though smaller and weaker, concentrated on fishing, privateering, coasting trade to western Europe, the slave trade and the West India Company. Both provinces favoured the navy over the army. The other five provinces were all more or less poor, agricultural, concerned with military threats across ill-defended frontiers, and therefore more interested in the army than the navy.

History had given the inland provinces a powerful voice in national politics, for Dutch independence had been won under the leadership of successive princes of the house of Orange-Nassau commanding the Dutch armies, and in the public eye the Princes of Orange had almost the status of a royal family. Constitutionally, they were merely noblemen elected to the provincial office of 'statholder' – but a prince who was statholder of a majority of provinces could command the national offices of Captain-General and Admiral-General. As commander-in-chief of both services, a Prince of Orange, particularly in wartime, could behave as much like a king as it was possible to do with only partial control of foreign policy, and none at all of finance. The Princes of Orange and the 'Republican' regents of Holland were the opposite poles of Dutch politics: the Orangists commanding the loyalty of the inland provinces and Zealand, plus the common people and middle classes in Holland; the Republicans controlling the money and the votes in the States-General. There was also a religious aspect of this political divide, for the Princes of Orange conformed to the Calvinist Dutch Reformed Church which dominated public life, but many of the Republican leaders belonged to the 'Remonstrant' or 'Arminian' group which professed a more 'high church' theology (therefore the more easily identified by English Independents as 'bad Protestants'). In November 1650 Prince William II of Orange died suddenly in the course of mounting something like a military coup d'état against Amsterdam. His heir was two days old, and the event allowed the Republicans to gain complete control of the Republic. It seemed providential on both sides of the Channel, for William II was Charles I's son-in-law, and his death removed one of the principal supporters of the Stuarts.

The Dutch constitution shaped the Dutch navy.[30] With no central government, there was no single national navy, but five provincial admiralties; nominally federal institutions, though in practice dominated by provincial interests. The Admiralty of Amsterdam was the wealthiest and politically most influential, but its rival the Admiralty of the Maze[31] at Rotterdam was the senior. Next in importance was the Admiralty of Zealand, with its headquarters at Middelburg and its naval yard at Flushing. There was a third Holland

Admiralty, that of the 'North Quarter',[32] which alternated its establishment every six months between Hoorn and Enkhuizen, and finally the little Admiralty of Friesland at Harlingen. Each of these admiralties had its own fleet and naval establishment, supported by its own revenues, but they did not exhaust the Republic's naval resources. The two great joint-stock companies, the East and West India Companies, each owned substantial fleets of well-armed ships which might, by negotiation, be made available to the Republic.[33] A number of municipal navies, the so-called *directieschepen*, provided convoy escorts for their own shipping, while privateering syndicates, especially in Zealand, put substantial forces to sea. An official list of the Dutch fleet issued in June 1652 is divided into not less than twenty-six sections.[34] There were numerous bitter and even murderous rivalries within the fleet and amongst its admirals: between Holland and Zealand, between Amsterdam and Rotterdam, between Orangist and Republican. Geography, moreover, divided all these forces into three groups. The ships of Amsterdam, the North Quarter and Friesland reached the North Sea through the Marsdiep by the island of Texel; a long voyage for the Amsterdam ships, passing over several awkward shoals. Rotterdam ships also had a tortuous passage but in deeper water, issuing into the open sea by one of two channels on either side of the island of Goeree.[35] The Zealanders alone, sailing from Flushing at the mouth of the western Scheldt, had easy access to the open sea. Rotterdam and Zealand forces had not far to go to combine, but the Texel is nearly 100 miles north, and an enemy might easily divide the Dutch forces.

The Dutch experience of naval war was the Eighty Years' War by which they had at length made good their independence from Spain. This war had been financed essentially from the profits of Holland's trade, including trade with the enemy which the Holland merchants regarded as economically indispensable. The navy's function had mainly been to protect trade by escorting convoys and blockading the Spanish North Sea privateer base of Dunkirk. Most of this had been done with armed merchantmen; the navy had few regular warships and none of great size. Only rarely had the Dutch had to fight regular naval battles against enemy fleets. The only occasion anywhere near home waters had been the great battle of the Downs, on 11 October 1639, when Tromp's fleet had destroyed the last major Spanish fleet ever to enter the North Sea; the day which may be said to mark the Netherlands' arrival as the leading maritime power in Europe, and the eclipse of Spain as a naval power for over a century.

The Downs is the broad anchorage which lies off Deal, enclosed by the Kentish coast to the west, and the Goodwin Sands to the east. At its northern end it can be entered from the North Sea or the Thames Estuary through the Gull Stream, and at its southern end from the Channel round the South Foreland. In the age of sail this anchorage was one of the crossroads of the world: during the prevailing south-westerlies ships from London and ports throughout the southern North Sea and Baltic lay here waiting for a fair wind down Channel, while ships which had come up the Channel for London waited their chance to get up the Thames. From the strategic point of view the Downs is the perfect position for warships to watch the upper Channel and southern North Sea. From the tactical point of view it is a trap in the prevailing wind, for the Gull Stream was too narrow for a large force to get through it in a hurry. A fleet lying in the Downs might be caught like a lobster in a pot by an enemy entering by the southern entrance with the wind behind him. It was just in this way that Tromp had won his great victory. Neither the Dutch who had won this battle nor the English who had witnessed it ever forgot it, and it exercised a powerful influence over both navies' strategy for the next fifty years.

As tension rose between the two countries during 1651, and Dutch diplomats in London strove to negotiate a settlement of the commercial issues surrounding the Navigation Act, the States-General voted to increase the Dutch fleet by not less than 150 ships, making a total of 226.[36] Proud of their status as the world's leading maritime power, they confidently expected to intimidate the Commonwealth. Instead they achieved the worst possible result: convincing the English that they were intent on war, by a measure which the admiralties were incapable of carrying into effect with speed, even though many of the new ships were taken up from trade. The Republican regents who now controlled Dutch policy were confident that the sort of navy and strategy which had served them so well in the past would suffice to keep trade flowing even if the English forced a war. This was rash, for the strategic situation of England was vastly more dangerous than Spain's had been. English observers like Captain Nicholas Foster of the *Phoenix* were frankly astonished that the States-General should risk a naval war,

> when (like an eagle's wings extended over her body) our coast surrounded theirs for 120 leagues from Scilly to the Maas in Holland one way, and as many from the Orcades thither the other way; and the wind blowing above three-quarters of the year westerly on the coast of England, made all our cape-lands and bays very good roads for ships to anchor at . . .[37]

Most Dutch trade routes passed close by the English shores, and the Republic (or at least Holland, its paymaster) was completely dependent on seaborne trade for food and livelihood. England, by contrast, was self-sufficient in food and had limited overseas trade. In the gloomy words of Adriaan Pauw, *raadpensionaris* of Holland and one of the Dutch diplomats in London, 'The English are going to attack a mountain of gold; we have to face one of iron.'[38] Tromp, unlike his political masters, was well aware that there was no hope of continuing trade as usual. In a note of April 1652, he argued that the Dutch fleet would have to be concentrated against the English fleet rather than dispersed to escort convoys.[39] Moreover there was a significant difference between the two navies. The English fleet which had fought the civil wars was in composition similar to the Dutch; it was a navy run by merchants, for merchants, and largely made up of armed merchant ships. The Commonwealth had inherited, however, the core of Charles I's Ship Money fleet of the 1630s; a force of great ships which had no Dutch counterparts. Tromp's flagship the *Brederode* was the only ship in the Dutch fleet of over fifty guns. There were fourteen English ships with more, and taking account of the heavier calibre of English guns, he reckoned that there were fifty English ships more powerful than his own.[40]

The final trigger for the outbreak of war was provided by the long-standing English claim to be saluted everywhere in the (undefined) 'British Seas' in acknowledgement of English 'Sovereignty'. This ambitious, not to say absurd, claim had long been a source of trouble with other nations,[41] but hitherto the States-General had avoided it by instructing their officers to yield the salute on the understanding that it was a courtesy, not an acknowledgement of any legal jurisdiction. Confident of their superiority, they chose this moment to give Tromp orders which were both stiffer in tone and vaguer in meaning: he was to yield the salute if the English forces were stronger, so long as 'the State shall not be trifled with'.[42] Tromp was not by nature rash or provocative, but such orders were fatal, in a period of high tension, when the exact form of the salute was unsure.[43] On 19 May 1652 Tromp and Blake met off Dover, and firing broke out over the issue of the salute. Though the facts were confused and disputed, it seems almost certain that Blake fired first.[44] Although greatly outnumbered, the English ships held their own in a confused action and took two Dutch prizes.[45] Even after the battle of Dover, Tromp remained conciliatory and the Dutch hoped to avoid war, but the English were enraged at what they regarded as a treacherous attack, and war was formally declared on 8 July.[46]

On both sides the political leadership was confident of victory, but dangerously vague as to strategy. While Tromp's fleet gathered strength, the English Council of State decided to send Blake to the Orkneys in the hope of intercepting rich homeward-bound Dutch East Indiamen diverted around Scotland. Apparently it was Blake's own choice to take the whole main fleet with him. He left behind only Sir George Ayscue, recently returned from Barbados, lying in the Downs with ten ships, though reinforcements including two of the biggest English ships were on their way down the Thames to him. Tromp saw his opportunity. On 10 July he was in sight of the Downs with over a hundred ships, but before he could attack a gale blew up and saved Ayscue. Instead Tromp was obliged by his orders to set off northward in pursuit of Blake, hampered by shortage of victuals and an outbreak of scurvy. On 25 July the two fleets were very close, near Fair Isle, when a violent gale scattered the Dutch. By the time it was over Tromp was missing over half his ships, but he had found the Indiamen, and with them he returned. Blake's fleet had ridden out the gale in Bressay Sound, and he too returned to the Thames when it became clear that the Dutch had departed. Both sides had risked disaster by sending their main fleets far away from the critical area of the southern North Sea, where everything of importance was at stake, and only good fortune had saved them. Though the responsibility was largely their own, the Republican leaders in the States-General were glad of an excuse to be rid of an Orangist admiral, and dismissed Tromp on his return.[47]

Before the main fleets had returned, Ayscue was sent down-Channel with about forty ships of various sizes to cover inward-bound merchantmen. Soon afterwards the Dutch sent a squadron after him with a similar mission. To command it they brought out of retirement a middle-aged Zealand merchant skipper named Michiel Adriaanszoon de Ruyter.[48] On 16 August the two squadrons met south of Plymouth. Ayscue was to windward with more and heavier ships, de Ruyter was hampered by his convoy. Ayscue twice 'charged' the Dutch from the windward, so that the two fleets passed through one another in no order. This tactic, which went back to the late Middle Ages, was still conventional; as yet neither side had issued fleet orders which went beyond generalities about keeping together for mutual support, and the normal form of fleet action was an indiscriminate mêlée.[49] In this case de Ruyter clearly had the better of it, though no ships were lost on either side: his convoy was saved, Ayscue retreated to Plymouth, and de Ruyter would have followed to attack him in port if a change of wind had not intervened. De Ruyter was then able to cruise for a week collecting inward-bound merchantmen before he turned for home. Blake was now in the Channel again, but de Ruyter skilfully avoided action and brought his convoy safely home at the end of September.[50]

Meanwhile, on 4 September, Blake had struck a blow in the still-continuing quasi-war with France. A French convoy sailing to relieve Dunkirk, under siege by Spanish forces, was taken off Calais, with the result that the city surrendered. Relations with France were yet further envenomed, but the French navy was a negligible force and there was nothing the French could do. In December they swallowed their pride and sent an ambassador to the regicide Republic.[51]

By 25 September Blake was back in the Downs with the main English fleet, and the Dutch were once more at sea under their new commander-in-chief Witte Corneliszoon de With. A fierce disciplinarian hated by all, de With was a very different character from the admired and beloved 'Daddy' Tromp,[52] or his next senior, the Orangist and Zealander Vice-Admiral Johan Evertsen, but he was a skilled tactician, a bloodthirsty fighter and (most important of all) a good Republican Hollander. Once more the Dutch were hoping to attack the Downs, and once again they failed. Worse, many of the ships scattered off the Shetlands in July had not yet returned, and they were outnumbered by about sixty-four against sixty-eight, beside the great disparity in force between the individual ships. Moreover morale in the Dutch fleet was poor, the men unpaid and mutinous.[53]

On 28 September the two fleets met north-east of the Downs, off the shoal called the Kentish Knock. The English had a south-westerly wind behind them and attacked in three squadrons, of which Rear-Admiral Bourne's had been delayed clearing the Gull and was separated from the others. Initially de With was able to concentrate on this isolated squadron, and the English attack was disrupted when the great Sovereign (Charles I's Sovereign of the Seas of 1637, now going to war for the first time) and Vice-Admiral Penn's flagship the James both briefly ran aground on the Kentish Knock itself. Soon, however, the great superiority of the English, and the disastrous morale of the Dutch, began to tell. Three Dutch ships were lost and at least nine deserted. The crew of the Brederode refused to allow de With to come aboard and he had to pull around the fleet in his boat looking for a flagship. Eventually he boarded the Indiaman Prins Willem, where 'I found a captain seventy years old, a sick crew, the pilot and several officers drunk . . .'[54] When the fleet returned de With caused uproar by blaming the defeat on cowardly Zealanders, meaning his immediate subordinates de Ruyter and Commodore Cornelis Evertsen as well as many of the captains.[55] Dutch confidence in their superiority to the English was now beginning to waver. 'Until now', the Swedish minister reported from the Hague, 'people claimed that the Dutch could sail, tack and fire faster than the English, but de With writes that they have found it otherwise.'[56]

Tromp was now persuaded reluctantly to resume command (with Johan

Evertsen as his second), though he foresaw that the Republican leadership did not trust him, and would not face up to the deficiencies of the fleet, still half paralysed by mutiny and mass desertion. What was worse, the success of de Ruyter encouraged the States-General to think that trade could be kept up as usual, and Tromp was now ordered to take a big convoy down Channel. On 23 November he was off Dunkirk with eighty-five warships escorting a convoy of over 450 sail, but bad weather then forced him to retreat. Seizing his chance, Tromp left his merchantmen behind and set sail with the fleet alone to seek a battle with the English. He well understood that only a decisive victory would clear away the English fleet and make it possible for Dutch trade to resume. Fortunately for him the English Council of State had no clearer strategic ideas than the States-General, its fleet was equally crippled by lack of pay and victuals, and twenty ships had been detached to the Mediterranean. Blake was lying in the Downs when the two fleets sighted one another on 29 November, but he was able to get to sea before Tromp could attack, and the two fleets met off Dungeness next day. Blake had only fifty-two ships, of which about twenty failed to come into action. The Dutch as usual concentrated on boarding, firing high and doing relatively little damage with their light guns, but though they only captured two English ships, the battle of Dungeness was an unequivocal Dutch victory. Blake retreated at first to the Downs, then further north to a less exposed anchorage off the Long Sand Head near the main channel up the Thames. Tromp, having cleared the Channel, returned to collect his convoy and sailed for the westward.[57] According to an old story, he now hoisted a broom to his masthead to signify that he had 'swept the Channel'. It cannot possibly be true: such vainglory would have been quite out of character, and the ordinary meaning of hoisting a broom to the masthead was that the ship was for sale.[58]

The Dutch underestimated their victory at Dungeness and were disappointed not to have achieved more, but in England the battle caused consternation. Blake's offer of resignation was declined, but his complaint 'that there was much baseness of spirit, not among the merchantmen only, but many of the State's ships' was taken seriously. Some captains were dismissed, Parliament voted increased pay for the Navy (to be found by paying off troops), and a new disciplinary code, the 'Laws of War and Ordinances of the Sea', was issued. It was largely concerned with treason, cowardice or neglect by officers, and for the first time the commander-in-chief now had the power to hold courts martial to punish them. Under the stress of defeat, the Rump was forced to concede to the Navy considerably more authority and money than before.[59]

On 30 January 1653 Tromp started for home from the Ile de Ré with seventy-five warships escorting a convoy of 150 merchantmen. Blake was waiting for him, his fleet spread across the narrow point of the mid-Channel between Portland and the Côtentin Peninsula. Blake's own squadron was at the northern and windward end of the line, and when Tromp appeared on 18 February near the English coast, he saw his opportunity and attacked Blake before the rest of the English fleet could beat up to windward. The Dutch fired high as they usually did, and later in the day the English squadrons began to close up. On the second day of fighting the Dutch began to suffer badly, but with great skill Tromp formed his ships into a rearguard covering the merchantmen ahead, and conducted a fighting retreat up Channel. Again Dutch morale and cohesion were poor, English frigates began to get among the convoy, and on the third day some of Tromp's ships were running out of ammunition. At nightfall on the 20th the Dutch were trapped against the French coast between Dieppe and Cape Gris Nez, their position apparently hopeless. Blake expected to complete his victory at dawn, but instead he found his prey escaped. Using the tide with great skill, Tromp had managed to extricate his fleet and convoy, rounding Cape Gris Nez in the night and getting away up the Flanders coast.[60]

For both sides the battle of Portland forced a painful reappraisal. The Dutch lost nine warships and twenty-four merchantmen sunk or taken, and Tromp forcefully pointed out to the States-General that for want of ammunition and discipline, among other necessities, the fleet had been within half an hour of complete catastrophe.[61] The English had yet again sent out no scouts and were again caught at the outset of the battle with their squadrons scattered. Thereafter their tactical illiteracy had made it impossible to take proper advantage of the weaknesses of the Dutch fleet. It is clear that some serious thought was now given to naval tactics, and probable that the principal thinker was Lieutenant-General George Monck, recently named as the third General at Sea to replace Popham, who had died in August 1651. Monck had been a pre-war officer of the English and Dutch armies, and was the first professional soldier to join the naval command. Portland was his first sea battle, and naval affairs were new to him, but he recognized chaos and indiscipline when he saw them. In the then state of naval tactics on either side, even the most gifted admiral had extremely limited opportunities of controlling his fleet in action. An extract from the journal of Captain Aert van Nes of Rotterdam, nicknamed 'Farmer Jim',[62] on the second day of the battle of Portland, illustrates the practicalities:

About noon the admiral signalled for me with a blue pendant at the mizzen peak ... but I couldn't get astern of him. Then the admiral hailed: 'Farmer Jim, Farmer Jim, run down to the merchantmen and tell them to escape E. by N. and E.N.E. . . . then go to Commodore de Ruyter and tell him to take station ahead of me.' I said 'Aye, aye, sir.' Then I went to de Ruyter and told him, from him I went after the merchantmen . . .'[63]

The English response was the 'Instructions for the better ordering of the Fleet in Fighting', issued just over a month later on 29 March 1653, which put the vice-admiral on the 'right wing', the rear-admiral on the 'left wing', and for the first time required each squadron 'to keep in a line with their chief'.[64] Ships out of station for any reason were to make every effort to get into the 'wake or grain' of the flagship (meaning the line prolonging her course astern or ahead). These orders are the first clear evidence of the line of battle, the classic fighting formation of sailing warships arranged in a single straight line, the better to deploy their gunfire.[65] It makes it likely that the English had now realized that their advantage lay in gunfire, and meant to fight in future on their own terms, not allowing the Dutch to come to close quarters and board. Unfortunately the orders are written in a military terminology which in the naval context is ambiguous, and leaves open the possibility that the Generals meant to approach the enemy in line ahead, but then bear up to attack in line abreast.[66]

After the battle of Portland there was a lull in the fighting while both sides reorganized. In May Tromp eluded the English fleet, sailed to the Norwegian coast to cover convoys coming home northabout, and having seem them safe into port went to look for the English in the Downs. They were not there, but on 2 June the two fleets finally met off the Gabbard shoal at the mouth of the Thames. Tromp had 104 ships, the English 105 under the command of Deane and Monck. According to their new orders, the English fleet formed in line ahead, and in the resulting gunnery duel the Dutch suffered heavily at a range at which their own, lighter guns were less effective. The following day the battle was resumed, the Dutch now having ammunition for only three hours' fighting. During this day Blake, who had been ill ashore, rejoined the English fleet with another thirteen ships, turning the Dutch defeat into a rout. Twenty Dutch ships were lost, and Tromp's flagship returned in a sinking condition. The English lost no ships, but Deane was killed. The disaster so often predicted by the Dutch admirals if their fleet was not better provided, above all with ammunition, had now occurred.[67] 'What use is it to equivocate, standing here before my sovereigns?' de With told the States-General. 'I can and must say that the English are now our masters and command the sea.'[68]

The English fleet now mounted a blockade of the Dutch coast, riding within sight of watchers on the steeple of the Groote Kerk in the Hague. Trade was at a standstill; the common people faced famine, the government feared an Orangist revolution. After a month English victualling collapsed under the strain of maintaining the fleet 100 miles from its bases and it returned to Solebay on the Suffolk coast. There Blake was sent sick ashore again, and the fleet returned under the command of Monck alone. On 16 July the English fleet was again on the Dutch coast, lying between the divided portions of the Dutch fleet.[69]

Tromp sailed again on the 25th, and with great skill succeeded in drawing Monck off the coast for long enough to unite his fleet. After two days of skirmishes, the two fleets fought off the Texel on 31 July. The English were again in line, and this time passed through the unformed Dutch fleet on opposite tacks four times in succession. By this time the Dutch had suffered badly and their fleet was disintegrating, though most of the captains did not yet know of the ultimate loss: Tromp was killed. De With managed to cover the retreat of the major part of the fleet, but there was no disguising the extent of the catastrophe.[70] 'The English fought with spirit and order, our people with neither,' reported the French minister at the Hague. 'The English have all the marks of honour: they have the prizes and the prisoners, and we have none.'[71]

Though the war continued to the end of the year, Dutch envoys were already in London seeking peace, and meeting a friendly reception. In spite of the devastation wrought on the Dutch economy by English naval activity, the English had as many reasons to welcome peace. Both sides had far outpaced their administrative and financial resources. English successes in home waters had been partly balanced by the Dutch elsewhere. In alliance with Denmark, the Dutch had closed the Baltic and cut off the supply of naval stores without which no English fleet could put to sea.[72] Indeed the English Navy could not have fought at all but for the punctual efficiency of Dutch merchants in fulfilling their existing hemp contracts after the outbreak of war, shipping the vital material in Polish ships to satisfy the Navigation Act.[73] In the Mediterranean the English squadron detached from the main fleet before the battle of Dungeness had been completely defeated by the Dutch, and a major fraction of England's overseas trade had been destroyed.[74]

Political considerations added to war-weariness on both sides. In the Hague the Republicans had an Orangist restoration to fear if the people suffered any further. In England there had been a political revolution during the war. Dissatisfaction with the Navy's performance after Dungeness and

Portland added to pressure on the Rump government, especially from religious radicals who regarded it as altogether too worldly and compromising. On 20 April 1653 a coup d'état led by the army's commander-in-chief General Cromwell expelled the Rump Parliament. The government was now dominated by extreme sects preaching a religious crusade against the Dutch as the first stage of the march on Rome. God, declared John Milton, was 'now finishing that great work, which by such visible signs, he hath made appear he hath in hand for the glory of his name, the felicity of these nations, and I believe for the blessed alteration of all Europe'.[75] The Fifth Monarchists in the naval administration greeted the new order with ecstasy, but the senior officers were more circumspect. Monck and Deane were associates of Cromwell's and made no difficulty, but the officer corps as a whole received the new regime with no more than guarded approval, and Blake, then sick on shore, said nothing.[76] Meanwhile the Navy's financial situation worsened steadily. In October there was a major mutiny among unpaid seamen at Chatham, who marched on London. There was fighting in the streets, Cromwell and Monck were threatened in person and Cromwell's Life Guard killed several seamen. The scene was unpleasantly reminiscent of the events of 1642 and 1648 when the seamen had previously intervened in national politics, in both cases in favour of Parliament and against arbitrary rule, and it underlined the instability and vulnerability of a military regime backed by a tiny minority of religious zealots, and wholly dependent on the Navy.[77] The negotiations with the Dutch aroused intense emotion among the sectaries, many of whom accused Cromwell of being the 'man of sin' for thinking of peace. But Cromwell was a complex personality, pulled several ways by the tensions within his government, and within himself. Cromwell the religious radical had expelled the Rump in April 1653. Eight months later it was Cromwell the social conservative who gave in to counsels of worldly prudence. To secure the future of the regime it was essential to find some basis of political stability, some form of government acceptable to the political nation, and only one had ever enjoyed the support of the majority of Englishmen. In the end Cromwell could not bring himself to take the crown, but the revolution of 12 December 1653 led shortly to his accepting the office of 'Lord Protector'.[78] England now returned to 'government by a single person', or, in plain Greek, monarchy. Thus the strains of the naval war it had started contributed to extinguishing the English Republic. The way was open for peace with the Dutch, but the sects never forgave Cromwell for betraying the New Jerusalem, and a part of him never forgave himself.

TWO

Cromwell's Hooves

Operations 1654–1659

The establishment of the Protectorate did nothing to solve the underlying dilemma of the military regime. Cromwell had 160 ships, eighteen foot and twelve horse regiments to maintain: too many to pay for by any politically acceptable means, but too few to sustain him in power by naked force. His first, carefully hand-picked, Parliament of August 1654 had to be dissolved when it demanded a reduction in the military establishment. The conquest of Scotland and Ireland called for more troops in garrison than it yielded extra tax revenue, making the overall situation worse. As before, the Navy remained politically suspect to the army, but militarily vital to its survival. By the spring of 1654 the three Generals at Sea (the plural form was first used officially in December 1653) were Colonel Robert Blake (only survivor of the original three), Cromwell's brother-in-law Major-General John Desborough, and the former vice-admiral William Penn, the first and only sea officer ever to be trusted with naval command by the army. George Monck went to command the army in Scotland in January 1654, Desborough (like Popham before him) concentrated on administration ashore, leaving Blake and Penn as active commanders-in-chief afloat.[1] The new vice-admiral was John Lawson, a sea officer of long experience, but more or less an Anabaptist in religion, and suspected of Leveller sympathies. In October 1654 Lawson and his captains in the Channel squadron received a petition from their ships' companies complaining of impressment and long-overdue pay. Resolving at a formal council of war that the petition was justified, they forwarded it to Cromwell. Undoubtedly they sympathized with their men's grievances (as well they might), but in the circumstances this was a political act not much short of a veiled threat. Cromwell dared not dismiss so popular an officer as Lawson (that was how half the fleet had been lost to the Royalists in 1648), but it was all the more urgent to find some employment for the Navy which would keep it out of politics.[2]

'God has not brought us hither where we are,' Cromwell informed his Parliament, 'but to consider the work that we may do in the world.'[3] For obvious political reasons, he wanted disaffected senior officers and unpaid soldiers and sailors to be found work in parts of the world well away from Whitehall. Once again, war seemed to be the only way out of the regime's political difficulties. The choice lay between France and Spain, and for much of 1654 Cromwell kept his options open. The unofficial war with France continued. Blake was sent to the Mediterranean with a squadron whose threatening presence forced the abandonment of a French naval expedition against Naples. English help was offered to the Huguenot (Protestant) rebels in France, then withdrawn when it looked as though it might risk a serious commitment. Instead Cromwell took up the Waldensians, a Protestant sect in the Alps who were persecuted by the Duke of Savoy. They were remote from any possibility of effective English help, and required only words.[4]

Once in the Mediterranean, Blake was drawn into war with Tunis. The three North African Regencies of Algiers, Tunis and Tripoli – the 'Barbary States' as they were known in Christian Europe – were nominally dependencies of the Ottoman Empire, but in practice semi-independent states which kept up a permanent state of war for motives very similar to Cromwell's. They too had soldiers (their Turkish garrisons) all too apt to intervene in politics if not distracted by a foreign war. The resulting system of warfare, the *corso*, was not piracy (though the term is still often used by Western writers) but public, declared war waged largely by private interests. Their political situation obliged the Regencies to be always at war against some of the Christian powers, but never against all, for the *corso* was primarily a system of slave-raiding, in which the profits came chiefly from ransoms and sales, and which therefore depended on commercial relations across the Mediterranean. In practice the Regencies made and observed treaties of peace with some scrupulousness, and were frequently enraged by breaches of faith on the Christian side.[5] Christian naval powers, obsessed with the misleading idea of 'Barbary piracy', had been mounting naval expeditions against the Regencies for centuries, but it was extremely difficult to make an impression on populous and strongly fortified cities on a dangerous lee shore. The English had already had some experience of this in the 1630s, but they still understood very little of the strategic, or indeed the moral, situation. In this case Tunis had gone to war because an English merchant ship had sold Tunisian passengers into slavery at Malta. This eminently justified retaliation, described by Blake as 'the barbarous carriage of these pirates', was his excuse for attacking them.[6]

Tunis itself was invulnerable, but in the bay of Porto Farina (El Bahira)

Blake found nine small warships sheltering under shore batteries, and on 4 April 1655 destroyed them all. The affair was, and usually still is, represented as a triumph against long odds, but a careful reading of the sources suggests that the defence was not formidable. The strategic profit of the victory was less than nothing, as the Dey of Tunis afterwards explained to Blake with sardonic amusement. The ships belonged not to him but to his overlord the Sultan, whose local power he was not sorry to diminish, and on whose goodwill the lucrative trade of the English Levant Company in Ottoman ports entirely depended. Having seriously damaged English interests, Blake was obliged to retreat with no concessions whatever. Visiting Algiers, the only port in the Western Mediterranean where he could buy victuals, he kept the peace and ransomed some English captives, paying well above the market price. Tunis and Tripoli continued to attack English merchant ships until in 1658 Captain John Stoakes, an officer of sense and moderation, was able to negotiate a peace.[7]

While Blake was in the Mediterranean, Cromwell and his Council of State had decided to go to war against Spain rather than France. On his way home he received orders for hostilities, and actually met a Spanish fleet off Cape St Vincent on 15 August 1655, but his cautious interpretation of ambiguous instructions deterred him from attacking, and he returned empty-handed at the beginning of October.[8] By the army especially, Spain was seen as a more Catholic country than France, therefore a more natural target for Englishmen, God's chosen instruments for chastising the Anti-Christ. It was also held indirectly responsible for the persecution of the Waldensians. 'What peace can we rejoice in,' General Fleetwood and his officers demanded, 'when the whoredom, murthers and witchcrafts of Jezebel are so many?'[9] Better still, as the renegade former Dominican friar Thomas Gage advised, 'the Spaniards cannot oppose much, being a lazy, sinful people, feeding like beasts upon their lusts, and upon the fat of the land, and never trained up to wars'.[10] Spain was well known to be fabulously wealthy, and to derive that wealth from silver and gold mined in the Americas. Nothing would be easier than to cut off that flow, and solve England's financial crisis at a stroke. The centrepiece of the plan was the 'Western Design', a major amphibious expedition to the Spanish Caribbean. With 3,600 regular troops, plus the support of the English colonists of Barbados and New England who, Cromwell believed, would flock to so agreeable a climate, this would suffice to take and hold Santo Domingo, or Puerto Rico, or Havana, or Cartagena, or perhaps all four of them.[11]

This delightful strategic prospect did not distract Cromwell from the political requirements of the operation. Though the army officers seem to have been good, the troops were made up by drafting from the regiments of the New Model Army those who would least be missed, on military or political grounds. The naval command was given to Penn, but he was subordinated to General Robert Venables, and both of them were limited by the authority of two 'civil commissioners',[12] who secretly reported to Cromwell on their activities and loyalty. None of this made for mutual trust, or simplified the command structure of the expedition, and experience was to prove that in moments of crisis Venables was very willing to defer to other authorities – not least his wife, who accompanied him. The administrative preparations were entrusted to a committee led by General Desborough, which left both services scantily equipped and victualled.[13]

The expedition approached the coast of Hispaniola in April 1655, alarmed to discover it 'rocky, and a great surf of the sea against it in so much that in many places we saw the beatings of the water appear afar off like the smoke of ordnance, the wind being but indifferent'.[14] On the 14th they got ashore at a place thirty miles from their target, the city of Santo Domingo. The country was almost waterless, and the soldiers had no waterbottles. Approaching the city four days later through thick bush, they were routed in an ambush by a few hundred local cowboys (*vaqueros*). Some of the officers died gallantly, and the 'sea regiment' of sailors preserved their discipline, but otherwise the affair was a disgraceful fiasco. Penn's ships had meanwhile bombarded the city, but its seaward defences were strong, and the ships kept a respectful distance. Having re-embarked the survivors of the army, Penn urged another attempt, but the army officers, Venables in particular, were too dejected to try.[15]

In one afternoon the invincible reputation of the New Model Army had been thrown away. The commanders dared not return to Cromwell without something to show for their labours, so they resolved to attack Jamaica. The island was apparently valueless, but for that reason the Spaniards had hardly settled or fortified it. On 11 May the English landed, and this time Penn personally took charge of the operation, 'for after the miscarriage at Hispaniola,' one of the civil commissioners reported to Cromwell, 'I have privately heard him say, "he would not trust the army with the attempt, if he could come near with his ships;" and indeed did, in the *Martin* galley, run in till she was aground before their breast-work in the bottom of the harbour . . .'[16] The Spaniards surrendered in six days, but this was only the beginning of the English difficulties. Jamaica was ideal for guerilla warfare and easily accessible from Cuba. It was almost uncultivated, and the troops were soon sickly and starving. To relieve the shortage of victuals Penn (and

Venables) took the bulk of the fleet home, arriving on 31 August 1655, when Cromwell put both commanders in the Tower.[17]

For some time it was doubtful if the English would be able to hold on to their new possession in the face of disease, starvation and Spanish attack. In the late 1650s, however, the infant colony discovered a means of livelihood and defence: buccaneering. The Spanish government still held to its original colonial policy, according to which all seas and lands west of the Azores and south of the Tropic of Capricorn were Spanish property in which the very presence of any foreigner (indeed, strictly any non-Castilian) was punishable by death. All Spain's treaties with foreign powers explicitly excepted this area, so that there was literally 'no peace beyond the line', even with countries with which Spain was at peace in Europe. Though there were now permanent French, Dutch and English settlements in the Caribbean, no trading vessel, however peaceful her intentions, could safely enter these waters without being prepared to defend herself. Yet there was much trade to be done, particularly with Spanish colonies which were very poorly served by the official shipping system. This situation generated a mixture of trade, smuggling and low-level hostilities, and gave ample opportunities to pirates and others who hoped to make their fortunes without the necessity of hard work. The buccaneers were originally a mixed collection of non-Spaniards who inhabited unsettled parts of the islands, living by hunting wild cattle. By the 1640s many had settled on the island of Tortuga, off the north coast of Hispaniola, and taken up a more active and lucrative life of raiding Spanish towns. Some buccaneers were also pirates, but the two trades were distinct, for most buccaneers were not seamen, and used ships chiefly as transport in their essentially amphibious warfare. Both groups depended on access to ports where they could sell booty and buy supplies, and the new English settlement of Port Royal, Jamaica, rapidly developed as their leading base in the Caribbean. Successive governors of Jamaica were very willing to legitimize their activities by granting privateering commissions against Spain. Their attacks were the island's best form of defence, and almost its only livelihood. The few warships of the State's Navy which remained on the station after Penn went home took a leading part in the same business. Its most notable exponent was Captain Christopher Myngs of the *Marston Moor*, who in the spring of 1659 returned from a raid along the 'Spanish Main' (the north coast of South America; modern Venezuela and Colombia) with booty worth £2–300,000, most of which was never declared to Governor D'Oyley's improvised prize court, but disappeared into the pockets of Myngs and his men.[18]

In England, meanwhile, Cromwell was faced with a war with Spain which had yielded nothing but shame and expense. Some of his illusions were gone, but he needed money more than ever, and still believed that 'six nimble frigates' would suffice to blockade the coast of Spain and cut off the flow of bullion.[19] Blake, the expert on that coast, and the only senior commander left in the Navy whom Cromwell could trust, was seriously ill. Lawson was appointed as his second-in-command, but however much Cromwell wanted him out of home waters, he was clearly alarmed that he might succeed to the command. Blake was therefore provided with a colleague, Colonel Edward Mountague, a reliable young Cromwellian who had never been to sea. His job was to remind Lawson and the sea officers (perhaps Blake too) who was master. Some of the captains expressed moral scruples about a war of unprovoked aggression, and about taking their unpaid men to sea again, leaving their families to starve. For Cromwell and Mountague, this was plain evidence of subversion, no doubt linked to a Leveller conspiracy which they had just suppressed in the army. 'It is not for us to mind state affairs,' Mountague warned the seamen bluntly, 'but to stop the foreigner from fooling us.'[20] Lawson and three captains, however, persisted in thinking for themselves, and resigned rather than serve in such circumstances.[21]

Blake and Mountague sailed without them, arriving off Cadiz on 20 April 1656. Briefly considering the possibility of taking Gibraltar (impracticable for want of troops), they were able to establish a base at Lisbon. Blake now settled to the exhausting and dispiriting business of blockade which he knew so well. 'The Spaniard uses his buckler more than his sword,' commented Philip Meadowe, English agent in Portugal, in July 1656. 'In the Dutch war we were sure of an enemy that would fight, besides good prizes to help to pay charges; but the Spaniard will neither fight nor trade.'[22] Occasionally the monotony was varied by Spanish galleys which looked out of Cadiz, 'but do no damage,' Captain Thomas Pointer wrote,

> unless it be in rousing us to expend a great deal of powder to no purpose, they always keeping without the range of our guns and English gunners are so unskillful – that they have spent in two days time above 3 or 400 shot – there has been no damage done on either side, but only expense of powder and shot.[23]

Then in September, while Blake and Mountague were at Lisbon, the news arrived that Captain Richard Stayner of the *Speaker*, left on watch off Cadiz with eight ships, had intercepted an inward-bound Spanish silver convoy. Two ships were taken, and three burned or sunk. Much of the treasure went down with them and the richest ship escaped, but an estimated £200,000 in silver was taken. When it heard the news, a euphoric Parliament believed the prizes might be worth £600,000 or even a million, sufficient to pay for the war. In fact only £45,000 ever reached England. The rest stuck to the fingers of Stayner's unpaid officers and men (not excepting Stayner's own). After this triumph Mountague came home with the bulk of the ships, leaving Blake at Lisbon. The ships needed a refit, and a Leveller-Fifth Monarchist rising (followed by the imprisonment of Lawson among others) persuaded Cromwell that he needed a strong force in the Channel. Mountague was also able to get essential supplies sent to Blake, who had repeatedly requested them in vain.[24]

Stayner's lucky success helped to confirm Cromwell in the idea that the naval war could still be made to pay. Unaware how difficult it is to intercept anything in the vastness of the sea; unaware that most of Spain's foreign trade was now in foreign ships, which 'we cannot hinder unless we should fight with all the world',[25] as Mountague warned; still dreaming of Gibraltar as a base from which to prey on Spanish wealth, Cromwell determined that Blake should keep up his blockade. As usual he was expected to do it with completely inadequate support. On 11 March 1657, after a storm off Cadiz, he set out his situation:

> some of the ships having lost their masts, boltsprits, and others are so broken and shattered in their works within, that they have spoiled a great quantity of their bread and powder, and are forced to keep their pumps continually going: And the frigates that came out last are so ill provided in twine, canvas and such like necessaries, that presently after their arrival they resorted to us for supplies, which we must buy at Lisbon or elsewhere as we can . . . I have acquainted you often with my thoughts of keeping out these ships so long, whereby they are not only rendered in a great measure unserviceable but withal exposed to desperate hazards, wherein though the Lord hath most wonderfully and mercifully preserved us hitherto, I know no rule to tempt Him . . .[26]

'We are all together and behold one another's face with comfort,' he assured Mountague, but in truth his situation was precarious, and he himself was dying.[27]

Nine days after writing those words, Blake met the merchantman *Catherine* of London whose master, David Young, had lost a hand fighting as a lieutenant in the Navy during the Dutch War. Young had left his voyage to bring Blake news of a Spanish convoy he had sighted in the Atlantic. Blake's captains wanted to send some frigates to intercept it, but there were no victuals for a cruise, and he refused to divide the force in case the main Spanish fleet should come out of Cadiz. Then in early April supplies at last arrived from England, and at the same time they received intelligence that the Spanish fleet was disabled. On 12 April Blake sailed with his whole squadron of twenty-three ships for Santa Cruz in the Canaries, where the Spanish ships had taken refuge. By now he was exhausted and in constant pain. His relations with his captains, whose desire for prize money he continually thwarted, were difficult, and they had trouble persuading him to allow them to attack. The seventeen Spanish ships (all but two armed merchantmen) were moored close inshore under the guns of the shore defences. On the morning of 20 April, Stayner led the attack with twelve ships, while Blake with the remainder provided covering fire. Afterwards Stayner reported:

> I knowing it not a time to neglect the business, I only gave them this verbal order, to follow me in a line . . . I stood upon the forecastle of our ship to seek a good berth for the better doing of our work. I perceived I might get in between the admiral and vice-admiral to our great advantage, which I did . . .

By coming close enough to the Spanish ships to shield them from the fortifications Stayner's squadron was helped to a complete victory: twelve ships burned and five towed off as prizes, which Blake with difficulty forced their captors to destroy. Stayner was the last away, and the *Speaker* suffered badly in her retreat:

> We had holes between wind and water four or five foot long and three or five foot broad, that we had no shift to keep her from sinking but by nailing hides over the holes, and nail butt staves along the sides of the hides, for we had eight or nine foot water in the ship that our pumps and bailing would hardly keep her free.

They had barely got out of range at dusk when all her masts fell overboard.[28]

Blake returned to blockade duty off Cadiz, until at the end of June 1657 he received orders to bring the bulk of the fleet home. On 7 August he died as his flagship entered Plymouth Sound. He was given a state funeral in Westminster Abbey, and left a reputation as high among his enemies as his friends. 'He was the first man who brought the ships to contemn castles on shore', wrote the Royalist Earl of Clarendon,

> which had been thought ever very formidable, and were discovered by him only to make a noise and to fright those who could rarely be hurt by them. He was the first that infused that proportion of courage into the seamen, by making them see by experience what mighty things they could do if they were resolved, and taught them to fight in fire as well as

upon water; and though he hath been very well imitated and followed, he was the first that drew the copy of naval courage and bold and resolute achievement.[29]

Much of this is true. Blake was the first modern English commander to lead his fleet in a series of close-fought and bloody battles. His courage, endurance and self-sacrifice inspired his own men and were remembered by later generations. Even Nelson reckoned himself inferior to Blake,[30] but this is hardly sustainable. Blake never learned much about naval tactics, during the Dutch War he was repeatedly surprised with his fleet divided, and his strategic judgement was fallible. His loyalty to the military regime of which he was a representative (or at least his silence in the face of its abuses) is perhaps admirable, though it betrayed all the ideals for which he had fought in the first Civil War – but the conduct of Lawson, who stood up to Cromwell on his men's behalf and refused to serve against his conscience, offers an alternative concept of devotion to duty.

The victory of Santa Cruz was not as unlucky for English interests as Porto Farina had been, but its value was political rather than strategic. No money had been gained for the English war-effort, and the Spanish crown directly profited, as the bullion landed before the battle included the large proportion customarily shipped in secret to avoid paying duty.[31] By the summer of 1657 Cromwell's war strategy against Spain was financially and politically bankrupt. The generals had assumed that Spain was vulnerable and incapable of striking back, and they discovered that the truth was almost the opposite. Though there was little the regular Spanish navy could do, the ports of Spanish Flanders – above all, Dunkirk and Ostend – had a long tradition of expertise in private warfare. Their privateers inflicted heavy losses on English merchant shipping. Having gained 1,200 to 1,700 prizes from the Dutch during the previous war, the English merchant fleet now lost 1,500 to 2,000 ships to Spain (mainly Flanders), many of which were sold straight back to the Dutch. Spanish trade was kept up in Dutch ships, and Cromwell could do nothing about it, for he needed Dutch friendship, and indeed Dutch shipping. He was now in a situation not dissimilar to Charles I's in the 1630s: he had built a large and expensive fleet to deter foreign powers, but in its absence English trade was exposed to heavy losses, which further weakened his political support.[32]

In strategic terms, a largely unsuccessful Spanish war pushed Cromwell towards France, whose long-term campaign against Spain he was in effect supporting. An alliance in March 1657 committed them to joint action in

Flanders. English troops fought alongside the French against the Spanish army at the battle of the Dunes on 4 June 1658 (going some way to redeem the reputation they had lost at Santo Domingo), after which Spain surrendered Dunkirk to the allies. This was the English share of the spoils, while the French helped themselves to the whole of Artois. England eliminated the greatest Spanish privateering base, but most of the ships moved down the coast to Ostend. France was clearly the main gainer from the joint enterprise. The English occupation of Dunkirk lasted three years; the French are in Artois yet.[33]

While the Spanish war continued, Cromwell's government slid into ever deeper financial and political trouble. In May 1657 his supporters (Mountague prominent among them), hoping it would open the way to a stable regime, strongly pressed him to accept the crown in name as well as in fact. The political Cromwell could see the force of their argument, but the religious Cromwell was obsessed with the Hispaniola disaster as a judgement of God on his iniquity, and dared not risk further wrath. A large part of the army, moreover, including many of his closest colleagues, were already disgusted by the conservative policy of the Protectorate, and threatened open revolt against King Oliver. At the last moment Cromwell drew back, and when he died on 3 September 1658 the future of the regime was as unsettled as ever. His son Richard, an inoffensive man with none of his father's personal authority, succeeded as Lord Protector. Mountague was one of his strongest supporters, but the army held aloof from the new government. Once again the two services were politically at odds.[34]

Meanwhile England had become embroiled in the war between Sweden and Denmark. It was not in English interests that either should control the Baltic completely, as the Dutch-Danish alliance had done during the Dutch War, and there was satisfaction when Charles X (Karl Gustav) of Sweden invaded Denmark from Germany, marched his army across the frozen Great Belt to Zealand[35] in February 1658, and imposed a peace (the Treaty of Roskilde) by which he gained the province of Scania. This was acceptable to both Dutch and English, for with the north shore of the Sound (the main channel into the Baltic) transferred to Swedish hands, it would be difficult for either Sweden or Denmark to shut foreigners out of the Baltic. Charles X did not stop there, however. By October 1658 his army was besieging Copenhagen and within reach of extinguishing Danish independence, when the Dutch sent a fleet to succour their ally. The Dutch-Danish fleet now cut off Charles X from Sweden, and threatened to transform his triumph into disaster. To balance the scales, an English squadron was sent into the Skagerrak under

Vice-Admiral William Goodson, which was very soon driven home by December weather, while Sir George Ayscue (unemployed since 1652) was lent to the Swedish navy. In April 1659 Mountague and the main English fleet arrived in the Sound, where he faced a delicate situation with a high risk of open war against the Dutch-Danish fleet. This was not his only problem: he had barely arrived when he learned that the army had taken advantage of the Navy's absence to overthrow the Protectorate.[36]

The political clock was now turned back to 1649, with the Rump Parliament recalled, the English Republic re-established, militants and sectaries once more advancing the 'Good Old Cause'. The new government appointed its friend Lawson to command the fleet at home, and sent Republican commissioners to Denmark in an attempt to keep control over their Cromwellian admiral. Mountague's diplomatic task was somewhat eased by an agreement between the Dutch and English governments to impose joint mediation on the warring powers (on the basis of the Treaty of Roskilde), which lessened the tension between the fleets on the spot. Politically, he maintained a studied loyalty to the Republican regime, and civil relations with its commissioners, though neither side trusted the other in the slightest, and he was already in secret contact with the exiled Royalists. In July there was a Royalist rising in England, but Mountague took no apparent notice and it was soon suppressed. In September he returned to England with his whole fleet, ostensibly because his victuals had almost run out. This was manifestly true, and the government was unable to back its acute suspicion of his political motives, but it was very happy to allow him to retire to the country, leaving the reliable Republican Lawson in command.[37]

The internal manoeuvres of 1659 did nothing to resolve England's profound political and financial crisis. One month after Mountague's return the army staged another coup d'état, expelling the Rump Parliament and installing a Committee of Safety of army officers (also diverting the Navy's inadequate income to pay their troops). This was too much for most adherents of the old Parliamentary cause. However little support the revived Rump retained among the political nation at large, it was at least the fragment of a freely elected Parliament and the last symbol of the legitimate grievances which had fuelled the first Civil War. Naked military rule was unacceptable. Both General Monck commanding the army in Scotland, and Lawson commanding the fleet, declared in favour of the Rump. So did the garrison of Portsmouth, which gave Lawson a secure base. For the moment Monck was too far away to do anything, but on 13 December Lawson entered the Thames with twenty-two ships, imposing a blockade on London. With the Navy's hand on its throat, the military regime collapsed, and on 26 December the Rump was restored. England was now ruled by a naval rather than a military republic, with Lawson as its Cromwell, but the country was deeply weary of all forms of Republicanism, extremism and arbitrary power.[38]

On 1 January 1660 General Monck with his army crossed the Tweed into England and began to march south. Facing him, the troops of General Lambert, leader of the recent military regime, dispersed rather than fight their old comrades. When Monck reached London in early February his political intentions were still cloaked, and Lawson was shocked when he declared for the return of the 'Excluded Members' – meaning all the survivors of the original 1640 Long Parliament who had been expelled because they would not consent to Republican or military rule. This restored Parliament appointed Mountague as General of the fleet, over Lawson's head. The moment was highly delicate. It was becoming gradually clear that Monck, Mountague and the Parliament were sliding towards restoring the monarchy as the only possible form of legitimate and stable government. Lawson was a convinced Republican and the officers of the fleet were as loyal to Republican and military rule as repeated purges could make them. The chances of avoiding civil war between army and Navy turned largely on Lawson's attitude. On 16 March the Long Parliament dissolved itself and issued writs for a new Parliament, freely elected. Perhaps it was at this moment that Lawson realized that the Republican cause was lost, and that futile struggle and bloodshed to restore it could not be justified. He had always been liked even amongst his opponents as a good-natured man and a plain dealer; now he reluctantly concluded that his duty (and also his own interest) was to work for stable government under the new order. The Navy was bankrupt, the men unpaid and almost starving; only a government enjoying popular support could hope to repair the situation. With great tact, Mountague enlisted Lawson's co-operation in yet another purge, discreetly removing the more extreme captains – meaning those with views close to Lawson's own. When the fleet sailed in May to bring Charles II from Holland, hastily cutting out the Republican harp from their jacks and replacing the State's arms on the sterns with the king's, the officers accepted the monarchy, and the men welcomed it with enthusiasm.[39] Nine years before Charles had escaped across the Channel in disguise aboard the smack *Surprise* of Shoreham, to apparently hopeless exile. Now he returned in triumph aboard the *Naseby* (hastily renamed the *Royal Charles*) at the head of a great fleet, to ride in triumph through the streets of London to the cheers of his reclaimed subjects.

In eleven years of violence and instability, the Commonwealth and Protectorate had never discovered a system of government, or taxation, which was acceptable to the political nation. In political terms the Republican experiment was an unqualified failure. But this political disaster was also the origin of England's naval greatness. These were the regimes which built the same tonnage of warships in four years (1651–5) as the monarchy had built in over half a century between 1588 and 1642. It was the fear and insecurity of a military dictatorship surrounded by enemies real and imagined which made England a first-class naval power. The soldiers could not do without the Navy, and yet they could not do with it. Repeatedly the fleet opposed the army in politics. Twice, in 1648 and 1659, it was instrumental in blocking the army's ambitions. Finally in 1660 its refusal to fight for the Republic opened the way for Charles II's restoration. It was a highly political and politicized service, sharing to the full the divisions of the age, often purged but never trusted by its military masters. Yet it was the Navy, not the army, which made Cromwell feared throughout Europe.[40] 'His greatness at home,' wrote the Royalist Clarendon,

> was but a shadow of the glory he had abroad. It was hard to discover which feared him most, France, Spain, or the Low Countries, where his friendship was current at the value he put upon it. And as they did all sacrifice their honour and interest to his pleasure, so there is nothing he could have demanded that either of them would have denied him.[41]

All this naval power was exercised to defend the regime, meaning the army. It was not applied on behalf of the people of England, Scotland and Ireland, crushed beneath Cromwell's hooves on the figurehead of the *Naseby*, and crushed by the taxes which paid for her. It was not applied on behalf of merchants and shipowners, whose trade was ravaged by Flemish privateers while the fleet was far away. In the eyes of its masters (or at least of some of them, some of the time), it was not applied for any worldly end, but for the building of the New Jerusalem and 'the ruining and the utter fall of Romish Babylon'.[42] All the purposes for which the new Navy had been created were hateful to the restored Stuarts who inherited it, and to most of their people. But the lesson they drew from the naval record of the Commonwealth and Protectorate was its right effect, not its wrong purpose. More than 200 years after the collapse of England's last empire – 200 years of precarious survival on the margins of Europe, 200 years of humiliation at the hands of the new great powers – the Navy had made England feared once more. This lesson the English did not forget.

THREE

A Looking-Glass of Calamity

Administration 1649–1660

B y the time of the outbreak of the first Civil War in 1642, English naval administration had had a settled structure for a century. There were two basic elements, the Admiralty and the Navy Board. The Admiralty – usually represented by the person of the Lord Admiral of England – was responsible, in consultation with the king and his ministers, for overall naval policy, command and discipline. The Lord Admiral himself commanded the main fleet, or named other admirals as his deputies. Under his orders, a small committee of permanent officials known as the Navy Board was responsible for building and maintaining ships, including running the dockyards and supplying naval stores. The Treasurer of the Navy, nominally a member of the Navy Board but practically independent, controlled the finances of the Navy. The essential task of supplying food and drink was the responsibility of one or more Victuallers, major contractors who undertook the whole business of supply for a fixed price per man per month. Finally, guns and ammunition and warlike stores were supplied (to the army as well as the Navy) by the Ordnance Board, an independent organization not subordinate to the Admiralty.

Parliament took over the Navy and its administration during the Civil War, appointing its own Lord Admiral or commander-in-chief to command at sea, but reserving the control of administration ashore to its own Admiralty Committee. The Navy Board became the Navy Commission with the addition of some members of Parliament (removed in 1643), and a Parliamentary Navy Committee was responsible for issuing money to the Treasurer. The basic structure of pre-war administration remained unchanged in principle, but it was substantially modified in practice by the tendency of the different committees and commissions to overlap in membership and function, so that a closely knit group of administrators effectively controlled everything. In the pre-war system, the supervision of the administrators by the Lord Admiral, and their own internal rivalries, had provided means of detecting malpractice which were now removed. The circumstances of the Civil War required a new Navy to be improvised, largely from chartered merchant ships. The Parliamentary naval administrators, who were nearly all shipowners or suppliers of naval stores themselves, were happily placed to provide what was needed.[1]

When the Independents seized power in the military coup d'état of December 1648, they appointed a 'Committee of Merchants', otherwise known as the 'Regulators', to eject their opponents from naval office. Both names were appropriate, for the Regulators were largely drawn from the 'New Merchants'.[2] The men who had fought the Civil War were predominantly Presbyterian in faith and moderate in politics, neither of which was now acceptable. The sea-going fleet, the Navy Commission and the Ordnance Board were purged of about two-thirds of their members. So was Trinity House, the chartered corporation which controlled pilotage on the Thames and acted as a point of reference on everything to do with merchant shipping. The subsequent political revolutions of 1653 and 1658 to 1659 did not attempt such wholesale changes to the working administration, which retained much of the personnel and style of the Commonwealth throughout the years of the Protectorate.

In March 1649 the Council of State appointed an Admiralty Committee whose leading figure was the veteran radical and Treasurer of the Navy Sir Henry Vane, long distinguished by his dominant personality – able, tireless and totally unscrupulous. The correspondence of Robert Coytmore, the committee's secretary, shows that he regarded Vane alone as its quorum, though the Generals at Sea were also members, and one of the three was usually left in London to speak for the fleet. The Parliamentary Navy Committee was led by the MPs Miles Corbett, Valentine Walton, Gregory Clement, and a group of generals including Cromwell and his son-in-law Henry Ireton; by 1650 Colonel George Thomson was its leading member. Vane and Walton amongst others were members of both committees. There was further overlap with the membership of the Navy Commission and the Regulators (which themselves shared offices and staff), and they in turn with the Prize Commission and Trinity House.[3]

This complex structure accurately reflected the regime's political priorities, and its political structure. As a system for managing the Navy, especially at the level of higher direction, it was less satisfactory, and the coming of the Dutch War soon revealed its shortcomings. Throughout the administration, men of proven ability and experience had been replaced by others chosen for religious and political loyalty. Robert Coytmore, for example, was a good Fifth Monarchist, but conceited, tactless and incompetent. Edward Popham complained that 'it is not unusual for Mr Coytmore to mistake winter for summer'. Though the Generals reported directly to the full Council of State, and the Admiralty Committee had no formal authority over them, they soon discovered that Coytmore was opening their private correspondence to each other. It seems very likely that he was informing his patron Vane, who never cared to be involved in any administration of which he was not entire master.[4] Herein lay one of the main obstacles to change, for Vane's was the loudest voice urging that large, amorphous and overlapping committees should be replaced by smaller and more effective bodies – meaning, as his enemies grasped at once, bodies more effectively controlled by Vane. As the Dutch War approached, Vane, as one of its leading opponents, began to lose ground. In January 1651 he was succeeded as Treasurer of the Navy (with generous compensation) by his deputy and rival Richard Hutchinson (Vane had nominated his own brother). When the war broke out in the summer of 1652 he and Walton walked out of the Admiralty, now dominated by their enemies. It was not the first time he had done this in the hope of obstructing a policy he disapproved of, and his absence did indeed weaken an already weak administration. The Council of State ordered its Foreign Affairs Committee to consider 'the state of the whole fleet' to relieve the Admiralty – but thirteen of its nineteen members were already members of the Admiralty Committee. The effect was to add yet another overlapping and ill-defined jurisdiction to the naval administration. Large amounts of very detailed work came to the Council of State itself for want of an efficient Admiralty organization.[5]

The real work of the war was done by the fleet at sea and the Navy Commission ashore, provided with too little money by the Rump Parliament, and too little direction by a government obsessed with political infighting and religious purity. By the summer of 1652 the Navy Commissioners were openly sarcastic about the incompetence of their superiors. 'We are glad to hear the whole business of the navy is under consideration,' they wrote to the Council of State, 'as hoping it will be for the better and not for the worse, wherein good advice would be taken and nothing done rashly which your Honours' wisdoms may prevent.'[6] The disaster of Dungeness caused an abrupt clearing of heads, and desks. Parliament removed the authority of its Navy Committee and voted money directly to the Navy Commission. A new Admiralty Commission of six (plus the three Generals) was created, headed by Vane, who threw all his unequalled energies into restoring the situation. Though the Admiralty Committee (and Coytmore, its secretary) still existed, power had passed elsewhere. 'Those in power,' George Thomson (one of the new Commissioners) recalled, were told that neither the Parliament nor Council . . . could manage the war . . . But if they committed that affair to a small number of three or four that understood their work, and had sufficient power given them they might yet recover what honour was lost . . . The Commissioners sat daily both early and late, and all persons had free and easy access to them that had any public business with them. They were private in their debates, not suffering any to be present at them, so that their counsels were kept secret. Their usual sitting was at White Hall, but if they thought their presence more needful at any other place, they hastened thither. They had daily an account in what readiness ships were in, and how men entrusted in that affair discharged their duties.[7]

Ruthless efficiency and secrecy were typical of all Vane's work. The Navy soon began to feel the benefit; but only for five months.[8]

Vane was an old enemy of Cromwell, and a foe to all sorts of dictatorship, except his own. On Cromwell's coup of 20 April 1653 Vane walked out again. The Fifth Monarchists (including Robert Blackborne, secretary of the Admiralty Commission, and John Poortmans, secretary of the Generals at Sea) rejoiced, but the Navy Commission and the Generals at Sea at once felt the removal of Vane's hand from the tiller. Thomas Smith, one of the Navy Commissioners, wrote privately to Vice-Admiral Penn asking for news of the whereabouts of the fleet, of which they had no official information. Richard Deane at Spithead complained that he too had heard nothing from the Admiralty,

which makes me question whether in the great revolution there be anybody takes care of us and of the naval affairs. I praise my God my trust is in Him and am not much solicitous though the world be turned upside down, only I say to you as also to our foreman that is gone into the country that you being the men who were the chief outward instruments in engaging me in this business and promising me what you did as to assistance and mutual confidence, you will not neglect me at such a time as this.[9]

In July the Admiralty was reinforced, almost entirely with soldiers. Its leading figure was now Cromwell's brother-in-law Major-General Desborough. By this time Cromwell himself was moving away from millenarian visions towards a more worldly and conservative concern for a bankrupt war-effort. With his second coup of December 1653 the evolution was complete. Another Admiralty Commission took office, composed entirely of soldiers without naval experience. Desborough and Penn were added to the Generals at Sea, whose commission for the first time allowed them to act as individual commanders-in-chief. The Lord Protector, as he presently became, had secured his control over the Navy, but once again a political revolution had removed everyone of experience from its higher direction.[10]

A series of Admiralty Commissions succeeded during the Protectorate, but their membership remained largely stable. The senior army officers were mostly busy members of the Council of State and not often present. Blake, Penn and Mountague were usually at sea, and Monck was in Scotland. Business was conducted by a group of five men (Colonel John Clerke, Major-General Thomas Kelsey, Lieutenant-Colonel Edward Salmon, Robert Beake and the New Englander Edward Hopkins) who by 1656 were all salaried – in effect, civil servants. The Admiralty was now a relatively unimportant administrative committee; it had acquired experience and stability at the price of losing political influence. There was nobody who carried weight in the Protectorate to argue for the Navy's needs, except Mountague when he was ashore. What money was available in a period of growing financial difficulty tended to be diverted to the army. By the spring of 1659 the Admiralty Commissioners were exhausted by the struggle and seeking to resign, when the fall of the Protectorate threw them out of office anyway. Sir Henry Vane returned to power with the Rump Parliament, but he seems to have been too busy dominating the Council of State to attend the Admiralty. In October the army seized power, expelling Vane and half the Admiralty Commission. By the end of the year it had virtually ceased to function, as had the Navy Commission, reduced by successive purges to a single London member. A new Admiralty was named by the restored Rump in February 1660, naturally reflecting its Republican principles, but its membership was modified to reflect first the return of the Excluded Members and then the new Parliament, and by the summer it, like the fleet at sea, was ready to welcome Charles II with more or less enthusiasm. No money at all had reached the Navy since the previous October, and even the most dedicated Republicans, of whom there were still many in the naval administration, found it hard to struggle for a regime which gave them nothing in return.[11]

Money was the rock on which the English Republic was first founded, and on which in the end it was wrecked. It was the capacity to impose taxes at ten times the pre-war level or more which allowed Parliament to sustain its war-effort during the Civil War. The most important of them were the Customs, the Excise and the Assessment. Only the Customs were an ancient revenue, traditionally assigned to the Navy. The Excise, imposed in 1643, was an indirect tax on the production of various items of common consumption, including food – the first national tax explicitly intended to fall on poor as well as rich. The Assessment, perfected in 1645 as the Monthly Assessment, was a land-tax developed from the pre-war Ship Money. These taxes sufficed to win the Civil War, but they were not sufficient to pay for the New Model Army. By the end of 1646 the army was owed over a million pounds in back pay, and Parliament was refusing to vote further taxes for it. By late 1648, when the army seized power, its debt had reached three millions. Royalist privateers, aided by the work of the Regulators in removing experienced officials, reduced the Customs receipts for the early months of 1649 to almost nothing. The Rump Parliament therefore increased taxes again: the Monthly Assessment rose to £90,000, eighteen times the level of taxation of a pre-war 'subsidy'. Some money was found from confiscating Royalist estates, and plans were made (though never carried out) to fell the royal forests, but nearly all the Commonwealth's income came from current taxes. It was never enough, and the Navy seldom had priority. In May 1650 Cromwell diverted £10,000 from the Navy to pay his troops and meet the threat of Leveller subversion, thus damaging naval credit. The same thing happened in the summer with the Irish expedition; by September Coytmore was writing 'Sea affairs go but slowly here, like the Egyptian chariots in the Red Sea'.[12] Nevertheless the financial situation had been stabilized by 1651. Some of the more unreliable regiments of the army were disbanded, and sales of cathedral lands paid off enough debt to stiffen the government's credit. In 1652 it proposed to spend £535,000 on the Navy (not including £237,000 in debts), and £1,328,579 (a 30 per cent reduction) on the army; on this basis the Commonwealth was more or less solvent, in that its credit sufficed to bridge the gap between income and expenditure, and it could put to sea a main fleet or 'Summer Guard' of just over 10,000 men, plus convoy escorts.[13]

All this was wrecked by the outbreak of the Dutch War in May 1652, without financial or administrative preparation. Parliament voted no additional money for the Navy until the defeat of Dungeness at the end of November, and never came near to matching naval expenditure and debt. By April 1653 the Navy Commissioners estimated that they would need £605,000 just for the current business of the next quarter. On 1 September they wrote to the Admiralty:

About two months since we sent an estimate to you of the charge of this summer's fleet wherein it appeared there would be £1,115,000 os. od. requisite to be paid between this and the last of December, without including the second rate ships intended to be built, or the winter guard. Since which time there hath been another engagement at sea whereby much prejudice hath been done to the hulls and tackle of the ships, which have both drained the stores and added much charge. Notwithstanding all this, finding no considerable provision made for money we conceived it necessary for us to lay before your Honours the daily clamours for want thereof, the vast and unreasonable charges the State is at in the price of commodities, besides the disreputation the State lies under, in having our contract broken, and credits laid low, whereas if your debts were paid and money were seasonably provided we might save you twenty in the hundred in price of commodity, and it is not imaginable what the advantage is in payment of mariners at their first coming into harbour, for whereas every 1000 men in your own ships that have been nine months out at sea £10,800 would pay them off, if they lie but one month unpaid it will cost the State £13,000 and if in merchants' ships about £14,000, which is £300 interest for £100 a year.[14]

Against all these charges Parliament had assigned only £600,000. In November 1653 Parliament was told that the Navy's debts amounted to £510,760, and its needs to next Lady Day (25 March 1654) £985,410, plus a further £300,000 for thirty new frigates; against which its anticipated revenue was £415,000. £2,160,000 was spent on the Navy during that year, plus £1,500,000 on the army, out of total State revenue of about £2,500,000. Throughout the war the Navy was forced to live from hand to mouth, with no proper financial planning or adequate provision. The Rump Parliament consistently refused to face up to the real cost of naval warfare. A 1654 report by the Revenue Sub-Committee insisted that the annual cost of the Navy 'at the greatest rate' amounted to £269,750; in reality it cost nearly three millions in the thirty months of the Dutch War. By the end of 1654, the Navy owed at least £600,000.[15]

This might have been thought a bad beginning for another war, but so convinced were Cromwell and his Parliament that a Spanish war must be profitable that they actually reduced taxes in 1655. Apart from the traditional Customs, no sure revenue was assigned to the Navy, and those sums which were voted were frequently raided by the army. By December 1655 the Navy's debts and current requirements together had reached £1,400,000. Customs revenue suffered severely from Spanish attacks on English shipping, while the total of all prizes taken by English ships over twelve months was £2,900. In October 1656 naval debt was reckoned at over half a million, and when Blake's fleet came home in November 1657 it had reached £994,500, with another million required for the next year. In 1658, with Navy bills waiting over a year for payment, the few remaining contractors still solvent and willing to do business with the government were charging the Navy 30–50 per cent over market rates. 'Unless there be a present supply of money to provide such necessaries as may be wanting, there will be a full stop to your affair', the Navy Commission warned in February 1659, 'for our credit is now gone, and it is not now only as to some stores but most . . .'[16] The political chaos of 1659 completed the ruin of the Navy's finances. In January 1660 the government was essentially bankrupt, and the Navy needed £2,157,883 to pay off its debts and fit out a Summer Guard.[17]

One of the reasons why the Navy was able to continue as long as it did was that the naval debt was disproportionately owed to the most vulnerable class of creditors: the officers and men of the Navy itself. Since ships' companies were paid only when their ships were put out of service (the autumn in most cases, as it was still unusual for fleets to operate all the year round), successive governments discovered that there was no easier way to save money in the short term (and of course, to waste it in the long term) than to keep ships in commission rather than pay them off. When they were paid, it was often in tickets rather than cash, which the men were obliged to pawn for whatever discount they could get. Many naval administrators and sea commanders complained of the injustice inflicted on their men ('we profess the equity of their desires is such that we know not what to answer them', as Deane and Monck wrote in 1653),[18] and hinted at the political risks of denying them ('conceiving the stopping of their money not to be the way to engage them', in the Navy Commission's words);[19] but the Admiralty suspected that complaints were 'set on as may be suspected by malignant spirits disaffected to the Parliament',[20] while sterner spirits like Major Nehemiah Bourne, Navy Commissioner at Harwich, tended to treat them as frivolous or malicious:

> The ungrateful and disingenuous spirit in the seamen I lament, who are neither sensible of what is the public or their private interest and concernment, but are below the beasts that perish. I hear that Ipswich and other parts are full of them, but here are few enough; they love not this air, since I have banished strong waters and sent some of them over the water.[21]

The new pay-scale instituted in 1653 had a good effect on recruitment for a short while, until the men discovered that they were no more likely to receive the new rates than the old. In the late 1650s the situation worsened rapidly. By the time Blake's fleet abandoned its blockade of the Spanish coast in the summer of 1657, only one of his ships had been paid within the past twenty months. In March 1659 there were ships, especially single ships on remote stations which posed no political risk, which had been unpaid for over four years. Men without money, even if they were still being fed, could not support their families, nor buy clothes for themselves, leaving them, as the crew of the *Bramble* complained in 1658, 'a spectacle of woe and a looking-glass of calamity'.[22] It is no wonder that by 1660 the English Republic had lost the loyalty of its seamen, and severely shaken that of its officers.[23]

The accumulating debts of the Commonwealth and Protectorate appear to be a story of unmixed political failure, but they concealed an important development. The new permanent taxes established in 1645 made it possible for the state to borrow at short term on the security of its revenues. From the 1650s the Treasury began to issue negotiable notes, payable 'in course' (meaning in numbered sequence of issue). The Navy Commission paid for its purchases by issuing similar Navy Bills on its own credit. Because these orders and bills were negotiable, contractors could discount them to speculators and financiers who were willing to hold them to maturity. Naturally suppliers inflated their prices to compensate for the discount, but so long as the State's credit was not stretched too far, it could still buy what it needed. Though there was nothing like a permanent national debt, the Commonwealth was the first moderately creditworthy English government in modern times. Its debts increased steadily during the Dutch and Spanish Wars, but the oldest debts were regularly repaid first, there was no default, and no complete collapse of the State's credit until 1658 and 1659. It was Cromwell's decision in 1657 to cut taxes in the middle of a major war which precipitated the eventual collapse. Though financial failure helped to destroy the Republic, its fiscal innovations survived it. Moreover these naval wars had an essential effect in educating public opinion. During the Dutch War there were still many members of Parliament who believed, as they had believed in 1640, that the Navy could and should live in peace and war from its own 'natural' revenue, the Customs, paid by the foreign trade which the Navy protected. This idea had proved to be unrealistic ever since 'Tonnage and Poundage' had first been voted to support the fleet in 1347, but Parliamentary optimism was proof against three centuries of experience. It was the lessons of the Dutch and Spanish Wars which finally persuaded the majority of the political nation that only permanent taxation could support permanent fleets.[24]

No aspect of naval administration was more vital in itself, nor more critically dependent on strong finance, than victualling. Blake's 1649 blockade of Lisbon presented an early challenge to the Victuallers, and the Dutch War was much worse. A weak Admiralty started the war disastrously by failing to anticipate what would be required. The technology of the age permitted beer to be brewed and meat packed only in the winter months, so that to victual a summer fleet it was necessary to 'declare' the proposed number of men, and issue the necessary money, in the preceding autumn. In June 1652, with operations already under way, the Council of State ordered the fleet to be victualled to October: 'conceive so much hath been signified to the Victuallers of the Navy,' they wrote lamely, 'but in case it be not, that so much shall be declared, and that all this victual should be put aboard together . . .'[25] It was nine months too late. In August the Council of State demanded a further 12,000 man-months of victuals, which the Victuallers agreed to supply in return for having their debt (£23,859 3s 8d) paid at once, their rate increased 12½ per cent to 8½d a man/day, and the balance of their account paid in monthly instalments.[26] Learning from experience, the Council ordered next year's supplies in good time, but the Victuallers still had to contend with the inadequacies of the Commonwealth Admiralty, which failed to appoint the necessary officers. 'The provision of victuals is now and will be within 3 or 4 days ready to be taken on board all the ships and frigates, and how it is to be received before any person be appointed to take charge of it we leave it to your grave wisdoms to consider of.'[27] The Admiralty also failed to realize that a contract for 'sea beer' did not cover the more expensive but durable 'strong beer'. The Victuallers' other difficulties included a severe shortage of the strong iron-bound casks necessary for beer and water which were to be stowed in the 'ground tier' at the bottom of the hold.[28] It seems that overall they managed to supply the quantity of victuals required, but there were numerous complaints of the quality, especially of the beer. In July 1653 Monck reported that 'The greatest part of the beer we had before, and is now come along with the *Reserve*, is not fit for men to drink for aught we hear as yet, having continual complaints thereof. The captain of the *Reserve* informs us that his men choose rather to drink water than beer'[29] – a shocking fact, for Englishmen drank water only in the last extremity. The same complaint came from Captain John Taylor, Master Shipwright at Chatham:

> the men have come to me . . . and showed me their beer, bread and butter, against which there is such an cry (and very justly), for it's such that in the dearest time that ever I knew I never saw so bad laid in by State nor mart. Here is witness the men do drink water rather than the beer, and the butter is most unfit for men of all the rest. And they must take pork now in harbour, which was salted before December last, as they say, or none.[30]

In April the Generals warned that 'the fleet with Vice-Admiral Penn is very defective in victuals, whatsoever the victuallers' instrument may report to the contrary, and do think if there be such shuffling to and again in this business we shall have a very hard game to play . . .'[31] Victualling failures were the major reason why it proved impossible to sustain a blockade of the Dutch coast that summer.

The victualling organization was run by the Navy Commission from 1649 to 1651, when the government managed to assemble a syndicate of Victuallers (led by Colonel Pride) prepared to venture their credit at the State's service. In 1654 the remaining Victualler, Thomas Alderne, was made a salaried official of the Navy Commission, and on his death in 1657 a board of Victualling Commissioners (Francis Willoughby, Nehemiah Bourne and Robert Thomson) was constituted under the Admiralty. There was never enough money available, and the steady weakening of the Navy's credit (political as well as financial) particularly affected Blake's fleet on the coast of Spain, but the Victuallers had some real achievements. By dealing direct in the provinces they undercut the London merchants and reduced the average cost of victuals by 39 per cent between 1649 and 1655. Admittedly this was a period of improving harvests, but overall food prices fell only 16 per cent in the same period. From 1658 the progressive collapse of the Navy's credit and administration affected the victualling with everything else, and by 1660 some ships' companies were starving.[32]

The radicals reconstructed the Navy Commission in 1649 with Parliamentary members, as in 1642, but once again complaints of malpractice from the sea commanders soon led to their removal to the Navy Committee. The five permanent officials who did the real work were in 1652 John Hollond, Captain Robert Moulton, Thomas Smith, Peter Pett and Major Robert Thomson. Hollond resigned and Moulton died in that year, leaving Smith as the only survivor of the pre-1649 Commission. In 1653 Colonel Francis Willoughby, Edward Hopkins and Major Nehemiah Bourne were added. Pett was permanently resident at Chatham, and during the Dutch War other resident commissioners were established at Portsmouth (Willoughby) and Harwich (Bourne). Permanent Agents, not members of the Commission, acted for it at other ports. In 1654 the Navy Commission was for the first time provided with a headquarters, in Mincing Lane near Tower Hill, where the Commissioners both lived and worked.[33]

This small body was responsible for the management of by far the largest fleets England had ever fitted out, sustained at sea for much longer periods than ever before. At the height of the Dutch War they were employing over 2,000 men in the dockyards. Between 1649 and 1654 they built eighteen ships in the dockyards and thirty-six by contract: 28,000 tons in five years. They worked hard, Sundays included, and their dedication and efficiency was widely admired, even by their Royalist successors. Not everyone thought as highly of Pett as he did himself, but Bourne showed remarkable energy and ability.[34] 'It is somewhat strange to me,' Monck commented,

> that twenty sail of ships should be so long a-fitting out from Chatham, Deptford and Woolwich where there are so many docks and so many instruments to give despatch, when there hath been fitted out from Harwich twenty-two sail of ships or more in half the time by Major Bourne, whose extraordinary care and diligence therein is worthy your knowledge.[35]

Extraordinary care and diligence, however, is not all that can be said of the Navy Commissioners. They and the Regulators formed a closely connected and intermarried group almost all of whom were shipowners and suppliers of naval stores. They came from the same parts of East Anglia, they worshipped together in the 'gathered congregations' of Stepney and Wapping, they had commercial and personal ties with New England, where many of them had taken refuge in the 1630s. Nehemiah Bourne, for example, shipmaster, merchant and brother of Vice-Admiral John Bourne, was the son of a Wapping shipbuilder and closely connected to the Rainsboroughs, the Haddocks, the Earnings and the Coytmores. All these families (except the Coytmores, originally from Caernarvonshire)[36] had come to Wapping from Leigh, Woodbridge, Aldeburgh and places nearby in Essex and Suffolk. In 1638 Bourne went to Massachussets, returning during the Civil War to become Major of the Suffolk regiment raised by Colonel Thomas Rainsborough, and largely officered by Americans. In 1645 he went back to the sea, in 1650 he was captain of the *Speaker*, and in 1652 Rear-Admiral of the fleet. He was probably recruited to the Navy Commission by Vane, former Governor of Massachussets; certainly he, Willoughby, Hopkins (ex-Governor of Connecticut) and the new Treasurer Richard Hutchinson had all been in New England with Vane. Bourne was a contractor and shipper of New England masts and tar, and the New Englanders pushed hard for the Navy to buy colonial naval stores (supplied by themselves) to replace the Baltic supplies unobtainable during the Dutch War.[37] Miles Corbett and Gregory Clements of the Regulators were suppliers of hemp and timber respectively. According to the Navy Commissioner John Hollond, the Regulators

> always carried something in their eye, either of private honour, profit, or revenge, that was the weight that set all the wheels of their zeal for public good a-going; and those things being compassed, the navy and its welfare did afterwards no more concern them or their care than the navy

of the great Turk . . . unless it were to settle a brother and a friend in two
or three of the best places thereof.[38]

Maurice Thomson (a Regulator), his brothers and partners Robert (Regu-
lator and Navy Commissioner) and George (of the Admiralty Committee),
all three shipowners and sponsors of the Navigation Act, dominated the
lucrative business of chartering 'merchant ships-of-war' to the state.[39] Thomas
Smith of the Navy Commission, the Victualler Captain John Limbery, Vice-
Admiral Richard Badiley and numerous other officials and officers from the
Council of State downwards owned ships in the State's service. Oliver
Cromwell himself was a timber supplier. Thomas Smith also supplied masts
and speculated in seamen's pay tickets, leading the crews of his ships to
complain that he had embezzled their wages. The Prize Commissioners bought
the prize goods which they sold in their official capacities.[40] 'I have often
acquainted you,' Coytmore warned Popham,

> that the State cannot have faithful service done by them [the Navy
> Commissioners] so long as many of them are owners of ships and practise
> the trade of merchandising, and some others of them are woodmongers
> and buyers and sellers of timber. If you will have the navy and Common-
> wealth faithfully served you must have the Commissioners free from
> such practices.[41]

Even when the officials avoided direct personal dealings, as Hollond
pointed out,

> All men know that if I be a merchant and a commissioner at the same
> time, that as a commissioner I am able to pleasure my fellow-merchant
> that deals with me for the State, either in price, time of payment, quantity
> or quality of the goods sold, and by that means engage the merchant to
> wash hands with me in the like civilities in my trade as a merchant at
> large . . .[42]

In the dockyards all the master shipwrights had private yards of their own
in which they built ships for the State. At Chatham, where Peter Pett was
Commissioner, his family remained in entire control of the yard, as they had
been for half a century. The complaints of William Adderley, appointed as
chaplain of the yard and vicar of Chatham in October 1649, led to an inquiry
which fully illustrated Adderley's point that 'It is not for the State's advantage
to have a generation of brothers, cousins and kindred, packed together in one
place of public trust and service.' But the Petts were equal to the challenge:
their influence in London was ample, and witnesses in the yard, like Thomas
Symonds, the Master House Carpenter, 'durst not discover for fear he should

be undone by the kindred . . . so knit together, that the devil himself could not discover them, except they did much impeach one the other, and they would be hanged before they would do so.' In March 1654 Adderley was dismissed, and the Petts were left in tranquillity.[43]

Naval historians have traditionally contrasted the corruption of Stuart naval administrators with the godly efficiency of the Commonwealth, when

> their dispatches were with all imaginable quickness, and every one endeavoured to exceed each other; and strove who should serve the public best, and cheapest . . . Indeed, it did behove them to bestir themselves, when they had the whole world upon their backs almost, at once, to deal with; and a discontent in their bowels, at the same time; yet you see, with what vigour and resolution, pains and industry they waded through it, to the terror and amazement of their enemies . . .[44]

In truth the most important difference between them was that arbitrary government provided the Navy with more money than the Stuarts had ever had: nearly £8 million between 1649 and 1660, compared to less than 3½ millions in the war years 1625–9, and less than one million from six years of Ship Money.[45] Whether or not one regards them as technically corrupt, the godly republican naval officials installed in 1649 (and for the most part left in office thereafter), certainly made sure that they were well rewarded for their work, whoever else went short. But their administration was effective overall, and some of its members (notably Nehemiah Bourne) were outstanding. It was responsible for some real reforms, including the abolition of all fees in favour of higher salaries in 1652.[46] It adopted imaginative solutions to its problems, such as the establishment of an industrial enterprise in the 'forlorn wilderness' of the Forest of Dean which exploited the local timber and iron to build ships and cast guns – something administratively easier because the Ordnance Board was in 1653 placed under the authority of the Admiralty.[47] It invested in some important additions to the Navy's 'infrastructure', including a ropeyard, new stores and the first dry dock at Portsmouth; another dry dock and more stores at Woolwich; a mast dock and three new wharves at Deptford.[48] When the Danes closed the Baltic during the Dutch War, it obtained vital supplies by ingenious expedients; requisitioning cargoes from Swedish, Hamburger, Lübecker and other neutral ships, importing masts from Scotland and from the Black Forest.[49]

Perhaps the most important of all the Commonwealth's innovations concerned the treatment of the sick and wounded. In the conditions of the age, any large gathering of men living together was likely to lead to disease, particularly 'camp', 'gaol' or 'ship' fever (the modern typhus), a cold-weather disease carried (as we now know) by ticks in dirty clothes, which attacked the ill-fed, ill-clothed and unwashed. Besides the inevitable disease, the Dutch War involved bloody fighting with large numbers of wounded being landed at short notice. Medical matters were initially one of the many responsibilities which by September 1653 had all but overwhelmed the Navy Commission; as they complained to the Admiralty:

> This office wants commissioners and clerks and a fit house as we have long ago intimated unto you by letter and word of mouth, but have no remedy. We believe that if it were taken seriously into consideration what a vast difference there is between setting out 30 sail as in former years, and now 200 and upwards, and have but the same help . . . The truth is we cannot without more help go through with this business . . .'[50]

The same day a new Board of Sick and Wounded was established to handle medical care ashore, and pensions for the wounded and widowed. Beds were commandeered in the London hospitals, and the old Savoy Palace and Ely House were turned into national 'military hospitals' for both services.[51] Both Dr Daniel Whistler, the energetic physician who acted as roving medical agent throughout the Dutch War, and Commissioner Willoughby at Portsmouth tried without success to get a hospital established there.[52] It was expensive to treat patients scattered amongst many pubs and lodging houses, 'besides the difficulty and charge otherwise of ordering their diet, nursing; the thronging of weak men into poor stifling houses; the temptations to them of drinking inordinately in victualling houses who have no other but strong drinks . . .'[53] Whistler never got his hospital, and for want of it, 'finding many healed almost, or slightly wounded, accounted it safe for them and less chargeable to the public to return them to their ships, where salt meat will not do more hurt than strong drink would here.'[54]

Worse problems were caused by large numbers of sick and wounded landed in the small East Anglian ports in the summer of 1653, to be lodged in farms and inns across the country. The Bailiffs of Yarmouth were described as 'very pitiful and careful of all sick and wounded men sent to them', and 'the seamen generally give a good character of the country people with whom they have been quartered for their care and tenderness over them', as Bourne reported, but the problem was lack of cash to pay innkeepers and farmers' wives who could not afford to wait the Navy's credit.[55] Even the celebrated volunteer nurse (and former spy) Elizabeth Alkin, 'Parliament Joan', who has been called the 'Florence Nightingale of the Seventeenth Century', was unable to get her expenses repaid.[56] Monck had the good sense to send some Dutch prizes into Yarmouth to be sold to raise money on the spot, 'for I do perceive they are not men of ability to forbear their money till it be returned from London'.[57] By this and other expedients the crisis was eventually overcome. In August 1653 the town of Ipswich had received 900 wounded men, and was owed £1,900, but by the coming of peace in March 1654 the town had been fully reimbursed for its claimed expenses of £3,838 9s 8d – perhaps more than fully, since the Sick and Wounded Board suspected they had been overcharged.[58]

The Sick and Wounded Board was a wartime expedient, which ceased to function in the late 1650s,[59] but like other innovations of the Commonwealth period, it established a precedent which was to be drawn on for over a century. The record of the Commonwealth and Protectorate was a paradox of mingled success and failure. As political experiments they were an unqualified failure, which left the English with an intense distaste for arbitrary government and all things military. For many contemporaries, however, the seamen's 'looking-glass of calamity' reflected not only the failures of an arbitrary regime, but England's renewed destiny at sea.

To account for this it is necessary to explain the position that sea power already occupied in the English national consciousness. The English national myth of sea power was based on the memory of Queen Elizabeth's naval war against Spain. It had been fought for England's freedom, against the mortal threat of Catholic tyranny. It had been a naval triumph, men believed, and would have been more so but for the Queen's hesitancy and parsimony. It had been fought at little public expense, and yielded enormous private profit. It had endowed English history with an ample stock of Protestant heroes. Above all, that part of the naval war which had seized the national imagination had been fought by private interests rather than by the crown, so that the prestige did not go to strengthen an image of royal power, but one of national liberty. It made English sea power the ideal expression of the nation in arms.

This did not apply to any sort of navy, used for any purpose, but to the natural English form of sea power, founded on the three elements of wealth, liberty and religion. In the public mind, English sea power was essentially involved in creating wealth, by promoting and protecting English trade, or by seizing the shipping of the enemy, 'to God's glory and our comfort'.[60] True English naval war was profitable in a general sense, if not (as some optimists still thought) in the specific sense of being financially self-supporting. Closely linked to that was its religious identification: true English sea power was applied in defence of Protestantism, against Catholic enemies, and there was a clear connection between war against Catholics at sea, and persecution of English Catholics at home. Thus, the public believed, Queen Elizabeth's subjects had pleased God and made England free and great. Much of the opposition Charles I had aroused sprang from his adoption of naval policies which supported royal rather than Parliamentary authority, and alliance rather than war with Spain. The Commonwealth and Protectorate, by contrast, adopted the naval policy which conformed to England's manifest destiny: aggressive war against Catholic Europe.[61]

This policy so perfectly fitted what the English political nation desired that the public almost persuaded itself that the war had been a success. This was the first English naval administration to keep fleets of hundreds of sail at sea over several consecutive years of war, to maintain substantial forces operational in winter as well as summer, and to send large fleets into distant waters for long periods. With much more money than its predecessors, it met and for a time overcame challenges which no previous English government could have thought of facing. The achievement did not last, but its brief administrative and naval triumphs offered a tantalizing glimpse of what might be possible to a stable and legitimate English government.

FOUR

The Melody of Experienced Saints

Social History 1649–1660

The Navy of the Commonwealth grew enormously in size, but it was not in most respects entirely new. The core of the fleet was the great ships inherited from Charles I. The essential structure of the naval administration remained intact; its upper reaches repeatedly purged, but the middle and lower levels much less affected. Thomas Turner, for example, Storekeeper of Deptford Dockyard in 1668, had started as a clerk in the Navy Office in the 1620s,[1] and there were many like him who contributed their experience to successive regimes. Only the seagoing officers of the Navy were really new. One captain alone of Charles I's Royal Navy chose to serve the Parliament: Sir George Ayscue. Many of the Parliamentary sea officers in turn defected to the Royalists in 1648, and two-thirds of the remainder were dismissed by the Regulators in 1649. Ayscue survived all these revolutions, only to be retired in 1652. His performance in the battle of Plymouth had been uninspired, but the real reason was probably that as a long-serving sea officer he had an independent base of support in the fleet which was a political threat: 'the two great exceptions are his extraordinary power with the seamen, and the General [Monck] cannot confide in him'.[2] For the most part, the Regulators had to find new captains, lieutenants and masters for a rapidly expanding fleet. They found them as far as they could in the same circles as they found administrators ashore – their own. The new officers were drawn in particular from the small merchants, shipowners and shipmasters, Republican in politics and Independent in religion, who had so strong an influence in the Common-wealth. It was difficult to find so many men so quickly from so small a pool, and it seems that active radicals and sectaries composed only about a quarter of the officer corps, but they dominated the senior positions and strongly affected the character of the whole service. The purges which followed the establishment of the Protectorate affected only the Admiralty and the highest ranks afloat, reaching no further down than those captains who, like Lawson, chose to identify themselves as active opponents of military rule. The officer corps as a whole remained until 1660 essentially that which the Regulators formed in 1649–50; a body notably more radical than the Cromwellian regime it came to serve, and still containing many active Republicans in 1660.[3]

It is possible to speak of officers' ranks in the seventeenth-century Navy only in a restricted sense. There were positions to which men were appointed, which stood to one another in a more or less defined relationship of authority, but they carried no permanent status in the Navy or in society. Though the captain of a ship was clearly senior to the lieutenant, a man might serve as captain one voyage and lieutenant the next. Army rank had greater and more permanent social prestige (especially under a military regime), so that those who had served in the New Model Army often continued to use their army ranks at sea. Nehemiah Bourne, for example, always preferred 'Major' to 'Rear-Admiral'. Apart from the collective Generals, the only quasi-permanent flag ranks were that of Penn and later Lawson as Vice-Admiral, Bourne as Rear-Admiral of the main summer fleet – in effect the old positions of Vice-Admiral and Rear-Admiral of England, deputies to the Lord Admiral. These were the only ones allowed flag-captains. Other 'admirals' were simply captains appointed to command particular squadrons, with vice-admirals and rear-admirals beneath them, and in the absence of any system of seniority within rank, they might find themselves having to establish their authority over captains of greater experience than their own.[4]

Within each ship, the officers were much the same as they had been in the 1630s. Under the captain was the master, in charge of navigation and shiphandling. The first three of the six Rates into which ships were classified (plus Fourth Rates from late 1652) were allowed one lieutenant, a position which seems often to have gone to ex-army officers or others with less seagoing experience. The lieutenant was senior to the master, but it was still not well defined which of the two had the better title to succeed to a vacant command. Three warrant officers headed professional 'departments' within the ship. The boatswain, always an experienced mariner, was in charge of rigging, ground tackle and their maintenance. The carpenter, trained by apprenticeship afloat or in a dockyard, was responsible for the hull and masts. The gunner took charge of guns and ammunition, and was in the seventeenth century often of better birth and education than the other warrant officers, sometimes a candidate for lieutenant or even captain.[5] The surgeon was also technically a warrant officer, though in terms of social position more like a civilian afloat, since few surgeons seem to have made a career in the Navy. Their pay and status were improved in 1652, and an ordinance of 1654 allowing former soldiers to follow trades without having to become freemen of the appropriate craft guilds, was used to allow former naval and military surgeons a short-cut to practice ashore, so that many surgeons came to start their careers with a spell of wartime naval service. All the warrant officers had mates, whose standing aboard was approximately equal to that of the senior petty officers, midshipmen and quartermasters.[6] In January 1653 the office of purser was divided, victualling becoming the responsibility of the ship's steward, and mustering the crew of a clerk of the cheque, each supposed to act as a control on the other. The experiment seems to have been unsuccessful, and in October 1655 pursers were revived. They had to give large sureties, and were generally landmen of a somewhat higher social class than other warrant officers, for which reason they often discharged their duties by deputy. John Weale, a purser of the 1650s who left a journal, was the son of a clergyman and subsequently became a lieutenant. With pursers were associated cooks, like-wise warrant officers, and with a higher social standing than they enjoyed in later centuries.[7]

Initially in 1649 the new officers were of necessity recruited directly, mostly from the same social milieu as the Regulators, and it seems to have been little more than accident who became captains and who masters. The great majority had experience as masters or mates of merchantmen, many were already middle-aged, and some were wealthy. They were seamen, pilots if not deep-sea navigators, reasonably educated and at least to some degree acquainted with business and paper-work. Some fighting record was an asset, especially for lieu-tenants. Many had New England connections, or came from East Anglian ports. Often captains were sent to waters with which they were familiar, or to protect the trade of their own home ports. Other things being equal, both Common-wealth and Protectorate preferred men of respectable birth, especially to com-mand the bigger ships, but they insisted on sea experience. Only the Generals were exempt from this requirement, and even they were conscious of what they had to learn. When Mountague was appointed he had a seaman build him a rigged model to teach him how to work a ship. Already a mathematician, he was soon taking his own sights; an uncommon skill for a seventeenth-century flag officer, and almost certainly unique among the Generals.[8]

As the Navy continued to expand, and the heavy casualties of the Dutch War had to be replaced, a primitive career structure began to develop, as far as it could without permanent rank. It was soon established that the most important commands would naturally go to those who had distinguished themselves in smaller ships. 'There are several honest and valiant men and commanders in the fleet,' Monck reminded the Admiralty in July 1653, 'whom

I have recommended to you for removes into the great frigates now abuilding next unto the flag ships, which I hope you are not forgetful of, for it will be a great discouragement unto them, for those who were never in the service to be preferred before them.'[9] Warrant officers, and senior petty officers such as midshipmen and master's mates, might all be candidates for lieutenant or master, and the ablest young men rose fast, producing a new generation of captains and even admirals in their twenties, some of them of very humble birth. Charles Wager was boatswain's mate of the *Tiger* in 1649 and Robert Clay her carpenter; both were captains before the Restoration. Christopher Myngs, the son of a shoemaker, began as Admiral Goodson's coxswain and was a captain at twenty-eight; Nicholas Heaton rose to command from the rating of trumpeter's mate. There was no formal test of eligibility for promotion, but able men, like Myngs, advanced on the patronage of their seniors, and the most successful seniors naturally had the luckiest followers. Of the seven captains whom Penn commanded in the Mediterranean in 1650–52, four (Lawson, Samuel Howett, Benjamin Blake and Joseph Jordan) became admirals, and two (Andrew Ball and John Mildmay) were already flag-captains when they were killed in action. Benjamin Blake, a brother of Robert, was one of the General's numerous kinsmen in the service, and Penn, Bourne and others also advanced their families.[10]

Generally it seems that senior officers did not lose sight of the need for ability, and were careful not to imperil their own reputations by defending incompetent relatives and connections. The outstanding example of abuse of patronage came not from an admiral but from Cromwell himself, who sent his nephew Thomas Whetstone with Penn to the West Indies with instructions 'to do him good as you find he deserves', by which Cromwell understood immediate promotion to be the flagship's lieutenant. When he learned that Penn had chosen a kinsman of his own (Richard Rooth) instead, he was not pleased:

> I did apprehend and took it as granted, that you would make my nephew Whetstone your lieutenant in this expedition; and I acquainted him and his friends therewith, who did depend thereupon. But I understand lately that my nephew is disappointed or at least delayed of that employment. Truly I have entertained such good hopes of the young man from these characters I have received of him, and that from yourself, that I should be loath he should be discouraged or neglected. And therefore I desire you to put your kinsman into some other command in the fleet, and let Whetstone be lieutenant to yourself according to your promise to me . . .[11]

Presently Penn was put in the Tower, and Whetstone was promoted captain, in which capacity he went out to the Mediterranean in 1657 as second-in-command to Captain John Stoakes. There his drunken and irresponsible behaviour caused serious embarrassment, until at length Cromwell's death permitted Stoakes to get rid of him.[12]

Like the naval administrators to whom they were so closely linked, the sea officers were not serving for nothing. In 1649 their pay was raised, while in December 1652, as part of the range of measures introduced after the disaster of Dungeness, the whole Navy received a new pay-scale, and a new system of prize-money was instituted, allowing both 'plunder' (private property and loose articles above the gun deck) as usual in privateers, and 10s a ton plus £6 13s 4d a gun for prizes, or £10 a gun for enemy ships sunk. The distribution between officers and men was left to 'the custom of the seas in that case'.[13] Not everyone was content with so much. There were numerous complaints of frauds and abuses by officers; embezzlement, private trade and smuggling, false mustering and illicit fees (for example from convoys).[14] Gunners had an evil reputation for selling the State's powder, and other warrant officers were not far behind. They had ample opportunity: the boatswain's stores of a First Rate were worth £331, and the carpenter's, £100, very few of which items were distinctively marked as the State's property. Theft from the dockyards was endemic; a search at Rochester in 1655 uncovered 300 tons of stores missing from Chatham.[15] Another problem was the tendency of captains to take unauthorized leave.[16]

None of this was unusual by the standards of the age, especially when officers' pay was so long in arrears that an honest man might starve for his virtue. Contemporaries were more impressed by the high standards of the State's officers than by their lapses. There were many examples of devotion to duty, and in particular many captains who forcefully took up their men's grievances over pay and conditions. When the crew of the *Maidstone* demolished the Victualling Office at Rochester in 1658, Captain Thomas Penrose refused to name any of the culprits, saying their food had been 'full of maggots, and so rotten no dog would eat it'.[17] 'The cries of poor men are very great,' wrote Captain Heaton from Plymouth in January 1660,

> and enemy's men-of-war are busy, but we can neither relieve the one, nor drive the other from our coast. Six of our frigates are in port, and lie only for want of victuals, and we expect 5 or 6 more every day, who are in the like starving condition with ourselves. If we should be forced, which God forbid, to turn all our men, which are many hundreds, on shore, they must steal or rob, having no money to relieve themselves and

poor families, being long without pay, as only two of our ships were paid 10 or 12 months since, and the rest have 26, 32, 42 and some 50 months' pay due.[18]

Captains drawn from the merchant service were socially relatively close to their men. Many of them had themselves risen from warrant or petty officer's rank, and had relatives in such situations. It was unremarkable for captains to drink and eat with warrant officers. Many captains had personal followings of men eager to serve with them, often drawn from their home ports. The mayor of King's Lynn, for example, sent up men who had volunteered to sail with Captain Seth Hawley. Nicholas Heaton recruited largely in his home town of Plymouth, John Coppin at Deal, Lambert Cornelius at Weymouth. Such ties between captain and crew could be close, even affectionate. When Captain Charles Thoroughgood of the *Worcester* was dismissed for cowardice in 1652, his officers and men demanded a court martial to clear his, and their, name.[19] The ship's company of the *Greyhound* in 1656 wrote to express their sorrow that 'our loving commander Captain Edmund Thompson is to leave us . . . which doth much grieve us to part from so honest a gentleman,' and asked for the master to succeed to the command.[20]

Not every captain was beloved, however, and it was mostly the smaller ships, some of which stayed in commission winter and summer, which had the chance to build up settled ships' companies. The majority of men were needed for the big ships, where no doubt discipline and social relations were more formal, and where casualties were heavy in the battles of the Dutch War. On the Essex coast after the battle of the Gabbard, 'the tide ever since brings in abundance of arms and legs, and dismembered bodies, a sad spectacle to behold' – and no help to recruitment.[21] In practice the Commonwealth Navy from the beginning relied heavily on force. Acts of February 1649 and March 1652 provided for 'impresting' seamen.[22] The word literally meant to issue an imprest, or advance of wages, by way of establishing a contract of employment, but the easy confusion of 'imprest' and 'impressed' (likewise 'prest' and 'pressed') was tending to shift its sense towards an implication of force. There were officers sent recruiting who understood the acts to cover volunteers alone, such as one Colonel Rous in Cornwall ('having received no orders more than to press such as would take their money . . . I could but persuade, not enforce any'), but this was unusually scrupulous.[23]

Most pressing was done at sea by ships' officers, and ashore by constables and pressmasters acting under the authority of the Vice-Admirals of the maritime counties (usually the Lords Lieutenant in another capacity). According to the acts they were permitted to take only mariners, sailors, watermen, surgeons, gunners, ship-carpenters, caulkers, coopers, hoymen (and carters, for the transport of victuals), who were to be given one shilling imprest, and 1½d a mile 'conduct money', or travelling expenses. In practice it was universally complained that the pressmasters took 'ploughmen, thatchers and hedgers', and released seamen for a bribe. In June 1653 it was reckoned that there were about 5,000 pressed landmen in the Navy.[24] 'It is able to pity any man's heart to see what poor creatures are pressed and sent hither,' wrote Captain Edmund Curtis. 'I believe the State was never so much abused by those that press men as they are now, and if they were not ill affected men that are employed for that purpose certainly they would not press such poor creatures and leave able seamen unpressed.'[25] Some pressmasters frankly admitted that they took

> all sorts of people (whether gentlemen or others) that come in our way, the watermen and seamen we pulled out of bed from their wives, and sent them . . . to the fleet in barges, two whereof being overladen, and the wind being high, were cast away . . . and all the men lost, which was a sad omen for the rest, who went as unwillingly as they would have done to the gallows.[26]

Men were as reluctant in the Spanish War for a different reason: 'I never see men so hard to get in my life; the seamen are so afraid to be sent to the West Indies as they said they had lief be hanged.'[27]

Pressmasters were supposed to receive the co-operation of local authorities, but in practice the authorities were very often on the seamen's side. As early as May 1652 the Council of State was threatening recalcitrant parish constables with impressment themselves.[28] At Bristol in May 1653 the pressmasters Thomas Hewitt and John Penny met

> open and public opposition against our proceedings and that by owners and merchants as to question our power we act by and whether there be any such power at present or not, and others they encourage the seamen that they may refuse to obey it upon which the seamen armed with clubs and staves saith if any impress by us come a near to be upon their own peril be it. In a word they are gone to such a height of boldness that our actions are attended with great danger and will so continue unless some speedy course be taken as your honours shall conceive most convenient. Again as I formerly wrote to you that several seamen after they had received their imprest and conduct money are carried away to sea, encouraged so to do by their masters and merchants, to the number of ten or more out of this city which I formerly gave you account of. Again

others make it a trade to receive impress and conduct money twice under pretence of volunteering. Again others having received impress and conduct money absent and hide themselves and go from one town to another and when we address ourselves to the magistrates it [is] to little or no purpose, to our great discouragement all the answer we receive from them is that we should bring them before them, and then they will do what not or nothing at all to them, which doth much encourage the offenders.[29]

From Plymouth Captain Richard Mill complained to the Admiralty that

I find little assistance from the justices of Cornwall and likewise in Devon, for I have not any from them! Mr. Trevill of Cornwall hath threatened me twice very highly before the view of the country, when I was in my business, came unexpected, and asked me whether that was the liberty of the subject to force men aboard, all that part of the country made very little appearance, and for the other of the justices, there is little appears from them. The constables act so slowly as they had counsel from the justices, for whereas there are in some places a considerable number of able men, sometimes they will bring in an old man or two. I have sent many hues and cries after men which have been imprest, but never a one at my knowledge taken, if any not above two . . . the seamen lie out in boats, some forty or fifty together, boys and women carry provisions to them, so that I am enforced to set shallops by water, and others by land to take them.[30]

At sea pressing was forbidden from outward-bound ships, 'being of very much prejudice to the trade and shipping of the nation', but in the emergency of a 'hot press', as in May 1652 and March 1653, merchant shipping might be embargoed until the main fleet was manned. The East Coast coal trade, a well-known source of good seamen, was convoyed to protect it from the Dutch, but the colliers often escaped their escorts to avoid having their men pressed.[31] Nehemiah Bourne, not a man to be trifled with, fired on a convoy to bring them to, 'they being some of them very angry and impatient to be delayed . . . but just now I have brought about forty of them to an anchor and we are digging for them where they have burrowed themselves'.[32]

Naturally many men evaded the press, or ran away before they could be conveyed afloat. Once at sea, for a summer's campaign in the majority of cases, there seems to have been little trouble, but if the fleet returned to port it was otherwise. When Monck and Blake came into Solebay in July 1653, Robert Blackborne, the Secretary of the Admiralty, went down to Suffolk.

In my passage betwixt Woodbridge and this place [Walberswick], I met many seamen with their clothes travelling towards London, who, upon examination, answered me that they had discharges from their captains, but could produce none. I fear the fleet's coming in will occasion the loss of very many of them, and in a great measure render the care and pains your Honours have taken for levy of mariners of little or no effect.[33]

There was frequent trouble when men were turned over from one ship to another without pay or leave, as Deane and Monck reported in March 1653.

Those which were turned over before to man the *Triumph* and other great ships at Chatham are continually about our doors complaining so that we cannot quietly walk the streets for them, continually crying to us to have their tickets paid, many of them having lost their clothes, and here is no money, and they tell us a little bit of paper is soon lost. We could wish that money might be had to pay them; and if possible, turning over from one ship to another might be avoided for the future, at least as much as may be, for we see it breedeth trouble and discontent.[34]

Leave seems to have been a regarded by volunteers as something like an entitlement, which it was dangerous to deny.[35] Serious problems arose among angry men held aboard ships in port for want of money to pay them off. 'I did well hope,' wrote Commissioner Peter Pett from Chatham in October 1653,

we should have dispatched the service with quietness and have done it till this morning, but even now comes the *Unicorn*'s company at least 200 of them, and with much peremptoriness in a mutinous way told me that they would not go aboard to do any duty till they had their money. I used all the arguments I could to please them in a fair way, and was assisted by Captain Lane and Captain Bourne, but nothing could prevail, therefore we must either submit to pay them which will not only in my opinion be very dishonourable to the service and beget an extreme ill precedent, and which I am confident will no way be pleasing to you, or else I shall humbly desire that a troop of horse may be forthwith sent down, which certainly will be of singular use.[36]

This was the incident which led to unpaid seamen attacking Cromwell in person, and there were ugly riots at Harwich and Portsmouth as well. The use of troops to avoid the 'dishonour' and 'ill precedent' of paying the men what they were owed became a frequent expedient, which of course did nothing to make the sailors (or their officers, who were in the same case and generally sympathized with them) love the army.[37] Nor did the employment of infantry afloat from 1653; an expedient to make up for shortage of seamen, which was highly unpopular with the seamen themselves.[38]

Discipline was one of the many costs of war which the Rump Parliament was reluctant to confront until the defeat of Dungeness left them no choice. Among the government's first reactions was to issue a code of 'Laws of War and Ordinances of the Sea', the later 'Articles of War', which remained in force with only minor revisions until 1749, and strongly marked the later Articles right up to the Naval Discipline Act of 1860. This is the more remarkable because these Articles of War were in no sense a coherent disciplinary code; they were a haphazard collection of measures almost entirely concerned with the misdeeds of officers, above all treachery and cowardice.[39] Article after article forbade communication with or assistance to 'any State, Prince, or other, being enemy or rebel to this Commonwealth', enjoined captains 'not to behave themselves faintly, nor yield to the enemy, or to cry for quarter', and threatened death to those who through 'cowardice, negligence or disaffection' should fail in action, or 'utter any words of sedition and uproar', or 'wilfully burn or set fire on any ship or magazine . . . not appertaining to an enemy'.[40] In this they faithfully reflected the concerns of the Commonwealth government in 1652. Blake's immediate reaction to the 'baseness of spirit' displayed during the battle (from which many ships returned having expended little or no ammunition)[41] was to doubt the loyalty of his captains, 'there being very great cause at present to suspect that our old enemies are again at work among us'.[42] More experienced senior officers had already pointed to a different problem: many of the new captains had been appointed to command their own ships, taken up for naval service, which gave them a powerful incentive not to risk their property in action. 'It is humbly conceived,' Penn wrote to Cromwell in June 1652,

> that the State would be far better served, if, as formerly, they placed commanders in all the merchant-ships so taken up; for, the commanders now employed being all part-owners of their ships (and fearing some not so clearly conscientious as they should be), I do believe will not be so industrious in taking an enemy as other men; especially considering, that by engagement they not only waste their powder and shot, but are liable to receive damage in their masts, sails, rigging, and hull, and endanger the loss of all, when they may be quiet, and receive the same pay.[43]

As far as the men were concerned, the main effect of the new Articles was to institute the practice of a 'private council of war', a petty court martial of ship's officers to try minor offences.

In general the discipline of the State's Navy was notably milder than that of the army; marked, in the opinion of the best modern study, by 'brisk paternalism' rather than severity. Though the Articles of War provided liberally for the death penalty, there appears to have been only one seaman hanged for an offence committed afloat between 1649 and 1660, to which should be added Captain Peter Warren, executed in 1652 for murdering one of his men.[44] The worst common offences, such as drunkenness and theft, were punished by whipping, disrating or dismissal. Meredith Price was dismissed as cook of the *Nightingale* in 1654, being 'much given to drink, swearing and railing, and his unhandsome ordering of meat has much disturbed and prejudiced the ship'.[45] The same year,

> At an anchor in Leghorn Road and this day were three seamen whipped from ship to ship two ordered to have 3 lashes apiece and the other four, one for stealing money on board the *Bridgewater* and one for striking his commander. He had 4 lashes and another for being drunk and fighting.[46]

This was one of the first recorded cases of 'flogging round the fleet', with the man put in a boat to receive so many lashes alongside each ship present. In 1658 a thief of ship's stores was given thirteen lashes alongside each of three ships and transported to Jamaica; his accomplices were flogged with him and had a corner of their ears cut off.[47] These were among the most severe punishments; at the other extreme we have a note of 'a private council of war on Barnaby Dennis who paid five shillings rather than he would be ducked'.[48] When officers abused their authority, as some did, the Admiralty was receptive to well-grounded complaints. A number of captains were dismissed as a result, while for lesser misjudgements others were reprimanded. 'It is necessary you should bear a command, and we would not weaken your hands in it,' Captain Edmund Curtis of the *Newcastle* was informed in 1658, 'though our advice be, that you would do it with that prudence and good temper of spirit as may not needlessly exasperate the ship's company, and make the service burdensome to them'.[49]

The new scale of pay which was another of the measures introduced after Dungeness has already been mentioned. For the first time it distinguished ordinary seamen from 'able seamen fit for the helm and lead, top and yard';[50] 'able' bearing the old sense of skilful.[51] 'Mariners come not into the service,' it was reported,

> neither is it likely, by what we have observed, that they will, unless some further encouragement be given to deserving men, the pay of a reformado that hath been twenty years a seamen being at present no more than an

ordinary waterman pressed from the Thames that never saw the sea before.[52]

Accordingly the 1647 rate of 19s a month was retained for ordinary seamen, while able received 24s a month. The new scale, like the Articles of War, had a long future, remaining in force until 1797. With it came the new system of prize-money and the entitlement to plunder already mentioned. This last was a reflection of what was more or less inevitable, or at least very difficult to prevent. It was before the new arrangements came into force that Captain Roger Martin reported taking 'a gallant ship, richly laden, having great store of silver; but what quantity I cannot give your Honours an account, for my men, entering her by storm, met with the silver, and plundered it before my coming on board'.[53] There were also new arrangements for the sick and wounded and a scheme of widows' gratuities, all to be paid out of the tenth share of all prize-money formerly given to the Lord Admiral.[54] The same fund paid for the first large issue of naval medals, mainly to officers.[55]

The common seamen of the 1650s appear very much in the character we know from the sixteenth or the eighteenth century: tough and resourceful, free-spending when they could get cash or credit, hard-drinking ashore and often afloat.[56] 'Some come tippling on shore, and then march away in their mad fits, some to privateers at Fowey, and some to their homes . . .', complained Captain Henry Hatsall, the Navy Commission's Agent at Plymouth, and the sailor Edward Coxere's memory of a visit to that port confirms the picture: 'We were all of us too wild and little considered the mercies we received, but took large liberty when ashore in drinking and sporting as the manner of seamen generally is.'[57] They were men of the world, accustomed to foreign parts and often foreign ships. 'I served several masters in the wars between King and Parliament at sea,' Coxere wrote.

> Next I served the Spaniards against the French, then the Hollanders against the English; then I was taken by the English out of a Dunkirker; and then I served the English against the Hollanders; and last I was taken by the Turks, where I was forced to serve then against English, French, Dutch, and Spaniards, and all Christendom. Then, when I was released from them, I was got in a man-of-war against the Spaniards, till at last I was taken prisoner by the Spaniards.[58]

All this in twelve years, during which he taught himself navigation and four languages.

Some seamen and rather more officers were married, and officers' wives figure from time to time in the records, sometimes tempting their husbands to stay ashore when they should have been at sea, sometimes aboard their husbands' ships, at least for the day if not in some cases for the voyage. Homosexuality seems to have been very rare, but the wandering life of the seamen (and sometimes their officers) did not always promote strict faithfulness in marriage, and there were some with wives in more than one port.[59] The parting was hard when ships sailed, especially for a distant voyage, like Penn's fleet sailing for the West Indies in December 1654, as the physician Dr Daniel Whistler recorded:

> This was a sad day with our married men, they hanging down their heads with a demure countenance, acting loath to depart, and some of them professing more love the one to the other in one half hour than they had performed in all the time of their being together. And many of our young men that had entangled themselves in love with some young virgin; who think it very hard and a great cruelty to leave a young virgin to whom he hath engaged and wholly devoted his heart. Others were weeping, and leaving and bequeathing unto them some pledge of their wanton love; receiving from them some cordial against sea sickness; as caps, and handkerchiefs, and shirts, to eye and wear when Neptune should most oppose them.[60]

'Loath to depart' was a popular sailors' song, but there was another kind of music in the State's Navy; 'the melody of experienced saints'.[61] The Puritans and Independents who dominated the Navy cared very much that they should serve according to the will of God. They held days of prayer before operations. 'We set this day apart,' Penn wrote,

> to seek the Lord for a blessing upon our designs. All the commanders, and several others of the officers and men, came on board me: our chaplain laid open the cause of our meeting, and made a large exposition on a psalm; and then the ministers of the *Swiftsure, Foresight,* and *Pelican* preached: the Lord, in mercy, hear us and own us![62]

At times the Lord was hard to find, especially on the 1655 Caribbean expedition. In Penn's squadron returning from Jamaica, on 13 July, 'being a day appointed for seeking the Lord, the *Paragon,* between nine and ten o'clock, in sermon-time, took fire in the steward's room; and burnt three or four hours, till at last she blew up'. The prayer and fasting were put off.[63] Since 'the Lord is a man of war', and 'his book the best handbook on war', in moments of perplexity Puritan commanders sought the guidance of the Holy Ghost by opening the Bible at random.[64] Seeking the Dutch in February 1653, they were given II Chronicles 20:16: 'behold, they come up by the cliff of Ziz' – which turned out to be Portland Bill.[65] They issued strict orders for the observance of the Lord's Day and the suppression of blasphemy, though it seems with mixed results.[66] 'There is such swearing at sea as if both hell, the damned and all the devils in it were let loose . . .' exclaimed the chaplain Daniel Pell; 'Were I a commander, if fair means and sweet persuasions would not prevail, I would hang them up at the mainyard.'[67] No admiral went so far, but Penn threatened a five-shilling fine or twenty lashes.[68] Commissioner Willoughby at Portsmouth called for junior officers ' "such as fear God, are faithful to the Commonwealth, and able to discharge their respective employments," which,' the Navy Commissioners replied drily, 'we know not how to answer, being not acquainted with three men of these capacities on the River.'[69]

Chaplains, of course, were key figures whose religious and political reliability was closely scrutinized, 'several persons having crept into the fleet under the name of chaplains, who promote opinions rather than godliness'.[70] Penn ordered his captains in 1655 'to take special care that no person be entertained on board your ship as chaplain but such as fear God, are well principled in religion, and whose life and conversation is agreeable to the rules of the Gospel'.[71] But the earthly rewards of a naval chaplain's position were scanty, the dangers considerable, the process of appointment haphazard, and the quality of the candidates very variable.[72] John Vincent of the *Jersey* was recommended by a brother officer in glowing terms:

> To speak truth take him to our sea by and large, take him as a scholar, take him as a godly man, an exemplary good liver, take him, as occasion be, as well with the sword in his hand as the word in his mouth, if I should but endeavour to set him forth, as we say, in his proper colours, my paper would shorter be full; to say all in this letter, take him every way I know too few such.[73]

On the other hand Robert Leonard of the *Constant Warwick* was dismissed by court martial in 1656 for coming off to the ship at Plymouth 'so drunk that they could not get him on board but were fain to hoist him in with the tackles'.[74] There were a number of ships where other officers or even seamen officiated as chaplains; a conservative clergyman took it as one of the three signs of a 'mad age' (the others being women preachers and women politicians). Simon Prior was 'minister and gunner' of the *Fame*, though her captain complained that he 'doth rather cause a confusion than a reformation amongst us [and] may cause great disquietness in our ship'.[75] In the 1650s several gunners joined the new sect of the Quakers, which provoked difficulties as they moved towards pacifism.[76]

How much lasting influence the 'saints' had on the Navy is difficult to estimate. After the Restoration it was fashionable to deride them as canting hypocrites, and there certainly were not a few trimmers who successfully mastered the pious language acceptable to their seniors.[77] But there were also many of profound faith, who served God and the Navy with equal devotion. One voice may speak for them: 'Your Honours' and the Commonwealth's faithful servant in the Lord', George Kendall, Clerk of the Survey of Deptford Yard, rebuking the Admiralty in July 1653 with the words of the prophet Micah,

> to present to your Honours the cry of some poor oppressed people which sounds daily in mine ears, wherein justice and mercy is required from you, for what is it that the Lord requires of man but to do justly and to love mercy and to walk humbly with the Lord. The complaint is very great amongst the seamen: first, for the withholding of their wages, which they have earned with the hazard of their lives, which causes the wives and children of many of them to suffer much hardship and disheartens them from the service. Secondly, for the violent pressing and carrying away those poor men whose wages is so stopped without any care taken for their distressed families in their absence. Thirdly, the bad provision is made for them at sea, being necessitated in many ships to feed upon unwholesome and stinking victuals, whereby many of them are become sick and unserviceable, and many are dead. Shall not their blood be required at the hands of those that, for their gain, undertake the victualling, though they be persons greatly in favour and may have an appearance of honesty and godliness? Certainly the great God of heaven and earth will make inquisition for blood if men do not. It cannot but be fresh in your memories how the arm of the Lord hath from time to time been made manifest in pulling down the mighty from their seats and breaking all unjust powers in pieces, and it is now the hopes of his people that truth shall spring out of the earth and righteousness shall look down from heaven, yea that it shall set us in the way of his steps. My humble advice is that seamen's wages be duly paid without stopping or diminishing any part thereof; that their families in their absence be preserved from perishing and special care be taken that their diet at sea be good and wholesome, and you will hereby engage them to a willing and cheerful service of you; that you shall not be put to such violent ways of compulsion as of late, which breeds much heart-burning between seamen and soldiers . . .[78]

It was not without risk for a junior official to remind the new military regime of the fate that injustice had brought on Charles I. Men like him may not be congenial to the modern reader, but they were not hypocrites or timeservers.

FIVE

Terrible, Obstinate and Bloody Battle

Operations 1660–1668

The Navy which the restored Charles II inherited in 1660, though dilapidated and virtually bankrupt, was by far the strongest point in an otherwise precarious regime. The hated army was disbanded, except for the king's Guards and the regiment of General Monck (now created Duke of Albemarle). Charles II intended to resettle the monarchy on as broad a basis of comprehension and toleration as possible, but the vengeful Royalists of the Cavalier Parliament limited his freedom, and in particular blocked his plan for religious toleration of Protestant dissenters. The result over the following years was to create the beginnings of a party political system, with Anglican Royalists supporting the crown, while Presbyterians, sectaries and other friends of the former Republic formed a disloyal opposition. For Charles, and most of his contemporaries, this looked dangerously like the opening moves of another civil war. His urgent priority was to cement the fragile unity of his kingdoms by strengthening the crown. Modern historians, who tend to dislike Charles, often accuse him of aiming to abolish Parliament and establish an autocratic, absolutist, even Catholic monarchy on the French model. He was undoubtedly impressed, as all Europe was, by the dazzling wealth and power of Louis XIV, and he was privately attracted by the Catholic church (into which he was secretly received on his deathbed), but it is less clear that he aimed to do any more than restore the traditional powers of the English crown as they had existed at his father's accession. For any project of strengthening his authority, the Navy was likely to be a prime instrument, and the only way of using it was a popular and lucrative foreign war, which gave him a good reason to listen to advocates of aggression.[1]

At first, however, the new government was pacific, preoccupied with reconstruction at home, and a new system of alliances abroad. Portugal, fighting since 1640 to re-establish her independence from Spain, secured an English alliance with a princess to marry Charles II, bringing the colonies of

Tangier and Bombay as her dowry. This naturally made Spain an enemy, and inclined France to be a friend – an inclination cemented by selling France Dunkirk, which Charles II judged to be indefensible at any cost he could afford. The Dutch feared the growing power of France and her evident ambitions on the Spanish Netherlands (modern Belgium), they were allied with Spain and at war with Portugal over the possession of Brazil. They therefore found themselves on the other side of this new alliance system, in spite of the lavish gifts with which they had, rather naively, hoped to buy Charles's friendship and the repeal of the Navigation Acts.[2] When Admiral Mountague, now created Earl of Sandwich, took a squadron to the Mediterranean in 1661 to attack Algiers (fruitlessly) and take possession of Tangier, he had tense encounters with a Dutch fleet under de Ruyter, cruising to support Spain against Portugal.[3]

In English domestic politics, Charles's first chief minister, the pacific Earl of Clarendon, progressively lost ground to court rivals gathered around the king's brother, James Duke of York, Lord Admiral of England. This group, many of whom had been ruined in the king's service in the 1650s, were the chief investors in the new Royal African Company, a venture intended to make quick fortunes trading and hunting for gold on the West African coast. Its first ships were sent out in 1660 under the former Royalist privateer Sir Robert Holmes, a tough and experienced seaman who already knew the waters. In dealing with the local people, he was instructed 'to express in all their demeanour and conversation the benignity and candour of the English nation' (a point which might possibly have been lost on the slaves he was also ordered to collect).[4] The Dutch West India Company was the dominant trading power in the area, in which it claimed a monopoly, but the Africa Company's court backers do not seem to have taken seriously the risk that any local fighting might spread. Charles's court in general neither liked nor respected the Dutch. They were notoriously Republicans, who had made peace with Cromwell on terms designed to exclude from power both the related houses of Orange and Stuart, who had given refuge to English Republicans after the Restoration, and were suspected of backing their plots. Moreover the English Navy had soundly defeated them, and many of the officers around the Duke of York looked forward to making their reputations and fortunes by doing so again. So did he. 'I must not forget to add his Royal Highness' own vigour,' his secretary William Coventry wrote of the causes of the war, 'who having been bred to arms, was willing to have an occasion to show his courage on sea as on land . . . this vigour of his Royal Highness broke the measure of those ministers who should otherwise have preserved the peace at any price.'[5] Though few English merchants stood to profit directly from war or wanted to fight for trade, there was widespread alarm that 'the Hollanders have taken a resolution to have the monarchy of trade of the whole world,' as John Evelyn put it, and would succeed if they were not opposed by force.[6]

The Dutch government was dominated, as it had been since 1653, by the towering figure of Johan de Witt, *raadpensionaris* of Holland. A great statesman of consummate ability and dedication, de Witt was the spokesman of the 'True Freedom', meaning the freedom of himself and his Republican associates to govern the state in its, and their, best interests, and to ignore the opinion of *het grauw*, 'the rabble', the opponents whom he himself reckoned to amount to 999 out of every thousand of the population. As was natural for a Republican Hollander, de Witt was a strong supporter of the navy, and at the end of the previous war with England he had forced through measures which created the first major Dutch fleet of purpose-built warships – a development of which the English were not sufficiently aware. In the judgement of Sir William Temple, long-serving English ambassador at the Hague, de Witt was 'a man of unwearied industry, inflexible constancy, sound, clear and deep understanding, and untainted integrity, so that whenever he was blinded, it was by the passion he had for that which he esteemed the good and interest of his state'.[7] His blindness was arrogance: he never doubted that his judgement was better than everyone else's on every subject (as it very often was), and he judged as a politician. To keep the Orangists from power he starved the army, and ensured that only Republican admirals were given high command. To preserve the superior status of Amsterdam, he kept all Dutch warships limited to the maximum draught which could clear the Pampus, the bar of the River IJ on which Amsterdam stands, though the other admiralties had deeper water available, and the admirals urged the need of the biggest possible ships to face the English.[8]

In Coventry's opinion, 'the Dutch war arose by strange accidental things concurring from several parts and parties without any intent to help each other'.[9] The immediate trigger, however, was undoubtedly the sending of Holmes to West Africa again at the end of 1663, with instructions to protect the Royal African Company's trade, which he interpreted as a licence to mount a devastating raid on the Dutch. Holmes, in Coventry's words, was 'a man of an understanding fit to make a war, and a courage to make it good; in the latter few go beyond him; in the former few come short.'[10] Before Holmes returned to Plymouth in December 1664, it was becoming clear what kind of war he had made.[11] De Witt had discovered Holmes's mission, and in spite of the dilatory and porous nature of Dutch government, found means to send swift and secret orders to de Ruyter in the Mediterranean to follow Holmes. His counter-stroke recaptured all that the Dutch had lost, and much more. Besides the seizure of all its trading posts but one, de Ruyter's booty from the Africa Company included 1,420 ivory tusks (weighing 16,959 lbs in total), 975 copper kettles and bowls, 14 chests of knives and rugs, sundry cloth, weapons, 3 tons of pepper, 30 bags of salt, 2,889 lbs of rice, and a clock. Continuing across the Atlantic, he made an unsuccessful attack on English shipping at Barbados, took many prizes elsewhere in the West Indies and raided the Newfoundland fishery before returning.[12] The tidings of 'our being beaten to dirt at Guinea by de Ruyter' reached England before Holmes did. ''Tis hard to say whether this news be received with more anger, or shame,' wrote Samuel Pepys, the young Secretary of the Navy Board, 'but there is reason enough for both.'[13] Both countries were now preparing for war. Sir Thomas Allin commanding the English squadron in the Mediterranean was ordered to attack the Dutch 'Smyrna convoy' homeward-bound from the Levant, which he did on 19 December 1664 off Cadiz, with only partial success, provoking the States-General to declare war on 14 January 1665.[14]

In both main fleets the choice of flag-officers and the organization of the fleets presented some tricky questions. Charles II had to choose between his brother the Lord Admiral (who had a gallant record as an army officer, but had never commanded at sea), Prince Rupert, Albemarle, Sandwich and Sir William Penn. His solution was to leave Albemarle ashore as acting Lord Admiral for administrative purposes, and organize the fleet into what was becoming the standard English formation of three squadrons, with York in command of the whole fleet and of the centre or Red Squadron, having Penn aboard the flagship to advise him. Prince Rupert became Admiral of the White, commanding the van or White Squadron, and Sandwich as Admiral of the Blue likewise commanded the rear. Each of the three had their Vice- and Rear-Admirals commanding the van and rear divisions of their respective squadrons, but the Vice-Admiral of the Blue, Sir George Ayscue, took the rear rather than van division so as to have a very senior admiral leading the line if the fleet should reverse course. With the conspicuous exception of the Duke of York, the English flag-officers were almost all experienced fleet commanders, mostly from the Cromwellian Navy. Though these 'flag ranks' were still only temporary appointments and not permanent ranks in the modern style, they fell into an established order of seniority: after the Duke came the Admirals of the White and Blue, then the three Vice-Admirals (Red, White and Blue in that order) and the three Rear-Admirals likewise. The Duke of York worked hard to unite his fleet; 'he ordered all the flag-officers on board with him every morning, to agree upon the order of battle and rank'.[15] The line of battle was arranged with some care, each flagship being assigned powerful 'seconds' ahead and astern to support her, and new Fighting Instructions were issued ordering captains to form a close-hauled line, keeping station half a cable (120 yards) apart, and not to leave the line either to capture enemies or assist friends: 'nothing but beating the body of the enemy's fleet can effectually secure the lame ships'. For the first time signals were established for tacking all together, or from the rear in succession, so that the fleet could quickly reverse order. Sandwich wanted to go further in the direction of 'professionalization' by excluding armed merchantmen from the line to make it shorter and handier as well as more powerful, but this was not adopted.[16]

The Dutch fleet organization, by contrast, reflected political rather than operational priorities. Rivalry between the admiralties had generated a plethora of flag-officers, to accommodate whom the fleet was divided into seven squadrons, each with three admirals or commodores. Most of the squadrons were made up of ships from mixed admiralties, commanded in many cases by admirals unknown to their subordinates, and there was no established order of seniority between them. Nor was there any arrangement of the squadrons in a line of battle, which the Dutch had not yet adopted. The overall commander-in-chief, Jacob van Wassenaer, Heer van Obdam, was an elderly cavalry officer who had won a victory over the Swedish fleet in 1658 (under the guidance of the able Captain Egbert Meeuwsen Cortenaer), but whose chief qualifications were that he was a Republican nobleman of proven courage, who did not represent any of the rival admiralties. This time Cortenaer, by now an admiral, commanded a squadron of his own, and Obdam had no professional adviser to hand.[17]

In the spring of 1665 the English fleet at first attempted to blockade the Dutch coast, hoping to intercept inbound convoys and de Ruyter's squadron, but as in 1653 the victualling arrangements soon collapsed under the strain, and the English retreated to the coast of Norfolk. The two fleets met off Lowestoft on 3 June; the Dutch with 107 ships, of which eighty-one were warships and eleven substantial Indiamen; the English with 100, including sixty-four men-of-war and twenty-four large merchantmen, but overall greatly superior in firepower. Initially the two fleets passed on opposite tacks at long range, then tacked again, the English to windward. The individual English squadrons soon got out of order, but each seems to have preserved a rough line. In the closing stages of the battle the English pressed the Dutch closer, and the firing grew so heavy that it could be heard in the Hague.

Thus we in the van, the Earl of Sandwich in the middle, the Prince Rupert in the rear, beat very hard upon them till 2 when they began to lask away 2 or 3 points from the wind; we followed them so close they were forced to go larger. At ½ past 2 they were some 4 or 5 points from the wind then Obdam blew up; by 3 they were all right before it, so that by 4 it became a confused rout . . .'[18]

Obdam was killed shortly before his flagship blew up, and the Dutch fleet disintegrated with rival admirals, each claiming to be the commander-in-chief, escaping in different directions. Their defeat would have been even heavier if the ensuing pursuit had not been called off during the night by one of the Duke of York's courtiers, acting without orders on a plea from the Duchess to keep him as far as possible out of danger.[19]

She was not the only one alarmed by the risks which the heir to the throne had run in a battle in which several courtiers had been killed at his side. After the battle Charles II ordered him ashore, and since Prince Rupert declined a joint command, Sandwich took the fleet to sea again in July, with Penn as his second-in-command. Their business was to exploit the victory of Lowestoft by intercepting Dutch trade, all of which was now forced to come northabout and through the North Sea. Specifically they were looking for de Ruyter, homeward-bound from West Africa and the Americas, and for a rich VOC convoy. The usual manning and victualling problems, compounded by plague in England, made prolonged cruising unattractive; 'besides if they should put it to hazard to go home, the sea is wide and night and fogs and flat coasts along the Dutch shore advantageous for them to escape us by'.[20] Sandwich therefore took the fleet north (narrowly missing de Ruyter on the way) to the coast of Norway, which was ruled by Denmark, therefore friendly to the Dutch and the obvious landfall for inward-bound Dutch shipping. He learned from the British minister in Copenhagen that King Frederick III was willing to break his alliance and escape from the tutelage of the Dutch at a profitable moment, when there was a rich Dutch convoy in one of his ports which could be taken by a joint Anglo-Danish attack and the proceeds shared. The prospect was not negligible, when a single laden Dutch Indiaman could be worth £250,000, or a quarter of Charles II's usual annual revenues. Discovering that the VOC convoy was in Bergen, Sandwich sent in a force under Rear-Admiral Thomas Teddeman to attack. Unfortunately, though Frederick III was indeed planning a treacherous attack on his ally, his orders to the governor of Bergen had not yet arrived, and when Teddeman attacked on 2 August he was beaten off by a determined defence by Commodore Pieter de Bitter and the Danish batteries. Instead of a strategic and financial coup, the defeat forced Denmark back into Dutch arms.[21]

The death of Obdam faced Johan de Witt with an unpleasant choice among three senior admirals: Witte de With, who hated everyone; Johan Evertsen, an able but Orangist Zealander whom de Witt was determined to ruin; and Cornelis Tromp, son of the great Maarten and like him a popular Orangist, but a very different character, 'who is not only unwise and unstable', as de Witt was warned, 'but shows great malice . . . a dangerous man . . . to whom no squadron should be entrusted, let alone the whole fleet'.[22] De Ruyter, widely respected and not politically active, was still at sea. Initially Tromp was chosen, then demoted as soon as de Ruyter returned, for which Tromp never forgave either of them. The fleet put to sea in August to cover the returning VOC ships from Bergen, with de Ruyter in command and de Witt himself aboard the flagship, 'to have the power of a Roman dictator in the fleet, and to represent the sovereignty of the State there and to act and command in all things as if the State itself were there', in the words of Sir George Downing, England's leading expert on Dutch politics.[23] Not content with political authority, de Witt interfered with operational planning and even pilotage. Few admirals would have tolerated it, but the mild-mannered de Ruyter formed a genuine partnership with him.[24]

The Dutch were scattered by a gale on the Dogger Bank. Most of them eluded the English, but on 3 September Sandwich captured a total of twenty-three prizes, including two rich Indiamen and their four escorts. Mindful of his unpaid men, and with verbal permission from the king, he authorized an immediate distribution of booty. This was politically disastrous, for he and his officers took their share, and his enemies were able to depict him as a corrupt profiteer. For the moment his naval career was ruined, and next year he went to Madrid as ambassador.[25]

For the 1666 campaign, Charles II wanted to balance the bold and skilful Prince Rupert with the more phlegmatic Albemarle. This was a risky policy, for they were extremely different characters, and their respective followers were bitter rivals, but the two admirals vindicated his judgement by maintaining a cordial working relationship. The first issue they, and the king's ministers, had to face was a strategic dilemma. On 16 January 1666 France declared war as a Dutch ally. The possibility was open that the French Mediterranean squadron under the duc de Beaufort would come north, combine with the smaller force at Brest, and come up the Channel to support their allies. Though in the event Beaufort's northward movements were extremely slow and cautious, English intelligence considerably overestimated the threat. Charles was less concerned about a French attempt to unite with the Dutch, which his fleet was well placed to prevent, than about reported plans to land troops in Ireland. It was this fear which led to the fateful decision to divide the main fleet, sending Rupert down-Channel with twenty ships on 29 May, while Albemarle remained in the Downs with fifty-six ships of the main fleet, well short of the seventy he regarded as the necessary minimum to face the Dutch. By now reports were coming in that the Dutch were nearly ready for sea, and both admirals were uneasy – but not uneasy enough to send out proper scouts to the Dutch coast. Albemarle wrote to Charles II hinting that if he met the enemy, honour would oblige him to fight whatever the odds, and that if the king wanted him to retreat he had better be given unequivocal orders. The king missed the point, but he did realize the danger of the fleet being trapped in the Downs, and ordered Albemarle north to the Gunfleet off Harwich, at the mouth of the main channel up the Thames, 'where you cannot be forced to do anything but what you choose'. Late on the 30th the changing intelligence picture caused Charles II to order Prince Rupert's recall, and the orders reached him off Portsmouth on 1 June. He still had no urgent news of the Dutch and no idea that the greatest naval battle of the age of sail was just beginning.[26]

Albemarle sailed from the Downs on 31 May, still unware that de Ruyter was very near and that he had only just escaped from the trap. Next morning, as he headed north to round the Long Sand Head, the Dutch were sighted to the eastward, to leeward. Though he could easily have escaped into the Thames, where powerful reinforcements would have joined him in a few days, Albemarle refused to run away from the enemy. The stiff breeze heeled the English ships so that their lee lower-deck ports had to be kept closed, while Dutch ships generally were stiffer, with higher freeboard, and profited from the leeward position. In such conditions the English advantage of firepower would be largely negated. What was more, de Witt had abandoned his opposition to bigger ships the previous year, and the Dutch now had growing numbers of big ships of seventy guns or more, some of them, like de Ruyter's new flagship the *De Zeven Provinciën* of eighty guns, equivalent to English Second Rates. Albemarle was advised to wait for easier weather next day, and would have done so, had the Dutch fleet (eighty-six ships against fewer than sixty English) not been found at anchor spread out in a manner which allowed them to be 'rolled up' from the windward end, much as Maarten Tromp had almost succeeded in doing off Portland thirteen years before. That had been Albemarle's first sea battle, and no doubt he had not forgotten it. Now he hastened to exploit his opportunity. Ignoring the odds and the risks, he bore down on the enemy in an improvised line.[27] Lieutenant Jeremy Roch of the *Antelope* was in it:

And then began the most terrible, obstinate and bloodiest battle that ever was fought on the seas, for rushing in amongst the thickest of them with our ship, being foremost, we fought through and all the rest followed us, so the Dutch presently cut, and came to sail. Then we tacked and fought our way through again and so we held on till 10 o'clock at night.[28]

Having the incomparable witness of Willem van de Velde the elder, who accompanied the Dutch fleet in a galliot and sketched every phase of the battle, we know more about the detail of this battle than of many in the twentieth century, and can be certain that Albemarle did not in fact close on the leading Dutch squadrons and crush them, but fought a conventional gunnery battle, at some range and disadvantage. By nightfall the two fleets, still in parallel, were approaching the Flanders coast, with Admiral Cornelis Evertsen's Zealand squadron now to windward. In tacking to the northward, the English van was left behind, Sir William Berkeley, Vice-Admiral of the White, was killed and his flagship taken. His Rear-Admiral, Sir John Harman, was trapped amongst the Dutch fleet by night, attacked by fireships which caused some of his crew to leap overboard in panic, but still managed to fight his way clear, 'conducting himself with notable fortitude like a true warrior', in the opinion of Dutch officers, and killing Evertsen in the process.[29]

Next day was fine: 'very hot,' Lieutenant Roch noted, 'more ways than one'.[30] The two fleets were reduced to fifty ships against seventy-seven. The English began by running down on the enemy and hauling up into line at close range, a new manoeuvre devised by Sandwich the previous year. The Dutch for their part were fighting in line of battle for the first time. For the next ten hours the two fleets repeatedly 'passed' on opposite tacks, individual ships and squadrons often cutting right through the enemy.

The manner of fighting at that time was, that each fleet lay in a line, and when the ships of one fleet lay to the northward, the heads of the other lay to the southward, the headmost ships of our fleet engaging first the headmost of theirs: so passing on by their fleet in a line, firing all the way, and as soon as the rear of one fleet was clear from the rear of the other, then each fleet tacked in the van, standing almost stem for stem one with another to engage again; by which means there was at least an hour's respite between every encounter.[31]

In the course of one of these engagements de Ruyter, heroically improvising communications, took his own squadron through the enemy line to rescue the trapped Tromp while leaving the bulk of his force to cover him to windward. By evening Albemarle's situation was growing desperate. He had only twenty-eight ships left in company which were fit for action. On the morning of the 3rd, a year to the day since Lowestoft, Albemarle was in full retreat. He was by no means routed, even now, but formed a line abreast with the fifteen heaviest ships to cover the remainder, using their heavy stern-chasers to keep the Dutch at a distance. Early in the afternoon Prince Rupert's squadron was sighted to the westward, and the two squadrons hastened towards one another.[32]

Navigation in the shallow waters of the southern North Sea was always tricky. The coasts are mostly low-lying, the best seamarks visible perhaps ten miles off in clear weather, which is not common in the North Sea. A good deep-sea navigator with a clear sky could fix his latitude (but not longitude) by observation to ten or twenty miles, but this was useless in waters where the pilot often needed to know his position to within a few cables, and where the available charts were in any case grossly inaccurate.[33] There was no substitute for caution, experience, and the lead, and in this crisis they failed. Unbeknown to the English pilots, the Galloper shoal lay between Albemarle and Rupert, and at about five o'clock Ayscue's flagship the *Royal Prince* ran hard aground. Terrified by approaching fireships, his men forced him to surrender. The flood tide subsequently floated her, but her rudder was disabled and de Ruyter ordered her burned – to the fury of Tromp, to whose squadron she had struck. 'And so we lost the second best ship in England, having ninety brass pieces of ordnance and eight hundred men, which was a great grief to all the rest of the fleet,' noted the sailor Edward Barlow. Even after fifty-six years' service, 'she was like a castle in the sea and I believe the best ship that ever was built in the world to endure battering,' wrote Charles's minister Sir Thomas Clifford, 'but she is gone and this is an ill subject to be longer upon'.[34]

The arrival of Prince Rupert's fresh ships and a few more from the Thames brought the English fleet up to about fifty-two ships, against about sixty-nine remaining Dutch. Both fleets reorganized overnight to adjust for their gains and losses, and prepared for a supreme effort on the 4th. In the course of heavy and confused fighting on successive passes, various squadrons on each side broke through the enemy line. Both Rupert and Albemarle succeeded in doing so from the leeward, but the initial English success was reversed by a desperate counter-attack by de Ruyter late in the day. The English standard ammunition allowance was forty rounds a gun, increased by special order to fifty shortly before this action, for those ships which could stow so much. By this time many of Albemarle's ships were running very short, and the nerve of some exhausted captains was failing. Prince Rupert's flagship was dismasted at the critical moment, and in the closing stages of the action the English were in full flight.[35]

In this great battle the English lost ten ships and about 4,250 men killed, wounded or captured – more than a fifth of those engaged. Ayscue was (and still is) the most senior English sea officer ever to have been taken prisoner in action. Two admirals (Berkeley and Sir Christopher Myngs) and ten captains were killed. At Sheerness John Evelyn, 'beheld that sad spectacle, namely more than half of that gallant bulwark of the kingdom miserably shattered, hardly a vessel entire, but appearing rather so many wracks and hulls, so cruelly had the Dutch mangled us: when the loss of the *Prince* (that gallant vessel) had been a loss to be universally deplored'.[36] Though de Ruyter was characteristically modest, the Dutch celebrated a great victory, and assumed that the English were crushed.[37] This was unwise, for the underlying balance of forces had not much changed, and the English were unlikely to make the mistake of dividing their fleet again. Though the Dutch had fought in line for the first time, the discipline and organization of the English fleet remained notably stronger. 'Nothing equalled the good order and discipline of the English,' wrote the comte de Guiche, a French observer aboard the Dutch fleet; 'never was line drawn straighter than that their ships formed . . . truly the admirable order of their fleet should always be imitated.'[38] Learning from experience, Albemarle and Prince Rupert issued additional Fighting Instructions soon after the Four Days' Battle, designed to strengthen the cohesion of the fleet further and develop ways to divide and overwhelm the enemy.[39]

In spite of the professional misgivings of the Dutch admirals, Johan de Witt had long dreamed of finishing the war by driving up the Thames to deliver a blow to the heart of English sea power. Early in July the Dutch fleet duly appeared at the mouth of the Thames, but de Ruyter judged it impossible and unnecessary to do more than mount a blockade. Meanwhile the English were preparing for action once more. On 22 July Albemarle and Prince Rupert sailed down the King's Channel in a single line nearly ten miles long. Three days later, on St James's Day, the two fleets met east of the Galloper, more or less where they had last parted. Under the fatal illusion that they were the stronger, the Dutch formed on the same tack as the English for a sustained gunnery duel. In fact their fleet was markedly weaker (seventy-two ships against eighty-seven better-armed English ships of the Fourth Rate and upwards) and its line was not well formed – partly because de Witt, alarmed by the heavy losses of flag-officers, had insisted on a 'snaking' line with the flagships lying further away from the enemy, an unworkable scheme which only disorganized and disheartened the fleet. In the resulting action the two rear squadrons (under Cornelis Tromp and Sir Jeremy Smith) became detached and fought a private battle, while the Dutch main body suffered an unequivocal defeat, though de Ruyter with his customary skill brought it home without disastrous losses (only two ships were taken, but four admirals were killed). On their return he accused Tromp of desertion, unleashing a quarrel so venomous that as a consequence Tromp was dismissed from the service.[40]

Casting about for a means of exploiting their victory, the English commanders-in-chief listened to a Dutch traitor, Laurens van Heemskerck, who reported that Dutch merchants stored rich goods on the islands of Vlie and Terschelling at the mouth of the Zuider Zee. Sir Robert Holmes was despatched with a squadron to raid them. Heemskerck proved to be an incapable pilot, but Holmes pressed a Danish seaman into service, and was rewarded with an unexpected coup: over 160 merchantmen lying in Vlie Roads, almost all of which he burned. 'Holmes's bonfire', on 9 August, cost the merchants of Holland the equivalent of over a million pounds; it was by far the most effective piece of English economic warfare against the Dutch in the three seventeenth-century wars.[41]

The two fleets sighted one another again on 1 and 25 September, but a combination of gales and bad English pilotage (including the third time that summer that English warships had been run on the Galloper) frustrated battle. By this time the Dutch, having successfully recovered their inbound VOC fleet, no longer had any need to cruise, and the English no longer had any money to. Acute financial and political crisis was seconded by plague, and the Great Fire of London from 2 to 6 September, which burned out much of the economic activity and tax revenue of the kingdom. By the end of the year peace negotiations had been opened, and Charles II had concluded that it would be impossible to send the main fleet to sea in 1667. At this point his hand was strengthened by unmistakably threatening French moves on the border of Spanish Flanders, giving the Dutch as much to fear from their ally as their enemy, so Charles put out secret feelers to Louis XIV. His gamble paid off: in July French armies invaded Flanders, and the Dutch were forced to concede moderate terms of peace.[42]

Meanwhile, however, Johan de Witt had been doing some gambling of his own. Early in June 1667 the Dutch fleet, commanded by de Ruyter but effectively guided by Cornelis de Witt, acting on his brother's behalf as political agent aboard the flagship, entered the Thames for his long-planned masterstroke. Overriding the admirals' misgivings, Cornelis de Witt drove the fleet forward. On 10 June the Dutch captured the unfinished fort at Sheerness, and began to feel their way up the Medway. On the 12th, de Witt and de

Ruyter personally directing the attack from a longboat, they forced the boom and blockships and advanced into Gillingham Reach, where the biggest ships of the fleet lay at anchor. The *Royal James*, *Royal Oak* and *Loyal London* were burnt by fireships. 'The destruction of these three stately and glorious ships of ours was the most dismal spectacle my eyes ever beheld,' wrote Edward Gregory, Clerk of the Cheque of Chatham Dockyard, 'and it certainly made the heart of every true Englishman bleed, to see such three Argos lost, whom six boats might have saved.'[43] Worst of all, the flagship *Royal Charles* (the former *Naseby*) was towed away in triumph as a prize. In all one First, three Second and three Third Rates (plus some smaller vessels) were taken, burned, sunk or scuttled as blockships. Only the *Royal Sovereign*, then at Portsmouth, escaped of the five principal flagships. Though the king's government was aware of the risk of paying off the fleet and had ordered the defences to be kept up, a combination of bankruptcy, complacency and incompetence had exposed the fleet to catastrophe. In strictly material terms things could have been much worse: the Dutch narrowly failed to destroy Chatham Dockyard, which would have taken a generation to rebuild; they never penetrated the upper Thames; and their only major landing operation, an attack on Landguard Fort defending Harwich, was repulsed with loss. But as everyone realized, the real significance of the Medway raid was political.[44]

The war had been launched on a wave of patriotic enthusiasm with a Parliamentary vote of £2,500,000, which the members of Parliament regarded as ample, and some courtiers thought would win the war and leave the king a handsome surplus. Neither Charles nor his ministers were so naive, but they certainly looked forward to the political gains of victory. Instead there came an Apocalypse of misfortunes; ruin, plague, fire and defeat, culminating in the humiliation of the Medway raid. Clarendon, who had opposed the war from the first, was ejected from office for losing it. Vengeful Parliamentarians, Royalists and Republicans together, mounted inquiries into the supposed misappropriation of the taxes voted for the Navy. 'We will not give any money, be the pretence never so great,' declared Sir Robert Brooke in the Commons Committee on Miscarriages, 'nay, though the enemy was in the River of Thames again, till we know what became of the last money given.'[45] The two Marine Regiments which had been added to the army for service afloat, so organized that their manpower could be discreetly expanded almost indefinitely, were sharply cut back in 1667. Public opinion was alarmed by the growing power of France and increasingly inclined to connect the court with ideas of Catholicism and absolutism. Parliamentary pressure effectively pushed Charles II into the anti-French 'Triple Alliance' of 1668 with the

Netherlands and Sweden. So far from exploiting naval success to gain in authority, as he had hoped, the king found his prerogative of war and foreign policy substantially invaded by Parliament.[46]

The war was almost as much of a disappointment from the commercial perspective. The English fleet had very few cruisers, and the imperative of facing the Dutch forced it to remain concentrated during the summer campaigning season. 'His Majesty's fleet have been masters of the sea this whole summer, and could not well have been so, if they had been carved into squadrons for the convoy of trade,' as Sandwich told the Merchant Adventurers' Company in November 1665, and the Levant Company received a similar response.[47] Those convoys which did sail were not necessarily well escorted. In June 1665 Cortenaer took a complete convoy carrying vital naval stores from Hamburg without firing a shot: 'It is reported that the captain made no resistance and was so overtaken with drink when they did take him that he should have been 2 hours aboard of the vice admiral's ship before he knew where he was.'[48] Dutch privateers were notably more successful than English ones, in spite of the enormous disproportion in the size of the merchant fleets at risk. A partial list mentions 360 English ships made prize, including over forty rich sugar or tobacco ships from the West Indies or Virginia. Danish privateers made further inroads, at least until the hard winter of 1666–7 froze them in port.[49] These years are significant for the solidifying in English Admiralty law of the new concept of a privateer – meaning a privately owned but publicly licensed warship cruising against an enemy in time of declared war – but the actual effectiveness of English privateers seems to have been very limited.[50] Only the Scottish merchant fleet, well placed to prey on Dutch shipping sailing northabout, may have profited from its participation in this war.[51]

In the Americas there were significant 'satellite' campaigns. While Holmes went to West Africa in 1664, Richard Nicholls crossed the Atlantic to capture the Dutch colony of New Amsterdam, renamed New York in the Duke's honour.[52] The West Indies was virtually the only theatre in which the French navy was active, and successful, until on 10 May 1667 off Nevis Commodore John Berry defeated a Franco-Dutch force under Abraham Crijnssen and Antoine Lefebvre de la Barre. Crijnssen went on to mount a destructive raid on the Virginia tobacco trade, but meanwhile another English squadron under Sir John Harman arrived and destroyed the French ships at Fort St Pierre on 25 June, after which he took the colonies of Cayenne and Surinam. None of this had any effect on the outcome of the war, the peace treaty having been signed already.[53]

At the same time the buccaneers of Jamaica continued their unofficial warfare. English relations with Spain were cool, Spanish officials still professed to exclude all foreign ships from the Caribbean, and successive governors of Jamaica found themselves, in the words of Lord Windsor in 1662, 'unwillingly constrained to reduce them to a better understanding by the open and just practices of force.'[54] The few men-of-war on the station were in the same business. Captain Myngs took the important town of Santiago de Cuba in October 1662 at the head of a force of over a thousand buccaneers, and followed it with Campeche four months later.[55] The outbreak of the Dutch war gave a new excuse, though the buccaneers preferred easy Spanish to tough Dutch targets. Henry Morgan, their rising star, ransomed Porto Bello for 100,000 pesos in June 1668. When the Fifth-Rate *Oxford* came out soon afterwards 'to restrain the buccaneers', she was immediately appropriated as his flagship for a great buccaneer assault on Cartagena, only aborted when she blew up, killing almost all on board except him. Just as Lord Sandwich in Madrid finally achieved a peace treaty in September 1667, Morgan's activities so enraged the Spanish government that they declared local war again in April 1669. That same month Morgan destroyed the Spanish Caribbean squadron in a battle on Lake Maracaibo.[56]

The Duke of York, candidly praising Dutch seamanship in bringing their whole fleet up channels which English pilots would not have attempted, inspired in Samuel Pepys in July 1667 the gloomy reflection that 'thus in all things; in wisdom – courage – force – knowledge of our own streams – and success, the Dutch have the best of us, and do end the war with victory on their side'.[57] It was undeniably true, but in the long perspective we can see that the future was not as bleak as it seemed immediately after the Medway raid. Much about the history of the war can be explained by a simple set of figures: the Dutch spent about £11 million, Charles II less than half as much. The Republic was richer, and Johan de Witt had stronger political support than the king.[58] In that sense Charles's policy was an entire failure, but it was based on a sound premise, that political power at home and naval power abroad depended equally on the ability to raise money. A government too weak for one would be too weak for the other, and of course for the king it was axiomatic that the power of the state was the power of the crown. He was bound to try to strengthen it when he could, and patriotic, popular and above all victorious naval war still offered the best prospect of success.

SIX

Protestant Liberty

Operations 1668–1687

Naval policy was not simply a matter of foreign affairs or grand strategy; it was intimately mixed up with religion and domestic politics. The deeply rooted English conviction that true, national and patriotic sea power was essentially and only Protestant presented Charles II and later his brother with a political problem analogous to that which their father had faced in the 1630s, for they too wanted to use sea power in the context of domestic and foreign policies virtually opposite to those which many in the House of Commons regarded as proper and natural.[1] Though Charles II was driven into the anti-French Triple Alliance in 1668, he did not give up hope of using a victorious Dutch war to strengthen the power of the crown. Parliament voted taxes to strengthen the Navy in response to the rising naval power of France, but the king was still looking in a different direction. In 1670 he concluded a secret treaty with Louis XIV, who gave him substantial subsidies to support English participation in his intended war against the Netherlands, in return for a vague undertaking to recognize the Catholic faith at some future date. Louis gained a client whom he could blackmail; Charles gained £225,000 a year during the war without Parliamentary strings. Together they planned to invade the Dutch Republic by land and sea and reduce it to a rump under the sovereignty of Charles's young nephew Prince William III of Orange, who (as both kings assumed) would co-operate in the overthrow of his Republican enemies. Charles's preparations were completed by the Stop of the Exchequer in January 1672, in effect a repudiation of crown debts in response to a credit crisis, which in the short term gave the king at least £1,300,000 in hand. Without Parliamentary grants or demands, Charles now had the resources for a short victorious war, and looked forward to a substantial strengthening of the crown as a result. His political preparations were completed by the Declaration of Indulgence in March, which granted religious toleration both to Protestant dissenters and to Catholics. Thus he enlisted the support of natural opponents, escaped the tutelage of the Anglican majority in Parliament, and partly satisfied his obligations to Louis XIV.[2]

All that remained was to win the war quickly, and it did not seem unduly difficult. 'This great Comet that is risen of late, the French King, who expects not only to be gazed at but adored by all the world' (Sir William Temple's words), had ordinary peacetime revenues of almost 100 million *livres*, equivalent to about £7,500,000 (more than seven times Charles II's income), which paid for an army nine times the size of the Dutch, and had built up a great navy from almost nothing: fourteen ships of the line in 1663 had become seventy-three in eight years.[3] In March an artificial quarrel over the acknowledgement of English 'Sovereignty of the Sea' provided a slight excuse for a declaration of war, three days after Sir Robert Holmes had launched an unprovoked and largely unsuccessful attack on a Dutch convoy in the Channel. De Ruyter was at sea soon after, and narrowly failed to prevent the meeting of the French and English fleets off Portsmouth on 5 May. The Duke of York returned to command the English fleet, probably because even a French admiral could serve under the command of a royal prince without humiliation. The allies' naval plan was simply to crush the Dutch fleet to open the way for a landing in Zealand, and they do not seem to have had any clear idea how to achieve it, beyond the imperative 'not to lie in the Downs by any means'.[4]

In fact they were lying in Solebay (Southwold Bay) on the Suffolk coast when the Dutch attacked on 28 May. The allies were expecting the attack and were more or less in formation, but still at anchor, the Blue Squadron (commanded by Lord Sandwich) to the north, the Duke with the Red Squadron in the centre, and the French, under the comte d'Estrées,[5] forming the White Squadron to the south. The wind was easterly, and the two English squadrons made sail on the starboard tack, heading north, but the Duke did not order the French to follow (perhaps he thought it too obvious), and they sailed on the opposite tack, heading south, marked by the weaker Dutch van. Two separate battles therefore developed, not reunited until the evening. In the northern battle the Dutch had the advantage. Sandwich was surrounded, his divisional admirals (Sir John Kempthorne and Sir Joseph Jordan) missed his signals in the smoke, and he perished when the *Royal James* grounded and was burned by a Dutch fireship. The Duke was in the thick of the fighting, and his First Captain was killed by his side. 'His Royal Highness went fore and aft in the ship and cheered up the men to fight,' wrote Captain John Narbrough,

> which did encourage them very much. The Duke thought himself never near enough to the enemy, for he was ever calling to the quarter-master

which cunded the ship to luff her nearer ... Presently when Sir John Cox was slain, I commanded as captain, observing his Royal Highness's commands in working the ship, striving to get the wind of the enemy. I do absolutely believe no prince upon the whole earth can compare with his Royal Highness in gallant resolution in fighting his enemy, and with so great conduct and knowledge in navigation as never any general understood before him. He is better acquainted in these seas than many masters which are now in his fleet; he is general, soldier, pilot, master, seaman; to say all, he is everything that man can be, and most pleasant when the great shot are thundering about his ears.[6]

Later in the action he was obliged to shift his flag twice. At the end of the day de Ruyter withdrew, having inflicted a sharp check on the allies with inferior forces (sixty-two ships against eighty-two), and put off any immediate plan of invasion. He had also provoked a violent quarrel in the French squadron, where d'Estrées accused his second, Vice-Admiral Abraham Duquesne, of failing to support him. Like almost all the officers of the infant French fleet, they had both been brought in from outside: d'Estrées an army officer and nobleman; Duquesne a merchant shipowner and one of the substantial minority of Protestants in the French navy; both of them inflexible and difficult characters. The allied fleet achieved nothing more that summer but an abortive cruise to intercept homeward-bound VOC ships.[7]

Meanwhile the French army was overrunning the Dutch defences with minimal opposition. In desperation the Dutch government opened the sluices to flood the low ground between the Zuider Zee and the Rhine, providing a last defence for Holland at the expense of the inland, Orangist provinces, which were abandoned to the enemy. (Zealand, composed of islands, was sheltered on the landward side but the intended target of the allied landings.) Emotions were now running very high. De Witt was forced from power, accused of treason, and on 28 June William III was named Captain-General and Admiral-General of the Republic. Disappointing Charles II's expectations, he threw himself wholeheartedly into its defence, though not neglecting his political interests. On 10 August the de Witt brothers were hideously murdered by an Orangist mob, organized by Cornelis Tromp with the foreknowledge of William III.[8]

De Ruyter was distressed at the killing of his friends, but his private sympathies were Orangist, and he worked cordially with William III, who confirmed him as commander-in-chief. It was much harder to accept the return of Tromp; 'a brave and valiant warrior', as de Ruyter warned the prince, 'but unsuitable either to command or be commanded, as he is too violent'.[9]

He did not mention that Tromp had tried to have him murdered in 1669, and organized a mob attack on his family while he was at sea in September 1672. Nevertheless de Ruyter agreed to serve with him in the interests of national unity, and William gave his 'princely word that Admiral Tromp will be kept under control'[10] – which he was, more or less. He quarrelled with other Dutch admirals, but not with the commander-in-chief, and made the conciliatory gesture (no doubt at the prince's prompting) of proposing the early promotion of de Ruyter's son Engel to rear-admiral.[11]

In 1673 the Dutch army under William III continued its desperate resistance against the French, assisted by men and guns taken from the fleet. In spite of the heavy odds against him, de Ruyter planned to take the offensive, blocking the King's Channel out of the Thames by sinking ships in the Swin, its narrowest point, and then dealing with the English Portsmouth squadron and the French. This plan was based on faulty intelligence and could never have succeeded. Remarkably enough, the Dutch were not aware that there were two other channels out of the Thames: the Barrow Deep, which the English fleet had used in 1666, and the Black Deep, which was unmarked and out of sight of land but could have been attempted in an emergency. The allied fleet was now under the command of Prince Rupert, the boldest pilot of all the English admirals, who appeared at the Swin just as de Ruyter did, and tacked his whole fleet through the narrows, with the ebb under them but the wind dead foul.[12]

To cover the Zealand coast on which the allies threatened to land, de Ruyter now retreated to the coastal waters known as the Schooneveld, off the island of Walcheren. This was a broad area of fairly open water, with an easy retreat either through the Deurloo and Spleet channels up the Scheldt, or via the Steendiep towards Rotterdam, but screened to seaward by scattered shoals which were not well known to the English. De Ruyter, a Zealander himself and familiar with these waters since his boyhood, had sufficient room to manoeuvre his smaller fleet, and sufficient navigational difficulties to perplex the enemy.[13] Prince Rupert arranged the allied fleet with his own Red Squadron in the van, the French White Squadron in the centre (perhaps so that it could not tack the wrong way), and the Blue Squadron (Sir Edward Spragge) in the rear. On 28 May the allies attacked, hoping to use their superiority (seventy-six ships against fifty-two) to achieve a crushing victory. Rupert was always a bold leader but not a very sophisticated tactician, and his Red Squadron fought a private battle with Tromp, while de Ruyter held off the rest of the allied fleet in a confused action, and subsequently relieved Tromp. At the end of the day the allies drew off with nothing gained.[14]

One week later, on 4 June, the two fleets fought again in the same waters. This time de Ruyter, seeing the allies extended and in disorder, attacked first. At this moment Spragge was actually aboard Prince Rupert's flagship, with a long trip back to his squadron, which was supposed to be leading the fleet. By the time Spragge had got back to his own flagship, Prince Rupert had changed his mind and taken the lead with his Red Squadron, throwing the whole fleet into some confusion. 'The Prince placing himself in the van,' Spragge complained,

the French in the middle, the line-of-battle, being of 89 men-of-war and small frigates, fireships and tenders, is so very long that I cannot see any sign the general admiral makes, being quite contrary to any custom ever used at sea before, and may prove of ill consequence to us. I know not any reason he has for it except being singular and positive.[15]

Once again de Ruyter's skilful tactics had held off the greatly superior allied fleet, which returned to the Thames with nothing achieved.[16]

The Dutch fleet appeared briefly off Harwich at the end of June, but serious sickness forced it back to the Schooneveld. The allies now decided to cruise off the Texel in the hope of drawing de Ruyter out into open water to defeat him and open the way for the intended landing. After some days of manoeuvres, in which the Dutch fleet was once again handled with much skill, the two fleets met off the Texel on 11 August. The disparity of force was even greater than before; eighty-six allied ships (of forty guns or more) against sixty Dutch. The two fleets were in parallel lines on the same tack, the shorter Dutch line to windward, and de Ruyter left much of the French White Squadron in the van virtually unmarked in order to concentrate on Prince Rupert in the centre, while Tromp and Spragge faced one another in the rear. As so often happened with the enormous fleets and primitive signals of the day, the battle split into separate actions. Tromp and Spragge, longstanding opponents, fought a private combat of great intensity, and during the afternoon Spragge, shifting his flag for the second time, was drowned when his barge was sunk by a chance shot. In the centre, where de Ruyter had managed to achieve almost equal odds, there was sharp action in the morning, broken off when each side steered to rejoin their rear squadrons. The French in the allied van, however, spent most of their energies trying to get to windward of the Dutch, in which they eventually succeeded, but then remained there watching the battle from a safe distance, in spite of Rupert's signals to rejoin the line. At the end of the battle de Ruyter was able to withdraw without loss, having once again frustrated the allies' invasion plans. This was virtually the end of the campaign; fighting against heavy odds, de Ruyter had saved his country in its hour of desperate need.[17] It has ever since been admired as a supreme example of courage and dexterity, as the English were the first to acknowledge. The Duke of York called de Ruyter 'the greatest [admiral] that ever to that time was in the world', and he was praised as much for his modesty and charity as for his courage and skill.[18]

For Charles II, the war had been a political disaster. The failure of the 1672 campaign had obliged him to resort to Parliament, whose price was the cancelling of the Declaration of Indulgence and the passing of the Test Act, which imposed religious tests designed to exclude Catholics from all public office. The principal victim was the Duke of York, now an acknowledged Catholic, who was forced to resign as Lord Admiral and commander-in-chief of the fleet. But the Duke remained heir to the throne, his second marriage to the Italian princess Mary of Modena in September 1673 threatened to beget a Catholic dynasty, and public disquiet was skilfully fanned by a covert Dutch propaganda campaign. Instead of strengthening his position, Charles II had succeeded only in persuading many of his subjects that he was aiming for Popery and arbitrary power. The battle of the Texel completed the ruin of his policy. Prince Rupert, never an enthusiast for the French alliance, loudly blamed d'Estrées for his failure, and the public was ready to believe that Louis XIV had ordered his admiral to leave the English in the lurch. Worst of all, from the two kings' point of view, Rupert's charges were more than confirmed in a violent denunciation of d'Estrées by his second-in-command, the marquis de Martel – one of the few long-serving sea officers in the French service, who resented a court favourite promoted over his head. Martel was imprisoned in the Bastille at once, but the alliance was irretrievably wrecked, and in February 1674 an Anglo-Dutch peace treaty was signed. France continued at war with the Netherlands, but Spain and much of Germany had now joined the war against her, and the French army was forced to evacuate all its conquests.[19]

For the French, and some of the English, war against the Dutch Republic was a war of gentlemen, men of honour and consequently courage, against the 'cheesemongers', tradesmen incapable of either. The Dutch were aware of these sneers, and amongst the numerous privateers which put to sea during this war, there were three named the *Getergde Kaasboer*, the 'Provoked Cheesemonger'. Dutch privateers, most of them from Zealand and many of them working out of Spanish ports, took at least 648 prizes during this war, the bulk of them English, and brought English trade to the Mediterranean virtually to an end.[20] 'There is no likelihood of any ships escaping the Dutch that adventure to sail towards any port of Spain or the Straits without convoy,' reported the English ambassador to Madrid, 'which neither must not be a small one.'[21] These losses confirmed the general impression in England that it had been the wrong war, against the wrong enemy, for the wrong motives. Even at its outbreak thoughtful Englishmen were ashamed of a war of naked aggression. After Solebay, John Evelyn wrote that 'the loss of my Lord Sandwich redoubled the loss to me, as well as the folly of hazarding so brave a fleet, and losing so many good men, for no provocation in the world but because the Hollander exceeded us in industry, and all things else but envy'.[22]

In distant waters the Dutch once again confirmed their supremacy. In the autumn of 1672, with the Republic facing ruin and conquest, the Admiralty of Zealand mounted with the utmost secrecy (the States-General was not informed) an expedition under the command of Commodore Cornelis Evertsen[23] to restore the province's finances by capturing a homeward-bound English East India convoy at St Helena. On the way out he encountered a larger English squadron going the same way, which forced him to abandon the plan and divert to the West Indies. There he met (to their mutual surprise) a squadron of the Admiralty of Amsterdam under Commodore Jacob Binckes. Agreeing to operate together, the two commodores mounted a destructive raid on the Chesapeake, and on 30 July 1673 recaptured New York (though it was subsequently returned at the peace settlement).[24]

In the East Indies both the allies were thrown on to the defensive by the local power of the VOC, which swept up most English and French shipping. A promising French trading initiative, which might in time have made a real contribution to national prosperity, was effectively written off in 1673 in favour of concentrating on the European war. Though the Dutch decided Bombay was too strong to be attacked directly, a squadron under Cornelis van Quaelbergen heavily defeated the East India Company's ships under William Basse off Masulipatam on 1 September 1673. In January 1673 Dutch forces from the Cape of Good Hope had taken St Helena, though an English squadron under Captain Richard Munden (the force that Evertsen had encountered) succeeded in retaking the island in May, and three prizes out of a VOC convoy which appeared soon afterwards.[25]

English overseas trade prospered again in the years after the Third Dutch War, especially those up to the Franco-Dutch peace of 1678, during which the English were neutral carriers. In foreign policy Charles II bent to the wind of public opinion. In November 1677 William III married his niece Mary (the Duke of York's daughter by his first, Protestant marriage), and the following year an Anglo-Dutch defensive treaty was concluded, which provided for joint naval operations by a common fleet under unified command. In domestic naval politics Prince Rupert occupied a key bridging position, as an outspoken supporter of an anti-French, Protestant, foreign policy, whose loyalty to the crown was beyond question. The Duke of York was replaced as Lord Admiral in 1673 by an Admiralty commission headed by Prince Rupert. A clever man and an able administrator, he provided real leadership, and reassured members of Parliament that the Navy was now on the right side.[26]

These developments in English politics were of course unwelcome in Versailles. To counter them the French ambassador bribed William Russell, Algernon Sydney and other leading members of the opposition, the 'Whigs' as they were nicknamed. As heirs of the Nonconformist, Republican interest of the 1650s, they were anything but natural friends of Louis XIV, but they served his purposes well by agreeing to demand immediate war with France, but refusing any money to pay for it. Thus they divided and paralysed English policy, and contributed to the atmosphere of paranoia which surrounded the revelation in August 1678 of the 'Popish Plot', in which it was alleged by Titus Oates (a former English naval chaplain dismissed for sodomy) that the Pope and the Jesuits had conspired to murder the king and replace him with the Duke of York. Less plausible charges and a less respectable witness would have been hard to find, but virtually nobody except the king himself kept a level head, and about thirty-five innocent people, Catholics or accused of being Catholics, were judicially murdered on Oates's word. Louis XIV fanned the flames by leaking details of the 1670 treaty. For a time it seemed that the opposition would succeed in excluding the Duke of York from the succession, and they threatened to restart the civil war if their demand was not granted. The Navy, allegedly filled by him with Catholic officers, was in the middle of the crisis. On inquiry the Catholic officers proved not to exist, but the public was not satisfied. Samuel Pepys, Secretary of the Admiralty, was put in the Tower on a charge of treason, and intense pressure was applied on his young clerk to supply the evidence to send him to the scaffold. In time, however, the tide of hysteria began to ebb. Sober men were appalled at the talk of civil war, and glad when Charles, benefiting from buoyant Customs revenues (and further French subsidies), was able to rule without Parliament. In June 1683 a Republican plot to murder Charles and James was uncovered; Russell and Sydney were executed for complicity in it, and the king's bastard son the Duke of Monmouth fled overseas to avoid the same fate.[27]

Charles II was now resettled on his throne, backed by the same Anglican Royalists who had restored him more than twenty years before. He had learned his lesson, and abandoned religious toleration, French alliance and other unacceptable policies. The crown was no stronger than before, but at least it was not much weaker, and the Navy was employed in the manner which Parliament regarded as proper.[28] In peacetime this was chiefly in the protection of trade, and it most needed protection against the Barbary States, and the Moroccan Atlantic port of Sallee. The Levant Company represented one of the most flourishing sectors of English foreign trade (it took up to a quarter of all English woollen exports), and another was the export to the western Mediterranean and Iberia of dried cod from the Newfoundland fisheries, and the import in return of dried fruit and wine. These trades were most exposed in the Mediterranean, but the cruisers of Sallee and Algiers were often met with in the Atlantic, and sometimes even in the Channel. In 1687 the Algerines took two mail packets to Holland and carried off a hundred passengers into slavery. Trade was protected by an uncertain mixture of convoys, cruisers, and direct attacks on the ports of the Barbary powers. There was as yet not much clear thinking about the advantages of these different methods, but experience was beginning to teach commanders on the spot some of the realities of the situation. The old prejudices against 'Barbary piracy' were thoroughly misleading. The best policy for a Christian trading power was to make itself sufficiently annoying as an enemy, and sufficiently attractive as a friend, to be elected as an ally of the Barbary States – and, equally important, to preserve those alliances by a faithful observance of their terms. Then the pressure of Barbary cruisers against the other Christian states with which they remained at war would become a tax on England's trading competitors. This simple realization was to become one of the essential bases of British commercial and naval operations in the Mediterranean throughout the eighteenth and well into the nineteenth centuries.[29]

Direct attacks on the Barbary ports were difficult and dangerous, but they formed an important element in the overall policy. Open war with Algiers, over various disputed prizes, was declared by Sir Thomas Allin in 1669, but he achieved nothing save a brief and fruitless blockade. In August 1670 six Algerine cruisers were driven ashore near Cape Spartel by a joint Anglo-Dutch squadron under Captain Richard Beach and Baron van Ghent. Next year, on 8 May, Sir Edward Spragge was able to destroy seven Algerine men-of-war in Bugia Bay (Bougie, Bejaïa), after which 'we got off into 9 fathom of water out of shot, and anchored, viewing all night our lovely bonfires, which, in my opinion, was the most glorious sight that ever I saw'.[30] This led to a treaty in which the Algerines made limited concessions.[31]

Sir John Narbrough bought a satisfactory agreement with Tunis in 1675 with supplies of guns and naval stores. With Tripoli he had more trouble, but on 14 January 1676 a daring boat attack by Lieutenant Cloudesley Shovell burned four men-of-war in harbour, and soon afterwards Narbrough sank four more in the open sea, which persuaded the Dey to a peace more satisfactory 'not only than was expected now but what was ever yet obtained by any prince from that nation'.[32] Later that year Narbrough was also able to conclude 'that chargeable and fruitless war with Sallee in which his Majesty hath been so long concerned,' as Pepys called it, 'so that (thanks be to God) that thorn is out of our foot'.[33] His worst problem was Algiers. Infuriated by the numerous bogus 'English' ships, all claiming benefit of the 1672 treaty, which their cruisers encountered, the Algerines declared war again in 1677. Narbrough had a maximum strength (early in 1679) of thirty-four ships, which was approximately as many as the Algerines, who cruised in small squadrons, sufficient to overwhelm all but the strongest convoy escort, and faster than anything in the English Navy. In December 1669 Captain John Kempthorne of the *Mary Rose* earned a knighthood by successfully fighting off an Algerine squadron of no less than seven ships which attacked his convoy off Cadiz. Acutely short of stores (partly because the Algerines captured his supply ships), with no base anywhere near the enemy, Narbrough found his campaign was crippled. 'A ship unfurnished is of no service but an unnecessary expense,' he warned the Admiralty in November 1678. 'They may sail to and fro, but to no purpose. It were better they were laid up in port. No ships whatever are better sailers than his Majesty's frigates when they are completely fitted, and if service be expected from them, they must be supplied with what is needful.'[34]

In theory the English had a base to supply all they needed: Tangier. In practice the colony from which so much had been hoped had three crippling disadvantages. In spite of an expensive garrison of 3,000 (later only 2,000) men it was exposed to constant attack by a formidable enemy: 'about 5,000 horse, able, dexterous, sober, valiant, incomparably well armed and clothed, and horsed', in the words of the first English governor, Lord Peterborough.[35] They killed his successor Lord Teviot in 1664, and the military situation of the colony was seldom better than precarious. The line of fortifications was too short to cover the town properly, but too long for the garrison to hold. Nor were the troops all of high quality. In 1681 Colonel Percy Kirke complained that 'of 33 gunners there is not 10 knows the gun from the carriage', and the Ordnance Storekeeper Francis Povey reported that his colleague the Firemaster 'is certainly a most ignorant person as to the knowledge of any ingredient except brandy'.[36] Worse, from the naval point of view, Tangier had no safe harbour. Impressively situated right in the Straits of Gibraltar, it offered only an exposed and dangerous anchorage. To remedy this the English undertook to build a mole, capable of withstanding the full force of the Atlantic seas. In

1683, after over twenty years of work, it was 479 yards long and contained 170,000 tons of stone, but it was still less than half complete, and there was disturbing evidence that the harbour was silting even as it was created. Most serious of all, Tangier was never a significant commercial port. An effective naval base had to be a place of trade, with a substantial population of merchants and contractors who could discount bills for cash, and supply victuals and naval stores; otherwise everything would have to be sent out from England at great expense, and nothing could be had at short notice.[37] In an endeavour to operate a small squadron Mediterranean-style, without the port and resources needed by regular warships, Charles II's government acquired two galleys for Tangier and some slaves to man them, but the galleys proved to be completely ineffective and were soon abandoned.[38]

In practice successive naval commanders-in-chief based their operations in the Mediterranean almost anywhere except Tangier. Allin and Spragge used Port Mahón; Narbrough used Leghorn and Malta when operating against Tripoli, then Leghorn, Port Mahón and Cadiz against Algiers. His successor Arthur Herbert used Cadiz and Gibraltar, bribing the Spanish governors for permission. A renewed campaign against Sallee from 1684 to 1688 was based on Lisbon and then Gibraltar. All of these places had disadvantages (Leghorn, the best place for stores, was also the furthest away, and 'bereaved . . . his Majesty of almost half the service of every ship that is forced to fetch her victuals and cleaning from thence'), but each could provide supplies or facilities unavailable at Tangier.[39]

Successive naval commanders-in-chief had a difficult task disposing their forces against so powerful and active an enemy as the Algerines. Blockade of the North African ports, on a dead lee shore for most of the year, with few local anchorages and hundreds of miles from any potential base, was quite fruitless, and even when ships were on station the fast Algerine cruisers could usually slip into port on moonless nights. Direct attacks on large and well-fortified cities were only occasionally useful. In time the best combination proved to be strong convoys mounted directly from England and back, reinforced by cruising squadrons at certain points. During the Dutch Wars a 'Soundings Squadron' cruised in the Western Approaches to see convoys safely into and out of the Channel, but against the Algerines the critical point was the Straits of Gibraltar, where the convoys could easily be attacked, and where Algerine ships homeward-bound with their prizes from Atlantic cruises might be intercepted.[40] In September 1677 Narbrough was 'cruising in the channel of the Straits' mouth so that no ships can pass but we see them; it's the only place to annoy the Algerines. I want extremely clean frigates that sail well, and provisions and stores to be lodged at Tangier . . . These Turks tell me there is five or six more in the Great Sea. I am laying in wait for them in the mouth of the Strait.'[41]

The techniques of convoy organization and escort became during these years one of the routine skills of the Navy. Convoys were organized in London in consultation with the merchants and shipowners, and before departure sailing orders were issued by the senior officer to his charges. At sea the escorts took station to windward of their charges, and at night one went ahead and one astern.[42] We have a charming picture in verse of an English convoy in the Mediterranean thanks to John Baltharpe, a petty officer of the *St David*:

> Sir John Harman he well known to Fame
> Appointed was to Guard the same:
> His care it was exceeding much,
> With them he always would keep touch:
> Make easie Sayl on Nights therefore,
> On Nights he bore the Light before
> His Chickens alwayes who close clings
> Under the shelter of his wings.
> On dayes perhaps they'l wander, yet keep sight
> Of their Rare Admirall if ought them fright
> As oft it hapneth, doth the Ravenous Kite;
> Under her wings they are at Night.[43]

By this time convoys were evidently a regular feature of naval service in the Mediterranean, at least in Baltharpe's eyes:

> As we go up, so they come down,
> And so our Convoys, they go round:
> No better way was ever taken,
> Nor will be when the same's foresaken.[44]

Convoys were often a sore trial to their escorts; slow, disobedient, straggling to the horizon even by day, but they were accepted as an ordinary part of a sea officer's duty.[45]

Herbert was possibly the most successful commander-in-chief in the Mediterranean (1679–83), and in 1682 he finally brought the Algerine war to a conclusion 'no less honourable for his Majesty than seasonable for his other affairs and commodious and beneficial for his subjects trading in all those seas'.[46] The treaty remained in force for 135 years. Herbert's was then the only large squadron operational, and the only source of promotion. This gave him the chance to build up a significant following of officers who owed their loyalty to him; the 'Tangerines' as they were sometimes known – ironically enough, since in 1682 Charles II finally decided to abandon Tangier. Herbert's violent temper and unsavoury private life did not make him everybody's favourite. Lord Dartmouth, who led the squadron which came out to evacuate Tangier, was his natural rival, and behind Dartmouth stood the Duke of York, who in 1685 succeeded to the throne as James II. This was in due course to give Herbert's following an unexpected political significance.[47]

Transatlantic trade might be convoyed on the European side of the Atlantic, but in the Americas local naval forces still consisted almost entirely of privateers.[48] In 1678 the government was advised that some ships were needed in the West Indies, in the face of a French squadron of six ships, 'inasmuch as between taking all, and losing all, there seems no middle way left', but next year it withdrew the two frigates from Jamaica which were the last English warships in the Caribbean. 'Your Lordships will know that good and well equipped frigates are the brazen walls of islands,' the Antigua Council wrote in 1680, but for the most part the islands had to do without them.[49] A few ships were sent to pursue pirates, and a flurry of interest was generated in 1686 by the remarkable success of the Massachusetts adventurer William Phips in salvaging a treasure of over £200,000 from a Spanish wreck off Hispaniola. Sir John Narbrough had a financial share in the expedition (characteristically well judged: £21,766 return on an £800 investment), later went out to protect the wreck site and actually died and was buried at sea there.[50]

In the Caribbean the buccaneers, having looted many smaller towns too often to leave anything worth stealing, achieved their most stunning success with Henry Morgan's sack of Panama in 1671, but even £30,000 was a disappointing financial return divided among 1,500 surviving participants. Investors were now tending to move into legal commerce and plantations, Spanish counter-measures increased, and the government of Jamaica made some serious attempts to discourage buccaneering.[51] In response the more desperate elements among the buccaneers mounted a series of raids across the isthmus of Panama into the Pacific, where they seized ships to raid down the coast of Spanish America. These little expeditions of the 1680s were the last major activities of the English-speaking buccaneers. Murderous, treacherous and ruthless as ever, they yet displayed extraordinary qualities:

> The buccaneers' daring in attack, their patience in enduring all sorts of toil and hardship, their perseverance despite the most terrible setbacks and their indomitable courage arouse our admiration; we might call them heroes, if virtue were not indispensable for true heroism.[52]

Though these raids were of no lasting significance in military or diplomatic terms, they have left a powerful imprint on the literature of several languages and occupy a permanent place in the European imagination, albeit a romantic place far removed from the cruel and sordid reality.[53]

On the death of Charles II in February 1685 his brother succeeded to the throne without trouble. When the Duke of Monmouth landed in the West Country in June 1685 his Protestant rebellion aroused only limited support and was defeated, as was the Earl of Argyll's rebellion in Scotland.[54] The fury of the Exclusion Crisis was passed, the opposition cowed, and buoyant trade was rapidly improving the crown's Customs revenues. James II's major weakness was his religion; to neutralize the fear and suspicion it was bound to arouse the bare minimum needful was to continue the Anglican, anti-French policies of his brother's later years. Instead he moved towards toleration for Catholics and Protestant Dissenters (even the hated Quakers benefited), and built up a large army, some of whose officers were Catholics. A few Catholic officers were also introduced into the Navy, and one flag-officer, Sir Roger Strickland, announced his conversion. These disastrous political blunders were enough to alienate most of James's natural supporters. Anglicans, Royalists, all those who supported royal authority and dreaded the return of civil war, were driven into opposing the king's policies, though not the king in person.[55]

Though in reality James's foreign policy remained cool towards France, people automatically connected his moves with those of Louis XIV, who continued steadily conquering territory and adding to the already terrifying power of France. Worse, from James's point of view, in October 1685 Louis revoked the Edict of Nantes, which had provided limited toleration for French Protestants. A flood of French Protestant refugees spread across Europe, loudly confirming what so many Englishmen and Scotsmen took for granted, that no Protestant was safe under a Catholic sovereign. Louis's arrogance and aggression made enemies of even his most reluctant neighbours. In 1686 a defensive alliance of both Protestant and Catholic princes was signed at Augsburg. The Dutch, who longed only to trade in peace, were infuriated by French measures to exclude their exports, and frightened by Louis XIV's unquenchable ambitions for conquest. All this while, James's second marriage had been childless, and his heirs remained his Protestant daughters Mary and Anne. Mary's husband Prince William III of Orange watched the situation in England with anxiety, but he knew that sooner or later he must succeed to effective power. Then, at the end of 1687, it became known that Queen Mary of Modena was pregnant. James's Declaration of Indulgence, issued in April

1687, had brought the political turmoil to boiling point, and now there was a serious risk that a Catholic dynasty would rule England for ever. The scene was set for a crisis which would really test the loyalty and efficiency of James II's Navy.[56]

SEVEN

Amazement and Discontent

Administration 1660–1688

The Navy of the Restoration was powerful, but bankrupt. In the spring of 1660, with some ships in commission which had been unpaid for over four years, the Navy owed over 1¼ million pounds. The Cavalier Parliament established a commission to disband the army and pay off the Navy's accumulated debts, which by 1663 had raised more than 2½ million pounds. Even so Charles II had to find at least £375,000 to discharge debts in his first four years on the throne, out of his ordinary income of one million a year, and it is not certain that all the naval debts of the 1650s were ever paid. Though the Parliaments of Charles II certainly had a more realistic idea of the cost of preparing for war than his father's had done, and made little difficulty about maintaining the Excise on beer and ale, even in the first flush of Royalist enthusiasm they never provided him with an income sufficient to maintain the fleet which he and they desired.[1] In commercial legislation they advanced on their predecessors. The new Navigation Act of 1660 was more practical and less rigid than its predecessor, and introduced the important concept of 'enumerated' (meaning selected) colonial products which could only be exported via Britain. Another act of 1663 applied the same principle in reverse, to goods imported into the colonies. In time these acts considerably stimulated English trade and shipping, and began the lucrative re-export trade in colonial products which was one of the foundations of English commercial prosperity in the eighteenth century.[2]

The naval administration of the revived Royal Navy followed precedent in most but not all respects. The king's brother James, Duke of York, was installed in the office of Lord High Admiral which he had nominally held since 1638,[3] and the Navy Board was reconstructed in a new form, with three Extra Commissioners in addition to the four Principal Officers of the pre-war board: the Treasurer (who in practice did not sit with the Board but with his clerks constituted a small financial department), the Controller (notionally the Navy's chief accountant), the Surveyor (in charge of purchasing stores) and the Clerk of Acts (the Board's secretary). Between the Lord Admiral and the Navy Board, the Admiralty and Navy Committee of the Privy Council acted mainly as a consultative body. There was a large measure of administrative continuity, concealing a major practical change which sets the years 1660 to 1688 apart from the rest of English naval history. Both Charles and James were keenly interested in the Navy, and in time they became expert in it. Unlike every sovereign before and after them, they were willing and able to transact much detailed and technical business themselves. The king's sea experience was chiefly as a yachtsman; effectively he invented yachting as a sport, initially with the *jacht* presented to him in 1660 by the Dutch government, soon replaced by English-built vessels more suitable for deep water offshore, several of them designed by himself. 'He understood navigation well; but above all he knew the architecture of ships so perfectly that in that respect he was exact rather more than became a prince', in one contemporary's opinion.[4] The Duke of York, as we have seen, became a capable fleet commander, and both the brothers were expert pilots for the Thames estuary. They came to know more about the seagoing Navy than all their ministers, many of their administrators, and some of their admirals. With strong and expert leadership from the top, English naval administration assumed new forms.[5]

Besides the king and the duke, the key members of the new naval administration were the duke's secretary William Coventry (also a member of the Navy Board from 1662), the Treasurer of the Navy Sir George Carteret, and the members of the Navy Board: the Controller Sir Robert Slingsby, succeeded in November 1661 by Sir John Mennes, the Surveyor Sir William Batten, and Sir William Penn, one of the extra commissioners. Both Slingsby and Mennes were Royalist gentleman who had served in the pre-war Navy and suffered for the king in exile. Mennes was an experienced seaman, an agreeable companion, a wit and poet (he introduced Pepys to Chaucer), but nothing in his previous career had prepared him for his new duties as the Navy's principal auditor, and he was sixty-one at the Restoration. Sir George Carteret was from a similar background: already a vice-admiral and Controller of the Navy in 1638, he had sheltered Charles II in his native Jersey until 1651, and later served as a French admiral. He was a gentleman of integrity, but had no specialized knowledge of finance. Penn was the distinguished Republican admiral, disgraced by Cromwell and easily accepted by the new regime, while Batten came from the same background but had led the Royalist naval revolt of 1648. Taken as a whole the administration was very strong in naval experience and loyalty to the crown, but weaker in administrative abilities. The Royalists had had little opportunity to acquire them in exile, and accountancy, insofar as it was recognized as a skill in the seventeenth century, was not one which a gentleman was likely to acquire anywhere, least of all at sea.[6]

The last member of the Navy Board was Samuel Pepys, the Clerk of Acts, a young man (twenty-seven in 1660) with almost no qualifications, jobbed into office by his cousin and employer, Lord Sandwich. Few of his contemporaries could have foreseen the extraordinary stature he was to acquire in the Navy of his own day, and to regain among the historians of the twentieth century. Forgotten after his death, rediscovered in the nineteenth century only as a diarist, he secured his modern reputation by leaving, not only his marvellously revealing diary, but his official papers in unequalled bulk and order. Thanks to him we know more about the administration of the Royal Navy of his day than of all earlier and many succeeding periods, but of course we see it through his eyes. Pepys very rapidly displayed the extraordinary gifts which so fully justified Sandwich's patronage. Endlessly diligent and painstaking, he had a prodigious appetite for fact and method. Soon he knew much more than any of his colleagues, indeed more than anyone in England, about stores and fittings, contracts and markets, accounts and statistics. As early as 1662 Coventry told him 'that I was indeed the life of this office'.[7] Relentlessly curious, he sought information from every source, questioned every expert, examined every paper. No detail was too small for him: the proper quality of bewpers for flags, the precise scope of a glazier's contract, the method of measuring blocks, the gauge of Stockholm and Russia tar, the sizes and patterns of hinges and fastenings. Master shipwrights might be unable to measure timber correctly, masters attendant ignorant of the proper widths of sailcloths, clerks of the cheque incapable of calculating wage costs, but Pepys made himself master of all.[8] 'No man in England was of more method,' Clarendon told him, 'nor made himself better understood than myself.'[9] So crushing was his omniscience, so compelling his sinuous prolixity, that it is easy to forget as one reads through his papers that brevity was not the only talent he lacked. He mastered things better than people, and his gifts were of the intellect more than the imagination. Though he had many private friends, though he formed powerful working relationships with those who appreciated his talents – notably Charles II, his brother the Duke, and James's secretary Coventry – he did not have the flexibility to accommodate himself to those he found uncongenial, and his relentless superiority made him an uneasy colleague. He was a rigid partisan, who formed his prejudices quickly and relaxed them seldom. Though he deplored factions among the sea officers, he gave them a poor example himself. Charles II, whose political judgement was greatly superior, sometimes found him an obstacle to unity and reconciliation. His narrow self-righteousness in dealing with sea officers was not the best way of promoting the tighter naval discipline which he so ardently desired. A more supple man, more generous in acknowledging the service and experience of others, might have been less isolated at the end of his career, and left an administration moulded to his ideals. As it was, the forms of government for which he had contested did not survive him, but he trained a generation of clerks who dominated naval administration for fifty years. A century after his death, this forgotten servant of a discredited regime was still warmly remembered in the Navy Office as 'a man of extraordinary knowledge in all that related to the business of that department, of great talents, and the most indefatigable industry'.[10]

Pepys's first great administrative battle was in 1663, over the Navy's contract for masts from the Baltic. There were only two merchants able to deal in the enormous quantities the Navy needed: William Wood and Sir William Warren. As Batten's son-in-law, Wood had apparently invincible claims. Pepys, having learnt every detail of the mast trade (with which none of his colleagues were familiar), was satisfied that Warren offered better quality and value, and did not hesitate to denounce his senior colleague's corrupt relationship with Wood, and get the contract removed from him. He never mentioned that he himself had received presents from Warren, but it is clear that Warren really did offer better value, and that Pepys allowed him no private favours. In spite of Mennes's complete failure to check any detail of Warren's vouchers, Pepys scrutinized them carefully and got several disallowed. There were aspects of his dealings which would not have borne public scrutiny, but he could honestly claim to be serving the king, saving him money, and tightening up the naval administration.[11]

The key figure in the naval administration of the 1660s was William Coventry (Sir William in 1665), the essential link between the Lord Admiral and the Navy Board from 1660 to 1667. Like Pepys, with whom he worked so closely, he had great administrative gifts, and his standards of public service were if anything higher. He himself pushed to have his income from fees replaced by a salary, which it was in 1664.[12] Unlike their less discerning colleagues, both Coventry and Pepys viewed the approach of the Second Dutch War with foreboding. 'We all seem to desire it, as thinking ourselves to have advantages at present over them; but for my part I dread it,' wrote Pepys in his diary.[13] Coventry doubted that trade would profit, 'setting aside our ability to go through with it, or rather taking that for granted – to which possibly some objections might be made from the posture of his Majesty's stores and treasure.'[14] That posture grew rapidly more feeble. In November 1664 Pepys calculated for the House of Commons that the war had already cost the Navy £852,700 extra, 'but God knows this is only a scare to the Parliament, to make them give the more money'.[15] Parliament did in fact vote £2,500,000, the largest single tax until the eighteenth century, but the twenty-five months from September 1664 to September 1666 cost £3,200,516, not counting depleted stores and inherited debts, leaving a deficit of £930,496. In April 1665, informed that the Navy needed at least £23,865 a week, 'my Lord Treasurer gave us', Pepys recorded, 'no answer but signs of amazement and discontent, with many protestations that this money in nature is not to be found, nor anything farther than what he had already allotted for the Navy, and with this uncomfortable answer dismissed us'.[16] Over the following year, war and plague reduced public revenue to about half its normal level. By March 1666 the funds available were only half the Navy's current requirements. In November (two months after the Great Fire had destroyed the commercial heart of the country) the Navy Board needed £179,793 at once, and owed £934,000.[17]

The results were inevitable. Big, creditworthy, merchants carried on supplying the Navy as long as they could borrow, inflating their prices accordingly. By the end of 1665 the premium for credit was 20–30 per cent. Small masts nearly doubled in price between September 1663 and May 1666; large masts rose 40–50 per cent. Hemp cost £42 a ton in October 1663, £57 by April 1666. Canvas was £15 8s a bale in February 1662, and £18 10s by October 1665.[18] 'This morning,' Pepys informed Coventry in July 1665,

> upon a pressing demand from Commissioner Pett for 1000 yards of kerseys, we sent for Mr Medowes, who declaring to us that the debt we owe him for that commodity arises to above £2000, and part thereof in bills of 12 months standing, and that he could not with any security to himself proceed to trust us farther unless we would add to his price 18d. per pound for what he should sell us, that thereby he might be in capacity of raising money from the goldsmiths, which he then knew he could of course compass and otherwise not; he pressed it publicly and with such absoluteness to the Board that (not knowing where else to be trusted) we were obliged to undertake for the getting him ready payment for this parcel or give him what he demanded in his price. I leave this to be reflected on at your leisure.[19]

Big merchants could afford credit, and at the worst they could afford to stop trading with the government. In 1665 Mrs Constance Pley of Weymouth, an importer of the prized Breton sailcloths called 'Noyals' and 'Vittery' (lighter and heavier canvas, from Noyal and Vitré respectively), though she had '£10,000 to pay and not 600 pence to do it with', was still willing to supply, 'as business is her sole delight in the world' – if she could have half her price in cash in advance. The next year only ready money would do, and by 1667 she had ceased doing business with the crown.[20] Many smaller suppliers went bankrupt. 'Just now is with me a poor oarmaker crying and wringing his hands for money,' wrote Commissioner Middleton from Portsmouth in March 1667,

> and desires to be a labourer in the yard to keep him from being arrested, for that he tells me he dareth not go home to his wife any more, for he shall be carried to jail by his timber-merchant; which request of his I granted, and is now entered a labourer, albeit the King oweth him for oars near £300.[21]

Middleton had no money to buy bricks:

> I have pulled down one chimney to fit the ship's furnaces and hearth; pray let me know by your next whether I shall pull down the chimney in the yard or the brick wall, for it is better that the chimney and wall be all down than that the ships should be continued here for want of money to buy brick, without which they cannot be fitted.[22]

Seamen and dockyard workmen went missing, or went hungry. In October 1665 Pepys wrote to Carteret that

> the yard at Deptford and the yards at Woolwich, both dock and rope yards, revolted yesterday wholly from their working, declaring they would work no longer without money, so that there is at this time not a wheel or a hammer going in all three yards, but of the officers and their servants.[23]

Next month Pepys told Coventry that

> the whole company of the *Breda* . . . are now breaking the windows of our Office and hath twice this day knocked down Marlow our messenger, swearing they will not budge without money. What meat they'll make of me anon, you shall know by my next. But, Sir, what will the consequence of this be, and how shall it be remedied?[24]

In March 1667 Pepys recorded in his diary, 'This day a poor seaman, almost starved for want of food, lay in our yard a-dying; I sent him half-a-crown – and we ordered his ticket to be paid.'[25] Next month Commissioner Taylor wrote from Harwich,

I am now sorry I have laid out so much of my own money to buy the beams; and I am more sorry to see men really perish for want of wherewithal to get nourishment. One yesterday came to me crying to get something to relieve him. I ordered him 10s. He went and got hot drink and something to help him, and so drank it, and died within two hours.[26]

At Portsmouth Middleton passed this brief epitaph on his workmen: 'Turned out of doors by their landlords, they perish more like dogs than men.'[27]

This was the financial background to the laying-up of the fleet and the Medway raid. After it a vengeful Parliament demanded to know what had become of their generous grants. 'God help the King and his cause if the Parliament shall give no more than they can be made understand reason for,'[28] Pepys had written early in the war, and Parliament took it for granted that only the grossest corruption could explain the inadequacy of the huge sums they had voted. Three bodies investigated: the Parliamentary Committee on Miscarriages (1667), the Public Accounts Committee (1668–9), and the Brooke House Commission (1667–9), a royal commission of salaried experts. Charles II was in no position to prevent his servants being interrogated, and the Navy Board was the bull's-eye of every committee's target. In this crisis the Board's spokesman and chief defender was Pepys; its youngest member, and the only one of no social, political or naval standing. From this test he emerged with his reputation as the indispensable expert firmly established. Though the Brooke House Commission, the most effective of the three, once or twice came near to transactions which Pepys greatly wished to cloak, they uncovered very little which was not more or less common knowledge in government: that Carteret's accounts were defective and Mennes's inextricably confused. Colonel George Thomson, who as a former Commonwealth Admiralty Commissioner was the Brooke House Commission's naval expert, proved no match for Pepys's detailed expertise. This committee's most explosive finding was that £514,518 8s 8½d had been spent 'for other uses than the war' – meaning other naval uses, mainly pre-war debts, but many chose to understand that this sum had been illegally diverted into the pockets of the king, his mistresses, or his naval administrators.[29]

Colonel Thomson was the spokesman for 'those pure angelical times' as Charles II sarcastically called them; 'those times concerning which people discourse in matters of the Navy as historians do of the primitive times in reference to the church',[30] as Pepys put it, and the apparent contrast with the godly and victorious Navy of Cromwell's time made naval administration a subject of high political sensitivity. In fact, though contemporaries were not disposed to believe it, Charles II's government had advanced on the

Commonwealth in administrative structures, in economy and almost certainly in honesty. Even Pepys, who privately admired his Republican predecessors, calculated (probably rightly) that they had spent considerably more money to keep up fleets of similar size. It was the Duke of York in 1662 who forbade naval officials to deal with the Navy on their own accounts, which struck at the fundamental weakness of the Commonwealth system. Restoration naval administration generated numerous accusations of corruption, because the many rivalries within and between courtiers, officials and sea officers gave motives for denunciations – but it does not follow that the discreet closed system of the saints, who prayed together and stayed together, was really more honest or economical.[31]

Moreover the strains and failures of the Second Dutch War stimulated some important innovations. In taxation it led to the revival of the Assessment (under the euphemism of the 'Royal Aid'), whose product was fixed by Act of Parliament and divided among the countries, so that the yield (very unlike the pre-war 'subsidies') was certain. This land tax was supplemented in 1667 by the Poll Tax, which fell on income from investments and employment. Together they were both more equitable, and a more effective base for borrowing. They allowed Sir George Downing, Secretary of the Treasury during the war, to introduce a form of credit instrument, secured on the new taxes and payable 'in course', which constituted a short-term system of national debt. In 1667 he extended this to peacetime revenues. At Coventry's urging the Navy Board instituted a similar system of paying its bills in course in 1665, though as Pepys pointed out, 'it implies an income in some near proportion to the expense', for want of which it was initially ineffective.[32]

Carteret was one of the casualties of the post-war Parliamentary investigations. He was replaced by Lord Anglesey, and he in turn in November 1668 by the joint-Treasurers Sir Thomas Osborne and Sir Thomas Littleton, who represented the Duke of York's court enemies, and treated the Navy Board with suspicion. They did serious damage to the Navy's still fragile credit by initially refusing to honour debts incurred before their appointment, but with experience they came to appreciate both the Board's efforts and the Navy's problems. New rules of September 1671, by which time Osborne was sole Treasurer, reduced his independence from the Navy Board and re-integrated naval finance and naval administration. Osborne was zealous, by this time knowledgeable, and did a good deal to regulate the finances of the Navy.[33]

After the war the Duke of York was anxious to reform the Navy Board and forestall his critics. To this end Pepys presented him in 1668 with a sort of denunciation of his colleagues, and their procedure: 'Most of the Board's time taken up in impertinent talk, confused discourses upon different matters at the same time or petitions, applications, and debates relating to the particular officers of some of the Board which ought to be despatched elsewhere.'[34] In brutal detail he explained that the formal requirements of the Duke's instructions were beyond human capacity, especially in wartime (Pepys's figures showed that the business of his office had increased sixfold since 1653), and broadly hinted that any instructions at all would be beyond the capacity of some of his colleagues, notably Mennes. But Mennes was an old Royalist who had suffered for his loyalty, and Charles II had a much clearer sense of the political value of rewarding loyalty than Pepys did. Moreover the obvious replacement was Penn, whom Pepys violently disliked and whose abilities he refused to recognize. As a result Mennes stayed in office, but no less than three extra members were added to the Navy Board: the Controllers of Treasurer's Accounts and Victualling Accounts (both in 1667), and a Controller of Storekeeper's Accounts in 1671, the year that Mennes finally died. In effect the auditing function was now divided into four.[35]

Naval administration developed in other respects during and immediately after the Second Dutch War. Following the Commonwealth precedent, Commissioners were appointed in 1664 to head the more distant dockyards: Colonel Thomas Middleton at Portsmouth, and Captain John Taylor at Harwich. Both of them were old servants of the Republic, and there was some debate over the safety of naming Taylor, who had been dismissed as master shipwright of Chatham in 1660 as a 'fanatic' (meaning an Independent in religion, hence probably a Republican in politics). Coventry, with the Duke of York's backing, insisted that 'his abilities are great and his dispatch hath heretofore been eminent . . . as to his being a fanatic, I have nothing to say for or against it, but I believe you will have need of all hands to the work now cut out',[36] and in the event Taylor's energy and loyalty proved the soundness of their judgement. After the war Middleton remained in office, adding another permanent dockyard commissioner to Peter Pett at Chatham. These yard commissioners were a curious hybrid feature of English naval administration which was to endure into the nineteenth century. Members of the Navy Board on detached service, their status was junior to their London colleagues, and they had no direct authority over the senior officers of the yards of which they were the heads. The master shipwright (in charge of shipbuilding and repairs, and hence the major part of the yard workforce), the masters attendant (responsible for ships afloat, moorings, yardcraft and pilotage), the clerk of the cheque (who kept the accounts) and the storekeeper, answered to the Navy Board in London, whose orders required three signatures to be valid. A yard commissioner could supervise, advise, warn and report, but he could not give direct orders. His power to control the situation depended more on force of character than formal authority, and there was ample scope for conflict with the senior officers. The Petts had run Chatham as a comfortable family business since James I's time. Though Commissioner Peter was dismissed as a scapegoat for the Medway disaster in 1667, his cousin Phineas Pett remained master shipwright, and clashed with the three succeeding Commissioners Captain John Cox (appointed March 1669), Thomas Middleton (May to December 1672) and Rear-Admiral Richard Beach.[37]

Another Republican innovation revived on the outbreak of war in 1664 was the Sick and Wounded Commission. Four, later five members, including Pepys's friend (and fellow-diarist) John Evelyn, each took responsibility for supervising the sick, wounded and prisoners ashore in a division of the country. The Board was devoted and efficient – Evelyn's accounting system aroused the admiration even of so rigorous a judge as Pepys – but like the rest of the naval administration it suffered acutely from want of money. The plague in East Anglia in 1665 and 1666 made things worse. The prisoners of war suffered worst of all, though right at the end of the war the Commissioners succeeded in establishing with the Dutch admiralties a system of mutual ransoming of prisoners. 'Consider with indignation,' Evelyn wrote to Pepys in September 1665, 'the misery, and confusion all will be in at Chatham, and Gravesend, where I was threatened to have our sick all exposed, if by Thursday next I do not send them £2000; and in what condition our prisoners at Leeds, are like to be . . . I am almost in despair, so you will pardon the passion . . .'[38] Evelyn pushed strongly for the building of a naval hospital, which he plausibly argued would in time save much money as well as many lives; but in 1666 there was no money available to make such an investment, and the Board had to continue with hired lodgings, inns and barns wherever it could find them. It worked closely and harmoniously with James Pearse, appointed Surgeon-General in 1664 to go afloat with the main fleet and supervise the surgeons and the hospital ships, of which one or two usually accompanied the fleet. When the Sick and Wounded Board was dissolved in March 1674 at the end of the Third Dutch War, Pearse and the Navy Board divided its residual functions. The Sick and Wounded Board also co-operated with the Chatham Chest, the Tudor naval charity which paid pensions or lump sums to wounded and disabled seamen. (The scale ran from £6 13s 4d cash grant and the same amount each year thereafter for the loss of one leg, or double for both; £15 a year for the loss of both arms; £5 a year for an arm disabled,

£4 a year for the loss of an eye, and so on.) In February 1666 another commission was established to distribute gratuities to the widows of those killed in action, on a scale ranging from £200 to the widow of a captain of a First Rate, down to £5 for the widow of an ordinary seaman in a Sixth Rate. It too was dissolved in December 1674, when its functions were transferred to the Navy Board.[39]

The Protectorate's Victualling Board was replaced in 1660 by Denis Gauden (formerly one of the contractors of 1650–54), as chief victualling contractor under the title of 'Surveyor-General'. He received 6d a man a day for ships in 'petty warrant' victuals in harbour, 8d for those at sea, and 8¾d for ships voyaging south of 27°N.[40] Though the royal administration did not commit the gross blunders of its predecessor at the outbreak of war, the victualling system soon began to feel the want of money as acutely as the rest of the Navy. By October 1665 Gauden was owed £425,933 6s 8d, including advances to pack next year's meat over the winter. Naturally the fleet commanders blamed Gauden for deficiencies, and in an endeavour to improve the situation (and come by another salary) Pepys proposed himself for a new position, also confusingly entitled 'Surveyor-General of Victualling', in effect an inspector-general of the system, with agents in the major ports. He held the position from November 1665 to February 1667, appointed good subordinates, threw himself into the work with his customary energy, and made useful improvements in the system; but he found no major dishonesty or inefficiency, and the basic problem of want of money was beyond his cure. Gauden seems to have provided victuals of good quality, but the quantity was never sufficient, and there was again a serious problem with shortage of iron-bound casks for the ground tier of beer, leading to damaged casks and lost beer. Shortages were made worse by ships kept in commission in order to avoid having to pay the men. After the war Gauden's accounts were found to be substantially accurate, and no better system of victualling could be proposed but to renew his contract in 1668 with the addition of some partners lest he should die in office.[41]

Pepys's most important and lasting contribution to the victualling system was a reform of the system of pursery. From (Pepys thought) about 1644, the pursers had been paid in proportion to the number of men borne on the ship's books, which gave them a powerful incentive to inflate the numbers by false mustering, often in league with captains who pocketed the corresponding wages. The short-lived experiment of 1653–5 with stewards and clerks of the cheque had been intended to deal with this by providing a cross-check, but the two had every incentive to co-operate in keeping up a mutually profitable system, and the Protectorate Navy had reverted to the former practice. The result, as Pepys discovered, was a system which not only encouraged the pursers to fraud but virtually enforced it, for 'a purser without professed cheating is a professed loser, twice as much as he gets.'[42] The muster-masters who were expected to check the accuracy of the ship's books met with all sorts of obstruction from the ships' officers. When the efficient Francis Hosier, muster-master at Gravesend, boarded the *Loyal Katherine*, 'I desired the boatswain to call up the men, but he was sitting in his cabin and giving out pint glasses of strong waters to the men, as I understood for 12d each, and he informed me that he could not find his men, there being such a throng . . .'[43] Under the pre-Civil War system, to which the Navy reverted at Pepys's urging, the purser was automatically allowed on his accounts the full value of the victuals for the ship's authorised complement (plus any supernumeraries allowed by official order) but nothing more. He had an incentive to economize (for example by issuing fresh food purchased locally, or giving the men money to buy on their own account, and saving the corresponding issue of expensive preserved foodstuffs), but much to lose by padding the musters, which would earn him nothing but awkward questions. Captains and pursers now had motive to expose one another's misdeeds, not to connive with one another. The system was designed to cause the purser to lose rather than gain by defrauding men of their victuals, and to put the captain on the men's side rather than the purser's if they had a grievance. Though by no means perfect, this system of pursery was an enormous improvement on the fundamentally corrupt and exploitative system of the Parliamentary and Republican Navy, and continued to work into the nineteenth century. It left the purser not a few opportunities of profit, and of dishonesty, but mostly in his associated businesses such as the sale of tobacco, sugar and brandy, rather than in pursery and victualling as such.[44]

It is worth noting in passing that the revived English system of pursery was markedly superior to those of foreign navies. In the Dutch navy the captains and even admirals – or rather, in practice, their wives and daughters – were responsible for victualling their own ships, and were expected to make a substantial part of their earnings thereby. The only check on their honesty was that they also recruited their own men, and stood to suffer from a bad reputation. French captains had no such check and also victualled their own ships, ruthlessly cheating their men, until in 1667 an English-style victualling contractor, the *Munitionnaire-Général*, was installed to prevent them. French captains continued to be responsible for victualling their officers, on a much more generous scale than the men. In the Spanish service the senior ranks were sold to the highest bidder, so captains and admirals busied themselves with private trade and paying passengers, as well as keeping their costs of victualling to a minimum.[45]

The Ordnance Board was continued in 1660, officially on its pre-Civil War footing of independence, though in practice it was much inferior in status to the Admiralty, especially an Admiralty headed by the Duke of York, and also to the Treasury. Since the artillery train of the army only occasionally took the field, and the engineers were still a small body of civilian consultants, the Board's work was overwhelmingly the supply of guns and warlike stores to the Navy and to forts (which used much the same patterns of guns and equipment as ships and belonged to the naval branch of the Ordnance service). Probably some administrative friction and delay would have been avoided if the Board had been formally subject to the Admiralty, as in the 1650s, but it seems to have worked efficiently during the Second and Third Dutch Wars, though of course affected by the general shortage of money. The Ordnance Board adopted payment 'in course' before the Navy Board.[46]

The administrative innovations of the 1660s were tested, in some cases to destruction, by the Third Dutch War. Even before the war broke out in 1672 the Navy's credit was still fragile, and dockyard wages were long in arrears. It was hard to stop the yardmen stealing stores or absenting themselves to work for others who would pay them. The same problems with contractors were repeated as in the previous wars, and again the victuallers ran into difficulties. Again money was acutely short for the sick and wounded, whose plight was made worse by the very cold summer of 1672. The 1672 Stop of the Exchequer wrecked Downing's fledgling scheme of public credit, but in other respects the acute but short-lived crisis of 1673 left relatively few financial and administrative scars.[47]

The real change wrought by the Third Dutch War was political. By handing over the Admiralty in July 1673 to a commission headed by Prince Rupert, which was in effect the existing Privy Council Admiralty Committee renamed, Charles made a political gesture of great importance. Instead of being entirely within the sphere of the king's prerogative powers, the Navy was now in a more neutral position, somewhere part-way between king and Parliament. Prince Rupert was a member of the House of Lords as Duke of Cumberland; and though in most respects the king's man, he was strongly identified with the anti-French foreign policy of the late 1670s. With Pepys the Secretary of the new Board, with Charles and his brother (Lord Admiral of Scotland since December 1672, when the previous holder of the office died) often present at its meetings (the king had a better attendance record than any member of the

Board), there was a large measure of continuity in the practical management of the Navy, but its political status had significantly changed.[48] The Navy Board's office near the Tower of London, having survived the Great Fire in 1666, was burned down on 29 January 1673, and Pepys's move to the new Admiralty a few months later may have suggested an amalgamation of the two, but the new political situation suggested otherwise. The less completely the king controlled the Admiralty, the more he needed the Navy Board to be distinct from it. Sir Christopher Wren was commissioned to design a new Navy Office on the same site, finally completed in 1684.[49]

Pepys was now a Member of Parliament as well as Secretary of the Admiralty, and the House of Commons, reassured that the Navy was now on the right side, was persuaded by him in 1677 to vote the unprecedented sum of £600,000 for a peacetime building programme of thirty ships of the line, intended to go some way to match the extraordinary growth of the French navy. Pepys spoke on behalf of his department almost in the manner of a modern cabinet minister; 'more like an Admiral than a secretary', as his enemies noted.[50] The building of so many big ships at once was a novelty, and for want of sufficient building slips in the dockyards, contracts had to be let with private shipbuilders, one of them as far away from the Navy Board's supervision as Bristol. It also raised new constitutional issues, for Parliament had voted not only the number and rate but even the dimensions of the ships, yet Charles thought 'that the principal consideration to be had as to the size of the ships be the pitching upon such dimensions as may render them by their force and build most capable of performing the service they are designed for' – meaning larger dimensions than Parliament had voted.[51] The Navy Board was afraid of being blamed by Parliament, either for departing from the wording of the Act, or for spending too much on each ship to complete the full thirty. In this case the king carried his point, but the incident was a tell-tale of the shifting balance of power over the Navy.[52]

In the turmoil of the Exclusion Crisis and the Popish Plot it shifted farther and faster. The king was forced to dismiss Prince Rupert's Admiralty Board in May 1679 and replace it with one drawn from cross-benchers and the more moderate members of the Parliamentary opposition. In effect he handed the Navy over to Parliament, if not completely to his opponents, as a guarantee that he was not intending to use the fleet in any bid for arbitrary power. The new Admiralty at once dismissed Pepys, who was so deeply stamped as the Duke of York's man, and replaced him, first with Pepys's able former clerk Thomas Hayter, and then, less happily, with John Brisbane, an indifferent correspondent quite ignorant of the Navy. Pepys, who nourished not a few dislikes, never hated anybody as much as the 1679 Admiralty, and devoted much of his formidable talents and his remaining twenty-four years of life to enlarging on its 'ignorance, debauchery, and other defects'.[53] He never appreciated how nearly fatal the Exclusion Crisis had been to the monarchy, and how little power Charles II retained to protect his servants. For Pepys, who lost his job and almost his life thereby, the dismissal of Prince Rupert's Admiralty Board was not the skilful manoeuvre of a desperate king, casting out a victim to distract the wolves closing around him, but a piece of frivolous cynicism by a monarch who could have retained it had he chosen to do so: 'No king ever did so unaccountable a thing to oblige his people by as to dissolve a commission of the Admiralty then in his own hand, who best understands the business of the sea of any prince the world ever had, and things never better done, and put it into hands which he knew were wholly ignorant thereof, sporting himself with their ignorance.'[54]

Pepys subsequently showed in convincing detail how much worse the performance of the 1679 Admiralty was than its predecessor. His figures were correct, but took no account of circumstances. In 1679 the Navy, thanks to the Opposition's efforts and Louis XIV's bribes, had been fully mobilized without any Parliamentary grants, so that the new Board inherited a financial crisis from which it never fully escaped, and a large fleet which it had to reduce in a hurry. The new Lords of the Admiralty may have been 'country gentlemen wholly ignorant of the business of the Navy',[55] as Pepys charged, but they were not fools, and they did their honest best to administer a small peacetime fleet with insufficient money. Moreover Charles II, 'a lover of the sea, and skilful in shipping',[56] continued to take some of the major decisions for them, and as his political position improved he filled vacancies on the Board with more friendly Parliamentarians. In 1683 this Admiralty was responsible for an important development when it replaced the last victualling contractors with a Victualling Board of salaried commissioners on the 1655 model. This was to remain the permanent form of naval victualling for a century and a half.[57]

In May 1684 Charles II was at last strong enough to dissolve the Admiralty Board and take the Admiralty into his own hands, with Pepys restored to favour as his 'Secretary of the Marine'. In all but name he was another secretary of state, a naval minister like Jean-Baptiste Colbert in France. The analogy certainly occurred to him, and to the king's enemies. Pepys's first action was to institute an inquiry into the management of the Admiralty and Navy Board since 1679. He presented his report to Charles on 1 January 1685. On 6 February the king died, and it was left to his brother James II to take it up.[58] On Pepys's recommendation, a special 'Navy Commission' was set up in April 1686 to restore the Navy to good condition, which Pepys undertook to do for £400,000 a year, while the existing Navy Board remained in order to clear up its accounts. In the thirty months of its existence this Commission seems to have very thoroughly restored the Navy, driven by Pepys's energy and fuelled by James's easier financial position. It repaired the thirty ships of 1677, which Pepys found decaying in reserve, and added fifty-four storehouses or other buildings to the dockyards.[59] The 1690 Public Accounts Committee, not friendly to the regime of James II, reported that

> The ships built, rebuilt and repaired by these commissioners were fully and well performed, and the buildings and other works by them erected and made during the continuation of the same commission were done with great exactness, sufficiency and frugality of expense in the managery and conduct thereof.[60]

Two themes sum up the naval administration of Charles II and James II: the struggle to make the administration of the Navy more efficient in spite of a constant, at times critical, shortage of money; and the contest between king and Parliament for the control of the fleet. Although it has long been customary to praise the godfearing honesty of the English Republic and condemn the corruption of Stuart administration (usually in the eloquent and numerous words of Pepys), Pepys's own example as well as the evidence he left make clear how greatly the probity and efficiency of Stuart naval administration advanced, and exceeded that of the English Republic. His own personal standards became higher as his career proceeded, perhaps especially after the fright the Brooke House Commission gave him. He did an enormous amount to improve the accounting standards of the Navy. His papers are full of instances of corrupt practices suspected, pursued, detected and prosecuted, and it is impossible to doubt that he left the system more honest and efficient than he found it.[61] Even in the 1660s there was nothing in the Navy to equal the gross, unashamed peculation of Pepys's friend Richard Cooling, the Lord Chamberlain's secretary, who 'told us his horse was a bribe, and his boots a bribe; and told us he was made up of bribes . . . and that he makes every sort of tradesman to bribe him; and invited me home to his house to taste of his bribe-wine.'[62] But by no means all the credit belongs to Pepys, and a similar rise in honesty and efficiency can be observed elsewhere, for example in the Treasury.[63]

The other theme of these years was power. Power over the Navy embodied power over the country, not because the Navy was really well equipped to interfere directly in domestic politics, nor because either Charles or James tried to use it in that way, but because it symbolized English liberty, political and religious, and because it required such large sums of money. James II was the last English sovereign to command an income which gave him a real possibility of governing without Parliament, and therefore of keeping full command of the Navy.[64] By 1686, with Pepys installed as Secretary of the Marine, the constitutional position of James II's Navy was not unlike that of Louis XIV's under Colbert and later Seignelay as *Secrétaires d'Etat pour la Marine*. Though Parliament had for a time gained substantial control over the Navy of Charles II, his brother had the fleet firmly back in his own hands. How firmly, events were presently to show.

EIGHT

Learning and Doing and Suffering

Social History 1660–1688

One issue has tended to dominate the social history of the Restoration Navy: the choice of captains and admirals. It is always encapsulated in the phrase 'gentlemen or tarpaulins': the question of whether the Navy's officers should be chosen from the nobility and gentry – the natural leaders of society, possessors of the hereditary military virtues of honour and courage, and principal supporters of the crown, but with few exceptions ignorant of seafaring – or from amongst professional seamen, the so-called 'tarpaulins' (from the oiled canvas of which seamen made their foul-weather coats), bred up to the sea and skilled in its ways. They had provided the Navy of the Commonwealth and Protectorate with almost all its captains, and therefore constituted the great part of the pool of available officers in 1660, but they had been chosen for their religious and political qualities as much as their professional abilities. They were, or had very recently been, 'fanatics', in the language of the Restoration, and Republicans. The choice was of high political sensitivity as well as practical significance. In fact there were two choices: one immediate, and one for the future. In the short term Charles II had to choose officers for the relatively small fleet retained in commission in 1660, and the much larger fleet prepared for war in 1664, largely from those who were then available. Beyond that, however, he had to set up a system (which the Protectorate had never done) to select and train the officers of future generations. For this he had to consider what qualities were needful, and how they could be nurtured. The two problems were distinct, and demanded different solutions, but both of them turned on the balance between political loyalty, social suitability and professional competence.

These were difficult issues at the time, and for two reasons they have been seriously misunderstood by subsequent generations and their historians. Being of obvious political sensitivity, the question of 'gentlemen or tarpaulins' was debated in the political world, amongst many people who had no specialized knowledge of the Navy. Precisely because the Navy was a national institution which commanded almost universal support, but very general ignorance, it provided a convenient rhetorical language for different political groups. To praise the good qualities of tarpaulin officers in Restoration England was indirectly to say what could not be said explicitly; to praise the English Republic which had chosen them, or at least to express discontent with the morality and efficiency of Charles II and his court. This rhetorical language of 'gentlemen versus tarpaulins' quickly took on a life of its own which long outlived the real problem in the Navy. We shall see that the real issue was almost completely solved in Charles II's lifetime, but the rhetorical debate was at its height around the end of the century, and had by no means died even in the 1740s. Historians from Macaulay almost to the present day have been unduly credulous in taking this political rhetoric at face value, as a comment on the real Navy; rather than what it actually was, a coded language used by politicians who knew very little about the Sea Service, but found it a perfect vehicle for conveying their views on national issues.[1]

The second reason for misunderstanding the 'gentlemen or tarpaulins' question is Samuel Pepys. Since his papers and his work as a naval administrator were rediscovered at the beginning of the twentieth century, they have exercised a dominant influence over the views of historians – and this was one of the issues on which his prejudices were strongest and most enduring. His patron Lord Sandwich, by origin a gentleman and a soldier, strongly disapproved of sea officers drawn from his own background. So did Pepys's mentor William Coventry. Himself a middle-class Londoner who had grown up with the victories of the Commonwealth Navy ringing in his ears, remote from the social values of the court and the Cavalier Parliament, Pepys readily accepted and never lost a deep-seated aversion to gentlemen officers. Though he was in time intellectually persuaded of the necessity of recruiting them, though he was a loyal servant of the king and his brother, he never to the end of his life ceased to collect disparaging anecdotes about gentleman officers, and always saw the Navy's administrative and disciplinary problems as springing from their social origins. He believed as profoundly as any of his contemporaries in hereditary virtues and vices; but in his case it was the virtues of middle-class professionals like himself; the vices of gentlemen, courtiers and those who aped their manners. Captain John Tyrrell, he declared in a characteristic judgement, was 'the only sober, diligent, modest and true bred seaman of any gentleman that I know in the fleet'.[2] Until recently historians were apt to accept Pepys's views as expressing all that needed to be said about the Restoration Navy. Now they are more aware that Pepys was a partisan, and that in this and other matters, he formed views in the 1660s which did not evolve as circumstances changed. In order to judge rightly the question of 'gentlemen or tarpaulins', it is necessary to put aside political rhetoric altogether, and to take some distance from the views of Samuel Pepys.[3]

In the spring of 1660, as we have seen, Mountague (as he then was) and Lawson removed some of the more aggressively Republican captains. As the Navy was reduced over the following twelve months or so, many more were paid off and returned, for the most part, to the merchant service from which they had come. Though only about 1 per cent of the officers refused the oath of allegiance to the crown, zealous Republican captains and Nonconformist chaplains were not re-employed. Those who were retained were joined by Royalist seamen like Thomas Allin, Richard Beach and Robert Holmes who had served in Prince Rupert's squadron or in privateers. The difficult choices came in the mobilization of 1664. With a war to fight, experience of the last war against the Dutch was at a premium, but so was loyalty, while at the same time a number of noblemen and courtiers pressed to be allowed to serve on the only field of honour which was available. Many old Cavaliers, moreover, had been exiled or impoverished for their loyalty, and hoped now to recoup their losses in by far the most important service the crown had to offer.[4] 'There are in his Majesty's service at sea,' Coventry noted,

> more than twenty captains who have served the king, so that his Majesty will have commanders enough of his own party to command the fleets herein proposed, whereby the fleet will be made safe for his Majesty's service against domestic dangers, though against foreign it must be confessed the former commanders are more capable.[5]

In this dilemma the Duke of York, characteristically deaf to political considerations, was all for the 'former commanders', the old Cromwellians. 'He perceived,' Pepys noted,

> it must be the old captains that must do the business, and that the new ones would spoil all. And my Lord [Sandwich] did very discreetly tell the Duke (though quite against his judgement and inclination) that, however, the King's new captains ought to be borne with a little and encouraged.[6]

The result was a senior officer corps of mixed origins, but dominated by veterans of the First Dutch War, including eleven of the seventeen flag-officers, and more than ninety captains. Already the officers' origins were more varied than the simple phrase 'gentlemen and tarpaulins' would imply. There were at least four identifiable groups: officers inherited from the State's Navy; those who had served the king or his father at sea in the 1640s and 1650s; gentlemen who had entered the Navy since 1660; and 'tarpaulins' who had done the same. Some fell into more than one group, and some fitted none at all. There were formerly Republican officers of high birth such as Sandwich and Ayscue, and Royalists who were socially obscure. 'Tarpaulins', in the sense of men who had made their first careers in merchantmen, included not a few of respectable family, and there were Royalist tarpaulins as well as old Republicans. Vice-Admiral William Goodson, Captain Joseph Ames and Captain Sir Robert Robinson were typical Cromwellian officers, all from Yarmouth. Sir Thomas Allin, the former Royalist privateer, came from the same social background but the rival seaport of Lowestoft ten miles to the south. Sir Robert Holmes and Sir Edward Spragge were minor Irish Protestant gentlemen who had likewise made their names as Royalist privateers. Much the same social mixture characterized the officers who entered after the Restoration. Captain Sir John Berry's father was a poor country clergyman. Sir John Kempthorne was the son of a lawyer who had been a Royalist officer in the Civil War. He was technically a gentleman, in that he inherited a coat of arms, but no money came with it, and he went early to sea to seek his fortune. He progressed from Topsham ships to the Levant Company, married the maidservant of the wife of the English ambassador at Constantinople, transferred to the Navy after the Restoration, and became in due course a vice-admiral. Charles Royden, the son of a minor Welsh gentleman ruined by his loyalty during the Civil War, went to sea as a common seaman, married a button-maker's daughter, and rose to be a rather unsuccessful captain. John Clements advanced in five years from a boatswain to a captain; as fast a rise and from as humble an origin as any Cromwellian officer.[7]

The most prominent social pattern in the Navy was not birth but connection. The Navy was made up of 'followings', senior officers bringing in their train colleagues and relatives whose careers they favoured. The most important patrons were of course at the top: Albemarle, Sandwich, Prince Rupert and the Duke of York himself, who tended to favour those who had long served with them. Others were surrounded by their relatives. Allin brought into the Navy his Ashby nephews, his brother-in-law and nephews the Utbers, and other kinsmen from the families of Anguish, Mighell and Leake. Many of these in turn went on to establish naval dynasties. Some followings were based on geography, most notably the 'Cockthorpe connection'. This little Norfolk village was the home of Sir Christopher Myngs, his follower Sir John Narbrough, and then Narbrough's protégé Sir Cloudesley Shovell. Shovell is another example of the social ambiguities of the post-Restoration entries. He was usually called a 'tarpaulin', because he came from East Anglia rather than the court, and because he went to sea young as a follower of one who himself had started as a boy in Cromwell's time, but Shovell's father, though not strictly a gentleman, was a prosperous local landowner. His contemporary George Rooke was both the third son of Colonel Sir William Rooke, a Kentish gentleman, and nephew of Lord Nottingham. He did not go to sea (as a follower of Spragge's) until he was nineteen, which clearly marked him as a gentleman officer – but his family had no more money than the Shovells, and they rose together as followers of Narbrough. Further afield than Norfolk and Kent, there was even a small group of Swedish officers, perhaps connections from Ayscue's service in Sweden.[8]

Both Charles and James worked hard to cement the unity of their fleet. The king assured the French ambassador that the ex-Republicans 'have all had the plague, but they are completely cured, and less likely to fall ill than the others'.[9] When the young Lieutenant Philip Mansell of the *Rainbow* taunted his captain, Willoughby Hannam, and Captain Jeremy Smith, 'with their having been rebels and served under Cromwell's commission', he was promptly court-martialled and dismissed from the service. 'His Royal Highness,' Sandwich noted,

> very graciously was pleased to express the King's Majesty's and his own displeasure against any recounting of former differences and parties. Said that all of the commanders were equally esteemed good subjects and officers and he doubted not but they would so approve themselves in all occasions, and he would severely reprehend any expressions of past divisions.[10]

The experience of the Second Dutch War went far to blur the past divisions. The old Cromwellian captains served loyally, and seven of them were knighted for good service (John Harman, Joseph Jordan, Christopher Myngs, Jeremy Smith, Thomas Teddeman, Roger Cuttance and William Jennings). Pepys was astonished to hear Lord Berkeley and other former Royalist exiles,

> cry up the discipline of the late times here, and in the former Dutch war . . . wishing with all their hearts that the business of religion were not so severely carried on as to discourage the sober people to come among us, and wishing that the same law and severity were used against drunkenness as there was then – saying that our evil-living will call the hand of God upon us again.[11]

A good many reputations, however, suffered from the misfortunes of the war. Sandwich and Penn were tainted by the prize goods affair, Teddeman was connected with the defeat at Bergen, and Albemarle blundered into the Four Days' Battle. Captain Edward Nixon, a veteran of the First Dutch War, was sentenced to death for cowardice. Amongst the new Royalist captains there were some like Sir Frescheville Holles, whom Penn called 'a conceited, idle, prating, lying fellow', and Batten, more succinctly, 'a very wind-fucker'.[12] But Holles was at least a gallant fighter, and the members of the Navy Board (Penn, Batten and Pepys, who recorded their opinions) disliked him because as an MP he asked some aggressive questions in the Commons in 1667 about their handling of contracts. There were other gentleman captains who were, or became, fine seamen, and distinguished themselves in battle, and there were 'tarpaulins' whose seamanship proved wanting.[13] The Duke of York went a long way to prefer professional experience to the usual claims of social rank. When the Duke of Buckingham, the most eminent of the noble 'volunteers' who went to sea with no specific naval rank, demanded to be admitted to the Council of War 'as being a Privy Councillor, and also for his quality sake', he was refused, though Captain the Earl of Marlborough, and the king's bastard son the Duke of Monmouth, were invited in addition to the nine admirals.[14]

The disappointments and recriminations of the war left the officer corps bitterly divided. Sir Robert Holmes and Sir Jeremy Smith, for example, blamed one another for the escape of Tromp after the St James's Day battle. As followers of Prince Rupert and Albemarle respectively, they were professional rivals, and once the main fleet was paid off their patrons were no longer able to suppress the dispute, which had to be settled by the king in person (largely in Smith's favour).[15] The quarrel, however, sprang from disappointment and professional jealousy, not political or social origins. Its background was the rivalry of men who already identified their careers with the Navy, and cared very much for the rewards of honour, rank and money which it had to offer. Destructive in themselves of morale and efficiency, such divisions yet marked an important stage in the evolution of a professional officer corps. Against them, moreover, must be set examples of officers who knew how to work efficiently together in spite of personal dislike or professional rivalry, starting with Albemarle and Prince Rupert in 1666. There were also many harmonious relations between officers of diverse backgrounds, such as Sir Frescheville Holles and his tarpaulin lieutenant Jeremy Roch. The first sea officers' club was formed in 1674 to dine weekly at the Vulture in Cornhill 'for the improvement of a mutual society, and an increase of love and kindness among them', its founding members a social cross-section of captains who clearly felt themselves united by their profession.[16]

In the Third Dutch War the officers were again drawn largely from the existing stock, with the addition of a small number of prominent noblemen of limited experience. Charles II made his own attitude towards them clear:

> I am not for employing of men merely for quality, yet when men of quality are fit for the trade they desire to enter into, I think 'tis reasonable they should be encouraged at least equally with others, and I assure you, this young man has been so industrious to improve himself and so successful in it, as he deserves some partiality in his case, to encourage others to do the like . . .[7]

What Charles well understood was the political value of recruiting great men to serve at sea, making naval service respectable and honourable, and cementing the Navy and the regime together. Moreover these new admirals had the timely virtue of standing apart from the professional disputes of the Navy, so that they could act as peacemakers. Lord Ossory, for example, was made a rear-admiral for the 1673 campaign. John Narbrough, whose experience and service gave him a strong claim to be a rear-admiral, consented to sail as Ossory's flag-captain and mentor. The Duke of York warmly appreciated Narbrough's generosity, Ossory fully acknowledged his contribution, and that autumn Narbrough received his rear-admiral's flag and a knighthood. Next year he went out to the Mediterranean as commander-in-chief, while Ossory was given command of the peacetime Channel fleet specifically to heal the divisions which Prince Rupert's recklessly partisan approach had done much to deepen. A compromise between political and naval imperatives had been made to work smoothly thanks to the good sense and professionalism of the officers concerned.[18]

With the return of peace the problems of the long term came to the fore. Apart from the brief mobilization of 1678, the Navy remained on a peacetime footing for fifteen years, from 1673 to 1688. The only important operational squadron was in the Mediterranean, and much of the limited promotion available was bestowed by Narbrough and Herbert as successive commanders-in-chief there. Meanwhile the Admiralty had three related problems: how to define seniority when there was no continuous service and no permanent rank; how to retain the services of experienced but unemployed officers who might be needed again; and how to choose and train young men to be officers in the future. The problem of seniority presented itself whenever ships found themselves in company with no designated commander-in-chief present. Even if there were a commander-in-chief present, the seniority of the captains under him was unsettled. Allin in 1664 simply appointed Captain William Poole of the *London* as his 'Captain-Lieutenant'. When in 1667 the English squadron in the West Indies planned to attack the French colony of Cayenne, the three captains drew lots to decide who should command. The problem frequently occurred in the Downs, because it was such a crossroads of the sea that ships came in at random, and a doctrine was slowly developed of identifying the senior captain there by date of first commission, giving him the title of 'commodore' (from the Dutch *kommandeur*, 'senior officer'), and a swallow-tailed broad pendant to distinguish him. As yet 'commodore' was simply a description of the senior captain present, not even a temporary rank, and the definition of seniority was itself uncertain. Pepys spent many years compiling a seniority list, but as late as 1688 the result was still unsatisfactory, as he warned Lord Dartmouth: 'though this may guide you very much, yet it is liable to as many defects as there may be gentlemen in the fleet, whose first commissions have happened to be granted to them by admirals or commanders-in-chief at sea.'[19] Further ambiguity surrounded the position of the commander-in-chief's 'First Captain' or 'Eldest Captain', often his senior adviser if not deputy, and regarded as having natural pretensions to promotion to flag rank. In the Duke of York's flagship in 1666, Penn as flag-captain acted as the Duke's expert adviser, and 'Captain' John Cox, the master, effectively commanded her.[20]

Unemployed officers were first provided for as 'volunteers', meaning, in this context, gentlemen supernumeraries allowed an able seaman's pay. Midshipmen extraordinary, first noted in 1669 and regulated in 1676, were similar but drew the higher pay of a midshipman. The system was unsatisfactory for all. The gentlemen officers had no work and almost no livelihood, while their captains tended to find them a nuisance.[21] They might have been of more use in wartime, for English warships had extremely few officers by modern standards. Most admirals commanded their own ships, and only the first three Rates were allowed two lieutenants (First Rates had three from 1678). Ships' companies of up to 1,000 were commanded by fewer than ten commissioned and warrant officers.[22] It was not unknown for a ship to lose all her commissioned officers in action. In 1667 Captain Henry Dawes of the *Princess* was killed in action with the Danish warships *Faisant* and *Haerderin*. His last words to his officers were: 'For God's sake do not yield the ship to those fellows!' They did not, but the lieutenant and master were killed in turn, and it was left to Richard Leake, the gunner, to bring her home.[23] In May 1689 the *Nonsuch* returned under the command of her boatswain, Robert Simcock, having taken two French prizes but lost her other officers.[24]

An alternative method of retaining unemployed officers was half-pay, first granted in 1668 to admirals who had served in the Second Dutch War. In 1674 it was extended to former captains of First and Second Rates, and in 1675 to former masters of the same ships, and to former commodores. From the beginning it was unclear whether half-pay was a reward for past, or a retainer for future, service. Superannuation, introduced for warrant officers in 1672, was clearly intended as a comfort in retirement, but it was entirely discretionary, and the Navy had to wait nearly two centuries for standard retirement pensions. In practice few officers benefited from either scheme. By 1687 there were two rear-admirals on half-pay, six captains and four masters, while six masters, two gunners and two surgeons had been superannuated.[25] Far more unemployed officers simply served in merchant ships in peacetime. This was normal for warrant officers and common for lieutenants and captains. Even Rear-Admiral Sir John Wetwang accepted a command from the East India Company in 1682. Some other commissioned officers reverted to warrant rank for the sake of the permanent employment on board ships in reserve, and one impoverished captain became a dockyard shipwright.[26]

An alternative livelihood for gentleman officers was the army, especially as it expanded under James II, and specifically the Marine regiment, which in spite of its naval connection, belonged to the army and was in most respects organized as a conventional foot regiment. It was easy to get leave from army regiments, so officers could push their naval careers when they had the chance without abandoning the security and status of an army commission. The first sea officer to acquire a commission in the Marines was Captain Francis Digby in 1671. He was followed by Captain George Rooke (lieutenant of Marines 1677, captain 1687). His brother Thomas, whose captain had made an enemy of his commander-in-chief Arthur Herbert, was court-martialled and dismissed the Navy on a flimsy charge of blasphemy, and joined the same regiment. George Byng, having fallen out with his captain, took refuge in the Tangier garrison, where Colonel Kirke made him an ensign.[27]

Both half-pay and superannuation had a long and important history ahead of them, but a still more important foundation of the sea officer corps was the process of entry and training of new officers. As early as 1661 Charles II instituted the rating of 'volunteer per order', taking the place and pay of one midshipman in each ship, 'to give encouragement to such young gentlemen as are willing to apply themselves to the learning of navigation, and fitting themselves for the service of the sea'.[28] These 'king's letter boys', as they were sometimes known, entered the Navy under the king's personal patronage; the channel by which most of the first generation of gentleman officers first went to sea. They were entitled to advance to the rate of 'midshipman ordinary' (meaning midshipman supernumerary to the ship's authorized complement), and so to lieutenant. Further regulations of 1676 fixed their age (not over sixteen) and increased the number of volunteers per order in each ship, to encourage 'the families of better sort among our subjects to breed up their younger sons to the art and practice of navigation in order to the fitting them for further employment in our service at sea'.[29] This was strong language for contemporaries. An 'art or practice' referred to the mechanical skill of a craftsman, or the acquired abilities of a middle-class professional. A gentleman was a gentleman precisely because he did not have or need to have such skills; to require gentlemen's sons, even younger sons, to learn an 'art or practice' in order to qualify themselves for the honourable service of the crown was socially revolutionary and politically all but subversive. Charles II and his brother took the requirement seriously. In December 1673, for example, Pepys received a certificate assuring him that Mr William Clinton, 'a gentleman and an understanding man', was fit to be a lieutenant, having been one year at sea and fought in three actions. 'I should very willingly have found it to have mentioned the other qualifications of a good sea officer beside that of valour, his Majesty being enough satisfied that that without sobriety and seamanship is lost, and too often proves rather fatal to the service than truly useful.'[30]

As yet the necessary degree of sobriety and seamanship was undefined. In December 1677 the critical decision was taken to oblige candidates for lieutenant to have served at least three years at sea, including one year as midshipman – then a working petty officer's rating – before passing an examination in seamanship conducted by senior officers. The concept of a qualifying examination was extremely rare, and the social implications of forcing gentlemen's sons to serve alongside seamen petty officers were bound to be extremely controversial. It has long been customary for historians to credit the innovation to Pepys, but this is a serious misunderstanding of his position. No decision of such political sensitivity could possibly have been taken by a civil servant alone. Pepys strongly supported the idea; as a good secretary he prepared the meeting and briefed his chairman – but the chairman was Charles II, and the decision had to be his. Present were the Admiralty and Navy Boards, most of the active flag-officers, and some captains of long experience. It is clear from Pepys's minutes that the desirability of qualifying service and an examination from the Navy's point of view was taken for granted. The discussion centred on whether it would be politically and socially feasible, and the king especially sought the views of the gentlemen officers. The turning point came when Captain George Legge was asked whether he had served one year as a midshipman: 'to which he answering no, but that it had cost him many an aching head and heart since to make up the want of it, that point was unanimously resolved on'.[31]

The lieutenants' examination, and even more the momentous decision to require qualifying service as a rating, was to be one of the keys to the long-term efficiency of the Navy. It seems so natural to the modern reader that it is easy to underestimate how completely it ran against the grain of seventeenth-century society. No other navy attempted anything comparable (though the Admiralty of the Maze, alone among the Dutch admiralties, instituted a navigation examination for its officers in 1698).[32] Pepys's prejudices against gentleman captains too easily blind us to the extent to which the culture of seamanship became deeply embedded in the Restoration Navy, among gentlemen as much as tarpaulins. 'Sir W. Booth observes very justly to me,' Pepys noted,

> that he would undertake to teach a man enough of the sea to talk as a seaman in a year, but to do the work and know the business his whole life is little enough, he answering to me that now he finds one thing or another to learn every day and that he did believe himself a better seaman after the first three years of his service than he knows himself to be now.[33]

The only way to learn seamanship, in Pepys's words, was 'to make themselves masters of it, by learning and doing and suffering all things'.[34] He deserves real credit for the decision, but the responsibility was entirely the king's. Some modern historians still dismiss Charles II as a lazy cynic who avoided hard work and difficult decisions.[35] In the naval context this judgement is unsustainable. As the then Secretary of the Admiralty told Queen Anne's husband thirty years later, 'however the reign of Charles II may have been exploded for other things, it cannot be so in relation to the Navy, for his Majesty's care extended no less to the officering the fleet with able seamen than to the maintaining of it with good husbandry'.[36]

It seems to be fairly clear that Charles II envisaged that his young gentlemen 'volunteers per order' would come to be the main if not sole source of future lieutenants, and hence in time of captains. Pepys accepted that 'volunteers will soon be our only lieutenants, and so captains', and the 1679 Admiralty Board continued the policy.[37] 'Tarpaulin' officers would still be promoted to command Sixth Rates, fireships and other small vessels without lieutenants or masters, in the quasi rank coming to be known as 'master and commander', but their careers would rise no higher. The officers' career structure would then have resembled that which the French navy adopted at the same time (and retained until 1791), with the critical difference that French gentlemen officers learned their profession in the classroom, and were not subjected to an examination. By 1688 almost all the rising generation of English sea officers were gentlemen who had entered as volunteers per order.[38]

All readers of Pepys's voluminous papers, especially his papers as Secretary of the Admiralty, will be familiar with his obsession with the corruption and indiscipline of the gentleman officers. His penetrating eye detected many misdeeds – drunkenness, absence without leave, debauchery, impiety, embezzlement and false mustering – but one above all concerned him: 'good voyages'. In the seventeenth century, and for long afterwards, international trade balances had to be settled in cash, and for obvious reasons merchants transmitting gold and silver overseas preferred to use well-armed warships. Though captains were forbidden to engage in private trade, an exception had to be made for specie, which they could carry for a fee of 1 per cent of its value. Pepys's complaint was that the carriage of specie, legitimate in itself, tempted captains to such illegitimate practices as diverting their course to promising ports, overcharging and shipping other goods. 'Upon the whole it is plain,' Pepys raged, 'that this business of money runs through and debauches the whole service of the Navy and is now come to the highest degree of villainy and infamy and nobody considers it.'[39]

Undoubtedly there were abuses, but the situation needs to be put in perspective. The carriage of bullion on commission, with all its attendant temptations, continued to be part of the Navy's functions throughout the eighteenth and nineteenth centuries without altogether destroying its operational efficiency. As late as the 1820s Sir Thomas Hardy made £18,000 by it in less than three years as Commander-in-Chief South America, and the practice was not forbidden until 1914.[40] The captains Pepys knew as Secretary of the Admiralty were almost all poor men, many of them representatives of families impoverished in the service of the crown. Their pay was too little to live on, and usually long in arrears. The Navy was at peace with major powers, though not with the Barbary States. In the circumstances they did not feel that 'good voyages' were a serious crime, and they resented pompous lectures from a comfortable bureaucrat who, as they well knew, was making £4–5,000 a year on fees for the issue of Mediterranean passes alone. They also resented his efforts to hold them to inflexible and unrealistic regulations which had more to do with bureaucratic forms than fighting efficiency. Pepys was in some ways the English Colbert, trying to do what his French counterpart succeeded in doing; to create an accountant's navy whose prime function was to balance the books and observe the formalities. Charles II, whose laxity Pepys never ceased to deplore, had a broader vision. He saw the necessity of rewarding loyal servants, if the Navy was to attract officers prepared to fight and die in his service. If he could not afford to do it himself, it was better that it should be done at the merchants' expense, even at the cost of tolerating a degree of dishonesty. It was typical of his rigid, disciplinarian brother James that he was fully persuaded by Pepys's arguments. In 1686 he forbade the carriage of bullion without order, in recompense granting captains generous 'table money' (an entertainment allowance), and the full value of their prizes. Unfortunately there were very few prizes, since there was no war in progress except against Sallee, and the additional allowances never materialized. When the hour struck in which James II needed devoted officers to fight for his throne, too few were to be found.[41]

It is easy enough to identify the weaknesses of the sea officers, because contemporaries were well aware of them. At the funeral of Captain Christopher Gunman in 1685 Evelyn gloomily noted that 'he was a sober, frugal, cheerful and temperate man; we have few such seamen left'.[42] Captains were accused of beating their warrant officers and the masters of merchant ships.[43] Captain Thomas Booth of the *Falcon* raised a drunken riot in Yarmouth in which a night-watchman was killed; Captain Thomas Penrose of the *Monck* lost his temper and pushed a man down stairs who was fatally injured.[44] Richard Thurston, master of the *Cambridge* in 1678, charged the lieutenants of his ship with 'drunkenness, swearing, revelling, ranting, defrauding, sheep-stealing, men-stealing, from other of his Majesty's ships in the night, discharging them for money or other considerable bribes . . .'[45] Warrant officers were universally suspected of embezzling their stores, so that the masters of merchant ships naturally approached a man-of-war's boatswain or gunner if they needed a coil of rope or a barrel of powder.[46] George Bradford, chaplain of the *Sweepstakes*, described by his captain as 'a gentleman recommended me by several worthy gentlemen' and 'very well approve[d] of' by the Bishop of London, went drinking ashore at every port: at Portsmouth he cheated the corporal of Marines at cards, at Dublin he danced naked around Trinity College, at Carrickfergus he and his wife pranced naked around the town 'catterwoolding' at one in the morning.[47] John Hacket was recommended by the Dean of Rochester on the grounds that 'he has been a sea chaplain for some years and unlike most of them is a sober well-tempered man'.[48] As for the medical men, seamen like Edward Barlow were not impressed:

> And the surgeons and doctors of physic in ships many times are very careless of a poor man in his sickness, their common phrase being to come to him and take him by the hand when they hear that he hath been sick two or three days, thinking that is soon enough, and feeling his pulses when he is half dead, asking him when he was at stool, and how he feels himself, and how he has slept, and then giving him some of their medicines upon the point of a knife, which doth as much good to him

as a blow upon the pate with a stick. And when he is dead then they did not think that he had been so bad as he was, nor so near his end . . .[49]

None of this should be exaggerated. Similar, indeed worse, stories could be told of any seventeenth-century public service in any country. The perform-ance of the English Navy in battle was at least equal to the Dutch, the leading maritime power of the age, admired by all for their honesty, efficiency and wealth. Against every colourful complaint one can set examples of gallantry, dedication and ability. Though the general standard of navigation was not high, there were some outstanding navigators, including Gunman and the pioneer hydrographer Grenville Collins.[50] It is notable how many English admirals were distinguished as seamen and pilots like Prince Rupert and the Duke of York, or as scientific navigators like Sandwich, Holmes and Nar-brough, observing magnetic variation and plotting their courses on charts on Mercator's projection.[51] 'Most of our navigators in this age,' Narbrough complained,

> sail by the plane chart, and keep their accounts of the ship's way accord-ingly, although they sail near the Poles; which is the greatest error that can be committed; for they cannot tell how to find their way home again, by reason of their mistake; as I have some in the ship with me now that are in the same error, for want of understanding the true difference of the meridian, according to their miles of longitude, in the several latitudes. I could wish all seamen would give over sailing by the false plane chart and sail by Mercator's chart, which is according to the truth of navigation; but it is an hard matter to convince any of the old navigators, from their method of sailing by the plane chart; shew most of them the globe, yet they will talk in their wonted road.[52]

John Baltharpe of the *St David's* gives us an admiring picture of his boatswain, Samuel Hatfield:

> With Silver Call, on Deck he stands,
> Winds it, make haste, aloft more Hands,
> Come on my Lads, look to your Gear,
> Be sure that we have all things clear.[53]

The picture of brisk efficiency is as worthy of remembrance as Pepys's com-plaints of embezzlement. Amongst chaplains we find Thomas Ken, later Bishop of Bath and Wells and one of the best-known churchmen of the age (though he was the last naval chaplain to become an English bishop until 1935). Thomas Dockwray, Spragge's chaplain in the *Victory* during the Second Dutch War, was celebrated in popular song:

His chaplain fell to his wonted work,
Cried 'Now for the King and the Duke of York!'
He prayed like a Christian and fought like a Turk . . .

Promoted Doctor of Divinity for gallantry in action at the St James's Day Fight, Dockwray was rewarded with a living at the end of the war, and returned to the sea in 1672 with an appointment as superintending chaplain, arguably the first ancestor of the modern Chaplain of the Fleet, only to be lost at Solebay in the burning of the *Royal James*.[54]

'The greatest difficulty and vexation in a war,' Coventry noted, 'is the manning of ships.'[55] The problem was even worse in the Second Dutch War than it had been in the First, for though the overall size of the fleets did not much increase, the average ship was considerably larger, and the adoption of fighting in line may also have made for larger crews. In 1666 Albermarle and Prince Rupert demanded increased complements in order to man ketches and tenders out of the big ships, and 'that we may be able to fight on both sides to destroy our enemies, and not to carry out ships for a show which will not be able to fight'.[56] Though attempts to take a census of seamen in the Elizabethan fashion failed, it seems that in wartime the Navy needed between a third and a half of the seafaring population over the summer. Its recruiting was concentrated in the Thames and East Anglia, but men were drawn in from all over the country.[57] In the *Bristol* on 1 March 1679 the chaplain noted, 'St Taffy's Day, and many in our ship do wear leeks.'[58]

From all parts of the country, popular captains drew men to follow them – often from their home ports, in the case of tarpaulin officers. At Chatham in 1672, Narbrough noted the volunteers appearing, 'some having respect for one commander, some for another and some for preferment &c.' He himself brought eight men with him, and when he turned over to another ship next year, 176 men and boys chose to follow him.[59] In the same way Kempthorne and other West-Countrymen recruited in Devon and Cornwall. Not all 'tarpaulins' were beloved, however – Allin, for one, was widely disliked – and many gentleman officers were popular and built up large followings. For all captains a good reputation on the lower deck was a valuable professional advantage. In 1669 Captain John Hayward of the *Foresight*, fitting out for the Mediterranean, was turning volunteers away at the same time as Captain Beach of the *Jersey* lying near by had sentries posted with drawn cutlasses to stop those few men he had found from running away.[60] Sir Edward Spragge caused some scandal by manning out of the London brothels with the help of a leading madam: 'as long as Damaris Page lived he was sure he should not lack men'.[61]

1a. Domestic life at sea: a sketch by Gabriel Bray of the sailmaker of the frigate *Pallas* with his mate in November 1774, sewing numbers on hammocks.

1c. A marine and a sailor of the *Pallas*, sketched by Bray, fishing off the anchor in Senegal Road, January 1775.

1b. Another of Bray's sketches, of a seaman of the *Pallas* leaning on a bowchaser. This gives a good idea of the sailor's characteristic working clothes: trousers, round jacket and round hat.

2a. John Crawford from Sunderland, nailing Admiral Duncan's flag (using a marlinspike as a hammer) to the maintopgallant masthead of the *Venerable*, after it was shot away during the battle of Camperdown. Daniel Orme met Crawford after the battle and drew him from life, but he evidently did not realize that the seaman had put on his best shore-going rig for the occasion; he is not likely to have been dressed like this in action.

2b. The wardroom officers of the *Gloucester* at dinner in 1812, painted by the chaplain Edward Mangin. The figures should be at least twice the size to fit the space.

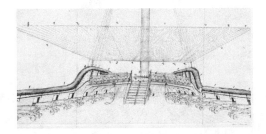

2c. The quarterdeck and poop of the *Venerable*, cleared for action, drawn by Benjamin Turner in 1799. With furniture and bulkheads removed, the captain's cabin is completely open. The netting overhead protects those on the quarterdeck from falling debris.

3a. Young Master William Blockhead on his first day afloat, 'Finding things not exactly what he expected ...' in the midshipmen's berth. One of a series of satirical prints by George Cruikshank after sketches by Captain Frederick Marryat.

3b. Another of the Cruikshank/Marryat series, showing Mr Midshipman Blockhead experiencing the delights of the middle watch in hard weather, without a greatcoat. Note the carronades on their pivoting slides, stowed against the bulwarks to make space. The officer of the watch (with speaking-trumpet) is sitting on a carronade slide while the black servant brings him something to keep out the cold.

3c. A barge and crew, drawn by Nicholas Pocock. As the officer passengers and the fancy paintwork suggest, these boats were for captains' personal use.

4a. A grisaille of the battle of the Gabbard, 2 June 1653, by Heerman Witmont. In the foreground, with the English Republic's 'Cross and Harp' colours at the main, is the *Resolution*, flagship of Deane and Monck, engaging Tromp's flagship the *Brederode*.

4b. The battle of Scheveningen, 31 July 1653, by Willem van de Velde the elder, the first official naval war artist in history. He can just be seen (lower left) seated amidships in the galliot provided for him by the Admiralty of Amsterdam.

5a. The surrender of the *Royal Prince*, aground on the Galloper, 3 June 1666, during the Four Days Battle, by Willem van de Velde the younger. Ayscue's white flag at the main is being struck; under the *Prince*'s stern is van de Velde's galliot, and off her port bow is Cornelis Tromp's temporary flagship the *Gouda*.

5b. The Medway Raid, June 1667, by Willem Schellinks, telescoping the events of several days. The view is from the Nore looking up the Medway, with Sheerness Fort burning in the lower left and Dutch boats' crews towing away the *Royal Charles* in the right centre, almost in line with Rochester Cathedral and Castle in the distance.

6a. The battle of Solebay, 28 May 1672, by Willem van de Velde the younger. This gives a realistic idea of the line of battle after some hours of fighting. In the foreground with the Royal Standard at the main is the Duke of York's second flagship the *St Michael*, and beyond her the burning remains of the *Royal James*.

6b. The battle of Quiberon Bay, 20 November 1759, by Dominic Serres the elder. The leading British ships, with Hawke's flagship the *Royal George* in the centre, are engaging the rear of the French line.

7a. An amphibious operation, the capture of Newport, Rhode Island, in December 1776, by Robert Cleveley, captain's clerk of the *Asia*, who was present. The ships are laying down a covering bombardment while the troops pull for the beach. In the right foreground is a flatboat carrying artillery.

7b. Barrington's defence of the Grand Cul de Sac, St Lucia, 15 December 1778, by the elder Serres. The British ships are anchored in a close line across the mouth of the bay, while d'Estaing's squadron attacks from the seaward. In reality Barrington had placed his squadron so skilfully, in relation to the wind and the coastline, that the French were not able to get as close as this.

8a. The line of battle as imagined by theorists: the battle of the Dogger Bank, 5 August 1781, engraved after Engel Hoogerheyden.

8b. A more realistic view of the same action by Thomas Luny.

In the Third Dutch War the Admiralty sought to encourage volunteers by guaranteeing that they should serve with the captains of their choice and not be turned over to other ships without their consent.[62]

The most famous example of an officer's following ('this extraordinary case – one of the most romantic that ever I heard of in my life, and could not have believed but that I did see it') comes from Pepys's diary. On 13 June 1665 he and Coventry went to the funeral of Sir Christopher Myngs, slain in the Four Days' Battle. As they got into their coach to leave,

> About a dozen able, lusty, proper men came to the coach-side with tears in their eyes, and one of them, that spoke for the rest, begun and says to Sir W. Coventry – 'We are here a dozen of us that have long known and loved and served our dead commander, Sir Christopher Myngs, and have now done the last office of laying him in the ground. We would be glad we had any other to offer after him, and in revenge of him – all we have is our lives. If you will please to get his Royal Highness to give us a fireship among us all, here is a dozen of us, out of all which choose you one to be commander, and the rest of us, whoever he is, will serve him, and, if possible, do that that shall show our memory of our dead commander and our revenge.' Sir W. Coventry was herewith much moved (as well as I, who could hardly abstain from weeping) and took their names; and so parted, telling me that he would move his Royal Highness as in a thing very extraordinary.[63]

Fireship service was exceptionally dangerous. Unfortunately it is not known what became of them.

In wartime volunteers never sufficed, and the Navy resorted to embargo and impressment. Embargoes, forbidding some or all merchant shipping to sail, were imposed in October 1664, December 1665, November 1666, March 1672 and December 1672. At the same time Lords Lieutenant of inland counties, and Vice-Admirals of maritime counties, were ordered to raise fixed numbers of men each. Many of the men they sent knew nothing of the sea, and there were numerous complaints of their ill-health and unsuitability. Commissioner Middleton at Portsmouth received

> men utterly unfit for service, some 50, 60, and even 70 years of age. No man will admit them into his ship; they cannot return without pay, and no one has power to send them home again, so they wander up and down the streets, starving and spreading infection in the town.[64]

Other press-warrants were issued to the mayors of seaports, and increasingly to the captains of ships. In the Thames Estuary, recorded Lieutenant Thomas Browne of the *Mary Rose* in 1666, many of the people on both shores are run up into the country as fearing the press, and some of our seamen have been so rude as to bring away not only common labourers, but farmers and constables, not sparing a Justice of the Peace from the Essex side.[65]

Much pressing was done at sea, out of coasters and homeward- (but not outward-) bound deep-sea ships, where seamen could always be found, at least by those who knew where they might be hidden. Shipwrights and caulkers were also pressed for the dockyards. The London Watermen's Company was supposed to supply a fixed quota of men, but the quality was so bad that in May 1666 their exemption from impressment was removed. 'The Masters of Waterman's Hall are good Christians, but very knaves;' wrote Commissioner Middleton, 'they should be ordered to send down ten or twelve old women to be nurses to the children they send for the king to breed'.[66] After repeated desertions, it was ordered in 1665 that pressed men be accompanied to the naval ports. The Deputy Lieutenants of Kent were instructed in 1666 'to leave a shilling at the house of each seaman, who shall be absent, with assurances, that if they appear not to serve his Majesty the next time they come to their houses, they shall be impressed',[67] but the financial crisis of that year led to the widespread abandonment of the shilling 'imprest money' which was held to make pressing legal, to the considerable alarm of Pepys.[68]

Neither he nor anyone else involved liked impressment:

But Lord, how some poor women did cry, and in my life I never did see such natural expressions of passion as I did here – in some women's bewailing themselves, and running to every parcel of men that were brought, one after another, to look for their husbands, and wept over every vessel that went off, thinking they might be there, and looking after the ship as far as ever they could by moonlight – that it grieved my heart to hear them. Besides, to see poor patient labouring men and housekeepers, leaving poor wives and families, taken up on a sudden by strangers, was very hard; and that without press-money, but forced against all law to be gone. It is a great tyranny.[69]

The same thing was repeated in the Third Dutch War, but this time the crisis was briefer, and there seems to have been a greater effort to regulate the process and respect legal forms, if only for fear of the growing power of Parliament. Extensive exemptions were issued; to colliers, fishermen, victuallers and transports, alum farmers, the Isle of Wight packets, vessels bringing stone to rebuild St Paul's Cathedral, the Archbishop of Canterbury's barge crew, and a man employed 'for picking of oysters for his Majesty's particular use'.[70] In June 1673 it was ordered that the masters of coasters might be taken, 'owing to the great want of midshipmen and such as understood the service'.[71] As before the Watermen's Company was a serious disappointment. Scottish seamen were exempt from impressment into the English Navy, but the authorities of the Royal Burghs were ordered to levy men, paying a bounty of 40s sterling.[72] Considerable numbers of landsmen were still coming aboard ships from one source or another. In July 1673 Narbrough mustered 701 men and boys in his ship, including 134 soldiers and 120 'trouncers and tradesmen which never were at sea and [are] unfit for sea service'.[73] The soldiers, both of the Marine regiment and others, were one of the more successful expedients. No longer the hated symbols of oppression they had been in the 1650s, the 'lobsters, viz. "red-coats"' seem to have been accepted afloat, and ships needed a lot of unskilled labour, as well as musketeers in action.[74]

The manning problem arose partly because the Navy was trying to obtain a large proportion of all the seamen in the country, at short notice and mainly from a limited area. It was made much worse by the Navy's well-earned reputation for paying late or never. The 1653 wage-scale remained adequate in peacetime, but it never kept pace with wartime inflation. In 1665 it was said that

> sickness and the colliers' great wages have taken many from us since we came in. The colliers give £8 and £9 per voyage, which is as much as 7 months' pay in the King's ships and may be performed in a month and no limbs hazarded: the security against being pressed being added, what hopes is there our men should stay with us or that others should come to us?[75]

Wages remained high throughout the 1670s, forcing the Navy to press even in peacetime. The king's service had certain advantages over merchantmen, including better victuals, medical treatment, and the possibility of prize-money and compensation for wounds. Merchant seamen's wages also suffered from fraud and arbitrary deductions, but for that the Admiralty courts provided an effective remedy. Numerous suits for the recovery of wages were brought there by common seamen, almost all either successful or settled out of court on the plaintiffs' terms.[76]

The crown, however, could not be sued, and no advantages of the Navy made up for the notorious fact that naval wages in wartime were usually far in arrears. In May 1667 the men of the *Pearl* and *Little Victory* refused to weigh anchor because they were between twenty-six and thirty-four months unpaid. In the same year the companies of two other ships petitioned 'that their families may not be starved in the streets, and themselves go like heathen, having nothing to cover their nakedness. Have fifty-two months' pay due, and neither money nor credit.'[77] Ships were kept needlessly in pay for months because there was no money to pay them off, just as they had been by the Commonwealth and Protectorate. When ships were paid it was often in tickets, exchangeable for cash at some remote and unspecified date, which seamen were obliged to sell or pawn at a heavy discount.[78] 'We do plainly see,' wrote Pepys in August 1667,

> that the desperate condition that we put men into for want of their pay makes them mad, they being as good men as ever were in the world, and would as readily serve the king again, were they but paid. Two men leaped overboard, among others, into the Thames out of the vessel into which they were pressed, and were shot by the soldiers placed there to keep them, two days since; so much do people avoid the King's service.[79]

This was the worst crisis of the era, however, and not a typical instance of naval life over a period of twenty-eight years (1660 to 1688), during most of which the Navy was at peace with major powers and ships were manned largely or entirely with volunteers. We are fortunate to have vivid glimpses of shipboard life, not only from the point of view of Pepysian bureaucracy, but from the journals of those who were there: the resourceful chaplain Edward Teonge, always ready to make the best of his new life (it was typical of him to preach one of his first sermons on Romans 8:28);[80] the eternal grumbler Edward Barlow rehearsing the sufferings of the sailor's 'hard and miserable calling'[81] with lugubrious relish; the supreme professional John Narbrough with his plain, lucid observation (penguins 'are short-legged like a goose, and stand upright like little children in white aprons, in companies together . . .');[82] the curious passenger John Covel delighting in the sailors' oddities; the cheerful doggerel of the working petty officer John Baltharpe with his lively descriptions of their daily life. Different writers give us different aspects of work aloft. Barlow naturally recalls shifting sails in a thunderstorm by night: 'and then we were to hang by our eyelids up in the air, when the ship rolled and tumbled so that we had much ado to hold ourselves fast from falling overboard, above us seeing nothing, and underneath us the raging of the sea.'[83] Narbrough's journal records working routine: 'This day the young men scraped the masts and blacked the mastheads and the yards.'[84] Baltharpe reproduces their repartee as they worked:

> Each Commendations of the other,
> Aloft they gave, some this, some t'other,
> Pastimes with Girles, they then discover.

The Purser they cry up a high,
For honest Man, but answer Lie;
Of Stewards honesty, and his Mate,
They loudly on the Yards do Prate . . .[85]

We hear of the pastimes and recreations of the sea. Off watch the seamen danced to harp or fiddle, and sometimes the officers too.[86]

If the weather be fair and will permit it, we seldom fail of some merry fellows in every ship's crew, who will entertain us with several diversions, as divers sorts of odd sports and gambols; sometimes with their homely drolls and farces, which in their corrupt language they nickname 'interlutes'; sometimes they dance about the mainmast instead of a maypole, and they have a variety of forecastle songs, ridiculous enough.[87]

Crossing the Equator, or entering the Mediterranean, the sailors demanded 'passage-money' from first-timers, on pain of being ducked from the yardarm.[88]

Regular gunnery practice was enjoined by the Duke of York's orders.[89] The extravagant salutes of the previous century were less fashionable, and only occasionally fired with shot 'as a token of more respect',[90] but they could still burn a lot of powder. On Oak-Apple Day, 'our ships, remembering the festival day, fired so many guns that they were buried in their own smoke'.[91] In February 1669 Allin in the Mediterranean met Rear-Admiral Willem van der Zaen of the Amsterdam Admiralty (killed in action with the Algerines less than a fortnight later),

who saluted after his old fashion 15. I answered 13; he again 9, we 7, he 7, we 5; he 5, we 3; he 3, we one; then he sent his lieutenant aboard with a present in a basket, which was 12 China oranges and 6 sweet lemons. I gave him 5 guns going off, which Van der Zaen answered 5 again and came aboard himself and caused us to fire in all about 100 guns.[92]

Charles II encouraged cheering ship as a less expensive alternative, and he and his brother were often greeted aboard their fleet by the men 'shouting and throwing away their caps', the officers manning the side and the ships dressed with flags. Narbrough was cheered away from his ship the *Prince* in 1672, though not all senior officers were so popular.[93] At Lisbon in 1662 Sandwich's squadron was illuminated in honour of Queen Catherine of Braganza:

Every ship had men sat upon the yards, a little distance, each man a large candle in paper lanterns in each hand. Upon every port sat a man, and all along the side that was next to the city; they stood so, till the candles were burned out, which made a glorious show.[94]

For the seaman, whose work was so peculiarly exposed to the weather, good, stout clothes were the tools of his trade. A professional seaman usually had a substantial collection to provide for different climates, and a sea-chest to keep it, with enough changes to shift into dry clothes when coming off watch. (Removing the chests into the hold or an accompanying tender was a major part of clearing ship for action.)[95] His clothes were not only important for health and comfort, but provided his bank, since they could easily be sold or pawned. Pursers had to keep a stock of 'slops' (official-pattern clothes) for sale to the men, who could charge them against their wages.[96] But not every seafarer was well equipped. Edward Teonge, the impoverished Warwickshire parson who went to sea to escape his creditors, pawned his only cloak to buy a hammock and arrived aboard his first ship with his few possessions on his back. 'Early in the morning I met with a ragged towel on the quarter-deck, which I soon secured. And, soon after, Providence brought me a piece of an old sail and an earthen chamber-pot: all very helpful to him that had nothing.'[97]

Teonge describes occasional invitations to dine at the captain's table with the relish of one who seldom ate well at home:

> This day our noble captain feasted the officers of his small squadron with four dishes of meat, viz. four excellent hens and a piece of pork boiled in a dish; a gigot of excellent mutton and turnips; a piece of beef of eight ribs, well seasoned and roasted; and a couple of very fat green geese; last of all, a great Cheshire cheese: a rare feast at shore. His liquors were answerable, viz. Canary, sherry, Rhenish, claret, white wine, cider, ale, beer, all of the best sort; and punch like ditchwater; with which we conclude the day and week in drinking to the king and all that we love; while the wind blows fair.[98]

Barlow, equally in character, fills pages with denouncing bad food in the king's ships and worse in merchantmen, but even he admits that the naval 'pinch-gut' or short-allowance money permitted men to buy fresh provisions for themselves.[99] Every seaman's memoir dwells lovingly on the delights of Mediterranean ports. At Messina, according to John Baltharpe,

> No soul alive did ever see,
> Such Traffique as on board had we,
> All sorts of things they put to Sale,
> Except it were strong Beer and Ale:
> Silk-stockings, Carpets, Brande-wine,

Silk Neckcloaths, also very fine:
Cabidges, Carrets, Turnips, Nuts,
The last a man may eat from Sluts:
Lemmons, Orenges, and good Figs,
Seracusa Wine also, and Eggs.
If you no Money had then they'd Truckar,
For Brande-wine out of their jar:
For Coats that's torn, and very old,
They Wine or Brande, then give would.
Strange 'twas to see such filthy Raggs,
As they would put into their Baggs:
With Brande, Brande, Brande Wino,
About they march most brave and Fino . . .[100]

After the reform of pursery we begin to hear of fresh food issued officially. Lying at the Nore in 1672, Narbrough noted with his customary precision,

> This day fresh meat came down for the whole fleet and a vessel laden with 3950 cabbages and 21½ bushels of carrots and 15 dozen and 9 bunches of turnips, for to be disposed of for the use of the fleet in the several ships for refreshing of the men . . . I made a dividend of my carrots and cabbages and turnips to the whole fleet, a cabbage for four men and a bushel of carrots for ten men.[101]

Narbrough was notably scrupulous in his handling of victualling. On an earlier voyage he records,

> Today the cooper found two butts of beer had leaked out: this day all of us drank water only, for it was ever my order that the meanest boy in the ship should have the same allowance with my self, so that in general we all drank of the same cask, and ate one sort of provision, as long as they lasted: I never permitted any officer to have a better piece of meat than what fell to his lot; but one blinded with a cloth served every man as they were called to touch and take, by which means we never had any difference upon that score.[102]

Characteristically, Narbrough also records in precise detail how the men fished, and what they caught.[103] He made his men wash daily and keep free from lice; not a negligible precaution, for Teonge buried a man 'as 'tis said eaten to death with lice'.[104] On a voyage of exploration, he cured men of scurvy with herbs and fresh meat.[105]

Discipline in the king's ships was more formal and becoming more severe than in merchantmen, which sometimes handed over troublemakers to the men-of-war, but the difference was not yet very great; flogging for desertion was regarded as an extreme brutality, and it was still possible to find a captain consulting with his warrant and petty officers on what to do in a crisis. It was not easy for seamen to complain against their own officers, but good captains frequently backed their men's grievances against the Navy, especially over their pay.[106] Whipping seems to have been most commonly resorted to for theft. A bad case in Allin's ship the *Foresight* in 1661 'had twenty lashes, but never shed a tear, a graceless rogue and an old thief'. At Spithead in 1678 a seaman of Henry Teonge's ship the *Bristol* 'had twenty-nine lashes with a cat-o'-nine tails, and was then washed with salt water, for stealing our carpenter's mate's wife's ring'. A man who struck a lieutenant was put in irons for two hours.[107] For letting a gun off by accident which killed the wife of a master the punishment was 'to be whipped and discharged the fleet'.[108] In Teonge's ships ducking seems to have been the usual penalty for overstaying leave, though one offender was pardoned at the pleas of officers, 'who alleged that he had injuries enough already, as having a wife a whore and a scold to injure him at home'.[109]

Not everyone left their wives at home, though it is difficult to estimate how many women were aboard when their presence was entirely unofficial. Sir John Mennes can hardly have been literally correct to complain in 1666 that the ships were 'pestered with women . . . as many petticoats as breeches',[110] but there are numerous orders to send the women ashore which suggest that they often accompanied their menfolk some way to sea.[111] Teonge records with a wry and uncensorious eye the scenes below decks the night before the sweethearts and wives were sent ashore.

> Hither many of our seamen's wives follow their husbands, and several other young women accompany their sweethearts, and sing 'Loath to depart' in punch and brandy, so that our ship was that night well furnished, but ill manned, few of them being well able to keep watch had there been occasion. You would have wondered to see here a man and a woman creep into a hammock, the woman's legs to the hams hanging over the sides or out at the end of it. Another couple sleeping on a chest, others kissing and clipping, half drunk, half sober or rather half asleep, choosing rather (might they have been suffered) to go and die with them than stay and live without them.[112]

What proportion of men were married is difficult to say, though the explosion of the *London* in 1665 killed about 300 men and left fifty widows.[113] Pepys collected stories, some of them no doubt true, of gentleman officers taking their mistresses to sea,[114] while 'his Royal Highness having forbidden Sir William Jennings to carry his wife in his frigate, she took her passage upon a merchantman in the fleet, which proved no small loss of time by reason the knight took all the opportunities of making visits'.[115]

Pepys attached importance to appointing good chaplains and maintaining a high moral tone in the fleet, but it is not quite clear how they were meant to achieve it. The chaplain's functions seem to have been essentially to say prayers once or twice a day, and preach occasionally; usually in port, though Teonge preached at sea. He once had a sermon interrupted by 'a very great school of porpoises on both sides of our ship, many of them jumping their whole length out of the water, causing much laughter'.[116] Communion services were virtually unknown: an inquiry in 1678 revealed that only one chaplain in the Navy had received Communion within the past twelve months.[117] The Navy does not seem to have been notably devout, but it was certainly patriotic enough to react with the usual English paranoia to the presence of a handful of Catholic officers in James II's Navy, most notably the convert Rear-Admiral Sir Roger Strickland, who was even alleged to have had Mass said aboard his flagship.[118] The traditional prejudice went with the seamen's traditional superstitions, as for example about the phosphorescence called 'corposanto' or St Elmo's fire: 'our men would hardly be persuaded but that they were not some *Hongoblins* or *Fairies*, or the enchanted bodies of witches, and we had many a fine story told to that purpose'.[119]

Charles II and James II ruled together for twenty-eight years, the space of a single generation, but together they achieved a remarkable transformation in their Navy, creating a loyal, coherent and reasonably united body of officers and men, with an established career structure for the officers. Professional ability replaced political correctness as the criterion for advancement. All this, however, was made possible by the two kings' keen personal interest in their Navy. It was still an open question whether its institutional structure was robust enough to survive them.

NINE

Mad Proceedings

Operations 1688–1692

Virtually all contemporaries regarded James II's position in the spring of 1688 as very strong. His policy of religious toleration had certainly aroused furious protest, but the English governing classes had been badly burned by the experience of civil war and military dictatorship, and were not prepared to start another great rebellion. However strongly people opposed the king's policies, not many disputed his right to rule. Amongst the minority who might have contemplated armed resistance, common prudence called to mind the fate of Monmouth's and Argyll's rebellions, and the presence of the king's large new army. The birth of a baby prince on 10 June promised to secure the future of the royal house.[1]

Across the Channel, however, the queen's pregnancy had already persuaded William III that he would have to act to safeguard his wife's inheritance, whatever the risk. Either James II would succeed, and hand on to his heir a powerful, possibly even a Catholic kingdom with an anti-Dutch foreign policy – or his Whig opponents would overthrow the monarchy and restore the English Republic. Either possibility would be a disaster for William himself, his wife and his country. The relentless advance of French power threatened a present return of the crisis of 1672 which the Republic had so narrowly survived. Without the active support of England it would take almost a miracle to preserve Dutch independence. William was convinced that desperate measures were called for, but his Republican adversaries, still deeply entrenched in the government of Holland, had no idea of gratifying the House of Orange with a reckless military adventure. Not for the first or last time, Louis XIV's blundering arrogance came to William's aid. In 1687 France abruptly cancelled the tariff concessions granted to the Netherlands by treaty, damaging and enraging the Amsterdam merchants who had hitherto been France's allies against the Orangists. Then in 1688 Louis sent his ambassador to the States-General to deliver a blunt warning not to dare to oppose his policies. Even the most pacifist members were outraged by these crude threats. Louis did not conceal his contempt for the 'cheesemongers', and had no idea that it mattered what his betrayed allies felt. His thoughts and plans were far away. His close ally the Ottoman Sultan Suleiman II had been forced to make peace with Austria. Before Austria could gather its strength against him, Louis planned a pre-emptive invasion of the Rhineland to punish the League of Augsburg for daring to ally against him. The only operational part of his fleet was in the Mediterranean ready to act against Pope Innocent XI, who had ventured to criticize his pro-Turkish and anti-Christian foreign policy. In September the French army invaded the Palatinate with a calculated display of brutality and destruction which alienated France's few remaining friends. At the same time all Dutch merchant ships in French ports were arrested. By these means Louis XIV achieved the apparently impossible; he rallied the Republicans of the States of Holland behind William III. Their final consent, however, came only in September, when the French army was irrevocably committed in the Rhineland; far too late in the season to mount a major seaborne operation with any regard for prudence.[2]

William had been actively preparing to intervene in England since early in the year, skilfully fomenting opposition to James II in England, and making all the military preparations he could in secret. In June he engineered an 'invitation' signed by seven Englishmen of some public standing. One of them was Admiral Arthur Herbert, who had publicly opposed James II's policy of religious toleration, on grounds of conscience. This caused some astonishment, Herbert's warmest admirers not having hitherto realized that he had one, and behind his declaration was perhaps jealousy at the rise of his rival Lord Dartmouth, who succeeded Strickland as commander-in-chief of the main fleet in September. By this time Herbert himself was in Holland, but his followers included a number of Dartmouth's leading captains.[3]

The Dutch forces assembled between June and October: a total of 463 ships, mostly small troop-transports but including forty-nine warships, carrying a total of 40,000 men, of whom over half were troops. Besides William's own Blue Guards, there were the Scots and English regiments of the Dutch army, plus Dutch, Huguenot, German, Swiss and Swedish regiments; there was even a unit of Laplanders. To make this possible the size of the Dutch army was multiplied four-fold. The whole force was at least double the size of the Spanish Armada of a century before, assembled in little more than a tenth of the time. William III was well aware that it was extremely dangerous to mount any naval operation, let alone a landing, in the season of the equinoctial gales, but there was no time to wait until the spring, by which time the French army might be on the Republic's inland frontier. Nor was there time to send the fleet to sea to win a victory and clear the way for the invasion convoy, and in any case it was essential to avoid starting a fourth Dutch War if William was to arrive in England in the guise of a religious saviour rather than a foreign conqueror. Arthur Herbert was appointed commander-in-chief of the Dutch fleet with instructions at all costs to avoid battle – but the odds against being able to evade a watchful English fleet less than a hundred miles away seemed almost insuperable, and Herbert was certainly prepared to fight.[4]

Both James II and Louis XIV had their attention elsewhere and were badly served with intelligence on Dutch preparations. It was not until late August that James II began to take the possibility of Dutch intervention seriously and ordered the main fleet to mobilize. Even then he initially thought France was a more likely Dutch target than England. It was hard for so experienced a seaman to take seriously the idea that professional naval men would risk a fleet, let alone an army, to the autumn gales, and he took it for granted that no troops would sail until the fleet had cleared the way by a decisive victory. It was therefore best for the English fleet to avoid battle with an enemy believed to be much superior, until the moment was right, but there was a risk of being caught by the sort of opening attack the Dutch had so often mounted in the past. The Downs, otherwise so well situated, were therefore out of the question. Learning that Dartmouth proposed to assemble the fleet at the Gunfleet, within fairly easy reach of the Thames and Medway yards, he recommended him to move further out, 'for fear he should be surprised while there by the sudden coming of the Dutch fleet, as being a place he cannot well get out to sea from, while the wind remains easterly'.[5] It would have been well for Dartmouth had he listened to a king who knew those waters much better than he did, but he preferred the convenience of the Gunfleet, and James was scrupulous in not overriding his admiral's judgement.[6]

The Dutch fleet sailed on 19 October and was almost immediately driven back into port by a gale. On 1 November it sailed again. The wind was hard easterly, and the initial course was to the north. William's intentions were, as usual with him, a close secret, and he may have had thoughts of landing on the Yorkshire coast (as James certainly anticipated), but an easterly wind made that impossible. Sometime about dusk on 2 November, with all the ships clear of the Flanders Banks but before the head of the fleet neared the dangerous shoals off the Norfolk coast, the decision was taken to reverse course and steer down-Channel. Dartmouth had sailed at almost the same moment as the Dutch, but the easterly gale prevented him from getting clear of the sands. At dawn on the 3rd the outliers of the Dutch fleet were actually in sight from his flagship, sailing south, but they were dead to windward and 'the ebb being almost spent, we could not weather the Long Sand Head and the Kentish Knock'.[7] By the time Dartmouth got to sea on the 4th, the Dutch were well down-Channel. On the 5th the wind veered south-westerly, blocking his further progress, and blowing the Dutch fleet neatly into Torbay. There William and his troops landed over two days of unseasonable calm.[8]

After the event, when there was so much to be gained by it, various English captains, all followers of Herbert and therefore not natural friends of Dartmouth, claimed to have formed a successful conspiracy to paralyse the English fleet. There is hardly any impartial evidence that this 'Tangerine conspiracy' existed. Dartmouth's councils of war were virtually unanimous, experienced officers like Strickland, who could not possibly have been secret friends of William III, concurring with more junior figures like Matthew Aylmer who subsequently claimed to have been conspirators. Given the false intelligence that the Dutch fleet was much the stronger, and the reasonable though false assumption that it would never risk the army at sea until it had won a victory, there was everything to be said for caution – and Dartmouth was naturally of a cautious, not to say hesitant, disposition. On 16 November, with better intelligence, his fleet sailed from the Downs to fight the Dutch, only to be prevented once more by bad weather. Even then the alleged conspirators did nothing more risky than secretly to send a junior officer (Lieutenant George Byng) with a verbal message to William III. William may well have hoped or even expected that the English fleet would be disabled by disaffection, but it is not at all clear that it really was. All the evidence is that his extraordinary triumph in the face of grave risks was indeed a matter of wind and tide. As a good Calvinist, he for one had no doubt that he had been predestined to succeed, and as a master of public relations he took care to spread the image of the Protestant saviour favoured by the Protestant wind, but the English seamen found it harder to identify the hand of God. ' 'Tis strange that such mad proceedings should have such success at this time a year,' Dartmouth wrote despondently to James II.[9]

William III was now ashore with his army, but his intentions were and still are obscure, though he had brought ammunition and supplies for a prolonged campaign. However many political leaders James II had alienated, very few joined William. The royal army lost a few senior officers but remained overwhelmingly loyal and substantially larger than the Dutch. Even among the minority who welcomed William, it is uncertain how many either desired or expected that he would seize the throne. The political crisis was resolved by a completely unexpected event. James II, whose bravery had been proved in a score of battles by sea and land, lost his nerve and ran away. Undoubtedly he meant to return, but it was the last and worst of his political misjudgements. His supporters' morale was broken by his desertion, while his enemies seized the chance to declare that he had abdicated the throne, and that his infant son was spurious. Both claims were manifestly false, but they gave William III his opening. An illegal 'Parliament' was summoned to do his bidding. Surrounded by Dutch troops, it obediently voted that Princess Mary had succeeded her father, and Prince William was joint sovereign.[10]

By April 1689, when they were crowned, the 'Glorious Revolution' had already fallen apart. The English, obsessed by fear of Catholicism, had imagined that nothing but love of the Church of England could have persuaded William III to risk his life and the Dutch Republic to spend over seven million guilders. Now they began to realize that their new king, though a Calvinist rather than a Catholic, was an ally of Catholic princes with reasons of state to be as tolerant in matters of religion as James II had been. It also began to dawn on them that he meant to involve them in an overseas war of ruinous expense. The first expense was a bill presented by the States-General for the whole cost of the invasion, computed as £663,752 (of which £600,000 was eventually paid). The bulk of the Anglican, loyalist political establishment had a very bad conscience about abandoning James II, and offered William at best a grudging tolerance. Many of the most eminent Anglican clergy refused to break their oaths of loyalty by swearing allegiance to the new king and queen. The true Whigs, on the other hand, had hoped for a restored Republic, while the Dissenters complained that William was able to extract from Parliament only limited toleration for them. Everyone charged him, very justly, with failing to persecute the Catholics.[11] In Scotland the Revolution was taken over by extremists completely out of William's control. Discarding constitutional figleaves, they openly declared James VII deposed for tyranny (thus making Scotland an elective monarchy), and demonstrated their superior purity and godliness by violent intolerance, including the execution of witches, Episcopalians and Englishmen.[12] The Anglican church, forced to concede toleration to Presbyterians in England, found their Scots co-religionaries were ruthlessly persecuted in return. In both kingdoms the active supporters of William III were a minority, and the political world was divided into numerous hostile groups, each with plausible reasons to suspect the loyalty of the others. From prudence or conviction many leading politicians, William III's supporters included, kept in contact with James II.[13]

Although he was in all but name a conquering sovereign whose troops occupied London, William III did not have the time or opportunity to impose his will completely. He had to get himself and the Dutch army home quickly, before the French took advantage of their absence, and he was obliged to compromise with English politicians. All his experience of the Dutch constitution, moreover, had taught him that government was an impenetrable labyrinth largely inhabited by enemies. His business was to avoid government and control power by acting in secret through a handful of trusted men in key positions. Though he was the son and husband of English princesses and knew English well, he insisted on corresponding exclusively in French or Dutch (both of which he wrote surprisingly badly), and only a few Englishmen joined his close advisers. For him it was normal that formal responsibility should be dispersed among many overlapping jurisdictions, while the jealousy and suspicion which marked the English political situation was much what he was used to at home. Though the letter of the English constitution was not radically changed in 1689, the manner in which it operated was. Naval administration was particularly affected by the removal of a king who knew a great deal about his Navy, and his replacement by one who took no interest in it at all.[14]

In foreign policy the situation in the spring of 1689 was confused. Louis XIV was at war with the League of Augsburg,[15] including the Dutch Republic, and with William III in person as Prince of Orange, but not officially with England or Scotland. King William III of England and Scotland had as yet no formal alliance with Prince William III, Captain-General and Admiral-General of the Dutch Republic. James II's followers controlled almost all Ireland, while in the Highlands of Scotland a Royalist army under the Viscount Dundee was in arms against the Edinburgh government. James II, whose strategic sense was so much better than his political judgement, meant to join his Irish and Scottish forces as the first stage of his campaign to regain his thrones. On 12 March 1689 French warships landed him in Ireland with some troops and money. Louis XIV, however, was busy elsewhere, he had not anticipated a naval war, and his Brest fleet was not ready for serious operations. William III cared equally little for Ireland, but had a better sense of the strategic value of sea power, and pushed the Anglo-Dutch negotiations which led to the convention of 19 April 1689, closely modelled on the abortive treaty of 1678, to create a joint Anglo-Dutch fleet. The ships were to be provided in the ratio five-eighths English to three-eighths Dutch, and the commanders-in-chief were always to be English. Naturally this was unpopular among the Dutch admirals, who on average were older and more experienced than their English contemporaries, but William was quite ruthless in putting the wider interests of alliance strategy first.[16]

At this point, on the threshold of a naval war which was to continue over much of the following twenty-five years, it is worth pausing for a moment to survey the three navies principally involved. The most superficially impressive in many ways was the great fleet which Colbert, Louis XIV's naval minister, built up almost from nothing in less than twenty years, and whose administration was codified in the nicest detail in 1689. Between 1672 and 1690, 216 million *livres* (about £16,500,000)[17] were spent on it, creating a fleet of over eighty ships of the line, at least equal in numbers to the English, and on average considerably larger and more heavily armed. Contemporaries were dazzled, as they were meant to be, and some historians still are, but the practical effectiveness of this great fleet was severely compromised. More than twice as much money was spent on shipbuilding as on the naval yards, which were quite inadequate to maintain the ships. Much of what was spent on the yards went on Colbert's new showpiece establishments at Le Havre – which had to be abandoned as an entire failure because of the hostile tidal system of the Seine – and at Rochefort, even worse situated twenty miles up a river too shallow to float large ships of the line. The French navy was almost unprovided with dry docks, so essential for the maintenance of big ships, and suffered badly from all sorts of industrial and technical weaknesses, notably in gun-founding. Its manning system, based on the compulsory registration of the coastal population for service one year in three, was widely admired abroad but never worked as intended, and never provided enough men to mobilize the whole fleet at once. The fleet itself, composed largely of big ships which drew too much water to enter any French Channel or North Sea port, was remarkably ill-adapted for war against the English and the Dutch. Above all, Colbert's navy was an accountant's navy, a bureaucrat's dream whose function was to obey the regulations and balance the books. Hardly anywhere in his voluminous instructions is there any mention of war.[18]

The Dutch fleet was the same redoubtable force which had so often fought the English. It had the same dispersed and ramshackle administrative system as before, and the admiralties still drew on the hypothecated ordinary revenues and the unequalled borrowing capacity which were the envy of every other naval administration. Nevertheless the system was under strain, and began to suffer badly by the early years of the eighteenth century. Financial exhaustion seriously affected even Holland, and effectively extinguished the Admiralty of Friesland. Bureaucratic decay and corruption (notably at Rotterdam) resisted attempts at reform, and the death in 1704 of Job de Wildt, Secretary of the Amsterdam Admiralty, removed the last figure with the influence and force of character to unify the system. The design of Dutch warships, which were notably slower and more leewardly than English, made problems for the allied admirals.[19]

The English Navy had been built up by Charles II and James II as a formidable force to fight the Dutch, as we have seen, but it was not perfectly adapted for the new strategic situation. Its ships of the line were very heavily armed, but lacked the seaworthiness and weatherliness for operations in the Atlantic – not least because they were overloaded with guns. The 'thirty ships' of the 1677 programme had hardly been tried at sea. There were few cruisers and little recent experience of protecting trade outside the Mediterranean; indeed there was a notable lack of senior officers with any recent fighting experience. The Navy's logistical system was largely based in the Thames and Medway, and it had no naval yard west of Portsmouth. The administration, for all Pepys's reforms, had never managed to keep large fleets operational for more than a few months even in the North Sea, close to its bases, and the victualling system was especially fragile. The financial resources of the English state had never matched its naval ambitions.[20]

Unlike their new sovereign, the English Parliamentarians were acutely worried by the situation in Ireland, and anxious that the Navy should frustrate James's campaign there. The Navy, however, was short of money after Dartmouth's midwinter cruising, and Parliament did not vote any until 25 April. Arthur Herbert, newly appointed commander-in-chief of the main fleet, did not get to sea until the beginning of April, leaving behind a number of ships which had mutinied for overdue pay. On 1 May (a week before war was declared) he encountered and fought a French fleet under the marquis de Château-Renault, which was landing troops in Bantry Bay at the south-western corner of Ireland. Herbert probably had nineteen ships of the line, all English, against twenty-four French. Initially the two fleets stretched up the bay in parallel lines, then tacked and sailed back out to sea. The French were to windward throughout and left Herbert's ships too much damaged to renew the action, but did not press their advantage and returned, first to the bay and later to Brest. It was a missed opportunity, followed by a violent quarrel between Château-Renault and his junior flag-officers, Job Forant and Jean Gabaret. For the English the action was equally unsatisfactory. Herbert's warning that 'though the battle is not always to the strong, yet the odds seem to be of that side' had been justified.[21] It took two months to repair his squadron at Portsmouth, during which Irish waters were completely uncovered. William III created Herbert Earl of Torrington, but neither of them was happy with the battle, and it was clearly his work the previous year which had earned him the title.[22]

Parliament and the public were intensely concerned at the Irish situation, and the almost complete lack of protection for trade against French privateers (between May and June there were only two English cruisers at sea in the Channel). James's forces were besieging Londonderry, the capture of which would open communications with Dundee's army in Scotland. Three French frigates under Captain Duquesne-Monnier were assigned to support him, two of them commanded by English officers who had followed James. No English warships opposed them, only two small cruisers, the *Pelican* and the *Janet*, which had been commissioned by the Scottish Parliament. On 10 July they were both taken by the French force in the North Channel. A larger French squadron would probably have won James's campaign, as both he and some French admirals urged, but Louis XIV was not much interested, and the Brest fleet did not sail until 5 August, when it cruised in the Bay of Biscay, well away from the enemy. Duquesne-Monnier was unable to prevent an Anglo-Dutch army under Marshal Schomberg landing near Belfast on 22 August. Torrington got to sea with the main Anglo-Dutch fleet in July and cruised in the Western Approaches, remaining at sea, at William III's insistence, until the end of September, by which time the fleet was extremely sickly, and the admirals thoroughly alarmed. To Edmund Dummer of the Navy Board it seemed 'a mighty boldness to advance with the Grand Fleet further westward of the Isle of Wight than the *[Royal] Sovereign* had been known to have been, since the time of her build',[23] without staying out into the autumn, 'the time of the year being so uncertain', as Admiral Edward Russell complained, 'long nights and a dark moon coming upon us, which are dreadful things at sea at this time of the year'.[24]

William III would never have invaded England if he had listened to admirals who pointed out inconvenient difficulties, and the more Torrington complained, the less the king trusted him. His chosen naval adviser was his Secretary of State the Earl of Nottingham, formerly a member of the 1679 Admiralty Board, a Tory politician of sanguine temperament who prided himself on his knowledge of the Navy. Behind Nottingham stood Russell, another sea officer who had deserted James II, but an old enemy of Torrington. Together they made plans for 1690. Though naval finance and victualling were in a state of collapse, there was no one in Whitehall now who cared much about such things. A substantial part of the fleet was in the Mediterranean under Vice-Admiral Henry Killigrew, and Nottingham assumed it would neutralize the French Toulon squadron. A small force under Rear-Admiral Sir Cloudesley Shovell was sent to the Irish Sea – much too small, as he pointed out, to stop the French controlling the Irish Sea if they chose, and cutting off the English army in Ireland. This was the more critical since William III himself landed in Ireland in June 1690 with fresh troops. None of this disturbed Nottingham and the Privy Council in London, advising Queen Mary in her husband's absence. Meanwhile the French elaborated grand but vague plans for the united Brest and Mediterranean fleets to enter the Channel.[25]

In May the French Toulon squadron succeeded in evading Killigrew off Cadiz, and on 13 June the united French fleet sailed from Brest and entered the Channel. Torrington sailed from the Nore ten days later, already gloomily convinced that the French would be stronger. On the 25th he sighted them off the Isle of Wight, and reckoned them almost eighty ships of the line (the true figure was seventy-five on the day of battle), against his own fifty-six. Torrington had been a lieutenant in the Four Days' Battle as well as the admiral at Bantry Bay; he knew the consequences of fighting against odds and being driven into port. On the other hand he was convinced that he did not have to fight. 'Most men were in fear that the French would invade, but I was always of another opinion, for I always said that whilst we had a fleet in being, they would not make the attempt.'[26] In London Nottingham, discreetly encouraged by Russell, saw no cause for alarm. The French fleet could not possibly be as large as Torrington claimed, and only the admiral's pessimism, defeatism or treachery could account for his reports. The final straw was Torrington's announced intention to retreat to the Gunfleet. No one had forgotten who had last retreated to the Gunfleet to keep his 'fleet in being' in the face of a threatened invasion, and they evidently did not trust God to be on their side a second time. Rather than risk a 'Catholic wind', Torrington was ordered to fight whatever the odds, and Russell was sent down to the fleet with secret orders to supersede him if he refused.[27]

Torrington received his orders on 29 June and called a council of war of his flag-officers, which concluded that they had no option but to obey. Next day the allies formed line of battle, and with the wind behind them, bore down to attack the French. We have no minutes of the council of war, and we do not know how Torrington meant to fight. Nor do we know whether Admiral Cornelis Evertsen[28] commanding the Dutch squadron, which formed the van, correctly understood Torrington's intentions, though he knew some English. It seems likely that Torrington meant to exploit the windward position and avoid disaster by fighting at long range. His squadron in the centre seems to have been to windward of the others, more distant from the enemy; possibly he meant his van and rear to cover the extremities of the longer French line, while he threatened the French centre, but the wind was light and the arrangement may equally have been accidental. At all events the Dutch squadron ran straight down into close action, leaving the leading division of the French fleet unmarked: 'a notable blunder, for professionals, which I saw at once I might exploit,' wrote Château-Renault commanding the French van.[29] The leading French division doubled on the Dutch squadron and inflicted heavy losses on them, including one ship captured, two sunk and many badly damaged. When the tide turned late in the afternoon, by which time there was almost no wind, Torrington ordered the Dutch to anchor and with his own squadron anchored to leeward, covering them from the French, who were slow to react and were carried out of action by the ebb. Over the next few days the defeated allied fleet retreated up the Channel, stopping the tides for want of wind. The French pursued with extreme caution in strict line of battle, but even so it was necessary to burn seven more Dutch and one English ship to avoid capture.[30]

The defeat of Beachy Head caused panic in England, and serious damage to the alliance. In the prevailing atmosphere of paranoia, no one attributed it to mistaken orders or overwhelming odds. Even before the battle, William, Mary and their ministers had been suspicious of Torrington; now they assumed that his deliberate treachery explained everything. 'In plain terms, by all that yet appears,' Nottingham informed William on 3 July, 'my Lord Torrington deserted the Dutch so shamefully that the whole squadron had been lost if some of our ships had not rescued them.'[31] Nottingham of course was anxious to shift the blame, but no one disputed his interpretation. Queen Mary wrote a grovelling apology to the States-General, offering to replace their lost ships, and William III assured them that Torrington would be punished. How to do it was not so obvious. Parliamentary impeachment would be slow and highly inflammatory of the political atmosphere, but the Admiralty Board struggled to avoid the responsibility. It took an Act of Parliament confirming the Board's power to try a peer before Torrington's court martial finally assembled at Chatham in December. To the outraged astonishment of William and his ministers, the court acquitted him. Most of its members were his old followers from the Mediterranean, there was no evidence of treachery, and the senior Dutch witness, Rear-Admiral Gillis Schey, contributed little but incoherent rage. Torrington's acquittal was popular among the English seamen, who regarded him as a political sacrifice to the Dutch (who 'through their own rashness and stupidity . . . were so roughly handled by the French fleet'),[32] and cheered him up the river to London. Next day William dismissed Torrington from the Navy, but he could do no more. Meanwhile the question of replacing him had proved no less difficult. The Admiralty Board wanted Russell, but he preferred influence to responsibility.

The Queen and her Council fell back on the Cromwellian expedient and chose a triumvirate of Killigrew, Sir John Ashby and Sir Richard Haddock.[33]

Meanwhile the much-feared French invasion had not happened, because no invasion had been prepared. The marquis de Seignelay, who had succeeded his father Colbert as naval minister, urgently needed the political credit of a glorious victory, but had thought no further. Four days before the battle, he had written to the commander-in-chief, the comte de Tourville:

> My confidence that you will gain a victory is such that I congratulate you in advance on the glory that you are going to acquire on that occasion; but since we must not stop there, I shall be content if you will let me know as soon as possible after the battle your thoughts on the employment of the fleet for the rest of the campaign.[34]

It was rather late in the year to be raising the question of strategy for the first time, particularly with an admiral whose many good qualities were undermined by a profound reluctance to take risks. Moreover Seignelay, like most people in the new English government, knew little of naval logistics, and was impatient with Tourville's excuses when he returned to port with victuals exhausted and a large proportion of his men sick. The sole profit of a great French victory was glory – and a raid which burned the village of Teignmouth[35] with several fishing boats.[36]

During the Channel campaign, the fate of nations was all to play for in Irish waters. William III defeated James II's army at the battle of the Boyne on the day after Beachy Head, and James subsequently withdrew to France, but William and his army remained in Ireland, dependent on lines of supply which Shovell was too weak to protect against serious attack. A fortnight before Beachy Head, James's Irish minister the Earl of Tyrconnel had assessed the naval situation with gloomy prescience:

> The want of a squadron of French men of war in St George's Channel has been our ruin, for had we had that since the beginning of May, the Prince of Orange had been confounded without striking a stroke, for he could have sent hither neither forces nor provisions, and Schomberg's army would have starved, if they did not desert him . . . It's to be feared their fleet will only triumph in the English Channel, for some days shoot a great many cannons into the English shore, and so return in August into their own ports.[37]

It was not the victorious French but the defeated allies who used the sea to support their Irish forces. Strenuous efforts were made to refit and strengthen the fleet, and on 17 September the joint admirals sailed with a substantial amphibious expedition which in one month succeeded in taking Cork and Kinsale, the two principal ports on the south coast of Ireland.[38]

For 1691 the three admirals were replaced by Edward Russell. As an outspoken enemy of the Stuarts he seemed politically safer than the other admirals, but until 1689 he had never commanded anything more than a single ship, and he was cantankerous and obstructive even in his most amiable moods. In France Seignelay died in the autumn of 1690, and his replacement, the comte de Pontchartrain,[39] saw more hope in attacks on allied trade than sterile fleet victory. Tourville was therefore sent to sea with orders to cruise between Ushant and the Scillies, intercept the rich allied Mediterranean convoy expected home in July, and fight the allied main fleet if it was encountered in more or less equal force. He was not to go far from Brest, especially not up the Channel. Even this was too bold for Tourville, who would have much preferred to stay in port. Not until 17 June was he finally forced to sea by imperative orders. Almost at once his scouts warned him of the approach of the Mediterranean convoy from one direction, and Russell's fleet from the other. Hastily abandoning waters so full of alarming opportunities, he fled into the Bay of Biscay. There Russell, with a smaller fleet, pursued him in late July, but Tourville's excellent scouting allowed him to evade the allies and return to Brest on 4 August. Meanwhile smaller French squadrons several times escorted troops and supplies to Ireland, where James's forces still held Limerick, but in the absence of the main fleet the communications of the English army were not disturbed, and Limerick finally surrendered on 13 October. The English government, seriously afraid that Parliament would vote to abandon the war as soon as Ireland was subdued, was desperate for a naval victory. To Russell's fury, he was therefore forced to keep the main fleet at sea into September, losing two big ships wrecked, when a smaller squadron of two-deckers could have protected trade and covered Ireland just as well.[40]

William III's English government was visibly weak and divided, and the Navy's loyalty was widely suspect. In France James II persuaded Louis XIV that the moment was ripe for decisive intervention, and a substantial French army was assembled on the Côtentin Peninsula. The plan provided for the Toulon squadron to arrive at Brest in the spring, permitting the united French fleet to sail in April to dominate the Channel before the English and Dutch could join forces. The troops would then be landed in Dorset. Though Tourville had not got to sea before June in the past three years, neither Louis XIV nor Pontchartrain took his logistical difficulties very seriously. They had to use Tourville, who was their only admiral with the seniority and experience to command the main fleet, but they were familiar with his excuses for inactivity, and they assumed that imperative orders were the solution to all the difficulties he raised. They finally forced Tourville to sea on 2 May, still without the Mediterranean ships and many of those from Atlantic ports.[41]

The threat of a French landing was known to William III, who was already planning one of his own in France, and strenuous efforts were made to prepare the allied fleet. Its different elements were assembled at St Helen's (the outer anchorage of Spithead, at the eastern end of the Isle of Wight). It was a bold decision to use an open anchorage only a few days' sail from Brest, and when the allies joined on 12 May, Tourville was already entering the Channel. Off Plymouth on the 15th he was joined by reinforcements bringing his strength up to forty-four ships of the line. The allied line eventually amounted to eighty-two ships, but Tourville had not received warning that the Dutch and English had joined, and was still expecting to meet an English force not much bigger than his own, and actively disloyal to William III. On 19 May, north-east of Cape Barfleur, Tourville sighted his enemy ahead and to leeward, and ordered an immediate attack. It is something of a mystery why he did so. His orders obliged him to fight even the united allied fleet, but only if he met it while covering his actual landing, which was not the case. It is true the orders contained phrases reflecting on his courage, but he had received similar orders in the past, and injured honour had never yet stung him into action. Perhaps the most likely explanation is the simplest: the morning was foggy, and he was committed to battle before he realized the odds against him.[42]

At first the battle went well for Tourville in spite of the odds. His fleet was concentrated and composed largely of big ships, it was handled with great tactical skill in a bold attack on the allied centre pressed to close range; Shovell 'never saw any come so near before they began to fight in my life'.[43] The allied line was extended, not to say scattered, and it was some time before the van and rear could work round to envelop the French. By evening, however, Tourville's situation was desperate, his line was disintegrating, and it was high time to disengage. During the night and the next day the main body of French ships retreated westwards, and on the 21st twenty-two ships were able to round Cape de la Hague[44] and escape through the Race of Alderney towards St Malo. Another group failed to round Cape Barfleur and took refuge in the bay of St Vaast-la-Hougue on the eastern side of the peninsula. The laggards of the main fleet, still anchored near Cape de la Hague when the tide turned on the morning of the 21st, were driven from their anchors by the force of the flood tide and swept back eastwards. Three big ships, including Tourville's badly damaged flagship the *Soleil Royal*, were beached near Cherbourg, and burned next day by English fireships. Twelve more were run close inshore at

St Vaast, where shore batteries and the invasion force camped near by gave them some protection. The English took time to prepare their attack, but on the 23rd and 24th boats and fireships burned all twelve ships of the line, besides some of the troop transports in harbour. The fighting was so close inshore that in one incident the bowman of an English boat pulled a French cavalryman off his horse with a boathook.[45]

The double battle of Barfleur-La Hougue was a notable allied victory, but in that age of discontent, few were happy with it for long. Russell thought the French ships and officers better than his own, and regretted that his subordinates Sir John Ashby and Philips van Almonde (commanding the Dutch fleet) had not risked a pursuit through the Race of Alderney to catch the rest of the French fleet before it reached St Malo. Russell's subordinate admirals quarrelled with him and with each other. Russell was angry at being made to keep his big ships out to the end of August, indeed constantly grumbling at the risks of taking them down Channel at all in 'weather fitting only for Laplanders to be at sea with'.[46] 'This storm,' he wrote to Nottingham at the end of June,

> has confirmed me in my former opinion, that no fleet of ships, being so many in number, nor of this bigness, ought to be ventured at sea but where they may have room enough to drive any way for eight and forty hours, or where they may let go an anchor and ride. In the Channel six hours, with a shift of wind, makes either side a lee shore, and had not Providence put it in my head in the morning early to bring to, but have run four leagues further over on the French coast, God knows what account you would have had of the fleet . . . This and a Dutch war are very different, for then bad weather was nothing, the fleet having it in their power to anchor, but now we keep the sea a thousand accidents attend it.[47]

The government in London, bombarding him with unrealistic and contradictory instructions, expected him to mount an immediate attack on St Malo. As Lord Carmarthen, his leading minister, warned William III,

> The omitting to endeavour it will be looked upon as an unpardonable crime in us not to advise and will have the worst consequences with a Parliament if it should fail for want of a due prosecution; amongst other ill humours which it will create, it will most certainly and unavoidably make them never give more for the support of any troops beyond seas.[48]

Ministers and Parliamentarians were very displeased to be told that its dangerous approaches and heavy fortifications made an attack impossible.[49]

Elsewhere in the world the first years of the naval war were equally disappointing. In the West Indies there were heavy losses to French privateers. Commodore Lawrence Wright arrived with thirteen warships and some transports in June 1690, but found it impossible to establish a good relationship with Christopher Codrington, Governor of the Leeward Islands, who demanded authority over both troops and ships. Codrington was a man of more energy than tact or talent, but his strategic ideas were sound: 'All turns on mastery of the sea. If we have it, our islands are safe, however thinly peopled; if the French have it, we cannot, after the recent mortality, raise enough men in all the islands to hold one of them.'[50] Together they succeeded in recapturing the island of St Kitts and the Dutch island of St Eustatius in July, but the arrival of a French squadron forced the abandonment of an attempt on Guadaloupe in May 1691. Wright presently went home on sick leave ('how justifiably I shall not say' was the comment of the Secretary of the Admiralty)[51] and was arrested on his return. In January 1692 Captain Ralph Wrenn arrived with reinforcements, and on 11 February was attacked off Barbados by the comte de Blénac. Though the French had double the numbers, Wrenn was able to cover the escape of his convoy and disengage without loss, but soon afterwards he and many of his men died of yellow fever, and the bulk of the squadron was sent home in April. In effect the two navies had cancelled one another out and achieved nothing.[52]

In New England there were virtually no regular warships present, but Sir William Phips, now Governor of Massachusetts, organized an expedition which captured Port Royal, Acadia (now Annapolis Royal, Nova Scotia) in May 1690. Emboldened by this success, the colony improvised an expedition with not less than thirty-two ships against Quebec. It arrived before the city on 6 October, very late in the season, and the chaotic 'siege' fell apart after only a week, but it failed by only a narrow margin, for if it had arrived even a week earlier it would have found no defence prepared. The English capture of Port Royal being more or less balanced by the French capture of Casco, in these waters too, neither side was able to do the other essential damage.[53]

This was the story of the opening years of the war at sea. The great fleets of which everyone had hoped and expected so much, proved to be difficult to use effectively in unforeseen circumstances. Governments whose experience was irrelevant and whose attention was elsewhere failed to produce any coherent naval policy, while the admirals found it easier to fight battles than to win them, and easier to win them than to achieve any lasting advantage. Only one naval operation was an unequivocal victory of enormous strategic consequences, one mounted in defiance of all common sense and professional experience, and achieved without fighting: the Dutch invasion of England in 1688.

TEN

Notorious and Treacherous Mismanagement

Operations 1693–1700

The allied victory at Barfleur-La Hougue in 1692 neither reassured the English nor deterred the French. In Versailles the prestige of the fleet and of Tourville its commander gained more from a gallant defeat than they had from a fruitless victory two years before. The French building effort continued unabated: 100,000 tons of ships, mostly the biggest classes, were added between 1691 and 1693, and the losses of La Hougue were made up within two years. The English, convinced by their own recent experience that invasions were easy, continued to fear a French attack in season and out of season, and continued to suspect the loyalty of admirals who made difficulties over landing in France.[1]

The favourite scheme of English ministers was for the allied main fleet to cover a landing to capture Brest, eliminating half the French fleet and most of the strategic threat against England. William III was working, in secret as usual, towards a quite different objective: the Mediterranean. The Dutch had long been accustomed to send squadrons there in wartime, and William appreciated strategic possibilities which lay beyond the mental horizon of most English ministers. Naval command of the Western Mediterranean was crucial to any war in which France was opposed to Spain on one side or any of the Italian states on the other, for in both cases the only route of an invading army was a single road squeezed between the mountains and the sea, and blocked by a series of fortresses. Command of the sea was needed to besiege or by-pass these fortresses, and to supply armies invading in either direction. This was the one essential service which England and the Netherlands could do for their exposed allies Spain and Savoy, without which there was every risk that they would be driven out of the war, allowing the French to double their armies in Flanders and advance on the Dutch Republic. Moreover William's naval advice came largely from the Amsterdam Admiralty, and Amsterdam dominated Dutch

Mediterranean trade, which would be greatly assisted by the presence of the allied fleet.[2]

At the king's insistence, the planned attack on Brest was postponed, and a strong squadron under Sir George Rooke was assigned to escort the long-delayed 'Smyrna fleet' of allied merchantmen bound into the Mediterranean. Rooke's voyage southward would be covered by the allied main fleet until he was safely past Brest. The king hoped Rooke's force would become the nucleus of a future Mediterranean fleet, but only Nottingham of all William's English ministers was entrusted with his strategic ideas. Russell, who refused to work with Nottingham, was replaced as commander-in-chief by another triumvirate: Henry Killigrew, Sir Ralph Delavall and Sir Cloudesley Shovell. As before, the primary object of dividing the command was political, the Williamite Shovell balancing Killigrew and Delavall, who represented the Tory majority in the Commons. The joint commanders had to plan their operation with very little intelligence, an acute shortage of victuals, and no hint of the king's strategy; moreover his orders forced them to sea before they could obtain any of what they lacked. They decided to cover Rooke as far as a point 150 miles south-west of Ushant, well past Brest, where they parted from him on 6 June. They considered going as far as Lisbon, but the Dutch admiral van Almonde, whose victualling situation was even more precarious than theirs, insisted on a speedy return to Torbay.[3]

Only when they were back in England did they learn that the French Brest and Toulon squadrons, blessed with greatly superior intelligence, had united off Cadiz and mounted a perfect ambush of the allied convoy as it rounded Cape St Vincent on 17 June. Fortunately for the allies, Tourville was as timid as ever. It took half a day to persuade him that he had intercepted a merchant convoy rather than the allied main fleet, and when he did send part of his force to attack, it was decoyed away by the Dutch squadron, and then delayed by two Dutch captains who sacrificed their ships to hold off the French and allow the convoy time to disperse; Rooke thought it 'one of the best judged things I ever saw in action'.[4] Three-quarters of the merchantmen escaped, but even so ninety-two were sunk or captured. The majority were Dutch, but the losses in London equalled those of the Great Fire of 1666. The French prizes sold for thirty million *livres*, equivalent to the entire French naval budget for 1692.[5]

The Smyrna convoy was a catastrophe for the unity of the alliance and the stability of William's English government. His English secretary William Blathwayt 'never saw the king so sensibly affected with any accident as this, which had all the worst consequences'.[6] English politicians reacted in their usual fashion: without reading the papers it had called for, the House of

Commons attributed the disaster to 'notorious and treacherous mismanagement'.[7] The king, who bore a substantial share of the responsibility, was happy to see the joint commanders-in-chief blamed for everything, but this was not enough to pacify the now Whig-dominated Parliament. William was forced to dismiss Nottingham as well, and appoint Russell as the new commander-in-chief. The Tories had now committed themselves to opposition, and the king was driven into the hands of politicians whom he detested, because they alone would support his Continental war. Most of the available admirals were either Whigs like Russell whom the king distrusted or Tories like Killigrew and Delavall whom Parliament distrusted. The unpartisan Rooke was a precious exception, so William made sure he was not blamed for the Smyrna convoy disaster.[8]

In spite of orders to bring his united fleet northwards, Tourville retreated to Toulon, reinforcing William's determination that the allied fleet should follow. He was forced to accept that the big ships needed refitting and victualling, but he succeeded in getting a strong squadron under Sir Francis Wheeler despatched on 29 November. William intended the squadron to be the nucleus of his Mediterranean fleet, but Parliament understood that its task was to collect and protect the survivors of the Smyrna convoy disaster. Both plans were wrecked with Wheeler's squadron near Gibraltar on 18 February 1694. The admiral went down with his flagship and two other battleships, the Levant Company lost more ships than it had the previous year, and the Dutch Vice-Admiral Gerard van Callenburgh, succeeding to the command, insisted on evacuating the Mediterranean. In London all attention was concentrated on the long-planned attack on Brest, but Wheeler's loss, and the news that the French Brest squadron had again sailed for the Mediterranean, forced a change of priorities. When Russell sailed on 2 June, he left a squadron to cover the Brest landing, but carried on southward with the main fleet. French intelligence, profiting as usual from the fact that so many Englishmen were prepared to betray their government, was fully informed of the Brest plan. When the landing was made on 8 June, it was repulsed with heavy loss.[9]

Russell sailed on into the Mediterranean, where the French army was besieging the fortress of Palamos on the road to Barcelona. Much was expected of him in England, but both Russell and Tourville knew that it was too late in the season. When he reached Barcelona early in August he was 1,600 miles from home, and four weeks from the autumn gales in the Channel. It was time to return at once, and Tourville looked forward to completing his campaign at leisure as soon as the allied fleet was forced to sail. William III had other ideas, but he knew how unpopular they would be, and kept them to himself until the last moment. Finally in early August, having failed to move his English ministers to take the decision, on his own authority he ordered Russell to remain as long as possible in the Mediterranean, and then to winter at Cadiz. The orders arrived just in time, and in spite of violent grumblings Russell obeyed them.[10]

A king who knew anything about naval administration would probably never have taken the risk. At virtually no notice, the English and Dutch naval authorities had to improvise naval yards at Cadiz, with stores and staff sent from home, and further supplies purchased locally, at a time of a rapidly worsening foreign-exchange crisis in England. Russell as usual was morose and abusive, but the administrative problems were overcome with remarkable success. The presence of the allied fleet so near to the Catalonian coast paralysed the French campaign, and kept Tourville's fleet in Toulon. Russell remained in the Mediterranean during the following summer, hampered by increasing shortages of men and worried by the damaging effects of the shipworm. The king forced him to delay his return until October 1695, ignoring the anguished complaints of both the admiral and the English government. Russell was so angry that he announced his intention of disobeying the order, and sent his letter overland through France and Flanders so that there was every chance that both William III and Louis XIV would read it, but as usual he did not carry out his threat. As the financial crisis deepened, the experiment of wintering the main fleet abroad was not repeated, but Rooke remained at Cadiz with thirty ships of the line over the winter of 1695–6.[11]

William's Mediterranean policy brought clear strategic benefits, though the risks were higher than the king cared to recognize. The fleet in the Channel, meanwhile, was achieving very little. After the costly disaster of Brest, enthusiasm for landings waned, but public opinion still demanded that the fleet do something, and took it for granted that loyal and determined admirals would have no difficulty in finding something successful to do. The only thing to be done was bombarding coastal towns. The French navy in the 1680s had introduced a new type of warship, the bomb vessel, which carried one or two heavy siege mortars firing explosive shells; a devastating but not very accurate weapon, suitable for use only against large, stationary targets. At Genoa in 1684 they had used them against the civilian population of an open city, a demonstration of terrorism which had horrified Europe and gone far to isolate France.[12] Now the allies were reduced to the same sort of warfare. First St Malo was bombarded in November 1693. In September 1694 Shovell was sent to attack Dunkirk with explosive fireships invented by the Dutchman Willem Meesters, which were a complete failure. These two places were at least major privateering bases, but Dieppe and Le Havre, attacked in July 1694, were only commercial ports. No informed observer thought these operations were of much military value. The Duke of Shrewsbury, one of the Secretaries of State, candidly told William III that, 'the designs we have on foot appear so frivolous that it is not very pleasant writing upon them'.[13] But the political pressure on the fleet to do something continued unabated, and in 1695 there were ineffectual attacks on St Malo, Granville, Dunkirk and Calais. Thoughtful Englishmen were disgusted. Losses of merchantmen, John Evelyn thought, were 'of infinite more concernement to the public than spending their time in bombing and ruining two or three paltry towns . . . an hostility totally averse to humanity, and especially to Christianity'.[14] Finally in July 1696 attacks were made on the little ports of St Martin de Ré and Les Sables d'Olonne, plus some insignificant islands off the coast of Brittany, by which time both the English war-effort and the English strategy were exhausted.[15]

In the same year, 1696, the French and Jacobites mounted their last serious joint plan, to assassinate William III and invade from Dunkirk. The scheme called for speed and secrecy, neither of which was achieved, but it did lead to the abrupt recall of Rooke's squadron from Cadiz (hastened home by financial crisis). By the summer the French plan had collapsed, and the allied fleet was concentrated in the Channel with nothing to do, and hardly anything to eat. 'Your speedy direction how our great and useless fleet should act would be very seasonable,'[16] Lord Godolphin wrote to the king on 12 June, but his only idea was the Mediterranean, which was financially and administratively out of the question. The French were bankrupt too, but with a final effort, they fitted out seven ships at Toulon for the summer of 1697, with whose help they took Barcelona in August.[17]

Both England and France found it frustrating to go to war in a novel strategic situation with fleets and ideas ill-adapted to it. Victories were hard to obtain and harder to translate into real advantage. By 1696 neither could afford to keep their main fleets in effective condition, and both were increasingly preoccupied with another form of naval warfare. Privately owned ships had always made war on enemy commerce for profit, but the circumstances of this war raised commercial warfare to new prominence. There were two distinct modes of privateering (and a range of combinations of both): full-time privateers cruised in the hope of taking prizes; while 'letters of marque', as they were called, sailed on their usual trades, but armed, as most long-distance merchantmen were, and prepared to profit from any windfalls that chance might put in their way. Privateering of either kind was of course a profit-making activity, in which the object was easy victims, not hard knocks and glory. Almost invariably, pure privateering in every country was a risky investment of last resort by shipowners whose peacetime trades were stopped and whose ships and capital would otherwise have lain idle. Ports whose trade prospered in wartime seldom bothered with privateering. Much of it was mounted against the coasting trade of the enemy from relatively small ports favoured by geography: from the Channel Isles, Zealand, the Basque ports and the Balearic Islands against France; from Dunkirk and St Malo against the allies.[18]

The strategic context of privateering was closely connected with the policy of blockade. Both English and Dutch governments attempted to cut off France, especially from imports of grain and naval stores from the Baltic, by forbidding all trade with the enemy. This was agreeable to the Zealanders, who mostly traded to the westward and in wartime specialized in privateering, but unacceptable to Holland, which dominated Baltic commerce and had always paid for war by trading with the enemy. In practice the prohibition was unworkable, if only because Holland's shipowners were practised in the use of neutral flags of convenience. The English legislation, which even forbade the import of prize goods taken from the enemy, had likewise to be relaxed. Moreover the attempt to control Baltic trade caused friction with Denmark and Sweden, both of which had respectable fleets with which they convoyed their own merchantmen through the allied blockade.[19] This friction was made worse by the traditional English insistance on the 'salute to the flag' in English waters. In August 1694 this led to a pitched battle in the Downs between Shovell and the Danish Captain Niels Lauritsen Barfød of the *Gyldenløve*, which came close to provoking war.[20] 'This is a very unhappy dispute,' Shrewsbury wrote,

> and fallen out in a most inconvenient time, when the great strength of our fleet is proposed to be kept at such a distance as will make the Danish marine force, added to what the French may put out, very uneasy to us; but at the same time, if this affront be passed over without a just resentment, it is not to be imagined what clamour it will create, and how the people, who are proud of their empire in the sea, will cry out that the honour of Eng[land] is sacrificed; and yet how far the allies will stand by us in such a quarrel is another question.[21]

In the opening years of the war, privateering on both sides was largely left to private shipowners. In France official attention began to turn to it as frustration mounted with the ineffectual performance of the main fleet in 1693 and 1694. Partly this movement was sponsored by Pontchartrain's political enemies, but there was a serious strategic argument underlying it, most cogently presented by the great military engineer Sébastien le Prestre de Vauban in his 1695 'Memorandum on Privateering' (*Mémoire sur la caprérie*). Vauban's argument was that the allied war-effort rested on the prosperity generated by seaborne trade, and could be ruined if the state managed the privateering war to mount a co-ordinated attack on it. The ground was prepared for his ideas by the disastrous harvest of 1693, leading to financial crisis and near-famine, which made the capture of allied Baltic grain convoys an urgent strategic requirement. From 1694 the French began to send out squadrons of up to a dozen ships, capable of overwhelming the most powerful convoy escorts. Some of these squadrons were composed entirely of royal warships, while others were a mixture of royal and private enterprise, with warships chartered to privateer owners on favourable terms, commanded in some cases by royal officers. As the crown's financial crisis deepened, these joint enterprises drew in capital from court investors and expertise from private shipowners to sustain the naval war.[22]

These powerful raiding squadrons achieved some striking successes. On 19 June 1694 the Flemish privateer Jan Bart[23] of Dunkirk overwhelmed the escorts of a Dutch grain convoy in the North Sea and captured it complete. Next year René Duguay-Trouin of St Malo took three English East Indiamen off the coast of Ireland, and the marquis de Nesmond with a royal squadron took two more, together costing the East India Company £1,500,000. Bart was the most successful of all the French privateer commanders; his base at Dunkirk was ideally placed to intercept North Sea shipping, and masked by shoals which made it almost impossible to blockade effectively. In May 1697 he took another entire Dutch convoy. Even when his attacks were driven off or his prizes recaptured, he imposed heavy costs in disrupted trade and a permanent blockade of Dunkirk.[24]

In the whole period from 1689 to 1713, the French took about 12,000 prizes of all sorts from their enemies, including about 4,000 English between 1689 and 1697. Many were fishermen or coasters, but fishing was a very big business in Holland and Zealand, while in England virtually all economic activity, especially commercial agriculture supplying the London market, depended on coastal shipping. The cumulative effect of losses and disruption was very great, while the privateering war also covered a remarkable growth in French overseas trade. Nevertheless the overall effectiveness of the French war on trade has long been disputed among historians. An older generation of French writers found in the exploits of privateer commanders the patriotic glory to make up for the disappointing performance of the main fleet, and evaded the question of whether privateering won wars. English-speaking historians from

A. T. Mahan onwards, on the other hand, tended to dismiss it as a frivolous diversion from the serious business of winning battles, and thus command of the sea. The events of this war do not support either argument. Plainly French commerce raiding did not in this case win the naval war outright, but neither did the clear victories of the battlefleets at Beachy Head and Barfleur. Possibly Vauban's ideas might have worked, if they had been fully applied, but he called for the royal fleet to tie down the allied fleet and overwhelm convoy escorts in order to open the way for the privateers. The French crown resorted to privateering mainly because it could no longer afford to keep up the royal fleet, and the more private capital financed the war, the more private interests fragmented strategy and dissipated effort. Undoubtedly French attacks contributed to the financial exhaustion which drove England to the negotiating table in 1697, but France was bankrupt too, and in both cases poor harvests and the financial weakness of the state (particularly the weakness of its credit) were more to blame than enemy action. The Dutch, who depended much more on foreign trade than the English, nevertheless finished the war in better financial health – partly because Dutch losses fell more on Zealanders and fishermen, both much exposed to attack from Dunkirk, than on the financial heart of the Republic in Amsterdam. Perhaps it may be said that commerce-raiding was the best available naval strategy for France in the later years of the war, given the weakness of the state, and that if the state had not been so weak, it might have been more effective.[25]

The one area in which the French war on trade was unquestionably effective was English domestic politics. As losses mounted, the protection of trade came to dominate Parliamentary discussion of the war. As usual, MPs attributed all misfortunes to treachery, and sought a remedy in removing control of the Navy from the admirals. After the Smyrna convoy disaster, the House of Commons attached to the 1694 Land Tax Bill a provision permanently allocating forty-three ships to 'cruisers and convoys' for the protection of trade. This was part of the Commons' longstanding campaign to win complete control of money bills. Faced with the alternative of rejecting the bill and crippling the war-effort, the Lords succumbed. This precedent gave the Commons the idea that naval affairs, especially the protection of trade, were a valuable political lever.[26]

The practical, as opposed to political, effect of these provisions was mixed. 'Convoys and cruisers' referred in contemporary usage to a series of cruising squadrons, normally five: one in the Western Approaches off southern Ireland, one near the Scillies, one off the Channel Isles, one based in the Downs and one on the East Coast. These squadrons provided cover for passing convoys, and from them local patrols (the 'cruisers') were detached, but they did not normally form convoy escorts themselves. The 1694 provisions in principle created virtually a second navy, large enough to make it difficult to find sufficient escorts for the convoys from the rest, especially in the face of attack from powerful squadrons, and in practice the Admiralty did not fully observe the legislation. For many Parliamentarians, 'Tonnage and Poundage' (the Customs revenue which had been allocated to the Navy since 1347) was understood as a straightforward fee for convoy protection (more or less like the Dutch *last- en veilgelden*, which was possibly what the Commons had in mind), and the escorts were even assigned to different ports and trades in proportion to the dues they paid. Though MPs were alert to the importance of trade (especially the coasting trade which affected most country land-owners), there were few shipowners in the House, and the practical difficulties of escort by a Navy very short of small cruisers were little understood. The Dutch had long experience of convoys and managed them well, but neither admirals nor Parliamentarians in England had any clear idea of the relative advantages, or different roles, of convoy escorts and covering forces. Initially the Admiralty Board knew as little as the rest, but as it began to take over responsibility for the trade war, it was forced to face the practical difficulties. Merchants were disorganized and could not agree when and where they needed convoys. When the sailing dates were fixed, it was hard to get the information to shipowners in time, especially those in provincial or colonial ports. Inward-bound convoys from the Americas or further afield needed to be met by additional escorts as they approached European waters, but contemporary communications and navigation made it impossible to fix meeting-points in the open sea. There were no established convoy signals or tactics, and escorts had no legal command over their charges.[27]

In the West Indies warfare continued to be dominated by the forces of nature. The campaigning season extended roughly from December to May, when the sickly season came, followed by the hurricanes in the autumn. The major local diseases in the Caribbean, both of African origin, were malaria and yellow fever. Malaria was endemic in rural areas, a debilitating disease which killed relatively few but conferred no lasting immunity. Yellow fever, carried (as we now know) by a different breed of mosquito, was an urban disease with a very high mortality. A typical outbreak left 85 per cent of those attacked dead and the rest immune, so it tended to lie dormant until a large number of people without immunity appeared. In ordinary circumstances it was more or less invisible, and in the 1690s it was a relative novelty, not yet familiar to military planners. Ideally a squadron from Europe should have sailed about September, but this was just when the European campaigning season ended with stores and victuals exhausted and ships in need of refit. In practice the weakness of English naval administration, especially victualling, always imposed delays, and by the time forces reached the West Indies their operations tended to extend into the summer. English squadrons had further to go than French, and lost more time by calling at Madeira to buy wine, the usual tropical substitute for beer. On average they took a fortnight longer than French squadrons, and arrived significantly more sickly as a result.[28]

All these factors were illustrated by the expedition of Sir Francis Wheeler, who reached the West Indies early in February 1693 with fifteen ships and 2,000 men, under orders to attack the French islands of Guadaloupe and Martinique before going on to New England to assist the colonials in another expedition against Quebec. In April he made landings in Martinique, did a good deal of damage and carried off 3,000 slaves, but his force was soon too sickly to do more. When he reached Boston he found Governor Phips knew nothing of the Quebec plan, and after a visit to Newfoundland he returned empty-handed. All he had achieved was to distract the French from taking advantage of the destruction of Port Royal, Jamaica, by an earthquake.[29]

In June 1694 Captain Jean-Baptiste du Casse, sea officer and governor of the French part of Hispaniola, landed in Jamaica and remained six weeks, doing much damage. The government was alarmed and prepared a relief expedition, but with the main fleet in the Mediterranean and forty-three ships reserved for 'convoys and cruisers', it could only find twenty to send with Captain Robert Wilmot. He sailed in January 1695, and in May landed in Hispaniola in concert with Spanish forces. Cap François was taken, and later Port-de-Paix, but by this time Wilmot was at odds with his Spanish allies and with the senior English army officer, yellow fever had broken out, and the force soon withdrew. More than three-fifths of the men died, and Wilmot joined them on the way home.[30]

Rear-Admiral John Nevill, who sailed in the autumn of 1696 with a squadron intended to replace Rooke at Cadiz, was diverted to the West Indies in pursuit of a major French expedition under the Baron de Pointis. Pointis and du Casse, in very uneasy co-operation, attacked Cartagena, which capitulated on 23 April 1697. One month later Pointis sailed, laden with booty, and almost immediately encountered Nevill. After a three-day chase, in which Nevill was greatly hampered by the poor quality of his spars and sails, Pointis escaped. The allies only captured his hospital ship, from which they caught yellow fever. Nevill called at Havana, whence he was supposed to escort Spanish treasure ships home, but the Spanish authorities refused even to allow him into port. By the time the allied squadron returned Nevill, his second-in-command and six captains were dead. Pointis meanwhile steered northward, eluded one British squadron at Newfoundland and another in the Western Approaches, and slipped into port exhausted, sickly and very rich. His success, and the fall of Barcelona consequent on the diversion of Nevill's squadron, had a significant effect on the peace negotiations.[31]

In northern waters the Canadian Pierre Le Moyne d'Iberville led a destructive war against the fur-trading posts of the Hudson's Bay Company most summers of the war, and burned English settlements in Newfoundland in November 1696. This attack forced the English to send a strong squadron under Commodore John Norris, and to attempt to fortify St John's, though official policy still discouraged permanent settlement in Newfoundland (which would tend to transfer the base of the fishery, with its supposed capacity to generate seamen, from North Devon to New England). At the end of the war the French in North America were in a strong position, though the governor, the comte de Frontenac, never obtained the troops he needed for his plan to take Boston and New York.[32]

For the English East India Company the accession of William III was a disaster on two fronts: abroad, because it was forced into a very uneasy alliance with its hated rival the VOC; at home, because the company had been so close to James II. The VOC at least undertook most of the burden of the war against French establishments in India, but this was more than counterbalanced by Whig encouragement of 'interlopers' to break into the company's monopoly, culminating in the formation in 1698 of a 'New Company' to take over the patent. Worst of all was the effects on its trade of American piracy. Though buccaneering in the Caribbean was now mainly a French activity (openly led and sponsored by du Casse), English piracy flourished in the northern colonies under the cover of privateering against France, and with the discreet encouragement of Whig political interests in London. New York in particular, where the authorities from the governor downward were deeply implicated, gained the reputation of a second Port Royal. The favourite hunting-ground of these Anglo-American pirates was the Indian Ocean, where trade was rich and European warships scarce. Basing themselves in Madagascar or other islands, they preyed especially on Indian ships. The 'Great Mughul' Aurangzeb, emperor of India, naturally complained to the English East India Company, which depended entirely on his licences to trade; while the VOC maliciously encouraged the Mughals to think that all pirates were English, and all Englishmen were pirates. In 1690 the company's trade was stopped in retaliation for English piracy. In 1695 the pirate Henry Avery took the Great

Mughal's own ship the *Ganj-i-Salwai*, carrying pilgrims to Mecca, whom the pirates raped and killed. This time the company had to undertake to escort Mughal shipping to get its privileges restored. Then three East Indiamen mutinied and turned pirate, and in January 1698 Captain William Kidd took the Indian ship *Quedah Merchant* (whose cargo belonged partly to a Mughal minister) off Cochin. By 1701 the East India Company was on the verge of destruction, but at home the political tide was turning against the Whigs, and the activities of men like Kidd were becoming an embarrassment. Arrested on his return to New York, he was hanged in London in May 1701.[33]

Financial exhaustion led to the peace of Ryswick in 1697, but settled none of its original causes. The ambitions of Louis XIV were plainly not extinguished, and the approaching end of the childless King Charles II of Spain provided an obvious flashpoint. English politicians, however, as usual viewed foreign affairs, if at all, only through the lens of domestic policy. Most of the English army was disbanded.[34] 'Everyone is very tranquil here,' wrote William III on 23 November 1700, three weeks after the death of Charles II,

> and they have very little notion of the great changes in the affairs of the world. It often seems to me a punishment from heaven that men here have so little sense of what goes on outside this island, although it would become them to take an interest for their own sake, as being reponsible for the affairs of the whole country.[35]

Insofar as the English perceived the risk of another war, it was in the Caribbean, where relations with Spain were poisoned by illegal trade and by the Scottish colony established on the Darien isthmus in 1698, and where France was taking an unmistakable interest. Obvious commercial interests drew Anglo-Dutch fleets to the Baltic in the summers of 1700 and 1701 to enforce peace between Sweden and Denmark. Since Frederick IV of Denmark was the aggressor, the allies acted in concert with the Swedish fleet, and in July 1700 Rooke and van Almonde bombarded Copenhagen.[36]

Next year the English Parliament passed the Act of Settlement, which amongst other provisions made a European war illegal without Parliamentary consent, forbade the appointment of any foreign-born person to public office, even if naturalized, and allowed no English monarch to leave the country without Parliamentary consent. These insulting measures reduced William III to the status of a Parliamentary lackey, and effectively withdrew England from the Anglo-Dutch alliance. It was still unclear, however, whether the English really could stop the world and get off.[37]

ELEVEN

An Additional Empire

Operations 1701–1714

A series of treaties between European powers had provided for a peaceful division of the Spanish empires on the death of Charles II. Louis XIV's grandson the duc d'Anjou would inherit the throne, but Charles's Austrian Habsburg cousins would gain valuable territory in Italy, which was what they really wanted, while the English and Dutch looked forward to improving their access to the trade of the Spanish Americas. None of them had any appetite for further war, even when it was revealed that in his will Charles II had left all his possessions to Anjou, and Louis XIV chose to accept the will and disavow the treaties. It took a characteristic display of Louis' blundering arrogance to create another coalition against France. French troops marched into the Spanish Netherlands, threatening the Dutch frontiers; French external tariffs were sharply raised, threatening their foreign trade; while French officials moved to take over the management of the Spanish American empire, with the obvious intention of excluding English and Dutch merchants. For the English, the final straw came when James II died in September 1701, and Louis, repudiating one of the clauses of the 1698 peace treaty, recognized his son as James III and VIII.[1]

For the 'Maritime Powers', England and the Netherlands, the War of the Spanish Succession was about access to the Spanish empire, not Spain itself. The allies adopted a candidate for the throne, the Archduke Charles of Austria, but they did not plan major campaigns in the Iberian Peninsula. The protection of the Netherlands required a campaign in Flanders, as in the previous war, but the allied fleets were expected to cut Spain's transatlantic links and force open the door for allied trade in Spanish America. They also needed to control the Western Mediterranean to cut Spain's links with her Italian empire, and support Savoy, a vulnerable ally in a key strategic position. In Spain itself the accession of Anjou as Philip V aroused little opposition except among the Catalans, traditionally loyal to the Habsburgs and hostile to Madrid. In the Spanish American empire, however, officials and colonists rebuffed French attempts to take over their trade. Dutch and English traders, though officially illegal, were accepted as honest and peaceful; but the French (the only European power still sponsoring buccaneers) were regarded as little better than pirates, and du Casse, the same who had sacked Cartagena, was the worst of all. In the Caribbean Spanish governors eyed French admirals come to 'protect' their silver home to Europe with an intense, and fully justified, suspicion. In these waters there therefore developed a sort of three-cornered war, in which French squadrons had as much trouble with their allies as their enemies. The weakness of the Spanish navy left the government in Madrid no choice but to rely on French warships to escort home the silver of the Americas, but every effort was made to ensure that it was landed in Spain rather than in France, whence (as Philip V's government quite rightly feared) very little of it would ever return. The French navy therefore mounted a series of large convoy operations over the course of the war. Though on strictly military grounds a few fast ships could have transported Spanish silver more safely, large squadrons were politically essential to demonstrate French commitment and overawe Spanish opposition.[2]

The first French squadron sailed in April 1701 under the marquis de Coëtlogon, but the Spanish governors would not even allow him to buy victuals, and he returned empty-handed. He was followed in September 1701 by Château-Renault, who had more success in collecting the Spanish convoy and seeing it back across the Atlantic. Vice-Admiral John Benbow sailed from England at the same time, but was too late to meet Château-Renault. In August 1702 another French squadron under du Casse, now a rear-admiral, arrived in the Caribbean. Benbow intercepted him on 19 August, off Santa Marta in what is now Colombia, and there ensued a desultory running battle lasting over six days. Benbow had seven ships of the line against four, but he was unsupported by several of his captains, and was eventually forced to draw off, badly wounded. He lived long enough to see Captains Richard Kirby and Cooper Wade court-martialled and condemned to death for cowardice. Benbow was one of the most respected admirals in the Navy, and the story of his last fight made a popular sensation which was remembered long after the campaign was forgotten.[3]

Meanwhile the allied main fleet under Sir George Rooke was preparing to sail. The plan was for a major amphibious landing to capture the port of Cadiz, which would at a stroke have cut off Spain's transatlantic trade, provided the allies with a base for Mediterranean operations, and the Archduke Charles with a foothold in Spain. Rooke, however, had no faith in a plan which involved leaving the Brest squadron between himself and home; he was ill, grieving for his wife, who had died just as they had sailed; and the fleet had insufficient victuals for prolonged operations. He put the troops ashore at Puerto Santa Maria, some distance from Cadiz, where their officers soon lost control and they fell to drinking, looting and desecrating churches. This was the end of any hope of military success, or of local support for the Archduke Charles: 'our fleet has left such a filthy stench among the Spaniards, that a whole age will hardly blot it out,' commented a local English merchant.[4] Presently the troops were re-embarked and the expedition sailed for home.[5]

At the same time Château-Renault was on his way back from the Caribbean. He hoped to make a French port, the Spaniards demanded a Spanish one, but Shovell had a squadron off Brest, and Rooke the main fleet off Cadiz, so to avoid them both Château-Renault steered for Vigo, on the north-western corner of Spain just north of the Portuguese border. The Galician coast here is penetrated by deep fjord-like inlets called *rias*, and the Franco-Spanish force took refuge at Redondela at the head of the *ria* of Vigo, which was blocked by a boom with batteries at either end. More or less by accident, Rooke learned where they were, and mounted an attack on 12 October. Marines were landed to take the batteries, and Vice-Admiral Sir Thomas Hopson's flagship the *Torbay* led the attack which broke the boom. There was heavy fighting, and the crew of the *Torbay* were almost asphyxiated by the explosion of an improvised fireship laden with snuff, but the result was a conclusive Anglo-Dutch victory from which no enemy ship escaped. Six French ships of the line were taken and the other six burned or wrecked. Nineteen Spanish ships of all sorts were burned or captured.[6]

Vigo was a great victory which rescued allied naval reputation and morale, and badly damaged the Franco-Spanish alliance. The French navy suffered heavily, and the Spanish navy was virtually eliminated, forcing Spain into a total dependence on French ships to keep up communication with the Americas. On the other hand most of the silver had been landed before the battle and was saved, indeed multiplied. Spanish revenues from the Americas had long been mortgaged in advance to foreign bankers, in this case mainly Dutch bankers. The Anglo-Dutch attack gave Philip V a perfect excuse to repudiate his debts and confiscate the money. Better still, he gathered much of the considerable proportion of silver which was usually smuggled. It was a disaster for Amsterdam bankers, and a financial windfall for Philip, only moderated by Louis XIV's insistence that Spain pay France for the lost French warships.[7]

In the longer perspective, the battle of Vigo had another consequence of great significance for England. On the accession of Philip V, Portugal, anxious to remain friends with its powerful neighbour, had signed an alliance with France. But the security of Portugal's overseas empire was even more important than the security of its inland frontier, and ministers in Lisbon were well aware that their own navy was incapable of assuring it; they had to have a good understanding with the dominant naval power in the Atlantic. The victory of Vigo reinforced the idea which Rooke's presence had already suggested; that France was not the right choice. In 1703 Portugal signed the 'Methuen Treaties' with England, the commercial provisions of which were to be an essential component of eighteenth-century Britain's prosperity. The discovery in the 1690s of rich gold mines in Brazil made Portugal a wealthy country without generating much economic development. Though the Portuguese government, following the textbook economics of the day, offically banned exports of bullion, the logic of the economic situation was that Portugal would import the textiles and manufactures it needed, and pay for them with Brazilian gold. The essential was that the convoys from South America be protected, even at the price of economic and naval dependence: 'The preservation of our overseas colonies makes it indispensable for us to have a good intelligence with the powers which now possess the command of the sea,' commented José da Cunha Brochado, Portuguese minister in London, 'the cost is heavy, but for us such an understanding is essential.'[8] The consequence throughout the eighteenth century was a flourishing trade in which English exports to Portugal were paid for with illegally exported gold, much of it carried in British warships whose captains found occasion to touch at Lisbon to pick up a profitable 'freight'. Portugal's only significant export trade was built up largely by the Scottish, English and Dutch merchants whose descendants still control it: the port wine trade, which provided English merchant ships with a return cargo and English dinner-tables with a patriotic alternative to French wines. Portuguese gold was an essential support for the British balance of payments, to set against the Baltic and East India trades which imported from countries where English products found few markets, and had to export silver to pay for them. The naval victory of Vigo therefore made an indirect but powerful contribution to Britain's long-term prosperity.[9]

In the short term the Portuguese alliance forced a major change in allied strategy, for Peter II's price for changing sides was an allied army to protect his frontier. Instead of a largely maritime war, the Maritime Powers now found themselves committed to extensive campaigning in Spain, with one army to the westward, based on Lisbon, and subsequently another in Catalonia. This was to prove a heavy and ultimately fruitless burden on their economies.[10]

The Mediterranean was now more important than ever, and thither Sir Cloudesley Shovell was sent in 1703, but he had only thirty-two ships, and arrived too late to achieve anything. He was delayed by the usual weakness of English victualling, and a new factor which was to become more common as the finances of the States of Holland weakened; the tardy arrival and short numbers of the Dutch squadron. Returning late and sickly to English waters, he was caught in the Channel by the Great Storm of 26–27 November, usually reckoned to have been the worst in two centuries, with winds of 150 knots. Shovell narrowly survived, but over 10,000 English seamen died; four ships of the line and nearly 100 merchantmen were lost on the Goodwin Sands in one night.[11]

Rooke and the main allied fleet in the Channel achieved little in 1703, meeting neither opposition nor opportunity. Three successive squadrons were despatched to the West Indies. The first, under Rear-Admiral William Whetstone, was ordered to reinforce Benbow in May 1701, and finally reached Jamaica in July 1702 after a fourteen-month struggle with bad weather and ill-found ships. A squadron under Captain Hovenden Walker arrived in the Leeward Islands in December 1702, and mounted an unsuccessful attack on the French island of Guadaloupe. Finally Rear-Admiral John Graydon took over the command in May 1703 with orders to collect the ships and return, making an attack on the French settlements in Newfoundland on the way. He failed in this attack, failed to fight du Casse's returning squadron which he met in mid-Atlantic, and returned sickly, worm-eaten and empty-handed, to be dismissed from his command. The whole two-year campaign had been fruitless and costly, and for the next three years the English Navy effectively abandoned the Caribbean to concentrate on the new strategic situation in Europe.[12]

William III was succeeded by his sister-in-law Queen Anne in March 1702. The replacement of a foreign general, strategist and statesman by an ill-educated Englishwoman who knew little of public affairs wrought many changes in the political world, but some things remained the same. Like William, Queen Anne disliked party politicians; like him, but for different reasons (she hated public assemblies, in which her poor sight caused her constant embarrassment), she preferred to work in private through trusted advisers – though unlike him, she presided at Cabinet and worked through rather than around her ministers. First among her confidantes was Sarah Churchill, Duchess of Marlborough, whose husband John was one of the senior army officers who had defected to William III in 1688. William had never entirely trusted him, but Anne did, and he soon occupied something of the position William had as *de facto* commander-in-chief of the allied armies in Flanders and chief strategist of the alliance. As a general he had talents which William had never possessed, and moreover he had a good working relationship with the equally brilliant Austrian general Prince Eugene of Savoy. As a strategist he followed William's policy, against the sense of the insular majority of English politicians, arguing that the coalition would collapse unless England made large contributions to an allied army in Flanders to defend the Dutch. As a result, he and the queen gradually found themselves forced, as William had been, into the arms of Whig politicians whom they distrusted, because no one else would support a Continental war.[13]

Marlborough had served afloat during the Third Dutch War, he had brothers in the Navy,[14] and he understood the value of sea power, but in 1704 he was preoccupied with the threat that the francophile Elector Maximilian II of Bavaria would open the way for French armies to march down the Danube to Vienna, destroying the Austrians and the alliance at a stroke. In an audacious move, kept a close secret (from English and Dutch politicians as much as the French), he marched the allied army 250 miles from Flanders across Germany to the Danube, and on 2/13 August he and Prince Eugene crushed the French army at the battle of Blenheim. Meanwhile Rooke had taken the allied main fleet into the Mediterranean, using Lisbon as an improvised forward base. The French too had concentrated their main fleet in the Mediterranean, and the two were briefly in sight off Minorca in May, but no action ensued. Having no landing force but the fleet's marines, Rooke evaded pressure from his allies to make another attempt on Cadiz, and in June the fleet failed to take Barcelona in spite of much local support. As some compensation, Rooke turned to Gibraltar, a small and ruinous fortress with a garrison of only 150 men. This was within the capabilities of the fleet, and on 24 July it was captured. It was a joint Anglo-Dutch operation, in the name of 'Charles III', the allied candidate for the Spanish throne, but the English had long been conscious of Gibraltar's strategic situation, and were already thinking of its future. Its immediate operational benefit, however, was negligible. Gibraltar had little trade, the anchorage was unprotected, and the only naval establishment was a small mole where a couple of Spanish galleys had sometimes sheltered. There was no question of basing a fleet there.[15]

The French fleet, now commanded by Louis XIV's bastard son the comte de Toulouse (Tourville had died in 1701), was too late to prevent the fall of Gibraltar, but advanced to fight for its recovery. On 13 August the two fleets met off Malaga, the French being to leeward, but between the allies and Gibraltar. The allies had fifty-three ships of the line (forty-one English and twelve Dutch) against, probably, fifty French. Rooke's 'Sailing and Fighting Instructions' of 1703 sum up the accumulated experience of half a century of Anglo-Dutch fleet actions, and the two fleets fought in what was now the conventional scheme of parallel lines. It was a hard-fought battle (the English casualties were proportional to those of Trafalgar), with two unusual features made possible by a flat calm. The French fleet was accompanied by galleys, which proved useful to tow damaged ships out of the line; while the allies, uniquely in a fleet action, used bomb vessels, which secured some damaging hits. At the end of the day neither side had a decisive advantage, but after a long bombardment of Gibraltar before the battle the allies were seriously short of ammunition. Some English ships had no shot left at all, though hasty redistribution during the night gave an average of ten rounds a gun (out of the standard allowance of forty) all round. Next day a shift of wind gave the French the weather gage and the opportunity to renew the action, but the majority of Toulouse's senior officers persuaded him that 'what we did yesterday will suffice for the reputation of the Navy and the king's arms',[16] and the French fleet returned to Toulon. Only a minority understood that they had fought for a tangible strategic objective, Gibraltar, which a final effort might well have regained.[17]

In England Tory politicians opposed to the war on the Continent tried to cry up Rooke and his battle as a counterweight to Marlborough and Blenheim.[18] The admiral, now in poor health, took no part in this, but profited from the opportunity to retire from active service.[19] Over the winter Franco-Spanish forces made a determined effort to recapture Gibraltar, whose situation was precarious. Supplies had to be shipped from Lisbon, where an allied squadron under Sir John Leake wintered, through a French blockade based on Cadiz. Leake's first effort arrived in November, just in time. On 9 March 1705 he returned with a bigger convoy, and an escort force including Portuguese as well as Dutch and English ships. This time he was able to intercept the French blockading squadron, commanded by Pointis, whose five ships of the line were all destroyed or taken. Their crews were lost too, which made this in some ways a more damaging defeat than La Hougue or Vigo, where the French ships were lost but their men saved. The siege was lifted and the immediate threat to Gibraltar removed.[20]

On 15 June the allied fleet under Shovell and van Almonde met at Lisbon. Joined to Shovell as joint commander-in-chief afloat, and sole commander-in-chief of English forces ashore, was the Earl of Peterborough. This talented if eccentric nobleman had no military or naval experience, and the intention of Queen Anne's government seems to have been to establish a political representative with authority over the strategic employment of English forces. Peterborough's powers, however, allowed him to interfere in operational decisions, which he did with enthusiasm. Shovell found him extremely tiresome. The allied fleet arrived before Barcelona in August, and though the allies were too weak for a siege, the admirals insisted on attempting an assault. To the soldiers' astonishment, it succeeded, providing 'Charles III' with a capital, and opening a second land front on Spanish soil.[21]

Unfortunately Barcelona was scarcely more useful as a fleet base than Gibraltar, and the allies were still forced to depend on the improvised resources of Lisbon. This gave the Franco-Spanish forces good prospects of retaking Barcelona before the allies could return, which they nearly did in the spring of 1706. At the last moment, on 27 April/7 May, just as the storming parties were preparing, the allied fleet (under Leake and Baron van Wassenaer) appeared. Toulouse and the French blockading squadron made good their escape, but the city was saved. Soon after, Cartagena, Alicante, Ibiza and Majorca were taken by the allies. On the western front, the Duke of Berwick was forced back by the Earl of Galway's[22] allied army, and on 27 June Galway entered Madrid. In the north Marlborough won another great victory at Ramillies in May and drove the French out of the Spanish Netherlands. Philip V retreated from Barcelona under cover of a total eclipse of the sun, and that summer it seemed that his grandfather the Sun King was in eclipse everywhere.[23]

Yet still the allies' efforts in the Mediterranean were crippled for want of a naval base. In 1707 they planned to solve the problem in the most radical possible manner, by capturing the French base of Toulon. The idea was that Prince Eugene would lead an allied army along the coast with the help of Shovell's fleet. This part of the plan worked, but Savoy's commitment to the project was equivocal, the defences of Toulon were strong, and as the siege proceeded Eugene became alarmed at the risk of being trapped by a relieving army. Early in August the allied army retreated, but even as it marched away, the ships achieved part of what they had come for. By destroying some coastal batteries they briefly cleared a way for English and Dutch bomb-ketches to get into range of the harbour, firing blind over an intervening ridge with the aid of observers ashore 'to show signals how the shells fell'.[24] This bombardment lasted only about eighteen hours, and sank two ships of the line, but it frightened the French into scuttling the remainder of the fleet in shallow water. The intention was to raise the ships when the danger was passed, and the wrecks were raised after the war, but only a few ever re-entered service. The allies now had undisputed control of the Mediterranean. It was at this point (not, as older histories used to say, after the battle of Barfleur) that the French government effectively abandoned its main fleet in favour of the privateering war.[25]

Still the allies had no winter base in the Mediterranean, and Shovell's fleet came home late in the season. Successive admirals since Russell had been grumbling about the risks of keeping out the big ships past the end of August, and for all its familiarity, the entrance to the English Channel was dangerous to navigators unable to fix their longitude. The usual practice of seamen making landfall after an ocean passage was to run down a parallel of latitude (i.e. a course due east or due west) to a safe landfall, some prominent feature which could been seen far off and safely approached. The mouth of the Channel is most unsafe, Ushant being foggy and 'surrounded with dangers in all directions',[26] the Scillies low-lying and also surrounded by reefs. Nor are they easily identified: in 1704 an inbound convoy mistook Scilly for Guernsey and had reached Lundy before they realized that they were on the wrong side of Cornwall. The Channel itself, lying roughly east north-east and west south-west, cannot be entered on a parallel of latitude, for a course due east clearing the Scillies by the small margin of ten miles leads straight on to the Casquets reef off Alderney.[27] The Scillies themselves were laid down about fifteen miles too far north on contemporary English charts, and there is a variable and unpredictable current tending to set ships to the northward. All these factors, compounded by remarkably careless navigation, were implicated in the great disaster of 22 October, when Shovell's returning squadron ran on to the outer rocks of the Scillies in the dark. The admiral and the ships' companies of three ships of the line were lost. Shovell was perhaps the only truly popular English admiral of the age, beloved by officers and men, respected by politicians of all parties. His death caused a profound shock, and led in due course to the 1714 Longitude Act, offering large prizes for a practicable method of fixing longitude at sea.[28]

Shovell's death was not the only loss to the allies in 1707, for in Spain Galway had been unable to maintain his hold on Madrid, and in April he was heavily defeated by Berwick at the battle of Almanza. Much of the allied position in Spain unravelled, so the need of a fleet – and therefore a fleet base – in the Mediterranean was as great as ever. The allied fleet, now commanded by Leake, arrived in May, and was soon active in supplying the allied army in Catalonia from Italy. In August Leake secured the surrender of Sardinia (part of the Spanish Mediterranean empire) to 'Charles III', providing an essential granary for Catalonia, and a usable naval base at Cagliari. There was, however, a much better and nearer one, which Marlborough and the queen's ministers had been thinking about for some time: Mahón, in Minorca,[29] by far the best harbour in the Western Mediterranean, and only 300 miles from Toulon. Leake arrived from Sardinia on 25 August and landed his marines. Soon afterwards Major-General James Stanhope arrived from Barcelona with troops, and in spite of the great strength of the island's main fortress, St Philip's, the conquest was completed in less than a month. Though it was made in the name of 'Charles III', the English intended from the beginning to keep the island for themselves.[30]

The capture of Mahón secured the allies' naval hold on the Western Mediterranean, but too late to affect the course of the war. The French fleet was past intervention, and the naval contribution to the war in Spain was mainly to control the export of grain from North Africa, which was supplied to the allied army in Catalonia and denied to the French. This was the main work of Sir George Byng in 1709, Sir John Norris next year, and Sir John Jennings in 1711, though Norris also attempted some raids on the coast of France.[31]

All the while that the Mediterranean dominated allied naval strategy, war at sea in English waters had largely been confined to the defence of trade. Then the 1707 Act of Union between England and Scotland inspired another French attempt to exploit Jacobite sentiment. It seemed a good moment to advance the cause of James VIII, with few troops in Scotland, and many people less than fully committed to the Union or to Queen Anne's government. Captain Thomas Gordon of the Scottish frigate *Royal Mary*, for example, was zealous in protecting Scottish merchantmen, but enjoyed a comfortable relationship with the Jacobite leader Lady Errol, who sent him a private signal to steer clear of Slains Castle whenever she had visitors from France.[32]

The French plan was for the royal squadron from Dunkirk under the comte de Forbin to sail in midwinter and land James in the Firth of Forth before allied squadrons could intervene. Dunkirk was all but impossible to blockade effectively even in summertime, Forbin was a bold and experienced commander, and the plan seemed to have a good chance of success even after the secret leaked out and the blockade was reinforced. At first all went well. Forbin got clean away on 9 March, with Sir George Byng in pursuit but far astern. Unfortunately Forbin seems to have had no idea of the strategic value of the expedition, and to have treated it with a carelessness verging on frivolity. He made his initial landfall at dawn on the 12th fifty miles too far north, past Stonehaven; a disastrous blunder which has never been explained. It was the evening of the 13th before the French were able to enter the Forth and anchor off Anstruther. Byng anchored near by off May Island later that night, unseen in the darkness. Even then there was time to land James and his troops, and the sacrifice of Forbin's small squadron would have been well worth it, but when he sighted Byng's squadron at dawn, he insisted on escaping to the northward. In the ensuing chase one French ship, the *Salisbury* (an English prize taken in 1703) was captured by her British namesake (built 1707), but the rest escaped, and Forbin refused another chance to land James. Thus the French threw away a good chance to create, at least, an effective diversion to Marlborough's plans, which after his victory at Oudenarde on 30 June/11 July, developed into an invasion of France.[33]

The naval war in the Caribbean revived in 1705. In April the enterprising Canadian Iberville mounted a destructive raid on Nevis, only to die of yellow fever at Havana on his way to attack Carolina. In May Rear-Admiral Whetstone arrived with an English squadron, reinforced in August by Commodore William Kerr, who later succeeded to the command. Kerr's squadron was immobilized by sickness and almost starved; he received no victuals from England until July 1707, and could do nothing to intercept the French squadron which du Casse had brought out to collect Spanish silver. Sir John Jennings arrived in December 1706, with the primary mission of persuading the Spanish governors to acknowledge the authority of 'Charles III'. In this he failed completely, and returned to England in May 1708, shortly followed by Kerr, who only got back by dint of borrowing men from the incoming British squadron. Kerr was then prosecuted in the common law courts, impeached by the House of Lords and dismissed from the Service for neglecting trade and demanding convoy fees.[34]

Kerr's relief was Commodore Charles Wager, who sailed in April 1707 with a squadron of seven ships of the line. He was followed by du Casse, who sailed from Brest in October, but spent only a short time in the Caribbean, leaving Havana in July 1708 with the Spanish silver from Mexico – but not the South American silver shipped from Porto Bello, which Wager had intercepted on 28 May. Like Benbow, Wager was abandoned by two of his captains, but he pressed home his attack with his own ship unsupported, took one and sank another of the Spanish ships. The Spaniards lost much money, and a good deal of what du Casse took home never reached Spanish hands. Wager returned to England in December 1709, but the British squadron remained on station.[35]

Further north there was desultory action on the Anglo-Spanish frontier throughout this war, with mutual raids from Carolina and Florida. The English twice attacked the Spanish port of Pensacola, and in 1706 a force of Spanish and French privateers raided Charleston. In these waters, moreover, especially North Carolina ('where there's scarce any form of government', as the Governor of Virginia alleged),[36] piracy was still a real problem. Massachusetts expeditions reached the French privateer base of Port Royal, Acadia, in June and August 1707, but were unable to make an impression on the French defences. On 1 October 1710 the Americans finally achieved a success in taking Port Royal (renamed Annapolis Royal), 'seven years the great pest and trouble of all navigation and trade of your Majesty's provinces on the coast of America'.[37]

In European waters another distraction was caused by the Great Northern War between the Baltic powers, which broke out in 1702. The belligerents of the Spanish Succession war were not directly involved, but all European navies depended more or less on mast timber and naval stores imported from the Baltic, while Baltic grain exports became progressively more essential both to England and France in the years of dearth from 1708. The Dutch moreover provided almost all the shipping which carried these goods. The Maritime Powers therefore needed to cover their shipping from Swedish and Russian attacks, while in the North Sea there were both French and allied grain convoys to be attacked and defended.[38] In the Baltic the Swedes were the main aggressors, and relations with England were not helped by the old irritant of the 'salute to the flag', which provoked a bloody action off Orfordness in July 1704 between Whetstone and the Swedish Captain Gustav von Psilander of the *Öland*.[39] In 1709 Norris took a squadron as far as the Sound to escort allied trade and intercept French. From 1710 Swedish privateers became more troublesome, but as long as the war against Spain lasted, the allies had no ships to spare to protect their trade within the Baltic.[40]

Inevitably, it was French privateers that presented the main threat to allied trade. The French continued the composite trade war which had been so effective in the previous war, with squadrons of royal warships, either equipped by the crown or chartered to private shipowners, used as the nutcrackers to break open convoy defences and expose the riches within. The commanders of these squadrons were the heroes of the French war on trade. In May 1703 the marquis de Coëtlogon intercepted a Dutch convoy under Captain Roemer Vlacq off Lisbon and sank or captured all five escorts: a notable victory, but a sterile one, for the escort's sacrifice enabled the entire convoy of over 100 sail to escape.[41] Unfortunately for the French this was too often the pattern. The chevalier de Saint Pol de Hécourt, commanding the Dunkirk squadron, in 1703 took the *Ludlow*, 34 (i.e. of thirty-four guns), and later the *Salisbury*, 52, which he took for his own command. He also inflicted heavy losses on the Dutch fishing fleet off Shetland. Next year he took another English ship of the line, the *Falmouth*, 58. 'It is to be desired,' commented a French official, 'that Monsieur de Saint Pol find fewer men-of-war and rather more Indiamen or rich interlopers, which would suit his poor owners much better.'[42] Instead he took a Dutch fifty-gun ship, the *Wulverhorst*, but once again the convoy had escaped by the time the escort was overwhelmed. Saint Pol's accounts for this loss-making cruise still had not been cleared up in 1718. In the same year 1704, Duguay-Trouin from St Malo took the *Coventry*, 54, and the *Elizabeth*, 70. Both English captains were sent to prison, one of them for life. Finally in October 1705 Saint Pol took an English convoy complete, three escorts and eighteen merchantmen, but was killed in the attack.[43]

His successor in command of the Dunkirk squadron was Forbin, a Gascon nobleman with many of the qualities traditionally associated with his country: bold, gallant and skilful; but also vainglorious and grasping. In May 1707 his squadron of eight ships of the line took two seventy-gun ships, the *Hampton Court* and *Grafton* with twenty-two ships of their convoy off Beachy Head, though more than half the merchantmen escaped. In the summer Forbin went north into the Arctic. Whetstone formed the escort of an allied convoy to Archangel, which he had left north of the Shetlands (further north than his orders required), before returning to other duties. Forbin intercepted the convoy off the Murman coast of Arctic Russia, but the local escort under Captain Richard Haddock saved it in a fog bank, and Forbin got only some stragglers. Then on 10 October off Ushant, the squadrons of Forbin and Duguay-Trouin by chance together encountered a convoy carrying troops to Lisbon. Between them they had twelve ships of the line against the five of the escort, though Captain John Richards had two three-deckers, the *Devonshire*, 90, and the *Cumberland*, 82. Duguay-Trouin did most of the fighting, in which the *Devonshire* was burned and three more escorts taken. Forbin arrived later and went straight for the convoy, taking ten (out of about 100). He made all the money, and with undamaged ships he returned early to port to claim all the credit.[44]

Against the undoubted successes of French squadrons must be set the many convoys which were successfully defended, or never attacked at all, and even the most celebrated French commanders were not always successful. In 1704 Saint Pol with six warships was frightened off a Virginia convoy of 135 sail under Captain John Evans, who formed a line of battle with his own four escorts and the ten biggest merchantmen.[45] In 1706 Duguay-Trouin intercepted a rich Portuguese Brazil convoy off Lisbon; one escort was taken, but the Portuguese warships saved the whole convoy.[46] His greatest exploit was the sack of Rio de Janeiro in 1711, which did return a profit, but overall Duguay-

Trouin's career cost his investors and himself a great deal of money.[47] His home port, St Malo, prospered in this war because it progressively abandoned privateering in favour of the extremely profitable interloping trade round Cape Horn to the 'South Sea', the Pacific coast of Spanish South America. Three ships which returned from Peru in May 1705 declared cargoes worth more than half the entire gross earnings of all the privateers of the port between 1702 and 1713.[48] In 1709 a convoy of seven ships escorted by Captain Michel Chabert came home laden with Spanish silver, of which Louis XIV received over four million *pesos*, and a quarter of a million found its way back to Philip V.[49]

The French privateering war certainly caused England heavy losses – the contemporary claim of 3,600 merchantmen taken during the war was probably not much exaggerated – but it is not at all clear that it was profitable, either economically or militarily. English foreign trade was more buoyant than in the 1690s, and better able to bear losses.[50] With experience, the organization of trade protection became gradually more effective, and imaginative. In 1709, in response to petitions from the Scottish Burghs, the local escorts on the east coast of Scotland were put under the operational command of the Lord Provost of Edinburgh, who for the rest of the war controlled the convoy system between Newcastle and the Orkneys and across the North Sea.[51] Moreover the efforts of allied privateers, especially from Zealand and the Channel Isles, have to be taken into account.[52]

As in the previous war, the French naval strategy was most effective in English politics. The heavy losses of 1707 caused an outcry in Parliament: 'Your disasters at sea have been so many, that a man scarce knows where to begin,' declaimed Lord Haversham in the House of Lords.

> Your ships have been taken by your enemies as the Dutch take your herrings, by shoals, upon your own coasts; nay, your Royal Navy itself has not escaped. And these are pregnant misfortunes, and big with innumerable mischiefs; your merchants are beggared, your commerce is broke, your trade is gone, your people and manufactures ruined . . .[53]

The result was the 1708 Cruizers and Convoys Act, which removed forty-three ships (nearly half of those between the Third and Sixth Rates) from Admiralty control and assigned them to specified home stations. As with the 1694 Act, the effect was probably to reduce the force available for convoy escorts in favour of cruising squadrons of doubtful effectiveness. Effectiveness, however, was not the main issue in Parliament, where Whig opponents of the government aimed to exploit back-bench disquiet to mount a coup against the Admiralty, and indirectly against Marlborough, whose brother Admiral George Churchill was blamed for mismanaging the naval war.[54]

In this case the Whigs profited from the situation, but overall the French war on trade acted in favour of Tory opponents of the Continental war, especially Marlborough's costly campaigns in Flanders. To aggrandize him, they argued, country gentlemen like themselves paid a heavy burden in Land Tax, too little of which went to protect England's true interests (notably in seaborne trade), and too much of which ended up in the pockets of City financiers, who profited from the war and paid nothing towards it. Most of the financiers were Whigs in politics, Jews or Nonconformists in religion, and French, Dutch or Portuguese in origin. Associated with them were England's Dutch allies, who were accused of bleeding England white in their defence, while they withdrew their stipulated quotas from the allied fleets and kept their own ships to escort their own convoys (frequently trading with the enemy). All the xenophobia so deeply rooted in English politics aroused MPs to demand a patriotic, profitable and English war at sea, of the sort which (as they believed) had never failed before. At the same time Tory attachment to the campaigns in Spain was fading, not only because the campaigns themselves were going very badly, but because the Archduke Charles unexpectedly succeeded to the Austrian throne on his elder brother's death in April 1711, and a re-creation of the sixteenth-century Habsburg empire under Charles VI seemed even less palatable than the Franco-Spanish connection under Philip V.[55]

The Tory government which took power in 1710 gave expression to these discontents. Subsequent historians have constructed a strategic tradition, the 'Blue-Water policy', to which the Tories were supposedly attached, but much of this is a modern rationalization of what had more to do with atavistic prejudice than rational calculation, and was to a large extent common ground among politicians of all parties. Mutual self-interest put the Whigs in bed with William III and later Marlborough, but they were not natural friends of kings and captains-general, nor of large armies and campaigns on the Continent; they were simply more realistic, or more prepared to compromise their principles for the sake of power. All English politicians were committed to the myths of English sea power, according to which a truly naval war, against a Catholic enemy, could not fail to succeed. The real distinction tended to be between those in opposition, who were wholeheartedly committed, and those in power, who were forced into some compromises with reality.[56]

Of the leaders of the 1710 Tory administration, Robert Harley was more level-headed than his colleague St John. In March 1711 Harley was stabbed (by a captured French spy who was being questioned by a Privy Council committee), and while he was recovering, St John was largely responsible for mounting a grand amphibious expedition against Quebec. This was a response to New England requests, but it was even more an expression of Tory ideology. The troops were taken from Marlborough's army in Flanders, and the ships were commanded by an impeccably Tory officer, Rear-Admiral Sir Hovenden Walker. To keep the expedition secret and avoid the 'tedious forms of our marine management',[57] as he put it, St John kept both the Admiralty and the Navy Board in the dark, allowing some of the ships to sail with only three months' victuals aboard in the expectation that they could be resupplied at Boston. When the expedition did arrive there at the end of June, with only a few days' warning, Walker was surprised to find that it was difficult to supply a force of over 12,000 men (greater than the population of Boston and its surrounding district) with provisions for a whole winter. Eventually they sailed at the end of July with three months' victuals, effectively gambling that they could conquer Quebec and find it full of food. Walker was worried about this, and further unnerved by the dangers of the St Lawrence without adequate charts or pilots – with reason, for on 23 August the fleet ran on the coast in the dark and seven transports were lost. On paper the force was still formidable, but Walker and his captains had had enough, and hastened to abandon the expedition.[58]

By the time it returned in October, the Tory government was in the process of withdrawing from the war. One month later Marlborough was dismissed from all his offices. At the same time the ministry published Swift's pamphlet *The Conduct of the Allies*, an official attack on the Dutch. 'No nation,' he proclaimed, 'was ever so long or so scandalously abused by the folly, the temerity, the corruption, the ambition of its domestic enemies; or treated with so much insolence, injustice and ingratitude by its foreign friends.'[59] Another pamphleteer ingeniously estimated that the Dutch had made a profit from the war of £12,235,847 5s 5d.[60] All this of course was meant to justify the British in abandoning their allies and withdrawing from the war. At the Treaty of Utrecht in 1713, Britain gained Gibraltar, Minorca, Acadia (renamed Nova Scotia), the whole of Newfoundland and St Kitt's (hitherto divided), and undisputed possession of Hudson's Bay. The Spanish Nether-lands were transferred to Austria, and as Britain's reward for betraying her allies, the French repudiated 'James III' and agreed to demolish the port and fortifications of Dunkirk. The reputation of 'perfidious Albion' was now well established in Europe, and as if to confirm it, Harley skilfully double-crossed the Jacobites, who provided a large part of his support, and engineered the peaceful succession of the Elector of Hanover when Queen Anne died on 1 August 1714.[61]

On most reckonings the material profit to England of almost twenty-five years of costly war against France was meagre. A small number of territories had been gained, two of them (Minorca and Gibraltar) of real, or at least potential, strategic value. The ambitions of Louis XIV had been checked, and Flanders (always so sensitive for England) safely confided to friendly hands. A Catholic dynasty had been removed, comforting English and Scottish Protestants at the price of a permanent threat to their security. Nothing so effectively destabilized a government as a legitimate pretender to the throne with support at home and abroad, so the price of Protestant liberty was eternal vigilance, and eternal expense. Less obvious than any of these changes, but in the long run most important of all, was the very rapid growth during these years of English foreign trade. The English domestic economy still depended overwhelmingly on agriculture and woollen cloth, but English (and now Scottish) merchants imported, and in large measure re-exported to Europe, greater and greater quantities of sugar and tobacco from the West Indian and American colonies, cotton from India and silk from China. These were long-distance 'rich trades', earning large profits but requiring large capital and advanced skills in banking, insurance and the management of shipping. Other shipowners traded in bulk goods with European ports: English cloth, timber and naval stores from the Baltic, salted cod from Newfoundland. All these trades, multiplied by the Navigation Acts, generated shipping and seamen as well as income. They went to build up what has been called a 'maritime-imperial' system, based on shipping and overseas trade much more than on extent of territory.[62] Eighteenth-century Englishmen were 'proud of their empire in the sea';[63] for them the word 'empire' still had the value of the Latin *imperium*, an abstract noun rather than a geographical expression.[64] 'Trade,' as Addison put it, 'without enlarging the British territories, has given us a kind of additional empire.'[65] To a greater and greater extent, Britain's real wealth was generated, and seen to be generated, from a maritime system in which overseas trade created the income which paid for the Navy, merchant shipping trained the seamen which manned it, so that the Navy in turn could protect trade and the country. Much was still to be learned about how best to do both, but few informed observers in 1714 would have disputed Lord Haversham's judgement that 'Your trade is the mother and nurse of your seamen; your seamen are the life of your fleet; and your fleet is the security and protection of your trade: and both together are the wealth, strength, security and glory of Britain.'[66]

TWELVE

Strife and Envy

Administration 1689–1714

The overthrow of James II brought an abrupt end to the naval system he and his brother had built up. Pepys resigned in March 1689, and no one person or institution replaced him as naval minister, rather a confusion of shifting spheres of influence. William III concerned himself with grand strategy, and sometimes took personal decisions, but he preferred to shelter behind his ministers. He presided at meetings of the Privy Council when he was in England, and the Council's Committees for Ireland and for Trade and Plantations also dealt with some naval and military business. In William's absence on campaign Queen Mary presided over the full Privy Council, and the smaller working committee coming to be known as the 'Cabinet', faithfully interpreting her husband's policy. After her death on 28 December 1694 a Privy Council committee known as the Lords Justices acted as regents in William's absence. Lord Nottingham, Secretary of State, dealt with naval business for both William and Mary until his dismissal at the end of 1693, and again between 1702 and 1704. Other secretaries of state had the same formal responsibilities but not the same close relationship with the sovereign, and did not claim so much knowledge of the Navy. William Blathwayt the Secretary at War acted as William's English secretary, accompanied him on campaign and dealt with much non-military business in addition to his official duties; Lord Godolphin, First Lord of the Treasury, acted as his representative on that Board; but William had no one at the Admiralty to whom he was close. Many naval responsibilities were delegated to Torrington and later Russell as commanders-in-chief of the main fleet, especially Russell when he was in the Mediterranean, but no one trusted Torrington, and Russell was an outspoken Whig who always behaved to the king with a truculent independence verging on open hostility. From 1694 he was First Lord of the Admiralty, from 1696 he was at home acting as a politician of rising influence (he became Earl of Orford in 1697), and as the

Whigs came to dominate William's government, he effectively eclipsed the Secretaries of State as naval minister, but he did not enjoy a relationship of trust with the king. William himself never recovered politically from the death of his wife, who provided his only claim to legitimacy and popularity, and he never succeeded in replacing Nottingham as a confidential channel of control over the Navy.[1] Queen Anne, for her part, did not attempt to make foreign or military policy in person, and the War of the Spanish Succession was managed by a small Cabinet dominated by Godolphin and Marlborough.[2]

The status of the Admiralty collapsed in 1689. It was natural for William III to treat it as a dependency of Parliament, as the Dutch admiralties were of the States-General, and equally natural for him to exclude it from real power. The Dutch admiralties at least exercised the important administrative responsibilities which in England belonged to the Navy Board, but the English Admiralty now had almost nothing to do. The Board William nominated consisted of a cross-section of mainly Whig peers and MPs. Initially Torrington was First Lord, and occasionally attended; a retired admiral, Sir John Chicheley,[3] was the Board's only other claim to naval expertise. It dealt with administrative details, and sometimes forwarded orders from Nottingham to ships at sea, but it rarely saw the king, and the only significant responsibilities it was offered were those it sought to avoid, notably the responsibility of court-martialling Torrington in 1690. At first the Tory majority in the Commons attacked it as part of the government, and held it responsible for the neglect of trade. In the quarrel between Russell and Nottingham which followed the battle of Barfleur, the Commons favoured Russell while the Lords closed ranks behind Nottingham. The Admiralty now became the Commons' instrument in backing Russell, and its status tended to rise as his did. In the 'cruisers and convoys' legislation of 1694, the Board was put forward as the Commons' stalking horse, its agency for gaining control of naval business, and by extension financial business. Instead of avoiding responsibility for the war and blaming one another for its misfortunes, the Commons and the Admiralty together now began to seek power over the Navy.[4]

The attitude of the House of Commons towards the Navy astonished those who remembered the reign of Charles II. It had always been enthusiastic about sea power in principle, but the context of an anti-Catholic foreign policy, and the terror of invasion from France or Ireland, made it generous in practice. In 1690, the Bishop of Salisbury reported, MPs 'dare not go back to their country if they do not give money liberally . . . we seem now not to be the same people that we were a year ago'.[5] As William and his 'Dutch War' became more and more unpopular among Tory MPs, they were even more inclined to vote against the army and for the Navy as the patriotic, national instrument of war. All parties, declared Colonel Robert Austen in the Commons in 1691, were 'unanimous that a fleet is necessary. 'Tis a great charge and necessary it should be so.'[6] Nevertheless Parliament supported the Navy essentially because it was the physical embodiment of England's political and religious freedom, not because members knew anything about it. Throughout this period they judged the Navy by ideological, not practical, standards, and their interventions in naval affairs were often ignorant and vindictive. 'The passion and violence of these men goes further than I could have thought possible,' William III wrote, 'it often seems like God's punishment on this country.'[7] In 1698, faced with a request to vote 10,000 seamen and 3,000 Marines, the Commons voted 15,000 seamen but struck out the Marine regiments altogether: as part of the army, they were symbols of tyranny, to attack them was to humiliate William, and their political significance mattered much more than their practical value. As war approached again, the naval votes increased sharply, but still the Marines were refused. MPs took it for granted that English warships were invincible, and that naval setbacks could only be accounted for by treachery.[8] The admirals naturally did not agree. 'The misfortune and vice of our country,' Shovell told Nottingham,

> is to believe ourselves better than other men . . . but experience has taught me that 'tis, without a miracle, number that gains the victory, for both in fleets and squadrons and single ships of near equal force, by the time one is beaten and ready to retreat the other is also beaten and glad the enemy has left him. To fight, beat and chase an enemy of the same strength I have sometimes seen but I have rarely seen at sea any victory worth boasting when the strength has been near equal.[9]

Parliament was ignorant partly because William III's government chose to keep it in ignorance, and the Admiralty was not excepted. Torrington did not always tell his colleagues where he was taking the fleet, and Nottingham excluded the Board from all knowledge of its activities. In August 1693 Pepys heard from a mutual friend who had been talking to Sir John Lowther of the Admiralty,

> observing to him between jest and earnest that we were at length come to one improvement in our conduct, namely, of being able to keep a secret, forasmuch as nobody could tell to this day whither our fleet's last orders were to carry them . . . Whereto Sir J. L. replied that none could know less of it than they of the Admiralty, the orders not only for their sailing but even for their victualling going from the Cabinet. And this he delivered by ways of complaint of their being no better treated than they

are in their office, but made when they are called to wait without, as the most ordinary attendants do.[10]

Russell and Sir John Trenchard, Secretary of State, worked out the 1694 assault on Brest between them. Only on the eve of his departure did Russell send Trenchard some information for the Board,

> for as yet I have taken no notice to them of the design. When you think it convenient, pray let them know both, it being for the service they should be acquainted with it, when you believe 'tis no longer necessary the names and qualities of the ships should be unknown.[11]

As late as 1696 the Admiralty was still relying on scraps of information picked up at the House of Commons.[12] That same year another body, the Council of Trade and Plantations (commonly called the Board of Trade), was established both literally and figuratively next door to the Admiralty, as a representative of shipowners' interests in the defence of trade.[13] This made ten persons or organizations claiming some responsibility for the operations of the Navy, without considering administration at all: the king, the Lords Justices, the Privy Council, the two Secretaries of State, two Houses of Parliament, the commander-in-chief of the main fleet, the Admiralty and the Board of Trade.

On 20 May 1699 Charles Sergison, Secretary of the Navy Board, had an interview with William III in which he pressed for the appointment of an Admiralty Board

> constituted of men of estate, quality, credit and reputation; of experience and diligence, zealous to your service, not leaning to faction or favours, and above all, men of temper – some of the last being so impatient of contradiction as hardly to be conversible, uncapable by that means of being informed, and consequently of ever being masters of a business so intricate as that of the Navy.[14]

He did not get his wish. Ten days later the Whigs fell from power, and a Tory Admiralty took office which was dominated by the Navy Board's unreasoning enemy Lord Haversham. This Board led the pursuit of Orford, accused of corrupt practices as commander-in-chief in the Mediterranean and as Treasurer of the Navy, but the ignorance and intemperence of its denunciations undermined its reputation. Finally, in January 1702, William lost patience and abolished the Board, appointing the Earl of Pembroke as Lord Admiral.[15]

Six weeks later, William was dead, and in May 1702 Pembroke was replaced by Queen Anne's husband, Prince George of Denmark. He was intelligent, conscientious and interested in naval affairs (his hobby, highly unusual in a seventeenth-century prince, was building model ships)[16] but he was also in bad health, diffident and inexperienced in public business, and the Council appointed to advise him did not altogether help. In particular the presence of Admiral George Churchill, an able administrator but an uncompromising and indiscreet Tory, was a source of growing weakness to his brother and Godolphin, struggling to maintain the non-partisan position the Queen desired, but increasingly forced into the arms of the Whigs. It suited the opposition to embarrass the queen and her government by blaming Prince George and his council for every naval misfortune, but in fact Queen Anne and her Cabinet continued to send important orders from a Secretary of State directly to admirals at sea without officially informing the Admiralty, whose business was still dominated by detail and routine. Prince George was not in the Cabinet, and after Nottingham left office for the second time in 1704, there was no one who could be identified as the minister responsible for the Navy.[17]

Prince George died in October 1708, prostrating the queen with grief, but relieving her government of a political embarrassment. He was replaced once more by Pembroke; no naval expert, but an experienced diplomat and just the sort of mild, apolitical figure whom the queen sought. He had no advisory council, which disposed of George Churchill, but unfortunately he was unqualified both personally and constitutionally to provide the Navy with political leadership. Meanwhile the Whigs pressed ever closer on the government. Queen Anne was finally forced to turn to them when Pembroke resigned in November 1709, and as Orford refused to serve as Lord Admiral, the Admiralty Board was restored with him as First Lord. Less than a year later the incoming Tory government retained the Admiralty Board, but could find no admiral of its own party to preside. The apolitical Sir John Leake and the Whig Sir George Byng were the leading naval members of the new Board, but Leake declined to be considered as First Lord or to join the Cabinet, so the Navy still had no political direction. The way was open for St John to take over and organize his expedition to Canada without professional intervention. When the Earl of Strafford was appointed as First Lord in 1712, he was explicitly warned that 'the employment of First Commissioner of the Admiralty brings your Lordship into Cabinet'.[18] This may be regarded as the moment when constitutional convention provided the Navy with a minister (albeit not an expert minister) for the first time since 1688.[19]

Less visibly, the constitutional relationship of Parliament with the Navy also developed during Queen Anne's reign. Parliament continued to harry unlucky admirals with accusations of treason. In 1707 Captain Sir Charles Hardy, acquitted by court martial of neglecting the protection of trade, was then brought before the House of Lords and dismissed. Whetstone was cashiered the same year because of Forbin's attack on the Russia convoy, although he had escorted it further than his orders required. The Cruizers and Convoys Act of 1708 was essentially a political coup by Orford and the Whig opposition, who were at least as much concerned to damage Prince George as to safeguard English shipping.[20] Nevertheless Parliament was less ignorant and prejudiced than before. So long as money was voted, ministers could ignore what Harley called the 'many murmerings, and hollow noises of distant winds'[21] emanating from the Commons, but they no longer thought, as William III had done, that it was either possible or desirable to keep MPs in complete ignorance. A series of inquiries into naval victualling, by both Commons and Lords, though partisan in intent, exposed the committee members to the detailed realities of naval administration. Parliamentary attacks on governments which themselves were ignorant of the Navy tended gradually to strengthen Parliament's knowledge and authority. There was a partial vacuum in naval policy-making, and Parliament was slowly drawn into it. Nothing was done to reduce royal prerogatives in principle, but in practice they were subtly eroded, to the extent that in 1713 Queen Anne announced that 'what force may be necessary for securing our commerce by sea . . . I leave entirely to my Parliament. Make yourselves safe, and I shall be satisfied,'[22] a phrase which would have been inconceivable from any previous monarch. Foreign policy and the army remained firmly within the monarch's personal responsibility, but the Navy was becoming a national service in constitutional form as well as in popular sentiment.[23]

All this while the routine work of the Admiralty Office continued. Much of it was copying orders and correspondence, maintaining records, and servicing the meetings of the Board, which were twice or thrice daily in wartime, sometimes late at night. In 1695 the Board was installed in a new building in Whitehall, providing space for lodgings for the Board members. In 1694 an 'establishment' of clerks was fixed, and the pay of the Secretary raised. Though not remotely comparable in importance to Pepys, the Secretary was now a person of some significance. An important milestone was the appointment in September 1694 of Josiah Burchett as joint Secretary. He was Russell's secretary, installed to keep his absent chief informed of what was passing at the Board of which he had just become head, but he survived the political circumstances of his appointment to become almost a feature of the constitution, and soon commentators noticed his pivotal position:

Whosoever cons the ship of the Admiralty, the Secretary is always at the helm. He knows all the reaches, buoys and shelves of the river of Parliament, and knows how to steer clear of them all. He is the spring that moves the clockwork of the whole Board, the oracle that is to be consulted on all occasions: he sits at the Board behind a great periwig, peeping out of it like a rat out of a butter firkin.[24]

When Burchett finally retired in 1742 he had been Secretary for almost half a century.[25]

Like the Admiralty, the Navy Board was severely shocked by the revolution of 1689, but whereas the Admiralty lost most of its responsibilities, the Navy Board lost only status. The work of managing dockyards, building ships and supplying stores remained as onerous and extensive as ever, but no longer were the Board members the honoured advisers of an expert sovereign. In 1699 Sergison complained to William III that they 'had been kept from his Majesty so long that they had almost forgot that they had a king'.[26] The Navy Board also had to suffer constant needling attacks from Boards of Admiralty which resented the uncomfortable fact that the junior board, unlike the senior, was composed of real experts with real jobs. Certainly no one could dispute the Navy Board's weight of experience. Sergison, Clerk of Acts from 1690 to 1719, had entered the Navy Office in 1671. Sir Richard Haddock was Controller of the Navy under six sovereigns, from 1682 to his death in 1715. Sir John Tippetts the Surveyor was only twenty years in office (1672–92), but his successors, like him, were all long-serving master shipwrights from the dockyards. No more than three Surveyors held office between 1672 and 1715; a single Controller of Treasurer's Accounts from 1691 to 1717. These men of long experience and large responsibilities, controlling an administrative machine of unequalled size (fifty-one clerks in the Navy Office alone in 1694; sixty-three by 1703), might well despise what Torrington called the 'insipid ignorants' of the Admiralty.[27] Important secrets were routinely concealed from the senior board, but the junior was always consulted. No wonder that Haddock, sounded on the possibility of promotion to the Admiralty in 1693, replied that 'I am capable of doing his Majesty far greater service as I am, than if I were at that board.'[28] If the Navy Board had a fault, it was a certain inflexibility natural in old men of long service (Haddock was eighty-five when he died in office). It was inclined to dismiss the suggestions of sea officers out of hand (partly because the Admiralty was inclined to back them to make trouble). Many captains, for example, requested that their longboats be replaced by yawls, which were smaller, lighter and more safely hoisted inboard. The Board's reply was that longboats had always been established, which must have been for a good reason: a perfect recipe for immobility.[29] It was the same with sails, where the experience of operating down-Channel soon persuaded flag-officers that ships needed more than they had had in the Dutch Wars, 'but 'twas answered by the Navy Board that two suits were the establishment, and if any ships had more, it was what ought not to be allowed'.[30]

Yet the outbreak of war in 1689 presented the Board with many new challenges. Its last major shipbuilding programme had been the 'thirty ships' of 1677, built in peacetime with money relatively easy. Now it embarked on an almost continuous expansion over twenty-five years, which increased the numbers of ships of the line (First to Fourth Rates) from 100 in 1688 to 131 in 1714, and of cruisers (Fifth and Sixth Rates) from eight to sixty-six. The net increase of thirty-one ships of the line and fifty-eight cruisers required the building of 159 ships of the line and 113 cruisers between 1691 and 1715.[31] This far exceeded the capacity of the dockyards, and necessitated building by contract in places as far away from the Board's supervision as Bursledon (where Mrs Ann Wyatt built the eighty-gun *Cumberland* in 1695) and the Humber.[32]

At the same time the new strategic situation directed urgent attention to the dockyards. After the battle of Bantry Bay it took two months to repair Torrington's squadron at Portsmouth, during which time the Channel was completely open. The double dock there could take nothing larger than a Third Rate and was the only dock on the coast; all the others (four double and five single docks) were on the Thames or Medway. Portsmouth, moreover, was over 200 miles straight to leeward of Brest. The search was on for a suitable site for a new yard to the westward. Kinsale was established as a cruiser base in 1694, but the bar of the Bandon made it impossible for ships of the line to enter and there was no question of a dockyard there. Tourville's 1690 Channel cruise strongly suggested that the new yard should not be too exposed to seaward, and the desirability of a site well to windward had to be balanced against the need to ship all its supplies from the Thames. Cork, Falmouth, Dartmouth and Milford Haven were all considered and rejected, and the choice fell on the eastern shore of the Hamoaze (the estuary of the Tamar and Tavy), three miles from Plymouth. There work began in 1691 on a new dockyard. Built on a grand scale, with a stone dry dock (the first in England) capable of taking First Rates, the yard cost over £67,000 by the time it was complete in 1700. The stone dock ('a knotty work, but to the kingdom the most beneficial it ere knew', in the words of Edmund Dummer, who designed it)[33] presented major technical challenges, and even worse was the new work undertaken in the soft ground of Portsmouth, where between 1690 and 1698 a large stone basin with stone docks opening off it was constructed.[34]

While this investment was going on, the ordinary working of the yards presented many difficulties. There were problems with the authority of the commissioners over the yard officers, and over the relations of both with sea officers.[35] It was hard to find skilled men for Portsmouth and Plymouth, remote from private shipyards, and it was sometimes necessary to resort to impressment. As usual the yard workmen, like seamen afloat, were among the first to feel the Navy Board's financial difficulties. There were riots at Plymouth in 1693, when the yard's wages were fourteen months in arrears, and again in 1698. 'The workmen will be forced to knock off,' Commissioner St Lo warned, 'their credit having for some time been on the rack, and victuals not to be gotten without ready money.'[36] Since yardmen, as crown servants, were protected from arrest for debt, unpaid wages constituted a sort of bondage from which the men could not escape. There was malnutrition and even starvation in the dockyard ports in the 1690s, and in October 1711 the yards were again over eighteen months in arrears.[37] George St Lo himself, energetic but hasty and tactless, caused some problems at Plymouth and later Chatham.[38] Overall, however, the yards evolved with some success to cope with the enormous increase in their business. In 1698 it was calculated that the capital value of Chatham Yard was nearly £45,000, and of Portsmouth over £35,000. By 1711 the yards (including ropeyards) employed a total of 6,488 officers and men in a wide variety of skills and trades, ranging from shipwrights (2,593), labourers (1,468), riggers (413), caulkers (256) and sawyers (245) down to locksmiths (six), wheelwrights (three) and trenail mooters (two).[39] Portsmouth, the biggest yard, employed 1,903 officers and men, with a further 119 in the ropeyard. It was followed by Chatham (1,213 plus 96 ropemakers) and Deptford (1,092). By way of comparison, William Johnson's shipyard at Blackwall, by some way the largest private yard in the country and the only one with a dock able to take a First Rate, employed thirty-two shipwrights in 1703.[40] With the sending of yard officers and artificers to Cadiz in 1694, the Navy Board became an international business for the first time, though as yet there were no permanent establishments overseas. As always, the yards faced challenges which no private undertaking knew or understood. Moreover they had a strong multiplier effect on employment, private investment and urban expansion. The dockyards had entered the industrial age a hundred years before the rest of the country.[41]

The Navy Board's contractors included both outside suppliers of goods, and master craftsmen within or alongside the dockyards, who enjoyed established positions and in some cases salaries, but supplied goods or services on exclusive contracts (normally 'for one year certain', terminable thereafter at six months' notice on either side) with fixed prices but unlimited quantities, according to demand. These standing contractors, sometimes one for each yard, in a few cases one for the whole Navy, included anchorsmiths, iron-mongers, glaziers and plasterers, braziers, plumbers, sailmakers, coopers, compass-makers, painters, tanners, turners, tilemakers, blockmakers and sup-pliers of colours (i.e. flags). The range of patterns they supplied is an index of the complexity of the dockyards' work. There were 132 items enumerated on the anchorsmiths' contracts, ten different types of ballast, 215 items supplied by the blockmakers, forty-eight types of colours, twenty-nine of cooper's wares, thirty-four types of fishing gear, 108 of glazier's and plasterer's wares, 115 species of ironwork and 178 of petty ironmongery, twelve patterns of oars, forty-three sorts of paint, sixteen of plumber's wares, 133 items of stationery, fifteen of tanner's goods, and three grades of sand.[42]

Amongst the goods supplied by outside contractors, sailcloth was a par-ticular problem, since the best came from Brittany, and the quality of English canvas was notoriously bad. In the short term the Navy Board had to rely on a combination of Ipswich canvas (much subject to mildew) with imports from Holland and Germany; but a bounty was offered in 1695 for English sailcloth of stipulated quality, refugee Huguenot weavers brought valuable skills, and by 1699 English producers were able to supply most of the Navy's peacetime requirement. By the time Rooke complained in 1704 of 'our English canvas according to its old custom flying away like dirt',[43] the problem was well on the way to being solved, and before the end of the war English producers could supply the Navy with as much good sailcloth as it needed.[44]

There was another sort of problem with slop contracts. Good, stout working clothes were essential to seamen's well-being, and as commissions increased in length, it became necessary to make them available aboard ship. These slops were supplied by contractors, issued by the purser and charged against men's wages. In the 1690s they included blue waistcoats and kersey jackets, white 'petticoat breeches' (a sort of canvas divided skirt) with red stripes, red caps and white neckcloths. Richard Harnage's 1706 contract speci-fied grey kersey jackets lined with red cotton, fifteen brass buttons and 'the buttonholes stitched with gold-coloured thread'; red kersey breeches, red flannel waistcoats, red or striped shag breeches, blue and white check linen shirts, linen drawers, leather caps, grey woollen stockings, gloves and mittens, shoes and brass buckles. In 1711 the range of sizes was increased from three to four, each bale of fifty suits being made up of eight of the smallest size, then seventeen, seventeen, and finally eight of the largest. It suited the Navy to draw contracts by which the clothes were shipped at the contractors' risk until the moment they were issued, though the bales passed out of their control as soon as they were delivered to the Navy Board. Aboard ship they were subject to many hazards: 'he verily believes it is impossible for pursers to prevent such damage, but that slops will become damnified either by the rats eating them or by water coming to them in leaky ships and in hot countries'.[45] Though pursers were allowed one shilling in the pound on slops issued undamaged, it was the contractor who bore most of the risk, with no control over conditions of storage. Damaged slops were returned for full credit in large and unpredictable quantities, 'so eaten or rotten that it hath not been presently discoverable whether the remains were parts of waistcoats or parts of breeches'.[46] What was issued was paid for long in arrears; in 1709 Harnage was owed £44,553 9s 1d for three years' supplies. So onerous were the terms of this business that no one would undertake it but by selling shoddy slops (as it was complained) at high prices. Public money was saved, and the risk was offloaded on to the contractor, but in the process the actual object of the exercise was lost sight of: giving the men access to the good clothes at fair prices which they needed.[47]

Naval stores from the Baltic lands presented different problems. The quantities required were large, and grew three- or four-fold between 1688 and 1714. As a natural result prices rose rapidly. In the fifteen months to the end of March 1689 the Navy paid £16,737 for hemp. In the financial year 1690–91 it was £49,933, and next year, £37,708. In the 1690s, moreover, the Board had to deal with a cartel among the hemp merchants.[48] Stockholm tar (actually produced in Finland, but shipped from Stockholm), the best product in its market, cost £6 a last in 1688, but £12 to £14 by 1694. In this trade the Swedish state monopoly Tar Company forced up prices. To combat it the Board patronized producers outside the Swedish empire in Russia, Norway and Courland,[49] but the damage to Finnish producers and Baltic shippers generally caused by the Great Northern War forced prices up to £17 5s a last of tar and £16 15s a last of pitch in October 1703. In 1704, the year tar briefly touched £36 the last, the Bounty Act established subsidies to colonial producers in New England. Their product was very expensive and unsatisfactory in quality, but the Board bought it because it helped to force down Swedish prices. Another problem was the Baltic shipping business, almost entirely in Dutch hands; the Board of Trade was established partly to manage this.[50]

Shipbuilding timber, especially plank and masts, was also imported from the Baltic, but here there was a wider range of producers, and New England came to dominate the small but valuable trade in 'great masts', large enough to make the lower masts of ships of the line. Some unsuccessful efforts were also made to develop Scottish masts after the Union of 1707.[51] For shipbuilding timber it was universally agreed that there was no good substitute for English oak, but it was becoming costly and difficult to find. It was not true, as contemporaries sometimes complained and historians sometimes repeat, that the supply was exhausted; the problem was the extremely high transport cost of whole trees moved by road, and the difficulty of finding them. Shipbuilding needed both 'standards' and 'compass timber'. Standards were tall, straight trees grown amongst underwood, usually in plantations combined with coppice, and might be for sale in parcels of a few score or even hundred trees at a time. Compass timber meant the crooks needed for 'knees' or brackets, and the curved pieces needed for futtocks. These came from oaks growing in the open, in parkland or hedgerows where the branches were free to spread. Few park owners would contemplate felling large numbers of trees at once (unless they were in urgent need of cash), while obtaining hedgerow oaks required going from farm to farm to buy a tree here and a tree there. The Royal forests tended to be managed, or mismanaged, in the interests of local officials and smallholders rather than the crown, and their yield was very disappointing. The Weald of Kent and Sussex contained the largest quantity of oaks in southern England, not far from the major dockyards, but its clay soil and notoriously bad roads meant that many of these trees were effectively inaccessible. In practice the Navy Board was reluctant to pay the transport cost of English oak growing more than fifteen miles or so from navigable water. In 1703, for example, it bought some oaks growing at Whinfell, south of Penrith, for £5 a load.[52] They were only twenty-five miles from the coast, but nearer forty by the only possible road. By the time they had been hauled to navigable water at Rockliffe, near Carlisle, shipped to Whitehaven and there transhipped to a seagoing vessel, the total cost had risen by more than 50 per cent – and the timber was still 500 miles from the nearest dockyard.[53]

The Victualling Board faced many of the same problems as the Navy Board with much weaker resources of experience, credit and reputation. The war of 1689 was already in progress before any money was voted to fight it, and it was much too late to prepare victuals. Urgent complaints arose almost at once from Torrington's fleet. 'I cannot but think some neglect has been in the provision', wrote Russell:

> The beef proves full of galls; though I do not know any harm in it, the men fancy 'tis poison, and in my one ship, several men has thrown over their provision, nor would they eat it till hunger made a necessity; and

no longer ago than yesterday, in several of the butts of beer, great heaps of stuff was found at the bottom of the butts not unlike to men's guts, which has alarmed the seamen to a strange degree.[54]

In November the House of Commons solved the problem in its own fashion by throwing the entire Victualling Board into the Tower. William III put pressure on the great Huguenot merchant Thomas Papillon to head a new Board, but even his honesty and good standing could not touch the essential problem. The Navy Estimates allowed 19s or 20s a man a lunar month for victualling, but the real cost of four weeks' naval victuals was about 23s, rising to 30s in years of bad harvests, and the number of men actually serving in the 1690s was sometimes as much as 40 per cent higher than that nominally voted. Prisoners of war were invariably, and troops transported overseas often, fed from naval stores without any additional vote to cover them. The Board resisted the adoption of a course, on the reasonable grounds that many of its suppliers were small men who could not wait for their money, but it had no cash for them, its credit ran away like water, and as the Board itself admitted, its accounts and methods of payment were in chaos.

> Through a continuance of many years in this disorder, the accounts . . . are perplexed and confused to such a degree as renders it now extremely difficult, if possible, to call the parties concerned to any tolerable account, either of cash or for those stores and provisions into which such cash hath been converted.[55]

The Smyrna convoy disaster of 1693, when the main fleet spent the entire summer on short allowance and was only briefly able to put to sea, was only the most prominent of the mishaps attributable to inadequate victuals, and it inspired another Parliamentary inquiry the following year.[56]

The new Victualling Board of 1701 brought about real improvements, especially in reducing its accounts to order, borrowing proper methods of record-keeping from the Navy Board, and starting an effective course. Some time after the Navy Board, the Victualling Board now adopted public advertisements for tenders, to make the best of its weak credit, but all its efforts were continually frustrated by poverty. Ships, even in home waters, were often on short allowance, but there was no cash to pay the men their 'shorto' (short allowance money) with which they might have made up the shortfall themselves. The quality of what was issued, especially the quality of salting and packing (and therefore the 'shelf-life'), was often poor. The Board's own establishments were inadequate and in the wrong place (the Thames rather than the South Coast), forcing it into a reliance on contractors who often delivered their products straight on board ship, with no check on quality or quantity but what the ship's own (frequently corruptible) officers could provide. For want of storage as well as brewing capacity the Board was repeatedly forced to brew in summer. Its credit weakened as the war continued. The new Victualling Course was already nine months in December 1702, fifteen months by December 1704, twenty-two months in December 1706, and twenty-nine months by December 1708. After a disastrous harvest, the Board had spent its entire annual vote before the end of July 1709, and its course reached thirty-three months that September – the point at which the Treasury marginally relieved it by decreeing that the interest in Navy and Victualling bills would be paid quarterly, rather than on maturity. Prices were still rising steeply, and the Board was paying at least 35 per cent above cash prices, when it could find sellers at all. In September 1710,

> this being the proper season of the year for making the large contracts for flesh, butter and cheese, for the two latter of which species as well as for salt we have made publication in the gazette appointing days for receiving tenders, but no persons came near us.[57]

By January 1711 the market price of beef oxen was 24s a hundredweight, and of hogs 35s, but the best tenders the Board could get for payment in bills were 42s and 65s respectively. Two months later all packing came to a halt when its coopers walked out, their pay fourteen months in arrears.[58]

Nevertheless the Victualling Board under Queen Anne was not an unmixed failure. The quality of the commissioners (a mixture of MPs, former sea officers, yard officers or other naval administrators) was higher than before, and many of them stayed long enough in office to acquire real experience. Its financial and administrative standards rose, and significant innovations were adopted, including (in 1704) the standard issue of fresh meat to ships in port. The first tentative efforts were made to set up regular victualling organizations overseas, in the Mediterranean and West Indies, to free squadrons from dependence on what they could carry from home. As soon as the war ended the Board began to tackle further reforms.[59]

Many of the same themes, of administrative disorder, and reform undermined by permanent financial crisis and intermittent political interference, distinguish the history of the Sick and Hurt Board as revived from 1689 to 1698. The standard form of the Navy Estimates did not recognize its existence, and its inadequate income was 'borrowed' from the votes for wages and victualling. Its accounts were described by the Navy Board in 1702 as 'so very irregular . . . that they could not be adjusted at this office', a defect attributed to the want of commissioners of 'naval education'.[60] Nevertheless it was involved in significant improvements, even if for the most part the initiative and the authority to carry them through came from above. The first naval physicians were appointed in 1691 at Russell's urging, to four home ports (Rochester, Deal, Portsmouth and Plymouth) and to the Red and Blue Squadrons of the main fleet (the Dutch formed the White). Greenwich Hospital was founded in 1694 as a home for disabled seamen, largely as a memorial to the beloved Queen Mary whose favourite project it had been.[61]

With the return of war a new Sick and Hurt Board was established in 1702 (maintained after the war until 1715), and although its responsibilities were still primarily administrative rather than medical, its members for the first time included two physicians. It had charge not only of sick and wounded seamen ashore, but of sick soldiers landed from ships, and for prisoners of war of all services. The notorious inadequacy of hired sick quarters (usually in inns) led it in 1704 to establish the first naval hospitals, run by contract. These too, however, were far from satisfactory. From Plymouth Captain Isaac Townshend reported,

> Having information that the hospital for sick and wounded at this place to which I had lately sent 60 men was very inconvenient and not fitting for their reception, I therefore this day sent one of my lieutenants and surgeons to it with command to give me an account of what they should observe touching the truth of that matter, who upon return do acquaint me that the rooms are very low and small having eight or ten beds in each, placed so close that you cannot easily pass from one to another and two in a bed, the light very little, not sufficient to give air, that some of the men were lying in their excrement and the linen in general very foul and scandalously nasty . . . I think men cannot reasonably be thought to recover so indifferently attended, pent up in such miserable lodging where they must certainly poison one another. It is an insufferable abuse to her Majesty's service: therefore in discharge of my duty to you and justice to the poor men I think myself obliged to tell you the hard usage they are under . . .[62]

Some hospitals were established overseas, and in 1711 the Navy's first purpose-built hospital was erected on an island in Port Mahón. The Board's finances were even more precarious than those of the rest of the naval administration. It had no course or bill system, but paid cash for everything, when it could get it. By September 1708 it was two years in arrears, and in the ten months to April 1711 it received no money at all.[63]

Prisoners of war presented a particular problem: to see them kept securely, in reasonable conditions would have been a real challenge even if money had been plentiful. Prisoner exchanges, either man for man or according a scale valuing each rank or rating in terms of numbers of seamen, lightened the administrative load, but required delicate negotiation; the object always being to recover as many English seamen as possible but return to France as few of the most useful categories as possible.[64]

In the long term one of the most significant developments concerned the Navy's relations with the rival medical corporations: the College of Physicians of London, the Barber-Surgeons' Company and the Society of Apothecaries. By demanding practical remedies for mass outbreaks of disease (something impossible and disreputable according to orthodox Galenic medicine), by distributing its official favours between the medical bodies, and by requiring (in 1709) that naval surgeons undergo a qualifying course in medicine (the physician's preserve), the Admiralty and Navy Board began to undermine the official divisions of the medical world. This effect was reinforced by an act of 1698 permitting 'discharged soldiers' to practise outwith guild regulations, which led to a growing number of ex-naval and military surgeons, trained to some extent as 'general practitioners', taking up practice ashore.[65]

Yet another organ of naval administration was the Transport Board, established in 1689 initially to handle the transport and supplies of the army in Ireland, though most of its work came to be the support of the British army in Flanders, and it also dealt with transatlantic expeditions. It was not clearly subordinate to the Admiralty, but often received orders from a Secretary of State via the Treasury, which could generate confusion. This board was finally wound up in 1702, after prolonged efforts to clear up its accounts. As the Navy Board declined to take on the transport service, another was then appointed, unofficially until it received a patent in 1710, and was finally wound up in 1717. The Transport Board had no Parliamentary vote, no course, no credit and very little order; but as with the other Boards, its administrative standards improved markedly under Queen Anne. In 1704 the Board received its first Parliamentary vote (£60,000, to set against the £263,040 it had spent since the beginning of the war). The appointment of the very efficient Thomas Colby (whose uncle of the same name was on the Victualling Board) as a third commissioner in 1705 led to the adoption of proper accounts and records, and payment in course.[66]

The Prize Commission was set up in 1689 to regulate the sale of naval prizes, and deduct the Lord Admiral's tenth share. It had frequent cause to complain of captains who sold their prizes irregularly (especially on foreign stations, where Vice-Admiralty courts were few and often corrupt), cheated their crews or failed to return the needful paperwork. Sea officers in their turn regarded the Commission as a racket (probably unfairly), and resented the fact that privateers seemed to be more favourably treated than themselves. They finally got what they wanted with the 1708 Prize Act (part of the Whig opposition's attack on the Admiralty), which abolished the Commission and the Admiralty tenth, awarding the whole value of prizes to the captors.[67]

The status of the Ordnance Board, working largely for the Navy but independent of it, was not changed in 1689. It continued to generate some administrative friction, especially over such demarcation questions as who was responsible for shipping guns from the gunwharf aboard ships afloat, but its real problem was the same as that of the naval administration: money. Its share of the naval vote varied from a minimum of 3.125 per cent (2s 6d out of £4) between 1698 and 1701, to a maximum of 8.23 per cent (7s out of £4 5s) from 1694 to 1697. With this it bought about 2,000 tons a year of guns and shot in the early 1690s, rising to a maximum of 5,240 tons in 1697–8. In 1689 it was paying £14 a ton for guns in a rough state, or £18 finished; by 1694 these prices had risen about 15 per cent. Between 1690 and 1696 it added about 2,900 guns to the Navy's stock, which by 1697 totalled 10,350. The new, lighter, gun establishment of 1703 called for the casting of 6,915 tons of new guns, costing about £100,000, but nothing extra was voted to cover it, and it was some years before the Board had the guns to meet the requirement (one reason why English ships remained over-gunned). Its gunwharves and stores were inadequate and in the wrong places, though building new gunwharves at Portsmouth (1705–10) and Plymouth (1719–20) improved the situation. Like the Victualling Board, it set up its first overseas agents in the Mediterranean and West Indies under Queen Anne.[68]

At the root of all the difficulties of naval administration over twenty-five years lay the evil of poverty. The Navy's problem was not that Parliament did not support it, but that it was too ignorant to do so effectively. No consolidated naval accounts were presented to Parliament or anyone else. The Treasurer of the Navy's 'declared account' showed only his personal financial relation with the Exchequer, and was always years out of date. Parliament seldom voted the whole sum mentioned in the Navy Estimates, assuming the crown would somehow make up the rest; furthermore it largely overestimated how much, and how quickly, the taxes it did vote would yield. Spending departments like the Navy Board received revenue from the Exchequer in the form of 'tallies' or assignments, but the tax funds assigned ranged from the reliable and prompt to the 'remote' and semi-fictional, and it was not unknown for them to be assigned twice. At Michaelmas 1693 the naval debt was £1,782,597, of which £1,483,804 represented a shortfall between revenue voted and received. The sums which Parliament had voted, and which it imagined had been received, were less than £300,000 short of the real requirement, and it was apt to attribute any further discrepancy to corruption. The form of the Navy Estimates itself did very little to clarify thinking. The small 'Ordinary' estimate was supposed to cover civil administration and the upkeep of ships in reserve. The 'Sea Service' estimate, which provided the bulk of the Navy's income, was expressed in terms of a number of men for a twenty-eight day month. The number was 7,040 in 1689, rose to 33,692 in 1694, then remained at 40,000 for the rest of the war and the whole of the next war from 1702 to 1712. This figure was purely a financial abstraction; it bore no fixed relation to the number of real men actually serving. The multiplier was £4 a man a month, except in 1691 and 1693 to 1697, when it was £4 5s. This figure was then divided in slightly varying proportions into four categories: wages (usually 30s), 'wear and tear' (27s to 30s), victuals (19s or 20s), and ordnance (from 2s 6d to 7s). The overall total was found by multiplying the monthly rate by the number of men voted, and that product by thirteen months and one day. In theory 'wages' went to the officers and men, 'victuals' to the Victualling Board, 'ordnance' to the Ordnance Board, and 'wear and tear' covered everything else. In practice only the Ordnance and Victualling Boards received what they were allocated, which was insufficient in both cases. Much of the 'wages' vote was borrowed by the Navy Board for more urgent requirements. Parliament sometimes made Extraordinary grants, particularly in these years for dockyard works at Portsmouth and Plymouth, but its last vote for new ships was in 1696. On a strict construction, 'wear and tear' covered only repairs, and thereafter naval officials were afraid of incurring Parliament's wrath by building ships without authority. They did not stop building in reality, but they increasingly covered their activities under the fiction of a static list of ships each of which periodically underwent a 'great rebuild'. All naval activities cost more money than was coming in. There was virtually no long-term system of borrowing, and the short-term credit of the Navy and the government wilted rapidly.[69]

The establishment of the Bank of England in 1694 did a great deal to stabilize short-term government credit. Essentially a group of wealthy and eminently credit-worthy Whig City financiers received a valuable monopoly of joint-stock banking in return for making a large loan to the government and buying up many outstanding tallies. The new corporation also issued 'bank notes' payable on demand, which circulated like money and had the effect of increasing both its own resources, and the liquidity of the economy.

For a short time the Bank worked, but by 1696 it was overtaken by a crisis. In this period all states depended on silver or gold coinage. If they ran a trade deficit, it could only be covered by exporting bullion and deflating the economy by reducing the volume of circulating coin. The English silver coinage was composed of hammered coins easily clipped by coiners, so that its real silver content was falling fast below its face values. For the first few years of the war the illegal profits in silver clippings made by the coiners pumped liquidity into the system and made it possible to send silver abroad to pay for the army in Flanders and the fleet in the Mediterranean, but this could not last. By 1696 public confidence in the coinage had evaporated (the golden guinea, notionally worth 21s 6d, was trading at up to 30s by 1695), economic activity was collapsing – and the harvest was a disaster. At the worst possible moment, the government was driven to call in the old coins and melt them into new silver coin with milled edges, impossible to clip. For some months any sort of coin was almost unobtainable, and the new issue of coinage, at double the weight but the same face value as the old, was necessarily much smaller. This had a severely deflationary effect on the economy, and made for an acute shortage of coin, especially the small change useful to the poor. Naval administrators, already sufficiently short of money in any form, found it impossible to find coin with which to pay cash. The Bank of England's credit collapsed, and the rival Tory Land Bank scheme proved a fiasco. In the long run the recoinage made a resumption of normal economic activity possible, but in the short term it completed the financial crisis which brought the war to an end in 1697.[70]

In finance as in naval administration, the years just before and during the War of the Spanish Succession saw important long-term reforms, masked by short-term crisis. In particular the Treasury began to issue the first long-term government 'funded' loans, meaning those whose interest was guaranteed by Act of Parliament to come from a named tax fund. Most of these funds were excises: reliable internal consumption taxes levied by the relatively efficient and uncorruptible officials of the Excise Office. At the same time the remark-able growth in English overseas trade, and especially the gold imports yielded by the Portugal trade, made it possible to finance a 'forward strategy', with troops and ships deployed overseas without draining the money supply. The problem of financing war was by no means solved, and by 1710 the naval debt had reached the unsustainable level of £5,747,822,[71] but the crisis of 1711, which forced both government and Parliament to study the national debt in detail, led to a large increase in funded debts, and special taxes to pay for them, including duties on coffee, tea, books, playing cards, calicoes, candles, coal, hackney coaches, linens, leather, paper, parchment, soap, silks and Irish salt. Harley, now Earl of Oxford, completed his fiscal triumph by floating the South Sea Company, a joint-stock company (and another Tory alternative to the Bank of England) which took over much of the outstanding government short-term debt in return for an allegedly lucrative trading concession in Spanish South America which Oxford obtained at the peace negotiation.[72]

This war ended, therefore, like the last one, in financial collapse, but it also heralded new fiscal practices which in the long run were to transform the capacity of the British state to make war. Particularly under Queen Anne, the efficiency of naval administration, and the level of Parliamentary knowledge and scrutiny, had grown considerably. Contemporaries, however, were more impressed by the scenes of financial catastrophe and political persecution through which they had lived, than by the clouded possibilities of a better future. Josiah Burchett, Secretary of the Admiralty, published two works after the war, his *Complete History of the most Remarkable Transactions at Sea*, and his epic poem, *Strife and Envy since the Fall of Man*. Both were clearly based on his experience as a naval official.[73]

THIRTEEN

Our Mob

Social History 1689–1714

The immediate effect of 1688 on the sea officer corps was the dismissal of Dartmouth (who died in the Tower in 1691), Strickland and four captains (Sir William Jennings, John Tyrwhitt, John Grimsditch and William Constable) who were suspected to be Catholics. In all 10–15 per cent of the 157 commissioned officers in Dartmouth's fleet resigned or were dismissed. Strickland, Jennings and six other captains followed James II into exile, and for the most part took service in the French navy. All were followers of Dartmouth or enemies of Herbert, who had little to hope for under the new regime. Most of the officers, however, seem to have taken a professional attitude to the revolution, in the sense that they thought first of their careers. In 1689 87 per cent of the captains serving had first been commissioned under James II, and in 1690 it was still 75 per cent after some heavy casualties and the intrusion of Williamite supporters such as Captain James Wishart, a Scotsman resident in Holland, who arrived in 1688 as a subaltern in the Dutch army.[1]

There was no wholesale political purge, then or later, but throughout William III's reign the mistrust and disloyalty of the political world were fully reflected in the officer corps, making it very difficult for any ambitious officer to avoid taking on his patron's politics. Though Russell does not seem to have been unduly partisan in his recommendations, he was certainly believed to be so, and widely disliked for political as well as personal reasons.[2] While Prince George was Lord Admiral, Churchill blocked the promotion of Whig officers like Byng and Norris who were followers of Russell, and the Tory administration in 1711 did the same.[3] A few admirals, notably Rooke, Leake and Shovell, tried with mixed success to remain neutral in politics, but both Rooke and Leake suffered for it. Admirals were subject to frequent Parliamentary interference, and as Shovell remarked, 'there is no storm as bad as one from the House of Commons'.[4] Doing one's best was no protection 'from censure in

London, where men judge of the wind and weather at sea as the smoke of their tobacco drives, and accordingly a man is pulled to pieces by common fame,'[5] Russell complained in 1691, and next year his own experience showed that even a victory did not guarantee approval.[6] 'Parliaments are grown into a habit of finding fault, and some Jonah or other must be thrown overboard if the storm cannot otherwise be laid,' declared William III's last Secretary of State James Vernon in 1697. 'But if the great Leviathan will be amused by an empty barrel it is a composition easily made.'[7] The officers whose careers suffered from Parliamentary censure did not find it so amusing. They included Killigrew in 1690, Delavall, Shovell and Killigrew again in 1693, Carmarthen in 1695, Sir John Munden in 1702, Rooke in 1703, Sir Charles Hardy and Sir William Whetstone in 1707.[8] While politicians, and elderly officers retired from the sea,[9] were still obsessed by the obsolete issue of 'gentlemen versus tarpaulins', nobody cared to draw attention to the very present problem of political interference.

The sense that careers depended more on friends in Parliament than on duty performed at sea contributed to other problems in the officer corps. Russell (himself the outstanding example of a political admiral) had a low opinion of the quality of the sea officers.

> Much the greater number has neither the resolution to do their duty nor the sense to distinguish when they do or do not . . . Our officers are most of them the scum of the seafaring mankind, who cannot get bread in any other service, by the help of friends get in to the King's service, without having any other merit but being very morose and unmannerly, which is taken for courage, and being dirty and slovenly, for seamanship.[10]

Some of this can be ascribed to the disdain of a duke's grandson for ill-bred 'tarpaulins', and to Russell's own sour temper, but the problem of cowardice was not imaginary. Even an admiral, Carmarthen, ran away from his own squadron when he took them for French.[11] After the battle of Barfleur the courage of some captains was suspected, and two lieutenants were dismissed for taking their ships out of line after their captains were killed.[12] The fierce convoy battles of these wars led to a number of captains and lieutenants being sentenced to death or dismissed from the Navy, besides lesser punishments.[13] Though many contemporaries wished to believe that cowardice was the mark of either gentlemen or tarpaulins (according to their prejudice) it seems in fact to have had little to do with social origin, but everyone's morale and *esprit de corps* were undoubtedly affected by the sense that ignorant and vindictive Parliamentarians were the judges of officers' efforts.

Beside these real problems, however, the Navy and its officers were evolving rapidly under the strains of prolonged war and rapid growth. To provide a full complement of commissioned officers for all the ships in service in the summer of 1690 required 109 captains, fifty-eight masters and commanders, and 202 lieutenants. By 1705 the equivalent figures were 144 captains, sixty-nine masters and commanders and 354 lieutenants; an increase of over 50 per cent in fifteen years.[14] The first official seniority list was issued in 1691, while in 1694 officers' pay was virtually doubled (though officers, like their men, were paid only at the end of a commission which might last several years), and a regular scale of half-pay was introduced for unemployed officers. In 1700 the pay-scales were reduced again, and half-pay was limited to the first fifty captains, 100 lieutenants and thirty masters on the list. Finally in 1713 new seniority lists were issued, with an establishment granting half-pay to all captains and lieutenants who 'stand fair to be employed when there shall be occasion', though it remained as unclear as ever whether half-pay was a reward for past service or a retainer for future services. At the same time Sixth Rate ships were allowed post-captains.[15]

No half-pay was provided for admirals on the 1700 scale, which led to the administrative expedient of 'dormant commissions' for flag-officers not serving, allowing more than one to each rank. In 1702 the White Squadron was revived after having been in abeyance since 1666, assigned first to the French and then to the Dutch squadrons. Since the Dutch squadron of the main fleet was still present, this completed the disruption of the old, logical structure of flag ranks belonging to the squadrons and divisions of the fleet (which had really only existed between 1653 and 1665). At Malaga, for example, Rooke commanded as Admiral of the Fleet, with Rear-Admirals of the Red (Byng) and White (Dilkes) as his divisional commanders, and his Captain of the Fleet (Wishart) lately made a Rear-Admiral of the Blue at his demand, although there was already another officer in that rank elsewhere. Shovell as Admiral of the White commanded the Van in two divisions, with a Vice-Admiral of the Blue (Leake) under him; and the Dutch, likewise in only two divisions, made up the Rear.[16]

At all levels, there was still confusion about relative rank and seniority. As late as 1700 it was still possible to find captains serving in the rank of lieutenant, and a lieutenant as a gunner. It was not quite clear whether masters and commanders (who had no half-pay establishment) were truly a distinct rank or merely a species of lieutenant, or possibly a species of captain. All masters and commanders, being 'commanders' in the then sense of the word (i.e. commanding officers of ships), were addressed as 'Captain', and to avoid

ambiguity the rank of full captain was called 'post-captain' (hence on promotion to it an officer 'took post' or was 'made post'). Within ranks both the
principle and practice of seniority were disputed. In 1692, for example, Captain
David Lambert of the *Breda* came into Spithead wearing a broad pendant to
find Captain George Mees of the *Ruby* flying one already, as Russell reported
to the Admiralty. 'Captain Lambert, it appears, expected to have had his post
from the date of his commission in 1664, since when, till he came into the
Newcastle, he has never been in the service.'[17] Captains claimed that those at
the head of the list had a prescriptive right to flag rank, but the Admiralty
denied it, and moreover insisted that it could promote admirals from what
seniority, and to what rank, it pleased. Sir Richard Haddock was promoted in
1690 directly from Captain to joint Admiral of the Fleet. He at least was a
captain of twenty-four years' seniority (and the serving Controller of the
Navy), but in 1708 Captain Lord Dursley, aged twenty-eight and with less than
seven years' seniority, was promoted Vice-Admiral of the Blue over the heads
of more than 100 captains. So experienced an officer as George Byng thought
that there was a rank of Admiral of the Red, which had never existed, while
the appointment of commander-in-chief and the rank of admiral of the fleet
were not distinct. The refusal of Dutch admirals to serve under English officers
not senior to them tended to force an artificial inflation of English flag ranks.[18]

Further confusion was added by those officers who held rank in both the
Navy and the army, not necessarily corresponding to each other. Shovell was
senior to Carmarthen as an admiral, but junior to him in the Marine regiment
to which they both belonged. Several sea officers used their Marine ranks at
sea, among them 'Colonel' Richard Kirby, shot for failing to support Benbow.
Others served in both capacities, alternately or even simultaneously. Captain
Charles Skelton, lost in the wreck of the *Coronation* in 1691, was both a
post-captain, commanding the ship, and a Marine captain, commanding her
Marine detachment. George Forbes (later Vice-Admiral and Earl of Granard)
served in the Navy during the Spanish Succession War with some distinction,
and was a post-captain by 1706, but he still found time to pursue military
careers in Holt's Marines and the Horse Guards. He fought as a sea officer at
Malaga in 1704, and as a cavalryman at Villaviciosa in 1710. After the war he
specialized in his naval career – insofar as a career can be called specialized
which made him at various times a Scottish MP at Westminster, an Irish
peer in Dublin, Governor of the Leeward Islands, British ambassador to
St Petersburg, and commander-in-chief of the Austrian navy.[19]

Charles II's new system for officer entry was severely disrupted by the
accession of a king who was not interested in the Navy. The 'king's letter', so

precious under Charles II and James II, now declined rapidly in value as intelligent young men sought patronage elsewhere. By 1708, when Prince George was sending Byng in the Mediterranean blank warrants for Volunteers per Order to fill up as he pleased, there was evidently no one left in London who was interested in their careers. The 'king's letter boy' no longer had any real connection with the sovereign, or even her husband. The natural consequence was that the numbers seeking to become officers by this route declined: they made up fewer than half of the 695 lieutenants commissioned between 1702 and 1712. For the same reason the regulations had to be clarified in 1702 to allow any person with the qualifying age and sea-time (in 1703 the age was fixed as twenty, and the sea-time increased to four years) to be examined for lieutenant.[20] In social terms the collapse of royal patronage reinforced the admirals' influence, and effectively ended any hope of making the officer corps socially exclusive, though even so well-informed a contemporary as Burchett did not immediately notice. 'Now the volunteers being grown mighty numerous and very chargeable to the Navy, and all the commission officers chosen out of them,' he lamented in 1711, 'there is no room left for the poor seaman of any sort, warrant officers and others (out of which many considerable officers have been produced, as namely Lawson, Harman, Kempthorne, Berry, Narbrough and Sir Cloudesley Shovell, to name no more) to hope for any preferment, which I take to be a discouragement to them.'[21]

As Burchett indicates, the flag-officers of his day were of diverse origins. There was a small but conspicuous group of noblemen like the Duke of Grafton, the Marquis of Carmarthen, Lord Berkeley of Stratton and Lord Dursley (later Earl of Berkeley), most of them first brought into the Navy (and in the case of Grafton, the world) by Charles II. But Benbow, possibly the son of a Shrewsbury tanner, started his career as a waterman's apprentice, while Sir Andrew Mitchell began in Scottish merchantmen and was pressed into the Navy in 1672. Sir John Leake was the son of the gunner who had saved the *Princess* in 1667. Sir John Jennings was the fifteenth son of a struggling Shropshire squire, and John Baker the stepson of a Deal carpenter.[22] With men like this dispensing the patronage, and the officer corps growing very rapidly, there was no room for the social exclusiveness which the French navy of the day was trying with mixed success to enforce.[23]

Men were, as always, the next most difficult essential of naval war to find after money, and when the new Admiralty asked the Navy Board in 1689 how to man the Navy, they could only reply that 'we are mightily at a loss what answer to make'.[24] The manning problem was indeed more intractable than ever before. The Dutch Wars had been short and largely seasonal. These wars were nine and ten years long respectively, increasingly fought all the year round, and with substantial forces, even at times the main fleet, in distant waters. Short-term solutions would not do – but long wars also opened new possibilities, in particular of training, which had been impossible in the brief crises of the earlier wars. The number of men borne on ships' books was already nearly 22,000 over the winter of 1689–90, and over 33,000 the following summer. It then rose steadily to a maximum of 48,500 in 1695, and was still nearly 45,000 in 1697. The figures for the next war were similar: 33,000 in 1702, the first full year of war, over 40,000 next year, 46,000 in 1706, and around 47,000 between 1709 and 1711.[25] London was by far the biggest English port and the home of the main long-distance trades, so it was naturally the focus of the Navy's manning effort. In 1702 London had about 12,000 men in deep-sea shipping, out of perhaps 40,000 seamen in the whole country. A local census of seamen and watermen along the Thames in 1691 showed that 56 per cent were in the Navy, 16 per cent were away on foreign voyages, and the remainder were mostly elderly. These figures suggest that in the second year of the war, both the Navy and the merchant fleet were already in serious difficulties.[26]

At first the Navy tried to avoid wastage by the novel expedient (possibly suggested by Shovell)[27] of systematically keeping the big ships in pay over the winters from 1691 to 1694 (as distinct from postponing the paying off of ship ad hoc to meet a cash crisis, as the Commonwealth had done), and allowing the men leave by turns while their ships were laid up. This was unpopular: the men regarded three months off a year as their birthright, and the combination of keeping them on the ships' books but allowing them leave simply promoted desertion. Moreover the move towards permanent service implied something even more distasteful: 'turning over' men from one ship to another, taking them from their shipmates and the officers who, in many cases, had recruited them, and forcing them to serve amongst strangers.[28] 'We think that the turning men over will be a general dissatisfaction,' the joint admirals warned the Admiralty in February 1694,

> and, we fear, of ill consequence, having observed by experience that nothing can be more grievous to the seamen than turning them out of one ship into another; and, admit you should think fit to continue this way of proceeding, we can have no prospect that the great ships can be manned in time.[29]

Another expedient to eke out the supply of seamen was to embargo or regulate foreign trades. Initially all merchant shipping was forbidden to sail between February and May, but this was unworkable and rapidly abandoned. Instead 'short-sea' traders to European ports were permitted to sail with protections for a limited number of men, and a system of controls was imposed on the Atlantic trades which limited the number of men to a figure about half the prewar employment. In 1690, for example, the London tobacco trade to the Chesapeake asked for 1,000 to 1,200 men and was allowed 400. This was impossible, and in 1691 the figure was increased to 800 plus 200 foreigners. These restrictions, added to French attacks, bore heavily on English overseas trade just when it was most needed to pay for the army and fleet deployed overseas.[30] As a pamphleteer put it in 1693, they were 'like stopping the circulation of a man's blood in his body ... For it's the foreign trade which makes this nation potent and happy, and not that within ourselves. It's from thence all our riches flow; 'tis that which brings the bullion and coin into the kingdom.'[31]

The reaction of Parliament was to distribute haphazard privileges and protections guided more by political influence than economic logic. Its especial favourites were those trades supposed to be 'nurseries of seamen', above all the Newfoundland fishery, which annually took several thousand landmen across the Atlantic to spend a summer line-fishing from small boats, or working ashore splitting and drying the cod – an experience believed on rather slender grounds to turn them into seamen.[32] The coal trade from the Tyne to London, which really did employ many good seamen as well as warming MPs' hearths, was heavily protected, but the results were not helpful for the Navy. 'The late proclamation, forbidding all pressing of men out of colliers,' Russell reported in 1691,

> proves already very fatal to the fleet, for no men that have been put sick on shore ever return, but so soon as they can crawl from their sick quarters, get up to London, and the profit of one voyage to Newcastle answers the loss of five months' pay in their Majesties' service. Several letters have been sent to the fleet to put the men upon running away now they may sail in colliers without the hazard of being pressed, and if some means be not found out to stop this, we must either let the men die miserably on board ship, or absolutely disable the fleet.[33]

Scottish seamen (or at least the crews of Scottish ships) were in principle not liable to impressment until the 1707 Act of Union, though efforts were made to get the burghs to levy men for the Navy.[34] The Lords Lieutenant and Vice-Admirals of English counties still received orders to raise men, but the results were costly and unsatisfactory. The gangs they employed were paid by quantity rather than quality, and liable to choose those most likely to pay a good bribe for their release. In each of the years 1693, 1694 and 1696 the English counties were ordered to raise quotas amounting to 8,100 men, but it is very uncertain if they actually did.[35] In the five years 1702 to 1707 they supplied a total of only 1,675 men, 'very indifferent and few of them seamen', at an average cost of 33s a head.[36] More and more recruitment, both of volunteers and by impressment, was therefore entrusted to ship's officers, who had to live with the results and were less likely to take the 'shacome-filthies, ragga-muffings and scrovies' of which Captain George St Lo complained.[37] From 1693 the Navy Board chartered small vessels as tenders to big ships, with which to press out of incoming merchantmen at sea. Ships' press gangs ashore often devoted much of their effort to recruiting volunteers. There was something of an annual rhythm to the work: volunteers were recruited in the spring, for particular ships; then in the summer and autumn, as merchant ships came home, the gangs pressed the unwilling who had to go where they were sent. An Admiralty order of 1703 specifically required that volunteers be allowed their choice of ship, and allowed captains turning over to take the 'usual number' of their personal followers with them.[38] This was the more important as entrusting recruitment to ships' officers gave the fullest scope for officers to exploit good reputations or local connections, especially those whose connections were away from the south-eastern counties where the Navy recruited so heavily. Jeremy Roch, for example, a Plymouth man given command of the *Charles Galley* in 1689, raised 200 men there in a week. This sort of recruitment carried obligations:

> My men being all, except about 20, of this part of the country, I could not deny them a day's time to see their friends, as many as had them near at hand, and being merry ashore, I had much to do to get them aboard and was forced to leave some behind, though a great many came after us some leagues at sea, for I tarried as long as I could.[39]

Leave to individual ships was often given, in wintertime sometimes for several weeks, and the captains of ships in port seem in many cases to have had an informal attitude to the subject.[40] Captain Rupert Kempthorne of the *Woolwich*, lying at Deptford in 1691, professed himself unable to lend another ship a working party,

> for I have not the men on board the ship, but have sent my officers to look for them and give them notice of it. As fast as I pick them up and have a conveniency to send them to you, you may be sure I will.[41]

Charles Sergison, the long-serving Secretary of the Navy Board, thought it impossible to prevent men 'straggling' ashore when their ships were in port.[42]

Every ship needed a minimum of skilled young topmen to work aloft, and of experienced petty officers to take charge on deck, but the size of a warship's company was dictated by the number of guns to be fought, and most of the work was simple pulling and hauling – of gun tackles in action, of the falls of the running rigging in working the ship – which called for disciplined team-work but little individual skill. The longer ships stayed in commission, the more chance there was to develop this teamwork. Until 1740 every ship had three authorized complements: a low figure, sufficient for peacetime, a medium for wartime, and a high for distant voyages. In 1701 it would have needed 48,000 men to man the whole Navy on the high scale, but only 28,000 on the low, and fewer still if ships had been commissioned simply to navigate without fighting. In 1691, for example, the *Royal Charles*, whose peacetime complement was 560, was brought around from Portsmouth to Woolwich by a navigating party of 360. There was therefore much scope to 'dilute' the skilled manpower, so the simplest of all mechanisms to ease the shortage of seamen was to recruit landmen. One experienced officer suggested that only half of a ship's company needed to be able seamen. However scarce seamen became, there were always poor labourers to whom the prospect of regular food, lodging and wages (albeit long in arrears) was attractive.[43] Merchantmen and privateers also recruited landmen in wartime, and wartime wage rates drew in foreigners.[44] Captain Woodes Rogers of the Bristol privateers *Duke* and *Duchess*, sailing for the Pacific in 1708, recorded that

> Our complement of sailors in both ships was 333, of which above one third were foreigners from most nations; several of her Majesty's subjects on board were tinkers, tailors, hay-makers, pedlars, fiddlers, &c, one negro, and about ten boys. With this mixed gang we hoped to be well manned, as soon as they had learnt the use of arms, and got their sea-legs, which we doubted not soon to teach 'em, and bring them to discipline.[45]

The Navy's manning problem was a subject of concern to many people in public life, and attracted the attention of pamphleteers and Parliamentarians alike. Unfortunately very few of them had a good grasp of the problem, and their recommendations tended to range from the helpful but marginal to the mischievous and fantastic. Nearly every commentator assumed that seamen were plentiful, and therefore concentrated on attracting them into the Navy, when the real problem was that the wartime demand for men greatly exceeded the peacetime supply, and the seaman's skills took a long time to learn. The government's official statistics reckoned that there were about 65,000 seamen in England around 1700, which was undoubtedly a substantial over-estimate even if it includes all sorts of inshore fishermen and part-time seafarers.[46]

An act of 1703 encouraged boys to become apprentices at sea, which was useful in the long term, but it also allowed adult seamen to declare themselves apprentices to avoid the press (a loophole stopped in 1705), and it protected the coal trade almost completely. Another act permitted debtors to get out of prison to serve in the Navy, which was modestly useful. A 1708 proposal to raise naval wages and limit those paid in merchantmen at least addressed one element of the problem, but the financial provisions were dropped and the main effects of the bill as passed were to wind up the Prize Commission and grant the whole value of prizes to the captors; and to forbid pressing in the Americas, which provided seamen with another privileged sanctuary, and caused the British naval effort in the West Indies to decline sharply. In any case the worst problem with naval wages was not that they were too low, but that they were too late. Wartime rates in merchantmen were certainly higher, but with some warships on foreign stations unpaid for four years, the nominal level of wages was almost irrelevant.[47]

The most radical solution proposed to the manning problem was the registration of seamen. In 1696 Russell managed to pilot through an act establishing a voluntary register, which was intended to create a reserve of 30,000 men, paid a retainer of £2 a year with double prize-money, exemption from impressment or turn-over, and various other privileges. Given time and money, the scheme might have worked, but it was passed at the worst moment of the war, when both money and manpower were extremely short, and as usual Parliament provided no fund to back its notional generosity. Nearly 20,000 men registered, but when they found that their allowances were unpaid and they were turned over just as before, their initial enthusiasm disappeared, and the scheme collapsed.[48] Another attempt was made in 1706 when Prince George encouraged Shovell to draft a bill providing for a compulsory register with generous provisions, but so controversial and expensive a measure had no chance of Parliamentary support, and only its incidental provisions survived. One of them required that men be paid when they were turned over, but as usual in this period the legislation did not provide any of the money it required to be spent, and the sole result was the issue of 'Parliament tickets', negotiable only at an extravagant discount.[49]

Probably the single most effective contribution to the manning problem were the Marine regiments. Initially disbanded as part of James II's army, they were revived in 1690, and supplemented in 1693 by no less than six ordinary foot regiments. Abolished in 1699 by a suspicious Parliament which saw every red coat as a symbol of Williamite tyranny, they were re-formed again in 1702, and paid off in 1713. Though the marines were useful as musketeers in action, and as landing parties when required (notably in the capture of Gibraltar, which was entirely the work of English and Dutch Marines), their everyday contribution to the Navy was essentially as a source of unskilled manpower for working the ships. They never provided the 'nursery of seamen' which optimists had hoped for, but they contributed between 3,000 and 5,000 men to the Navy. Their great weakness was administrative: the military structure of proprietary regiments managed by their colonels was completely unsuitable for the small Marine detachments paid on their ships' books, and their financial affairs were from the beginning chaotic and corrupt. The military authorities blocked all the Navy Board's attempts to impose naval accounting standards and administrative systems.[50]

From the beginning both the quantity and quality of naval manpower, 'this raff and scum' as Rooke called it,[51] was the subject of frequent complaint by admirals.[52] 'Possibly our mob may prove the better of the two,' he wrote doubtfully in 1696, 'but whether this is a sufficient ground to venture our all upon, I must submit to wiser men's determinations . . .'[53] The sources give an impression, however (although no statistical stiffening can be given to it), that the problem was less acute during the Spanish Succession War. Complaints were fewer, and there seems to have been a greater effort to regulate the process of impressment; certainly there are a good many orders to release pressed men on either legal or compassionate grounds. Probably recruitment by naval parties produced more, and more suitable, men than the civil authorities had done, and undoubtedly the Navy's requirement could be more easily found when the English (and from 1707, Scottish) merchant fleet was growing fast.[54]

Before leaving the subject of manning, it is worth making a brief comparison with the French *système des classes*,[55] by which the seafaring population of coastal districts was registered for compulsory naval service, one year in three. This was widely admired in England,[56] and inspired both the 1696 and 1706 schemes, but so aggressive a symbol of arbitrary government as compulsory registration proved quite unacceptable to Parliament. Aside from its political disadvantages, however, the French system in the light of modern research reveals numerous practical defects. French Flanders and the Basque country, lying on the frontiers of France, were exempt, and the seamen of Provence, which was not, often escaped to Italian ports. The men of big commercial ports like Bordeaux and Nantes were scarce aboard warships, presumably because merchant shipowners found means to keep them off the registers.[57] The burden of service therefore fell disproportionately on the small ports and fishing villages of Brittany and Normandy, and did not reach many of the deep-sea sailors who would have been most useful. The system did nothing to increase the total supply of seamen, which, even on paper, was incapable of manning the main fleet without largely stopping seaborne trade. The revocation of the Edict of Nantes led to the flight of about 9,000 Protestant seamen, many of them the precious petty and warrant officers on which every ship's efficiency depended. In practice to man the French fleets of 1690 to 1707 required calling up most or all of the registered men simultaneously, and since this was extremely unpopular, it was necessary to use violent compulsion. In terms of inhumanity, there was little to chose between English and French methods. In terms of efficiency, the *système des classes* was capable of manning limited forces more quickly than the English could, a significant advantage in the early stages of mobilization, but it tended to exhaust France's smaller stock of seamen more quickly, and it did not provide the incentives to recruit and train landmen which existed in England.[58]

Of the daily lives of seamen it is necessary to speak with caution, for at the beginning of the eighteenth century, as now, the exceptional was newsworthy but the commonplace went unrecorded. Though sometimes represented by modern writers as a miserable proletariat, professional seamen were in fact not untypical of the skilled working classes of their day. They were predominantly literate, often surprisingly well educated, especially in languages, which they picked up on their travels, and in mathematics, which was the essential qualification for any ambitious boy who hoped to advance either in merchantmen or men-of-war. Most of them were the sons of seafarers, 'bred to the sea', but newcomers were attracted by travel and adventure. It was a young man's trade; few started later than fifteen or sixteen, and a seaman in deep-sea shipping was old at forty, though coasters tended to employ more of the oldest and youngest. Many older seamen were married, and it seems that on marriage they often settled in London, where there were many opportunities for a woman to earn a living while her husband was at sea.[59] For their sake Russell refused to sail in 1694 until his ships were paid: 'I could not bring myself to carry ships to sea, and the men unpaid, when hundreds of poor women was waiting for their husbands' money, to support their children and families.'[60] At least a few women went to sea in the Navy, officially or unofficially. Some officers took their mistresses: when Wheeler's squadron touched at Newfoundland in August 1693 a settler of Bay Bulls bought 'one of the officers' misses' for £100 to make his wife.[61] The Marine regiments followed military practice in permitting three men of every company to marry 'on the strength', whose wives and children accompanied them to sea.[62]

The problems of the Victualling Board, and the quality of its products, have already been described, yet, in the view of the long-serving naval physician Dr William Cockburn,

> whatever a sailor may complain of in the Royal Navy, his victuals are a great deal better, and his allowance larger, than in any navy or merchant-ships in the world. Their drink is as good table-beer as any family in England can drink; and the quantum is what they will.[63]

This was perhaps a somewhat optimistic view, at least as regards the beer, but even the morose Barlow thought the quality of naval food was one the reasons why it was irrational to desert to a merchantman.

> Many times they run away and leave eight or ten months' pay behind them and lose it, they being very foolish, for before they can make the money good again, their voyage is many times at an end. And their Majesties' ships are better victualled than most merchant ships are, and their pay surer, and there they have no damage to pay; and if they lose a leg or an arm they have a pension for it, and their work is not so hard, neither do they wear out so many clothes; all which things they find in most merchant ships.[64]

The increasing issue of fresh provisions did something to make up for the quality of the Victualling Board's packing and salting, while if the men could get their short-allowance money they could lay in stores for themselves. They could indeed do it without money if they were not watched: Leake in the Mediterranean had trouble with his men stealing grapes and cabbages ashore. Another crew bartered old clothes at the Cape Verde Islands for oranges, lemons, coconuts, pineapples, bananas, hens, hogs, goats and monkeys.[65] It was well understood among seamen that such provisions prevented scurvy.[66] The naval chaplain John Swanne noticed the effect of decent food on 'poor boys, thin and meagre and helpless, coming into the navy who have formerly lived hard . . . having everything in a plentiful manner at sea they thrive extraordinarily, beyond what anyone can imagine, and shoot up to be men on a sudden, after a prodigious manner'.[67]

Seafaring was a hard life, but not exceptionally deadly. It has been calculated that the mortality among English merchant seamen overall in these years was about 4.5 per cent a year to disease, 1 per cent to shipwreck and 0.5 per cent to accidents. In European and Atlantic trades the death rate was well below 1 per cent – much healthier than ashore – but it rose to about 10 per cent in East Indiamen and up to 25 per cent in slavers.[68] In the Navy there were a number of serious epidemics. In September 1689 Torrington reported 599 dead and 2,588 sick in his fleet, 'and this at an anchor where the men are not exposed to the weather as they are at sea'.[69] Russell's fleet wintering at Cadiz in 1694–5 lost considerably, while squadrons in the West Indies were repeatedly struck by yellow fever. Shovell returned from the Mediterranean in 1703 with 1,500 men dead and more ill than his three hospital ships could hold. These, however, were exceptional events and mortality was usually much lower. Hospital ships were no answer to the incapacity of contemporary medicine and surgery in the face of epidemic disease, but at least they provided some specialized care (including women nurses) and allowed infectious cases to be isolated from ship's companies.[70] James Christie, surgeon of the *Jefferys* hospital ship, claimed that 'we lose not so many in proportion as candid physicians in London own, viz. one of every five sick, and think that they come off well to boot'.[71] Dr Cockburn reckoned there were four deaths by illness or accident for every one killed in action. Leake stated that his flagship the *Prince George* in the Mediterranean lost 43 per cent of her complement over the years 1704 to 1706, but if true this was an extraordinarily high figure. At almost the same time the journal of Henry Watson, surgeon of the *Tiger* under his command, records 212 cases of 140 individuals (out of a complement of 250) over ten months, of whom seven died. These included one killed falling from aloft and one by a powder explosion, nineteen other injuries, 145 fever cases, 47 other ailments, and no killed or wounded in action. The death rate from all causes was 3.2 per cent a year of the ship's complement.[72]

Off-watch, seamen had time to relax, especially in men-of-war with their large crews. Music, reading and gambling were common pastimes.[73] Some ships had bands – 'trumpets, hautboys, and violins' in the case of the *Duchess*.[74] Drinking was universal. Good officers usually managed to keep their men more or less sober at sea, but in port it was impossible: 'Thus it is that seamen, having escaped drowning, drown their cares,' observed Captain Stephen Martin, 'and thus it is necessary that it should be, else no man would persevere in that kind of life.'[75] Wise captains like Thomas Phillips did not make unnecessary work, but allowed their men to relax: 'they are such a sort of people, that if they have justice done them, a good word now and then, and be permitted their little forecastle jests and songs with freedom, they will run through fire and water for their commander, and do their work with the utmost satisfaction and alacrity'.[76]

Discipline in the Navy was by now somewhat more severe than in merchantmen, but most contemporaries who complained about it were making a political point about the cruelty and cowardice of gentlemen captains rather than a dispassionate observation.[77] Rhetoric aside, men could expect to be whipped for theft and mutiny in both warships and merchantmen – even on occasion in privateers, whose discipline was notoriously relaxed – and similar punishments were awarded by magistrates ashore.[78] Many of the Navy's worst disciplinary problems were in any case with quarrelsome and abusive officers, not men.[79]

Seamen had no great reputation for religion, and Marius d'Assigny, a French Protestant refugee turned naval chaplain, denounced the 'impiety that reigns at sea where no manner of respect is shown to God, religion or ministers, where cursing and blasphemy is modish and the Devil is more respected and bears a greater sway than the Almighty Creator of all things'.[80] A more temperate observer, the purser Henry Maydman, thought the chaplains were the problem, 'for the maritime people are not naturally over zealous, yet they can often produce better temperance, chastity, modesty, honesty, courage &c than appears in some of these sparks which are taken from the altars of the universities'.[81] These are not impartial comments, however; both of them were implicitly invoking the ghost of the Commonwealth Navy to rebuke their contemporaries. There is no doubt that the demonstrative piety of the 1650s was out of fashion, but it not so easy to say that the real moral and religious standard of the average ship's company had collapsed. The Society for the Promotion of Christian Knowledge, founded in 1699, took a great interest in the spiritual welfare of seamen, and Shovell, Benbow and Rooke among others promoted its work. One chaplain suggested that 'the giving of a little tobacco to be joined to the good advice and instruction, if done with a due air of concern, will have wonderful effects', but the Society declined to finance this good work.[82]

FOURTEEN

Great Frigates

Ships 1649–1714

The Parliamentary forces fought the civil wars of the 1640s with a miscellaneous fleet mostly composed of armed merchantmen. The 'great ships' inherited from Charles I were of relatively little use to them, and the biggest of all, the *Sovereign* (ex-*Sovereign of the Seas*) and *Resolution* (ex-*Prince Royal*) spent most of the wars laid up. In the new strategic situation of 1649, with fast cruisers from Dunkirk and elsewhere wreaking destruction on English shipping, neither great ships nor armed merchantmen were ideal. Many of these raiders were of the typical Dunkirker type known as 'frigates'. As usual this protean word, which sows confusion in so many periods of naval history, was in the process of changing its meaning. The Dunkirker frigates were small, lightly built ships, long and low, with large crews but minimal armament, designed for short-range, high-speed operations against weakly defended targets. The first large English frigate is generally reckoned to be the *Constant Warwick*, built in 1645 as a private warship for a syndicate of Parliamentary officers led by the Earl of Warwick, but almost at once chartered, and later bought, for the State's Navy. Like the Dunkirkers she was very fast and very lightly built, 'trembling in the sea as the Turkish privateers do', in the words of Sir Phineas Pett, son of her builder.[1] The *Constant Warwick* was an outstanding success, soon imitated, but the pure frigate did not fulfil many English requirements. The need was for ships with as much as possible of the frigate's speed, combined with the robustness and stowage necessary to keep the sea and cruise for long periods. Thus the English frigate began to grow rapidly into a sort of frigate-like ship in a range of sizes, the word being applied ever more loosely until even the great *Sovereign* (after having her upperworks reduced in 1651) might be described as 'a delicate frigate (I think the whole world hath not her like)'.[2] Other languages like French acquired a verb 'to frigate', meaning to build long and low, and a corresponding adjective, so that Seignelay could report in 1672 that the English 'generally frigate their big ships much more than in Holland or France'.[3] The new fleet which the Commonwealth built in the early 1650s (fifty-four rated ships in the six years 1650–55) consisted largely of various sizes of ships loosely described as 'frigates'.[4]

The largest of these were the two-decker 'great frigates' of the Third Rate, of which the first was the *Speaker*, launched in April 1650, which may be regarded as the ancestor of English two-decker ships of the line for the next hundred years. Originally planned to carry forty-four guns, she was completed with fifty, and was carrying sixty by 1655, which put her clearly among the 'great ships' of the day. Frigate hulls were long and unhandy, ill-adapted to the continuous manoeuvre of Elizabethan gunnery tactics. Building ships in the frigate style which were large enough to fight in pitched battles implied a new idea of tactics, concentrated on broadside gunnery, with little expectation of hand-to-hand fighting. Admirals of an older generation like Ayscue objected to the great frigates precisely because they were too low, and consequently vulnerable to boarding. The design was in fact modified from 1650 by the addition of a forecastle, without which the new ships had proved very wet in a head sea, but it is clear that the English had decisively committed themselves to the idea of gunnery action before the outbreak of the First Dutch War, and well before the first experiments with the line of battle. The old Elizabethan tactic, in which a ship approached the enemy, fired off all her guns in turn and then withdrew to reload, was still being used (this seems to have been more or less how Ayscue fought the battle of Plymouth in 1652), but it was increasingly common for English ships to close their opponents and batter them broadside-on. From this it was only a short step to organizing the whole fleet in a line of battle. In the First Dutch War there were more naval battles in fifteen months than there had been in northern waters over the previous 150 years, and the tonnage of English warships built in the five years 1651 to 1655 was equal to all that added in the fifty-five years from 1588 to 1642. The result was a rapid development of ideas and designs which by the mid 1650s had transformed the 'great frigate' into the earliest form of what was later called the ship of the line. In just over ten years, the English Republic increased its fleet from the thirty-nine ships of 1649, to the 156 of 1660, of which no less than seventy-five were of the Fourth Rate or above, and reckoned able to lie in the line of battle.[5]

The growth of the English fleet was not so rapid under Charles II, but the size of English ships continued to increase, not least to match the new Dutch ships built during the Second Dutch War. Charles II's first shipbuilding programme in 1664 included two new three-decker Second Rates and ten

Third and Fourth Rates. A further ten ships were ordered in 1666, but the financial crisis stopped all but three of them. The king took a personal interest in these designs, and encouraged the movement to greater dimensions. The Navy Board as yet had no shipbuilder on it to impose any central control, and the king's knowledge of naval architecture was at least as good as that of many of the constructors. Francis Bayley of Bristol, one of the most successful of them, was all but illiterate and still built without draughting on paper at all. Charles realized well before some of the professionals, who were still wedded to the 'frigate' hull form, that more guns could only be carried with acceptable freeboard and stability by increasing the ships' beam.[6]

By the time of the next major English building programme, the 'thirty ships' of 1677, Sir John Tippetts was Surveyor of the Navy, the first shipwright to occupy the position which became established as that of the Navy's principal warship designer. Sir Anthony Deane, another eminent shipwright, was also on the Navy Board, but even so Charles II's personal influence, as we have seen, once more operated to increase the dimensions of the ships. The twenty Third Rates of this group were built as something like a class, and efforts were made to standardize the dimensions of their masts and spars. Their hull form, a successful expansion of the old frigate style with the beam necessary to carry a heavy armament, remained the basis of the design of English two-decker ships of the line up to 1755.[7]

As size and armament increased rapidly, all navies encountered difficulties in maintaining sufficient freeboard to keep the lower batteries usable in a seaway, and sufficient stiffness for ships to stand up to their canvas. In Allin's ship the *Plymouth*, 60, in 1664, 'we got in our guns before the bulkhead of the gunroom and the guns next the bulkhead in the gunroom; they lay always ploughing in the water when we bore sail'.[8] Even when designs were initially satisfactory, they tended to be loaded with more and more guns over their careers. In 1672, for example, the *Fairfax*, originally built for fifty-two guns in 1653 and then rated at sixty, was actually mounting seventy-two.[9] Even new ships had sometimes to be 'girdled' with extra planking on the waterline to increase buoyancy and stability. Narbrough commented on his ship, the new First-Rate *Prince* of 1670,

> The ports amidships are 3 ft 5 in free from the water. I do believe the ship will bear a good sail, for she stands at her bearing. Girdling the ship would make her one of the finest ships in the whole universe, for it would make her much more floatier and carry her guns higher, and she would bear the better sail and be a better and securer ship to receive shot, and I believe it will not prejudice her sailing.[10]

The new *Royal Charles* of 1673, built to replace the flagship lost in 1667, 'proves a mere table', as Prince Rupert complained, 'ships water with the least breath of wind, and in great gales her topsails may overset her'. Richard Haddock his flag-captain agreed: 'her only fault is she is tender-sided, in all respects otherways the best ship in the world'.[11] There were similar problems in other navies. The new *Excellent*, Tourville complained in 1680, 'has her main battery submerged and the scuppers not two inches clear of the water',[12] and this was a common complaint of French ships of this period. Only the Dutch, especially the Amsterdam ships with their full, square sections and flat floors, were stiff and able to carry their guns high – though the same hull form made them slow and leewardly. Even the Dutch had failures amongst their biggest ships: the Zealand-built *Koning Willem*, 90, of 1692, was too tender to open her lower gunports or carry her topsails in any reasonable wind.[13]

Such defects, serious enough in the North Sea, were much worse in the heavy weather of the open Atlantic to which war against France called the Dutch and English navies. Under the expert guidance of Charles II, the Royal Navy had evolved rapidly to match the circumstances of the Dutch Wars. Now an equally rapid evolution was called for to face another strategic situation, but there was no one to guide it. William III was not interested, and in the chaos of competing jurisdictions which ran the Navy of the 1690s none of his ministers or officials had the knowledge to understand, or authority to impose, the necessary changes. No Surveyor could have done it without powerful government and Admiralty support, and it did not help that Sir John Tippetts died in 1692, replaced by the able but young and largely unknown Edmund Dummer. In 1690 Parliament voted money to build seventeen Third Rates and ten Fourth Rates, specifying not only the tonnages, as in 1677, but the number of guns as well. This generated a major problem, for the figures were not based on actual designs or expert assessment. In particular, it was impossible to build satisfactory eighty-gun Third Rates of only 1,100 tons as the Act demanded. But in the atmosphere of suspicion which pervaded English politics, admirals and naval administrators alike understood how dangerous it was to thwart the will of Parliament. The result was a bad class of ships; cramped, weak, unstable and overgunned, which in effect abandoned the developments of Charles II's reign and reverted to the 1650s, just when the strategic situation required movement in the opposite direction. Their structural weakness was to an extent remedied by connecting the quarterdeck and forecastle to make a complete upper deck, thus deepening the hull and converting them into quasi three-deckers, but in all other respects they remained an unhappy class. Then from 1696 to 1745 Parliament voted no more money for shipbuilding, and the Navy's needs were increasingly met by 'great rebuilds' of existing ships, which were largely or entirely broken up and reconstructed, sometimes on the old bottom, sometimes merely incorporating some of the old timbers. Great rebuilds were not completely inflexible, and it was common for the dimensions of the new ship to exceed those of the old, but they constituted another brake on change just when the strategic situation demanded rapid evolution.[14] To all this should be added the psychological effect on the ship designers of a regime which punished initiative and blocked development. 'It seems a matter very worthy enquiry,' noted Pepys,

> how far the emulation among builders (both the King's and private men) is now [1694] kept alive in proportion to what it always was during the reigns of our two last princes. Whose personal concernments for and knowledges in that affair led them not only to the giving a liberty, but even encouraging all men of that trade, beginners as well as old practisers, and even assistants and foremen as well as master-builders, nay, down to the very barge-maker and boat-maker, to bring their draughts to them, and themselves vouchsafed to administer occasion of discoursing and debating the same and the reasons appertaining thereto. Not only to the great and universal encouragement of the men, but improvement of their art to the benefit of the state.[15]

This seems to be a just comment. The techniques of naval architecture continued to develop in England under the later Stuarts, and both French and Dutch designers tried to adopt the English practices of draughting designs on paper, and making blocks and models for the guidance of shipwrights, but after 1688 innovation in ship design was stifled.[16]

Another discouragement to progress was the development of the Establishments which classified ships into the six Rates according to the number of their guns.[17] The idea of classifying ships went back to Tudor times, but it had been largely abandoned in the miscellaneous fleets of the 1650s. It was Pepys, characteristically, who in connection with the 1677 building programme drew up a 'solemn, universal and unalterable' classification of the Navy, providing the number and weight of guns for each ship, and calculating the complements from the guns' crews. Seven men were allowed to a 42-pounder, five to a 32-pounder, four to an 18-pounder and so on, which was half a gun's crew in each case, or enough to man one broadside for continuous firing. This was the final administrative recognition that the age of the line of battle had arrived.[18] In practice, as Sir Thomas Chicheley the Master of the Ordnance pointed out, the ordance establishment could not be fully applied, 'in that the

Office of the Ordnance cannot gun his Majesty's ships otherwise than as the natures and weights of the guns his Majesty is at present master of will admit.'[19] Neither this nor the lighter 1703 establishment (equally theoretical, for the same reason) imposed any restriction on ship design. Their intent was simply to standardize armaments with a view to administrative and operational convenience, perhaps also easier relations between the Admiralty and the Ordnance Board.[20]

The establishment adopted by Prince George's Admiralty in 1706, however, went much further in fixing the leading dimensions of each class of ship. In principle the Navy was now committed for ever to a range of existing classes, with no provision for development or adaptation to circumstances. In practice the new rules were never slavishly followed, and were replaced by a new establishment in 1719, but they constituted another obstacle to change. At that moment, with the last operational French fleet about to be scuttled at Toulon, it hardly mattered, but with hindsight it is clear that the weakness of English naval government had needlessly hampered the essential process of evolution in ship design to meet new strategic realities. The result was that English warships, compared gun for gun, were notably smaller, and in some cases weaker, than their foreign contemporaries. An English eighty-gun ship had a broadside of only 1,104 lbs, compared with the 1,560 lbs of a Portuguese eighty. A Spanish eighty was the same size as an English ninety, and had almost as heavy a broadside: 1,440 lbs, against 1,642 lbs for a ninety-gun ship on the 1702 establishment. Only the Baltic navies, with severe limitations on draught, continued to build ships no larger than English.[21]

If English ship design stagnated and even regressed from the 1690s, innovation seems to have continued in matters which were beneath Parliamentary scrutiny. In the 1670s the problem of the boring shipworm in tropical waters had been addressed by the adoption of thin lead sheathing on the underwater hull. This ran into an unexpected, and with the knowledge of the time inexplicable, problem, which we can now identify as electrolytic corrosion. In the *James*, for example, 'the ruther being loose they unhung it and hoisted it upon deck where they found the pinckle irons quite consumed and eaten by the salt of the lead or some other matter which corrodes from the lead that eats the iron and nails'.[22] This, ultimately unsuccessful, innovation was adopted with Charles II's active interest and encouragement.[23] By contrast, an important and eminently successful technical development happened some time in the 1690s without generating any interest, or even record. Since the sixteenth century, ships had been steered with a whipstaff, a vertical lever connected to the inboard end of the tiller, handled by a steersman who stood on the deck above the tiller flat, with a limited view of the sails through a small hatch cut in the deckhead above his head. The whipstaff was fragile, unmanageable in heavy weather, and allowed only restricted helm movement (about 7° either side of amidships). At some date in the late 1690s, English ships began to adopt the steering wheel, which doubled the arc of movement of the rudder, and allowed the ship to be steered by up to ten men in heavy weather, standing on the quarterdeck, beside their officers, with a clear view of sails and binnacle. It was exactly the sort of detailed technological innovation which made an essential and often vital difference to the performance of warships. Though it was quickly reported by French naval intelligence, the French navy was thirty years behind in adopting it.[24]

The rig and rigging of ships offers similar contrasts. Reef-points, which for some still obscure reason had fallen out of use in the mid-sixteenth century, returned to topsails in the 1640s, and replaced bonnets on the courses soon afterwards, making it easier to shorten or make sail as the weather changed. At about the same time the adoption of staysails helped to balance the sail plan when sailing close-hauled. Early in the eighteenth century jibs set on a jibboom began to replace the cumbersome spritsail topsail as man-oeuvring sails to push the ship's head about when tacking or wearing. All these developments tended to make ships easier and safer to handle, with smaller crews in proportion to their size.[25] At the same time there was steady progress in the quality of English cordage, which was lighter for a given strength than French, with reduced weight and windage aloft and less friction running through the blocks. It was already true, as it was throughout the eighteenth century, that the English Navy was much more interested in such matters of practical technology than in the theoretical science which carried so much prestige in France. It was also true already that the efficiency of French naval intelligence provided ministers in Versailles with a flow of accurate reports on English naval technology, but the conservatism of French officers and dockyards continually frustrated their attempts to copy it. French shipbuilders, for example, fastened their ships with iron spikes where English and Dutch shipwrights used wooden trenails – lighter, and much more durable. Because iron and oak react badly on one another, the working lives of French ships tended to be prematurely ended by 'nail-sickness'. Colbert and several of his successors were correctly informed about this, but they were unable to change French shipbuilding practice.[26]

In spite of its early interest in frigates, the English Navy built relatively few cruising warships in the seventeenth century. Ships down to the Fourth Rate were thought of primarily as ships of the line. Scouting was neglected by many admirals, convoy escort was more common in peacetime than in war, and the remaining functions of small warships were relatively limited. In battle small frigates had an important role in beating off enemy fireships, and covering the advance of friendly fireships. Since fireships were small, and for obvious reasons often old and decrepit, they were easily sunk by the gunfire of big ships, and their best chance was to approach under cover of smoke or confusion. Even so they were usually effective only against grounded or disabled ships, and they often acted more as a psychological than a practical weapon, spreading panic among threatened crews. The small warships' limited functions did not call for high speed or long range, and there was a tendency for English Fifth and Sixth Rates to be miniature versions of the ships of the line rather than a distinctive cruising design, many of them mounting their guns on one and a half or two decks. The convoy warfare of the 1690s greatly increased the demand for escorts and led to large building programmes which raised the proportion of 'cruisers' from just over one for every five ships of the line in 1680, to one for two in 1700. The requirement, however, was for a powerful armament to fight off French raiders rather than for speed, so like their larger sisters, English cruisers tended to be cramped and over-gunned. Genuine cruisers, of high speed and long range, as yet scarcely existed in the English Navy, and were not common elsewhere.[27]

The only ships in the English Navy which were really built for speed were the yachts. This new type, initially derived from the *jaght Mary* presented to Charles II by the Dutch in 1660, was almost equivalent to a Sixth Rate in size, and was used not only to convey messages and important people, but for scouting and other cruiser-like functions. Because Charles II and his courtiers raced their yachts in peacetime, much attention was given to their speed, and their designs contributed to some of the more successful hull forms of eighteenth-century British cruisers. To them can be added the unusual and successful *Peregrine Galley* of 1700, subsequently converted into a royal yacht, and one of several small and fast ships designed, or at least influenced, by the Marquis of Carmarthen.[28]

The only other completely new type introduced into the late seventeenth-century Royal Navy was, as we have seen, the bomb vessel. The first English bomb, the *Salamander*, was built in 1687, and was ketch-rigged like her French models, but by 1695 the English were building ship-rigged bombs the size of Sixth Rates, which had the advantage that when they were not needed for bombardment, they could land their mortars and operate as small cruisers. The manning arrangements of bombs were unique in British service, in that the firing of the mortars was directed by a party of artillerymen supplied by the Ordnance Board. This Board also attached a tender to each bomb which carried spare shells, and aboard which the artillerymen slept.[29]

The ability of English ironfounders (almost entirely in the Weald of Kent and Sussex) to cast large quantities of light and medium guns had been an important component of English sea power since Tudor times, and it continued to be throughout the seventeenth century. The rapid expansion of the State's Navy in the 1650s rested on the ability of the Wealden gunfounders to supply very large quantities of iron guns, especially the culverins and demi-culverins (roughly 18-pounder and 9-pounder) which armed the majority of English ships. The Ordnance Board ordered 3,360 guns, almost all iron, between 1650 and 1653. The largest naval guns, the 42-pounder full cannon or 'cannon of 7' (meaning 7-inch calibre), were at the extreme limit of blast-furnace capacity and were still normally cast in the more costly brass, though an experimental batch of iron cannon of 7 was accepted in 1657. Guns were cast in several patterns and lengths for each calibre, but the majority were of the lighter patterns known as drakes (guns with a tapered bore, fired with reduced charges) and cutts (short-barrelled pieces). Almost all were cast in the lighter and stronger 'fine metal', costing £26–30 a ton against only £17 6s for 'coarse metal'. As the Ordnance Board reported in April 1653,

> we humbly conceive the fine to be far tougher and more free from honeycombs and not subject to break, and when they do they rend like brass and do not fly into several pieces as the others do, and therefore are not so dangerous to the men and ships. They are also much lighter and so of much greater ease to the ships.[30]

The steady fall in the weight of individual guns of a given calibre was an important factor in making possible the rising number of guns carried by English ships in the seventeenth century.[31]

The Ordnance Board continued to push forward the technical standards of its founders after the Restoration. In 1668 it began ordering iron cannon of 7 (weighing about three tons each) to mount on the lower gun decks of the biggest ships. In spite of the superior prestige of brass guns, the whole 1677 programme, including the First-Rate *Britannia*, was armed entirely in the cheaper iron to keep within the Parliamentary grant. For the same reason Prince Rupert's new invention the 'Rupertinoe' gun was rejected. This was a pattern of gun which was first cast, then annealed in a furnace and machined on a lathe to finish it, giving a piece of very high quality, but costing more than twice as much as an ordinary iron gun. Though technically successful, they were too expensive to be widely adopted, and only three ships, the *Royal*

Charles, Royal James and *Royal Oak* of 1671–4 were armed with them. Drakes were falling out of favour at this period, probably because they were quite easy to blow up by loading them with the full charge of a normal gun of the calibre, though it was many years before they were all replaced.[32] During the Second and Third Dutch Wars the bigger English ships were equipped with 'fire shot' or incendiary shells for some of their guns, with an 'engineer' from the Ordnance Board to look after them. Two Dutch ships, the *Hof van Zealand* and the *Duivenvorde*, were destroyed by them in the Four Days' Battle.[33]

Throughout this period Wealden gunfounding was dominated by the Browne family, though they had numerous competitors and subcontractors. The Brownes were finally driven into bankruptcy in 1682 by the crown's unpaid debts, but their furnaces (notably the two biggest blast-furnaces at Horsmonden and Ashburnham) continued to cast for the Navy under new ownership. The Ordnance Board undertook no gunfounding itself. In the early 1690s it was buying about 2,000 tons of guns and shot a year, rising to a maximum of 5,240 tons in 1697–8. Between 1690 and 1696 about 2,700 guns were added to the Navy's stock, which in 1697 totalled just over 10,000 guns of all ages and calibres. The Board was paying £14 a ton for rough cast guns in 1689, or £18 for finished guns, which prices had risen about 15 per cent by 1694. Shot cost £10–11 a ton. Small arms were bought by the Ordnance Board from numerous manufacturers in London, and increasingly Birmingham. Sulphur was imported from Italy, while saltpetre, still scarce in the 1650s, was imported from India by the East India Company.[34]

It is paradoxical, at first sight, that the political revolution of 1689 which led to a long-term increase both in the size of the English Navy, and in the political and financial support for it in Parliament, should have had such an unfortunate effect on its technical capacity, especially in ship design. In fact the underlying cause of both developments was the same. As Parliament moved to take control of the Navy, it naturally ensured that naval policy was congruent with its own priorities. Confidence and enthusiasm gradually replaced the suspicion with which Parliament had regarded the naval ambitions of the Stuarts – but the very movement which propelled the Navy into the centre of national life distanced it from the expert leadership which had been provided by the later Stuarts and their servants. A Navy which was the darling of the political nation was a Navy controlled by ignorant amateurs. In the long run, a successful Navy needed to combine political support with technical autonomy, but in 1714 the machinery to make this possible did not yet exist.

FIFTEEN

Pride and Prejudice

Operations 1715–1744

When Queen Anne died on 1 August 1714, her Tory supporters dominated Parliament and English politics. If only her half-brother 'James III' had been prepared to embrace the Church of England, as his supporters urged him to, he would probably have succeeded her. The Whig supporters of the Elector of Hanover[1] were certainly a minority, but they were united and determined, and the religious issue narrowly tipped the balance in their favour. The vast majority of Englishmen, however, were convinced supporters of legitimate monarchy, and accepting the accession of George I according to the provisions of the Act of Settlement of 1701 meant disinheriting more than fifty legitimate heirs to the thrones of England and Scotland, senior descendants of the Stuarts, on no other grounds than their faith. Even if Whigs and foreigners had been naturally popular among the Tory majority of the political nation, this repudiation of a fundamental political principle would have been very difficult to swallow. It made the whole of Britain what Scotland in effect already was; an elective monarchy, a crowned Republic like Poland, where Parliament made up the rules as it went along. In Scotland the Union was already highly unpopular, even under a Stuart queen. Moreover it became rapidly clear that Hanoverian Britain was going to be a one-party state. Every monarch since 1660 had aimed for a comprehensive political system embracing all loyal subjects; George I, and later George II, ruled through the Whigs alone and excluded all Tories from confidence or even contact. Though active Jacobites, in the sense of people prepared to risk their lives to restore the Catholic Stuarts, were probably relatively few even in 1714, British governments for forty-five years treated the bulk of their subjects with an undisguised suspicion which was not calculated to win their loyalty.[2]

Foreign observers from solid monarchies not undermined by rival dynasties or Parliamentary politics viewed Britain's seeming instability and weakness with pity and contempt. In the summer of 1714 many confidently predicted civil war in, or between, England and Scotland. On both sides of the Channel it was obvious that Britain's strategic situation was profoundly weakened by internal disunity, and the presence of a legitimate alternative claimant to the throne. This vulnerability was the basic factor in British naval strategy in the first half of the eighteenth century. With a small army, a disloyal population and many enemies abroad, Britain under George I and George II had little to depend on except the Navy. Fear was the main determinant of foreign policy, and fear dictated a large fleet in home waters.[3]

It was needed almost at once, for in the summer of 1715 serious rebellions in favour of James III and VIII broke out in both England and Scotland. The Marquis of Carmarthen, one of the most senior and able of the British admirals, was now commanding his ships, and in December (just over seven years since he had failed in his last attempt) James landed in Scotland. British ships in the Channel managed to prevent some ships from sailing with assistance for him, and covered the passage of Dutch troops to assist their allies, but the eventual defeat of the rebels owed a great deal to the incompetence of their own leaders, especially the Earl of Mar in Scotland. The Hanoverian regime survived, but its confidence was not entirely restored.[4]

What immediately strengthened its position was diplomacy rather than naval or military strength. Louis XIV died in August 1715, leaving an exhausted country to his five-year-old great-grandson Louis XV. France, Britain and Hanover were each in different ways vulnerable. This opened the way to a Franco-British alliance which lasted from 1716 to 1731. It was an important, indeed formative period, which gives the lie to the idea, widespread in the eighteenth century and since, that Britain and France were 'natural and necessary enemies'.[5] In strategic terms the alliance implied among other things that the two countries remained rivals for access to the trade of the Spanish empire, as they had been during the war. More immediately, however, they had a common interest in enforcing the terms of the 1714 peace settlement on Spain, the only belligerent which refused to accept them, mainly because Philip V's second wife, the forceful Italian princess Elizabeth Farnese, could not stomach the loss of Spain's Italian empire to Austria. Though the Spanish navy was only in the early stages of recovery from the disasters of the previous war, a large amphibious expedition was despatched in 1717 to conquer Sardinia, and a second to Sicily in the following year. This aroused a 'Quadruple Alliance' of France, Britain, Austria, the Netherlands and later Savoy; but the French Mediterranean fleet had not recovered from the Toulon disaster ten years before, the Dutch admiralties were financially exhausted, and only the far-away British were in a position to enforce the alliance's demands.[6]

Initially, therefore, the Spaniards were unopposed. Not until the summer of 1718 did a British fleet under Sir George Byng appear, with orders to force a Spanish withdrawal from Sicily. His position was delicate, for war was not yet formally declared and the alliance was still under negotiation. Byng, however, had a robust attitude to responsibility; his maxim was 'that a commanding officer should only call a council of war to screen him from what he has no mind to undertake'.[7] When the Spaniards refused to re-embark their army, he proceeded to attack at once, correctly anticipating approval from home. The Spanish fleet, with only fourteen ships of fifty guns or more against Byng's twenty-one, was anchored in Paradise Roads, off Messina, where deep water and strong offshore currents made it difficult to attack. If the commander-in-chief Antonio de Gastañeta had followed the advice of his Irish subordinate Rear-Admiral George Camocke (one of James II's former officers) he would have stayed there, but instead he fled southward out of the Straits of Messina and formed a line of battle, which fell apart when Byng caught up and attacked. The resulting action, the battle of Cape Passaro on 31 July/11 August, was consequently an untidy chase in which the more numerous and more heavily armed British ships achieved an inevitable victory. Seven Spanish ships of the line, including three flagships, were captured.[8] Part of the Spanish force took refuge inshore, pursued by a squadron under Captain George Walton. A few days later Byng received from him a report on the movements of the Spanish army ashore, with a laconic sentence, apparently added as an afterthought, describing his own activities: 'We have taken and destroyed all the enemy's ships upon this coast, the number as per margin.'[9] Cape Passaro was a crushing victory, but it demonstrated the limitations as much as the strengths of sea power, for the Spanish army was not dislodged and British ships were forced into a lengthy and arduous blockade of Sicilian ports. It took two years of military and naval pressure by the whole alliance, culminating in a French invasion of Spain, to force an eventual, and as it proved only temporary, Spanish withdrawal from Italy.[10]

The naval part of the War of the Quadruple Alliance was not entirely confined to the Mediterranean. British privateers, including some from the New England colonies in the West Indies, cruised against Spanish shipping with modest results.[11] A two-ship British privateering expedition, partly manned by former buccaneers, was despatched to the Pacific under the command of Captains John Clipperton and George Shelvocke. There were some survivors from the usual squalid tale of greed, strife and betrayal, but the voyage yielded no financial or military profit.[12] In Northern waters a Spanish attempt in March 1719 to land 5,000 men in Scotland to raise a Jacobite rebellion in co-operation with Sweden was dispersed by a gale, but what was meant to be a diversionary force of 1,000 Spanish and Scottish troops was successfully landed in the Highlands. Spanish troops briefly garrisoned Eilean Donan Castle, which was blockaded by British warships, but the main body met superior Hanoverian forces as they marched up Glenshiel, and surrendered at once. The expedition was all over by June 1719. In October of that year a British force of 4,000 men under Lord Cobham and Vice-Admiral James Mighels in retaliation occupied Vigo for ten days, advanced inland as far as Pontevedra and even levied a contribution on Santiago de Compostela before withdrawing.[13]

To explain Sweden's interest in Jacobite rebellion it is necessary to revert to the Great Northern War, which was going very badly for her. Much of her northern empire in Estonia, Livonia and Courland had already been lost to Russia, and from 1712 most of her territories in Germany were overrun by Prussia and Denmark. Hanover then bought from Denmark her conquests of Bremen and Verden, giving her for the first time an outlet to the sea – and making Sweden an enemy. The peace of 1714 allowed the British and Dutch to devote attention to the protection of their Baltic trade from the belligerents of the Northern War. A joint squadron was organized, under Admiral Sir John Norris and Rear-Admiral Lucas de Veth, who met at the entrance to the Sound in June. As soon as they compared their orders difficulties became obvious. Dutch policy was strictly neutral, British policy was more or less neutral, but Hanoverian policy was not neutral at all – and Norris had both official orders from the Admiralty (to convoy allied trade) and private orders from George I (to fight alongside the Danish fleet against Sweden) which contradicted them. British foreign policy was now being distorted in the interests of a foreign monarch: exactly what the Act of Settlement had in theory forbidden. Fortunately Norris, in spite of appearances (he never learned to spell the simplest English words), was a finished diplomat familiar with the Baltic, who managed to navigate through the situation without losing his credit with the Admiralty, the allies or the king. There was no hope of reconciliation with Sweden, however (George I as Elector of Hanover was officially at war with Charles XII from October 1715), and Sweden naturally took up the Jacobite cause.[14]

The same difficulties recurred in 1716, with a Dutch squadron now under Captain Hendrik Grave. The new Russian fleet was in the southern Baltic this summer, with Tsar Peter I in person acting as its second-in-command, and a scheme was prepared for a joint Danish, Russian, Prussian, British and Hanoverian seaborne invasion of Scania. The natural candidates for the naval command were Norris and the Danish admiral Ulrik Christian Gyldenløve, but neither would serve under the other, so Peter the Great was nominated commander-in-chief. By this time, however, the astonishing rise of Russia was worrying her allies almost as much as her enemies, and neither Danes, British nor even Hanoverians were enthusiastic about the great expedition. By September, with the prospect of a winter campaign, nor was Tsar Peter, and it never sailed.[15]

By 1717 British opinion was turning against Baltic commitments, partly because it seemed risky to send so many ships far away when the regime faced real threats at home, but Swedish involvement with the Jacobites justified George I in sending another squadron, this time under Sir George Byng. (Norris was busy on a diplomatic mission to Tsar Peter, then visiting the Netherlands.) Byng's orders were carefully balanced, envisaging the possibility of action either against Sweden or Russia, but in practice the Swedes stayed in port, the Danes failed to co-operate, and Byng's main work was protecting trade.[16] By this time Sweden was clearly exhausted, and the strategic picture was dominated by fear of Russian expansion. Norris was back in the Baltic every summer from 1718 to 1721, but besides the protection of trade his priority was now to cover the Swedish coast from just the sort of Russian landing in which he had been supposed to participate in 1716. Although his force was clearly superior to the Russian sailing fleet, the geography of the Baltic made the task very difficult. In effect there are two Baltics, and two different navies are required to control it. The relatively deep and open waters of the southern and central Baltic are the domain of regular warships like Norris's. Much of the upper Baltic, the east coast of Sweden, the opposite shores of Finland and Estonia, and the Åland Islands between them, are covered by a dense archipelago of thousands of islands divided by numerous narrow and shallow channels (the 'leads'), where deep-sea warships could not penetrate. Here naval warfare was conducted by shallow-draught, oared vessels; it was the last stronghold of the galley, which in the Baltic flourished until it was finally superseded by steam power. Both Sweden and Russia maintained separate inshore navies distinct from their deep-water fleets. The Swedish *skärgårds-flottan* was based in Stockholm against Russia, while the sailing fleet was 250 miles south in Karlskrona, facing Denmark. Norris could control the southern and central Baltic, but it was possible for the Russian galley fleet to pass in safety by the leads along the Finnish coast, through the Åland Islands and all the way to Stockholm, only once, briefly, emerging into deep water to round

Hangö Head,[17] the southernmost promontory of Finland. Hangö was a point of great strategic significance, and the scene of several important naval battles, including the great Russian victory over Sweden of 6 August (NS) 1714 which had established Russian dominance of the inshore waters and created Norris's problem.[18] In July 1720 the Russian galleys won another victory, at Gränhamn in the Ålands, actually in sight of Norris, who was powerless to intervene. When the war ended the following year Sweden was shorn of all her overseas empire except Finland in the north, and the ports of Stralsund and Wismar on the Pomeranian coast.[19]

In the years following the Northern War, British squadrons continued to be often and actively employed for diplomatic purposes. Sometimes these stopped only just short of war, but arguably the Navy was a more effective deterrent when it did not often fight, for real battles, like Byng's in 1718, might expose the limitations as well as the strengths of sea power. In 1726, for example, at a time of tension with Spain, Russia and Austria, one fleet watched Ostend, another entered the Baltic to check the Russian fleet, and yet a third blockaded Porto Bello in the Caribbean to stop South American silver being shipped to Spain. 'It is indeed a reflection which must afford his Majesty a great deal of comfort and satisfaction . . .,' commented Lord Townshend, one of the Secretaries of State, in August 1726,

> that whilst one of his fleets is preserving the tranquillity of the North against the ambitious and pernicious designs of the Czarina, and another is keeping the Spanish treasure in the West Indies and thereby preventing the Emperor and Spain from disturbing the peace of the South, the very report of a third squadron going out has caused such alarm and confusion in the Austrian Netherlands, and has put Spain, in the low and miserable condition of their finances, to the trouble and expense of marching their troops and fortifying their seaport towns.[20]

His complacency was not fully justified, for though the deterrence was successful, it was also costly. It needed large fleets and skilful leadership; notably, in these years, that of Sir Charles Wager in the Baltic in 1726 and on the coast of Spain in 1727, while the Spaniards besieged Gibraltar and open war was barely averted. A plain, quiet, amiable man, marked by his upbringing among the New England Quakers, Wager was a shrewd strategist, and all the more effective as a diplomat because he never raised his voice, and never said anything he did not mean. In 1729 he commanded the Anglo-Dutch fleet assembled at Spithead in a further display of force which eventually brought Spain to a settlement.[21] The Navy's worst experience of deterrence was that of

Francis Hosier's Caribbean squadron in 1726 and 1727. The admiral himself, both his successors, eight captains and more than 3,000 of his men died of tropical disease.[22] Nor was his blockade entirely effective, for Spanish historians are unanimous that the silver was diverted up the coast to Mexico and shipped home from Vera Cruz without being intercepted, but by the time it arrived the Spanish government's war plans had had to be abandoned.[23]

Though quite large squadrons like Hosier's were sometimes sent overseas for particular objectives, very few ships were as yet permanently stationed abroad. From 1713 there were usually two or three 'station ships' distributed among the American colonies, and the number rose to nine in the early 1720s, mainly to suppress 'the unspeakable calamity this poor province suffers from pirates', as the governor of South Carolina put it in June 1718.[24] The authorities in North Carolina were on friendly terms with notorious pirates like Edward Teach ('Blackbeard'), and at times there was something like open war between the provinces, with pirates blockading Charleston, and both South Carolina and Virginia mounting naval expeditions into Pamlico Sound and the Cape Fear River. The pirates, however, could not long resist co-ordinated efforts by warships on the coast and colonial authorities denying them shelter and supply in port.[25] By the mid-1720s piracy in the Americas was virtually extinct, and the main complaint of the Admiralty was that 'the captains of his Majesty's ships stationed in America have of late years taken a very unwarrantable liberty of lying in port with their ships for the greatest part of the time they have remained abroad, to the dishonour of his Majesty's service, and the disservice of the colonies for whose protection they were appointed'.[26] In his first year on the Carolina station in 1725, Captain George Anson was three months at sea out of twelve – but there was not now a great deal to do at sea, and those who found useful things to do were not necessarily encouraged. Captain George Gascoigne of the *Alborough* spent five years charting the dangerous coast of the Carolinas, but the Admiralty took no interest in his surveys, which remained unpublished.[27]

During the 1720s and 1730s important developments were taking place in the Spanish and French navies, little noticed by contemporary Englishmen and not much by modern historians. The disasters of the War of the Spanish Succession had reduced the French fleet to a small force (thirty-one ships in 1721, the same as 1661)[28] and almost eliminated the Spanish; now they began to be rebuilt in quite new forms. From 1714 to 1754 four successive Spanish naval ministers – Bernardo Tinajero, José Patiño, José Campillo y Cosio and the Marqués de Ensenada – pursued a coherent long-term plan for the reconstruction of a Spanish navy whose function was to preserve the two

Spanish empires (in Italy and the Americas) by guarding their communications and keeping a balance of power between Spain's colonial rivals, France and Britain. The fleet was meant to escort trade and deter amphibious expeditions; there was no intention of fighting the British for overall command of the seas (which would risk another Cape Passaro to no essential purpose), only to make Spain a valuable alliance partner, and to impose unacceptable risks on would-be aggressors, at an economical cost. Intelligent long-term investment in Spanish dockyards allowed a fleet to be constructed of well-built ships which gave long service at relatively low expense. By establishing a major naval yard in the West Indies, at Havana, and basing a permanent squadron of ships of the line there, Spain very steeply increased the difficulty for foreign naval powers of mounting expeditions against Spanish America. The ships required for this policy were large, strongly built but lightly armed, designed for long-range cruising and convoy escort rather than fleet action. The Spanish navy had weaknesses which its leaders worked patiently to remedy, but some of which (notably a severe lack of seamen) they were never able to overcome. Nevertheless it was a fleet rationally designed to meet Spain's needs, growing in size and effectiveness throughout the eighteenth century, which both British and French contemporaries were unwise to underestimate.[29]

We know about Spanish naval policy, because Spanish ministers laid out coherent plans and Spanish historians have investigated them, but with France the situation is more obscure. The comte de Maurepas, who inherited the position of naval minister in 1723 at the age of twenty-two and remained twenty-six years in office, was clear that 'trade generates the wealth and consequently the power of states; navies are absolutely necessary to sustain seaborne trade'.[30] Though he does not appear explicitly to have declared that he was rebuilding the French navy essentially for colonial and commercial warfare against Spain, rather than to fight France's then-ally Britain, the evidence suggests this. Almost as soon as he took office, French dockyards began building ships of the line, each to their own designs (for French naval architecture was not centralized), but all to a common plan. There were virtually no three-deckers; instead the fleet was composed of very large two-deckers, whose design implies that they were intended for long-range fast cruising in trade-wind latitudes. Unlike Spanish ships, however, they were heavily armed but lightly built, with high maintenance requirements and short working lives, and Maurepas invested very little in French dockyards, so that large expenditure on shipbuilding was needed to keep up quite a small fleet.[31] It is unclear whether Maurepas, whom many contemporaries regarded as a lightweight ('clever and means well, but does not know what colour the sea is', was his secretary's verdict),[32] realized this weakness of his policy.

The revival of French and Spanish sea power, and the end of the alliance with France in 1731, gradually weakened Britain's naval supremacy, and contributed to the decision to remain neutral in the War of the Polish Succession from 1733 to 1735. In spite of its name much of this war was fought in Italy, where Spain was again trying to rebuild her empire. Both Sir Robert Walpole, George II's chief minister, and Wager, First Lord of the Admiralty from 1733, were confident of British naval superiority (in 1734 Wager told the king 'that we were at present stronger than any nation at sea, perhaps than any two'), but they preferred to mobilize the fleet and negotiate from strength rather than go to war, and it was much more difficult to spare a fleet for the Mediterranean with the Channel to guard against France. The Spanish navy was still weak, but in these more favourable circumstances it was strong enough to achieve what it had failed to get fifteen years before. At the end of the war Spain gained Milan, and established the satellite kingdom of the Two Sicilies, embracing Sicily and southern Italy.[33]

Meanwhile British relations with Spain were deteriorating in the Americas. The British South Sea Company had been formed to exploit the trading concession known as the Asiento which Harley had obtained from Spain at the peace of 1714. The Asiento ('contract') was to supply slaves to the Spanish Caribbean, plus one trading vessel a year – a concession which the British meant from the first to exploit to open up as extensive a commerce as they could manage in the teeth of Spanish legislation. The result was a smuggling trade, illegal in Spanish eyes but officially supported by British governments. In the Caribbean, where the pirate and buccaneer traditions were not extinct, licensed illegality attracted bad characters on all sides. The Spanish government, unable to finance an official customs service, sold licences to private vessels to act as *guarda-costas* – in effect ill-regulated peace-time privateers which lived off the smuggling system, employing all sorts of fraud and violence which British traders often reciprocated. Spanish regulations regarded the possession of Spanish coin as sufficient proof of illegal trade, but the Spanish silver dollar (the famous *pieza de ocho reales* or 'piece of eight') was the international currency of the Americas, and it was all but impossible to trade without using it. British governments and public opinion were bombarded by numerous protests against Spanish misdeeds, some of them justified, but Spain had as much reason to complain. Naval commanders-in-chief convoyed the smugglers in return for a 5 per cent fee, disguised as freight for carrying bullion. British warships shipped private cargoes, in defiance of Admiralty regulations as well as Spanish law; in 1722 Captain John Waldron of the *Greyhound*, officially stationed at New York, was murdered while trading on the coast of Cuba. Directors of the South Sea Company were deeply involved in illegal trade, defrauding their own shareholders as well as the Spanish crown.[34] 'It is without doubt irksome to every honest man to hear such cruelties are committed in these seas,' wrote Rear-Admiral Charles Stewart from Jamaica in 1731,

> but give me leave to say that you only hear one side of the question; and I can assure you the sloops that sail from this island, manned and armed on that illicit trade, has more than once bragged to me of their having murdered seven or eight Spaniards on their own shore. To prevent these cruelties has been one reason for allowing convoy to that trade . . . Villainy is inherent to this climate, and I should be partial if I was to judge whether the trading part of the island or those we complain of among the Spaniards are most exquisite in that trade.[35]

This is the context in which Captain Robert Jenkins of the *Rebecca* suffered off Havana in 1731 when he was boarded by the notorious *guarda-costa* Juan de Leon Fandino. The story that Jenkins appeared in the House of Commons with his severed ear in a jar is a myth, but as a respectable merchant seaman who had really suffered from unprovoked brutality, he provided a convenient case for the enemies of Walpole and his policy of peace with Spain to revive in the late 1730s. Neither government desired war, and their disputes over the Caribbean trade were settled in the Convention of the Pardo, agreed in January 1739, but the South Sea Company refused to sign, and British public opinion was by now violently agitated. Opposition was supported by Tories but led by dissident Whigs gathered around the Prince of Wales, the 'Patriots' as they called themselves, who mounted a brilliant campaign appealing to all the old certainties of the English naval myth. The public remained almost as convinced as Cromwell's government had been over eighty years before that Spain was wealthy, effete and vulnerable.[36] A 'mad and vain nation . . . warmed and hardened by pride and prejudice'[37] identified with the traditional idea of national naval superiority which dictated that a war against Spain must necessarily be easy, glorious and profitable. Poets and musicians added their references to the glories of Queen Elizabeth's reign. Shakespeare was evoked and imitated; the young Tory writer Samuel Johnson contributed to the campaign; and in their masque *Alfred*, first played in the garden of the Prince of Wales's house at Cliveden in 1740, James Thomson and Thomas Arne conjured up a once and future golden age in which the tyranny of 'Don

Roberto' would be ended, and British sea power restored: 'Rule, Britannia, rule the waves; Britons never will be slaves'.[38] The Navy, 'as essential to our Safety & Wealth as Parliament or Magna Charta', was the guarantor of freedom, virtue and conquest.[39]

Thus the government was forced into a war with Spain in October 1739. Hoping to avoid it until the last minute, it had done little to prepare, and only in the West Indies were there any British forces ready to act. Walpole's government, however, and in particular Wager, had at least given thought to the strategy of a commercial war with Spain, which of necessity had to be based on seaborne attacks on Spanish trade and possessions. Ministers shared many of the opposition's ideas on how to do it, but they had a much more realistic idea of the difficulties. Wager, who knew the Caribbean well, understood that the Spanish defensive system of fortifications backed by a naval squadron in Havana was designed to force attackers to mount large, costly and slow-moving expeditions likely to be crippled by tropical diseases before they could achieve anything. Instead he favoured keeping the bulk of the fleet at home, sending abroad only small, fast-moving naval forces to mount destructive raids against the many vulnerable points of a far-flung empire, in the Caribbean, the Far East and the Pacific.[40]

Only in the Caribbean was such a force already available. Vice-Admiral Edward Vernon was one of the ablest officers of the day, but his appointment to the Jamaica command in July 1739 aroused some astonishment, for he was also a well-known and noisy opposition politician. But both Wager and old Sir John Norris, still active at nearly eighty and advising the Cabinet on strategy, insisted on Vernon's merits: 'He is certainly much properer than any officer we have to send,' Wager advised, 'being very well acquainted in all that part of the West Indies and is a very good sea officer, whatever he may be, or has been, in the House of Commons'.[41] Vernon had repeatedly told the public that he could take a Spanish colonial fortress like Porto Bello with half a dozen ships, and this was not empty rhetoric, for he shared Wager's ideas on the strategy of small squadrons hitting hard and moving fast. On 20 November 1739 he appeared off Porto Bello with six ships, and at dawn next morning they attacked. Carefully planned and boldly executed, Vernon's attack was a complete success, and the defenders surrendered in twenty-four hours. Though there were no rich galleons in port, Vernon stayed three weeks to raze the fortifications, wrecking the official Spanish system of regulated commerce confined to the annual commercial fair there, and opening the way for more dispersed 'free' trade in future.[42]

Few British governments have ever won so striking a success in the opening weeks of a war, and none have got so little credit for it. Vernon was one of the opposition, and for them his victory became 'our honest admiral's triumph over Sir Robert and Spain' – in that order – and the first of the inevitable triumphs to follow.[43] Ministerial talk of logistical difficulties or tropical diseases could be dismissed as obvious nonsense. British ships and seamen were invincible – Vernon had proved it – and if they were not, it could only be because the treacherous Walpole was in Spanish pay. The government was unable to resist the public clamour for a major expedition to the Caribbean.[44] Vernon and Wager were equally unhappy. Vernon wondered if the Victualling Board could sustain a major force so far from home, and was seriously concerned both about the Spanish fleet at Havana, and about a potentially hostile French squadron in the Caribbean with unknown orders. This danger was real, more real than he knew, for in August 1740 the French admiral the marquis d'Antin sailed for the West Indies with twenty-two ships of the line and orders to unite with the fourteen ships of the Spanish admiral Don Rodrigo de Torres and attack Vernon without warning. At that point Vernon had ten ships, and even if the twenty-five coming out to reinforce him under Rear-Admiral Sir Chaloner Ogle had arrived in time he would have been barely equal. Luckily for Vernon, both French and Spanish squadrons were in a bad state; Torres's orders were to cover Spanish treasure home through the Florida Straits, not to work with the French; and d'Antin had to go home in January 1741 when his victuals ran short.[45]

The same month Ogle's squadron reached Jamaica, bringing with it the great expeditionary force of 8,000 troops whose target had been left to be chosen by the commanders-in-chief on the spot. One of the two, Major-General Lord Cathcart, was already dead, and his second in command, Brigadier Thomas Wentworth, though an experienced and level-headed staff officer, had none of Vernon's force of character and long experience of command. From the beginning Vernon dominated the expedition, and bullied the soldiers into doing what he wished. In some ways this was a good thing, for Vernon was by far the soundest strategist available, and he was absolutely right that naval requirements had to take priority in the West Indies, but his ruthless exploitation of the army, his unscrupulous skill in claiming credit for every success and blaming the soldiers for every failure, eventually destroyed any possibility of harmonious combined operations. At first, however, all went well. Cartagena, with a good harbour and well to windward of both the British base at Jamaica and the potential Spanish threat at Havana, was strategically the right choice to attack, and the expedition arrived on 4 March, with about two months of reasonably healthy weather before the rainy season began. The British did not appreciate, however, that the fortifications had been substantially rebuilt since the French had mastered them in 1697, and were strengthened by four Spanish ships of the line. The result was an arduous campaign as the British fought their way through the outer defences of the city, culminating in a disastrous assault on the fortress of San Lazar on 9 April. Five days later the British began to withdraw. They had come close to victory, and it seems likely that more effective co-operation would have carried the day. Much credit also is due to an heroic defence led by the one-eyed, one-armed and one-legged veteran Vice-Admiral Don Blas de Lezo.[46]

After Cartagena the expedition, now very sickly, returned to Jamaica and then sailed to 'Cumberland Harbour' (Guantánamo Bay) in Cuba to mount an overland attack on Santiago de Cuba forty-five miles away, a project which Vernon regarded as a dangerous waste of time, and effectively sabotaged. After this relations with Wentworth irretrievably broke down, and by the time the expedition returned to Port Royal at the end of November it had only 2,000 troops still fit for service.[47] Though Vernon did not leave the Caribbean until October 1742, this was the end of any major amphibious operations. He left Ogle as commander-in-chief, with nineteen ships of the line divided between the Leeward Islands and Jamaica, but his tasks were mainly defensive. Rear-Admiral Charles Knowles took a small squadron to attack the town of La Guaira on the coast of what is now Venezuela in February 1743, and the nearby Puerto Cabello in April, but neither attack prospered. In October the two West Indian stations were formally divided, Ogle remaining at Jamaica while Knowles became commander-in-chief in the Leeward Islands.[48]

The Porto Bello operation was not quite the only expression of Wager's strategic ideas. Two other expeditions were planned in 1739, to the Far East to attack the Philippines, and into the Pacific to attack Panama at the same time as Vernon was taking Cartagena, thus cutting the Spanish empire in two. The Philippine plan had to be dropped for want of forces, but the Pacific expedition went ahead, under the command of Captain George Anson. After many delays, he sailed in September 1740 with six warships and two supply vessels. Besides the ships' companies, he carried a landing force supposedly of 500 soldiers, but actually made up of garrison troops and Chelsea Pensioners, all of whom died on the voyage. As a fighting force, the squadron was destroyed by the horrific three-month struggle to round Cape Horn against the fierce gales of the Southern Ocean. 'The weather was still stormy with huge deep, hollow seas that frequently broke quite over us, with constant rain, frost or snow,' wrote the purser Lawrence Millechamp. 'Our decks were always full of water, and our men constantly falling ill with the scurvy; and the allowance of water being but small reduced us to a most deplorable condition.'[49] Two ships turned back, a third was wrecked, and the shattered squadron which assembled in the Juan Fernández Islands in July had lost two-thirds of its men to scurvy. Nevertheless Anson determined to do what he could. Proceeding north up the coast of Chile, he took a few prizes and raided the small town of Paita. Arriving off Acapulco too late to intercept the inward-bound annual 'galleon' from Manila, he determined to return home as Drake had done, across the Pacific. The squadron was now reduced to two ships, the *Centurion* and *Gloucester*. On the long passage westwards scurvy broke out again, the sinking *Gloucester* had to be burned for want of men to save her, and the *Centurion* herself narrowly escaped disaster. With difficulty Anson was able to get his ship repaired and obtain a few replacement men at Canton, and in April 1743, still with less than half the *Centurion*'s normal complement, he sailed, ostensibly for England, but actually meaning to make a final attempt to intercept the westbound 'Manila galleon'. Now at last he achieved a real victory: on 20 June off Cape Espíritu Santo the *Centurion* met and took the *Nuestra Señora de Covadonga*, carrying 1,313,843 pieces of eight and 35,682 oz of virgin silver. Anson returned to Canton where he sold his prize, and thence to England, where the *Centurion* arrived without further incident in June 1744. More than 1,300 members of the original expedition had perished, and 145 now remained to see England again.[50]

Anson's voyage is remembered as a classic tale of endurance and leadership in the face of fearful disasters, but to the British public of 1744 it was the treasure of the galleon, triumphantly paraded through the streets of London, which did something to restore battered national self-esteem. Virtually nothing else had happened since the fall of Porto Bello to flatter English illusions about a naval war with Spain. In June 1740 a British overland expedition from Georgia unsuccessfully attacked the Spanish fort at San Agustín in Florida, in conjunction with a naval blockade. In June 1742 a Spanish seaborne force from Havana landed in Georgia, but this attack failed likewise.[51] There was some privateering, mainly by New England ships in the Caribbean.[52]

In the Mediterranean a British fleet under Vice-Admiral Nicholas Haddock was supposed to blockade Cadiz, prevent a Spanish army being transported from Barcelona to Italy, and stop the French fleet from Toulon supporting its Spanish allies. For this range of tasks his force was completely inadequate (thirteen ships of the line against twenty-seven of the French and Spanish together), but when in November 1741 the allies transported the Spanish army to Italy, the Duke of Newcastle, Secretary of State, publicly threw the whole blame on Haddock. In April 1742 he suffered a nervous breakdown and returned to England 'melancholy distracted'.[53] His replacement, Vice-Admiral Thomas Mathews, was fully occupied trying to intercept supplies from Spain to the Spanish army in Italy, but the possibility of the French fleet entering the war forced him to keep his fleet concentrated, and limited his scope to blockade the Italian coast or protect British trade. The only unequivocal success of British sea power in the Mediterranean came in July 1742 when Mathews detached Captain William Martin with a small squadron, including four bomb vessels, to 'bring the king of the Two Sicilies to a just sense of his errors' in having sent his army to join his father's campaign in northern Italy. On 8 August Martin anchored off Naples, the entire capital under his guns and the royal palace directly on the waterfront, and gave Charles IV half an hour to withdraw from the war – which he did. No more economical demonstration of naval power has ever been given – but in the fullness of time it was to have some unintended consequences.[54]

The lesson of the War of Jenkin's Ear was that the medical and logistical difficulties of large-scale operations in the Caribbean were beyond British resources, and that the mere threat of French assistance tied up too many ships in home waters to allow effective campaigning against Spain in the Mediterranean. Spain suffered no essential loss in the war except Porto Bello, and was able to pursue her military ambitions in northern Italy with only limited interference. The advance of a French army towards Hanover in 1741 forced George II as Elector to declare himself a neutral in the crisis then developing in Germany, which effectively wrecked the possibilities of building an anti-French coalition, and demonstrated how easily the French could now apply pressure on Britain in a way the Navy was powerless to oppose.[55] Very little indeed was now left of the gross illusions with which the British public had gone to war. Sir Robert Walpole, who had striven to avert a war some of whose evils he foresaw, fell from power in February 1742 as a result of its disappointments. In 1744 he had the melancholy satisfaction of watching from the opposition benches of the Lords as his former opponents struggled with a failing war effort and the imminent prospect of French intervention.

SIXTEEN

A Strong Squadron in Soundings

Operations 1744–1748

Almost as soon as Britain went to war against Spain, much of Europe began to slide into the concurrent but distinct wars collectively known to historians as the 'War of the Austrian Succession'. Prussia fought Austria for the possession of Silesia (1740 to 1742 and again 1744 to 1745); Spain fought Austria in Italy for the duchies of Parma and Piacenza (1741 to 1748); France and Bavaria fought Austria (1741 to 1742); and Prussia fought Saxony (1744 to 1745). Britain was not directly involved in these wars, but Austria was a British ally, Prussia and Spain were French allies, and by the time France formally joined Spain against Austria in 1743, tension was already acute. In February 1744 France declared war against Britain.[1]

British attitudes to a French war, like a Spanish one, were rooted in a semi-mythical past, and made sense only in relation to domestic politics. It was taken for granted that Louis XV's ambitions posed as great a threat to Europe as Louis XIV's had done, and that it was the duty and interest of every European power to unite in a grand coalition against France, always built around Austria and the Netherlands but naturally under British leadership, what British politicians called the 'Old System'. Armies on the Continent were no more popular with the British public than they had been in William III's time, and the British idea of the proper strategy in a war against France was for the allies to sustain the burden of the war in Europe, while Britain concentrated on the war at sea, and took the profits of successful sea power. 'The most effectual way to assist our allies will always be to prosecute the war by sea and in America,' declaimed the MP and Jamaica planter William Beckford. 'We may conquer from our enemies, they can conquer nothing from us, and our trade will improve by a total extinction of theirs.'[2] Only a handful of British statesmen appreciated that this prospect looked more attractive in London than in Vienna, Berlin or the Hague. 'I am astonished at English policy,' wrote Frederick II of Prussia. 'They think of the whole of

Europe as existing only to serve them. They never consider other people's interests, or use any arguments except money.'[3] The Hanoverian connection, moreover, poisoned both diplomacy and domestic politics. The vulnerability of Hanover severely weakened George II's diplomatic position, and his refusal to risk his beloved electorate chilled potential allies. In England Hanover was the perfect symbol of everything the public detested in foreign policy, and opposition politicians, Whigs as much as Tories, won easy popularity with the public, and unpopularity with the king, by denouncing it.[4] The 'Patriots' distinguished themselves by their offensive references to 'that family whom we have raised from a petty dominion . . . whom from want and weakness we have exalted to a throne', as the young Lord Sandwich put it in 1743.[5]

War, therefore, and especially a French war, sharply revived the tension present in the British political system since 1714 if not 1689, between the prejudices of the British political nation, and the European outlook of the king. This was one of the reasons Walpole had tried so hard to avoid war, and why the war when it came brought in a period of acute political instability. Since it was a disappointing naval war, the Admiralty was an obvious weak point of the ministry. In the 1741–2 Parliamentary session a new Cruizers and Convoys Act, modelled on that of 1708, narrowly failed to pass after the Admiralty had conceded most of its provisions. Soon afterwards, in February 1742, Walpole fell and a new government was formed, partly of former opposition Whigs, led by Lord Carteret, who was attractive to George II because he spoke German and shared the king's Continental outlook. Foreign policy was still the king's prerogative, not Parliament's, but no government could expect to be popular which adopted a 'Hanoverian' foreign policy. In this ministry Sir Charles Wager was replaced by Carteret's follower Lord Winchilsea, the first civilian politician at the head of the Admiralty since the Earl of Strafford in 1714. Sir John Norris, the Admiral of the Fleet since 1734, refused to serve under a civilian novice half a century his junior, and Winchilsea had no naval colleague of weight and experience, so as Britain slid towards war with France, the Admiralty continued to be the weak point of an unpopular government.[6]

Among the many things calling for its attention was the situation in the Mediterranean, where Admiral Mathews had orders to prevent, if necessary by force, the (still officially neutral) French fleet from supporting the enemy Spanish fleet. Since the Spaniards had taken refuge with the French in Toulon, Mathews' task was to blockade that port from a precarious anchorage in the nearby Hyères Islands. The admiral had an excellent fighting record and a clear strategic grasp of the situation, but his faults included an autocratic style of command and a violent temper, and he was on poor terms with his second in command, Vice-Admiral Richard Lestock, whom he several times asked the Admiralty to transfer elsewhere. Lestock too was a good officer, a follower of Vernon who shared his intelligent interest in tactics, but it would have been well if Winchilsea had grasped the nettle and parted the two admirals. He may have been deterred by political considerations, Lestock being a connection of the opposition 'Patriots' who would certainly denounce the Admiralty for persecuting their man if he were moved.[7]

The result was unfortunate. On 8 February 1744 the Franco-Spanish fleets sailed from Toulon, intending to catch Mathews with a surprise attack on his anchorage, but he was warned by his frigates at once. The French were commanded by Vice-Admiral Claude Court de la Bruyère (who was a few days short of his seventy-eighth birthday); the Spaniards by Rear-Admiral Don Juan José Navarro. In very light winds, the fleets closed one another slowly, but by the evening of the 10th the allies were in a rough line heading southward, the French leading and the Spaniards some way astern, with the British fleet more or less parallel to the eastward and windward. Mathews in the centre was much nearer the enemy than Lestock in the rear or Rear-Admiral William Rowley in the van,[8] and in spite of signals to close up into line, Lestock was still further away at dawn on the 11th. He continued to ignore Mathews' signals, and at 11 o'clock the commander-in-chief lost patience and led his division to attack. The result was a partial action; hot around Mathews' and Navarro's flagships and distant in the van where the French were scarcely engaged, while Lestock's division took no part at all. The Spanish flagship was badly damaged, and one Spanish ship, the *Poder*, surrendered to Captain Edward Hawke of the *Berwick*, but when the French tacked towards the close of the day and threatened to cut Mathews off he had to break off the action and abandon the prize. Next day Mathews chased the allies back towards Toulon, Lestock's division now in the lead, but he called off the pursuit, fearing to be drawn to leeward, away from the Italian coast he was meant to blockade, and worried too that the French Brest fleet, known to have sailed for an unknown destination, might be about to appear. In strictly military terms the battle of Toulon was a frustration rather than a disaster (though Mathews' absence repairing damages at Port Mahón in March did allow Spanish supplies to get through to their army), but the apparent cowardice of Lestock aroused violent emotions both in the Navy and in the political world, and the repercussions continued to influence action and opinion for forty years.[9]

Meanwhile the British were facing another crisis in home waters. The

French declaration of war had been timed to coincide with an invasion, mounted from Dunkirk with the cover of a squadron from Brest. The operation was prepared in great secrecy and the British did not suspect until the last moment. Their defences were in some disarray. An acute shortage of seamen hampered the Channel squadron, the three-deckers 'designed to form a home guard' were unable to sail,[10] and Winchilsea's Admiralty was so widely distrusted that all ships in home waters were temporarily put under the command of the eighty-four-year-old Norris as Admiral of the Fleet, reporting directly to the Cabinet – which ignored his warnings of French preparations. Fortunately for the British, French planning too was less than realistic. They counted on support from two British captains, neither of whom seems to have been Jacobite, and one of whom was dead;[11] and they were sure Norris was lying in Portsmouth when he was actually in the Downs. Vice-Admiral the comte de Rocquefeuil, commanding the covering squadron of fifteen ships from Brest, was off Dungeness on 24 February when he was considerably alarmed to sight Norris approaching with a superior force. The gale which saved Rocquefeuil also wrecked the invasion convoy in Dunkirk Roads, and the French abandoned their project for the moment.[12]

The news of the battle of Toulon arrived in England soon afterwards, and unleashed a violent controversy. Lestock, having been sent home, was soon available to conduct his own defence, which he did with some skill, blaming Mathews' clumsy and ambiguous signals, and his haste in attacking without waiting to form the line. Since the signal book was notoriously clumsy and ambiguous, and Mathews was notoriously hasty, this was a plausible line. By the autumn, with both admirals back in England, preparations for courts martial were in progress.[13] Meanwhile, however, Carteret's ministry was in deep political trouble, not least because of its naval misfortunes, and in November he and his friends were forced out of office. In their place the ministry recruited the 'New Allies', opposition Whigs associated with the 'Patriots', and even some Tories. The 'New Allies' specifically demanded, and obtained, the Admiralty. Just after Christmas 1744, the Duke of Bedford became First Lord, accompanied by his followers the Earl of Sandwich and Captain George Anson, newly returned from his voyage round the world and the hero of the hour.[14]

Bedford, Sandwich and Anson, who in turn followed him as First Lords of the Admiralty, were between them in charge of the Navy (with one short break) from 1744 to 1762, and were responsible for a range of reforms and developments in tactics, discipline, ship-design and administration which substantially reshaped it. They took office deeply dissatisfied with the performance of the Navy in many areas, but the situation which most urgently called for action was the battle of Toulon. There had already been courts martial on some captains (notably Captain Richard Norris of the *Essex*, son of Sir John, who was acquitted in the teeth of clear evidence of cowardice) which suggested that the sea officers would close ranks and protect one another. The 'New Allies', and the old opposition, were determined that it should not happen again, and insisted on a Parliamentary inquiry which preceded the naval courts martial. The Commons made some effort to investigate impartially, but MPs were well out of their depth in naval tactics, and the cool and articulate Lestock appeared before a lay audience to better effect than the angry and apparently muddled Mathews. At least one member of the new Admiralty Board, George Grenville, was on Lestock's side, and the Commons took the same line. The ensuing courts martial could not but be influenced. Mathews was condemned, with some slight plausibility, for failing to mount a close attack, and failing to pursue the enemy. Lestock was completely acquitted, with no plausibility at all. Much falsified evidence was presented on his behalf and accepted by the court. All this provided another bad precedent, to renew those of the 1690s, for political interference in naval discipline. It taught those who were minded to learn that gallantry was less important than formal adherence to the line of battle, and that cowards with political friends had nothing to fear.[15]

While the Toulon inquiry and trials were going on in 1745 and 1746, the country and the new Admiralty were passing through repeated crises. The Jacobite rebellion which the French had failed to support in 1744 broke out the following year with virtually no help from the French navy. Antoine Walsh, a Nantes shipowner of Irish descent who had made a fortune in the slave trade, provided the ships which carried Prince Charles Edward Stuart to the Highlands, where he landed in July. By September he was in Edinburgh, and on the 21st the British army was routed at Prestonpans, just outside the city. On 4 December the Jacobite army reached Derby, only 145 miles from London. The greater part of the British army was facing the French in Flanders. The Navy had narrowly failed to intercept the prince, and could do little to check the rebellion.[16]

What the new Admiralty had done was to appoint Vernon to command in the Channel. He was a former political associate, his misfortunes in the West Indies could be blamed on Walpole and the army, and his abilities were real. He acted with energy and skill, all the while bombarding the Admiralty with his opinion on strategy, and narrowly watching French preparations, for the success of the Jacobites had spurred France into another invasion plan.

Unfortunately for the Jacobites, French priorities were elsewhere, the forces committed were small, and the planning was even more haphazard than before. The Jacobite army retreated from Derby on 6 December, but the French were not ready until a month later. The intention was to embark from Boulogne to land at Dungeness; only at the last moment did the duc de Richelieu learn that his whole force could not clear Boulogne on one tide, and that if ships sailed from France at high water, it might be low water by the time they reached England. There were a few critical days when the wind served and Vernon was to leeward in the Downs, during which a determined general prepared to run big risks might have got at least part of the force to England, but the mercurial Richelieu was not the man.[17]

By this time Vernon's relations with the Admiralty had reached breaking point, as it became clear that the admiral enjoyed being a politician at least as much as a sea commander. He took a high line with the Board, and demanded the same authority as Norris had had, including the right to appoint his own officers. 'I am sorry to say I think my old friend delights too much in pen and ink and many words,'[18] Knowles wrote privately to Anson from the Downs on Christmas Day 1745, by which time Anson and his colleagues were painfully aware of it. Vernon had frequently threatened to resign, and now they took him at his word. He then published two anonymous pamphlets, entitled *A Specimen of Honest Truth from an Honest Sailor* and *Some Seasonable Advice from an Honest Sailor*, which printed his correspondence with the Admiralty, much of it highly secret. When he refused to acknowledge his authorship, he was dismissed from the Navy.[19]

British sea power began to act more effectively against the rebels as they retreated northward early in 1746. In December 1745 Lord John Drummond landed at Montrose with 1,200 French troops of the *Royal Ecossais* regiment, but thereafter ships on the East Coast under Rear-Admiral John Byng inter-cepted much, though not all, of the money and supplies sent from France to the rebels, on which they depended after they abandoned Lowland Scotland and could no longer collect its taxes. The loss of the *Prince Charles*, driven ashore on the Sutherland coast on 25 March 1746 by the *Sheerness*, denied the Prince the money she was carrying and forced him to fight the Duke of Cumberland's army in disadvantageous circumstances at Culloden on 16 April. That defeat doomed the Jacobite cause. Throughout the rest of that year British warships patrolled both coasts of Scotland, and on 3 May there was an action in Loch nan Uamh between three British cruisers and two French privateers sent by Walsh to rescue the Prince. This attempt failed, but in September another French ship finally carried him back to France.[20]

In 1744 and 1745 the naval war against France had yielded little satisfaction, some relief, and a good deal of alarm and despondency; but it also produced one unexpected triumph. The great French fortress of Louisbourg on Cape Breton Island was one of the showpieces of Maurepas' colonial policy (for he was responsible for the colonies as well as the navy), and one of the reasons for suggesting that his policies were not wholly based on logical rigour. Fortresses usually guarded key bridges, passes or road junctions, and were designed to allow a small garrison to pin down a large army for a siege of, typically, six to eight weeks; long enough for a relieving force to appear, or at least for the enemy to waste much of the campaigning season for limited gains. Louisbourg failed on both counts. It did little to block the way to Canada or anywhere else, for the Cabot Strait into the Gulf of St Lawrence is seventy miles wide, and the French, unlike the Spaniards at Havana, never based a squadron there to act as an effective deterrent. Nor could the fortress defend itself for long enough, since a relieving force could scarcely reach it until the next campaigning season, and there are no tropical diseases to aid the defenders in that bleak climate. Louisbourg's value was more economic than military: its rich cod fishery gave a livelihood to about a quarter of all French seamen. This fishery the New Englanders coveted, and in January 1745 the General Assembly of Massachusetts resolved to mount an expedition against it. Troops the colonials could raise themselves, and transports to carry them, but for warships they had to appeal to the British admirals in the West Indies, Vice-Admiral Thomas Davers at Jamaica, and Commodore Peter Warren in the Leeward Islands. Davers refused, but Warren, overriding the unanimous opinion of his captains gathered in a council of war, came at once with four ships. On 24 March the expedition sailed from Boston, on 30 April the troops were put ashore near Louisbourg, and on 17 June the fortress surrendered. Warren is an informative contrast to Vernon as naval commander of an amphibious expedition. He had the same outstanding powers of command, but very unlike Vernon he impressed all who met him with 'his great civility and good nature'.[21] Throughout a long and difficult siege, which might so easily have been wrecked by disputes between soldiers and sailors, Englishmen[22] and colonials, Warren worked harmoniously with all.[23]

On both sides of the Channel the capture of Louisbourg diverted naval attention to North America. In France Maurepas devoted all the French navy's resources to recapturing the fortress in which he had sunk so much of his political capital – leaving nothing to support the Jacobites. A great expedition of ten ships of the line, twelve other warships and forty-two transports carrying 3,500 troops was prepared at Brest under the command of his young kinsman

Vice-Admiral the duc d'Enville, an officer of the French Mediterranean galley force who had apparently never been to sea under sail. After prolonged administrative delays it finally sailed in June, still lacking many things essential to success, notably adequate provisions for a transatlantic voyage. Most of the officers were ignorant alike of navigation and geography, and had only a vague idea of the whereabouts of the great natural harbour of Chebucto in Nova Scotia,[24] their first destination. By the time the bulk of the scattered fleet finally gathered there after three months at sea, it was already crippled by sickness. D'Enville died a week after arrival, and his next in command tried to kill himself. This left the force in the hands of the marquis de La Jonquière, an officer of courage and experience, but by this time it had disintegrated beyond hope of any offensive operations. On the voyage home shortage of food and water reduced one ship to cannibalism.[25]

The capture of Louisbourg, like Porto Bello and Anson's return, aroused great enthusiasm in Britain because it was not only a success, but a success which confirmed the stereotypes in which the political nation believed. It gave credibility to a maritime strategy just as the allied campaign in Flanders was going badly. Bedford, as a prominent member of the 'New Allies', insisted on an expedition to conquer Canada as his price for consenting to a continued British commitment on the Continent. In February 1746, moreover, the ministry had been strengthened (in Parliament, if not with the king) by the ejection of Carteret's remaining supporters and their replacement by more of the 'Patriots', including the young William Pitt, which further tilted the political balance towards a maritime war. By June 1746 the Canada expedition was ready, under the command of Lieutenant-General St Clair and (the newly acquitted) Vice-Admiral Lestock. By this time, however, it was very late in the season for a transatlantic operation, and the news that d'Enville's fleet had sailed for an unknown destination made it seem too risky to send a large force far away. The Cabinet therefore decided on an autumn landing on the coast of France, after which the force would be available for Canada in the spring of 1747. Early in September the expedition sailed for the French East India Company's port of Lorient in southern Brittany. The two commanders were unhappy: the season of the equinoctial gales was about to begin, there was no safe anchorage on that coast, and they had virtually no intelligence about Lorient. Nevertheless the troops were put ashore on 20 September and advanced towards the town. By chance they encountered the only, slight, defences it possessed, and retreated at once. Had they but known, the French had already decided to surrender; moreover Lorient had no seaward defences, and Lestock could have sailed straight into the port to disembark the troops

on the quayside. The operation was a complete and almost farcical failure –
but it nevertheless provides a significant contrast with what was happening to
d'Enville's force on the other side of the Atlantic at the same time. The British
expedition was healthy and well fed, it was withdrawn without achievement,
but also without loss, and professional relations between general and admiral
remained smooth throughout.[26]

Besides the d'Enville expedition, the French navy's main preoccupation
in the Atlantic was the protection of trade, above all the rich trade with the
West Indies which made up the major part of France's overseas commerce.
Between 1716 and 1740 its annual value had risen from twenty-five to sixty
million *livres*, and the single colony of Saint Domingue[27] was now the richest
in the world.[28] Initially Maurepas hesitated to organize convoys, which were
unpopular with merchants because of the delays they imposed. In the Caribbean, however, where the British had two permanent squadrons and the
French none, French merchantmen suffered serious losses. This mattered not
only for the value of their homeward cargoes of sugar, coffee and other
colonial products, which at the worst would bear delay, but for their outward
cargoes of foodstuffs without which the islands' slave populations would
starve. A vigorous British commander-in-chief, like Knowles in the Leeward
Islands in 1744, raised the real danger of famine.

Neither side was happy with the results of the convoys of 1744 and 1745.
The British Leeward Islands squadron was torn between cruising to windward
of the French islands to intercept French shipping, or to windward of Barbados
to cover inward-bound British shipping from enemy privateers. Commodore
Fitzroy Henry Lee, Knowles's successor, did not have the strength to do both,
and was violently attacked for neglect of duty by the colonists and their
influential friends in London, who got his successor sent out with orders to
court-martial him. British planters were reluctant to support the conquest of
French sugar islands, which would only introduce formidable competitors
into the market protected by the Navigation Acts, and interrupt their lucrative
clandestine trade with the enemy; they therefore much preferred complaining
about French privateers to capturing their bases. The Jamaica squadron did not
have the same strategic dilemma as the Leeward Islands, since the Windward
Passage was the best place both to watch French ports and to cover British
trade, but the Spanish Havana squadron of ten ships of the line severely
hampered successive British admirals, without even having to put to sea, by
obliging them to keep their squadrons concentrated and near their base.[29]

The French on their side suffered serious losses, but their well-escorted
convoys proved invulnerable. In 1745, therefore, Maurepas adopted a new

policy of compulsory convoy, paid for by a levy of 5 per cent on outward and 12 per cent on homeward cargoes. The plan was to run three convoys a year, though in the event only four sailed between 1745 and 1747. In spite of delays and some losses imposed by the British Caribbean squadrons, these convoys were notably successful, and the few interceptions did not redound to the credit of the Royal Navy. Off Cap Nicolas at the northern end of the Windward Passage in August 1746 Captain the comte de Conflans escorting 131 merchantmen met Captain Cornelius Mitchell with four ships of the Jamaica squadron, but thanks to his skill and Mitchell's timidity, Conflans was able to extricate his convoy after a running fight of ten days with the loss of only one merchantman. In the same waters in March 1747, Captain comte Dubois de la Motte drove off Captain Digby Dent from his convoy. In both actions the attackers were equal in numbers to the escort, but were unable to profit from the situation.[30]

In home waters a Western Squadron had been created early in 1745 under Vice-Admiral William Martin, with sixteen ships of the line (including four Dutch). His primary function was to cover British convoys in the Western Approaches, which he did with success, but his orders tied him closely to the movements of these convoys, and he had few frigates. He was unable to trouble the French convoys, Prince Charles Edward's voyage to Scotland, or d'Enville's expedition. In the summer of 1746 Anson (now a Vice-Admiral) took over this command with more ships and looser instructions, and cruised long into the winter in the vain hope of intercepting d'Enville's ships returning from Canada.[31] On 26 December, still far at sea, 'Ushant bearing North-East by East 70 leagues', he wrote to Bedford on learning that the French had escaped him, 'From what I have felt this last fortnight I think whoever happens to have success at sea cannot be too well rewarded, for I would not suffer the same anguish of mind, that I have done upon this disappointment for all the honours, riches and pleasures this world can afford.'[32]

Throughout 1745 and 1746 a debate had been taking place between Bedford, Sandwich, Anson and Vernon about the proper functions of this Western Squadron. None of them laid out a comprehensive strategy, but as usual Vernon's ideas were the clearest and broadest:

> I have always looked upon squadrons in port, as neither a defence for the kingdom, nor a security for our commerce; and that the surest means for the preservation of both, was keeping a strong squadron in Soundings, which may answer both these purposes, as covering both Channels and Ireland, at the same time it secures our commerce.[33]

The basis of Vernon's strategy was the prevailing westerly winds, and the absence of any major French naval base in the Channel. Any French invasion force, such as the one Vernon spent much of 1745 watching, must either sail without escort, or be covered by warships entering the Channel from the westward. A fleet cruising in the Western Approaches lay to windward of the Channel and all the French Atlantic ports, perfectly placed to intercept such a force, while at the same time covering British trade both homeward- and outward-bound. Anson agreed, but was thinking also of intercepting French convoys, and rather favoured keeping the main fleet in port until intelligence indicated that they were ready to sail: 'the French can never be so much annoyed, nor this kingdom so well secured, as by keeping a strong squadron at home, sufficient to make detachments, whenever we have good intelligence that the French are sending ships either to the East or West Indies'.[34] Both admirals wanted to concentrate the main fleet, but Lord Sandwich at the Admiralty argued that a sufficient force could be kept together for home defence without losing opportunities to damage the enemy: 'by immediately recalling them [cruisers], we shall fall into the same trap which has, during the whole war, been so successfully laid for us, of giving way to every sudden alarm, and by that means have missed every advantage fortune would have thrown in our way'.[35]

These were different aspects of a strategy which was not clearly explained on paper until the twentieth century, and which, perhaps, only Vernon and the taciturn Anson really understood at the time. In essence it provided for a single, powerful squadron cruising in the Western Approaches to discharge all of Britain's most essential naval tasks: safeguarding against invasion, protecting trade, intercepting enemy ships and squadrons, watching and if necessary even blockading enemy ports. That was the theory: the practice required excellent intelligence, a large force of frigates to report the enemy's movements, highly seaworthy ships with an administrative system capable of keeping them supplied for long periods at sea, and a considerable measure of luck to intercept enemy squadrons in an area of about 150,000 square miles stretching from the Fastnet to Finisterre. If the squadron stayed at sea together for as long as possible, it increased its chances of fighting a decisive action if it met an enemy fleet, but it increased the wear and tear on the ships, especially if it stayed out in the autumn, the season of the equinoctial gales, but also of the rich convoys coming home from the West and East Indies. An autumn cruise might protect the trade at the cost of crippling the squadron for months. If the ships were dispersed in small groups on cruising stations trade might be better protected, but there was a risk of defeat in detail. If the squadron lay in port it kept in the best condition to meet the enemy, but the worst position to do so. The choice of port was also difficult: Spithead or St Helen's (off Portsmouth) were convenient but too far up Channel; Torbay was dangerously exposed either to enemy attack or to a south-easterly wind; Cawsand Bay at the mouth of Plymouth Sound was a cramped and even more exposed anchorage, while the Hamoaze off Plymouth Dockyard itself took far too long to get in and out of. The idea of the Western Squadron was not new – Sir Francis Drake had proposed something similar in 1588 – but these and many similar questions had to be answered before it could be made to work in practice. In 1747, for the first time, the Western Squadron began to work.[36]

Two French convoys were preparing to sail that spring, for India and Canada, but the convoy of the *Compagnie des Indes*, which sailed first in March, was driven back by bad weather and an encounter with British cruisers. This alerted the British; Anson was given all the ships that could be assembled with substantial freedom to deploy them where he chose, and in April he sailed for the Bay of Biscay. In the usual westerly winds French ships sailing from Brest, Lorient or Rochefort were almost bound to stretch south-westerly across the Bay past Cape Ortegal or Finisterre. On 3 May, north of Cape Ortegal, he intercepted the two French convoys, now combined. The marquis de La Jonquière formed a line of battle with his six ships of the line and three Indiamen, but Anson had fourteen ships of the line, and the result was never in doubt.

> They behaved all very well and lost their ships with honour and repu-
> tation, but I can without vanity say that our ships were better disciplined
> and made a much hotter fire upon them, than they did upon us, and it
> was easy to judge whose fire was best before the gross of my fleet got up,
> and they were superior in strength to my ships that engaged them.[37]

This complete little victory was the first real vindication of the Western Squadron. La Jonquière's sacrifice, however, covered the escape of many of the merchantmen.[38]

In June there was a further success in the same waters when Captain Thomas Fox commanding six ships of the line and two frigates separated from Anson's force intercepted Dubois de la Motte's convoy from the West Indies (the same which had driven off Dent). This time the escort did not make a stand, and the British took forty-eight out of 160 merchantmen.[39] By now Anson was ashore, and his second-in-command Warren was command-ing the Western Squadron, but in the autumn he in turn was obliged by illness to depute sea-going command to the newly promoted Rear-Admiral Edward

Hawke. Both Warren and Anson were uneasy about giving an inexperienced officer so much responsibility,[40] and he was provided with precise orders where to cruise. These orders were mysteriously 'mislaid', and reached Hawke only on 15 October – the day after, following his own intelligence and judgement, he had met a French outward-bound West India convoy, about 200 miles west of Ushant. The marquis de l'Etanduère's escort of eight ships of the line formed a line of battle to hold off Hawke's fourteen as long as possible, and the sacrifice of six of the eight allowed most of the 250 merchantmen to escape, but Hawke was able to warn the Leeward Islands squadron in time for it to intercept some of these on arrival.[41]

The two battles of Finisterre (as they are known in English) were a triumph for the new strategy of the Western Squadron. 'Sir Peter Warren says,' wrote the Duke of Newcastle,

> we have more French ships in our ports, than remain in the ports of France; and that he will carry the challenge, to fight them, with their own ships . . . I believe we have done their trade and marine more hurt this war than in all the foregoing ones: and it was high time to do it, for they were growing powerful rivals to us, in both.[42]

At once the improved situation in European waters began to have effects overseas. In the Leeward Islands a new British commander-in-chief, Commodore George Legge, arrived in April 1747 with sufficient strength to institute a more effective blockade, and by the end of the year the French islands were on the verge of starvation. At the same time Rear-Admiral Knowles at Jamaica was able to suppress much of the trade of Saint Domingue, and on 1 October 1748 he intercepted a Spanish squadron under Vice-Admiral Reggio going from Vera Cruz to Havana. Each side had seven ships of the line; one Spaniard was taken and another sunk.[43]

In the East Indies in 1745 the British squadron under Commodore Curtis Barnett had cruised with success against French trade, causing heavy personal loss to Joseph Dupleix, the head of the *Compagnie des Indes* on the Coromandel Coast. The enraged Dupleix, with a much larger army at his disposal, besieged the British capital of Madras. Barnett meanwhile had died, his successor Captain Edward Peyton fought an indecisive action on 25 June 1745 with the French ships under Captain Bertrand Mahé de la Bourdonnais, and then abandoned Madras, which surrendered in September. A new British commander-in-chief, Commodore Thomas Griffin, arrived at the end of 1746, and was able to save the British fort at Cuddalore from a French assault – greatly helped by dissension between Dupleix and La Bourdonnais which paralysed the French squadron. Griffin then blockaded the French capital of Pondicherry throughout the summer of 1747, while the French awaited the naval reinforcements that would restore their supremacy. Now, however, the influence of the Western Squadron began to be felt even on the other side of the world; only three ships under Captain Jean-Baptiste Bouvet de Lozier had escaped from Anson's victory, and reached Mauritius in October 1747. In June 1748 Bouvet was able to get urgently needed supplies into Pondicherry in spite of the presence of Griffin's squadron near by, the Vice-Admiral (as he had then become) demonstrating a complacency and lack of energy which might have exposed him to defeat at anchor, and later led to accusations of cowardice. Meanwhile Rear-Admiral Edward Boscawen had sailed from England in November 1747 with six warships and a landing force intended to attack Mauritius or the French possessions in India. Very unusually, he was explicitly named as commander-in-chief of both services. Frustrated at Mauritius by heavy surf, he arrived on the Coromandel Coast at the end of July 1748 and renewed the siege and blockade of Pondicherry. This was abandoned when the monsoon broke at the beginning of October, and soon afterwards the news of peace arrived.[44]

The rise of the Western Squadron made an important contribution to tactics as well as strategy. Once again many of the ideas came from Vernon, but it was Anson, Warren and Hawke who worked them out in practice. All naval tactics were severely affected by the limitations of signalling. The joint Anglo-Dutch signal book of 1689, which with modifications remained in British service for a century, consisted essentially of references to paragraphs of the Fighting Instructions.[45] Neither Instructions nor signal books were arranged in a logical sequence, or indexed. Many of the signals did not explicitly convey any order, but drew the recipient's attention to instructions which themselves were obscurely or ambiguously worded. Though admirals could and did add signals to meet anticipated tactical situations, there was no means of making any signal which had not been pre-arranged. When circumstances arose in action which did not fit those envisaged in the Fighting Instructions, an admiral's only recourse was to select the signal or combination of signals which seemed least inappropriate and hope that his captains would guess his meaning. The signals, moreover, were conveyed by combinations of flags or pendants hoisted in specific positions, and guns fired to windward or leeward. In order to understand a signal it was necessary to have a view of the flagship from broad on the bow or quarter: in a line ahead keeping tolerable station the flagship's signals would be impossible for most of the squadron to take in. The guns which formed an essential element of many signals were naturally difficult to distinguish in action. In close action gunsmoke often grew so thick that officers could not see the length of their own ships, let alone observe signals from a flagship which might be several miles away.[46]

For these and other reasons the critical use of naval tactics was before a battle, not during it, in the initial manoeuvres when an admiral might hope to keep control of his squadron and gain a decisive advantage. Once action was joined, it was the training and initiative of individual captains which counted. This was why Mathews' autocratic style of command would probably have failed even if Lestock had done his best. Vernon, by contrast, devoted much trouble to training his squadrons and informing his captains, and Anson did the same. 'I will follow your advice,' Warren wrote to him a few days after the first battle of Finisterre,

> and be very communicative with the captains of our squadron; I always thought it very necessary to be so and a thing that would be very much for the king's service to let them know one's scheme, or plan of operation.[47]

Both of them stressed the importance of fighting at close range in order to gain a decisive result:

> I am glad you told his Majesty that you and I had recommended the engaging the enemy close on all occasions. I dare say where we happen to be we shall show such an example as all officers must follow that have spirit or any regard to honour or reputation.[48]

Hawke absorbed these lessons, and in due course passed them on to a new generation of officers.[49]

By the end of 1747 the news of the naval war was at last encouraging, but everywhere else the situation was grim. In Flanders, in particular, the French armies under Marshal Saxe had conquered the Austrian Netherlands and stood poised to overrun the Dutch Republic. From unreasonable optimism in the spring of 1747, the British government had sunk into something like panic by early 1748. Fortunately France was almost bankrupt, and agreed to a peace on the basis of the restitution of conquests. The French withdrew from the Low Countries and restored Madras, but the British had to give up Louisbourg. Those who knew how the war was going were thankful to have got off so lightly, but the British and American public saw the only fruit of a maritime war thrown away to redeem the failures of allied armies on the Continent.[50]

A dispassionate analysis of the British war effort in the wars of 1739 to 1748 would have to report a large measure of weakness. Apparent naval superiority over Spain had proved remarkably difficult to translate into lasting victory, in spite of the isolated successes of Vernon at Porto Bello and Anson over the Manila galleon. Naples had been intimidated, but Madrid had not. The French seemed to have made up on land for all they had lost at sea, including Louisbourg. Though important developments in the capacity to sustain long-range operations were taking place in the 1740s, they were largely hidden from the public eye. The battles of Finisterre were the only victories in which the public could take unalloyed pleasure, the only obvious signs that Britain's battered national myth of naval destiny might have a basis in fact. Here, at least, people were not mistaken, for the Western Squadron was to be the foundation of British naval superiority in European waters, and eventually the world. Almost sixty years since William III had overturned the Royal Navy's strategic situation by sending it to war against France, the British were at last beginning to learn how to exploit the facts of geography to command the seas.

SEVENTEEN

A Scandal to the Navy

Operations 1749–1758

The years following the peace of 1748 were a time of taking stock in British strategy, and because politics and strategy were so intimately linked, it is necessary to explain something of the political structure and personalities of the time. The office of 'prime minister' did not then exist, and the phrase was not in use in its modern sense. The job of a modern British prime minister – to lead the government and preside over the Cabinet – belonged to the king, insofar as it existed. His ministers, most of whom were peers, dealt separately with the business of their departments, and reported to him individually.[1] There was no constitutional requirement for ministers to reach a common view. One minister, Henry Pelham, complained in 1747 that

> he did not know where the government lived; that there was none; they met indeed, and talked, and then said, 'Lord! it is late; when shall we meet to talk over this again?' and that the king was quite insensible, and would do nothing, saying it was their business.[2]

Yet it was essentially his business, foreign affairs and war, which ministers dealt with – things largely outside the competence of Parliament, which spent much of its time on local and particular matters. The great issue on which government and Parliament met was finance, the granting of taxes, now clearly understood as the responsibility of the House of Commons. For this reason the minister for finance, the First Lord of the Treasury (for the Treasury Board was in commission throughout this period), was often in the Commons, where he was sometimes the only and always the senior Cabinet minister. He therefore had to act as leader of the House and principal government spokesman as well as finance minister. Those who possessed the talents to master this demanding combination tended to carry more weight than their relatively junior political or social position would justify. When peers presided at the

Treasury, the junior office of Chancellor of the Exchequer had to be held by a commoner of ability who could justify the government's financial policy to the House of Commons.[3]

The other senior members of an eighteenth-century Cabinet were the Lord Chancellor, usually the Lord President of the Council and the Lord Keeper of the Privy Seal, and the two Secretaries of State, for the Northern and Southern Departments, who divided foreign affairs on the basis of geography; the Southern Secretary taking southern and western Europe (including France and Spain), while the Northern Secretary took Germany, Russia and Scandinavia. The Secretaries, being also the official channel for the king's formal commands to all parts of government, were regarded as senior to most of their political colleagues, and had some responsibilities for domestic affairs. The Southern Secretary, as the senior of the two, usually conveyed the king's commands to military commanders-in-chief, colonial governors and the Board of Admiralty. Only the authority of a Secretary of State could unify the three branches of the British armed services: the Navy, represented by the Admiralty and the other naval boards; the army, a loose collection of horse and foot regiments on the separate British and Irish establishments over which the Secretary at War exercised some administrative supervision; and the Ordnance Board, responsible for the artillery and engineers as well as the supply of munitions to the other services.

> Every one who is at all acquainted with the constitution of this government must know that all warlike preparations, every military operation, and every naval equipment must be directed by a Secretary of State before they can be undertaken. Neither the Admiralty, Treasury, Ordnance, nor Victualling Boards can move a step without the king's command so signified.[4]

Though the authority of the Admiralty Board had already risen considerably since 1714, and First Lords like Wager and Bedford (though not Winchilsea) were clearly understood as the responsible ministers for the Navy, formal commands still reached them from a Secretary of State. Only a Secretary, moreover, could exercise authority over a combined operation, so the amphibious expeditions of the eighteenth century were controlled by one of the Secretaries, usually the Southern Secretary, to whom both admiral and general reported directly. At the beginning of the operation there was a formal hand-over of authority over the warships from the Admiralty to the Secretary of State, though it was understood that the admiral should keep the Board informed of what he was doing.[5]

Outstanding among the finance ministers of the eighteenth century was Henry Pelham, First Lord of the Treasury from 1743 to his death in 1754, who earned the rare combination of the confidence of the king, the respect of the House of Commons and the trust of the financial world. Pelham's elder brother the Duke of Newcastle was Secretary of State for one or other department from 1724 to 1754, then his brother's successor as Treasury minister until 1756, and again from 1757 to 1762. Though not without talent, especially as a political manager, the jealous, vain and timid Newcastle was often a trial to his brother and his colleagues. The Pelhams, together with the great jurist the Earl of Hardwicke, Lord Chancellor from 1737 to 1756, represented the surviving core of Walpole's party, and Walpole's policy. They accepted the necessity of some sort of Continental commitment in time of war, as an inescapable consequence of Britain's strategic situation, and of the Hanoverian succession. Newcastle therefore concentrated his post-war diplomatic efforts on attempts to rebuild the 'Old System'. 'A naval force,' he assured Hardwicke in 1749,

> though carried never so high, unsupported with even the appearance of a force upon the Continent, will be of little use. It will provoke, but not effectually prevent ... France will outdo us by sea, when they have nothing to fear by land, and they can have nothing to fear there, if we can have nothing to oppose them.[6]

By this he meant that his diplomacy was the core of Britain's defence. Bedford, Sandwich, Pitt and others drawn from the Whig opposition of the 1730s disagreed: they were identified with the ever-popular English idea of a maritime war as the natural and painless British strategy. They had begun their political careers linked with the Prince of Wales – always under the Georges the natural connection for politicians who wanted to oppose the ministry without being linked to the Jacobites. When the prince died in 1751, some of the opposition regrouped around his younger brother the Duke of Cumberland, a potential regent in case George II (sixty-seven in the spring of 1751) should die before his thirteen-year-old grandson came of age.[7]

Politics and strategy were closely linked – but it is important to understand that strategy in the modern sense did not really exist. The word only entered the English language in the early nineteenth century, as a borrowing from French, then used chiefly in its Greek sense to refer to the art of the general.[8] Eighteenth-century British statesmen did not know the word, and consequently had no distinct concept of the thing. Navies and armies existed, and they had of necessity some ideas about how to use them, but those ideas tended to be pragmatic, often detailed, not based explicitly on any developed theory. For contemporaries, British policy towards the outside world was a single, large subject which embraced diplomacy, commerce and war. Each of these aspects of national policy had naval implications, and could be seen to influence the employment of British fleets and squadrons, but contemporaries were not in the habit of isolating the naval implications of policy. It was in many ways a strength of their approach, and of the British constitution which put such wide responsibilities in the hands of the Secretaries of State, that it encouraged a unified approach to foreign policy, but it was a weakness in that it discouraged study of the practical application of policy in wartime.

The Navy itself was in no condition to supply the want of any specifically naval policy-making. Modern navies apply much of their effort to planning for war in every foreseeable situation, and justify their existence largely in terms of their readiness for war. Eighteenth-century navies were not blind to the need to be ready for war, but for many reasons advance planning was both more difficult and less urgent for them.[9] No navy had anything in the nature of a modern naval staff, nor was there any forum for the discussion of strategy, or indeed of any other aspect of naval affairs. There were no institutions of higher study for the profession of arms, and no idea of encouraging officers to study it. Intelligent admirals hoped their officers would read history and other books, but there was no professional literature they could suggest that dealt with strategy. There were numerous manuals on navigation, gunnery, naval architecture and other technical subjects; and a growing interest in tactics and signalling;[10] but the literature on naval warfare in general consisted of a handful of works translated out of French, none of which dealt with strategy in any coherent fashion.[11]

The five years between the end of the war and Henry Pelham's death were dominated by his efforts to restore the government's financial stability. The war had left debts which terrified the political world. 'We have exerted ourselves to the utmost,' Pelham wrote in February 1748, 'I wish we may not find we have already exceeded our abilities. Our whole depends on our credit, that begins to stagger, and if it should be stretched the least further I am satisfied it would break.'[12] He therefore demanded sharp reductions in the naval vote; by 1750 it was down to 8,000 men, and Sandwich's insistence on a minimum level of naval strength was one reason for his dismissal in 1751. His successor was Anson, whose already powerful political position as a public hero had been greatly strengthened by his marriage to Hardwicke's daughter in 1748. He was now part of the Pelhamite inner core of British politics, and it was evidently understood when he was appointed that he would not upset

Pelham's policy of retrenchment.[13] This policy was notably successful in its own terms – Pelham was able to reduce the Land Tax from four to three shillings in the pound in 1752 – but also controversial. The war, the 1745 rebellion and the French invasion schemes had left a heightened sense of national vulnerability. Newcastle's instinct to rebuild an anti-French coalition was very much a minority reaction; for most of the British political nation, the war inspired a renewed interest in sea power, and therefore a renewed concern for the welfare of the Navy. The myths of a triumphant war against Spain had been severely battered, but the re-emergence of France as the major enemy had diverted attention away from Spain, and enough had been done against France, at Louisbourg and the battles of Finisterre, to encourage the advocates of naval war.[14]

In France people drew different lessons from the war. Some persuaded themselves that the Jacobites were stronger than ever, commanding leading politicians, 'the wisest heads and richest towns of England'.[15] Many seem to have accepted with remarkably little questioning that it had been right to abandon France's pacific foreign policy to go to war against Austria in 1741 and Britain in 1744, and that it would be proper to fight Britain again at some suitable opportunity. Nobody seems to have asked whether the French navy was structurally equipped for such a war, though it was obvious enough that it was too small. Maurepas assessed his own policy in characteristically detached tones in 1745:

> My enquiries into the reasons which led to the adoption of the extreme policy of reducing the navy to a lower state than ever before, have convinced me that they were much less influenced by the need of economy than by the foreign policy of the Regency . . . since these reasons no longer applied after the Regency, it seems that the navy should subsequently have been rebuilt to its former level.[16]

French ministers did not doubt that their country, whatever its short-term wartime financial difficulties, was inherently better able to bear the burden of victory than Britain. 'Everything here is real: fertile land, precious goods, clinking cash; a lack of credit would not affect any of this.'[17] With three times the population and number of soldiers of Britain (to say nothing of a vastly more stable political and financial structure), France, they thought, was self-evidently the superpower of Western Europe. French overseas trade, briefly checked by the reverses of 1747, continued to grow rapidly after the war. Less noticed was the fact that much of this trade was under foreign flags, and that the pool of French seamen available to man the navy was not growing.

Moreover no French Pelham had tackled wartime debts, which continued to cripple post-war naval reconstruction.[18]

Another European power forced to reconsider her position by the Austrian Succession War was the Netherlands. Although never a declared belligerent, the Republic had fought against France, and come very close to disaster as a result. All parties were badly shaken, and very reluctant to be drawn into war against France again if safe and profitable neutrality could by any means be preserved. The British for their part had been very dissatisfied with the quality and quantity of the Dutch contribution to the allied war-effort, ashore and afloat, and had lost most of their remaining illusions that the Republic was still a great military or naval power. Her strategic significance in Europe now rested largely on her still-dominant position in the carrying trades, especially the Baltic trade. The Anglo-Dutch treaty of 1674 allowed either party to ship any cargo except munitions of war, narrowly defined to cover little more than arms and ammunition, through a blockade by the other. Naval stores were explicitly made free, so there was nothing to stop Dutch merchantmen supplying the French navy with as much timber, hemp and tar as it needed. This, and on the other side the quasi-piratical activities of British privateers, had generated a great deal of friction, but a pragmatic solution was developed in the 1740s. Dutch merchantmen met on the high seas were stopped and searched, but no attempt was made to seize cargoes of naval stores for French dockyards; instead the cargoes were bought by the British crown. The French suffered, but Dutch shippers received their contract price and were not dissatisfied. The Navy Board, however, was unhappy at being forced to buy (and then sell at a loss) overpriced goods of a quality far inferior to what it demanded for British service.[19]

Henry Pelham's death in 1754 produced a new political situation, and coincided with a new threat from abroad. Newcastle took his brother's place, but could not supply his talents, nor speak for the ministry in the Commons, where the most persuasive voices (notably William Pitt) were distasteful to the king or his ministers. Newcastle was obliged to call on Henry Fox (who became Southern Secretary in November 1755) and his patron Cumberland, but the ministry still lacked strength and stability.[20] Meanwhile a dangerous situation was developing in North America, where French officials in Canada were intriguing with the Indian tribes and pushing into the Ohio valley, west of the Allegheny Mountains and behind the British colonies. To London this seemed unequivocal evidence of aggressive intent, though it is unclear how far French ministers had in fact planned or foreseen what their subordinates were doing. Aiming to negotiate a settlement from a position of strength, they sent a minister to London, and thirteen ships of the line carrying troop reinforcements to Louisbourg and Quebec. The British government likewise did not desire war, but a weak ministry and a divided Cabinet could not agree on what the French intended, or how to react.[21]

The result was a messy compromise, intended to defeat French aggression in North America by a display of overwhelming force, while at the same time avoiding war in Europe. At Cumberland's insistence a substantial military expedition under Major-General Edward Braddock was to strike over the mountains into the Ohio Valley and roll the French frontier back to the Great Lakes. Vice-Admiral Boscawen was despatched in April 1755 with eleven ships of the line and orders to intercept and seize any French ships carrying troops to America, if necessary by force. Ministers knew that the French were using warships fitted as troopships, with their main battery of guns dismounted, but they seem to have hoped that he could seize or attack even warships without provoking war. In the event the French squadron lost company in the fogs of the Grand Banks, and Boscawen only found three of them. One escaped, and two were captured after stiff fighting. 'It gives me much concern that so little has been done, since any thing has been done at all . . .' commented Hardwicke when he heard. 'Voilà the war begun.'[22] Worse news arrived soon afterwards. Approaching the French position of Fort Duquesne on the Ohio, Braddock's force had been ambushed by French and Indian troops and routed.[23]

Both sides now feared that war was unavoidable, yet hesitated to commit themselves completely. In June Rear-Admiral comte Duguay was sent out with the Brest squadron of nine ships to cover homebound trade, with orders to commit limited hostilities only, which led to the capture of the British frigate *Blandford*. At the same time Hawke was at sea with the Western Squadron with equally ambiguous orders; to detain French ships of the line, but not to fire first or to bother with smaller warships. In August he was reinforced and sent new orders to bring in French merchant ships as well. As a result many prizes and prisoners were taken, but neither Duguay's squadron nor the French warships returning from North America were intercepted, and French cruisers continued to report meeting British warships which did not attack. In Versailles ministers were baffled, and in September the *Blandford* was sent back to Britain as an earnest of peaceful intentions. By this time, however, the British government had decided that peace was irretrievable, and by the end of the year the French had come to the same conclusion. In January they delivered an ultimatum in deliberately unacceptable terms, and both sides regarded themselves as committed to war, though the actual declaration did not come until May. Thus Britain and France blundered into a war – the Seven Years' War as it is known, though it actually lasted almost nine years – which neither had prepared for or desired. Britain's natural strengths at sea and overseas had come to little. The only counterbalance to disaster in North America was the almost accidental capture of 5,500 French prisoners aboard the seized merchantmen, of whom about half were able seamen. This was equivalent to the crews of about five ships of the line: a real blow, but not a crippling one.[24]

With Anson First Lord of the Admiralty, there was no doubt that British naval strategy would be based once more on the Western Squadron, which was at sea under Hawke in the spring of 1756. Ministers soon realized, however, if they had not known before, that the facts of geography which made the strategy of the Western Squadron possible had also left it one major weakness. From the Western Approaches it could cover all the French Channel and Atlantic ports: the naval bases of Brest and Rochefort, the commercial ports of Le Havre, St Malo, Nantes and Bordeaux, and the establishment of the *Compagnie des Indes* at Lorient. What it could not in any way cover was the French Mediterranean naval base of Toulon. For France, a fleet divided between two seas was always a weakness, but it was also an opportunity, for the Toulon squadron was a sort of strategic wild card which France could play in any part of the world, unless the British were strong enough to detach an equivalent squadron at least as far as Gibraltar. Such strength might be built up, with time and good fortune, but at the start of every eighteenth-century war, the Toulon squadron severely embarrassed British naval planners.

The possession of Minorca increased rather than diminished British strategic difficulties. The superb harbour of Port Mahón was admirably situated as a base of operations against Toulon, but the island was a liability. Even with a substantial garrison there was no possibility of defending every landing place. The people remained stubbornly indifferent to the blessings of British rule and could not be relied upon for any help. The island could only feed itself in good years; troops and ships had to be victualled from overseas (usually Algiers). As a result British Mediterranean squadrons found their operations hampered by the necessity of defending their base and its communications. In peacetime the Royal Navy left only a few ships in the Mediterranean, and in the spring of 1756 there was nothing to protect Minorca but an understrength garrison.[25]

The intelligence reaching London indicated two simultaneous French threats. On the Channel coasts of France a major invasion force was assembling, but there were also clear indications of an amphibious expedition preparing at Toulon, possibly (but not certainly) against Minorca. Either operation might be a feint to cover the other, and French ministers were free to delay their choice until the last minute.[26] As the British fleet slowly mobilized (all the more slowly because of the sickly state in which Boscawen's ships had returned from North America), it was not at all clear that there would be enough ships available to meet both threats. In this dilemma ministers were sure that home defence was the Navy's essential priority. 'I think it would be a dangerous measure,' Anson wrote to Hardwicke in December 1755, 'to part with your naval strength from this country, which cannot be recalled if wanted, when I am strongly of opinion that whenever the French intend anything in earnest, their attack will be against this country.'[27] All available ships were therefore added to the Western Squadron. Not until March did the British feel strong enough to make a detachment to the Mediterranean. As usual on the outbreak of war, there was a scarcity of admirals with experience of wartime command but not disabled by age. The obvious choice, the only one with extensive experience of those waters (and apparently the only one who asked for the job), was Vice-Admiral the Hon. John Byng, youngest son of Sir George (later Lord Torrington). At the end of March Byng took command of a squadron of ten ships of the line, and on 6 April he sailed, with orders to collect a regiment from the Gibraltar garrison on his way to reinforce Minorca. He had on board many of the officers of both garrisons, who had been on leave, as eighteenth-century British army officers usually were in peacetime.[28]

Meanwhile the French, observing British preparations, had concluded that Channel invasion was too risky, and on 15 March the decision was taken to try an attack on Minorca. Four days after Byng, Vice-Admiral the marquis de La Galissonière sailed from Toulon with twelve ships of the line escorting 176 transports carrying 12,000 men commanded by the duc de Richelieu. On Easter Sunday, 18 April, the French troops landed without opposition at Ciudadela. Having committed themselves to the landing only at the last minute, the French had collected no intelligence about Minorca, and were alarmed to confront defences which they had not anticipated. The British garrison under the eighty-four-year-old Lieutenant-General William Blakeney had retreated into Fort St Philip, a fortress of great strength which commanded the entrance to Port Mahón. Richelieu found himself committed to a lengthy siege, driving his trenches through solid rock, and completely dependent for ammunition, food and even water on seaborne supply which enemy warships might easily interrupt. La Galissonière's ships had no port of refuge, and were only victualled to the end of June.[29] On 20 May Byng's squadron was sighted approaching. 'Gentlemen,' remarked the Duke to his officers, watching from the shore,

> there is a very interesting game being played out there. If Monsieur de La Galissonière defeats the enemy, we may continue our siege in carpet slippers – but if he is beaten, we shall have to storm the place at once, at any cost.[30]

Meanwhile in London, ministers were growing worried by the tone of placid despondency in Byng's letters. The final straw was his letter of 4 May from Gibraltar (received on the 31st), announcing that he had not embarked the troops from the garrison since his mission was hopeless and Minorca was bound to be lost. 'This man will not fight!' George II exclaimed when he read it. On 16 June Sir Edward Hawke sailed with a single ship, under orders to take over the squadron from Byng.[31]

By this time it was too late. Byng's squadron, now with thirteen ships of the line, met La Galissonière's twelve and attacked, but it was handled with notable incompetence and only a few of the British ships, not including the flagship, were seriously engaged. The battle was a disappointment, but the British force was substantially intact and there was still everything to play for. The French position was so precarious that Byng needed only to cruise in the vicinity or let loose his frigates against the unescorted merchantmen bringing Richelieu's supplies. The only hope for the French was for Byng to withdraw all British ships from the Western Mediterranean, and this he obligingly did. 'What a scene Byng had open to him, and to throw it all away!' exclaimed Boscawen when he heard.[32] On 28 June, after an heroic resistance, Blakeney was forced to surrender.[33]

Byng was astonished to be relieved by Hawke when he reached Gibraltar, 'having no suspicion that his conduct was not highly praiseworthy'.[34] He returned home in a mood of righteous indignation, to find the Navy and the public furious against him. For the British public any admiral who failed had betrayed the national trust. Sea officers were more informed critics, but even they all condemned him. 'No doubt but Mr Byng's behaviour on the late occasion off Mahon must anger and surprise you and every thinking man in the kingdom,' wrote Captain Samuel Faulknor. 'Sad indeed: he's brought more disgrace on the British flag than ever his father the great Lord Torrington did honour to it.'[35] 'What a scandal to the Navy, that they should be premeditated cowards that have been so long bred to arms,' was Boscawen's comment,[36] and even those who did not accuse Byng of physical cowardice spoke of gross misconduct.[37]

Byng had few defenders for his own sake, except a handful of his loyal followers led by the eccentric and always wildly partisan Captain Augustus Hervey, but naturally the opposition exploited the public outrage at the disaster to attack the government, which it blamed for sending Byng with insufficient force. As a result of the loss of Minorca, the government fell in December 1756, and was replaced by a ministry formed by William Pitt, and consisting largely of his own numerous relatives, the Pitt-Grenville 'cousinhood'. Pitt's ministry had every political motive to exculpate his 'gallant worthy friend' Byng[38] and shift the blame on to their predecessors, and they appointed a friendly president to Byng's court martial, which opened shortly after they had taken office. The admiral himself expected a complete acquittal. The weight of professional opinion, however, was overwhelming. Byng was convicted, not of cowardice, but of 'failing to do his utmost to take or destroy the enemy's ships', one of the many provisions of the Articles of War which still reflected the political fears of the English Republicans of 1653, and which carried an automatic death penalty. Nobody expected him actually to be executed, and the government had no desire that he should be, but the admiral was certainly unlucky in his friends. Hervey concocted mad escape plots implying French or Jacobite connections. Voltaire sent Byng a clandestine letter from Richelieu expressing admiration for his conduct, which was inter-cepted by ministers and raised further suggestions of treason. Finally when the new First Lord of the Admiralty, Pitt's tactless and arrogant brother-in-law Earl Temple, presented the Board's request for clemency to George II, he implied that the king, as a coward himself, ought to have compassion on the admiral.[39] That sealed Byng's fate, and he was shot on his own quarterdeck on 14 March 1757. Since a surprising number of historians, seemingly unaware of the fall of the Newcastle ministry, have attributed Byng's death to political persecution,[40] it is worth repeating that he died while his political friends were in office, and in spite of their efforts to save him from the anger of the king, the fury of the public, and the disgust of his naval colleagues.[41]

These unpopular efforts were partly responsible for the dismissal of Pitt's ministry in April 1757. For the next twelve weeks there was effectively no government. Only at the end of June was the ministry reconstructed as an uneasy alliance of Pitt and Newcastle. Hardwicke, though no longer Lord Chancellor, remained an indispensable source of political strength and judi-cious advice in Cabinet, and was able to force his son-in-law Anson (now unpopular and blamed by many for the loss of Minorca) back into the Admiralty. The new government, taking office in some disarray well into the campaigning season, hastened to do something to demonstrate that they had the war under control. A reinforcement for North America was announced, but inexperienced ministers, many of them political enemies of one another, reduced both the raising of troops and the organizing of transports to confusion. Lord Barrington, the Secretary at War, mislaid some of his new regiments and only discovered their whereabouts by accident. On the Continent, meanwhile, the Duke of Cumberland, commanding the Anglo-Hanoverian army, was driven back by the French and forced to surrender on terms which left Hanover under enemy occupation.[42]

The Western Squadron, having spent much of 1756 watching Brest, made two cruises in January and again in March 1757, but missed three French squadrons going to the West Indies or Canada. This allowed the French to assemble at Louisbourg a force which by the end of June amounted to eighteen ships of the line under Vice-Admiral comte Dubois de la Motte. The British plan had been to mount another Anglo-American assault on the fortress, and the troops had been conveyed from New York to Halifax, but Vice-Admiral Francis Holburne had only fifteen sail of the line and the assault had to be abandoned. Holburne's fleet was then dispersed and badly damaged by a storm. Fortunately the elderly and inactive French admiral did nothing to exploit the situation, but the British campaign had entirely failed without his intervention.[43]

The new Southern Secretary of State William Pitt, anxious to satisfy the public and demonstrate his own maritime credentials in what remained of the year 1757, pushed for the Western Squadron to undertake some amphibious attacks in the style of Vernon at Porto Bello. The choice fell on Rochefort, well inland up the River Charente but allegedly ill defended. By the time the force entered Aix Roads at the mouth of the river it was already the end of September and the sea officers were thinking nervously of equinoctial gales. Captain Richard Howe of the *Magnanime* bombarded and subdued the Ile d'Aix battery covering the mouth of the river 'with such cool and steady resolution, as has (most justly) gained him the universal applause of Navy and army',[44] in the words of Captain George Rodney, but then the assault hung fire. With inadequate and confusing intelligence, Major-General Sir John Mordaunt was not prepared to land unless the Navy could assure his retreat, and Hawke could not guarantee that the weather would permit re-embarkation over open beaches. So the attack was abandoned, and the force returned; the army and Navy in a bad temper with one another, Pitt humiliated and angry with both.[45] One important thing it had achieved, though the British were scarcely aware, was to expose Aix Roads to casual attack, making the principal assembly point for French overseas convoys unusable, and forcing them to gather at Brest where they could not be supplied locally.[46]

1756 was not only a year of political turmoil in Britain, but of the 'diplomatic revolution' in Europe, meaning the collapse of the 'Old System' which Newcastle had cherished for so long. Weary of an alliance which exposed the Austrian Netherlands and did nothing to sustain her interests in Germany, Austria abandoned the British connection and linked with France instead. Austria's enemy Prussia as a result became available as a British ally. Since the ruthless aggression of Frederick the Great had surrounded his country with enemies, he needed all the friends he could get, so Prussia fortuitously made up for the British allies lost by Newcastle's bungling diplomacy. Another consequence of the alliance between Austria and France (and the neutrality of Spain) was that the Western Mediterranean ceased to be a theatre of war. The British had no need to maintain a fleet there, which meant that the loss of Minorca, however humiliating, was of very little strategic consequence. Britain's Levant trade, though declining, still had to be protected, but the Royal Navy did not re-enter the Mediterranean in strength for thirty years. Partly as a consequence, Algerine sea power revived. The British remained careful to keep on good terms with a state capable of damaging its trade and starving Gibraltar, but local (especially Spanish and Italian) shipping suffered.[47]

Instead the British government found itself under pressure from Frederick the Great to send a squadron to the Baltic to protect East Prussia from Russian invasion. It was deeply reluctant to do so, not only because the ships were needed elsewhere, but because Britain did not wish or need to become embroiled in a Baltic war against Russia, still less to provoke Prussia's enemies Denmark and Sweden into restricting the shipment of naval stores. Frederick, however, was difficult to refuse. His western army under the talented Prince Ferdinand of Brunswick made it possible for George II to repudiate Cumberland's surrender and take the field again, and in the course of 1758 Ferdinand's joint Prussian-Hanoverian army was to drive the French out of Hanover altogether. It was impossible not to make at least a token British contribution, and 9,000 British troops joined Ferdinand's army that summer.[48]

The British government's strategic dilemma mirrored its internal divisions. Newcastle was pleased to revive 'Continent measures', as he wrote to Anson in July:

> It is with pleasure I see them now coming into fashion again; they are the only true solid ones, from whence any great and real advantage can

come . . . It is a great point for continent politicians (as you and I are) that 9,000 men are sent into Germany. We must play a little with expeditions, to make *that* go down.[49]

He was no less pleased at the discomfiture of his colleague and rival Pitt, who had won office by promising the public the maritime war they yearned for, and now found himself having to justify another British army on the Continent. Pitt's answer was the 'expeditions' to which Newcastle refers; coastal raids designed to reassure his supporters of his commitment to a maritime war, and pacify Frederick the Great by drawing French forces away from Germany to guard the coast, without sending British troops or ships far away from home.[50]

On 5 June warships under Captain Howe (covered to the westward by the main Western Squadron) landed 9,400 men in Cancale Bay, from which they marched nine miles westward to St Malo. The fortified city itself proved to be inaccessible without a regular siege, but in the port of St Servan just up the river the British were able to burn at least eighty privateers and merchantmen, plus four warships on the stocks, before returning to Cancale to re-embark, having spent a week on French soil without loss, and virtually without opposition. The force then cruised along the coasts of Normandy, considering or at least alarming places from Granville to Le Havre, before on 7 August landing near Cherbourg. The great dockyard port was not constructed until the nineteenth century, but Cherbourg was a fortified town, and both port and fortifications were destroyed. The British army stayed over a week without being seriously threatened, and again re-embarked on the 16th without loss. Next month another and more ambitious attempt was made against St Malo, this time approaching from St Lunaire just to the west, with the intention of carrying the troops across the Rance estuary in landing craft. This, however, proved impossible, heavy weather made the beaches at St Lunaire impracticable, and the British troops retreated towards the cove of St Cast twelve miles away, the nearest landing place sheltered from a westerly gale. This time French forces were nearer and more alert, the march was handled with remarkable carelessness, and in the final stages of the embarkation the British rearguard was overrun, with the loss of 800 men, mostly prisoners.[51]

Pitt's coastal raids have been the subject of much attention from historians, as much for their symbolic value as for their strategic significance. From the late nineteenth century until the mid twentieth they served as prime examples of Pitt's strategic genius in identifying and exploiting the 'British way in warfare',[52] the use of sea power as a strategic lever to multiply the value of small bodies of troops. More recently the pendulum of historical opinion (following modern politics as usual) has swung back from sea power and empire towards the 'Continental Commitment', and it has been fashionable to decry Pitt's raids as militarily negligible, serving to bolster his political position rather than to advance the war-effort.[53] Both positions, it may be suggested, were exaggerated. We no longer need to see eighteenth-century naval operations through the late nineteenth-century imperial spectacles which have distorted so many views of them. Coastal raids against a major power were not a war-winning strategy by themselves. Nor, however, need we deny that these raids were an economical and generally successful use of available forces which could not have been deployed elsewhere. They had great political and diplomatic value in humiliating France, and really did tie down large bodies of troops (134 infantry battalions and 56 cavalry squadrons, according to a recent French historian) which might otherwise have faced Prince Ferdinand in Germany.[54] Their political impact was all the greater in the summer of 1758, when the British public in three years of war had still been fed almost no news but of disappointments and disasters. At long last, however, this was about to change.

EIGHTEEN

Myths Made Real

Operations 1758–1763

'In this country,' remarked Voltaire, 'it is thought good to kill an admiral from time to time, to give courage to the others.'[1] There was more truth in the epigram than perhaps he knew, for the execution of Byng had a profound effect on the moral climate of the Navy, and sharply reversed the effects of the battle of Toulon. The fates of Mathews and Lestock had taught officers that misconduct with support in high places had nothing to fear; the fate of Byng taught them that even the most powerful political friends might not save an officer who failed to fight. Many things might go wrong with an attack on the enemy, but the only fatal error was not to risk it. Byng's death revived and reinforced a culture of aggressive determination which set British officers apart from their foreign contemporaries, and which in time gave them a steadily mounting psychological ascendancy. More and more in the course of the century, and for long afterwards, British officers encountered opponents who expected to be attacked, and more than half expected to be beaten, so that they went into action with an invisible disadvantage which no amount of personal courage or numerical strength could entirely make up for.[2]

For the French navy this psychological burden was added to a traditional doctrine which regarded the completion of the 'mission' as more important than battle or victory, and tended to deprecate or sneer at fighting. 'Do you know what a naval battle is?' asked Maurepas. 'Two squadrons sail from opposite ports, they manoeuvre, they meet, they fire; a few masts are shot away, a few sails torn, a few men killed, a lot of powder and shot wasted – and the sea remains no less salty than before.'[3] The admirals agreed with the courtiers. 'Too often these naval battles produce much more noise than profit,' Vice-Admiral the comte d'Estaing remarked, a generation later,[4] and his contemporary Rear-Admiral comte Barras de Saint-Laurent explained that 'it is a principle of war that one should risk a great deal to defend one's own position, but very little to attack the enemy's'.[5] At the end of the century the theorist Captain Joseph d'Audibert de Ramatuelle summed it up:

> The French navy has always preferred the glory of achieving and safe-guarding a conquest to the glory, perhaps more brilliant, but less substantial, of taking a few ships of the line. Thus it has kept more closely to the object of war.[6]

More accurately, it kept to the object of convoy war, in which context the British too believed in the primacy of the 'mission'. British officers were always strictly ordered to remain with their convoys and not to be tempted on any account to abandon them. The difference was that, for the British, this was understood as a disagreeable but essential exception to the general rule that an officer's first duty was always to defeat the enemy. French officers generally sailed under orders which defined battle as the exception, to be risked only in particular and unusual circumstances when the objects of the operation could not otherwise be attained. As a result they tended to be psychologically unprepared to take opportunities of victory when they offered. The Spanish navy suffered from the same problem. In both cases the doctrine of the 'mission' made a good deal of sense for navies mainly designed to defend colonies and trade. It was much less helpful to navies which, wisely or unwisely, had been committed to naval war against Britain in which there was little to be achieved by remaining on the defensive.[7]

During 1758, good news began to reach Britain from various parts of the world, and in many cases the psychological effect of the battle of Minorca and the death of Byng was clearly discernible. After heavy losses at the beginning of the war, the French had restarted West India convoys in 1757. In October 1757 Captain the comte de Kersaint was lying at Cap François with five ships of the line and a convoy ready to sail for home, while the port was blockaded by three smaller ships under Captain Arthur Forrest. On the 21st Kersaint sailed to clear a path for the merchantmen, and Forrest immediately attacked. In spite of the odds, the result was tactically indecisive, and both sides retreated to port for repairs. Since Forrest's base, Port Royal, lay 300 miles to leeward, it was Kersaint who profited, getting his convoy safely away on 12 November long before the British ships returned. Strategically, one can therefore say, Forrest and his colleagues were wrong to fight when their mere presence would have made it very difficult for Kersaint to sail his convoy. Morally, however, it was a tonic to British naval confidence that 'our captains were too gallant to be terrified at their formidable appearance', as Forrest's commander-in-chief Rear-Admiral Thomas Cotes reported.[8]

In the Mediterranean the effort of manning La Galissonière's squadron had exhausted Toulon's resources, and it was not until November 1757 that Rear-Admiral La Clue Sabran sailed for the West Indies, having taken over a year to man six ships of the line. Finding his way barred by Admiral Henry Osborn with the British Mediterranean squadron (now based at Gibraltar), La Clue took refuge in Cartagena to await reinforcements. On 28 February 1758 Osborn was cruising off the port when he intercepted Rear-Admiral Duquesne de Menneville (the former Governor-General of Canada who had done so much to start the war) coming with three sail of the line from Toulon. Duquesne's ships scattered with the British in pursuit. The *Orphée*, 64 was taken by three British ships, and another small French ship of the line was driven aground, while Duquesne's flagship, the eighty-gun *Foudroyant*, was chased into the night by the *Monmouth*, 64. Their respective broadsides were 1,164 lbs against 1,944 lbs,[9] but the *Foudroyant* had been La Galissonière's flagship at Minorca, and the *Monmouth*'s captain Arthur Gardiner had been Byng's flag-captain. He knew Anson's opinion that Byng and his officers had dishonoured the Navy that day, and he redeemed his honour with his life. When the *Foudroyant* surrendered to Robert Carkett, the *Monmouth*'s First Lieutenant, at one o'clock in the morning, she had suffered 134 killed to the *Monmouth*'s thirty. The capture of this ship, against these odds, did a lot to restore the Navy's reputation as well as Captain Gardiner's posthumous honour.[10]

The East Indies were so far from Europe that fighting there always tended to be partly disconnected from strategy elsewhere. Moreover, the European East India companies were more concerned with their own rivalries, and their relations with the Indian princes, than with the quarrels of their respective sovereigns in Europe. In the mid-1750s both British and French companies were trying to end, not extend, their existing proxy war with one another's Indian allies. When Rear-Admiral Charles Watson arrived at Bombay in 1755 his first task was to second the East India Company's own little navy, the 'Bombay Marine', in a campaign against Mahratta sea power on the Malabar Coast, where Angria (the Mahratta admiral) was a standing threat to coasting trade, and sometimes even to the big East Indiamen. The Company's ships had already taken the Mahratta port of Severndroog in 1755; in February 1756 Watson and Lieutenant-Colonel Robert Clive launched an amphibious assault on Angria's main base of Gheria. This succeeded, where all previous assaults had failed, because Watson had adequate charts, surveyed especially for the operation, which allowed him to work his big ships through the shoals and alongside Angria's fortifications. This operational chart-making was to be one of the keys to British success in amphibious operations all over the world, and it was the more noteworthy in that the Royal Navy had as yet no reputation for hydrography in general. Watson needed it again in December 1756 when his ships forced their way up the River Hooghly to recapture Calcutta, taken five months before by Siraj-ud-Dowla, Nawab of Bengal.[11]

By this time the European war had reached India, and Watson next bombarded and took the French fort of Chandernagore upstream. Soon afterwards he died, leaving Rear-Admiral George Pocock in command, and Pocock was still in the Hooghly in the autumn of 1757 when Commodore Charles Steevens reached Bombay on the other side of India with reinforcements. They met at Madras early in 1758, and soon afterwards Rear-Admiral comte d'Aché de Serquigny appeared. The Coromandel Coast of southern India, where the European 'factories' or trading settlements lay close to one another in a line from south to north (windward to leeward during the summer), has no harbour, and warships could safely operate there only during the south-west monsoon in the spring and summer when the wind is offshore. By mid-September, when the coming of the north-east monsoon is heralded by a period of violent storms, European squadrons withdrew; the British usually to Bombay, and the French to Mauritius. Command of the sea during the trading season, April to September, made it possible to trade, blockade and sustain military operations along the coast. To gain it the two admirals fought on 29 April, off Cuddalore, and 3 August, off Negapatam. The two squadrons were roughly matched, Pocock with seven small ships of the line, d'Aché with one ship of the line and eight Indiamen, approximately equal to British fifty- or sixty-gun ships. In both cases d'Aché disengaged, leaving Pocock's ships too much damaged aloft to pursue, and the two squadrons withdrew in September with no major advantage on either side. At the same time the first action demonstrated what might be regarded as a more equivocal consequence of Byng's (and Lestock's) conduct, which was to be shown on various occasions up to the end of the century: British admirals' alertness to the possibility of cowardice among their captains. In this case Pocock's three rear ships failed to get properly into action, mainly it seems from a combination of slow, foul ships and baffling winds, but all three were court-martialled and two dismissed, though Pocock himself came to think one of the sentences harsh.[12]

Next spring d'Aché was reinforced by three ships of the line. Unfortunately this was more than Mauritius could feed, and by the time he had gone to Madagascar for rice, it was the beginning of September before he reached the Coromandel Coast, determined to land supplies at the principal French factory of Pondicherry and leave at once. Pocock managed to bring him to a fierce but indecisive action on the 10th, in which d'Aché himself was badly wounded, but soon afterwards the French admiral achieved his mission and sailed again for Mauritius. In the 1760 season d'Aché never reached India at all, as his squadron was held back to cover his base from a rumoured British attack, and then overwhelmed by a typhoon. This left the British squadron under Pocock's relief Steevens to support the siege of Pondicherry. This he continued long past the change of the monsoon, even when five of his ships were wrecked in a storm on 1 January 1761, until a fortnight later Pondicherry finally surrendered, leaving France no important foothold in mainland India.[13]

Long before this, the tide of the war on both sides of the Atlantic had begun to turn. British plans for 1758 included a renewed assault on Canada by sea and land. The seaborne attack on Louisbourg was for the first time spearheaded by a squadron which wintered, frozen-in, at Halifax, in order to be off the French port early in the season. This prevented some, though not all, supplies from reaching the garrison until the main force under Boscawen arrived, after an extremely bad passage, early in June. With twenty-one ships of the line (not counting two fifties) and 12,000 troops under General Jeffrey Amherst the British had an overwhelming superiority, and once the risky initial landing in Gabarus Bay on the 7th had succeeded, the course of the siege was predictable. It was already far advanced on 21 July when three of the five French ships of the line in port were burned by the besiegers' mortar bombs. On the night of the 25th boats from the British squadron burned a fourth and captured the last, exposing the harbour side of the town to immediate attack. Within a few hours Louisbourg had surrendered.[14] Given that the British had chosen to take Louisbourg before advancing up the river towards Quebec, and that their inland campaign had mixed fortunes, the French had at least held the fortress long enough to give Canada a year's grace, but the French navy had been able to give it only limited succour. Dubois de La Motte's squadron had returned from Louisbourg in November 1757, unscathed by the Western Squadron but in the grip of a terrible typhus epidemic. It lost a quarter of its strength: 4,000 men were landed sick at Brest, and from them an epidemic spread throughout western Brittany. Overall more than 4,000 seamen died afloat or ashore; heavier losses than France suffered in any battle this war. Manning a squadron from Brest for 1758 was acutely difficult after this.[15]

Ever since they first established permanent West Indies squadrons in the 1740s the British had derived much advantage from having ships on station, their crews accustomed to the climate, even when the French squadrons which came out with convoys were as strong. Against the local privateers, however, no absolute success was possible. The Windward and Leeward Islands lie so close together that British merchantmen perforce passed within easy range of the French islands, especially Martinique, whose numerous coves sheltered scores of little sloops and schooners ready to dart out when the coast was clear. At least 1,400 British merchant ships were taken in the West Indies during this war by French privateers, mostly from Martinique. The loss of ships bringing provisions from North America fed the French plantations, almost starved the British islands, and halved the number of merchantmen registered in Maryland in five years.[16] The only effective solution was to capture the privateers' base, and by the end of 1758 (thanks to the ships released by the fall of Louisbourg) the British squadrons had been raised to a strength which made this a realistic ambition. By January 1759 Commodore John Moore commanding in the Leeward Islands had ten ships of the line and a landing force of 6,000 men. On the 16th the British landed on Martinique, but found the defences too strong and withdrew after three days. Moving immediately to their alternative target, they landed on Guadaloupe on the 22nd. A month later, a third of the troops were already sick, but the death of General Hopson on 27 February put the military command into the hands of a younger and more vigorous man, Brigadier John Barrington, whose ruthless destruction of crops and plant soon brought the French settlers to surrender. The capitulation was signed on 1 May, and a relief expedition from Martinique arrived one day too late. This operation added to the British possessions a little colony whose sugar production of 80,000 hogsheads a year was said to exceed that of all the British Leeward Islands together. The British public was overjoyed, the Guadaloupe planters gained a market which easily reconciled them to British sovereignty, but British sugar-growers were extremely unhappy at the competition.[17]

The French response was to order the Toulon squadron to the West Indies to retrieve the situation, and on 5 August 1759 La Clue Sabran sailed. Boscawen, commanding the British Mediterranean squadron, was refitting at Gibraltar when La Clue's ships were sighted passing through the Straits. In less than three hours Boscawen got to sea in pursuit. The forces were eleven British (sixty guns and upwards) against ten (mostly larger) French, but during the night part of La Clue's squadron lost company, and he had only seven ships with him when Boscawen caught up with him next morning, 18 August, south of Cape St Vincent. The resulting action was a stern chase in which the rearmost French ship, the *Centaure*, 74, made a heroic resistance and for some time delayed Boscawen's attack. In the end three French ships were taken and two were driven ashore near Lagos and burned. La Clue himself was badly wounded but survived.[18]

In North America the British plan for 1759 was to attack Canada on three fronts. One part of the army would advance up the Hudson Valley and along Lake Champlain, while the other part crossed Lake Ontario and descended the St Lawrence, the two converging on the French capital of Montréal and tying down the defending forces, while a seaborne expedition coming up the St Lawrence would tackle the dangerous navigation and heavy fortifications of Quebec. This force entered the river in June, Vice-Admiral Charles Saunders with twenty ships of the line (and many smaller) escorting 8,000 men under Major-General James Wolfe. The navigation of the river proved to be much easier than the French had supposed, and the expedition arrived before Quebec at the end of June. Here things began to go wrong. The sloth and timidity of the British forces inland had relieved the marquis de Montcalm, the French governor, of immediate fear for his capital, and allowed him to concentrate his army (12,000 men, mainly colonial militia) in Quebec, whose defences facing downriver were very strong. Young Wolfe (he was only thirty-two), though an outstanding regimental officer, soon showed himself to be a neurotic and vacillating general. The technique of brutal devastation which he had learned in Scotland in 1746 stiffened the Canadians' resistance, while he wasted the short season in a series of ill-managed frontal assaults. Meanwhile Saunders sent officers (including James Cook, the master of the frigate *Mercury*) by night to survey the river upstream, past the city. On 18 July, covered by a new battery on the opposite shore, the first British warships forced their way upstream. This transformed the strategic situation, for Quebec's lines of communication lay up the river (and the road which ran beside it) to Trois Rivières and Montréal, and the possibility was now open for British troops to land in the heart of the French position and force Montcalm to fight in the open. For most of the thirty miles between Quebec and Trois Rivières the river bank was low and unguarded, but Wolfe overruled his brigadiers and insisted on an extraordinarily dangerous and needless alternative: to land by night just above the city. The sea officers thought it unlikely that they could find the precise landing spot on a swift current in the dark. The soldiers greatly doubted if they could then scale a 100-foot cliff with a French post on the top. Nevertheless, with great skill and luck, the troops were put ashore in the right place, the French sentries had by chance been withdrawn a few hours earlier, and at dawn on 13 September the British army was drawn up on the Heights of Abraham facing the city. Even then Montcalm's position was very strong: he outnumbered Wolfe, he was behind fortifications, and his best troops were not far up country, ready to take the British in the rear. But Montcalm, too, though gallant and attractive, was not a gifted general. He distrusted all Canadians, and resolved to come out and fight at once before his militia could run away. In the ensuing battle the French were broken, both generals were killed, and Quebec surrendered soon after. No campaign better illustrates the maxim that wars are won by those who make the fewer blunders.[19]

In 1758 and 1759 British fortunes had sharply improved in most parts of the world except in home waters. The Western Squadron spent much of 1758 under Anson's command once more, but scurvy and victualling problems limited him to six weeks at sea, though he once victualled at sea from transports on the coast of Brittany. In October 1758, now under Saunders, the squadron again failed to intercept French ships entering and leaving Brest. It was clear to British ministers that the Western Squadron had to do better. It was all the more clear as it became evident that the French government, with its naval strength and colonial position weakening fast, had decided to solve its troubles at a stroke by invading Britain. Once again the English Jacobites were to play their part, and again there were unrealistic hopes of Spanish, Swedish and even Russian participation. By unorthodox financial manoeuvres enough money was borrowed to keep the French navy at sea for another summer. The plan was for the invasion force to sail with the main fleet, which had to come from Brest and Rochefort. It was, however, impossible to assemble the army at Brest, which always depended on food and raw materials imported by coastal shipping from the rest of France, and which by the spring of 1759 was already severely short of timber and unable to feed extra mouths. It was therefore decided to assemble the army around Vannes, in southern Brittany, where it could be fed, and where the inland sea of the Morbihan provided anchorage for transports. It followed that the Brest fleet had to sail down to collect the transports before returning to the English Channel.[20]

It followed for the British that Brest was now the key point. Intermittent cruises in the Western Approaches would not suffice; it was necessary for the Western Squadron to be continually off Brest or very near it. Never before had the Royal Navy faced the dangers of a close blockade of Brest, and the geographical situation needs to be explained, for wind, tide and navigation were as always the limiting factors in naval operations. Brest dockyard lies on a narrow river, the Penfeld, issuing on to a huge enclosed roadstead, which itself communicates with the sea by a narrow channel, the Goulet, lying almost east and west with high ground on both sides. Outside the Goulet are two anchorages, Berthaume Bay on the north and Camaret Bay on the south side, themselves screened from the open Atlantic by extensive reefs and islands through which there are three passages. To the westward the Iroise is open but scattered with dangerous pinnacle rocks. To the northward the narrow and rock-strewn Four with its formidable tide-race leads into the English Channel. To the south the Chaussée de Sein, a long chain of reefs and islands (known to the English as the 'Saints' or 'Seams'), stretches westwards into the Atlantic. Through it there is one deep but very narrow channel, the Raz de Sein, with the Tevennec rock in the middle of the channel at its northern end. The tide runs through the Goulet at three knots, the Four at four and a half knots and the Raz at seven knots. None of them could be passed except with the tide, and as it is twenty-five miles from the Goulet to the Raz it required exact timing to pass both on the same ebb (or, inward-bound, on the same flood), so that squadrons often had to anchor at least one tide in Berthaume or Camaret Bay. The distances are such that there is no one position from which a fleet could watch all three channels out of Brest except close in with the Goulet where they meet, but neither is there any ground high enough for watchers on the mainland of Brittany to see far enough out to sea to locate a blockading squadron in the offing.[21]

In the prevailing south-westerlies it was easy for French ships to enter the Goulet, but to leave required an easterly or northerly wind; commonest in the late winter and spring, between January and May. At other times of the year the chance to sail from Brest usually came when one of the regular depressions blew in from the Atlantic over the British Isles, causing the wind in the Channel to veer northerly and easterly. Overall it is possible to sail from Brest on about 40 per cent of the days in the year. Because they were often sailing in northerly winds, and because they often wished to avoid the British, the French tended to use the Raz de Sein more often than the other channels.[22]

For a different reason inward-bound squadrons often came the same way. It has been explained why Ushant was a dangerous landfall. No sane navigator, unsure of his position after weeks at sea, would head straight for Brest – least of all a navigator plotting on the *Neptune François*, the official French chart atlas from 1693 until 1822, which lays down the port thirty-five miles out of position. Instead French ships usually came in from the Atlantic on the parallel of Belle Isle, an excellent bold landfall, from which a south-westerly wind would carry a ship on the port tack to Lorient and Brest, or on the starboard to Nantes, Rochefort and Bordeaux. Alternatively they might first make Cape Finisterre or Cape Ortegal to fix their position and then strike north-eastward across the Bay to Belle Isle. From Belle Isle ships approached Brest from the south-east, past the headland of Penmarc'h and through the Raz de Sein. For the British this meant that any close watch on Brest required a squadron between the Seams and the Penmarks (to use English names), in which position the Breton coast is a deadly lee shore and the only possible escape in a westerly gale would be down into the Bay of Biscay, away from home. The only reasonably safe position for a British squadron watching Brest is west or north-west of Ushant, with the Channel open to leeward, but from here it is impossible to see the Raz de Sein.[23]

These were some of the difficulties Sir Edward Hawke faced when he sailed with the Western Squadron in May 1759 under orders to keep as close to Brest as possible. There he developed a system by which the main squadron was kept in relative safety to seaward of Ushant, but in constant touch with an inshore squadron of two small ships of the line under a bold and skilful captain (Augustus Hervey) lying off the Black Rocks at the inner end of the Iroise, near enough to the Goulet to see anything coming in or out of Brest. Another small squadron was detached into the Bay to watch Rochefort and the French transports in the Morbihan. Initially Hawke was to return at intervals to Torbay for victuals and water, but by August he had thirty-two sail of the line, enough to take turns to visit port and still keep twenty or so on station permanently. At the same time a regular system of replenishment with fresh provisions at sea was developed, with transports carrying live cattle, vegetables and beer. This presented many practical difficulties, with deep-laden merchantmen beating up from Plymouth to the blockading station dead to windward, and coming alongside to trans-ship their cargoes in exposed anchorages or even the open sea. Great determination and expense were necessary, but as a result Hawke was able to keep his ships continually healthy and on station throughout the summer and autumn.[24] The naval physician James Lind, like all professional observers, was astonished at what was now possible.

> It is an observation, I think, worthy of record – that fourteen thousand persons, pent up in ships, should continue, for six or seven months, to enjoy a better state of health upon the watery element, than it can well be imagined so great a number of people would enjoy, on the most healthful spot of ground in the world.[25]

It had never been possible for a fleet at sea to remain healthy for so long.

With the French fleet commanded by the comte de Conflans believed to be ready to sail, Hawke remained at sea throughout the autumn, but was repeatedly blown off station by gales, to the alarm of the government – but not of Hawke. 'Their Lordships may depend upon there being little foundation for the present alarms,' he wrote from Plymouth Sound on 14 October. 'While the wind is fair for the enemy's coming out, it is also favourable for our keeping in; and while we are obliged to keep off, they cannot stir.'[26] A month later he was blown into Torbay by another gale, and on the same day he sailed, so did Conflans from Brest, 200 miles away. On 16 November, approaching Ushant, Hawke met the victualler *Love & Unity* who told him that the French were at sea. They were unlucky with the wind, which blew them not only out of Brest but far to the westward before they could shape a course for the Morbihan. On their own account, they were also suffering cruelly from a shortage of seamen, with only 70–80 per cent of their established number of able seamen, and a third of those mere *novices*, equivalent to British 'ordinary seamen'. In fact most of Hawke's captains would have thought themselves very well off with that manning: the real difference was between ships which had been continuously at sea for many months during which they had worked up their crews to a high state of efficiency, and those which had not left port.[27]

The Morbihan, where the French transports lay, is itself within the great bay of Quiberon, which is screened from the open Atlantic by the Quiberon Peninsula, prolonged by a chain of islands ending at the southern end in the rocks called the Cardinals (*les Cardinaux*), with the bulk of Belle Isle further to seaward providing more shelter. On the 20th Conflans' twenty-one ships of the line were approaching Belle Isle when their lookouts sighted Hawke's twenty-three ships astern. The scene was dramatic. Both fleets were driving eastwards before a rising gale, the French shortening sail, Hawke's ships shaking the reefs out of their topsails. Before them in the fading light of a winter's afternoon lay a dangerous coast of which they had no reliable charts. Conflans was confident that the British would not dare to follow him into Quiberon Bay, underestimated the rate at which Hawke's ships were closing, and chose to lead a headlong escape rather than form a line of battle. By mid-afternoon the leading British ships were already in action against the French rear as Conflans rounded the Cardinals to lead into the bay, when the wind suddenly veered two points, heading the French and throwing them into confusion. As the night came on, a fierce battle was fought in heavy seas. Trying to open her lower-deck gunports, the *Thésée* flooded and went down. The *Superbe* was sunk by two broadsides from Hawke's flagship the *Royal George*. The final reckoning the following morning was one French ship taken and six (including Conflans' flagship the *Soleil Royal*) wrecked or sunk, with the survivors scattered up and down the coast and three trapped in the Vilaine river with their guns thrown overboard. Two British ships were wrecked, but their crews were rescued.[28] 'When I consider the season of the year,' Hawke reported, the hard gales on the day of action, a flying enemy, the shortness of the day, and the coast we are on, I can boldly affirm that all that could possibly be done has been done. As to the loss we have sustained, let it be placed to the account of the necessity I was under of running all risks to break this strong force of the enemy.[29]

No British admiral ever ran such navigational risks or gained so dramatic a victory. The threat of invasion vanished, and French sea officers fell into rage and despair. 'I do not know everything about it,' Captain S. F. Bigot de Morogues of the *Magnifique* wrote, 'but I know too much. The battle of the 20th has annihilated the navy and finished its plans.'[30] 'This is a consequence of what we have seen for a long time,' another survivor wrote, 'blunders, proofs of ignorance and then folly, plenty of zeal but no ability, plenty of gallantry but no sense, arrogance without prudence. That sums up what has just happened.'[31]

For William Pitt 1759 was a year of personal as well as national triumph, the year which finally gave substance to the English national myth of sea power which he had so long proclaimed. There was paradox, however, even in the triumph. Prince Ferdinand's decisive victory at Minden in August was also popular, and Pitt found himself taking credit for a Continental war as well as a naval war. By 1761 18,000 men, a quarter of the British army, were fighting in Germany. The finances of the French navy were halved to support the army in Germany; the new minister would not even feed the dockyard cats. At sea the absence of the French navy meant that there were few targets left. Brest was almost empty, and needed no blockade beyond cruisers to stop coasting trade. Instead a squadron established itself in the comfortable anchorage of Quiberon Bay to watch the French transports in the Morbihan, and the three ships still in the Vilaine, while another lay in Aix Roads off Rochefort. Friendly relationships were developed with the islanders: on the Ile d'Aix the British landed to buy vegetables and play cricket, while the Ile Dumet in Quiberon Bay was established as a market garden for the fleet. These squadrons remained until the end of the war, though two of the French ships of the line from the Vilaine finally escaped in fog in November 1761.[32]

The only excitement in home waters was the cruise of the Dunkirk privateer François Thurot, whose joint-stock amphibious expedition to Ireland was originally intended to coincide with the 1759 invasion. He sailed from Dunkirk in October 1759 with five frigates, evading the British Downs squadron and cruising for some time in Norwegian waters before arriving in the North Channel in February 1760. There he occupied the little port of

Carrickfergus for several days, and might have threatened Belfast had he still been on speaking terms with the senior officer of troops. On 28 February, off the Isle of Man, he was intercepted by three British frigates. Thurot was killed, and his three remaining ships taken.[33] In Canada the removal of Montcalm revived French resistance, the British forces in Quebec were defeated, and the city was only narrowly saved by relief ships in the spring of 1760. Eventually, however, even the caution and inefficiency of General Amherst's circuitous approach on Montréal could not save French Canada, which surrendered in September.[34]

The following month, October 1760, George II died, to be succeeded by his twenty-two-year-old grandson George III. This tended to worsen tension within the ministry, between Pitt who wanted to push on to further conquests abroad, and his Cabinet colleagues who looked to a victorious peace. The first fruit of this tension was the expedition of April 1761 against Belle Isle. Surrounded by cliffs, the island was a difficult target, but it was far enough offshore to be easily isolated by Commodore Augustus Keppel's fleet. The first landing failed, but a week later at a different spot the troops got ashore. The French garrison was then besieged in the citadel of Palais for forty days before being forced to surrender on 7 June. The occupation of a part of metropolitan France was an intolerable humiliation for Louis XV and, as Pitt intended, a major obstacle to peace. The disagreements within the ministry, however, were not resolved, with the aggressive Pitt opposed by more pacifist colleagues, including George III's favourite the Earl of Bute.[35]

In October 1761 Pitt resigned, but the impetus of the war continued. In January Rear-Admiral George Rodney led a second and successful attack on Martinique, with 16,000 troops drawn partly from Canada under Major-General Robert Monckton. The island surrendered in a month, soon followed by the remaining French possessions in the Lesser Antilles. 'We are highly obliged to the inhabitants for their pusillanimous defence,'[36] was Rodney's comment, and the knowledge of how prosperous the planters of Guadaloupe now were under British rule was one of the reasons. A relief force of seven ships of the line under Rear-Admiral the comte de Blénac-Courbon had been fitted out at Brest with great difficulty, but he reached Martinique the day after it fell, and spent the next six months at Cap François, immobilized by damaged ships and sickly crews.[37]

British relations with Spain were now an issue of growing concern. For over forty years, Spain's prudent policy had avoided entanglement in France's quarrels while slowly building up the Spanish navy into an effective deterrent force. The war of 1739 had shown the strengths of Spain's strategy of defence in depth. The Seven Years' War brought a dispute over captured merchantmen to irritate Anglo-Spanish relations, but it did not change Spain's national interests. What did change was the death of King Ferdinand VI in August 1759. His heir, Charles III, was his half-brother of Naples, the same who had been humiliated by Captain Martin in 1742 and had never forgotten the lesson. He brought to the Spanish throne a hatred of the British and a high sense of the value of sea power. Spain now began to slide towards an aggressive foreign policy, and the death of the prudent and peace-loving Queen Maria Amalia in September 1760 removed another obstacle to war. In August 1761 a treaty between Spain and France bound Spain to go to war by May 1762 if no peace had been concluded by then. In the event the British discovered the treaty and declared war themselves on 4 January.[38]

Two days later the Cabinet decided to attack the heart of Spanish Caribbean power: Havana. The plan was drawn up by Anson, and it was a bold scheme even with so powerful a navy to support it, for there was barely six months before the onset of the rainy season, and no one who remembered Vernon at Cartagena could doubt what that would mean for troops ashore. The great expedition, under Sir George Pocock and Lieutenant-General the Earl of Albemarle, sailed from England only two months after the decision had been taken. In the Leeward Islands Pocock collected more troops from North America and most of the forces which had just taken Martinique, leaving some ships to blockade Blénac in Cap François. The boldest element of Anson's plan was for Pocock to use the Old Bahama Passage along the north coast of Cuba, a dangerous channel unknown to British navigators, and regarded by the Spaniards, who had charted it accurately, as impracticable for big ships. Normally all deep-water shipping passed along the southern side of Cuba, rounded Cape Corrientes and beat 200 miles up the coast to Havana, assuring the Spanish capital of ample warning of its approach. Using the Old Bahama Passage, with the guidance of a running survey made by one of Pocock's frigates, allowed the attacking force to run straight downwind towards its target.[39]

Meanwhile in Havana, neither warnings from Madrid of approaching war, nor intelligence from various sources of British plans, had shaken the complacency of the governor, Don Juan del Prado, and the admiral, the marqués del Real Transporte.[40] The governor applied to be transferred to Florida, on the grounds that he would have no opportunity to distinguish himself in action commanding a place which no one would dare to attack. Even when the British ships were actually in sight he refused to believe the danger.[41] Meanwhile Real Transporte's ships were all laid up, 'unrigged as though for the winter'.[42] With fourteen ships of the line in Havana (and another seven elsewhere in the Caribbean) against Pocock's nineteen, he could at least have severely complicated the British situation. Instead he sank three ships to block the harbour entrance, and thereby bottled up the remainder where they could do no good. Having failed to oppose the British landing on 7 June, del Prado also failed to defend the hill of La Cabaña which overlooks the city. The British occupied it at once, and could probably have taken the city soon afterwards if they had tried. They certainly should have tried, for with the rainy season imminent, they had to move fast. Instead Albemarle insisted on a regular siege of the only strong point of the defences, the fortress of El Morro at the mouth of the harbour. Defended with desperate gallantry by Captain Don Luis de Velasco of the *Reina*, the Morro held out until it was stormed on 30 July, and Havana finally surrendered on 13 August 'with its dependencies' (which the British understood to mean the whole island of Cuba) and twelve ships of the line, plus two on the stocks. By this time so many of the British army were sick or dead that the operation was on the verge of collapse; out of 11,000 men first landed, with 3,000 subsequent reinforcements, only 3,000 were still in action. The operation which Anson had planned as a swift and painless coup de main, almost finished as another Cartagena, and perhaps would have done had del Prado and Real Transporte been more alert.[43]

Anson died in June 1762, and never knew of the fall of Havana, nor of the last conquest of the war, which he had planned at the same time. With the scanty resources available on the spot, and with only unenthusiastic support from the East India Company (whose local officials stood to lose some very lucrative private trade), the British commanders in India improvised an expedition against the Spanish capital in the Orient, Manila. They were an oddly matched pair: the plain sailor Rear-Admiral Samuel Cornish, who was reputed to have set out in life as a common seaman,[44] and Colonel William Draper, who had started his career reading for Holy Orders, and proceeded from a Cambridge fellowship to the Grenadier Guards. Draper had about 1,700 men, including one infantry battalion and an artillery company;

> the rest are a composition of deserters of all nations, whom I take with me more to ease the fears and apprehensions of the people at Madras, than from any service I can expect of them. But I have no choice: these or none; such banditti were never assembled since the time of Spartacus.[45]

Cornish had seven ships of the line, some frigates and transports, most of them in poor condition.

OPERATIONS 1758–1763 · 287

The *Lenox* is become very weak and leaky and is much broke; the others by age are constantly complaining, their timbers many of them quite rotten and in general so bad that I am afraid to inspect into their complaints.[46]

They sailed at the end of July. It was essential to move fast, before the Spaniards heard, or the monsoon broke, or the ships sank. 'I have little to say in my justification for venturing on such a slight foundation,' wrote Draper,

> but that the zeal and ardour of all the gentlemen of the Navy and the few under my command bid me hope for success. We have unanimity for our base; I build much upon it. The place is large but not very strong: the inhabitants very numerous, but not used to war.[47]

This was an accurate estimate. The British entered Manila Bay on the evening of 23 September,[48] and Draper's motley little army stormed the city on 6 October. Much plunder was obtained, and Cornish's ships were repaired in the dockyard at Cavite, but the conquest brought no lasting benefit to Britain. For a few months the British tried to establish their rule over the Philippines, until the news of peace arrived from Europe, and for several years they vainly tried to collect the ransom of four million dollars which had been promised on the surrender of the city. Otherwise the expedition left little but the memory of an operation which for luck and daring has seldom been matched.[49]

The peace settlement, ratified in February 1763, represented an unparalleled triumph for Britain, but also, in the eyes of William Pitt (now in opposition) and many others, an unparalleled and unjustified act of renunciation, inspired by the conviction expressed by the Duke of Bedford, who negotiated the peace:

> The endeavouring to drive France entirely out of any naval power is fighting against nature, and can tend to no one good to this country, but on the contrary must excite all the naval powers in Europe to enter into a confederacy against us, as adopting a system viz. that of a monopoly of all naval power, which would be as least as dangerous to the liberties of Europe as that of Louis XIV was, which drew almost all Europe upon his back.[50]

To the intense relief of the British sugar-planters, who had lobbied very hard on the subject, Britain returned Martinique and Guadaloupe, and instead took Canada, which had always been a dead loss to the French crown. Louisbourg and Cape Breton Island were retained, but France was still allowed access to the Grand Banks fishery, which was believed to be so essential to naval manpower.[51] Of Britain's other conquests from France, Belle Isle, St Lucia in the West Indies, Goree in West Africa[52] and the settlements in India (to remain unfortified) were all restored. Spain received Havana and Manila, but ceded Florida and Minorca in return. In addition the French handed Louisiana to Spain as a notional compensation for her sacrifices in the allied cause.

To explain Britain's triumph in the Seven Years' War, after so many disappointments before, it is necessary to look at the practical capabilities of government, the army, and in particular the Navy. Much of this comes under the heading of administration, of which more presently, but there were developments in professional competence which were of long-term importance. Many of them went back to the 1740s, when Vernon, Anson, Warren and Hawke had laboured to improve the training and cohesion of their squadrons. Further lessons were learned from the early disasters of the war, the Rochefort expedition as well as Minorca. British capabilities in amphibious operations, always the most difficult of all operations of war, rose rapidly with the frequent opportunities of practice from 1758 onwards. A number of officers (notably Augustus Keppel) made their careers as specialists in assault landings. Anyone who has studied the great amphibious operations of the 1940s will find much that is familiar in the careful plans of assault convoys and landing operations drawn up in the 1750s.[53] Relations between admirals and generals, between sailors and soldiers, became notably harmonious and efficient. 'During this tedious campaign, there has continued a perfect good understanding between the army and Navy,' reported Saunders from Quebec;[54] and Pocock at Havana professed it,

> almost impossible for me to express or describe that perfect harmony that has uninterruptedly subsisted between the fleet and the army from our first setting out, indeed it is doing injustice to both to mention them as two corps, since each has endeavoured with the most constant and cheerful emulation to render it but one.[55]

These were not conventional civilities, but recognitions of an indispensable condition for victory.[56]

The organization of trade defence was also better than in previous wars. Convoys were more numerous, the Admiralty's tact in consulting merchants about them smoothed the practicalities and gained it a reputation for fair dealing. Particularly trusted groups such as the Bristol Society of Merchant Venturers were even allocated a warship under their own control. Sailing dates which had been worked out with London merchants were communicated to provincial ports via the newspapers, particularly the new specialist shipping paper *Lloyd's List*. Convoy escorts were supplemented by co-opting 'letters of marque' and placing them on the escort screen; by this date it had become common for convoy commanders to issue plans allocating each escort a station around the convoy. Many British privateers, initially commissioned at the outbreak of war with France (and again with Spain), found business dropping rapidly away as enemy shipping was swept from the seas, and were chartered to the Navy as 'armed ships', employed as convoy escorts.[57] Colonial shipping trading between the colonies was not protected by Admiralty convoys, though some of the American colonies (in particular Massachusetts) had their own small warships to protect their trade. As in previous wars many American ships went privateering in the West Indies; but this was less lucrative when French trade there had collapsed so badly, and positively dangerous when combined with illegal trade to the French islands.[58]

As British supremacy at sea became more of a reality during this war, the question of neutral shipping became more acute. If, as neutrals claimed, 'free ships made free goods', they could carry what they liked through a British blockade and British naval power would be deprived of much of its effect. International law in these questions was unsettled, though in some cases bilateral treaties (like the Anglo-Dutch treaty of 1674) defined respective rights. The British government, though anxious to exploit its naval superiority, had many reasons of prudence and diplomacy to remain on good terms with neutral powers, especially those like Sweden and Denmark which controlled indispensable supplies. What this meant in practice was that the High Court of Admiralty tried to lay down clear rules which ensured Britain's essential interests, but left neutrals room to trade profitably. Sir James Marriott, Judge of the High Court of Admiralty from 1778 to 1799, frankly stated British policy to be to keep 'as nearly to the Law of Nations, as the necessity of the case will allow, which necessity the most powerful in war are generally the best judges of . . . we are now judges of what shall be esteemed munitions'.[59] Thus by the 'Rule of the War of 1756', the High Court of Admiralty declared that it would not admit neutrals to carry trade in wartime which was forbidden to them in peace; while the rule of the 'continuous voyage' treated cargoes as having been shipped from their port of origin, even if they had been unladen and reladen at a neutral port *en route*. These rules prevented Dutch and Danes carrying on France's colonial trade when French ships could not. Neutral shipowners lost a lucrative opening, but they were not denied their usual trades, including those guaranteed to the Dutch by the treaty of 1674, and they could live with clear rules.[60]

British privateers, which ignored the rules and whose activities often approached both piracy and blackmail, really threatened good relations with neutral powers, but it was politically difficult for Pitt to restrain these perfect expressions of the English naval tradition. The roseate memory of the Elizabethan age, installed deep in the public consciousness, endowed privateers with a political significance out of all proportion to their real value to the war-effort, and made it very difficult for politicians to touch them. An act was passed in 1759 to limit small Channel privateers, which had a particularly ugly reputation, and two letters of marque were revoked during the war, one for piracy and the other for firing on a warship's boat. Overall, however, the government's response was notably timid, and it did not dispute the privateers' grandiose claims of their contribution to victory, though in reality the Navy took more than twice as many prizes, including almost all enemy warships and privateers.[61]

For the first time, the British had concluded a war with extensive gains of territory overseas. A new sort of empire was now growing to rival the invisible empire of trade which they had long been building up. Another way of expressing the situation is to say that Pitt was the first man who had turned the old national myth of sea power into reality. Hitherto all the popular conviction had been on the side of a naval war, but all the political reality had dictated a Continental connection. With a good deal of help from Frederick the Great, Pitt had shown that a naval war really could be made to work, and by doing so he had permanently altered the balance of political possibility in Britain. A new young king, who ostentatiously identified with Britain rather than Hanover, confirmed the shift. It is at this level, of strategic vision and political conviction, that Pitt truly changed the course of British history. It is not true, as an older generation of historians believed, that he was a talented leader of war in practical matters of planning and administration. He left those to others, of whom Anson was the most important. Neither Pitt's genius nor his position as Secretary of State sorted with details. He was an orator and rhetorician, not a practical politician nor a systematic thinker: 'an Inigo Jones in politics', in the words of the diplomat James Harris, 'a man of great ideas, a projector of noble and magnificent plans'.[62] The most powerful of his great ideas was also the oldest and least original: the English national destiny to gain wealth and power by waging victorious war at sea. British statesmen and admirals like Cromwell, Charles II and Vernon had tried to realize this vision, but their hopes had been shipwrecked by the massive practical difficulties of sustaining and projecting effective sea power. William III, Marlborough and the governments of early Hanoverian Britain had preferred the comfortable familiarities of military and political engagement on the Continent. Pitt took the old myth of English naval destiny, and turned it from an easy slogan for opposition politicians remote from responsibility into a working strategy for overwhelming victory.

NINETEEN

The Great Wheels of Commerce and War

Administration 1715–1763

In 1693 the allied main fleet barely managed to remain at sea a fortnight, and returned sickly and starving to leave the Smyrna convoy to its fate. Sixty-five years later Hawke was able to stay continually at sea for six months, keeping his men healthy and well fed far into the winter. Behind this striking contrast lie administrative developments which laid the foundations of naval success. No professional skill or strategic vision would have been of any avail if means had not been developed to keep squadrons at sea for long periods in home waters, and long voyages overseas. Moreover it was precisely in these matters of administration that the British opened a decisive superiority over their enemies, above all France.

Behind all naval activity, of course, lay finance, and that in turn divided into the capacity to tax, and the capacity to borrow. The first funded loans in Queen Anne's reign had shown the way to borrow long-term at low interest, and the 'Financial Revolution' was virtually completed in 1715 by the issue of the first undated or perpetual annuities, which offered funded interest payments (at 5 per cent), but gave the holder no right to demand repayment of the principal. (The Treasury could redeem at will, so that if interest rates later fell, as they did, the stock could be replaced by cheaper issues.) It was coming to be understood that government stock was an investment instrument for the public as well as a means of raising money for the state, and that the stock exchange allowed any investor to reclaim his capital when he needed. This was to be decisive for the British government's capacity to borrow in the future, but it did not solve the problem of the legacy George I's government inherited of over £40 million in older loans at interest rates of between 6 and 9 per cent. The total interest bill was over two and a half millions a year, of which £882,566 was accounted for by 'irredeemable' annuities paying very high rates for the whole lives of the holders. The 1717 Conversion Acts funded almost ten million of older loans into 5 per cent government stock, but the

'Irredeemables' remained a particular problem. Meanwhile in France the Scottish financier John Law was pushing a bold and far-sighted scheme to expand the economy by issuing paper currency, and at the same time to convert some of the French public debt into Mississippi Company stock. Technically sound but vulnerable to ignorance and fraud, this scheme soon collapsed into inflation, ruining many and blackening the reputation of public investment in France, but not before it had encouraged a similar speculative fever in England. Inflated by unscrupulous manipulators working on public credulity, this 'bubble' drove the price of South Sea Company shares to unsustainable heights before the inevitable collapse late in 1720. In the process the holders of 'irredeemable' annuities were persuaded to convert into South Sea stock, so that the collapse liquidated one of the British government's most expensive obligations. Like the Law scheme, it was a serious blow to public confidence, but in the long run less severe, mainly because the circulation of paper currency in England remained very limited and there was no inflation. Some of the monied classes were ruined, but the stock exchange was reformed as a result, and the long-term economic life of the country was not badly damaged. The political effect of the bubble was to drive a generation of politicians out of office and open the way for the rise of Robert Walpole, who became First Lord of the Treasury in 1721.[1]

The Walpole era was one of peace, but the Navy was not neglected, and a large fleet was maintained in reserve. At the same time, as we shall see, important administrative reforms were undertaken – but nothing which would disturb political tranquillity or excite the passions of members of Parliament. This meant that the form of the Navy Estimates remained unaltered, and in practice the sums voted went into a single fund to be drawn on as needed. Ships were built and repaired, though no money for shipbuilding was asked for or granted between 1696 and 1745, and the only Extra estimate for repairs, in 1743, was refused. A new Admiralty Office rose between 1723 and 1726 (replacing the ill-constructed 1695 building), but though members of Parliament presumably noticed it as they walked down Whitehall, they did not inquire how it had been paid for without a Parliamentary vote. So long as opposition was interested in opposing, not understanding, government made sure that the naval estimates looked plausible, not realistic. The system of paying ships at the end of a commission ensured that there was always a large 'float' of wage credit, so unpaid wages were borrowed to cover the essentials for which Parliament voted too little, or nothing at all – until in 1745 the number of ships paying off equalled those commissioning, and the trick became impossible. The payment of bills 'in course' was now routine, and Navy Bills were a recognized short-term investment, which bore interest after six months (at 5 per cent from 1714 to 1748, then 4 per cent until 1783). They were freely transferable, selling for a varying discount on face value, and the length of the 'course' increased or decreased as the Navy Board spent more or less than its current income. Both the discount and the Course of the Navy were printed in the financial press, and suppliers had only to check the current prices and adjust their bids accordingly. They could then hold the bills in which they were paid to maturity, but most contractors preferred to use their capital in their businesses, and instead discounted their bills on the Exchange to speculators who specialized in them. The effect was to allow the Navy Board (and the Victualling Board, whose bills moved in parallel) to run its own public debt system, outside Treasury control. So long as the Course did not get so long as to threaten investors' confidence, the Navy could increase its short-term debt as much as it needed. In 1722, 1728, 1734, 1747 and 1749 Parliamentary grants paid off some of the accumulated naval debt, or converted it into government stock, the interest rate on which, thanks to Pelham's skilful management, had fallen to 3 per cent by 1749. In theory the Navy was perpetually underfunded; in practice it always had enough, and it had every incentive not to draw attention to the illogicality of a system whose effect was to allow the Navy complete freedom to spend its income as it wished, and a considerable measure of elasticity to increase it when it needed. The Treasury had no control over the Navy; in 1725 its attempt to find out how many ships were in commission was sharply rebuffed. This did not lead to waste and corruption, for naval administrators, uneasily aware that their system was in some sense illegal, were anxious not to attract Parliamentary scrutiny. Moreover the financiers who held large sums in Navy Bills were in effect investors in the Navy who followed its administration with keen attention. This provided a strong incentive for the Navy Board to manage its business frugally in order to safeguard its credit.[2]

They ordered these things differently in France. A poor state in a rich nation, dependent on politically costly forms of taxation, it borrowed proportionately much more of its expenditure than Britain. Financial obligations regularly exceeded income, though it seems the French crown ran a small surplus in a few years in the 1660s, and possibly the 1730s. By 1697 debt service was already absorbing over a quarter of the revenue of the state. The proportion rose steadily through the eighteenth century until by the 1780s it was over half. The French crown was a notoriously untrustworthy debtor, and moreover continued throughout the eighteenth century to use self-amortizing loans which paid back both capital and interest. The result was that France paid at least 50 per cent higher real interest rates than Britain. A multitude of different tax funds with inconsistent or non-existent accounts made it almost impossible to get a clear idea of the national finances, and there was no finance minister to try. Individual ministers had their estimates approved by the king, but the *Contrôleur-Général des Finances* was essentially a book-keeper with no authority to construct a national budget or limit ministers' expenditure to what had been approved. The French navy depended on the two *Trésoriers-Généraux de la Marine*, notionally paymasters and accountants, but in fact bankers who covered the gap between tax revenues received and expenses undertaken, by floating public loans and issuing private unsecured notes of hand. Since naval authorities could and did draw on them without consulting the minister, neither he nor they had easy means of forecasting or controlling expenditure. When things went well they made monopoly profits by means the crown could not afford to investigate, for when things went badly only their credit kept the navy afloat. The same was true of the *Munitionnaire-Général*, the victualling contractor (or in reality, banking syndicate) which supplied both the victuals and the money to buy them. The navy, like the state, tended to run steadily further into debt, in peace as well as war. At the outbreak of war in January 1756 it already owed 14.5 million *livres*, of which a third was in highly speculative unsecured notes. By June 1758 the debt was 42 million, more than the current year's estimated expenditure. The news of the fall of Quebec bankrupted the entire system, and by 1760 naval activity had almost ceased.[3]

The British Admiralty (another institution with no parallel in France) achieved in the Walpole years the stability which had so long eluded it. The Board was headed by a succession of respected admirals: Orford (1714 to 1717), the Earl of Berkeley (1717 to 1727), Lord Torrington (1727 to 1733) and then Sir Charles Wager (1733 to 1742), who came to occupy a recognized position in the second rank of government ministers. The professional expertise of these First Lords of the Admiralty made their situation unusual among ministers, most of whom were chosen as representatives of property and interest rather than personal ability. Winchilsea in 1742 to 1744 showed what might happen to a First Lord who lacked authority in the Navy, and Bedford too was not a perfect advertisement for civilian rule. He was an intelligent man who knew his own mind, but he had no taste for routine administration, and he loathed London. In January and February 1745 the new First Lord attended every meeting of the Admiralty Board, but by August he was down to one in seven. His usual idea of a wartime working week was to come up from Woburn on Tuesday or Wednesday morning and return on Thursday afternoon. He expected to be consulted on important decisions, by post, but he was deaf to pleas to attend the Admiralty or the Cabinet. His Board functioned well because Anson supplied naval expertise, and Sandwich, administrative ability.[4] Sandwich then succeeded in 1748, just at the end of the war, and Anson followed him for most of the period from 1751 until his death in June 1762. By this time the exceptional nature of the First Lord's position among ministers was securely established. 'Capacity is so little necessary for most employments,' Henry Fox reminded a colleague in March 1757, as they discussed how to replace Pitt's ministry, 'that you seem to forget that there is one where it is absolutely so – viz. the Admiralty . . . The First Lord of the Admiralty must be a man of real ability and great application.'[5]

Admiralty Boards usually included one or more sea officers junior to the First Lord amongst the political placemen, but there was no position analogous to the modern First Sea Lord as professional head of the Navy. During the Walpole era there were other senior admirals at the Board, including Torrington and Wager before they became First Lords, Sir John Norris (1718 to 1730), and Sir John Jennings (1718 to 1727), but this was not automatic: Anson was visibly the dominant naval member of Bedford's Board when he was still only a captain. When he became First Lord in 1751 he had Boscawen as senior naval colleague, who remained on the Board till his death ten years later. Major naval operations were still officially the province of the Secretary of State, and the Admiralty's recognized importance sprang from the First Lord's authority rather than the Board's. He settled important naval questions with his colleagues in Cabinet. Board business was largely routine. In the first month of the Bedford Board it made just under 700 minutes, of which 32 per cent concerned individual ships, 28 per cent concerned individual officers, 10 per cent other named persons (ratings, civilian employees, passengers, prisoners of war), and only 4 per cent touched on strategy, diplomacy or the movement of whole squadrons.[6]

The Admiralty was the centre of the naval system rather than its head. Here all the lines of communication and authority met, and the smooth functioning of the Admiralty Office was essential to the effectiveness of the apparently disorganized collection of different naval boards and authorities. Institutional memory was one of its most important contributions, and it was early (though not unique) in establishing a regular career structure for its staff. At the head of the Office, the Secretaries of the Admiralty carried the authority of unequalled experience. In one century, from 1694 to 1794, there were sixteen Secretaries of the Treasury, seventy-six Under-Secretaries of State – and four Secretaries of the Admiralty. Josiah Burchett, Secretary for forty-eight years, the servant of two Lords Admiral and twenty-eight Boards, was succeeded in 1742 by Thomas Corbett, and he by John Clevland in 1751. Lord Halifax only agreed to take Anson's place as First Lord in 1762 on condition that Clevland would stay in office, and Newcastle had no doubt who would really be running the Admiralty: 'It is plainly a stop-gap, and shows a great want of hands; however as I hope . . . he will be directed by Clevland, he may do tolerably well.'[7] When Clevland died next year he was followed by Philip Stephens from 1763 to 1795, who then served another eleven years as a member of the Board. Corbett had been eleven years at sea and twenty-seven in the Admiralty when he became Secretary; Clevland, whom Anson brought from the Navy Office, had worked there for twelve years, broken by twelve years as Clerk of the Cheque of Plymouth Dockyard. Stephens was Anson's former secretary, and had twenty-four years' experience divided between the Navy Office and the Admiralty. These men had long professional service, and long personal memories. When Stephens began in the Navy Office in 1739, the Surveyor had started his career under Charles II, and the Secretary of the Admiralty had been trained by Pepys. Sixty-seven years later when Stephens finally retired, he could claim that two generations of civil servants linked the Navy of Rupert and Monck to the Navy of Nelson; the Restoration to the Regency.[8]

An important addition to the Admiralty's responsibilities was made by the transfer of the army's Marine regiments (revived on the outbreak of war in 1739) to Admiralty control in 1747. Once again their regimental structure had proved entirely unsuitable to naval requirements, and their financial affairs fell into chaos. Admiralty control of itself, however, did only a little to cure the problem. The Board itself wanted to complete the transfer by adopting a permanent, non-regimental structure, but at the war's end the Marines were again disbanded to save money.[9]

The Navy Office was much bigger than the Admiralty, but was likewise an established 'civil service' in miniature. There were a few dismissals, presumably on political grounds, in 1714 and 1715, including one of the Commissioners, but this was the last occasion of the century when politics upset the Office's established routine. One senior clerk, John Russell, lately promoted Extra Commissioner to assist the Controller, described his working week in 1748:

> On Mondays: collect and abstract all bills of exchange, yards, and all Navy Bills for the week past, and examine the same with the Comptroller of the Treasurer's Account. Tuesday examine all invalids and sign their tickets for payment. Wednesday: all day at the Pay Office. Thursday: with the Comptroller receiving petitions of poor seamen run on ships' books,

and relieving such as appear just. And examine the transport accounts, a very p—[page torn] duty, all in my office. Friday, all day at the Pay Office. Saturday: examine all imprest and contingent accounts for the Week. And attend the Board every night to dispatch orders and letters till 9 o'clock. And you know besides all this, that I am at calls, where ever a Commissioner is wanted; am just come from Woolwich paying off the *Rainbow*.[10]

The clerks were expected to work regular hours (by no means automatic in eighteenth-century government); nine to two and four to eight in the 1740s, with at least three clerks staying on as late as the Board sat, or until ten at night on the three days each week that the post went out. For this they were well paid. In 1748 Richard Morris, a junior Navy Office clerk, calculated that

My place in this Office (including some private matters) is worth about £80 a year, which with odd jobs I do for the Duke of Somerset, Earl of Londonderry, some merchants &c, out of office hours, make together my present income above £100 a year, without any great hurry or confinement.

Evidently he still had some leisure, even in wartime:

I had also the sole care of collating and correcting the Welsh Bible lately published by the Society for Promoting Christian Knowledge, under direction of the Welsh bishops; a work of incredible labour, that took up all my vacant hours for four years together.[11]

In an emergency the Navy Office worked much longer hours. When accounts of stores and provisions were needed for a Cabinet meeting one day in 1758, the clerks were ordered to work all night to produce them.[12] By contrast, in the Ticket Office (part of the Treasurer of the Navy's department) there were complaints in 1759 that the clerks were all gone by three o'clock.[13]

Much of the Navy Board's work continued to be the supervision of the dockyards, which were still growing in size and complexity. The total employment in the home yards was 6,487 in 1711, and 9,618 in the peace-time year of 1730. They were increasingly specialized in different functions. Deptford, the furthest upriver, built smaller ships, was the headquarters of the naval transport service, and acted as a depot from which naval stores were distributed to yards and squadrons at home and abroad. Woolwich, likewise constrained by the width and depth of the Thames, concentrated on building, and its ropeyard was a major producer. Chatham was affected by the silting of the Medway and the difficulty of navigating up and down the river, in which the sixty-gun *Pembroke* capsized with heavy loss of life in 1744. The biggest ships were no longer laid up there, and the yard specialized in building and major repairs. Busy at times of mobilization and demobilization, at other periods it often lent workmen to other yards. Sheerness, on the deep-water anchorage of the Nore at the junction of the Thames and Medway, was excellently situated but cramped, malarial and lacked fresh water. It did a great deal of work on cleaning and repairing the smaller classes of warship. The maintenance of the seagoing fleet was largely the work of the south-coast yards: Portsmouth the biggest, but Plymouth growing as the Western Squadron rose in importance. In wartime they had little time to spare for shipbuilding, though some ships were kept on the stocks to occupy the shipwrights during the neaps. Ships of the line could only dock on the fortnightly springs when the tidal range was greatest, so for three or four days the docks would work night and day. Weed and barnacles naturally grow on a ship's submerged hull, steadily reducing her speed, so ships which hoped to retain their speed had to dock frequently to clean their underwater hulls, and in wartime the docks were in heavy demand, especially at springs. They could dock, bream, scrape and pay a Third Rate in two tides. During the neaps smaller ships could be docked, or big ships might remain in dock for major repairs, and there was always work to be done on ships afloat, but overall the neaps were a relatively slack time in which some building might be done.[14]

The great size of the dockyards exacerbated the real problems of managing them, and above all of managing the workforce. Private yards employed men on 'task work' (piece work), and only when there was work to be done. The old and sick were turned away. The dockyards had a completely different policy, employing men on quarterly wages, from apprenticeship to old age. 'Here are indeed many persons belonging to the yard who have behaved well that are grown old in the service,' as the Deptford yard officers reported in 1744, 'but are capable of performing several light works upon which they are employed to the advantage of the Crown.'[15] Winter or summer, in peace or war, there was always something to do in the yards, and in wet weather the shipwrights would move indoors to work on masts or boats. Every yard had a surgeon, and the injured were entitled to the benefits of the Chatham Chest. Though there were usually reductions at the end of a war, well-behaved men could make a secure and comfortable career in the dockyards, rising in some cases to positions of considerable status and authority. These privileges made up for the higher nominal wages in private yards in wartime, and made a dockyard job very desirable. The threat of dismissal should therefore have been effective in preserving discipline, but in practice it was not. Collectively, if not individually, the yard men were a repository of skill and experience which could not be replaced (especially at Portsmouth and Plymouth, where there were few private yards near by), and they knew their value. 'They set the great wheels of commerce and war in motion . . .' wrote the shipwright and Methodist pamphleteer William Shrubsole in 1770, 'without which the pulse of civil society would stand still.'[16] Their collective organization and discipline repeatedly defeated the attempts of yard officers or the Navy Board to impose unwelcome innovations. The most notorious of the privileges they preserved was the right to take 'chips', supposedly as many waste scraps of timber as could be held under one arm, in practice usable pieces of some size and quantity, not infrequently concealing more valuable items like copper or ironwork. More significant was the right, as the men conceived it, to work 'extra', meaning overtime, of one or two 'tides' (of one and a half hours) or a 'night' (five hours). The working day was twelve hours; two tides were worth as much as half a day at ordinary rates, and a night was equal to a whole day's earnings. Often it was really necessary to work very long hours, especially at springs, when ships in dock had to be worked on night and day, but it was also possible for yard officers to match the high wartime wages of private yards by allowing more or less fictitious 'extra'. Such concessions, made at times of crisis, were difficult to claw back later, and the officers did not always try very hard. There was a deep-rooted spirit of community in the yards, whose managers often felt more sympathy for the men's appeals to equity and tradition than for the Navy Board's appeals to economy. The result, in the opinion of many contemporaries, was that the yards worked well, but they did not work hard. Though it was, and is, difficult to establish their 'productivity' from eighteenth-century statistics, it is reasonable to suppose that it could have been higher.[17]

Bedford and his Admiralty colleagues certainly supposed it. In the Walpole era long-serving naval First Lords had built up excellent relations with the Navy Board, which neither of them wished to upset by radical innovations. Taking office in 1744 after the collapse of the Caribbean campaigns and the débâcle of Mathews and Lestock, Bedford's Board wanted to change many things, and they were not reluctant to provoke a confrontation with the Navy Board in the process. Bedford was thirty-five and Sandwich, twenty-six. Dominating the Navy Board sat Sir Jacob Acworth the Surveyor, sixty-one years in service and disinclined to allow noble amateurs to teach him how to run the dockyards. The new Admiralty bombarded the Navy Board with requests for information about finance, shipbuilding, recruitment, dockyard employment, timber policy, ship design and many other matters. Some of these requests the Navy Board refused, and many it ignored. The

Commissioners of the Navy were appointed by the Admiralty, but they could not be dismissed except for gross misconduct, and it was painfully clear that Acworth did not intend to make a vacancy. Though the Bedford Admiralty made progress with other parts of its reforming agenda, it got almost nowhere with the dockyards.[18]

Sandwich, with his keen administrative sense, understood that the strength of the Navy Board's position was its monopoly of information. In 1749, with the war over, Pelham demanding economies and himself now First Lord, Sandwich resolved on a new approach to the problem. On 9 June, less than three months after Acworth's death, the Admiralty Board,

> taking into their consideration the number of men borne in the several dock and ropeyards, the great expense attending the same, and that the works are not carried on with the expedition that might be expected from them, which must arise from the remissness of the officers, or insufficiency of the workmen, or both,

decided to visit the yards themselves.[19] The Navy Board never did this, and it provided an obvious means of outflanking their monopoly of information. On their visitation the Lords of the Admiralty met with much food for thought, and action: stores neglected, accounts years in arrears, standing orders ignored – as well as some departments which were in a good state of order and efficiency. They did not meet with all the yard officers, for some of them were absent without leave, or present but too old to work. At Woolwich, 'intending to discourse with the Master Attendant on the bad condition the ships and moorings lay in, [we] found him incapable of business or performing any sort of duty'.[20] Sandwich was particularly interested in the possibility of introducing task work into the dockyards, about which he questioned the yard officers closely. The result of the 1749 visitation was another stream of Admiralty orders to the Navy Board, but once again the response was slow. In 1751 Sandwich fell from office, and next year the Navy Board bluntly announced that it was 'against any innovation, more especially the attempting to build anything whatever by task'. Anson's Board ordered 890 men to be dismissed from the yards in 1753 to save money, but he was content to allow disruptive plans of reform to sleep, and there were no more visitations for a generation.[21]

The relative merits of building in the dockyards and private yards was always a matter of controversy. Contemporary statistics suggested that private builders were cheaper, but the Navy Board insisted that they were also worse, that their ships had shorter lives and higher maintenance requirements.

Undercapitalized shipbuilders, dependent on the Navy Board's progress payments for working capital, could not afford to buy seasoned timber, nor take the time to build to the dockyards' high standards. They retorted that the Navy Board and its officials were scarcely impartial judges. These were, and are, difficult questions to settle, but in practice circumstances rather than principles tended to dictate policy. In wartime the dockyards could not build enough ships and it was essential to resort to private builders, especially for frigates and smaller men-of-war, but not only for these. One of Britain's major assets in a naval war was a private shipbuilding industry capable of building ships of the line. When ships were urgently needed, the Admiralty had to turn to the private builders, as it did particularly during the Seven Years' War.[22]

The French, by comparison, had no private shipyards capable of building ships of the line, unless the *Compagnie des Indes* at Lorient is regarded as private, and the naval yards were very poorly equipped. As late as 1750 the French navy had built only four dry docks, of which one had been abandoned and the other three did not work properly.[23] Its first fully functional dry docks, the Formes de Pontaniou at Brest (one double and one single), were not completed until 1756, and they were not deepened to take a three-decker until the 1780s.[24] As a result the French navy was forced to depend for most of the century on careening its ships for cleaning and underwater repairs. In this laborious and dangerous process the ships had to be stripped of guns and stores, the masts strengthened, and then the ships 'hove down' alongside a careening wharf fitted with suitable holdfasts, by heavy tackles run to the mastheads, in order to expose first one side of the hull and then the other. The process imposed grave strains on the hull even when it went well. Ships were usually weakened by it, sometimes seriously damaged or even sunk. The British, with sixteen dry docks in the home dockyards at the beginning of the century, rising to twenty-four at the end, never needed to heave ships down in home waters (though small cruisers away from the dockyard ports were still cleaned by grounding to work at low water).[25]

The Navy Board's procedures for buying naval stores were by now well established. Great care was taken to keep the markets competitive, though the system of 'standing contractors', while highly responsive to fluctuations in demand, was arguably not the cheapest.[26] When new products appeared, like 'Incombustible or Extinguishing Tar, that destroys Sea Insects' in 1752, or Mr Lewis's Improved Plantation Tar in 1755, the Board assessed them with careful comparative trials.[27] In 1759 it gave a major standing contract to Walter Taylor, a blockmaker of Southampton, who had designed machinery which helped him to produce smaller, lighter, and cheaper blocks with lower friction.

Besides saving money, Taylor's blocks saved topweight aloft and work on deck, making it possible for bigger ships to be handled without bigger crews. It was precisely such incremental technical improvements which contributed so much to the superior performance of British ships, and it was typical that in spite of the fullest information supplied by French naval espionage, including examples of the machines themselves, the Taylor system was not made to work in a French dockyard until 1795.[28]

The import of naval stores from abroad continued in this period without major interference. Pitch and tar came from Sweden; shipbuilding timber and masts from the eastern Baltic ports of Russia, Poland and Prussia; sawn softwood timber and small masts from Norway. The small but valuable market for great masts was partly served from New England, together with the subsidized pitch and tar which helped to keep Swedish prices down (and in the case of pitch now rivalled the Swedish product in quality).[29] The Navy Board bought bar iron only from Sweden, with a little from Spain, America and Russia, which it then passed to British contractors to work up into iron fittings for shipbuilding. The different qualities of iron depended on the ores from which it was made, and iron from British ores did not have the needful qualities. In particular only 'Oreground' iron from the Dannemora mines was suitable for steel production. This allowed the Swedish government monopoly, the *Jernkontoret*, to maintain a high price. English iron was adequate for pigs of ballast, of which the Navy Board bought 1,000 tons a year by the Seven Years' War.[30] Slops continued to be supplied on a single standing contract. There were new contracts in 1725, 1731 and 1740, with the prices increased in an endeavour to improve quality, but for the contractor it remained a hazardous business, and in 1744 he was £121,000 in arrears. Finally in 1758 the Navy Board took over the issue of slops at its own risk.[31]

In 1714 George Atkins, Storekeeper at Mahón, enjoyed the solitary distinction of being the Navy Board's only established officer overseas, but in the post-war years the Navy's establishments overseas grew rapidly. By 1739 there were naval yards at Gibraltar and Mahón in the Mediterranean, Jamaica and Antigua in the West Indies, all of which expanded rapidly in the 1740s.[32] In 1729 work began on an entirely new yard at Port Antonio on the north coast of Jamaica, intended to replace Port Royal with its vulnerability to fire and earthquake. In practice the disadvantage of a sickly bay remote from the main trading port was never overcome, and the new yard was abandoned in 1749. Meanwhile Port Royal had escaped fire and earthquake, but was hardly a model naval establishment, as Rear-Admiral Charles Knowles the commander-in-chief complained in 1748:

I will venture to affirm that had inconveniences and obstructions been studied in the disposition of the several magazines in this harbour, they could not have been accomplished more effectually. The ships careen at Port Royal; send for their stores (7 miles) to Kingston; for their provisions (5 miles) to New Greenwich; for their water (12 miles) to Rock Fort; and for their ordnance stores (5 miles) to Mosquito Point; so that every different officer's stores are situated as far asunder as the length and breadth of the harbour will admit them to be placed. And when the breezes blow ships may wait several days and cannot send a boat to any one of them, let the urgency of the case be never so great, whereas they might all (except the water) [have] been connected together at Port Royal very commodiously . . .[33]

However Knowles, who was already well known to the Navy Board for his freedom in undertaking expensive engineering works without getting approval beforehand, soon began the process of consolidation.[34]

The difficulty of financial control was for the Navy Board one of the major problems with overseas yards. Captains and admirals were happy to spend public money, with a good chance of retrospective Admiralty approval, while the Navy Board's own officials, remote from oversight, all too easily succumbed to dishonesty.[35] Nevertheless such issues had to be faced, for naval yards overseas were indispensable to the strategy of the mid-century wars, with permanent squadrons stationed abroad and big expeditions sent out from home. No European power except Spain possessed anything comparable, and they were an essential support of growing naval dominance. In tropical waters, where 'the heat of the climate . . . [makes] wood and iron decay much sooner than in any other part of the world', as Rear-Admiral Cotes explained, ships required more maintenance than at home.[36] The destructive boring of the shipworm in the West Indies presented particular dangers. Ships were 'sheathed' with extra thicknesses of plank as a measure of protection, but the worm swiftly ate through the sheathing, which had to be replaced at frequent intervals. Docks would have been of the utmost value, but none of these naval yards had a dock, and since there is almost no tide in the Mediterranean, and too little in the West Indies to ground ships, it was necessary to rely on careening to work on ships' hulls underwater, with all the attendant disadvantages. The *Princess Mary* was dismasted twice in thirteen months trying to heave down at Jamaica. It was reckoned that a ship of the line spending three years in the West Indies and hove down once a year would be in as bad a state as one which had spent eight to twelve years in home service without refit. 'When a ship is broke,' Commodore James Gambier wrote in 1772, there is no bringing her to her sheer again without a dock . . . and when once her sheer is broke, she will ever be leaky at sea, because the whole frame becomes elastic, and can never be prevented till she is put into a dock, and stripped, and the frame put into its original position.[37]

The only British dry dock overseas did not belong to the Navy (though warships freely used it), but to the East India Company at Bombay, where the tidal range was just sufficient to dock ships of the line. Opened in 1754, made double during the Seven Years' War and triple in 1773, it was an essential support of British naval supremacy in the Indian Ocean.[38]

Even more important than yards and squadrons overseas was the supply of stores to them. In the 1690s the Navy Board had expected squadrons to carry their stores with them, but the high consumption in tropical conditions frequently immobilized ships for want of spars and cordage. In Queen Anne's war the Board began sending out storeships, but it still allowed too little, and chronic shortages persisted. Things improved in the 1740s, but there remained serious failures both of quality and quantity. Vernon still had ships 'on a single bottom' (unsheathed), which it was a real struggle to keep afloat. After only eight months in the Caribbean the *Prince Frederick* had to be hove down not less than six times, 'but I thank God I can acquaint their Lordships that she is in a condition now to swim home upon a tallowed bottom'.[39] It took on average nine months between demanding stores in the West Indies and receiving them, so without intelligent anticipation problems were inevitable, but it was difficult to predict the consumption of naval stores when a single unlucky gale might use up a year's supply of masts and cordage. Poor co-operation between the Navy Board and the Admiralty meant that laden storeships waited months for convoy from Deptford to Spithead, and then often missed the West India convoys. Finally in the Seven Years' War the two boards had the system working smoothly. The mean time for a storeship to get from the Thames to Spithead fell to thirty-eight days. Further supplies, especially of masts, were shipped by contractors directly from North America. As a result there were no serious shortages in the West Indies during this war.[40]

The Victualling Board's affairs improved after the crisis of 1711. A new 'course' was started, the Board's credit revived, and in 1715 its business was 'branched' so that each Commissioner was responsible for one department. Next year the Board issued new instructions for salting and packing meat which seem to have led to a marked improvement in quality. There was no change in the essentials of this already ancient technology, but packing in summer was forbidden, while close attention to detail, and to the highest quality of raw materials (notably salt), yielded a sharp fall in complaints of spoiled meat. The same instructions were reissued in 1736, 1764, 1766 and 1784. Payments of 'shorto' likewise fell away as deficiencies of supply became rarities; in the war of 1739 to 1748 they were one-tenth of what they had been thirty years before. It became a settled policy that any salt meat still in store after two years was to be sold. In the eight years 1750 to 1757 the quantities of victuals issued by the Board, and the proportions condemned (by panels of ship's officers, who had no interest in concealing deficiencies), were as follows:

Bread	54,642,437 lbs	0.3%
Beer	110,049 tuns	0.9%
Brandy	351,692 gals	nil
Beef	4,498,486 lbs	0.06%
Pork	6,734,261 lbs	0.03%
Pease	203,385 bus	0.6%
Flour	6,264,879 lbs	0.3%
Suet	809,419 lbs	0.1%
Raisins	705,784 lbs	0.1%
Oatmeal	138,504 lbs	0.9%
Vinegar	390,863 gals	nil
Stockfish	166,943 lbs	7.9%
Oil	71,668 gals	0.4%[41]

With the exception of stockfish, which was being phased out because it was hard to preserve (and unpopular with the men), there was no item of which as much as 1 per cent was condemned, an astonishing figure considering the limitations of the technology and the hazards to which the full casks were exposed after issue.[42] It was now settled policy that salt meat was to be replaced by fresh whenever possible in port, and even at sea, and likewise biscuit with baked bread. Though the Victualling Board was not unaware that fresh meat was cheaper, the primary motive was the health of the ship's companies, and much of the saving was applied to issuing 'roots and greens' whenever fresh meat was served. The anti-scorbutic value of fresh meat and vegetables, derided by medical science then and for long afterwards, was well known among seamen.[43]

The Victualling Board's greatest difficulty in the early Hanoverian period was its cramped site on Tower Hill, and in particular its inadequate wharfage. The crisis of 1740, when the victualling organization was overwhelmed by sudden mobilization after a bad harvest, in the midst of a winter which froze the pickle in the casks and the transports in their berths, was in this connection a blessing in disguise, for it drew attention to the problem, and released funds for capital investment. In 1743 the Board was able to lease the Red House estate in Deptford and build a large complex of stores and mills, besides adding new breweries to the victualling yards at Portsmouth and Plymouth. This allowed it to do nearly all of its own brewing, packing and milling, reducing dependence on contractors and giving higher quality at lower cost.[44] Abroad, the rising scale of operations presented new challenges. Allowing captains and pursers to victual their own ships was a certain recipe for fraud and expense. Initially the Board's preferred solution was to establish a local victualling organization headed by its own senior official, the Agent-Victualler, either accompanying the squadron (as in the Baltic expeditions early in George I's reign), or permanently established ashore wherever there was a naval station. The alternative was for a private contractor to take responsibility for a station, which in principle was cheaper, but more vulnerable to dishonesty. The firm of Mason & Simpson, contractors for Jamaica, were overwhelmed by the demands of Vernon's fleets (of which they were given little notice), and the Board had to take over. By the end of the 1740s, however, the Board was satisfied that contractors gave the best value, and that its procedures of accounting and oversight were adequate to prevent abuses. During the Seven Years' War there was only one Agent-Victualler overseas (at Gibraltar), and another afloat with the East Indies squadron. In this war the ships and troops in the West Indies were entirely supplied by contractors who drew their supplies, not from London but from the cheaper and nearer markets of New England and Ireland.[45]

British naval victualling is a remarkable story of rising standards, making ever more extended operations possible. 'This ship has now been at sea twelve weeks, which is longer than I ever knew any first-rate ever at sea . . .' wrote Boscawen to his wife in September 1756. 'At the beginning of the Spanish War our cruisers would not keep the sea above a fortnight, till one or two of them were broken for it, now three months is but a common cruise.'[46] Soldiers and passengers remarked with pleasure on the goodness of naval food.[47] What was more remarkable is that higher standards came at steadily falling expense. It cost approximately the same to provide excellent victualling for 70–85,000 men during the Seven Years' War, as it had to provide quite inadequate victualling for 40–50,000 men during the War of the Spanish Succession half a century before. In 1758, a year of high prices, the Board fed 70,000 men for £913,905; it had spent £942,879 on 48,000 men in 1710.[48] In France, by contrast, the story is of an inefficient, corrupt and costly system progressively dis-integrating under the strains of the mid-century wars. Its greatest strength, ironically, was the apparent weakness that both the French navy and the French West India colonies were largely fed from Ireland, a trade so vital to both parties that false flags and other covert means were found to keep it going even in wartime.[49]

Beyond naval operations, the work of the Victualling Board has a wider significance for the agricultural and economic history of Britain. The Board was the largest single purchaser on the London markets for agricultural products, and its policy of managing the markets so as to encourage the growth of large firms, while at the same time promoting competition, was at least influential, and possibly critical, in the growth of a sophisticated and integrated national and eventually international agricultural market. The British economy was unique in that there were few peasants, in the sense of subsistence farmers. Even small producers in remote parts were accustomed to serving a national market, exporting their goods (usually by coastal ship-ping) to London, being paid by bills which they could discount locally, investing their savings in the financial markets. Long before the industrial revolution began, a commercial and agricultural revolution had taken place which made the British economy the most sophisticated in the world, and which linked internal commerce to international trade flows. The growth of a national agricultural market was fundamental in this, and the work of the Victualling Board in pushing it forward is a subject which agricultural and economic historians have been unwise to ignore.[50]

The Sick and Hurt Board was reconstituted in 1740, and for the first time continued in peacetime at the end of this war. As before, it was essentially an administrative body responsible for running the naval medical service ashore, with limited responsibilities for the fleet afloat.[51] It was not a source of medical advice, which the Admiralty sought from the best authorities, usually meaning the College of Physicians of London. In retrospect it can be seen that this was only occasionally helpful. With few exceptions physicians had no acquaintance with naval medicine, and they were trained in a strictly theoretical school which placed a high value on *a priori* reasoning and regarded empirical observation as the mark of a charlatan – the word 'empiric' in the medical jargon of the day meant a quack. As a result medical men with relevant experience, or naval men familiar with the inherited wisdom of seafarers, were too often dismissed in favour of the latest medical theories. Dr James Lind, first physician of Haslar Hospital and the leading naval doctor of the 1750s and 1760s, started his career with some useful observations on scurvy, then

steadily moved away from them towards more orthodox positions. A generation later the cautious and non-committal reports of Captain James Cook
were taken to reinforce the currently fashionable medical doctrine of 'iatro-
chemistry', which once again led directly away from a solution to the problem
of scurvy.[52]

The significance of scurvy, however, has been grossly exaggerated. It has
been seriously suggested that a million British seamen died of it in the
eighteenth century – a figure which implies that every man who ever served
in the Navy died of scurvy approximately twice.[53] In fact true scurvy, uncompli-
cated by other diseases, was a killer only on very long ocean passages, and its
effect on normal naval operations was to limit the length of time a squadron
could stay at sea. Hawke's blockading squadron in 1759, supplied with fresh
provisions at sea, broke through the hitherto accepted limitations, and at the
end of the Seven Years' War scurvy was no longer a serious problem in British
warships.[54] Moreover it is necessary to be cautious in discussing a disease
whose name was used by doctors as a catch-all term for anything they could
not identify or cure. In the words of Edward Strother, 'it is yet a sufficient
answer to patients when they enquire into their ailments to give this return
to a troublesome enquirer, that their disease is the scurvy, they rest satisfied
that they are devoured with a complication of bad symptoms'.[55]

The real killers at sea were fevers, especially typhus (to use the modern
name) in cold weather, and malaria, yellow fever and other tropical diseases
in warmer climates (though malaria was also endemic in marshy parts of
England, including Sheerness Dockyard). Typhus, the 'gaol fever', 'camp fever'
or 'ship fever' of the eighteenth century, was above all the disease of cold and
dearth. A serious epidemic over the hard winters of 1739–41 wrecked the
Navy's mobilization, with men falling sick faster than they could be recruited.
The same thing happened again in 1755–6. We now know that typhus is
carried by lice in dirty clothes. Medical opinion then rejected such an 'exploded
doctrine',[56] but the prevailing notion of disease as transmitted by 'corrupted
air', indicated by bad smells, directed attention to cleanliness. Throughout
the eighteenth century British naval officers' fanatical attention to the cleanliness of their ships and men aroused the astonishment of visiting foreigners,
but it had unquestionably good results in limiting disease. By the mid-century
typhus occurred mainly among new recruits, not yet clothed and washed by
the Navy, hence especially at times of mobilization. There was no British
equivalent to the crippling epidemic of La Motte's squadron in 1757.[57]

The typhus epidemics naturally called attention to the deficiencies of the
naval hospitals, which were provided by contractors, and the sick quarters or

lodgings, which were usually pubs. The expensive remedy was for the Navy to build its own hospitals, and in January 1745 the first Parliamentary vote was granted to begin a new hospital at Haslar outside Portsmouth. When finally completed in 1761 it had a maximum capacity of 2,000 patients; more than four times the size of Guy's and St Thomas's in London, the next biggest hospitals in England.[58] At a cost of over £100,000 (double the cost of the Admiralty building in London) Haslar provided for the highest standards of medical care, careful segregation of infectious diseases, and (not least) careful guard against the risk of desertion. Haslar, and even more the second naval hospital at Stonehouse near Plymouth (finished in 1762), the first to be built on the 'pavilion' system with separate blocks isolated from one another, became a model studied and copied all over Europe.[59]

On overseas stations the evils of contract hospitals and sick quarters were even more evident, and at Jamaica the same solution was attempted. At New Greenwich near Kingston a new hospital was built in 1740, an enclosed quadrangle with a guarded gate 'and a lieutenant's guard constantly mounted for keeping them in good discipline and preventing Captain Punch invading them, a formidable enemy to their health and their morals', as Vernon remarked with satisfaction.[60] Unhappily, as Knowles reported in 1748, it proved to be a disaster which had to be abandoned, 'being situated in the middle of a bog and the most unhealthy part in all the country. Few men have recovered that has been sent there yet, and most of them have deserted.'[61]

The Ordnance Board continued to patronize the Wealden ironfounders as it had for 300 years, for in spite of their small scale and obvious inefficiency, they had access to the most suitable ores. In the 1750s the Board began awarding some contracts to foundries elsewhere, but initially the quality of their guns was alarmingly poor. Moreover there was a hidden problem with northern iron ores which were contaminated with sulphur, producing 'hot-short' iron, which developed weaknesses when heated. This fault was not revealed when guns were proofed cold, and led to numerous gun explosions during the 1770s. What was worse it coincided with a bad period in British gun design. The Armstrong pattern guns of 1732 had serious weaknesses, and new patterns issued in 1743 and 1761 barely kept pace with the improvement in the quality of gunpowder which was taking place at the same time.[62] Powder was a crown monopoly, and the Ordnance Board arranged the import of saltpetre from Bengal, and sulphur from Sicily and Iceland, but the actual manufacturing was done by private firms under contract. The Board had difficulty in maintaining quality, as well as in keeping firms active in a hazardous trade which was only profitable in wartime, for which reason it bought the Faversham powder mills in 1759.[63] Overseas the Ordnance faced many of the same problems as the Navy and Victualling Board, and like them had by the Seven Years' War reached a level of practical efficiency which ensured that British forces seldom ran short of essentials.[64] Once again the contrast with France is instructive. There the fragmented iron industry had great difficulty casting guns in the number and quality the French navy required. In the 1750s the adoption of the method developed by the Swiss gunfounder Jean Maritz of casting a gun solid and boring it out on a lathe represented an important technical advance, but French industry was still incapable of meeting the navy's requirements.[65]

In Britain two fundamental transformations were in progress, in naval administration and in the economy at large. Naval establishments represented in many respects so many islands of the nineteenth century in the eighteenth-century countryside. These enormous and complex enterprises faced challenges of management and control which were as yet unknown to private business, or to any other part of government. It seems that they transferred relatively few skills to the national economy, which still had little need of them, but their very large-scale purchases of goods and services of high quality at keen prices provided a powerful engine driving the growth of the national agricultural market, and certain international trades such as timber imports. Around them the British economy was still agricultural and commercial rather than industrial, but increasingly sophisticated and integrated. The geography of the British Isles gave most districts access to coastal shipping, and only the efficiencies of water transport (which contemporaries reckoned to cost at most about one-twentieth of road transport)[66] made possible a national market, integrated directly into international markets. Even small ports gave direct access to overseas markets, and exposed local business to the requirements of international trade. In the early eighteenth century the little Dorset port of Lyme Regis, for example, was importing sugar from the West Indies and tobacco from Virginia and in return exporting drapery, canvas, gloves, saddlery, hats, gowns, kerseys, soap, earthenware, nails, ironware, shoes and beer bottles, among other things, the products of craftsmen and small businesses in the surrounding towns and villages of Dorset, Devon and Wiltshire.[67] Though France was a bigger country with a larger population and greater wealth overall, it had nothing like the integrated British national economy, and its great commercial ports were linked to foreign countries rather than to the interior of France. At the same time the rising productivity of agriculture, feeding into a national market which allowed producers to profit from every increase in output, fed a growing population with no increase in the number working on the land. All this contributed powerfully to the growth of a sophisticated economy with developed banking and insurance systems, which consistently generated the ample, indeed surplus investment capital essential to finance both war and economic growth.

※━◆━※

TWENTY

Disagreeable Necessities
Social History 1715–1763

I can't but think it honest advice for his Majesty's service, that some parliamentary provision should be provided for the Crown's obtaining the voluntary service of our seamen, that those who are to be depended upon for the defence of our present royal family, our religion and liberties, should not be the only persons in this country that appear to have no liberty at all.

Vernon's thoughts were cogent, as usual, but as the Admiralty pointed out, politically unrealistic:

Their Lordships . . . are as much averse to the present methods of pressing as any man can be, and wish some better method was established to man his Majesty's ships. But until the legislature has done so, their Lordships think it their duty and also of all his Majesty's officers to exert their utmost diligence to procure men to serve his Majesty at sea, according to the present methods, how disagreeable soever they may be; and not to expose the nation to danger from reasons of private tenderness.[1]

For the eighteenth-century Navy the manning problem was always the critical factor which limited operational possibilities and damaged social relations. Both the Admiralty and outside critics continued to search for solutions, most of which involved the registration of seamen on the French model, or the creation of some sort of reserve on a retainer or half-pay basis. Walpole took a close interest, and was behind the Parliamentary bill of 1720, and the unpublished scheme of 1727. Further bills were introduced with no better success in 1740, 1741, 1744, and 1749. All of them foundered only partly on Parliament's distaste for expense, either to the taxpayer or to the shipowner. More fundamentally, compulsory schemes were rejected as incompatible with English liberties. According to the myth of English sea power in which the political nation so devoutly believed, liberty and the Navy were intimately associated. The symbiosis of trade and sea power provided the Navy's man-power by an automatic mechanism which required no government inter-vention. Consequently there could be no manning problem; or if there appeared to be, it was only because of Walpole's malice and tyranny. 'It is not only to enslave, for the best part of their lives, upwards of 150,000 free born subjects, and to invest the crown with an absolute power over them;' declared Lord Gage of the 1740 bill, 'but also, thereby to give the crown a farther power of influencing of the elections throughout England.'[2] Jenghis Khan, James II and the Spanish Inquisition had attempted nothing so wicked. The modest 1749 plan to establish a voluntary reserve of 3,000 men was denounced by Lord Egmont as intending 'to circumscribe public liberty, and augment the number of those, whom ministers desired to reduce to a state of slavery'.[3] Even Parliamentarians who accepted that there was a real manning problem were not prepared to solve it by strengthening the power of the state. For them the press gang was a lesser evil, so long as its powers were strictly circumscribed, and fell on a politically insignificant class, the seamen.[4]

In the Seven Years' War the story was much the same. Parliament rejected another registration scheme in 1758, and the same year a bill sponsored by Pitt passed the Commons which would have allowed a writ of *habeas corpus* to be used to get any pressed man out of the Navy.[5] The most original and useful contribution to the manning problem was made by a private charity, the Marine Society, founded in 1756 with the main object of sending unemployed or orphan teenagers to sea as officers' servants. It calculated that the wartime Navy needed about 4,500 boys as servants, of whom about 1,000 were 'young gentlemen' intended to be officers. Many of the remainder the Society sup-plied, and as its boys nearly all came from non-seafaring families, they probably represented a real increase of several thousand to the 'pool' of naval recruitment. The Society also provided free working clothes to over 10,000 naval recruits (not all its own), which seems to have had a significant impact on the typhus problem.[6]

Parliament's refusal to confront the manning problem forced the Navy to rely on the old methods. Though the civil authorities were still ordered to raise men, impressment was now very largely in naval hands, and in 1745 the first 'Regulating Captains' were appointed to impose order on ships' press gangs ashore, the beginnings of what by the Seven Years' War had become an organized 'Impress Service' covering much of England. Individual ships still provided many of the press gangs ashore, but the Regulating Captains imposed common standards, forcing gangs to release men who were not seamen, or had valid 'protections' (certificates of exemption), or belonged to other ships, as well as preventing them releasing those who had bribes to offer. This at least smoothed some of the worst injustices and inefficiencies of the system, but the lavish and haphazard issue of protections by Parliament, the Admiralty, the Navy Board, and other naval and even civil authorities created insoluble difficulties. In 1741 14,800 men were said to be protected, out of about 35,000 employed in seagoing merchantmen and inland navigation just before the war. By 1757 there were 50,000 protections in circulation, easily enough to cover every seafaring man not already in the Navy.[7] Protections exacerbated the crises at the peaks of mobilization, in 1740, 1745 and 1756, and so did illness. In the typhus epidemic of 1739–40 25,000 men fell ill, of whom 2,570 died and 1,965 deserted from hospital. At the same time Vernon's ships in the West Indies were losing about one-fifth of their men every year to disease and desertion combined. In 1755–6 typhus again hit mobilization, and over 2,000 men died. The Admiralty was driven to desperate expedients. In the spring of 1739 and 1740 embargoes were imposed on all outward-bound merchant shipping, and on the second occasion they were deliberately used as a means of forcing shipowners to 'compound' for a certain proportion of protections; forty out of 100 men for an East Indiaman, for example. The remaining sixty would have to be foreigners, landmen, or seamen liable to impressment. In 1745 the Admiralty pressed every sixth man from non-statutory protections, promising them release after four months' service.[8]

The legal position of impressment was clarified by Broadfoot's Case of 1743, in which a seaman of that name was indicted for murder for shooting an unarmed gangsman. The judge mustered an impressive range of legal opinion to support the legality of impressment in principle, but he also held that in this case the gang was acting illegally because its lieutenant (to whom the press warrant was directed) was at that moment absent. He therefore directed the jury to bring in a verdict of manslaughter rather than murder. This judgement outraged the public, which demanded that Broadfoot be acquitted as a defender of English liberty.[9] Many magistrates agreed, and in some parts of the country press officers and their gangs faced prosecution, fines, and sometimes imprisonment. Even in Plymouth, a town as susceptible to Admiralty pressure as any in England, the Mayor imprisoned a Marine detachment for arresting deserters, and ignored requests to release them. The Admiralty would defend its officers in court if it was quite sure of its legal ground, but there were cases of impress lieutenants being left to rot in gaol for years, or even for life. There were also physical risks, of course; in 1756 a press lieutenant lost an eye in an affray.[10]

Magistrates and local authorities who openly or covertly opposed impressment did so in the name of the 'liberty of the subject', but 'liberty' and 'privilege' have always been close neighbours, and in practical political terms, the issue was one of local power against central. The English political system ensured the 'liberties of Englishmen' by keeping the state weak, and local authority strong. A press gang was an instrument of state power operating in the localities, and therefore a direct threat to the autonomy of magistrates and corporations, to which they reacted sharply. Hence the common practice of impress officers applying to magistrates to endorse their warrants. There was no legal necessity to do so, but it was politically very wise, and many magistrates would support, or at least tolerate, the activities of a press gang so long as their authority had been invoked. In other cases, notably London during the Seven Years' War, magistrates who would not permit the presence of a press gang, were prepared to press for the Navy themselves. In seaports there were economic interests at stake, since naval recruitment forced up the price of skilled labour for the shipowner, but the political issue was always central. It was the liberty of the magistrate, not the seaman, which mattered. This meant that in towns, counties and colonies where there was strong local government, willing to accept responsibility (and to spend money in bounties or other incentives), it was often possible for the Navy to reach an accommodation. In Bristol, for example, the Society of Merchant Venturers, representing the merchants and shipowners of the city, agreed to provide a fixed number of seamen in return for an exemption from impressment ashore. Hence this recruiting song for the Bristol privateer *Blandford* in 1746:

> Here is our chief encouragement, our ship belongs to Bristol,
> Poor Londoners when coming home, they surely will be press'd all:
> We've no such fear when home we steer with prizes under convoy,
> We'll frolic round all Bristol town, sweet liberty we enjoy.[11]

This was disingenuous, since pressing afloat was not restricted (Broadfoot's Case arose from an incident in King Road at the mouth of the Avon), but it did express a real benefit to the shipowners and seamen of Bristol. In Liverpool, by contrast, a weak local authority in terror of the mob refused to take any responsibility, and pressing ashore and afloat contributed to the endemic violence of the port.[12]

At sea, where most impressment took place out of inward-bound ships as they approached port, seamen had limited opportunities of evasion, and armed resistance was not unknown. In such cases the masters of the merchantmen would profess to have been unable to prevent 'mutineers' seizing arms to resist the press gang, and then escaping ashore. The law, however, was quite clear that a man who deserted at any stage in a voyage, even twenty-four hours from home, forfeited all his wages. If half the crew ran away as the ship approached port, the owners stood to multiply the profit of the voyage – a consideration which tended to dissolve the master's powers of discipline. The Admiralty found by experience that there was no prospect of prosecuting masters in such a case, however open the appearance of connivance. Indeed most resistance to impressment was in practice protected by the law, though when the Bristol privateer *Sampson* fired on a warship's boat and killed four men, the Admiralty managed to have her letter of marque revoked.[13]

In the Americas seamen were often very scarce, and ill-drafted legislation made the situation worse. The Act of 1708, the 'Sixth of Anne', forbade pressing in the Americas, but it was not clear if it was perpetual (as the colonials believed), or expired with that war; and equally whether it applied to the Navy only, or to the civil authorities as well. An Act of 1746, intended to clarify the situation, exempted the West Indies from pressing but not America, which naturally inflamed colonial opinion there, especially in New England. The following year there was a major riot against impressment in Boston. In practice it was usually possible to press at sea out of incoming merchantmen in the West Indies, and the manpower problems there were mainly due to sickness and desertion. Vernon reckoned that during his West Indian command 500 men had deserted from the naval hospital at Jamaica, 'which I believe have all been seduced out and gone home with the homeward bound trade, through the temptation of high wages and thirty gallons of rum, and being generally conveyed drunk on board their ships from the punch houses where they are seduced'.[14] It was most difficult to press American seamen out of colonial ships. Pressing ashore in any colony was problematic without the active support of the colonial governor, and sometimes with it as well. On occasions like the 1745 Louisbourg expedition in which the colonies took the lead, the Navy could rely on some backing, but at other times local political and commercial interests predominated. However the Navy had no large forces based on American ports except briefly in 1745–6 and 1757–8, and the issue of impressment in New England was of more significance to colonial politics than naval operations.[15]

The difficulties of recruitment were one side of the naval manning problem; the other was the prevention of desertion. The first half of the eighteenth century was a period of stable or falling prices, so that the naval wage, fixed as long ago as 1653, remained competitive in peacetime into the 1760s. In wartime, however, when all sorts of seamen were very scarce and wages in merchant ships rose sharply, the Navy was at an acute disadvantage. Parliament never contemplated trying to match wartime wages, and it is not clear if it had done how quickly the money would have increased the supply of skilled seamen, who took years to train. Moreover the Navy, like merchantmen, paid only at the end of a voyage, and by the mid-century a naval 'voyage' might last as long as three or four years. All that Parliament would vote was an Act of 1728 which provided means for men to pay a proportion of their wages to their wives every six months (though they themselves still had to wait until the end of the commission), and replaced 'rigging wages' in harbour with full sea pay. Another Act of 1758 improved the mechanism of 'remittances' to wives, and required that men turned over from ship to ship be paid their wages up to six months before. These two Acts provided a real benefit to the minority of seamen who were married, but few men took advantage of them. Paying men on turn-over put money in their pockets and encouraged them to run away to spend it. Seamen were no more coldly calculating than any other class of men, and often threw away more money in accumulated wages by desertion, from merchantmen as well as warships, than they could rationally have hoped to earn at the highest wartime wages. In practice the Navy was usually able to retain the loyalty of men who had become members of a settled ship's company, with officers and shipmates they knew. Men who ran away tended to do so when they were 'turned over' to a strange ship, or in their first few months aboard a new ship. Often they ran back to their former officers, elsewhere in the Navy, rather than to merchantmen. During the Seven Years' War the ships of the Navy were losing, on average, about 7 per cent of their men a year to desertion, but a significant proportion of this was movement from ship to ship within the Navy.[16]

Sea officers well understood the value of social stability afloat, but in the crises of naval manning the Admiralty was driven to expedients which destroyed it. Turning men over to strange ships 'breaks their hearts', as Admiral Philip Cavendish wrote in 1741.

> Pressed men to be sure, it is right to dispose of them to the ships that want them. But the turning over volunteers, and men that have belonged to ships some time, and like the ship and their officers, I dare say that won't advance the Service at all.[17]

Even more than in the seventeenth century, when few ships were long in commission, every captain had a 'following' of junior officers and men: large or small, weak or strong according to his own reputation. Professional success at sea, where everything depended on teamwork, rested largely on the size and quality of a captain's following, so captains were very anxious to keep the men they had gathered, and the men themselves were equally anxious not to be forced to serve with strangers. Officers and followers were bound together by mutual dependence as well as respect and liking. An officer had to look after his people; he had to advance their careers, get them their wages and prize-money, and protect them when they got into trouble. Whether his private feelings were warm or cold towards his people, every captain knew that he needed them. Even the most senior officers took pains to care for their followers; after thirty years as an admiral, Norris was still corresponding with individual seamen and attending to their interests. Admiralty regulations permitted captains to take their own servants with them when they turned over to another ship, but whenever possible they stretched this. Commodore Charles Steevens, turning over from the *Elizabeth* to the *Grafton* in the East Indies in 1759, managed to take no fewer than seventy petty officers and 259 seamen, but this was only possible under a friendly commander-in-chief (Pocock) a long way from the Admiralty's watchful eye. However good and necessary followings were, they hampered the efficient use of manpower and might prevent unlucky or unpopular captains from getting to sea at all, so compromises had to be forced.[18]

The impossibility of refusing one's followers was one of the main reasons why leave was so often given. Obviously it was risky, when desertion was a problem, but it was also essential for health and morale, and dictated by common humanity. Everyone knew that some men would return late from leave, and some not at all, but official attitudes to 'straggling' ashore were relatively relaxed. In 1745 the soldiers manning the road-block at Petersfield on the Portsmouth–London Road had orders to arrest all seamen going away from Portsmouth without tickets of leave, but those going towards Portsmouth were to be allowed through even if their leave had expired. Norris asked his flag-captain not to mark absentees 'R' (for 'run') on the ship's books 'till there be a moral certainty of their not intending to return', and to take off the 'Rs' of those who did.[19] Men who were arrested as 'stragglers' or deserters seldom suffered any punishment beyond having the captor's reward charged to their wages. The Admiralty well knew that 'crimps' or dealers in seamen often persuaded drunken men-of-warsmen to desert, or simply abducted them. It regarded the crimps as far more guilty than the seamen, but enticing men to desert from the Navy (unlike the army) was no offence in law, and there was little that could be done to stop them – except of course to restrict leave. Vernon, who always insisted on granting leave whenever possible, nevertheless warned one of his captains at Port Royal in 1740,

9a. The *Brunswick* fighting the *Vengeur du Peuple* (to starboard) and the *Achille* during the battle of the First of June 1794, by Nicholas Pocock. In this celebrated action the *Vengeur* was so badly damaged that she sank soon after surrender. Pocock was a professional seaman before he became an artist, and was present at the battle; this is a rare painting which gives a realistic impression of smoke.

9b. The frigate *Mermaid* driving the French corvette *Brutus* ashore on the coast of Grenada, 10 October 1795; engraved after Pocock.

10a. The inshore squadron of St Vincent's fleet drying sails at anchor off Cadiz during the blockade following the battle of St Vincent, 1797, by Thomas Buttersworth. The town and the enemy fleet are visible in the background.

10b. The opening of the battle of the Nile, 1 August 1798, as the *Goliath* crosses the head of the French line, painted by Cooper Willyams, chaplain of the *Swiftsure*.

11a. The battle of Copenhagen, 2 April 1801, engraved after Pocock. On the disengaged side of the British line in the foreground two bombs are firing on the Trekroner Fort.

11b. Commodore Dance's convoy fighting Linois off Pulo Aor, 15 February 1804, painted and engraved by William Daniell. The French are to the left, with the Indiamen forming their line of battle in the centre.

12a. The battle of Trafalgar, 21 October 1805, by Pocock. The view is looking down the allied line from near the head, just as the two British columns to the right (Nelson's the nearer and Collingwood's the farther) cut through it.

12b. The capture of the Dutch West Indian colony of Curaçoa on 1 January 1807 by four British frigates under the command of Captain Charles Brisbane of the *Arethusa*. This watercolour is by Brisbane himself.

13a. The floating out of the eighty-gun three-decker *Cambridge* from her building dock at Deptford Dockyard, 21 October 1755, by the dockyard shipwright John Cleveley the elder. The new First-Rate *Royal George* is shown anchored in the stream.

13b. Portsmouth Harbour from the Gunwharf, 1770, by Dominic Serres the elder. The harbour entrance is to the left, with Spithead beyond, and the bulk of Haslar Hospital is visible in the background.

14a. An anonymous drawing of Woolwich Dockyard, about 1770, with a bomb-ketch in the foreground.

14b. A model of the *Bellona*, 74, probably made to demonstrate copper sheathing to George III. It shows her on the slip ready for launching, though in fact she was almost twenty years old in 1779.

15a. Blackwall Yard, 17 July 1784, with the *Adventure*, 44, being launched, by Francis Holman. This single private shipyard has four ships of the line, two forty-fours, two Indiamen and another merchant ship in various stages of construction, besides several ships refitting in dock.

15b. A perspective of Deptford Dockyard in the 1790s, by Nicholas Pocock. The large number of ships in Ordinary moored in the stream suggests a date before the outbreak of war.

16a. Plymouth Dockyard in 1798, also by Pocock. The southern (right-hand) half of the yard was all newly constructed. The town of 'Plymouth Dock' (the modern Devonport) is already growing up around the dockyard, though there is still open country between it and Plymouth proper in the distance.

16b. The Admiralty Boardroom, 1807, by Augustus Pugin, with the figures added by Thomas Rowlandson. The First Lord sits at the near end of the table, the Secretary at the other end with the Reader standing beside him. Note the rolled charts, and the tell-tale from the wind-vane on the roof.

'Apprehending many ill consequences from the account you gave me yesterday of your permitting your men a general liberty to frequent the town, from their destroying their health in punch houses and giving opportunities for their being seduced to desert the public service.'[20] Norris had problems at Lisbon with men allowed ashore to play cricket (always a source of disorder in the eighteenth century) getting into fights with the locals.[21]

Manning problems, in all navies, gave particular significance to the usual practice of exchanging prisoners of war. Sometimes prisoners were returned wholesale, with an account kept of which side was in credit, to be made up at the peace by paying a lump sum in ransom. The British often followed this method in the colonies, where the administrative burden of enemy prisoners was intolerable, and especially in the West Indies, where the colonial authorities were so deeply involved in clandestine trade with the enemy that they deliberately manipulated prisoner exchange as a means of starving the Navy of manpower, and warning the enemy of its movements. For this reason the control of prisoners of war in the colonies was transferred to the Navy in 1761. At home, where the British expected to hold many more prisoners than the enemy, they usually preferred to exchange 'man for man'. In practice this was not applied literally, but by a table which valued officers of different ranks in terms of a number of seamen. This allowed the system to be managed to return the least valuable enemy prisoners (commissioned officers) first, and keep back the most valuable (warrant and petty officers) to be exchanged last. The French navy's inability to protect transatlantic trade, and its traditional recourse to heavily manned privateers, both led to damaging losses of these key people which had a disproportionate effect on naval capability. Some of these losses were permanent, for though both sides attempted to hold their prisoners in humane conditions, typhus was an ever-present threat in eighteenth-century prisons, and the conditions of French prisoners worsened after 1759 when a bankrupt administration sent no more money to feed them, and they became dependent on the charity of the British government and public collections. About one French prisoner in eight died during the Seven Years' War; 8–9,000 men out of about 60,000 held at one time or another.[22]

The greatest number of men in the Royal Navy during the War of the Spanish Succession was 48,000. At the height of the next war, in 1747, the figure was as much as 58,000, and in 1760 it was over 85,000. The 1747 figure, it has been calculated, was 62 per cent of the total stock of British seafarers (including those in inland navigation), and by 1760 the proportion had risen to 67 per cent. The Navy was larger in each successive war, demanding a large and growing proportion of the total seafaring population (which itself was growing), and the size of individual ships was also increasing.[23] This alone would have put the discipline of the Navy, and all its social conventions, under increasing strain. We should be very cautious, however, of adopting the twentieth-century image of a 'strictly ordered, hierarchical society repressing all deviance'.[24] Contemporaries were far more impressed by the Navy's relaxed, not to say chaotic discipline. By modern standards the authority of a sea officer was weak, and ships functioned at sea on an implicit basis of co-operation and consent which sprang from the experience of seamen bred from boyhood to the necessity of teamwork for survival. In port, where there was no 'functional discipline' to sustain them, officers' powers of command over their ship's companies were notoriously feeble.[25]

One Admiralty reaction to the growing size and continued indiscipline of the Navy was to impose more detailed regulation on the internal affairs of ships. The *Regulations and Instructions relating to his Majesty's Service at Sea*, first published in 1731, were largely a codification of orders issued at various dates in the past as far back as 1663, but they still marked a significant move by the Admiralty to bring sea officers under closer control. Many of the regulations prescribed the very numerous accounts and papers which all officers, but above all the captain and purser, had to render. Keenly aware of the risks and temptations of handling public money and stores, ever conscious of the risk of Parliamentary inquiry, the Boards now demanded from ships' officers an unceasing flow of accounts and certificates. To pass his accounts a captain had to return more than sixty separate sets of books and accounts to different offices. The slightest discrepancy between them would stop his pay. Nor did the *Regulations and Instructions* limit themselves to accounting. They told captains how to rate their men and when to practise gunnery, to keep their ships clean and well-ventilated, to issue fresh meat and vegetables but not fruit or neat spirits, to encourage fishing but discourage blasphemy and forbid women. They bade captains 'show themselves a good example of honour and virtue to their officers and men', and, taken literally, they regulated many details of a ship's daily routine.[26]

In reality, of course, not every regulation was obeyed, and much shipboard life was still completely unregulated, but the tendency was slowly towards uniformity and central control. An important development was the introduction during the Seven Years' War of the 'divisional system', apparently invented and certainly popularized by Vice-Admiral Thomas Smith. His simple but powerful idea was to divide the ship's company into divisions allocated to the lieutenants and warrant officers, who were responsible for their discipline and cleanliness. Instead of an undifferentiated mass of men whom the officers could not (in a big ship) know by name, the divisional system ensured that every man was known as an individual to at least one officer. The bigger the Navy grew, the more professional seamen, who knew how to look after themselves and keep clean, were supplemented in wartime by landmen who did not, the more essential it was for discipline, health and humanity that a mechanism be found to preserve human relations between officers and ratings. The divisional system provided both for the welfare of the men, and their control by the officers. It reinforced discipline and was implicitly centralizing, though it was not imposed by the Admiralty, and it spread only by force of example. Closely connected with it was the new practice of captains keeping a public Order Book of their own internal ship's regulations. Lord Howe was an influential early proponent of the divisional system, and his 1759 order book in the *Magnanime* seems to have been copied by many captains.[27]

The fragility of officers' real authority, the serious and growing difficulty of recruiting and retaining men in wartime, made it ever more important for captains to gain their men's affections by humane treatment. 'It is his indispensable duty,' as Captain Christopher O'Brien advised,

> to see that the poor seaman be not wronged of his due, nor the service carried on by noise, stripes or blows; a method so inhuman, so unlike the officer, and so contrary to all true discipline, ought to be suppressed as soon as attempted . . . and not the ship made a prison of, but where the service requires immediate and constant attendance, or liberty is too much abused.[28]

It is implicit in this comment that some officers did carry on the service by 'noise, stripes or blows', but to understand the 'wooden world' of a ship it is necessary to distinguish different sorts of blows, in different circumstances. Casual violence and corporal punishment were commonplace in the eighteenth century, many members of a wartime ship's company had to be trained fast in the basics of communal living and working, and it was commonly accepted that a boatswain's mate with a rope's end was a salutary encouragement. Professional seamen did not object, so long as it was applied with discrimination: not on themselves, but on landmen, Marines and other inferior persons ignorant of the seaman's business. Nor did they complain if the captain had dirty, lazy or thieving men flogged, for they disrupted the crowded world of the ship's company, and threw extra work on their shipmates. Seamen accepted that officers had to punish, and did not care to serve with weak or lazy captains whose ships were disordered, uncomfortable and dangerous. Everything depended, however, on the discriminating judgement of the captain in bestowing encouragement, and punishment, on those who really deserved them. All successful naval discipline rested on an implicit alliance between the officers and the professional seamen, or at least the reasonably sober and reliable seamen. Indiscriminate violence undermined it, and the first sign of a brutal captain was often a disordered ship. 'The want of good order and discipline on board the *Superb* under your command'[29] was attracting admirals' (in this case Vernon's) disapproval almost as soon as she was commissioned by Captain the Hon. William Hervey in 1740. 'There is no government in that ship,' complained Cavendish. 'The men run away with the boats and won't obey their officers. Something must be done or that ship is lost to the Service.'[30] Something was in 1742, when Hervey was court-martialled and dismissed the Navy for ill-treating his officers and men. He was a fine seaman with a creditable record, and he was the son of an earl, but he had wrecked the system of mutual respect on which all naval discipline ultimately rested.[31]

Mutiny was part of this system of relations; it was the safety valve which blew when complaints were not heeded. Mutiny in the Hollywood style, the piratical seizure of a ship on the high seas, occurred occasionally in merchantmen and privateers, but was almost unknown in the Navy. The only example in this period was the mutiny of the *Chesterfield* in 1748. The ship was anchored off Cape Coast Castle in West Africa, her captain and most of the officers dining ashore with the governor, when the first lieutenant, Samuel Couchman, seized the ship, announcing his intention of turning pirate. Two days later the ship's company, led by the boatswain, recaptured the ship. Couchman and the lieutenant of Marines were shot; Roger Gastril the boatswain was appointed Master Attendant of Woolwich Yard.[32] This spectacular case of officer-led mutiny was completely untypical of commonplace lower-deck mutinies, which invariably took place in port, and were in the nature of a strike or demonstration over one of a small list of traditional grievances, usually overdue pay, bad food or unpleasant officers. Commonly the order to weigh anchor would be refused – sometimes quietly, sometimes with some shouting and disorder, but never with violence – in order to draw authority's attention to an unanswered complaint. In most cases authority smoothed over the matter as quickly as possible by conceding the demand. The Admiralty's reaction to a typical mutiny can be read in two Board minutes:

> [10th March 1746] The company of the *Sunderland* having mutinied and refused to go to sea with Captain Brett, resolved that Captain

Crookshanks be ordered to repair down to Plymouth and take the command of the ship in the room of Captain Brett.

[11th March 1746] The Lords thinking proper that the captain and company of the *Sunderland* should be parted, in regard to the present dissension between them and the mutiny of the men, they have sent down Captain Crookshanks to command her . . . resolved that Lieutenant Kirley be directed to get the men on board, and the ship ready for sea, and he is to be acquainted that if any disturbance happens and the men do not come to their duty, it will be imputed to him as the cause of it.[33]

If it were within the captain's power to settle a mutiny which was liable to be 'imputed to him', authority might never hear of it at all.[34]

All the serious problems of naval discipline were with officers, not ratings. Army officers like Major George Lestanquet, who went out in the *St Albans* to the West Indies in 1741, were appalled at naval behaviour.

This day about noon, Captain Knight disapproving something one of his lieutenants named Long [did] . . . the lieutenant resented it in a public manner upon the quarter deck in the presence of all the ship's company; damned his captain, and told him he did not want him for anything, and would not be used so. I think he was very wrong, and do not understand such discipline.[35]

In the aftermath of the battle of Toulon the new Bedford Admiralty Board faced a crisis of authority and discipline. Apparently guilty officers had been acquitted by courts martial made up of their fellow-captains, 'led away by their private prejudices or narrow principles, to the discredit of themselves, and to the ruin of their profession', in Sandwich's words.[36] It was in the nature of a court martial, made up of captains, that it might side with a captain accused, against whatever discipline the admiral, or the Admiralty, wished to impose. Then a Lieutenant George Fry of the Marines was convicted on doubtful grounds by a court martial in the West Indies. The Admiralty cancelled the sentence, but Fry brought a civil action against Sir Chaloner Ogle, who had presided at the trial. The common lawyers had always hated martial law, and Sir John Willes, Chief Justice of Common Pleas, awarded Fry £1,000 damages and encouraged him to sue each member of the court in turn. This he did, proceeding next against Rear-Admiral Perry Mayne, who was at that moment, in May 1746, presiding over Lestock's court martial. Mayne and the other members adjourned the trial, issuing angry resolutions against Willes, and he in turn ordered them imprisoned for contempt of court. The discipline of the Navy appeared to be collapsing in uproar, and the Admiralty feared that no captain would now risk sitting on a court martial,

> which coming once to be known among the common seamen and Marines, it is easy to foresee what scenes of riot and disorder his Majesty's ships of war may come to be, and what fatal consequences may be apprehended from such a failure of discipline and government over his Majesty's forces by sea.[37]

It seemed urgently necessary to gain two slightly contradictory points: to establish a court martial's legal independence from interference, and to restrict its freedom to award as little punishment as it pleased. There was also a problem with the jurisdiction of courts martial, which according to the Articles of War applied only to persons in 'actual service and full pay ... in or belonging to the fleet', so that naval discipline in any form did not extend to officers on half-pay (including the Impress Service), or to warrant officers of ships in Ordinary.[38]

The weaknesses of courts martial bore on another of the Admiralty's problems, cowardice. The conspicuous failures of Richard Norris and others at Toulon were followed by a series of actions reflecting further discredit on the Navy. In May 1744 the *Northumberland*, 64, rashly engaged two French ships of the same size in the Bay of Biscay, and surrendered soon after the captain was killed. Three months later off Cape St Vincent the *Solebay* surrendered to a French squadron without a fight. Next year the *Anglesea* was surprised off Kinsale by a French ship which she had taken for a friend. The captain and master were killed, the first lieutenant was sick ashore, and the second, Baker Phillips, surrendered. He was shot for cowardice. Then in April 1746 the *Solebay* was recaptured with great gallantry by the Bristol privateer *Alexander*, to the further humiliation of the Navy. In 1747 the Spanish *Glorioso*, 74, coming home from the West Indies, was twice intercepted by British ships. Off the Azores she drove off the *Warwick* while the senior officer, Captain John Crookshanks of the *Lark*, watched from a safe distance. Later the *Glorioso* beat off the Bristol privateers *King George* and *Prince Frederick*, blew up the Fourth-Rate *Dartmouth*, and was finally taken after a six-hour action by the *Russell*, 80, which, 'being very old and weak and receiving five shot between wind and water', almost sank in the process. Though in the end the *Glorioso* was captured, Spanish officers and British privateersmen came off with more credit than the Navy.[39]

To improve the status and *esprit de corps* of the sea officers, the Admiralty instituted two linked novelties: rank and uniform. Hitherto naval ranks had no definition in military terms, and still indicated a temporary employment as much as a permanent position in society. Fixing officers' ranks was meant to 'animate them to support the dignity of their rank by a proper deportment and distinction', and to avoid embarrassment and ambiguity in their relations with other services at home and abroad. It also moved some way towards establishing master and commander as a permanent rank, equivalent to major, though it still had no half-pay establishment. A proposal of 1730 to institute a permanent rank of commodore had failed, but at least a commodore now ranked unequivocally with a brigadier-general, while a post-captain over three years' seniority ranked with a colonel.[40] At the same time as rank came another innovation long requested by officers: a uniform. The design was largely worked out by a group of Anson's followers, though some officers came to regret having chosen the middle-class colour of blue instead of the more martial and distinguished red.[41] Uniform had social as well as professional value; although the Admiralty considered providing one for warrant officers ('to be of plain blue cloth, and the coat lapelled with the same'),[42] it was as yet only granted to commissioned officers, and to midshipmen, 'to distinguish their class to be in the rank of gentleman, and give them better credit and figure in executing the commands of their superior officers'.[43] Officers were supposed to adopt the uniform at once, but even in flagships uniformity came slowly. At Portsmouth in 1749 the Admiralty found 'the gentlemen on the quarter deck not being dressed in the uniform, many of whom had blue trimmed with white, but almost every one made in a different manner'.[44]

Another difficulty which the new Admiralty wished to address was the choice of admirals. In 1743 George II had reluctantly agreed that there might be more than one in each rank, and by the end of 1747 the total had reached twenty-one: one Admiral of the Fleet (Norris), six Admirals, six Vice-Admirals and eight Rear-Admirals. Subtracting the elderly, unfit and unsuitable, this left a very narrow range of choice for active commands. Moreover there was no recent precedent for promoting admirals except from the top of the captains' list, and passing captains over for promotion caused constant complaint, so that many of the candidates for flag rank were already elderly, unfit or unsuitable. Anson meant to solve this problem by imposing compulsory retirement schemes both for captains and admirals, but the idea of forcing an admiral to give up his commission was too radical for the age, and the captains' scheme went ahead only in disguise. In July 1747 a new rank was created, Rear-Admiral 'without distinction of colours', to which were promoted twenty captains on the explicit understanding that they were superannuated. It was now possible for the Admiralty to reach as far down the captains' list as it desired, taking some as active Rear-Admirals, and providing the rest with 'an honourable retreat from service' as 'Yellow Admirals'.[45] What was still impossible was to select admirals from younger captains not near the top of the list, but during the Seven Years' War Anson did a lot to circumvent this restriction by freely creating commodores. This policy reached its extremity in 1761 when Commodore Augustus Keppel commanded a fleet of sixty-three sail with two junior commodores under him. Though still only thirty-six, he was a post-captain of seventeen years' seniority, and had been a commander-in-chief, off and on, for twelve of them.[46]

The most pressing issue remaining for the Admiralty at the end of the war in 1748 was the linked problem of cowardice among officers, and the jurisdiction of courts martial. The Fry case in particular was behind the 1749 Navy Bill in which the Admiralty proposed a revision of the Articles of War. One of its provisions, applying martial law to officers on half-pay, aroused determined opposition and split the Navy. Some of this was inspired by the Prince of Wales and his political friends, exploiting an opportunity to embarrass the government, but there were real professional concerns which turned even some of Anson's followers against the bill. Subjecting half-pay officers to martial law would allow any Admiralty to force them to serve anywhere against their will, but gentlemen of honour expected to dictate the circumstances in which they would serve; they were still remote from the nineteenth-century ideal of duty. Perhaps Wager, an admiral who inspired trust and affection, might have carried the point, but Sandwich was a civilian politician, one of those who had subjected Mathews, Lestock and their captains to political inquiry in 1745, and his bill aroused alarm. In the end it passed with the obnoxious provision removed. What survived among other changes was an increase in the number of offences for which a court martial had no discretion to vary a sentence of death. Byng was to suffer as a result.[47] In principle the Admiralty now had some, though not all, of the means it had sought to impose courage and discipline, and during the Seven Years' War the example of Byng, and the leadership of Anson, visibly strengthened the sea officers' professional standards. Much about their working lives remained unlike any modern profession, but the structure of the sea officer's career must await another chapter.

TWENTY-ONE

The Battle of the Legislature

Operations 1763–1779

I t is more obvious in retrospect than it was at the time that the extraordinary triumph of the Seven Years' War altered Britain's strategic perspective. For the first time the public came to believe that colonies were a strength in themselves, not merely valuable as a source of trade. 'Colonies' meant British America, a single economic unit stretching from Labrador to Barbados, for the few British colonies elsewhere in the world scarcely figured in public consciousness. The value of the American plantations was both misunderstood and exaggerated. It was seriously suggested that there were as many as 50,000 American seamen, without whom the Royal Navy could not be manned, though the British government's own figures suggested between 3,000 and 5,000, not many of them engaged in transatlantic trade or easily available to British warships.[1] Others like Frederick Hervey, Bishop of Derry, still believed that 'the existence of Great Britain without the fishery of Newfoundland, that certain appendage to America and that indispensable nursery of your maritime force, is as romantic as a *château d'Espagne*.'[2] This new appreciation of the importance of the colonies combined with a sense that they needed reform. A corrupt and self-seeking colonial elite, it seemed, had preferred trading with the enemy to supporting the war-effort. George Grenville, First Lord of the Treasury from 1763 to 1765, was a determined financial reformer confronting a colossal wartime debt, and anxious to levy taxation on the colonies to pay for a permanent garrison, now for the first time established in North America.[3]

As Britain turned outwards to the world beyond Europe, enthusiasm grew for a new style of exploration. Expeditions like Lieutenant James Cook's to the Pacific in 1768 to observe the 'transit of Venus', and Captain Constantine Phipps' Arctic voyage of 1773, were accompanied by civilian scientists and had as much to do with scientific as geographical discovery. This was an international movement in the spirit of the Enlightenment, ostensibly for the benefit of all mankind, but there were also purely national motives discreetly veiled from public view. It seemed obvious that the unknown parts of the world, the Pacific especially, would soon be explored as navigational techniques improved, and British ministers wanted to make sure that Britain was not left out of whatever commercial or strategic benefits might be brought to light. This was the primary motive for Cook's second Pacific voyage of 1772 to 1775, during which he disproved the theory of a southern continent in temperate latitudes which had obsessed geographers for 2,000 years, and for his last voyage of 1776 to 1779, in which he met his death, which dispersed the theories of a navigable North-West Passage through Canada.[4]

Government turned towards colonies and distant oceans partly because it turned away from Europe. It had always been a reflex of British diplomacy to seek allies against France, but in the post-war world they were not to be found. Humiliated France no longer aroused much alarm, and the Continental powers were in any case much more concerned about the rise of Russia. This moved the centre of European diplomatic gravity to the East, and left Britain dealing with inland powers which had little to hope or fear from sea power. Her natural friend was Russia, their link the trade in naval stores which was so lucrative to Russia and so essential to the Royal Navy. Russia herself was now a sea power whose growing significance was underlined in 1770 by the voyage of a Russian squadron to the Mediterranean, where it won the crushing victory of Chesme over the Turks. Britain secured a commercial treaty with Russia in 1766, but no military alliance was available at a reasonable price.[5] Diplomatic weakness was made up by naval strength. In a series of incidents with France and Spain in 1764 and 1765 over colonial rights in Newfoundland, the Turks Islands and the Honduras coast in the Caribbean, and the Gambia river in West Africa, Grenville's government employed naval power, and the threat of naval mobilization, as an effective deterrent and forced its opponents to retreat.[6]

Naval deterrence worked, but it did not make Britain any less isolated or disliked, and it depended on a resolute government prepared to use it. In 1765 the Grenville ministry was replaced by one led by the marquess of Rockingham and composed, as it seemed, mainly of his friends from the turf; 'Persons called from the *stud* into the *state*, and transformed miraculously out of jockies into ministers'.[7] Next year Pitt returned to power, now ennobled as the Earl of Chatham, but without a war to demonstrate his supreme talents as a strategist. Contemptuous as always of everyday politics and politicians, he made no attempt to recruit allies, and observed the progressive collapse of his ministry with lofty disdain. The Duke of Grafton, who followed him in 1768, was still idler and less businesslike than his former colleague Rockingham.

Rockingham had sometimes forgotten to attend Cabinet meetings; Grafton came but slept. Five years of weak leadership soon undermined the impression made abroad by Grenville's firm deterrence. Failure to obtain the Manila ransom promised by Spain, or to prevent France's acquisition of Corsica in 1768, encouraged ministers in both countries, and the progress of the popular radical politician John Wilkes, attended by widespread rioting, provided further evidence of what Frederick the Great called the 'instability of our measures and sudden changes in our administrations, which made it almost impossible to transact business with us with any sort of security'.[8]

This is the background to the crisis of 1770, when Spain ejected the infant British colony from the Falkland Islands. This act was inspired not only by a sense of Britain's weakness, but by the backing of the French minister the duc de Choiseul, who had been planning a naval war of revenge ever since he became naval minister in 1761.[9] He had since organized a series of espionage operations to collect information on possible landing beaches in England, and now he saw an opportunity to launch the united Bourbon monarchies on a decaying Britain.[10] In London, however, there was a new prime minister, Lord North, and a government ready to mobilize the Navy. By the end of 1770 war seemed to be imminent, and it was only averted at the last moment when the French government drew back, dismissing Choiseul and obliging Spain to abandon its claims on the islands.[11]

The Falkland Islands crisis had important political consequences in Britain. It greatly strengthened the position of Lord North, and allowed him to replace several inherited ministers. One of them was Sir Edward Hawke, First Lord of the Admiralty since 1766. The great admiral had been a conscientious administrator who had managed the mobilization effectively, but his political naivety had added no strength to a weak ministry, and he was now old and ill.[12] In his place North installed Lord Sandwich, who now returned for a third time as First Lord, to the Admiralty where he had begun his political career twenty-six years before. North and Sandwich were to preside over the country and the Navy for the next twelve years, into and through the American War of Independence. The failures of that war in the end drove them both from office, and damned their reputations for posterity, so it is important to stress just how successful the North ministry was in the early 1770s. North admirably combined the two qualities needed of the eighteenth-century prime minister; he was a master of finance and an outstanding leader of the House of Commons,[13] where his skill, integrity and unfailing good humour commanded widespread respect. His firm handling of the Falkland Islands crisis led to a period in which Britain's reputation abroad seemed secure. The French navy was thrown into chaos by the mismanaged reforms of the new naval minister Bourgeois de Boynes, while judicious demonstrations of British naval strength supported British diplomacy in parts of the world as far apart as India and the Baltic.[14]

This happy situation was disturbed in the mid-1770s by political crisis in the American colonies, but that crisis only reinforced the impregnable position of the North ministry in British politics. It is hardly possible to sum up in a paragraph the issues which sustain the historians of half a continent, but a few words about the causes of the American troubles are needed. All Englishmen believed that the only real threat to their liberty came from the power of the crown, and Parliament's authority, specifically its control of finance, was their essential defence. The colonists disputed Parliament's right to tax them, and by doing so they attacked the citadel of English liberty, aligning themselves with absolutism and (for older observers) Jacobitism. Though they pretended to oppose the excessive power of the crown, it was obvious that George III was, as he claimed, 'fighting the battle of the legislature'.[15] In the 1760s the American dissidents had had many respectable friends in British politics, but as the crisis worsened and the issues became clearer their position became increasingly exposed. Lord Chatham until his death in 1778, and the Rocking-ham Whigs who made up the main opposition to North, still professed to support the Americans in resisting the 'power of the crown', but both their known principles and their practice when in government entirely contradicted them, and they carried little conviction among the independent majority in Parliament. Most members of Parliament found the American arguments absurd and sinister; only the popular radicals outside Parliament, supporters of John Wilkes and others, wholeheartedly endorsed the American cause, and even they were able to do so only because they were safely remote from responsibility.[16] 'Numbers undoubtedly will not be wanted in either House,' commented Sandwich in 1775, 'as the nation seems more unanimous against the Americans, than I ever remember them in any point of great national concern since I have known Parliament.'[17]

As the colonists took arms and the American crisis slid into open violence in 1774 and 1775, therefore, the North ministry was forced to take action by king and Parliament as much as by its own convictions. The difficulty was what to do. The issues at stake were political rather than military: they concerned the relations of government and governed within the British world, and they demanded a political solution, but that in turn was impossible until order was restored. Riots were commonplace in the eighteenth century, and in the absence of a police force British governments were used to sending soldiers to suppress them. Police action to restore order among Englishmen was what they contemplated; it is quite anachronistic to think in terms of two different nations going to war. Only Lord Barrington the Secretary at War, daunted by the scale and remoteness of the problem, argued for the alternative of a naval blockade, to hit the New Englanders in their pockets, and cut them off from external relief. There were obvious reasons to reject his plan. From the political perspective, it would rather encourage than suppress rebellion. Practically, the numerous small ports on the New England coast were beyond the capacity of the North American squadron to cover, and an effective blockade would have to have been mounted in the West Indies.[18]

The Caribbean was critical to any strategy for dealing with North America. The wind and current systems of the North Atlantic are circular and clockwise, so that ships bound from European ports to the Americas naturally fetched a great arc to the southward, down to latitude 15°N or thereabouts, to pick up the easterly trade winds for an easy run across the Atlantic. They then passed not far from the West Indies and the Bahamas to approach American ports from the south. The West Indies were therefore more or less on the direct route to America, and most colonial shipping traded with the islands. The natural route for supplies from Europe to the rebels, who initially had no domestic production of arms and ammunition, was via French, Dutch and Danish islands in the West Indies. British warships could search American ships met at sea in the Caribbean, but an effective blockade would have required direct action against neutral ports, with a high risk of provoking war at the worst possible moment. For these reasons blockade was not a practicable strategy.[19]

Throughout the American War, British strategy was influenced and constrained by political tension within the ministry, and in particular between North, Sandwich, and the new Secretary of State for the Colonies, Lord George Germain, who took office in November 1775. This third secretaryship, created in 1768, assumed a new importance with the American rebellion. Germain was the responsible minister for political and military activities in the colonies, including combined operations with the Navy and the transport of troops and military supplies across the Atlantic. He was an energetic and able administrator with the king's support, but in other respects he was an unfortunate choice. Cold, arrogant and isolated, distrusted and distrustful, Germain habitually intrigued to undermine other ministers. His strategic ideas were limited to promoting action in the Americas, his own department, and subverting British arms in the rest of the world. Despised by the public as the general who had been disgraced for cowardice at the battle of Minden, he was privately suspected of being a homosexual surrounded by young men who were employed to spy on his colleagues (and one of whom was thought to be employed by the French to spy on him).[20]

Germain's principal (though not only) rival was Sandwich, as First Lord of the Admiralty the other leading war minister. He had been a minister when Germain had been a subaltern, and North a schoolboy. Three times First Lord of the Admiralty, twice Secretary of State, he added unequalled experience to the first-class mind and determined energy which marked all his public life. Only the Admiralty, however, of all Cabinet posts, was ever filled on ability. Cabinet ministers in general, then as now, were chosen to balance interests, and Sandwich's political interest was weak. He was poor by the standards of an English peer, a crippling practical defect in the expensive business of high politics, and a damaging moral blemish which implied dependence if not corruption. Anson's control of the Navy in the previous war had been fortified by his wealth, his political connections and his professional standing as the 'Father of our Service'. Sandwich lacked all three.[21]

Given Sandwich's political weakness, and Germain's political methods, tension within the Cabinet was inevitable. What made it really damaging was North's inadequacy as a war leader. It has been explained that the eighteenth-century constitution did not provide for a minister to lead the Cabinet, but at least in wartime, unity of policy demanded one, and North's many talents did not extend in this direction – as he himself saw clearly, for self-knowledge was one of his many attractive qualities.

> In critical times it is necessary that there should be one directing minister, who should plan the whole of the operations of government, and control all the other departments of administration so far as to make them co-operate zealously and actively with his designs even though contrary to their own. Lord North . . . is certainly not capable of being such a minister as he has described.[22]

'Government by departments was not brought in by me,' he remarked after the war; 'I found it so, and had not the vigour and resolution to put an end to it'.[23] Chronically indecisive and easily flustered in moments of crisis, he 'only wanted one quality to make him a great and distinguished statesman', as his colleague Henry Dundas remarked, 'despotism and violence of temper'.[24] Without it, continual infighting between Cabinet ministers, especially Germain and Sandwich, was reflected by indecision in the formation of strategy.[25]

At first the problem was not acute, for the crisis was almost entirely within

Germain's department. The Cabinet had intended that the troops sent to Boston in 1775 would solve the problem at a stroke. Next year the situation was worse; Boston had to be evacuated, Quebec was narrowly saved from a rebel army, and much larger forces were despatched, the ships commanded by Vice-Admiral Lord Howe, the army by his brother Major-General Sir William. Together they mounted a complex amphibious operation of unprecedented scale, landing the army on Long Island, crossing to Manhattan, and routing the rebel army. Only General Howe's pessimistic caution allowed it to escape envelopment and surrender. Unfortunately this proved to be the pattern of operations. The Navy did all that was asked to supply and move the troops, but no decisive victory was obtained, and the crisis deepened into 1777, with promises by Germain that one more push with more troops and more ships to support them would extinguish the rebellion.[26]

For 1777 Germain planned a grand strategy by which Howe's army would advance up the Hudson from New York, cutting the rebels in two, while another force under Lieutenant-General John Burgoyne came down from Canada to meet them. Howe, however, decided to go off in the opposite direction, shipping the army by sea to the head of Chesapeake Bay where they landed and advanced on Philadelphia. Howe was rewarded with the capture of the rebel capital, but meanwhile Burgoyne was stopped in the wild country of upper New York and forced to surrender at Saratoga. Neither general emerged with credit from this disaster, but Germain, who was responsible for overall strategy and should have co-ordinated their movements, was primarily to blame.[27]

As the American crisis deepened, the Navy's responsibilities grew. No previous British government had ever attempted to maintain a large army 4,000 miles away, and never before had the soldiers found themselves unable to buy food and fodder and hire waggons locally. By July 1776 the Navy and Victualling Boards had taken up over 146,000 tons of transports, 46,000 tons more than the maximum of the previous war. This took no account of transports chartered by the Ordnance Board or the Treasury (in effect Germain), which was responsible for victualling troops overseas. The Navy and Victualling Boards had long experience of this business and conducted it with frugal efficiency, but the Ordnance Board went its own way, and Germain's guiding principle was to organize everything in his department differently from the Navy. Naval transports sailed under convoy, so Germain sent his unescorted. The Navy Board tendered at a fixed price, so Germain outbid it and cleared the market.[28]

Transports needed to be protected because in 1777 the rebels began to send out privateers, and even regular warships. In May Captain John Manley sailed from Boston with a squadron of two frigates and nine assorted privateers, enough to have rolled up much of Howe's scattered squadron if it had been boldly handled, but fortunately Manley was a timid leader and his force was soon neutralized.[29] Other American privateers caused losses to merchant shipping and transports in American and West Indian waters, though the claimed figure of 300 prizes is probably exaggerated. Most significant was the handful of American privateers in European waters, not so much for their military effectiveness as their real political impact, and their success in envenoming relations between Britain and France, where they were based.[30]

As the American crisis developed from 1775 to 1777, Sandwich's attention had been focused elsewhere. However troublesome the American rebels might be, however much the Navy's assistance was needed to deal with them, they were Germain's problem, and they posed no military threat to Great Britain. France and Spain were Sandwich's real worry, for the longer the crisis lasted, the higher the risk that they might seek to exploit it. North's policy throughout was of appeasement (and economy), trusting that Germain would solve the American crisis without the need of naval mobilization. In May 1776 the comte de Vergennes, the leading French minister, got a secret decision to send aid to the American rebels and to build up the French navy as quickly as possible to a war footing. British intelligence knew within a month, but Sandwich had great difficulty in persuading his colleagues to adopt even limited countermeasures. For the next fourteen months the process continued, with the French consistently ahead, and the British response cautious and tardy in spite of all Sandwich could do to alert ministers to the threat across the Channel. Because of it, Sandwich refused to allow Howe any ships of the line; the biggest ships in America were small forty-four- and fifty-gun two-deckers, and the whole battlefleet was retained at home. The greatest problem, even when full mobilization was finally agreed in August 1777, was that so many of the men needed to man the ships of the line were already absorbed by warships and transports in American waters. Moreover almost all the Navy's frigates were overseas, and the emergency building programme of frigates which customarily accompanied mobilization had not started. Sandwich's failure to persuade his colleagues of the need of early mobilization ensured that the Royal Navy would go to war at a crippling disadvantage.[31]

The French government saw an irresistible opportunity, but Vergennes' thinking on how to exploit the opportunity does not seem to have been very clear. Like many British commentators, he regarded the American colonies as the source of most of Britain's wealth and most of the Royal Navy's manpower.

Deprived of them, Britain would be enfeebled and dependent on France, which would again assume its natural position as the dominant power of western Europe. He had no natural enthusiasm for Republican rebels, and it has been argued that he meant to double-cross the Americans from the first.[32] It is certain that he meant to wage war by indirect means and in distant waters, avoiding anything so risky as direct confrontation with the Royal Navy – even though that implied a long war, such as in the past had soon exhausted France's resources. He was clear, however, that France needed the support of Spain to have any hope of naval victory.[33]

The news of Saratoga made it obvious that North's gamble with appeasement had failed, and war with France could not be long delayed. This would be a real war, potentially a mortal threat to Britain, which reduced the American rebellion to a sideshow. Whoever won the Franco-British war could settle the fate of the colonies at leisure afterwards. 'The object of the war being now changed, and the contest in America being a secondary consideration',[34] ministers decided to withdraw most of their forces from North America to the West Indies, leaving only two or three ports to be held as naval bases. The same strategic logic called for a revival of the Western Squadron, which had served Britain so well in the two previous wars. Here, once again, was the crucial position where naval dominance could be built up to ensure Britain's safety at home, and superiority abroad. Failure to mobilize in time had made the situation more dangerous than before, so it was all the more important to concentrate on the critical point. Vergennes' greatest fear was that the British would do so.[35]

With the help of hindsight, and two centuries of writings on strategy, all this is much clearer than it was to Lord North's Cabinet in the spring of 1778. They had to consider not only the French fleet preparing at Brest, but also the unknown intentions of the Toulon squadron, which might join that of Brest to enter the Channel as it had in 1692, or mount an operation against Minorca as it had in 1756, or (as Germain feared) cross the Atlantic. On the one hand there was a real risk of invasion, on the other the danger that Howe's squadron (with no ships of the line) would be crushed by the French, forcing the surrender of the army in America. Beyond the immediate threats lay the question of a long-term strategy, for detaching ships of the line to North America, as Germain demanded, implied emasculating the Western Squadron which had served Britain so well. Sandwich alone seems to have had some understanding of the strategic issue, but he had neither the professional nor the political weight to overrule Germain's insinuations (backed by the king) that his 'defensive attitude' would lead to disaster. The result was an anguished debate and a messy compromise leading to the worst of both options. Sand-wich was forced to agree to detach a large part of the main fleet to America, but only when it was certain that the Toulon squadron was indeed going that way. Admiral comte d'Estaing sailed from Toulon with twelve ships of the line on 13 April, but he did not pass the Straits of Gibraltar until 17 May, and Vice-Admiral John Byron was not detached with his thirteen until early June.[36]

Meanwhile Sandwich had faced the tricky choice of a commander-in-chief for the main fleet. It has been observed that with the limited flag list of the day, it was often difficult to choose admirals for major commands, especially after years of peace. Moreover Sandwich was under political pressure: from Germain, demanding a right of veto over senior appointments; and from John Robinson, Secretary of the Treasury and the government's chief political manager, demanding men 'who . . . carry with them public opinion' – meaning opinion where it mattered, in the House of Commons.[37] Howe being in America, the only obvious choice was Keppel, who had plenty of experience in high command, albeit mainly in combined operations. The problem with Keppel was that he had spent the peace acting as manager of the Rockingham Whigs, so he was strongly identified with the government's opponents, and (as events were to prove) liable to be manipulated by colleagues of stronger character and fewer scruples than his own, who could see profit for their party in discrediting the ministry. Sandwich was determined, however, that politics should not influence the choice. Keppel agreed to serve, and under him were appointed Vice-Admirals Sir Robert Harland, who had Rockingham connections, and Sir Hugh Palliser, Sandwich's Admiralty colleague and therefore a government man, but also a friend of Keppel who was able to act as a bridge between them.[38] Naval opinion was reassured: 'They are tough fellows and will do well,' wrote Captain John Jervis of the *Foudroyant*.[39]

Sandwich found Keppel hard to manage. Though he too opposed any detachment from the main fleet, his correspondence was too despondent in tone and obscure in expression to be of much use in Cabinet. He incessantly demanded promotion for his friends and reinforcements for his fleet. He lamented his 'most anxious and critical situation that ever an officer who had character to preserve was placed in'.[40] Having been forced to accept the loss of Byron's ships, he demanded orders permitting him to retreat in the face of a superior enemy, and used them in June to run away from a rumour, exposing a rich West India convoy, and damaging the government.[41]

In July Keppel was at sea again, reinforced to twenty-nine ships of the line, including seven three-deckers. At the same time the French fleet sailed from Brest, thirty ships of the line (including only two three-deckers) plus two fifty-gun ships, under Vice-Admiral comte d'Orvilliers. In spite of delayed mobilization, Sandwich had managed to achieve a decisive superiority at the critical point, but detaching Byron's squadron had thrown it away. Vergennes knew France might never have another opportunity. Keppel's fleet was still somewhat superior, but French officers had benefited from several peacetime training squadrons, and when the two fleets met on 27 July they had the better of the initial manoeuvring for advantage. 'The French behaved more like seamen, and more officerlike than was imagined they would do, their ships were in very high order, well managed, well rigged and . . . much more attentive to order than our own,' reported Lieutenant John Blankett of Keppel's flagship the *Victory*.[42] Keppel tried to force an attack with his own fleet in some disorder, the French fired high, and Palliser's rear division, which was most closely engaged, was too badly damaged aloft to renew the action. 'Two fleets of equal force never can produce decisive events,' commented Jervis, 'unless they are equally determined to fight it out, or the commander in chief of one of them bitches it, so as to misconduct his line.'[43] The indecisive battle of Ushant was a huge relief to the French, who treated it as a triumph, and a disappointment to the British, but Keppel's relations with Sandwich, Harland and Palliser remained good. The Rockinghams put it about that his fleet had been crippled by shortage of masts and stores. The claim was quite false, and Keppel contradicted it in private, but allowed his party to profit from it in public. In the autumn he put to sea again to cover incoming convoys, and returned in October, tired and disappointed, to find a new and ugly political situation developing.[44]

An opposition newspaper had published a letter from an anonymous officer of Keppel's flagship, blaming Palliser for the lost opportunity, and hinting at cowardice. No officer could overlook a slur to his honour, least of all one of Palliser's obscure social origins, who had nothing but his professional character to depend on. He asked Keppel to contradict the story, and he declined. There is no evidence that Keppel knew in advance about the letter (probably written by his young cousin Lieutenant George Berkeley), or privately agreed with it, but by adopting the charge, for clearly political motives, he raised an uproar. It looks very much as though Keppel himself was now little more than a glove-puppet for the extremists of the Rockingham party. The least damaging way out of the situation would have been for Palliser to ask for a court martial on himself to clear his name, but the Rockinghams blocked that by demanding it in Parliament, thus making it a political issue. Instead Palliser demanded a court martial on Keppel, not for political abuse of his authority, which was not mentioned in the Articles of War, but for misconduct in action – the very charge for which Byng had been shot. Petrol was poured on the flames which Sandwich was urgently trying to quench, and even moderate observers began to believe the Rockinghams' claims of a government plot to persecute their hero. Keppel's court martial was attended by a crowd of opposition noblemen, intimidating the witnesses and rejoicing in Keppel's inevitable acquittal. Palliser was then court-martialled in turn, and likewise acquitted, but the tide of hostility against him was such that he was forced out of the Admiralty and his naval career was ruined.[45]

The Keppel–Palliser affair generated a degree of political excitement in the early months of 1779 which at times verged on hysteria, dividing the fleet and badly damaging the government, but its worst effects were soon over. By May Captain R. B. Walsingham could report from Portsmouth that 'we are as quiet here as if we had never had a court martial; these violent party affairs soon subside', and the opposition admiral Sir John Ross 'very cheerfully' accepted a command.[46] Keppel was the hero of a brief hour, but his naval career was ruined, and sober reflection soon spoiled his public reputation, even in his own party. The majority of the admirals and captains of the fleet behaved, like Harland, with 'great decency and moderation' regardless of their private feelings. Only a handful of extremists, notably Jervis ('a good officer, but turbulent and busy, and violent as a politician'), attempted to keep the flames burning.[47] Nevertheless the affair left the Channel Fleet (though not the whole Navy) badly disunited for much of 1779, and was not forgotten on some quarterdecks even twenty years later.[48]

When Byron sailed on 9 June 1778, he took the risk of the direct crossing to North America, against the prevailing westerly winds, which given luck with wind and weather might have allowed him to catch up with d'Estaing, who was only three weeks ahead. Unfortunately 'Foul-Weather Jack' was not often lucky with the wind, and certainly not this time. His fleet was shattered and scattered by a heavy gale, and Lord Howe was left to face d'Estaing's squadron by himself. By this time Howe had seven small sixty-four-gun ships of the line, two fifties and some frigates, all sickly and short-handed; the odds in firepower were about two to one. As d'Estaing approached New York on 11 July, he found Howe's ships skilfully moored inside the island of Sandy Hook in a position to rake any ship which tried to enter the harbour. Moreover d'Estaing's American pilots were unsure if there would be enough water for his big ships to cross the bar. For eleven days d'Estaing hesitated, and then he sailed away. In August he tried to dislodge the British garrison from Rhode Island, with equal lack of success, and he had achieved nothing when he sailed from Boston at the beginning of November, bound for Martinique.[49]

At the same time a large British troop convoy carrying 5,000 men, escorted by a small squadron under Commodore William Hotham, sailed from New York for the West Indies to attack the island of St Lucia, strategically placed to windward of Martinique. The two forces proceeded south on parallel courses, unaware of each other's presence until d'Estaing captured a stray troop transport. He had an easy triumph within his grasp, but the master of the prize persuaded him that the convoy was bound for Antigua instead of the obvious, and correct, destination of Barbados, where it arrived safely on 10 December. Rear-Admiral Samuel Barrington, commanding in the Leeward Islands, was waiting for it, and that same afternoon he and Major-General James Grant agreed their plans. On the 13th troops landed at St Lucia, while the squadron (four ships of the line, three fifties and three frigates) anchored in the Grand Cul de Sac. The following afternoon d'Estaing's thirteen ships of the line were sighted approaching, but they did not attack the exposed British force at once. During the night Barrington moored his ships in a close line across the head of the bay, the transports within. D'Estaing attacked twice on the 15th but could make no impression; then landed his troops and was heavily repulsed.[50]

In January Byron appeared in the islands, still in pursuit of d'Estaing, but his ships were shattered and sickly, and he achieved little in the next six months. In July 1779 d'Estaing covered an expedition against the British island of Grenada, which brought on a battle between the two squadrons on the 6th. Byron's bold but disorganized attack went wrong; several ships were badly damaged and only saved from capture by d'Estaing's timidity. Soon afterwards d'Estaing left the station to mount an attack on the British position at Savannah, in Georgia, which was a bloody fiasco, and by the end of 1779 he was back in Europe having achieved nothing in eighteen months cruising and fighting around the western hemisphere.[51]

Meanwhile in Britain the Keppel–Palliser affair was used by the opposition to attack Sandwich and the handling of the naval war, bringing on a crisis in Parliament. The illness of the Earl of Suffolk, Northern Secretary of State, who died in March, suggested a solution: 'if the faction got into the fleet should render it possible that Lord Sandwich will be less able than a new person to manage that department, then to advance Lord Sandwich to the Northern Seals', as the king proposed, and find a less controversial figure for First Lord of the Admiralty.[52] The obvious choice was Lord Howe, lately back from America with his reputation enhanced by the defence of Sandy Hook. He had wide support in the Navy, and he was politically uncommitted. Unfortunately his brother the general was at odds with Germain, each blaming the other for

Saratoga, and the admiral was engaged in his brother's cause. What this meant in practice was that Howe was willing to serve in return for promotion for himself and his brother, the sinecure office of Treasurer of the Navy (worth £4,000 a year), and the dismissal of Germain. Even in an age when officers were expected to look after their own interests, this was a breathtaking proposal. Money and promotion might have been arranged, but there could be no question of gratifying the admiral by removing a minister who still enjoyed the king's support. 'If Lord Howe would have come cordially into the Admiralty it might have been a popular appointment,' the king commented, 'but as he has added conditions that it would be disgraceful to grant, I am clear Lord Sandwich fills the Admiralty much better than any other man in the kingdom would.'[53] Unfortunately the crisis brought out the worst of North's vacillation. For seven months he agonized over filling the vacant secretaryship, or resigning himself, while Cabinet meetings were paralysed. 'Will your Lordship in this place allow me to lament the state of our Cabinet meetings,' Sandwich wrote in September, 'and to point out to you how absolutely necessary it is that you should take the lead among us, and not suffer any question to be agitated there that is not decided and carried into execution'.[54] In this situation, with politics and public life in turmoil, the ministry palsied and his own future in doubt, Sandwich had to find a replacement for Keppel to command the Channel Fleet. Again Howe would have been the obvious candidate, but since his terms were unacceptable, Sandwich had to look elsewhere, and the command went to Admiral Sir Charles Hardy, an officer with a long and respectable career whose age (sixty-two) and seniority put him above jealousy, and whose popularity and relaxed manner were well calculated to calm the heats of faction.[55]

The British blunders of 1778 encouraged Spain to enter the war. France had already lost naval supremacy in European waters; the overall balance of forces in 1779 promised to be about sixty-six ships of the line against ninety British. Spain could offer at least fifty ships of the line, enough to gain a crushing advantage. Spanish ministers were more hard-headed about the American crisis than the French. They knew what they wanted (the recovery of Minorca, Gibraltar, Florida and the Honduras coast, in that order), they saw how to achieve it (a swift, decisive stroke while their advantage lasted), and what to avoid (a long war in which the underlying British strength could be brought to bear). Their contribution was indispensable, so they controlled French strategy, and they had no time for Vergennes' indirect approach or vague hopes that the British financial system would collapse and avoid the risks of a battle. To the alarm of French ministers and admirals, the Combined

Fleet was committed to a Channel campaign for 1779, leading to a landing in force to seize Portsmouth.[56]

When Hardy sailed in June 1779 it was not yet certain that Spain would go to war, but by August he was facing fearful odds: sixty-six ships of the line in the Combined Fleet against thirty (eventually thirty-nine) British. It was generally agreed that even a modest superiority in numbers gave a sailing fleet the huge advantage of doubling and crushing one end or other of the enemy line (as the French had done at Beachy Head in 1690); there was no precedent for a fleet surviving such odds as Hardy faced. Keppel had been unnerved by a much less threatening situation, and Hardy in addition had to cope with a barrage of conflicting advice. Some (notably the king, and Captain Lord Mulgrave, who was both Hardy's subordinate and the senior naval member of the Admiralty Board) urged him to fight at once; some urged him not to risk a disaster. Some (including Sandwich) begged him to stay at sea; some begged him to come into port. In the face of all these pressures Hardy remained his own man, calm and cheerful, always insisting that he would fight at a moment of his own choosing, when he had drawn the enemy far up the Channel. That moment never came. In foggy weather, the two fleets only once sighted one another, and on 11 September the Combined Fleet returned to Brest. Possibly a greater admiral than Hardy, or one better informed of his enemy's difficulties, might have risked and won a battle against long odds, but at the lowest estimate he showed sound judgement and great moral courage, and his fabian tactics saved the country from the threatened invasion.[57]

They were greatly assisted by the failures of the French navy. Prolonged delays, largely in French dockyards, had prevented the allies from joining until 23 July. The Spanish ships were properly stored for the campaign, but by the time they entered the Channel early in August the French were almost out of food and water, and reduced to begging supplies from their allies to stay at sea. Without pilots or adequate charts they were terrified of going up the Channel, and incompetent scouting left them quite ignorant of Hardy's whereabouts. Though the Spanish ships were fairly clean and healthy, the French ships were filthy as usual, and crippled by a deadly epidemic which left at least 8,000 men sick or dead.[58]

By sending d'Estaing's squadron across the Atlantic in the spring of 1778 the French threw away more than all the advantage of early mobilization, and ran a big risk which might have been exploited. If Howe had been left to fend for himself, which in the event he had to do anyway, and Byron's ships had remained with Keppel's fleet, as Keppel and Sandwich wanted, the balance of naval power in home waters would have been transformed. The battle of Ushant would have been fought at odds of at least five to three, had d'Orvilliers put to sea. More likely he would have stayed in port, and Keppel could have established a loose blockade of Brest, in the best position to intercept French forces sailing for the Americas. Either way the naval war would have taken a potentially decisive turn in Britain's favour, earlier than it had done in the previous war. This was the decision indicated by logic and tradition, this was the bold concentration which might have yielded early victory.

It did not happen because ministers (like modern historians) could not get America out of their minds. If the king and Cabinet had been prepared to admit the logic of abandoning most of America until France was defeated – and the logic of abandoning Germain which went with it – the French folly in splitting their fleet when they might have united it would have opened the chance of a decisive victory before Spain could enter the war. True, decisive victory early in a war was rare, but at the available odds it was far from impossible, and it was the best chance of retrieving the blunder of late mobilization. Instead, the British imitated the French, sending Byron's squadron on a costly wild-goose chase half across the world, in waters beyond effective communication from London and without dry docks, where it could neither be controlled, directed nor repaired. With him vanished the only chance of driving France out of the war and depriving the American rebels of support. Evacuating most of America would certainly have allowed the rebels to consolidate and the loyalists to suffer, but for the most part that had already happened, and concentrating at home was the only hope of establishing conditions by which the rebellion might one day have been defeated. Instead a hesitant and divided government dissipated its naval strength on the strategic periphery, and abandoned the initiative to the enemy.

—•◆•—

TWENTY-TWO

Distant Waters

Operations 1780–1783

T he alarms of 1779, especially the presence of the Franco-Spanish Combined Fleet in the Channel, seriously weakened the North government, but the opposition found it difficult to profit without being tainted by connection with the extremist friends of America who openly rejoiced in their country's defeats (several well-known Rockingham Whig noblemen among them), or with subversive radical politicians outside Parliament. The anti-Catholic Gordon Riots in June 1780, during which destructive mobs controlled London for several days, frightened all shades of political opinion, and the equivocal behaviour of several opposition leaders (notably Lord Shelburne) during the riots did them further damage. Though North explored the possibility of gaining the Rockinghams for the coalition that summer, the king vetoed their demand to put Keppel into the Admiralty, and the ministry continued in the same form, rather gaining than losing strength during 1780 and 1781.[1]

Byron's fruitless cruise around the Americas did not remind the Cabinet of the virtue of concentrating their forces in European waters. For the moment they stuck to their decision to leave American waters as a sideline, but instead they concentrated on the West Indies. The plan for 1780 was to send out a strong squadron which on its way would relieve Gibraltar, now under siege by a Spanish army. Though some ministers (Sandwich in particular) were sceptical, the British public was deeply persuaded of the value of Gibraltar (and Minorca which depended on it), and the ministry felt obliged to give it a high priority.[2] Sandwich took the risk of choosing Admiral Sir George Rodney to command the squadron. Rodney was an intelligent and aggressive admiral with an outstanding fighting record in the previous war, a stern disciplinarian with high professional standards, and moreover a former MP who supported the government. The risk arose from his unpopularity in the Navy, and his very well-established reputation for dishonesty. All admirals

were concerned to handle promotions in ways which supported their authority, most officers had joined the Navy to make their fortunes, and not a few
bent the rules with more or less judgement and discretion. Rodney was unique,
however, in repeatedly and flagrantly misappropriating public money and
abusing his powers of patronage in ways which could not possibly be overlooked even by the most friendly Admiralty Board. Partly as a result he was
several times bankrupted, and in 1778 was living in France to escape from his
creditors. Only a loan from a generous French nobleman allowed him to
return.[3]

Rodney sailed from Portsmouth on Christmas Eve 1779 with eighteen
ships of the line and a large convoy. As he rounded Cape St Vincent on
16 January he encountered a Spanish squadron under Don Juan de Lángara,
which attempted to escape and was pursued into the night. The result of the
'Moonlight Battle' was the capture or wreck of six of the eleven Spanish ships
of the line, plus the successful relief of Gibraltar and Minorca. Leaving most
of his ships to return to the Channel Fleet, Rodney pressed on the Leeward
Islands, where he arrived in March 1780.[4]

Given the odds Lángara's only hope had been escape, and Rodney's victory
was assisted by an important technical innovation. The British had been
experimenting for more than thirty years with copper instead of wood sheathing against the shipworm. The advantage was lightness and durability; the
disadvantage was cost, and a serious problem of corrosion in the underwater
ironwork of the hull, including the rudder irons and the heavy bolts which
fastened together keel, stem and sternpost. The cause of this corrosion (electrolytic action) was not then understood, but it was known that it could be
prevented by establishing a watertight seal between the hull and the copper.
By 1779 the Controller of the Navy, Captain Charles Middleton, had identified
a technique, based on coating the bare hull with lacquered brown paper
before coppering, and persuaded Sandwich to undertake the cost and risk of
coppering the entire Navy. By 1780 coppered ships were joining the fleet, and
Rodney's squadron was partly made up of them. Coppering transformed
tactical as well as strategic possibilities, for copper turned out not only to keep
out the worm, but to repel fouling. In spite of the British advantage in dry
docks fouling was a constant problem, and doubly so in the Caribbean where
there were no docks and the weed grew twice as fast. Copper remained
naturally clean and bright, and coppered ships were reckoned to be at least a
knot faster as a result – a huge tactical asset in ships whose best speed under
fighting sail was only five or six knots. Ships which had been the slowest could
now outpace the entire uncoppered fleet. 'To bring an enemy to action,'

Rodney wrote, 'copper bottom ships are absolutely necessary,'[5] and a French officer, the chevalier de Cotignon, ruefully echoed him: 'the English sail much faster than us, especially now that they are sheathed in copper and we in oysters'.[6] What was more, coppering eliminated the need to dock frequently for cleaning and minor refits, and Middleton reckoned that it effectively increased the available fleet by one-third.[7]

Rodney arrived in the West Indies at about the same time as Vice-Admiral the comte de Guichen. Their forces were almost equal (twenty-one and twenty-two ships of the line respectively), though the bulk of Rodney's ships, having been some time in the Caribbean, were in poor condition. On 17 April they fought an indecisive action off Martinique. Rodney had an intelligent plan for mounting a concentrated attack on the enemy's centre and rear, which in other hands might have worked. Unfortunately Rodney's style of leadership wrecked his chances of victory. His behaviour towards other officers was cold and arrogant; he treated all his subordinates, including his junior flag-officers, as fools and automata, to be communicated with only by signals to which he demanded unquestioning obedience. In this case he had instituted a new signal to be hoisted 'when the commander in chief means to make an attack upon the enemy's rear', but like many of the old signals it did not explain how the captains were to realize the admiral's intention, and when it was hoisted in conjunction with the standard signal for each ship to engage her opposite number in the enemy line, the British line spread out to engage the French ship for ship. The result was an indecisive action, for which Rodney blamed everyone but himself. There were two further, slighter actions on 15 and 19 May, when Rodney gained some advantage.[8]

In North America there were now no large British forces, but there was one piece of unfinished business springing from the decision to hold a series of naval bases for the benefit of the wider war. There was no such British base between New York and Antigua, and to fill the gap an expedition was mounted from New York against Charleston by Vice-Admiral Marriot Arbuthnot and General Sir Henry Clinton. Clinton was an officer of some talent, undermined by a paranoid distrust of everyone he had to deal with, and it is to Arbuthnot's credit that they were able to work effectively together, at least for a while. This expedition was an unexpected triumph, for the rebels committed a large part of their field army to the defence, which surrendered with the town on 12 May.[9] By August Clinton and Arbuthnot were back in New York, considering, and disagreeing about, how to tackle a French squadron of six ships of the line under Rear-Admiral the chevalier de Ternay which had just arrived at Rhode Island. Then, on 14 September, something extraordinary happened: Rodney appeared at New York, demanding to take over the North American station. Ever since the 1740s the Navy had divided American waters into geographical 'stations', and there was neither precedent nor possible justification in his orders for a commander-in-chief to abandon his own station to occupy another. Rodney ordered the elderly Arbuthnot to sea to blockade Rhode Island, while he settled himself ashore at New York to amass as much of Arbuthnot's prize-money as possible, and took the opportunity to promote his fifteen-year-old son a post-captain. Arbuthnot did not directly disobey Rodney, who was the senior, but he naturally sent furious protests home, while Rodney, with the considerable art of which he was master, despatched unctuous letters to all his influential correspondents accusing Arbuthnot of greed and spite, and congratulating himself on his wisdom and virtue. The hurricane season over, Rodney sailed again for the Leeward Islands at the end of November, taking with him two of Arbuthnot's frigates and all his naval stores. The incident was over by the time the correspondence reached London, and Sandwich had to handle the victor of the Moonlight Battle with caution, but it still seems extraordinary that neither he, nor the Cabinet, nor Germain, who was so keen to establish his authority over the appointment of admirals, intervened to support Arbuthnot. Rodney was privately warned not to interfere with other people's patronage and prize-money, but the central issue of authority was fudged, and the official relationship of the four American stations (Jamaica, the Leeward Islands, North America and Newfoundland) was left dangerously uncertain.[10]

In Rodney's absence the West Indies had been struck by two hurricanes, one of which was reckoned the worst for a century, and moreover took an unusual track. The last convoy home from Jamaica was caught; two ships of the line and six frigates were lost, and most of the survivors were dismasted. The British, however, had already withdrawn most of their forces from the Caribbean. Spain was the real loser, for that able and energetic general, Bernardo de Gálvez, had taken the risk of mounting his invasion of Florida in the hurricane season, and the expedition from Havana was largely destroyed.[11]

At home Sandwich was again faced with the necessity of finding a new commander-in-chief for the Channel Squadron when Sir Charles Hardy died in May 1780. Barrington was recently returned from the West Indies, his reputation enhanced by his defence of St Lucia against d'Estaing, but he refused the proffered command. His motives were not political but personal. Always easy and popular with his equals and subordinates, Barrington was touchy and suspicious in his relations with authority. He had taken offence at not being praised for his action in sufficiently glowing terms, and it seems had some fear of the responsibility of being commander-in-chief. He accepted the second command, under Admiral Francis Geary. 'An honest man and a good plain officer,' in Hawke's words,[12] Geary was one of the most popular admirals in the Navy, with a long career behind him as everybody's ideal second-in-command, cheerful and efficient. Older, but also fitter, than Hardy (he was seventy, but lived another sixteen years) he had many of the same virtues as a level-headed peacemaker.[13] He did not have to face the Combined Fleet in the Channel, but he was ordered on prolonged cruises to the south-west, designed to cover British convoys and keep the French and Spaniards apart. Like the Western Squadron in 1746 and 1757, he lacked the forces to maintain a standing blockade, and enemy squadrons (Guichen's and Ternay's among them) had little difficulty in avoiding him. Moreover his prolonged cruising out of range of home ports led to a serious outbreak of scurvy. A lucky encounter with a Portuguese brig with a cargo of lemons helped, but in August the fleet was forced into port, with Geary and several of the admirals ill.[14] In its absence the Spanish main fleet under Don Luis de Córdoba achieved a notable success, intercepting an outward-bound West India convoy off the Azores and taking fifty-five out of sixty-three sail. It was the worst convoy disaster since 1693; 1,350 seamen and 1,255 troops were made prisoner, and several London underwriters went bankrupt.[15] While Geary was ashore Barrington was ordered to take the fleet to sea, and flatly refused to obey. This was little better than mutiny, and seemingly a deliberate attempt to divide the fleet against the government, so he was dismissed, and once again Sandwich had to find a new commander-in-chief. This time he turned to Vice-Admiral George Darby, a 'plain but valuable man' in Mulgrave's judgement,[16] who commanded the fleet with unostentatious firmness and competence for the remainder of 1780 and 1781.[17]

1780 was also the year of a diplomatic and strategic crisis caused by the alliance of Baltic powers known as the Armed Neutrality, which proposed to put pressure on the naval powers (meaning Britain) by denying them their essential supplies of naval stores. Russia alone supplied the Royal Navy with over 90 per cent of its hemp for cordage, and (now that the New England forests were unavailable) almost 90 per cent of the largest masts, and the alliance was essentially a Russian project which Denmark and Sweden were forced to join. The Danes, however, skilfully subverted Catherine the Great's plan. A few days before the alliance came into force in July 1780, they signed an agreement with Britain which conceded the British definition of naval stores as contraband, in return for the right to carry foodstuffs through a British blockade. Thus Denmark secured her own export and carrying trade by sacrificing Russia's exports to France and Spain. In practice the Russians found that they needed to export at least as much as the British needed to import, and the main effect of the Armed Neutrality was to neutralize the Baltic and spare the British the necessity of protecting their shipping beyond the North Sea.[18]

The position of the Netherlands was critical to all British attempts to block Baltic naval stores from reaching France and Spain, since Dutch ships still dominated the Baltic trade, and the 1674 treaty still gave them complete rights to carry naval stores through a British blockade. The Dutch government was deaf, however, to any mention of the Anglo-Dutch military treaty of 1678, with its provisions for mutual assistance, and blocked the British practice of buying Dutch cargoes destined for French dockyards which had smoothed difficulties in previous wars. Relations were further worsened in 1779 by the operations of the American Captain John Paul Jones out of Dutch ports, and in December a Dutch convoy under Rear-Admiral Graaf van Bylandt was brought into Portsmouth by force. With French encouragement the Dutch became increasingly intransigent, the extent of their secret help to the American rebels was discovered, and in December 1780, shortly before the Netherlands planned to join the Armed Neutrality, the British declared war. Their intention was both to stop the flow of naval stores to France, and to advance the Orangist (and traditionally anglophile) party in Dutch politics.[19] In the event neither objective was achieved. The Dutch found means to avoid the British blockade in the Channel by shipping naval stores by inland waterways from Dutch ports, through the neutral Austrian Netherlands into France. Large numbers of Dutch merchantmen transferred to neutral flags (mainly Danish and Prussian) to continue trading. The effect on Dutch politics was to damage the Prince of Orange and encourage the francophile 'Patriot' party. On the other hand Dutch merchant ships provided rich and defenceless prizes, especially in distant waters, and generated a short-lived British privateering boom. Playing a weak diplomatic hand with little skill, the Dutch had provoked a war which was for them an unmixed disaster.[20]

The news of the Dutch War reached Rodney in the Leeward Islands in February 1781, soon after he had been reinforced by a new second-in-command, Rear-Admiral Sir Samuel Hood. With the news came orders to seize the Dutch island of St Eustatius, centre of a flourishing entrepôt trade between Europe, the islands and the American colonies. Proclaiming righteous indignation against treasonable dealings by British subjects with enemies and rebels – some of which was undoubtedly going on – Rodney looted everything he could find in the crowded warehouses of the island. Public and private

property, enemy, neutral or friend, were all indiscriminately pillaged, and Jewish merchants (many of them American loyalists) were especially badly treated. Some of his loot Rodney sold to the enemy himself, some he tried to order the Navy Board's local representative Commissioner Laforey to buy on public account, but most he loaded on to a convoy which he sent home. In May these ships were captured in the Western Approaches by Rear-Admiral the comte de La Motte-Picquet with a squadron from Brest; the prizes were valued at 4,717,195 *livres* 19s 7d, or about £215,000. Having no possible legal defence for much of what he had done, Rodney was in due course sued and condemned to heavy damages, which he could not pay.[21] The end result was to ruin the admiral; the immediate consequence was to transfer the trade to Danish islands, and divide Rodney's forces at a critical moment, allowing a major French fleet to reach Martinique unscathed in April – indeed, offering Vice-Admiral the comte de Grasse an opportunity to fight Hood at considerable advantage, though he preferred a distant skirmish. In June Grasse was able to capture Tobago. Rodney encountered him by night, but avoided the opportunity of another moonlight battle. This failure to neutralize the major French fleet in the Western Hemisphere was to have unfortunate consequences.[22]

Elsewhere in the world the Navy had mixed fortunes that summer. An expedition originally intended against Spanish South America, and diverted on the outbreak of the Dutch War against the Cape of Good Hope, sailed in March 1781 under the command of Commodore George Johnstone. Not far behind him was a French squadron sailing for the East Indies under Captain the bailli de Suffren. On 16 April Suffren attacked Johnstone's ships in the roadstead of Porto Praya in the Cape Verde Islands. Neither officer showed to great advantage: each had warning of the other's presence but neglected to inform his captains, so that both attack and defence were muddled. Johnstone's ships had rather the better of the action, but Suffren got first to the Cape and landed reinforcements for the garrison, which frustrated the object of the British expedition. Johnstone had the substantial consolation prize of finding six Dutch East Indiamen in Saldanha Bay near Cape Town. They were set on fire by their crews, but with great boldness and seamanship the commodore in person led the boarding parties which saved all but one.[23] In May Gálvez succeeded at the second attempt in taking Pensacola and West Florida.[24] In July another Spanish expedition captured Minorca, a place still of symbolic (if not much practical) value, and the base of a flourishing Mediterranean privateering fleet under British colours.[25] In August there was better news from the North Sea, where a squadron under Vice-Admiral Hyde

Parker escorting a convoy encountered the Dutch fleet under Rear-Admiral Johan Arnold Zoutman on a similar mission near the Dogger Bank. There were seven ships on each side, and one Dutch sixty-four-gun ship sank after the action. The battle was tactically a hard-fought draw, but strategically a British victory, since the Dutch fleet gave up attempting to cover convoys from the Baltic for the rest of the year.[26]

The siege of Gibraltar was now in its third year, the garrison once more in urgent need of supplies, so the Cabinet decided to risk sending Darby's fleet south escorting a relief convoy. The resupply of Gibraltar in April was successful, but ministers understood that it carried high risks. While Darby was away Grasse sailed for the West Indies, Suffren for the East Indies, and La Motte-Picquet sallied out to capture the St Eustatius convoy. The ministry hoped that the Spanish fleet, perhaps joined by Grasse, would fight for Gibraltar, giving Darby the chance of a decisive action, but the allies did not care to risk battle even with a substantial advantage. In August, however, another Franco-Spanish Combined Fleet approached the Channel, and Darby, outnumbered almost two to one, moored his squadron in a double line across Torbay, much as Barrington had defended the Grand Cul de Sac at St Lucia in 1778. By this time the whole squadron was coppered, and the Cabinet was sufficiently confident that Darby could avoid being forced to fight when he did not choose, to order him to sea to find and shadow the enemy. In the event they returned to port and he never found them.[27]

The unprecedented opportunities of a coppered fleet encouraged some officers to radical thoughts. Rear-Admiral Richard Kempenfelt, who had been Captain of the Fleet to Hardy and Geary and was now one of Darby's divisional commanders, suggested that only a 'flying squadron' of twenty or so coppered ships now needed to be kept permanently at home. The bulk of the fleet, unhindered by the need to dock and refit, could go out to the Caribbean for the winter and return to European waters in the spring.[28] Kempenfelt was a clever officer of wide reading and intellectual tastes; if even he had failed altogether to grasp the strategic lesson of the previous two wars, it should warn us not to assume that it ought to have been obvious to the Cabinet. At the tactical level, however, he was quite right about the opportunities open to coppered ships, and he showed he could translate theory into practice when he was sent out in December with twelve ships of the line to intercept a French convoy bound for the Caribbean. When he made contact on the 12th he found that Guichen had twenty-one sail of the line, but had carelessly allowed the escort to fall to leeward of the convoy. Before he could cover it Kempenfelt's ships had broken up the convoy and taken twenty prizes.[29]

There were few in London prepared to take much comfort from Kempenfelt's success, for very bad news had arrived three weeks before from a part of the world where nothing important was supposed to be happening: North America. The capture of Charleston, originally intended solely as a naval base, had opened to Germain the attractive prospect of subduing the southern provinces, which were believed to be strongly loyalist in sentiment. This proved to be an illusory hope. British troops could campaign, generally with success, but the re-establishment of royal authority remained remote, and there were now significant British forces operating in the interior, far from the coast, for the first time since Burgoyne's army in 1777. Moreover, just as in 1777, Germain had failed to establish whether Clinton in New York was the overall commander-in-chief, or merely the senior general in America. Early in 1781 Brigadier Benedict Arnold led an amphibious expedition from New York into Chesapeake Bay. Having destroyed the town of Richmond, he fortified the small port of Portsmouth, where he was presently threatened by the movement of part of the rebel army. The only French warships in North America remained the squadron at Rhode Island, temporarily commanded by Captain the chevalier Destouches after Ternay's death in December 1780, and still blockaded by Arbuthnot. In March Destouches escaped and headed south. Arnold was evidently at risk, and Arbuthnot pursued with an energy which belied his age. Each squadron had seven ships of the line. On the 16th, off Cape Henry, Arbuthnot caught up with the French and fought a confused and tactically unsatisfactory action, which achieved its purpose. Destouches returned to Rhode Island, and Arnold's troops were saved.[30]

Like the Spanish siege of Pensacola, which was going on at the same time, this little campaign might have served as a warning to the British of the consequences of losing command of the sea even for a short while, but it seems only to have reinforced a conviction among the generals (and Germain) that the Navy would always rescue them if they got into difficulties. Meanwhile the British army in the southern colonies under General Earl Cornwallis was marching into Virginia, and in the Caribbean, as the hurricane season approached that summer, the main fleets began to leave. Rodney sent Hood with ten ships of the line to reinforce North America, expecting that Grasse would do the like, but he himself went home for the winter, to recover his health, and no doubt to defend himself over the St Eustatius affair. Hood arrived at New York on 28 August to confront an unexpected crisis. Arbuthnot having gone home, the North American squadron was temporarily commanded by his second Rear-Admiral Thomas Graves, who was senior to Hood. In the Chesapeake Cornwallis, like Arnold before him, had fortified himself in a suitable seaport (Yorktown), and was complacently waiting for the Navy to collect him. It was beginning to become clear that this might not be as easy as he thought. Both General George Washington's American 'Continental Army' before New York, and the French troops which Ternay had brought to Rhode Island, were on the move, possibly towards Virginia. Hood feared that part of Grasse's fleet would join with the Rhode Island squadron (now commanded by Rear-Admiral comte Barras de St Laurent) to cut off Cornwallis by sea. On 31 August Graves and Hood sailed with their combined force of nineteen sail of the line to stop them. The Admiralty in London, Clinton in New York and Rodney, now on his way home across the Atlantic, each possessed critical pieces of intelligence which they had not passed on. Put together, they might have told Graves that the French threat was more serious than he realized. Grasse had come north with his entire fleet of twenty-six ships of the line, which anchored at the mouth of Chesapeake Bay on the 29th. On 5 September Graves and Hood appeared off the Chesapeake, and Grasse came out to fight. Graves was outnumbered and several of his ships were in a poor state; one of them had to be abandoned in a sinking condition soon afterwards. Nevertheless he had some chance of driving the French off, and he knew he had to take it. Unfortunately the situation called for initiative and tactical flexibility from Hood, commanding the rear division, and in his recent career as Commissioner of Portsmouth Dockyard and then Rodney's second, he had not had much chance to develop either. Only the British van and centre were heavily engaged, and the French were able to return to the Chesapeake while the British retired to New York to repair. Even then Graves did not know that Barras's squadron (with the French army siege train) had not yet arrived to increase the enemy numbers, that Washington's army was on the march southward, that Clinton was not going to do anything to intercept it, and that Cornwallis was not going to do anything to escape. A second relief expedition sailed from New York on 19 October, twenty-five ships of the line against thirty-six, but it was too late. Cornwallis had surrendered the previous day.[31]

All concerned reacted in character to the news of this disaster. Hood wrote to his influential friends blaming Graves's signals for his own failure to come into close action. Graves avoided recrimination and accepted responsibility. Rodney falsified his correspondence to prove that he had foreseen everything and forewarned everyone. Lord North exclaimed, 'Oh God! It is all over.' Militarily it was not, for the loss even of 6,000 troops, in a subsidiary theatre of a war which was to be decided at sea, was not an irretrievable catastrophe. Politically, however, North was right: Parliamentary confidence in the ministry, and his own confidence in himself, were fatally wounded, though the government did not actually collapse until March 1782.[32]

Meanwhile the naval war in the Americas went on. Grasse, Barras, Graves and Hood all returned to the West Indies in November. In January Grasse's fleet covered a French landing on the island of St Kitts. A fortnight later, on the 25th, Hood came to the island's rescue. With great tactical skill he lured Grasse out of his anchorage in Basseterre Roads and slipped in himself, anchoring under fire in a position from which his inferior force (twenty-two ships of the line against thirty) could not easily be dislodged. Two French attacks the following day were repulsed. Unfortunately Hood had only a few troops, and ashore the French siege of the British garrison on Brimstone Hill proceeded unhindered. On 13 February it surrendered, putting Hood in great danger of being trapped between enemy shore batteries and the enemy fleet. Next day officers from each ship were summoned to Hood's flagship to rate their watches by the admiral's chronometer, and at eleven at night, without noise or signal, each ship cut her cable and made sail. The French observed nothing, and at dawn the anchorage was empty.[33]

Less than six months after his equivocal performance at the battle of the Chesapeake, Hood had made his reputation as a brilliant tactician, but he could not save the island, and he did no more than slightly delay the enemy plan to mount a massive Franco-Spanish invasion of Jamaica. Rodney returned from England in February, and took up the watch of the French fleet from St Lucia. On 8 April Grasse sailed from Martinique, thirty-six ships of the line accompanied by a large troop convoy, heading for Cap François and his rendezvous with the Spaniards. Rodney, with thirty-seven ships, followed at once, and there ensued four days of manoeuvring with little wind, Grasse embarrassed by a series of collisions in his fleet which cost him time and ships. The last straw was the dismasting of the *Zélé* (Captain Gras-Préville's third collision in three days and his fourteenth in just over a year), which brought on a battle on the 12th. The two fleets passed on opposite tacks in light airs under the lee of Dominica, and at the height of the battle, in thick smoke, a shift in the wind threw both lines into confusion, taking the British aback so that some ships paid off on to the other tack and led through the French line in three places. This 'breaking the line', subsequently much argued over by tactical theorists, was unintended and unfortunate. It led to the ships around Grasse's flagship being cut off and surrounded, but it allowed the bulk of the French fleet, hitherto trapped between the British and the land, to escape to leeward. At the end of the day the British had taken five French ships, including Grasse and his three-decker flagship the *Ville de Paris*, but to Hood's fury the exhausted Rodney countermanded the pursuit of the remainder. Still, Hood took two of the escapees later, and the Jamaica expedition was abandoned.[34]

Materially, the battle of the Saintes was a clear but by no means overwhelming British victory. Psychologically, it had a disproportionate effect on both sides of the Channel, where it was seen to mark the moment at which the British recovered their old superiority at sea. In Britain it was greeted with extraordinary national rejoicing, while the French navy was torn apart by mutual recriminations and a series of courts martial reminiscent of the Keppel–Palliser affair.[35] A fortnight before the battle a new government headed by Rockingham had taken power in Britain. Keppel was the First Lord, and one his first decisions was to dismiss Rodney. Then the news of the Saintes arrived. At first the new ministers were unmoved, but when the scale of the public reaction became clear, they panicked and tried too late to recall the order, finishing up offering palpably insincere congratulations through gritted teeth. Rodney was rewarded for two great victories with a barony; the contrast with Keppel's new viscountcy was rather glaring. To replace him Keppel chose Admiral Hugh Pigot, one of his political friends who had refused to serve throughout the war; apart from a brief commission during the Falkland Islands mobilization of 1770 he had not been at sea for nineteen years. Scurrilous but not implausible rumours suggested that his real qualification for the job was that the new Foreign Secretary Charles James Fox owed him £17,000 in gambling debts which he could not otherwise repay.[36] As commander-in-chief in the Leeward Islands Pigot proved to be amiable, idle and corrupt. Discipline grew slack, and opportunities to defeat both French and Spanish fleets were thrown away. The new government was committed to peace with the American rebels, but victory over the French and Spaniards, and they in turn were still planning a dangerous expedition against Jamaica. Unfortunately neither the ministry, nor Keppel, nor Pigot was equal to the challenge. Middleton the Controller read in the newspapers about their plans to ship troops from America to the West Indies, and had to explain to the new Admiralty Board that such a move required some time to assemble a transport force.[37]

Pigot's appointment was only the first of many embarrassments which Keppel brought on a weak ministry. Sandwich had made himself unpopular by the rigorous political and professional impartiality with which he awarded promotions; Keppel's exclusively political and at times vindictive handling of patronage aroused disgust. He tried to eject Palliser from his retirement post as Governor of Greenwich Hospital, and tried to avoid responsibility for doing so. He dismissed George Jackson the Second Secretary of the Admiralty (who had officiated as judge-advocate at his court martial in 1779), the first political removal of an Admiralty official since 1690. Unlike every previous First Lord, he made the closing months of the war, when the Navy already had too many officers, the occasion for a promotion boom, concluding with eighteen captains on the day he resigned in January 1783.[38]

Rockingham was a feeble leader, and left a ministry in disarray on his death on 1 July 1782. His successor, the Earl of Shelburne, was possibly the cleverest man in public life, and certainly the most distrusted. His isolation was completed by the resignation of Fox, the ministry's best speaker in the Commons. Shelburne soon learned to manage the Navy by dealing directly with Middleton and leaving Keppel on the sidelines, but his government was visibly disintegrating by the end of the year.[39]

In home waters the war continued throughout 1782. The Rockingham ministry secured Howe's services to command the Channel Fleet by paying his price: promotion to full admiral and an English viscountcy for himself, and his brother made Lieutenant-General of the Ordnance.[40] Barrington became his second, and in April took his division to sea to intercept a French convoy sailing for the East Indies. So large a proportion of the active fleet was in the West Indies that the Channel Fleet had to serve both for a Western Squadron and in the North Sea, which Howe visited in May on rumours of activity from the Dutch. Next month he was back to the westward to face another Combined (but in fact mainly Spanish) fleet of over forty ships of the line under Córdoba, which had already intercepted a British convoy on its way north. Early in July Howe with twenty-five sail of the line was off the Scillies, with the enemy fleet to windward, between him and an incoming British Jamaica convoy. With considerable daring he took his fleet through the dangerous channel between the Scillies and Land's End to gain the weather gage and go in search of the convoy, though in the event he encountered neither it nor the enemy. The Combined Fleet's third approach to the Channel frightened Keppel considerably and embarrassed the new ministry, but achieved nothing beyond a temporary British retreat from the North Sea and the stopping of all Baltic convoys for six weeks.[41]

Meanwhile the great siege of Gibraltar was approaching its climax. On 13 September an assault supported by a flotilla of floating batteries of a novel design was a complete failure, but still the garrison's supplies were low and once more the British government resolved to risk sending the Channel Fleet south. Howe sailed on 11 September with thirty-five ships of the line, expecting to meet the Combined Fleet of about fifty in Gibraltar Bay. In fact he had already seen his storeships into Gibraltar and was returning when he met the allies off Cape Spartel on 20 October. Córdoba had forty-six ships and the weather gage, but his attack was not pushed to close range, and there was no decisive battle. Howe's reputation as a tactician was heightened by his skill in passing a convoy into Gibraltar in the face of a superior enemy. The allies lost their last and closest chance of naval victory, and the war in home waters was virtually over, though hostilities did not cease until February 1783.[42]

Only in the East Indies was the war at sea still in progress, and to explain this remote campaign it is necessary to go back to 1780, when a small British squadron under Vice-Admiral Sir Edward Hughes was supporting the East India Company's army in its war against Hyder Ali, Nabob of Mysore, a powerful French ally. The capture of the Dutch port of Negapatam in November after a dangerous amphibious operation, and the destruction of Hyder Ali's fleet off Mangalore on 8 December by the combined forces of Hughes's squadron and the Bombay Marine, effectively eliminated Mysore sea power. During 1780 and 1781 Hyder Ali received hardly any assistance from the French squadron commanded by Rear-Admiral Thomas d'Orves.[43] Reinforced by Suffren's squadron, the French finally sailed from Mauritius in December 1781. In February 1782 d'Orves died, and Suffren (now Rear-Admiral) succeeded to the command. He was a very different character from his predecessor, and indeed all French admirals of the day. A Provençal who never learned to speak proper French, slovenly and foul-mouthed, trained as a corsair in the navy of the Knights of Malta, Suffren was a bold and aggressive fighter but scarcely a team player. Always popular on the lower-deck (at least of Toulon-manned ships), he was hated by many of his captains, whom he humiliated with his violent and sarcastic temper, telling them nothing before action and blaming them for everything afterwards. Hughes his opponent was a complete contrast. An orthodox tactician, a safe pair of hands whose sound judgement and long experience on the station had earned the trust of the Admiralty and the East India Company, he lacked Suffren's meteoric brilliance, but he was a leader, not a bully. He knew how to make himself respected and obeyed.[44]

Suffren arrived on the Coromandel Coast in February 1782, soon after Hughes had captured the Dutch port of Trincomalee on the east coast of Ceylon, the finest harbour in the Bay of Bengal. Suffren knew that everything depended on his gaining command of the sea at once, and with eleven ships of the line against Hughes's nine, he attacked off Madras on 17 February. At first the attack went well, but half the French ships failed to come into close action, and Hughes was able to retrieve the situation. Something similar happened with a second action on 12 April off Provedien on the coast of Ceylon. Refitted with stores sent by the Dutch from Batavia and the Danes from Tranquebar, Suffren again fought Hughes off Negapatam on 6 July, and again both squadrons were considerably damaged without decisive result. Then Suffren achieved a real victory in capturing Trincomalee on 25 August. Hughes arrived too late to save it, but the two squadrons fought again off the bay on 3 September. As usual the better order and discipline of Hughes's squadron made up for his inferior numbers (twelve against fourteen ships of the line), and the result was indecisive. Hughes retreated to his remote but well-equipped base of Bombay, while Suffren refitted in the port of Atjeh on the northern tip of Sumatra with materials supplied by the Dutch. In March 1783 Suffren was back at Trincomalee to receive reinforcements from France. On 20 June 1783, off Cuddalore, the two squadrons (now eighteen British, all coppered, against fifteen French) fought for the last time, again with no decisive result. Soon afterwards the news of peace arrived to put an end to this campaign, unique in naval history for the intensity and balance of the fighting. After the war the French, anxious to forget their other admirals, built up Suffren into an heroic legend which still finds echoes, but it was Hughes's solid defensive campaign which thwarted him and saved the British positions in India.[45]

The unwisdom of North's government in failing to mobilize against the French threat until much too late, failing to adopt the strategy of concentration at the essential point which had served so well in two previous wars, and repeatedly dispersing their strength in remote parts of the world, might have led to much worse disasters than it did. Eighteenth-century communications did not allow fleets on the other side of the Atlantic to be controlled in any effective manner, either locally or from home, and the result was a series of undirected random cruises in which British and French squadrons blundered aimlessly around the New World, occasionally encountering one another in strength and circumstances which were completely unpredictable. As the war developed and Britain's peril from French and Spanish invasion fleets in the Channel grew greater, ministers took more and more of their ships and scattered them further and further away from the only waters where their presence might have have won the war, and their absence nearly lost it. In the circumstances the Navy did well to save Britain from invasion, and to save thirteen of the twenty-six British American colonies, together with Gibraltar and India.

TWENTY-THREE

The British Lion Has Claws

Operations 1784–1792

At home and abroad, the independence of the thirteen North American colonies in 1783 was taken to mark the end of Britain's brief and precarious period as a major power. The loss of the colonies would inevitably mean the loss of the transatlantic trade, and hence of the financial resources, seamen and sea power which they had sustained. The Archduke Leopold told his brother Joseph II of Austria that Britain now ranked no higher than Denmark or Sweden in the European scale, and it was widely assumed that this was only the beginning of a process of disintegration which would gather pace as more colonies escaped, and the notorious instability of British domestic politics reasserted itself.[1] To prove the point, the Shelburne ministry spent the whole of its short life tearing itself apart, and finally fell to pieces in April 1783. It was succeeded by an improbable combination of Lord North and his followers with Fox and the Rockingham Whigs, nominally headed by the Duke of Portland. Keppel returned to the Admiralty, where Howe had been First Lord for three months. The king loathed Fox, a notorious libertine whose support of the American cause had earned him the reputation of a closet Republican, and made no secret of his dislike of the ministry which had been forced upon him. This alone would have seriously weakened it in Parliament, and in December it fell over a bill promoted by Fox to reform the East India Company in a manner calculated, it seemed, to put the Company's wealth and political influence in his own hands. George III worked actively to overthrow his own ministers, a clear breach of the constitution and another sign of a system in collapse. Their replacement was a minority 'mince-pie administration', as the wits called it, seemingly unlikely to last beyond the twelve days of Christmas. It contained few politicians of weight and experience, and was headed by the twenty-four-year-old William Pitt, who brought very little but his father's name and a growing reputation as an orator. With the king against the politicians, and the public talking of civil war, the general election of April–May 1784 was seen to mark a 'crisis of the constitution'. The result was unequivocal. The political nation, always disposed to put king before faction, disliked Fox and his friends as much as George III did, and voted overwhelmingly for the new government. When the new Parliament assembled in May, young Pitt was secured in power, and Fox was back in the political wilderness.[2]

The American War was unlike its predecessors in that all the belligerents except the Dutch were able to maintain their foreign trades. The British convoy system survived the strain of a war in which there was no overall command of the sea surprisingly well. Convoy organization was tightened. As we have seen, there were several disasters when convoys were intercepted by enemy squadrons sufficiently strong to overwhelm the escorts, particularly when the main fleet was absent relieving Gibraltar, but the great majority of convoys were successfully protected. Sea officers did not enjoy convoy duty ('How can I pretend to answer for the safety of ships commanded by such a set of mules?', complained Captain Thomas Pasley. 'Thus is a captain of a man-of-war's character sported away, who happens to have the misfortune to command a convoy'),[3] but they knew they had to do it. The Channel Fleet was forced to devote much of its efforts to covering convoys outward or homeward, and the necessity of cruising in the autumn, the season of the equinoctial gales, to cover convoys returning from the East and West Indies, had a significant effect on the fleet's capacity. In particular it made it very difficult for expeditions to the West Indies to sail early enough to catch the campaigning season. The sugar islands themselves suffered severely from shortage of food which normally came from North America. Nevertheless the essential trade was kept up, and with its aid the resourceful North was able to finance the war.[4]

It helped that French privateering, at least from French Atlantic ports, was at a low level, mainly because French shipowners had no incentive to find other uses for their ships, since the British failure to gain command of the sea in European waters allowed French convoys too to run with limited interference. Most of the French privateering effort in this war was with small vessels against local trade, either from the West India islands (where it had much to do with acquiring food imports and covering illegal trade), or from Dunkirk, which was effectively a specialized fishing and privateering port with limited deep-sea trade. At the end of the war French transatlantic trade, above all with Saint Domingue, resumed its rapid rise.[5]

American independence presented Britain with an acute dilemma of trade policy. Splitting British America divided an economic unit; it cut off the West

India islands from their source of food and timber. If the government allowed the barriers of the Navigation Acts to stand, excluding shipping from the United States, the sugar islands would starve. If it opened the trade to American ships, there would be no hope of regenerating the seaman so essential to British sea power, and a real risk of losing the islands to the United States with which they were politically as well as economically linked.[6] The abolition of the Board of Trade and the Colonial Secretary of State by the Whigs in 1782, in the name of reducing the power of the crown, weakened the government's capacity to make informed decisions on such matters, and throughout 1783 and 1784 ministers' attention was elsewhere. While government hesitated, admirals and governors in the West Indies turned a blind eye to American ships rather than ruin the colonies they were supposed to protect. Into this delicate situation sailed three young frigate captains – the brothers Wilfrid and Cuthbert Collingwood and their friend Horatio Nelson – determined to enforce the law and incidentally hoping (vainly, in the event) to make a lot of money from seizures half the value of which came to them. They managed to do a considerable amount of damage to the economy of the islands before they were stopped, but the row drew Pitt's government's attention to the issue, and forced it to a decision.[7] The Board of Trade was revived in 1786, and a new Navigation Act, 'a Bill for the increase of Naval Power', definitively shut out American ships from the West Indies and forced British planters to import from Ireland or Canada. They faced at least a tripling of their costs to support British sea power.[8] As a small compensation, the Admiralty despatched an expedition to the Pacific to bring back specimens of a new food plant, the breadfruit tree, which it was hoped would provide the West Indian slaves with a nutritious and almost labour-free addition to their diet. Unfortunately Lieutenant Bligh and the *Bounty* came to grief, and though his second voyage succeeded, it turned out that the slaves would not eat the breadfruit.[9] Government was forced to modify its position, and in 1787, 1792 and 1794 concessions were made to American imports in American ships. Nevertheless the West India planters' political interest was in decline. Now opposed to British shipping and sea power with which they had hitherto been identified, their capacity to defend the threatened institution of slavery itself was weakening.[10]

In spite of the destructive divisions opened by the Keppel–Palliser affair, the Royal Navy emerged from the American War in surprisingly good condition. The large-scale amphibious operations mounted during the war, notably at New York in 1776 and Charleston in 1780, showed that it had not forgotten the skills learned during previous wars, and new ones were developing. In the Channel Fleet in particular, new ideas of tactics and signalling were under development, which were to bear fruit in the 1790s. Signals which could be hoisted in any position from any available mast were easier to read, and the number of available signals was increased. Kempenfelt and Howe were leaders of this movement, but unfortunately Kempenfelt was drowned when the *Royal George* foundered in 1782, and Howe used it to impose a highly centralized system of command which limited captains' initiative in action. Still more unfortunately, he himself redrafted and combined the signal book and Fighting Instructions, enveloping the whole in his own impenetrably obscure prose. As a result the potential for more flexible and articulated tactics was still to be realized when war broke out again in 1793.[11]

The French navy emerged from the American War with its prestige and self-esteem restored, but informed observers inside and outside the service still had many reasons for disquiet. The regular officers violently resented the outsiders from the army (d'Estaing was a general turned admiral), the *Compagnie des Indes* and elsewhere who had been forced into the navy after the Seven Years' War to teach them their business. Discipline was poor, and standards of seamanship and navigation left much to be desired; army officers taking passage on board warships during the war had tended to be very unimpressed by what they had seen. Two reforming ministers, Gabriel de Sartine (1774–80) and the marquis de Castries (1780–86) attempted to improve the education and training of the officers, to address standards of cleanliness and health, and to rejuvenate the manning system which had only with acute difficulty supported the fleets.[12] Spanish ministers, who had some reason to feel that their navy had performed better than the French, were engaged in similar efforts.[13]

At the same time both countries participated in the remarkable naval arms race which marked the 1780s. In tonnage terms, the French and Spanish navies together were about 17 per cent superior in ships of the line to the British in 1785, and in five years that superiority doubled, to 34 per cent. In terms of numbers, the figures in 1785 were sixty-two French and sixty-one Spanish ships of the line against 137 British; in 1790, seventy-three French and seventy-two Spanish against 145 British. In five years of heavy peacetime expenditure, the Bourbon powers had achieved a battlefleet equal in numbers, and composed of larger ships, in spite of the fact that the British themselves were also expanding. This naval arms race extended even to quite minor powers. Dutch battleship strength almost doubled between 1780 and 1785. The Two Sicilies built up a powerful little fleet centred on a squadron of six new ships of the line.[14]

Pitt's triumph of 1784 transformed British politics. Very unlike his father in everything except his powers of oratory, the younger Pitt proved to be a great prime minister as the eighteenth century defined the job: someone who could manage the Commons, manage the money and manage the king. So long as his main opponent was Fox, whom the public distrusted and the king loathed, his hold on power was secure. Only in the new century, towards the end of his short life and long career, did the political situation shift against him. For the ten years between the end of the American War and the outbreak of the French Revolutionary War, Pitt was free to devote his talents to restoring financial stability. In 1784 there was £14 million outstanding in Navy and Ordnance Bills, all of which had been converted into government stock by the following year. This re-established the Navy's short-term credit. Pitt's new Sinking Fund, which promised in time to pay off the whole national debt, and his 1785 Commission on Fees in Public Offices, which promised to save money by administrative reform, secured public confidence in government and government credit. Though the crown was running a surplus to invest in the Sinking Fund, the Navy Estimates were not reduced, nor did members of Parliament demand that they should be after the alarms of the American War. The peacetime establishment of manpower rose to 18,000 in 1784 (which translated into Navy Estimates of roughly £2,250,000), and 20,000 in 1788. Also in 1784 Pitt secured an extraordinary vote of £2,400,000 for shipbuilding. In 1786 Howe was able to report that the Navy had twenty guard ships in commission and sixty ships of the line ready for immediate mobilization. By 1790 he expected to have twenty more, and Middleton later claimed that in that year 'there were upwards of 90 sail of the line in good condition with every article of their stores provided'.[15]

The situation was very different in France. Such figures as French ministers could extract from the morass of government accounts gave them the impression that France's financial position was secure, and that Britain was about to collapse under the burden of public debt. They were right that Britain had paid more to fight the American War, and had higher overall debts – but paying only half the real interest rate of France, it could support the debt on a smaller proportion of national income. Pitt's government was running a surplus, and its credit was solid. Post-war French governments were running a large deficit, much of it to finance naval expansion. Insoluble financial problems led to the call of the Estates-General in 1789, which unleashed the French Revolution. It used to be argued that the cost of the American War, or even the Seven Years' War, had been responsible, but it now appears that it was these post-war debts which finally sank the French monarchy.[16] Spain too floated her naval expansion in the 1780s on unsustainable borrowing, though Spain's capacity for internal reform was greater, and in 1798 the Ministry of Finance finally managed to gain effective control over the naval budget. The result was an abrupt halt to Spain's remarkable rise to naval greatness. The naval share of national expenditure fell from 23 per cent in 1796 to 10 per cent in 1800: no ship of the line was launched between 1798 and 1820.[17]

Pitt's care in looking after the Navy was the more remarkable in that Lord Howe remained as First Lord of the Admiralty for his first five years in office. Devoid as ever of political gifts, 'austere, morose and inaccessible',[18] Howe made himself equally disliked by the Navy and his political colleagues. Pitt managed the Navy by his close connections with Middleton at the Navy Board, which he often visited. Howe disliked Middleton and maintained only distant official relations with him, so that the Admiralty's contribution to the naval reforms which Middleton and Pitt were pushing forward was to block them when it could. So isolated was it from the rest of the government that in 1786 Howe actually led his colleagues in voting against a government bill. Two years later he caused the ministry further damage by his handling of promotions, putting various senior captains (Middleton among them) on the list of 'yellow admirals', in spite of good services in the American War, and good friends in the Commons. Possibly justifiable in itself, certainly defensible by a more popular or politically adroit minister, Howe's decision was the last straw for his colleagues, who were happy to force him out of office.[19] 'Lord Howe richly deserves what he has got, and if the effects were solely to be centred in his Lordship, I should feel glad that his shameful list had been exposed and censured,' commented Pitt's cousin the Duke of Buckingham.[20]

Pitt needed a First Lord whom he could trust, and who would add strength, in the words of his cousin William Wyndham Grenville, 'by connecting the department of the Admiralty with the rest of the administration, which has never yet been the case under Pitt's government, even in the smallest degree'.[21] He chose his elder brother Lord Chatham, who certainly united the ministry, and was intelligent, but 'almost proverbial for enervation and indolence'.[22] Chatham crippled the work of the Admiralty by taking important correspondence home and forgetting it. When he left office, the incoming Secretary of the Admiralty recorded, 'many hundred packets, carried into the house of the First Lord, were found there unopened'.[23] The reforms which Howe had resisted, Chatham neglected.[24]

Soon after Chatham took office in July 1788, the government was shaken by the Regency crisis, when the first of George III's periods of serious illness (madness, as it was then thought) seemed about to make the Prince of Wales effectively king, and his friend Fox prime minister. The king's recovery in January 1789 spoiled their hopes, but the episode had some effect in reviving political divisions in the Navy, since several of Fox's friends and the Prince's courtiers were naval politicians in the style of Keppel, who alleged that they had been denied promotion on political grounds.[25] When the fleet mobilized in 1790 with the detested Howe as commander-in-chief, Captain the Duke of Clarence reported to his brother the Prince of Wales that

> Party runs very high, and they are sadly disunited; the arrival of Lord Howe is looked for hourly, and does not serve to increase the good humour ... Sir John Jervis ... has highly disobliged all the admirals and particularly in the most pointed manner, and, without the least provocation, Sir Alexander Hood ... Jervis is determined to oppose Lord Howe in everything.[26]

Pitt was quite prepared to use the Navy on which he lavished so much attention, and it was mobilized for diplomatic purposes three times in four years. In 1787 there was a crisis in Dutch politics when the anti-Orangist 'Patriots' seized power, and appealed to France to support them. They also manhandled the Princess of Orange, a Prussian princess, which aroused the Prussian army as well as the British Navy against them. War seemed likely for a time, but financial collapse forced France to abandon her friends, so the House of Orange was restored to power, and both Prussian and British prestige boosted at French expense. Behind the British interest in Dutch politics was a new concern for the strategic value of Dutch colonies. The American War had shown how the availability of Dutch ports at the Cape, Ceylon and Sumatra had transformed the operational effectiveness of the French Indian Ocean squadron. Moreover after 200 years of leaving the Dutch East Indies in the capable hands of the VOC, the Dutch navy sent its first squadron to the Indian Ocean in 1783, a force powerful enough to disquiet the British East India Company. The British were therefore anxious that the Netherlands should not again become an ally or satellite of France.[27]

Two years later another crisis broke over news that a British fur-trading post at Nootka Sound on the west coast of what is now Vancouver Island had been dismantled by the Spanish authorities, who claimed the whole known west coast of North America as part of their colony of California. At first Pitt's government knew almost nothing of what had happened, nor even where Nootka Sound was, but as a precaution it began mobilizing the Navy that autumn, and by the height of the crisis in the spring of 1790 a formidable fleet was already assembled. At the same time public excitement was aroused, the old myths of popular anti-Spanish and anti-Catholic sentiment were once again displayed, and Pitt was driven to appease public opinion, and outflank Fox, by claiming a general right to trade in any Spanish territory it pleased, regardless of Spanish law. This claim he knew to be indefensible, and expected would lead to war, but the weakness of France, now in political turmoil, left Spain unsupported. By July, when Howe's fleet at Spithead numbered forty-three sail of the line, Spain was forced to give ground, and in October she conceded most of Britain's claims. 'English diplomacy [is] at a height even greater than that of 1787,' commented the Under-Secretary J. B. Burges. 'In one word, we are vastly pleased, and hope that Europe in general will profit by the hint now given that the British lion has claws and teeth, and can shake his mane to a good purpose.'[28] This stinging humiliation of the Bourbon powers, so soon after the American War, was a further boost to Pitt.[29]

Perhaps it made him over-confident, for in 1791 he tried naval deterrence in less favourable circumstances, mobilizing to force Russia to retreat from the fortress of Ochakov on the Black Sea, acquired from Turkey in 1788. Behind this sudden interest in a place which Pitt could not find on the map was the memory of the Armed Neutrality of 1780, and the desire to escape what Daniel Hailes, British minister in Warsaw, called 'a very embarrassing dependence on a very imperious and capricious woman'.[30] But Catherine the Great was not vulnerable to British sea power, Parliament was unenthusiastic about an issue remote from British interests, and Pitt was obliged to retreat.[31]

Europe was not the limit of British naval interests in the years after the American War. The British were cured of their obsession with colonies as such, but their interest in trade was redoubled by the need to replace the transatlantic trade which had been, or was bound to be, lost with American independence. There were four strands to this new interest in remote parts of the world, above all the Pacific, which were not yet occupied by European powers and might be exploited to Britain's benefit. The first was the defence of Britain's remaining trade, especially the East India Company's trade. The second was the possibility of discovering peoples or regions offering materials of value. The third was the hope of establishing bases useful in wartime, particularly those from which expeditions could be despatched to open up Spanish South America, whose unproductive wealth and neglected commercial opportunities were an article of faith among British policy-makers. In pursuit of one or more of these ideas, surveys of the Indian Ocean were set in motion which identified harbours of potential importance in Diego Garcia in the Chagos Archipelago (midway between Mauritius and India), the

Andaman Islands and Nancowry Island in the Nicobars (both on the windward side of the Bay of Bengal in winter-time). The East India Company founded a new establishment at Penang at the entrance to the Malacca Straits. An expedition under Captain George Vancouver was sent to survey the north-east corner of the Pacific, where the hunt for sea-otter pelts had provoked the Nootka Sound crisis. Government encouraged the whale fishery in the southern oceans, which employed fifty British whalers by 1790. The botanist Sir Joseph Banks, President of the Royal Society and a sort of unofficial minister of science, encouraged the search for economically valuable plants like breadfruit and improved strains of cotton.[32]

The fourth strand of imperial policy derived from an aspect of the British judicial system, which had a large number of capital crimes, and sentenced many criminals to death, but executed only a small minority of them. Most death sentences were commuted to transportation to a remote and unpleasant part of the world, namely Virginia.[33] When that ceased to be available in 1775, the convicts were temporarily accommodated in hulks moored in the Thames and elsewhere. Ten years later the supply of hulks was exhausted and the convict situation urgently called for a solution. Having canvassed and abandoned various less distant possibilities, the government decided to establish a penal settlement in New South Wales, which Cook had reported to be fertile and largely uninhabited. In May 1787 Captain Arthur Phillip sailed in command of the 'first fleet' to establish the new colony. It is a matter of controversy among Australian historians whether the government's motives were primarily penal or strategic.[34] By abolishing the Colonial Secretary of State in 1782 and rearranging the other Secretaries' responsibilities into Home and Foreign departments, the Rockinghams had reduced colonial and military business to a minor sideline of the Home Office, and Pitt's Home Secretary Lord Sydney did not have many talents to spare for them, so decisions tended to be guided by expediency rather than grand design. It is certain that the new colony was expensive, and the administration was interested in anything which might offset, or at least justify, its cost. There were hopes of the Norfolk Island pine, 'truly stately, and in appearance awfully magnificent', as a source of masts; but unfortunately it turned out to 'snap like a carrot'.[35] The New Zealand flax plant proved equally disappointing as a source of sailcloth. What was left was the superb natural harbour on the shores of which the new colony's capital of Sydney was founded. This was potentially of great strategic value, and was later considered in connection with expeditions to South America, but in the colony's early days, when it depended on Britain for everything including food, there was no question of basing any squadron there.[36]

In the aftermath of the Seven Years' War, fumbling British governments had rapidly dissipated what seemed an unassailable position of power and prestige. After the unparalleled disaster of the American War, Pitt's administration achieved the opposite. By the early 1790s there was no more talk of Britain's decay and collapse. The Dutch, Spanish and even Russian 'armaments' had shown British sea power to be revived and rejuvenated. It was clear by then that the economic consequences of American independence had been minimal (except to the West India planters). Trade continued to flow, and grow, in its old channels without the Navigation Acts. In 1700 10 per cent of British exports went to the Americas; by 1798 the figure was 57 per cent. British merchants still offered American consumers the goods they wanted, and American exporters the prices (and credit terms) they needed. British ships and British seamen in ever-growing numbers still earned their living in the transatlantic trades.[37] Above all the international strategic situation was transformed from 1789 by France's political disintegration. Radicals in Britain rejoiced at the dawn of a new era of freedom, but the dominant sentiment was astonishment and delight that the country's only serious rival had committed political suicide. As French public life slid from reform into anarchy and violence, some began to regret the collapse of civilized society, but no one seriously proposed to interfere. 'It is surely in our interest, and there can be no doubt of its being our plan to preserve a strict neutrality,' wrote Burges.

> We have felt too strongly the immense advantages to be derived by this country from such a state of anarchy and weakness as France is at present plunged in, to be so mad as to interfere in any measure, which, may, even remotely, tend to put France into the situation, where a long and sensible experience has taught us she had the power to injure us. When she had the power . . . she never wanted the will.[38]

As he approached his tenth year in power, Pitt had reason to be satisfied at the astonishing change in Britain's international standing and prospects. In February 1792, introducing another year's financial estimates to the House of Commons, and looking forward to a future of reducing debt and falling taxation, Pitt declared,

> unquestionably there never was a time in the history of this country, when, from the situation of Europe, we might more reasonably expect fifteen years of peace, than we may at the present moment.[39]

Nine weeks later the European war began.

TWENTY-FOUR

Plans of Improvement

Administration 1763–1792

There is no doubt that the Navy Estimates fell to abnormally low levels under Anson in the early 1750s, and Sandwich's schemes to improve the management of the dockyards were allowed to sleep. Mobilization in 1755–6 was relatively slow – certainly slower than in 1778–9 – and total strength was kept up by a large wartime programme of emergency building; over 100 ships of all sizes, mostly from private yards.[1] Informed contemporaries were not deceived by the triumphant results of the Seven Years' War into thinking that all was well with the infrastructure of the Navy. When Sandwich returned to the Admiralty in April 1763 he began by investigating the mobilization of 1755, and the Navy's cycle of shipbuilding and replacement. Five months later he was moved to be Secretary of State, and the Earl of Egmont continued his work. The key problem was that the Navy had grown faster than the capacity of the dockyards. From 109 seagoing ships in 1690, the fleet had increased by 1765 to 266; more than doubling the numbers and tripling the tonnage in a period in which the number of men employed in the yards at the height of each successive war had not quite doubled, from 4,300 to 8,500, and the physical equipment of the yards in docks, slips and buildings had grown much less. In fact almost all the increase, in both men and structures, had occurred at the beginning of the century with the building of Plymouth Dockyard.[2] As a result the yards had less and less capacity for shipbuilding, though it was generally believed that yard-built ships were both cheaper and more durable. The more ships were hastily, and in some cases shoddily, built by private yards, the sooner they needed to be replaced, the greater the burden of maintenance which fell on the yards during their lives, and the worse the overall problem.[3]

Egmont instituted an overall 'plan of improvements' for the dockyards, which envisaged spending £731,410 on Portsmouth and Plymouth, beginning with new storehouses constructed in brick to be as far as possible fireproof.

At the same time he led the first Admiralty visitation of the yards since 1751, paying particular attention to management and productivity. He ordered the Navy Board's standing orders to be collected and codified, and instituted a superannuation scheme to retire the oldest artificers. Having obtained votes totalling four and a half millions to pay off the Navy and Victualling Course, Egmont skilfully outflanked Grenville's attempts to impose economies by dealing directly with the king, and shutting the Treasury out. When Grenville fell, Egmont was left in place by the Rockingham administration, but found Chatham impossible to work with, and resigned in September 1766.[4]

Hawke his successor was a conscientious administrator who, in financial terms at least, was notably more successful than Anson. Before the war real naval expenditure (allowing for fluctuations in debt) had barely exceeded one million a year at best, but Hawke never had less than £1,625,470. Without Egmont's political weight and sophistication, however, and a member of a weak and almost leaderless government, Hawke was less successful in other respects. He failed to get the votes to carry on Egmont's dockyard scheme. Hawke's Admiralty made no visitations of the dockyards itself, but instructed the Navy Board to do so in 1767 and 1769, which achieved little. The Admiralty ordered the Navy Board to enforce its standing orders, but the Navy Board had neither the means nor inclination to do so, and the Admiralty was in no stronger a position to enforce its own commands. One significant innovation was introduced in 1768 when Hawke's colleague Charles Jenkinson drew up the first 'Plan of Expense', a sort of naval budget which offered the possibility of greater financial and hence management control.[5]

When Sandwich became First Lord again in January 1771 he dropped this innovation. Like Egmont, he was in the business of getting higher real expenditure for the Navy by exploiting the ignorance of Parliament and the Treasury, and 'Plans of Expense' revealed too much, in particular how much he had saved from the incomplete Falkland Islands mobilization. Sandwich's real expenditure in the early 1770s was never less than double Anson's peacetime figure. For 1772 the Admiralty obtained Estimates for 25,000 men, 9,000 more than in 1771, which it used to pay off debt and accumulate a quiet surplus. This sort of manoeuvre was a traditional consequence of the artificial form of the Estimates, but it was beginning to arouse new suspicion in Parliament. The 1770s saw the rise of the 'economical reform' movement, patronized by the opposition Whigs, which argued that much, or even most government expenditure was a corrupt attempt to subvert English liberties by buying votes, and consequently that liberty was best preserved by reducing all public expenditure indiscriminately. Though there were sinecures in the government's gift, some of them used for political purposes, the basic assumption of 'economical reform' was largely fantasy, but in British politics, conspiracy theories always found a willing audience. The Treasurer of the Navy being the only public accountant exempt from producing vouchers and outside effective Treasury control, the Navy Estimates were an obvious target for suspicious minds, and an embarrassment to the North government as it got into increasing trouble over the conduct of the American War. Estimates for repairs, which were impossible to predict accurately, were a particular bugbear. They usually cost more or less than estimated, and it was not uncommon for ships which were estimated not to be repaired at all, and ships to be repaired which had not been mentioned in the Estimates. The same was sometimes true of shipbuilding: £37,600 was voted between 1778 and 1783 to build a ship called the *Caesar* which was never begun.[6] In a 1778 debate Lord Mulgrave for the government admitted that 'the Estimate was the usual mode of raising money, but it was never meant to state the purposes the money was to be applied to,' which provoked Edmund Burke into throwing the Estimates at Lord North, 'exclaiming that it was treating the House with the utmost contempt, to present them with a fine gilt book of Estimates, calculated to a farthing, for purposes to which the money granted was never meant to be applied.'[7]

Sandwich needed to increase the Navy Estimates in the early 1770s because he faced a crisis. It was clear that a large proportion of the existing fleet was nearing the end of its life all at once. Beyond this short-term crisis loomed the long-term problem of the inability of the yards to build more than a fraction of the ships the Navy needed. Sandwich resumed Egmont's investment in the yards,

> but neither this or any thing else that can be devised, will enable us to keep up the proper number, unless it is contrived to give them a greater duration than that which we have experienced of late years, nor is it in my opinion possible for any nation to keep up a fleet so built.[8]

The only way out was to find means of building ships with longer working lives, reducing both the shipbuilding and repair burden, and to increase the productivity of the yards to deal with the work which remained. In political terms Sandwich's difficulty was that few Parliamentarians understood, or wished to understand, these technical issues, and that in order to deceive the French he was being less than candid about how many ships he had in repair anyway. Moreover it was difficult to explain the problem of block obsolescence without blaming either Anson, for hasty wartime building, or Hawke, for inadequate peacetime maintenance, and either suggestion gave much offence to the Navy. It has recently been argued that the real origin of the problem lay further back, in the 1730s, a decade of unusually mild winters in southern England. Frost is the natural enemy of dry rot, and without frosts the large fleet which Walpole was keeping in reserve seems to have been badly affected. The result was a major problem of block obsolescence in 1748–9. It was to tackle this that Sandwich fought and lost his battle for higher expenditure in 1751. Fifteen years later, at the end of the Seven Years' War, the next generation of ships became obsolete all at once; Egmont chose to repair rather than replace, thus shortening the cycle, and in the early 1770s it repeated itself again. Sandwich was determined to break out of the trap by building a fleet which would last.[9]

One part of his strategy was to build ships slowly and carefully, using seasoned timber and allowing the ships themselves to season on the stocks. This slowed the rate of building just when he needed a lot of ships, so he was obliged to order ships from private yards almost at once, but the new contracts required the private builders, too, to allow the ships time to season in frame. Given time, he intended to reach the happy state of having the whole fleet of ships of the line built in the dockyards. To make that possible, he had to solve another difficulty; a serious shortage of timber in the yards. He achieved this by increasing the Navy Board's allowance for transport costs (thus widening the 'catchment area' open to exploitation), and developing new sources abroad. This was not so much because he immediately needed alternatives to the Navy's reliable and traditional suppliers in Polish and Russian ports, but to spread his risks, and keep the timber merchants on notice that he could undermine any cartel. Sandwich's objective was to keep in the dockyards three years' consumption of timber, carefully stored so that it could season under cover, and managed so that the oldest timber was used first. This sounds simple and obvious, but it had never been systematically attempted before.[10] At Chatham in 1774, Sandwich recorded his

> very pleasing sensation to observe all the seasoning sheds filled, and the whole face of the yard covered with timber, ranged in proper order, and so disposed, that in consequence of the directions that have been given, those pieces that have been the longest in store may be always first expended.[11]

Sandwich was in Chatham on visitation, as he was every year from 1771 to 1778. He knew the dockyards much better than any First Lord before or since, and much better than the Navy Board.

> In the various offices in which I have had the honour of serving the
> Crown, I have always found that till I understood the business thoroughly
> myself, I was liable to imposition, and fearful of taking any thing upon
> myself; and therefore I have ever made it my first object to get free from
> these shackles, as fast as I could, by making myself master of what I was
> to undertake.[12]

Knowledge was power, but Sandwich had learned from experience, and did
not try to use it to confront the Navy Board. Instead he carefully involved it
as an ally in his projects, and always brought some members of it with him
on visitation. His chief asset was Captain Hugh Palliser, lately appointed
Controller when Sandwich took office, an officer of outstanding ability. In
1775 Palliser was promoted to Rear-Admiral and then moved to the Admiralty
Board, a very unusual reward for exceptional service. His replacement, Captain
Maurice Suckling, was also an able man but a less successful choice, mainly
because he was seriously ill within two years of appointment.[13]

The second part of Sandwich's long-term strategy was to improve the
productivity of the yards. He restarted Egmont's superannuation scheme,
though it was still treated as a privilege for the deserving rather than a universal
entitlement, and many elderly shipwrights remained to lower the output of
the yards. The same comment applied to apprenticeships, which should
logically have been one of the most promising means of expanding the yards'
skilled workforce, but which Sandwich did not increase until 1782, just as he
left office. Most of his energy was devoted to his bold and imaginative attempt
to introduce task work. In principle this offered the men a large increase in
wages and the Admiralty a large increase in output. In practice not everyone
stood to gain, and everything depended on the very complex details of pricing
jobs and measuring work, which were difficult to get right first time. Little
effort was expended on explaining the scheme to the men, and several of the
senior yard officers (notably Israel Pownall, Master Shipwright of Plymouth)
were hostile. Moreover one of the most attractive features of task work from
the Admiralty's point of view was that it regained official control of the work
process and put the artificers in the power of their officers. The men could
see this as well as Sandwich could. The result was that when the scheme was
implemented in the spring of 1775, the river yards adopted it, but Portsmouth
and Plymouth went on strike. Going on visitation that summer, Sandwich
found himself having to reason with angry crowds of shipwrights. As the
troubles of America grew, the Admiralty had to buy industrial peace with
concessions. Not until after the end of the war did Portsmouth and Plymouth
accept task work, and in the event Sandwich's successors found it achieved

less than he had hoped. In the context of weak authority and entrenched trade privileges, it was almost as liable as day work to be perverted to the mutual convenience of the men and their officers.[14]

Suckling died a week before the battle of Ushant in July 1778. A good Controller was badly needed, and Sandwich's choice was surprising: Captain Charles Middleton, a little-known Scotsman with a difficult character and a hitherto unremarkable career. It is possible that a shared enthusiasm for the music of Handel first drew them together. However the connection was established, Sandwich never made a better choice, for Middleton was to be one of the most influential figures in shaping British naval history for almost thirty years. He resembled Sandwich in being a first-class administrator with a voracious appetitite for paperwork, but in every other respect they were completely unlike. Sandwich was polite, urbane, detached, with the tolerance born of indifference to religion and scepticism towards all universal claims. Middleton was narrow-minded, intolerant, priggish, and devoted to the novel and alarming doctrines of the Evangelical movement. Long experience as a politician had given Sandwich a deep knowledge of men and affairs; Middleton was content to know the mind of God. Sandwich was an excellent judge of men, familiar with their weaknesses as well as his own. Middleton saw all difficulties in simple, personal terms: everybody else was the problem, and he was the solution. He had to the fullest degree the unscrupulousness of the truly high-minded. No doubtful transaction ever shook his conviction that he was right, and God was with him.[15] In his own 1782 statement of the qualities needful in a Controller we have his assessement of himself:

> As the whole conduct of the Board must naturally depend on his exertion, he in his professional line should have a comprehensive knowledge and extensive abilities; in his principles he should be conscientious and upright; in his conduct impartial, firm and decisive; in the expenditure of public money, provident and liberal; in receiving information open, and in giving a fair trial to whatever promises improvement, candid and patient. In short, as in the management of this department, the serviceable state of the whole Navy and the expenditure of public money required in it depends, his knowledge and his care must extend to everything connected with it, and therefore to his professional line he must join great application and method, and a general knowledge of business and accounts.[16]

Middleton's talents really were very great. 'The Controller is the most indefatigable and able of any in my time,' Robert Gregson, one of his clerks, wrote in 1782. 'The load of business he goes through at the Board, at the

Treasury, the Admiralty, and his own house, is astonishing, and what I am confident no other man will be able to execute.'[17] But he was not an easy man to work with. When things went wrong, it was always someone else's fault, and the fault was always cast in terms of morality. In moments of stress he addressed Sandwich in insulting language, accusing him of idleness and corruption. As Sandwich's political position weakened during the war, Middleton intrigued behind his back with Germain. His aim was invariably to gain more power for himself, and his ultimate objective was to get the Controller a seat on the Admiralty Board. With the whole machinery of naval administration under his hand, Middleton was confident of being able to dominate any civilian First Lord, if not to succeed as First Lord himself. Few politicians would have tolerated Middleton for long, and perhaps none but Sandwich could have harnessed his unequalled talents while restraining the destructive and ignoring the offensive sides of his character. Together they formed a powerful administrative team, uniting the Admiralty and the Navy Board as they had not been united since the seventeenth century, and perhaps were never to be again.[18]

Sandwich's long-term shipbuilding plan was an early victim of the American War. Once full mobilization was belatedly ordered, shipbuilding contracts had to be widely distributed, and even repairs were for the first time contracted out. For want of dockyard capacity some ships lay awaiting repair for long periods, worsening their condition and adding to the overall load. Coppering the entire fleet added another huge burden to the dockyards (eighty-two ships of the line, fourteen fifties, 115 frigates and 102 sloops or cutters had been coppered by the end of 1781), though by the end of the war it was yielding a large dividend by freeing the docks from regular cleaning and frequent refits. After the war, when Middleton had leisure to recalculate the Navy Board's timber estimates, he discovered that the three years' supply which Sandwich had laid in was in reality only two, but it was enough. At the worst crisis of the war the yards never ran short of seasoned timber – in January 1782 they were turning it away because all the stores were full – and the ships constructed during the war proved to be notably well built and durable. The same was true of naval stores. There were serious problems with the accuracy of the available figures, but once again the actual stocks proved to be ample. 'Our stores are in abundance,' one of the Lords of the Admiralty wrote in September 1781, 'and I have no fear of their failing us for these three years, such has been our diligence to purchase and complete them.'[19] The loss of masts from North America, which had supplied about one-third of the largest sizes before the war, caused temporary problems, but Russia easily made up the difference, and the yards could always manufacture 'made masts' from smaller sticks, which were as good though more expensive.[20]

One of Middleton's greatest triumphs was the coppering of the fleet, which illustrates both his administrative gifts, in a matter which lent itself to his characteristic centralizing drive, and Sandwich's readiness to undertake bold and visionary schemes. They were lucky to adopt it just as the new Parys Mountain copper mine in Anglesey glutted the British market, for a single Third Rate needed about fourteen tons of copper plate and fastenings, at a cost of around £1,500.[21] They were lucky, too, that the war ended when it did, for around 1782 it was becoming clear that there was something badly wrong with Middleton's method. After the battle of the Chesapeake, reported Captain Lord Robert Manners,

> We felt severely the danger of keeping coppered line of battle ships long out without looking at their bottoms, as the *Terrible*, one of the finest seventy-fours we had, by her exceeding bad state even before she left the West Indies, and by the firing of her own guns, and the enemy's shot in the action, was found in so desperate a state that she was ordered to be scuttled and set on fire.[22]

A number of ships sank suddenly two or three years after they had been coppered, including the famous *Royal George*, which foundered at anchor at Spithead in August 1782. But for the peace, the result might have been a catastrophe, but in the event there was time for a thorough investigation to reveal that the 'waterproof' paper seal failed as ships' hulls worked in a seaway, allowing electrolytic action to corrode the iron fastenings, hidden under the copper. Fortunately a solution was developed: bolts and fittings of hardened, annealed copper. At considerable cost the entire fleet was docked to replace iron fastenings with copper. Coppering shows the weaknesses as well as strengths of Middleton as a reformer, whose solution for all problems was to take personal control, and who did not admit the possibility of being wrong. In truth he adopted his method on the basis of hasty trials and a good deal of wishful thinking, ignoring the considerable experience of corrosion problems available in the dockyards, and he defended it obstinately long after there were obvious grounds for alarm.[23]

After the war Middleton had the time to tackle some of the major reforms which had been impossible in wartime, but he found the political climate less congenial. Keppel showed no desire to work with him, and when Middleton intrigued with Shelburne behind his back, he found the minister more interested in economical reform than in boosting the Controller's power. Howe treated him with his remote icy politeness, went on a visitation of the dock-yards in 1784 without telling the Navy Board, and vetoed all Middleton's proposals. Some of these might have been of great importance, notably his plan to roof over the dockyard building slips so that ships could be built in the dry. This was eventually adopted in the nineteenth century, but it could have extended Sandwich's work on the longevity of the fleet in time to have had a real impact on the Napoleonic War. Middleton was able to achieve a great deal in matters entirely within the Navy Board's authority, such as store-keeping, accounting and the codification of the Board's standing orders, but without Admiralty support his grand schemes were still-born.[24]

One small but significant development in these years was the first naval order for English wrought iron. The Navy Agent and man of business Henry Cort came into possession of Fontley Forge near Fareham by foreclosing on a loan, and in partnership with the Pay Office clerk Adam Jellicoe began to take on naval contracts. In connection with a Victualling Board order for iron hoops, Cort invented a rolling mill, which was subsequently used in the production of the drawn copper bolts for refastening coppered ships. A 1782 Navy Board contract to convert scrap iron into ballast pigs led to his development of the coal-fired 'puddling' process, which in conjunction with the rolling mill produced the first English wrought iron as trustworthy as Swedish metal. In 1784 Cort became the first British ironmaster to sell the Navy wrought iron for anchors. The partnership collapsed in 1789, when Jellicoe was discovered to have been borrowing official funds to sustain it and killed himself, but in its short life it had laid essential technological foundations for the nineteenth-century British iron industry.[25]

Middleton's other achievements in the late 1780s were the fruit of his close working alliance with Pitt, behind Howe's back. Advised by Middleton, Pitt effectively carried forward much of Sandwich's work in rebuilding the fleet. It had ended the American War, unlike every previous and subsequent one, in good material condition (the coppering problem aside) and Pitt's steady investment progressively improved it. In 1786 he moved the Navy Board from its cramped office by the Tower into the new government offices at Somerset House, where for the first time it worked alongside the Victualling Office, Sick and Hurt Office and Navy Pay Office, and where Pitt himself often visited. Middleton's plan was to rationalize the business of the Navy Board, where most of the work fell on a few (led by himself), while other members had little or nothing to do. The weakness of yard management, and the age of many yard officers, meant that a mass of detail came to the Board for decision. Middleton intended to deal with this by breaking the Board up into three committees to deal with correspondence, accounts and stores, he himself being chairman of all three. Nor had he forgotten his long-term ambition to get to the Admiralty.[26]

His intended vehicle was the 1785 Commission on Fees in Public Offices, Pitt's instrument for drawing the fangs of the 'economical reform' movement. He developed a close but discreet connection with the chairman, the banker Francis Baring, and John Dick, another of the members, and fed them his plans for reforming the Navy Office and installing himself at the Admiralty. Baring was deaf and Dick blind, but Middleton was happy to act as their eyes and ears. Having secured the removal of Howe in July 1788, Middleton was confidently looking forward to the adoption of his schemes when the Regency crisis interfered. Afterwards he found Chatham indisposed to strenuous reforms. Finally in March 1790, with no sign of action from Pitt or Chatham, he resigned in frustration. Though he continued to keep open the unofficial channels he knew so well, at sixty-three he seemed to have retired from public business for good.[27]

Compared to the turbulence experienced by the dockyards and the Navy Board, other parts of the naval administration worked relatively smoothly during and after the American War, with no major reforms or disruptions. The Victualling Office coped efficiently with the demands of the war, including the victualling of unprecedented forces across the Atlantic without the help of the New England market from which it had formerly drawn so much. When the victualling of troops overseas was transferred to it from the Treasury, the result was a marked improvement in both efficiency and economy. Some political noise was generated over an alleged fraud by the Board's corn factor Christopher Atkinson, dismissed in February 1781, but he was identified and attacked as a protégé of Sandwich, and it is not clear how guilty he really was.[28]

The Ordnance Board was forced by the experience of the American War to confront the weaknesses of its gun designs. Thomas Blomefield, the Inspector of Artillery, introduced a new 'hot proof' which led to the condemnation of many existing guns, and in 1787 the Board adopted his new standard gun patterns for the Navy. These were excellent designs, but rearming the whole Navy was a massive undertaking, and reliable guns were in short supply until the late 1790s. At the same time new technology transformed the gunfounding industry. In 1775 the ironmaster John Wilkinson patented a method of boring guns from the solid (apparently an improvement on the Maritz method, already known in Britain), which the Board adopted. This expensive innovation hastened the collapse of the Wealden industry, already unable to compete with the lower costs of coal-fired furnaces. In the late 1780s many new foundries were established elsewhere in England and Scotland to profit from the rearmament of the Navy.[29] Blomefield's new gun designs were all the more timely because the quality of gunpowder was improving fast during and after the American War, thanks to experiments by Major William Congreve and the Cambridge chemist (and in 1782 Bishop of Llandaff) Richard Watson. These yielded more powerful and durable powder, which was manufactured more cheaply in the Board's own mills at Faversham and later Waltham Abbey.[30]

Behind the strategic misjudgements and failures of the American War, therefore, the administrative structure of the Navy was in many respects already strong, and yet capable of reform and renewal. Across the Channel, French ministers were interested in reform too, but faced many difficulties. Without any institutions comparable to the Admiralty or Navy Board, French naval administration had no central repository of professional expertise, and had to form policy on the basis of very inadequate information. French Atlantic dockyards depended heavily on the Baltic for masts and timber, but they were forced to use Dutch shippers and agents, while nearly all the exporting firms in the Baltic ports were British. These merchants did not refuse to supply the French navy, but somehow it always got the worst goods at the highest prices. One of the major advantages of Toulon as a building yard was that it had reasonably reliable sources of timber in Corsica, Albania and the Black Sea, and Italian or Turkish (in reality Greek) merchants and shippers to supply it.[31]

The French iron industry was collectively substantial but technically backward, scattered in small and often remote units. The state devoted much money and energy to importing British technology, but the industry as a whole was resistant to innovation. William Wilkinson, brother of the English ironfounder and like him a radical Nonconformist who was happy to express his opposition to the North government and the American War, built the new Indret foundry in 1777, but it depended on imports of English pig-iron. After the war he established another forge on a coal-field at Le Creusot, but in practice both coal and iron-ore were scarce, the quality of output was poor, and the works collapsed altogether in 1814. Similar problems attended the copper industry, which suddenly became of high strategic importance for coppering ships. France imported copper from Sweden, but could not get enough, and attempts to smuggle it from Britain failed. In 1781 the Wilkinsons helped to set up the Romilly copper foundry and after the war supplied it with the latest equipment (until Pitt's 1785 Tools Act blocked the export of sensitive technologies), but still the French lagged behind Britain. In all these cases, moreover, advanced industry existed only to supply the state and had no other markets, so its life depended on the precarious financial health of the French navy.[32]

The Spanish navy had many of the same problems and solutions, but more consistent long-term planning. Ferrol was the Spanish Brest, which depended on the Baltic for many supplies, especially masts, and on coastal shipping for the remainder. The establishment of Havana yard, which by the mid-century was building a third of all Spanish warships from tropical hardwoods, contributed to the outstanding longevity of Spanish ships, and so did heavy investment in the naval yards. In 1754 the Spanish navy built the first dry docks in the tideless Mediterranean, at Cartagena, and in 1774 it solved the problem of pumping them out by installing the first steam engine in a dockyard. By the early 1780s there were also two docks at Ferrol and three at Cadiz, emptied by steam engines of Spanish construction. The long-established Spanish iron industry, mainly in the Basque country, produced about 2,500 tons a year in the mid-century, for which the navy was the largest customer (towards the end of the century it was using up to 1,200 tons a year of nails alone), but the foundries' technology was tending to fall behind that of Sweden and Britain, and in 1784 a Basque espionage expedition was despatched to investigate the Scottish iron industry. In 1767 the Irishman John Dowling built the first Spanish steel works, and in 1791 a new government steel foundry was established at Sargadelos near Ferrol. Copper was imported from Sweden and Hungary until the Rio Tinto mine opened in 1784. The German Georg Graubner established a copper foundry in 1771 which supplied Cartagena, and the other yards had them soon afterwards. The Algeciras copper mill in 1793 installed the first Spanish rolling mill. Overall Spanish efforts to build up domestic industry and keep up with foreign technology were at least as successful as French, and in key respects such as dry docks much more successful, but in this as in everything else the Spanish navy reached its apogee in the mid-1790s.[33]

All over Europe, navies were expanding, pushing against the limits of financial, industrial and technical capacity. Very soon, though none of them knew it, they were to confront perils of a completely new order. It was to be no more a question of success or failure, victory or defeat, but of the survival or extinction of states. In this new struggle, very much was to depend on the solidity and strength of each navy's infrastructure, and its flexibility to respond to unprecedented stresses.

TWENTY-FIVE

A Golden Chain or a Wooden Leg

Social History 1763–1792: Officers

T he fact that the Navy was largely demobilized in peacetime was the single dominant factor in almost every aspect of its life. The manning problem was almost solely due to the fact that the Navy did not employ in peacetime the men it needed in war. Many of its operational and practical difficulties arose from the fact that it was effectively a part-time profession for senior officers, who tended to spend the first part of each war relearning what they had forgotten since the last. The careers of sea officers (the phrase 'naval officers' in the eighteenth century referred to the civilian officials of the Navy Board) were dominated by the fact that almost all promotion took place in wartime. Only a tiny minority of the lucky and well-connected could hope to be promoted in peacetime. In the peacetime years of 1784 to 1788, for example, there were an average of only nine new lieutenants made each year. Yet officers, especially junior officers, did not last. The mean seniority of serving lieutenants in wartime was only about five years, and those still serving past fifteen years' seniority were very rare. In 1759 Hawke recommended Lieutenant Robert Taylor, who, 'if I am not mistaken, is the oldest lieutenant now employed, a sober, diligent, good officer'.[1] Nineteen years after his first commission, he really was almost the 'oldest' (meaning most senior) on a list of serving lieutenants the vast majority of whom had been promoted since the outbreak of the Seven Years' War. After the end of a war age, death or the necessity of earning a living rapidly thinned the ranks of available officers, especially lieutenants, and ensured that at every major mobilization, including those like the Falkland Islands or Nootka Sound Armaments which did not lead to war, there was an acute shortage. The result was very large numbers of promotions: 303 new lieutenants in 1790, including over 150 on a single day, 22 November 1790. As wars continued, the shortage would ease and the rate of promotion slow, but at the end of every eighteenth-century war there were too many officers, and promotion stopped until the cycle recommenced again. More precisely, promotion stopped at the end of every war except the American War, when Keppel added a large number of his political friends to the already swollen lists.[2]

For the future sea officer, the most important means of ensuring a success-ful career was to be born at the right moment, ideally about twenty years before the outbreak of a major naval war. Having gone to sea at a suitable age (no older than fourteen), obtained the necessary experience (six years at sea from 1729, of which two had to have been spent in the Navy as a midshipman or master's mate) and passed the lieutenant's examination, the young man would be ideally positioned to profit from the inevitable promotion boom at the beginning of the war. At higher ranks the same applied, for there was always a similar, though smaller demand for new commanders, captains and admirals. The unluckiest officers were those who qualified as lieutenants towards the end of a war but failed to get their commissions. They were condemned to 'midshipman's half-pay' – 'nothing a day, and to find them-selves', as the bitter jest had it, hence the stock image of the midshipman blacking shoes for a meagre living.[3] Those who had their commissions at least had their half-pay, but lieutenants, commanders and captains who stood fair for promotion but just missed it before the peace were similarly unlucky, and might well be too old to pursue their careers by the time war returned. On the occasion of George III's visit to Portsmouth in 1773, an analysis was made of the service records of the officers of the two flagships *Barfleur* and *Dublin*. Ten years after the end of the Seven Years' War, the five lieutenants of the *Barfleur* had between fourteen and seventeen years' seniority. The first three lieutenants of the *Dublin* had between eleven and fourteen years' seniority, and a total of seventy-five years' naval service between them. Only one lucky young man, Lieutenant John Manley, fourth of the *Dublin*, had been promoted in 1770 during the Falkland Islands crisis. Perfectly positioned to profit from the promotion boom of the American War, Manley reached post rank in October 1782 just as it ended, and in due course died a vice-admiral. Amongst the young gentlemen of the two ships, the disappointments of peacetime were even more marked. There were twelve young men on the two quarter-decks, with between seven and eighteen years' service each, who had already passed for lieutenant, and eight more who had exceeded the qualifying sea-time (more than doubled it in four cases). Three of these twenty were promoted on the occasion of the king's visit, and thirteen more achieved commissioned rank during the American War, between 1775 and 1781, by which time they had accumulated an average of nearly seventeen years' service each. Yet these were lucky persons in all respects except their dates of birth; followers of admirals, in several cases noted as possessing influential patrons ashore. It was the glories and opportunities of wartime ('either a golden chain or a wooden leg', in the words of the ambitious young master's mate John Morris in 1739)[4] which tempted young men to join the Navy, but that was often too late. Logically it would have been wiser to strive to enter in peacetime when nothing much was happening, but that was hardly in human nature, especially not the nature of boys, and in peacetime young gentlemen were scarce.[5] 'Alas, how many sail round Cape Disappointment!', the seaman William Spavens lamented, and often from the sole disadvantage of the wrong date of birth.[6]

Since most young men went to sea young enough to have the qualifying sea-time for lieutenant before they reached the qualifying age of twenty, it was not unknown for them to gain a year or two with a false baptismal certificate. Authority was aware of this, and the rules were bent with some discrimination to accelerate the promotion of young men of outstanding talent, usually at times when lieutenants were in short supply. Those like Rodney who abused the convention were brought up smartly.[7] The regulations on sea-time were seldom bent, but there was an important exception, well established by the time of the American War, which concerned young gentlemen's education. Boys who had gone to sea around twelve were unlikely to be advanced mathematicians, and had limited hopes of becoming such at sea. Usually boys learned their essential navigation in one of the schools which specialized in mathematics, often after two or three years at sea. The brothers Jahleel and Edward Brenton, for example, of a Rhode Island loyalist family, went to sea with their father in 1781 aged eleven and seven, then at the end of the war were sent to a 'maritime school' in Chelsea to learn navigation and to France for the language, before resuming their naval careers.[8] It became an accepted convention that during this schooling the boys might be borne for up to two years on the books, not of a seagoing ship, but of a ship under refit, a guardship or yacht, so that their 'sea-time' should be building up while they studied. This was within the letter of the regulations, and balanced the need both for practical seamanship and for advanced mathematics.[9]

Mathematics had been needed for navigation since the late Middle Ages, but the 'discovery of the longitude' in the 1760s called for more serious studies than before. Two methods became available more or less at once. Chronometers were simple to use and required only a straightforward observation, but they were not widespread until far into the nineteenth century. The Navy first supplied them in small numbers, to ships in distant waters only, from the 1790s, but they were not a standard issue until the 1840s. Until then officers bought their own. They cost sixty to a hundred guineas, plus five or ten a year for cleaning and repair, and a single chronometer was not reliable: for real security a ship needed three, so that if one went wrong the error could be detected. Few officers, and very few masters, could afford even one; in 1802 only 7 per cent of British warships had a chronometer. In practice therefore the method of 'lunar distances' was preferred, which called for advanced mathematics, but no instrument more expensive than the essential quadrant (costing about three guineas in the 1760s) necessary for all observations, or, better, the new sextant (twelve guineas) which could measure angles up to 120°. Lunars served either by themselves, or to rate the chronometer for those who had one. Even so lunars were not a panacea. They could only be observed about twenty days in each lunar month, and of course all observations require a clear sky, and all calculations are subject to error. Crossing the Atlantic in 1776, Howe took a lunar which put them 300 miles west of their true longitude; they nearly ran on Nantucket Shoal when they thought they were off Long Island. Merchant ships were still crossing the Atlantic without chronometers, charts or sextants far into the nineteenth century, and all but the most daring navigators still made their landfalls by latitude sailing. In 1782 Cook's old pupil Captain James King, escorting a convoy to the West Indies, horrified the merchantmen by approaching Barbados from the north-east, trusting solely to lunars.[10]

The social origins of sea officers were very varied. At the top of the social scale there were a minority of young men, sons of gentlemen and even noblemen, whose position in society gave them the strongest grounds for expecting to reach commissioned rank. At the other end there were many boys who lacked the basic literacy and advanced numeracy which every lieutenant had to have. Between these extremes was a very wide range of social situations from which boys might become commissioned officers, warrant officers, masters or mates of merchantmen – in fact almost every rank from admiral to common seaman. It was quite normal for captains and admirals to have near relations by blood or marriage who were warrant officers or officers of merchantmen. Some officers moved from merchantmen into the Navy, while in peacetime others moved in the opposite direction to earn a living or augment their sea-time. Often it seems to have been little more than luck who finished up at what level in which service.[11] Some British officers served in the navies of foreign powers, especially the Russian navy, which in the years after 1715 was boosted by a number whose reputation for Jacobitism (or in the case of Captain John Deane, cannibalism) suggested a fresh start abroad. Catherine the Great recruited more in the 1760s, mainly Scots, including Samuel Greig from Inverkeithing, who stayed to become one of the great Russian admirals.[12]

A significant development in the late eighteenth century was the emergence of the first quasi-professional specialization amongst commissioned officers, the transport agents. These were officers employed afloat and in uniform by the Navy Board to control and organize merchant ships on charter to the government. Their position was in several respects uncomfortable and ambiguous, because they looked and behaved like sea officers, but were in law only naval officers, not liable to naval discipline. Nevertheless the huge transport force of the American War required a lot of management, and the status of transport agents rose from being a job only for elderly lieutenants. Officers of ability were needed, and commanders-in-chief found means to promote senior transport agents to commander or even captain.[13]

A few examples of naval careers spread over the length of the eighteenth century may illustrate their diversity. Peter Warren, born in 1703, was the third son of a bankrupt Irish Catholic small landowner. Following a common survival strategy of their class, the Warrens brought up their younger sons as Protestants, and Peter followed his uncle Matthew Aylmer, who had already converted in the same way and prospered in the Navy. That in turn connected him with Aylmer's son-in-law Sir John Norris, who ensured that his wife's cousin was employed through the peacetime years, mainly in the Americas, though they were at Copenhagen when Norris made him post in 1727. By good luck with prizes and seizures, judicious investment in local commerce, and a fortunate marriage with a New York heiress, Warren was already a wealthy man when the battles of the War of the Austrian Succession gave him a fortune in prize-money. When he died at the early age of forty-eight in 1752 he was worth about £160,000.[14]

Arthur Forrest, a former master's mate who had served his time for lieutenant in the Navy, was master of a merchantman in the Jamaica trade when in 1740 Vernon recruited him as a pilot on the Cartagena expedition. Declining £50 for his services, Forrest asked instead for perferment, so Vernon made him lieutenant and put him in command of a sloop to teach the masters of the squadron the pilotage of Port Royal. Thereafter Forrest pursued a naval career largely in the Caribbean, where he made his business interests mesh with his sea service and became a substantial Jamaica planter. 'A very brave, sensible, candid man', he made his naval reputation by his 1757 action with Kersaint in the Windward Passage, and died commodore commanding at Jamaica in 1770.[15]

Mark Moore, born in Boston, Massachusetts in 1739, left Harvard at fifteen to join the Navy, and before the end of the Seven Years' War had served successively as midshipman, able seaman in a West Indiaman, second mate of a slaver, lieutenant in the Swedish navy, second lieutenant of a British privateer, acting lieutenant in the Navy commanding a tender, lieutenant in the Portuguese navy, mate of a brig in the New England timber trade, midshipman in the Navy again, and master of a Bristol trading brig – after which he swallowed the anchor and became an actor-manager.[16]

George Keith Elphinstone, fifth son of the Scottish peer Lord Elphinstone, was born in January 1746 in the midst of the Jacobite rebellion in which his entire family was deeply involved. Having neither money nor influence, his father sent him to sea in 1761 'to acquire his education and business together and without expense'. In 1766 he sailed as fourth mate of the *Triton* East Indiaman, commanded by his brother, before returning to the Navy and getting his commission during the Spanish Armament of 1770. He was posted in 1775, and was high enough on the captains' list to reach flag rank in 1794, just as a great war started which was to provide almost unlimited employment for a reliable admiral (who was a friend of the Prince of Wales), and raise him in due course to the peerage.[17]

Bartholomew James, ninth child of an unprosperous Falmouth merchant, went to sea in a Post Office packet at fifteen in 1767, and transferred to the Navy at the time of the 1770 mobilization. He contrived to remain employed until he received his commission in 1779, but was still only a lieutenant at the end of the war in 1783. Having failed in business as a brewer, he was helped by naval friends to buy a share in a merchantman, in command of which he traded to the West Indies from 1787 to 1793. On the outbreak of war in 1793 he took command of a Jamaica privateer, which was taken up as a government transport for the West Indies expedition next year, when Lieutenant James became a transport agent. Thereafter he pursued his naval career, effectively retiring from the sea in 1799 with the rank of captain and a modest fortune.[18]

William Prowse, a Devon man probably born in the same year as James (1752), served before the mast during the American War, rose to be a master's mate and was made lieutenant in December 1782. He spent much of the ensuing peace in merchantmen, but was well placed to prosper when war broke out in 1793, was posted in 1797, and reached rear-admiral in retirement in 1821. Prowse was lucky in being born at the right moment and in fighting in at least seven battles (including St Vincent and Trafalgar), but he seems to have been a worthy character who rose from obscurity through solid reliability rather than brilliance.[19]

Edward Pellew, five years younger, was the son of a packet commander. He went to sea as servant to a fellow Cornishman, Captain John Stott, was thrown out by him as a troublemaker, but survived this disaster to rise eventually to be an admiral and a peer. In his own words 'pock-marked, ugly, uninteresting and uneducated', Pellew was also tough, brave, skilful, lucky and unscrupulous. He made lieutenant a few months before the French war broke out in 1778, was posted before the end of it, and was knighted for taking the first prize of the next war. As we shall see, Pellew knew how to take his political chances, but his rise was mainly the consequence of luck and talent, including the all-important luck of being born at the right moment.[20]

The majority of all sea careers began in boyhood, but some did not transfer to the Navy until relatively late, and those who reached commissioned rank from humble circumstances always tended to be older. The future Commodore William Boys was twenty-eight when he entered the Navy and thirty-five when he received his first commission. It was, however, possible to leave it too late: Gregory Bowden was not allowed to take the lieutenant's examination in 1745 because he was fifty-five and had not been in the Navy for thirty-one years. A few entered the Navy direct when already adults. Charles Cotton initially went to Lincoln's Inn but thought better of the law, joined the East India Company at eighteen and transferred to the Navy the next year, in 1772. This was perfect timing, and as his father was an MP and baronet, there was no risk of his merits being overlooked: he was a post-captain at twenty-six, with barely enough sea-time to qualify as a lieutenant.[21]

The fact that the great majority of sea officers went to sea in boyhood and had only a technical and professional education, had two related disadvantages which were obvious to thinking contemporaries. The first was that the typical young officer, however skilful a seaman and navigator, had very little general education. The future Admiral Sir Edward Codrington went to sea aged thirteen in 1783, and reached lieutenant in 1793. 'I have repeatedly heard him say,' his daughter recorded, 'that during those nine years (so important for the formation of character) he never was invited to open a book, nor received a word of advice or instruction, except professional, from anyone.'[22] It was possible to reach flag rank with barely a primary education; in the worst cases ignorant and monoglot admirals had to take on wide strategic and political responsibilities for which they were completely unqualified. Howe told George III

> that he thinks in our service the attention is carried so long alone to seamanship that few officers are formed, and that a knowledge of the military is necessary to open the ideas to the directing large fleets.[23]

Since the Admiralty had almost no control over the process of entering and training future officers, it could take no official action in the matter, but it was generally understood that boys or young men who hoped to reach high rank would do very well to read, travel and learn languages. The best opportunity to do this naturally came in peacetime, and to those who could afford it, so the right date of birth, and at least a little money, smoothed the path to command.[24] 'Read – let me charge you to read,' was Captain Cuthbert Collingwood's advice to a midshipman in 1787.

> Study books that treat of your profession, and of history. Study Faulkner's Dictionary, and borrow, if you can, books which describe the West Indies, and compare what you find there with your own observations. Thus employed, you will always be in good company. Nature has sown in man the seeds of knowledge; but they must be cultivated to produce fruit.[25]

The only means of education at the Admiralty's disposal was the Royal Naval Academy at Portsmouth, established in 1737 on the abolition of the volunteers per order. It admitted only the sons of noblemen and gentlemen and cost £70 or £80 a year, beyond the pocket of most officers, though in 1773 fifteen free places for officers' sons were created. However, the total was only forty places, the Academy was badly run and seldom full, and it had little impact on the Navy as a whole. Whatever the 'academites' learned at their desks, they were not absorbing seamanship or making the vital personal contacts on which their careers would depend, so informed parents tended to avoid it.[26]

Related to education was the social issue of the behaviour and status of a gentleman. A lieutenant's commission, 'which is an independency and the rank of gentleman in every society and in every country',[27] made a young man an officer and a gentleman overnight, but when he buckled on his sword, he did not necessarily put on the manners of a gentleman as easily. Even those of good family were not likely to acquire much polish in the boisterous atmosphere of the midshipmen's berth, and polite society was apt to view the sea officers with some disdain. Writing to the Duke of Rutland from Portsmouth in 1782, Major the Hon. H. F. R. Stanhope reported that

> Mulgrave is at the head of a party of young men, consisting of Keppel, Berkeley, Bertie Conway, the Finches &c, &c. I live with them entirely. They are all perfectly good-humoured and very hospitable, but not very polished in their manners.

How different, Stanhope went on, from the duke's late brother, Captain Lord Robert Manners, who had 'all the good breeding of a fine gentleman, a character totally unknown here'![28] Thus did Eton and the Grenadier Guards condescend to a group of sea officers, every one of whom was the son of a peer.[29]

Already, however, the social status of the Navy was rising – as witness the presence of Manners and Lord Charles Fitzgerald in the Navy during the American War, where dukes' sons had been unknown since Charles II's time. What changed everything was George III's decision to send his younger son Prince William Henry to sea in 1779. To send the prince to sea to learn his profession like any boy of no family, and under orders to be treated in the same way as them, was socially radical, even revolutionary. 'The young man goes as a sailor,' the king insisted, 'and as such, I add again, no marks of distinction are to be shown unto him; they would destroy my whole plan.'[30] The sea service did not now lack prestige, though it might still lack polish. (Prince William's own contribution to polite society was 'a foul mouth and a strong head ... his vast repertoire of dirty stories made him the terror of every genteel drawing-room'.)[31] A small but telling index of the Navy's rising social status is the amount of money young gentlemen's fathers were expected to find for their mess bills. A captain's servant's pay (just under £12 a year) went to the captain, and a boy needed something for pocket money and to contribute to the mess's purchase of food and drink to supplement the official rations. In 1733 a peer's son was sent to sea with five guineas; in 1748 John Jervis's father gave him £20 to launch him on his career, and when that ran out left him to live on an able seaman's pay. Elphinstone claimed that his father gave him £5 and told him to make his fortune. For most of the century £20 a year seems to have been regarded as ample, but in 1779 Rodney called for at least £30 (admittedly in a period of inflation, and from a duke's son), and during the French wars of the 1790s and early 1800s captains were asking anything from £30 to £60 a year, sometimes including something to add to the ship's schoolmaster's pay in order to obtain a good man, suitable to educate gentlemen's sons.[32]

The mechanism which regulated naval careers at every level was patronage, the normal machinery of eighteenth-century society. Captains rated or dis-rated their own people, often chose their warrant officers, and had a substantial voice in the selection of commissioned officers. An admiral normally chose his flagship's officers, and a commander-in-chief overseas appointed officers to fill vacancies, subject to the Admiralty's approval. The Board itself, dominated by the First Lord, appointed all commissioned officers in home waters, and had a substantial and growing influence on appointments overseas. Every sea officer, certainly every captain and admiral, had a 'following' of junior officers who attached themselves to him and as far as possible followed his fortunes. As he rose, he drew his followers with him to higher ranks, and they in turn began to collect followers around them to repeat the process. It was a very successful mechanism for selecting and advancing on merit, because it was very much against an officers' interest to weaken his following and damage his reputation by advancing incompetents. It was also a mechanism which identified and promoted good men very fast, as far as post rank, after which all progression was by seniority. Many post-captains were in their twenties and thirties, already experienced seamen but still full of the boldness and physical stamina of youth. The youngest captains in turn reached the top of the list and became available for flag rank around their late forties, but most British admirals were older. At every rank up to post British officers were ten or twenty years younger than their equivalents in the French navy, but French admirals of the Revolutionary and Napoleonic Wars had been promoted fast to replace a vanished generation, and were in many cases younger than their British opponents.[33]

So much for internal, naval patronage, but politics might also influence officers' careers. Politics in the eighteenth century was not the full-time activity of a semi-professional class, but a normal, almost automatic consequence of any position of even moderate authority or eminence in national or local life. Captains and admirals were almost bound to have political commitments, at least at a local level, and many were active in national politics, members of Parliament, or closely related to them. They were involved in political patronage, the bestowal of jobs, contracts and favours in ways which cemented their own authority and that of the crown. When officers were also politicians, and when civilian ministers were First Lords of the Admiralty, naval and political patronage inevitably overlapped, and professional merit was apt to be coloured if not overridden by political considerations. It was understood that sea officers had to demonstrate real professional competence and experience, but it was a matter of judgement how far other factors might also be taken into account. On the whole the captains and admirals, whose own professional credit was at stake, were good at insulating officers' careers from outside interference; meaning that they themselves acted as a filter, receiving recommendations from political and personal connections, but adopting only those candidates whose abilities justified their endorsement and strengthened their professional authority. At the Admiralty, political admirals of character and independence like Wager and Anson were able to do this to great effect.[34]

Civilian First Lords, however well intentioned and well informed, were more exposed to political pressure. The Hon. Samuel Barrington, for example, had passed his examination and was an acting lieutenant five and a half years after he went to sea, and was confirmed in the rank (with back-dated seniority) a year later in October 1746. Immediately his brother Lord Barrington, a junior Admiralty Lord, pestered Bedford to make him a commander. The duke and his colleagues were reluctant, but there were precedents, and they felt unable to refuse a member of the government. Barrington was made a commander in one month, and reached post rank the following year, at the age of eighteen. He really was a good officer, lucky to start his career at the right moment, but it was largely political influence which had got him so far and so fast. Bedford and his colleagues were capable of mounting determined resistance to political interference when they felt on sure ground, but even a duke did not have unlimited room for manoeuvre.[35]

Lord Sandwich during the American War, at a time of violent political divisions, experienced in an acute form all the disadvantages of a civilian minister disposing of naval patronage. Modern research has demonstrated beyond any doubt the rigorous impartiality with which Sandwich distributed promotion on grounds of professional merit alone – but that made him no friends except the king. The admirals preferred their civilian chiefs to be remote and not too well informed. They were uncomfortable with a politician of thirty years' experience who knew the Navy and its officers as well or even better than they did, and, officer-like, had even built up a naval following of his own. It was an equivocal satisfaction to the admirals that Sandwich chose good men, when they were the ones who should have controlled the choice. For civilian politicians, especially peers, Sandwich was one of themselves who refused their reasonable requests by referring to an alien and incomprehensible code. Thus he explained to Lord Berkeley in 1779:

> The candidates for promotion in the Navy are so numerous, that it is absolutely necessary for me to hold the same language to all who address themselves to me upon that subject, and I am obliged to have the most strict attention to the seniority of those who either by themselves or friends solicit preferment. The rule of seniority indeed usually gives way in cases where officers have the good fortune to distinguish themselves in battle, but I cannot agree with your Lordship that exertions on harbour duty, though very meritorious, should give the same pretension. There are many young men of fashion in the Navy who are equally solicitous for preferment and their friends are equally pressing; your Lordship will find on enquiry that my answer to all of them is the same, whatever their connections may be.[36]

For many contemporaries, especially Rockingham and his noble friends, this was proof of 'corruption', as the eighteenth century understood the word (meaning any perversion of the right order of society, not necessarily for financial motives), for there could be no honest reason to deny the natural leaders of society what was theirs by right. The king might order his son to receive no special treatment, but dukes like Rutland or Leinster had no idea of suffering such an indignity: 'that would be trifling too much with one of the first families in the kingdom,' as Lord Robert Manners indignantly exclaimed.[37] Friends of government expected special treatment and were outraged not to receive it. 'Sea officers are apt to be discontented if everything is not done according to their wish,' Sandwich observed, 'they are exceedingly jealous of one another, and ready to find fault with everybody's conduct but their own.'[38] Honour and envy were nearly related. A gentleman was the only proper judge of what was needful to sustain his honour, and an officer's honour might be offended, in his own eyes, by any order which threatened to lower his consequence, to limit his power and influence, to direct his career or operations in some direction less advantageous than he felt he deserved. Honour required that a captain or admiral should have every opportunity to vindicate his courage and conduct, that is to say that he should have the best possible ship or squadron on the best possible station. A man of nice honour had the right to demand it, and he expected his demand to be met. Tedious, unspectacular duty in obscure or unprofitable situations was inherently dishonourable, to be rejected by a gentleman as a matter of principle, so officers declined or accepted appointments as they pleased, and as they were still legally entitled to do. The situation of First Lord of the Admiralty carried much power, as W. W. Grenville remarked, for 'the patronage annexed to it is so considerable as to be a real object, in a political point of view, to any person engaged in a public line of life, where the acquisition of friends is always an important point.'[39] Without authority, however, the power served only to make enemies, and in their different ways Sandwich, Keppel and Howe all showed how difficult it was for either politicians or admirals to combine political and professional authority over the Navy. As a result, the balance between political and professional influences on officers' careers remained uncertain as the century drew towards its close.[40]

The attraction of a sea officer's career was straightforward. In an age when the eldest son invariably inherited whatever property a family possessed, and younger sons even of the greatest families had to make their way in the world, the Navy offered a respectable livelihood with minimum barriers to entry and almost unlimited possibilities of wealth and honour for a lucky few. It was arduous and dangerous, but for younger sons whose lives could be risked there was nothing to equal it.[41] Its character was marked by the nature of shipboard society, in which all ranks and ratings lived crammed in the narrow space of the 'wooden world', dependent on a high degree of organization and co-operation for comfort and survival. The complex machinery of the sailing ship depended on very skilled men working as a team, and the skills of the young topmen aloft were as vital as those of the officer on the quarterdeck. Future officers began their careers as ratings, and were expected themselves to have mastered the topmen's skills. This made the Navy socially unique. Gentlemen were the natural leaders of society because of who they were, not what they had learned; they were precisely those who did not need to master a trade or profession. Gentlemen officers who had spent their teenage years working aloft, who had been taught common skills like knotting and splicing by common seamen, were unusual creatures in eighteenth-century society. The idea of gentlemen's sons running errands and carrying powder to the guns astonished foreign observers. 'To be bedded worse than hogs, and eat less delicacies'[42] was not the proper fate of boys of good family, even in the boisterous austerity of the public schools, still less to be flogged and turned before the mast with the common seamen.[43]

In this unnatural world, where the order of civil society was subverted, the proper distinctions of dress were difficult to maintain. Commissioned officers' uniforms, with cocked hat, tight breeches, tail coat and sword, expressed their status as gentlemen, men who did not need to work. Seamen wore the characteristic 'short clothes' of their trade, with 'round hats' or caps, 'round jackets' cut off below the waist, and loose 'trousers' which could be rolled up when the decks were washing down. These clothes, very unlike the 'long clothes' worn ashore, were comfortable and safe for work aloft.[44] Officers at sea, however, also worked, and even captains often went aloft, so uniform had to be adapted, if not abandoned. Richard Vyvyan, a chaplain boarding the *Nonsuch* in the Channel in 1780, 'enquired for the captain, and was told that a person dressed, or rather *undressed* in a white jacket, night cap and flannel trousers on the quarter deck was Sir James Wallace'.[45] Even Prince William Henry as a captain in 1786–8, though a notorious martinet and stickler for detail, confined himself to ordering his officers to wear blue, 'and they will recommend themselves by wearing uniform coats or jackets'. The reference to jackets implies that they already had an unofficial 'uniform' jacket, in the seamen's style, a century before the 'monkey jacket' was officially adopted, and he explicitly allowed trousers as a substitute for breeches at sea.[46] All this was normal during the Great Wars, though more in frigates than line-of-battle ships, still less flagships, and certainly not ashore.[47] In the crack frigate *Aurora* in the 1790s, on sighting a strange sail, 'Captain Digby was as usual one of the first at the mast-head with his round jacket and trousers, his glass slung across his back', as one of his midshipmen remembered, but a lieutenant who appeared in trousers at the Admiralty in 1815 was sent home to dress properly.[48] In boats at Spithead, Colonel George Landmann recalled,

> lieutenants were not easily distinguished from petty officers – indeed sometimes not from civilians, particularly when they omitted the cocked hat and sword, by no means uncommon, and substituted a round hat and a short dirk, not so long as a carving-knife, and especially when over all was worn a plain great coat or brown camlet boat cloak, lined with green baize.[49]

The rising status of warrant officers was marked in 1787 by their first official uniform. In reality there were two distinct groups of warrant officers. Pursers and surgeons were sea officers with fair pretensions to be gentlemen, but something of the character of civilians who had joined the Navy, if not as adults, at least later in their teens than many of the commissioned officers, and tended to be better educated. The pursership of a frigate was described during the American War as 'advantageous as to income and also genteel'.[50] Chaplains, though officially only ratings, belonged socially to the same category, they and some of the surgeons being the only university graduates afloat. Not that chaplains often were afloat: for much of the eighteenth century a naval chaplaincy was regarded as a sinecure, and Sandwich caused consternation by demanding that chaplains do duty. 'When you were so good as to apply for me for this chaplainship, neither you nor I thought that in consequence of obtaining it I should be obliged to be near the ship or on board,' Percival Stockdale complained to his patron David Garrick in 1776.[51] These gentlemanlike warrant officers increasingly hoped to be treated as such, to be allowed to dine in the wardroom and wear a uniform which distinguished them from boatswains, gunners and carpenters. These three formed the other group of warrant officers, those who had unequivocally risen from the lower deck. Boatswains and gunners were almost always former working petty officers and common seamen. Carpenters were often former dockyard shipwrights, and always learned their trade as apprentices, but they too were socially distinct from the 'gentleman' warrant officers. All three were key officers on whom much of the efficiency of a ship depended, and good boatswains in particular, first-class seamen able to carry authority with the men from amongst whom they had risen, were scarce and precious. In 1745 Hawke made an acting boatswain of 'my best boatswain's mate, who was a boy with me under Captain Durrell in the *Scarborough* ... men of that profession being very scarce that are good for anything'.[52] A generation later in 1780 Captain John Colpoys of the *Orpheus* requested that Barlow Fielding his boatswain be allowed to exchange into another ship to make a fresh start. He was a good seaman but black and 'wants that great requisite (in a boatswain) of making himself of consequence among the people, who have, I find, taken a dislike to the man's colour'.[53] Finally the masters were in a category of their own: technically warrant officers but unchallenged members of the wardroom, closely related in terms of pay and status to the senior lieutenants, and their equals or superiors in professional knowledge.[54]

Professional knowledge was perhaps the outstanding characteristic of British officers. Though in many cases uneducated and unpolished, they were distinguished from their social equals ashore, and their equals in foreign navies, by their very long sea experience. If they had a characteristic weakness, it was the vice of the age: drink. All memoirs mention it with frequency, and generally in a tone of amused toleration.[55] Thus the surgeon James Ker sketched the officers of the *Royal Oak* in 1779:

> Our first lieutenant, that little sottish-looking man, has turned out a very brisk, able officer and one who does not want either good sense or learning. Unfortunately, when not immediately engaged in the duties of his profession, he is but too apt to yield to the baneful delights of the private bottle ... the master, a shrewd old fellow who never failed to visit the bottle as duly as did the sun the world. By frequent repetition of a trifle of what-not he so bedimmed his eyes and got so top-heavy that we used to con him to bed after his having thrown the knives and forks at us.[56]

Officers started on this course young. It was a boy of eleven who wrote home, 'Wine is no luxury to me, for I have two glasses at dinner every day and two at supper, which is my half allowance, I not liking grog.'[57] After dinner was often when the boys skylarked in the rigging. The son of the first lieutenant of the *Grampus* in 1787 was playing after dinner on the mizzen topsail yard, 'having had his glass of wine', when he fell to his death at his father's feet.[58]

TWENTY-SIX

Dividing and Quartering

Social History 1763–1792: Men and Manning

The manning problem in the American War was more severe than ever before, because a large proportion of Britain's naval manpower was already committed to the transport force, the naval squadron and the extensive amphibious and inland operations in North America, before the main fleet mobilized at all. At the height of the war in 1781 there were 105,000 men in the Navy and (briefly) as many as 20,000 in privateers, out of an estimated total of only 140,000 British seafarers, which itself was roughly double the pre-war figure. It is possible that the total available seafaring manpower may have been more than has been supposed, but even so the massive expansion in wartime was only possible because many non-seamen, or former seamen, or foreigners were drawn to sea by high wartime wages. Without landmen it would have been impossible to man the Navy in wartime, but Kempenfelt considered that 'young landmen, with proper attention, may, in three months, if half that time at sea, be made to know every rope in the ship, to knot and splice, hand and reef, and be perfect in the management of the cannon and small arms', and that included most of the work of the ship.[1] Impressment by itself did nothing to increase overall manpower, because it applied only to British seamen. Its effect was to ensure that the Navy retained some of the scarce and essential professional seamen, above all topmen. In economic terms it increased the effective supply by forcing men to work twelve months of the year who were accustomed in peacetime to take two or three months a year ashore.[2]

Always controversial, impressment was doubly divisive during the American War because the war itself had some elements of a civil war, even in Britain. Wilkite radicals outside Parliament took up the American cause and opposed impressment, at the same time as they professed to back the Navy and the war against France and Spain. They tried to bridge the contradiction by insinuating that impressment was not really a means of manning the Navy at all, only a pointless expression of arbitrary power. The argument was less than cogent, but that did not reduce the practical difficulties presented by hostile magistrates opposing all naval recruitment in London, which was by far the biggest seaport. At the most acute stage of the manning crisis in 1779, the government temporarily suspended all statutory protections, though the protected men were discharged the following year. As before, however, impressment was really effective afloat rather than ashore, and the opposition of London magistrates was less damaging than the efforts of shipmasters. Even the East India Company helped its men to avoid the press, to the extent of issuing them with firearms.[3]

It has been calculated that 230–235,000 men were recruited for the Navy from 1776 to 1783. The Impress Service was responsible for half the total: 116,357 men, of whom 72,658 were paid bounty as volunteers, and the majority of the remaining 43,699 must have been pressed. The other half must have been made up of men recruited at sea, officers, Marines, volunteers privately recruited by officers and other sources. The best estimate is that about 80,000 men, one-third of the total, were pressed, divided equally between sea and shore.[4] Though impressment ashore was violently controversial, and sometimes violently opposed, on close observation much of it seems to have been a matter of negotiation. The Impress Service, as we have seen, negotiated with local authorities. Liverpool, more co-operative than in the previous war, was offering additional bounties of ten guineas for an able seaman and five for a landman by 1779. Many Impress officers were local men themselves. Captain James Alms in Sussex, for example, was the son of the Duke of Richmond's steward at Goodwood. In the three years to the end of 1779 he raised 570 men of whom just under half (243) were pressed, and another third were volunteer landmen.[5] Individual seamen negotiated with press officers. Many of them 'volunteered' when escape became impossible, gaining a bounty and their choice of ship. Men might be allowed to 'enter for the ship' days after being pressed, when they had decided they liked her and wanted to stay. A man with friends or inside information might volunteer for a ship fitting out and get a protection for a couple of months – good for some leave. For the Impress officers, who were paid by results, volunteers were worth more, and abandoned any claim to exemption and discharge. The Admiralty disapproved of the extra expense of these eleventh-hour 'volunteers', but was powerless to stop the trade.[6] So many men, however, gained the volunteer's 'right' to choose his ship that in 1777 the Admiralty, as Sandwich explained, found it necessary to make a regulation to confine that option to such men as enter with an offer of the particular ship in which they wish to serve; the other mode of allowing them to choose at large was so much abused that we were obliged to stop it; otherwise we should have had no disposable men which in times of equipment are what are most wanted.[7]

Even those who were unequivocally pressed seem very often to have regarded it as an incident of their profession, soon to be got over ('However I was young and had the world before me, did not fret much, and was willing to go to any part of the world,' wrote William Richardson),[8] though perhaps not many were as enthusiastic as George Price, a pressed man who wrote home '. . . this leaves us all in good spirits for a man of war is more like a gin shop than any thing else'.[9]

One species of 'impressment' which was prominent in public debate in the eighteenth century, and has been much studied since, is the recruitment of criminals and vagrants. An aspect of the English naval myth in which the political world believed was that the Navy, as a truly national force, should have a healing and cleansing effect on society, freeing it of 'idle and reprobate Vermin by converting them into a Body of the most industrious People, and even, becoming the very nerves of our State'.[10] Naval acts of Parliament, whatever their other content, often included provisions by which magistrates might send such persons into the Navy, and it is sometimes implied that dealing with criminals and undesirables was a real, or even the real, objective of impressment.[11] There is no doubt that many people would have liked impressment to have served this function, and that it suited the opposition to North's government to allege that this was another example of arbitrary power. In practice, however, nothing in any of these acts obliged the Navy to accept magistrates' offerings, and it was invariably reluctant to do so. A few criminals did find their way into the Navy, but the Navy wanted none except smugglers, who had valuable skills.[12] 'I am in my conscience convinced', wrote Sandwich, 'that receiving these wretches into a ship crowded with men is excessively dangerous to the health of the crew, and will occasion desertion and villainy to increase; besides the captains and officers are against receiving them.'[13]

Volunteers remained the basic source of naval manpower, and even in a period when inflation was reducing the real value of the naval wage, the peacetime labour market normally supplied the Navy with all the men it needed. The memoirs of seamen who served in both merchantmen and the Navy suggest that less work, better food, more certain payment and fairer treatment in the Navy made up for the difference in nominal wages.[14] Captain

Phillip going out to New South Wales in 1785 had his pick of volunteers, 'all young men that were called seamen, 160 in number, no boys or women allowed,' in the words of Jacob Nagle, who was one of them.[15] Personal connections were as always the best way to recruit. When John Stott was given a command during the Falkland Islands crisis, he at once got leave to go down to Penzance 'where he represents he has a prospect of procuring many men to complete the complement of the ship'; young Ned Pellew was one of those he collected.[16] Twenty years later Cuthbert Collingwood was putting together a ship's company by writing to his young officer followers to come to him and bring volunteers with them. Even after volunteers' freedom to choose a ship was restricted in 1777, officers could still nominate their followers, and Sandwich strongly encouraged captains to man their ships by their own efforts, as he explained in the House of Lords:

> Such a mode of procuring men creates a confidence between the commanding officer and the seaman. The former is in some measure bound to act humanely to the man who gives him a preference of serving under him; and the latter will find his interest and duty unite, in behaving well under a person from whom he is taught to expect every present reasonable indulgence, and future favour. These, and other instances of a similar nature which have come to my knowledge, have enabled me to point out one thing that might, in my opinion, be the means of furthering the naval service; that is, trusting less to the assistance of the Admiralty board, and giving every possible encouragement to the captains appointed to the command of ships to complete their own crews.[17]

The disadvantage came when these captains transferred to other ships and begged to be allowed to take their large followings with them. Sandwich understood how desirable it was in principle 'that every ship should form a regular ship's company, which will be much broken into if we go on borrowing and lending',[18] but it was impossible to allow popular captains to take all the best men and leave the unlucky or unpopular with none. The popular captains were naturally annoyed ('the disgust of the seamen to the Navy is all owing to the infernal plan of turning them over from ship to ship, so that men cannot be attached to their officers, or the officers care two-pence about them,' complained young Captain Nelson in 1783),[19] and Sandwich found refusing this sort of request another easy way to make powerful enemies.[20]

As in all previous wars, the high 'turn-over' of men meant that the total number recruited during the American War was more than double the maximum number serving at any one time. There was roughly one case of desertion for every three men recruited. The annual desertion rate peaked at over 16 per cent in 1776, double the figure for the previous war, but again it has to be understood that manning records were kept only for individual ships, and movement from ship to ship cannot be distinguished from escapes from the service as a whole. People deserted to the Navy as well as from it, in spite of its serious financial disadvantage in wartime.[21]

Sickness was another major drain on manpower, and a major component of 'turn-over'. The resurgence of scurvy in the Channel Fleet does not seem to have caused many deaths, but it removed many men to hospital, and forced Geary into port in August 1780 with 2,400 men (one in seven) ill. The real killers were fevers, especially typhus, influenza and dysentery. There were, however, significant developments taking place in the health of the Navy. The first 'slop-ships' were instituted in 1781, in which new recruits were washed and issued with fresh clothes before being drafted to their ships. This had an immediate effect in reducing the incidence of typhus. In 1780 Rodney took with him to the West Indies the fashionable physician Sir Gilbert Blane, who was appointed physician to the squadron. With Rodney's support he instituted a regime which stressed cleanliness of ships and men, ventilation, avoidance of 'land air' and filthy clothes, fresh fruit and vegetables against the scurvy. 'A true seaman is in general cleanly, but the greater part of men in a ship of war require a degree of compulsion to make them so,' he wrote; 'and such is the depravity of many, that it is not uncommon for them to dispose of their clothes for money to purchase spirituous liquors.'[22] Blane's measures were little more than the common practice of officers and the common wisdom of seamen for generations, but they were applied with rigour and the full support of the commander-in-chief, and Rodney's fleet was lucky to have no land operations to undertake. As a result, by the time of the battle of the Saintes in April 1782, the death rate in the fleet was down to 1.4 per cent a year; it must have been the healthiest body of British subjects in the world.[23] Blane's work was important not only for what he achieved but for who he was and how he did it. It was a radical novelty that a physician should prefer folk wisdom to classical learning, and bolster his arguments with an unapologetic appeal to experience expressed in statistics: 'It has appeared from our reasonings concerning the nature of medical investigation, that important practical truths can be ascertained only by averages expressive of the comparative results of numerous individual facts.'[24] This was the origin not only of improvements in the health of the Navy in later years, but also of the nineteenth-century public health movement and the modern science of epidemiology.[25] Blane, who went aboard the prizes after the battle of the Saintes, is yet another witness to the still very poor standards of hygiene and health in French warships.[26] A French visitor to a British frigate after the war made the same observation: 'It is kept in such scrupulous cleanliness that we were astonished: I saw nothing like it on a frigate in Toulon. They blame the uncleanliness of the French, and say it causes more casualties than the English. They wash the entire ship every day.'[27]

Prisoners of war were less of a net advantage to the British in this war than before, because the French convoy system was working efficiently. As a result there were fewer French merchantmen taken, and fewer French privateers at sea, whose losses were always the largest drain on the French naval manpower pool. Better administration on both sides of the Channel also greatly reduced losses to disease amongst prisoners. Nevertheless by the end of the American War both French and Spanish naval manpower was virtually exhausted.[28]

A seventy-four-gun ship of the line berthed 500–600 men on the lower deck, in a space about 165 feet long and forty-five feet across. Here they hung their hammocks to sleep, and slung their mess tables to eat. In principle every hammock was allowed fourteen inches width, which at sea, though not in port, would allow each man twenty-eight inches to sleep in a ship keeping two watches, with the hammocks slung starboard and larboard watches alternately. A 'seventy-four' had thirteen guns a side, of which two were in the gunroom aft, where the gunner and various junior officers berthed and messed, with cots or bunks because the sweep of the tiller overhead made it impossible to sling hammocks. On the rest of the gun deck a hundred or so six-man messes had to find space to eat between the guns.[29] 'Men are nowhere so crowded in so small a space as in a ship of war,' Captain Philip Patton observed,[30] and crowding was perhaps the greatest hardship of the sea life. Certainly seafaring was physically arduous and dangerous, but the Navy was much less arduous and dangerous than merchantmen and fishing boats, or indeed than trades ashore like mining. The determining feature of life in the Navy was the inescapable psychological pressure of the crowd, and the constant necessity for self-discipline and meticulous organization for comfort and safety. 'It is the confined bird-cage-like space which seamen are obliged to live in,' Captain Francis Liardet wrote, 'which in a measure creates the excitement and uncontrollable spirit when they first go on shore, after having been any length of time without leave.'[31] Even today, when warships are very large and crews are very small, there is something of the same release of tension on going ashore after weeks at sea. In the eighteenth century the alternation of tension and relaxation was fundamental to naval life.

Wise officers therefore relaxed the tight order of shipboard life when it was safe to do so, as Jacob Nagle records:

> Mr Bradley, first lieutenant, gave the ship's company a frolic . . . as much as we pleased to drink and carousing on the quarter deck and dancing and shouting and so great a noise on board of us, the captain of the *Swan* man of war thought there was a mutiny.[32]

On 'crossing the line' of the Tropics or the Equator there was a traditional ceremony when men dressed up as 'King Neptune' and his court came aboard to tax all newcomers 'a bottle and pound' (of spirits and sugar, to make flip) on pain of a ducking.[33] Captain Thomas Pasley of the *Sybil*, crossing the Equator in 1780,

> Mustered the ship's company to know who had and who had not crossed the Line before; found only 44 officers and all that had. Stopped a day's allowance from every one that had not, except those that chose ducking in preference . . . added to the liquor stopped a few gallons, to make double allowance to all, and my liberty even to get drunk if done without noise or quarrelling. Sailors are indeed unaccountables: grog is with them the liquor of life, their *summum bonum*.[34]

This was on a long ocean passage, when the men were drinking watered spirits in place of beer, but even in home waters when beer was freely issued, spirits seem to have been available in most ships, and officers often gave them out as a reward.[35] Brandy was the usual choice, or rum in the West Indies; 'that destructive liquor, Geneva' was less favoured, and the naval physician Thomas Trotter claimed that 'during my residence at Plymouth Dock, towards the conclusion of the late war, I had the satisfaction of getting 200 gin-shops shut up. They were destroying the very vitals of our naval service.'[36]

This was an unusual, not to say quixotic, effort. Most officers and men relaxed in port, and for the men like the officers, relaxation invariably involved drink. Lieutenant James Gardner, an Irish officer serving with an Irish crew ('very quiet when not disturbed'), records with relish the fights between his ship's company and others, and there are other witnesses of similar incidents.[37] Relaxation also of course implied leave. 'The British sailor should sometimes enjoy the society of his mistress, and be permitted to drink his skin full of liquor, and there is no service afterwards that he will not cheerfully undertake,' Captain John Inglefield advised.[38] As before, the Admiralty gave leave to captains, and captains gave leave to their own men, providing them with 'tickets' to prove that they were ashore legitimately. 'Those who are found wandering on shore without such certificates will be deemed stragglers, and

if absent more than twenty-four hours taken up as deserters' in the words of
Captain J. T. Duckworth's order book.[39] In the closing years of the American
War coppering was a new enemy to leave, for it eliminated the frequent
docking which had hitherto been the natural opportunity for it. When ships
were desperately needed and hard-driven, it was natural for the men to be
driven hard as well. Some officers thought about the consequences, but it
seems not many.[40]

In foreign ports captains allowed their men ashore, or allowed bumboats
to approach the ship, in order that their men should replenish their mess
stores.[41] At English Harbour, the naval yard at Antigua, which was free of
sharks, the market women would swim out to ships with fruit and vegetables
to sell floated in a tub before them.[42] At Maio in the Cape Verde Islands,
Captain Pasley, 'allowed a free and general market, both on board and at the
watering place, of which the sailors made most excellent use: very few messes
had less sea stock than three or four pigs, as many fat goats, and half a dozen
of fowls.'[43] For this reason ships often had a great deal of livestock aboard,
and water for the beasts could be a problem.[44] When Rodney's fleet cleared
for action before the battle of the Saintes, one seaman recalled, 'cows, sheep,
hogs, ducks, hen-coops, casks, wood &c were seen floating for miles around
us'.[45] What never left the ship unless she sank was her native population of
rats, often more numerous than the ship's company. In one month in 1800
the rats aboard the *Montagu* destroyed 19 bushels of peas, 60 lbs of flour,
152 lbs of butter, 1,232 lbs of bread, 1,362 lbs of meat, 2,381 lbs of rice and
cheese and 176½ gallons of wine. In the same year the gunner of the *Indefatigable* discovered that rats had eaten 1,361 filled cartridges in the magazine,
leaving her only forty-two. Rats had their attractions nevertheless, at least to
midshipmen, to whom they provided good hunting, and 'nice and delicate
eating . . . full as good as rabbits'.[46]

At sea the comfort and happiness of the crew very much depended on the
organization of the ship, and the tendency was still for captains (and in the
case of Howe, an admiral) to issue order books regulating daily life in steadily
increasing detail.[47] In part this was because they were no longer content to
leave so much to the petty officers to manage in their own fashion. 'Last war,'
Inglefield wrote, referring to the American War,

> there is no doubt that the internal discipline of His Majesty's ships was
> in general brought to as great a degree of perfection, almost, as it is
> capable of receiving . . . This general improvement proceeded from a
> method adopted in every branch of an officer's and sailor's duty, by
> dividing, and quartering the officers with the men, and making them

responsible for that portion of duty allotted them, without noise, or the brutal method of driving the sailors like cattle, with sticks. Whether it were to make or shorten sail, to manoeuvre the ship, to keep the men clean clothed, clean bedded and berthed, this method was practised . . . By a just proportion of labour falling to the lot of each man, instead of the management of it being entrusted to the partiality and brutality of boatswains' mates, the men were kept in better temper; and were less harassed and fatigued in their spirits, as well as in their bodies.[48]

This growing distaste for casual violence was a discernible trend, but certainly not universal. Nagle served in the brig *St Lucia* in 1782, with a scratch crew and a young commander, where 'nothing was to be done without knocking down and thrashing in every duty that was to be done'.[49] The men, like their officers, seem to have been becoming more sensitive to the issue. In the *Hannibal* in 1794 'the men a few days after being on board, finding the boatswain's mates did not carry canes, entered'.[50] The men particularly resented being struck by midshipmen, and some captains would disrate or arrest a midshipman for doing so. Another deterrent to abuse of authority was the real risk of an officer being caught ashore, especially after dark, by men with a grievance.[51] For the historian it is always difficult to generalize about discipline when so much depended on an individual captain, but perhaps a fair summary was the advice given by Joshua Davis, an American seaman impressed during the American War, to his fellow-countrymen who might find themselves in a similar situation: stay quiet and sober, and 'you will stand a good chance of receiving favours from your officers'.[52] 'I should think myself criminally culpable and divested of all humanity was I to neglect pleading the cause of so many brave and to their country valuable men,' as Duckworth wrote in 1780, which was probably a fair indication of motive. Humanity came first, but he had not forgotten how valuable the men were to their country, and to himself.[53]

A different light, however, can be cast on naval discipline in this period by considering mutiny. Mutinies still occurred which were never reported to authority, because the captains were not anxious to draw attention to their problems, or because the officers regarded them as justified.[54] What was new was that some mutinies occurred during the American War, for entirely traditional reasons and within the traditional rules, which were suppressed by authority and the leaders severely punished. This happened to the mutineers of the *Defiance* in May 1779, objecting to a new captain (Maximilian Jacobs) who was a foreigner with an unsavoury reputation; it happened to the men of a squadron ordered to North America in April 1780 who mutinied for pay, though they proved their legal entitlement under the 1758 Navy Act; and it happened to the men of the *Santa Monica* next year who complained 'of being knocked down with speaking trumpets, handspikes, blades and oars'.[55] There does not seem to have been any formal change of official policy, but it is understandable that in the desperate situation of this war when every ship was needed at sea, and at a time of acute political tension, the more relaxed attitudes of an earlier generation went overboard. What is harder to understand is the severity with which some of the Portsmouth mutinies of 1783 were suppressed. These were classic 'demobilization' mutinies such as had occurred at the end of previous wars when everyone wanted to be paid off at once. There was no serious operational pressure, and with a little patience and understanding the problems would have solved themselves as the conditions of the peacetime labour market returned. Instead both Howe's and Keppel's Admiralties showed a marked absence of patience and understanding, and six men were hanged. It looks as though authority was rewriting the old rules.[56] One far too notorious mutiny need not long detain us. The seizure of the *Bounty* in the Pacific by one of her watchkeeping officers in 1791, like the officer-led mutiny of the *Chesterfield*, was a completely untypical affair which tells us only about the persons concerned. Lieutenant Bligh was an outstanding seaman with an ungovernable temper and no idea how to get the best out of his officers; Fletcher Christian was a weak and unstable young man who could not stand being shouted at.[57]

A growing number of captains (Bligh among them) now kept three watches rather than two, allowing each man one uninterrupted night's sleep in three. This meant fewer hands to work the ship without calling the watches below, so thoughtful admirals like Howe gave notice of when they intended to tack or wear, and tried to avoid it at night. With striking unanimity, captains of very varying disposition, including those like Prince William Henry who had a bad reputation for vexatious trifles, insisted that 'the people [are] never to be interrupted at their meals but on the most pressing occasion'.[58]

The Navy was conservative in its habits, and both officers and men continued to dine at noon or soon after well into the nineteenth century, long after fashionable dinners ashore had drifted later in the day. The men were allowed three-quarters of an hour for breakfast and an hour and a half for dinner.[59] The surgeon James Ker, evidently not overworked in a healthy ship, described his daily routine aboard the *Elizabeth* on passage to the West Indies in 1778 thus:

Until we get into warm weather our time for rising is seven or half after seven o'clock. Breakfast at eight. At nine I see my patients which takes up half an hour or an hour. From that to eleven generally read or write in my cabin, then take a walk on deck, give the captain an account of the sick. After having stretched my limbs, see what the admiral is doing and what the fleet, how we steer and how the wind blows, I come down to my cabin again and take up a book again till the drum beating 'The Roast Beef of Old England' warns me to dinner, of which I have generally a fore-feeling in my stomach. After despatching this necessary piece of business and the grog being finished, the remainder of my time till supper is spent variously in reading, writing, card-playing, backgammon, walking or conversation as humour leads. From supper time at 8 o'clock till bed-time is spent in chit-chat over our grog drinking.[60]

Most officers had much more to do. Apart from navigating and working the ship, keeping her clean and organized, there were constant drills and practices. Gun-drill was stressed by almost all admirals, though it was usually 'dry', without powder or shot, and Boscawen seems to have been unusual in training his men to fire at a mark, which implied a fighting range of several hundred yards. Howe stressed the importance of a high initial rate of fire, something whose tactical value was to be of great importance in the coming Great Wars.[61]

There seems to have been a slow increase in formality in naval life. Drums were beaten at mealtimes, sometimes at dawn and dusk. Ceremonies were observed of hoisting colours at dawn, firing the evening gun, and firing royal salutes ('Spithead Fights') on important occasions. The divisional system was usually marked on Sunday by a muster of the whole ship's company, the officers in correct uniform and the men wearing their best clothes, clean and shaved. 'The sailors made a very decent and sedate appearance, and were remarkably well clothed and neat in their apparel. About 450 of them attended divine service this morning,' recorded Howe's secretary Ambrose Serle aboard the *Eagle* going out to North America in 1776.[62] A church service, however, conducted by a chaplain at sea, was still very rare during the American War. Captains had long dressed their barge crews in some sort of livery, even if it was only a distinctive cap, and a few captains (inevitably led by Prince William Henry) were moving towards imposing some sort of uniform on the whole ship's company. A growing number of ships possessed bands, and captains were beginning to go to pains and expense to acquire musicians. Music was excellent for morale, especially in the evenings when the men danced and the boys skylarked.[63]

The single major innovation in the manpower and social life of the Navy in the mid-eighteenth century was creation of the permanent corps of Marines under full Admiralty control in 1755. 5,700 men were organized in fifty independent companies divided between three divisions, at Portsmouth, Plymouth and Chatham. There were hardly any ranks above major, and most of those which existed were sinecures given as rewards to senior sea officers. Marine commissions were not purchased, the social standing of Marine officers was somewhat below that of both army and Navy, and the Marines had little of the sea officers' character of professional experts. Most seem to have been middle-class boys, with relatively few born gentlemen and no peers. Their half-pay was too small to live on, so like junior sea officers they had to seek jobs in peacetime, though Second Lieutenant Robert Binsley was struck off in 1766 'for having engaged himself as an actor at one of the theatres'.[64] Promotion was slow and usually by seniority, but some started as second lieutenants no older than ten or twelve, and the early war generation of the 1790s rose fast. Relations with the sea officers were not always easy. They resented idle Marines with nothing to do but play the flute and disturb their watchkeeping messmates; Marines resented the superior rank and prospects of the sailors. A row between Captain Sir James Wallace and Lieutenant James Bourne in 1782, which led to Bourne assaulting his captain in the street and being sent to prison, aroused some ill-feeling among Marine officers who identified with their colleague.[65]

The private Marines were similar to British infantrymen of the day, mostly from southern and Midland England, with a proportion of Irishmen, and (during the Great Wars) a considerable number of foreigners, many of them former (non-French) prisoners of war. Their work was mainly to pull and haul as part of the unskilled workforce of the ship, and to provide sentries guarding sensitive parts of the ship (the magazines, some storerooms, the captain's cabin). In action they fought as infantrymen, and they were available to do the same in landing parties if required. They were encouraged to learn the seaman's trade, but it was forbidden to order them aloft against their will. Like landmen in general, they were the butt of seamen's jests and scorn, and might therefore side with the officers against the seamen if there were trouble, but this was by no means automatic. Since there were often not enough Marines, ordinary infantrymen were sometimes drafted on board men-of-war, where they seem to have mastered their duties quickly enough. Some at least enjoyed the change of scene, and the plentiful naval rations. 'A man may live here very well, no man being stinted to beer, for he may drink what he pleases,' noted Corporal William Todd aboard the *Thetis* in 1757.[66] The 97th Foot fought with distinction at the Dogger Bank action in 1781, the soldiers filling the places of wounded seamen in the guns' crews.[67]

As before there were often a number of women amongst those living aboard. Their presence was unofficial, and they made their own arrangments with the purser for food, but many captains were content that they should be there. The wives of warrant and petty officers, older than the young men who made up the bulk of the ship's company, might have a steadying influence, and there were many practical ways in which they could make themselves useful, and earn an income aboard, by washing, sewing or looking after children. In 1780, by Admiralty order ('there being no precedent for the relief of persons not borne on the ship's books') a seaman's wife was awarded a Chatham Chest pension for a wound received in action.[68] In 1794 some Irish landmen sent for their widowed mother to join them afloat. Young women running away to sea in disguise to follow their sweethearts – a theme beloved of eighteenth-century romantic fiction – occasionally existed in real life. Sometimes officers kept their mistresses aboard, but this seems to have been mainly in peacetime, and in small or distant ships, remote from an admiral's eye. In port things were always more relaxed, and a captain's wife and children might live aboard a guardship. The men always had women aboard in port if they did not have leave to go ashore. In the West Indies women slaves came aboard; 'poor things! and all to obtain a bellyful of victuals'.[69] One related subject beloved of some modern writers deserves a brief mention: homosexuality seems to have been rare, intensely disliked by the men, and very difficult to conceal afloat.[70]

Unfortunately there has been virtually no research undertaken into what one might call the female half of the naval community as a whole: not the minority of women who went to sea, but the wives and mothers who stayed at home, bringing up small children, earning their living as best they might while their menfolk were at sea, enduring years of absence and uncertainty. They represent an enormous void of ignorance, and our knowledge of the social history of the Navy will never be complete until someone fills it.[71]

TWENTY-SEVEN

Science versus Technology

Ships 1714–1815

It was for long an article of faith among naval historians that eighteenth-century British warships were inferior to their French and Spanish opponents, because British shipwrights remained wedded to craft traditions, while their Continental rivals were men of education who applied mathematics and science to the solution of their problems. This judgement flattered, and sometimes still flatters, a range of agreeable prejudices. It fitted the eighteenth-century upper classes' admiration for France as the home of social glamour and prestige. It expressed British sea officers' conviction that as men of honour they were both morally and practically superior to civilian technicians; it magnified their courage and judgement when they won, and excused their failures when they lost. It also increased their earnings when they were trying to sell their prizes to the Navy Board with a glowing endorsement of their virtues.[1]

There are, nevertheless, several good reasons to reject the inferiority of British design out of hand. It is essentially an explanation of how France and Spain won the naval wars – which is not what we need to explain. In the century from 1714 more than half of all French warships (ships of the line and frigates) ended their careers sunk or captured, and the proportion rose steadily. In just over twenty years of warfare from 1793 to 1815, the French built 133 ships of the line and 127 frigates; and lost 112 and 126 respectively to enemy action or stress of weather. On average they lost a ship a month for twenty years.[2] At first sight this does not suggest superior design. Moreover the comparison between 'good' French and 'bad' British design rests on the naive assumption that the two were directly comparable, that British and French designers were building the same size and types of ship, to fulfil the same functions – in other words that the strategic situations of the two countries were the same. This in fact is what many naval historians do assume: that the Bourbon powers, and subsequently Revolutionary and Imperial France, built their navies, and had to build their navies, to mount a frontal challenge to Britain for command of the sea, so that the opposing fleets may be considered as mirror images of one another. Command of the sea was the only thing worth striving for in the 'Second Hundred Years' War', and Britain was the only enemy worth mentioning: in this view the historical function of the French and Spanish navies was to provide the Royal Navy with suitable opponents. These assumptions are extremely unsafe. As we have seen, there are good grounds for thinking that Maurepas and Patiño were not planning to fight pitched battles with the British, and did not need ships designed for that purpose. The proper question to ask of all ship designs is not how well they compared with one another, but how well they corresponded to each country's strategic priorities, and how wisely those priorities had been chosen.[3]

Nor is it very useful to ask how 'scientific' the designs and designers of different countries were. It is still possible to encounter historians who put weight on the changing titles of the shipbuilders. In France 'master carpenters' (*maîtres charpentiers*) became 'master constructors' (*maîtres constructeurs*) and then simply 'constructors', before advancing to 'constructor-engineers' (*ingénieurs-constructeurs*) and finally becoming known as 'naval architects' (*architectes navales*), whereas in Britain warships were still being designed in the mid-nineteenth century by persons styled 'master shipwrights'. The retention of a name drawn from the vulgar tongue, it is implied, must obviously indicate an unlettered craftsman confined to traditional rules, while a name derived from Latin must bespeak logic and education, and one based on Greek marks the summit of enlightened science. Perhaps it is still necessary to point out that the different titles of shipbuilders tell us something about their social aspirations, but nothing whatever about their working methods. Though British ship designers, like British professionals in comparable subjects such as architecture and engineering, continued to learn their business by apprenticeship until well into the nineteenth century, and though they were expected to spend a period working with their tools to understand the fundamentals of shipwrightry, the training they received in the mould lofts and drawing offices of the dockyards seems to have been in most respects as sophisticated as anything available in France.[4]

There was, however, a real and important difference between Britain and France in attitudes towards 'natural philosophy', meaning science and fundamental knowledge in general. Mathematics lay at the heart of contemporary science, but mathematics was not an intellectually or socially neutral language. The mathematics of the 'philosopher' was pure mathematics: geometry, algebra, calculus. It was pure because it was abstract, and because it was essential to true science, that process of deriving universal truths from first principles, which Cartesianism prescribed. In social terms, this was the mathematics of the gentleman; one fully qualified for philosophy because he had no necessity to earn a living. It was very different from the vulgar utility of what in English was called 'mixed mathematics', the working calculations of men who had to work: men like bankers, tradesmen and navigators. The primacy of theory over practice, and of science over technology, was characteristic of France in the eighteenth century. The philosopher-mathematician alone was qualified to unravel the knottiest problems, and by tracing the fundamental machinery of nature he demonstrated his superior intellectual and social standing. 'Tracing' is the precise word, for geometry was a pure form of pure mathematics, and those whose subject could be expressed in geometrical terms enjoyed the highest scientific standing. It was a fundamental article of the Enlightenment faith that the philosopher was entitled and obliged to correct the work of the craftsman – this indeed was part of the official duties of the French *Académie Royale des Sciences*. As philosophers, gentlemen and mathematicians, its members were necessarily superior to mere practical experience. In naval architecture as in other domains, it was the duty of officers and philosophers to correct the vulgar errors of the shipwrights, by the application of pure mathematics.[5]

The result was a series of studies by Leonhard Euler, Pierre Bouguer and others, deriving their prestige precisely from their remoteness from practical shipbuilding. The foundations they laid were built upon over the next two centuries to develop the modern science of naval architecture, but in the eighteenth century they had little to offer the shipwright. Most of their effort was devoted to the fashionable subject of hydrodynamics, and particularly the problem of the resistance of water to a moving hull, but since they ignored the existence of skin friction, which we now know to constitute virtually the whole of resistance at the speeds of which these ships were capable, their work had no practical value. More useful study was devoted to hydrostatics, which yielded the important definition of the metacentre, but French efforts to apply it in practice were not uniformly successful. The *Scipion*, *Hercule* and *Pluton*, launched at Rochefort in 1778 by François-Guillaume Clairin-Deslauriers, were among the first large French warships to have been designed on the basis of stability calculations. Unfortunately the sums were wrong, and the ships were too tender to carry sail. Much of their stowage had to be replaced by ballast before they could go to sea, sharply reducing their usefulness. Whatever else 'science' may have been doing in the eighteenth century, it was not an unmixed blessing to French naval architects.[6]

One further general point about warship design needs to be made. Though ships may not have been directly comparable, naval architecture was highly competitive. Constructors constantly studied the designs of rivals at home and abroad, looking for ideas to borrow. In France and the Netherlands, so much less centralized in naval administration than Britain, these comparisons were often internal, between the rival traditions of the Mediterranean and Atlantic yards of France, and the admiralties of the United Provinces, but everywhere they were also international. All European navies were deeply involved in technical espionage, and in peacetime the French navy made a practice of sending its most talented constructors on extended visits to foreign, especially British, ports to learn everything they could. There is a particularly full and impressive report from the 1737 visit of Blaise Ollivier, master shipwright of Brest, with detailed comments on British and Dutch shipbuilding practice, much of which he admired and some of which he copied. All the European navies engaged in similar activities. In wartime they studied prizes; in peacetime they fished in the international market for warship designers. In 1727 the Admiralty of Amsterdam secured the services of three English shipwrights, with whose help it adopted 'English-style' designs – though naturally Rotterdam and Zealand declined to follow suit. In 1748 Ensenada, preparing to reform Spanish naval construction, sent Captain Jorge Juan on a major mission of industrial espionage to England. 'His journey will be most useful to us,' the minister wrote, 'for in technical matters we are extremely ignorant, and what is worse, without realizing it.'[7] Juan returned with both information and a considerable number of shipwrights and artificers for the Spanish yards. English or Irish shipwrights became master shipwrights of Cadiz, Havana, Cartagena, Guarnizo and Ferrol. Throughout the eighteenth century the Danish navy, undoubtedly the world leader in technical intelligence, systematically collected copies of secret warship designs from every admiralty in Europe.[8]

What seems to have been rare if not completely unknown in any navy was the literal copying of complete designs. Though statesmen and sea officers, impressed by foreign ships and ignorant of naval architecture, sometimes ordered ships to be built after the lines of a prize, it was in practice difficult if not impossible to do so. British hulls, for example, were more heavily timbered than French, so that a ship built in a British dockyard to the exact lines of a French design would displace more and float deeper. To maintain the same draught and freeboard, the British designer would have to adjust the lines, and so the ship would no longer be the same. In such cases the British designer might allow his superiors to believe that he had 'copied' a French design, or he might attempt to educate them in the complexities of naval architecture. Besides the lines, many other aspects of a foreign design would be changed to reflect British practice and requirements. The result might be a ship greatly influenced by foreign models, but it was never a slavish copy.[9]

All these general considerations form a necessary background to any history of British warship design in the eighteenth century, but for thirty years, from the accession of George I in 1714 to the outbreak of war with France in 1744, British warships evolved slowly with little influence from outside. There were no Parliamentary votes for shipbuilding, so the practice of 'great rebuilds' continued, though some of these 'rebuilt' ships were constructed years after their former selves had been broken up, in different dockyards, and without necessarily using any old timbers. The 1719 Establishment in principle dictated dimensions in detail, but in practice there seems to have been a slow but steady growth in dimensions. Some ships were built to the Admiralty's 1733 proposal for a new and larger establishment, though it was never officially adopted, and the Ordnance Board blocked the heavier armaments which the Admiralty also wanted. Then the capture of the Spanish seventy-gun *Princesa* in April 1740, which took three British seventies six hours of hard fighting, caused considerable shock in Britain, and led to the adoption of a slightly larger 1741 Establishment, in conjunction with the heavier 1733 armament scheme. Soon afterwards the outbreak of the French war brought further shocks.[10]

The main conservative forces affecting the British fleet were political and financial rather than technical. Neither the Navy nor Ordnance Board was enthusiastic about novelties which Parliament was not likely to favour, and still less likely to pay for. The Walpole administration kept up a large fleet, on paper and to a considerable extent in reality, and no one in the political world looked beyond numbers of ships to consider issues of quality and size. The Establishments were more an expression of this situation than an obstacle in themselves. The redoubtable Sir Jacob Acworth, Surveyor of the Navy from 1715 to 1749, did not take kindly to interference in the Navy Board's business. 'I have been in the Service fifty-seven years,' he commented in April 1740 on complaints from Mathews,

> and remember that the ships in King Charles's time always decayed as fast, I am sure much faster, than they do now. But at that time, and long since, officers were glad to go to sea and would not suffer their ships to be complained of and torn to pieces in search for hidden defects.[11]

The admirals resented it, and many would have agreed with Vernon that 'the arbitrary power a half-experienced and half-judicious Surveyor of the Navy had been entrusted with had in my opinion half ruined the Navy'.[12] But Acworth was no unthinking reactionary. He designed a number of ships whose underwater lines were based on theoretical concepts developed by Sir Isaac Newton. They were not a great success – a little more conservatism might have spared the Navy an unhelpful intervention from abstract science – but in many respects Acworth was a designer of talent. His ideas about the unhappy three-decker eighty-gun ships of the 1690s, and indeed about all the older British designs, stressed the importance of reducing topweight to improve stability and weatherliness. This was completely sound, and the admirals' reactions may not have been unconnected with the fact that the tophamper Acworth wanted to remove consisted largely of their cabins.[13]

The Bedford Admiralty arrived in December 1744 determined to reform British ship design together with everything else. Their chosen instrument of reform was a committee of senior officers under the chairmanship of Sir John Norris, directed to draw up a new establishment, and specifically to replace the three-decker eighties with a two-decker seventy-four-gun design. Although the committee consisted mainly of members of the Board or known opponents of Acworth, it was entirely dependent on him and the master shipwrights for technical advice, and proved as much a brake as a spur to progress. It moved some way in the direction of greater size, but flatly refused to abandon the small three-decker. The ships of the 1745 Establishment turned out to share many of the deficiencies of their predecessors: cramped, crank, overgunned and leewardly.[14]

This impasse was broken by the sensation caused by the prizes of the two battles of Finisterre, above all the new French seventy-four *Invincible*. Maurepas' new fleet was built around these seventy-four-gun two-deckers, with a lower-deck battery of twenty-eight 36-pounders and a main-deck battery of thirty 18-pounders. Though the *Invincible* was by no means the largest in her class (the *Magnanime*, taken next year, was considerably bigger) she was 50 per cent larger in tonnage than the standard British seventy-gun Third Rate, and fired a broadside 75 per cent heavier.[15] The differences between these British and French ships arose almost entirely from the difference of size. Naval architecture is a question of balance: if two competent designers build rival ships of the same tonnage and type, one can only gain a marked advantage in any one quality, such as speed or armament, by sacrificing the others. Even a modest increase in size, however, permits a significant improvement in quality all round, and a 50 per cent increase ought to translate into overwhelming superiority. But increased size naturally means increased cost. British naval agitation to match or copy French designs was not so much a technical as a political campaign, directed at Parliament, to finance bigger and more expensive ships.[16]

The Finisterre victories came too late in the war to have an immediate effect, but in 1750 the Sandwich Admiralty secured the Privy Council's authorization to vary the 1745 Establishment as they thought fit, which effectively marks the end of the British shipbuilding establishments. In 1755, just as the outbreak of the Seven Years' War released the Navy Estimates from peacetime financial limits, Anson was able to appoint a Surveyor of the Navy of his own mind, Sir Thomas Slade. From this date the Navy was in process of rapid transformation into a superficially French-style line of battle based on seventy-four-gun two-deckers.[17]

There remained important differences, however, between British and French warships. British ships continued to be somewhat smaller in tonnage and shorter, but more heavily timbered and fastened. Their rig and lines performed best in going to windward, and in heavy weather. They were built to stand the strain of prolonged sea-time at all seasons, they were stored for long cruises, and they were built to fight. They were also built to last; relatively cheap to construct and maintain, they were the rational choice of a navy which meant to surpass its enemies both in numbers and in stamina. Their rig, masts, sails, cordage, blocks, pumps, cables, steering gear and fittings of every kind were greatly superior in design and quality. French ships of all classes were lightly built of inferior timber, fastened with nails instead of trenails, but their very long hulls were highly stressed in a seaway. In fine weather these 'battle-cruisers' with their long hulls and taunt rigs were fast off the wind, but their performance fell off rapidly when close hauled, or when wind and sea rose. What was worse French designers seem to have had something of an obsession with reducing the depth and weight of the hull, which made their ships light and buoyant, but directly weakened resistance to hogging, sagging and racking strains. Worst of all they actually believed that the working of the timbers increased the speed of the ship. Consequently these ships had high building costs, high maintenance costs and short working lives, which made France's low investment in docks and yards all the more expensive. In close action French ships with their light scantlings were a death trap.[18]

Some French observers were aware of some of the deficiencies of their designs.[19] A warship, one constructor declared,

> ought to be fast, so everything is normally sacrificed to that. They are
> lightly timbered in order to be buoyant and carry their guns high; they

have fewer and weaker fastenings because the play of the timbers makes for speed ... it is to be feared that these principles lead the king's constructors to build ships of the line which lack some of the qualities of a real man-of-war. They are afraid of losing their reputations, because the height of success for them is a fast ship which carries her guns high.[20]

French dockyard officers had to pick up the pieces, literally. The constructors, complained the comte de Roquefeuil, commanding at Brest in 1771,

are all frauds. They build ships which are very light, very long and very weakly fastened because they sacrifice everything to speed and that is the way to get it. The first cruise gives the ship and her builder their reputation ... [afterwards] we have to rebuild them here at great expense for a second commission by which time they have lost their boasted speed.[21]

It is not even clear that sacrificing so much to hull forms which were fast in certain circumstances was actually the best way to get high speed in practice. Modern studies suggest that the possible differences in hull form, within the inherent limitations of wooden ship construction, cannot account for the wide differences in recorded performance. The smoothness of the underwater hull, which was a matter of cleaning or coppering (and hence of docks), and the infinite variations of rig and trim which were under the captain's control, were almost certainly worth more. This explains how frequently British ships were able to catch French ones even in conditions which should have favoured them, and why French prizes taken into British service seem generally to have been faster after capture than before. Moreover prizes were usually significantly altered. The ships were always rerigged and rearmed, and the holds (especially of frigates) were rebuilt to give increased stowage to allow for prolonged cruising. The hanging of the decks, the siting of hatchways and magazines, the stowage of boats and booms, the position and design of pumps and capstans were often changed. These alterations produced substantially different ships.[22]

Mention of frigates calls us back to the other important innovation in mid-eighteenth-century warship design. The new French battle-fleet of two-decker sixty-fours, seventy-fours and eighties were unquestionably built to a common plan imposed from Versailles, though the actual hull designs differed from yard to yard. Small cruisers, however, were beneath the minister's notice, and the constructors were left to build more or less what they thought fit. It seems therefore that the *Médée* of 1740, commonly regarded as the first of the 'true' or classic frigate type which formed so prominent a part of all navies by the late eighteenth century, was a product of Ollivier's unaided genius. The essence of the frigate in this sense was a small two-decker cruising warship mounting no guns on the lower deck. This made it possible to carry a battery of relatively heavy pieces on the main deck, high above the waterline, where they could be fought in bad weather, as well as lighter guns on quarterdeck and forecastle.[23] This general arrangement was not new, in French or British service. In 1689 Torrington had proposed

> that these new frigates should for rendering them more useful for their Majesty's service, be built in such a manner that they should have but one size of ordnance flush, and that to be upon the upper deck, whereby they will be able to carry them out in all weathers.[24]

The resulting class of Fifth Rates were soon overloaded with guns, in the British style. They were succeeded in 1719 by a class of Sixth Rates carrying a battery of twenty 6-pounders (ten ports a side) in the same arrangement, but they too tended to become overloaded with guns as British officers watched with concern the growth in the power and size of foreign warships. When the outbreak of war with France in 1744 exposed British trade to attack by French warships and privateers, the small, slow and cramped British cruisers aroused widespread dissatisfaction in the Navy.[25] Once again it was French prizes which provided the leverage to dislodge the Navy Board's opposition. 'As all our frigates sail wretchedly,' Anson wrote to Bedford in April 1747,

> I entreat your Grace that an order may be immediately sent from your Board to the Navy Board to direct Mr Slade the Builder at Plymouth to take off the body of the French *Tyger* with the utmost exactness, and that two frigates may be ordered to be built with all possible dispatch, of her dimensions and as similar to her as the builder's art will allow; let Slade have the building of one of them.[26]

The Navy Board mounted a stout defence of the small forty-gun two-decker as superior to French cruisers like the privateer *Tigre* to which Anson referred, and they had some grounds to do so, for the French designs had all the characteristic French weaknesses, being very long and flimsy. When Ollivier's *Médée* was taken in 1744 the Navy Board refused to buy her, so she was sold as a privateer, and soon afterwards fell apart in the open sea.[27] This was not what the Navy wanted, and in spite of Anson's request for exact copies of a prize, this was not what it got. The visible superiority of French cruisers, at least in speed, provided the Bedford Board with the leverage it needed to overcome the Navy Board's resistance, and the co-operation of dockyard shipwrights of a younger generation than Acworth provided the technical backing – but what they produced were not exact copies of French designs. It is clear from the surviving correspondence that during the 1740s the shipwrights were carefully comparing prizes with the fastest existing British designs (notably the yacht *Royal Caroline*), and using the untutored enthusiasm of Anson and his colleagues to back a move from the old short two-deckers to the first British 'true frigates', with longer hulls (eleven or twelve ports a side) giving a twenty-two- or twenty-four-gun battery, initially of 9-pounders. These very successful ships were inspired by French prizes in a political as much as a technical sense. The differences of British from French design philosophy and performance were even clearer in the case of frigates than of ships of the line.[28]

Using the standard shorthand method by which all navies classified their ships by the number of guns, the early British frigate classes were mostly twenty-eights, which were followed in the Seven Years' War by thirty-twos. In the case of frigates, however, the number of guns is not a good measure, partly because it included the light guns on quarterdeck and forecastle which could easily be changed, but mainly because it concealed the most important factor, the calibre of the main battery. Though a thirty-two does not sound much more powerful than a twenty-eight, the twenty-eights had a 9-pounder main armament and the thirty-twos, 12-pounders, giving a broadside 50 per cent heavier. These ships in turn were followed in the American War by the first 18-pounder frigates, rated as thirty-sixes or thirty-eights, but with more than double the broadside of the twenty-eights. It is therefore most useful to refer to frigates, as many contemporaries did, by their main battery calibre, and especially to distinguish the 18-pounder 'heavy frigates' from their predecessors.[29]

The smaller cruisers known as sloops developed in parallel with the frigate, of which they were essentially miniature versions with one less deck, carrying their battery on the open upper deck. By the time of the American War many of the smaller sloops were rigged as brigs rather than ships. The two-masted rig economized significantly in manpower and was perfectly satisfactory for most purposes, though more vulnerable to damage in action. As an alternative it was possible to rig vessels of this size (200 tons or so) as cutters or schooners, which were even more economical in manpower, but whose very big sails required expert handling. Smallest of all sea-going warships were the gunbrigs and gunboats, built in considerable numbers for Channel patrols and local defence during the Great Wars.[30]

The Royal Navy's transformation in the 1750s and 1760s into a superficially French-style fleet based on seventy-four-gun line-of-battle ships and 12-pounder frigates was a belated recognition that the Dutch Wars were over.

Political rather than technical weakness had arrested, or at least slowed, the evolution of British warships into types suitable for the oceanic warfare of the eighteenth century. The ships which Sir Thomas Slade designed during his fifteen years as Surveyor (1755–1771) were admirably adapted to Britain's strategic requirements. Seaworthy, weatherly and tough, with stowage for long cruises, they were the ships needed to dominate European waters in all weathers, and to reach out if necessary to distant waters. By common consent, Slade was the greatest British naval architect of the century. His First Rate the *Victory*, one of the fastest three-deckers in the world, was the darling of British admirals for half a century, constantly kept in repair when a lesser ship might have been broken up and replaced. The Navy was still building ships to Slade's designs well into the nineteenth century, and it was generally agreed (even by themselves) that his successors, though competent designers, never matched his genius.[31]

It is important to understand, however, that at no stage from the 1750s was the Navy building as many ships as it needed. As the century progressed and the dockyards came to be devoted almost completely to repairs, prizes made an essential contribution to keeping up the numbers of the Royal Navy.[32] Even if French ships were unsatisfactory, it was necessary to use them, and the Navy Board reduced its prices in proportion to their lower usefulness. There was moreover a high political value in filling one's fleet with obviously foreign names, every one an advertisement for a victory. Many of these names became traditional in British service, even names like *Foudroyant* and *Téméraire* which mean nothing in English. At this day (2004) the Royal Navy still has three ships in service named after Louis XIV.[33]

While the British were evolving new warship designs with the help of foreign borrowings, the Spanish navy was doing the same. The English and Irish constructors recruited in the 1740s were replaced twenty years later by French builders, as Spain's foreign policy became aligned with France's, and they in turn were succeeded in the 1780s by Spanish naval architects whose products were regarded by many British officers as the finest in the world. Spanish ships of the line were big, handsome, very well built and long-lasting, though not particularly fast.[34] Meanwhile the French navy was not evolving. In the American War France had succeeded for the first time in imposing the sort of long-range cruising war, with a maximum of movement and a minimum of fighting, which favoured French designs. This confirmed the French navy's already high sense of the superiority of its ships, and led in 1786 to the adoption of what amounted to an establishment, fixing the designs of all French warships. This was a political and scientific rather than technical or administrative move, the ultimate triumph of the gentleman philosopher (in this case the ex-artillery officer and geometer the chevalier de Borda) over the dockyard shipwrights. Borda could not design a ship himself, but he found a talented young constructor in need of a patron, Jacques-Noël Sané, who was ready to do what he was told. The Borda-Sané 'establishment' ossified French warship design into the 1820s.[35]

Only a few French experts seem to have had some awareness of the dangers of immobility. Captain the comte de Kersaint, who visited England in 1785, urged that:

> We must copy the workmanship of their shipwrights whose exact joints contribute so much to the longevity of their ships; we must copy the seamanlike proportions of their masts, the cut of their staysails, the strength of their rigging, the perfection of their blocks and cordage. We need their capstans, their cables, above all their anchors which hold better than ours. We must study their shiphandling, and copy their distribution of men for working ship. We must try to adopt their discipline and internal organization, that spirit of order and obedience without which there can be no navy or army.[36]

Sané's rival Pierre-Alexandre Forfait, who was in England in 1788, admired many details of British shipbuilders' work, and regarded them as 'more expert than ours' in construction, if not design.[37] He was especially dissatisfied with the extremely taunt French rigs, which were demanding in manpower, and destructive of the seakeeping, stability and weatherliness of the ships. All this was true, but the official Borda-Sané line was that the French navy had achieved perfection, and nothing could or should be changed.[38] On a summer's day in light airs a French ship fresh off the stocks still showed to fine advantage: 'I never saw vessels sail as they,' as Captain Lord Cochrane wrote to his commander-in-chief, explaining how his sloop had been captured: 'everything is calculated for the Mediterranean, light sails, small ropes, prodigious masts and yards . . .' – but this was a recipe for disaster in heavy weather.[39]

The transformation of the British fleet in the mid-century required something like a revolution in attitudes. Afterwards, the Admiralty and Navy Board seem to have been more open to technical innovations great and small, including new types of ship and vessel. The 1757 landings on the coast of France, for example, revealed that ships' boats were inadequate for large troop landings. On 7 April 1758 the Admiralty approved a design for a new type of 'flat-bottom boat' or landing craft. On the 26th the Board saw the first boat in action at Woolwich, and ordered twenty to be built for the forthcoming expedition. On 23 May the flat-boats were ready at Portsmouth, and on 8 June they led the landing at Cancale. From the issuing of the first sketch design for the new type to its first use in action had taken two months. These flat boats became a standard part of the equipment of all British amphibious operations.[40]

In guns, as we have seen, the Ordnance Board grappled for much of the century with the problems of poor design, compounded by the industrial and technical consequences of the collapse of the Wealden iron foundries. There was no change in the basic patterns of naval guns until the American War, but there was a valuable technical innovation: gunlocks. Great guns had been fired since the sixteenth century with a linstock, which was a length of burning slowmatch held in a stick. Having pierced the cartridge in the gun, and poured priming powder into the touch-hole, the gun-captain touched his linstock to the priming powder to fire the gun. This was slow and dangerous and made accurate shooting from a moving ship impossible since the gun had to be fired from the side and did not reliably go off at once. Gunlocks were first issued not later than 1745, but spread only slowly, mainly it seems because they could not be fitted to the older patterns of gun. As late as the American War it seems to have been unusual for a ship's whole armament to be fitted with locks. The gunlock, which was simply a modified form of the firing mechanism of a flintlock musket, was used in conjunction with a quill or tin tube filled with priming powder, which was pushed down the touch-hole to pierce the cartridge. With no loose priming powder the process of priming was quicker and safer, and the gun could be fired with a lanyard by the gun-captain standing in the rear, beyond the recoil but positioned to sight along the gun. This was an important aid to fast and disciplined firing, still not generally adopted in the French navy at the time of Trafalgar.[41]

The first important innovation in gun design was also introduced during the American War. One of the new foundries established in the 1760s, at Carron, near Falkirk, developed an entirely new type of gun intended for the defence of merchant ships. The 'carronade' was a short, light gun with a large calibre but a very small charge. It could easily be handled by a few men, the small charge meant low recoil forces and allowed a simple swivel mounting, and at short range the large shot with low muzzle velocity had a formidable 'smashing' effect. Loaded with grape or canister instead, the carronade was a deadly weapon against boarders at close quarters. The Carron Company built up a healthy market during the American War among merchant ships seeking defence against privateers. It was harder to persuade the Navy that it might have a use for a short-range gun, and to persuade the Ordnance Board to deal again with a company which had acquired a reputation for incompetence and sharp practice. The company overcame these disadvantages with the powerful advocacy of Charles Middleton, a fellow-Scot (and possibly a shareholder). He in turn persuaded Sandwich, and in the teeth of determined opposition from the Ordnance Board and many of the admirals, they succeeded in having carronades mounted in a number of ships, usually in place of the light guns on quarterdeck and forecastle. The result was some spectacular victories, notably in September 1782, when the new 18-pounder frigate *Hébé* surrendered to the elderly forty-four *Rainbow*, which had been experimentally rearmed entirely with carronades. This was the fruit of surprise, and experience was to show that a ship with no long guns was very vulnerable to being attacked at long range, but as a supplement to a conventional main battery, especially for frigates, the carronade was a considerable addition of strength. Moreover French gun-foundries were unable to match the carronade for more than twenty years. Here, as in so many other areas of naval warfare, it was British technology rather than French science which made the difference in war.[42]

The new Blomefield guns, and the new carronades, had reached the whole Navy by the end of the French Revolutionary Wars, though as late as the battle of Copenhagen in 1801 there were serious casualties from the bursting of guns of the old Armstrong pattern. The new cylinder gunpowder was on general issue from 1803, its greater explosive force requiring a reduction in powder charges. During the Napoleonic War a number of experimental lightweight guns were produced, intended to combine some of the advantages of carronades and long guns, but in action they proved unsatisfactory.[43] A completely new weapon in European warfare was the rocket, as designed by William Congreve, and first tried in action against Boulogne in 1806. The rocket proved to be exceedingly inaccurate, but an effective incendiary weapon against large fixed targets, and frightening to horses or inexperienced troops.[44]

During the Great Wars with France, while French warship design stagnated, British designs continued to develop. During the six years (December 1794 to February 1801) that Lord Spencer was First Lord of the Admiralty, there was a clear tendency for the size of British ships to grow. Under his successor John Jervis, Lord St Vincent (1801–4) there was a reaction to smaller, more old-fashioned designs, and a leaning to French inspiration. Partly this was no doubt a difference of generations: Spencer was a young civilian with no inherited prejudices; St Vincent was an old admiral of the generation formed by the experiences of the 1740s. St Vincent was also a Whig, identified with the traditional francophilia of the nobility at a period when Pitt and George III had captured patriotic Britishness. The generally poor performance of these French-inspired designs, and those of the exiled French engineer

Jean-Louis Barrallier, finally discredited French ideas. They were particularly unsuitable for blockade stations because their narrow holds could not stow sufficient for the cruises of twenty weeks or more which were becoming commonplace. The big building effort of the Napoleonic War, necessary to replace the ships of the Anson–Sandwich generations as they finally wore out, was mostly based on adequate if uninspired British-style designs.[45]

The most important innovations of these years were in building practice rather than design. The shortage of compass timber and knees, and the urgent need to strengthen older ships for extended lives, led to the adoption of a number of novelties from Gabriel Snodgrass, master shipwright of the East India Company, especially the use of diagonal riders, bolted down in the hold over the existing structure of old ships to stiffen the frames. This in turn was an essential element of the 'system' adopted by Robert Seppings, Surveyor of the Navy from 1813 to 1832, whose diagonal timbering allowed new ships of much greater length to be built without loss of rigidity. Also during the Napoleonic Wars many knees were replaced by iron plates bolted through simple chocks (wooden blocks). 'Wall-sided' ships, with vertical topsides rather than the traditional tumblehome, saved on compass timber for the toptimbers, gave more room within board, greater stability at large angles of heel, and a better spread for the rigging. Shortage of timber inspired the softwood-built 'fir frigates', which were light and fast but had very short working lives. More successful was the building of ships in teak at Bombay Dockyard during the Napoleonic War. Though difficult and expensive to work, teak is a superb shipbuilding timber which is virtually immune to rot and amenable to iron fastenings. During the lifetime of the master shipwright Jamsetjee Bomanjee the management and quality of workmanship of Bombay yard was very high, but after his death in 1821 the building programme was brought to an end by mismanagement, corruption, and the exhaustion of the Malabar teak forests.[46] Other important innovations were in fittings. Davits made it much simpler and safer to put a boat in the water. New patterns of anchors, and the first chain cable, improved ships' chances of surviving an onshore gale. Iron water-tanks, fitted permanently in the bottom of the hold in place of the traditional tiers of casks, saved the men much time and labour in watering, eased the ship by carrying weight lower in the hull, and saved space in the hold for other stowage.[47]

The Spencer Admiralty was notably open to experimental designs. These included the double-ended sloops of Samuel Bentham, and Captain John Schank's sloops with sliding keels, none of which were unequivocal successes, though the problem with Schank's keels was maintenance rather than performance. Most radical of all was Lord Stanhope's *Kent Ambinavigator*, which if she had worked would have been the world's first steam warship.[48] The American engineer Robert Fulton, having failed to interest the French authorities in his ideas for submarines, and his 'catamaran' (a sort of floating mine), came to Britain in 1804. The Admiralty was interested, and the 'catamaran' was demonstrated in a trial, but failed completely in action.[49]

Another important innovation of the Spencer years was the widespread use of troopships. It had long been a common practice of the French navy, sometimes imitated by the British, to fit ships of the line temporarily as troopships by landing their lower-deck guns. Such ships were often described by the French term *armé en flûte* ('fitted as a transport'). The usual British practice was to move troops overseas in chartered transports drawn from the merchant fleet. The disadvantage was the long delays involved in chartering, assembling and moving merchantmen under convoy. During the Great Wars the strategic situation often required Britain's small forces of troops to be moved fast over long distances. Beginning in the 1790s, the Navy therefore built up a large force of naval troopships. These ships were drawn from the old two-decker classes of forty-fours and fifties, now too small for the line of battle and outclassed as cruisers by the new heavy frigates. To them were added prizes, some former East Indiamen, and some old Third Rates, too weak to carry their main armament but still fit for service in a less demanding role. With their lower-deck guns removed, the troopships had a spacious troop-deck suitable for infantry (moving cavalry and artillery was always more difficult). Under naval command, they could be assembled and moved swiftly. Their main-deck guns were equivalent to the armament of a frigate (though the crews were smaller), so that troopships could look after themselves against anything below a ship of the line. There were also some naval store-ships converted in a similar manner, which accompanied overseas squadrons operating in hostile waters.[50]

We shall see that the Royal Navy experienced some unpleasant shocks when it went to war against the United States Navy in 1812. These were sometimes attributed to superior American ship design, but in fact the seagoing ships of the US Navy were frigates and sloops very similar to their British contemporaries. The US Navy was constructed in the 1790s to meet a threat from Algiers, and its three biggest ships were intended to outclass Algerine 18-pounder frigates. These were the 24-pounder frigates *United States*, *Constitution* and *President*; powerful ships with the scantlings of a small ship of the line. Though not fast (the *President* perhaps excepted) or good seaboats, they were well adapted to act as the 'capital ships' of a small navy. There were a few similar ships in both British and French service, either built as such or 'razees', cut down from two-deckers by removing a deck, but the major navies tended to have limited use for a slow cruising warship which cost as much as a ship of the line.[51] To match the big American ships the Royal Navy hastily built or converted a number of 'super-frigates' of its own, including some remarkable razeed seventy-fours which carried a 36-pounder main battery with 42-pounder carronades on quarterdeck and forecastle. These ships were the idea of Captain John 'Magnificent' Hayes (one of a family of shipwrights, and originally trained for the same profession), who took the first of them, the *Majestic*, to American waters in 1814, and had the satisfaction of taking the *President* soon afterwards.[52]

The only US warships which were to an extent original were the least successful part of the fleet, the gunboats, whose inspiration was political rather than professional. Thomas Jefferson, President of the United States from 1801 to 1809, believed fervently that armies and navies were 'pillars of corruption', destructive of the political purity of the Republic, and that 'gun-boats are the only *water* defence which can be useful to us, and protect us from the ruinous folly of a navy'.[53] Much derided by subsequent American naval historians writing in support of a deep-water battlefleet, the Jefferson gunboats were in fact serviceable craft, useful for local defence in conjunction with properly sited batteries. They had little effect on the outcome of the war, because they were the product of an ideological and strategic vision which proved to be quite erroneous.[54]

If there is a single lesson which can be drawn from the study of warships and their weapons, it is that the only useful measure of quality is fitness for purpose, and that the strategic judgement of what functions a navy is meant to fulfil, is even more important than the technical skill of the designer. British ships were more successful not because British warship designs were individually outstanding (though some of them were), but because the British had achieved by the 1760s, and never subsequently lost, a fair balance between their strategic requirements and the ships they built to meet them. France built ships with some good qualities, and Spain built ships with many good qualities, but in both cases their governments committed their navies to wars which they had not been designed to fight, and were not equipped to win. Traditionally minded French and Spanish naval historians have often excused their defeat as inevitable, given the disproportion of forces and resources. In fact France and Spain combined were superior in strength for much of the American War and the Great Wars. It is not unreasonable to guess that the same amount of money, spent on ships more suitable for the purpose, might have built fleets capable of beating the Royal Navy. It has to be realized, however, that the ships were the expression of an ethos as much as a strategy. It was not merely ship design which France and Spain would have to have changed, but the very structure of their navies, their training, organization and discipline – and if it had been possible to change all these things, then they might have won even with inadequate ships, as the Royal Navy did in the 1740s.

TWENTY-EIGHT

Order and Anarchy

Operations 1793–1797

Prussia and Austria went to war to overthrow the French revolutionaries in April 1792, but the British did not join them. The Continental situation began to seem more menacing in the autumn, when the French army checked the allied advance, and the French government called on the oppressed subjects of monarchs everywhere to revolt, but it was the French invasion of the Austrian Netherlands in September which really alarmed Whitehall, and even then it was the French who declared war on Britain on 1 February 1793. In 'this most important struggle between all the order and all the anarchy of the world',[1] Pitt's government had no official view about the anarchy and violence of French politics. Its essential war-aim was deeply traditional, to keep a hostile power out of the Low Countries, to which end an expeditionary force under the king's son the Duke of York was despatched to join the allied army in Flanders.[2]

British strategic thinking, however, was not confined to the Netherlands. The core of Pitt's government was a triumvirate of himself, Lord Grenville the Foreign Secretary, and Henry Dundas, since 1791 the Home (and therefore also military and colonial) Secretary. Dundas was the author and advocate of a strategy designed to emasculate French power for ever by striking at its root in the colonies. Without the French West Indian colonies – above all Saint Domingue – which generated two-fifths of French foreign trade and two-thirds of its deep-sea shipping, French sea power could not survive, and French military strength would be fatally undermined. 'This country,' he believed, 'having captured the French West India islands and destroyed their existing fleet, may long rest in peace.'[3] While the French navy was in chaos, and the French army fully occupied on the Continent, Dundas meant to do to France exactly what France had tried and failed to do to Britain fifteen years before. A great expedition to the West Indies was therefore prepared, and sailed at the end of November 1793.[4]

Meanwhile, unexpected strategic opportunities had opened elsewhere. Since November 1792 the French government had been controlled by the radicals of the Jacobin faction, whose answer to dissent was the guillotine. The dockyard towns were islands of metropolitan radicalism in the more conservative countryside of France, controlled by extremists who had also taken over the French navy, destroying its discipline and much of its organization, and driving most of the officers into exile. In the summer of 1793 there was a Royalist revolt in the Vendée in western France, and a widespread reaction against the radicals elsewhere, including Toulon, where the local Jacobins were ejected from power in July. It soon became clear, however, that the Jacobin government in Paris was not going to be dislodged. By the end of August a government army was advancing towards Toulon, where 50,000 starving refugees were trapped between the guillotine and the sea. In desperation the municipal leaders appealed to Lord Hood, commanding the British squadron blockading the port. Ever bold and sanguine, Hood did not hesitate to make a quick decision on a question whose political and strategic delicacy would have given many admirals pause. He offered British support to the Toulonnais if they would declare for a Bourbon restoration and permit him to occupy the town, which they reluctantly accepted. The British government, though embarrassed by the commitment to the Bourbons, was overjoyed to learn that half the French fleet was in its hands and a second front in France had been opened. Meanwhile Hood had to improvise the defence of the town. Toulon is surrounded by mountains and eminently defensible, but he had only a fraction of the needful troops, of several nationalities and varying quality. His principal allies the Spaniards co-operated, but the destruction of the Toulon fleet (leaving the British to dominate the Mediterranean) was not high on their list of strategic priorities, and the major reinforcements Hood needed did not appear. The French army pushed ever nearer to the town, and by early December it was clear that the place could not be held. On the night of the 18th–19th the allies withdrew, taking with them several thousand refugees and three French ships of the line under Royalist officers. The remainder of the fleet, the dockyard and stores, were supposed to be destroyed by British and Spanish naval parties, but in the confusion of an unplanned withdrawal the work was not completed. Nine ships of the line and the main stores were burned; thirteen more (and five frigates) escaped with varying degrees of damage, as did the giant *Dauphin Royal* then under construction. Nevertheless the destruction of the timber stocks painfully built up over years was possibly the single most crippling blow suffered by the French navy since Quiberon Bay.[5]

This is the moment to introduce the officer entrusted with the British share of the task of destruction, Captain Sir William Sidney Smith. Knighted for heroism in Swedish service, lately returned (still on half-pay) from a visit to Turkey, Smith was a colourful figure whose vainglory and indifference to the conventional naval virtues of seamanship and subordination disgusted many officers, especially senior officers. His extraordinary courage, independence and linguistic talents showed to best advantage in the irregular operations on the margins of diplomacy and espionage in which he spent much of the war. Conventional officers tended to blame him for the failure to destroy the whole of the Toulon fleet, but Lieutenant R. W. Miller, who was with him that night, found him 'a glorious fellow, cool, vigilant, intrepid, humane, with a mind whose compass took objects in every point of view at once'.[6] With Smith we may introduce the young Corsican artillery officer Napoleon Buonaparte, who first made his name in the French army during the siege of Toulon. The two of them were destined to meet on a future occasion.

Both Toulon and the Royalist revolt in the Vendée presented the British government with opportunities which it was anxious to exploit, but the only immediate source of troops for either was the West India expedition, then almost ready to sail. There were voices in the British government warning of the dangers of dissipating effort, but they did not sound loudly in the ears of Pitt, always optimistic, and never a master of detail. Dundas as Home Secretary was the responsible minister for military affairs: he was also President of the Board of Control (in effect minister for British India), Treasurer of the Navy, government political manager of Scotland, and shared with Pitt the leadership of the House of Commons. He admitted to being 'rather overloaded'. No British minister except the First Lord of the Admiralty, and to an extent the Master-General of the Ordnance, had access to detailed expert advice on military matters, and neither the amiable but torpid Earl of Chatham, nor the talented but unpopular and isolated Duke of Richmond, carried much weight in the government. As a result the West India expedition was halved to make up forces for Toulon and the Vendée, neither of which arrived in time.[7]

The expedition arrived in the Caribbean early in 1794. Its commanders, Lieutenant-General Sir Charles Grey and Vice-Admiral Sir John Jervis, were excellently chosen; familiar with the waters and with combined operations, friends (and Whig political colleagues) of one another. Together they acted with energy and success. Martinique was taken in March, St Lucia and Guadeloupe next month, and Port-au-Prince, capital of Saint Domingue, in June. By the beginning of the sickly season all the French Windward Islands[8] were in British hands, and it seemed only a matter of time before the rest of Saint Domingue followed. The French planters, who had rapidly adjusted to the commercial opportunities of British rule a generation before, were Royalist in sentiment, and horrified by the emancipation of their slaves which the French government decreed in February 1794. It might have seemed hard to alienate them from British rule, but Grey and Jervis were equal to the challenge – as the naval surgeon Leonard Gillespie reported:

> The French say, they expected to find, under an English government, an end to confiscation and oppression, and a peaceable enjoyment of their properties. But to their great regret, they find their situations very little bettered; and a change only from one set of oppressors to another.[9]

By their ruthless looting and extortion, Grey and Jervis disgusted all classes in the islands, while their seizure of American merchant ships threatened war with the United States. Then in June 1794 French warships from Rochefort landed a thousand troops on Guadaloupe, where the angry locals supported them, and an energetic commander, the young Victor Hugues, led them to victory. Grey's troops began to fall victim to the climate, while Hugues recruited negro and mulatto regiments to the Republican cause.[10]

Meanwhile in home waters the main Channel Fleet was again commanded by Lord Howe – George III's favourite admiral if no one else's. The lesson of the American War had been well learned, and no one disputed the importance of keeping the main fleet together in home waters; but the question of where in home waters was as open as it had been fifty years before. Howe disapproved of close blockade, and kept the fleet in Spithead except when outward- or inward-bound convoys had to be covered. The French fleet in Brest was known to be in turmoil, and when it sailed in the summer of 1793 to operate against the Royalists in the Vendée, it was soon paralysed by mutiny. In October two delegates of the Jacobin government, Pierre Louis Prieur 'de la Marne' and André Jean-Bon St André, arrived in Brest to take over the town and the fleet. With ruthless energy and frequent executions, they brought the fleet into order and discipline, if not complete efficiency. It sailed in May 1794, commanded by Rear-Admiral Louis Thomas Villaret-Joyeuse, accompanied by Jean-Bon St André, with a determination to fight, and a confidence in the inevitable victory of Republican virtue, which the Royal Navy had not encountered in the French before.[11]

Their mission was to cover the passage of a large convoy from the United States carrying colonial products from the West Indies, and grain which the Jacobin government urgently needed to feed Paris. Howe was informed of all

this and at sea in good time, but the scouting of British frigates was unsuccessful, and the French convoy was never located. The two main fleets did
encounter one another, and after four days of skirmish and manoeuvre during
which Howe skilfully gained the weather gage, they fought a fleet battle on
1 June; twenty-five British against twenty-six French ships of the line. This
was Howe's opportunity to put his new signals and tactics into practice. His
intention was to employ a new manoeuvre by which the line of battle would
close the enemy from the windward, and at a given moment turn together to
cut through the enemy line at many points and engage from the leeward side,
preventing escape. In spite of supplementing his signals with frigates carrying
messages by word of mouth Howe failed to get many of his captains to
understand him, and only part of the British fleet carried out the manoeuvre
as intended, but with an enemy willing to stand and fight he was able to bring
on the desired close action, and the result was an unequivocal victory. Seven
French ships of the line were taken (one of which sank soon afterwards), with
4,200 men killed or wounded and 3,300 taken prisoner: the heaviest losses the
French navy had suffered in one day since 1692. For British officers who had
last been in action in the American War, the 'Glorious First of June' (as it was
later remembered, partly because it was fought so far out in the Atlantic that
there was no nearby land to give it a name) was a great day – but it was no
disgrace for the French, who had fought with 'a savage ferocity' (in the words
of Collingwood, who was there), and who had achieved their strategic objective
of covering their convoy.[12]

The aftermath of the battle, moreover, left many British officers dissatisfied. The elderly and cautious Howe, advised by his equally cautious Captain
of the Fleet Sir Roger Curtis, refused to chase the retreating French as they
towed off several likely prizes. At Chatham's insistence Howe's despatch
named captains who had distinguished themselves, which infuriated those
not named, many of whom had fought gallantly but had not happened to be
in sight of the flagship. To make resentment worse a gold medal for the battle
was then issued only to those captains whom Howe (or Curtis, as many
suspected) had selected, and when George III came down to the fleet to
honour the admiral, the captains were not invited to meet him.[13]

In the Mediterranean Hood was not disheartened by the defeat of Toulon,
but turned his attention to the conquest of Corsica. In principle he had
available the British troops which had been sent, too late, to reinforce the
garrison of Toulon. In practice relations between the two services were
disastrous. Hood was as ever bold and enterprising, with a clear grasp of the
strategic and diplomatic situation, easily assuming the status of supreme

commander over both services which he had never been granted. Cautious to the point of sloth, resentful of the admiral's and the Navy's superiority, the army officers declined to be drawn into operations for which they did not have orders. Hood therefore set about conquering Corsica with the Navy alone (including a quantity of infantry embarked as Marines, whom he used as his private army). The siege of Bastia (April to May 1794) was entirely a naval affair, though a new army commander, General Charles Stuart, co-operated with bad grace in the siege of Calvi (June to August). In these operations young Captain Horatio Nelson among others distinguished himself and was wounded. At the same time military advice was in part vindicated. Hood's decision to attack Bastia was based on Nelson's judgement that a small garrison could be quickly overwhelmed. In fact the garrison was not small; the place was too strong to be stormed and the soldiers were right that it would have to be starved out. An independent observer of the campaign, Sir Gilbert Elliot, the Scottish lawyer who had been sent out as British political agent to Toulon and finished up as viceroy of Corsica, admired Hood, but could see that there was no future in his style of command in combined operations. Effective co-operation was needed, not another Vernon to keep the army in subservience.[14] Comparing the two services, however, Elliot had no doubt he preferred the Navy for his son: 'The character of the profession is infinitely more manly. They are full of life and action, while on shore it is all high lounge and still life.'[15]

At home in Britain there were important political developments in July 1794. The Whig opposition split; the moderate majority under the Duke of Portland joined the government, leaving in opposition only Fox and about forty of his followers who were still more or less friendly to the French Revolution. Places had to be found for the leaders of the Portland Whigs. Pitt therefore revived the third Secretaryship of State, now styled 'Secretary for War', for Dundas, leaving the Home Office for Portland.[16] Earl Spencer, another of the Whig peers, initially became Lord Privy Seal. In December there were further changes, aimed more specifically at improving the management of the war, and among them Spencer swapped offices with Lord Chatham. The new First Lord of the Admiralty, aged thirty-five and without any experience of public office or naval affairs, was cultivated, charming and somewhat diffident. He was not part of Pitt's inner circle, but his Admiralty Board included two dominant, not to say domineering, naval men, Hood and Sir Charles Middleton (whom Pitt had brought out of retirement in May). Both were close associates of Pitt, accustomed to managing a weak First Lord, and expecting to carry on in the same way. Spencer was very soon to find that

Dundas had similar ideas. His first year in office was marked by the efforts of the admirals on one side, Dundas and the army on the other, to control the new First Lord.[17]

Howe, now sixty-eight and unwell, continued at the king's insistence to command the Channel Fleet, which continued to spend much of its time in port. On the last day of 1794 the Brest fleet sailed for an unmolested cruise of thirty-four days, during which it lost four ships of the line to stress of weather, but took over a hundred British prizes including one ship of the line, and sent a reinforcement of six ships of the line into the Mediterranean. In early February 1795 Howe sailed to cover an outward-bound convoy of over 600 sail, but he was soon driven back to Torbay. This capacious anchorage on the Devon coast, often used by the Channel Fleet, is safe in the prevailing westerlies, but dangerously exposed in the rare event of the wind backing southeasterly and blowing up. On 13 February this happened, and for a day the fleet was in imminent danger of destruction. In the end their cables held, but Howe's health and nerve were broken. He retired to Bath, where he continued to issue orders and collect the commander-in-chief's prize-money, while his second-in-command, Admiral Lord Bridport, did the work. This situation might have strained the warmest friendship, and the two admirals were not on good terms. Nor did they agree on strategy, as Bridport believed in prolonged cruising rather than awaiting intelligence in port.[18]

With an inexperienced First Lord, and both Howe and the Admiralty issuing orders to the Channel Fleet, the movements of British squadrons were dangerously ill co-ordinated. In June 1795 the expedition to relieve the Royalists in the Vendée finally sailed without Bridport, at sea, being aware of its movements. Villaret-Joyeuse from Brest was able to get between the two, but instead of the convoy he intercepted another squadron under Vice-Admiral William Cornwallis on 16 June. With five ships of the line against nine Cornwallis had to conduct a fighting retreat, but with great skill he brought off his squadron without loss. On the 22nd Villaret-Joyeuse was actually in contact with the British troop convoy, but meanwhile Cornwallis's report had guided Bridport, who intercepted the French off the Ile de Groix next day. Villaret-Joyeuse fled into Lorient, losing three ships, and might have lost more but for Bridport's reluctance to chase inshore, since the French had to wait for high water to get into the port. In the end the expedition to the Vendée was a naval success, as much by luck as judgement, followed by a military catastrophe in which many of the French Royalist troops were massacred.[19]

Throughout the first three years of the war, while the Channel Fleet spent so much of its time at anchor, most of the available frigates were detached in independent squadrons. The two best-known, under Captains Sir Edward Pellew and Sir John Borlase Warren, were based on Falmouth. Composed mainly of new heavy 18-pounder and even 24-pounder frigates, with the best young captains and a free hand to cruise, these squadrons won a large share of glory and prize-money, while their effect on French coasting trade reduced Brest by 1795 to near starvation. They were not often in company with the main fleet, and had neither need nor opportunity to practise scouting, but there were plenty of compensations for the lucky captains. In a not-untypical year, 1793, the 18-pounder frigate *Phaeton*, under Captain Sir Andrew Snape Douglas, took a frigate, a corvette, two large privateers and a merchantman worth £300,000. With his characteristic audacity Sir Sidney Smith, commanding the *Diamond*, took his ship into the Goulet by night in January 1795, hailing the French ships in his faultless French to ask for news, and returning without detection with the latest information.[20]

When Spencer became First Lord, Hood was home from the Mediterranean on leave. On the news that the Toulon fleet had been reinforced from Brest, he demanded an equivalent addition to his own squadron, in language which led Spencer to dismiss him from both the Mediterranean command and the Admiralty Board. For all his ability Hood was seventy years old, inflexible and incapable of working with the army – but the real issue was political rather than professional. Hood appealed to Pitt and Dundas to put Spencer in his place, only to find that he had mistaken his man; Spencer meant to be his own First Lord.[21]

In Hood's absence the Mediterranean squadron was commanded by Vice-Admiral William Hotham, a competent and popular officer but lacking Hood's buoyancy and drive. 'Admiral Hotham is a gentlemanlike man,' Sir Gilbert Elliot wrote, 'and would, I am persuaded, do his duty in a day of battle. But he is past the time of life for action; his soul has got down into his *belly* and never mounts higher now, and in all business he is a piece of perfectly inert formality.'[22] On 13 and 14 March off Cape Noli Hotham did his duty in pursuit of the Toulon squadron, but with worn-out and undermanned ships, far from a friendly base, he did not choose to push his advantage. Captain Nelson's *Agamemnon* was the leading ship, and took a major share in the capture of two French ships of the line, but he was not satisfied. 'Admiral Hotham seems to have given the business up and thinks we have done enough, whilst Goodall and myself think we have done nothing in comparison to what we might.'[23] Four months later on 13 July there was another partial action between the two fleets, the British pursuit called off by Hotham when the escaping French neared the land.[24] On this occasion his second Vice-Admiral

Samuel Goodall 'is described as kicking his hat about the deck in a frenzy of rage when he was called off.'[25] 'The risk might have been great but so was the object,' Nelson commented. 'Had Lord Hood been here he never would have called us out of action but Hotham leaves nothing to chance.'[26]

In the West Indies the British situation continued to deteriorate during 1795, with revolts in Grenada, St Vincent and St Lucia inspired by Victor Hugues, and an unrelated rebellion in Jamaica. Both army and Navy were now suffering severely from the climate, especially yellow fever. But in Europe the situation was worse; every British military campaign had failed, every British ally except Austria had withdrawn from the war. French troops conquered the Netherlands in January 1795 and established the 'Batavian Republic'. Victory in the West Indies was all the more essential now that it was nowhere else to be found. The government therefore prepared a great new expedition, straining every nerve to raise fresh troops. In the ten months from August 1795 35,000 men were sent to the West Indies. The new Transport Board was faced with the task of chartering 100,000 tons of merchant shipping – about one-seventh of the entire British merchant fleet – in two months.[27]

Ministers had to find commanders for these forces, and given the acute dearth of experienced talent in the higher ranks of the British army, Dundas had the harder task. His choice was his kinsman Major-General Ralph Abercromby, sixty years old, not an easy man to work with, but still a junior general with little appropriate experience. With the example of Hood before him, Dundas was determined to have an accommodating admiral, and approved of the choice of Rear-Admiral Hugh Christian, an expert in military transport with whom Abercromby was able to work. He did not at once appreciate that Christian was intended to command the expedition only out to the West Indies, where he would become second-in-command to Admiral Sir John Laforey in the Leeward Islands. Laforey was not popular in the army, and Dundas feared that Abercromby would refuse to serve with him, so he demanded that Laforey be dismissed to make room for Christian. To remove a blameless (albeit somewhat unenterprising) senior admiral, in favour of a very junior one who was visibly the army's candidate, was an explosive proposition, both in the Navy at large, and on the Admiralty Board, where it raised once more the question of who was master. Middleton, now the senior naval lord and ambitious as ever to dominate the Board, immediately seized on this issue, on which he was sure to be backed by the admirals. He refused to sign the order to relieve Laforey. Faced with the choice of dictation from Middleton or Dundas, Spencer forced Middleton's resignation, but avoided a complete submission to the army. Laforey was moved sideways to the Jamaica command, Christian was allowed to be acting commander-in-chief of the Leeward Islands, but warned to expect a more senior admiral to take over early in 1796.[28]

Spencer had managed to assert at least part of his authority, but the Navy was alarmed by the suggestion that the army now had some sort of veto over the appointment of admirals. Inter-service relations were already in a very delicate state for another reason. In the summer of 1795 an infantry officer serving afloat as a Marine in the Mediterranean squadron was dismissed from his ship by a naval court martial for insubordination to his captain. The army chose to back his case, which went up to the law officers and the king before being dismissed. The Duke of York as commander-in-chief of the army then issued (apparently without consultation) regulations for soldiers serving afloat, which appeared to remove them from naval discipline altogether. The regulations arrived at Portsmouth in October as the West India expedition was assembling, and caused a furore. All the eight admirals then in port, and all the captains but one, signed a furious letter of protest. Spencer was able to defer the issue by persuading the duke not to publish his new regulations, but the 'admirals' mutiny' did nothing to strengthen his authority, or naval discipline in general.[29]

Meanwhile the assembling of the expedition proceeded in the teeth of a hard winter and repeated gales. Christian finally sailed in November, only to be struck by further gales which drove the whole expedition back into port at the end of January 1796 with heavy loss of life. By the time it was ready to sail again, in March, the new commander-in-chief was ready to go with it: the talented but eccentric and cantankerous Cornwallis, who had led the 'admirals' mutiny', and was in no mood to accommodate Spencer in anything. Soon after sailing his flagship was damaged in a collision in yet another gale and forced back to Portsmouth. Spencer ordered Cornwallis to proceed to his station in a frigate, and the admiral flatly refused. He was therefore removed from the command and court-martialled, but acquitted – no court of sea officers would convict the Navy's hero who had stood up to military interference. It was left to Christian to take the convoy out to the Leeward Islands, where it finally arrived in April 1796, near the end of the campaigning season.[30]

The only part of the whole world in which British naval and combined operations were entirely successful in 1795 was the East Indies. On the news of the French conquest of the Netherlands, the East Indies squadron and troops of the East India Company were able to seize Trincomalee and Malacca in August 1795, followed by Colombo and most of the Spice Islands early in 1796. In all these cases it was the strategic value of the ports as naval bases which was uppermost in ministers' minds, and the most strategic point of all was the Cape of Good Hope. 'What was a feather in the hands of Holland,' Dundas was advised by Captain John Blankett, 'will become a sword in the hands of France.'[31] An expedition to seize it (in the name of the exiled Prince of Orange) sailed under Rear-Admiral Sir George Elphinstone and Major-General John Craig in March 1795, and after some hard fighting the colony was captured in September. To complete the success, a Dutch squadron under Rear-Admiral Engelbertus Lucas sent out the following year to recover the Cape was trapped in Saldanha Bay in August 1796 and forced to surrender without fighting.[32]

Everywhere else 1796 was for the British a year of struggle. In the West Indies Abercromby was able to stabilize the situation and recapture most of the Leeward Islands, but Guadaloupe remained in French hands to threaten the British islands and their trade, and only a few towns could be held in Saint Domingue. All this was achieved at a very heavy cost: about 14,000 men killed, almost all by yellow fever, dysentery and malaria. Britain's only field army was largely consumed in the West Indian campaigns of the 1790s. It has been calculated that 43,750 white British troops died in the West Indies between 1793 and 1801, just over half of those who had been sent, to which must be added between 19,000 and 24,000 men of the Navy and the transports.[33] In the Mediterranean a new commander-in-chief, Jervis, raised the fleet to a high state of morale and efficiency, but he could do nothing to save a dis-integrating strategic situation. During the summer of 1796 the French army under Bonaparte (now a general, and using a more French form of his name) overran much of northern Italy. Spain, guided by the francophile minister Manuel de Godoy, allied with France in August on terms which left France in effective control of Spanish policy, and in October declared war. There were now few friendly ports open to British ships in the Mediterranean, and it was more and more difficult to keep the squadron operational. Corsica was threatened, and in October the British garrisons were with much danger and difficulty evacuated to Elba. The same month Jervis's second Rear-Admiral Robert Man suffered some sort of a nervous breakdown and returned to England without orders, taking part of the squadron with him and leaving the rest acutely exposed. By this time the government had decided that it was no longer possible or useful to keep a fleet in a sea where there were no allies left to support. By December Jervis's squadron was based on Lisbon to watch the Straits of Gibraltar.[34]

In home waters the situation grew steadily more difficult. A French invasion flotilla was preparing in Dunkirk. A second blockade in the North

Sea had to be mounted to cover the Dutch fleet. Meanwhile the main Channel Fleet continued to be managed by the uneasy triangular relationship between the Admiralty, Howe and Bridport. Late in 1796 intelligence indicated that the Brest fleet was preparing for an expedition carrying troops to an unknown destination, which was in fact Ireland. In face of this threat the Channel Fleet moved some way towards close blockade, maintaining part of its strength at sea west of Ushant all the time. In late December 1796 Vice-Admiral John Colpoys was at sea with a squadron of fifteen sail of the line, while Sir Edward Pellew, with his own ship the *Indefatigable* alone, was well up the Iroise watching Brest. Since the French in Brest had at least double Colpoys' strength, and Bridport with the main fleet was 200 miles to leeward in Spithead, the British situation was exposed.[35]

Meanwhile the French had their own difficulties. The organization and discipline of the fleet had slid further under the 'Directory' which succeeded the fallen Jacobin regime in August 1795. The navy's reputation among informed Frenchmen was of fathomless incompetence and cowardice. The triumphant generals of the French army, who had beaten every nation in Europe, took it for granted that nothing would be achieved at sea until they took command.

> Our hateful navy cannot and will not do anything . . . What a bizarre mixture! The commissioned officers chaotic and divided, organized indiscipline in a fighting service . . . arrogance, ignorance, vanity and folly.[36]

That was the opinion of the twenty-eight-year-old General Lazare Hoche, commanding the expedition at Brest. His first step was to dismiss Latouche-Tréville, a relic of the Jacobins, and appoint Vice-Admiral Justin Morard de Galles, who like most former royal officers had been imprisoned under the Jacobins and in fear of his life, and was by no means enthusiastic about facing fresh dangers.[37]

The French sailed in thick weather on 16 December; seventeen sail of the line, thirteen frigates and some transports carrying nearly 15,000 troops. At the last moment Hoche insisted that they take the Raz de Sein rather than the Iroise, with the result that one ship was wrecked with heavy loss of life, and the rest were scattered in fog and darkness. Hoche and Morard in a frigate never regained contact with the rest of the expedition, which arrived in Bantry Bay in a blizzard on the 22nd. After a week of continuous gales they abandoned hope and returned to Brest. Pellew had observed the French sailing and hastened to warn Colpoys, but the admiral was not on his rendezvous; he had retreated to Spithead to ride out the gales. When the French returned, Pellew again, this time with another of his frigates, intercepted the seventy-four-gun *Droits de l'Homme*, chased her through the night and drove her ashore near Brest. Bridport and Colpoys knew nothing about the threat until it was all over, defeated by bad weather and French incompetence with almost no help from the Royal Navy.[38]

The Admiralty and the public were badly shaken, but worse was to follow. On 22 February 1797 three French frigates landed 1,500 troops on the coast of Wales near Fishguard. The soldiers were mostly liberated criminals commanded by an American adventurer, and within twenty-four hours they had surrendered to the local militia without firing a shot. In military terms the expedition was pure comic opera, but its consequences for the government in London were not at all funny. The news that French troops were ashore on the British mainland caused a run on the banks. Gold was already short, mainly because so much had been exported to subsidize Britain's allies, or spent on importing grain after the bad harvest of 1795–6, and the Bank of England was forced to suspend the convertibility of its notes. This temporary measure (which lasted until 1821) can be seen in retrospect to have been thoroughly helpful. The note issue continued to be managed with prudence; neither the credit of the Bank nor the value of the currency were seriously damaged. Going off the gold standard allowed the British economy during the course of the wars to be gently reflated, ensuring maximum production and employment. At the time, however, what was visible was an acute financial crisis which threatened the government's ability to continue the war, and even to maintain the fabric of society.[39]

Amidst the gloom there was only one piece of good news. Jervis's 'Mediterranean' fleet was now shut out of the Mediterranean, but his aggressive determination had not slackened, and Spanish politics gave him an opportunity. Godoy was no friend to the Spanish navy, and had a low tolerance for unwelcome information. Two successive commanders-in-chief of the main fleet, one of them (Vice-Admiral José de Mazarredo) the most talented Spanish admiral of his generation, were dismissed for warning that it was not ready for war with Britain. Their successor, Vice-Admiral José de Córdoba, was ordered to sea to cover a convoy carrying quicksilver (essential for silver production in the American mines), and thereafter to participate in a French scheme for the invasion of Britain. Córdoba knew he was liable to be intercepted by Jervis, but he believed there were only ten British ships to face twenty-nine of his own. Jervis, who had excellent intelligence and efficient scouting frigates, knew exactly Córdoba's movements and strength. He also knew the inefficiency of the Spanish fleet (lately a British ally), and he knew, as he remarked, that 'a victory is very essential to England at this moment'.[40]

On 14 February, in foggy weather, Jervis intercepted the Spanish fleet off Cape St Vincent. The actual odds that morning were fifteen British ships of the line against twenty-three and five transports, though in the thick weather the British counted them all as men-of-war. 'They loom like Beachy Head in a fog. By my soul, they are thumpers,' called down Lieutenant Henry Edgell of the *Barfleur*, who had gone aloft to get a better view.[41] The main body of eighteen Spanish ships of the line and one transport were to windward, with five more ships of the line detached to leeward escorting four transports. Quickly forming a line, Jervis cut through the gap between the two parts of the Spanish fleet and tacked in order to attack the main body from the rear and windward. His intention was to follow the traditional British tactic of rolling up an ill-formed enemy from the rear, which had served so well in the Finisterre battles, at Quiberon Bay and Rodney's 'Moonlight Battle' of 1780. Before the bulk of his fleet had tacked, however, his movement was disrupted by an attack from his other side by Vice-Admiral Juan Joaquín Moreno commanding the convoy escort, and soon afterwards Córdoba ordered his own squadron to bear up to attack the British rear. The effect would have been for each squadron to be chasing the other's tail, and if the Spanish ships had reacted smartly to the order it would have gone far to retrieve their situation. Jervis ordered his rear division to tack to block this move, but Vice-Admiral Sir Charles Thompson missed the signal. Of Thompson's division only Commodore Nelson in the *Captain* took in the signal and turned out of line, soon followed by his friend Collingwood in the *Excellent*. This checked Córdoba's move and gave the main body of the British fleet time to overwhelm the Spanish centre. Later in the action the *Captain*, already crippled, encountered two badly damaged Spanish ships which had collided. Nelson himself led one of the boarding parties which seized the *San Nicolas*, and from her went on to board the three-decker *San Josef*. Several other British ships went after the great *Santísima Trinidad*, an old and unsuccessful ship, but notionally the only four-decker in the world. She had actually struck her colours when another Spanish ship came up and towed her off 'in a masterly style'.[42] Nevertheless Jervis had gained a complete victory, taking four prizes from a greatly superior enemy.[43]

A victory at such a moment, against such odds, accompanied by such conspicuous heroism (Nelson was probably the first British flag-officer to lead a boarding party in person since Sir Edward Howard in 1513) could not fail to arouse public enthusiasm, and Nelson took some care to ensure that his own name should not be overlooked – to the disgust of some of his brother officers. Partly as a result, many myths grew up around the battle, notably that Nelson alone had saved the day by 'disobedience', and single-handed had captured two Spanish ships. In fact his bold initiative was in response to the admiral's known intentions, and only in the most technical sense without orders; while the *San Nicolas* and *San Josef* had already been battered by four other British ships before Nelson gave them the *coup de grâce*: 'the resistance they made was not great, a sort of scuffle in which a few lives were lost,' wrote Colling-wood, who was one of the four.[44] Nelson deserved his fame, but the victory was a triumph of teamwork. As a result the Spanish fleet became extremely shy of putting to sea, and the overall British naval situation was considerably eased.[45]

Apart from this battle there was no other good news in the spring of 1797. In April Britain's last ally, Austria, opened negotiations with France. Pitt was anxious to follow her example, seeing no possibility of financing a war which seemed to be hopeless and endless. Grenville, on the other hand, insisted that there could be no lasting peace with a government without faith or law. The nature of French government in fact was very relevant to Britain's strategic dilemma. The 1795 constitution established an executive 'Directory' and a bicameral parliament of which one-fifth was re-elected every year. The Direc-tory was Republican, but the 'Councils' were becoming progressively more Royalist. Meanwhile all parties looked with hope or fear towards the victorious French armies and their leaders, especially Bonaparte, then setting up a satellite republic in northern Italy, and Hoche, planning to do the same in the Rhineland. The legislators would have been content to buy peace by giving up most of France's conquests, but the armies lived and depended on continued conquests, which made the generals famous, wealthy and dangerous. The Directory was incompetent, venal and visibly failing, and the British govern-ment's extensive espionage operations in France kept it fully informed of French politics.[46]

This is the context in which to locate a curious incident in April 1796 when Sir Sidney Smith, still commanding the *Diamond* in the Channel, and deeply involved in contacts with the French Royalist underground, was captured in a boat action at the mouth of the Seine. With him in the boat were 'midship-man' J. W. Wright, whose naval career seems to have been only a cover for full-time intelligence work, and a leading Royalist agent disguised as Smith's servant. Smith was not treated as a prisoner of war but taken to Paris and installed in the Temple prison, where he lived in comfort, with complete freedom of communication, and some freedom of movement. A Royalist coup d'état was in preparation. The French police were deeply penetrated by both British and Royalist agents, and the audacious Smith used (or just possibly engineered) this accident to install himself in Paris to participate. Unfortunately he, the British government, and the majority of Frenchmen, were to be disappointed. On 4 September, '18 Fructidor' in the Revolutionary calendar, a Republican counter-coup seized power in Paris and imprisoned the moderate and Royalist leaders. With them passed the remaining elements of idealism and internationalism in French policy. The Directory was now controlled by cynical and in several cases corrupt men whose interests were not served by peace. Bonaparte was not officially among them, but of all Frenchmen he had the most to gain from continuing the war, and his luck did not desert him. A fortnight after the Fructidor coup, his rival Lazare Hoche died of consumption at the age of twenty-nine. Smith was now stranded in Paris until he escaped in February 1798, almost certainly with the connivance of Georges Pléville le Pelley, the Minister of Marine, of whose connections with the Royalists he knew too much.[47]

Pitt had prevailed on his colleagues to open peace negotiations with France, but Fructidor proved Grenville right. Nothing could be agreed with a government which had no interest in peace, and which could not control its own armies. Britain was condemned to continue the war, however distant the hope of victory. The best of Britain's small army were dead in the West Indies. Then, on Easter Sunday, 16 April 1797, came the worst news of all: the Channel Fleet in Spithead had mutinied. 'Our only hope is a submission to the enemy,' wrote Edmund Burke. 'If they demand Portsmouth as a cautionary town it will be yielded to them; and, as to our Navy, that has already perished with its discipline for ever.'[48]

———•◆•———

TWENTY-NINE

Infinite Honour

Social History 1793–1802: Men and Manning

No serious study of the manning of the Navy during the Revolutionary and Napoleonic Wars – the 'Great Wars' as contemporaries called them – has ever been written, and much about the subject remains conjectural. It looks as though the initial mobilization proceeded relatively easily, and that most of those raised in the first two years were volunteers. In September 1794, when the total number of seamen and Marines borne had reached almost 86,000, Lord Chatham had increased the Navy by almost 70,000 in two years, and in the two years to January 1795 there were 62,800 volunteers, half of them able seamen.[1] Information from individual Regulating Captains commanding districts of the Impress Service up and down the country agrees. Admiralty instructions for Impress officers were now to encourage men to volunteer even when they were facing impressment as an alternative. In effect this created two classes of volunteer: 'spontaneous' volunteers, many of them followers of particular officers, who were not to be diverted from their intended ships; and other volunteers, who received bounty and advance wages, but went where they were sent. The official bounty for volunteers was £5 for able seamen, £2 10s for ordinary seamen and £1 for landmen, but in most seaports this was increased by local bounties paid for by public subscription. In 1793 London and Liverpool were offering £2 extra for an able seaman and £1 for an ordinary. Many other places did likewise, even inland towns like Wrexham, which promised two guineas and one guinea 'to those Ancient Britons, natives of this country, who are ready to come forward and defend the wooden walls of Old England, against her natural and inveterate enemy'.[2] In this war (unlike the American) few local authorities sympathized with the enemy, though one conspicuous exception was Portsmouth, dominated throughout this period by a Unitarian radical Whig group led by Sir John Carter, whose relations with the Home Office were guarded.[3]

Local efforts to support naval recruitment opened the way for local agreements with the Admiralty, bodies like the Watermen's Company of London or the authorities of Orkney agreeing to supply a set number of men in return for exemption from the press. Such arrangements were ideal from the Admiralty's point of view, avoiding all the unpleasantness and political damage of impressment by delegating a large share of naval recruitment to the local authorities which carried out so much of government in Britain. A particularly interesting example occurred on the Tyne, a nursery of early trade unionism among the seamen of the coal trade. In October 1792 they went on strike for an increase of 10s in the winter wage of £2 10s for a voyage to London and back. The strike was illegal, troops and ships were assembled, but the officers of both services and the city fathers of Newcastle on Tyne made little secret of their sympathy for the seamen. With rigorous discipline the strikers kept the peace, while the authorities exerted heavy pressure on the shipowners. In the middle of this came the mobilization, when the Impress Service was set up on the Tyne by Captain Peter Rothe, a local man, and a local hero for his support of the seamen's cause, who was able to establish a working relationship with the seamen's leaders, implicitly closing ranks against their common opponent, the shipowners.[4]

Local agreements inspired a government scheme to establish a national system of local recruitment, known as the Quota Acts. There were three Acts of Parliament for 1795 and two for 1796 which levied fixed numbers of men for the Navy, and in some cases the army, from various combinations of English, Welsh and Scottish local authorities (none of the acts applied to Ireland).[5] These recruits were implicitly to be volunteers, since no mechanism for compulsion was provided in the acts, only means to raise money with which to pay bounties. Criminals or vagrants were explicitly excluded. Those authorities which failed to meet their quotas were to pay fines instead. Connected with these Acts was the 1795 Navy Act[6] which established an improved mechanism by which men could 'allot' a portion of their pay to be drawn once a month by a named relative, the intention being to ensure that married men recruited under the Quota Acts did not leave their families destitute to become a charge on the poor rates.[7] The 1795 Port Quota Act was rather different from the other four, being directed to ad hoc committees in the seaports, representing shipowners, who were to find a total of just under 20,000 men, every able seaman counting for two. If no able seamen had been recruited under this act, no recruit had opted for the army who had the choice, and every quota had been filled, the five acts together would have raised just under 40,000 men for the Navy. The 1795 acts, which coincided with a time of dearth and unemployment, appear to have been fairly successful, but the 1796 acts proposed much smaller quotas, and produced so few men that the scheme was then abandoned. Overall it seems likely that the Quota Acts raised up to 30,000 men for the Navy.[8] Possibly no more than one-sixth were seamen, but the remainder were overwhelmingly young working men from a cross-section of the usual country trades, mostly from the counties they were recruited for or near by. Though there were some from more distant parts, only 3 per cent were Irish.[9] There is no evidence at all of the criminals or educated troublemakers often alleged to have been recruited by these acts; these were respectable working men in need of a job.[10] Mention of the Irish leads to a related suggestion made by some Irish historians that the 1796 Insurrection Act of the Irish Parliament had filled the fleet with tens of thousands of political prisoners, members of the United Irishmen (an officially non-sectarian but Protestant-led middle-class revolutionary movement) or the Defenders (a rural Catholic resistance movement). Large and vague estimates have been offered, but the best figure at present available seems to be 115 men belonging to one or other movement sent into the Navy from 1 September 1795 to 1 June 1797, after which the Admiralty refused to receive any more.[11] Ordinary criminals, vagrants and above all thieves, remained as unpopular with the naval authorities as ever, but minor offenders for riot, drunkenness and the like, and seamen criminals not guilty of theft, were sometimes accepted.[12]

All this is necessary background to the great naval mutinies of 1797. First, however, we must consider a number of lesser mutinies which took place in the opening years of the war. As in the past, the majority of mutinies were settled informally. Returning from the battle of 1 June, the men of the *Orion* got drunk and mutinied for leave. There was talk of a court martial for the leaders, 'but Captain Duckworth had them before him today', Midshipman William Parker wrote to his father, 'and said as he was of a forgiving nature he gave them into the hands of the ship's company, that he restored them to him with love for the services they had done him'.[13] Next month some of the men of the *Barfleur* mutinied against being drafted into another ship, 'but the temperate and good management of Captain Elphinstone settled the business quietly', as Collingwood reported.[14] About the same time there was a demonstration aboard Cornwallis's flagship the *Minerva* in the East Indies against the young flag-captain John Whitby punishing men for swearing. 'Though the punishment was light, it displeased the men very much,' according to William Richardson, who was one of them. Alerted by the protest, Cornwallis intervened and stopped the practice.[15] In the Mediterranean the men of the *Berwick* mutinied over lean beef. 'The officers at last prevailed on them to return to their duty, and Sir John Collins being an easy man, no examples were made,' recorded J. A. Gardner, one of his junior officers.[16] Next year in the same fleet, Nelson

> came here two days ago and found a most unpleasant circumstance; a mutiny on board the *Windsor Castle*, Admiral Linzee's ship. The crew wishing to change their captain and first lieutenant, the officers have been tried at their own requests and most honourably acquitted but the admiral notwithstanding has removed them and forgiven the ship's company who richly deserved a halter. I am of opinion 'tis mistaken leniency and will be the cause of present innocent people being hanged.[17]

Two years later Nelson himself quelled a mutiny by force of character when the crew of the frigate *Blanche* (Jacob Nagle among them) refused to receive Captain Henry Hotham, 'bearing the name of such a tartar by his own ship's crew that our ship mutinised and entirely refused him'.[18] More serious was the mutiny of the *Defiance* in the Firth of Forth in September 1795 against five-water grog 'as thin as muslin and quite unfit to keep out the cold' (according to John Nicol, whose ship was lying near by), as a result of which five men were hanged.[19] Most serious of all, in the light of subsequent events, was the *Culloden* mutiny of December 1794. The ship had grounded the previous month, and the men claimed she was unseaworthy. A surrender was negotiated, not by the *Culloden*'s own hot-tempered Captain Thomas Troubridge, but by another officer, Captain Thomas Pakenham, who was well known for his humane sympathies. It was afterwards believed by seamen throughout the Navy that Pakenham had given his word that the men would not be punished, but the Admiralty broke it, and five men were hanged. After this no seaman would believe an officer's word of honour. An essential bond of trust had been severed.[20]

In February and March 1797 Howe, still nominally commanding the Channel Fleet from Bath, received by post a number of anonymous petitions purporting to come from various ships of his fleet (which was then at sea), requesting higher pay. On his own account he did not take them very seriously, but he made some inquiries in the fleet, apparently without informing Bridport, and unofficially passed the petitions to the Admiralty. Similar petitions had already been received there, and ignored. In this case Lord Spencer sent the petitions to Bridport for his comments.[21]

By the time he received them it was too late. The fleet returned to Spithead on 30 March. After waiting two weeks for a reply, the seamen put their plans into motion. Only in the last few days did it become obvious to their officers that something was afoot. Bridport from the start advised negotiation and conciliation, but the Admiralty's reaction to the rumour of discontent was to order the fleet to sea. This gave the signal for the outbreak of the mutiny on 16 April.[22] The mutiny consisted essentially of a collective refusal to obey the order to weigh anchor. For the next week the fleet was immobilized by the mutineers while a body of elected delegates, two from each ship, negotiated first with Bridport, and later with the Board of Admiralty itself led by Lord Spencer. Although a few unpopular officers were sent ashore, no violence or disorder occurred, and the mutineers did not interfere with the ordinary routine of their ships. On the 19th, indeed, the Grand Duke of Württemberg, who was in England for his marriage to Princess Charlotte, paid a state visit to the fleet accompanied by Spencer and the Lords of the Admiralty, the mutineers politely manning the yards and firing the appropriate salutes.[23] The mutineer delegates denied any political motives and proclaimed their loyalty to the king. They insisted throughout on their readiness to sail immediately if the French fleet put out from Brest, and would not allow frigates and convoy escorts to join them, lest trade should suffer. Their principal demands were for an increase of wages, unchanged since 1652 and seriously eroded by the inflation of the past thirty years, together with various improvements in the quality and quantity of victuals and the treatment of the wounded. Though they did not say so, it is clear that a major grievance was the operation of the bounty system, especially the extra bounties paid under the Quota Acts, which had the effect of giving latecomers, mainly landmen, far more than the seamen who were really valuable. This outraged their sense of fair play.[24] Most of the men's demands were eventually conceded, and with the arrival of a royal pardon on Sunday the 23rd the first Spithead mutiny was officially over.[25]

The necessary legislation was now set in motion, but the motions of Parliament were too slow for the seamen, who became increasingly suspicious that they had been deceived again. On 7 May the mutiny broke out anew. This time there was violence, though not from the mutineers: Colpoys ordered the officers of his flagship the *London* to fire on the mutineers, several of whom were killed. The enraged men nearly hanged the admiral and one of his officers in retaliation, but were dissuaded by two of the leading delegates. Colpoys, Vice-Admiral Gardner, ten captains and 100 other officers (about one-fifth of the total) were now sent ashore and the mutineers took effective command of the fleet, but the remaining captains and admirals, including Bridport, remained aboard. (Captain Sir Richard Bickerton had his wife living aboard throughout the mutiny.) Two days later the necessary Act of Parliament finally passed the Lords and received the royal assent. Lord Howe had at last been allowed to resign his command in April, but he now came to Portsmouth on behalf of the king to persuade the mutineers that their demands really had been granted. In addition they now insisted that a list of named unpopular officers (about half of those who had been sent ashore) should be replaced, and this Howe (without authority) conceded. The reconciliation was completed with ceremonies on 15 May, culminating in a banquet given by Howe for the delegates of the fleet. Two days later Bridport was able to sail to take station off Brest.[26]

Meanwhile another mutiny had broken out among the ships at the Nore. This anchorage was a focal point where ships coming from Chatham and the river yards, or those returning from sea, often spent a few days. It was also a major distribution centre for new recruits, and an old line-of-battleship, the Sandwich, lay permanently off Sheerness as guardship and floating barracks. There was a flag-officer, Vice-Admiral Charles Buckner, to supervise the business of the port, who flew his flag in her. There was no fleet at the Nore, accustomed to operating together, simply a transient population of ships most of which stayed there only briefly. There were only three ships of the line and some frigates there when mutiny broke out on 12 May. Initially it aroused little alarm; only after twelve days, when it became clear that the concessions made at Spithead were not going to satisfy the new mutineers, did the Admiralty react. The Nore mutineers demanded not only the same concessions given at Spithead (which in reality had already been granted to the whole Navy), but more regular pay, advance wages for pressed men, a right to leave in port, a more equitable distribution of prize-money, a standing pardon for returning deserters, and an effective veto on the appointment of officers.[27] Neither at Spithead nor the Nore did the mutineers mention either impressment or flogging as grievances, and the mutineer leaders themselves flogged men for drunkenness.[28] To cement their cause the Nore mutineers imposed rigorous discipline, stopping all communication with the shore in order that the men should not discover the concessions made at Spithead, and not hesitating to fire on ships which offered to leave the anchorage. The Board of Admiralty arrived on the scene on 28 May, but from the beginning they refused to make further concessions, and stopped shore supplies to the mutineers. They must have known that the new mutiny had little of the public support of the old and virtually none of the leverage. The Channel Fleet was the country's principal strength and only safeguard against invasion; the small group of ships at the Nore had limited opportunity to do mischief, and several of them were visibly reluctant to remain in the mutiny. On 30 May the frigates Clyde and San Fiorenzo escaped under fire from the mutineers.[29]

The Nore mutiny was then on the verge of collapse, but it was saved by the mutiny of Admiral Adam Duncan's North Sea Squadron off Yarmouth on 27 May, after which most of his squadron sailed to join the Nore mutineers. This was another crisis, potentially worse than the Spithead mutinies, for Duncan's task was to blockade the Dutch fleet in the Texel, which (unlike the French in Brest) was known to be ready for sea and preparing for an expedition. For some days Duncan was reduced to keeping up a pretence of blockade with two ships only. Moreover the reinforced Nore mutineers became increasingly extreme in their attitudes as their situation grew more difficult. For three days they attempted a complete blockade of the Thames, and when that failed they discussed sailing their ships to an enemy or neutral port. But supplies were short, more and more ships found means to desert the mutineers, and when they gave the signal to sail on 9 June no ship obeyed it. After fighting on board, all the mutinous ships had been recaptured by loyalist seamen by 13 June, and the last of the great mutinies was over.[30]

The 'terrifying scene' of the great mutinies, as Lady Spencer called it, 'the most awful crisis that these kingdoms ever saw', in the words of Lord Arden, one of the Lords of the Admiralty, demanded explanations, and contemporaries rushed to offer them.[31] Only obliquely and privately did authority admit that the men had real grievances, above all (in Spencer's words) that 'the wages were undoubtedly too low in proportion to the times',[32] and they took it for granted that only outside subversion could account for the mutinies. The French or the Corresponding Societies (the main centres of political agitation, if not subversion, in Britain) were the obvious candidates, but others favoured the Foxite Whigs, the United Irishmen, the Defenders or the Methodists. In every case the Quota Acts (and the Insurrection Act) provided the obvious mechanism by which designing landmen had been introduced into the Navy to corrupt the simple sailors.[33] Modern historians have taken up the theme with enthusiasm, each according to their taste and interests identifying a different group of subversives, but all agreeing that outsiders brought in by the Quota Acts must have been responsible.[34] As a variation on this theme a contrast has been proposed between the 'unpolitical' (benign, morally justified) Spithead mutinies, and the 'political' or 'revolutionary' (malign and dangerous) mutinies on the East Coast.[35]

The idea that the mutinies were led by outsiders suits many theories, but it is difficult to reconcile with the evidence which has long been in print, and still more difficult to square with the unpublished research now available.[36] The delegates of the fleet at Spithead put their names to documents and negotiated publicly. We know who they were, their ages, ratings and places of birth. Without exception they were able seamen or seamen petty officers with long experience at sea; none of them was a Quota man, and only four out of thirty-three were Irish.[37] Though the fact was long since disproved, it is still sometimes repeated that Valentine Joyce, the delegates' spokesman, was a Belfast tobacconist and a Quota man.[38] In fact he was born in Jersey, had been a seaman all his life, and on his own statement had served in the Navy since he was eleven. His family lived in Portsmouth where his father was serving in the garrison.[39] It is only possible to believe that the mutiny was really led by Quota men if one believes that the delegates were straw men concealing the real leaders[40] – or the real leader, that shadowy Macavity of the Channel Fleet, the mysterious genius who 'must' have organized the mutiny but who covered his tracks so perfectly that no trace of his existence survives.[41] Here we are in the presence of the conspiracy theory in its purest form, in which the entire absence of evidence only serves to prove the fiendish cunning of the conspirators.

At the Nore the situation is more obscure. For obvious reasons the leaders of this mutiny were not keen to be identified afterwards: some escaped, others concealed themselves, and we cannot be sure that the twenty-nine men eventually hanged were the true leaders. Richard Parker, the nominal leader or spokesman of the mutineers, was a Quota man of some education, besides being a former professional seaman and inferior officer in the Navy, but it appears very unlikely that he could have been the real organizer. He is reported to have been mentally unstable, he had not been at sea for years, and he only arrived aboard the *Sandwich* twelve days before the mutiny broke out.[42] The men who have been identified as being most likely to have been the real leaders were long-serving petty officers and seamen, none of them Quota men and only a few of them Irish. This mutiny was clearly badly planned and disunited from the first, perhaps a hasty response to the news from Portsmouth. Evidently neither means nor ends were properly thought out, and as the situation fell apart desperate men resorted to violence – but this by itself is no evidence of political subversion, and these mutineers also declared their loyalty.[43]

The men of the North Sea fleet had real grievances of long-overdue pay, and in some ships lack of leave, but they showed 'marked civility and deference' to their officers, in the words of Lieutenant William Hotham of the *Nassau*, and insisted that their delegates 'are not to be understood as ringleaders of a mutinous assembly, but as men appointed by the majority of each ship's company, in order to prevent confusion and obtain as speedy a regularity of affairs as possible'.[44] In the course of the mutiny they fired the customary salutes for the king's birthday and the anniversary of Charles II's restoration. As the mutineer leaders at the Nore became more extreme, the North Sea ships became more reluctant, the delegates consulted their officers and in due course chose their moment to desert the mutiny. Lieutenant Edward Brenton of the *Agamemnon* remembered that

> The seamen, generally speaking, throughout the mutiny, conducted themselves with a degree of humanity highly creditable not only to themselves, but to the national character. They certainly tarred and feathered the surgeon of a ship at the Nore; but he had been five weeks drunk in his cabin, and had neglected the care of his patients . . . The delegates of the *Agamemnon* showed respect to every officer but the captain; him, after the first day, they never insulted, but rather treated with neglect.[45]

After it was over Vice-Admiral Onslow returned aboard his flagship the *Nassau* to find all his property and valuables untouched, while the mutineers of the *Inflexible* carefully replaced some of Captain Ferris's crockery which they had accidentally broken. This does not look like the work of revolutionaries bent on smashing the fabric of civil society.[46]

During and after the mutinies the government conducted secret inquiries aimed at exposing links with subversives at home or abroad. These reports stated unequivocally that the mutinies were not organized or inspired from outside, though there was a possibility of subsequent contact with the Corresponding Societies or even the Whigs.[47] Officers who witnessed the mutinies at first hand, like Lieutenant Philip Beaver of the *Monarch* at Spithead, had no doubt that they were led by seamen whose conduct they frankly admired.

> They have demanded nothing but what to every unprejudiced person must appear moderate and just, and they have conducted themselves with a degree of prudence and decency which I thought them incapable of . . . I had always great respect for an English seaman; I like the character now better than ever.[48]

Far away with Jervis off Cadiz, Nelson thought the same: 'for a *mutiny* . . . it has been the most manly that I ever heard of, and does the British sailor infinite honour'.[49]

The 1797 mutinies fundamentally changed the attitudes of officers and men throughout the Navy, but it is helpful to distinguish short-term and long-term changes. In the immediate aftermath of the mutinies, the men were disturbed and excited, and the officers were badly frightened. No captain now knew where he stood. 'You must persuade them, but you cannot force them to return to their duty. I believe the majority are well disposed ... and do not know their own strength,' wrote Captain Graham Moore of the frigate *Melampus.* 'I go on much in the old way and have been under the necessity of punishing a number of men since we left Spithead. Each time I was expecting a riot, but all went off quietly.'[50] The weaker captains lost their nerve, and the tougher ones reacted with severity to the slightest sign of trouble. None were tougher than Sir John Jervis, now Earl St Vincent, and to his squadron blockading Cadiz were sent many ships whose discipline was most shaky. In July 1797, for example, the men of the *St George* mutinied, ostensibly to free three men convicted of buggery, 'as an execution for such a horrible offence would bring disgrace on the ship'.[51] This was on a Friday. The captain and officers suppressed the trouble at once, a court martial sat next day, and the convicted men were hanged on Sunday morning immediately before prayers. Jacob Nagle was a witness:

> The inside division of line-a-battle ships was engaged by the [Spanish] gunboats, the other division had their pennant up at the mizzen peak for prayers, and the other division had the yellow flag hoisted a-hanging of two men, all at one time on a Sunday morning.[52]

When Vice-Admiral Thompson (he who had missed the signal at the battle five months before) protested at this profanation of the Sabbath, St Vincent seized the opportunity to get rid of him.[53] The captain of the *Romulus* calmed a mutiny by promising that no one would be punished and the ship sent to England. St Vincent kept his word; but he broke up the ship's company and distributed them to other ships before she went home.[54] In May 1799 there was a mutiny in Pellew's ship the *Impetueux* in Bantry Bay, the men protesting at excessive flogging and demanding a new captain, second and fourth lieutenant; 'our first lieutenant his going on leave who has ever been a father to the ship's company'. Pellew was refused a court martial by two admirals, Bridport and Sir Charles Cotton, and even St Vincent grumbled at being made 'hangman to the fleet'. Three men were hanged, but the two lieutenants complained of were put ashore, 'their continuance in the ship being judged highly dangerous to her safety'.[55]

In some of the mutinies planned or attempted in the late 1790s there is evidence of the activities of the United Irishmen, who after the 1797 mutinies tried to exploit the opportunity which they had not noticed before. After the failed Irish rebellion of 1798, however, the United Irishmen themselves changed character and became an aggressively Catholic movement, taking oaths 'to kill or destroy the Protestants'.[56] This was a bad way to enlist the support of a ship's company, and most of these plots were betrayed or suppressed by other seamen.[57] The mutiny of the frigate *Hermione* in September 1797 was a spectacular and unique event, and one of the very few which apparently conforms to the popular stereotype of a brutal captain driving his men to extremities. In fact the conduct of Captain Hugh Pigot was not simple brutality, but inconsistent and irrational brutality. Men could put up with a good deal so long as they knew where they stood, but Pigot was completely unpredictable. Worse, he directly attacked the moral foundations of shipboard society. In the final incident which triggered the mutiny, he threatened to flog the last men down from aloft. They would necessarily be the yard-arm men, the most skilful topmen, with the dangerous and critical job of passing the reef-earrings. Pigot was punishing men for being the best, and when three men fell to their deaths in their haste to get down, he called to 'throw the lubbers overboard'. It was the worst insult in the seaman's vocabulary, and this final degradation drove the men mad. They seized the ship and murdered most of the officers.[58]

Edward Southcott, the master, was one of the few to survive. 'All the best men were the principals of the mutineers,' he said afterwards, and it was true of all mutinies.[59] At Spithead in 1797, as an old seaman remembered, 'There weren't so many let into the secret of the mutiny as was at first imagined; but then they were chiefly petty officers and able seamen, who possessed a strong influence over all hands, fore and aft.'[60] John Mullen, captain of the forecastle, who led the *Adamant* mutiny in June 1798 was described by Captain William Hotham as 'one of the finest and best behaved men in the ship and had never had an angry word said to him or a lash upon his back'.[61] It was the same with the mutiny of the *Téméraire* in Bantry Bay in 1801, demanding to go home on the news of peace rather than to the West Indies. The leaders, in Edward Brenton's view, 'were the noblest fellows, with the most undaunted and prepossessing mien, I ever beheld – the beau ideal of British sailors'.[62] Organizing a mutiny was a supreme test of character and leadership. Only those who were really admired by their shipmates would be followed. Authority very much wished to believe in the alternative explanation of outside agitation, which would absolve it of ignoring genuine grievances, but this was wishful thinking. Almost without exception, mutinies were led by petty officers or long-serving leading hands, the natural aristocracy of the lower deck.

It was precisely these men, experienced, responsible, fully alive to the necessity of organization and teamwork at sea, who were the officers' essential allies in establishing discipline. For this reason St Vincent's policy of favouring and encouraging the Marines to sustain authority against mutiny was extremely dangerous. It worked, in the short run, for the Marines like other landmen had always been the butt of seamen's disdain, and their resentments could be turned to account. What he was doing, however, was dividing the ships' companies, setting the officers against their natural supporters, and undermining the petty officers' authority with their men. As Captain Philip Patton pointed out,

> The effect of connecting *landmen* with the officers of ships as the confidential class is completely overturning the natural order of things . . . It will be highly dangerous to bring the Marines to act against the real seamen at any time, as no ship can be made safe if they are discontented.[63]

The Marines deserved their improved status and the title 'Royal' which St Vincent obtained for them in 1802, but it would have been better for the Navy if they had won it in action against the enemy.[64]

——————•◆•——————

THIRTY

The Second Coalition

Operations 1797–1801

I n the aftermath of his victory off Cape St Vincent, Earl St Vincent (as he became in June) blockaded the Spanish fleet in Cadiz. With Austria out of the war, there was no prospect of re-entering the Mediterranean, and even his base at Lisbon was uncertain, as the Portuguese government came under heavy French pressure. St Vincent kept his fleet in a high state of health and efficiency by rigorous training and discipline, taking great care to supply it with fresh food. Though exposed to the full force of the open Atlantic, his blockading technique in good weather was to anchor so close in that the ladies of Cadiz could easily be seen taking the air on their flat roofs. This also permitted discreet communication with the town. 'Small boats come off during the night,' wrote Captain John Markham of the *Centaur*.

> So confident are we in the integrity of these poor Spaniards, that the officers have by their means got their linen washed in the town. We receive fresh beef, mutton, fowls, eggs, and vegetables from Portugal and Tangiers.[1]

In the immediate aftermath of the mutinies, the admiral was at least as concerned to occupy his men as to fight the Spaniards. At night he sent boats even closer inshore, and in early July, attempting to push a bomb vessel within range of the Spanish ships, he brought on a series of vicious hand-to-hand boat actions. Nelson was conspicuous in this fighting and narrowly escaped death. It was extraordinary that a rear-admiral should risk his life in a lieutenant's place, but there were good reasons. Discipline and morale were shaky, there had been examples of cowardice among both officers and men in the boats, and it was necessary that a flag-officer should lead from the front.[2]

For the same reasons St Vincent now sent Nelson with a small squadron to attack Santa Cruz de Tenerife in the Canary Islands, where a Spanish merchantman laden with treasure was reported. Without troops this was a hazardous operation, but the Navy had rushed the defences of small ports before, and this was no moment for inactivity. Two landing attempts on 22 July, however, only succeeded in alerting the defences. Then a deserter's information persuaded the captains to make another attempt, and Nelson consented. This time the plan was for a direct frontal assault of the town in darkness, relying on speed to overwhelm the strong defences. Everyone knew it was very risky, and their assessment of the defences was optimistic. Though the governor General Antonio Gutiérrez had fewer than 800 regular troops and about as many local militiamen (mostly without firearms), the defenders were well led, well trained and in good heart. Even so if the whole British force of 1,000 had rushed the mole, as planned, they might have succeeded, for it was defended by fewer than 100 men. Unfortunately the defences were alert, strong currents swept the boats along the shore, and only a few, including Nelson's, reached the mole. As he stepped from the boat he was badly wounded, and his right arm was later amputated. In the town Captain Troubridge and the survivors of the landing parties were able to negotiate a surrender by which they were returned to their ships. After a chivalrous exchange of letters between Nelson and Gutiérrez, the defeated British force sailed away on 27 July.[3]

The precedent St Vincent had hoped Nelson would be able to follow was the British capture of Trinidad in the West Indies, which took place on 18 February 1797. The Spanish defences were weak, the governor disgusted to find himself allied with French Republicans, and the British commanders, Abercromby and Rear-Admiral Henry Harvey, had a respectable landing force which justified Spanish surrender. On 18 April they landed at San Juan in Puerto Rico, hoping to repeat their success, but here the Spanish defences and leadership were of higher calibre, and on the 30th the British were forced to re-embark. This was the last possible target in the Caribbean which the surviving British striking force might have been able to capture. In May 1798 all but two places that the British still held in Saint Domingue were evacuated, and they too were abandoned in September in return for an agreement with the negro leader Toussaint l'Ouverture to leave Jamaica unmolested. For the rest of the war the British had to stand on the defensive in the West Indies, though in 1799 they managed to take the small but valuable Dutch colonies of Surinam and Curaçao.[4]

In France the Directory was so preoccupied with its own political crisis during 1797 that it was not even aware of the British naval mutinies until they were over, and the mutineers' willingness to fight the enemy was not tested.

When an enemy fleet did put to sea in October, it was the Dutch rather than the French, and for political rather than strategic reasons. Vice-Admiral Jan Willem de Winter did not mean to risk a battle to no purpose, and was returning to port when Duncan's squadron intercepted him on the 11th. The Dutch were heading north up the coast of Holland, already almost within sight of the Texel and safety. Duncan had no time to form line of battle but attacked from his cruising formation in two groups, intending to perform 'Lord Howe's manoeuvre'. Like Howe, he found that only some of his ships were able to understand the signal and carry it out, but he brought on a close action in which the van and rear of the Dutch line were overwhelmed and crushed. Each side had sixteen ships in the line, the British slightly superior in weight of armament, but the Dutch suffered a complete defeat in spite of fighting with great determination. Three admirals (including de Winter), nine ships of the line and two frigates were taken; the British had never won a victory remotely equivalent against more or less equal forces.[5]

The victory of Camperdown, gained by a fleet which had been in mutineers' hands four months before, was a powerful moral and political tonic, which eased the strategic problem of controlling the North Sea, and for the first time bestowed on the Royal Navy something of the aura of invincibility which now hung about the French armies on land. To celebrate it, St Vincent and the First of June the government organized a solemn Thanksgiving Service in St Paul's Cathedral in December, attended by George III in person.[6] Looking at the war as a whole, however, the most that could be said of the naval victories was that they had prevented a bad situation getting any worse. In October 1797 at the peace of Campo Formio, Austria effectively changed sides and joined France (or rather Bonaparte in person, who was negotiating against the instructions of his own government) in partitioning Europe, taking parts of southern Germany, Venice and Istria to make up for the loss of Belgium and Lombardy, and at the same time repudiating the British loan with which she had been fighting. In the new year French armies 'liberated' Switzerland and Rome. A French invasion force under Bonaparte's command was assembling in the Channel ports.[7]

With few troops and no allies, the most that Britain could now do in Europe was the occasional raid, such as the plan proposed in the spring of 1798 to blow up the locks at Ostend at the seaward end of the ship-canal to Bruges, thus blocking an important inland port and assembly-point for invasion forces. This was the scheme of Captain Home Popham, a plausible young officer with a chequered reputation, whose excellent services as the Duke of York's naval liaison officer in Flanders at the start of the war had gained him early promotion, but who had never commanded a warship. Dundas adopted him and his project, and pressed Spencer to appoint him in command. Once again Dundas was trying to control Spencer, and the army was trying to control the choice of naval commander for a combined operation. 'I am not without apprehensions,' wrote Spencer, 'that his being placed in command of a squadron on this occasion may give great disgust and offence to the profession who are sufficiently irritable in these matters.'[8] Nevertheless Spencer contrived to give him local command, and Popham planned and executed the raid with great skill on 20 May. Unfortunately, after the locks had been destroyed, a gale blew up which prevented the re-embarkation of the troops, who were forced to surrender.[9]

At the end of May a large-scale rebellion of the United Irishmen broke out in Wexford and elsewhere in Ireland. Fortunately for the British, the French were taken by surprise, and were not interested in investing any real effort in Ireland. On 6 August 1,000 men under General J. A. Humbert sailed from Rochefort to land in Mayo, but the rebellion was over before he left France, and so small a force could do no more than create a temporary diversion. On 16 September Commodore J. B. F. Bompard with ten ships and a mere 300 men sailed from Brest to reinforce Humbert, but he had already surrendered, Bompard's ships were intercepted on the coast of Ireland and only three escaped.[10]

In both Britain and France, strategic attention was on the Mediterranean, not the Atlantic. In February 1798 Bonaparte abandoned the invasion of Britain as impracticable, and instead forced on a reluctant Directory a favourite scheme of his own for an expedition to Egypt. 'Everything's worn out here,' he complained, 'I haven't enough glory. This little Europe cannot provide enough.'[11] The strategic rationale, insofar as there was one, was to replace France's lost colonies, and perhaps in the long term to open communication with India. The political temptation for the Directory was to be rid of their most dangerous subordinate, and the Army of Italy which was devoted to him. From the Army of the Rhine, Hoche's old command where Bonaparte was not worshipped, came General J. B. Kléber, in his own words to see 'if that little bugger's got any guts',[12] and perhaps also to keep him under observation. Financed by looting the city of Berne, the expedition was a remarkable feat of improvisation. Over 30,000 troops were carried by 300 transports, escorted by seven frigates and thirteen ships of the line. Three of these were old and in poor condition, but the rest were new and powerful ships, including the 120-gun flagship *Orient* (the *Dauphin Royal* of 1793), the largest warship in the world. The flag-officers, Vice-Admiral F. P. de Brueys d'Aigalliers, Rear-Admirals P. C. de Villeneuve, A. S. M. Blanquet du Chayla and Denis Decrès, were all former noble officers of the *ancien régime*, released from prison on the fall of the Jacobins, who brought professional experience without much of the resolution and enterprise of their Republican predecessors. The soldiers despised and as far as possible ignored them, while Bonaparte was in personal command of the fleet. None of them seems to have anticipated much danger from the Royal Navy, which had not been present in the Mediterranean for eighteen months.[13]

British ministers were well aware that the expedition was preparing, and had a good deal of intelligence pointing towards the Levant, which they found very difficult to believe. Of all the many areas of the world in which a powerful French army under a talented general might have done Britain harm, there was hardly one which was further from any British interests or French prospects than Egypt. Only Dundas, whom Grenville begged in vain to think 'with a map in your hand, and with a calculation of distances',[14] took the idea seriously, mainly because he seriously believed that a French army could march swiftly and easily from Egypt to India. His colleagues were more concerned by the reviving possibility of a new alliance with Austria, which would certainly be impossible without a fleet in the Mediterranean to protect the flank of an Austrian army in northern Italy, and Austria's dependent ally the Two Sicilies. As a first step more information was urgently needed. At the end of April 1798, Nelson, recovered from his wound, rejoined St Vincent off Cadiz and almost at once was detached with three ships of the line and three frigates to watch Toulon. Soon afterwards the government at last made up its mind to risk stationing a proper fleet in the Mediterranean again, leaving home waters with no strategic reserve whatever. On 24 May St Vincent received a reinforcement of eight sail of the line, and the same day he detached ten to join Nelson.[15]

Meanwhile Nelson had met with disaster: in the early hours of 21 May his flagship the *Vanguard* was completely dismasted in a gale. The other ships in company did not suffer severely, and the accident must be attributed to bad seamanship, either by Nelson himself (who was not the outstanding seaman of his generation), or his young flag-captain Edward Berry (whose subsequent career was a catalogue of gallant bungling interspersed with longer and longer periods of unemployment).[16] It came at the worst possible moment, for the day before the storm, the French expedition had sailed from Toulon. While the *Vanguard* repaired her damage in a Sardinian bay, the French passed unseen. As soon as she was fit for sea, Nelson hastened to the rendezvous where his frigates had been ordered to wait ten days for him. He arrived on the eleventh day, 9 June; they had left to seek him elsewhere, and they never found him. Two days earlier Troubridge had joined him with the reinforcements. Nelson now had a fleet to command, for the first time, and an enemy to seek, but he had no information where the French had gone, and no frigates to help him find them.[17]

First looking on the Italian coast, Nelson headed south on information that the French had been seen steering towards Malta. South of Sicily on 22 June a neutral merchantman informed him that the French had taken Malta from the Knights of St John and sailed again on the 16th for an unknown destination. They had not appeared in Sicily, the obvious target, the wind ruled out anywhere to the westward, so in the teeth of probability Nelson decided they were bound for Egypt. Calling back the ships then chasing some sails in the distance, lest the fleet become separated, he pushed for Alexandria with all speed. What he did not know was that the neutral's information was in one critical respect wrong: the French had sailed from Malta on the 19th, not the 16th. The distant sails were actually the outliers of their fleet, and the two flagships were then only sixty miles apart. On 28 June the British squadron sighted Alexandria, only to find the port empty and no news of the French. On the 30th he sailed again, sick at heart at having wrongly guessed the enemy's intentions. Next day the French fleet, which had proceeded more slowly, and on a more northerly course, anchored off Alexandria and prepared to land its troops. On 20 July Nelson was back at Syracuse, where the fleet watered and victualled, but found no information. On the 24th he sailed, still convinced the French must be somewhere in the eastern Mediterranean, and meaning to search in the Aegean. Then at last, on the 28th, he received definite intelligence that the French were in Egypt. At noon on 1 August the British were close enough to Alexandria to see the harbour crammed with French transports, but no sign of the men-of-war. The only other anchorage on the coast was Aboukir Bay twenty miles to the northward. By mid-afternoon the French fleet was in sight, anchored in the bay in a single line.[18]

Bonaparte had ordered the fleet to a position convenient for the army's purposes, and seemingly did not much care what happened to it, though he subsequently falsified the record to conceal his responsibility. Brueys and his officers, sensing that they had been abandoned, seem to have been seized with a sort of despairing torpor. He had seen Hood defend Frigate Bay at St Kitts in 1782; perhaps he overrated the possibilities of fighting at anchor, but he certainly knew what precautions had to be taken, and had neglected them all. His ships were lying at single anchor, leaving room to swing, mostly without springs to cant their broadsides to bear on an attacker. Though he now knew that British warships were back in the Mediterranean, he had no scouts out, and even when the British came in sight, he persuaded himself that they would not attack that day. But the wind was blowing into the bay, so, accepting the risks of fighting in shoal water and gathering darkness, Nelson ordered an immediate attack, the ships forming a rough line as they stood in. Rounding the island of Aboukir which marked the southern entrance of the bay, they hauled up to reach the head of the enemy line. Captain Thomas Foley of the *Goliath*, the leading ship, observing the French ships lying at single anchor, on his own initiative crossed the head of the line and came down the inshore side, where the French had not even cleared for action. The next three ships did the same, while Nelson and the rest of the fleet took the outside berth. Brueys had stationed his weakest ships at the head of his line on the ungrounded assumption that it could not easily be attacked: instead they received an overwhelming onslaught without the rest of the fleet to leeward being able to help them. The British worked methodically down the line until they came to the *Orient*. She seriously damaged the *Bellerophon* which was driven out of action, but then caught fire herself. Late that evening she blew up with an explosion which stunned both French and British and brought all fighting to a halt for some time. Later the action resumed, but all through the night Villeneuve's rear division made no attempt to come to their comrades' assistance. Next morning, when most of the British ships were too much damaged to follow, Villeneuve made his escape with two ships of the line and two frigates. He left behind eleven battleships and two frigates taken or sunk, by a squadron of thirteen ships of the line (one of which ran aground and did not get into action) and one fifty-gun Fourth Rate.[19] 'Victory is certainly not a name strong enough for such a scene,' Nelson wrote to his wife.[20]

An officer was despatched overland to India to warn the East India Company that Bonaparte was in the Orient. Rear-Admiral Peter Rainier, commanding in the East Indies, did not take the threat very seriously, but it had some effect in distracting attention from plans against Mauritius, Manila and Java, and a small squadron under Captain John Blankett was sent out from Britain to the Red Sea.[21] Nelson's despatches home were lost when the *Leander*, 50, met and was taken by another survivor of the battle, the seventy-four-gun *Généreux*, with the result that rumours of the battle circulated throughout Europe for some time before definite news. The French landing was known in Britain long before. Ministers were depressed; Dundas proclaimed the inevitable loss of British India, and blamed Spencer for choosing an inexperienced young admiral. The contrast when a victory of such stunning completeness was announced was overwhelming: Spencer fainted on hearing the news. All over Europe Britain's potential allies heard of the battle with an enthusiasm which promised a new coalition against France.[22] Turkey declared war on the invader of her dominions, and Russia sent a squadron under Admiral F. F. Ushakov from the Black Sea to co-operate against France. Accompanied by a Turkish squadron under Cadir Bey, Ushakov occupied the Ionian Islands (former Venetian possessions in French hands since 1797) and laid siege to the French garrison of Corfu.[23]

The Two Sicilies was the most exposed of all countries to French aggression, and the most intensely relieved at the victory. When Nelson finally reached Naples aboard the crippled *Vanguard* on 22 September, he was received by the court and people amid scenes of enthusiasm barely short of hysteria. The British minister, Sir William Hamilton, was prominent in the rejoicing, and his theatrical wife still more so. Under their care Nelson, who had been badly concussed in the action, began to recover from his wound and from the intense strain of the previous months. But this 'country of fiddlers and poets, whores and scoundrels'[24] irritated him, and on 15 October he sailed with some relief to take care of the blockade of the French garrison of Malta, where the islanders had risen against their new masters and confined them to the fortifications. On 5 November he was back in Naples, dealing with high policy and diplomacy in conjunction with Hamilton and Queen Maria Carolina, the real head of her husband's government, which was dominated by a small group of her favourites, mostly brought in from Austrian service. The queen advocated an aggressive foreign policy, intended to provoke French attack and force Austria into war. Daughter of the Empress Maria Theresa, sister of two emperors and mother-in-law of the reigning emperor, the queen was happy to treat her husband's kingdom as a pawn in a private foreign policy designed to overthrow the French Republicans and avenge her murdered sister Queen Marie-Antoinette. She used Lady Hamilton to manipulate Sir William, who had long since become an uncritical admirer, and Nelson had no idea how unpopular the queen and her policy were among informed Neapolitans. His orders were to support British allies, and he readily fell in with, and encouraged, the queen's policy. Overbearing King Ferdinand's misgivings, Nelson lent his support to the offensive. On 28 November Leghorn surrendered to his ships, and next day the king entered Rome in triumph. One week later the French counter-attacked, and the Neapolitan army instantly disintegrated. By the end of the year the court had been evacuated to Palermo, and a French satellite republic was erected in Naples. What was worse, Austrian ministers were infuriated by his blatant attempt to force them into war, and the prospects of another coalition receded. When all excuses have been offered for Nelson's disastrous venture into strategy and diplomacy, it remains an outstanding example of the dangers of promoting admirals on professional ability alone, without education or knowledge of the world.[25]

In home waters Bridport and the Channel Fleet continued their watch on Brest throughout 1798 and 1799. Unlike Howe, Bridport believed in extensive cruising, but his blockade was still relatively loose, the condition of his ships was deteriorating after five years of war, and he was chronically short of frigates. As a result French squadrons, like Bompard's in September 1798, still found opportunities to sail unobserved even in summer-time. Spencer was anxious to replace Bridport, as 'his energy and other qualifications are nearly passed by', but could not find a suitable candidate.[26] In the spring of 1799 the French fleet in Brest was known to be preparing for sea, probably for the Mediterranean, but ministers were so sensitive about Ireland that Bridport was ordered to regard it as his first priority. On 26 April, Vice-Admiral Eustache Bruix sailed. One British frigate saw him, but her signals were missed in the fog, and Bridport moved north to cover Ireland. By the time it became clear that Bruix had gone south, he had a week's lead. He also had more ships than had been anticipated.[27]

St Vincent's Mediterranean squadron now had the Mediterranean to look after once more, but it was still blockading Cadiz. As Bruix approached, the old admiral himself was ill ashore at Gibraltar, leaving his second-in-command Vice-Admiral Lord Keith off Cadiz. On 3 May Bruix appeared off Cadiz with twenty-four ships of the line (including five Spanish which had joined from Ferrol on his way south). Mazarredo had twenty-eight inside the port, and Keith with fifteen was caught between the two, in a rising onshore gale. He formed a line of battle and awaited the French attack, but it never came. Bruix's orders were very much in the traditional French form; they allowed the possibility of action without enthusiasm. Abandoning the prospect of victory and inevitable delay, Bruix pushed on into the Mediterranean, where his primary objective was to relieve Bonaparte's army in Egypt. So far he had pursued his mission with boldness and skill, and he had everything to play for if he kept his nerve, for the allied forces were scattered all over the Mediterranean. Rear-Admiral J. T. Duckworth had four ships of the line at Minorca (captured by the British the previous November); Nelson had three off Malta and four off Naples, supporting a Royalist revolt assisted by Russian and Turkish troops which was in the process of overthrowing the 'Partheno-pean Republic'. In the vicinity were also four Portuguese and three Neapolitan ships of the line; in the Levant Sir Sidney Smith had two more, and Ushakov had twelve at Corfu, which had lately surrendered. It was urgent to concentrate before Bruix defeated them all in detail, and Keith concentrated on Minorca. Meanwhile Bruix had suffered a collision which persuaded him to steer for Toulon, where he found new orders. Austria had re-entered the war, the French army in Italy was in headlong retreat, and he was ordered to convey supplies for it to Genoa. Keith pursued him up the Ligurian coast, getting almost within sight before he was forced back by headwinds and misconceived orders from St Vincent, still commanding ashore. Bruix, now abandoning the idea of succouring the army in Egypt, returned to the Atlantic, bringing Mazarredo's fleet with him. Together they entered Brest on 8 August, while Keith, still in pursuit, arrived a week later. Bruix's cruise had been a brilliant failure. Tactical skill combined with irrational and unpredictable changes of strategy had baffled British pursuit, but he had made absolutely nothing of his opportunities to change the course of the war at sea.[28]

At the height of the crisis one admiral and his ships were conspicuously absent from Keith's fleet. Nelson had refused three direct orders from Keith to join him. By this time he was in thrall to Lady Hamilton, and through her Queen Maria Carolina had effectively taken command of the admiral and his squadron, which were absorbed in Neapolitan affairs. Officers who loved and admired him were horrified at the sudden change in his personality and conduct, while Spencer in London grew more concerned the more he heard.[29]

By March 1799 Russia and Austria were fighting France, but Austria was not allied, or even particularly friendly, to Britain, and the erratic Tsar Paul I of Russia was the only link binding the three. While Austrian and Russian armies drove the French back on all fronts, the British searched for some way of making an effective contribution with only a small army, and a perennial shortage of shipping for large troop movements overseas. This was the inspiration for the Anglo-Russian expedition to North Holland, which landed at Den Helder on 27 August. Immediately it achieved an important success: the main Dutch fleet lying near by, many of whose officers were Orangists, surrendered without firing a shot. Ashore the Duke of York's army did well at first, but there was no general Orangist rising, and by the onset of winter it was clear that there was not going to be any break-out. In October the duke negotiated an armistice which allowed the evacuation of his army. Meanwhile the Austrians and Russians had been defeated, and Russia soon abandoned the war.[30]

In the spring of 1799, while Bruix was cruising about the western Mediterranean, Sir Sidney Smith had been left with two ships of the line to watch Bonaparte, who was advancing north up the Syrian coast. Not content with observation, Smith captured the French siege train and took an heroic part in the Turkish defence of the medieval walls of Acre. 'The town is not, nor ever has been, defensible, according to the rules of art;' he wrote, 'but according to every other rule, it must and shall be defended.'[31] In May Bonaparte retreated, massacring prisoners and poisoning his own wounded as he left. There was no more glory to be had in Egypt, and in Europe there were new opportunities, with the Directory tottering, and the French armies retreating on all fronts before the Austrians and Russians. On 23 August Bonaparte sailed aboard a small corvette, and reached France unnoticed by any allied warships. This was probably not pure luck. As so often in his career, Smith (whose brother was acting British minister in Constantinople) was combining a naval with a quasi-diplomatic role, charged with secrets not known to admirals or even cabinet ministers, among them Bonaparte's contacts with the Royalists. Unfortunately the plan misfired. Bonaparte did indeed overthrow the Directory in November, only to instal, not Louis XVIII, but himself as 'First Consul' and effective sovereign.[32]

When Bruix returned to Brest in August, for a week (until Keith arrived) he had the numbers to overwhelm Bridport and control the Channel. Soon British command was re-established, but the whole episode made Spencer still more dissatisfied with Bridport's management. With over forty sail now in Brest, conveniently but also dangerously close to home, it was doubly necessary to prevent any more unpleasant surprises. Moreover a really close blockade offered the possibility of starving a port which had never been able to feed a large squadron from local resources. It was difficult for a civilian who had never seen Brest to dispute what was possible with the commander-in-chief, but Spencer was looking for an admiral of another mind, and in April 1800 he found one: St Vincent. 'You will have heard,' wrote Pellew,

> that we are to have a new commander in chief, heaven be praised. The old one is scarcely worth drowning, a more contemptible or more miserable animal does not exist. I believe there never was a man so universally despised by the whole Service. A mixture of ignorance, avarice and spleen.[33]

Not everyone was so pleased, for St Vincent brought with him the 'discipline of the Mediterranean Fleet'. Perceptive observers like Spencer and Collingwood were concerned that 'there are a great many ships where the reins of discipline are held very loosely, the effect of a long war, and an overgrown navy'.[34] St Vincent meant to change things. He had long believed that 'the officers in general, with very few exceptions, are so licentious, malingering and abominable that their conduct must bring about another mutiny',[35] and he took an unmistakable pleasure in imposing the most arduous and dangerous possible form of blockade, as much for its effect on them as on the enemy. In easterly winds he kept the whole fleet off the Black Rocks ('New Siberia') at the head of the Iroise by day, off Ushant by night, with an inshore squadron yet further in, just off the Goulet, and another off the Penmarks. In westerlies and in winter the cruising station was only a little further out. This was extremely hazardous; casualty rates rose rapidly, and many captains and admirals could not stand the strain for long. St Vincent filled his letters to the Admiralty with dismissive remarks about the feeble nerves of his subordinates, always contrasted with the unflinching rigour of the Navy's greatest admiral. He required the fleet to tack and wear in close order, close inshore, at least once every night with the captain and every officer on deck. He required two lieutenants to be on watch at all times. Himself needing little sleep, he rose with a telescope at three in the morning to see which of his captains was not on deck at first light. When officers were summoned to the flagship he refused to shorten sail for the boats, but watched them with amusement struggling for hours in his wake. Only the absolute minimum time was allowed ships in turns to visit Torbay for fresh food and water, not including any leisure on shore. When St Vincent fell ill in October 1800 and continued his command from the shore, he took up residence at Tor Abbey overlooking Torbay, which left even less scope for lingering at anchor. The Channel Fleet's sea-time, especially sea-time close off Brest, sharply increased. The *Boadicea* was twenty-three weeks on the blockade station in 1800, and several others twenty weeks or more.[36]

The human and material cost of St Vincent's blockade was high, but it was effective in restricting coastal trade, and perhaps also in psychological terms. Service under him was 'a fine school of humility', as Collingwood put it,[37] and many officers were worn out and dispirited. The best of them, however, responded to his injunction to 'rub out *can't* and put in *try*',[38] and were exhilarated by a powerful sense of professional superiority over an enemy who no longer controlled even his inshore waters. A British chart was prepared of the approaches to Brest. In June 1800 the *Mars* painted ship at anchor just off the Goulet as though she had been at Spithead. In September the inshore squadron began to take shelter during gales in the almost landlocked Douarnenez Bay just south of Brest.[39]

While the reputation and self-confidence of the Navy rose, that of the army fell yet further. In August 1800 an attempt was made to seize the Spanish dockyard of Ferrol. The troops were landed without serious opposition and marched near enough to the yard to view its weak defences, whereupon the commanding general insisted on withdrawal. It was now difficult to find British generals who inspired anything but contempt among sea officers.[40]

In allowing Sir Sidney Smith in the Levant the independence which so well suited his talents and tastes, Pitt in London had not considered the practicalities of command and responsibility. To operate without offending either St Vincent and Nelson, his naval superiors, or Lord Elgin the new British ambassador in Constantinople, Smith would have needed superhuman restraint and self-effacement, and his many good qualities did not stretch far in that direction. There was trouble during 1799, and a great deal more in January 1800, when Smith on his own initiative participated in an agreement, the Convention of El Arish, by which he undertook to allow the French army passage home from Egypt. As usual his thinking was political. The French troops now hated the general who had abandoned and betrayed them, and Kléber, who had succeeded to the command, made little secret of his intentions. 'That bugger has left us his breeches full of shit,' he told his officers. 'We're going to get back to Europe and stuff them in his face.'[41] Smith's plan was to help him, but Elgin and Keith (who had relieved St Vincent in the Mediterranean command), thinking in military terms, were appalled. The British government, finding that Tsar Paul had taken against the convention, also withdrew its consent, and the French stayed in Egypt, where Kléber was assassinated in June 1800.[42]

The French government now planned another relief expedition, as a reduced copy of Bruix's cruise of 1799. On 23 January 1801 Ganteaume with seven ships of the line escaped from Brest without detection and headed south. Like Bruix he got into the Mediterranean but took refuge in Toulon instead of taking the clear route to Egypt to land his troops. Eventually he did get as far as the coast of Egypt, but fled at the sight of British sails and achieved nothing.[43]

To explain the presence of another British fleet in the Levant it is necessary to go back to the summer of 1800, when Dundas persuaded his colleagues to send Abercromby with 20,000 troops – virtually Britain's whole disposable force – to the Mediterranean, in the hope of finding a suitable target. Their first idea was to land near Cadiz in October, but Keith, the naval commander, was deeply unenthusiastic about an unprotected coast, with yellow fever raging on shore. By this time British admirals assumed that the British army would run away at the first difficulty, and were not disposed to risk their ships on the soldiers' account. In this case it was well Keith did not, as an onshore gale blew up the day after they sailed, but the episode left the army 'the scorn and laughing-stock of friends and foes', and inter-service relations in a poisonous condition which augured ill for any future operations.[44]

Dundas's next plan was to use Abercromby's force to conquer Egypt from the French. On the basis of sketchy information and much wishful thinking he convinced himself and his colleagues that the French army was down to 13,000 men, ready to surrender at the first excuse, and that Abercromby with 15,000 indifferent troops could do the job. Only Sir Sidney Smith, with his usual mastery of the intelligence picture, came anywhere near the true figure of over 30,000 French troops in Egypt, and no one believed him. An opposed landing is the most dangerous of all military operations, and after their performance at Cadiz no dispassionate observer, knowing the true strength of each side, would have given Abercromby and Keith the slightest chance of success. Yet everything went right for them. They had the good luck to face an incompetent French general, and the good sense to spend a month in a deserted bay on the Turkish coast practising the landing operation, which was left to the management of more junior officers who worked well together. On 8 March 1801 the British landed in Aboukir Bay in the teeth of prepared defences (Captain A. I. F. Cochrane acting as the Navy's first 'beachmaster'), and on the 21st they defeated the French in a decisive battle outside Alexandria. Abercromby was mortally wounded, but at last the British army had shown that it could fight, and in due course the entire French army in Egypt surrendered.[45]

In conjunction with Abercromby's landing, another force was sent from India to land at the head of the Red Sea. It arrived too late to affect the outcome of the campaign, but it was still a remarkable example of strategy on a global scale. To support it a squadron under Popham came out from Britain to the Red Sea, where in his usual manner he operated with talent and energy, exceeding his instructions and ignoring his commander-in-chief. Other British plans in the Indian Ocean, notably the hope of taking the very troublesome French privateer base of Mauritius, were hampered by the distraction of Egypt, and the deficiencies of the Cape as a naval base which was unable to feed any considerable squadron.[46]

In almost every respect, 1800 was a year of unrelieved difficulty for the British government. In June Bonaparte, once more commanding the French armies in Italy, reversed the Austrian successes and with the narrow victory of Marengo turned the tide of the war. In February 1801 at the peace of Luneville Austria was again driven out of the war, recognizing French satellites in Switzerland and most of northern Italy. In January France and Spain agreed to force Portugal to abandon her old alliance with Britain or face invasion. In Britain 1 January 1801 marked the Act of Union between Britain and Ireland, intended to make possible a political settlement of Ireland based on emancipation of the Catholics. Like so many of Pitt's policies, it was the hasty product of the inner triumvirate acting without much research or information, and it immediately ran on to a large and well-charted rock. George III was advised that Catholic emancipation would break his coronation oath, and refused his consent. On this issue Pitt fell from power.[47]

His replacement was Henry Addington, a successful Speaker of the House of Commons whom few had considered as socially or politically of Cabinet rank. Grenville, Dundas and Spencer also left the government, though they did not immediately join the opposition, and Addington's Cabinet was widely regarded as lightweight. He chose St Vincent as the new First Lord of the Admiralty in the hope that a naval hero would lend his administration some essential prestige, and initially thought that he could combine the Admiralty and the Channel Fleet. St Vincent was personally and politically closer to the Foxite Whigs than the government he had joined, and Addington was presently to discover that he had taken on a great deal more than he expected or desired.[48]

By the autumn of 1800 Tsar Paul had abandoned the war and was moving towards a pro-French position of 'armed neutrality' on the model of 1780. The immediate crisis, however, was with Denmark, and arose from Danish miscalculation of how far it was safe to claim a right to convoy Danish merchant shipping through a British blockade without being searched. Knowing Britain's dependence on timber and naval stores from the Baltic (also on grain after yet another disastrous harvest), the Danes believed that they were in a position to push their advantage. The British were not anxious for trouble with neutrals, but in the face of what looked like aggression, they felt obliged to act. In July 1800 a Danish convoy was forcibly brought into port to be searched for contraband, and with a British squadron lying off Copenhagen in August, the Danes agreed to allow their convoys to be searched. No other move was made to restrict Denmark's very profitable wartime shipping, and in the short term both parties were content, but Denmark was drawn further into the Russian camp.[49]

By the end of 1800 open conflict with the Armed Neutrality was imminent. St Vincent advised Spencer that 'Sir Hyde Parker is the only man you have to face them. He is in possession of all the information obtained during the Russian Armament, more particularly that which relates to the navigation of the Great Belt.'[50] One of the last acts of Spencer's Admiralty before St Vincent took over was to appoint Parker to command the fleet assembling for the Baltic, with Nelson, now home from the Mediterranean, as his second. Spencer and St Vincent still had faith in Nelson, at sea and away from Emma Hamilton, and looked to him to inspire the elderly Parker, but after recent events there could be no question of giving him an independent command again. In March Denmark went on to the offensive, putting an embargo on British shipping and occupying Hamburg and Lübeck, and the same month St Vincent hurried Parker to sea. Parker had an obvious reason for delay (he had just married a young woman of twenty-four) and just possibly another, less obvious, for a handful of members of both outgoing and incoming administrations, not including Spencer or St Vincent, knew something of a plot against the life of Tsar Paul, which might put an early end to the Armed Neutrality. It is hard to believe, however, that they can have had very definite foreknowledge and still have allowed the fleet to sail. As far as the admirals were concerned, the only question was whether to strike at Denmark, the nearest and most vulnerable member of the alliance, or ignore the Danish and Swedish fleets to pass up the Baltic and attack that part of the Russian fleet which was laid up in Reval, while the remainder was still frozen in Kronstadt. This would have been the boldest and safest course, tackling the real core of the alliance rather than the reluctant Danes and Swedes, but it was too bold for Parker. After much hesitation over the two alternative entrances to the Baltic, the Sound or the Great Belt, he agreed to risk the passage of the Sound, where the much-feared Danish batteries did them no damage, and the Swedes did not fire at all. On 30 March they anchored in sight of Copenhagen.[51]

The month lost by Parker's idling had allowed the Danes to put the defences of Copenhagen into a formidable condition, but fortunately for the British they had moored their ships along rather than across the channels leading towards the city, so that they could be attacked one after the other as at the Nile. Their fleet was divided into two squadrons under separate command, and only the Crown Prince, commanding the defences in person, had authority over both. Moreover the line of unrigged ships and floating batteries along the King's Deep in front of the city (Commodore Olfert Fischer's command) was strongest at the key point off the dockyard where the Tre Kroner fort marked the angle of the two channels, and weakest at its further, southern end. Nelson saw that that end could be attacked by a fleet which came up the Hollands Deep, rounded the end of the Middle Ground shoal and came back down the King's Deep. It would not be necessary to subdue the strongest part of the defences in order to get bomb vessels within range of the city and force a negotiation with the Danes. On 1 April Nelson was detached to attack with twelve smaller ships of the line, while Parker with the bigger ships waited offshore. That evening he anchored at the southern end of the Middle Ground. At dawn the next morning, with a favourable southerly wind, the British ships weighed anchor to attack.[52]

Almost at once things miscarried. Without reliable charts or pilots, the British thought the deepest part of the channel was further from the Danish ships than it was, and kept too far to seaward. One ship grounded before the action began, and two more grounded on the farther side of the channel, at very long range. The remaining nine fought at the relatively long range of a cable (240 yards), reducing the effectiveness of their gunnery, though subsequent sounding showed that they could have run right alongside the Danish line, and even doubled it, as at the Nile (a possibility which frightened the Danes). The Danish defences were stronger than anticipated, and their guns were served with great gallantry. The result was a slow and hard-fought victory, with several ships suffering severely before the superiority of British gunnery began to tell. Fortunately the strongest part of the Danish defences around the Tre Kroner fort to the north was largely or entirely out of range, and Commodore Steen Bille's squadron in the main channel, though fully rigged and manned, was not ordered into action. Parker, whose eight ships were supposed to have worked up towards the town to check such a move, advanced so slowly that he could have done nothing to assist. Nevertheless time was on Nelson's side. By 1.30 p.m. British gunnery had clearly mastered the southern defences. Fischer had abandoned his burning flagship, twelve more ships were largely or completely out of action, and the way was open for the British bomb vessels to get within range of the city. At this point Parker, still four miles away, hoisted the signal of recall, made 'general' (i.e. directed to each ship individually). Had the signal been obeyed it would have transformed victory into catastrophe, for Nelson's ships could only have withdrawn across the face of the undefeated northern defences, in front of which several of them subsequently ran aground when attempting this move after the cease-fire. Angry and agitated at his superior's folly, Nelson turned to his flag-captain and said, 'You know, Foley, I have only one eye – and I have a right to be blind sometimes . . .', and, putting the telescope to his blind eye: 'I really do not see the signal.' Fortunately Nelson's captains, seeing that he had not repeated Parker's signal, copied him in disobeying the commander-in-chief.[53]

Soon afterwards the Danes accepted Nelson's proposal of a cease-fire. Virtually ignoring Parker, Nelson now negotiated in person with the Crown Prince, effective head of the Danish government. Nelson wanted a truce of sixteen weeks, sufficient to sail up the Baltic and deal with the Russian fleet. The Danes feared that this would be enough for the Russians to deal with them, but eventually agreed to fourteen, having heard (some time before the British did) of the murder of Tsar Paul, and correctly guessing that Russian policy might change. Physically and emotionally exhausted, and convinced that further fighting was unlikely, Nelson was preparing to return to England on sick leave when on 5 May Parker received orders to hand over his command to Nelson and himself return to England. The arrival of unofficial accounts of the battle soon after Parker's despatches had convinced ministers that he had to be replaced at once, and revived their confidence in Nelson. The prospect of command and activity revived Nelson himself, as it always did. On the 6th he took command, and next day he sailed for Reval. There he found the new Russian government conciliatory, and with no further need of fighting in the Baltic, he returned to England, landing at Yarmouth on 1 July.[54]

The new First Consul had once again taken personal command of invasion forces assembling around Boulogne. The port was too small and quite unsuitable for the purpose, while the landing craft, copied from the Swedish *skärgårdsflottan*, were unfit for the open waters of the English Channel. British officers who had observed the preparations were not impressed, but the public was alarmed, and Addington's ministry needed to reassure them. On 27 July 1801 Nelson was appointed to command the local anti-invasion forces in the Channel. The appointment of a vice-admiral and public hero to what was essentially a captain's command quieted public alarm, and incidentally kept Nelson busy and away from Emma Hamilton. He undertook his new command with his customary energy. On the night of 15 August he organized a boat attack on French invasion craft moored at the mouth of Boulogne harbour, but the enemy were forewarned, and the attack was driven off with loss.[55]

One month before, two notable actions had been fought in the Straits of Gibraltar. Rear-Admiral C. A. Durand de Linois, with three ships originally detached from Ganteaume's squadron, was coming from Toulon hoping to find Cadiz open, but on discovering his mistake, took refuge at Algeçiras, across the bay from Gibraltar. There he was attacked on 6 July 1801 by Rear-Admiral Saumarez from Cadiz with five ships of the line. Linois had moored his ships inshore under cover of batteries, but the wind dropped as the British approached and the attack failed badly. One ship grounded and was captured, the rest were driven off with damage. On the 12th Vice-Admiral Moreno arrived from Cadiz with five ships of the line to escort Linois, and the allies sailed for Cadiz that afternoon. The forces were now ten ships of the line against Saumarez's six, but one on each side was too badly damaged to sail. In the ensuing night action, one French ship was captured, two Spanish three-deckers fought one another and both blew up, and another French ship narrowly escaped after fighting off several British attackers. Saumarez had retrieved his reputation with a remarkable victory against odds, which had strategic consequences in confirming Spanish disgust with their French alliance. They demanded their fleet back from Brest, and relaxed the pressure on Portugal.[56]

This was one of several factors which propelled Britain and France to negotiate the Peace of Amiens, signed in October 1801 and ratified the following March. For Britain it was a peace of financial, political and strategic exhaustion. Nothing had been gained for which the war had been fought, but there seemed to be no promising strategy left to carry it on. By reconquering Egypt and knocking out the Armed Neutrality Britain had at least demonstrated a capacity to survive. Possibly the Consulate might prove to be a stable French government interested in lasting peace, though many people in and out of government were not convinced. At the negotiations Britain returned most of her overseas conquests (except Trinidad and Ceylon), in return for assurances of goodwill from Bonaparte which the Addington administration very much wished to believe.[57]

THIRTY-ONE

A Great and Virtuous Character
Administration 1793–1815

The reforms instituted by Pitt in the aftermath of the American War were still incomplete when the Revolutionary War broke out in 1793, and at the Admiralty the replacement of Chatham by Spencer as First Lord in 1794 removed a dam to reform. This existing momentum of change then came under extra pressure from the necessities of war, and from the ideology of 'economical reform', which was still alive among the Foxite Whigs.

First of the necessities of war was of course money. The British had fought each of their eighteenth-century wars on borrowed money, and the ever-growing capacity to borrow was fundamental to British survival in war. The proportion of the cost of each war raised from current taxation fell from 49 per cent in the War of the League of Augsburg to only 19 per cent in the American War. All the rest came from borrowing. In each war finance ministers believed that they had reached the limits of what the markets would bear, and each time they were proved wrong. But they were right that there must be a limit somewhere, and in the late 1790s Pitt finally reached it. The financial crisis of 1797 was three-fold: a crisis of liquidity, met by suspending gold payments; a crisis of government credit, which demanded increased revenue; and a crisis of taxation, which had to be surmounted to provide it. Almost all the new taxes on which government loans had been secured for a century were indirect taxes, mainly excises. The principal direct tax, the Land Tax, had been levied on a fixed assessment since 1692. By 1797 real income from land was grossly underestimated, and no other income was taxed at all. As a rough proxy, Pitt's government taxed the distinctive possessions of the rich: horses, dogs, servants, carriages, coats of arms and even hair powder. In 1798 these self-assessed taxes were tripled or more, and when that brought in less than half the seven millions predicted, the case for radical reform became irresistible. In 1799 Pitt introduced the first income tax, which reversed the financial trends of a century. Over the length of the Great Wars 58 per cent of the cost of the wars was met from taxation, more than at any time since Charles II's reign, and the proportion of direct to indirect taxes exceeded one-third for the first time since Queen Anne's reign. Between 1800 and 1815 taxation paid for 70 per cent of the cost of the war. It was this additional direct taxation, paid only by the wealthy, which made possible the great war for the defence of liberty and property. By comparison with the American War, government debt trebled, but tax receipts in money terms increased by more than five-fold, reaching the unprecedented figure of 20 per cent of national income.[1]

In France the picture was completely different. The early Revolutionary governments paid for war by printing paper money, the *assignats*, whose value had collapsed by 1796. This experience of inflation confirmed Napoleon's unsophisticated conviction that paper money and government borrowing were bad, and that any war-effort (meaning the British) which depended on them was fundamentally weak and vulnerable. He instituted a sound silver coinage (the *franc de germinal* of 1803) and a system of direct taxation which was supposed to cover all government expenditure. In practice his government only once ever balanced its books, in the peace year of 1802, and the Napoleonic war-effort was financed by looting and extortion of the occupied territories, and by unofficial borrowing 'off the balance-sheet'. Though he preached sound government, he never provided sound finance, and never could have done unless he had been willing to restrain his ambitions. As it was, the Napoleonic Empire depended, politically and socially, on continual war to finance continual war, to feed the emperor's ambitions and endow the new military aristocracy which supported his throne. The system was incapable of stability.[2]

The British financial crisis of 1797 very much concerned the Navy, which mutinied for more pay in the middle of it, and led to a limited reform of the archaic mechanism of the Navy Estimates. The traditional figure of £4 a man a month, which for 1797 yielded an estimate of £12,935,496 (against an actual expenditure of £14,065,980), was for 1798 raised to £7, giving a more realistic, or at least less unrealistic, estimate of £13,254,116 10s, and for the first time providing votes for various services which had not officially been mentioned to Parliament before. It was, however, a limited reform entirely on government terms. The recommendations of the 1785 Commission on Fees remained un-published, and when the Commons Select Committee on Finance attempted to investigate Admiralty salaries, Spencer sent them smartly on their way.[3]

Within the naval administration, some important changes were intro-duced in 1794, both to improve the management of the war, and to demonstrate to the Portland Whigs that Pitt was serious about reform when necessary. To relieve the overworked Navy Board and remove the wasteful competition of different transport services a Transport Board was created. This was not universally popular. The Board dealt with troop movements and came partly under Dundas as Secretary of State, so that it could be seen as another Trojan horse full of soldiers. Moreover most of the new Transport Commissioners were Scots, and several were associates of Sir Charles Middleton, which raised a different suspicion. From May 1794 Middleton was on the Admiralty Board, but not in the situation he had so long sought, for being no longer Controller, he no longer controlled the Navy Board. Knowing him, the new Controller (Sir Andrew Snape Hamond from 1794 to 1806) and his colleagues had reason to be on their guard against attempts to undermine their authority. Nevertheless the Transport Board was efficient and probably essential to the great expeditions to the West Indies and elsewhere mounted during this war. In 1795 it took over responsibility for prisoners-of-war from the overworked Sick and Hurt Board.[4]

Another Middletonian innovation was the appointment of Samuel Bentham as Inspector-General of Naval Works in April 1796. Bentham came of a family of shipwrights and had been trained in naval architecture before making a successful career as a military contractor in Russia (he liked to be known by his Russian rank as 'Brigadier-General Sir Samuel Bentham'). He was energetic, ambitious and had original ideas (better known today in the form written up by his brother Jeremy) about the importance of individual responsibility in business and administration. His connections included his stepbrother Charles Abbot, chairman of the Commons Finance Committee. With his subordinates the Architect, Chemist and Mechanist (from 1799 the distinguished engineer Simon Goodrich) Bentham formed a miniature naval board, of which he was the political head and they were the technical brains. The Inspector-General was an employee of the Admiralty with wide powers in the dockyards, in other words an instrument to interfere with the Navy Board's responsibilities. In the event Middleton left the Admiralty over the Laforey affair six months before Bentham was appointed, but Bentham worked for ten years as Inspector-General. His position made friction with the Navy Board inevitable, and the projects he sponsored often hampered the everyday work of the yards in the short term, but he was nevertheless the force behind a series of important inventions and innovations. He rebuilt the main basin at Portsmouth with deeper docks to take bigger ships, and introduced caissons to replace dock gates. He encouraged the installation of steam engines to drain these docks, and to power machinery which included sawmills, rolling mills for copper plates, and the block mills invented by Marc Brunel and manufactured by Henry Maudslay. These block mills are generally regarded as the world's first assembly line of machine tools, an epoch in the industrial age, and for the Navy a remarkably productive investment which by 1808 was producing 150,000 blocks a year. The last of the Brunel-Maudslay block machines ceased working only in 1983. Bentham urged the construction of a new dockyard on deeper water at Northfleet or the Isle of Grain to replace the old Thames and Medway river yards, but it was his own invention of the steam dredger in 1802 which saved the Navy's existing investment, in Chatham especially, and allowed the old yard to continue to handle all but the biggest warships until it finally closed in 1984.[5]

As First Lord of the Admiralty Spencer was courteous, efficient and open-minded, popular in the Navy and among his colleagues. 'Our Board is like one family,' recorded William Marsden the (Second) Secretary. 'Business may, in former times, have been conducted as well in the Admiralty department, but certainly never so pleasantly or so smoothly.'[6] St Vincent was an extreme contrast, violent and bigoted. So far from being open to new ideas, he brought to the Admiralty a museum of attitudes many of which belonged in the seventeenth rather than the nineteenth century. He was an uncompromising supporter of 'economical reform', for whom all government expenditure was inherently corrupting. Brought up in one of the few Hanoverian families in Staffordshire, the most Jacobite county in England, he suspected all Scotsmen as the natural tools of arbitrary despotism. He advocated the abolition of the British army (the Guards and the artillery excepted) as a danger to liberty, and its replacement by the Royal Marines.[7] For St Vincent it was an article of faith, requiring neither argument nor evidence, that 'the civil branch of the Navy is *rotten to the very core*'.[8] Radical surgery was urgently needed. Fortunately the man of the hour was at hand, and the Peace of Amiens gave him his opportunity.

> It is a moment and crisis such as this, that a country learns the value of a MAN. Upon *one* temper, the constitution of a *single* mind, and the firmness of a single wrist, depend sometimes the fate and glory of an Empire . . . the great Chief, who possessed the most minute and accurate knowledge, not only of their general state, defects, and sufficiency, but of the inside of every ship, and the composition of every company![9]

When Addington recruited the admiral to lend reputation to his government, he did not realize that he was getting 'a Patriot-Conqueror and a Statesman-Reformer . . . that great and virtuous character' whose mission was to crush 'the harpies and hydras that sting, and pollute, and prey upon the public', in short to bring civil war to the civil departments of the Navy.[10] These phrases are amongst the most restrained and coherent in an extraordinary pamphlet subsequently produced for St Vincent, which defends his conduct in office in tones of unbridled megalomania. Addington managed to suppress the pamphlet, but it was too late to suppress its hero.

The only specific instances of malpractice in the naval administration which St Vincent ever produced were those already uncovered and dealt with before he took office. There probably were few others of importance. The most thorough modern study finds only twenty-three allegations of dishonesty against any naval employee or contractor between 1772 and 1821, of which only nine were proved.[11] In practice St Vincent's charges can be reduced to two: that nobody did any work in the dockyards (he seriously argued that only 10 per cent of the work paid for was performed), and that all contractors were corrupt. The first was easy to establish to his satisfaction, for the yards' lifetime employment practices meant that there were many relatively unproductive boys and old men. Moreover the inflation and dearth of wartime years had been met in the traditional fashion by stretching overtime and task work rates. Going on visitation to the dockyards in 1802, St Vincent and his colleagues forced down real wages, and made it their business to dismiss as many yard officers and men as possible, including many elderly men without pensions. In conjunction with a scheme of Bentham's, he also got rid of most of the apprentices. A particular target for St Vincent was the 'mutineers' who had petitioned for an increase in wages to meet the extreme scarcity and high prices of the previous winter. The Cabinet begged for restraint, the Law Officers advised him that petitioning was no crime, but he ignored them all. By the time that the war broke out again in May 1803 he had wrecked morale and efficiency, reduced the yards' workforce by a fifth, and badly damaged their capacity to recruit.[12]

St Vincent's broader objective, as Marsden wrote,

> is to get rid of the Navy Board. They are not faultless. Like most other boards and public offices they have left many things undone; but the visitation did not bring home to them any act of corruption or malversation. It was then tried to drive them out by the most abusive letters that ever were written from one Board to another; but they were too prudent to gratify our gentlemen in this way.[13]

St Vincent installed a personal representative on the Navy Board 'so that the Admiralty might have at least one man there upon whose honesty and intelligence their lordships could rely' – to report on his colleagues.[14] He put a representative on the Sick and Hurt Board with the same instructions. The First Lord attempted to entrap the Controller, abusing him for not using his initiative to issue shipbuilding contracts, and when he did so, trying to have him dismissed for acting without authority. He then refused to have any personal dealings with Hamond apart from summoning him to receive orders, and Hamond naturally declined to act again without written order. This breakdown of trust at the heart of British naval administration went far to make the system unworkable. Spies and informers were encouraged in the dockyards, and as far as he could St Vincent installed his own immediate followers in key positions. He urged Bentham to inform against the yard officers, and the yard commissioners to deny the authority of the Navy Board. For two years he impounded the accounts and stores records of the yards, seeking evidence to incriminate the officers, and meanwhile paralysing their work.[15]

St Vincent's methods with contractors were of a piece. He insisted on applying the letter of timber contracts in the most rigid possible fashion in order to find excuses to reject timber as substandard. Since timber is a natural material and continually variable, precise contracts were unworkable without a degree of common sense and mutual accommodation, which he forbade. He also refused to recognize that prices were rising, so the contractors refused to supply and the Navy ceased to buy. By June 1804, with a new war in progress, the Navy Board reckoned that it had less than a quarter of its annual requirement of sailcloth, deals and copper in stock, and only half a year's hemp and plank. To solve the timber crisis and drive prices down, St Vincent stopped all shipbuilding for the Navy in private yards, just at the moment when a major shipbuilding programme was urgently needed.[16]

The centrepiece of St Vincent's 'reforms' was the Commission of Naval Enquiry, set up in December 1802 to get rid of the junior naval boards, when he found that he did not have the power to dismiss them all out of hand, and they would not resign. His objective was an inquisition with power to demand evidence under oath, so as to investigate, incriminate and convict all at once, but the Lord Chancellor forbade it. 'The commission will, in fact, be a sort of protection to the inferior boards, which have been in the situation of a toad under a harrow,' Marsden commented. 'To crush them was the object of the bill, and the frauds in the dockyards (which we are daily detecting and punishing) are only the pretext.'[17] The other object was to abolish task work, which St Vincent particularly hated. In practice the commission based much of its work on the 1785 Commission on Fees, and most of its reports rehearsed matters which were already in the public domain.[18]

War broke out again three months after the Commission began its work, and the uproar which St Vincent had already generated within naval administration soon spread to national politics as the damage he had done became obvious. On this issue Pitt and Spencer moved from neutrality towards the Addington government into open opposition. They were, however, hampered by considerations of political tactics, for Fox, Grenville and their respective parties, colleagues in opposition, were friends to 'economical reform' and disposed to give St Vincent the benefit of some doubt. Pitt and Spencer therefore attacked St Vincent for neglecting Channel defences against invasion, on which he was much less vulnerable, and could call on the support of some distinguished admirals, including Nelson and Pellew. In Pellew's case the speech was a strictly business proposition: 'I find . . . I am older than I was [he was forty-seven] and can't get to the mast head so well as I used. I want to be an admiral for I am tired [of] squaring the main yard.'[19] He received his reward for political support in 1804 when he was appointed commander-in-chief in the East Indies. Meanwhile the commission became more aggressively partisan, seeking to bring charges of corruption (which it leaked to friendly newspapers) against St Vincent's numerous personal enemies, many of them people on whom Addington depended for Parliamentary support. It attacked John Dick, Storekeeper at Jamaica and formerly personal secretary both to Hamond, and to Middleton's nephew James Gambier. (St Vincent particularly despised Middleton as a corrupt Scotsman.) The commission brought charges (based, as a Parliamentary inquiry subsequently established, on evidence fabricated by St Vincent's secretary) against Captain Sir Home Popham, well known for his connections with Pitt. In a bizarre development, one of Popham's junior officers, visiting the Admiralty to apply for promotion, was on St Vincent's personal orders seized by a press gang and carried off to sea – because, it was suggested, he refused to give evidence against his captain.[20]

There is no doubt that St Vincent's bigotry and megalomania did great damage to naval administration, and discredited the cause of reform. His obsession with individual malefactors (so characteristic of the seventeenth century) diverted attention away from the genuine structural problems of weak dockyard management, and weak leadership of the Navy Board. Hamond, though honest and conscientious, was not a strong Controller, and contractors really were taking advantage of him.[21] In politics, so far from being an accession of strength, St Vincent greatly contributed to the collapse of the Addington ministry and the return of Pitt in May 1804. Pitt's new ministry was weaker than his first, most of the Whigs, including Grenville and his followers, remaining in opposition, but Dundas, now created Viscount Melville, took over the Admiralty. His first priority was to restore harmony and co-operation in the naval administration (to which end Bentham was sent on leave to Russia), but it was not possible to stop there. Melville was his own man, but Middleton was his kinsman and a longstanding associate of Pitt who had the ear of the new administration and was anxious to take up the cause of structural reform once more. In December 1804 the government therefore established the Commission for Revising and Digesting the Civil Affairs of the Navy, commonly known as the Board of Revision, with Middleton as its chairman. It was partly intended as a political antidote to the partisan work of the Commission of Naval Enquiry, but mainly as a genuine instrument of administrative change, and the natural successor of the Commission on Fees of 1785 and the Select Committee on Finance of 1797.[22]

Meanwhile the Commission of Naval Enquiry was still hunting for the misdeeds of St Vincent's opponents, and at last it found something significant. In its tenth report, of January 1805, it showed that Alexander Trotter, Paymaster of the Navy in the 1790s, had kept public money in a private bank account at Coutts Bank, opposite the new Navy Pay Office in Somerset House, rather than in his official account, a mile away in the Bank of England. This was contrary to an Act of Parliament promoted by Melville when he had been Treasurer of the Navy, and Trotter's immediate superior. It was a gift for St Vincent and the Whig opposition, who forced Melville's resignation, and mounted the last ever Parliamentary impeachment. This entertained the political nation for most of 1805 and 1806, leaving little attention to spare for the war. Eventually Melville was acquitted, but he never resumed his political career.[23]

Pitt had to find a new First Lord in a hurry, and with limited political options he was driven to adopt a stop-gap. Thus it was that Sir Charles Middleton finally at the age of seventy-nine attained the position which he had coveted for so long, and a peerage with it. His appetite for detail was now sated, or at least limited to the Board of Revision, of which he continued to be chairman. At the Admiralty Lord Barham confined himself to 'the general superintendence and arrangement of the whole', above all to the big issues of strategy, of which there were quite sufficient in the spring of 1805. He left his colleagues to deal with the routine administration of the Board, but he was by no means an aged figurehead. He regularly worked a ten-hour day, issued secret orders in his own hand, and did not hesitate to overrule 'my confidential assistant' (and nephew) Admiral James Gambier, the 'First Sea Lord' (a phrase Barham appears to have coined).[24]

The death of Pitt in February 1806 ended his government, and Barham's public life. In Pitt's place came the strained coalition of Grenville's 'New Whigs' and Fox's 'Old Whigs' with the followers of Addington (now Lord Sidmouth), which was nicknamed (not without sarcasm) the 'Ministry of all the Talents'. Grenville was Prime Minister and Fox Foreign Secretary, until he died after five months in office. Almost the only thing on which the 'Talents' were agreed was the idea of 'economical reform', but they had no formed idea what to do with the naval administration, and they had the sense to send St Vincent back to sea. Charles Grey and Thomas Grenville, their successive First Lords, seem to have been daunted by the magnitude of their task. 'The difficulties of this immense machine press heavily upon me,' Grenville complained.[25] The 'Talents' was the only Whig-led ministry between 1783 and 1830; thirteen months out of nearly half a century during the rest of which the Whigs had ample time to mature their grievances and nourish a political mythology in which they were the only champions of reform. St Vincent's legacy to them was the conviction that the reform of the Navy was at the centre of the reform of society, and the essential reform was to destroy the subordinate naval boards. In the shorter term St Vincent's activities helped to fragment the pattern of British politics and lead to a succession of weak governments, preoccupied with their own survival as much as fighting the war. The administrations of the Duke of Portland and Spencer Perceval which followed the 'Talents' between 1807 and 1812 were formed of Pitt's old followers without the support either of Sidmouth's or of Melville's block of Scottish MPs. The weakness of government during these years was partly offset by the weakness of the opposition, disunited and discredited by their performance in office, but only in 1812, after Perceval's murder, did Lord Liverpool form a strong government which united all parties except the radical Whigs.[26]

The 'Talents' permitted the Board of Revision to continue its work discreetly, though Barham himself retired from active participation. Its final reports came out in 1808 and 1809, and under Charles Yorke, First Lord from 1810 to 1812, a great deal was done to implement detailed reforms in yard management, especially financial controls and methods of wage payment. 1808 was also the year in which Bentham's office was amalgamated with the Navy Board under the title of Civil Architect and Engineer, a change which so much disgusted him that he seldom came to work, and in 1812 was retired on a large pension. Nevertheless these were productive years for the installation of new machinery and equipment in the yards. Wooden buildings were replaced by fireproof construction entirely of stone and iron. A new building yard was established at Pembroke in 1809 to exploit reserves of timber and manpower well away from the established yards. A training school for future 'shipwright officers' was established at Portsmouth in 1810. Two years later work began on a massive breakwater across the centre of Plymouth Sound, designed to remedy the great deficiency of the western yard, whose inner anchorage, the Hamoaze, was very difficult to get in and out of under sail, while the outer anchorage in Cawsand Bay was distant, cramped and exposed. At Sheerness, of which it was reported in 1808 that 'the great bulk of the yard may be said to be a wreck', the building of a completely new yard began in 1813. In the same years the building slips in all the yards began to be roofed over, as Middleton had proposed thirty years before.[27]

The great work of the dockyards was of course the maintenance of the fleet. At the outbreak of the Great Wars in 1793 both ships and yards were in good condition, and effort could be devoted to an initial building programme. By 1800 the strain of war, and particularly of close blockade, had greatly increased the proportion of ships in dockyard hands. The situation was hardest in waters like the Mediterranean where fleets had to keep themselves in repair, far from a dockyard or even a friendly port. In 1797 there were 108 ships of the line and 293 frigates and smaller vessels in commission, 82 per cent of the total in each case. The figures, both of the total numbers of ships, and the proportion available for service, were very sharply lower in 1804 and 1805. 'I wish we had peace, and could lay our ships up in dock,' Marsden wrote in January 1805. 'They are worn down like post-horses during a general election.'[28] At the time of Trafalgar, two-fifths of the ships of the line were out of commission, and only eighty-three were available for sea service. Of these eighteen were fit only for home waters, and none of the remainder had more than five years' estimated life left. There was also an acute shortage of frigates, and of men to man them. Some of this is due to the usual difficulties of mobilization, some of it represents the natural life-cycle of ships built in Sandwich's time, but all the problems were made much worse by St Vincent's disruption. To make up for the lost ground prodigious effort and expenditure were necessary, with a great increase in contract shipbuilding, at higher prices. Many technical corners had to be cut, to save time and timber, and extend the life of old ships. At every stage continued victories were essential, for the Royal Navy consistently built fewer ships than its enemies, and never less than a quarter of the British fleet was made up of prizes. By 1809 there were 113 British ships of the line in commission, the largest figure ever. The battlefleets had scarcely increased since the initial mobilization twelve years before, but the total number of cruisers of all sizes had multiplied more than three-fold to 596, as the Navy strained to exploit the command of the seas which the battlefleets had gained. For the first and last time in history, a single navy possessed half of all the world's warships.[29]

The Admiralty Office, especially the fees and salaries earned by its clerks, had been the earliest concern of the Commission on Fees before the war, and continued to be a popular target of the economical reformers. They particularly objected to the quasi-sale of offices, by which clerks paid their predecessors fixed sums on entry to office, and to salaries supplemented by fees, which rose steeply in wartime. Philip Stephens as Secretary of the Admiralty received £1,184 4s 2d in fees in 1784; in 1797 the figure was £4,340, and at every level wartime incomes at least trebled the peacetime figure. Under pressure from successive inquiries, the Admiralty moved towards the abolition of fees and premia, but only in return for generous salaries and pensions, appropriate to 'constant and laborious services'.[30] The Secretary's wartime salary from 1800 was £4,000, double the First Lord's. The Admiralty knew the dangers of entrusting secrets to ill-paid clerks; it sought people of high calibre and it expected them to work hard.[31]

During this period a distinction came to be made between the Second Secretary, the permanent official formerly just called the Secretary, and the First Secretary, a member of the government, appointed by the Prime Minister rather than the Board. This distinction was formalized in 1807, but had been understood for some time before. On the fall of the Addington ministry in 1804, however, it was the Second Secretary, St Vincent's personal secretary Benjamin Tucker whom no one could trust, who was ejected, and the First Secretary, the distinguished orientalist William Marsden, who was begged to stay. In 1806 the Whigs put Tucker back in for fourteen months, but with that exception John Barrow was Second Secretary from 1804 to 1845, a worthy successor to the long-serving Secretaries of the eighteenth century. He and Marsden read, answered and filed every letter which came into the Admiralty on the day of receipt. When the news of Sir John Duckworth's victory in the West Indies in February 1806 reached the Admiralty, Marsden recorded,

> I had a terrible day of it – was knocked up at three o'clock in the morning, when I had got about an hour-and-half's sleep, called up Mr Grey at four, having by that time arranged and docketed my papers, and drawn out a bulletin. I then worked till seven, and lay down in hopes of getting a little sleep – but it would not do; so I returned to the office, and worked there till Mr Grey's dinner was ready.[32]

Later in the war a subsequent Secretary, the forceful Irish politician and man of letters J. W. Croker, was still opening all incoming post himself. He spoke of himself as the 'servant of the Board', but Yorke said that 'it was precisely the other way'.[33]

Only one product of naval administration was more important than the maintenance of the ships; the maintenance of the men. We have seen that the capacity to keep ships' companies healthy for long periods at sea had steadily improved throughout the eighteenth century, but the Great Wars imposed unprecedented demands. The whole blockading strategy, above all the close blockade adopted by St Vincent, depended completely on the ability to keep men healthy for months at sea. The basic victualling requirement was not negligible. A Third Rate with a crew of 590, stored for five months, stowed 41 tons of biscuit, 407 tuns of beer, 23 tons of beef, 12 tons of pork, 10 tons of pease, 4 tons of oatmeal, 2 tons of butter and 4 tons of cheese. For six months the Channel Fleet of 36,000 men consumed 2,925 tons of biscuit, 1,671 tons of beef, 835 tons of pork, 626 tons of pease, 313 tons of oatmeal, 156 tons of butter, 313 tons of cheese, and 32,000 tuns of beer. An elaborate accounting system kept track of all this food throughout the cycle of issue and consumption, in order to predict requirements as well as eliminate dishonesty. From the Victualling Board's headquarters at Deptford it was 180 miles by sea to Portsmouth, and another 215 from there to the blockading station off Ushant, nearly all of it against the prevailing wind. Careful planning and meticulous organization were needed to ensure that these distant ships did not run short.[34]

The problem which these preserved foods did not cure was scurvy, and there were essentially two complementary approaches to dealing with it. The orthodox opinion among naval men, and by the end of the century among most doctors, was that a healthy diet, including fresh meat and vegetables, was indispensable. The alternative was lemon juice, but this was generally regarded as a medicine for the treatment of scurvy rather than a substitute for a proper diet. Dr Thomas Trotter, Physician of the Channel Fleet, demanded 5,000 lbs a day of green vegetables for the fleet in May 1795. 'I wanted it to be given in large allowance to the different messes of the seamen; and that the fresh beef broth should be full of greens, or other pot-herbs. The lemons we could only consider for the cure.'[35] Virtually from the outbreak of war, squadrons on the coast of France received shipments of cattle and vegetables, and were encouraged to buy their own from the Breton islanders, but there were still outbreaks of scurvy, which were treated when the squadrons came into port. There was a serious outbreak in the summer of 1795, after which the Admiralty ordered bullocks, sheep, potatoes, cabbages and onions from Plymouth and Cork for the blockaders. In March 1796 the Admiralty ordered that all ships coming into port were to have fourteen days' fresh beef and 50 lbs of cabbages and 10 lbs of onions for every hundred men.[36]

Lemon juice was available as a standard issue to ships going on foreign voyages from the outbreak of the war. In 1794 Rainier's flagship the *Suffolk* made a nineteen-week passage to India without suffering any scurvy at all. The Sick and Hurt Board supplied the juice, and it also put forward the controversial argument, opposed by Trotter, that lemon juice might be regarded as an item of diet as well as a medicine.

> From our own observations, and the experience of ages, we have been led to consider fresh limes and lemons, or the juice of those fruits, properly prepared for keeping, as the most powerful antiscorbutic in nature, and know of no instance in which (when administered genuine) it has failed to cure the disease, even in its most advanced stages, either on board ship or on shore. It is also well ascertained that a certain proportion of lemon juice taken daily, as an article of seamen's diet, will prevent the possibility of their being tainted with the scurvy, let the other articles of their diet consist of what they will.

The Board therefore proposed the general issue of lemons, 'as the best sub-stitute for fresh fruit and vegetables, and the most powerful corrective of the scorbutic qualities of their common diet'.[37] The attraction of this argument was obvious, for lemon juice, though not cheap, was far easier to store and ship than fresh vegetables or live oxen. By 1800 the supply of lemon juice was sufficient for general issue in home waters. St Vincent was an early convert, and when Trotter put up resistance, he was replaced with Dr Andrew Baird, 'an invaluable treasure' who supported the juice.[38] Fresh food was still issued whenever it could be had, but it was certainly the general issue of lemon juice which virtually eliminated scurvy from the Channel Fleet by the end of 1800, and made possible the very long and arduous cruising which St Vincent demanded. Everywhere in the Navy the disease became very rare; it accounted for only 2 per cent of British naval patients in the Edinburgh Royal Infirmary between 1795 and 1800, for example (compared with 25 per cent of seamen from the Russian North Sea Squadron).[39]

The combination of fresh food and lemon juice was standard throughout the Navy for the rest of the Great Wars. In 1807 the Admiralty ordered vegetables on foreign stations to be issued only to the sick, but this order aroused widespread protest and was soon withdrawn. In 1808 the Victualling Board's standing orders were to issue all ships in port with 5 lbs of fresh beef a man a week, replacing half the salt beef and all the salt pork – but ships coming in from long cruises were to receive their whole meat ration of 7 lbs a week as fresh beef. Vegetables were to be issued on the scale of ½ lb a man a day of cabbage or greens, and one-tenth of a pound of onions. Every man was to receive a fluid ounce of lemon juice and an ounce of sugar daily, to be made into 'sherbet' or lemonade (though in practice, it seems very often to have been made up into punch with spirits).[40]

In the Mediterranean, during the long years when nearly all its northern ports and shores were in enemy hands, great tenacity was needed to keep ships' crews healthy during very long cruises. Nelson, who was a gifted administrator as well as a great leader, devoted enormous pains to the victualling of his ships. He scoured the Mediterranean for fresh beef, onions and oranges. After Spain entered the war in December 1804 the devoted Agent-Victualler, Richard Ford, was buying food as far away as South Russia. Individual pursers were responsible for obtaining very large quantities. In the first three months of 1804, for example, the *Gibraltar* bought 4 oxen and fodder, 54,610 lbs of fresh beef, 43,971 lbs of bread, 3,746 lbs of rice, 7,380 gallons of wine, 11,000 onions, 4,320 bundles of leeks, 2,184 cabbages and fourteen pumpkins to feed about 600 men. Nelson was able to exploit British protection of Sicily to set up a contract to buy 30,000 gallons of lemon juice a year at one shilling (later 1s 6d) a gallon, which compared with 8s for inferior juice shipped from England. Eventually the Sicilian lemon groves supplied the entire Navy. 'The great thing in all military service is health,' Nelson wrote, 'and you will agree with me, that it is easier for an officer to keep men healthy, than for a physician to cure them.'[41] In the first three years of the Napoleonic War, there were only 110 deaths from all causes in a squadron of 6,500 men. When Dr Leonard Gillespie joined the *Victory* as Physician to the Mediterranean Fleet in January 1805, when most of the ships had been twenty months at sea, he found almost nothing to do. There was one man in the flagship's sick-berth, and only a handful ill in the whole fleet.[42] Presently the squadron moved rapidly to Alexandria, back the whole length of the Mediterranean, chased to the West Indies and back across the Atlantic, arriving after two years at sea and a voyage of almost 10,000 miles, as Nelson reported, 'in the most perfect health, and only require some vegetables and other refreshments to remove the scurvy'.[43]

Such very long cruises, and unplanned movements over thousands of miles, were only possible because victualling and health had been brought to a degree of perfection never known before. Other diseases besides scurvy had also been sharply checked. The use of 'slop ships' in which new recruits were washed and clothed reduced, though it never entirely eliminated, typhus. A voluntary campaign of vaccination (the Admiralty never felt that it was morally justified in making it compulsory) effectively defeated smallpox.[44] The real killers remained the tropical fevers, above all yellow fever, which continued to baffle both theory and practice. Medical explanations ranged from damaged coffee beans to the phases of the moon. All tropical waters – or rather, tropical lands, for the open sea was healthy everywhere – remained dangerous to Europeans.[45] Naval surgeons made some important advances in anatomy (which they had socially acceptable opportunities of studying), and in the treatment of wounds, especially in swift treatments, for shock and loss of blood were always the main killers of the wounded. Unfortunately it was an iron-clad naval tradition that the wounded were treated strictly in the order they reached the surgeon, regardless of the seriousness of their condition. Without triage, men bled to death who might have been saved, while the surgeons' time was occupied with trivial or hopeless cases.[46]

The Sick and Hurt Board never resolved a basic difficulty over its functions. In the past it had been an essentially administrative body, running the naval hospitals. During the 1790s its professional prestige rose, it was increasingly regarded as a source of expert medical advice, and in 1796 it took over the examination and appointment of naval surgeons, from the Surgeons' Company and the Navy Board respectively. At the same time, however, its administrative reputation steadily declined. In 1795 a captain and three lieutenants were appointed to each of the naval hospitals to impose naval discipline on establishments which had hitherto been entirely civilian-run, and in particular to keep spirits out of the hands of the nurses and patients. The work of the Board itself was damaged by a series of professional and personal quarrels. Dr William Blair fought with Sir Gilbert Blane, who was appointed by Spencer in 1795, and Dr John Harness fought with Dr Baird when St Vincent appointed him as his man on the Board. All the while the Board's administration was falling into chaos. Harness blamed St Vincent for reducing the staff, but it seems also to have been the case that in their new capacity as inspecting physicians the Commissioners spent their time visiting naval hospitals rather than superintending the work of their clerks. When Barham investigated in 1805 he found uncleared accounts going back forty years, to a value of over £2,500,000. As a result the Board was amalgamated with the Transport Board next year. The physicians continued to serve as the 'Medical Committee', but the administration of the naval medical service was entrusted to more competent hands.[47]

In naval administration real change was arrested by the doctrinaire attacks of St Vincent and the Whigs. In material terms Trafalgar was the worst point of the naval war, when the condition and number of the Navy's ships had been reduced by sudden demobilization and reckless devastation. Regardless of its strategic effects, the great victory was essential to redress the material odds and make up some of the ground which St Vincent had lost. Under more stable and pragmatic governments, the physical condition of the Navy slowly recovered, and real administrative reforms were progressively introduced. The high point of sustained investment in new buildings, equipment and ideas came towards the end of the war, especially under the Liverpool government, and continued into the peace.

THIRTY-TWO

A Thinking Set of People

Social History 1803–1815: Men and Manning

B y the time the war resumed in 1803, after the brief peace of Amiens, the immediate agitation generated by the great mutinies had died down. Officers no longer feared a Jacobin massacre, and had had time to digest the lessons of 1797. A long-term evolution in attitudes to naval discipline is evident, of which the essential component is that there *were* attitudes to naval discipline: matters which had been taken for granted before were now the subject of much thought and comment, by both officers and ratings. Among them was the value which seamen set on their dignity and self-respect. Skilled seamen were precious, and they knew their worth. They expected officers to treat them with respect. 'They are very far from being inferior to other men, either in generous or in elevated sentiments,' wrote Philip Patton. 'They are, like landmen, fully sensible of the eternal obligations and immutable effects of justice, they are open to the dictates of common sense and uncommonly alive to every generous and to every noble feeling.'[1] When they had occasion to complain of ill-treatment, it was often the shame ('terming damned useless trash and degrading us beneath brutes', in the words of a petition from men of the *Centaur* in 1812)[2] as much the brutality which they dwelt on. 'We thought our character stand fair in the opinion of all concerned,' claimed the men of the *Canopus* in 1806, 'and we cannot possibly bear being cut in pieces by one who knows not our merit or demerit.'[3] They resented casual insults, especially to their professional abilities.[4] An exception tending to prove this rule was Sir Richard Strachan, who (as William Richardson recorded) called his men 'damned mutinous rascals'.

> Yet the sailors liked him for all that, as they knew he had a kind heart, and thought no more of it when his passion was over. They gave him the name of 'Mad Dick', and said that when he swore he meant no harm, and when he prayed he meant no good. However, he was a brave, zealous

and active officer, and was always very lenient to a prisoner when tried by court-martial.[5]

Amongst thinking officers two strands of opinion may be distinguished. The socially and politically conservative deeply regretted that the folly of Lord Howe and the Admiralty had provoked the great mutinies and shown the seamen their strength. They feared the consequences to society if common men, afloat or ashore, learnt to act collectively and politically. Collingwood was one of them:

> How unwise in the officers, or how impolitic in the administration, that did not attend to, and redress the first complaints of grievance, and not allow the seamen to throw off their obedience and to feel what power there is in so numerous a body. What is conceded to them is not received as a provision which justice makes them, but as what they have extorted, and they now know how they may extort, what in justice they have not the same claim to.[6]

These officers objected to cheap postage being allowed to seamen, since reading and writing was bound to encourage men to think, and they even deplored allowing the men to subscribe to patriotic collections, a political act which should have been limited to the propertied classes.[7] They took care of their men partly because they were now aware of the dangers of not doing so. 'It has always been a maxim with me,' Collingwood wrote, 'to engage and occupy my men, and to take such care for them that they should have nothing to think of for themselves beyond the current business of the day.'[8] Yet these officers, many of whom were Evangelicals or influenced by the new piety, were also animated by a deep sense of duty towards their men, often expressed in language evoking biblical images of the fatherhood of God. One of these pious officers was Commander James Nash of the troopship *Revenge*. In 1811 Private William Wheeler of the 51st Foot took passage in her to Lisbon to join Wellington's army. He had already been at sea once before, under a flogging captain who had given him a very bad idea of naval discipline, and he was charmed by the contrast.

> The captain goes by the name of 'Father'. Cursing and swearing is not allowed. The good feeling existing between the captain and sailors was fully displayed last Sunday morning, when the ship's company assembled for the captain's inspection. It was truly pleasing to see the good old man, their 'Father' as the men have justly named him, walking through the ranks of sailors, who all appeared as clean as possible, with health

and contentment glowing in their faces. As he passed the men he seemed
to impart to each a portion of his own good nature . . .'[9]

Collingwood looked after his men with scrupulous care, and insisted that his
officers address them with courtesy, and by name.[10] 'How attentive he was to
the health and comfort and happiness of his crew!' one of them wrote. 'A man
who could not be happy under him, could have been happy nowhere; a look
of displeasure from him was as bad as a dozen at the gangway from another
man.'[11] As for Collingwood's own feelings, we have the witness of a friend who
met him in the street one day and was astonished to find him in tears: 'He
said that a few days before his ship's company were paid off – that he had lost
his children – all his family – that they were dear to him, and he could not
refrain.'[12] The senior officers of a generation before had been accustomed to
a sort of rough intimacy with their men which had disappeared by the end of
the century (and would have been foreign to so reserved and formal a man as
Collingwood in any age), but they would never have felt this intense personal
commitment.[13]

In contrast to this conservative, paternalistic strain of opinion we may set
another, more liberal, which urged that seamen be treated as intelligent adults
and at least potential citizens. In the opinion of Captain Anselm Griffiths,
'seamen are nowadays a thinking set of people and a large proportion of them
possess no inconsiderable share of common sense, the most useful sense after
all'.[14] 'I am sure that the reasoning faculties of seamen are not done justice to
by many who command them,' Captain C. V. Penrose wrote, 'for they are by
no means to be despised.'[15] Sir Alexander Ball thought 'that no body of men
can for any length of time be safely treated otherwise than as rational beings;
and that, therefore, the education of the lower classes was of the utmost
consequence to the permanent security of the empire, even for the sake of our
navy'.[16] Officers of all shades of opinion united in insisting that men were not
to be worked unnecessarily, especially not for drill or show, and that good
officers avoided 'worrying tricks of brief authority' and 'vexatious niggling'.[17]
'Having obtained and established energy, zeal, respect, sobriety and cleanliness, what can be wanting?' asked Griffiths. 'The captain whose object is to
command a cheerful and contented crew will be satisfied with these.'[18]

One difficulty in the way of all these ideas, pointed out by Captain William
Hoste among others, was that 'no absolute monarch can be more *despotic*
than a captain of a man-of-war, *if he pleases*. No character, and, indeed, no
creature existing, has it so much in his power to render the lives of those
under his command either miserable or happy.'[19] In the absence of any

common system of naval discipline, every captain had his own ideas, and many writers noted how the change from one to another was often troublesome. Few had the sensitivity to introduce novelties gradually.[20]

After the Great Wars ideas continued to evolve – and this lays a trap for the historian, for in the 1830s radical politicians (in Britain and the United States) adopted naval and military discipline, and in particular flogging, as a convenient rhetorical shorthand for a range of social and political targets. This created a market for polemical books and pamphlets in the form of memoirs describing naval discipline in lurid terms. Some of these memoirs were genuine, or at least incorporated genuine material, but they must be used with caution, for they express attitudes which were unknown until well after 1815.[21] (A similar caution applies to another genre of memoir, the religious narratives written from an Evangelical perspective, which stress the depravity of the author's life before his conversion. Naval life was not really as depraved as the convention of this sort of story requires.)[22] Throughout the period of the Great Wars flogging was accepted by virtually everybody as a normal and unremarkable practice everywhere in society. It is telling that one could joke about flogging; it had not yet become a sensitive subject.[23] Seamen knew and valued the necessity of good discipline afloat, for the comfort and safety of all. 'In all my experience at sea I have found seamen grateful for good usage,' wrote Richardson, 'and yet they like to see subordination kept up, as they know the duty could not be carried on without it.'[24] They never objected to flogging so long as it was not abused, and no lower-deck writer of the time uses the violent language of Thomas Hodgskin, an ex-officer with a guilty conscience, describing naval discipline as 'one universal system of terror; no obedience, but what was forced, no respect, but what was constrained'.[25]

The question of what was abuse was the most sensitive barometer of naval opinion. In 1794 a petty officer was court-martialled and convicted for refusing an order to 'thrash the men up',[26] but after 1797 tolerance for 'starting' (chasing men to their work with a cane or rope's end) fell rapidly amongst both officers and men, and it was forbidden by the Admiralty in 1809. It did not completely disappear even then, as evidence the fact that captains' order books continue for some years to mention it ('The highly improper practice of what is called starting the men, is most peremptorily forbidden').[27] Aboard the guardship at Plymouth in 1809 the Irish recruit Henry Walsh noted, 'It is indeed disgraceful to mankind for to behold those boatswain's mates how the[y] drive those men like as many slaves,'[28] but this must have been a very late example.[29] In the same year another landman, Robert Clover of the bomb vessel *Thunder*, was positively lyrical about his officers: 'a set of men who are at once an ornament to human nature, and a credit to the Service they are engaged in: the best of usage prevails, and a boatswain or his mate dare as well be damned as strike a man, or use abusive language to him'.[30]

Similar sensitivities were shown about flogging. Hardly anyone thought it could be dispensed with altogether, but it was increasingly the mark of a good officer to keep flogging to a minimum (at least in British service; it is worth noting in passing that the young United States Navy flogged at least twice as much, and did not abolish starting).[31] In June 1797 Captain James Burney told Lord Spencer that 'I served in a ship where every one of the maintopmen were stripped and flogged at the gangway for no other reason than that another ship in company got her topgallant yards up first.'[32] It is not clear when, if ever, this incident took place, but in the aftermath of the mutinies the story was clearly offered as a scandalous abuse of authority.[33] In reality flogging seems in most cases to have been confined to a minority of troublemakers, mostly punished for offences against the peace and order of shipboard life rather than the officers' authority as such. Fewer than a tenth of men were ever flogged, and few of them twice, for flogging clearly worked, in the sense of deterring men from re-offending.[34] In 1804 Nelson sharply reproved a lieutenant-commander who had flogged every man of his ship's company for failing to reveal a culprit: 'I cannot approve a measure so foreign to the rules of good discipline and the accustomed practice of his Majesty's Navy.'[35] The 1806 *Regulations and Instructions* removed the maximum of twelve lashes which had hitherto limited a captain's powers of punishment in theory, though not for many years in practice. This suggests rising official tolerance of severity, but in reality the movement was all the other way. 1806 was also the year that running the gauntlet was forbidden. In 1811 punishment returns were instituted, followed immediately by the first Admiralty orders requiring captains to justify excessive punishment.[36] Another indicator of changing sensibility is the number of officers who revealed in private, if not in public, their revulsion at having to witness flogging.[37] Collingwood regarded excessive flogging as 'big with the most dangerous consequences, and subversive of all real discipline'. He consciously trained himself to rely on it less and less until in the end he could manage his ships without flogging at all.[38] Other officers did the same, seeking out alternative punishments which were more likely to reform than degrade.[39] It was now a commonplace that officers rather than men were to blame for bad discipline. 'It has always appeared to me that good officers make good men,' Griffiths wrote. 'Idle officers spoil the best ship's company.'[40]

Courts martial continued to award sentences of several hundred lashes, but these need to be understood in the context of contemporary judicial practice. Eighteenth-century British society made up for the extreme difficulty of catching criminals by theatrically severe punishments, but only a bare minimum were ever carried out. Hundreds of crimes carried the death penalty in courts ashore, but most death sentences were commuted to transportation, preserving the deterrent effect (it was hoped) but demonstrating the judges' compassion – and persuading the juries to convict, which could otherwise be difficult. There were no juries in courts martial, but in other ways they behaved similarly. A sentence of several hundred lashes was a statement about the severity of the crime, but officers knew that the presiding surgeon would halt the punishment after a hundred lashes or so, and that the remainder was commonly remitted on petition. When men were sentenced to death, it was usually thought sufficient to hang one or two (often chosen by lot) and pardon the remainder. Only St Vincent carried out all sorts of sentences in full.[41]

Two dramatic incidents may be chosen to illustrate changing attitudes to naval discipline during the Napoleonic War. One was the extraordinary case of Robert Jeffery, a troublesome seaman of the brig *Recruit* who in 1807 was marooned on an uninhabited islet in the Caribbean, where he would have died had he not fortunately been rescued by an American merchantman. When these facts became known they created a public furore which destroyed Captain the Hon. Warwick Lake's career and considerably embarrassed the government.[42] The other is the mutiny of the frigate *Nereide* in 1808. This ship was in the East Indies, where the crew twice petitioned Pellew, the commander-in-chief, against the severities of Captain Robert Corbet. They then refused to weigh anchor unless to sail to the Cape of Good Hope, where undoubtedly they expected to find a more sympathetic commander-in-chief, Vice-Admiral Albemarle Bertie. Corbet suppressed the mutiny with his customary vigour and presence of mind, and in due course a court martial was held at the Cape, which condemned ten men to die. Bertie, evidently feeling he could not overlook mutiny altogether, hanged one of the ten and reprieved the others. He then immediately brought a court martial against Captain Corbet for cruelty, and for good measure added another on a similar charge against one of his own captains. Although Corbet's prosecutors were nominally the men of the *Nereide*, it was obvious that the admiral was behind them. This put the captains who formed the court in a dilemma, which is broadly hinted at in the record. Corbet had an outstanding fighting record and a plausible defence, but they were clearly very unhappy at his methods of discipline. On the other hand they were equally unhappy at the admiral's attempts to interfere in a captain's prerogative to manage his own ship, and they must have been aware that any one of them might be the next to be caught between a complaining crew and a reforming admiral. So they compromised on an acquittal accompanied by a reprimand. When the Admiralty heard it was openly critical of Corbet, and took the opportunity to forbid starting.[43]

Corbet was far away on a foreign station, where he was killed in action the following year, but it became normal for such cases to ruin an officer's career. The court martial might convict, or it might acquit with a strong recommendation to change his conduct, as in the case of Captain Robert Preston of the *Ganymede* in 1811, but in a period of high officer unemployment the result was likely to be the same. A lieutenant-commander removed from his cutter the same year was 'given to understand (although not officially) that until my character was freed from the unfavourable effect of the imputations thus cast upon me by the seamen there could be no hope of my ever again being honoured with employment in the service'.[44] In the *Alfred*, according to Henry Walsh,

> some of the ship's company wrote a letter to the Board of the Admiralty and acquainted the government of the cruelty the captain had exercised over the ship's company since he first joined her. In some days our captain got an answer which obliged him to read it to the ship's company. He was very much reprimanded in it for his former misconduct, and requested that he would conduct himself more better with regard to the usage of the ship's company hereafter.[45]

This story seems to have grown in the telling, and Captain Horton was not in fact officially censured, but it shows how the men understood the power of a complaint to damage an officer's career.[46]

Behind most disciplinary problems lay alcohol. 'It is observable and deeply to be lamented,' wrote Lord Keith in 1812,

> that almost every crime except theft originates in drunkenness, and that a large proportion of the men who are maimed and disabled are reduced to that situation by accidents that happen from the same abominable vice. It is an evil of great magnitude, and one which it will be impossible to prevent so long as the present excessive quantity of spirits is issued in the Royal Navy.[47]

It is ironic that officers became more aware of the evils of drink at the same time as the Navy officially issued growing quantities of spirits. Beer was and remained the official drink of the British seaman, the daily ration of which was not abolished until 1831, but in practice it was becoming increasingly common to issue wine or spirits instead, even in home waters, where beer had hitherto been the usual issue. There was no decision of policy to issue spirits – the official 'rum ration' cannot be dated before 1844 – but the practical difficulties of embarking and stowing beer, during a war in which ships were spending very long periods at sea with only brief visits to port, were tending to force a growing use of spirits. A Third Rate had to load between fifty and 100 tuns of beer, mostly in butts weighing half a ton each. They had to be stowed in the bottom of the hold and the ship was not stable without them; embarking beer was not an evolution to be undertaken casually at sea.[48]

Half a pint of spirits replaced a gallon of beer, and was normally issued half in the morning and half in the evening, in the form of 'three-water grog' (diluted with three parts of water). That made up only two pints of liquid, not enough for a working day, and implied that the men were drinking water at other times – a silent social revolution, though it must have become easier when iron water-tanks replaced wooden casks and improved the quality of drinking water. The official issue of spirits was supplemented by other sources: from officers, who gave liquor as a reward, and from men, who smuggled it aboard. Spirits formed the currency of shipboard, the matter of an extensive trade, control of which cemented the authority of the petty officers. To get drunk was the birthright and hallmark of real sailors, who when they were given leave 'hasten to the first tavern and drink themselves into a state of helpless infirmity; which not to do would be symptomatic of cowardly lubberliness, or worse'.[49] If leave were refused, the men at least expected an issue of grog to console them. The only way to limit drunkenness in a ship issuing spirits in place of beer was to increase the proportion of water, but this was perceived by the men as an insult and a punishment – not least because it was used as a punishment by captains seeking an alternative to flogging. Captain Patrick Campbell told his men that 'he was really tired and annoyed by continually flogging of men, only for that beastly habit of drunkenness, so ill becoming an Englishman'.[50] He therefore extra-watered the culprits' grog – but this made it impossible to do the same to the well-behaved. Captains were now sensitive to the legitimate demands of their men, and it was dangerous to exclude spirits from the list. Spirits in place of beer were in any case an official entitlement which could be extra-watered, but could not be denied even to defaulters. In practice most captains allowed men of good character access to extra liquor, at least at selected moments.[51]

The failure of the Quota Acts forced the Navy to rely on its traditional methods of recruitment, including (in May 1798) the suspension of all statutory protections for five months.[52] Captains were still encouraged to recruit their own men from among their own followers, but as before, when a captain came to change ships and sought to take his followers with him, it became a privilege reserved to the well-connected under Chatham, and allowed only in limited numbers by Spencer and his successors.[53] In 1805 Melville proposed a manning scheme based on the 1795 Port Quota Act which would have imposed quotas on shipowners in proportion to their tonnage, with an embargo on their shipping until the seamen were provided, and protections for the remainder when they had been. This would have avoided the need of much if not all impressment. More ambitiously, he also wanted a national register of seamen to be selected for naval service by ballot. Whether either scheme (the second especially) would have been acceptable to Parliament is uncertain, but in the event Melville's fall killed them, and his successors did not take up the ideas.[54] Instead impressment continued in its traditional form, modified whenever possible by agreements with local authorities. To encourage them, the Admiralty would apply whatever pressure it could. In 1806 Rear-Admiral James Vashon commanding the Impress Service in Scotland suggested that withholding letters of marque from the ships of Greenock and Port Glasgow would 'induce them to enter into a compromise of sending some men into the service instead of making it a rendezvous for all the deserters from the Navy'.[55] On the Tyne and Wear the seamen and keelmen came to agreements with the Impress Service which exempted them from the press in return for an annual quota of men.[56] In 1810 an agreement with the East India Company offered protections for a fixed number of seamen in proportion to the ships' size, the overplus to be peaceably yielded (by no means the universal practice of Indiamen).[57]

As always, the press gang was after the best men, prime seamen, and it usually succeeded. It was proverbial in the Navy that most of the petty and warrant officers (to say nothing of the press gangs) had themselves been pressed. The Navy promoted these valuable men because they were good candidates, and because promotion would secure their services. Offers of advancement were an essential part of the bargaining process which often accompanied impressment.[58] They were part of the unofficial or clandestine economy of manpower which went on below the surface of official regulations. Other examples were the ways in which captains and even admirals encouraged the desertion of useless men,[59] and manipulated the system to acquire more able seamen than they appeared to have. Commander the Hon. William Cathcart, commissioning the sloop *Renard* in 1802, gave his new recruits their advance wages, took their clothes as a surety and then allowed them to go on leave without entering them on the ship's books until they returned. This was risky but effective. 'They go on shore and tell the rest that the captain is a bloody good fellow, lets them go on shore when they please, and that gets numbers off, out of which I pick the best.' Meanwhile his weekly returns to the port admiral understated his real manning situation and gained him time to fit out.[60] Port admirals themselves were often suspected of 'hoarding' skilled men, and captains at sea might well have more able seamen than their ships' musters appeared to indicate. 'Schemes of complement' were drawn up which prescribed the essential minimum of petty officers and able seamen, but only rigorous inspection by divisional flag-officers would ensure that they were being followed. As this was a guaranteed source of unpopularity, many admirals preferred not to look under that particular stone.[61]

   Although no large-scale analyses of ships' muster-books have been undertaken, it is possible to give some idea of the composition of a typical ship's company. A sample of 4,474 men from ships commissioning at Plymouth in 1804–5 shows 47 per cent English, 29 per cent Irish, 8 per cent Scots, 3 per cent Welsh, 1 per cent from the Isle of Man and the Channel Isles, 5 per cent from the Americas and 6 per cent from the rest of the world. The most important counties of origin were in descending order London, Dublin, Devon, Cork, Lancashire, Gloucestershire and Kent, but London and Devon contributed considerably higher proportions of able seamen than the others. Overall, 35 per cent were petty officers, able seamen or idlers, and 65 per cent ordinary seamen, landmen or boys – a ratio of skilled to unskilled men which had almost exactly reversed since the American War thirty years before.[62] Among just under 21,500 officers and men in the thirty-three British ships and vessels present at Trafalgar, there were 1,482 born outside Britain and Ireland, including 373 from the USA, 136 from Italy, eighty-three from Sweden, sixty-six from the Isle of Man, sixty-four from the Channel Isles, and so on down through fifty-seven from France, to one each from Greece, Mexico and Sardinia. The counties represented started with London, Devon and Dublin. The median age was twenty to twenty-four, and the ages ranged from three boys of ten, to one man over sixty-five.[63] Analyses of individual ships give a similar impression. The St Domingo, 74, at about the same date had a ship's company of just under 600 men, of whom 212 (38 per cent) were seamen, and another twenty-seven 'seafaring men' (fishermen, sailmakers, shipwrights and the like). The median age was between twenty and twenty-five; and the range was from five boys of eleven, to fifteen men aged between forty-five and sixty. This ship was reckoned well manned.[64] In 1810 the new First Rate Caledonia, Pellew's flagship in the Mediterranean, had only 208 seamen and forty-two other 'seafaring men' out of 751 seamen and marines, and a total ship's company, including officers and boys, of about 900.[65]

It was possible to make an efficient ship's company with barely a quarter of them seamen, because ships spent long periods at sea and long hours in drill and training. Nevertheless critics argued that the Navy's training effort was incomplete, and in particular that the boys were neglected. In 1794 the Admiralty abolished the old rating of 'captain's servant' and made up captains' pay to compensate for the lost wages. In its place were created three classes of 'boy', of which 'Boy First Class or Volunteer' was explicitly reserved for young gentlemen intended to become officers, and the remainder were divided into second and third class according to age. These boys were meant to be the Navy's future topmen, but in practice many of them were acting as domestics, and were not encouraged or even allowed to go aloft. Not enough captains took the time and trouble to see their boys properly trained, and Collingwood was unique among admirals in recruiting boys for his fleet and taking a personal interest in their training.[66]

The basic reason for the manning difficulties of the Navy was the same as it always had been, the scarcity of seamen. The difference in the Great Wars was that they went on long enough for the supply of seamen to adjust to the demand. Though it took time to train a good seaman, it certainly did not take twenty years. It would be logical to expect, therefore, that the manning crisis should have eased as the wars continued. It did not, in part no doubt because the Navy continued to increase to its maximum size of just over 140,000 between 1808 and 1810, but also for other and preventable reasons. In spite of the pay increases of 1797 and 1806 the Navy was still at a financial disadvantage compared to wartime wages in merchantmen, but on the other hand it had the advantages of better food and conditions. More could certainly have been done to train boys and landmen. The critical issue which many contemporaries identified, however, was leave.

With surprising unanimity seamen accepted impressment as unavoidable, but they very deeply resented not being trusted with occasional liberty. They resented it all the more because it was visibly unnecessary, since many captains did trust them, and earned the loyalty of their men.[67] 'That ship which gives the most leave will ever have the least desertion,' wrote Captain Griffiths, and he himself discreetly gave his men leave even when his flag-officer had forbidden it.[68] Captain William Parker of the frigate *Amazon* gave regular leave and in eight years only ever lost one man.[69] A good captain, Admiral Patton wrote, will convince his men that 'they will never be confined when duty will admit of their being absent'.[70] 'A real sailor is a fine fellow,' Captain

Francis Liardet wrote, 'and if you make a point of giving him leave on every possible occasion, he will seldom take full advantage of it; but deprive him of the liberty of going on shore, and he will most surely make a grievance of it to the fullest extent.'[71] When Captain Edward Leveson-Gower took over the frigate *Promte*, which had suffered heavy desertion under his predecessor, he gave twenty-four hours' leave, ten men at a time, 'having said that his ship should never be called a prison ship'. They all returned, William Richardson among them, 'for we thought it would be very ungrateful now to desert, when we had got a captain who would give us liberty'.[72] Captain Charles Penrose thought St Vincent's policy of limiting the time of refits was a serious mistake. Three weeks would be better than eight days, 'and during that time, every officer and man should have leave to go on shore, unless confined on board for bad conduct. *This is the way to prevent desertion.*'[73] This message gradually took effect. Even St Vincent thought that ships returning from several years abroad should give general leave, and in 1806 the First Lord of the Admiralty was urging him to allow his men more leave. By 1809 it seems to have been standard practice to give forty-eight hours' leave when a ship was paid, and a fortnight's leave on paying off at the end of a commission.[74] If leave had been made a standard practice earlier in the war, it might have done a lot to limit the Navy's manning problems. Leave of course reduced the effective manpower pool, but even a modest reduction in desertion would have made up for that. In the first two years of the Napoleonic War 5,662 able seamen, 3,903 ordinary seamen and 2,737 landmen deserted.[75] Even allowing that a proportion of these will have run from ship to ship, and most of them deserted to rejoin the national pool of manpower from which the Navy recruited; even allowing that men were at the same time deserting to the Navy as well as from it;[76] these figures still represent a terrible cost, to the men themselves and to the war-effort, which more generous leave might have greatly reduced. The real disadvantage – or advantage – of general leave was that it would have very sharply exposed the bad captains. Humanity and liberty were bound together. This is probably the real reason why it had to await the humanitarian movement of naval opinion during the Napoleonic War.

Impressment had no friends, least of all among sea officers. 'It is impossible to describe the terror, the anxiety, the cruelty, the injustice, and the grievous wrongs inflicted on society in general, by the continuance of this shameful practice,' wrote Captain Edward Brenton.[77] It very ill agrees with the modern idea of an all-powerful state imposing an equitable obligation on all. It has to be said, however, that the British state, remaining weak and leaving much of government (including military recruitment) to the localities, succeeded without imposing universal conscription in raising very large forces. In 1809 there were 141,000 men in the Navy and over 300,000 in the army and embodied (i.e. mobilized) Militia, together between 11 per cent and 14 per cent of the adult male population, without including the part-time Local Militia and Volunteers. The army alone was three times the size of Napoleon's in proportion to the population from which it was recruited.[78]

Prisoners of war were an important component of the manning situation on both sides of the Channel, for the Great Wars were the first in which prisoners were not exchanged. The French Revolutionaries first decreed in 1794 that all British and Hanoverian prisoners of war were to be murdered out of hand. Only one sea officer carried out the order, and though he was promoted for it, he was not copied. British prisoners in Revolutionary France suffered from brutality and administrative chaos, but they were not actually massacred. Under the Directory exchanges briefly resumed, and then stopped for good. Napoleon refused either to exchange or to pay for the keep of French prisoners in Britain. As a result a very large administration had to be created to look after the men at least some of whom might otherwise have been exchanged to man French warships. By 1814 there were over 80,000 French prisoners in Britain, one-third of them from privateers. The district around Brest alone had lost 28,000 seamen in seven years. At first they were kept afloat in hulks, but from 1803 the policy was to disperse prisoners inland, away from the dockyard ports. The officers lived on parole in country towns, the men were housed in purpose-built camps. The biggest were Perth, Valleyfields (south of Edinburgh) and Norman Cross (near Peterborough), each of which held 7,000 men. The permanent prison of Dartmoor, begun in 1806, held 6,000. Some hulks were still used, partly as a punishment for those who had attempted to escape, but they were insanitary and extremely costly to run. The mortality among prisoners in Britain was 1 or 2 per cent a year, but in the hulks about double that. Overall the British administration, initially overwhelmed by the numbers, was by 1803 reasonably efficient and humane, though at the level of camp guards and local contractors there was corruption and exploitation.[79]

The structure of the Navy during the Great Wars was complicated by the addition of several specialized, shore-based services. The stations of the Admiralty Telegraph, a visual signalling chain established from London to Portsmouth, Deal and Sheerness in 1796, Plymouth in 1806 and Yarmouth in 1808, were each commanded by a lieutenant. So were the coastal signal stations.[80] Other 'shore jobs' suitable for elderly or disabled lieutenants were to command harbour hulks, hospital and prison ships. The Impress Service employed substantial numbers of officers and men: eighty-four lieutenants in 1795; thirty-six captains (or commanders) and ninety lieutenants in 1797; twenty-seven and sixty-eight respectively in 1805. More served with the Sea Fencibles, a sort of coastal militia of fishermen and boatmen established in 1798, and restarted in 1803 (when it was amalgamated with the Impress Service), for local defence against invasion. Its military value was questioned, but it employed quite a lot of officers – in some cases as a cover for other activities such as espionage.[81] A new force was added to the Royal Marines in 1804 when the Royal Marine Artillery was created to replace the detachments from the Royal Artillery which had hitherto manned the bomb vessels' mortars, as a result of disciplinary trouble with the soldiers.[82]

Of the daily life of the Navy at sea enough could be said to fill another book, and there is space to mention only a few aspects. The dangers to health and morale presented by very long periods at sea made it important that the men should have every opportunity to buy food and comforts for their messes. In foreign ports men invariably bought fruit, vegetables and livestock.[83] In the East Indies, where the men had little cash, 'there being no regular distribution of "rhino" in this country' (the comment of John Collum, surgeon of the *Terpsichore* in 1802), they swapped salt beef for yams, pumpkins and sweet potatoes.[84] When Nelson's fleet touched at Sardinia in 1805 the locals set up a market, 'which of course met with a most welcome reception from 12,000 men, with plenty of money, and no means for two years before of spending it', recorded Marine Lieutenant Marmaduke Wybourn of the *Repulse*.[85] At sea the blockading squadrons were served by small vessels selling their wares around the fleet.[86] The Guernsey schooner *Goodrich*, for example, sailed from St Peter Port for the blockading station off Brest in 1809 with a cargo of wine, coffee, sugar, cognac, gin, playing cards, chocolate, rum, mustard, hams, tobacco, tea, 'knit jackets', cloth and buttons, soap and cheese.[87] The presence in her cargo of 3,150 gallons of spirits explains why some admirals disapproved of these vessels.[88] Messes were almost always allowed to buy livestock, though attitudes to pigs varied. Some captains thought them too dirty, St Vincent forbade them, but Captain William Lobb of the frigate *Crescent* allowed his men as many as they pleased, running freely about the main deck, as long as they were washed daily; they must have been the cleanest hogs in the fleet.[89] Just before Christmas 1812, Captain Edward Codrington of the *Blake*,

> was amused upon going round the ship last Sunday, to see a whole sheep roasting in the galley, stuffed with potatoes and onions. It seems the mess to which this belonged had bought it, like many others, for a Christmas

dinner; but it being agreed that there was no certainty of what might happen in the intervening time, they determined 'to have a good *blow-out* while they were all stout and hearty.' The prize-money has done the ship great credit, owing, perhaps, in some measure, to the power I have here of preventing the introduction of extra liquor. For, besides good clothing, every mess-place in the ship is ornamented with gold, according to their several tastes, at their own expense, and with some degree of uniformity in the shelves, broken by the little variety of their own paintings and ornaments; which, marking contented choice rather than the hand of power, the whole produces a very pleasing effect.[90]

This domestic sense seems to have been something new among the seamen.[91]

The new style of officership led to the regulation of daily life with growing precision, and watch and station bills might now include stations for entering and leaving harbour; mooring and unmooring; bending, loosing, reefing, furling, making and shortening sail; tacking and wearing; sending up and down topgallant yards; striking and getting up lower yards; hoisting boats in and out. Regular days and times were allocated for sail and gun drill, and washing days. Cleanliness remained an obsession, and virtually all ships were cleaned daily, but sweeping was tending to replace scrubbing decks on some days of the week to reduce the evils of damp.[92] All good officers aimed to work their ships with the minimum of noise, 'so that when a loud and general order comes from the mouth of the captain every man may hear and comprehend', as the order book of Captain Edward Riou of the frigate *Amazon* explained.[93] For this reason the Navy did not allow shanties, though a fiddler was traditional when weighing anchor. Aboard the frigate *Alceste* in 1806, the seaman William Pemberton remembered, 'All seemed riot, confusion, desperation; but all was silent; for all was obedience to a sure design; it was order, precision, exactness, and familiarity with the action.'[94] 'When conducting any manoeuvre of the ship,' wrote Captain Thomas Louis,

> I strictly caution against noise either on deck or aloft. Nothing tends so much to cause it as the unnecessary repetition of orders. The officer commanding on the forecastle should be the only voice heard. I expect the people, at least the captains of the tops, will thoroughly understand what they are ordered about and render further orders unnecessary, and that the officers will consider abuse or bad language as a downright contradiction to this order.[95]

The first lieutenant of the *Unité* under Captain Patrick Campbell had only to order 'Make sail' and the rest followed automatically, while Captain Thomas

Hardy was said to be able to work the *Victory* in total silence, by hand signals alone.[96]

Though the work of the ship was highly disciplined and regulated, all writers insisted on the importance of allowing the men to relax whenever possible, and the large crews of men-of-war made considerable leisure possible. 'When the larboard watch is on in a morning I can sleep till 7 or 8 o'clock and sometimes longer which I could not do in an Indiaman,' wrote one pressed man.

> We have very little work to do and plenty of men to assist when any work is to be done . . . I find it the very reverse of what it was represented to me to be, for when we have done our duty we may go to the fire to sleep, to read, write or anything.[97]

St Vincent was a particular friend to the 'make and mend', a sort of half-holiday for the men to sort out their clothes and sea-chests: 'every sailor knows a little about his needle . . . and can cut clothes, particularly trousers'.[98] 'Thus employed,' wrote Edward Brenton, 'I have always seen the men cheerful and happy, rummaging their chests and bags, clearing out their berths and greatly increasing their little comforts below.'[99] Swimming alongside the ship was popular in fine weather, usually in a sail triced up to a couple of studding-sail booms, since many sailors could not swim, and the danger of sharks had to be considered.[100] Off-watch, many men read or told stories, and in the evenings in good weather dancing and singing were almost universal.[101] 'Every moonlight night the sailors dance,' Collingwood wrote, 'and there seems as much mirth and festivity as if we were in Wapping itself.'[102] Aboard the *Revenge*, as Private Wheeler recorded,

> Two evenings a week is devoted to amusement, then the boatswain's mates, with their pipes summons 'All hands to play'. In a moment the scene is truly animating. The crew instantly distribute themselves, some dancing to a fiddle, others to a fife. Those who are fond of the marvellous, group together between two guns and listen to some frightful tale of ghost and goblin, another party listens to some weather-beaten tar who 'spins a yarn' of past events, until his hearers' sides are almost cracked with laughter. Again is to be found a select party immortalizing the heroes of gone by days by singing songs to the memory of Duncan, Howe, Vincent, and the immortal Nelson, while others whose souls are more refined are singing praises to the GOD of Battles. Thus my time is passed in the midst of health, pleasure and contentment.[103]

Music had always played an important part in shipboard life, and there was all the more of it as it became fashionable for captains to take pride in having a good band, if necessary paying professional (often military) musicians out of their own pockets.[104] Young William Richardson, whose ship was lying in the Moray Firth in 1794 as escort to transports embarking troops of a Highland regiment, was astonished to see on the moonlit quarterdeck 'Highland gentlemen and ladies dancing in their Highland dresses to the music of our little band, consisting of a clarionet, a violin and a pipe and tabor'.[105] Captain Charles Paget had an Irish piper with 'Union pipes'.[106]

With music often went amateur theatricals, encouraged by many captains and admirals (notably Nelson) as antidote to the boredom of long weeks on blockade.[107] Aboard the frigate *Diamond* off Brest in 1806, 'the crew danced or got up a kind of farce, which was farcical enough'.[108] Big ships could do better. In the Mediterranean in 1807 the *Royal George* had not less than three acting companies performing on alternate nights, nicely graded by social rank: the wardroom officers doing Shakespeare's *Henry IV*; the midshipmen producing the 'genteel comedy' *The Poor Gentleman*; while the lower deck played Foote's 'broad farce' *The Mayor of Garrett*.[109] In the *Ocean* off Cadiz the same year, Collingwood wrote,

> We have an exceedingly good company of comedians, some dancers that might exhibit at an opera, and probably have done at Sadler's Wells, and a band consisting of twelve very fine performers. Every Thursday is a play night, and they act as well as your Newcastle company.[110]

A visitor to Admiral Durham's flagship the *Bulwark* in Basque Roads in 1813 was invited to a performance of O'Keefe's *Wild Oats*, followed by a hornpipe, and again that popular favourite, *The Mayor of Garrett*. The gun deck was fitted with scenery, drop curtain and footlights. During the dancing the admiral whispered to his guest, 'Don't stare so: it is a real woman, the wife of a fore-topman.'[111]

She was not alone. Though some captains and at least one admiral (the austere Collingwood) still forbade women aboard their ships, it seems to have been an unusual position by the time of the Great Wars, and there are numerous passing references to the presence of the wives of warrant officers and ratings. Captains' order books, like that of the *Indefatigable* in 1812, sometimes prescribe regulations for 'the women belonging to the ship'.[112] The whimsical memoir of Aaron Thomas claimed that 'it is the rules of the king of England's Navy to permit every sailor to have a woman aboard, if they choose', which was certainly not true.[113] The only women borne officially on the ship's books were those 'married on the strength' of foot regiments serving as marines, which included twenty women at the battle of St Vincent.[114]

Unofficially, however, there were at least a few women aboard most ships. Many of them evidently made a living by washing, and St Vincent threatened to send them home for wasting fresh water and giving captains an excuse to return to port, but even he made no move to ban women as such.[115] In the *Goliath* at the battle of the Nile, one woman was killed and several wounded, and a baby was born. Four of the nineteen men killed left widows who were aboard the ship, which if the casualties were exactly proportional to the whole ship's company would suggest that there were at least 100 wives aboard. After the battle the four destitute widows were entered by Captain Foley on the ship's books in the rating of 'dresser' (i.e. nurse), which he appears to have invented for the purpose.[116] Christian White of the *Majestic* was another woman who fought and lost her husband in this battle.[117]

Ships with married couples aboard, by no means all of them elderly, also had babies. Nelson stood godfather to a baby of the *Minotaur* born off Leghorn in July 1800.[118] In 1812 a seaman and his wife were both killed in action aboard the sloop *Swallow*, leaving a three-week-old orphan. There was no other nursing mother aboard, but the child was saved, suckled by the wardroom goat.[119] When the first naval campaign medal, the Naval General Service Medal, was finally issued in 1847 to all men and boys who could show that they had been present at one of a long list of actions large and small, one of the few surviving claimants for the battle of the First of June 1794 was Daniel Mackenzie of the *Tremendous*. Since his name was on the ship's books, his claim was clearly valid, so the medal was duly issued, engraved with his name and rating: 'Daniel T. Mackenzie – Baby – H.M.S. *Tremendous*'.[120]

The majority of women at sea lived openly as women, but there were a few women disguised as men and serving as seamen.[121] At the 1807 court martial which condemned Lieutenant William Berry to death for sodomy one of the principal witnesses was a young woman who appeared in court dressed as a seaman.[122] 'William Brown', the black captain of the main top of the *Queen Charlotte*, was discovered to be a woman in 1815 after eleven years aboard.[123]

THIRTY-THREE

Honour and Salt Beef

Social History 1793–1815: Officers

The sea officer's career began in childhood. By fourteen or fifteen a boy should have enough education and experience 'to enter into the glory and honour of his profession'.[1] Nineteen, Croker told a mother in 1812, 'is more than six years too old to begin a sea life'.[2] Of a sample of 100 officers who passed their lieutenant's examination in 1793, at least thirty-eight were not older than twelve when they first went to sea. Four were under eight years old, and the youngest was less than five.[3] These were the boys who were to become midshipmen, and since that elastic word was still changing its meanings, it is well to distinguish them. There were still midshipmen in the Navy in the original, seventeenth-century sense: senior petty officers, experienced seamen who had risen as far as they were going to go. More numerous were the young gentlemen, or would-be gentlemen, in their late teens or twenties, who served as junior officers immediately under the lieutenants whose ranks they hoped soon to join. Somewhere between these two groups were the disappointed midshipmen, embittered and often hard-drinking men in their thirties or even forties who had hoped and failed to get a commission. These were the 'oldsters' whom Thomas Huskisson remembered, 'whose pretensions were so highly valued by themselves that it was nearly twelve months before they condescended to take further notice of us youngsters than to inform us that "grog" was very bad for us, and they would oblige us by drinking our allowance themselves'.[4] The 'youngsters' were boys, still too young to exercise more than nominal responsibility, but increasingly called 'midshipmen' in the new sense of the word as a synonym for the older 'young gentleman'. Any of these might or might not be rated 'midshipman' on the ship's books, without it having any effect on what they were actually doing. One young man only discovered by accident that he had been rated midshipman when he happened to see the relevant page of the muster-book; it was a bureaucratic detail which nobody had bothered to tell him.[5]

A significant innovation was the institution in 1794 of the new rating of 'Boy 1st Class or Volunteer' for 'young gentlemen intended for the sea service', though it had little immediate impact.[6] Captains continued to find their own volunteers, the Admiralty had no involvement in the selection of the Navy's future officers, and young men of very varied origins still found their way on to the quarterdeck. The sons of warrant officers and the like were quite common, not a few commissioned officers had begun before the mast, and a significant minority had been pressed (twice, in the case of Lieutenant James Hodgson).[7] On the quarterdeck of the *Victory* at Trafalgar, John Quilliam the first lieutenant had been pressed, and John Pasco the signal lieutenant was the son of a Plymouth Dockyard caulker. Captain Alexander Wilson had been Lord Bridport's coxswain; Rear-Admiral Troubridge was the son of a pastrycook. There was a mulatto captain, and a vice-admiral who had been flogged round the fleet for desertion.[8] By establishing the rating of volunteer, however, the Admiralty proclaimed that it was possible, and desirable, to identify the future officer in childhood, at the moment at which he joined the Navy. Since he could not yet have acquired any professional knowledge, and since no attempt was made to test whatever qualities he might possess, the only basis of the distinction between the three classes of boy was that implied by the wording of the Order in Council; that is, between gentlemen and the rest. Just as the French navy abandoned its tradition of choosing officers from the nobility in favour of the career open to talent, the British Navy started moving in the opposite direction.[9]

Because of the wide range of age, experience and ability, and the entire absence of any official training scheme or curriculum for the boys, there was an enormous variety in what they might be doing. We meet a midshipman of fourteen taking charge of a watch, and another of the same age still sucking his thumb. There were boys of eleven or twelve risking their lives in a boat action one day, and playing marbles on the poop or building a model ship the next. It was commonly remarked that there were different types of midshipmen in different ships: sophisticated and hard-swearing in ships of the line, slovenly and ill-bred in the little sloops and brigs, but an elite in the frigates, smart and proud of facing early danger and responsibility.[10] Frederick Chamier commanded a boat in a landing operation for the first time at thirteen, and was greeted by his captain on his return: 'You are fairly a sailor now; been drunk, been aloft, and been in action. Take your hands out of your pockets, youngster, or I shall order the sailmaker to stitch them up.'[11] It was a tough life, especially for boys from comfortable homes, and beginning it was a shock for everyone. 'I had anticipated a kind of elegant house with guns in the windows,' recorded Chamier;

> an orderly set of men; in short, I expected to find a species of Grosvenor Place, floating about like Noah's Ark. Here were the tars of England rolling about casks, without jackets, shoes, or stockings. On one side provisions were received on board; at one port-hole coals, at another wood; dirty women, the object of sailors' affections, with beer-cans in hand, were everywhere conspicuous; the shrill whistle squeaked, and the voice of the boatswain and his mates rattled like thunder in my ears; the deck was dirty, slippery, and wet; the smells abominable; the whole sight disgusting; and when I remarked the slovenly attire of the midshipmen, dressed in shabby round jackets, glazed hats, no gloves, and some without shoes . . .'[12]

Many boys kissed their mothers goodbye at ten or twelve, and returned as men if they returned at all. William Hoste left his Norfolk parsonage at twelve to follow his neighbour Captain Nelson, and came back ten years later as a post-captain. When Abraham Crawford left his home in County Waterford at thirteen he had never seen the sea on which he was to make his career.[13] The eighteen-year-old Commander William Parker, writing home from the West Indies in 1800, described himself for the benefit of his sisters who had last seen him as a boy of twelve: 'I am thin, well tanned by the sun, and want a great deal of English polishing; so, whenever I return to England, I must put myself entirely under your directions to learn me *good* breeding, which sailors, you know, are not remarkable for.'[14]

There were two views on how the future officer might acquire some education. Many, like Collingwood, thought the essentials were best learned in a proper school ashore.

> Has he been taught navigation? If his father intended him for the sea, he should have been put to a mathematical school when twelve years old. Boys make very little progress in a ship without being well practised in navigation; and fifteen is too old to begin, for very few take well to the sea at that age.[15]

Too often, Collingwood complained, the boys came to sea knowing nothing, or the wrong things.

> He is as well-bred, gentlemanly a young man as can be, and I dare say an excellent fox hunter, for he seems skilled in horses, dogs, foxes and such animals. But unluckily . . . these are branches of knowledge not very useful at sea. We do not profit by them off Ushant.[16]

St Vincent agreed: 'It is a lamentable thing that youths intended for the Navy do not receive a suitable education before they embark.'[17] The alternative was to study afloat, but this was not generally easy. The 'unintellectual mediocrity' of an average wardroom made up of 'snorers, chessmen and soakers' was not likely to foster a good education.[18] There were many ships in which the officers read nothing but the Navy List, and the boys received more gin than instruction, or passed their time 'sleeping, playing, and walking the decks with their hands in their pockets'.[19] There were some captains, however, who took pains with their youngsters, and made sure to get a competent mathematician as schoolmaster. Captain J. T. Duckworth of the *Orion* – 'the very best man in the Navy for training youth', in St Vincent's opinion – had 'a very scientific schoolmaster'.[20] Captain W. P. Cumby required all his boys to master longitude by chronometer and lunars, and if they did not, would mark their certificates that it was by 'wilful neglect'.[21] Such captains took equal care that the boys learn seamanship. Anselm Griffiths had an old seaman teach his youngsters two hours a day. Francis Cole 'made all the boys assist in fitting the rigging (we were all covered with tar!) but it did us a great deal of good', as Abraham Crawford remembered.[22] William Parker in the *Alarm* obtained 'a most clever astronomer', and had his midshipmen follow a regular syllabus of practical instruction: Monday at the lead or on the mizzen topgallant yard; Tuesday small arms practice; Wednesday knotting and splicing; Thursday on the mizzen-topsail; Friday at the great guns; Saturday with the boatswain.[23] The best of these captains, moreover, were men of culture, and anxious that their young men should follow their example. George Elliot had 'a very little Latin, much less Greek, and could not write a correct line of English, when I went to sea, at nearly eleven years old', but one of the lieutenants 'took a sort of charge of me, kept my books, and made me read in his cabin'.[24] In the frigate *Niger* young William Parker found that 'Captain Foote has a vast number of books, so I had a fine choice. In general I read Shakespeare's plays. Captain Foote desired me to read those which were taken from the History of England, and I compared them to the History, which was very amusing.'[25] 'Give him a hint how necessary it is he should be acquainted with history in general,' Hoste wrote home about his young brother. 'He is so fond of the practical business, that I am obliged to exert fraternal authority to get the theory.'[26] These captains were far from a majority, but they included many of the outstanding officers of the day, and their example led in 1806 and 1812 to new regulations which raised the status of the schoolmaster, and permitted chaplains to take on the role in addition to their own. 1806 was also the year when the Royal Naval Academy at Portsmouth was expanded, reformed and

17a. Jamsetjee Bomanjee, Master Shipwright of Bombay Dockyard 1792–1821, engraved after G. Bragg. He is holding the plans of the *Minden*, 74, built at Bombay in 1810, and in his waistband is the silver rule presented to him by the East India Company in 1804. One of the ships he built, the *Trincomalee* of 1817, is still afloat.

17b. After his first great naval battle, the Duke of York commissioned from the court painter Sir Peter Lely a series of thirteen portraits of the 'Flagmen of Lowestoft', the senior officers who had fought with him. Like the majority of them, Sir Jeremy Smith was a former Republican.

17c. James Duke of York himself, soon after he became King James VII and II, by Nicolas de Largillière.

17d. Samuel Pepys, by Sir Godfrey Kneller.

18a. Edward Vernon, by Charles Philips.

18b. Edward Boscawen, by Sir Joshua Reynolds, wearing the first flag-officer's full-dress uniform.

18c. Lord Howe, by John Singleton Copley.

18d. Sir Cloudesley Shovell, by Michael Dahl.

19a. A marble bust of Nelson, by John Flaxman, 1805.

19b. Rear-Admiral Sir John Jervis (the future Lord St Vincent), by Sir William Beechey.

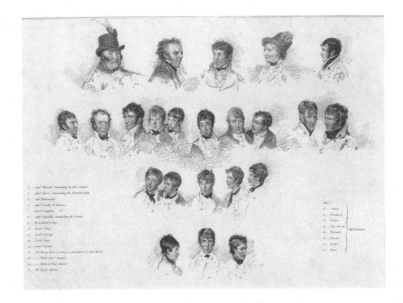

19c. A group of officers serving under Commodore Sir Samuel Hood in the Leeward Islands early in 1805, by John Eckstein. The second, third and fifth from the left in the top row are respectively Commander James Maurice commanding the *Diamond Rock*, Captain Murray Maxwell of the flagship *Centaur* and Commander George Bettesworth of the sloop *Curieux*.

20a. The Fourth-Rate *Adventure* of 1646, originally one of the fast frigates of the Parliamentary Navy, drawn by the younger van de Velde about 1675, by which time she had main-deck guns mounted in the waist to make her a two-decker.

20b. The *Charles Galley* of 1676, a successful fast cruiser built for Mediterranean operations against the Algerines, painted by the elder van de Velde. Apart from two ports aft in the gunroom, and one right forward, the lower deck is unarmed, in the style of the 'true frigate' of a century later, but the row of sweep-ports (and the name) indicate that she could be rowed in a calm.

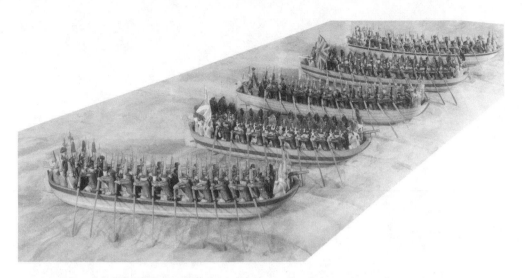

21a. Models of flatboats, the landing craft of the eighteenth century.

21b Men of war leaving Plymouth Dockyard, 1766, by Dominic Serres.
The view is looking across the Hamoaze, from the Cornish side near
Torpoint towards the dockyard, before the hill in the right background
was levelled to make the southern extension.

22a. George III reviewing his fleet at Spithead, 22 June 1773, by John Cleveley the younger. The royal yacht (and the commissioner's yacht to port) are passing between a double line of guardships.

22b. A homeward-bound West India convoy in September 1782, by Robert Dodd, with the damaged merchantman *Lady Juliana* in the foreground, in tow of the frigate *Pallas*.

23a. The *Ramillies* shortening sail in a squall, 1782.

23b. The dangers of close blockade: this is the wreck of the *Magnificent* on the Boufoloc Rock off Brest, 25 March 1804, by J. C. Schetky.

24a. The frigate *Triton* getting her convoy under way from St Helen's in 1808, by Pocock.

24b. The 'ship *Harriet* James Baillie Commander', by Nicholas Cammillieri, 1815. Merchantmen like her were not only the foundation of Britain's trade and prosperity, but frequently employed on military operations. The number 660 painted on her bows shows that she was on charter to the Transport Board.

renamed the Royal Naval College, though the war ended before this innovation made any impact on the Navy.[27]

Many of the best captains for training youngsters were in frigates, and frigates, with continual cruising and activity, were the best schools of service. Their officers and men were recognized (not least by themselves) as a professional elite, honed by independent cruising and frequent action. The majority of the Navy, however, were manning ships of the line, many of them tied down on tedious blockade duty. With the rising social status of the Navy, captains were under growing pressure to take, and keep, young men who were not all cut out for naval life. None seems to have suffered more than Collingwood, almost unique as an admiral who took a personal care of the youths of his flagship. One mother

> writes to me that her son's want of spirits is owing to the loss of his time when he was in England, which is a subject that need give her no concern, for if he takes no more pains in his profession than he has done, he will not be qualified for a lieutenant in sixteen years, and I should be very sorry to put the safety of a ship and the lives of the men into such hands. He is of no more use here as an officer than Bounce is, and not near so entertaining.[28]

Bounce was the admiral's dog. 'I have recommended to his mother to take him from the sea,' Collingwood wrote of another young hopeful. 'Perhaps he might make an apothecary. If he did poison a patient now and then, better that than lose a whole ship's company.'[29]

Though a large number of officers had been made by Keppel's political promotions in 1782, and at the time of the 1787, 1790 and 1791 mobilizations, the outbreak of war in 1793 found the Navy short of junior officers as usual, and the best possible basis for a successful career was as ever to be born at the right moment.[30] Officers who received their first commissions between 1790 and 1794, perfectly placed to profit by the Great Wars, enjoyed the most successful careers of the whole eighteenth century; half of them were promoted within nine years. George Cockburn, for example, was an acting-lieutenant of twenty in July 1792, confirmed in January 1793. He then rose from tenth lieutenant of the *Victory* to first, then to commander and captain, all in thirteen months.[31]

Those young officers who did advance in their profession had to pass the lieutenant's examination and produce certificates showing that they were at least twenty years old and had not less than six years' sea service. All these tests were real. The examination was regarded as formidable, especially when

Hamond was Controller of the Navy ('whose character for turning mids back frightened me not a little,' W. S. Lovell recalled),[32] though the actual failure rate was only about 5 per cent. In addition candidates were regularly rejected because their proofs of age or service were deemed to be suspicious.[33] At the same time, as we have seen, it was acceptable for a proportion of 'sea-time' to have been passed in harbour, and some candidates were certainly younger than twenty. George Elliot, for instance, passed on 6 August 1800 with a certificate from the minister of his home parish (Minto in Roxburghshire) stating him to have been baptized on 2 June 1779, though he had in fact been born in Swanage on 1 August 1784. He was barely sixteen – but he had been at sea since he was ten, he had already distinguished himself in two battles, and he had been taking charge of a watch for more than a year.

> If I was not as efficient as was desirable, I suspect I was equal to at least two of the lieutenants, who had just been made from common seamen, and were neither used nor very fit to command. Four out of our five lieutenants were made in that way, the distress for officers was so great – two were efficient, *one very good*, the other two very much otherwise.[34]

Brought up by an outstanding captain (Thomas Foley), recommended by St Vincent and Nelson, young Elliot had all the qualities the Navy needed, and the examiners who turned away other boys as too young passed over his proof of age with discriminating negligence.[35]

There is no doubt that some candidates for promotion started with advantages. First among them were the 'children of the service'. There was no subject on which admirals were more entirely in agreement than the propriety and justice of favouring the sons of sea officers. Nelson considered 'the near relations of brother officers, as legacies to the Service'.[36] St Vincent felt the same: 'It is not necessary to remind your Lordship of young Peter Parker, nor of Sir Roger Curtis's son, as they are children of the service – therefore are to fill the first vacancies.'[37] Rear-Admiral Sir Peter Parker had looked after young Lieutenants Nelson and Collingwood at Jamaica during the American War. Thirty years later they pushed forward his grandson, a lieutenant at sixteen, and a post-captain in a Trafalgar vacancy before he was twenty. 'I have made advantage of our calamities,' Collingwood wrote, 'and having lost two excellent men, I have endeavoured to replace them with those who will in due time, I hope, be as good.'[38] Charles Adam, nephew of Lord Keith, went to sea at ten, was a lieutenant at eighteen, a post-captain at nineteen, and before he was twenty-one had justified his patrons with a notable victory over a French frigate in the Indian Ocean.[39] These two were outstanding young men, but not every admiral's kinsman did so well. Pellew's brutal and incompetent brother Israel was a continual embarrassment, and his favoured sons were not much better.[40] 'Do me all the kindness for my son you can,' Pellew wrote from the East Indies to a friend on the Admiralty Board. 'I may live to return it to one of yours, for you see the wheel goes round and round.'[41] It did, but more scrupulous admirals tried to take merit into account as well.

The Navy's rising social status was shown by the number of successful admirals who reached the peerage. Some admirals of earlier generations had been made peers for political reasons, but during the Great Wars the Navy participated in the growth of what has been called a 'service elite', in which men were rewarded because of what they had done professionally, rather than who they were. This implied a new underlying ideal, one in which duty was beginning to infiltrate the concept of honour.[42] Thus Hood, Bridport, St Vincent, Nelson, Collingwood, Keith, Gardner, Gambier and Exmouth (Edward Pellew) all served in the Navy with the peerages they had earned at sea, while Saumarez and Duncan were ennobled on or after retirement. At the same time the Navy's new social standing was marked by the presence of younger sons of the established aristocracy; not only the sons of impoverished Scottish or Irish peers anxious to make their fortunes, of whom there had always been a few, but members of the highest and wealthiest families of the English nobility. Attitudes towards them were equivocal. 'This vast overflow of young nobility in the Service makes rapid strides to the decay of seamanship, as well as subordination,' St Vincent complained, 'and I wish with all my heart we had no captains with seats in Parliament.'[43] 'A sprinkling of nobility was very desirable in the Navy,' he told George III,

> as it gives some sort of consequence to the service; but at present the Navy is so overrun by the younger branches of nobility, and the sons of Members of Parliament, and they so swallow up all the patronage, and so choke the channel to promotion, that the son of an old officer, however meritorious *both* their services may have been, has little or no chance of getting on.[44]

Nelson agreed about the destructive effects on discipline of the 'Honourables': 'Orders are not for them – at least, I never yet knew one who obeyed.'[45] Collingwood likewise complained of inexperienced officers of good family who tried to make up their own deficiencies at the expense of their men, 'endeavouring to conceal, by great severity, their own unskilfulness and want of attention, [they] beat the men into a state of insubordination'.[46] 'There may exist,' he commented on the mutiny of the sloop *Danaë*, commanded by the twenty-year-old Lord Proby, 'a degree of violence when severity is substituted for discipline which is insupportable . . . The truth is, in this great extensive navy, we find a great many indolent, half-qualified people, to which may be attributed most of the accidents that happened.'[47]

It is indeed possible to find examples of noblemen who received more favour than they deserved. 'I hope Lake will soon be promoted,' wrote Keith in 1803, 'the prince is very desirous he should.'[48] Son of one of the Prince of Wales's courtiers, eventual heir to an earldom, Warwick Lake had the most favourable winds to propel his career − until he wrecked it by marooning Robert Jeffery. A duke's son was in an even stronger position. 'We must send Lord William Fitzroy to some foreign station where he may be likely to obtain promotion,' St Vincent wrote in 1803; 'the sooner the better, as his Grace of Grafton is very exigent.'[49] Fitzroy passed from lieutenant to captain in less than four years, survived insinuations of cowardice, but was finally dismissed the service for brutality in 1811.[50] For contemporaries outside the Navy, like Mrs Charlotte Nugent, it was normal that the natural leaders of society should receive proper respect, and disgraceful if they did not.

> Lord Townshend wrote to Lord Barham to ask him to make him [Lord James Townshend] a lieutenant. What would you say if I assert that this was refused? When you consider Lord Townshend's services, his respectability, is it not incredible? Lady Townshend is very indignant, but likewise hurt to death about it.[51]

By conventional standards an eminent marquis and his wife had every reason for indignation. But there is another side to this story. Lord James was promoted lieutenant the following week, having apparently served the regulation six years, and he soon proved to be, in Hoste's words, 'as good a seaman and officer as ever stepped the quarter-deck'.[52] He joined outstanding frigate captains like Lord William Stuart ('a gallant enterprising young man', St Vincent thought),[53] Lord Henry Paulet,[54] Lord Mark Kerr ('so delightful a youth,' St Vincent wrote, 'that I hope he will not long continue idle'),[55] the Hon. Frederick Maitland (whom the famous frigate captain Michael Seymour called 'the best cruiser I ever met with'),[56] and the Hon. Charles Paget (described by Duncan as 'a very fine young man and an active officer').[57] All of these had real merits, though no doubt their rank in society helped to ensure that they were not overlooked. As George III remarked, when Maitland's cousin John distinguished himself in action, 'being a man of good family will I hope also be of advantage in the consideration, as it is certainly wise as much as possible to give encouragement, if they personally deserve it, to gentlemen.'[58] The most detailed studies do not agree whether the sons of the nobility were favoured beyond their deserts.[59] The question is complicated by the fact that many of them were also related to senior officers, and might as well be counted as 'children of the service'. 'Your son,' Collingwood told Lord Radstock,

> is as promising an officer as any in the service; the labours of his duty have made him skilful, and he has no tricks or vices to set against his good qualities. He is young, but he has as much knowledge as half the veterans; and, above all, he never expects the service to bend to his convenience.[60]

Young Commander Waldegrave was the son and grandson of peers, but also the son of an admiral.[61]

The sons of peers were a special group within the larger category of those having influence in the civilian or political world outside the Navy. As we have seen, such civilian 'interest' had always been brought to bear on naval careers, when senior officers were prepared to back it, but it was now an established convention that commanders-in-chief overseas, even so far away as the East Indies, could dispose only of vacancies caused by death or court martial. All others belonged to the First Lord of the Admiralty, who provided every commander-in-chief with a continuously renewed 'Admiralty list' of candidates. The First Lord therefore controlled, and was known to control, most of the promotion in the Navy, and it was harder for civilian First Lords of the Admiralty than it was for admirals to insulate professional criteria from political ones, even when they understood the need to do so. Lord Spencer was in a particularly exposed situation. As a Whig peer, he had been brought up to believe that it was essential for the liberties of Englishmen that the power of patronage should as far as possible be removed from the crown and its servants (such as admirals) and put into the hands of the independent guardians of political liberty (Whig peers). Unlike Sandwich, he did not bring to office thirty years' experience of the Navy and its peculiar conventions. 'An able and virtuous man with a princely fortune', St Vincent called him, 'the justest and ablest man that ever presided at this Board.'[62] Naval opinion generally gave him credit for ability and good intentions, but it was impossible to avoid noticing the numerous Spencer connections – Lady Spencer's connections in particular – whose sea careers prospered under his direction. Edward Fellowes, 'a very promising young man and a very near relation of Lady Spencer's', rose from midshipman to captain in twenty months.[63] Jervis in the Mediterranean looked after others, 'for I feel I ought to devote the first fruits of the Spanish War in the Mediterranean to Lady Spencer'.[64] 'I am extremely obliged to you for your attention to all my numerous recommendations,' Spencer replied,

> and I trust you will not think me unreasonable (when you consider my situation here as to applications of that sort) if I continue to keep up my list. I have now only to mention the name of one young officer, but he is so respectably connected that I cannot avoid bring him forward to your notice. I mean Lieutenant Henry Heathcote, son of Sir William, the Member for Hants; his father is so anxious about him that it will give me great satisfaction to hear he is of the sort which you are not unwilling to favour.[65]

Jervis was not unwilling, and the young man was a post-captain in ten months. Spencer promoted the Hon. Charles Herbert, a lieutenant at eighteen and a post-captain at twenty,

> on the never-ceasing importunities and remonstrances of Lord Carnarvon, who made such an outcry about his son's disappointments that I thought it absolutely necessary in a political view to gratify him.[66]

As a result he had to put off Commander William Lukin, nephew of his friend and political colleague William Windham, but he made up for it later when, as he explained to St Vincent, 'I was under an engagement to Windham to move his nephew into an 18-pounder frigate and I wished to take the opportunity of giving the *Thames* to a young relation of mine.'[67] None of this was unprecedented, or by most contemporary standards unjustified, and until Spencer's handling of naval patronage is studied in detail it is not possible to say with any confidence whether he significantly altered the balance of political or social to professional qualifications for advancement.[68]

St Vincent was a Whig politician too, and in practice receptive to the claims of the aristocracy both as commander-in-chief and as First Lord, but when he came to office he announced an entire change of policy: no further promotions of commanders or captains until appointments could be found for existing officers. 'The system is undoubtedly just and highly honourable to him,' commented the *Times*, 'but if the noble Lord can pursue such a rigorous and impartial line of conduct for a long continuance, it will be more than any of his predecessors have been able to accomplish.'[69] 'The list of post-captains and commanders so far exceeds that of ships and sloops,' St Vincent told Keith in September 1801,

> I cannot, consistently with what is due to the public and to the incredible number of meritorious persons of those classes upon half-pay, promote except upon very extraordinary occasions, such as that of Lord Cochrane

and Captain Dundas, who have the rank of post-captain; nor can I confirm any of the appointments made by commanders-in-chief upon foreign stations, except the vacancies are occasioned by death or the sentences of courts martial.[70]

As was his wont, St Vincent contrasted his own rectitude with his predecessor's laxity:

The circumstances of the war, and the numerous connexions of the Spencer family, have contributed to swell the list of post-captains and commanders to an enormous size, insomuch I have determined not to promote to those ranks, except in cases of extraordinary merit and service, until the worthy on half-pay are provided for.[71]

St Vincent was not, however, quite as rigorous towards his own friends and connections as he wished people to think. 'The officers of the *Ville de Paris*,' he wrote to one applicant in April 1801, 'remain as they did when I left her; and my own nephew, commander of the *Stork* sloop, who is reputed an officer of uncommon merit and acquirements, stands as he did before I came into office; and I have refused to promote at the request of four princes of the blood.'[72] What he did not mention was that he had tried unsuccessfully to persuade Spencer to promote his nephew just as he left office, and that he himself was encouraging overseas commanders-in-chief to create false vacancies by bogus resignations.[73] A few months later he made his nineteen-year-old nephew post himself, 'for there is no gratification equal to that derived from pushing the fortunes of deserving men'.[74] The Peace of Amiens gave him the excuse for a large promotion, modelled on Keppel's of 1782: 'I agree with you that the Board should be governed by former practice at the close of such a successful naval war as we have witnessed.'[75] When the war resumed, St Vincent adopted the same austere promotion policy, in public. On 18 May 1803 he assured the Marquis of Douglas, 'I have not forgot Lord Cochrane, but I should not be justified in appointing him to the command of an 18-pounder frigate when there are so many senior captains of great merit without ships of that class.'[76] Douglas might have been surprised to read what St Vincent had written the previous day to the commander-in-chief at Halifax:

This will be delivered to you by Captain Fane of the *Driver*, son of Mr Fane, Member of the County of Oxford, who is sent out to you with a view to his being promoted to the rank of post-captain . . . Captain Fane is a near relation of mine and every way worthy your good offices and protection.[77]

St Vincent was not quite breaking the conventions he had inherited, but he was certainly indulging himself for a young cousin whose career, though respectable, was not remotely as distinguished as Cochrane's.

Behind St Vincent's public austerity lay a growing realization that there was a crisis in the naval career structure. As early as 1797 Lord Spencer was concerned that 'all the frigates we have coming forward are nearly engaged, and the town of London, as well as Portsmouth and Plymouth, swarm with young captains who on every account ought to be employed, but whom I am, for want of ships for them, under the necessity with great regret to keep in idleness'.[78] There is no doubt that he was right. The number of captains and commanders was growing faster than the supply of ships for them to command. There had always been elderly and unfit officers on the lists, for whom half-pay served as a substitute for the retirement pension scheme which did not exist, but the proportion of officers unemployed began to rise from about 1795, and the unemployment was concentrated among the newly promoted, who were presumably the youngest and fittest. Between 1795 and 1800 captains serving fell from 69 per cent to 48 per cent of those listed, and were down to 41 per cent by 1810. Commanders serving were only 40 per cent of those listed in 1800, but recovered to 51 per cent in 1805, before falling again to 44 per cent in 1810. Over the same five years, 1805 to 1810, the number of commanders increased from 422 to 608, and the number of ships for them from 121 to 246; that is to say that the number of sloops doubled in five years, but the proportion of commanders who could be employed still fell. Lieutenants were the least, or last, affected by the trend: 71 per cent were serving in 1805, which was within the historic range, but by 1810 the proportion had fallen to only 60 per cent.[79]

The rank of commander (as distinct from the generic term, then meaning 'captain' or 'commanding officer') was established in 1794, from which date direct promotion from lieutenant to post was no longer possible. This left an anomaly: all commanders were still captains of sloops (and therefore addressed as 'Captain'), though they were frequently much younger and less experienced than the first lieutenants of line-of-battle ships who were now unequivocally their juniors. In other respects establishing the rank of commander made little difference. It had long been very unusual to skip the rank of master and commander, but it remained common to pass through it very rapidly. The employment of commanders was always difficult, because the number of commanders' commands in the Navy was always less than half the number of post-ships. However quickly lucky officers passed through the rank, it was difficult to find commands for all the commanders who sought them. The more it became usual, and from 1794 compulsory, for the future post-captain to have passed through the rank of commander, the greater the likelihood that commanders would have to be promoted, not because they were needed in that rank, but solely to assure a supply of post-captains for the future.

There were in fact two distinct groups of commanders: young (sometimes very young) officers rising fast, for whom it was a brief stepping-stone to post-rank, and men promoted late in their careers who went no further. We may guess that this latter group was disproportionately made up of older men who had reached commissioned rank from warrant rank or the merchant service. During the Great Wars, commanders become more numerous relative to captains, and the young 'high-flyers' decline as a proportion. A significant factor here was the Admiralty's decision on the outbreak of war to reclassify troopships as commanders' rather than lieutenants' commands. Fully justified by their size and importance, this change considerably increased the numbers of commanders' commands, and avoided some problems of military discipline by ensuring that a troopship would normally be commanded by an officer senior to the senior officer of troops embarked. There was some tendency for the two groups of commanders to command different sorts of ships: the dashing young men taking the cruisers, the glory and the prize-money; the middle-aged taking the troopships. Late in the Napoleonic War, however, the Admiralty began to regard troopships as a suitable apprenticeship for frigate command.[80]

During the Napoleonic War promotion to commander or captain usually entailed a period of unemployment. Officers who lived on their pay were even driven to decline promotion. Commander James Hillyar, who supported his mother and sisters, refused a post-ship in 1803, 'because,' as Nelson explained, 'although he might thus get his rank, yet if he were put upon half-pay, his family would be the sufferers'.[81] Officers were now taking command of ships who had been long enough ashore to have forgotten their profession, something hitherto confined to the outbreak of war after years of peace. In January 1808, for example, Captain Thomas Brodie took command of the new frigate *Hyperion*. Although a captain of 1802, Brodie 'had not had his foot on board a ship since he was a lieutenant' (as one of his officers recorded), 'and was consequently "rather rum in his nauticals", as the common phrase went respecting him'.[82]

The obvious question to answer is, how did the Navy come to have too many officers? In the present state of knowledge a definite answer is impossible, but some causes can be identified. Since would-be officers began their careers under the patronage of captains and other officers, and the Admiralty had no official knowledge of them until they presented themselves for examination as lieutenant, it had no means of regulating their numbers. Nor did it directly control the examination (which was conducted by the Navy Board at home, and by panels of captains convened by commanders-in-chief abroad), and no attempt was ever made to limit the number who were examined, or who passed. The Admiralty was not formally under any obligation to commission any more of these young gentlemen as lieutenants than there was employment for, but one can understand that the presence of numerous qualified candidates created at least an expectation of advancement, if not a sense of entitlement. The traditional cycle of war and peace which had roughly balanced supply and demand over the long term gave way in the 1790s to over twenty years of almost continuous war. In 1790 a full-scale mobilization succeeded by a period of peace allowed the Admiralty secretariat to overhaul the half-pay lists, striking out large numbers of officers who had not responded to the proclamation calling for their services, so that the proportion genuinely available for service was probably higher than usual on the outbreak of what was to be a war more than twice as long as ever before.[83] In these circumstances the Navy's traditional system of promotion, run as it always had been run, was very likely to produce too many officers.

There was, moreover, a particular problem with midshipmen, lieutenants and commanders, for the only reward for gallantry or good service by junior officers was promotion. Ratings were sometimes given money, captains might be given a medal or a knighthood, and admirals a peerage, but for junior officers promotion was the only distinction normally available. Contemporaries identified the problem. Private medals, available to junior officers and even ratings, were issued by philanthropists including Nelson's prize agent Alexander Davison, the industrialist Matthew Boulton, and St Vincent himself, but the Admiralty forbade them to be worn with uniform, and in most cases they rewarded presence at a general action rather than individual distinction. An official order of 'naval and military merit' was proposed but shelved because of George III's illness.[84] In the absence of any system of decorations, 'all we get is honour and salt beef', as Nelson put it.[85] The only tangible reward was promotion. Gallantry in action was the only exception St Vincent would admit to his ban on promoting new commanders and captains.[86] The problem was that in a long war there were many examples of gallantry – and all the more of them as young officers realized that this was their only chance of promotion. The number of those it was just to reward bore no relation to the number it was possible to employ. The practice of advancing all the first lieutenants of the ships of the line which had fought in a fleet action, instituted in 1794, had a particularly devastating effect on the Commanders' List.

St Vincent, Camperdown and the Nile between them increased it by more than a third in two years. In 1801 St Vincent found 'almost all the first lieutenants who were made commanders on the battle of the Nile, several of those of St Vincent, of Camperdown, of Lord Bridport's action before L'Orient, upon half pay; and I feel myself bound, by every principle of justice, to bring them forward in the first instance'.[87] Presently the battle of Copenhagen added another batch of deserving candidates for whom little could be done.

Further down the scale there was a fast-growing problem of 'passed midshipmen', qualified for lieutenant but unable to get commissions. From 1804 to 1814 the Admiralty used the term 'sub-lieutenant' for passed midshipmen and master's mates who were appointed as watchkeeping officers in gunbrigs and gunvessels, whose only commissioned officer was the lieutenant in command. Unfortunately it was not a rank and conferred no useful status; rather the reverse, since the gunbrig lieutenants had a bad reputation.[88]

Unlucky officers naturally resented their misfortunes and looked for someone to blame. The 'Honourables', and Spencer who had promoted many of them, were an obvious target. 'Your encouragement for those lieutenants who may conspicuously exert themselves,' Nelson told St Vincent, 'cannot fail to have its good effect in serving our country, instead of their thinking that if a vessel is taken, it would make the son of some great man a captain, in place of the gallant fellow who captured her'.[89] Perhaps Spencer did advance the wrong men, but it does not appear that he was guilty of promoting too many. The annual rates of promotion under the first four First Lords during the Great Wars can be laid out in a simple table:

	Captains	Commanders	Lieutenants
Chatham (1793–4)	46.8	72.2	316.2
Spencer (1794–1801)	50.7	95.4	268.3
St Vincent (1801–4)	61.5	75.8	236.7
(1802 excepted)	23.1	44.4	209.5
Melville (1804–5)	14.5	42.5	177.3[90]

There was a sharp increase in promotions of captains and commanders in the peace year of 1802, when St Vincent indulged himself with the precedent of 1782, but otherwise the rate of promotion was falling as successive First Lords took account of supply and demand. By the time of Trafalgar, however, it was too late. It would have needed a complete stop to all promotions (except perhaps of lieutenants) for years to correct the situation, and that was in practice impossible. 'With regard to patronage,' Barham complained, when I read over the claims before me – from admirals and captains for their children, from the king's ministers, members of parliament, peers, and eminent divines – I do not know when I am to make another [commander]. Under these circumstances it is impossible that any person in my situation should give satisfaction. If I steer clear of injustice I shall think myself fortunate.[91]

Political realities had not disappeared. In May 1805 Pitt instructed him to appoint Captain Edward Codrington to the *Orion*.

The captain is brother of the member for Tewkesbury, and[92] has not recently attended, although an uniform supporter; the cause, I have been privately told, is that he conceives he has been treated with inattention in respect to his brother. Mr Codrington is a respectable country gentleman, with a large fortune, and it seems desirable that he should be gratified.[93]

Four years later Collingwood told a follower,

Lord Mulgrave knows my opinion of you, and the confidence I have in you; but the truth is, that he is so pressed by persons having parliamentary influence, that he cannot find himself at liberty to select those whose nautical skill and gallantry would otherwise present them as proper men for the service. A hole or two in the skin will not weigh against a vote in Parliament, and my influence is very light at present.[94]

Mulgrave did his best to accommodate Collingwood, but in the circumstances it was inevitable that most officers were disappointed most of the time.

The traditional balm to the wounded naval spirit was prize-money, or (for captains) the less dangerous and even more lucrative 'freight' of bullion. Glory, honour and patriotism were powerful forces, but there was hardly anyone in the Navy who was indifferent to money, and there was a good deal of it about. The single Vice-Admiralty Court of Jamaica condemned prizes worth £2,300,000 during the Revolutionary War. Between 1803 and 1810 the ships of the Navy on home stations were taking about £1 million a year in prizes. The Convoys and Cruizers Act of 1708 laid down a division of prize-money which was in force for a century. The commander-in-chief took one-eighth, the captain a quarter, the master and lieutenants, the warrant officers and the petty officers one-eighth each, and the remaining quarter was divided among the 'private men', seamen and marines.[95] Even this inequitable distribution gave the seamen significant windfalls. The Nile netted every man £7 18s, Trafalgar £9 9s 6d, and Strachan's action of November 1805 (when all the prizes were brought home), £10 13s – roughly half a year's pay on the 1797 scale.[96] Prize-money went a long way to make a happy ship. When the first lieutenant of the brig-sloop *Helicon* restowed her in 1810 and made her very fast, 'This favourable change produced a corresponding one in all on board. The prospect of prize-money exerted its never-failing influence; the men were more cheerful, desertions became more rare, look-outs were better kept . . .'[97] Captain Henry Digby of the frigate *Aurora*, operating from Lisbon in the 1790s, made a practice of selling all his prizes out of hand without waiting for condemnation by an Admiralty court, and distributing the proceeds at once. This was legally risky, but extremely popular, and gained Digby all the volunteers he needed. Captain Patrick Campbell was doing something similar in the Adriatic during the Napoleonic War, ransoming prizes for cash and distributing it at once to avoid the delay and expense of the Malta Vice-Admiralty Court.[98]

It was captains and admirals, however, who could really make their fortunes. Only a minority actually did so, but a frigate captain cruising on good ground, or the commander-in-chief of an overseas station, had excellent prospects. In eight years commanding frigates during the Revolutionary War Captain J. S. Yorke took at least fifty-six prizes, of which thirty-four whose accounts survive earned him over £30,000. His pay was £146 a year. The four frigates which took the Spanish register ships *El Tetys* and *Santa Brigida* in 1799 shared £652,000 net. The admiral got £81,000, four captains £40,730 each, and every seaman received £182 4s 9¾d – ten years' pay. In 1803 Commander William Parker brought home £150,000 in diamonds from Lisbon, earning 1 per cent 'freight'. Two years later he made over £24,000 from prizes in a single cruise.[99] On 22 February 1805 Capt. the Hon. Charles Paget wrote to his brother announcing that he had made a rich prize: 'my *whack* of prize money at a moderate calculation will be about fifty thousand pounds, which for a younger brother is not a bad fortune to have made'.[100] Two days later he anchored at Spithead and hastened to London to speak to his sweetheart. They were married on 7 March, and within a fortnight he was regretting his haste.[101]

In the East Indies officers' pay bills could only be cashed at a discount of about 20 per cent, but the East India Company paid generous allowances which more than made up the difference: £3,000 a year for the commander-in-chief, £500 for a captain, and so on down to free tea and sugar for the ships' companies. Two successive commanders-in-chief each made about £300,000 in prize-money during their careers, Rainier entirely and Pellew largely on this station. Keith in the Mediterranean made just under £67,000 in less than three years.[102] It was for this that admirals faced the risks of a tropical climate or, like H. C. Christian at the Cape in 1798, separation from a sick wife and a beloved family: 'With my West India prize-money also, I hope we may be enabled to take tolerably good care of our dear girls. The boys will, I trust, be taken care of. This is my most anxious wish, and the reflection that strengthens and supports me in the sacrifice I have made – namely, that I am working for them.'[103]

Against the captain's prize-money has to be set the risk of failure and damages in the Admiralty courts, which he bore alone. Seizing an ostensibly neutral merchantman, which might or might not prove to be enemy property, required nice judgement and experience, to say nothing of commercial knowledge and the ability to interpret ship's papers in many languages, some or all of which were likely to be false.[104] Mistakes were easy and expensive. 'Law is a bottomless pit and I have no inclination to fathom its depths,' in the words of one commodore declining to get involved with a Danish prize.[105] Moreover captains were expected to 'keep a table', and admirals had to feed and entertain their staff and numerous official visitors. When St Vincent was reappointed to the Channel Fleet in 1806 he spent £700 on his initial outfit alone; sixteen months of his official allowance of 'table money' at 30s a day. Pellew spent £3,250 fitting out for the East Indies. As commander-in-chief in the Mediterranean from 1799 to 1801 Keith was spending about £8,000 a year on entertainment, or more than four times his pay.[106] Nelson on the same station kept an excellent table ('three courses and a dessert of the choicest fruit, together with three or four of the best wines, champagne and claret not excepted', noted Gillespie)[107] and was never lucky with prizes:

> I believe I attend more to the French fleet than making captures; but of what I have, I can say as old Haddock did, 'It never cost a sailor a tear, nor the nation a farthing'. That thought is far better than prize money; not that I despise prize money, quite the contrary. I wish I had one hundred thousand pounds at this moment, and I will do everything consistent with my good name to obtain it.[108]

A new division of prize-money was promulgated in 1808, in which the seamen and marines divided a half between them (petty officers and able seamen benefiting particularly), and the admiral and captain were reduced to one-twelfth and one-sixth respectively. This aroused strong protests from the captains.[109]

Prize-money was always divisive, and freight (which was largely unregulated) more so. They frequently led to disputes and law suits, notably that between Nelson and St Vincent. They maintained civil relations in spite of it, but not everyone did.[110] 'In no community, considered collectively, does a vindictive spirit manifest itself more generally or exhibit its effects to a later period of existence than among naval men,' considered John Cunningham, surgeon of the *Sceptre* in 1803, and there was a proverb 'that if a captain in the Navy were to be roasted, another would always be found ready to turn the spit'.[111] Prize-money added to the grievances of lack of promotion. It was something of an obsession with officers that their hard-earned prize-money was swallowed up by the inefficiency and corruption of Vice-Admiralty Courts and prize agents. This grievance was not entirely imaginary, but it was greatly exaggerated.[112] None were more obsessive about this subject than Lord Cochrane, who pursued a feud with the Malta Vice-Admiralty Court for releasing a Maltese privateer which he had seized. Cochrane, however, is a very unsafe witness, in this and everything else, and he himself had a well-established reputation for dishonesty which culminated in 1815 in a conviction for Stock Exchange fraud which finished his naval career. His Radical friends passed it off as political persecution, but the evidence was very strong.[113]

Cochrane was unique, but the element of desperation which marks his later career was not. It shows in the reckless gallantry of young officers pushing boat attacks – to the alarm of admirals who saw lives hazarded for negligible military advantages.[114] It was one reaction to the strains of naval service in the years after Trafalgar, when the Navy's public standing had never been higher, but its opportunities of glory and wealth seemed to be drying up. The situation called for real qualities of leadership from commanders-in-chief, which not all of them possessed. St Vincent had shown one way to get officers to do their duty, but there were serious disadvantages in his approach, visible to contemporaries like C. V. Penrose:

> a system of discipline and management, for which, when he began it, perhaps there was a good deal of reason, as he found a lax sort of command the order of the day. But when occasion has once put power in the hand of man, it is I believe only a Washington who has known how to relinquish it.[115]

There was never a clearer case of the corrupting influence of power, nor the dangers of dividing to rule an organization which needed to be united. St Vincent tried to entrap officers into committing offences, and took an unmistakable and growing pleasure in humiliating them in front of their men, which undermined their authority and subverted all real discipline.[116] 'It was an invariable rule with St Vincent *not to do what anybody asked*, and to do things at the last possible and most inconvenient moment,' wrote George

Elliot, 'and it made no difference whether the sufferer was friend or foe.'[117] Nelson's style was the opposite. 'It was his art to make all under him love him, and own his superiority without a ray of jealousy.'[118] He had in a very high degree the talent of the great commander to inspire and encourage people who did not know him personally. 'He was easy of access, and his manner was particularly agreeable and kind. No man was ever afraid of displeasing him, but everybody was afraid of not *pleasing* him.'[119] That was the opinion of Edward Codrington, and his fellow-captain George Duff thought the same. 'He is so good and pleasant a man, that we all wish to do what he likes, without any kind of orders.'[120] None of the admirals who came after him equalled his genius as a leader of men. Collingwood, a greater man in some respects, was beloved in his own ship but had neither taste nor talent to reach out to the whole fleet.[121]

Separation had always been one of the hardships of the sea service, and it was particularly hard in the blockade years of the Great Wars. 'The delight of receiving letters is only known in its full extent to those who are and have been long in a foreign country,' wrote Lieutenant Edward Napier, 'perhaps it is one of the most powerful sweeteners of life.'[122] In 1803 Duckworth calculated that he had been ten years at sea, and not seen his daughter for six years.[123] In 1805 Captain G. J. Hope had been fourteen months at home in eight years, and the same year Codrington wrote home that 'Captain Rutherford told us yesterday, declaring that it was d–d foolish for a sailor to marry – that he had been in that happy state for nine years, one only of which he had been with his wife!'[124] Collingwood complained that 'my family are *actually strangers to me*'.[125] When he died in 1810 he had not seen his wife and daughters since the outbreak of war seven years before, nor the garden he loved so much.

> Tell me how do the trees which I planted thrive? Is there shade under
> the three oaks for a comfortable summer seat? Do the poplars grow at
> the walk, and does the wall of the terrace stand firm?[126]

In 1811 Captain Benjamin Hallowell reckoned to have been home ten months in eighteen years as a captain.[127] Next year his friend Codrington mused on his condition in a letter to his wife on their wedding anniversary: 'here I am solitary amidst numbers, deprived equally of solitude and of society'.[128]

There was a radical solution to the problem of loneliness, which some married officers began to adopt during the Napoleonic War. St Vincent, of all people, set the fashion. Though he hated officers to marry, he had the Wynnes, an English refugee family with three teenage daughters, living aboard his flagship in the Mediterranean for over a year, and took great pleasure in the girls' company ('the old gentleman is very partial to kisses, he abuses all those who do not salute the ladies and always obliges all the gentlemen that are present to kiss us').[129] When the inevitable happened and the eldest married Captain Thomas Fremantle, he raised no objection to their living together aboard Fremantle's frigate. Betsy Fremantle took part in the council of war before the disastrous attack on Santa Cruz in 1797; it is possible that her presence inhibited a frank discussion of the risks.[130] She was not the only captain's wife of her generation living aboard a cruising frigate in wartime. In 1799 Captain C. J. M. Mansfield of the *Dryad* had his wife and two small daughters with him at sea. Mrs Mansfield had a dress with epaulettes, like a captain's uniform, though her shipmates remarked that her powers of command did not extend to her children.[131] In 1799 Bridport heard with 'astonishment and concern' that one of his captains had his wife and children aboard.[132] They were ordered home, but during the Napoleonic War it was not unknown to meet wives afloat, especially in semi-combatant situations like coastal passages, or aboard troopships.[133] Captain Francis Austen had his wife and children aboard with him in the Baltic in 1812, and as he was Rear-Admiral Sir Thomas Williams' flag-captain the admiral can hardly have been unaware. Popham had one of his daughters with him off the North Coast of Spain. The following year Captain J. A. Gordon, boarding the *Venerable*, was astonished to find that Commodore David Milne had his wife, two children and a maid aboard. Milne blandly professed to be unaware that wives were forbidden at sea, 'but we all agree that if we thought a cruise would do either of our wives any good, the best way would be to take her, and let the Admiralty find it out, if they can!'[134]

It was the warrant officers who did best out of the Napoleonic War. Commissioned officers' prospects were blasted and their prize-money reduced, but the situation of the 'gentlemen' warrant officers improved. Surgeons received a proper uniform in 1805, with the all-important sword which marked them as gentlemen, and masters and pursers followed in 1807. At the same time they were officially recognized as being of 'wardroom rank'. Masters' pay was increased, and the new position of 'First Master' created for the master of the flagship.[135] Pursers' acceptance as gentlemen was marked by the not infrequent occasions when they took a lieutenant's place in action.[136] All this indicated that a division was slowly opening along a fault-line which the haphazard rank and rating structure of the Navy had not clearly recognized before; between those who were gentlemen by birth and those who were not. This was to become the central organizing principle of the ranks and ratings of the Navy after 1815.

THIRTY-FOUR

Gain and Loss

Operations 1803–1805

The Peace of Amiens satisfied no one for long. The hereditary First Consul for life (as he became in August 1802) was happy to receive back Britain's recent conquests, but he had no interest in a lasting settlement, and French aggression and expansion continued unchecked. The nebulous assurances on which the Addington ministry had depended soon proved to be worthless, and the British hand-over of Malta (whose fate had been left particularly uncertain by the treaty) was stopped. Since Russia also had an interest in the island this provided Bonaparte with an excellent occasion for war, calculated to divide his most dangerous enemies. The British declared war in May 1803, sooner than Bonaparte had intended, when many French warships and merchantmen were overseas and vulnerable. At sea the Royal Navy moved first, but on land French armies soon added Hanover to their conquests. In May 1804 Bonaparte proclaimed himself 'Emperor of the French' under the title Napoleon I.

France had the strategic initiative, and without allies, Britain necessarily stood on the defensive. There were two points at which it was both possible and essential to block Bonaparte's expansion: the English Channel, and the central Mediterranean narrows. In May 1803 a French army marched to southern Italy, threatening Sicily, Greece and Egypt. Beyond them lay the East – and Britain had returned the Cape of Good Hope, commanding the other route to India. To prevent French advance into the Levant and beyond, it was necessary to hold Malta and keep a fleet in the western Mediterranean basin; but Malta itself was too far from Toulon to be useful as a base for a blockade, and to feed Malta it was necessary to draw on both Sicily and North Africa. The Mediterranean fleet, and Nelson its commander-in-chief, therefore had to combine both an offensive watch on the French fleet in Toulon and the defensive care of Sicily and Malta. The British dockyards were far away, and their stores were empty anyway, but St Vincent airily assured Nelson that he would not need them.

I have no idea under the vigour of your character that there will be an imaginary difficulty; real ones cannot exist. In short, cordage may be manufactured at sea; caulking and every other refitment, which in England requires dock yard inspection, your Lordship knows is much better performed by the artificers of the squadron; and barring accidents by shot, there is nothing that cannot be provided for.[1]

Toulon was impossible to blockade closely, as frequent winter gales blew squadrons offshore, and from the hills behind the port it was easy to tell where or whether the enemy was on station. Nelson insisted that he was not attempting a blockade, only watching the port from a distance with the intention of intercepting when the enemy should sail – but this was chancy even with many scouts, and like all the British squadrons, 'I am distressed for frigates, which are the eyes of a fleet.'[2] Nelson based his squadron on the remote anchorage known to the British as 'Agincourt Sound' in the Maddalena Islands. From there he kept an unbroken watch on Toulon for almost two years, continually at sea, keeping his men in good health and spirits, scrimping naval stores and patching his old ships.[3]

Meanwhile Bonaparte had taken command of the army assembling around Boulogne for the invasion of Britain. Opposite him Lord Keith commanded the North Sea and the Narrow Seas as far west as Selsey Bill, while on shore the Duke of York – never a lucky general in the field, but an outstanding strategist and organizer – planned the defence of Britain if the enemy should get ashore. Weak ministries in London, responding to public alarm, mounted or proposed a series of ingenious attacks on the invasion ports, several of them sponsored by Popham or Sidney Smith, but none of them particularly successful.[4]

Napoleon took the invasion preparations even more seriously than the British public. Sums which would have paid for thirty-five Third Rates were expended on the hopeless task of converting Boulogne, Etaples, Ambleteuse and other still smaller and less promising creeks into major ports. In the end Boulogne gained a new basin, capable of holding 1,000 landing craft, but the harbour still dried almost completely at low water, the bar was passable only two and a half hours either side of high water, and the open roads were quite untenable in the prevailing westerlies. In twelve months' effort the maximum number of landing craft ever sailed on one tide was 100. 'Let us be masters of the Straits but for six hours, and we shall be masters of the world,' Napoleon declared in July 1804.[5] Two weeks later, against the protests of his admirals, he ordered a trial embarkation in blowing weather during which thirty craft were wrecked and several hundred men drowned. 'A romantic and epic dream,'[6] he described the experience, and carried on dreaming at other people's expense. By the spring of 1805 he had assembled a grand total of 1,064 officers, 163,800 men, 19,635 riding horses and 3,742 artillery horses, plus three million rations, 600 oxen and a flock of 3,000 sheep. Medals had been struck and monuments erected to commemorate the glorious conquest of England. (The 'Napoleon Column' still stands on the cliffs outside Boulogne, though its inscription has subsequently been adjusted.) In the port, however, he had only half as many landing craft as he imagined, and his idea of the time and conditions necessary for the operation was completely divorced from reality. Simply to embark and put to sea would have required somewhere between five and eight days (estimates vary) of fine, calm weather. To cross the Channel under oars would have taken at least two days more, but a fair wind would have raised surf on the landing beaches, and the invasion craft could not face much wind anyway. There was no question of them facing even the smallest warship; their every encounter with the Royal Navy outside the range of shore batteries was a disaster, and it is impossible to imagine how they could have evaded contact if they had put to sea. In September 1804, for instance, Keith's subordinate Rear-Admiral Sir Thomas Louis had four small two-deckers, four heavy frigates, ten sloops, four bomb vessels and fourteen gunboats, luggers and cutters to patrol the short stretch of Channel between Dungeness and Boulogne, and this was only one-sixth of the 218 ships and vessels under Keith's command. Napoleon's admirals had no illusions about what Denis Decrès, his Minister of Marine, privately called the emperor's 'bizarre, shifting and contradictory projects',[7] but they knew that their professional opinion counted for nothing, and none of them had the courage to tell him the truth.[8]

With a French invasion preparing, the close blockade of Brest was of great importance, and St Vincent put it in the hands of Cornwallis. 'A man of very reserved habits and manners; of few signals, and fewer words', who 'never laughed, and seldom smiled, and kept his officers at an awful distance',[9] the austere Cornwallis kept nearly as close a blockade as his predecessor without the same obvious pleasure in imposing discomfort. Coasting trade to Brest was severely restricted. As early as June 1803 the dockyard was reported about to stop shipbuilding for want of timber, by February 1805 traffic had almost ceased, and great efforts were made to complete the Brest–Nantes Canal (opened in 1806). In October 1803 Collingwood was commanding the Inshore Squadron, 'a station of great anxiety and required a constant care and look out, that I have often been a week without having my clothes off, and sometimes up on deck the whole night'.[10] The same month Cornwallis received warning of a French expedition planned for Ireland – but unlike Bridport four years before, he was specifically ordered not to leave the mouth of the Channel open by chasing off to Ireland unless he was sure the French had really gone that way. The same point was made by instructions issued by Melville in the summer of 1804. The great difficulty of the blockade was that there were too few ships to maintain it, for by demobilizing the fleet and disrupting the dockyards St Vincent had eliminated any margin of superiority. 'The French Navy is daily increasing, both at Toulon and Brest,' Nelson wrote in July,

> whilst ours is as clearly going down-hill. It will require all Lord Melville's abilities to get our fleet ahead of that of the French. We made use of the peace, not to recruit our Navy, but to be the cause of its ruin.[11]

In September 1804 Melville calculated that he had seventy ships of the line available in home waters, of which Cornwallis had forty-four, which sufficed to keep seven on station off Rochefort, another seven off Ferrol, and sixteen off Brest – to watch twenty-one inside. There was no margin to spare for losses, and Cornwallis was ordered to run no undue risks with winter gales.[12]

> You have not the means of sustaining the necessary extent of naval force, if your ships are to be torn to pieces by an eternal conflict with the elements during the tempestuous months of winter, and allow me to remind you that the occasions when we have been able to bring our enemy to battle and our fleets to victory have generally been when we were at a distance from the blockading station.[13]

The squadron off Ferrol was needed to watch five French ships of the line, returning from the West Indies on the outbreak of war, which had taken refuge there. Spain was still neutral, and it was worth Britain making every effort to keep her out of the war when the Spanish fleet held the balance of power. This made the blockade of Ferrol a matter of diplomatic as well as operational delicacy. Pellew handled it with great skill, establishing a convenient anchorage in a neighbouring bay where he maintained cordial relations with the Spaniards, and a close watch on the French. In May 1804 he handed over to Rear-Admiral the Hon. A. F. I. Cochrane, a talented officer with his family's established talent for making enemies, and relations with the Spaniards soon broke down. Cochrane assured Melville that Spain was determined to go to war, and only awaited the arrival of a squadron of frigates bearing treasure from South America to declare it. This intelligence determined the Cabinet to seize this treasure. Four frigates under Captain Graham Moore successfully intercepted the Spanish squadron off Cadiz on 6 October: three ships were captured and a fourth blew up, killing among others the wife and daughters of a returning Spanish governor. The operation was well executed, but whether it was wise or right is another question. If the attack had to be made, it would have been better in overwhelming force, to which Spanish officers might decently have surrendered without bloodshed. As it was, Rear-Admiral Bustamante, an officer of honour and ability, could not possibly avoid fighting, unprepared as he was. This attack, delivered without warning or declaration of war, in which many innocents perished, was bound to blacken Britain's reputation, inflame Spanish feelings, and make war swift and certain which otherwise might have been deferred, though probably not avoided.[14]

The Spanish declaration of war in December 1804 transformed Napoleon's strategic calculations, doubling his fleet to 102 ships of the line, against eighty-three British in seagoing condition. Moreover, though Napoleon would certainly not have admitted it, the quality of the Spanish navy was in several respects, especially the professional calibre of its officers, clearly superior to that of the French. The promising French officers brought forward by the Jacobin government ten years before had been got rid of, and replaced by former noblemen, experienced but demoralized and cynical, who were prepared to serve as the emperor's lackeys. Vice-Admiral Latouche-Tréville, the last of Napoleon's senior sea officers with a mind of his own, died commanding the Toulon fleet in August 1804. After that the French navy was dominated by the *quarteron d'Aboukir*, the 'Nile Quartet', as they were known: Decrès, Bruix, Ganteaume and Villeneuve, all men indelibly associated with the catastrophe of 1798, who could be relied upon not to offend the imperial ears with unwelcome truths.[15]

Even before the Spanish fleet was available, Napoleon was planning naval operations. In July 1804 Latouche-Tréville was to take the Toulon fleet via Rochefort and Cherbourg to Boulogne. This plan was cancelled on the admiral's death. It was followed by no fewer than eight major plans involving the co-ordinated movements of many fleets, ordered in the twelve months between September 1804 and September 1805. All of them addressed the central problem of Napoleon's naval strategy: the fleets available to him were superior in total numbers, but divided between Toulon, Cartagena, Cadiz, Ferrol, Rochefort, Brest and the Texel. The first essential was therefore to unite all, or as many as possible, of these squadrons. All Napoleon's plans had certain features in common. They assumed that blockaded squadrons would be able to escape at a moment of the emperor's choosing, and make long sea passages at high speed to very precise timetables. They assumed that wind, sea and tide would obey his requirements. They assumed that the enemy would do nothing and understand nothing, or only those things which suited Napoleon's convenience. Finally, these plans had one more factor in common; each was cancelled before the orders for the previous one had been carried out, or even received. The result was progressively deepening confusion, with different squadrons attempting to conform to different plans at the same time, and the emperor himself (who had no naval staff, and used Decrès as a mere secretary) growing muddled and careless.[16]

Napoleon's third scheme of December 1804 was the first which generated actual operations. It called for the Toulon fleet, now commanded by Villeneuve, to cruise to South America and the Caribbean, where it would meet the Rochefort squadron and return to French Channel ports. The British blockading squadrons would meanwhile have been decoyed to the West Indies or somewhere else, leaving the coast clear. On 11 January 1805, in very bad weather, Rear-Admiral Missiessy succeeded in getting out of Rochefort with four ships of the line and 3,500 troops, setting course for the West Indies in accordance with this plan. On the 14th Villeneuve sailed from Toulon – and two days later, unknown to either of them, Napoleon cancelled the plan. In the Mediterranean Nelson fell back on Sicily, the essential position to block the way to the Levant. Once assured by his cruisers that the French had not gone westward, Nelson swept around the whole basin of the eastern Mediterranean to be sure they had not got past him in that direction. Back at Malta on 19 February, he learnt that Villeneuve, damaged by bad weather, had returned to Toulon.[17] As soon as he was back in port, Villeneuve wrote to Decrès asking to resign his command. 'I should like to point out to you that about all one can expect from a career in the French navy today is shame and confusion ... under no circumstances do I intend to become the laughing stock of Europe by being involved in further disasters.'[18] 'I really believe your admiral does not know how to command,' Napoleon wrote privately to General Lauriston, commanding the troops embarked, whom he used as a sort of military commissar or shadow commander-in-chief,[19] with orders 'constantly to renew our admirals' energy and resolution to carry things through, without allowing themselves to be deterred as easily as they usually are'.[20] But Napoleon and Decrès did not have, and clearly did not really want, an admiral of spirit to command the fleet, and Villeneuve himself was ordered to remain.

At the end of February Napoleon issued a new invasion scheme, the fifth. Under this Ganteaume was to sail from Brest, collect the French and Spanish ships from Ferrol, and meet Villeneuve from Toulon at Martinique, where Missiessy would also be waiting. The combined fleet (under Ganteaume's command) would then return across the Atlantic to cover the invasion, arriving off Boulogne between 10 June and 10 July. On 30 March 1805 Villeneuve sailed once more from Toulon with eleven ships of the line, evaded Nelson's watch and passed through the Straits of Gibraltar. Off Cadiz he ignored Sir John Orde's squadron of five ships of the line, and Orde, leaving his cruisers to shadow the enemy, immediately fell back on the Channel Fleet off Brest, correctly judging that the proper response to the French plans, whatever they might be, was to concentrate on the strategic point. 'In bringing to England the large ships under my command, I shall afford an opportunity to dispose of them anew: by which little can be risked, and much might be gained if the enemy's blow is aimed at England or Ireland.'[21] Villeneuve collected the Spanish Cadiz squadron under Vice-Admiral Don Federico Gravina and sailed for Martinique on 10 April. Two successive despatch vessels having been lost on passage, Nelson had had no orders or information from home for five months, and lost some time before he picked up the scent. He did not pass the Straits until 6 May, and only on 11 May, having obtained good intelligence of Villeneuve's movements, did he set off in pursuit across the Atlantic. He was chasing eighteen ships of the line with eleven, and he was one month behind. The other parts of Napoleon's scheme had meanwhile miscarried. Ganteaume in Brest, ordered to sail but forbidden to fight, never got past the British blockade, while Missiessy at Martinique gave up waiting for the third plan to be fulfilled and sailed for home on 28 March.[22]

The British government was by no means mesmerized by Napoleon's schemes in the spring of 1805. It hardly noticed them in the excitement of domestic politics, which led to Melville's resignation on 8 April. What attention ministers could spare for the war-effort was devoted to their own strategy and diplomacy. An alliance with Russia was signed in April, gained partly with a promise that Britain's small field army would be committed to the Mediterranean. The troops under Lieutenant-General Sir James Craig sailed on 19 April, with an escort of two ships of the line under Rear-Admiral John Knight. There was no First Lord of the Admiralty in office, and the precious convoy had been gone ten days before ministers realized that neither Nelson nor Orde had received warning to expect it, and that the Toulon fleet was at sea, presenting a grave danger to the convoy and Britain's whole Mediterranean strategy. The papers reached Pitt at two o'clock in the morning of 30 April, soon after the Commons rose, and he found Barham still awake after his first day at the Admiralty. They knew Orde had left the mouth of the Straits, and they did not know where Nelson had gone at all, so they ordered fourteen sail of the line under Collingwood to be detached from the Channel Fleet to

Cadiz, there to act as intelligence might suggest. Luckily the perils of the situation had been avoided by intelligent initiative. As Knight came south he learned of the French fleet and took refuge in Lisbon, arriving just in time to counter intense French pressure on the Portuguese government to repudiate the British alliance. Villeneuve knew nothing of the convoy and had gone off across the Atlantic, so presently Knight sailed again, meeting Nelson off Cape St Vincent who added a three-decker to strengthen the escort. Then the convoy ran into further trouble. Ministers ordered the troops to land at Gibraltar and the escorts to return to strengthen Sir Robert Calder's weak squadron off Ferrol, not realizing that there was plague in the Gibraltar garrison, and six Spanish ships of the line ready for sea at Cartagena. Fortunately the Spaniards did not know that Nelson had left the Mediterranean, and Collingwood appeared before they found out. He sent the convoy on under sufficient escort, and the troops arrived safely at Malta in July.[23]

Villeneuve and Gravina reached Martinique on 16 May. The allies now had overwhelming naval and military strength in the Leeward Islands, as indeed they had had for most of the time since Missiessy arrived in February, but almost nothing was done to exploit it. The allied fleet lay at anchor waiting for Ganteaume, and its only achievement was to recapture the Diamond Rock. This isolated pinnacle rock stands off the coast of Martinique near the capital, Fort de France, and the prevailing winds force shipping to pass close by it to fetch the port. In January 1804 it was seized by Commodore Samuel Hood and armed with four heavy guns, including two 18-pounders on the 600-foot summit. Commissioned as a sloop under Commander James Maurice, the Diamond Rock blockaded Fort de France for eighteen months, only surrendering to overwhelming force when its ammunition ran out and an earth tremor cracked its water cistern.[24]

While this operation was in progress Villeneuve received fresh orders; Napoleon's seventh plan. This required him to capture a long list of British Caribbean colonies while waiting for Ganteaume, and then to collect the allied ships from Ferrol before proceeding to Boulogne. Villeneuve sailed on 4 June, and almost at once captured part of a British convoy, but from the prizes he learned that Nelson had arrived in the West Indies. Immediately forgetting all his orders, he sailed at once for Europe. Nelson was delayed by some false intelligence which sent him in the wrong direction, but even so he sailed in pursuit only two days behind, on 13 June. At the same time he sent the brig Curieux to warn the Admiralty; she sighted the allied fleet in her passage and observed that they were steering a course for Ferrol. Nelson returned to his proper station, arriving at Gibraltar on 20 July.[25]

Although Napoleon fondly supposed that British squadrons would easily be lured off station to the West Indies, ministers in London and British admirals at sea all thought Villeneuve was likely to be back, and most of them correctly interpreted the French plan as a feint to cover an invasion. The immediate question was where Villeneuve and Gravina were heading for, and the arrival of Commander Bettesworth of the *Curieux* at the Admiralty on 8 July supplied the answer. Barham ordered Cornwallis to lift the blockade of Rochefort, and send that squadron to join Calder off Ferrol. A week before Villeneuve and Gravina arrived (with twenty ships of the line), Calder was waiting for them with fifteen. When they met on 22 July in fog, the action was partial and confused. The Spaniards did all the fighting and lost two prizes. Next day the two fleets were still in sight and the weather was clear, but Calder was to leeward with much damage to spars and rigging. On the 24th, however, he had a good chance to renew the action and did not take it, though it was clear to many British officers (including most of his captains) that to cripple the allied fleet when the opportunity offered was worth any loss to Calder's squadron. Instead Villeneuve took refuge in Vigo, later moving to Ferrol on 2 August.[26]

Next day Napoleon arrived at Boulogne to wait for him. He still supposed that his flawless combinations had baffled the enemy, that Villeneuve would very soon appear off Brest in overwhelming force, defeat Cornwallis and liberate Ganteaume. He was unwilling to believe that Ganteaume could only sail from Brest on a wind which would make it impossible for Villeneuve to come to him, or either of them to get up Channel. He was unwilling to believe that any wind which would move the battleships would be too much for the landing craft. He was unwilling to believe that the enemy might take a hand, though Ganteaume had had the nerve to hint as much. Above all he was unwilling to believe that his clockwork admiral might think for himself, but this was how the invasion scheme finally collapsed. The nearer he got to the British squadrons the lower Villeneuve reckoned his chances of success, and after his action with Calder he despaired altogether. On 11 August he sailed from Ferrol heading south, back towards the Mediterranean. As he came south, Nelson was steering north, still in pursuit, but a northerly wind forced him out into the Atlantic and the two fleets did not meet. Nelson and Calder having in turn fallen back to join Cornwallis, he had thirty-six ships of the line off Brest, more than sufficient to block any possible Franco-Spanish combination. Villeneuve was quite right to despair. On 18 August Nelson arrived home for his first shore leave in twenty-seven months, the Combined Fleet took refuge in Cadiz on 21 August, and Collingwood took up the blockade.[27]

Napoleon had intended that the invasion of Britain should dispose of his chief enemy and forestall another coalition against him. On 23 August he finally faced the reality that he had failed in both. The invasion was impossible, and both the Austrian and Russian armies were on the march. On the 26th the Grande Armée broke camp at Boulogne and moved towards the Rhine. A fortnight later Napoleon issued his ninth and last fleet plan, ordering the Combined Fleet into the Mediterranean to cover troop movements in southern Italy which formed a minor part of his plan of campaign against Austria. Though he heard that the British blockade of Cadiz had been reinforced, he did not bother to change these orders, which exposed the fleet to a very high risk of battle and defeat, in pursuit of an objective of negligible strategic importance. It has been suggested that his action can only be explained by wounded vanity, a subconscious desire to punish the hated navy for its failure to contribute to his glory.[28]

On 28 September Nelson arrived off Cadiz to resume his command. He did not expect the enemy to come out, but Collingwood, with his superior strategic grasp, believed they would. On 8 October the senior officers of the Combined Fleet meeting formally in a council of war rejected the emperor's orders, though for form's sake they offered to sail if the British fleet should be weakened. None of them wished to fight a battle to no purpose, while for the Spaniards action against the Two Sicilies was repugnant – and Gravina was a Sicilian himself. Ten days later the unexpected event happened: six ships of the line, in need of water and provisions, were detached from Nelson's squadron to Gibraltar, leaving him markedly inferior. At the same time Villeneuve learned that his relief would be arriving very soon. Nelson was keeping his fleet over the horizon, with frigates watching the port. On the morning of the 19th they reported that the Combined Fleet was getting under way, and by the afternoon of the 20th the whole fleet was at sea, heading for the Straits. Nelson closed from the seaward, but still out of sight.[29]

It is sometimes implied that Nelson fought the battle of Trafalgar surrounded by a 'band of brothers' (to use his own favourite Shakespearian quotation) who were thoroughly familiar with him and his system. In fact only five of his twenty-seven ships of the line had formed part of the Mediterranean Fleet during the previous two years, only eight of the captains had ever served with him before, and only five had ever fought a line-of-battleship in a fleet action.[30] Most of them had never met him when he took over command three weeks before the battle, but all of them knew his reputation, and all were immediately attracted by his charm. 'Lord Nelson is arrived!' wrote Captain Codrington of the *Orion* on the 29th. 'A sort of general joy has been the consequence, and many good effects will shortly arise from our change of system.'[31] 'Lord Nelson, I believe,' thought Captain W. G. Rutherford of the *Swiftsure*,

> is generally thought to be merely a fighting man; but he is a man of amazing resource and abilities . . . The privations this little fleet of eleven sail has gone though has been great; but it has been with cheerfulness, because Lord Nelson commanded them . . . If you do not know Lord Nelson, he is the most gentlemanlike, mild, pleasant creature that ever was seen.[32]

These were officers who had the opportunity to meet the admiral in person, but his influence was felt everywhere. 'Though we had before no doubt of success in the event of an action,' wrote Henry Walker, a midshipman of the *Bellerophon*, 'yet the presence of such a man could not but inspire every individual in the fleet with additional confidence. Every one felt himself more than a match for any enemy.'[33]

Nelson had passed his career in a period of tactical innovation and experiment, and he was always an eclectic borrower of new ideas. 'He possessed the zeal of an enthusiast,' Collingwood wrote, 'directed by talents which Nature had very bountifully bestowed upon him, and everything seemed, as if by enchantment, to prosper under his direction. But it was the effect of system, and nice combination, not of chance.'[34] Above all it was the effect of flexibility.

> Without much previous preparation or plan he has the faculty of discovering advantages as they arise, and the good judgement to turn them to his use. An enemy that commits a false step in his view is ruined, and it comes on him with an impetuosity that allows him no time to recover.[35]

Before the battle he circulated a plan of attack in three divisions, the third to be kept to windward under a trusted officer with discretion to throw it into action at the decisive point: 'I think it will surprise and confuse the enemy. They won't know what I am about. It will bring forward a pell-mell battle, and that is what I want.'[36] In the event, with only twenty-seven against the enemies' thirty-three, Nelson went into action in two columns. Contrary to all precedent, both he and Collingwood in their powerful flagships were at the head of their respective columns instead of in the middle, and the British went into action under full sail including studding-sails, so that many men were busy handling sail who would otherwise have been manning the guns, but they closed much faster than the enemy can have expected. Even so their progress was slow in the light airs, and there was time to prepare for battle, for meals to be eaten and last letters written, and for Nelson to 'amuse' the fleet with Popham's newly introduced 'telegraph' system, which for the first time allowed an officer to compose signals in his own words: 'England expects that every man will do his duty.'[37]

During the night Villeneuve had attempted to form line of battle from his cruising formation of three columns, with Gravina commanding a detached 'squadron of observation' ahead and to windward. Seeing the enemy bearing down towards his rear on the morning of the 21st, Villeneuve ordered his fleet to wear together, thus reversing its formation and direction. This further disorganized an already loose formation, and introduced a pronounced curve in the Combined Fleet's line. Possibly against Villeneuve's wishes, Gravina's squadron bore up to support the rear (as it now was) of the line, instead of keeping its station to windward. The Combined Fleet was now steering northwards, back towards Cadiz, and Nelson probably interpreted the move as a last-minute scramble for safety. Perhaps this caused him to modify his tactics, for instead of turning parallel to the enemy at the last minute to perform 'Lord Howe's manoeuvre', as he had proposed beforehand, Nelson's column held on, initially towards the enemy van, then suddenly altering course to starboard to cut nearly vertically through the middle of the Combined Fleet. Collingwood's column, approaching on a line of bearing, had already cut diagonally into the rear. The unconventional head-on approach was dangerous but besides gaining time, it concealed Nelson's intentions from the enemy until the last moment. Initially fighting at a great advantage against the isolated leaders of the British columns, the centre and rear of the allied line were now subjected to a growing onslaught as ship after ship came into action. Gravina's squadron, absorbed into the rear and engaged by Collingwood's ships, was not in a position to take any initiative, and the unengaged van under Rear-Admiral P. E. Dumanoir le Pelley, which was, did nothing until the battle was already lost. Firing began about noon, and the battle was virtually over by about five o'clock, with seventeen prizes in British hands, and another burned.[38]

'In case signals can neither be seen or perfectly understood,' Nelson had written, 'no captain can do very wrong if he places his ship alongside that of an enemy.'[39] This was no mere general exhortation but a precise reference to an important tactical issue. There were three inter-related questions of naval gunnery: range, rate of fire and target, and different tactical situations called for different answers to them. For the historian the subject is difficult to study, for contemporary estimates of rates of fire tend to be few and vague, while ranges were judged by eye and expressed by terms such as 'musket shot' or 'pistol shot' which had no agreed definitions. It seems clear that at least as far back as Vernon, Anson and Hawke, most British admirals had stressed close range and a high rate of fire. Attacking Porto Bello in 1739, one of Vernon's ships, the *Hampton Court*, 70, fired 400 rounds in twenty-five minutes, which suggests each gun fired about one round every two minutes, and this is probably near the upper limit of any ship's performance.[40] At the end of the century, after the introduction of gunlocks, a few exceptional ships could do better than this: after several years' training Collingwood's flagship the *Dreadnought* could fire her first three broadsides in three and a half minutes.[41] There was no question, however, of being able to sustain such a rate of fire. Men running out guns weighing up to two tons each could not support such an effort for long. The captain who trained his men to fire so fast was planning to close to very close range before opening fire, or the guns' crews would be exhausted before the shot began to tell. 'I do not wish the ships to be bilge and bilge,' said Howe at the First of June, 'but if you can lock the yardarms so much the better, the battle will be the sooner decided.'[42] That implies a fighting range of about twenty feet. The tactic called for very high discipline, for the men had to lie silent, 'all as quiet below as house-breakers', being fired at as they approached, and the captain was the most exposed of all.[43] (At Trafalgar Hargood of the *Belleisle*, second in Collingwood's line, had his men lying between the guns for protection and still suffered fifty casualties before he fired a shot.) Then a devastating volume of fire at close range would probably settle (though not necessarily finish) the action in half an hour or less. At Trafalgar many British broadsides were fired double-shotted, which had the effect of reducing the muzzle-velocity and increasing the short-range 'smashing' effect of the shot.[44]

By contrast a captain who emphasized target practice – slow, deliberate shooting – was contemplating a long action, with less danger to his men and himself, but much less prospect of a decisive result, for both the accuracy and the destructive force of smooth-bore guns firing solid shot fell off rapidly at ranges over 200 yards or so. At the Minorca action in 1756 the French seventy-four *Guerrier* claimed to have fired 659 rounds in three and a half hours; engaged on one side, this implies about five and a half rounds an hour from each gun. At the Saintes another French ship fired 1,300 rounds in six hours, or about six rounds an hour from each gun; faster would have been impossible, it was claimed, considering the heat and the casualties. That may well have been true, over that time, but the form in which the claim is expressed implies a different concept of a gunnery battle.[45]

Related to this was the question of firing high or low. It is something of a misunderstanding to talk of firing on the 'up roll' or 'down roll'; steam ships roll regularly, but on a wind a ship under sail pitches and heaves more than she rolls.[46] Accurate shooting required precise timing as the ship moved in six dimensions,[47] and demanded well-trained guns' crews. Many who are recorded as firing high were probably just firing wild, sending as many shot into the sea as into the air.[48] Nevertheless a tactical choice was available: firing into the enemy hull, especially at close range, promised a rapid decision by killing men and disabling guns. Firing high, to cripple masts and yards, was the logical choice of the weaker party which meant to escape, or the slower party which sought to prevent the enemy escaping. Sometimes British ships had tactical reasons to fire high or French ships to fire low,[49] but by the end of the century there was a powerful British naval convention of firing low and fast from the closest possible range. French captains, on the other hand, including those like Captain Lucas of the *Redoutable* (the ship which fought the *Victory* and killed Nelson) who had their men thoroughly trained and could have chosen otherwise, continued to believe in firing high, as French gunnery manuals were still recommending well after the war.[50] 'An English shot would kill twenty of our men; a French shot in reply would cut a line or make a hole in a sail.'[51] There are many cases of French and Spanish shot going completely over British ships. At Trafalgar the *Principe de Asturias* fired so high that she shot away the *Defiance*'s main truck, but only killed one man.[52] To hit the main truck (say 180 feet above the water-line) with guns which could only elevate about 7° with the quoins removed, she must have been firing at not less than 350 yards, or perhaps just firing wildly in the heavy swell.[53] Conversely, in the *Bellerophon* engaging the *Aigle*,

> our fire was so hot that we soon drove them from the lower deck, after which our people took the quoins out and elevated their guns, so as to tear their decks and sides to pieces. When she got clear of us she did not return a single shot while we raked her; her starboard side was entirely beaten in.[54]

This was the sort of result Nelson wanted, and this was why he urged his captains to the closest possible range – but not all of them listened. Sir Edward Berry of the *Agamemnon* for one, ranged the battlefield shooting indiscriminately at long range, firing into some British ships and fouling the range for others.[55] As a result captains like Codrington of the *Orion*, who was next astern, had difficulty finding an enemy which they could close. For him Berry was an example of how not to do it: 'Having repeatedly pointed out to my men the waste of shot from other ships, I now had a fine opportunity of convincing them of the benefit of cool reserve.'[56] Though the British fleet as a whole was substantially outnumbered, most of the fighting was done by the leading dozen or so ships at very close range, inflicting casualties and damage out of all proportion to what they received. Collingwood's *Royal Sovereign* fought eight enemy ships of the line, of which one alone, the Spanish three-decker *Santa Ana*, suffered double her losses. The *Colossus* fought three enemy ships of the line and suffered the heaviest casualty rate in the British fleet, but still inflicted two and a half times her own losses. Overall the British lost 449 killed and the Combined Fleet probably about ten times as many. The French and Spanish ships were more numerous and more heavily manned; they were fought in most cases with desperate gallantry and in many cases with some skill. So complete a defeat in spite of so many advantages can only be explained by the crushing superiority of British gunnery tactics.[57]

At every level of society, amongst those who knew him personally and those who knew only his name, the news of Nelson's death at Trafalgar was received as a personal grief. Collingwood, most reserved and private of men, wept, and so did many other officers and men. 'My heart, however, is sad, and penetrated with the deepest anguish,' wrote Captain Henry Blackwood of the frigate *Euryalus*. 'A victory, such a one as has never been achieved, yesterday took place . . . but at such an expense, in the loss of the most gallant of men, and best of friends, as renders it to me a victory I never wished to have witnessed.'[58] A boatswain's mate of the *Victory* was unable to pipe the men to quarters for tears. Joy in 'our victory, in which we gained and lost so much', as Collingwood put it,[59] was almost submerged by the universal sense of loss. The immortal hero was hailed as an undying inspiration to his countrymen. Very soon he was being painted at the moment he was struck down in compositions closely modelled on the deposition of Christ from the Cross. His funeral became a national act of celebration and mourning such as the death of kings had never aroused.[60]

At sea the battle did not extinguish every cause of concern for the Admiralty. Four ships of the allied van under Dumanoir had escaped into the Atlantic, and somewhere out there Captain Zacharie Allemand with the five ships of the line of the Rochefort division had been cruising since July as part of Napoleon's seventh naval scheme. In turn both squadrons threatened some important convoys, including a very rich East India convoy bringing home two commanders-in-chief, Admiral Peter Rainier and Major-General Sir Arthur Wellesley, and an outward-bound expedition under Sir Home Popham and Major-General Sir David Baird on its way to recapture the Cape of Good Hope, which sailed from Cork at the end of August. Allemand narrowly missed both of these, but also evaded every one of the British squadrons, and returned to Rochefort on Christmas Eve after 161 days at sea, having taken forty-three merchantmen (half of them neutrals) and three men-of-war. Meanwhile Rear-Admiral Strachan, stationed off Cape Finisterre with four ships of the line to watch for him, intercepted Dumanoir instead, chased him half across the Bay of Biscay and captured all four of his ships on 4 November.[61]

Trafalgar more than made up the naval supremacy which Lord St Vincent had lost. At the end of the campaign Britain had an unchallenged command of the sea, in quantity and quality, materially and psychologically, over all her actual or potential enemies, which she had never known before. Yet the death of Nelson was a heavy price to pay, and it was not clear what it had bought in terms of the war as a whole. The very day Villeneuve and Gravina sailed from Cadiz, the Austrian army surrendered at Ulm. On 2 December Napoleon won a great victory at Austerlitz over the Austro-Russian armies and destroyed the coalition Pitt had laboured to construct. Seven weeks later Pitt himself was dead. Whatever Trafalgar had won, it had not won the war. Nor had it saved Britain from invasion, for Napoleon's invasion schemes had already collapsed under the weight of their own absurdity so completely that even the emperor had noticed. It has for some time been fashionable among British (though not French) historians to dismiss the victory as essentially marginal, or at best as the means of allowing Britain to survive until at last armies and allies could be found to win the war.[62] But if a sea power could not commit her forces to the critical point somewhere in central Europe, neither could she risk them there. Trafalgar certainly was the means of survival, which is not a negligible achievement in a war which no other nation survived unscathed. Trafalgar achieved more than that, however. Napoleon had no sooner thrown away his fleet than he realized how much he needed it to break out of the strategic limitations of his situation, and spent the rest of his reign in a futile and immensely costly attempt to reconstruct it. He at least had no idea that sea power is irrelevant to great continental armies. We shall see, moreover, that Trafalgar was also the guarantor of Britain's economic prosperity, which allowed her to continue at war and to subsidize her allies at war, while Napoleon ground up and consumed the resources of France and all western Europe to feed his military ambitions.[63]

The greatest of all losers from Trafalgar, however, was not France but Spain. Drawn into a parasitic alliance by which France bled the monarchy to feed Napoleon's ambitions, the Spaniards sacrificed at Trafalgar the fleet which alone maintained Spain's status as an imperial power, and a great power. The colonial elites of the Spanish empire had long been restive under metropolitan rule, but as long as the Spanish fleet protected them from the danger of European enemies – above all of the British, who alone still had the capacity to mount major amphibious operations across the Atlantic – their dreams of independence were unrealistic. After Trafalgar Spain had no hold on them – still less when events were soon to demonstrate that they could defend themselves. Forty-five years after Charles III had committed Spain to a francophile foreign policy, France had finally sucked Spain dry.

THIRTY-FIVE

A Continental System

Operations 1806–1811

The Ministry of the Talents came to power in Britain in February 1806 after Pitt's death, just as the Third Coalition was collapsing. Fox, and to a lesser extent his colleagues, were more interested in making peace than war, and when peace proved unobtainable, they had no clear idea what to do next. With no Continental allies, nor much enthusiasm for acquiring any, the new ministers groped for a strategy while distant events overtook their half-formed plans, and distant admirals were left to fend for themselves. They removed Cornwallis to make way for (but also no doubt to get rid of) their colleague St Vincent. At seventy-one he took up his old command only on condition that he be allowed to live ashore in wintertime, but he had not lost his old vigour, at least of language:

> We gibe between Ushant and the Black Rocks in the day, stand off at night, and in at four o'clock in the morning . . . I cannot approve of the rendezvous of my predecessor 'seven leagues south-west of Ushant' and intend to change it for 'well in with Ushant' during an easterly wind.[1]

As before all other officers fell below his standards, especially those appointed by his political opponents:

> What animals this offal of Pitt is composed of! Signal after signal with guns, which has been almost incessant ever since my arrival on this station, having produced no effect, I yesterday gave out a strong injunction both to this and the inshore squadron . . . and we are pretty well dressed this morning.[2]

In reality, however, the old admiral was less formidable than before, because he had lost all political credit, even with his friends in office.[3]

Napoleon's first thought after Trafalgar was to use his surviving ships of the line to make up powerful raiding squadrons, like Allemand's. To this end two squadrons escaped from Brest in December 1805: Rear-Admiral Corentin de Leissègues with five ships of the line initially carrying supplies for the French West Indies, and Rear-Admiral Jean-Baptiste Willaumez with six to cruise in the Atlantic. On 6 February 1806 Leissègues's squadron was destroyed off San Domingo by Duckworth with six ships of the line (originally detached in search of Allemand), which took three French and drove the other two ashore. Rear-Admiral Cochrane, who had formed part of this squadron, met Willaumez off Tortola in July, but with only four ships against six and a large convoy to look after he did not choose to force an action, and Willaumez escaped. He stayed at sea eight months, but all he had to show for the cruise was a handful of small prizes when his squadron, shattered by a hurricane, took refuge in an American port in October.[4]

The most promising area for French naval commerce-raiding was as usual the Indian Ocean, where Mauritius was remote from British attack but perfectly situated on the routes of the Indiamen. On the outbreak of war Rear-Admiral Linois had a powerful squadron of one ship of the line and three frigates. Having raided the East India Company's establishment at Bencoolen in Sumatra, Linois took up a position at the southern end of the South China Sea to await the Company's homeward 'China Fleet'. Nathaniel Dance, the commodore or senior master of the convoy, and his officers, had some warning of the danger, but with no escort they could only hope to bluff their way past, as two previous East India convoys had done in recent years. In January 1797 Rear-Admiral Pierre Sercey's frigate squadron had been frightened off an East India convoy in the Bali Straits which he mistook for warships in a bad light at long range, and in January 1799 Rear-Admiral Don Ignacio Maria de Alava commanding the Spanish Manila squadron of two ships of the line had declined to attack the British escort of another near Macao.[5] Linois met Dance's convoy off Pulo Aor, near the modern Singapore, on 14 February 1804, and the Indiamen put their plan into action. Forming a line of battle, they tacked and stood boldly in to the attack. After a short action with the leading three Indiamen, Linois fled, and Dance hoisted the signal for the 'general chase' – a unique event in naval history, for a convoy of merchant ships to chase a squadron of warships – before re-forming his convoy for the dangerous passage of the Malacca Straits. Subsequently Linois reported that he had heroically fought off eight British ships of the line, and later French historians have laboured to excuse his mistake, but his officers do not seem to have been fooled, and it is extremely difficult to believe that he was. At long range an Indiaman might indeed pass for a small ship of the line, but the moment she tacked or fired the difference between 150 Lascars and 600 men-of-warsmen (to say nothing of the difference between an

Indiaman's armament and a battleship's) would be instantly apparent, and Dance's ships were in action for at least half an hour, within long gunshot range (say half a mile). Linois had thrown away a prize worth at least £8 million through mere timidity.[6]

Linois continued to cruise in the Indian Ocean for the next two years, taking a number of valuable individual prizes including five Indiamen, and supplying Mauritius by bringing in prizes laden with food. Nevertheless by the end of 1805 the island could no longer feed his squadron, and on his passage home he was taken by a British squadron off the Canaries in March 1806. Meanwhile the affairs of the British East Indies squadron had been thrown into confusion, not by the enemy but by domestic politics. Sir Edward Pellew reached his new station in the autumn of 1804, though it was some time before he met Rainier and took over the command. Meanwhile Pitt had returned to power, and his new ally Sidmouth insisted on a suitable job for Rear-Admiral Troubridge, lately St Vincent's colleague at the Admiralty. The solution was to divide the East Indies station on the longitude of Ceylon, giving Troubridge the eastern half and Pellew the western. Politically it was a master-stroke, satisfying Sidmouth's claim while punishing his supporter Pellew and setting two anti-Pittite political admirals at one another's throats. From the point of view of the war the decision was utterly irresponsible. Pellew was certain to resent having the richer half of his command taken away, Troubridge had a notoriously violent temper, and the prospect of harmonious co-operation between them was remote. But the rhythm of the monsoons obliged the British forces to spend part of each year on the Coromandel Coast (in Troubridge's station) and part on the Malabar Coast (in Pellew's), where the only dockyard was. There was no practical way of dividing the two. When the two admirals met at Madras in August 1805 Pellew effectively ignored the Admiralty's orders and took Troubridge under his command, where he remained, in a state of unsuppressed fury. When the Whigs returned to office early in 1806, they restored Pellew to his sole command, and transferred Troubridge to the Cape of Good Hope, which (as we shall see) had by then been captured. His flagship the *Blenheim* was an old ship which had been badly damaged by grounding and was unseaworthy. Pellew intended to replace her, but Troubridge seems to have been all but mad with rage and desperation to escape to his new command, and insisted on sailing at once in spite of the written protests of her captain. She was lost on passage with all on board, on or about 1 February 1807. Thus perished one of the most outstanding officers of his generation, the favourite of Nelson and St Vincent, but his death at least left the East Indies command once more united and undisturbed in the capable hands of Sir Edward Pellew.[7]

The Popham-Baird expedition captured the Cape with little difficulty in January 1806. Popham (taking the opportunity to promote himself an established commodore) displayed his usual talent in managing troops and landings, combined with his equally characteristic energy, ambition and lack of judgement. British governments had long been interested in the supposed wealth and neglected commercial potential of South America; Popham himself had been involved in projecting expeditions, and was a friend of the South American would-be independence leader Francisco Miranda. He easily convinced himself and Baird that they could and should mount an unauthorized expedition to South America, confident that his patron Pitt (whom he believed to be still alive and prime minister) would pardon a successful initiative. Popham sailed in April 1806 with a reinforced regiment commanded by Baird's second, Major-General William Beresford. They arrived in the River Plate in June, and by good luck and surprise Beresford took Buenos Aires on the 28th. The news reached London in September, and the Talents Ministry turned with pleasure to a more agreeable subject than the European war. Like Popham they easily assumed that the fall of the city of Buenos Aires automatically involved the whole viceroyalty of which it was the capital: the modern Argentina, Uruguay, Paraguay and Bolivia combined, including the great silver mine of Potosí in the Andes. Popham had already sent the manufacturing towns of England a prospectus setting out the limitless commercial opportunities of this new British empire. The first of several relief expeditions with troops and stores sailed for the River Plate in October 1806, and meanwhile ministers were planning to improve on their new acquisition by conquering the whole of Spanish America. Then in January 1807 came an unwelcome injection of reality: the news (which Popham had suppressed for as long as he dared) that after less than seven weeks of British rule the citizens of Buenos Aires had recaptured their city and made Beresford's men prisoners. By now, however, too many hopes and reinforcements had been invested for the ministry to draw back. In February 1807 an expedition capably led by Brigadier-General Sir Samuel Auchmuchty and Rear-Admiral Charles Stirling captured Montevideo on the north bank of the estuary, but Lieutenant-General John Whitelocke's assault on Buenos Aires in July was a catastrophe, with half the attacking force killed or captured. To extricate his prisoners Whitlocke agreed to evacuate the entire region. Meanwhile British merchants lost heavily attempting to penetrate a country of which they knew even less than the soldiers did. The main long-term consequence of Popham's disastrous initiative was to do further damage to the flimsy reputation of the British army, and give an enormous boost to the self-confidence of the Spanish colonial leaders, who had defended themselves with the enthusiastic support of their people, in spite of limited help from regular troops and none at all from the Spanish navy.[8]

The River Plate expeditions extinguished what remained of the Talents' reputation as a war ministry, though they fell in March before the full extent of the fiasco became clear. The new ministry was fully occupied by the war in Europe, where Russia and Prussia were again in the field against Napoleon. In June 10,000 men were sent to the Swedish port of Stralsund on the Prussian coast to act on the flank of the French armies, but they had barely sailed when the news arrived of the decisive French victory at Friedland on 14 June, followed by the sudden treaty between Napoleon and Tsar Alexander I at Tilsit on 7 July. This reduced Prussia to a rump state, and the British government had early intelligence of secret clauses which supposedly called for the coercion of Denmark and Sweden and the expulsion of Britain from the Baltic.[9] In the face of this grave threat the new government determined to act fast. An ultimatum was presented to the Danish government, and in the absence of a clear answer an expedition (utilizing the Stralsund troops) was landed on Zealand to attack Copenhagen. After a bombardment in which part of the city was destroyed, the Danes surrendered and their fleet (fifteen ships of the line and fifteen frigates) was removed to Britain. Ironically George Canning and Viscount Castlereagh, the new Foreign Secretary and Secretary for War who planned the expedition, had moved too fast, because the British ultimatum arrived before the demands which Napoleon was indeed intending to present to the Danes. A few weeks later and French aggression might have forced Denmark into the arms of Britain, as Danish strategic planning tacitly anticipated. As it was, this apparently unprovoked British attack on an inoffensive neutral aroused widespread disgust in Europe, and indeed among British officers like Captain Charles Paget:

> The Danes have done nothing hostile towards us, and surely we cannot be so unprincipled as to attempt the island of Zealand without some fair pretext … Would it be justifiable without any previous hostile act on their part, to take their fleet from them, on the plea of preventing it being a means ultimately of Buonaparte to execute his plan of invasion?[10]

This was precisely Canning's justification, this and the making it impossible for France to seal the mouth of the Baltic.[11]

After Trafalgar Collingwood was left commander-in-chief of the Mediterranean, though both he and his fleet spent most of their time off Cadiz (the

Mediterranean station extended as far as Cape St Vincent), because the main threat came from the Atlantic. Collingwood was a worrier, who did not know how to delegate or to relax: 'I assure you I have more confinement at my table and letters than an attorney's clerk,' he told his sister in April 1806. 'There is no end of it and I am not the better for having no exercise.'[12] He was also a master of strategy and diplomacy, instinctively alert to the attitudes and interests of foreign powers. Almost alone among British admirals, he understood and sympathized with the outlook of the North African states, on which his ships depended greatly for food and water. 'I have always found that kind language and strong ships have a very powerful effect in conciliating people,' he wrote, and his judgement in balancing the two was unequalled.[13] His strategic vision was all the more important as poor communications and weak ministries left him without instructions for long periods, obliged in effect to run a large share of British foreign policy and war planning by himself. (Almost literally by himself: his staff consisted of his secretary and one clerk, increased in 1808 to two.) Soon after Trafalgar a Russian squadron from the Baltic under Vice-Admiral D. N. Senyavin entered the Mediterranean to protect the Ionian Islands from the French in Venice and Dalmatia. Senyavin was an anglophile who had served six years in the Royal Navy, and Collingwood was able to maintain good relations with him, while the energetic frigate captain Patrick Campbell harried the French in the upper Adriatic. Collingwood had much more trouble with Sir Sidney Smith, operating off French-occupied Calabria and just as completely in the pocket of Queen Maria Carolina in Palermo as Nelson had been seven years before. In July 1806 Collingwood's ships landed 3,000 British troops under Major-General John Stuart (Craig's successor in command of the British Mediterranean expeditionary force) to win a small but complete victory over the French near Maida in Calabria. It was the story of Egypt in 1801 repeated in miniature. The French were much stronger than Stuart supposed, only Smith had good intelligence and nobody believed him, but the British infantry redeemed the general's misjudgements. The affair was of no strategic importance, but a real boost to the shaky morale and reputation of the British army.[14]

As Russia moved back to war against France in the autumn of 1806, Turkey moved the opposite way, and Britain was reluctantly driven to regard her as a potential enemy. In November the government ordered Collingwood to send Vice-Admiral Duckworth with six ships of the line up the Dardanelles to Constantinople to put pressure on Turkey. Possibly it might have worked if done sooner, but without a landing force Duckworth could apply little pressure and was at risk of being trapped. Though an excellent fighting seaman, the admiral was not the obvious choice for subtle diplomacy, and he was ordered to be guided by the British ambassador Charles Arbuthnot, who was ill and depressed. What was needed was an unconventional negotiator of charm and daring who knew the court and language of Turkey – and by a remarkable coincidence, just such a person was third in command of Duckworth's squadron. Sir Sidney Smith, if anyone, might have pulled it off, and Pitt might have tried him, but neither the Whig government nor the admirals had any time for him. Duckworth got his ships past the batteries and into the Sea of Marmara, but achieved nothing off Constantinople. On his way back several ships were damaged by the 'Dardanelles guns', huge bombards, the oldest of which had been cast in 1453 for the siege of Constantinople. The *Windsor Castle* was hit by a marble shot weighing over 800 pounds. This fruitless operation was followed by a British landing in Egypt in March 1807, which confirmed Turkey as an enemy, and involved the British troops in many difficulties, without advancing the war against France at all.[15]

After Duckworth's departure Senyavin blockaded the Dardanelles, and near by on 1 July 1807 he won a clear victory over the Turkish fleet. At Tilsit, however, Alexander I agreed to abandon the Mediterranean and transfer the Ionian Islands to France. Senyavin was left to make his own way back to the Baltic. He and Collingwood were now near-enemies, but neither wished to provoke hostilities. 'We must take care,' Collingwood advised one of his captains, 'that those nations whose hearts are really with us, and who on the first happy change would be openly on our side, may not, by any intemperate act of ours, be thrown into the hands of the enemy.'[16] Senyavin likewise looked forward to a future Russo-British alliance, and had no hope of fighting his way home anyway. In November 1807 he was driven into the Tagus by gales. There he found himself in the middle of another crisis. The Portuguese government was under intense French pressure, with a French army under General Junot approaching through Spain. As Franco-Spanish forces invaded, Sir Sidney Smith arrived with a British squadron to persuade the Portuguese royal family and fleet to escape under British protection to Brazil rather than submit to France. He succeeded at the last possible moment: the Portuguese ships crossed the Tagus bar on 30 November as Junot's advance guard entered Lisbon. Less than a month later Senyavin learned that Russia had allied with France against Britain, but he resisted all Junot's pressure for co-operation, and for eight months of 1808 he lay at anchor, maintaining discreet contact with Sir Charles Cotton's British blockading squadron off the Tagus.[17]

The grand strategy of war changed in 1807. Like the British, Napoleon was forced to adopt an indirect strategy by his inability to mount direct attacks, and he chose economic warfare. The Berlin Decrees of November 1806 and the Milan Decrees of December 1807 together established the 'Continental System' of economic blockade, which was intended to achieve several, not entirely compatible, objectives. Napoleon's economic ideas were primitive. Real wealth, for him, consisted of land, people and industry producing for home markets. Trade, and still more finance, were essentially parasitic activities, and an economy built on them was necessarily flimsy, exploitative and vulnerable. His first object was simply to ruin Britain by denying her European markets for exports and re-exports. He also aimed to deny her strategic imports such as Baltic naval stores. At the same time he aimed to ruin Britain in mercantilist fashion by forcing her to trade on disadvantageous terms, that is, to import goods (such as Baltic naval stores) which could only be paid for by exporting bullion. He was unconcerned by the prospect of denying trade to his own subjects, especially his non-French subjects. The Continental System directly affected the war on land as well as at sea, since it required a united continent, and forced Napoleon to conquer any country, even if friendly, which did not choose to participate in his economic warfare. Portugal was the first victim. The British response was a series of Orders in Council which declared all ports under French control to be blockaded, and permitted trade with them only on British terms. The effect of all these measures was to outlaw neutrality at sea, permitting ships of every nation to trade only on the terms of one or other belligerent. The only important neutral shipowning power not yet under French domination was the United States, but there the measures were resented more in principle by President Jefferson and his Republican party than in practice by the New England shipowners, who were for the most part opposition Federalists, and whose inflated wartime profits reconciled them to a great deal of inconvenience. Jefferson's response was the Embargo Act of 1807, intended to punish both belligerents by denying them US exports, but in practice punishing principally his own compatriots, the merchants and shipowners.[18]

At the beginning of 1808 the Duke of Portland's ministry could congratulate itself on some achievements in its first eight months in office. The Whigs' disastrous ventures in South America and Egypt had been liquidated. Bold and ruthless action had removed two fleets from Napoleon's hands, and kept the access to the Baltic open. Nothing, however, could remove the building yards, nor the rich resources of the Baltic lands, with which Napoleon intended to build a fleet of 150 sail of the line. Moreover the Copenhagen attack had turned Denmark into Napoleon's most angry and determined ally. In the absence of friends there was nowhere in Europe where Britain's small army could act, and hardly anywhere else. The Cabinet considered Iceland, Greenland, Norway, Kronstadt, Walcheren, Brest, Vigo, Cadiz, Ceuta, the Azores, the Mediterranean or Spanish America, but all it actually achieved was the peaceful occupation of the Portuguese island of Madeira. Britain's only ally was the unstable Gustavus IV of Sweden, whose world-view was based on a deranged interpretation of the Book of Revelation. In April a British squadron under Vice-Admiral Saumarez and 10,000 British troops under Lieutenant-General Sir John Moore were sent to support Sweden against actual Russian invasion in Finland, and threatened Franco-Danish invasion across the Sound. No plans had been agreed beforehand, and relations between the king and the talented but abrasive Moore soon broke down completely, so the troops returned empty-handed. The Russians overran Finland with some ease. The great fortress of Sveaborg was surrendered without a fight and most of the *skärgårdsflottan* with it, exposing Stockholm to a Russian seaborne invasion through the leads. Saumarez took his squadron to cruise off Hangö Head, the one point where he could block such an advance, and there on 25 August the Swedish-British fleet fought a partial action against the Russian sailing fleet, in which the British ship of the line *Implacable* cut off and took the Russian *Sevolod* in full view of the Russian fleet. Though the Swedish fleet was crippled by scurvy, this action was sufficient to drive the Russians into port and protect Sweden.[19]

Marshal Bernadotte's planned Franco-Danish invasion of Sweden from the south was frustrated by a very unexpected development. Spain was now openly a French puppet state, its royal family in prison in France and Napoleon's brother installed on the throne, but in May 1808 a rebellion against French rule broke out in Madrid. In July a French army of 22,000 men surrendered to the Spaniards at Baylen; the worst defeat Napoleon's troops had yet suffered, and a shocking blow to French prestige. It was Napoleon's practice to make up his armies with large contributions from his vassal states, and most of Bernadotte's troops in Denmark were Spanish. On the news of the rebellion in Spain a British agent (the Scottish Benedictine monk Dom James Robertson disguised as a cigar merchant) made secret contact with the Spanish general, the marqués de la Romana, and an audacious plan was worked out by which the bulk of his troops (over 10,000 men) were secretly removed from Danish territory in August by British ships and conveyed back to Spain to join the war against Napoleon.[20]

The Spanish revolt cut off Junot in Portugal, where the starving population rebelled with Cotton's encouragement. Early in August a British force of 10,000 men was landed on the Portuguese coast to support them. Collingwood, who knew the British army of old, was not optimistic:

I hope Sir Arthur Wellesley will not be a teaser. I have seen so much of it . . . that indeed I would never let a soldier out of England – they are deadweights on the necks of those who have to care for them. And as for 'expeditions', I wonder how the word got squeezed into the line of service. I would as soon send a tortoise on expedition.[21]

Wellesley, however, was different. On 21 August he defeated Junot at Vimiero. That evening he was superseded by a senior general who vetoed the pursuit and negotiated a convention by which the French army was evacuated in British ships. That infuriated the government, but it liberated Portugal quickly, and at the same time Cotton was able to negotiate with Senyavin a peaceful settlement by which the Russian ships were interned at Portsmouth.[22]

That autumn Sir John Moore led a British army into northern Spain. When Napoleon himself marched into Spain to crush the rebellion, Moore boldly struck at his rear, and in the depth of winter was forced to retreat over the mountains into Galicia. Transports were made ready to receive him at Vigo, but at the last moment he sent word that his exhausted and hard-pressed troops were diverting to Corunna. With great skill and considerable luck with the weather the transports were brought round to Corunna (an open bay dangerous for a large fleet in wintertime), and on 16 January Moore fought a successful action which gained enough time for an evacuation. He himself was killed, but that night the troops were successfully brought off.[23]

Throughout 1808 Collingwood had to hold the Mediterranean with a bare minimum of hard-pressed ships. Early in the year Napoleon concerted a plan to capture Sicily and drive the British from the sea. Ganteaume from Toulon managed to get to Corfu and back, narrowly avoiding interception, but Sicily was never seriously in danger. When the Spanish revolt broke out Collingwood's good personal relations with Spanish admirals, which went back to their chivalrous exchanges in the aftermath of Trafalgar, helped to open immediate co-operation. The French warships still in Cadiz were seized, and later the Spanish provisional government was established in that island city which the Royal Navy could help to defend. Spanish warships were removed to the safety of Minorca, once more available as a base for the Royal Navy. From Mahón frigates and smaller craft ranged along the coast of Catalonia in support of the rebels, none with more daring and success than the frigate *Impérieuse* under the brilliant Lord Cochrane. In the Levant Collingwood skilfully nursed relations with the Turks, potential allies again now the Russians had changed sides, who finally made peace in January 1809. Ministers in London had such confidence in him that they seldom bothered to write, except to refuse his requests for leave. They were anxious to exclude

Admiral the Duke of Clarence, Prince William Henry, who fancied the command for himself, and they had no compunction in keeping the exhausted admiral on the station he managed so well.[24] 'I am not bilious, my dear Mary,' he wrote to his sister in March 1809, 'but worn down with fatigue and many vexations. I have not strength of body to support the arduous business I have to conduct, but my active mind will allow me no rest, and I am wearing down very fast.'[25] Yet throughout 1809 there was no slackening in his work or his fleet's. He took the initiative in seizing the Ionian Islands from the French and sending a frigate squadron up the Adriatic. 'We are carrying on our operations in the Adriatic and on the coast of Italy with great éclat,' he wrote to Rear-Admiral Thomas Sotheby in June 1809.

> All our frigate captains are great generals, and some of the brigs are good brigadiers. They have taken seven forts, garrisons, or castles, within the two last months; and scaling towers at midnight, and storming redoubts at mid-day, are become familiar occurrences . . . It is really astonishing; those youths think that nothing is beyond their enterprise, and they seldom fail of success . . . This activity and zeal in those gallant young men keep up my spirits.[26]

In September Collingwood intercepted and destroyed a French convoy running supplies into the besieged garrison of Barcelona. The next one had to go by land, with an escort of 8,000 troops to cover it from Spanish irregulars. It was almost his last service. In February 1810 he was at last allowed to resign his command, but he died on the passage home.[27]

In February 1809 a squadron escaped from Brest, failed to make its intended port of Lorient, and arrived instead in Aix Roads at the mouth of the Charente, making a total of eleven ships of the line there. The dangers of getting up the river to Rochefort had always forced the French to depend on this anchorage, not fully protected from either the weather or the enemy, and the British determined to mount an attack with fireships. The fleet was commanded by Admiral Gambier, but although he had several highly competent and distinguished subordinates, the command of the actual attack was instead given to Lord Cochrane. Cochrane had a brilliant record, but no contemporary imagined that it was professional merit which had influenced a weak government to take a plum command away from deserving seniors, and give it to a junior captain who happened also to be an MP and heir to an earldom. Violent resentments were aroused in the fleet, to add to the natural antipathy between the pious, elderly, and safe Gambier, and the bloody-minded radical Cochrane. The result was a wasted opportunity in which

Cochrane's initial success was not followed up by the main fleet. Nevertheless the French lost four ships of the line and a frigate wrecked or burned, while seven others escaped only by throwing their guns overboard. Unlike the honourable defeat of Trafalgar, this battle was marked by panic and cowardice which had a very bad effect on French naval morale.[28]

After the high hopes aroused by the Spanish rebellion, 1809 was a year of military disappointments. Marshal Soult's invasion of Portugal was defeated, Wellesley advanced into Spain and in July won another victory at Talavera (for which he was made Viscount Wellington in September), but he was still unable to maintain his position. Austria re-entered the war, and the British government decided to assist her by opening a second front so close to home that it would be safe to use part of the home defence army. The initial plan was to occupy the Dutch island of Walcheren at the mouth of the Scheldt, with its dockyard town of Flushing where five ships were building for the French navy. This was then expanded to a much more ambitious plan to push far up the Scheldt to the inland port of Antwerp, which Napoleon had made into a major shipbuilding centre. This would have required exact inter-service co-operation and great speed, but the first three months of the year were largely taken up with a Parliamentary inquiry into corrupt army promotions allegedly made by the Duke of York, which cost the army its outstanding administrator. Then the inexplicable choice of Lord Chatham as commander-in-chief cast a pall of sloth over the military part of the expedition. By the time it sailed on 28 July the Austrian defeat at Wagram was already known, and in the end all that was achieved was the capture of Flushing, at the cost of 4,000 soldiers dead and nearly 10,000 ill of 'Walcheren fever' – malaria – caught in the marshy islands of Zealand. In the aftermath of this disaster the government disintegrated in mutual recrimination, Canning and Castlereagh fighting a duel.[29]

The only part of the world in which British arms were entirely successful in 1809 was the West Indies, where the Spanish revolt isolated the remaining French colonies. The Spaniards took the last French foothold in Saint Domingue, while between February 1809 and February 1810 the British took Martinique, Guadaloupe and all the remaining Dutch or French colonies, leaving no French overseas possession outside the Indian Ocean.[30]

There Mauritius and Réunion (Ile de Bourbon) had survived thanks to their extreme remoteness and the distractions which had diverted several previous British plans of attack. Their weakness was that Mauritius depended on Réunion for food, and the two islands together could barely feed themselves without adding ships as well. With the Cape once more in British hands, they were subjected to an increasingly effective blockade. Here alone in the whole world, there were still French warships at sea in a good state of efficiency. In waters where there were no ships of the line, and very valuable British trade at stake, the frigates of French captains like Jacques Hamelin, Pierre Bouvet de Maisonneuve the younger, Victor Duperré and Albin Roussin, represented a serious threat, and encouraged the British to mount a serious campaign against them. This was possible because of the great conquests of Marquis Wellesley (and his brother Sir Arthur Wellesley) as Governor-General of India from 1798 to 1805, which (at the cost of almost bankrupting the East India Company) had created a new British Indian empire and a British Indian army. By persuading their Indian troops that they might make sea voyages without losing caste, the British acquired in the East what they never had in Europe: a major field army available for overseas operations. The first stage was the capture of Réunion in July 1810. Next month the campaign suffered a dramatic reversal when a bold attack on French ships moored among the reefs of Grand Port on Mauritius went badly wrong and led to the loss of four British frigates – the only French naval victory of the Napoleonic War. Within a few weeks, however, Commodore Josias Rowley had re-established British supremacy in the waters around the island, and in December a large expedition arrived with 6,800 troops. The landing on a dangerous coast was handled with great professional skill, and with overwhelming force ashore the French garrison surrendered soon afterwards. So dangerous a naval base was never again suffered to return to French hands.[31] In July 1810 Napoleon annexed the Batavian Republic, and with an energetic governor in Batavia, Field-Marshal Herman Daendels, the Dutch colonies seemed to present similar dangers. Accordingly expeditions were despatched to take Amboyna and Banda in 1810, and Java itself in 1811. This was effectively the end of the war in the East.[32]

Napoleon's economic warfare initially had a substantial impact in reducing British exports and damaging the British economy, but the Spanish revolt soon blew an enormous hole in the Continental System, opening not only Spain and Portugal but their entire colonial empires to British trade. In the North Saumarez, who commanded in the Baltic every season from 1808 to 1812, set up and maintained a system which covered British trade with outstanding success, though all of it had to pass through hostile Danish waters for 300 miles between the Skaw and Bornholm. The Great Belt is only three miles wide, and enemy ports were nowhere more than thirty miles away, yet convoys of up to 1,000 sail were regularly passed through with little or no loss. Between June and December 1809 2,210 merchant ships were escorted through the Great Belt without any loss at all. The worst moment came early, when a belated convoy in January 1809 was lost in the ice in the Malmö Channel. The

Danish navy had nothing left bigger than brigs and gunboats, but (in some contrast to the French navy under Napoleon) it remained resolute and effective, never missing an opportunity to attack. Nevertheless its achievement was strictly limited. The high point of Danish success was in July 1810 when Captain Lorentz Fisker with five brigs of the Norwegian division captured an entire convoy of forty-seven sail off the Skaw. Next year came a worse disaster for the Royal Navy, when the last homeward convoy was delayed until November, and three ships of the line were wrecked with the loss of 2,000 men – more than four times the British deaths at Trafalgar.[33]

Almost from the start, both economic blockades had to be modified and compromised. The British licensed those trades which they wished to promote, or could not avoid. After yet another bad harvest in 1809 Britain actually imported grain from the Continent, with the encouragement of Napoleon in his mercantilist mode.[34] Under the French flag even coastwise trade was now almost impossible; in 1810 a convoy from the Scheldt to Le Havre and Cherbourg took thirteen months to complete a two-day voyage.[35] Yet France needed goods which could only come from overseas, so licences were issued and ships put to sea which the French government knew would come under British control as soon as they passed out of gunshot. Even the Danes, perhaps Napoleon's only truly enthusiastic allies, were obliged to compromise with reality. Preserving Norway for the Danish crown was at the heart of Frederick VI's policy, but Norway was fed by grain from Jutland which could only be shipped across the Skagerrak with British licences, and only paid for by exporting Norwegian timber to Britain.[36] Everywhere in Europe merchants whose livelihoods were at risk penetrated the system with every kind of false flags and papers, while the British established commercial depots at Malta, Gibraltar, Heligoland, Lissa, and elsewhere from which a flourishing clandestine trade passed into Europe. Bogus privateers coloured imported cargoes as fictitious captures. Soldiers and officials even at the highest levels of the Napoleonic system were eminently corruptible, and many honest men, not otherwise disloyal, had no patience with measures openly designed to support Napoleon's ambitions by beggaring his subjects, and particularly his non-French subjects. Behind the official façade, the Continental System was dissolving the political glue of the Napoleonic regime. Amsterdam had eighty sugar refineries in 1796, and three by 1813. Before the war this had been the centre of the francophile 'Patriot' movement, the natural home of Napoleon's natural supporters in Holland – but no longer.[37] The British economy suffered too, but its main components survived and flourished, while imports of strategic materials were never blocked. Hemp was the only essential Russian product which Britain could not replace from elsewhere, but by 1810 British hemp stocks were so high that imports were forbidden except against matching Russian purchases of British goods.[38]

In response to Napoleon, Britain in effect abandoned the Navigation Acts and the Admiralty Court practice of a century. Instead of strictly scrutinizing the papers and ownership of foreign merchant ships and cargoes, and restricting British commerce to British ships, the government now accepted that many of the trades which it wanted to sustain could only be carried on clandestinely, and that destination rather than ownership, real or apparent, was now the only important test. All and any ships were therefore allowed to trade so long as they sailed under British convoy for the whole voyage, ensuring that they went to or from a British or friendly port. British harbours and convoys were filled with foreign-owned and manned merchantmen flying neutral or even enemy flags.[39] British warships were instructed to bring in merchantmen found sailing alone, but to take under their convoy whatever ship requested it, 'notwithstanding all the documents which accompany the ship and cargo may represent the same to be destined to any neutral or hostile port, or to whomsoever such property may belong'.[40] As the strategic situation evolved, both sides in effect changed their strategy, the British with the Orders in Council of April 1809, Napoleon with the Trianon Decrees of August 1810. These regulations tended to move away from blockade towards regulated trade, and both were in part bids for American support. Before and after, however, having physical control of the seas, the British could enforce their system where Napoleon could not, and in any case high wartime freight rates made shippers very willing to comply with British restrictions.[41]

Economic warfare was in effect a new application of the world-wide British convoy system which had been in place since 1793, and was made compulsory for most British trades by the 1798 and 1803 Convoy Acts. These acts for the first time gave escort commanders some legal powers to enforce the obedience of their charges. Licences were issued to fast ships to sail independently, but their losses were much higher than those of ships in convoy, and they were forbidden in 1812. 'Effectual protection can only be given to British commerce by a rigid adherence to the convoy system,' the chairman of Lloyd's declared in 1814.[42] In a sample of 132 convoys between 1793 and 1797, four were attacked. Out of 5,827 ships escorted, 398 straggled from their convoys, and thirty-five were lost. Careful calculations by the Secretary of Lloyd's suggested that over the whole period 1793 to 1815 British merchant losses were about 2 per cent a year from all causes net of recaptures, but in deep-sea trades as much as 5 or 6 per cent, half to marine causes and half to enemy action. In the English

Channel in 1808 losses to all shipping, escorted or independent, were only 1½ per cent. The convoy system was co-ordinated with the Admiralty by 'conferences' of merchants in particular trades, and by Lloyd's for the ship-owning and marine insurance businesses as a whole. Lloyd's was also a centre of shipping and naval intelligence from all over the world.[43]

The cost of this extensive system of trade defence was the principal achievement of the French war on trade, both by privateers and men-of-war. Actual losses were never sufficient to cause the British real anxiety, even in the Indian Ocean where French attacks were most effective. Powerful raiding squadrons like Allemand's, which had the potential to do real damage, lacked the intelligence to locate their targets. French Mediterranean privateers had some commercial success at the expense of neutral shipping, but in the Atlantic ports virtually no one seems to have made any money from it. As in every naval war, French privateers drained the stock of French seamen into British prisons: 42,000 were taken during the Revolutionary War, which in principle was two-thirds of the skilled manpower needed to man the French navy, and there were 27,000 French seamen in Britain in 1814.[44]

When Saumarez arrived in the Baltic in 1808 Sweden was Britain's only ally, but the loss of Finland and the removal of Gustavus IV by a palace coup in March 1809 threw Sweden into French hands. Then the heir to the throne died, and, seeking a replacement acceptable to Napoleon, the Swedes adopted Marshal Bernadotte, who arrived as Sweden's effective ruler in 1810. The British government took it for granted that yet another European state had been absorbed into Napoleon's empire, and were not at all surprised when Sweden declared war in November 1810. Only Saumarez refused to accept that things were quite as they seemed from a distance, and insisted on following his own policy of conciliation, ignoring the fears, and at times the direct orders, of ministers. Knowing Sweden's dependence on foreign trade as well as its vulnerability to France, in constant contact with the Swedish court, he distinguished its public declaration of war from its private declarations of friendship. Swedish ports continued to be discreetly open to British trade, and Swedish merchants continued to supply Saumarez's ships with all they needed. Throughout three years of nominal war, the bleak roadstead of Vinga Sound fourteen miles off Gothenburg remained the centre of the British Baltic convoy system. 'A most dreary situation,' as it was described in 1811 by Captain David Milne of the *Impetueux*,

> but very convenient anchorage for our fleet, being very secure, and plenty of water in the small islands, or rather rocks, the hollows of which, where

there is any soil, the different ships have made into gardens and have raised great plenty of vegetables for the use of the officers. The fleet is supplied in a private manner from Gothenburg with plenty of everything.[45]

By maintaining peace with a declared enemy, Saumarez was able to keep open the Baltic trade, which supplied Britain with essential naval stores and opened wide breaches in Napoleon's Continental System all along the southern shore of the Baltic. Bernadotte for his part played a dangerous game with skill, double-crossing his old master and preparing for a post-war settlement in which his future kingdom (he succeeded to the throne in 1818) was to make up for the loss of Finland by gaining Norway from Denmark.[46]

In the Peninsula Wellington was forced back on Lisbon in the autumn of 1810. Ministers still had no confidence in the British army and nervously prepared for evacuation, but Wellington was a former Chief Secretary of Ireland, and his brother was Foreign Secretary, so he had the political as well as military credit to stand his ground. His main political worry was the effective accession of the Prince of Wales to the throne in February 1811 as Prince Regent, which for a time threatened the recall of the Whigs, who had never believed in the Peninsular campaigns. Wellington had prepared a strong defensive position, the Lines of Torres Vedras, stretching from the Tagus to the sea, but his whole strategy depended on sea communications to feed what in the end amounted to 420,000 military and civilian mouths, British, Portuguese and Spanish. At a time of dearth in Britain, much of the grain he needed came from the United States, and cattle from North Africa, but there was an acute shortage of silver to pay for these imports, and a naval mission had to be despatched to South America to obtain some. All this was organized by Admiral George Berkeley in the Tagus, freely ignoring his orders to satisfy the general's demands. They had their reward in March 1811 when the starving French army began to withdraw into Spain.[47]

Thereafter Wellington's army was able to advance steadily inland, but it continued to depend absolutely on seaborne supplies. The French armies in Spain, living off the country as French armies did, were dispersed and vulnerable to guerilla attack. They had 260,000 men in the Peninsula, but at least two-thirds of these were tied down in garrisons, foraging and protecting lines of communication against Spanish irregulars. Wellington's British and Portuguese army of about 50,000, sustained by conventional supply lines which ran straight back to Lisbon and the sea, could be kept concentrated, and sometimes outnumbered the armies the French could gather on the battlefield.[48] In the Mediterranean during 1810 and 1811 Collingwood's successor Cotton was essentially on the defensive, except for operations on the coast of Catalonia in support of the Spaniards, and in the Adriatic against the French in Italy and Dalmatia. Here the island of Lissa was an important centre of clandestine trade into Europe. On 13 March 1811 Rear-Admiral Edouard Dubordieu with a force of six French and Italian frigates attempted to capture the island, bringing on a battle against four British frigates under Captain William Hoste. Hoste was an old follower of Nelson who went in to action flying the signal 'Remember Nelson', but it was Dubordieu who adopted Nelson's tactics, coming down from the windward in two columns. It was a mistake: Dubordieu was killed and half his ships wrecked or captured.[49]

Throughout the years after Trafalgar, Napoleon was pouring large resources into a new battlefleet to replace the one he had thrown away. Brest was virtually abandoned in 1810 because of the British blockade, but a new building yard was established at Antwerp, whose situation at the leeward end of the Channel was a worry. British governments watched Napoleon's efforts warily, as they were prudent to do, and maintained the operational strength of the Royal Navy at rather over 100 ships of the line, but they did not divert money or manpower from the frigates and other cruisers whose numbers continued to increase. Some modern historians have been impressed by Napoleon's efforts, and have taken his claims and ambitions much more seriously than they deserve.[50] In fact much of the building effort, like all Napoleon's naval plans, was based on fantasy. Hastily constructed of green timber to obsolete designs, many of these ships were rotten before they were ever commissioned. Shipwrights were scarce and scarcely paid, so the building quality was poor. A number of the ships built at Antwerp proved to be either unstable or too big to get through the lock gates, and had to be broken up in the basin where they had been launched. In 1811 the French empire had seventy-two ships of the line on paper, but at best only fifty-five might have been made seaworthy, and perhaps thirty were of some military value. Eleven were built at Venice and Trieste, but the only one which actually put to sea, the *Rivoli*, was captured within thirty-six hours, and there is little reason to expect that the others would have fared much better. Morale and discipline remained very poor, especially among the officers, and the remaining seamen hated Napoleon's solution, which was to dress them as soldiers and drill them in 'naval battalions'. Much as an efficient fleet might have done to increase Napoleon's strategic options, there is nothing to suggest that he ever had any realistic idea how to obtain one.[51]

THIRTY-SIX

No Greater Obligations

Operations 1812–1815

Napoleon's Continental System was a serious threat to Britain, but only so long as he could impose it on the whole of Europe. The revolt of Spain and Portugal, the defection of Sweden and Turkey all weakened it. Another large rent was torn in its fabric at the beginning of 1811 when Tsar Alexander I, tiring of a policy which so obviously served French rather than Russian interests, opened his ports to neutral shipping, which in practice meant American ships trading on British account. Thereafter relations with Napoleon worsened, and in the spring of 1812 he prepared to invade Russia. The strategic motive for the attack arose entirely from the Continental System; had there been no economic warfare against Britain there would have been no need to make an enemy of Russia. The French army crossed the Russian frontier on 24 June. On 7 September it won a costly and limited victory at Borodino, and a week later it entered Moscow, but the Russians did not offer Napoleon the chance of a decisive battle, and he had no means of sustaining his army where he was. In mid-October Napoleon began his retreat from Moscow. French armies were not equipped for retreat, psychologically or practically, even in easier conditions than a Russian winter. Between 500,000 and 570,000 men, out of an original strength of about 650,000, died or were captured. Meanwhile the Tsar had sent his Baltic Fleet to winter in British ports, a powerful gesture of confidence which greatly encouraged ministers in London. There Lord Liverpool, who succeeded the murdered Spencer Perceval in June, had put together the strongest and ablest ministry since the fall of Pitt in 1801.[1]

In the Peninsula, Wellington's armies continued their methodical advance, and the Navy continued its active support along the Mediterranean and Biscay coasts of Spain. Between 1808 and 1811 Britain had already sent 336,000 muskets, 100,000 pistols, 60,000,000 cartridges and 348 artillery pieces to Spain or Portugal, and ships on both coasts were continually landing arms and money to support Spanish irregulars. In eight months from May 1812 a single ship, the *Blake* on the Mediterranean coast, landed over 8,000 muskets and 600,000 cartridges. At the same time Sir Home Popham on the Biscay coast, enthusiastically co-operating with Spanish guerillas, helped to tie down thousands of French troops and capture Santander. This then became Wellington's supply base, shortening his lines of communication by land and sea. Army and Navy co-operated well, though the following year the irritable Wellington complained that not enough had been done to help him during the difficult siege of San Sebastian, and an emollient officer had to be sent to his headquarters to explain that there were limitations on what ships could do on that dangerous coast. Wellington freely conceded, however, that 'if anyone wishes to know the history of this war, I will tell him that it is our maritime superiority gives me the power of maintaining my army while the enemy are unable to do so' – which was the evident truth.[2] In June 1813 his decisive victory at Vitoria effectively ended the French presence in Spain (Catalonia excepted), and finally re-established the reputation of the British army.[3]

The greatest single difficulty in keeping Wellington in the field was not troops but gold. The Peninsular campaigns cost £3 million pounds in 1809, £6 million in 1810, and £11 million in 1811, much of which had to be spent in the country, and therefore in gold or silver, which by 1811 was desperately short. Moreover the grain which fed Wellington's army did not come from Britain, where the harvests had failed as usual. The major part came from the United States, and in American ships.[4] This was one of the reasons why the worsening diplomatic relations between Britain and the United States were a matter of concern. The most important factor in this friction was the young Republic's position as a neutral trader caught between two belligerent powers. From 1810, as the Continental System weakened, Napoleon made efforts to win over the Americans by promised or pretended concessions. The British likewise, conscious that American grain fed Wellington's army and American ships carried British trade, weakened the force of the Orders in Council, and finally abolished them in June 1812, to favour both the Americans and those industries and districts at home which were suffering as a result of the commercial war.[5]

In the United States, the Republican Presidents Thomas Jefferson (1801–9) and James Madison (1809–17) inclined to friendship with France. The opposition Federalists (from whom the British took their picture of American politics) called them 'Jacobins', which was scarcely true, but they instinctively assumed that French victory was in American interests. They also assumed in the summer of 1812 that French victory was imminent. A war against Britain would therefore be a war on the winning side, but Madison believed that the United States alone held a knife at Britain's throat. He believed that American ships and exports were vital to Britain's survival. He believed (as all Americans did) that Canada, whose population was only one-tenth of that of the United States, could easily be overrun; he believed that Canadian food fed the West Indies, and Canadian masts kept the Royal Navy at sea. He therefore negotiated from what he took to be a position of overwhelming strength, for, in Jefferson's words, 'Providence has placed their richest and most defenceless possessions at our door.'[6] Behind him Congress was belligerent, though it saw no necessity to vote any money to build up the armed forces. A prominent group of Republicans known as the 'War Hawks' loudly supported a war to conquer Canada in order to get the lands of Britain's allies, the Indians of the 'Old North-West'.[7]

One subsidiary issue of which relatively little was made at the time concerned the impressment of seamen from American merchant ships by the Royal Navy. It had always been the wartime practice of Britain, and other maritime nations, to reclaim their subjects from foreign ships. The difficulty with the United States arose from the difficulty of distinguishing the nationality of people who looked and sounded more or less the same. Moreover the law of Britain and most other countries defined nationality by birth, but the United States permitted nationality to be gained by a period of residence. There were therefore many people who were British in the eyes of English law and American in the eyes of United States law. This would have been a substantial difficulty in any circumstances, but it was compounded by the refusal of Jefferson and Madison to issue any official citizenship documents. Their position was that all persons aboard American ships were to be regarded as US citizens without further evidence. This claim, unsustainable in US or any other law, was designed to make negotiations impossible. Behind it lay the advice of Albert Gallatin, the long-serving Secretary of the Treasury, who calculated that 9,000 men, half the seamen in American deep-sea merchant ships, were British subjects. The prosperity of the US economy (and the revenues of the US government, which came largely from Customs) depended on them. Since no agreement could possibly keep acknowledged British subjects in foreign service against their sovereign's wishes, it was necessary to avoid an agreement. When two American diplomats actually reached one with the friendly Whig government in 1807, Jefferson refused to send it to Congress for fear it might pass.[8]

In the absence of official documents, US consuls issued unofficial ones, which were often respected, but left numerous occasions of dispute. Even the most scrupulous consuls had to depend on unverifiable declarations for their evidence of citizenship, and by no means all were scrupulous in a business which earned large fees. British officers in turn, desperate for men and convinced with some reason that there were many British deserters sailing under the US flag, had all the excuses they required to treat any document with scepticism. The result, according to modern research, was that about 6,500 US citizens were pressed into the Royal Navy, of whom about 3,800 were subsequently released.[9] All this, however, was only an irritant to diplomatic relations. For Jefferson and Madison it was a minor issue, one of many illustrations of Britain's dependence on US goodwill. The sufferers were seamen, who were of little political consequence, and shipowners, who were not anxious for any remedy which would interrupt their profitable wartime trading, and were mostly Federalists anyway. Instead of respecting the Embargo Act and putting pressure on Britain, they had removed their ships to ports in Canada or Florida and carried on trading illegally, which did not dispose the Republican administrations to make extra efforts on their behalf.[10]

A single incident of impressment at sea had real significance. The Talents Ministry appointed one of their own to command in North America, the Whig MP Vice-Admiral George Berkeley, who had a record of irresponsibility going back to the Keppel–Palliser affair. At his orders, the USS *Chesapeake* was stopped by force by HMS *Leopard* in June 1807 to remove some British deserters. Berkeley could claim a precedent, for earlier that year US soldiers had boarded a British warship under repair in an American port to retrieve some British subjects who had deserted from their service. Nevertheless it was all but an act of war to fire on a warship, and went far beyond anything justified by Berkeley's orders or intended by British ministers. Other admirals were aghast: 'exceedingly improvident and unfortunate,' was Collingwood's comment.[11] The affair generated violent emotion in the USA and much embarrassment to the British government, which had to apologize and disavow its admiral.[12]

By 1812, however, this was past history. The British government felt with some reason that it had met all the substantial grievances of the USA, and was surprised when Congress declared war in June. For some time it was assumed that the war was a mistake, which would be retrieved when full information reached Washington, and British officers were instructed to stand on the defensive.[13] There was no question of diverting troops or ships from the real war against Napoleon to an accidental enemy which seemed incapable of doing any damage, except possibly to Canada. Sir John Borlase Warren was sent to take over the North American station with contradictory orders to negotiate and blockade, but he had too few ships to cover British trade and watch the extensive coastline of the United States. In any case he had limited reason to interfere with American merchant shipping, so much of which was trading on British account. Many American ships were licensed by the British because they were supplying Wellington's army. Madison imposed an embargo on trade with the enemy, but its main effect was to convert legitimate trade into smuggling and lose the Customs revenues, and it did not apply to Portugal. For the British both strategic and political considerations suggested treating the Federalist ports of New England very lightly, and they in return supplied British squadrons offshore, British troops in Canada and the main British naval base of Halifax with everything they needed.[14]

The Republican administration expected nothing from the US Navy, which Gallatin called 'unproductive, wasteful and destructive'.[15] It only agreed to commission the seagoing ships for a few months to cover returning US merchantmen, and the Customs revenue they generated. By then it was confidently expected that the invasion of Canada would have won the war. Things did not run according to plan. On 16 August General William Hull surrendered the principal US army to the Canadian militia at Detroit.[16] In the face of this humiliating disaster there was one gleam of consolation, from an unexpected direction. Three days later General Hull's nephew Captain Isaac Hull of the *Constitution* captured the British 18-pounder frigate *Guerrière*. By the end of the year two more British 18-pounder frigates had been taken, the *Macedonian* by the *United States* and the *Java* by the *Constitution*. These actions were followed in the first part of 1813 by others between sloops and brigs, which yielded further victories for the US Navy. These single-ship actions caused a sensation on both sides of the Atlantic. The American public was naturally delighted to celebrate victory, and the US government was happy to divert attention from the collapse of its war strategy. In Britain the Navy and the public were shocked to discover that they were not invincible. People who thought the Navy was being ruined by aristocrats, or brutal discipline, or slack discipline, or the wrong sort of discipline, hastened to attribute blame accordingly.[17] The Admiralty issued an implicitly critical circular reminding captains of the importance of gun drill.[18] Later historians have tended to adopt one or other of these monocausal explanations, but there is in fact no reason to impose any single interpretation on these different actions. In the case of 18-pounder frigates in action with 24-pounder ships, the disparity of force is a sufficient explanation. In a few cases, mainly small vessels in the West Indies, where there had been no serious fighting for several years, there is reason to doubt the efficiency of the British men-of-war. The loss of the brig-sloop *Peacock* to the US ship-sloop *Hornet* in February 1813 was attributed by the court martial to 'want of skill in directing the fire, owing to an omission of the practice of exercising the crew in the use of the guns for the last three years,'[19] and her shooting seems to have been wild. Most of these actions, however, were settled by individual skill and luck, some one way and some the other, as one would expect between more or less evenly matched opponents.[20] A more interesting question, which the Admiralty circular does not address, concerns gunnery tactics rather than gunnery drill. The rational tactic for a weaker ship meeting one of the big US 24-pounder frigates was either to escape, or to keep at long range and fire high to disable masts and spars, which it seems both the *Guerrière* and *Macedonian* attempted. This sort of long-range gunnery was not the British tradition, and the Ordnance Board had recently ceased to issue dismantling shot, which the US Navy used to good effect.[21] Nevertheless the US frigate *Essex*, armed entirely with carronades, was taken by the *Phoebe* in March 1814 in a long-range action which exploited the US ship's weakness.[22]

One British officer who was keenly interested in the unfashionable subject of long-range gunnery was Captain Philip Broke of the 18-pounder frigate *Shannon*, who practised his men in all forms of gunnery, and even fitted his guns with a system of his own invention by which they could be laid on the orders of an officer on deck or aloft, on a target obscured from the gun captains by smoke or darkness. This however played no part in the *Shannon*'s victory over the USS *Chesapeake* off Boston on 1 June 1813, an action between similar ships fought at close range and decided very quickly. By now it was the US Navy which was over-confident, and Captain James Lawrence who was careless. Specifically neither he nor his first lieutenant noticed that the boatswain had failed to sling the topsail yards in clearing for action. One of the first broadsides cut the *Chesapeake*'s foretopsail tye, the yard came down with a run, the ship luffed up and was repeatedly raked, and most of the officers were dead within ten minutes.[23] A warship is a complex system, and the failure of any component may involve the failure of all. Contemporaries, however, and to a surprising degree subsequent historians, have tended to interpret these actions in moral rather than technical terms, as indicators of national virtue or decline, which is to load them with far more significance than they can possibly bear. Even in strictly military terms they were of limited importance, but they were among the factors which led both British and Americans to revise their strategy in 1813.

For Madison the conquest of Canada was still the only option. The natural line of advance, up the Hudson valley and Lake Champlain to Montreal, was ruled out by the refusal of the New England states to co-operate. The Great Lakes covered the frontier westward, and it was now obvious that the command of the lakes (which General Hull had not considered) was essential to attack or defence. In practice only Lake Ontario was critical, for command of its waters would allow the Americans to attack the fortress of Kingston commanding the head of the St Lawrence, or the British (had they had the troops and the inclination) to invade upstate New York or the Ohio valley. The western lakes were too far from the centres of European settlement to have much effect on the war by themselves. For the rest of the war Lake Ontario was the scene of a remarkable inland building race in which the two fleets kept pace with one another. At the end of the war Commodore Sir James Yeo had a three-decker, 102-gun flagship, and his opponent Commodore Isaac Chauncy had two ships almost as large under construction. No decisive battle between them happened, for Yeo was on the defensive and had nothing to gain, while Chauncy, whose naval yard at Sackett's Harbour was very close to the enemy, was too cautious to risk the victory which he needed. On Lake Erie to the westward Commander O. H. Perry won an American victory in September 1813, which had no effect on the main campaigns, but cut off Britain's Indian allies in Ohio and Michigan.[24]

The disadvantage of Warren's inability to blockade the northern US ports was that American warships and privateers were able to get to sea. The privateers did extensive damage to British trade in the West Indies, and for a time forced up insurance rates as high as 30 per cent, usually with a rebate of a third or more for convoy. These were local effects, however; overall British marine insurance rates were no higher between 1812 and 1814 than they had been in 1810 and 1811. Lloyd's reckoned that 1,175 British ships had been taken by Americans during the war (less 373 recaptured), but British overseas trade was growing rapidly throughout. Canadian privateers in turn, particularly from Liverpool, Nova Scotia, preyed on the coasters which carried most American inter-state trade.[25]

The victories of the US Navy naturally attracted British counter-measures. Convoy escorts were strengthened, 18-pounder frigates were forbidden to take on the three big American ships alone, and the number of British warships on the North American coast increased. It was not a univerally popular station, as Edward Napier's journal makes clear:

Found the month of April, on and about St George's Bank, extremely unpleasant and changeable from *bad* to *worse*; very cold, with damp, penetrating fogs, constantly and alternately changing to rain with the wind from west round by south to east, when it hardens into snow and sleet, which continues till it veers to the westward of north, a sure indication of hard frost; thus the comforts of a winter cruise on the coast of North America are inexhaustible.[26]

By the summer of 1813 the British watch on the major American ports was sufficient to hamper the US Navy considerably. In June Commodore Stephen Decatur with the *United States* and two other ships was prevented from leaving New York and driven into New London. The local population were anything but sympathetic, and kept the British fully informed of Decatur's position. He was even less popular when attacks by explosive devices organized from New York provoked Warren into stopping coastal shipping. The British offshore were supplied with everything they needed, as recorded by Captain Sir Thomas Hardy of the *Ramillies*:

> Fortunately for us Block Island has no guns in it, therefore we get plenty of water and stock from it and we also get our linen washed there. The inhabitants are very much alarmed and of course they are most completely in our power, but as long as they supply us we shall be very civil to them.[27]

The Nantucket Quakers declared formal neutrality, and all along the New England coast places which committed no hostilities were left in peace by the blockaders, who had no difficulty in watering and buying provisions. 'Sent the boats armed to procure oxen,' wrote Napier. 'Arms are put in to save appearances, for the people are willing enough to supply us with whatever we want.'[28] Off Provincetown in Cape Cod Bay they found harbour and welcome in onshore gales.[29]

After the summer of 1813 the US Navy's opportunities were nearly gone. Only small warships still managed to get to sea, with fewer and fewer successes. Decatur's frigates were laid up at New London. The *Essex* cruised successfully against British whalers in the remote Pacific until early 1814, but she was the last American warship of any size at sea. In June 1814 Isaac Hull, now commanding Portsmouth Navy Yard, was told by the Secretary of the Navy that it was not worth defending as the ships were now valueless. The *President* escaped from New York in January 1815 but was captured within a few hours.[30]

The United States marched on Montreal in 1812 just as Napoleon marched on Moscow. By the summer of 1813 it was beginning to dawn on Washington that both war-efforts might have taken a wrong turning. In September Russia, Prussia and Austria united against France, and the following month their armies decisively defeated the French in the 'Battle of the Nations' at Leipzig. Britain spent not less than £10 million in a year supporting the new alliance. Wellington's armies crossed the French frontier in October, and by the end of the year the Austrians and Prussians were on French soil too. Refusing all offers of peace from his Continental enemies, who as late as February 1814 were prepared to leave him his throne, and the 1792 frontiers of France, Napoleon held on until the disintegration of his regime forced him to abdicate in April.[31]

As Napoleon slid to defeat, the situation of his friends across the Atlantic grew more uncomfortable. Whereas the American contribution to feeding Wellington's armies had still been of importance at the beginning of 1813, by the end of the year the markets of most of Europe were once more open to British trade. Madison chose this moment to impose a total embargo on American shipping, when it could do no harm to anybody except Americans. US licensed flour exports, nearly all to the Peninsula, had been nearly a million barrels in 1812 and 1813, but fell to 5,000 in 1814. Total US exports were worth $45 million in 1811, and $7 million in 1814, by which time the insurance rate on Boston ships sailing for foreign ports had reached 75 per cent, coastal shipping was at a standstill, and some people in the New England states were contemplating secession.[32]

For the British the American War was a tiresome irritant, which they wished to end by bringing home to Madison's government the reality of its situation, without diverting major forces from the final effort to defeat Napoleon. To this end the local naval commander, Rear-Admiral George Cockburn, mounted seaborne raids around Chesapeake Bay during 1813, finding he could move everywhere and penetrate far up the rivers without meeting serious opposition. Early in 1814 a new commander-in-chief, Sir Alexander Cochrane, was impressed by Cockburn's work and determined to expand it. The British were careful to attack military targets rather than civilians or private property, but they were aware that the political situation was different from New England: the Chesapeake country was close to Washington both geographically and politically. Cockburn's men did good business with the peaceable, but did not hesitate to punish places which offered resistance. They also welcomed runaway slaves.[33]

Cochrane and Cockburn were both tough and skilful, Cockburn now thoroughly acquainted with the Bay. In the summer of 1814 the first regiments from Wellington's army, liberated by the defeat of Napoleon, arrived to provide them with a powerful landing force. In August they mounted an expedition up the Potomac River towards Washington. This was at least as far inland as Antwerp and the soldiers had misgivings, but Cockburn knew his enemies. He drove the project forward and accompanied the troops when they landed. In the event the American defences were cowardly and disorganized, and only the guns manned by the US Navy put up any determined resistance. President Madison was nearly captured, and when the British entered Washington on the evening of 24 August Cockburn and General Ross were able to dine on the victory banquet he had left behind in the White House. They then burned the public buildings of the capital and returned to their boats, having spent nine days in enemy territory and encountered minimal resistance. This was achieved with fewer than 5,000 men, and there were many more to come across the Atlantic.[34]

Some of these troops went to Canada, where Lieutenant-General Sir George Prevost moved cautiously southward along the Lake Champlain route until his advance was stopped by a US naval victory at Plattsburg on 11 September. Other troops went to the Gulf of Mexico for an attack on New Orleans which was intended to open the Mississippi and make possible a new link with Britain's Indian allies. The initial landing force, however, put ashore in a bad position before the general arrived, was heavily defeated on 8 January 1815. These final battles might or might not have proved decisive had the war continued, but in the event they proved to be unnecessary. Even before losing his capital Madison had recognized the reality of his situation and despatched a mission to Europe, which in December concluded peace with Britain. The British were happy to be rid of a pointless and costly war. The United States abandoned all her war-aims, but at least she had narrowly avoided complete defeat and dismemberment. It remained to construct a myth which might allow Madison's futile and humiliating adventure to be remembered as a glorious national triumph.[35]

Britain spent most of 1814 negotiating a peace settlement with her European allies. She was in a strong position, having contributed an army of 150,000 men to the final campaigns against Napoleon, as large and as good as any of the allied armies, and paid for 425,000 more. She might have retained the French and Dutch colonial empires, which were entirely in her hands, but she did not choose to. The small Dutch territory of Guiana, which was an important cotton producer, was the only colony retained on economic grounds. The other places Britain kept – Malta, the Cape of Good Hope, Ceylon and Mauritius – were all of strategic, not economic, importance. They were the naval ports from which the trade of the world might be safeguarded. A generation before, the British had flirted with the idea of an overseas empire, and burned their fingers badly in America. They were not to be caught the same way again. Trade, not territory, was the key to Britain's prosperity: seaborne trade secured by naval power. The mortal danger to Britain had come, as it had always come, from a dominant European power controlling the Low Countries and able to build up a powerful fleet in the Channel. Britain's primary aim in the peace settlement was to ensure that no future Napoleon, or Louis XIV, could conquer Flanders and build a fleet at Antwerp. A powerful new Kingdom of the Netherlands was therefore created, ruled by the House of Orange and embracing the old Dutch Republic, the Austrian Netherlands, Liège and Luxemburg. To be truly a great power, it needed an empire, and so the East Indies were returned to safeguard Britain's situation in Europe. 'The establishment of a balance of power in Europe,' a secret article of the peace treaty declared, 'requires that Holland should be established on a scale to make her capable of preserving her independence by her own resources.'[36] British colonial promoters like Stamford Raffles complained at the loss of Java, but the British government wanted trade and security, and knew that a restored Dutch empire was no real danger to either. In the words of a Cabinet memorandum, 'the Dutch are dependent upon British support and could never in the long run constitute a serious threat to British commercial interests in South-East Asia'.[37] Martinique and Guadaloupe were returned to France for similar reasons, to give the restored Bourbon monarchy some dignity and consequence, but not enough power to be dangerous – to make France 'commercial and pacific' rather than 'military and conquering', as Castlereagh told the House of Commons.[38] Having achieved Dundas's old dream of destroying French sea power, Britain could afford to be generous. Besides, Britain had acquired a new overseas empire, but not from its European enemies. It was in India that the conquests of Cornwallis and Wellesley carved out a new empire for the East India Company, which by 1818 had annual tax revenues of £18 million (one-third of Britain's) and an army of 180,000 men. This empire was self-supporting, though its trade and connection with Britain of course depended entirely on command of the sea.[39]

The 1814 peace treaty allowed Napoleon to retire as sovereign of the Italian island of Elba. It was not in his character, however, either to retire or to keep his promises. In March 1815 he returned to France and forced Louis XVIII from his throne. The allies were obliged once more to mobilize against him – an embarrassment for the British, since most of Wellington's experienced regiments had gone to America. Napoleon had to shatter his enemies before they could re-form their victorious coalition, so he hastened to a campaign in the Low Countries. Having narrowly failed to divide and defeat them in detail, he faced the Anglo-Dutch forces under Wellington (assembled to keep the

French out of Antwerp) and the Prussian army under Field-Marshal Blücher. After this defeat at Waterloo no one gave him a second chance. The Navy had little to do in the last campaign against Napoleon except re-establish the blockade, but it was on hand in July 1815 when he reached the coast, hoping to escape to the United States. On the 14th, when it became clear that he had no hope of evasion, he surrendered to Captain F. W. Maitland of the *Bellerophon*. On 7 August he sailed for his last exile on St Helena, from which British sea power could ensure that he would never escape.[40]

Napoleon's final defeats, in 1814 and 1815, were the work of a coalition of powers which were rivals as well as allies. They had the same interest in the balance of naval and colonial power as the British had in the balance of power on the Continent. They did not desire to crush France absolutely, but to retain her as a substantial naval and commercial power capable of limiting Britain's ambitions. As late as 1813 they offered Napoleon terms, including the retention of Antwerp, which would have been a serious threat to Britain. Even in 1814 he might have saved his throne. He lost everything because he would not limit his ambitions or keep his promises. In the end his European enemies were convinced that they would never be secure so long as the 'Chaka Zulu of Europe' remained at large, with his insatiable appetite for his neighbours' armies and cattle.[41] For their own survival they crushed France and consented to a peace treaty which secured Britain unchallenged naval supremacy.[42] 'There is no mortal to whom Great Britain has greater obligations than this blackguard,' declared the Prussian Field-Marshal Gneisenau,

> for it is the events which he has brought about which have raised England's greatness, security and wealth so high. They are lords of the sea, and neither in this dominion nor in world trade have they any rivals left to fear.[43]

Conclusion

I t is many years since British historians felt comfortable in celebrating their country's triumphs. Once upon a time, Britain's incontestable naval and commercial supremacy in 1815 would have been explained as the predestined fruit of national virtue, religious truth and political freedom. Among professional historians all three explanations would nowadays arouse varying degrees of amusement, distaste and embarrassment, but no modern consensus of opinion has emerged to replace them. For many years the tendency has been to ignore or belittle the fact as well as the consequences of British naval supremacy. Not many would go so far as to dismiss it outright as a convenient myth, or imply that Napoleon won the Napoleonic War,[1] but a number of intellectual strategies have been devised to ignore it. The first generation of major naval historians, writing at the end of the nineteenth century, were naturally concerned to trace how the Navy had made the Empire, since it was self-evidently the Empire which made Britain great. Taking their cue from them, many modern writers implicitly assume that the functions of the Navy were essentially aggressive, to win territory overseas. It seems for them to follow that sea power is nowadays both uninteresting, except to specialists in imperial history, and morally disreputable, something the honest historian ought to pretend does not exist.

Among strategic and military historians, by contrast, it is very generally accepted that sea power was an essentially defensive force, necessary but not sufficient for Britain's ultimate victory. All Britain's successful wars, they argue, were won by, or at least could not have been won without, European allies and a British army on the Continent. Though great land powers were capable of defeating sea powers, the reverse was never possible. The ultimate triumph of 1815, therefore, was primarily due to Wellington and the British army, as well as Marshal Blücher and the Prussian army. The Navy had held the Channel against invasion, but it could do no more.[2] This argument has been most powerfully and elegantly presented by scholars who had themselves fought as soldiers in the analogous campaign against Germany in 1944 and 1945.[3] Only recently has it been extended, or subverted, by a new presentation of sea power as a form of strategic depth, like the Russian plains a means of riding the blow of an attack, retreating to avoid defeat and prepare ultimate victory. In this view sea power faced by land power is still essentially defensive, but the defence is a kind of elasticity which as it retreats, gathers strength for the return blow. It is the means of buying time, and giving the enemy scope to commit mistakes and over-extend himself.[4]

British sea power has also been interpreted in terms of economic history, as an aspect of Britain's rise as an imperial and industrial power. This approach tends to make naval power appear as an inevitable product of impersonal historical forces, bound to rise as the British economy rose, and bound to fall as it declined. An essential component of success in the era of dispersed maritime empires, it was doomed to irrelevance as the twentieth century brought in the age of great land empires bound together by railways rather than shipping. Their competition transformed a seaborne empire, and the Navy which protected it, into a burden rather than a strength.[5]

All these explanations have force, but they are not altogether compatible with one another, and none of them now looks completely persuasive by itself. In the twenty-first century all but one of the great land empires has broken up, and both economic prosperity and international power are at least as closely linked to seaborne trade and sea power as they were in the eighteenth century. As to armies on the Continent, it is unquestionable that a Continental victory requires a Continental commitment, so long as one understands victory in the terms of 1815 or 1945: the physical conquest of the enemy territory, and the overthrow of his regime. Total wars of this sort, however, have been unusual in history. Most wars are fought at more limited cost, for more limited objectives. British wars for overseas trade or possessions, and strictly defensive wars against overseas enemies, could be conducted largely or entirely at sea and overseas – as they were in the English case up to 1688. Only rarely did the threat of a Napoleon or a Hitler force British participation in a European coalition war. It was dynastic engagements which enforced a Continental commitment for the century after 1688, not British national interests. Without foreign monarchs, there would have been infrequent need, or no need, to have armies and allies on the Continent. The foreign monarchs, of course, were recruited for religious reasons. Protestantism, and very little else, recommended William III and George I to their new subjects. Thus the Reformation, which had wrecked England's strategic security in the sixteenth century, continued to undermine it in the eighteenth. It is true that the one eighteenth-century war which Britain fought without Continental allies, the American War, was a partial defeat, but it is not at all safe to assume that the lack of allies was responsible, when there are other and better explanations.[6] For most of the eighteenth century, the Continental Commitment was essentially for the benefit of the Church of England, not the Royal Navy.

It is paradoxical that Protestantism, which was a strategic weakness for England and Britain, was for the same reason an essential strength to British sea power. This was not because Protestant seamen were braver or wiser than those of other faiths; it was because the governing classes of Britain were obsessed with the Popish menace. It is sometimes suggested, particularly by foreign historians, that British naval supremacy rested on the British people's unique consciousness of the importance of the sea. It may be doubted if in reality there ever was a time when the average ploughboy or mill-lass thought a lot about sea power, but what mattered was that the political nation, those who informed opinion and took decisions, were deeply convinced that their religious freedom, and hence their political freedom and material security, depended on it completely. Few of them knew much about the Navy, and many of them were profoundly ignorant of it, but they knew that they needed it. This more than anything else accounts for the strong, consistent and broad-based political support for a costly Navy which distinguishes Britain from all other European powers, naval powers included. It is impossible to imagine that a Catholic England would have been, or felt, so isolated and imperilled. It was because she became Protestant that she had so many reasons to build up a fleet, and so few opportunities for soldiering in Europe, long before she had any significant overseas trade or possessions. Fear provided the motive to maintain a fleet whose primary purpose was always defensive.[7] As Henry Maydman wrote in 1691,

> England must resolve to be at the constant charge, of keeping a great Fleet in continual Action, if ever the Nation hopes to have any Peace or Tranquillity; for it is only the Navy under its Monarchical Government, as in Church and State Established, by God's Assistance, can bring any lasting Peace or Happiness to this Nation.[8]

As these lines suggest, the significance of sea power to British history lies at least as much in domestic politics and the growth of the state as in foreign policy and war. Political theorists at least as far back as Aristotle have linked navies and democratic forms of government,[9] and it used to be customary to connect the Revolution of 1688 with England's rise to naval greatness.

Unfortunately for this argument, it is beyond doubt that the powerful English fleet of the 1690s was not originally the product of Whig revolution, or even Stuart monarchy, but of Republican government and military dictatorship.[10] The State's Navy of the 1650s, like the fleets of Spain in the late sixteenth century, France in the late seventeenth, Germany in the late nineteenth, and Russia in more than one period, all show that autocratic, militarized states are perfectly capable of building large and efficient navies, often with astonishing speed – but they do not seem to be capable of sustaining their creations. The English Republic (and the English army which dominated it) took barely ten years to create the most formidable navy in Europe, and then to collapse. Spanish sea power enjoyed a brief period of strength in the 1590s followed by a steep decline. Louis XIV's fleet rose to be the largest in the world in less than thirty years, and had largely disappeared within another thirty. The fleet that Tirpitz built on borrowed money ran out of credit in the budget crisis of 1912. All these cases can be well explained by the argument that the temporary influence of a dominant favourite or the capricious will of the All-Highest was no substitute for the solid support of entrenched interest groups.[11] 'Naval strength is not the growth of a day, nor is it possible to retain it, when once acquired, without the utmost difficulty, and the most unwearied attention,' wrote the pioneer economist Sir John Sinclair in 1782.[12] Only the unwavering support of the political nation, sustained over decades if not centuries, could build up a dominant sea power.

The importance of 1689 to naval history was not that Parliament created English sea power, but that it began to take it over. In the short term the consequences of replacing strong and expert Stuart leadership with incompetent and fractured Parliamentary administration were disastrous, but in the long term it mattered very much that the Navy and the money finished up together in the hands of the House of Commons. There has been much disagreement among historians and political scientists over the nature of British government. It has been argued that British government or British bureaucracy were uniquely efficient,[13] and strikingly inefficient;[14] that the country was surprisingly militarized, and unusually free of military influence.[15] It has been described as unique in combining the 'urban, capital-intensive' path to modernity with a strong central government.[16] For some scholars, England was different because it had a strong Navy, and it had a strong Navy because it was different.[17] For others England was different because it had a strong Parliament, and it had a strong Parliament because it was different.[18] Neither observation seems to have quite the explanatory force we need.

It is helpful in this context to divide eighteenth-century British government into two parts: the crown's and Parliament's. The crown's government, which included the army and foreign affairs, was based on a balance of central and local forces, the powers of the crown checked by those of the nobility and gentry. It was traditional if not archaic, dispersed and inefficient. Parliament's government was quite different; highly centralized and precociously professional. Here were found the Treasury and the revenue-collecting departments, especially the Customs and Excise, and here too was the Navy. Studying one side or the other of government produces entirely different conclusions. The location of the main revenue-raising and revenue-spending departments on the efficient, Parliamentary side of British government is one of the most distinctive and important features of British constitutional development. Because Parliament captured the Navy, it was able to realize the character of British sea power as the ideal expression of the nation in arms which was founded on the folk-memory of the Elizabethan age. It made the Navy an expression of the liberty of the people, where the army was an expression of the power of the crown. The Stuarts could never have done this, however wisely they had managed the Navy.[19]

Parliamentary control made possible the astonishing rise in the level of real taxation in Britain after 1688. From 1688 to 1815 Britain's gross national product increased about three-fold, and tax receipts about fifteen-fold. By 1810 they had reached almost one-fifth of gross national product. The British government was consistently spending about twice the proportion of national income which was available to French governments, yet because most British taxes (until income tax) were indirect and inconspicuous, the French believed themselves to be much more heavily burdened. The Navy was normally the largest single consumer of British public revenue, and the army was its only rival.[20]

The British state's unequalled capacity to raise revenue was the indispensable foundation of sea power, but its significance is not solely military. Getting and spending so large a proportion of national income made the state the principal actor in the economy, and it was the economy which made Britain great. By the later eighteenth century, before the industrial revolution had begun, Britain was already one of the two great international trading powers. There is much disagreement among economic historians as to how the British economy grew and what factors gave rise to the industrial revolution, but chronology alone makes it clear that Britain was a great power before she was an industrial power. By 1815, when her main commercial rival, France, had destroyed herself and much of Europe with her, Britain was incontestably the dominant world trading power – but the industrial revolution was still in its early stages, and only water-powered cotton mills were yet making a major contribution to the economy. In the period in which Britain rose to greatness, there were only three significant economic activities in the British Isles: agriculture, foreign trade and war.[21]

Attempts have been made to downplay the significance of one or all of these, but it is hard to believe that they were not all three essentially involved in Britain's economic growth. Foreign trade, especially the rich colonial and East India trades, generated the liquid capital which paid for wars. At least until the 1790s the British economy was producing more investment capital than it could absorb, which was how the government was able to borrow steeply rising sums at stable or falling interest rates. Since it is probable that the peacetime economy was not running at full capacity, wartime expenditure financed by borrowing had little inflationary effect, and Britain's eighteenth-century wars were at least partly paid for by mobilizing unemployed capital and labour. The effect of the state, especially the state in wartime, was to stimulate the economy. 'In many ways, this two-way system of raising and *simultaneously* spending vast sums of money acted like a bellows, fanning the development of western capitalism and of the nation-state itself.'[22] The economic burden of war was therefore remarkably low, except when large armies like Marlborough's and Wellington's campaigned overseas and had to pay for what they purchased locally in cash. What was spent on the Navy was nearly all spent in Britain, or spent overseas in buying from British merchants who remitted their profits home.[23]

Foreign trade and the Navy therefore formed two elements of a single symbiotic system, exactly as eighteenth-century writers never tired of explaining. The Navy protected trade and protected the country. Trade generated the seamen to man the Navy, and the money to pay for it. Overseas possessions had a subordinate role in this system, as sources of trade, but only in the atypical years of the mid-century did the British become obsessed with colonies for their own sake, and the débâcle of the American War cured them of that. The eighteenth-century British were not keeping up a Navy to conquer a colonial empire. Integrally involved with the international trade system was the financial system. Few of Britain's overseas trades balanced by themselves, but the system as a whole was balanced by bills exchanged on London: a massive and complex system of international credit payments. Combined with banking, brokerage and insurance, it made London the centre of a financial empire which earned large sums in 'invisible' trade, and articulated the national and international trading system. The capital markets were an essential part of the financial world, and their foundation was government stock, the indispensable investment instrument which drew capital to London from all over the British Isles, and indeed all over the western world. As the dominant borrower, and as an enormous purchaser of goods and services at home and abroad, the state in general and the Navy in particular were at the heart of this commercial and financial system.[24]

The financial system in turn linked international trade with domestic agriculture, whose rapid productivity growth made possible the rise of the economy as a whole. From 1600 to 1800 the population of England almost tripled, but the agricultural workforce stayed about the same and the country remained broadly self-sufficient in food. By 1800 only one-third of the British population (compared to two-thirds in France) was on the land. Even in the hard years of the Great Wars, when fourteen harvests failed out of twenty-two, few people were ever in serious want, and both the economy and the population continued to grow very fast. A prosperous rural population formed a large consumer market for nascent domestic industries, while those displaced from the land provided the manpower which fought the wars, at a low cost to the productive economy. All this was made possible by the growth of an efficient national agricultural market, in which, as we have seen, the Victualling Board was heavily involved. This national market depended on coastal shipping, for only the efficiencies of water transport were capable of integrating so large an area as the British Isles. The agricultural market also spread the financial system to the remotest corners of the British Isles, and drained the surplus profits of farmers and landowners into the London capital markets. In this way agriculture too contributed capital and skills to the 'maritime imperial' system.[25]

It has been argued that the industrial revolution, when it came, heralded the end rather than the beginning of Britain's economic supremacy, for it was based on technologies which could easily be exported. The commercial and agricultural revolutions of the seventeenth and eighteenth centuries, on which Britain's economic supremacy was first established, derived from 'social efficiencies' of British society which were difficult or impossible for foreigners to copy.[26] These were precisely the aspects of society which also favoured sea power. Only flexible and integrated societies could surmount the very considerable difficulties of combining the wide range of human, industrial, technical, commercial and managerial resources required to build and fight a seagoing fleet. Nations in which public policy was based on a broad consensus of interests, in which numerous private businesses serviced and influenced government, in which land and trade overlapped, were best equipped to sustain a navy. Middle-class participation in public life, professional skills, commerce, industry and private finance directly favoured and were favoured by navies. Sea power was most successful in countries with flexible and open social and political systems. They were the same which favoured trade and industry, and for the same reason, for a navy was the supreme industrial activity. The armed forces of early modern states were the blueprint of their modern societies: a complex, integrated, industrial world for the naval powers; a rigid, archaic world of great landed estates for the military powers.[27] Open societies were best at naval warfare for the same reason that they were later best at meeting other challenges of the modern world, because a navy was an image of the modern world in miniature. 'Warfare on the British model was a triumph for an enterprising and acquisitive society, not an authoritarian one.'[28] Britain did not simply survive centuries of warfare relatively unscathed because of geographical and historical accident,[29] to profit from the industrial revolution because there were no competitors left undevastated by war. Naval warfare was Britain's apprenticeship for commercial and industrial supremacy.

Much of this argument still rests on suggestive connections rather than established proofs, for economic and agricultural historians on one side, and naval historians on the other, have built few bridges between their subjects.[30] Some attention has been given to the subject of technological 'spin-off' from the Navy to industry, concluding that it was significant in only a few cases.[31] What cannot be gainsaid by any impartial observer is the impact of war on history, economic as well as political and social. In 1790 France was on most measures as likely as Britain to become the great industrial and commercial power of the nineteenth century. The devastation wrought by Napoleon's ambitions ended that hope for ever – but it was not an inexplicable accident that Britain alone was spared.[32] Having at last learned to master the facts of geography and turn them to their advantage, the seventeenth-century English and eighteenth-century British made their Navy the guarantor of their freedom and security. It did not come easily or naturally; it required great skill, long experience and ceaseless vigilance. Freedom from foreign invasion, conferred by sea power, provided the security which alone made long-term investment and economic growth possible. In this way if no other, naval supremacy was the indispensable foundation for prosperity. Add to this the preservation of the lives and liberties of the people, and the strictly defensive achievements of sea power would have been central to British history even if it had never made any other contribution.

The achievements of British sea power were national ones, the product of government and society as much as of the Navy as an institution. Without the courage and professional abilities of officers and men at sea they would have been impossible, but the most crucial developments in the period covered by this volume were not naval but financial and administrative. It was the capacity of naval administration ashore, above all the Victualling Board, which transformed the operational capabilities of British fleets at sea. The seamanship of officers and men and the capabilities of their ships (though perhaps not their discipline) were probably adequate in the 1650s to have achieved much of what the Navy actually did during the Great Wars, but their operational range was completely inadequate, and the government was incapable of paying for the limited operations they did undertake. Only when ships could be kept at sea with healthy crews for long periods could the possibilities of naval power be fully exploited. Thus the final achievement of naval supremacy, after so many false starts and disappointments, was truly a national achievement which drew on the economic and social resources of the three kingdoms to sustain professional sea power at war. One small detail missing from the 1815 peace treaty marked what Britain had now won. There was no claim to the 'salute to the flag'. The empty boast of 'sovereignty of the sea' which had embarrassed English diplomacy and troubled the peace of the Narrow Seas for 500 years was quietly dropped. There was no more need of it, now that Britain had incontestably gained the real command of the ocean.[33]

CHRONOLOGY

Covering a period in which the events of naval history are recorded in considerable detail in standard works, this Chronology is intended only as an outline. Since most of the events it mentions are also in the main text, or are otherwise well known to history, references have been supplied sparingly.

1649

Jan 17: Treaty of Kilkenny makes an alliance between the Royalists and the Irish rebels.

Jan 20: Prince Rupert with the Royalist squadron sails from Helvoetsluis for Ireland.

Jan 29: Prince Rupert arrives at Kinsale.

May 22: Blake establishes a blockade of Kinsale.

Aug 15: Cromwell lands at Dublin with an English army.

Oct 17: Prince Rupert sails from Kinsale.

1650

Mar 10: Blake blockades Prince Rupert in the Tagus.

Apr 27: Defeat of Montrose's Scottish Royalist force at Carbisdale.

Jul 16: Prince Rupert fails to break Blake's blockade of the Tagus.

Sep 3: Cromwell defeats the Scottish army at Dunbar.

Oct 12: Prince Rupert and the Royalist squadron sails from the Tagus.

Nov 5: Most of the Royalist squadron is driven ashore and destroyed at Cartagena.

1651

Mar: Penn's squadron enters the Mediterranean in vain pursuit of Prince Rupert. Surrender of Waterford to Parliamentary forces.

Jun 1: The Royalist garrison of the Isles of Scilly surrenders.

Jul: English amphibious operation across the Firth of Forth.

Aug 6: Charles II invades England with the Scottish army.

Sep 3: The Scottish army defeated by Cromwell at the battle of Worcester; Charles II escapes in disguise.

Sep 30: The *Constant Reformation* founders in a gale off the Azores, Prince Rupert narrowly escaping.

Oct 31: Surrender of the Isle of Man to Parliamentary forces.

Dec 12: Surrender of Jersey.

Dec 19: Surrender of Guernsey.

1652
Jan 11: Barbados surrenders to Sir George Ayscue.
Apr: Galway surrenders to Parliamentary forces; the last Royalist port in the British Isles.
May: Prince Rupert's ships in the West Indies.
May 19: Battle of Dover.
Aug 16: Battle of Plymouth.
Aug 28: Dutch defeat English Mediterranean squadron off Elba.[1]
Sep 4: Blake captures French relieving convoy off Dunkirk, which is forced to surrender to its Spanish besiegers.
Sep 28–9: Battle of the Kentish Knock.
Nov 30: Battle of Dungeness.

1653
Feb 18–20: Battle of Portland.
Mar 4: Dutch destroy English Mediterranean squadron off Leghorn.[2]
Mar 4: Prince Rupert enters Nantes, ending three years cruising.
Apr 8: De With unsuccessfully attacks a convoy of colliers off Scarborough.[3]
Apr 20: Cromwell seizes power from the Rump Parliament.
Jun 2–3: Battle of the Gabbard.
Jul 31: Battle of the Texel.
Oct 5: Mutiny in ships at Chatham.
Dec 12: Dissolution of Barebone's Parliament, leading to establishment of the Protectorate.

1655
Apr 4: Blake's squadron destroys nine Turkish warships in Porto Farina.
Apr 14: English landing in Hispaniola, leading to failed attack on San Domingo.
May 11: English landing in Jamaica.
Aug 31: Penn's fleet returns to England from the West Indies.

1656
Apr 20: Blake mounts blockade of Cadiz.
Sep 9: Stayner intercepts a Spanish convoy off Cadiz.

1657
Apr 20: Blake and Stayner destroy a Spanish squadron in Santa Cruz de Tenerife.
Aug 7: Blake dies at sea off Plymouth.

1658
Feb 26: By the Treaty of Roskilde, Denmark surrenders Scania to Sweden.
Feb 28: Goodson intercepts Dutch ships intended for a Royalist invasion.[4]
Jun 4: Franco-English military victory over Spain at the battle of the Dunes, followed by the surrender of Dunkirk.
Sep 3: Death of Oliver Cromwell.

Oct: Goodson sent to the Skagerrak to support Sweden and counterbalance the Dutch-Danish fleet.

1659

Apr: Mountague sent to support Sweden against the Dutch-Danish fleet.
May 6: English occupation of St Helena.[5]
May 7: Restoration of the Rump Parliament, followed by the return of the Commonwealth.
Oct 12: English army expels the Rump Parliament.
Dec 26: Restoration of the Rump with naval backing.

1660

Feb 21: Restoration of the Long Parliament of 1640.
Mar 16: Long Parliament dissolves itself and calls a free election.
Apr 25: Convention Parliament meets and invites Charles II to return.
May 29: Charles II enters London.

1661

Jul 29: Sandwich's fruitless demonstration against Algiers.

1662

Oct 8: Captain Christopher Myngs captures Santiago de Cuba.
Oct 17: Charles II sells Dunkirk to France.

1663

Oct: Sir Robert Holmes sails for West Africa.

1664

Aug 27: An English expedition captures New Amsterdam (renamed New York).
Oct: De Ruyter reaches the West African coast and recaptures Goeree.
Dec 19: Sir Thomas Allin attacks a Dutch convoy off Cadiz, leading to the outbreak of the Second Dutch War.

1665

May 20: Dutch capture an English convoy from Hamburg on the Dogger Bank.
Jun 3: Battle of Lowestoft.
Aug 2: Battle of Bergen.
Sep 3: Sandwich takes rich Dutch prizes on the Dogger Bank.

1666

Jan 16: France declares war on England.
Apr 23: The French capture St Kitts.
Jun 1–4: Four Days' Battle.
Jul 25–26: St James's Day Fight.
Aug 9: Holmes's Bonfire.
Sep 2–6: Great Fire of London.
Nov: The French capture Antigua.

1667
May 10: Battle of Nevis.
Jun 9–14: Medway Raid.
Jun 25: Battle of Fort St Pierre.
Jul: French invasion of Flanders.

1669
Apr 27: Morgan defeats the Spanish Armada de Barlovento in Lake Maracaibo.
Dec 29: Captain John Kempthorne knighted for defending his convoy against an Algerine squadron.

1670
May 22: Secret Anglo-French Treaty of Dover.
Aug 18: Anglo-Dutch victory against an Algerine squadron near Cape Spartel.

1671
Jan: Buccaneers under Sir Henry Morgan sack Panama.
May 8: Spragge destroys an Algerine squadron off Bougie.

1672
Jan 2: Stop of the Exchequer.
Mar 13: Holmes's attack on a Dutch convoy marks outbreak of Third Dutch War.
May 28: Battle of Solebay
Jun 28: William III restored to power in Netherlands.
Aug 10: De Witt brothers murdered.

1673
May 28: First battle of Schooneveld.
June 4: Second battle of Schooneveld.
Jul 30: Dutch capture New York.
Aug 11: Battle of the Texel.
Sep 1: VOC defeats the English East India Company off Masulipatam.

1674
Feb 9: By the Treaty of Westminster England withdraws from the Third Dutch War.

1676
Jan 14: Shovell's attack on Tripoli.

1678
Jul 16: Anglo-Dutch naval alliance.
Aug 13: Outbreak of the Popish Plot agitation.

1682
Apr: Herbert's treaty with Algiers.

1685

Feb 6: Death of Charles II.
Jun 14: Surrender of the Earl of Argyll's rebel squadron in the Kyles of Bute.[6]
Jul 6: Defeat of Monmouth's rebel army at Sedgemoor.
Oct 18: Revocation of the Edict of Nantes.

1686

Jun–Jul: Undeclared Anglo-French war in Hudson's Bay.

1688

Sep 25: France declares war on the League of Augsburg and invades the Palatinate.
Oct 19: Dutch invasion fleet sails, but is blown back into port.
Nov 1: The Dutch invasion fleet sails again.
Nov 5: William of Orange lands in Torbay.
Dec 25: James II flees the country.

1689

Feb 12: William and Mary proclaimed King and Queen of England.
Mar 12: James II lands in Ireland.
Apr 19: Anglo-Dutch naval agreement.
May 1: Battle of Bantry Bay.
May 7: England declares war on France.
Jul 28: Relief of Londonderry.
Aug 22: Anglo-Dutch army lands in Ireland.

1690

May 11: Sir William Phips takes Port Royal, Acadia (i.e. Annapolis Royal, N.S.).
Jun 30: Battle of Beachy Head.
Jul 1: Battle of the Boyne.
Jul 16: A squadron under Lawrence Wright takes St Kitts
Aug: Dutch and English East Indiamen fight French East Indiamen off Madras.
Sep 17: English naval expedition sails to take Cork and Kinsale.
Oct 6–8: Phips's unsuccessful attack on Quebec.
Dec 8–10: Court-martial and dismissal of Lord Torrington.

1691

May 13: English attack on Guadeloupe abandoned.
Oct 13: Surrender of Limerick, last Irish city in Jacobite hands.

1692

Feb 11: Wrenn's squadron fights the French off Barbados.
May 19: Battle of Barfleur.
May 22–24: Battle of La Hougue.

1693

Apr: Wheeler twice raids Martinique.

Jun 17: Smyrna Convoy action.

Nov 16–19: English bombardment of St Malo.

1694

Feb 18: Wheeler's squadron wrecked near Gibraltar.

May 17: Du Casse lands in Jamaica, remaining six weeks.

Jun 8: English landing near Brest driven off with heavy loss.

Jun 19: Bart captures a Dutch grain convoy in the North Sea.

Jul 12–13: Allied bombardment of Dieppe.

Jul 15: Allied bombardment of Le Havre.

Aug 12: Shovell and Barfød fight over the 'salute to the flag'.

Sep 12–16: Shovell bombards Dunkirk.

Oct 3: Le Moyne d'Iberville takes Ft York, Hudson's Bay.

Oct: Russell with allied main fleet winters in Cadiz.

Dec 28: Death of Queen Mary II.

1695

May 19: Wilmot temporarily captures Cap François and later Port-de-Paix.

Jul 5: Allied bombardment of St Malo.

Jul 27: Allied bombardment of Dunkirk

Aug 17: Allied bombardment of Calais.

    The pirate Henry Avery takes the Great Mughul's ship *Ganj-i-Salwai*.

1696

Apr 3: Shovell bombards Calais.

Jun 7: Bart takes a Dutch convoy on the Dogger Bank.

July 15: Lord Berkeley's squadron attacks Biscay islands.

1697

Apr 23: Pointis and du Casse take Cartagena de Indias.

May 26–27: Pointis eludes pursuit of Nevill in West Indies.

Aug: French capture Barcelona.

Sep 10: Treaty of Ryswick.

1698

Jan 30: The pirate William Kidd takes the *Quedah Merchant* off Cochin, causing a crisis in the East India Company's business.

Nov: Establishment of the short-lived Scottish colony of Darien.

1700

Jul 9 and 14: Anglo-Dutch-Swedish fleet bombards Copenhagen.

Nov 1: Death of Charles II of Spain opens Spanish Succession question.

1701

Jun 12: Act of Settlement regulates succession to the throne of England.
Sep 6: Death of James II: Louis XIV recognizes his son as King of England.

1702

Mar 8: Death of William III, accession of Queen Anne.
Apr 23: War declared against France.
May: Sir J. Munden fails to intercept French squadron bound for West Indies.
Aug 19–25: Benbow's last fight.
Aug 26–Sep 7: Leake attacks French settlements in Newfoundland.
Aug 15: Rooke lands an allied army near Cadiz.
Oct 12: Battle of Vigo.

1703

Jan 17: Saint Pol-Hécourt captures the *Ludlow* in the North Sea.
Apr 10: Saint Pol-Hécourt attacks an English squadron capturing two vessels.
Nov 26–27: The Great Storm; twelve English warships with over 1,500 lives lost.

1704

Mar 12: Dilkes captures two Spanish ships of the line and an armed merchantman off Lisbon.
Jul 24: Duguay-Trouin captures an escort and twelve merchant ships from an English convoy.
Jul 24: Rooke's Anglo-Dutch fleet captures Gibraltar.
Jul 26: Whetstone and Psilander fight off Orfordness over the 'salute to the flag'.
Aug 2: Battle of Blenheim.
Aug 13: Battle of Malaga.

1705

Mar 9–10: Leake defeats Pointis's attempt to assist siege of Gibraltar.
Apr: Iberville raids Nevis.
Sep 23: Shovell, van Almonde and Peterborough take Barcelona.
Oct 20: Saint Pol-Hécourt is killed taking an English convoy in the North Sea.

1706

Feb 1–22: French raids on St Kitts and Nevis.
Apr 27: Leake and Wassenaer raise siege of Barcelona.
Jun 1: Near St Helena, Desaugiers captures two English East Indiamen.
Jun: Fairborne supports siege of Ostend.
Aug 25: Leake takes Alicante.
Sep 9 and 14: Leake takes Ibiza and Majorca.
Sep: William Kerr fails to take San Domingo.

1707

Mar 21: *Resolution* driven ashore by a French squadron near Ventimiglia and burned.
Apr 14: English defeat at Almanza.

May 1: Union of England and Scotland under the name of Great Britain.

May 2: Forbin takes part of a convoy off Beachy Head.

Aug 11: Prince Eugene and Shovell fail to take Toulon, but the French fleet is scuttled.

Oct 10: Forbin and Duguay-Trouin take the *Cumberland* and twenty-two English merchantmen off Ushant.

Oct 22: Shovell wrecked in Scillies.

1708

Mar 13: Byng thwarts French invasion of Scotland.

Apr 26: Cassard captures an English convoy and escort off the coast of Ireland.

May 28: Wager intercepts a Spanish convoy in the Caribbean and takes the *San Josef*.

Aug 13: Surrender of Sardinia to the allies.

Sep 18: English conquest of Minorca.

1709

Feb: St John's, Newfoundland taken by the French.

Apr 7: Byng fails to relieve Alicante.

Apr 18: Cassard attacks an English convoy off Tabarka.

Oct 26: Duguay-Trouin captures the British ship of the line *Gloucester* sixty.

Dec 29: Cassard captures the *Pembroke*, 60, and *Falcon*, 32, near Corsica.

1710

Jun: Norris defeats French attack on Sardinia.

Oct 1: Port Royal, Acadia (renamed Annapolis Royal) taken by New Englanders.

1711

Apr 17: Archduke Charles succeeds as Charles VI of Austria.

May 4: Walker expedition sails for Canada.

Aug 23: Walker expedition to Quebec loses several ships wrecked and turns back.

Sep 11: Duguay-Trouin captures Rio de Janeiro.

1713

Mar 31: Treaty of Utrecht.

1714

Jul 26: Russian victory of Hangö over Sweden exposes Finland and Sweden to seaborne attack.

Aug 1: Death of Queen Anne and accession of George I.

1715

Aug 20: Death of Louis XIV of France.

Sep 6: Outbreak of Jacobite rising in Scotland.

Dec 22: 'James III' lands at Peterhead.

1717
Aug 22: Spanish expedition lands in Sardinia.

1718
Jul 22: Quadruple Alliance of France, Empire, Britain and Netherlands is signed.
Jul 31: Battle of Cape Passaro.

1719
Jun 11: Surrender of Spanish expeditionary force to Scotland in Glenshiel.
Oct 10: British landing at Vigo.

1720
Feb 6: Peace between Spain and Quadruple Alliance.
Jul 27: Battle of Gränhamn.
Oct: Collapse of the 'South Sea Bubble'.

1726
Hosier blockades Porto Bello.

1727
Feb: Spain besieges Gibraltar.
Jun 11: Death of George I and accession of George II.

1728
Feb 24: Undeclared war with Spain concluded.

1739
Oct 8: Outbreak of war with Spain.
Nov 22: Vernon takes Porto Bello.

1740
Jun: Unsuccessful British attack on San Agustín, Florida.
Sep 18: Anson's squadron sails for the Pacific.

1741
Mar 4: British land at Cartagena de Indias and begin unsuccessful siege.

1742
Apr 16: Mathews establishes a loose blockade of the Spanish and French fleets in Toulon.
Jun 7: Fruitless Spanish attack on Georgia.
Aug 8: Captain Thomas Martin forces the Two Sicilies out of the war.

1743
Feb 18: Knowles attacks La Guaira.
Apr 24: Knowles attacks Puerto Cabello.
Jun 20: Anson takes the Manila galleon.

1744
Feb 11: Battle of Toulon.

Feb 24: Norris and Rocquefeuil parted by a gale off Dungeness, which also wrecks the French invasion plan.

Mar 4: War between France and Britain.

Jun 15: Anson returns from his voyage round the world.

1745

Mar 20: British bombardment of Savona and San Remo.

Apr 30: New England expedition lands near Louisbourg.

Jun 17: Louisbourg surrenders.

Jun 25: Peyton fights an indecisive action with Mahé de la Bourdonnais off Madras.

Jul 23: Prince Charles Edward lands in the Highlands.

Sep 21: Jacobite victory at Prestonpans.

Dec 4: Jacobite army at Derby.

1746

Apr 16: Battle of Culloden.

May 3: Action in Loch nan Uamh.

Jun 11: D'Enville's disastrous expedition sails to recapture Louisbourg.

Jun 25: Battle of Negapatam.

Aug 4: Mitchell fails to attack Conflans' convoy in the Windward Passage.

Sep 10: The French capture Madras.

Sep 20: Fruitless British landing at Lorient.

Dec 5: British occupy the Lérins Islands.

1747

Jan 23: British bombardment of Antibes.

Mar 25: Dubois de la Motte drives Dent away from his convoy in the Windward Passage.

May 3: First battle of Finisterre.

May 16: French recapture Lérins Islands.

Jun 20: Fox intercepts Dubois de la Motte's convoy in the Bay of Biscay.

Oct 14: Second battle of Finisterre.

1748

Jun 11: Griffin fails to prevent Bouvet de Lozier from reinforcing Pondicherry.

Aug 19: Boscawen begins the (unsuccessful) siege of Pondicherry.

Oct 1: Knowles's action with Reggio off Havana.

Oct 7: Peace of Aix-la-Chapelle ends the War of the Austrian Succession.

1755

Apr 2: Capture of Mahratta stronghold of Severndroog by East India Company forces.

Jun 10: Boscawen intercepts part of a French squadron carrying troops to North America.

Jul 9: Braddock's defeat at the Monongahela River.

1756

Feb 13: Watson and Clive capture Mahratta port of Gheria.

Apr 18: French landing in Minorca.

May 20: Byng's action with La Galissonière off Minorca.

Jun 20: Siraj-ud-Dowla, Nawab of Bengal, takes Calcutta from the East India Company.

Jun 28: Surrender of Minorca.

1757

Jan 2: Watson and Clive recapture Calcutta.

Mar 14: Execution of Byng.

Sep 8: Cumberland surrender the Anglo-Hanoverian army to Richelieu at Klosterzeven.

Sep 13: Holburne's fleet off Louisbourg is scattered by a hurricane.

Sep 23: Bombardment and capture of Ile d'Aix.

Oct 21: Forrest's action with Kersaint off Cap François.

1758

Feb 28: 'Moonlight' battle off Cartagena.

Apr 29: Battle of Cuddalore.

Apr 30: British capture of Senegal.

Jun 5: British landing near St Malo.

Jun 7: British landing near Louisbourg.

Jul 26: Surrender of Louisbourg.

Aug 3: Battle of Negapatam.

Aug 7–15: British landing at Cherbourg.

Sep 3–11: British landing near St Malo.

Dec 31: British capture Goree, West Africa.

1759

Jan 16: Abortive British landing on Martinique.

Jan 22: British landing on Guadeloupe.

Apr 8: British capture Masulipatam.

May 1: Surrender of Guadeloupe to Britain.

Jul 4: Rodney bombards Le Havre.

Aug 1: Battle of Minden.

Aug 18–19: Battle of Lagos.

Sep 10: Battle of Pondicherry.

Sep 13: Battle of the Heights of Abraham, leading to the surrender of Quebec.

Nov 20: Battle of Quiberon Bay.

1760

Feb 28: Defeat of Thurot off the Isle of Man.

Sep 8: Capture of Montreal and surrender of French Canada.

Oct 15: Death of George II and accession of George III.

1761
Jan 15: Surrender of Pondicherry.
Apr 8: Belle Isle landing.
Jun 7: Surrender of Belle Isle.

1762
Jan 4: War breaks out with Spain.
Mar 1: Surrender of Martinique.
Jun 7: British landing near Havana.
Jun 20: Ternay briefly captures St John's, Newfoundland.
Aug 13: Surrender of Havana.
Oct 6: British capture of Manila.

1763
Feb 10: Peace of Paris ends the Seven Years' War.

1768
May 15: France gains control of Corsica.
May 25: Cook sails on his first Pacific voyage.

1770
Jul 5: Russian naval victory of Chesme over Turkey.

1771
Jan 22: Spain cedes Falkland Islands to Britain, averting war.

1773
Dec 16: Boston 'Tea Party'.

1774
Sep 5: Meeting of the Continental Congress in Philadelphia.

1775
Apr 19: Fighting between American rebels and British troops in Massachusetts.
Jun 17: British troops defeat American rebels at Bunker Hill, Boston.

1776
Mar 17: British evacuate Boston.
May 2: France secretly decides to aid the American rebels at the risk of war.
Jul 4: American rebels declare independence.
Sep 15: British amphibious operation captures New York.

1777
May 21: Manley's rebel squadron sails from Boston.
Aug 22: Full British naval mobilization against France is ordered.
Sep 27: British capture Philadelphia.
Oct 17: Burgoyne capitulates at Saratoga.

1778

Feb 6: Franco-American alliance signed.

Apr 13: D'Estaing sails from Toulon.

Jun 9: Byron sails for North America.

Jul 22: D'Estaing abandons his plan to force Howe's defence of New York.

Jul 27: Battle of Ushant.

Aug 8: D'Estaing attacks Rhode Island.

Aug 10: Action between Tronjoly and Vernon off Pondicherry.

Sep 7: The French take Dominica.

Oct 18: Pondicherry taken by the British.

Nov 4: D'Estaing sails from Boston for Martinique.

Dec 13: British capture of St Lucia.

Dec 15: Barrington repels d'Estaing's attack on St Lucia.

1779

Jan 30: The French recapture Senegal.

Jun 16: Spain declares war and besieges Gibraltar.

Jul 6: Battle of Grenada.

Aug 14: British naval victory over a rebel squadron in the Penobscot River.

Aug 16: The Franco-Spanish Combined Fleet approaches Plymouth.

Sep 23: *Bonhomme Richard*, Capt. J. Paul Jones, captures the *Serapis* off Flamborough Head.

Oct 9: D'Estaing's assault on Savannah is repulsed.

Dec 18: La Motte-Picquet and Hyde Parker skirmish off Martinique.

Dec 30: Dutch convoy under Bylandt is brought into Portsmouth by force.

1780

Jan 16: Moonlight Battle.

Mar 10: Russian declaration of 'armed neutrality'.

Mar 14: Spaniards capture Mobile.

Apr 17: Rodney and de Guichen fight off Martinique.

May 12: Charleston captured from the rebels.

May 15: Action between Rodney and de Guichen.

May 19: Action between Rodney and de Guichen.

Jun 2–8: Anti-Catholic Gordon Riots in London.

Aug 9: Córdoba takes a British West India convoy off the Azores.

Sep 14: Rodney takes over the North American station.

Dec 8: The British defeat the Mysore fleet off Mangalore.

Dec 20: Britain declares war on the Netherlands.

1781

Jan 6: Abortive French attack on Jersey.

Feb 3: Rodney captures and pillages St Eustatius.

Mar 16: Battle of Cape Henry.

Apr 6: Darby relieves Gibraltar.

Apr 16: Porto Praya action between Johnstone and Suffren.
Apr 29: Grasse fights Hood off Martinique.
May 2: La Motte-Picquet takes the St Eustatius convoy in the Western Approaches.
May 11: Spain captures Pensacola and West Florida.
Jun 2: Grasse takes Tobago; Rodney avoids a night action.
Jul 21: Johnstone captures Dutch East Indiamen in Saldanha Bay.
Aug 5: Battle of the Dogger Bank.
Aug 18: Spain occupies Minorca.
Sep 5: Battle of the Chesapeake.
Oct 18: Surrender of Cornwallis's army at Yorktown.
Nov 13: British combined operation captures Negapatam.
Dec 12: Kempenfelt captures part of de Guichen's convoy in the Bay of Biscay.

1782
Jan 11: Hughes captures Trincomalee.
Jan 25–26: Hood repels Grasse from Basseterre Roads.
Feb 17: Battle of Sadras.
Apr 12: Battle of the Saintes. Battle of Provedien.
Apr 21: Barrington takes most of a French convoy intended for the East Indies.
May 8: Spaniards capture the Bahamas.
Jul 6: Battle of Negapatam.
Aug 25: Suffren captures Trincomalee.
Sep 3: Battle off Trincomalee.
Sep 13: Disastrous Spanish assault on Gibraltar using floating batteries.
Oct 20: Howe fights partial action off Cape Spartel in the course of relieving Gibraltar.

1783
Jun 20: Battle of Cuddalore.
Sep 3: Peace of Versailles.

1787
May 13: The 'First Fleet' to New South Wales sails.
Jun 28: Arrest of the Princess of Orange, leading to Prussian intervention in the Dutch 'Patriot' crisis.

1789
May 5: Estates-General of France assemble.
Jul 14: Fall of the Bastille.

1790
Oct 28: Spain yields to British demands over Nootka Sound incident.

1792
Apr 20: France declares war on Austria, starting the French Revolutionary Wars.
Sep 20: Battle of Valmy halts Prussian invasion of France.

Nov 6: French victory over the Austrians at Jemappes, followed by the conquest of the Austrian Netherlands.

Nov 19: France offers assistance to revolutionaries everywhere.

1793

Feb 1: France declares war on Britain.

Feb 13: Formation of First Coalition of Britain, Austria, Prussia, the Netherlands, Spain and Sardinia against France.

Aug 28: Hood occupies Toulon.

Nov 26: Grey–Jervis expedition sails for the West Indies.

Dec 19: Allied evacuation of Toulon.

1794

Feb 7: British landing in Corsica.

Mar 22: Capture of Martinique

Apr 4: Capture of St Lucia.

Apr 20: Surrender of Guadaloupe.

May 22: Surrender of Bastia.

Jun 1: Battle of First of June.

Jun 4: Capture of Port-au-Prince.

Jul 11: Portland Whigs join the British government.

Aug 10: Surrender of Calvi.

Dec 31: Brest fleet sails for an Atlantic cruise.

1795

Jan: French conquest of the Netherlands.

Feb 13: Channel Fleet almost wrecked in Torbay.

Mar 13–14: Hotham's action off Cape Noli.

Jun 16: Cornwallis's retreat from Villaret-Joyeuse.

Jun 17: British expedition to aid the French Royalists in the Vendée sails.

Jun 23: Ile de Groix action.

Jul 13: Hotham's second action.

Aug 17: Capture of Malacca.

Aug 23: Directory replaces the Jacobin regime.

Aug 26: Capture of Trincomalee.

Sep 16: Capture of the Cape of Good Hope.

Oct: The 'admirals' mutiny'.

Nov 16: Christian's convoy sails for the West Indies, but is soon blown back by gales.

1796

Jan 29: Christian driven back into port.

Aug 17: Capture of Lucas's Dutch squadron in Saldanha Bay.

Aug 19: Secret Treaty of San Ildefonso between France and Spain.

Oct 5: Spain declares war on Britain. British evacuate Corsica.

Dec 16: Hoche expedition sails from Brest.

Dec 22–29: French fleet in Bantry Bay.

1797

Jan 28: Sercey's squadron is frightened off an East India convoy in the Bali Straits.

Feb 14: Battle of St Vincent.

Feb 18: Surrender of Trinidad.

Feb 22: French landing at Fishguard.

Apr 16: Outbreak of the Spithead mutiny.

Apr 18–30: Failed British assault on San Juan, Puerto Rico.

Jul 4: Boat action off Cadiz.

Jul 22–23: Nelson's unsuccessful attack on Sta Cruz de Tenerife.

Sep 4: Coup d'état of Fructidor forestalls a Royalist seizure of power in France.

Oct 11: Battle of Camperdown.

Oct 17: Peace of Campo Formio; Austria makes peace with France, leaving only Britain of the First Coalition.

1798

Apr: Outbreak of undeclared 'quasi-war' between France and the USA.

May 19: Bonaparte's expedition sails from Toulon.

May 20: British raid on Ostend.

May 26: Outbreak of rebellion in Ireland.

Jun 12: French expedition captures Malta.

Jun 21: Irish rebels defeated at Vinegar Hill.

Jun 28: Nelson reaches Alexandria for the first time.

Jul 1: French begin landing in Egypt.

Aug 1: Battle of the Nile.

Aug 22: General Humbert lands in Mayo.

Sep: Final British evacuation of Saint Domingue.

Nov 14: British capture of Minorca.

Nov 29: The Neapolitan army enters Rome.

1799

Jan 27: Alava is frightened off an East India convoy near Macao.

Mar 19: Bonaparte begins siege of Acre.

Apr 26: Bruix sails from Brest.

May 3: Bruix passes Cadiz without attacking Keith.

May 20: Bonaparte abandons the siege of Acre.

Jun 1: Formation of Second Coalition of Britain, Russia, Austria, Turkey, Portugal and the Two Sicilies against France.

Aug 8: Bruix re-enters Brest with the combined French and Spanish fleets.

Aug 23: Bonaparte sails from Alexandria to return to France.

Aug 27: Anglo-Russian landing in North Holland, and surrender of the Dutch fleet.

Oct 18: Duke of York signs armistice and agrees to evacuate North Holland.

Nov 9: Brumaire Coup: Bonaparte overthrows the Directory and installs himself in power.

1800

Jan 24: Convention of El Arish.
Apr 21: St Vincent takes command of the Channel Fleet.
Jul 25: Arrest of a Danish convoy.
Aug 26: Failed British attack on Ferrol.
Aug 29: British fleet off Copenhagen forces an agreement with Denmark over neutral trade.
Sep 5: French garrison of Valetta surrenders.
Sep 30: Franco-American war is ended.
Dec 16: Formation of second Armed Neutrality.

1801

Jan 1: Act of Union between Britain and Ireland.
Jan 23: Ganteaume sails from Brest.
Feb 9: Peace of Luneville: Austria is driven out of the war.
Mar 8: British landing in Aboukir Bay.
Mar 12: Parker and Nelson sail for the Baltic.
Mar 14: Resignation of Pitt's government.
Mar 21: Battle of Alexandria.
Mar 23: Assassination of Tsar Paul I.
Apr 2: Battle of Copenhagen.
Jul 6: Battle of Algeçiras.
Jul 12: Battle of the Straits.
Aug 15: Nelson's unsuccessful attack on French landing craft off Boulogne.
Oct 1: Preliminaries of Peace of Amiens signed.

1802

Mar 27: Peace of Amiens concluded.

1803

Apr 30: USA purchases Louisiana and New Orleans from France.
May 18: Napoleonic War begins.
Oct 19: Secret Franco-Spanish military alliance.
Dec 2: Establishment of the 'Armée d'Angleterre' at Boulogne.

1804

Jan 7: The British capture the Diamond Rock.
Feb 14: Battle of Pulo Aor.
May 10: Pitt forms a new government.
May 16: Bonaparte declares himself Emperor of the French.
Oct 6: Spanish treasure ships attacked off Cadiz.
Dec 12: Spain declares war on Britain.

1805

Jan 11: Missiessy sails from Rochefort for the West Indies.
Jan 14: Villeneuve sails from Toulon.

Mar 28: Missiessy leaves Martinique to return to France.

Mar 30: Villeneuve sails again from Toulon.

Apr 8: Melville resigns as First Lord of the Admiralty to face impeachment.

Apr 10: Villeneuve and Gravina sail from Cadiz for the West Indies.

Apr 19: British troop convoy sails for the Mediterranean.

May 11: Nelson leaves the Spanish coast in pursuit.

May 16: Villeneuve and Gravina reach Martinique.

Jun 11: Franco-Spanish fleet leaves the West Indies.

Jun 13: Nelson sails in pursuit.

Jul 17: Allemand sails from Rochefort.

Jul 20: Nelson arrives at Gibraltar.

Jul 22: Calder's action.

Aug 3: Napoleon arrives at Boulogne to take command of the invasion of Britain.

Aug 9: Third Coalition of Britain, Russia and Austria is completed.

Aug 11: Villeneuve sails from Ferrol for the Mediterranean.

Aug 21: Combined Fleet enters Cadiz.

Aug 26: The Grande Armée breaks camp at Boulogne and sets out towards the Rhine.

Aug 28: Popham–Baird expedition to the Cape sails from Cork.

Sep 28: Nelson resumes command of the Mediterranean Squadron off Cadiz.

Oct 19: The Combined Fleet sails from Cadiz.

Oct 20: Austrian army surrenders at Ulm.

Oct 21: Battle of Trafalgar.

Nov 4: Strachan's action.

Dec 2: Napoleon defeats Russian-Austrian army at Austerlitz, driving both out of the war.

Dec 13: Leissègues and Willaumez sail from Brest.

1806

Jan 10: Capture of the Cape of Good Hope.

Feb 6: Duckworth's victory off San Domingo.

Feb 11: Ministry of the Talents takes office, following the death of Pitt.

Mar 13: Linois is taken off the Canaries.

Jul 4: Battle of Maida.

Jun 28: Beresford captures Buenos Aires.

Aug 12: Buenos Aires retaken by local forces.

Nov 21: Berlin Decrees.

1807

Feb 3: Auchmuchty captures Montevideo.

Feb 19: Duckworth passes the Dardanelles.

Mar 17: British landing in Egypt.

Mar 24: Fall of the Ministry of the Talents.

Jun 22: *Leopard–Chesapeake* incident.
Jul 7: Whitelocke's attack on Buenos Aires fails disastrously.
Jul 7: Franco-Russian agreement at Tilsit.
Sep 7: British attack on Copenhagen leads to the surrender of the Danish fleet.
Nov 30: The French army occupies Lisbon: the Portuguese fleet and royal family sail for Brazil.
Dec 17: Milan Decrees.
Dec 26: British occupation of Madeira.

1808

May 2: Spanish revolt against French rule.
Aug 1: British troops land on the coast of Portugal.
Aug: La Romana's troops are removed from Denmark.
Aug 21: Wellington defeats Junot at Vimiero.
Aug 25: Anglo-Swedish fleet fights the Russians off Hangö Head.

1809

Jan 16: Battle of Corunna and evacuation of Moore's army.
Feb 24: Surrender of Martinique.
Apr 11: Basque Roads action.
Jul 6: Battle of Wagram.
Jul 13: British capture of Senegal.
Jul 28: Wellesley's victory at Talavera. Walcheren expedition sails.
Sep 26: Collingwood defeats French convoy bound for Barcelona.
Oct 14: Peace of Schönbrunn: Austria driven out of the war.
Nov 13: East India Company forces destroy Ras-al-Khaima.
Nov 19: Spanish defeat at Ocana leads to French conquest of all Andalusia except Cadiz.
Dec 23: Final British evacuation of Walcheren.

1810

Feb 6: Capture of Guadeloupe.
Feb 19: Surrender of Amboyna.
Jul 9: The Netherlands is annexed to the French empire.
Jul 9: Capture of Réunion.
Jul 19: Norwegian ships take a British convoy off the Skaw.
Aug 9: Capture of Banda Neira, Moluccas.
Aug 23: Battle of Grand Port.
Oct 10: French army stopped by the lines of Torres Vedras outside Lisbon.
Nov 17: Sweden declares war on Britain.
Dec 3: Surrender of Mauritius.
Dec 10: France annexes Hamburg, Bremen, Lübeck and Hanover.
Dec 31: Alexander I opens Russian ports to neutral shipping.

1811

Mar 13: Battle of Lissa.
Mar 5: French army retreats from Torres Vedras towards Spain.
Aug 4: British landing on Java.
Sep 18: Surrender of Java.
Dec 24: Loss of the *St George* and *Defence* on the Jutland coast.

1812

Jan 19: Wellington takes Ciudad Rodrigo.
May 11: Murder of Spencer Perceval leads to formation of Lord Liverpool's administration.
Jun 18: USA declares war on Britain.
Jun 24: French army invades Russia.
Aug 12: Wellington enters Madrid.
Aug 16: US army surrenders at Detroit.
Aug 19: USS *Constitution* captures the *Guerrière*.
Sep 7: Battle of Borodino.
Oct 19: Napoleon begins to retreat from Moscow.

1813

Jun 1: *Shannon–Chesapeake* action.
Jun 21: Wellington wins battle of Vitoria, driving French from northern Spain.
Sep 9: San Sebastian surrenders to Wellington.
Sep 10: US victory of Put-In Bay, Lake Erie.
Oct 8: Wellington's army enters France.
Oct 16–19: Battle of Leipzig.
Nov 8: Allied peace terms offering Napoleon his throne and France's 1792 frontiers are rejected.

1814

Mar 30: Allied armies enter Paris.
Apr 11: Abdication of Napoleon.
May 4: Napoleon arrives on Elba.
Aug 24: British capture Washington.
Sep 11: US naval victory of Plattsburg, Lake Champlain.
Nov 1: Opening of the Congress of Vienna.
Dec 24: Treaty of Ghent ends the War of 1812.

1815

Jan 8: Battle of New Orleans.
Mar 1: Napoleon returns to France.
Jun 18: Battle of Waterloo.
Jul 7: Allied armies enter Paris.
Jul 14: Napoleon surrenders to the Royal Navy.
Aug 7: Napoleon sails for St Helena.

Notes

1. Spalding, *Badiley*, pp. 100–119. Elias, *Schetsen* III, 138–46.
2. Spalding, *Badiley*, pp. 199–212. Elias, *Schetsen* VI, 3–12.
3. *FDW* IV, 328–39. Elias, *Schetsen* IV, 166–70.
4. Venning, *Cromwellian Foreign Policy*, pp. 146–7.
5. William Foster, 'The Acquisition of St Helena', *EHR* XXXIV (1919), pp. 281–9.
6. W. E. May, 'The Navy and the Rebellion of the Earl of Argyle', *MM* LVII (1971), pp. 17–23.

SHIPS

In Appendix II of *The Safeguard of the Sea* an attempt was made to list all English royal warships in service between 1509 and 1649, but it is neither possible nor necessary to do the same for the years 1649 to 1815. The ships are far too numerous to list individually, and all the essential information about them is available in reliable reference books.[1] Instead it is possible to provide much better information about the numbers and tonnage of ships of different types available at different dates. By far the most complete and accurate statistics of this nature are those compiled by Professor Jan Glete, with whose generous permission they are reproduced here. These figures he has compiled for all the navies, so that accurate international comparisons are available for the first time. In order to make them, however, he has had to discard the rating systems and tonnage measurements of the day, which varied from time to time and country to country. Instead he has imposed standard measures, based on estimated displacement in metric tons – a measure unknown in the seventeenth and eighteenth centuries, and a system of tonnage measurement used only by some navies. Readers should be aware, therefore, that the tonnage figures in his lists cannot generally be compared with those in contemporary sources. Their great advantage is that they can be compared with each other.

A further caution is necessary. Published and unpublished lists of the size of different navies in this period vary very greatly. Partly this is because historians have not always been sufficiently critical of figures calculated on different bases, or intended to mislead, or affected by administrative practices such as the British 'rebuild' system of the first half of the eighteenth century[2] which had the effect of padding the lists with fictitious ships. More fundamentally, however, there was an intrinsic problem which made it impossible for contemporary naval administrators, however well informed, to predict what proportion of their ships could be made available for service. In all navies the majority of ships were out of commission in peacetime, and their massive hulls easily concealed decay which was not revealed until they were taken in hand to fit out for sea. Mobilization always produced unpleasant (and occasionally pleasant) surprises. Moreover navies naturally tended to fit out first those ships which were in the best condition, and how far down the list they proceeded to repair ships in poorer condition was a function of how urgent was the need, and how much money and manpower happened to be available. No navy ever had all its ships available for service, and the proportion which might be made fit for service was variable and unpredictable. At the height of the Seven Years' War the Royal Navy had three-quarters of its ships at sea or ready for sea, which was probably near the maximum figure which was sustainable for any length of time. A further uncertainty is introduced by the difficulty of classifying old ships reduced to less demanding forms of service such as troopships or hospital ships. At the close of the French Revolutionary War in 1801, for example, the Royal Navy had a notional total of 192 ships of the line, but of these five were serving as troopships, twenty-nine were commissioned only as harbour hulks, a further twenty-nine were in Ordinary (probably too rotten even for harbour service), and eighteen were building – leaving 111 of the line in seagoing commission as such.[3] The following tables give maximum figures including all ships notionally available on the last day of each five-year period. The numbers actually ready for immediate sea service would in all cases have been substantially lower.

In these tables English, later British, ships from 1681 follow the English rating scheme, according to which First to Fourth Rates were reckoned fit to lie in the line of battle. Before 1681 Professor Glete does not attempt to distinguish 'ships of the line', but for the purposes of this table I have arbitrarily included ships of 500 tons displacement and upwards as 'ships of the line' from 1650 to 1680. The small Fourth-Rate fifty-gun two-deckers are included as line-of-battleships up to 1790. English Fifth and Sixth Rates (or ships of below 500 tons up to 1680) are classified in the modern term as 'cruisers'; from the mid-eighteenth century these are the classic frigates. Equivalents in other navies which used different rating schemes are based on basic type (ship of the line or cruiser) and tonnage. In all navies cruisers below 100 tons displacement (to 1680), 300 tons (to 1790) and thereafter 500 tons have been omitted. These 'steps' up in minimum tonnage naturally have the effect of producing equivalent 'steps' down in the total numbers. The 'major fleets' are essentially those most relevant to British policy and strategy, omitting others such as Portugal, Sweden, Algiers and the Ottoman Empire which were numerically significant. The US Navy's strength was sixteen cruisers in 1800, eleven in 1805, nine in 1810 and seven (plus three ships of the line) in 1815. Ships on the Great Lakes are not included in either British or US strength.

Numbers of Major Fleets, 1650–1815

	Ships of the Line				Cruisers			
Year	England	France	Netherlands / Spain[4]	Denmark / Russia[5]	England	France	Netherlands / Spain	Denmark / Russia
1650	46	18	21	23	26	14	41	20
1655	82	17	67	19	51	6	34	9
1660	76	21	64	14	55	5	33	2
1665	90	32	79	22	53	15	36	6
1670	69	84	95	27	35	36	34	10
1675	73	102	80	24	37	32	30	10
1680	95	89	62	33	20[6]	28	23	11

	Ships of the Line						Cruisers					
	England	France	Netherlands	Spain⁴	Denmark	Russia⁵	England	France	Netherlands	Spain	Denmark	Russia
Year	*England* *France*		*Netherlands* *Spain⁴*		*Denmark* *Russia⁵*		*England* *France*		*Netherlands* *Spain*		*Denmark* *Russia*	
1685	98	94	72		33		20	29	23		11	
1690	83	89	52		27		26	32	21		11	
1695	112	119	72		27		46	30	42		10	
1700	127	108	83		32		49	31	29		10	
1705	122	105	79		36	0	66	32	28		11	3
1710	123	94	86		39	4	57	24	33		13	6
1715	119	62	71	9	36	28	63	12	24	13	15	8
1720	102	27	56	11	24	33	52	6	18	15	16	11
1725	106	39	44	16	25	35	46	6	20	11	13	10
1730	105	38	38	39	25	38	45	7	18	11	9	10
1735	107	43	42	44	28	34	43	7	25	13	9	10
1740	101	47	35	43	26	20	43	7	24	12	7	9
1745	104	45	33	31	28	28	67	23	27	6	8	6
1750	115	45	34	15	30	32	79	21	20	5	12	8
1755	117	57	29	39	28	27	74	31	25	22	9	8
1760	135	54	28	49	30	24	115	27	29	23	12	4
1765	139	59	30	41	31	22	91	23	29	16	12	8
1770	126	68	31	55	31	27	76	35	44	21	14	10
1775	117	59	26	64	33	34+0	82	37	38	28	15	14+6
1780	117	70	26	59	34	31+0	111	58	40	34	16	14+10
1785	137	62	47	61	32	44+3	133	57	38	37	18	23+12
1790	145[7]	73	48	72	32	51+7	131	64	36	46	16	30+22
1795	123	56	28	76	30	50+11	160	65	30	51	13	27+13
1800	127	44	16	66	28	54+13	158	43	6	41	9	24+10
1805	136	41	15	40	20	35+12	160	35	10	26	11	10+6
1810	152	46	13[8]	28	2	33[9]+10	183	31	7	17	0	10+4
1815	126	52	19	16	2	33+15	151	31	14	15	3	13+8

Source: Glete, *Navies and Nations* II, 522–675

Notes

1. Colledge, *Ships of the Royal Navy* and Lyon, *Sailing Navy List.*
2. Explained in Ch. 27.
3. Schomberg, *Chronology* IV, 109.
4. No figures available before 1715.
5. Baltic fleet (from 1705) + Black Sea fleet (from 1775). I have omitted the Sea of Azov fleet, 1696–1727.

6. An apparent fall caused by some ships of over 100 tons being too small for the new Sixth Rate.

7. Including fifteen fifties which hereafter are treated as crusiers.

8. In July 1810 the French satellite Kingdom of the Netherlands was suppressed and its navy incorporated with that of France.

9. Or twenty-five excluding Senyavin's squadron interned under British control.

FLEETS

The figures provided in Appendix II permit direct comparison of the strength of different navies, but for the reasons explained there, they exaggerate the forces actually available for sea service. To give a realistic impression of the forces which were deployed at different times requires a series of 'snap-shots' taken at different dates.

1654,[1] Preparing for War with Spain

'General Blake's Squadron': 29 ships (1×60 guns, 2×54, 3×50, 1×46, 2×40, 6×36, 1×34, 1×32, 1×30, 1×24, 2×22, 3×16, 1×14, 1×12, 1×10, 2 pinnaces).

'General Penn's Squadron': 38 ships (1×60, 4×54, 3×44, 3×40, 1×36, 5×30, 2×28, 5×24, 7×20, 3×18, 2×12).

Guards and Convoys: Bristol 1 (36); to Morlaix 1 (40); 'at the colliery' 1 (14); Downs 3 (48, 44, 14); between Rame Head and Cork 3 (2×36, 1×34); between Isle de Batz and Ushant 4 (1×36, 2×34, 1×32); off Cape de la Hague and Cape Barfleur 2 (2×48); convoy to Hamburg 1 (22); Newfoundland 4 (36, 32, 28, 22); mouth of the Channel 2 (34, 32); Ireland 8 (32, 22, 2×20, 18, 12, 10, 8); Scotland 9 (29, 28, 4×22, 12, 10, 1 unknown); New England 3 (50, 2 unknown); Weymouth 1 (46); herring fishery 1 (22); Jersey 1 (32); 'coming into the River' 2 (36, 26); Newcastle 3 (30, 26, 24); Severn 2 (26, 12); Harwich 1 (36); Portsmouth 6 (50, 40, 2×36, 30, 22); Scillies 2 (10, 6), Hope 2 (36, 38), Chatham 13 (100, 80, 2×52, 2×50, 2×36, 34, 2×28, 27, 1 pinnace); Woolwich 3 (70, 42, 12); Deptford 4 (30, 16, 14, 1 shallop).

[Charles Dalton, 'The Navy under Cromwell: Its Strength and Cost, 1654', *JRUSI* XLIV (1900), pp. 1181–6].

June 1666, Four Days' Battle

Rates	1st	2nd	3rd	4th	5th	6th	Merchant	Fireships
Main Fleet, White (Ayscue)								
Van (Berkeley)		1	1	3			2	
Centre	1	1	2	3	1			1
Rear (Harman)		2	1	2				
Red (Albemarle)								
Van (Jordan)		2	2	2				1

Rates	1st	2nd	3rd	4th	5th	6th	Merchant	Fireships
Centre	1		1	3	1			
Rear (Holmes)		1	2	4				1
Blue (Smith, absent)								
Van (Teddeman)		2	1	2			1	
Centre		1	1	3				1
Rear (Utber)		1	2	1			2	
Joined 3–4 June				5				1
Detached (Prince Rupert)								
Van (Myngs)		1	1	5				
Centre	1		2	4				4
Rear (Spragge)			2	4				
Thames and Medway	1	1	3	7	1		12	3
Portsmouth			2	5				
Plymouth and thereabouts			1	4	11			
Other home waters				3	10			1
Convoy to Barbados				1	1			

Source: Fox, *Distant Storm*, pp. 370–4.

1 July 1690, War with France

Rates	1st	2nd	3rd	4th	5th	6th	Fireships	Others
Main Fleet (Torrington)	2	6	25	7	2	4	17	3
[Mostly in the Downs, but many smaller detached on convoys or cleaning]								
Irish Sea (Shovell)				3	3	8		
Convoys and cruisers, guardships and refitting				18	7	16		2
Mediterranean (Killigrew)		1	4	7	1	2	1	1
West Indies (Wright)			1	9	2	1	2	
Jamaica						1		
New England					1			
Virginia						1		

Source: PRO: ADM 8/2.

July 1696, War with France

Rates	1st	2nd	3rd	4th	5th	6th	Fireships	Others
Main Fleet (Berkeley)	6	8	19	3		6	7	
Cruising in Soundings (Nevill)			4	1			1	
Channel (Benbow)			2	5	3	1	2	
Other cruisers			2	5	3	4		
Home convoys			6	4	8	5	1	
Fishery protection					1	4		
Refitting, cleaning, guard-ships, in port			2	3	8	7	4	
East Indies				5		2	1	
Hudson's Bay				1		1		
Convoys to:								
Iceland				1			1	
Portugal				1	1			
Leeward Ids				1		1		
Spain				1				
Virginia				3	2		1	
Barbados				1	1			
Jamaica				2				
New England					1	1		
Canaries					1		1	
Newfoundland					1			
New England				1				
Mediterranean		1	7	1	1			
West Indies				3	4	2		

[12 yachts, 3 ketches, 6 storeships, 4 hospital ships, 18 bombs; all in home waters or with main fleet]

Source: PRO: ADM 8/4.

June 1707, War with France

Rates	1st	2nd	3rd	4th	5th	6th	Fireships	Others
Mediterranean (Shovell)	1	2	22	9	4	4	4	12
Convoy to Lisbon and then to cruise in Soundings (Hardy)			6	5	3			
Off Dunkirk (Whetstone)				9	1			
Home ports, local convoys and patrols	1	2	5	9	16	14	2	21

Rates	1st	2nd	3rd	4th	5th	6th	Fireships	Others
'Going on Foreign Service'								
Archangel				2	1			
New England				1				
Virginia				2				
Leeward Ids					1	1		
Newfoundland				1		1		
Jamaica							1	
Jamaica (Wager) to relieve:			1	3	2			
Jamaica (Kerr)			1	3	1	1		3
Barbados, to relieve				1	1	1		
Barbados, to be relieved				2		1		
Newfoundland				2	1	1		
Leeward Islands, to relieve				1	1	1		
Leeward Islands, to be relieved					2	1		
St Helena and the Cape				3				
Smyrna and Scanderoon			1	3				
New England				1	1			
New York					1	1		

Source: PRO: ADM 8/10.

July 1727, Naval Deterrence

Rates	1st	2nd	3rd	4th	5th	6th	Others
Plantations (Hosier)			3	8	1	2	2
Barbados					1		
Leewards Islands					1		
Virginia					1		
Carolina						1	1
New York						1	
New England						1	
Newfoundland				1	1		
Ordered to West Indies					1		3
Coast of Spain (Wager)			7	7		2	6
Baltic (Norris)			12	3		1	5
Ireland						2	1
Home waters and ports			1	5	3	3	12

Source: PRO: ADM 8/16.

July 1731, Tension with Spain

Rates	2nd	3rd	4th	5th	6th	Sloops	Yachts
Plantations etc.			1	3	12	4	
Mediterranean			1	1	3	1	
'Designed for the Mediterranean'	1	6	5	1			
Ordered home				2	5		
Newfoundland			1		2		
Ireland					1		1
Home service		3	4	4	4	9	7
Fitting out as guardships		3	1				
Total	1	12	13	12	27	14	8

Source: *BND* No. 210, pp. 364–5.

January 1741, War with Spain

Rates	1st	2nd	3rd	4th	5th	6th	Sloops	Others
At Home	3	6	10	15	4	15	10	15
West Indies (Vernon and Ogle)			15	19	3	6	3	14
Mediterranean (Haddock)			3	7		4		4
Convoys				2	3	3		
South Seas (Anson)				3	1	1	1	
North America				1	1	4	1	
Africa				1				
Total in commission	3	6	28	48	12	33	15	33
Ordinary and building	4	7	13	14	11	2	3	1
Grand Total	7	13	41	62	23	35	18	34

Source: Schomberg, *Chronology* IV, 17–25.

July 1757, Seven Years' War

Rates	1st	2nd	3rd	4th	5th	6th	Sloops	Others
East Indies			4	4		3	1	
Plantations		1	11	17	6	14	10	4
Mediterranean		2	7	5	2	3	2	

Rates	1st	2nd	3rd	4th	5th	6th	Sloops	Others
Convoys and cruisers	2	1	5	12	4	22	29	13
At home	1	8	11	6	3	5	1	20
Total	3	12	38	44	15	47	43	37

Source: *BND* No. 222, pp. 383–4.

1778, American War

Rates	1st	2nd	3rd	4th	5th	6th	Sloops	Others
At home		7	38	5	7	5	14	18
East Indies (Vernon)			1		2	3		
Africa				1				
Leeward Islands (Young)			1		3			
Jamaica (Gayton)			1		4	1		
Mediterranean (Mann)			1	1	2	2		
North America (Howe)			6	5	18	25	16	13
Newfoundland (Montagu)			1	1		3	5	7
In commission		7	45	15	27	44	41	38
Ordinary	3	2	37	9	11	8	6	
Building	1	4	5	3	3	1	2	
Grand Total	4	11	87	27	41	53	49	38

Source: Schomberg, *Chronology* IV, 54–62.

May 1804, Invasion Threat

	Ships of the line	Fifties	Frigates	Sloops	Bombs	Gunbrigs	Gunboats	Cutter and schooners	Armed ships
Channel Fleet									
(Cornwallis)	33		11	2				10	
Off Brest	20		5	1				5	
Off Rochefort	5		1					1	
Off Ferrol	7		2	1				1	
Ireland									
(Gardner)			6	5				6	

	Ships of the line	Fifties	Frigates	Sloops	Bombs	Gunbrigs	Gunboats	Cutter and schooners	Armed ships
Mediterranean (Nelson)	13	1	11	10	3		6	2	
Off Toulon	12		6						
Cruising and detached	1	1	5	10	3		6	2	
Convoys to and from St Helena	2		1						
East Indies (Rainier)	6	2	7	5					
with the admiral	6	1		1					
cruising		1	7	4					
Jamaica (Duckworth)	6		7	11				7	
Leeward Ids (Hood)	2	1	4	9				8	
North America (Mitchell)		1	2	2					
Newfoundland (Gambier)		1	3	1				3	
North Sea (Keith)	21	6	29	26	12	25		32	19
Off the Texel (Thornborough)	8		2	1		1		3	
Off Heligoland			1	1		1			
Off Helvoetsluis			2					2	
Hollesley Bay	1					6			
Off Flushing (Smith)		1	2	3				2	
Yarmouth (Russell) and Scotland (Vashon)	1	1	1			4		3	7
Humber	1		1						
'Stationary but ready'	4	2	5			3			

	Ships of the line	Fifties	Frigates	Sloops	Bombs	Gunbrigs	Gunboats	Cutter and schooners	Armed ships
Off Boulogne (Louis)		1	5	3	7	3		4	
Dungeness and Downs	5	1	4	4	4	6		5	
Cruising and convoys			4	8		1		4	3
In port and fitting	1			2	1			6	9
Off Le Havre			2	3				3	
Jersey and Guernsey (Saumarez)		1	7	4		4		9	
Fitting out, convoys, other	5		37	17	3	11		5	22
Total in commission	88	13	125	92	18	40	6	82	41

Source: *SVL* II, 552.

Note

1. Probably in the summer, when the Dutch War had ended but Blake was preparing to sail for the Mediterranean and Penn for the West Indies. I have silently corrected some obvious misreadings of proper names, which do not inspire confidence in the accuracy of the figures.

RATES OF PAY

The 1647 wage scale[1] was slightly adjusted in 1649 by the issue of permissible, but not obligatory 'rewards'.

1649 Scale of Sea Pay

By the 28-day month[2]	1st Rates £ s d	2nd Rates £ s d	3rd Rates £ s d	4th Rates £ s d	5th Rates £ s d	6th Rates £ s d
Captain	21 0 0	16 16 0	14 0 0	10 10 0	8 8 0	7 0 0
Lieutenant	4 4 0	4 4 0	3 10 0	–	–	–
Master	7 0 0	6 6 0	4 13 4	4 4 0	3 14 8	Captain acts
Master's Mate or Pilot	3 5 4	2 16 0	2 16 0	2 6 8	2 2 0	2 2 0
Boatswain	3 10 0	2 16 0	2 9 0	2 4 4	2 2 0	1 12 8
Master Carpenter	3 3 0	3 3 0	2 6 8	1 19 8	1 19 8	1 15 0
Master Gunner	3 3 0	3 3 0	2 6 8	1 19 8	1 19 8	1 15 0
Boatswain's Mate	1 10 4	1 10 4	1 10 4	1 8 0	1 8 0	1 8 0
Carpenter's Mate	1 8 0	1 8 0	1 8 0	1 5 8	1 5 8	1 5 8
Gunner's Mate	1 8 0	1 8 0	1 5 8	1 5 8	1 5 8	1 3 4
Quartermaster	1 15 0	1 8 0	1 8 0	1 8 0	1 8 0	1 8 0
Quartermaster's Mate	1 8 0	1 5 8	1 5 8	1 5 8	1 5 8	1 5 8
Quarter Gunner	1 3 4	1 1 0	1 1 0	1 1 0	1 1 0	1 1 0
Seaman	0 19 0	0 19 0	0 19 0	0 19 0	0 19 0	0 19 0

Sources: *CJ* VI, 173 and BL: Add. MSS 18772 f. 12v. Both give rates by the day, which I have converted.

The shock of the defeat at Dungeness produced substantial increases in 1653, together with an allowance in lieu of prize-money of 10s a ton and £6 13s 4d for every carriage gun for every prize, or £10 a gun for men-of-war sunk or destroyed, 'to be shared and divided amongst them proportionably according to their respective places and offices'.[3]

1653 Scale of Sea Pay

By the 28-day month	1st Rates £ s d	2nd Rates £ s d	3rd Rates £ s d	4th Rates £ s d	5th Rates £ s d	6th Rates £ s d
Captain	21 0 0	16 16 0	14 0 0	10 10 0	8 8 0	7 0 0
Lieutenant	4 4 0	4 4 0	3 10 0	3 10 0	–	–
Master	7 0 0	6 6 0	4 13 8	4 6 2	3 17 6	Captain acts
Master's Mate or Pilot	3 6 0	3 0 0	2 16 2	2 7 10	2 2 0	2 2 0
Midshipman	2 5 0	2 0 0	1 17 6	1 13 9	1 10 0	1 10 0
Boatswain	4 0 0	3 10 0	3 0 0	2 10 0	2 5 0	2 0 0
Carpenter	4 0 0	3 10 0	3 0 0	2 10 0	2 5 0	2 0 0
Gunner	4 0 0	3 10 0	3 0 0	2 10 0	2 5 0	2 0 0
Purser and Clerk of the Cheque	4 0 0	3 10 0	3 0 0	2 10 0	2 5 0	2 0 0
Surgeon	2 10 0	2 10 0	2 10 0	2 10 0	2 10 0	2 10 0
Steward	2 0 0	1 16 8	1 10 0	1 10 0	1 6 8	1 5 0
Cook	1 5 0	1 5 0	1 5 0	1 5 0	1 5 0	1 4 0
Boatswain's Mate	1 15 0	1 15 0	1 12 0	1 10 0	1 8 0	1 6 0
Carpenter's Mate	2 0 0	2 0 0	1 16 0	1 14 8	1 12 0	1 10 0
Gunner's Mate	1 15 0	1 15 0	1 12 0	1 10 0	1 8 0	1 6 0
Quartermaster	1 15 0	1 15 0	1 12 0	1 10 0	1 8 0	1 6 0
Master Trumpeter	1 10 0	1 8 0	1 5 0	1 5 0	1 5 0	1 4 0
Other Trumpeters	1 4 0	1 4 0	–	–	–	–
Quartermaster's Mate	1 10 0	1 10 0	1 8 0	1 8 0	1 6 0	1 5 0
Surgeon's Mate	1 10 0	1 10 0	1 10 0	1 10 0	1 10 0	1 10 0
Corporal	1 15 0	1 12 0	1 10 0	1 10 0	1 8 0	1 5 0
Yeoman of the Jeers, Sheets, Halliards and Tacks	1 12 0	1 10 0	1 8 0	1 8 0	–	–
Coxswain	1 12 0	1 10 0	1 8 0	1 8 0	1 6 0	–
Carpenter's Crew	1 6 0	1 6 0	1 5 0	1 5 0	1 5 0	1 5 0
Quartermaster's Gunner	1 6 0	1 6 0	1 5 0	1 5 0	1 5 0	1 5 0
Armourer	1 5 0	1 5 0	1 5 0	1 5 0	–	–
Gunsmith	1 5 0	1 5 0	–	–	–	–
Yeoman of the Powder Room	1 2 4	[same in all rates; also Steward's Mate, Cook's Mate, Coxswain's Mate, Swabber, Cooper]				
Able Seaman	1 4 0	[same in all rates]				
Ordinary Seaman	0 19 0	[same in all rates]				
Grommet	0 14 3	[same in all rates]				
Boy	0 9 6	[same in all rates]				

Source: *FDW* III, 274, 285 and 319.[4]

1686 Establishment of Sea Pay and Complement

By the 28-day month	1st Rates		2nd Rates		3rd Rates		4th Rates		5th Rates		6th Rates		Lg. Yachts		Sm. Yachts and Sloops	
	No	£ s d	No	£ s d	No	£ s d	No	£ s d	No	£ s d	No	£ s d	No	£ s d	No	£ s d
Captain[6]	1	21 0 0	1	16 16 0	1	14 0 0	1	10 10 0	1	8 8 0	1	7 0 0	1	7 0 0	1	7 0 0
Lieutenants	3	4 4 0	3	4 4 0	2	3 10 0	2	3 10 0	1	3 10 0	1	2 16 6		–		–
Master	1	7 0 0	1	6 6 0	1	4 13 8	1	4 6 2	1	3 17 6		Captain acts				
Boatswain	1	4 0 0	1	3 10 0	1	3 0 0	1	2 10 0	1	2 5 0	1	2 0 0	1	2 0 0	1	2 0 0
Gunner	1	4 0 0	1	3 10 0	1	3 0 0	1	2 10 0	1	2 5 0	1	2 0 0	1	2 0 0		Boatswain acts
Purser	1	4 0 0	1	3 10 0	1	3 0 0	1	2 10 0	1	2 5 0		Captain acts				
Carpenter	1	4 0 0	1	3 10 0	1	3 0 0	1	2 10 0	1	2 5 0	1	2 0 0	1	2 0 0	1	2 0 0
Cook	1	1 5 0	1	1 5 0	1	1 5 0	1	1 5 0	1	1 5 0	1	1 4 0	1	1 4 0	1	1 4 0
Mates and Pilots	6	3 6 0	5	3 0 0	3	2 16 2	2	2 7 10	2	2 2 0	1	2 2 0	1	2 2 0	1	2 2 0
Surgeon	1	2 10 0	1	2 10 0	1	2 10 0	1	2 10 0	1	2 10 0	1	2 10 0	1	2 10 0		–
Midshipmen	18	2 5 0	14	2 0 0	10	1 17 6	7	1 13 9	3	1 10 0	2	1 10 0	1	1 10 0		–
Yeomen of the Powder Room	2	2 5 0	2	2 0 0	2	1 17 6	1	1 13 9	1	1 10 0	1	1 10 0		–		–
Carpenter's Mates	2	2 0 0	2	2 0 0	1	1 16 0	1	1 14 0	1	1 12 0	1	1 10 0		–		–
Quartermasters	8	1 15 0	6	1 15 0	4	1 12 0	4	1 10 0	2	1 8 0	1	1 6 0	1	1 6 0		–
Boatswain's Mates	2	1 15 0	2	1 15 0	1	1 12 0	1	1 10 0	1	1 8 0	1	1 6 0		–		–
Corporal	1	1 15 0	1	1 12 0	1	1 10 0	1	1 10 0	1	1 8 0	1	1 6 0		–		–
Yeomen of the Sheets	4	1 12 0	4	1 10 0	2	1 8 0	2	1 8 0	1	1 6 0		–		–		–

By the 28-day month	1st Rates		2nd Rates		3rd Rates		4th Rates		5th Rates		6th Rates		Lg. Yachts		Sm. Yachts and Sloops	
	No	£ s d	No	£ s d	No	£ s d	No	£ s d	No	£ s d	No	£ s d	No	£ s d	No	£ s d
Coxswain	1	1 12 0	1	1 10 0	1	1 8 0	1	1 8 0	1	1 6 0	–	–	–	–	–	–
Coxswain's Mate	1	1 4 0	1	1 4 0	1	1 4 0	1	1 4 0	1	1 4 0	–	–	–	–	–	–
Quartermaster's Mates	4	1 0 0	4	1 0 0	4	1 8 0	2	1 8 0	1	1 6 0	1	1 5 0	–	–	–	–
Surgeon's Mates	2	1 0 0	2	1 0 0	1	1 0 0	1	1 0 0	1	1 0 0	1	1 0 0	–	–	–	–
Master Trumpeter	1	1 0 0	1	1 8 0	1	1 5 0	1	1 5 0	1	1 5 0	1	1 4 0	–	–	–	–
Ordinary Trumpeters	5	1 4 0	5	1 4 0	5	1 4 0	5	1 4 0	–	–	–	–	–	–	–	–
Quarter-Gunners	8	1 6 0	6	1 6 0	4	1 5 0	4	1 5 0	2	1 5 0	1	1 5 0	–	–	–	–
Ordinary Carpenters	10	1 6 0	8	1 6 0	6	1 5 0	4	1 5 0	2	1 5 0	1	1 5 0	–	–	–	–
Steward	1	1 5 0	1	1 5 0	1	1 5 0	1	1 3 4	1	1 0 8	1	1 0 0	1	1 0 0	–	–
Armourer	1	1 5 0	1	1 5 0	1	1 5 0	1	1 5 0	1	1 4 0	1	1 4 0	–	–	–	–
Gunsmith	1	1 5 0	1	1 5 0	–	–	–	–	–	–	–	–	–	–	–	–
Steward's Mate	1	1 0 8	1	1 0 8	1	1 0 8	1	1 0 8	–	–	–	–	–	–	–	–
Gunner's Mates	2	1 15 0	2	1 15 0	1	1 2 0	1	1 0 0	1	1 8 0	1	1 6 0	–	–	–	–
Captain's Clerk	1	2 5 0	1	2 0 0	1	1 7 6	1	1 3 9	1	1 0 0	1	1 0 0	1	1 10 0	–	–
Sailmaker	1	1 8 0	1	1 8 0	1	1 8 0	1	1 8 0	1	1 8 0	1	1 8 0	–	–	–	–
Able Seamen		1 4 0	[same in all rates; also Cook's Mate, Cooper, Swabber]														
Ordinary Seamen		0 19 0	[same in all rates; also Barber]														
Grommets		0 14 3	[same in all rates]														
Boys		0 9 6	[same in all rates]														

Source: Tanner, 'Administration' XIV, 274.

The 1653 wage-scale remained substantially in force for the rest of the century. In 1666 wages for flag-officers were established as 50s and 40s a day for the vice-admiral and rear-admiral 'of the Fleet' (meaning the full admirals commanding the Van and Rear Squadrons), with 30s and 20s respectively for vice-admirals and rear-admirals 'of a squadron'. These translate into £70 or £56 a month for a full admiral, £42 for a vice-admiral, and £28 for a rear-admiral. At the same date the lower scale of harbour or 'rigging' wages was promulgated. Such scales continued to be issued until 1728.[5]

In 1686 a new Establishment was promulgated, which laid down the numbers of officers and petty officers for each rate, as well as making some variations in wage rates.

In February 1694 the new government, no doubt anxious to buy the loyalty of those who had so recently served James II, ordered the sea pay of flag-officers, captains, lieutenants, masters and surgeons to be doubled (though at the same time the number of servants allowed to captains and admirals was reduced).[7] In 1700 almost half this increase was removed (except from surgeons and their mates), but the number of servants was again increased. From this date the Admiral of the Fleet was allowed fifty servants, an admiral thirty, vice-admiral twenty and rear-admiral fifteen. A captain was allowed four for every hundred men of the ship's company, boatswains, gunners and carpenters two each, and all other officers down to the cook one each.[8] The masters took their servants' wages, less whatever allowance they chose to give the boys. This more than doubled a captain's pay, at least in wartime, with a full complement and every servant's berth filled.[9]

1700 Establishment of Sea Pay

By the day		
'Admiral and Commander-in-Chief'	£5 0s 0d	[i.e. Admiral of the Fleet]
Admiral	£3 10s 0d	
Vice-Admiral	£2 10s 0d	
Rear-Admiral	£1 15s 0d	[Also Commander-in-Chief's First Captain]
Physician	£1 0s 0d	[when afloat; shore appointments £200 p.a.]

By the year		
Admiral of the Fleet's Secretary	£300	[All secretaries' pay to cover under-clerks, writers etc.]
Admiral's Secretary	£200	[when commander-in-chief]
Vice- and Rear-Admiral's Secretary	£150	[when commander-in-chief]

Commodore's Secretary	£100	[when commander-in-chief]
Admiral's Secretary	£100	[when not commander-in-chief]
Vice- and Rear- Admiral's Secretary	£50	[when not commander-in-chief]

By the 28-day month	1st Rates			2nd Rates			3rd Rates			4th Rates			5th Rates			6th Rates & smaller		
	£	s	d	£	s	d	£	s	d	£	s	d	£	s	d	£	s	d
Captain[10]	28	0	0	22	8	0	18	18	0	14	0	0	11	4	0	8	8	0
Lieutenant	7	0	0	7	0	0	5	12	0	5	12	0	5	12	0	5	12	0
Master	9	2	0	8	8	0	6	6	0	5	12	0	5	2	8	4	0	0
Boatswain	4	0	0	3	10	0	3	0	0	2	10	0	2	5	0	2	0	0
Gunner	4	0	0	3	10	0	3	0	0	2	10	0	2	5	0	2	0	0
Carpenter	4	0	0	3	10	0	3	0	0	2	10	0	2	5	0	2	0	0
Surgeon	5	0	0	[same in all rates; plus 2d a head of the whole ship's company]														
Purser	4	0	0	3	10	0	3	0	0	2	10	0	2	5	0	2	0	0
Second Masters and Pilots[11]	3	10	0	[same in all rates]														
Master's Mates	3	6	0	3	0	0	2	16	2	2	7	10	2	2	0	2	2	0
Surgeon's 1st Mates	2	10	0	[same in all rates]														
Midshipmen	2	5	0	2	0	0	1	17	6	1	13	9	1	10	0	1	10	0
Master at Arms	2	5	0	2	0	0	1	17	6	1	13	9	1	10	0	1	10	0
Schoolmaster[12]	–			–			1	17	6	1	13	9	1	10	0	–		
Captain's Clerk	2	5	0	2	0	0	1	17	6	1	13	9	1	10	0	1	10	0
Surgeon's 2nd Mates	2	0	0	[same in all rates]														
Carpenter's Mates	2	0	0	2	0	0	1	16	0	1	14	0	1	12	0	1	10	0
Sailmaker	1	15	0	1	15	0	1	15	0	1	14	0	1	12	0	1	10	0
Quartermasters	1	15	0	1	15	0	1	12	0	1	10	0	1	8	0	1	6	0
Boatswain's Mates	1	15	0	1	15	0	1	12	0	1	10	0	1	8	0	1	6	0
Gunner's Mates	1	15	0	1	15	0	1	12	0	1	10	0	1	8	0	1	6	0
Yeomen of the Powder Room	1	15	0	1	15	0	1	12	0	1	10	0	1	8	0	1	6	0
Corporal	1	15	0	1	12	0	1	10	0	1	10	0	1	8	0	1	6	0
Yeomen of the Sheets	1	12	0	1	10	0	1	8	0	1	8	0	1	6	0	1	6	0
Coxswain	1	12	0	1	10	0	1	8	0	1	8	0	1	6	0	1	6	0
Quartermaster's Mates	1	10	0	1	10	0	1	8	0	1	8	0	1	6	0	1	5	0
Surgeon's 3rd–5th Mates	1	10	0	1	10	0	1	10	0	–			–			–		
Trumpeter	1	10	0	1	8	0	1	5	0	1	5	0	1	5	0	1	4	0
Sailmaker's Mates	1	8	0	[same in all rates]														
Quarter-Gunners	1	6	0	1	6	0	1	5	0	1	5	0	1	5	0	1	5	0
Carpenter's Crew	1	6	0	1	6	0	1	5	0	1	5	0	1	5	0	1	5	0

By the 28-day month	1st Rates £ s d	2nd Rates £ s d	3rd Rates £ s d	4th Rates £ s d	5th Rates £ s d	6th Rates & smaller £ s d
Steward	1 5 8	1 5 0	1 5 0	1 5 0	1 5 0	1 5 0
Armourer	1 5 0	[same in all rates]				
Sailmaker's Crew	1 5 0	[same in all rates]				
Gunsmith	1 5 0	1 5 0	–	–	–	–
Cook	1 5 0	1 5 0	1 5 0	1 5 0	1 5 0	1 4 0
Steward's Mate	1 0 8	1 0 8	1 0 8	1 0 8	–	–
Able Seamen	1 4 0	[same in all rates]				

[Also Midshipmen Ordinary, Cook's Mate, Coxswain's Mate, Yeoman of the Boatswain's Store, Swabbers, Coopers, Captain's Cook]

Ordinary Seamen	0 19 0	[same in all rates]				

[Also Shifter, Barber, Gunner's Tailor]

Chaplain	0 19 0	[same in all rates; plus 4d a head of the whole ship's company]				
Landmen and Servants	0 18 0	[same in all rates]				

These are gross rates, from which 1s 6d was deducted from all ranks and ratings (6d for the Chatham Chest, 4d for the chaplain, 2d for the surgeon; and from 1696 6d for Greenwich Hospital). From 1732 commissioned officers also paid 3d a month to the Charity for the Relief of Sea Officers' Widows.

Sources: Merriman, *Sergison Papers*, pp. 207–8; and *Queen Anne's Navy*, pp. 313–14. *History of the Russian Fleet under Peter the Great . . .* ed. Cyprian A. G. Bridge (NRS Vol. 15, 1899), pp. 149–53.

The 1700 pay-scale remained in force with minor variations for almost the whole of the century. When servants were abolished in 1794 officers' pay was increased by £11 8s a year for each servant forgone.[13] Early in 1797 lieutenants' pay was increased to a flat rate of £7 a month in all rates of ship (plus compensation for a servant).[14] This increase was one of the triggers for the great mutiny, which gained a general increase in ratings' (but not officers') pay of 5s 6d a month for petty officers and able seamen, 4s 6d for ordinary seamen, and 3s 6d for landmen. The new rates were as follows:

1797 Scale of Sea Pay

By the 28-day month	1st Rates £ s d	2nd Rates £ s d	3rd Rates £ s d	4th Rates £ s d	5th Rates £ s d	6th Rates & smaller £ s d
Master's Mates	3 11 6	3 5 6	3 1 8	2 13 4	2 7 6	2 7 6
Surgeon's 1st Mates	2 15 6	[same in all rates]				
Midshipmen	2 10 6	2 5 6	2 3 0	1 19 3	1 15 6	1 15 6
Master at Arms	2 10 6	2 5 6	2 3 0	1 19 3	1 15 6	1 15 6
Schoolmaster[15]	–	–	2 3 0	1 19 3	1 15 6	–

By the 28-day month	1st Rates £ s d	2nd Rates £ s d	3rd Rates £ s d	4th Rates £ s d	5th Rates £ s d	6th Rates & smaller £ s d
Captain's Clerk	2 10 6	2 5 6	2 3 0	1 19 3	1 15 6	1 15 6
Surgeon's 2nd Mates	2 5 6	[same in all rates]				
Carpenter's Mates and Caulkers	2 5 6	2 5 6	2 1 6	1 19 6	1 17 6	1 15 6
Sailmaker	2 0 6	2 0 6	2 0 6	1 19 6	1 17 6	1 15 6
Quartermasters	2 0 6	2 0 6	1 17 6	1 15 6	1 13 6	1 11 6
Boatswain's Mates and Sailmaker	2 0 6	2 0 6	1 17 6	1 15 6	1 13 6	1 11 6
Gunner's Mates	2 0 6	2 0 6	1 17 6	1 15 6	1 13 6	1 11 6
Yeomen of the Powder Room	2 0 6	2 0 6	1 17 6	1 15 6	1 13 6	1 11 6
Corporal	2 0 6	2 0 6	1 17 6	1 15 6	1 13 6	1 11 6
Yeomen of the Sheets	1 17 6	1 15 6	1 13 6	1 13 6	1 11 6	1 11 6
Coxswain	1 17 6	1 15 6	1 13 6	1 13 6	1 11 6	1 11 6
Quartermaster's Mates	1 17 6	1 15 6	1 13 6	1 13 6	1 11 6	1 11 6
Surgeon's 3rd–5th Mates	1 15 6	1 15 6	1 15 6	–	–	–
Sailmaker's Mates	1 13 6	[same in all rates]				
Quarter-Gunners	1 11 6	1 11 6	1 10 6	1 10 6	1 10 6	1 10 6
Carpenter's Crew	1 11 6	1 11 6	1 10 6	1 10 6	1 10 6	1 10 6
Steward	1 11 2	1 10 6	1 10 6	1 10 6	1 10 6	1 10 6
Armourer	1 10 6	[same in all rates]				
Sailmaker's Crew	1 10 6	[same in all rates]				
Gunsmith	1 10 6	1 10 6	–	–	–	–
Cook	1 10 6	1 10 6	1 10 6	1 10 6	1 10 6	1 9 6
Steward's Mate	1 6 2	1 6 2	1 6 2	1 6 2	–	–
Able Seamen	1 9 6	[same in all rates]				
Ordinary Seamen	1 3 6	[same in all rates]				
Landmen	1 1 6	[same in all rates]				

Source: PRO: ADM 7/678 No. 23.

The pay of the standing warrant officers (boatswain, gunner, carpenter and purser) was increased in 1802. In 1805 masters and surgeons were given uniform and rank with but after lieutenants, and their pay also was increased. Physicians also benefited in the same way. The resulting rates were as follows:

1802 and 1805 New Rates of Warrant Officers' Pay

By the 28-day month	1st Rates £ s d	2nd Rates £ s d	3rd Rates £ s d	4th Rates £ s d	5th Rates £ s d	6th Rates £ s d	Sloops £ s d	Smaller £ s d
Master	12 12 0	11 11 0	10 10 0	9 9 0	8 8 0	7 7 0	6 6 0	5 5 0
Second Master	5 5 0	5 5 0	5 5 0	–	–	–	–	–
Physician	£29 8s to £58 16s according to seniority							
Surgeon	£15 8s to £25 4s according to seniority							
Assistant Surgeon	£11 18s [same in all rates]							
Boatswain	4 10 0	4 0 0	3 10 0	3 0 0	3 0 0	2 15 0	2 15 0	
Gunner	4 10 0	4 0 0	3 10 0	3 0 0	3 0 0	2 15 0	2 15 0	
Carpenter	5 10 0	5 0 0	4 10 0	3 0 0	3 0 0	2 15 0	2 15 0	
Purser	4 10 0	4 0 0	3 10 0	3 0 0	3 0 0	2 15 0	2 15 0	

Plus servants or compensation in lieu in each case except Assistant Surgeon.

Sources: PRO: ADM 7/678, Nos. 29–35. *KMN* III, 33.

In 1807 a new pay-scale was issued, the first complete revision since 1700. Besides increasing pay, this considerably increased the number of petty officers' ratings by recognizing the captains of parts of ship, who had long been chosen from among able seamen, but had not hitherto been paid extra for their responsibilities.

1807 Scale of Sea Pay

By the 28-day month	1st Rates £ s d	2nd Rates £ s d	3rd Rates £ s d	4th Rates £ s d	5th Rates £ s d	6th Rates £ s d	Sloops £ s d
Captain	32 4 0	26 12 0	23 12 0	18 4 0	15 8 0	16 16 0	16 16 0
Lieutenants	8 8 0 [same in all rates, but £9 2s 0d in flagships]						
Master	12 12 0	11 11 0	10 10 0	9 9 0	8 8 0	7 7 0	6 6 0
Second Master	5 5 0	5 5 0	5 5 0	–	–	–	–
Surgeon	£15 8s to £25 4s according to seniority						
Assistant Surgeon	£11 18s [same in all rates]						
Carpenter	5 16 0	5 6 0	4 16 0	3 6 0	3 6 0	3 1 0	3 1 0
Boatswain	4 16 0	4 6 0	3 16 0	3 6 0	3 6 0	3 1 0	3 1 0
Gunner	4 16 0	4 6 0	3 16 0	3 6 0	3 6 0	3 1 0	3 1 0
Purser	4 16 0	4 6 0	3 16 0	3 6 0	3 6 0	3 1 0	3 1 0
Master's Mates	3 16 6	3 10 6	3 6 8	2 18 4	2 12 6	2 12 6	2 12 6
Midshipmen	2 15 6	2 10 6	2 8 0	2 4 3	2 0 6	2 0 6	2 0 6
Clerk	2 15 6	2 10 6	2 8 0	2 4 3	2 0 6	2 0 6	2 0 6
Schoolmaster	2 15 6	2 10 6	2 8 0	2 4 3	2 0 6	2 0 6	2 0 6
Armourer	2 15 6	2 10 6	2 8 0	2 4 3	2 0 6	2 0 6	2 0 6
Master at Arms	2 15 6	2 10 6	2 8 0	2 4 3	2 0 6	2 0 6	2 0 6
Carpenter's Mates	2 10 6	2 10 6	2 6 6	2 4 6	2 2 6	2 0 6	2 0 6
Caulkers and Ropemakers	2 10 6 [same in all rates]						

By the 28-day month	1st Rates £ s d	2nd Rates £ s d	3rd Rates £ s d	4th Rates £ s d	5th Rates £ s d	6th Rates £ s d	Sloops £ s d
Quartermasters	2 5 6	2 5 6	2 2 6	2 0 6	1 18 6	1 18 6	1 18 6
Boatswain's Mates	2 5 6	2 5 6	2 2 6	2 0 6	1 18 6	1 18 6	1 18 6
Sailmaker	2 5 6	2 5 6	2 5 6	2 4 6	2 2 6	2 0 6	2 0 6
Gunner's Mates	2 5 6	2 5 6	2 2 6	2 0 6	1 18 0	1 16 6	1 16 6
Yeoman of the Powder Room	2 5 6	2 5 6	2 2 6	2 0 6	1 18 0	1 16 6	1 16 6
Armourer's Mate	2 5 6	2 5 6	2 2 6	2 0 6	1 18 0	1 16 6	1 16 6
Corporal	2 5 6	2 5 6	2 2 6	2 0 6	1 18 0	1 16 6	1 16 6
Caulker's Mate	2 6 6	2 6 6	2 6 6	2 6 6	–	–	–
Yeomen of the Sheets	2 2 6	2 0 6	1 18 6	1 18 6	1 16 6	1 16 6	1 16 6
Coxswain	2 2 6	2 0 6	1 18 6	1 18 6	1 16 6	1 16 6	1 16 6
Quartermaster's Mates	2 0 6	2 0 6	1 18 6	1 18 6	1 16 6	1 15 6	1 15 6
[Also Captains of the Forecastle, Foretop, Maintop, Afterguard and Waist]							
Sailmaker's Mates	1 18 6	[same in all rates]					
Quarter Gunners	1 16 6	1 16 6	1 15 6	1 15 6	1 15 6	1 15 6	1 15 6
Carpenter's Crew	1 16 6	1 16 6	1 15 6	1 15 6	1 15 6	1 15 6	1 15 6
Sailmaker's Crew	1 16 6	[same in all rates]					
Gunsmith	1 15 6	1 15 6	1 15 6	–	–	–	–
Steward	1 15 6	1 15 6	1 15 6	1 13 10	1 10 2	1 9 6	1 9 6
Cook	1 15 6	1 15 6	1 15 6	1 15 6	1 15 6	1 14 6	1 14 6
Steward's Mate	1 5 2	1 5 2	1 5 2	1 5 2	–	–	–
Chaplain	0 19 0	[same in all rates]					
Able Seamen	1 13 6	[same in all rates; also Midshipmen Ordinary, Volunteers per Order, Cook's Mates, Coxswain's Mates, Yeomen of the Boatswain's Store, Cooper and Captain's Cook]					
Ordinary Seamen	1 5 6	[same in all rates]					
Landmen	1 2 6	[same in all rates]					
Boys 1st Class	9 0 0 p.a.						
Boys 2nd Class	8 0 0 p.a.						
Boys 3rd Class	7 0 0 p.a.						
Some obsolete ratings have been omitted.							

Sources: Lavery, *Nelson's Navy*, pp. 326–7. *KMN* III, 33.

The only persons who did not benefit from any of the increases between 1797 and 1807 were the chaplains, and their position was finally improved by regulations of 1812 which provided them with a salary of £150 a year (plus compensation for one servant). In addition those qualified and willing to act also as schoolmasters received another £20 a year plus £5 deducted from the pay of each young gentleman under instruction.[16]

Notes

1. Rodger, *Safeguard*, p. 503.
2. For the purposes of the Navy Estimates a year contained thirteen months and one day, or two days in leap years, but rates of pay seem very often to have been expressed in annual terms by simply multiplying the monthly rate by thirteen and ignoring the odd day.
3. *FDW* III, 276.
4. Powell and Timings, *Rupert and Monck*, pp. 178–9 has a version from 1665 with some variations, some and probably all of which are clearly transcription errors.
5. Tanner, 'Administration', XII, 62–3. Turnbull, 'Administration', pp. 399–401. *BNA*, p. 183.
6. Master and commander of Sixth Rates and below.
7. *BAW*, p. 110.
8. Merriman, *Queen Anne's Navy*, pp. 313–14.
9. *WW*, p. 351 gives a table of complement as it stood in the 1750s, when the number of servants ranged from fifty-two (worth £42 18s a month net of deductions) in a 100-gun First Rate, down to eighteen (worth £14 17s) in a twenty-gun Sixth Rate.
10. Master and commander of sloops etc., and of Sixth Rates until 1713.
11. In 1797 second masters were established in line-of-battleships at £4 10s a month (PRO: ADM 7/678 No. 22).
12. From 1702. Plus £20 annual bonus.
13. Lewis, *Social History*, pp. 305–7, whose calculations seem to be somewhat perplexed. At 16s 6d a month net a servant's pay should have amounted to £10 14s 6d a year.
14. PRO: ADM 7/678 No. 21.
15. Plus £20 a year.
16. PRO: ADM 7/678, unnumbered note.

ADMIRALS AND OFFICIALS

1. Admiralty and Navy Commission, 1652–59

There was no formal order of precedence in the Commission. The first Commission was dominated by Sir Henry Vane Jr for its five months of existence, until April 1653. The succeeding Admiralty Commission was dominated from July by Major-General John Desborough. He remained a member until September 1656, by which time the Commission had ceased to be a policy-making body, but its working head from about 1654 was Colonel John Clerke.

[Sources: as in Ch. 3, especially Hammond, 'Administration'.]

2. Lords High Admiral

1660, Jun	James, Duke of York.[1] Resigned July 1673.[2]
	[1673–1684, Admiralty in commission.]
1684, May	Charles II took the office into his own hands.
1685, 6 Feb	James II succeeded his brother and kept the office in his own hands.
1688, 11 Dec	By legal fiction James II abdicated, leaving the Admiralty vacant.
	[1689–1702, Admiralty in commission.]
1702, 26 Jan	Thomas Herbert, 8th Earl of Pembroke.
1702, 20 May	George, Prince of Denmark.[3] Died 28 Oct 1708.
1708, 29 Nov	Earl of Pembroke.
	[1709–1827, Admiralty in commission.]

[Source: Sainty, *Admiralty Officials*, pp. 20–22.]

3. First Lords of the Admiralty

1673, 9 Jul	Prince Rupert.
1679, 14 May	Hon. Sir Henry Capel.
1680, 19 Feb	Hon. Daniel Finch, later Lord Finch and 2nd Earl of Nottingham.
	[Board dismissed 19 May 1684.]
1689, 8 Mar	Admiral Arthur Herbert, later 1st Earl of Torrington.
1690, 20 Jan	Thomas Herbert, 8th Earl of Pembroke.
1692, 10 Mar	Charles, 3rd Lord Cornwallis.

1693, 15 Apr	Anthony Carey, 5th Viscount Falkland.
1694, 2 May	Admiral Edward Russell, later 1st Earl of Orford.
1699, 31 May	John Egerton, 3rd Earl of Bridgwater.
1701, 4 Apr	8th Earl of Pembroke.
[1702–1709,	Senior Members of the Lord High Admiral's Council:
1702, 22 May	Admiral of the Fleet Sir George Rooke.
1705, 11 Jun	Vice-Admiral Sir David Mitchell.
1708, 19 Apr	David Wemyss, 4th Earl of Wemyss.]
1709, 8 Nov	1st Earl of Orford.
1710, 4 Oct	Admiral of the Fleet Sir John Leake [first on the Board patent, but refusing to act as First Lord].
1712, 30 Sep	Thomas Wentworth, 1st Earl of Strafford.
1714, 14 Oct	1st Earl of Orford.
1717, 16 Apr	Admiral James Berkeley, 3rd Earl of Berkeley.
1727, 2 Aug	Admiral of the Fleet George Byng, 1st Viscount Torrington.[4]
1733, 21 Jun	Admiral Sir Charles Wager.
1742, 19 Mar	Daniel Finch, 8th Earl of Winchilsea.
1744, 27 Dec	John Russell, 4th Duke of Bedford.
1748, 26 Feb	John Montagu, 4th Earl of Sandwich.
1751, 22 Jun	Admiral George Anson, 1st Baron Anson.
1756, 17 Nov	Richard Grenville, 2nd Earl Temple.
1757, 6 Apr	8th Earl of Winchilsea.
1757, 2 Jul	1st Baron Anson.
1762, 17 Jun	George Montagu, 3rd Earl of Halifax.
1762, 18 Oct	Hon. George Grenville.
1763, 20 Apr	4th Earl of Sandwich.
1763, 16 Sep	John Perceval, 2nd Earl of Egmont.
1766, 15 Sep	Vice-Admiral Sir Charles Saunders.
1766, 11 Dec	Admiral of the Fleet Sir Edward Hawke.
1771, 12 Jan	4th Earl of Sandwich.
1782, 1 Apr	Admiral Hon. Augustus Keppel, later 1st Viscount Keppel.
1783, 31 Dec	Admiral Richard Howe, 1st Viscount Howe.[5]
1788, 16 Jul	John Pitt, 2nd Earl of Chatham.
1794, 19 Dec	George John Spencer, 2nd Earl Spencer.
1801, 19 Feb	Admiral John Jervis, 1st Earl of St Vincent.
1804, 15 May	Henry Dundas, 1st Viscount Melville.
1805, 2 May	Admiral Charles Middleton, 1st Lord Barham.
1806, 10 Feb	Hon. Charles Grey, later Viscount Howick.
1806, 29 Sep	Thomas Grenville.
1807, 6 Apr	Henry Phipps, 1st Lord Mulgrave.[6]
1810, 4 May	Charles Philip Yorke.
1812, 25 Mar	Robert Dundas, 2nd Viscount Melville [to May 1827].

[Source: Sainty, *Admiralty Officials*, pp. 20–33.]

4. Senior Naval Lords

All Lords of the Admiralty were members of the government and sat in one or other House of Parliament. There was no established position of 'Senior Naval Lord' or 'First Sea Lord', and the only naval lords who were unequivocally at the head of the Navy were those who were First Lords. Most Admiralty Boards also included one or more other sea officers, however, and some of these were professionally active and influential. This list is of sea officers who were junior Lords of the Admiralty (or junior members of the Lord Admiral's Council, 1702–8), and can be identified as having taken a lead on naval issues. On some Boards there was no such person, and on others, two or more, not necessarily the most senior naval members. It will be understood that who was active, and what issues were naval rather than political, are matters of historical judgement. This is not to be understood as a list of holders of any specific office.

1682–4 and 1689–90	Rear-Admiral Sir John Chicheley.
1683–4	Vice-Admiral Arthur Herbert.
1690–91	Admiral Edward Russell.
1690–99	Captain Henry Priestman.
1693–4	Admiral Henry Killigrew.
1693–4	Vice-Admiral Sir Ralph Delaval.
1694–1702	Vice-Admiral, later Admiral of the Fleet Sir George Rooke.
1699–1705	Vice-Admiral Sir David Mitchell.
1699–1708	Captain, later Admiral George Churchill.
1704–7	Admiral Sir Cloudesley Shovell.
1706–8	Vice-Admiral, later Admiral Sir Stafford Fairborne.
1708–14	Admiral, later Admiral of the Fleet Sir John Leake.
1708 and 1710–14	Rear-Admiral, later Admiral Sir James Wishart.
1709–21	Admiral Sir George Byng, later Admiral of the Fleet and 1st Viscount Torrington.
1718–30	Admiral, later Admiral of the Fleet Sir John Norris.[7]
1718–33	Vice-Admiral, later Admiral Sir Charles Wager.
1742–3	Admiral Philip Cavendish.
1743–4	Vice-Admiral Sir Charles Hardy.
1744–51	Rear-Admiral George, later Admiral Lord Anson.
1751–6 and 1757	Admiral William, later Sir William Rowley.
1751–61	Rear-Admiral, later Admiral Hon. Edward Boscawen.
1756–7	Rear-Admiral, later Vice-Admiral Temple West.
1756–63	Vice-Admiral, later Admiral Hon. John Forbes.
1763–5	Captain Richard Howe, 4th Viscount Howe.
1765–6	Vice-Admiral Sir Charles Saunders.
1765–6	Rear-Admiral Hon. Augustus Keppel.
1766–70	Rear-Admiral Sir Peircy Brett.

1771–5	Captain Hon. Augustus John Hervey, later Rear-Admiral and 3rd Earl of Bristol.
1775–9	Rear-Admiral, later Vice-Admiral Sir Hugh Palliser.
1777–82	Captain Constantine John Phipps, 2nd Lord Mulgrave.
1783–9	Captain, later Rear-Admiral Hon. John Leveson-Gower.
1788–95	Vice-Admiral Samuel Hood, 1st Viscount Hood.
1794–5	Vice-Admiral Sir Charles Middleton.
1795–1801, 1804–6, 1807–8	Captain James, later Admiral Lord Gambier.
1795–1801	Rear-Admiral, later Vice-Admiral William Young.
1801–4	Captain, later Rear-Admiral Sir Thomas Troubridge.
1801–4 and 1806–7	Captain, later Rear-Admiral John Markham.
1807–12	Vice-Admiral, later Admiral Sir Richard Hussey Bickerton.
1807–9 and 1820–28	Captain, later Vice-Admiral Sir William Johnstone Hope.
1808–13	Rear-Admiral, later Vice-Admiral William Domett.
1810–18	Captain, later Vice-Admiral Sir Joseph Sydney Yorke.
1812–18	Rear-Admiral George, later Sir George Johnstone Hope.

[Source: Sainty, *Admiralty Officials*, pp. 21–33.]

5. Secretaries of the Admiralty

Secretaries to the Lords Admiral, Admiralty Boards and Commissions. From 1795 these are the First Secretaries, MPs and members of the government.

Admiralty Committee of the Council of State, Mar 1649–53: William Jessop (1642–53), Robert Coytmore (1645–53) and Robert Blackborne (1650–53).[8]
Admiralty and Navy Commission, Dec 1652–Apr 1653: Blackborne.
Admiralty Commission, 1653–9: Blackborne.

1660, Jul	Hon., later Sir, William Coventry.
1667, Sep	Matthew Wren.
1672, Jul	Sir John Werden.
1673, Jun	Samuel Pepys.
1679, May	Thomas Hayter.
1680, Feb	John Brisbane.
1684, May	Pepys.
1689, Mar	Phineas Bowles.
1690, Jan	James Southerne.
1694, Aug	William Bridgeman.

1694, 26 Sep	Bridgeman and Josiah Burchett.
1702, 20 May	Burchett and George Clark.[9]
1705, 25 Oct	Burchett.
1741, 29 Apr	Burchett and Thomas Corbett.
1742, 14 Oct	Corbett.
1751, 30 Apr	John Clevland.
1763, 18 Jun	Philip Stephens.
1795, 3 Mar	Evan, later Sir, Evan Nepean.
1804, 21 Jan	William Marsden.
1807, 24 Jun	Hon. William Wellesley Pole.
1809, 12 Oct	John Wilson Croker (to 29 Nov 1830).

[Sources: Aylmer, *State's Servants*, pp. 234–8 and 265–7. Sainty, *Admiralty Officials*, p. 36.]

6. Second Secretaries of the Admiralty

From 1795 two aspects of the job of Secretary were distinguished; the politician and MP becoming First Secretary, the permanent head of the Admiralty Office the Second Secretary. Earlier this title had been occasionally used as a synonym for 'Deputy Secretary', usually a wartime promotion of the Chief Clerk.

1795, 3 Mar	William Marsden.
1804, 21 Jan	Benjamin Tucker.
1804, 22 May	John Barrow.
1806, 10 Feb	Tucker.
1807, 9 Apr	Barrow, later Sir John Barrow (to 28 Jan 1845).

[Source: Sainty, *Admiralty Officials*, pp. 36–7.]

7. Controllers of the Navy

No member of the Navy Commission appears to have acted particularly as Controller under the Commonwealth and Protectorate. The 1686 Navy Commission likewise consisted of six undifferentiated 'Commissioners for Current Business'.

1660, 31 Aug	Sir Robert Slingsby.
1661, 28 Nov	Sir John Mennes.
1671, 15 Apr	Admiral Sir Thomas Allin.
1680, 28 Jan	Thomas Hayter.
1682, 2 Feb	Captain Sir Richard Haddock [1686 continued as a special Commissioner to clear arrears of accounts on the suspension of the Navy Board].
1688, 12 Oct	Haddock reappointed.
1715, 16 Mar	Rear-Admiral Sir Charles Wager.

1718, 23 Apr	Captain Thomas Swanton.
1723, 9 Feb	Vice-Admiral James Mighells.
1734, 27 Apr	Captain Richard Haddock.
1749, 27 Mar	Captain Savage Mostyn.
1755, 28 Feb	Captain Edward Falkingham.
1755, 25 Nov	Captain Charles Saunders.
1756, 24 Jun	Captain Digby Dent.
1756, 29 Dec	Captain George Cockburne.
1770, 6 Aug	Captain Hugh, later Sir Hugh Palliser.
1775, 12 Apr	Captain Maurice Suckling.
1778, 7 Aug	Captain Charles, later Rear-Admiral Sir Charles Middleton.
1790, 29 Mar	Captain Henry, later Sir Henry Martin.
1794, 25 Sep	Captain Sir Andrew Snape Hamond.
1806, 3 Mar	Captain Henry Nicholls.
1806, 20 Jun	Captain Sir Thomas Boulden Thompson (to 24 Feb 1816).

[Source: Collinge, *Navy Board Officials*, p. 21.]

8. Surveyors of the Navy

After Hollond's resignation no member of the Commonwealth Navy Commission appears to have acted particularly as Surveyor. From the mid-eighteenth century it became customary to have two, and eventually three joint Surveyors.

1648–Dec 1652	John Hollond.
1660, 20 Jun	Vice-Admiral Sir William Batten.
1667, 25 Nov	Colonel Thomas Middleton.
1672, 5 Sep	John, later Sir John Tippetts
	[1686–88 retained as commissioner of old accounts.]
1688, 12 Oct	Tippetts reappointed.
1692, 9 Aug	Edmund Dummer.
1699, 22 Sep	Daniel Furzer [to death 17 Mar 1715].
1706, 19 Oct	Furzer and William Lee [to 16 Nov 1714].
1715, 6 Apr	Jacob, later Sir Jacob Acworth.
1746, 11 Jul	Acworth and Joseph, later Sir Joseph Allin.
1749, 16 Mar	Allin.
1755, 4 Sep	Thomas, later Sir Thomas Slade and William Bately.
1765, 28 Jun	Slade and John, later Sir John Williams.
1771, 22 Feb	Williams.
1778, 11 Apr	Williams and Edward Hunt.
1784, 13 Dec	Hunt and John, later Sir John Henslow.
1786, 7 Dec	Henslow.
1793, 11 Feb	Henslow and William, later Sir William Rule.
1806, 20 Jun	Rule and Henry Peake.

1813, 14 Jun   Peake (to 25 Feb 1822), Joseph Tucker (to 1 Mar 1831) and
Robert, later Sir Robert, Seppings (to 9 Jun 1832).

[Sources: Hollond, *Discourses*, pp. xviii–xix. Cogar, 'Politics', pp. 128–30. Collinge,
Naval Board Officials, p. 22.]

Notes

1. Acted from the Restoration by virtue of his patent of 1638, confirmed by another
of 29 Jan 1661.

2. As Lord High Admiral of England, but remained Lord Admiral of Scotland.

3. Lord High Admiral of Great Britain following the Union of the Crowns, 28 Jun
1707.

4. A new title; there is no connection with Arthur Herbert.

5. 4th Viscount in the Irish peerage.

6. 3rd Lord in the Irish peerage.

7. Norris was occasionally called to advise the Cabinet in the 1740s.

8. Jessop and Coytmore had started as secretaries to the Earl of Warwick, Lord
Admiral 1643–5 and 1648–9.

9. Private Secretary to Prince George of Denmark, Lord High Admiral.

MANPOWER

There do not appear to be any usable statistics of naval manpower earlier than 1688, and those which are available from that date present some problems. It is difficult to say on what basis the figures were compiled, and the discrepancies between different sources suggest that they were not compiled on the same bases, nor necessarily on consistent bases. The difference between the two main statistical series for the eighteenth century (those printed by the Hardwicke Commission in 1859, and those compiled by Lloyd from a variety of manuscript sources) is greatest in years when the Navy was either mobilizing or demobilizing, which suggests the difference between maximum and mean figures. Other discrepant or frankly incredible figures are doubtless due to clerical errors. In this table, 'seamen' covers all the officers and men of the sea service, those 'borne' were entered on a ship's books, and those 'mustered' were actually present on board. New recruits might be mustered but not yet borne until they reached their first ships, while men absent from their ships for any reason would be borne but not mustered. I have discarded the numbers of men voted by Parliament, which are cited by many historians, because (as explained in Ch. 12) these are an accounting fiction.

Total Seamen and Marines Borne and Mustered

Year	Borne (1)	Borne (2)	Mustered (1)	Mustered (2)
1688	12,714			
1689	22,332			
1690	31,971			
1691	35,317			
1692	40,274			
1693	43,827			
1694	47,710			
1695	48,514			
1696	47,677			
1697	44,743			
1698	22,519			
1699	15,834			
1700	7,754			
1701	22,869	20,916		19,632
1702	33,363	38,874	30,973	34,650
1703	40,805	43,397	33,896	38,871

Year	Borne (1)	Borne (2)	Mustered (1)	Mustered (2)
1704	40,433	41,406	31,081	38,873
1705	43,081	45,807	36,646	41,734
1706	46,125	48,346	39,091	44,819
1707	45,055	44,508	40,274	40,121
1708	44,529[1]	47,138	42,072	44,668
1709	47,647	48,344	42,406	41,885
1710	46,493	48,072	42,872	43,950
1711	46,735		43,516	
1712	38,106		35,991	
1713	21,636		19,725	
1714	13,098	49,860[2]		12,062
1715	13,475	13,475		
1716	13,827	13,827		
1717	13,086	13,806		
1718	15,268	15,268		
1719	19,611	19,611		
1720	21,188	21,118		
1721	16,746	15,070		12,576
1722	10,122	10,122		9,582
1723	8,078	8,078		7,723
1724	7,037	7,037		6,637
1725	6,298	6,298		6,001
1726	16,872	16,872		15,408
1727	20,697	20,697		19,105
1728	14,917	14,917		13,682
1729	14,859	14,859		13,892
1730	9,686	9,686		9,187
1731	11,133	11,133		10,504
1732	8,360	8,360		7,887
1733	9,682	9,684		9,056
1734	23,247			
1735	28,819			
1736	17,010			
1737	9,858			
1738	17,668	17,668		16,817
1739	23,604	23,604		21,516
1740	37,181	37,181		32,006
1741	47,121	32,329		39,013
1742	44,283	40,479		35,149
1743	49,865	44,342		38,908
1744	53,754	47,202		43,537
1745	53,498	46,766		42,723

Year	Borne (1)	Borne (2)	Mustered (1)	Mustered (2)
1746	58,011	59,750		46,021
1747	58,508	51,191		48,200
1748	59,596	44,861		41,377
1749	18,602			
1750	12,040			
1751	9,972			
1752	9,771			
1753	8,346			
1754	10,149	10,149		9,797
1755	33,612	33,612		29,268
1756	52,809	52,809		50,037
1757	63,259	63,259		60,548
1758	70,694	70,518		70,014
1759	84,464	84,464		77,265
1760	86,626	85,658		
1761	80,954	80,675		
1762	84,797	84,797		81,929
1763	38,350	75,988		
1764	20,603	17,424		17,415
1765	19,226	15,863		
1766	16,817	15,863		
1767	15,755	13,513		
1768	15,511	13,424		
1769	16,730	13,738		
1770	19,768	14,744		
1771	31,310	26,416		25,836
1772	26,299	27,165		
1773	21,688	22,018		
1774	19,928	18,372		
1775	19,846	15,230		15,062
1776	31,084	23,914		
1777	52,836	46,231		
1778	72,258	62,719		
1779	87,767	80,275		74,479
1780	97,898	91,566		82,751
1781	99,362	98,269		
1782	105,443	93,168		95,095
1783	65,677	107,446		
1784	28,878	39,268		
1785	22,183	22,826		
1786	17,259	13,737		13,478
1787	19,444	14,514		

Year	Borne (1)	Borne (2)	Mustered (1)	Mustered (2)
1788	19,740	15,964		15,946
1789	20,396	18,397		
1790	39,526	20,025		
1791	34,097	38,801		
1792	17,361	16,613		
1793	59,042	69,868		69,416
1794	83,891	87,331		73,835
1795	99,608	96,001		
1796	112,382	114,365		106,708
1797	120,046	118,788		114,603
1798	119,592	122,687		114,617
1799	120,409	128,930		
1800	123,527	126,192		118,247
1801	131,959	125,061		117,202
1802	77,765	129,340		118,005
1803	67,148	49,430		
1804	99,372	84,431		
1805	114,012	109,205		
1806	122,860	111,237		119,627
1807	130,917	119,855		
1808	139,605	140,822		
1809	144,387	141,989		
1810	146,312	142,098		
1811	144,762	130,866		
1812	144,844	131,087		138,204
1813	147,087	130,127		
1814	126,414			
1815	78,891			

Sources: cols. 1: HC 1859 Sess. 1 VI, 362; HC 1868–9 XXXV, 1177–9; Johnston, 'Parliament and the Navy', p. 502; cols. 2: Lloyd, *British Seaman*, pp. 286–90.

Notes

1. 41,529 in HC 1868–9 XXXV p. 1177.
2. This must surely be a clerical error; perhaps the figure belongs to 1711.

NAVAL FINANCE

Much more is now known about the finances of the English government and the English Navy under the Interregnum, but substantial uncertainties remain. The figures below derive from the accounts of the Treasurers of the Navy, and do not include the unknown sums which were paid for naval goods and services directly from central revenues by the issue of Exchequer tallies. 'Expenditure' is the total accounted for by the Treasurer; 'Outstanding Debt' is the sum outstanding at the end of each year, and 'Real Expenditure' is the sum of net expenditure plus the increase in the debt. Unpaid naval debt incurred before 1650 is not included; in 1660 a total of £10,501 was still outstanding for the years 1640–49. Expenditures for accounting periods of more than a year have been expressed as an annual rate.

Naval Finance, 1649–60

Year	Expenditure[1]	Outstanding Debt	Real Expenditure
1649–50[2]	£ 493,932 p.a.	£ 116,461[3]	£ 610,393 p.a.
1651	347,572	222,434	453,545
1652	531,361	324,840	633,767
1653	1,335,100	439,667	1,449,927
1654	1,101,844[4]	455,612	1,117,789
1655	580,241	462,762	587,391
1656	732,486	496,145	765,869
1657	572,748	704,561	781,164
1658–60[5]	433,296 p.a.	1,048,447	570,850 p.a.

Sources: Wheeler, *World Power*, p. 45; and 'Navy Finance', p. 462.

There are relatively few financial statistics available for the later Stuart period, when the Navy's income came from a confusing and shifting mixture of the king's personal revenue and Parliamentary grants. The best record is the cash 'Issues' of the Exchequer to the Treasurer of the Navy, to which may be added 'Issues' to the Ordnance Board, which in this period was largely concerned with naval weapons (except perhaps in the years 1686–8, when James II built up a substantial army). There appear to be no coherent statistics of naval debt in this period, and the expenditure of the Parliamentary commission which discharged the debts of the Commonwealth navy is not included. In this table the Issues are recorded for Exchequer years beginning at Michaelmas (29 September), and are rounded to the nearest pound. These figures may be compared with actual expenditures by the Treasurer of the Navy.

Exchequer Issues to the Navy and Ordnance, 1660–88

Year	Navy	Ordnance[6]	Total
1660–61	£ 149,952	£ 10,101	£ 160,053
1661–2	521,040	52,800	573,840
1662–3	325,561	102,899	428,460
1663–4	330,205	55,227	385,432
1664–5	1,108,291	229,894	1,338,185
1665–6	1,164,341	277,321	1,441,662
1666–7	677,614	40,835	718,449
1667–8	486,591	50,353	536,994
1668–9	1,007,920	40,638	1,048,558
1669–70	289,583	28,636	318,219
1670–71	200,897	27,923	228,820
1671–2	721,370	127,044	848,414
1672–3	727,126	172,950	900,076
1673–4	865,312	118,790	984,102
1674–5	549,106	50,214	599,320
1675–6	237,560	94,041	331,601
1676–7	516,711	68,800	585,511
1677–8	659,535	186,272	845,807
1678–9	518,966	53,017	571,983
1679–80	561,717	112,847	674,564
1680–81	331,932	25,067	356,999
1681–2	362,875	40,788	403,663
1682–3	350,973	105,975	456,948
1683–4	367,289	43,339	410,628
1684–5	305,155	54,800	359,955
1685–6	367,736	65,000	432,736
1686–7	476,508	101,905	578,413
1687–8	448,182	112,328	560,510

Source: Chandaman, *English Public Revenue*, pp. 350–63.

Naval Expenditure, 1660–1689

Period	Expenditure	Annual Average
7 Jul 1660–31 Dec 1664	£1,814,653	£403,256
1 Jan 1665–31 Dec 1669	3,916,130	783,226
1 Jan 1670–31 Dec 1674	2,616,852	523,370
1 Jan 1675–31 Jan 1680	2,470,022	494,004
1 Feb 1680–31 Dec 1684	2,561,748	521,740
1 Jan 1685–4 Apr 1689	1,807,351	425,259

Source: Wheeler, *World Power*, pp. 55 and 59.

The figures from 1689 to 1815 derive from a Parliamentary report of 1869 which gives both Parliamentary votes and the accumulated naval debt (i.e. on the Course of the Navy and Victualling) at the close of each year. Grants to pay off naval debt are included, and in this table I have treated naval debt funded into government stock (or in 1711, South Sea Company stock) as grants. Though no money was actually voted in these cases, the transfer of debt from the Navy's to the Treasury's books was from the Navy's point of view equivalent to a grant. From these figures it is possible to calculate real naval expenditure by adding an increase in naval debt to the Parliamentary votes, or subtracting a reduction. The resulting figures are more useful than Parliamentary votes alone, which give the misleading impression of peaks of naval spending in those (in many cases peacetime) years in which large sums of naval debt were paid off or funded. These figures assume that Parliamentary grants were paid in full, in the years they were voted, which however was not always true in the 1690s. Note also that the Navy had some non-Parliamentary sources of income, such as the sale of old stores (only from 1811 included in the Parliamentary vote). For comparison I have added an independent calculation of true naval expenditure for the years 1745 to 1781 made by Dr Ruddock Mackay from Treasury documents.

Naval Finance, 1689–1815

Year	Parliamentary Votes	Accumulated Naval Debt	Net Expenditure	Mackay
1689	£1,198,648	£ 567,542	£1,766,190[7]	
1690	1,612,976	–	1,900,608[8]	
1691	1,791,694	–	2,079,326	
1692	1,575,890	–	1,863,522	
1693	1,926,516	1,430,439	2,214,148	
1694	2,500,000	1,564,856	2,634,417	
1695	2,382,712	1,663,078	2,480,934	
1696	2,516,972	1,758,009	2,611,903	
1697	2,372,197	2,075,233	2,689,421	
1698	1,539,122	2,245,957	1,709,846	
1699	1,296,383	1,440,368	490,794	
1700	956,342	1,334,233	850,207	
1701	1,380,000	1,264,722	1,310,489	
1702	2,209,314	1,525,522	2,470,114	
1703	2,209,314	1,576,694	2,260,486	
1704	2,080,000	2,266,865	2,770,171	
1705	2,230,000	2,640,938	2,604,073	
1706	2,234,711	3,211,937	2,805,710	
1707	2,210,000	3,562,751	2,560,814	
1708	2,210,000	3,628,505	2,275,754	
1709	2,200,000	4,969,247	3,540,742	

Year	Parliamentary Votes	Accumulated Naval Debt	Net Expenditure	Mackay
1710	2,200,000	5,655,536	2,886,289	
1711	7,862,592	800,961	3,008,017	
1712	2,260,000	425,471	1,884,510	
1713	1,200,000	1,011,098	1,785,627	
1714	1,068,700	1,100,040	1,157,642	
1715	1,146,748	696,671	743,379	
1716	984,473	1,043,337	1,331,139	
1717	947,560	764,038	668,261	
1718	910,174	1,072,697	1,218,833	
1719	1,003,133	1,450,258	1,380,694	
1720	1,397,734	1,503,688	1,451,164	
1721	789,250	1,506,581	792,143	
1722	1,607,894	777,057	878,370	
1723	736,389	1,078,573	1,037,905	
1724	734,623	721,776	377,826	
1725	547,096	1,255,491	1,080,811	
1726	732,181	1,630,794	1,107,484	
1727	1,239,071	1,937,023	1,545,300	
1728	1,495,561	1,188,960	747,498	
1729	996,026	1,335,061	1,142,127	
1730	863,787	1,396,724	925,450	
1731	742,034	1,445,843	791,153	
1732	698,885	1,624,101	877,143	
1733	748,283	1,873,951	998,133	
1734	2,452,670	693,503	1,272,222	
1735	1,768,914	491,361	1,566,772	
1736	1,037,436	494,939	1,041,014	
1737	799,201	507,555	811,817	
1738	1,292,886	346,945	1,132,276	
1739	856,689	824,684	1,334,428	
1740	2,157,688	1,301,526	2,634,530	
1741	2,718,786	1,936,571	3,353,831	
1742	2,765,574	2,351,843	3,180,846	
1743	2,653,764	2,573,509	2,875,430	
1744	2,521,085	3,349,823	3,297,399	
1745	2,567,084	4,022,328	3,239,589	3,033,334
1746	2,661,535	5,506,144	4,145,351	3,339,096
1747	3,780,911	5,473,374	3,748,141	3,541,886
1748	3,640,352	5,459,677	3,626,655	3,430,565
1749	5,179,878	1,866,752	1,586,953	1,586,954
1750	1,021,521	1,716,923	871,292	871,693

Year	Parliamentary Votes	Accumulated Naval Debt	Net Expenditure	Mackay
1751	1,056,599	1,675,793	1,015,469	1,015,429
1752	1,794,561	944,901	1,063,669	1,063,670
1753	810,207	1,132,206	997,512	997,411
1754	910,889	1,296,568	1,075,251	1,074,850
1755	1,714,289	1,688,791	2,106,512	2,677,569
1756	3,349,021	2,238,010	3,898,240	3,898,239
1757	3,503,939	3,462,967	4,728,896	4,828,896
1758	3,874,421	4,575,429	4,986,883	4,986,882
1759	5,236,263	5,391,830	6,052,664	6,052,664
1760	5,609,708	5,228,695	5,446,573	5,448,534
1761	5,594,790	5,607,961	5,974,056	5,973,095
1762	5,954,292	5,929,125	6,275,456	6,276,374
1763	8,017,186	4,046,899	6,134,960[9]	4,246,752
1764	2,094,800	3,926,915	1,974,816	1,974,817
1765	4,313,636	2,484,595	2,871,316	1,503,647
1766	2,722,283	1,456,921	1,694,609	1,694,612
1767	1,869,321	1,203,072	1,615,472	1,625,470
1768	1,526,357	1,339,158	1,662,443	1,652,442
1769	1,924,669	1,092,848	1,678,359	1,668,356
1770	1,622,067	1,497,454	2,026,673	2,036,675
1771	3,082,500	1,195,410	2,780,456	2,780,455
1772	2,070,665	1,535,383	2,410,638	2,410,637
1773	1,885,573	1,886,780	2,236,970	2,237,050
1774	2,104,917	1,886,100	2,104,237	2,104,258
1775	1,684,060	2,698,579	2,496,539	2,496,537
1776	3,227,056	3,624,420	4,152,897	4,152,896
1777	4,210,306	4,003,574	4,589,460	4,589,458
1778	5,001,896	5,175,607	6,173,929	6,173,928
1779	4,589,069	8,157,878	7,571,340	7,771,339
1780	7,003,284	10,372,628	9,218,034	9,018,034
1781	8,936,277	11,318,451	9,882,100	9,882,099
1782	8,063,206	14,207,414	10,952,169	
1783	6,483,833	15,510,768	7,787,187	
1784	9,099,669	10,792,887	4,381,788	
1785	12,055,309	1,712,490	2,974,912	
1786	2,434,327	1,608,204	2,330,041	
1787	2,286,000	1,892,650	2,570,446	
1788	2,411,407	2,216,651	2,735,408	
1789	2,328,570	2,370,439	2,482,358	
1790	2,433,637	1,818,020	1,881,218	
1791	4,008,405	2,301,280	4,491,665	

Year	Parliamentary Votes	Accumulated Naval Debt	Net Expenditure	Mackay
1792	4,985,482	2,745,991	5,430,193	
1793	3,971,915	5,444,366	6,670,290	
1794	7,432,783	7,108,074	9,096,491	
1795	7,806,169[10]	10,788,985	11,487,080	
1796	11,779,349	4,158,744	5,149,108	
1797	24,629,202[11]	6,458,490	26,928,948	
1798	13,449,389	5,556,034	12,546,933	
1799	13,654,013	5,992,288	14,090,267	
1800	13,619,080	8,705,886	16,332,678	
1801	15,857,037	9,073,071	16,224,222	
1802	13,833,574	3,103,648	7,864,151	
1803	10,211,378	4,037,308	11,145,038	
1804	12,350,606	3,933,099	12,246,397	
1805	15,035,630	5,911,588	17,014,119	
1806	15,864,341	5,520,208	15,472,961	
1807	17,400,377	4,993,549	16,873,718	
1808	18,317,548	4,625,324	17,949,323	
1809	19,578,467	5,916,401	20,869,544	
1810	19,829,434	5,591,823	19,504,856	
1811	20,935,894	4,890,774	20,234,845	
1812	20,442,149	6,057,913	21,609,288	
1813	21,212,012	8,562,291	23,716,390	
1814	19,312,071	6,361,076	17,110,856	
1815	19,032,700	3,694,821	16,366,445	

Sources: HC 1868–9 (366) XXV, 1177–9. Mackay, *Hawke*, pp. 305–6.

Notes

1. Maurice Ashley, *Financial and Commercial Policy under the Cromwellian Protectorate* (London, 2nd edn 1962), p. 48, gives slightly different figures.

2. The period 13 May 1649 to 31 Dec 1650.

3. New debt for 1650.

4. £2,968,305 over the three years 1652–4, against £3,034,981 received by the Treasurer over the same period: Hammond, 'Administration', p. 97.

5. The period 1 Jan 1658 to 7 Jul 1660.

6. Tomlinson, *Guns and Government*, p. 177, gives a table of Ordnance Office expenditure, 1660–1714, calculated in a different way and for different periods, but broadly corroborating these figures.

7. Attributing the whole accumulated naval debt to that year, for want of better information, though undoubtedly some of it was incurred in 1688.

8. As there are no figures for the Course of the Navy for 1690 to 1692, I have divided the total increase between 1689 and 1693 into equal annual instalments.

9. In this year £2,888,209 of Navy, Victualling and Transport Bills were funded, and in 1765 a further £1,367,670. The large discrepancy between my figures and Mackay's is evidently because I have treated these as *de facto* grants, and his sources have not.

10. Including a vote of £184,615 from the Irish Parliament.

11. This includes £11,595,529 in naval debt funded into government stock. The figures for the naval debt, however, suggest that at least some of this ought to be attributed to 1796, which would smooth out the implausibly extreme fluctuation of net naval expenditure in 1796 and 1797.

REFERENCES

Introduction

1 Lediard, *Naval History*, Preface [n.p.].
2 *Rethinking Leviathan: The Eighteenth-Century State in Britain and Germany*, ed. John Brewer and Eckhart Hellmuth (Oxford, 1999).

1 A Mountain of Iron

1 Hutton, *British Republic*, pp. 1–22. Worden, *Rump Parliament*, pp. 2–12.
2 Michael Seymour, 'Warships' Names of the English Republic, 1649–1660', *MM* LXXVI (1990), pp. 317–24. Capp, *Cromwell's Navy*, p. 5. Evelyn, *Diary* III, 149–50. Cromwell became commander-in-chief in January 1650.
3 Rodger, *Safeguard*, pp. 425–6.
4 Göran Behre, 'Gothenburg in French War Strategy 1649–1760', in *Scotland and Scandinavia 800–1800*, ed. Grant G. Simpson (Edinburgh, 1990), pp. 107–18, at pp. 107–8.
5 Junge, *Flottenpolitik*, pp. 131–2. Capp, *Cromwell's Navy*, pp. 42–3. Wheeler, 'Prelude to Power'.
6 Cogar, 'Politics', p. 74.
7 Capp, *Cromwell's Navy*, pp. 48–54. Brenner, *Merchants and Revolution*, pp. 553–5.
8 Firth and Rait, *Acts and Ordinances* II, 17. Powell, *Blake*, pp. 77–8. Baumber, *General-at-Sea*, pp. 68–71; and 'Civil Wars and the Commonwealth', pp. 278–80. Penn, *Memorials* I, 289–91 (quoted p. 289). Junge, *Flottenpolitik*, pp. 112–13.
9 Perrin, *British Flags*, pp. 63–4. *FDW* III, 189.
10 Baumber, 'Civil Wars and Commonwealth', p. 255.
11 *CSPD* 1649–50 p. 202, 22 Jun 1649.
12 Not 1st, as stated in Rodger, *Safeguard*, pp. 426 and 472.

13 Anderson, 'Royalists at Sea in 1649', pp. 320–25. Warburton, *Prince Rupert* III, 264–79.
14 Powell, *Blake*, pp. 81–9. *LRB* pp. 8–49 and 71–4. Anderson, 'Royalists at Sea in 1650', pp. 325–37; and 'Operations of the English Fleet', pp. 409–10. Baumber, 'Civil War and Commonwealth', pp. 302–14. Gardiner, *Commonwealth and Protectorate* I, 106–33.
15 Initially as a subordinate senior officer, appointed by the triumvirate of which he was one. Popham arrived with reinforcements in May to make up a quorum.
16 Anderson, 'Royalists at Sea in 1650'; and 'Operations of the English Fleet', pp. 411–15. Baumber, 'Civil Wars and Commonwealth', pp. 324–40. HMC *Leyborne-Popham*, pp. 61–71. C. R. Boxer, 'Blake and the Brazil Fleets in 1650', *MM* XXXVI (1950), pp 212–28. Powell, *Blake*, pp. 90–103. Penn, *Memorials* I, 298–300. *LRB* pp. 54–65 and 74–89. 'Prince Rupert at Lisbon', ed. S. R. Gardiner, in *Camden Miscellany X* (CS 3rd S. 4, 1902). Warburton, *Prince Rupert* III, 313 (quoted).
17 Powell, *Blake*, pp. 104–7. *LRB* pp. 65–70 and 90–95. Baumber, 'Civil Wars and Commonwealth', pp. 341–4. Anderson, 'Royalists at Sea in 1650', pp. 157–68; and 'Operations of the English Fleet', pp. 418–20.
18 Gardiner, *Commonwealth and Protectorate* I, 306. Junge, *Flottenpolitik*, pp. 124–6. Capp, *Cromwell's Navy*, p. 70. (The figures for losses differ slightly between these authorities.) Gigliola Pagano de Divitiis, *Mercanto inglesi nell'Italia del seicento: Navi, traffici, egemonie* (Venice, 1990), p. 72.
19 Anderson, 'Royalists at Sea, 1651–1653'.
20 J. S. Wheeler, 'The Logistics of the Cromwellian Conquest of Scotland', *W&S* X (1992), pp. 1–18. Gardiner,

Commonwealth and Protectorate I, 257–61 and 291–6. Baumber, 'Civil Wars and Commonwealth', pp. 315–21.

21 J. R. Powell, 'Blake's Reduction of the Scilly Isles in 1651', *MM* XVII (1931), pp. 205–22; and *Blake*, pp. 108–20. *LRB*, pp. 95–104 and 112–36. Baumber, 'Civil Wars and Commonwealth', pp. 346–52. C. D. Curtis, 'The Presence of Tromp during Blake's Reduction of the Scilly Isles in 1651', *MM* XX (1934), pp. 50–66.

22 J. R. Powell, 'Blake's Reduction of Jersey in 1651', *MM* XVIII (1932), pp. 64–80; and *Blake*, pp. 121–33. *LRB*, pp. 111–12 and 136–42. Baumber, 'Civil Wars and Commonwealth', pp. 355–58. Jane H. Ohlmeyer, 'Irish Privateers during the Civil War, 1642–50', *MM* LXXVI (1990), pp. 119–31, at p. 130. Gardiner, *Commonwealth and Protectorate* II, 66–9.

23 J. R. Powell, 'Sir George Ayscue's Capture of Barbados in 1651', *MM* LIX (1973), pp. 281–90. Baumber, 'Civil Wars and Commonwealth', pp. 360–64.

24 Worden, *Rump Parliament*, pp. 18 and 165.

25 Jones, *Britain and the World*, pp. 64–5; and *Britain and Europe*, p. 47. Haley, *The British and the Dutch*, pp. 78–9. Israel, *Dutch Republic*, pp. 610–11 and 714; and 'Spain, the Spanish Embargoes', pp. 207–10. Boxer, *Dutch Seaborne Empire*, pp. 74–5.

26 Haley, *The British and the Dutch*, p. 89. Brenner, *Merchants and Revolution*, pp. 626–9; 'Civil War Politics', pp. 100–105; and 'The Social Basis of English Commercial Expansion, 1550–1650', *JEcH* XXXII (1972), pp. 361–84. Groenveld, 'English Civil Wars', pp. 559–61. Firth and Rait, *Acts and Ordinances* II, 559–62. Israel, *Dutch Republic*, p. 715. Junge, *Flottenpolitik*, pp. 150–55. J. E. Farnell, 'The Navigation Act of 1651, the First Dutch War, and the London Merchant Community', *EcHR* 2nd S. XVI (1964), pp. 439–54. Capp, *Cromwell's Navy*, pp. 75–6. Jones, *Anglo-Dutch Wars*, pp. 112–13. *FDW* I, 48–50 and 81. Junge, *Flottenpolitik*, pp. 147–65.

27 See particularly the works of Pincus and J. R. Jones cited below.

28 Pincus, *Protestantism and Patriotism*, pp. 14–97, 129–31 and 138–48.

29 Israel, *Dutch Republic*, is the best introduction.

30 Bruijn, *Varend Verleden*, provides an accessible introduction to Dutch naval administration. See also his *Dutch Navy*, 'Political and Social Economic Setting', and 'Mercurius en Mars uiteen'. Elias, *Schetsen* II, 9–12, and 40; III, 38–42; IV, 100–109 and 120–21; V, 15–19 and 132–6.

31 In modern spelling the Maas, the river on which Rotterdam stands.

32 'Het Noorderkwartier'; otherwise West Friesland, which in spite of its name is part of Holland and nowhere near Friesland.

33 Alfred Staarman, 'De VOC en de Staten-Generaal in de Engelse Ooorlogen: een ongemakkelijk bondgenootschap', *TvZ* XV (1996), pp. 3–24, at pp. 3–9.

34 *FDW* I, 260–66; cf. *GNZ* I, 51–3 for a list of 1653 arranged according to a different scheme.

35 Aseart et al., *Maritieme Geschiedenis* II, 83–4.

36 Elias, *Schetsen* II, 1–40. *FDW* I, 57–169.

37 *FDW* I, 31–2. The Orcades = the Orkneys.

38 'De Engelsche gaen tegens een gouden Berg aen; de onse ter contrarie tegen een Ysere': Aitzema, *Staet en Oorlogh* III, 721. The same phrase had been applied to Spain in 1638: M. G. de Boer, *Het Proefjaar van Maarten Harpertsz. Tromp, 1637–1639* (Amsterdam, 1946), p. 97 n.1.

39 J. C. M. Warnsinck, 'Tromp's "Considerations" of 1652', *MM* XXI (1935), pp. 452–3. Cf. Elias, *Schetsen* II, 33, and *FDW* I, 100–102 (misdated).

40 Elias, *Vlootbouw*, p. 83.

41 Rodger, *Safeguard*, pp. 380–83.

42 'De Staet geen kleynigheyt zou komen te lyden': Elias, *Schetsen* II, 55.

43 *NZW* I, 417–18. Fulton, *Sovereignty*, pp. 398–9 and 770–72.

44 A. A. van Schelven, 'Het begin van den Slag bij Dover, 29 Mei 1652', *BMHG* XLVII (1926), pp. 235–48. *The Life of Cornelius van Tromp, Lieutenant-Admiral of Holland and Westfriesland . . .* (London, 1697), p. 21.

45 Powell, *Blake*, pp. 143–4. Elias, *Schetsen* II, 60–63. Prud'homme van Reine, *Schittering en schandaal*, pp. 140–43. Contemporary narratives in *FDW* I, 192–9, 205–21, 227–8, 250–56, 276–85 and 295–8; HMC *Portland* I, 651–2; Penn, *Memorials* I, 421–2; *GNZ* I, 1–2.

46 Powell, *Blake*, pp. 145–54. Elias, *Schetsen* II, 65–6.

47 Powell, *Blake*, pp. 155–61. Elias, *Schetsen* II, 113–29. *FDW* I, 301–302, 345–99 and 415–31. Prud'homme van Reine, *Schittering en schandaal*, pp. 149–53. Baumber, *General-at-Sea*, pp. 128–34.

48 Prud'homme van Reine, *Rechterhand*, is a good modern biography of the great Dutch admiral, but there is little of value in English beyond the perceptive sketch by A. van der Moer in Sweetman, *Great Admirals*, pp. 82–111.

49 *FDW* I, 321 and IV, 34–8. Corbett, *Fighting Instructions*, pp. 88–90. Rodger, 'Broadside Gunnery'.

50 Powell, *Blake*, pp. 162–4. Baumber, *General-at-Sea*, pp. 135–43. Elias, *Schetsen* III, 57–60. *FDW* II, 2–3, 105–12, 121, 142–53, 188–211. *NZW* I, 424–7. Brandt, *De Ruiter*, pp. 25–9. Prud'homme van Reine, *Rechterhand*, pp. 62–3. Le Fevre, 'Ayscue', p. 195.

51 Powell, *Blake*, pp. 165–8; and 'Blake's Capture of the French Fleet before Calais on 4 September 1652', *MM* XLVIII (1962), pp. 192–207. Baumber, *General-at-Sea*, pp. 139–40. Capp, *Cromwell's Navy*, p. 71. C. D. Curtis, 'Blake and Vendôme', *MM* XXI (1935), pp. 56–60. *LMF* V, 191–3. *MMF* I, 194–5.

52 'Daddy' loosely renders the Dutch 'Bestevaer'. Prud'homme van Reine, *Schittering en schandaal* is a modern life of Tromp and his son Cornelis.

53 Baumber, *General-at-Sea*, pp. 143–5. Elias, *Schetsen* III, 33–75. Warnsinck, *Drie zeventiende-eeuwsche admiraals*, pp. 57–8. Blok, *De Ruyter*, pp. 51–2. Roos, 'Johan Evertsen', pp. 123–31.

54 'Een capiteyn bejaert van 70 jaren en sieck volc, de loots en verscheyde officieren droncken . . .': De With to States-General, 20 Nov NS 1652, in Elias, *Schetsen* III, 77, trans. in *FDW* III, 53.

55 Powell, *Blake*, pp. 171–6. Baumber, *General-at-Sea*, pp. 145–9. Elias, *Schetsen* III, 73–87. *FDW* II, 217–364. Penn, *Memorials* I, 446–50. 'T Leven en Bedrijff van Vice-Admirael de With, Zaliger', ed. S. P. L'Honoré Naber, *BMHG* XLVII (1926), pp. 47–169. Prud'homme van Reine, *Rechterhand*, pp. 64–7. Warnsinck, *Drie zeventiende-eeuwsche admiraals*, pp. 83–7.

56 'Man hafwer här för detta sustinerat att Hollenderne skulle myckitt snällare och snarare kunna segla, wända och skiutha än de Engelske, men de Witte skrifwer att nu hafwa befunnet contrarium': *GNZ* I, 25, H. Appelboom to A. Oxenstjerna, 13 Oct NS 1652.

57 Powell, *Blake*, pp. 181–91. Baumber, *General-at-Sea*, pp. 154–8. Elias, *Schetsen* IV, 1–71. *FDW* III, 91–95, 106–8, 116–20, 143–5, 167 and 199–266. Penn, *Memorials* I, 458–60. Prud'homme van Reine, *Rechterhand*, pp. 68–70; and *Schittering en schandaal*, pp. 164–5. Warnsinck, *Drie zeventiende-eeuwsche admiraals*, pp. 140–42.

58 Edgar K. Thompson, 'Lashing Broom to the Fore Topmast', *MM* LIX (1973), pp. 441–2. The source of the story is the unreliable life of Monck by his army chaplain: Thomas Gumble, *The Life of General Monck, Duke of Albemarle . . .* (London, 1671), p. 57.

59 *FDW* III, 92, Blake to Admiralty, 1 Dec 1652 (quoted); and 293–301 (the new 'Laws and Ordinances'). Powell, *Blake*, pp. 192–206.

60 Powell, *Blake*, pp. 207–22. Baumber, *General-at-Sea*, pp. 170–78. Elias, *Schetsen* IV, 80–94. *FDW* IV, 2–230. Penn, *Memorials* I, 474–7. *NZW* I, 446–55. *LRB* pp. 204–5. R. C. Anderson, 'The English Fleet at the Battle of Portland', *MM* XXXIX (1953), pp. 171–7. Prud'homme van Reine, *Rechterhand*, pp. 72–3; and *Schittering en schandaal*, pp. 166–9.

61 Prud'homme van Reine, *Rechterhand*, p. 73. Elias, *Schetsen* IV, 91.

62 'Jonge Boer Jaap', 'Young Farmer Jim'. The van Nes family is typical of the Dutch navy of the time in that there were a large number of them who are easily confused:

eight sea officers, all belonging to the Admiralty of the Maze, of whom one (Jan Jacobse) was nicknamed 'Oude Boer Jaap', and two (Jan Jacobse his brother and Aert Jansse his nephew) were successively nicknamed 'Jonge Boer Jaap'. *NZW* I, 769–75 attempts to disentangle the family.

63 'Naer de middag seynde de admyrael met de blauwe wimpel van de besaensroe om mijn . . . maer ick cost niet achter hem comen. Doen riep de admyrael: "Boer Jaep, Boer Jaep, loop eens naer de coopvaerders en seght eens tegen haer alsdat sij O.t.N. ende O.N.O. heen loopen . . . ende loopt eens naer de commandeur De Ruyter ende seght hem dat hij hier vóór mijn loopt." Ick seyde: "Ick sal het doen, mijnheer." Doen liep ick naer De Ruyter ende seyde dat hem ende daervandaen liep ick naer de coopvaerders . . .': Bruijn, *Varend Verleden*, p. 93.

64 Printed (with the accompanying Sailing Instructions) in *FDW* IV, 262–74, Corbett, *Fighting Instructions*, pp. 99–104 and (a 1654 issue) Penn, *Memorials* II, 76.

65 Much needless confusion has been generated by modern writers failing to distinguish the line of battle from other forms of the line ahead, and other sorts of line. On all this see Rodger, 'Broadside Gunnery'.

66 A. H. Taylor, 'Sandwich and the Ship of the Line', *NR* XLI (1953), pp. 134–43. Powell, *Blake*, pp. 225–7. Palmer, 'The "Military Revolution" Afloat'. *FDW* IV, 18, 34–8, 209–10. Lavery, 'The Revolution in Naval Tactics', p. 170. Tunstall, *Naval Warfare*, pp. 16–21. *NZW* II, 87–118. Baumber, *General-at-Sea*, pp. 182–4, argues for the second interpretation.

67 Powell, *Blake*, pp. 236–9. Baumber, *General-at-Sea*, pp. 183–4. Elias, *Schetsen* V, 46–120. *FDW* V, 5–146. Penn, *Memorials* I, 491–8. *NZW* I, 467–70. Prud'homme van Reine, *Rechterhand*, pp. 76–80; and *Schittering en schandaal*, pp. 180–83.

68 'Wat helpt het dat ik zwyg? Ik ben hier voor myn Opperheeren. Ik magh, en moet het zeggen, d'Engelschen zyn nu meester van ons, en dienvolgens van de zee': Brandt, *De Ruiter*, pp. 51–2. Aitzema, *Staet en Oorlogh* III, 829 gives slightly different wording.

69 Powell, *Blake*, pp. 241–4. *FDW* V, 147–62. Prud'homme van Reine, *Rechterhand*, pp. 77–8; and *Schittering en schandaal*, p. 183.

70 Powell, *Blake*, pp. 244–6. Baumber, *General-at-Sea*, pp. 184–6. Elias, *Schetsen* V, 140–212. *FDW* V, 162–429. Penn, *Memorials* I, 501–40. *GNZ* I, 83–4.

71 'Les Angloys se batent avec ordre et coeur, les nostres avec faute de cela . . . Touttes les marques de l'honneur sont demurées aux Angloys, ils ont des navires, des prisonniers, nous n'en avons nul': *GNZ* I, 83–4, Gentillot to Servien, 20 Aug NS 1653.

72 R. C. Anderson, 'Denmark and the First Anglo-Dutch War', *MM* LIII (1967), pp. 55–62. Elias, *Schetsen* III, 89–96. Lind, *Kong Frederik den Tredjes Sømagt*, pp. 52–8.

73 Powell, *Blake*, p. 152. The States-General did not forbid trade with the enemy until Dec 1652: Elias, *Schetsen* IV, 109–16.

74 Elias, *Schetsen* III, 116–70 and VI, 2–41. Corbett, *Mediterranean* I, 212–32. *NZW* I, 462–6. Anderson, 'First Dutch War in the Mediterranean'. Spalding, *Badiley*, pp. 53–230. Warnsinck, 'Een Nederlandsch Eskader in de Middellandsche Zee'. F. W. Brooks, 'Captain Henry Appleton', *Yorkshire Archaeological Journal* XXXVI (1946), pp. 357–65.

75 Pincus, *Protestantism and Patriotism*, p. 118.

76 Powell, *Blake*, pp. 230–31. Baumber, *General-at-Sea*, pp. 187–8. Pincus, *Protestantism and Patriotism*, pp. 115–18. Penn, *Memorials* I, 489–91. Worden, 'Cromwell and the Sin of Achan', pp. 125–34. Capp, *Cromwell's Navy*, pp. 122–5. Cogar, 'Politics', pp. 140–50.

77 Cogar, 'Politics', pp. 157–9. Rodger, *Safeguard*, pp. 414 and 425–6.

78 Pincus, *Protestantism and Patriotism*, pp. 119–71. Capp, *Cromwell's Navy*, pp. 126–8. Hutton, *British Republic*, pp. 62–5.

2 Cromwell's Hooves

1 Venning, *Cromwellian Foreign Policy*, p. 15. Ollard, *Cromwell's Earl*, pp. 38–40. Powell, *Blake*, p. 248. Firth and Rait, *Acts and Ordinances* II, 812–13. Derek Hirst, 'The English Republic and the Meaning of Britain', in Bradshaw and Morrill, *The British Problem*, pp. 192–219, at pp. 218–19.

2 *CCSP* II, 405–6. Capp, *Cromwell's Navy*, pp. 135–7. Junge, *Flottenpolitik*, p. 266. Binns, 'Lawson'.

3 Crabtree, 'Protestant Foreign Policy', p. 178; cf. Capp, *Cromwell's Navy*, p. 86.

4 Battick, 'Cromwell's Navy', pp. 30–34, 85–96, 112–14 and 186; and 'Cromwell's Diplomatic Blunder', pp. 283–6. Venning, *Cromwellian Foreign Policy*, pp. 38–44 and 65. Powell, *Blake*, pp. 252–6; and 'Blake and Mountagu', p. 341. Corbett, *Mediterranean* I, 236–55.

5 Fisher, *Barbary Legend*. Peter Earle, *Corsairs of Malta and Barbary* (London, 1970). Panzac, *Les Corsaires barbaresques*, pp. 11–112. J. de Courcy Ireland, 'The Corsairs of North Africa', *MM* LXII (1976), pp. 271–83. López Nadal, *El comerç alternatiu*.

6 *LRB* p. 295, to John Thurloe, 18 Apr 1655.

7 Fisher, *Barbary Legend*, pp. 216–27. Battick, 'Cromwell's Navy', pp. 124–32 and 288. Powell, *Blake*, pp. 262–4; and 'Weale Journal', pp. 108–9. Corbett, *Mediterranean* I, 260–71 and 292–5. *LRB* pp. 294–5 and 319.

8 Powell, *Blake*, pp. 269–72. *LRB* pp. 307–9. Corbett, *Mediterranean* I, 272–3. Battick, 'Cromwell's Navy', pp. 169–77.

9 *TSP* III, 466.

10 *TSP* III, 60.

11 Battick, 'Cromwell's Navy', pp. 144 and 148; 'Cromwell's Diplomatic Blunder' and 'Cromwell's Western Design'. Korr, *New Model Foreign Policy*, pp. 89–97. Venning, *Cromwellian Foreign Policy*, pp. 46–73 and 87. Junge, *Flottenpolitik*, p. 231. Burchett, *Complete History*, pp. 385–9. Crabtree, 'Protestant Foreign Policy', p. 178. R. C. Thompson, 'Officers, Merchants and Foreign Policy in the Protectorate of Oliver Cromwell', *Historical Studies Australia and New Zealand* XII (1965–7), pp. 149–65, at pp. 151–3.

12 A third never joined the expedition.

13 Firth, *Venables Narrative*, pp. x–xl. Penn, *Memorials* II, 37–46. Taylor, *Western Design*, pp. 9–11. Venning, *Cromwellian Foreign Policy*, p. 81.

14 R. H. Boulind, 'The Strength and Weakness of Spanish Control of the Caribbean, 1520–1650: The Case for the *Armada de Barlovento*' (Cambridge Ph.D. thesis, 1965), p. 545, quoting NMM: WYN/10/1.

15 Wright, 'Spanish Narratives'. Penn, *Memorials* II, 49–94 and 123. Firth, *Venables Narrative*. Taylor, *Western Design*, pp. 26–30. Rodríguez Demorizi, 'Invasión inglesa'. Incháustegui Cabral, *El Plan Antillano*. Battick, 'Rooth's Sea Journal', p. 13.

16 Penn, *Memorials* II, 51, Gregory Butler to Cromwell, Jun 1655.

17 Taylor, *Western Design*, pp. 38–128. Penn, *Memorials* II, 31–3 and 99–107. Battick, 'Cromwell's Navy', pp. 155–9.

18 Haring, *Buccaneers*. Bradley, *Lure of Peru*. Bridenbaugh, *No Peace beyond the Line*. Taylor, *Western Design*, pp. 131–93. Pawson and Buisseret, *Port Royal*, pp. 20–21. Dyer, 'Myngs in the West Indies'.

19 Battick, 'Cromwell's Navy', p. 248.

20 There seems to be no good source for this well-known phrase, often misattributed to Blake, but it certainly expresses the substance of Mountague's message.

21 Ollard, *Cromwell's Earl*, pp. 40–43. *LRB*, pp. 393–6. Cogar, 'Politics', pp. 196–208. Powell, *Blake*, pp. 274–6; and 'Blake and Mountagu', pp. 342–5. Baumber, *General-at-Sea*, pp. 213–14. Harris, *Sandwich* I, 90–91.

22 *TSP* V, 216; to the Secretary of State John Thurloe, 16/26 Jul 1656.

23 Powell, 'John Bourne', p. 112.

24 Firth, 'Blake and the Battle of Santa Cruz', pp. 228–31. Powell, *Blake*, pp. 287–91; and 'Blake and Mountagu', pp. 346–68. Penn, *Memorials* II, 153–8. Manwaring, 'Two Letters', p. 335. Otero Lana, *Los corsarios españoles*, p. 300.

25 *TSP* V, 171, to J. Thurloe, 30 Jun 1656.

26 *LRB* p. 383, to Admiralty Commission.

27 9 Feb 1656: *LRB* p. 382, and Manwaring, 'Two Letters', p. 338.

28 Firth, 'Stayner's Narrative', pp. 132–5 (both quotations); also *BND*, pp. 215–16. Other accounts of the battle in Dewar, 'Blake's Last Campaign'; Firth, 'Blake and the Battle of Santa Cruz', pp. 234–44; *LRB*, pp. 455–60; Powell, *Blake*, pp. 299–305, and 'Weale Journal', p. 146; Baumber, *General-at-Sea*, pp. 234–5; *AE* V, 26.

29 Clarendon, *Rebellion* VI, 38.

30 *DLN* II, 379.

31 Otero Lana, *Los corsarios españoles*, p. 300. Venning, *Cromwellian Foreign Policy*, p. 140.

32 Capp, *Cromwell's Navy*, p. 103. Jones, *Britain and Europe*, pp. 51 and 55. Baetens, 'Flemish Privateering'. Otero Lana, *Los corsarios españoles*, pp. 298–305. Hammond, 'Administration', pp. 305–11. Cogar, 'Politics', p. 191.

33 Battick, 'Cromwell's Diplomatic Blunder', pp. 289–97. Capp, *Cromwell's Navy*, pp. 100–101. *LMF* V, 224. Korr, *New Model Foreign Policy*, pp. 182–94. Robert Stradling, 'Catastrophe and Recovery: The Defeat of Spain, 1639–43', *History* LXIV (1979), pp. 205–219, at p. 214.

34 Hutton, *British Republic*, pp. 70–74. Korr, *New Model Foreign Policy*, pp. 185–7. Worden, 'Cromwell and the Sin of Achan', pp. 140–45. Harris, *Sandwich* I, 102–11. Venning, *Cromwellian Foreign Policy*, pp. 138–151. Capp, *Cromwell's Navy*, pp. 150–51 and 331.

35 The Danish island of Zealand, or Sjælland, on which Copenhagen stands; not to be confused with the Dutch province.

36 Roberts, 'Cromwell and the Baltic'. Capp, *Cromwell's Navy*, pp. 106–9. Anderson, *Naval Wars in the Baltic*, pp. 81–91; and *Sandwich Journal*, pp. xi–xxvi.

37 Ollard, *Cromwell's Earl*, pp. 67–71. *CCSP* IV, 246. Capp, *Cromwell's Navy*, pp. 333–40. Cogar, 'Politics', pp. 228–34.

38 Capp, *Cromwell's Navy*, pp. 342–50. Cogar, 'Politics', pp. 236–50. Binns, 'Lawson', p. 104.

39 Capp, *Cromwell's Navy*, pp. 353–65. Cogar, 'Politics', pp. 251–8. Ollard, *Cromwell's Earl*, pp. 80–81. Binns, 'Lawson', pp. 104–5. *GNZ* I, 260. Poynter, *Yonge Journal*, p. 38.

40 Venning, *Cromwellian Foreign Policy*, pp. 240–45. Korr, *New Model Foreign Policy*, pp. 196–211. Glete, *Navies and Nations* I, 184. Aylmer, *State's Servants* p. 335.

41 Clarendon, *Rebellion* VI, 94.

42 *TSP* III, 61, quoting T. Gage.

3 A Looking-Glass of Calamity

1 Rodger, *Safeguard*, pp. 421–4.

2 William Reid, 'Commonwealth Supply Departments within the Tower and the Committee of London Merchants', *Guildhall Miscellany* II (1960–68), pp. 319–52, prints the fragmentary minute-book of this body, without recognizing what it was.

3 Hammond, 'Administration', pp. 21–49. Capp, *Cromwell's Navy*, pp. 45–55. Cogar, 'Politics', pp. 25–48 and 74–82. Junge, *Flottenpolitik*, pp. 109–18. Aylmer, *State's Servants*, pp. 145–7. Rowe, *Vane*, pp. 158–62.

4 Cogar, 'Politics', pp. 27–8. HMC *Leyborne-Popham*, pp. 22–4, quoting (p. 22) Popham to Vane, 18 Jul 1649. Rowe, *Vane*, p. 159.

5 Hammond, 'Administration', pp. 51–4. Cogar, 'Politics', pp. 27–32, 56–8 and 108–10. *FDW* I, 240–43. *BND* No. 138, pp. 236–7. Rowe, *Vane*, pp. 169–77.

6 *FDW* II, 129; 24 Aug 1652.

7 Cogar, 'Politics', p. 121, quoting BLO: Clarendon MS 47 ff. 178 and 181–2.

8 Hammond, 'Administration', pp. 55–60 and 78–9. Capp, *Cromwell's Navy*, pp. 79–80. Cogar, 'Politics', pp. 116–40. Junge, *Flottenpolitik*, pp. 200–202. Rowe, *Vane*, pp. 178–88.

9 *FDW* IV, 368, to the Admiralty Commissioners John Salwey and Richard Carew, 22 Apr 1653. 'Our foreman' is Vane.

10 Hammond, 'Administration', pp. 60–62. Capp, *Cromwell's Navy*, pp. 122–8. Cogar, 'Politics', pp. 140–62. Firth and Rait, *Acts*

and Ordinances II, 708–11 and 812–13. *FDW* IV, 382–3. Rowe, *Vane*, pp. 189–90. Hollond, *Discourses*, p. 120.

11 Hammond, 'Administration', pp. 66–75. Cogar, 'Politics', pp. 168 and 223–58. Capp, *Cromwell's Navy*, pp. 341–2 and 363–5.

12 HMC *Leyborne-Popham*, p. 42, to E. Popham, 27 Sep 1650.

13 Wheeler, 'Navy Finance', pp. 459–60; and *World Power*, pp. 40–46, 64–5 and 94–139. Wheeler, 'Financial Operations', pp. 330–31 (Hammond, 'Administration', p. 87, gives slightly different figures). Capp, *Cromwell's Navy*, pp. 9 and 37–43. Sara Morrison, 'Fell, Sell or Save? The Dilemma in English Forest Policy, 1649–1660' (Western Ontario MA dissertation, 1996).

14 *FDW* VI, 43.

15 Wheeler, 'Financial Operations', pp. 332–9. *FDW* III, 304–6; IV, 57–8 and 296–7. Capp, *Cromwell's Navy*, p. 10. Cogar, 'Politics', pp. 113 and 154. Hammond, 'Administration', pp. 84–98. Junge, *Flottenpolitik*, pp. 314–29. Charles Dalton, 'The Navy under Cromwell: Its Strength and Cost, 1654', *JRUSI* XLIV (1900), pp. 1181–6.

16 Cogar, 'Politics', p. 217, quoting BL: Add. MSS 9300 f. 79.

17 Hammond, 'Administration', pp. 98–110. Cogar, 'Politics', pp. 174–212 and 251–2. Junge, *Flottenpolitik*, pp. 314–29. Wheeler, 'Navy Finance', pp. 462–5. Maurice Ashley, *Financial and Commercial Policy under the Cromwellian Protectorate* (London; 2nd edn 1962), pp. 47–8. *BND* No. 139, p. 237.

18 *FDW* IV, 306, to the Admiralty, 5 Apr 1653.

19 *FDW* II, 133, to Council of State, 25 Aug 1652.

20 Cogar, 'Politics', p. 131, quoting BLO: Rawlinson MS A.227 ff. 10–11.

21 *BND* No. 163, p. 282, to the Admiralty, 10 Nov 1653. 'Over the water' means to confinement in Landguard Fort.

22 Capp, *Cromwell's Navy*, p. 276.

23 Hammond, 'Administration', pp. 111–15. Capp, *Cromwell's Navy*, pp. 275–82. Cogar, 'Politics', pp. 132–3 and 209–10.

Aylmer, *State's Servants*, pp. 143–4. *ARN*, pp. 316–20. Deane, *Deane*, pp. 401, 422 and 604. *FDW* III, 73, 164–5, 279–80, 286–8 and 377. Tedder, *Navy of the Restoration*, pp. 12–14.

24 Wheeler, 'Navy Finance'; and *World Power*, pp. 50–52, 140–41 and 148–62. Rodger, *Safeguard*, p. 125. Cogar, 'Politics', pp. 174–5.

25 *FDW* I, 294.

26 *FDW* II, 74–6. Wheeler, 'Navy Finance', p. 463.

27 *FDW* III, 383, P. Pett and N. Bourne to the Admiralty, 16 Jan 1652.

28 *FDW* III, 384 and 395; V, 279–80. HMC *Portland* II, 87.

29 *FDW* V, 256, to the Admiralty, 5 Jul 1653.

30 *FDW* V, 274, to the Admiralty, 11 Jul 1653. 'Mart' = market.

31 *FDW* IV, 387, R. Deane and G. Monck to the Admiralty, 29 Apr 1653. 'Instrument' = agent, representative.

32 *ARN*, pp. 325–8. Cogar, 'Politics', pp. 170 and 253. Hammond, 'Administration', pp. 257–68. Junge, *Flottenpolitik*, pp. 166–9. Wheeler, 'Navy Finance', pp. 462–3. Baumber, 'Civil Wars and Commonwealth', pp. 286–93.

33 *ARN*, pp. 346–352. Baumber, 'Civil Wars and the Commonwealth', pp. 281–3; and 'Parliamentary Naval Politics', p. 407. Cogar, 'Politics', pp. 43–8.

34 *ARN*, pp. 362–8. Oppenheim, 'Navy of the Commonwealth', p. 59. Hammond, 'Administration', pp. 118–37. Cogar, 'Politics', p. 131.

35 *FDW* V, 301, to the Admiralty, 20 Jul 1653.

36 Robert Coytmore the Secretary of the Admiralty Committee came of the Caernarvonshire branch of the same family and was Bourne's cousin: Aylmer, *State's Servants*, pp. 265–6. Chaplin, 'Nehemiah Bourne', pp. 31–3. Eames, 'Sea Power and Caernarvonshire', p. 47; and 'Sea Power and Welsh History', p. 242.

37 Capp, *Cromwell's Navy*, pp. 303–4. Chaplin, 'Nehemiah Bourne'. Junge, *Flottenpolitik*, pp. 172–6.

38 Hollond, *Discourses*, p. 120.

39 Deane, *Deane*, p. 631, R. Deane and G.

Monck to the Admiralty Commission, 31 May 1653.

40 Baumber, 'Civil Wars and Commonwealth', p. 283. Aylmer, *State's Servants*, pp. 247–50. Junge, *Flottenpolitik*, pp. 181–3. Hammond, 'Administration', pp. 147, 153 and 325. Capp, *Cromwell's Navy*, pp. 50–51. Andrews, *Ships, Money and Politics*, pp. 58 and 200–202. *FDW* III, 164–5 and 279–80. Cogar, 'Politics', p. 52. Marsh, 'Navy and Portsmouth', p. 125.

41 HMC *Leyborne-Popham*, p. 46, 18 Oct 1649.

42 Hollond, *Discourses*, p. 310.

43 Hammond, 'Administration', pp. 133. *ARN* pp. 365–6. Cogar, 'Politics', pp. 92–8 (quoted pp. 95 and 93) and 170–72. Aylmer, *State's Servants*, pp. 157–8.

44 Maydman, *Naval Speculations*, pp. 55–6. Historians have long been influenced by *ARN*, whose own sympathies were strongly Republican.

45 Wheeler, *World Power*, pp. 32, 35 and 49.

46 Hammond, 'Administration', p. 23. Cogar, 'Politics', pp. 47 and 55.

47 Aylmer, *State's Servants*, p. 41. Frank H. Harris, 'Lydney Ships', *Transactions of the Bristol and Gloucestershire Archaeological Society* LXVI (1945), pp. 238–45 (quoting the shipwright Daniel Furzer, p. 238). Hammond, 'Administration', pp. 272–6. *ARN*, p. 361.

48 *ARN*, pp. 362–8. Hammond, 'Administration', pp. 118–19. Dietz, 'Dikes, Dockheads and Gates', pp. 145–6. Marsh, 'Navy and Portsmouth', pp. 120–21. Rodger, *Safeguard*, p. 71, tries to scotch the hardy myth of the 1496 Portsmouth dock.

49 Hammond, 'Administration', p. 146. Junge, *Flottenpolitik*, p. 172. *FDW* III, 369.

50 Hammond, 'Administration', p. 35, quoting PRO: SP 18/40 No. 142, 29 Sep 1653.

51 Hammond, 'Administration', pp. 224–6. *KMN* II, 9 and 19–26. *FDW* VI, 89–93. *ARN*, pp. 320–22. Gregory Robinson, 'Wounded Sailors and Soldiers in London during the First Dutch War (1652–1654)', *HT* XVI (1966), pp. 38–44.

52 *KMN* II, 14. *FDW* III, 320 and IV, 220.

53 *FDW* IV, 241, to Sir H. Vane, 21 Mar 1653.

54 *FDW* IV, 232, to the Council of State, 16 Mar 1653. These were men wounded at the battle of Portland.

55 *FDW* V, 270 and 343, Peter Pett and N. Bourne to the Admiralty, 10 and 30 Jul 1653.

56 G. E. Manwaring, ' "Parliament Joan", The Florence Nightingale of the Seventeenth Century', in *The Flower of England's Garland* (London, 1936), pp. 75–90. *KMN* II, 52. *FDW* IV, 104–5 and V, 247–8. *ARN*, p. 323 n.2.

57 *FDW* V, 300, to the Admiralty, 20 Jul 1653.

58 A. G. E. Jones, 'The Sick and Wounded in Ipswich during the First Dutch War, 1651–1654', *Suffolk Review* I (1956), pp. 1–7.

59 *KMN* II, 26.

60 *English Privateering Voyages to the West Indies 1588–1595*, ed. K. R. Andrews (HS 2nd. S. Vol. 111, 1959), p. 339 n.4, quoting the account book of the London privateer owner Thomas Middleton for the voyage of the *Vineyard* in 1603.

61 Rodger, 'Myth of Seapower'; and *Safeguard*, pp. 353–63, 379–86, 393–4 and 411–14.

4 The Melody of Experienced Saints

1 Aylmer, *State's Servants*, p. 267.

2 *FDW* V, 340, quoting a newsletter of July 1653.

3 Capp, *Cromwell's Navy*, pp. 53–6, 132–3, 138–43 and 296–8.

4 Capp, *Cromwell's Navy*, pp. 190–94. *FDW* III, 374–6 and 406.

5 Capp, *Cromwell's Navy*, pp. 171–2 and 201–4. *ARN*, pp. 358–60. *FDW* I, 11 and VI, 250. Penn, *Memorials* I, 427. Battick, 'Rooth's Sea Journal', p. 3.

6 *KMN* II, 74. Capp, *Cromwell's Navy*, pp. 201–11.

7 Hammond, 'Administration', pp. 197–8. *FDW* III, 373–4 and 383. Capp, *Cromwell's Navy*, pp. 206–8. Powell, 'Weale Journal'. Tanner, *Further Pepys Correspondence*, pp. 103–5.

8 Capp, *Cromwell's Navy*, pp. 155–67.

Powell, *Blake*, p. 291. Ollard, *Cromwell's Earl*, p. 41.

9 *FDW* V, 301–2, 20 Jul 1653.

10 Rodger, *Safeguard*, p. 409. *FDW* I, 6, 13 and 23. Capp, *Cromwell's Navy*, pp. 171–85.

11 HMC *Portland* II, 88–9, 27 Nov 1654 and 15 Jan 1655.

12 Capp, *Cromwell's Navy*, pp. 188–9. M. L. Baumber, 'The Protector's Nephew: An Account of the Conduct of Captain Thomas Whetstone in the Mediterranean, 1657–1659', *MM* LII (1966), pp. 233–46.

13 Appendix IV. Firth and Rait, *Acts and Ordinances* II, 9–13. *FDW* III, 269 and 285–8.

14 Tomlinson, *Guns and Government*, p. 49.

15 Capp, *Cromwell's Navy*, pp. 196–201 and 231–8, Hollond, *Discourses*, pp. 129–32. Hammond, 'Administration', p. 198. *ARN*, pp. 356–60.

16 *FDW* IV, 44 n.1; V, 331–2.

17 Capp, *Cromwell's Navy*, pp. 214–15, 242 and 289–90. Hendra, 'Penrose'.

18 *CSPD* 1659–60, p. 338, to the Admiralty, 31 Jan.

19 Capp, *Cromwell's Navy*, pp. 215–18. *ARN*, p. 319. *FDW* I, 249–50 and III, 313.

20 Capp, *Cromwell's Navy*, p. 217.

21 Capp, *Cromwell's Navy*, p. 81.

22 Firth and Rait, *Acts and Ordinances*, II, 9–13 and 578–80.

23 *FDW* IV, 163.

24 Hammond, 'Administration', pp. 176 (quoted) and 178. Hollond, *Discourses*, pp. 49–51.

25 *FDW* III, 400, to R. Coytmore, 21 Jan 1653.

26 Cogar, 'Politics', p. 136, quoting BLO: Clarendon MS 45 f. 204.

27 Hammond, 'Administration', p. 183, quoting PRO: SP 18/124 No. 18.

28 *FDW* I, 188.

29 *FDW* V, 37, to Navy Commission, 14 May 1653.

30 *FDW* V, 333–4, 27 Jul 1653.

31 Penn, *Memorials* I, 415 (quoted). *FDW* I, 140–41 and 186–7; IV, 233–5, 290 and 317–18.

32 *FDW* IV, 348, to the Navy Commission, 14 Apr 1653.

33 *FDW* V, 259, to the Admiralty, 6 Jul 1653.

34 *FDW* IV, 284, to [the Admiralty?], 30 Mar 1653.

35 Capp, *Cromwell's Navy*, pp. 248–9.

36 *FDW* VI, 107, to the Admiralty, 5 Oct 1653.

37 Capp, *Cromwell's Navy*, pp. 282–92. Cogar, 'Politics', pp. 133 and 157–9. Hammond, 'Administration', pp. 180–81 and 205–6. Hollond, *Discourses*, p. 128. *FDW* I, 129; III, 128 and 438; IV, 218; V, 295; VI, 128–30, 168 and 172–3. Powell, *Blake*, p. 247.

38 *ARN* p. 315. Hammond, 'Administration', p. 177. Powell, *Blake*, p. 203. Capp, *Cromwell's Navy*, pp. 272–4. Penn, *Memorials* I, 473. *FDW* III, 424; IV, 201 and 252–4. Eric Gruber von Arni, 'Soldiers-at-Sea and Inter-Service Relations during the First Dutch War', *MM* LXXXVII (2001), pp. 406–19.

39 Rodger, *Articles of War*, pp. 8–11. *ARN* pp. 311–12. *FDW* III, 267–8, 272 and 279–301.

40 *FDW* III, 293–9, quoting Arts. III, XII, XV and XXXI.

41 *FDW* III, 315–16.

42 *LRB*, pp. 197–8, to Navy Commission, 23 Jan 1653.

43 Penn, *Memorials* I, 427, 2 Jun 1652. Cf. *FDW* III, 394.

44 Capp, *Cromwell's Navy*, pp. 220–30 (quoted p. 221). *FDW* II, 262 and III, 37.

45 Eames, 'Sea Power and Caernarvonshire', p. 47.

46 Powell, 'Weale Journal', p. 98.

47 Hammond, 'Administration', p. 200. *ARN* p. 357 records a man sentenced to ten lashes alongside each flagship in 1653.

48 Battick, 'Rooth's Sea Journal', p. 6.

49 Capp, *Cromwell's Navy*, pp. 223–4.

50 *FDW* III, 274, Admiralty Committee report, 20 Dec 1652.

51 Always abbreviated in ships' muster-books as 'Ab'. Some time in the nineteenth century this began to be rendered 'A.B.', whence the absurd construction 'able-bodied seaman', coined presumably by someone who thought ordinary seamen were cripples.

52 *FDW* III, 148, 'Deputed Commissioners' to the Council of State, 9 Dec 1652.

53 *FDW* III, 100, to the Speaker, 2 Dec 1652.

54 Hammond, 'Administration', pp. 216 and 229.
55 *ARN* p. 328. Powell, *Blake*, p. 246.
56 Capp, *Cromwell's Navy*, pp. 243–9.
57 *CSPD* 1655, p. 135, Hatsall to Col. J. Clerke, 19 Apr 1655. Coxere, *Adventures*, p. 40.
58 Coxere, *Adventures*, p. 37.
59 Capp, *Cromwell's Navy*, pp. 249–57. Thompson, 'Haddock Correspondence', pp. 3–4.
60 Whistler's journal, 26 Dec 1654, in Firth, *Venables Narrative*, p. 144.
61 Capp, *Cromwell's Navy*, p. 306.
62 Penn, *Memorials* I, 318, 14 Dec 1650.
63 Penn, *Memorials* II, 126. Battick, 'Rooth's Sea Journal', p. 20.
64 Timothy George, 'War and Peace in the Puritan Tradition', *Church History* LII (1984), pp. 492–503, quoting (at p. 496) Alexander Leighton, *Speculum belli sacri; or the looking-glasse of the holy warre* (1624); cf. Exodus 15:3.
65 *FDW* IV, 94.
66 Capp, *Cromwell's Navy*, pp. 293–8. Penn, *Memorials* II, 64. Battick, 'Rooth's Sea Journal', p. 15. Amos C. Miller, 'John Syms, Puritan Naval Chaplain', *MM* LX (1974), pp. 153–63.
67 Capp, *Cromwell's Navy*, p. 323.
68 Penn, *Memorials* II, 64.
69 Deane, *Deane*, p. 607. 'The River' is the Thames.
70 Scott, 'Naval Chaplain', p. 50, quoting an order of 1654. Capp, *Cromwell's Navy*, pp. 319–21. Cogar, 'Politics', pp. 177–9.
71 Penn, *Memorials* II, 66.
72 Capp, *Cromwell's Navy*, pp. 307–19.
73 Powell, 'Weale Journal', p. 159, J. Weale to Hugh Peters, 22 Jan 1656.
74 Scott, 'Naval Chaplain', p. 49.
75 Capp, *Cromwell's Navy*, pp. 298 and 316. Deane, *Deane*, p. 540. Hammond, 'Administration', p. 245, quoting PRO: SP 18/202 No. 41.
76 Capp, *Cromwell's Navy*, p. 306. *ARN* p. 358. Hendra, 'Penrose', p. 18.
77 Smith, *Chaplains*, p. 17. *ARN* p. 371.
78 *FDW* V, 276–7. Besides Micah 6:8, he uses Psalms 9:12, Luke 1:52, Psalms 2:9 and 85:11 and 13.

5 Terrible, Obstinate and Bloody Battle

1 Speck, *Reluctant Revolutionaries*, pp. 28–31. Jones, *Charles II*, pp. 6–8 and 69. Hutton, *Charles the Second*, p. 254.
2 Israel, 'Emerging Empire', pp. 423–9. Corbett, *Mediterranean* II, 300–310. Jamieson, 'Tangier', pp. 9–11. Anderson, *Sandwich Journal*, pp. xxx–xxxi. Nicolaas Japiske, *De verwikkelingen tusschen de Republiek en Engeland van 1660–1665* (Leiden, 1900), pp. 55–7.
3 Corbett, *Mediterranean* II, 316–23. Jamieson, 'Tangier', pp. 13–15. Anderson, *Sandwich Journal*, pp. xxxiv–xxxv and 91–4.
4 Ollard, *Man of War*, p. 64.
5 Turnbull, 'Administration', p. 121, quoting Longleat: Coventry MSS Vol. 102 f. 12.
6 Jones, *Anglo-Dutch Wars*, pp. 89–93 and 145–9; *Britain and the World*, pp. 71–5; and *Britain and Europe*, pp. 57–8. Loades, *England's Maritime Empire*, pp. 202–3. Hutton, *Restoration*, pp. 215–16. Haley, *The British and the Dutch*, pp. 95–6. Wilson, *Profit and Power*, pp. 91–5 and 125–6. Davies, *Royal African Company*, pp. 41–3 and 64. Pincus, 'Popery, Trade and Universal Monarchy'; and *Protestantism and Patriotism*, pp. 222–317 (quoted p. 300).
7 Haley, *Temple*, p. 289.
8 Rowen, *John De Witt: Statesman*, pp. 28–30, 68, 119–21 and 182–3. Jones, *Anglo-Dutch Wars*, pp. 45–51, 70–71 and 78–9. Haley, *Temple*, pp. 39–44. Elias, *Vlootbouw*, pp. 103–57.
9 Davies, *Gentlemen and Tarpaulins*, p. 133, and Ollard, *Man of War*, p. 85 (giving slightly different readings).
10 Ollard, *Man of War*, p. 86.
11 Ollard, *Man of War*, pp. 87–130.
12 Oudendijk, *Johan De Witt*, pp. 87–8. Brandt, *De Ruiter*, pp. 294–361. *NZW* I, 604. Prud'homme van Reine, *Rechterhand*, pp. 130–38. Warnsinck, *Abraham Crijnssen*, p. 51. Blok, *De Ruyter*, pp. 178–98. Rowen, *John de Witt, Grand Pensionary*, pp. 461–2. G. S. Graham, 'Britain's Defence of Newfoundland', *CHR* XXIII (1942), pp. 260–79, at p. 265.

13 *DSP* V, 352–3. Tanner, *Further Pepys Correspondence*, p. 34, S. Pepys to Sandwich, 22 Dec 1664.

14 Anderson, *Allin Journals* II, xii–xv and 221–223; *Sandwich Journal*, p. xlv. Corbett, *Mediterranean* II, 340.

15 *Original Papers containing the Secret History of Great Britain*, ed. James Macpherson (London, 1775, 2 vols.), I, 28.

16 Fox, *Distant Storm*, pp. 87–93. Anderson, *Sandwich Journal*, pp. 174–8, 195–8 and 222. Corbett, *Fighting Instructions*, pp. 108–13, 122–9 (quoted p. 127). Tunstall, *Naval Warfare*, pp. 21–5. Taylor, 'Sandwich', pp. 137–8. Harris, *Sandwich* I, 287 and 298–9. Ollard, *Cromwell's Earl*, p. 129.

17 R. C. Anderson, 'Dutch Flag-Officers in 1665–7', *MM* XXIV (1938), pp. 40–48. Bruijn, *Dutch Navy*, p. 86. Fox, *Distant Storm*, pp. 95–8 and 360–67. *NZW* I, 559. Roos, 'Johan Evertsen', p. 132.

18 Pearsall, *Second Dutch War*, p. 9, quoting 'Observations on the battle', possibly by Penn.

19 Warnsinck, 'De laatste Tocht van van Wassanaer'. Fox, *Distant Storm*, pp. 108–26. Anderson, *Allin Journals* I, 234–44; and *Sandwich Journal*, pp. xlviii–lvi and 182–228. Harris, *Sandwich* I, 206–308. Prud'homme van Reine, *Schittering en schandaal*, pp. 241–4. *GNZ* I, 190–97. *NZW* II, 11–26. Penn, *Memorials* II, 322–51. *DSP* VIII, 491–2.

20 *GNZ* I, 253, 'Lord Sandwich's Narrative'.

21 Warnsinck, *Pieter de Bitter*. Harris, *Sandwich* I, 314–35. Anderson, *Sandwich Journal*, pp. 247–65. *NZW* II, 47–9. Jones, *Anglo-Dutch Wars*, pp. 160–63. Tedder, *Navy of the Restoration*, pp. 133–7. *GNZ* I, 250–58. Fox, *Distant Storm*, pp. 128–34. Ollard, *Cromwell's Earl*, p. 135. Barfod, *Niels Juels flåde*, p. 20. Lind, *Kong Frederik den Tredjes Sømagt*, p. 243. Jones, 'Dutch Navy', p. 19.

22 'Niet alleen onverstandigh ende capricieus is maer daeronder oock groote malitie toont . . . een dangereus mensch . . . aen dewelcke geen esquadre, ick laete staen een heele vloot, toevertrout behoort te worden.' *Brieven aan Johan de Witt*, ed. Robert Fruin and N. Japiske (HG 3rd S.

Vols. 42 and 44, 1919–22) II, 242 and 244, N. Vivien to J. de Witt, 13 and 14 Aug 1665.

23 *GNZ* I, 277, to Arlington, 28 Jul NS 1665.

24 Oudendijk, *Johan De Witt*, pp. 107, 122–3 and 128–9. Blok, *De Ruyter*, pp. 210 and 214. *NZW* II, 44–5. Prud'homme van Reine, *Rechterhand*, pp. 155–62; and *Schittering en schandaal*, pp. 247–9. Warnsinck, *Drie zeventiende-eeuwsche admiraals*, pp. 153–6. Bruijn, 'Cornelis Tromp', pp. 180 and 183. Fox, *Distant Storm*, pp. 147–9.

25 Harris, *Sandwich* II, 3–12. *GNZ* I, 266. Anderson, *Sandwich Journal*, pp. 277–82. Fox, *Distant Storm*, pp. 137–40. Ollard, *Cromwell's Earl*, pp. 137–47.

26 Fox, *Distant Storm*, pp. 163–210, has much the fullest and best analysis. Documents are in Powell and Timings, *Rupert and Monck*, pp. 55, 185–8, 201–7, 210–12, 216–17 and 221–31 (quoted p. 225); *GNZ* I, 298–301, 306–7, 317 and 332–4; *DSP* VII, 179–80; HMC *Hodgkin*, p. 54. See also *LMF* V, 441–54; Anderson, *Allin Journals* II, xvi–xviii; Corbett, *Mediterranean* II, 343–8; Hutton, *Restoration*, p. 242; Sue, *Marine Française* I, 567; Mémain, *Rochefort*, pp. 398–9; J. R. Powell, 'Talbot and the Division of the Fleet in 1666', *MM* LIII (1967), p. 136. For the Thames channels see Rodger, 'Weather', p. 181.

27 Fox, *Distant Storm*, pp. 154–8 and 216–34. Documents on the battle as a whole are in Powell and Timings, *Rupert and Monck*, pp. 231–60; Van Foreest and Weber, *De Vierdaagse Zeeslag*; *GNZ* I, 332–43; Penn, *Memorials* II, 388–91; Barlow, *Journal* I, 117–22. Other descriptions in *NZW* II, 66–84; Prud'homme van Reine, *Rechterhand*, pp. 167–74, and *Schittering en schandaal*, pp. 254–7; Taylor, 'Four Days Fight'.

28 Ingram, *Three Sea Journals*, p. 48. 'Cut' means cut their cables, to make sail in a hurry.

29 Fox, *Distant Storm*, pp. 235–58. Grove, *Til Orlogs under de Ruyter*, p. 94, prints a vivid narrative of the boarding of Berkeley's flagship. [Harman] 'met een zonderlinge standvastigheit als een eerlyk

soldaat hadt gequeeten': Brandt, *De Ruiter*, p. 483. This was Cornelis Evertsen the Elder, younger brother of Jan.

30 Ingram, *Three Sea Journals*, p. 49.

31 *GNZ* I, 335, quoting an anonymous 'Account of the Battle'.

32 Fox, *Distant Storm*, pp. 260–76.

33 Rodger, 'Weather', pp. 179–81.

34 Barlow, *Journal* I, 120. Powell and Timings, *Rupert and Monck*, p. 254, Clifford to Arlington, 5 Jun 1666.

35 Fox, *Distant Storm*, pp. 292–314.

36 Evelyn, *Diary* III, 441, 17 Jun 1666.

37 Fox, *Distant Storm*, pp. 316–21. Boxer, 'De Ruyter through English Eyes', p. 237.

38 'Rien n'égale le bel ordre et la discipline des Anglais, que jamais ligne n'a été tirée plus droite que celle que leurs vaisseaux forment . . . A la verité l'ordre admirable de leur armée doit toujours être imité . . .': Corbett, *Fighting Instructions*, pp. 118–19.

39 Powell and Timings, *Rupert and Monck*, p. 104. *GNZ* I, 414–15. Corbett, *Fighting Instructions*, pp. 129–37. Penn, *Memorials* II, 569–611. V. Vale, 'The Dating of the Duke of York's Supplementary Orders, 1672', *MM* XXXVIII (1952), pp. 223–4; cf. C. R. Boxer in *MM* XXXIX, 63. Weber, 'Single Line Ahead'. Van Foreest and Weber, *De Vierdaagse Zeeslag*, pp. 11–12 and 158–70. Taylor, 'Four Days Fight', pp. 297–9.

40 Prud'homme van Reine, *Schittering en schandaal*, pp. 260–64; and *Rechterhand*, p. 166. *BND* No. 128, pp. 217–19. Pearsall, *Second Dutch War*, pp. 27–8. Fox, *Distant Storm*, pp. 334–40. *NZW* II, 123–30. Powell and Timings, *Rupert and Monck*, pp. 261–79. *GNZ* I, 419–38. Bruijn, 'Cornelis Tromp', pp. 185–7.

41 Ollard, *Man of War*, pp. 148–58. *NZW* II, 147–8. Pearsall, *Second Dutch War*, pp. 32–3. Anderson, *Allin Journals* I, 281–3; and 'Latter Part of the Year 1666', pp. 18–24. Fox, *Distant Storm*, p. 342. *GNZ* I, 463–5. Powell and Timings, *Rupert and Monck*, pp. 122–4.

42 Fox, *Distant Storm*, pp. 344–6.

43 *GNZ* I, 580.

44 Rogers, *The Dutch in the Medway*, gives the best overall account in English.

Oudendijk, *Johan De Witt*, pp. 156–60. *NZW* II, 174–201 and 749–65. Jones, *Anglo-Dutch Wars*, pp. 173–7. *GNZ* I, 529, 555–7, 573–81 and 595–603. Powell and Timings, *Rupert and Monck*, pp. 282–8. Turnbull, 'Administration', pp. 132–3. Haley, *Temple*, pp. 46–53 and 121–3. Van Waning and van der Moer, *Dese Aengenaeme Tocht*. Geyl, 'Tocht naar Chatham'. Tanner, 'Administration', XII, 40. James, *Memoirs*, pp. 57–8. Davies, *Gentlemen and Tarpaulins*, pp. 147–51. D. A. Crofton, 'The Dutch in the Medway, June 9–13, 1667', *JRUSI* XXIX (1885–6), pp. 935–49. Hussey, *Suffolk Invasion*.

45 *DSP* IX, 88.

46 Chandaman, *English Public Revenue*, pp. 210–12. Pincus, *Protestantism and Patriotism*, pp. 348–427. Hutton, *Restoration*, pp. 218 and 270–75. Haley, *Temple*, pp. 162–3. Edye, *Royal Marines*, pp. 6–93.

47 Harris, *Sandwich* II, 26–7. Wilson, *Profit and Power*, p. 131.

48 *GNZ* I, 206, quoting an (English-language) Rotterdam newsletter. Cf. Fox, *Distant Storm*, p. 107, who identifies the captain as Anthony Archer of the *Good Hope*.

49 Bruijn, 'Dutch Privateering', p. 89. Barfod, *Niels Juels flåde*, p. 24.

50 Rommelse, 'English Privateering'. Marsden, 'Early Prize Jurisdiction'; and *Law and Custom*, II, 407–8. Tracy, *Attack on Maritime Trade*, pp. 33–4.

51 Eric J. Graham, 'The Scottish Marine during the Dutch Wars', *SHR* LXI (1982), pp. 67–74.

52 Henry L. Schoolcraft, 'The Capture of New Amsterdam', *EHR* XXII (1907), pp. 674–93. C. H. Wilson, 'Who Captured New Amsterdam?', *EHR* LXXII (1957), pp. 469–74.

53 Warnsinck, *Abraham Crijnssen*, pp. 54–70 and 148–66. Crouse, *West Indies*, pp. 17–84. Frank Fox, 'Hired Men-of-War, 1664–67', *MM* LXXXIV (1998), pp. 13–25 and 152–72, at p. 17. *LMF* V, 459–71.

54 Marsden, 'Early Prize Jurisdiction', p. 54.

55 Dyer, 'Myngs in the West Indies',

pp. 185–6. Pawson and Buisseret, *Port Royal*, pp. 23–4. Taylor, *Western Design*, pp. 212–20. C. H. Firth, 'The Capture of Santiago, in Cuba, by Captain Myngs, 1662', *EHR* XIV (1899), pp. 536–540. HMC *Finch* IV, 387, Sir C. Shovell to Nottingham, 12 Aug 1692.

56 Earle, *Sack of Panamá*, pp. 49–130. Pawson and Buisseret, *Port Royal*, pp. 25–8 and 42. Thornton, *West-India Policy*, pp. 67–110. Haring, *Buccaneers*, pp. 100–154. Bassett, 'Caribbean', pp. 1–84.

57 *DSP* VIII, 359–60.

58 Hutton, *Charles the Second*, p. 249. Glete, *Navies and Nations* I, 189. Chandaman, *English Public Revenue*, pp. 210–11.

6 Protestant Liberty

1 Rodger, 'Myth of Seapower'.

2 Jones, *Anglo-Dutch Wars*, pp. 92–9; *Britain and the World*, pp. 95–103; and *Britain and Europe*, pp. 61–2. Chandaman, *English Public Revenue*, pp. 222–8. Boxer, 'Third Anglo-Dutch War', pp. 70–73. Hutton, *Charles the Second*, pp. 286–90. Haley, *Temple*, pp. 26–34 and 278–87.

3 Haley, *Temple*, pp. 26 and 53 (quoted). Hutton, *Charles the Second*, p. 289. Glete, *Navies and Nations* I, 187–91. Villiers, *Marine Royale* I, 58–59 and 63–4.

4 Anderson, *Third Dutch War*, pp. 4–11. Ollard, *Man of War*, pp. 175–7. Fulton, *Sovereignty*, pp. 467–86. *BND*, pp. 197–8 (quoted p. 198).

5 This is Jean, comte, later duc, d'Estrées (1624–1707), like the Duke of York a Lieutenant-General in the French army. He should not be confused with his son Victor-Marie, marquis de Cœuvres, later duc d'Estrées (1660–1737), also an admiral.

6 Anderson, *Third Dutch War*, pp. 96–7, Narbrough's Journal. The version in Dyer, *Narbrough*, pp. 102–3, and 'Narbrough and Solebay', p. 225, is not quite accurate. 'Cunded' = conned. Brandt, *De Ruiter*, p. 675, quotes an unnamed English officer, a survivor of the *Royal James*, saying almost the same thing

of de Ruyter: 'Is dat een Admiraal! Dat's een Admiraal, een Kapitein, een Stuurman, een matroos en een soldaat. Ja die man, die Heldt, is dat alles te gelyk.'

7 Anderson, *Third Dutch War*, pp. 11–22, 93–103, 164–86 and 395–7 (better transcripts than HMC *Dartmouth* III, 13–23). Sue, *Marine Française* II, 366–422. Thompson, 'Haddock Correspondence', pp. 12–19. Villette-Mursay, *Mes Campagnes de mer*, pp. 145–6. Tunstall, *Naval Warfare*, pp. 32–4. Dyer, 'Narborough and Solebay'. *LMF* V, 532–46. *GNZ* II, 116–18. *NZW* II, 340–45. Vergé-Franceschi, *Duquesne*, pp. 253–60. Dessert, *Tourville*, pp. 78–83 and 87–91.

8 Prud'homme van Reine, *Schittering en schandaal*, pp. 294–308.

9 'Een vaillant en braef soldaet, maer niet bequaem om te commandeeren noch om gecommandeert te worden, alsoo hij te furieus was': Prud'homme van Reine, *Schittering en schandaal*, p. 313.

10 '. . . prinselijk woord, dat de Heer L. Admirael Tromp mag weesen gereguleert': Prud'homme van Reine, *Schittering en schandaal*, p. 313.

11 Prud'homme van Reine, *Schittering en schandaal*, pp. 330–31; and *Rechterhand*, pp. 247–58. Bruijn, *De Oorlogvoering ter Zee*, pp. 8–9 and 15–18; and 'Cornelis Tromp', p. 188. Warnsinck, *Schooneveld*, pp. 9–13. Japiske, *Correspondentie van Willem III* II, i, 297.

12 Warnsinck, *Schooneveld*, pp. 3–6. Anderson, *Third Dutch War*, pp. 27–9. Bruijn, *De Oorlogvoering ter Zee*, pp. 23–5 and 40. Powell and Timings, *Rupert and Monck*, pp. 41–2, 90, 265 and 288. Rodger, 'Weather', p. 181.

13 See the chart in Warnsinck, *Schooneveld*, p. 32.

14 Anderson, *Third Dutch War*, pp. 29–36, 300–302, 319–21, 334–5, 371–7 and 398–400. Warnsinck, *Schooneveld*, pp. 41–59. Prud'homme van Reine, *Rechterhand*, pp. 261–3. *NZW* II, 371–81. Tunstall, *Naval Warfare*, p. 35. Bruijn, *De Oorlogvoering ter Zee*, pp. 51–6. Japiske, *Correspondentie van Willem III* II, i, 237–9. HMC *Dartmouth* I, 20–23.

Thompson, 'Haddock Correspondence',
pp. 19–20. *GNZ* II, 235–53.

15 Anderson, *Third Dutch War*, p. 327,
Spragge's Journal.

16 Anderson, *Third Dutch War*, pp. 37–41,
303–4, 321–3, 336, 378–9 and 387–9.
Warnsinck, *Schooneveld*. Prud'homme
van Reine, *Rechterhand*, pp. 264–5.
Tunstall, *Naval Warfare*, p. 36. Bruijn, *De
Oorlogvoering ter Zee*, pp. 59–60, 118–20
and 165–6. Japiske, *Correspondentie van
Willem III* II, i, 244–5. *GNZ* II, 262 and
270–73.

17 Anderson, *Third Dutch War*, pp. 45–54,
354–62, 381–6, 390–94 and 400–405.
BND No. 129, pp. 219–22. *NZW* II,
410–24. Sue, *Marine Française* III, 23–40.
Bruijn, *De Oorlogvoering ter Zee*,
pp. 89–90, 152–5, 184–5 and 205–9. HMC
Dartmouth III, 27–33. Prud'homme van
Reine, *Rechterhand*, pp. 267–72. Tunstall,
Naval Warfare, p. 37. *GNZ* II, 288 and
297–362.

18 Chappell, *Pepys's Tangier Papers*, p. 314
(quoted). Boxer, 'De Ruyter', pp. 12–15;
and 'De Ruyter through English Eyes'.
Haley, *Temple*, p. 308.

19 Jones, *Charles II*, pp. 102–13; and *Anglo-
Dutch Wars*, pp. 97–100, 199–213 and
222–5. Boxer, 'Third Anglo-Dutch War',
pp. 85–91. Sue, *Marine Française* III,
23–65. Morrah, *Prince Rupert*, pp. 372–6.
Masson, *Histoire de la Marine* I, 112–13.
Ekberg, *Louis XIV's Dutch War*,
pp. 157–71. *LMF* V, 562–76. *GNZ* II,
336–42. Dessert, *La Royale*, p. 233; and
Tourville, pp. 94–5.

20 Bruijn, 'Dutch Privateering'.

21 Israel, 'Emerging Empire', pp. 437–8,
quoting Sir William Godolphin. 'The
Straits' are the Straits of Gibraltar, as a
figure for the Mediterranean.

22 Ollard, *Cromwell's Earl*, p. 255. Evelyn,
Diary III, 605–6 and 620 (quoted).

23 This is Cornelis Corneliszoon Evertsen,
called the Youngest until his father was
killed in 1665, and thereafter the Younger,
to distinguish him from his cousin-
german Cornelis Janszoon Evertsen,
called the Younger in his uncle's lifetime,
and thereafter the Elder. It is essential not
to confuse the three Cornelis Evertsens

with one another, or with any of the
numerous other members of the family
who commanded ships and squadrons of
the Admiralty of Zealand. Doeke Roos,
*Twee eeuwen varen en vechten; het
admiralengeslacht Evertsen (1550–1750)*
(Flushing, 2003) deals with the family as a
whole.

24 De Waard, *De Zeeuwsche Expeditie*.
Shomette and Haslach, *Raid on America*.

25 G. J. Ames, 'Colbert's Indian Ocean
Strategy of 1664–1674: A Reappraisal',
FHS XVI (1989–90), pp. 536–59. Boxer,
'Third Dutch War in the East'. G. C.
Kitching, 'The Loss and Recapture of
St Helena, 1673', *MM* XXXVI (1950),
pp. 58–68. *LMF* V, 498–525.

26 K. H. D. Haley, 'The Anglo-Dutch
Rapprochement of 1677', *EHR* LXXIII
(1958), pp. 614–48. Davies, 'Imperial
Navy', pp. 27–9. Hope, *British Shipping*,
p. 192. Chandaman, *English Public
Revenue*, pp. 234–9. O'Malley, 'Whig
Prince'. *CPM* prints the records of the
1673–9 Admiralty Board.

27 Jones, 'French Intervention'. Davies,
'Political Crisis'. Tanner, 'Pepys and the
Popish Plot'; and *Pepys's Naval Minutes*,
p. 181. Ollard, *Pepys*, pp. 272–92.

28 Speck, *Reluctant Revolutionaries*,
pp. 36–40. Childs, '1688', pp. 406–7.

29 Hornstein, *Restoration Navy*, pp. 33–52
and 101–3. Baltharpe, *Straights Voyage*,
pp. xiii–xx. Ollard, *Pepys*, p. 313. Panzac,
Les Corsaires barbaresques, pp. 11–112.

30 HMC *Dartmouth* III, 6, Spragge's
journal.

31 Anderson, *Allin Journals* II, xl–xlvii and
97–210. J. C. M. Warnsinck, 'Luitenant-
Admiraal Willem Joseph Baron van
Ghent', in *Van Vlootvoogden en Zeeslagen*,
pp. 347–81. Baltharpe, *Straights Voyage*,
pp. xxvii–xxxviii.

32 Dyer, *Narbrough*, pp. 151–3. *CPM* III, 64,
121, 179, 186 (quoted: S. Pepys to Duke of
York, 13 Apr 1676). Harris, *Shovell*,
pp. 61–3. Jamieson, 'Tangier', p. 71.

33 *CPM* III, 286 and 294, S. Pepys to R.
Rooth, 10 Oct, and Sir J. Narbrough,
14 Oct 1676.

34 Pagano de Divitiis, *Il commercio inglese*,
p. 267. Hornstein, *Restoration Navy*,

pp. 104–28 and 166–79 (quoted pp. 175–6); in 'Tangier and Exclusion', p. 341, she cites the same letter with a different date. G. A. Kempthorne, 'Sir John Kempthorne and his sons', *MM* XII (1926), pp. 289–317, at pp. 300–302.

35 Routh, 'Occupation of Tangier', p. 65.

36 HMC *Dartmouth* I, 72–3 and 61, Kirke and Povey, both to Col. George Legge, 10 Dec and 17 May 1681.

37 Routh, 'Occupation of Tangier'; and *Tangier*, pp. 343–64. Jamieson, 'Tangier', pp. 128–34. HMC *Dartmouth* III, 40–46.

38 A. Jamieson, 'The Tangier Galleys and the Wars against the Mediterranean Corsairs', *AN* XXIII (1963), pp. 95–112. G. E. Aylmer, 'Slavery under Charles II: The Mediterranean and Tangier', *EHR* CXIV (1999), pp. 378–88.

39 D. W. Donaldson, 'Port Mahón, Minorca: The Preferred Naval Base for the English Fleet in the Mediterranean in the Seventeenth Century', *MM* LXXXVIII (2002), pp. 423–36. Hornstein, *Restoration Navy*, pp. 158–208; and 'Tangier and Exclusion', pp. 331–62 (quoted pp. 343–4).

40 Middleton, 'Chesapeake Convoy System', p. 183. Hornstein, *Restoration Navy*, pp. 59–89.

41 Dyer, 'Journal of Grenvill Collins', p. 205. The 'Great Sea' is the Atlantic.

42 Anderson, *Allin Journals* I, 63–94. Hornstein, *Restoration Navy*, pp. 54–8 and 91–2. *CPM passim*, e.g. IV, 536–7 and 663. Teonge, *Diary*, pp. 34–6.

43 Baltharpe, *Straights Voyage*, pp. 29–30 (original spelling).

44 Baltharpe, *Straights Voyage*, p. 56.

45 Anderson, *Allin Journals* I, 63–4, 92–4 and 146.

46 Hornstein, *Restoration Navy*, pp. 134–54. Pagano de Divitiis, *Il commercio inglese*, p. 279, quoting Sir Leoline Jenkins, Secretary of State, to English consuls, 8 May 1682.

47 Le Fevre, 'Tangier and Glorious Revolution'. Davies, *Gentlemen and Tarpaulins*, pp. 185–95.

48 Hornstein, *Restoration Navy*, pp. 31 and 61–2; and 'The English Navy and the Defense of American Trade in the Late Seventeenth Century', in Reynolds, *Global Crossroads*, pp. 103–20. Chapin, *Privateer Ships and Sailors*, pp. 29–49.

49 Bassett, 'Caribbean', p. 314, quoting PRO: CO 1/42 No. 65. Thornton, *West-India Policy*, pp. 237–42 (quoted p. 237).

50 Earle, *Wreck of the Almiranta*. Cyrus H. Karraker, 'Spanish Treasure, Casual Revenue of the Crown', *JMH* V (1933), pp. 301–18. Earle, *Pirate Wars*, pp. 135–46.

51 Zahedieh, 'Hopeful Trade'. Earle, *Sack of Panamá*. Esquemeling, *Buccaneers*, pp. 127–223.

52 'Causa admiración la audacia para acometer, la paciencia para soportar toda clase de trabajos y penalidades, la constancia, á pesar de los más terribles contratiempos, y el valor indomable de los filibusteros, á quienes podríamos calificarlos de héroes, si para el verdadero heroísmo no fuera indispensable la virtud.' F. González Suárez, Archbishop of Quito, *Historia general de la República del Ecuador* (Quito, 1890–1903, 7 vols.) IV, 346.

53 Esquemeling, *Buccaneers*, pp. 289–475. Bradley, *Lure of Peru*, pp. 103–56. Spate, *Pacific* II, 132–57. Burney, *History of the Buccaneers. A Buccaneer's Atlas: Basil Ringrose's South Sea Waggoner*, ed. Derek Howse and Norman J. W. Thrower (Berkeley, Calif., 1992). P. K. Kemp and Christopher Lloyd, *The Brethren of the Coast: The British and French Buccaneers in the South Seas* (London, 1960). Various writers have re-created the buccaneers as utopian socialists, homosexuals and other modern stereotypes, and they continue to inspire the still more fertile imaginations of the film-makers.

54 W. E. May, 'The Navy and the Rebellion of the Earl of Argyle', *MM* LVII (1971), pp. 17–23.

55 Speck, *Reluctant Revolutionaries*, pp. 6–78. Childs, '1688', pp. 406–11. Davies, *Gentlemen and Tarpaulins*, pp. 199–208. Chandaman, *English Public Revenue*, pp. 256–61. On James's policies in general see John Miller, *James II: A Study in Kingship* (London, 1978).

56 Sonnino, 'Louis XIV's Wars', pp. 122–4. Israel, 'Emerging Empire', pp. 439–41.

Jones, *Britain and Europe*, pp. 70–84; and 'French Intervention', pp. 15–19.

7 Amazement and Discontent

1 *CPM* I, 98. Tedder, *Navy of the Restoration*, p. 4. Turnbull, 'Administration', p. 403. Chandaman, *English Public Revenue*, pp. 196–9 and 204–5. Wheeler, *World Power*, pp. 51–2 and 167–9.

2 Chandaman, *English Public Revenue*, p. 13. Ralph Davis, *English Overseas Trade 1500–1700* (London, 1973), pp. 35–7. O'Brien, 'Inseparable Connections', p. 55.

3 *CSPD* 1637–38 p. 351.

4 Gilbert Burnet, *History of His Own Time*, ed. M. J. Routh (Oxford, 1823, 6 vols.) I, 159.

5 Turnbull, 'Administration', pp. 18–24, 37–40, 62–70 and 142–3. Tanner, 'Administration' XII, 19–20. *DSP* X, 2–3 and 56–8. *CPM* I, 245–7. Anderson, *Third Dutch War*, p. 107. James and Shaw, 'Admiralty Administration', p. 19 n.4. Sainty, *Admiralty Officials*, p. 20. Collinge, *Navy Board Officials*, pp. 1–3 and 18–24.

6 *DSP* X, 21–2, 27–8, 53–4, 77–8, 243–4, 312–13, 398–9. Callender, 'Mennes'. Turnbull, 'Administration', pp. 207–38. Aylmer, *Crown's Servants*, pp. 46–7 and 179–83.

7 *DSP* III, 171.

8 Latham, *Pepys and the Second Dutch War*, pp. 25–35, 70 and 72. Tanner, *Further Pepys Correspondence*, pp. 26–7 and 208–13. Chappell, *Pepys Shorthand Letters*, p. 8. Knighton, *Pepys and the Navy*, published after this chapter was written, is now the first thing to read about him.

9 *DSP* VII, 60.

10 HC 1806 V, p. 5, 1st Report of the Board of Revision, which I take to echo what they had learned in investigating the Navy Office.

11 Latham, *Pepys and the Second Dutch War*, pp. xxxi, 9–13, 88–9, 148–54 and 166–76. Tanner, *Further Pepys Correspondence*, pp. 6–10, 15–19 and 20–25. *DSP* X, 137 and XI, 55. Turnbull, 'Administration', pp. 295–9. Pool, *Navy Board Contracts*, pp. 26–8.

12 *DSP* X, 77–8. Turnbull, 'Administration', pp. 310–19. Vale, 'Clarendon, Coventry'.

13 *DSP* V, 137, 30 Apr 1664.

14 Pearsall, *Second Dutch War*, p. 7.

15 *DSP* V, 330.

16 Tanner, *Further Pepys Correspondence*, p. 42, to W. Coventry, 15 Apr 1665.

17 Tanner, 'Administration' XII, 31–2; *Further Pepys Correspondence*, pp. 150–54. Hutton, *Restoration*, pp. 218 and 237. Chandaman, *English Public Revenue*, p. 212.

18 Turnbull, 'Administration', pp. 353–4.

19 Tanner, *Further Pepys Correspondence*, p. 48.

20 Turnbull, 'Administration', pp. 356–7. Chappell, *Pepys Shorthand Letters*, pp. 30–31. Pool, *Navy Board Contracts*, p. 31, quoting PRO: SP 29/138, 10 Dec. 1665.

21 Tanner, *Further Pepys Correspondence*, p. 170, to S. Pepys, 31 Mar 1667. Crown employees were to an extent protected from arrest for debt.

22 Tanner, *Further Pepys Correspondence*, pp. 172–3, to S. Pepys, 7 Apr 1667.

23 Chappell, *Pepys Shorthand Letters*, p. 67, 14 Oct 1665.

24 Tanner, *Further Pepys Correspondence*, p. 74, 4 Nov 1665.

25 *DSP* VIII, 109, 12 Mar 1667.

26 Tanner, *Further Pepys Correspondence*, p. 172, to S. Pepys, 4 Apr 1667.

27 *CSPD* 1664–5 p. 522, to S. Pepys, 17 Aug 1665.

28 Tanner, *Further Pepys Correspondence*, p. 58, to Sir P. Warwick, Secretary of the Treasury, 8 Oct 1665.

29 Tanner, 'Administration' XII, 41–8. Turnbull, 'Administration', pp. 155–61, 370–76, 417–21 and 476–509. Latham, *Pepys and the Second Dutch War*, pp. xxiii–xxxix and 269–435. Ollard, *Pepys*, pp. 200–224. Ranft, 'Political Career of Samuel Pepys', pp. 368–9. Chandaman, *English Public Revenue*, pp. 210–12. Aylmer, *Crown's Servants*, pp. 62–3 and 260. E. S. de Beer, 'Reports of Pepys's Speech in the House of Commons, March 5th, 1668', *MM* XIV (1928), pp. 55–8. Chappell, *Pepys's Tangier Papers*, pp. 335–7, prints Pepys's 'Journal of my

Proceedings in the Business of the Prizes', 1665, one of the items he was most anxious to conceal.

30 Latham, *Pepys and the Second Dutch War*, p. 371.

31 *BND* No. 141, pp. 239–41. Penn, *Memorials* II, 265–8. Turnbull, 'Administration', pp. 90–92. *DSP* VII, 307 and IX, 484. Aylmer, *Crown's Servants*, p. 181.

32 Chandaman, *English Public Revenue*, pp. 146–7 and 216–17. Wheeler, *World Power*, pp. 56–7. James, *Memoirs*, pp. 136–41. Turnbull, 'Administration', pp. 101–2, 166, 314–15, 361–5 (quoted p. 361).

33 Balleine, *Carteret*, pp. 132–6. Latham, *Pepys and the Second Dutch War*, pp. xx–xxi and 190. Tanner, 'Administration' XII, 49 and 98–9. Turnbull, 'Administration', pp. 146–74 and 188–205.

34 Latham, *Pepys and the Second Dutch War*, p. 140.

35 *CPM* I, 28–34. Tanner, 'Administration' XII, 41–5. Turnbull, 'Administration', pp. 93–5 and 207–40. Collinge, *Navy Board Officials*, pp. 18–24. Latham, *Pepys and the Second Dutch War*, pp. 191–4.

36 Tanner, *Further Pepys Correspondence*, p. 29, quoting Coventry from PRO: SP 29/104.

37 Turnbull, 'Administration', pp. 69–70, 115 and 461–8. *CPM* I, 15–16. Saville, 'Royal Dockyards'. Aylmer, *Crown's Servants*, p. 181. Ehrman, *Navy*, pp. 103–4. N. Macleod, 'The Shipwright Officers of the Royal Dockyards', *MM* XI (1925), pp. 355–69. Note that there are at least six Phineas Petts and seven Peter Petts of note. On the ramifications of the Pett family see A. W. Johns, 'Phineas Pett', *MM* XII (1926), pp. 431–42; the genealogies in *The Autobiography of Phineas Pett*, ed. W. G. Perrin (NRS Vol. 51, 1918), pp. l–li, are erroneous.

38 La Bédoyère, *Particular Friends*, p. 33. This is Leeds Castle, Kent, not the town in Yorkshire.

39 Shaw, 'Hospital Ship'; and 'Sick and Wounded'. James, *Memoirs*, p. 112. Tanner, *Further Pepys Correspondence*, pp. 116–18; and 'Administration' XII,

64–6 and 688–90. *CPM* I, 133–8 and IV, liii. La Bédoyère, *Particular Friends*, pp. 36, 64–5, 79 and 308. *KMN* II, 84–144. *GNZ* I, 269. Turnbull, 'Administration', pp. 50–51.

40 The latitude of the Canary Islands; this would cover all transatlantic voyages as well as those to the South Atlantic or the Indian Ocean.

41 Tanner, *Further Pepys Correspondence*, pp. 51–79; and 'Administration' XII, 37–9. *CPM* I, 152–6. Chappell, *Pepys Shorthand Letters*, p. 71. Powell and Timings, *Rupert and Monck*, pp. 42–3, 48, 132–3, 137–8, 142–3 and 166–74. *GNZ* I, 492–5. Turnbull, 'Administration', pp. 42–3 and 427–50.

42 *DSP* VI, 306. This well-known quotation is often misused to describe the post-1666 system of pursery.

43 Edye, *Royal Marines*, p. 40.

44 Tanner, *Further Pepys Correspondence*, pp. 93–111 and 189–90. It is extraordinary that this very important development does not seem to have been noticed by any modern historian. *WW*, pp. 87–98, describes pursery in detail as it was in the mid-eighteenth century, essentially in this system. *DSP* X, 286 is mistaken in crediting Pepys with the invention of muster-masters, which went back to 1627.

45 Bruijn, 'Mercurius en Mars uiteen', pp. 103–4. Mémain, *Rochefort*, pp. 902–3. Etienne Taillemite, 'Les Problèmes de la marine de guerre au XVIIe siècle', *XVIIe Siècle* Nos. 86–7 (1970), pp. 21–37, at p. 26. *GNZ* II, 30–31. Angel Guirao de Vierna, 'El professional del mar: reclutamiento, nivel social, formacion', in *España y el Ultramar hispanico hasta la Ilustración* (Madrid, 1989), pp. 97–112, at pp. 107–9.

46 Tomlinson, *Guns and Government*, pp. 20–46, 144–58 and 164. Latham, *Pepys and the Second Dutch War*, p. 120.

47 *CPM* I, 104–7, 117–19 and 156–8; II, 228–30. Saville, 'Royal Dockyards'. Albion, *Forests and Sea Power*, pp. 221–3. Turnbull, 'Administration', pp. 367–8 and 450–51. Anderson, *Third Dutch War*, p. 146. La Bédoyère, *Particular Friends*, p. 79. *KMN* II, 116–26. Tanner, *Further*

Pepys Correspondence, p. 266; and 'Administration' XII, 50–51. Chandaman, *English Public Revenue*, pp. 224–9.

48 *CPM* I, 38–42 and II, xi–xiv. Tanner, 'Administration' XII, 680. Ollard, *Pepys*, pp. 228–31. Grant, *Scots Navy*, pp. xxiv–xxvi. *BND* No. 143, pp. 242–4.

49 T. F. Reddaway, 'The Temporary Navy Office, 1673–84', *Transactions of the London and Middlesex Archaeological Society* XIX (1958), pp. 90–94; and 'Sir Christopher Wren's Navy Office', *BIHR* XXX (1957), pp. 175–88.

50 Tanner, 'Administration' XII, 693–7. *BND* No. 151 pp. 255–7. Ranft, 'Political Career of Samuel Pepys' (quoted p. 373). 'Admiral' here means Lord Admiral.

51 *CPM* IV, 415, quoting Charles II from the minutes of the Admiralty Board of 5 May 1677.

52 *CPM* I, 46–55; III, 380–82; IV, 406–7, 413–15 and 431–4. *CPM* II, 234 (of 1674) is another example of fear of Parliamentary censure.

53 Tanner, *Pepys's Naval Minutes*, p. 133.

54 Davies, 'Pepys and the Admiralty'. *CPM* I, 60 (quoted). Tanner, *Pepys Private Correspondence* I, 5–9.

55 Tanner, *Pepys's Naval Minutes*, p. 357.

56 Evelyn, *Diary* IV, 409.

57 Davies, 'Pepys and the Admiralty'; and 'Political Crisis', pp. 277–88. *CPM* I, 58–64 and 180–82. Pepys, *Memoires*, pp. 1–12. Tanner, 'Administration' XIV, 285–6. *BND* No. 144, pp. 244–5.

58 Ranft, 'Political Career of Samuel Pepys', pp. 373–4. *CPM* I, 66–7 and 77–8. Tanner, *Pepys's Naval Minutes*, pp. 167 and 232; and 'Administration' XIV, 55. Bryant, *Pepys* III, 207.

59 Coleman, 'Naval Dockyards', p. 141. *CPM* I, 80–89. Pepys, *Memoires*. Tanner, 'Administration' XIV, 56–65 and 261–6. Chandaman, *English Public Revenue*, pp. 256–61. Ehrman, *Navy*, pp. 205–10.

60 *CPM* I, 96. But Johnston, 'Parliament and the Navy', pp. 111–13, notes that Pepys had some influence on this committee.

61 Ollard, *Pepys*, pp. 254–5. Turnbull, 'Administration', pp. 263–4 and 413. *DSP* I, 308. Latham, *Pepys and the Second*

Dutch War, pp. 5, 19, 43–6, 53–5, 59, 64, 68, 95–108, 113–14, 117, 126, 199 and 217–18. *CPM* I, 185–7; II, 273–4; IV, 60 and 134–5. Tanner, *Further Pepys Correspondence*, pp. 122–3 and 131.

62 *DSP* VIII, 369.

63 Tomlinson, *Guns and Government*, pp. 34–8. Chandaman, *English Public Revenue*, pp. 213–16. Wheeler, *World Power*, pp. 56–8. *DSP* X, 109.

64 Chandaman, *English Public Revenue*, pp. 259–61.

8 Learning and Doing and Suffering

1 Glass, 'The Image of the Sea Officer'. Rodger, 'Myth of Seapower'.

2 Le Fevre, 'Tyrrell', p. 153.

3 Davies, *Gentlemen and Tarpaulins*, pp. 36 and 146. Latham, *Pepys and the Second Dutch War*, pp. 221–7. *DSP* II, 114; IV, 169–70 and 196; VII, 10 and VIII, 304. Ollard, *Pepys*, pp. 246–7. *CPM* I, 200–204. Chappell, *Pepys's Tangier Papers*, pp. 121–3, 150 and 212.

4 Capp, *Cromwell's Navy*, pp. 371–85. Davies, *Gentlemen and Tarpaulins*, pp. 30–33 and 130–6.

5 Ollard, *Man of War*, p. 137.

6 *DSP* III, 122.

7 Davies, *Gentlemen and Tarpaulins*, pp. 5–6 and 28–30; 'Devon and the Navy' I, 176; 'Wales and Mr Pepys's Navy', p. 109. Capp, *Cromwell's Navy*, p. 384. McDonnell, 'Irishmen in the Stuart Navy', p. 87. Kempthorne, 'Kempthorne'. Anderson, *Allin Journals* I, xi–xiii. *DSP* X, 67.

8 Davies, *Gentlemen and Tarpaulins*, pp. 24–5 and 30–31. Dyer, *Narbrough*. Peter Le Fevre, 'Sir Cloudesley Shovell's Early Career', *MM* LXX (1984), p. 92. Hattendorf, 'Rooke and Shovell', pp. 43–5. Harris, *Shovell*, pp. 2–7. Svensson, *Svenska Flottans Historia* I, 467 and II, 153. I place little reliance in the anecdote of Rooke's origins told by W. C. Boulter, 'A Contemporary Account of the Battle of La Hogue', *EHR* VII (1892), pp. 111–14.

9 'Ils avoient tous eu la peste, mais qu'ils étoient parfaitement guéris, et moins

susceptibles de maladie que les autres':
Penn, *Memorials* II, 301.

10 Anderson, *Sandwich Journal*, p. 173.

11 *DSP* VI, 45–6.

12 *DSP* VIII, 275.

13 Capp, *Cromwell's Navy*, pp. 384–5.
Ollard, *Man of War*, p. 169. Vale,
'Clarendon, Coventry', pp. 116–18.
Ingram, *Three Sea Journals*, p. 49. Davies,
Gentlemen and Tarpaulins, pp. 38–42.

14 Anderson, *Sandwich Journal*, pp. 179–80.

15 Ollard, *Man of War*, pp. 147 and 164.

16 Davies, *Gentlemen and Tarpaulins*, pp. 38
(quoted) and 63–6. Ingram, *Three Sea
Journals*, pp. 27–74. E. Altham, *Historical
Memoirs of the Royal Naval Club . . .*
(London, 1925), pp. 3–5.

17 HMC *Finch* II, 167, to Lord Finch, 13 Mar
1682, commenting on John, Lord Berkeley
of Stratton, who had just succeeded to the
title on the death of his brother, already a
captain. In spite of Charles's partiality, he
was not made a lieutenant until 1685, and
captain of a small vessel in 1686.

18 Dyer, *Narbrough*, pp. 127 and 135. Davies,
Gentlemen and Tarpaulins, pp. 161–75.

19 HMC *Dartmouth* I, 162.

20 Dyer, *Narbrough*, pp. 41–2. *CPM* II, 400
and 413–14; III, 98, 147–8, 209, 295 and
311; IV, 88–9. Chappell, *Pepys's Tangier
Papers*, pp. 132, 154, 158–9, 187, 191 and
215. Anderson, *Third Dutch War*, p. 295;
Allin Journals I, 142 and 226. Davies,
Gentlemen and Tarpaulins, pp. 60–62.
Perrin, *British Flags*, pp. 102–9.

21 *CPM* III, xxx–xxxi; IV, 90, 100 and
307–8. May, 'Midshipmen Ordinary and
Extraordinary'. *BND* No. 170, pp. 293–5.

22 Fox, *Distant Storm*, p. 21. Davies,
Gentlemen and Tarpaulins, p. 11. In 1672
Captain Richard Haddock of the *Royal
James* told his wife he had nearly 900
aboard, and the Duke of York's flagship
'1000, I believe, and upwards':
Thompson, 'Haddock Correspondence',
p. 11.

23 Fox, *Great Ships*, p. 73. Barfod, *Niels Juels
flåde*, p. 24. Martin-Leake, *Leake* I, 5.

24 Laughton, *Studies*, p. 277. *LMF* VI,
54–5. Malo, *Les Corsaires dunkerquois* II,
85. Powley, *King William's War*,
p. 151.

25 Davies, *Gentlemen and Tarpaulins*,
pp. 53–4. *BND* No. 169, pp. 292–3. *CPM*
I, 145–9.

26 Davies, *Gentlemen and Tarpaulins*,
pp. 58–9.

27 Edye, *Royal Marines*, p. 129 and
Appendix, pp. xxii–xxiv. Davies,
Gentlemen and Tarpaulins, pp. 59–60.
Tunstall, *Byng Papers* I, xxi–xxiii.
Hattendorf, 'Rooke and Shovell',
pp. 46–9. HMC *Finch* II, 127. Smith,
Chaplains, facing p. 47. Peter Le Fevre,
'The Dispute over the *Golden Horse* of
Algiers', *MM* LXXIII (1987), pp. 313–17.

28 *BND* No. 165, p. 283; W. Coventry to Sir
R. Stayner, 7 May 1661.

29 *BND* No. 170, p. 293.

30 *CPM* II, 232 and 185, S. Pepys to Capts. R.
Rooth and H. Killigrew, 24 Jan 1674 and
22 Dec 1673.

31 *CPM* IV, 493–4, 535–6 and 543–5 (quoted
p. 544). Ollard, *Pepys*, pp. 251–4.

32 Bruijn, *Varend Verleden*, p. 144. Rodger,
'Honour and Duty'.

33 Chappell, *Pepys's Tangier Papers*, p. 233.

34 Chappell, *Pepys's Tangier Papers*, p. 234.

35 Ollard, *Pepys*, pp. 230 and 315. Hutton,
Charles the Second, pp. 221 and 302.

36 Lloyd, *British Seaman*, p. 100, quoting
Josiah Burchett.

37 Davies, 'Pepys and the Admiralty', p. 42.

38 Merriman, *Queen Anne's Navy*,
pp. 310–11.

39 Latham, *Pepys and the Second Dutch War*,
pp. 200, 229–30 and 247–8. Tanner,
Further Pepys Correspondence, pp. 356–7;
'Administration' XIII, 45 and XIV, 281–3.
Howarth, *Pepys Letters*, p. 68. *DSP* VII,
212, 333 and 409; VIII, 141. *CPM* I, 193–9;
III, 55 and 132; IV, 60–61 and 494.
Chappell, *Pepys's Tangier Papers*, pp. 139,
141, 144–6, 159–60 and 174–84 (quoted
p. 184).

40 Derek Severn, 'Nelson's Hardy', *HT*
XXVIII (1977), pp. 505–12, at p. 511.
Dillon, *Narrative* II, 272–3.

41 Davies, *Gentlemen and Tarpaulins*,
pp. 41–52, 180–84 and 228–31. Ollard,
Pepys, p. 231. Glass, 'The Profession of
Sea-Officer', pp. 69–84. Pepys, *Memoires*,
and Tanner, 'Administration' XIV, 275–6,
print the allowances of table money,

which nearly doubled a captain's pay. *CPM* I, 210–19. On Colbert see (with different viewpoints but similar conclusions) Etienne Taillemite, *Colbert, Secrétaire d'Etat de la Marine et les réformes de 1669* (Paris, 1970), and Dessert, *La Royale*.

42 Evelyn, *Diary* IV, 432.

43 Thornton, *West-India Policy*, pp. 235–6. Anderson, *Third Dutch War*, p. 151. Tanner, *Further Pepys Correspondence*, p. 37. Latham, *Pepys and the Second Dutch War*, p. 134. *CPM* III, 227.

44 *CPM* IV, 494–5. Hendra, 'Penrose', p. 20.

45 *BND* No. 175, p. 302, to the Navy Board, 18 Nov 1678.

46 Barlow, *Journal* II, 302.

47 Curry, 'English Sea-Chaplains', p. 7 (quoting Captain Charles Royden). Ollard, *Pepys*, pp. 248–9.

48 Smith, *Chaplains*, p. 22 (quoted). Taylor, *Sea Chaplains*, p. 489.

49 Barlow, *Journal* I, 213–14.

50 P. M. Cowburn, 'Christopher Gunman and the Wreck of the *Gloucester*', *MM* XLII (1956), pp. 113–26 and 219–29. Mountfield, 'Greenvile Collins'. Dyer, 'Journal of Grenvill Collins'.

51 Tanner, *Pepys's Naval Minutes*, p. 112. Anderson, *Sandwich Journal*, pp. 135, 151 and 153. Anderson, *Third Dutch War*, pp. 72–3, 107, 122, 132, 205 and 278. Ollard, *Man of War*, pp. 84 and 123–4.

52 Robinson, 'Narbrough's Voyage', pp. 85–6.

53 Baltharpe, *Straights Voyage*, p. 19.

54 Chappell, *Pepys's Tangier Papers*, p. 4. Taylor, *Sea Chaplains*, p. 555. Firth, *Naval Songs and Ballads*, p. 75. Scott, 'Naval Chaplain', pp. 57 and 60. *DNB sv* Samuel Speed attributes the story to the wrong man at an imaginary battle.

55 Davies, *Gentlemen and Tarpaulins*, p. 67.

56 Powell and Timings, *Rupert and Monck*, pp. 53 and 79.

57 Davies, *Gentlemen and Tarpaulins*, pp. 67–9.

58 Teonge, *Diary*, p. 241; cf. Davies, 'Wales and Mr Pepys's Navy'.

59 Anderson, *Third Dutch War*, pp. 59 and 339.

60 *BND* No. 173, p. 299. Davies, *Gentlemen and Tarpaulins*, pp. 69–70 and 98–9; and 'Devon and the Navy', p. 176. Baltharpe, *Straights Voyage*, p. 87. Le Fevre and Harding, *Precursors of Nelson*, 'Introduction', pp. 8–9. Latham, *Pepys and the Second Dutch War*, p. 215. Ollard, *Man of War*, p. 205.

61 Latham, *Pepys and the Second Dutch War*, p. 217.

62 *CPM* II, 43 and 196.

63 *DSP* VII, 165.

64 *CSPD* 1664–5 p. 240, 6 Mar 1665.

65 *BND* No. 167 pp. 291–2, to his father Sir Thomas Browne, 16 Jul 1666.

66 *CSPD* 1667–8 p. 364; to the Navy Board, 29 Apr 1668.

67 Powell and Timings, *Rupert and Monck*, p. 94.

68 Turnbull, 'Administration', pp. 45–8 and 378–92. Latham, *Pepys and the Second Dutch War*, pp. 203–6. Davies, *Gentlemen and Tarpaulins*, pp. 71–7; and 'Devon and the Navy', pp. 176–7. Baltharpe, *Straights Voyage*, pp. 12–15. Tanner, 'Administration' XII, 36 and XIV, 284. Fox, *Distant Storm*, pp. 24–5 and 89–91. Powell and Timings, *Rupert and Monck*, pp. 46–7, 66–8 and 78. Anderson, *Sandwich Journal*, p. 222. James, *Memoirs*, pp. 106–111, 135–6 and 145–6.

69 *DSP* VII, 189–90.

70 *CPM* I, 123–6 and 132; II, 233 (quoted) and 234; IV, xlvii–xlviii.

71 Robinson, 'Admiralty and Naval Affairs', p. 31.

72 James, *Memoirs*, p. 274. Grant, *Scots Navy*, pp. xix–xx.

73 Anderson, *Third Dutch War*, p. 340. The *Oxford English Dictionary* offers no plausible contemporary meaning of 'trouncer'.

74 Davies, *Gentlemen and Tarpaulins*, p. 76. Teonge, *Diary*, p. 209.

75 Tedder, *Navy of the Restoration*, p. 118.

76 Davies, *Gentlemen and Tarpaulins*, pp. 78–85. Barlow, *Journal* I, 83 and 89–90. Steckley, 'Litigious Mariners'. Earle, *Sailors*, pp. 31–8. *Courts of Admiralty in Colonial America: The Maryland Experience, 1634–1776,*

ed. David R. Owen and Michael C. Tolley (Durham, N.C., 1995), pp. 2–3 and 11.

77 Schoenfeld, 'Restoration Seaman', pp. 279–80.

78 Turnbull, 'Administration', pp. 405–9. Latham, *Pepys and the Second Dutch War*, pp. 207–9.

79 *DSP* VIII, 394.

80 'And we know that all things work together for good to them that love God . . .': Teonge, *Diary*, p. 63.

81 Barlow, *Journal* I, 112.

82 Robinson, 'Narbrough's Voyage', p. 59.

83 Barlow, *Journal* I, 164–5.

84 Anderson, *Third Dutch War*, p. 69.

85 Baltharpe, *Straights Voyage*, p. 37.

86 Chappell, *Pepys's Tangier Papers*, pp. 8, 11 and 13. Baltharpe, *Straights Voyage*, pp. 21–2.

87 Bent, 'Covel Diaries', p. 103.

88 Bent, 'Covel Diaries', pp. 105–6. Chappell, *Pepys's Tangier Papers*, p. 15. Barlow, *Journal* I, 181.

89 James, *Memoirs*, p. 83. Tedder, *Navy of the Restoration*, pp. 67–8.

90 Bent, 'Covel Diaries', p. 129.

91 Teonge, *Diary*, p. 208. 29 May was the anniversary of Charles II's restoration.

92 Anderson, *Allin Journals* II, 88. *NZW* II, 219–21.

93 Anderson, *Allin Journals* I, 264 (quoted). Barlow, *Journal* I, 101. Anderson, *Third Dutch War*, pp. 65, 68, 78, 84, 108 and 189. Baltharpe, *Straights Voyage*, pp. 53–4. *GNZ* II, 94.

94 Poynter, *Yonge Journal*, p. 49; cf. Anderson, *Sandwich Journal*, p. 132.

95 Anderson, *Allin Journals* I, 270 and II, 84; *Third Dutch War*, p. 68. Teonge, *Diary*, p. 42. Bent, 'Covel Diaries', p. 129.

96 Earle, *Sailors*, pp. 34–5. Teonge, *Diary*, p. 53. Tedder, *Navy of the Restoration*, pp. 69–70.

97 Teonge, *Diary*, p. 31.

98 Teonge, *Diary*, p. 44.

99 Barlow, *Journal* I, 54, 59–60, 68–9, 83, 127–8 and 213. Baltharpe, *Straights Voyage*, pp. 23, 38, 59–63. Poynter, *Yonge Journal*, p. 48.

100 Baltharpe, *Straights Voyage*, pp. 67–8.

101 Anderson, *Third Dutch War*, pp. 148–9.

102 Robinson, 'Narbrough's Voyage', p. 14. The transcript in Dyer, *Narbrough*, p. 66, is not entirely accurate.

103 Anderson, *Third Dutch War*, pp. 119, 128 and 130.

104 Robinson, 'Narbrough's Voyage', p. 20. Teonge, *Diary*, p. 248.

105 Robinson, 'Narbrough's Voyage', pp. 27 and 58.

106 Earle, *Sailors*, pp. 148–61. Chappell, *Pepys's Tangier Papers*, pp. 173 and 237. Anderson, *Allin Journals* I, 3. Davies, *Gentlemen and Tarpaulins*, pp. 95–101. Barlow, *Journal* I, 161–2.

107 Anderson, *Allin Journals* I, 6, 60 (quoted), 121, 241; II, 206. Teonge, *Diary*, p. 220 (quoted).

108 Anderson, *Sandwich Journal*, p. 146.

109 Teonge, *Diary*, pp. 79 and 196.

110 *KMN* II, 91.

111 Powell and Timings, *Rupert and Monck*, pp. 13, 30 and 48. Teonge, *Diary*, p. 37.

112 Teonge, *Diary*, p. 29.

113 Evelyn, *Diary* III, 408.

114 Latham, *Pepys and the Second Dutch War*, pp. 229–30, 247–8. Howarth, *Pepys Letters*, p. 68. *DSP* VII, 333.

115 *Tangier at High Tide: The Journal of John Luke 1670–1673*, ed. Helen Andrews Kaufman (Geneva and Paris, 1958), p. 65.

116 Teonge, *Diary*, p. 49.

117 Tanner, 'Administration' XIV, 282. *BND* No. 171 pp. 295–6. *CPM* I, 205; IV, 400–402 and 544–5. Anderson, *Allin Journals* I, 58; and *Third Dutch War*, p. 77. Chappell, *Pepys's Tangier Papers*, pp. 4 and 6. Scott, 'Naval Chaplain', pp. 57–76. Davies, *Gentlemen and Tarpaulins*, pp. 104–10.

118 Gooch, 'Catholic Officers'. Davies, *Gentlemen and Tarpaulins*, pp. 104–16. That Strickland had Mass said aboard his ship has been generally credited (except by Powley, *Revolution of 1688*, p. 26), but I have never seen first-hand evidence. Catholic canon law forbade the saying of Mass in a ship at sea, though it might have been possible at anchor.

119 Bent, 'Covel Diaries', p. 127; cf. *BND* No. 167, p. 291.

9 Mad Proceedings

1 Childs, '1688'. Speck, 'Orangist Conspiracy', pp. 453–5.

2 Baxter, *William III*, pp. 225–6 and 230–31. Israel, 'The Dutch Republic and the "Glorious Revolution" ', pp. 34–8; and 'Emerging Empire', pp. 439–41. Sonnino, 'Louis XIV's Wars', pp. 122–5. Jones, 'French Intervention', pp. 5–6 and 15–19. Symcox, *French Sea Power*, pp. 72–4. Meyer, *Béveziers*, pp. 3–7 and 31–2. Masson, *Histoire de la Marine* I, 110 and 118–22. Rose, *England in the 1690s*, p. 115. Hoak, 'Anglo-Dutch Revolution', pp. 25–6. Carswell, *Descent on England*, pp. 25–33, 172–3 and 233.

3 Speck, 'Orangist Conspiracy'. Le Fevre, 'Torrington', pp. 26–8. Ware, 'Torrington', pp. 83–4.

4 Hoak, 'Anglo-Dutch Revolution', pp. 17–18. Van der Kuijl, *De glorieuze overtocht*, pp. 23–37. Groenveld, 'Une flotte très considerable'. Israel and Parker, 'Providence and Protestant Winds', pp. 337–8 and 351. Japiske, *Correspondentie van Willem III* I, i, 57–8; ii, 610–16. *NZW* III, 36–55. Jones, 'Protestant Wind', p. 201. Israel, 'The Dutch Republic and the "Glorious Revolution" ', p. 33. Haley, *The British and the Dutch*, pp. 136–8.

5 HMC *Dartmouth* I, 165, S. Pepys to Dartmouth, 17 Oct 1688.

6 Tanner, 'Naval Preparations', pp. 272–4. Ehrman, 'Pepys's Organization', pp. 211–17. Burchett, *Complete History*, pp. 408–14.

7 HMC *Dartmouth* III, 56, Journal of Grenville Collins, master of Dartmouth's flagship *Resolution*.

8 HMC *Dartmouth* I, 262–3. Jones, 'Protestant Wind'. Japiske, *Correspondentie van Willem III* I, ii, 623–4; II, iii, 45 and 53. *NZW* III, 55–65. Powley, *Revolution of 1688*, pp. 41–80. Anderson, 'Combined Operations'; and 'Prince William's Descent'. Pearsall, 'Invasion Voyage'.

9 Le Fevre, 'Tangier and the Glorious Revolution'. Laughton, *Torrington Memoirs*, pp. 26–7. Davies, 'James II, William of Orange'; and *Gentlemen and Tarpaulins*, pp. 207–15. Burchett, *Complete History*, p. 414. Powley, *Revolution of 1688*, pp. 95–7. M. J. Sydenham, 'The Anxieties of an Admiral: Lord Dartmouth and the Revolution of 1688', *HT* XII (1962), pp. 714–20. Tunstall, *Byng Papers* I, xxxiv–xxxviii. Ollard, *Pepys*, p. 342 (quoted); the version in HMC *Dartmouth* I, 267 is slightly modernized.

10 Holmes, *Great Power*, pp. 176–89. Childs, '1688', pp. 414–21. Beddard, 'Whig Revolution', pp. 12–16, 73–4 and 94–6. Morrill, 'Sensible Revolution', pp. 82–7.

11 Van der Kuijl, *De glorieuze overtocht*, pp. 45–50. Israel, 'General Introduction' to *Anglo-Dutch Moment*; and 'The Dutch Republic and the "Glorious Revolution" ', pp. 39–42. Jones, 'William III and the English'. Bruijn, 'William III and his Two Navies', p. 119.

12 The master and two mates of the English merchantman *Worcester* hanged on a trumped-up charge of piracy; but this was in 1704, when the political context had somewhat evolved. See Goldie, 'Divergence and Union', p. 237; and Grant, *Old Scots Navy*, p. 253.

13 Goldie, 'Divergence and Union'. Morrill, 'Sensible Revolution', p. 99; and 'British Problem', p. 38. Rose, *England in the 1690s*, pp. 210–15.

14 Jones, 'William III and the English', pp. 18–20. Ehrman, *Navy*, pp. 269–73. Baxter, *William III*, p. 307. Clark, *Dutch Alliance*, pp. 143–4.

15 This is known as the War of the League of Augsburg; otherwise the War of the English Succession, the Nine Years' War, or King William's War, besides other names in other languages.

16 Symcox, *French Sea Power*, pp. 76–85. Pilgrim, 'French Naval Power', pp. 324–7. Warnsinck, *De Vloot*, pp. 6–7. Clark, *Dutch Alliance*, pp. 37–39. Bruijn, 'William III and his Two Navies', pp. 116–20. Ehrman, *Navy*, pp. 245–59. Powley, *King William's War*, pp. 44–119. Israel, 'The Dutch Republic and the "Glorious Revolution" ', p. 40. Van Schelven, *Almonde*, pp. 52–4.

17 At thirteen *livres* to the pound sterling.
18 Dessert, *La Royale*. Pilgrim, 'French Naval Power' and 'Colbert-Seignelay Naval Reforms'. Taillemite, 'Une Marine Pour Quoi Faire?'; also 'Colbert et la marine', in *Un nouveau Colbert*, ed. Roland Mousnier (Paris, 1985), pp. 216–27; and 'Colbert et l'Ordonnance de 1689: synthèse d'une œuvre legislative', *CHM* No. 17 (1988), pp. 2–38. Acerra, *Rochefort* I, 32–84 and 220–21; III, 602–8 and 627. Acerra and Zysberg, *L'Essor des marines*, pp. 20–24, 50–51, 61–4, 79–81 and 102–4. Meyer, 'La Marine française de 1545 à 1715'. Masson, *Histoire de la Marine* I, 66–79 and 176. Jean Peter, *Les Manufactures de la Marine sous Louis XIV: la naissance d'une industrie d'armement* (Paris, 1997), p. 306. Rodger, 'Form and Function'. Jean Meyer, 'States, Roads, War and the Organization of Space', in Contamine, *War and Competition between States*, pp. 99–127, at p. 110. Symcox, *French Sea Power*, and Villiers, 'Marine de Colbert', are still somewhat dazzled by Louis XIV's navy: recent French writers like Taillemite, Meyer, Masson, Acerra and Dessert are in varying degrees more sceptical.
19 *NZW* III, 89–97, 147–55 and 721–49. Bruijn, *Varend Verleden*, pp. 129–42; *Dutch Navy*, pp. 99–110; and *Admiraliteit van Amsterdam*, p. 9. Warnsinck, *De Vloot*, pp. 6–7 and 15–19.
20 Davies, 'Navy on the Eve of War'. Ryan, 'William III and the Brest Fleet'. Duffy, 'Devon and Naval Strategy' I, 182–5. John B. Hattendorf, 'The English Royal Navy', in *The Age of William III and Mary II: Power, Politics and Patronage 1688–1702*, ed. Robert P. Maccubbin and Martha Hamilton-Phillips (Williamsburg, 1989), pp. 127–32.
21 HMC *Finch* II, 200, to Nottingham, 17 Apr 1689.
22 *LMF* VI, 47–50. Ehrman, *Navy*, pp. 245–46 and 265–6. Powley, *King William's War*, pp. 133–45. Villette-Mursay, *Mes Campagnes de mer*, pp. 148–50. Symcox, *French Sea Power*, p. 84. Meyer, *Béveziers*, pp. 49–51. HMC *Finch* II, 206. Duffy, 'Western Squadron',

p. 61. Calmon-Maison, *Château-Renault*, pp. 119–22.
23 Duffy, 'Devon and Naval Strategy' I, 182. The *Royal Sovereign*, ex-*Sovereign of the Seas*, was launched in 1637. The same reflection was current aboard her in 1691: Barlow, *Journal* II, 419.
24 Lawson, 'Public Opinion', pp. 16–32 and 298–300. *LMF* VI, 51. Symcox, *French Sea Power*, pp. 83–9. Grant, *Scots Navy*, pp. 2–3 and 26–9. Powley, *King William's War*, pp. 148–9, 166–90, 240–42, 247–55 and 280–97. Aubrey, *James Stuart's Armada*, pp. 33–41. Kerrigan, 'Ireland in Naval Strategy', pp. 170–72. Masson, *Histoire de la Marine* I, 126–28. HMC *Finch* II, 247, E. Russell to Nottingham, 19 Sep 1689 (quoted).
25 Ehrman, *Navy*, pp. 321–30. Lawson, 'Public Opinion', pp. 35–42. Symcox, *French Sea Power*, pp. 91–7. Meyer, *Béveziers*, pp. 59–69. HMC *Finch* II, 273. Powley, *King William's War*, pp. 346–50.
26 Ehrman, *Navy*, p. 350.
27 Burchett, *Complete History*, pp. 422–5. Ehrman, *Navy*, pp. 343–9. HMC *Finch* II, 282, 315–18, 331–2, 381 and 439. Warnsinck, *De Vloot*, pp. 72–4 and 94–5. *BND* No. 121, pp. 201–2. Le Fevre, 'A Sacrifice to the Allies', pp. 55–6.
28 This is Cornelis Corneliszoon Evertsen the Younger, formerly the Youngest, the same who had commanded the Zealand squadron in the West Indies in 1672–3 and negotiated the 1678 Anglo-Dutch naval agreement.
29 '. . . Une faute bien considérable, pour les gens du métier, dont je vis bien d'abord que je profiterais': Calmon-Maison, *Château-Renault*, p. 132.
30 *LMF* VI, 67–76. Laughton, *Torrington Memoirs*, pp. 44–7. Meyer, *Béveziers*, pp. 77–90. Edye, *Royal Marines*, pp. 320–21. Delarbre, *Tourville*, pp. 340–41. Burchett, *Complete History*, pp. 425–7. Warnsinck, *De Vloot*, pp. 94–126. Villette-Mursay, *Mes Campagnes de mer*, pp. 197–8. Taillemite and Guillaume, *Tourville et Béveziers*, pp. 73–82 and 86–90. Calmon-Maison, *Château-Renault*, pp. 130–36. *NZW* III,

196–217. HMC *Portland* VIII, 29–32. Dessert, *Tourville*, pp. 234–9.

31 HMC *Finch* II, 334.

32 Phillips, 'Journal', p. 199.

33 Ehrman, *Navy*, pp. 352–366. Lawson, 'Public Opinion', pp. 51–8. *NZW* III, 217–24. James, 'Lords Commissioners', pp. 76–91 and 272–4. HMC *Finch* II, 342–3, 351, 382–3 and 493–5. Aubrey, *James Stuart's Armada*, pp. 50–54. Warnsinck, *De Vloot*, pp. 127–37. Krämer, *Maison d'Orange-Nassau* I, 70–73.

34 'L'espérance certaine que j'ai du gain de la bataille me donne lieu de vous féliciter par avance de la gloire que vous aurez acquise dans cette occasion, mais comme il ne faut pas en demeurer là, je serai bien aise que, aussitôt après le combat, vous me fassiez savoir ce que vous pensez de l'emploi de la flotte pendant le reste de la campagne . . .': Delarbre, *Tourville*, p. 183 n.2.

35 Not Tynemouth, as some French writers suppose.

36 Symcox, *French Sea Power*, pp. 99–102. Meyer, *Béveziers*, pp. 91–4 and 119–21. Jean-Luc Suberchicot, 'Contrainte sanitaire et grandes escadres: la flotte de Tourville à Béveziers', *XVIIe Siècle* XLIX (1997), pp. 455–78. Delarbre, *Tourville*, pp. 183–7 and 342–7. Masson, *Histoire de la Marine* I, 129–133. Coquelle, 'Les Projets de descente' XV, 436–9. Dessert, *Tourville*, pp. 226–33 and 240–47.

37 'Letter Book of Richard Talbot', ed. Lilian Tate, *Analecta Hibernica* IV (1932), pp. 99–138, at p. 130, to Queen Mary of Modena, 26 Jun NS 1690.

38 Symcox, *French Sea Power*, pp. 96–8. Pearsall, 'War at Sea'. Burchett, *Complete History*, pp. 428–33. Mulloy, 'The French Navy and the Jacobite War'. Ehrman, *Navy*, pp. 369–70. Kerrigan, 'Ireland in Naval Strategy', pp. 170–73.

39 This is Louis Phélypeaux, comte de Pontchartrain, 'Secrétaire d'Etat de la Marine' 1690–99; not to be confused with his son and successor Jérôme, also comte de Pontchartrain, in office 1699–1715.

40 Lawson, 'Public Opinion', pp. 59–74. *LMF* VI, 89–92. Ehrman, *Navy*, pp. 375–82. Symcox, *French Sea Power*,

pp. 111–16. *MF* I, 169–71. James, 'Lords Commissioners', pp. 94–6. Delarbre, *Tourville*, pp. 363–71. Burchett, *Complete History*, pp. 433–49. HMC *Finch* III, passim. Aubrey, *James Stuart's Armada*, pp. 63–72. Mulloy, 'The French Navy and the Jacobite War', pp. 28–30. Masson, *Histoire de la Marine* I, 134–7. Villette-Mursay, *Mes Campagnes de mer*, pp. 201–3. Dessert, *Tourville*, pp. 258–69.

41 *LMF* VI, 97–103. Toudouze, *La Bataille de la Hougue*, pp. 20–26. Aubrey, *James Stuart's Armada*, pp. 77–80 and 89. Masson, *Histoire de la Marine* I, 137–9. Taillemite and Guillaume, *Tourville et Béveziers*, pp. 29–31. Dessert, *Tourville*, pp. 269–80.

42 Krämer, *Maison d'Orange-Nassau* I, 275–6. Aubrey, *James Stuart's Armada*, pp. 79–89. Toudouze, *La Bataille de la Hougue*, pp. 27–32. *MF* I, 178–9. Masson, *Histoire de la Marine* I, 141–9. Delarbre, *Tourville*, p. 197. Villette-Mursay, *Mes Campagnes de mer*, pp. 217–18. Dessert, *Tourville*, pp. 274–82.

43 Allyn, *Narrative*, p. 33.

44 The north-west corner of the Côtentin Peninsula. Both contemporary Englishmen and modern writers have frequently confused it with the small seaport of 'La Hogue', more correctly St Vaast-la-Hougue, just south of Cape Barfleur, which forms the north-eastern corner of the peninsula.

45 Toudouze, *La Bataille de la Hougue*, pp. 34–62. Aubrey, *James Stuart's Armada*, pp. 90–123. Ehrman, *Navy*, pp. 395–7. Symcox, *French Sea Power*, pp. 120–23. HMC *Finch* IV, 47–177. *NZW* III, 301–22. Burchett, *Complete History*, pp. 461–9. Villiers, 'Marine de Colbert', pp. 175–94. HMC *House of Lords* IV, 210–12. Villette-Mursay, *Mes Campagnes de mer*, pp. 206–18, 250–54 and 350–52. *LMF* VI, 104–28. Allyn, *Narrative*, pp. 25–55. Laughton, 'Commissioner's Note Book', pp. 168–201. Granier, 'Coëtlogon', pp. 117–19. Martin-Leake, *Martin*, p. 18. Van Schelven, *Almonde*, pp. 83–92. Dessert, *Tourville*, pp. 282–7.

46 HMC *Finch* IV, 285, to Nottingham, 3 Jul 1692. Cf. Allyn, *Narrative*, p. 46, who

confirms that the weather really was very
bad.
47 HMC *Finch* IV, 270–71, 30 Jun 1692.
48 *CSPD* 1691–2 p. 326, 14 Jun 1692.
49 Aubrey, *James Stuart's Armada*,
pp. 109–10. HMC *Finch* IV, 177–8,
189–92, 206, 285, 348–51, 377 and 410.
Lawson, 'Public Opinion', pp. 82–108.
Ehrman, *Navy*, pp. 400–402. Denman,
'Political Debate', pp. 69–74. Burchett,
Complete History, pp. 470–76. James,
'Lords Commissioners', pp. 100–103.
Aubrey, *James Stuart's Armada*,
pp. 133–53.
50 *CSPC* 1689–92 p. 537, to Carmarthen,
12 Sep 1691.
51 Burchett, *Complete History*, p. 458.
52 Moses, 'British Navy and the Caribbean',
pp. 13–27. Buchet, *L'espace Caraïbe* I,
162–8. Bassett, 'Caribbean', pp. 362–72.
Lawson, 'Public Opinion', pp. 249–64
and 269–74. *LMF* VI, 243–7. Hrodej, *Du
Casse* I, 96–121. Burchett, *Complete
History*, pp. 451–60. HMC *Finch* III,
83–5. Morgan, 'British West Indies',
pp. 383–92. Glass, 'The Profession of Sea-
Officer', pp. 170–73.
53 Baker and Reid, *New England Knight*,
pp. 84–102. Ernest Myrand, *1690: Sir
William Phips devant Québec* (Quebec,
1893). Chapin, *Privateer Ships and Sailors*,
pp. 102–5. *LMF* VI, 257–61. Guttridge,
Colonial Policy, pp. 50–52. Robert de
Roquebrune, 'Le Siège de Québec en 1690
par l'amiral Phipps et la victoire du
Comte de Frontenac', *Neptunia* 65 (1962),
pp. 8–12. W. T. Morgan, 'Some Attempts
at Imperial Co-operation during the
Reign of Queen Anne', *TRHS* 4th S. X
(1927) pp. 171–94. Graham, *North
Atlantic*, pp. 68–75.

10 Notorious and Treacherous Mismanagement

1 Glete, *Navies and Nations* I, 220–22.
Villiers, *Marine Royale* I, 64. Jones,
'Limitations of British Sea Power',
pp. 36–7. Lawson, 'Public Opinion',
pp. 111–14. Masson, *Histoire de la Marine*
I, 142–3. Johnston, 'Parliament and the
Navy', pp. 11–12.
2 Lawson, 'Public Opinion', pp. 114–25.
Ehrman, *Navy*, pp. 491–9. Guy Rowlands,
'Louis XIV, Vittorio Amadeo II and
French Military Failure in Italy, 1689–96',
EHR CXV (2000), pp. 534–69. Frits
Snapper, 'Oorlogsinvloeden op de
overzeese handel van Holland 1551–1719'
(Amsterdam doctoral thesis, 1959),
pp. 196–7 and 328–30; also 'Koning-
Stadhouder Willem III en de
commerciëel-financiële structuur van de
republiek', *TvZ* VIII (1989), pp. 19–24, at
p. 21.
3 Anderson, 'Smyrna Fleet', pp. 95–108.
Hattendorf, 'Rooke and Shovell',
pp. 55–6. James, 'Lords Commissioners',
pp. 104–12. Lawson, 'Public Opinion',
pp. 116–29. *House of Lords MSS* I, ii–x.
Ehrman, *Navy*, pp. 500–502. Van
Schelven, *Almonde*, pp. 99–101.
4 *House of Lords MSS* I, 220. They were
Captains Philip Schrijver of the *Zealand*
and Jan van der Poel of the *Wapen van
Medemblik*.
5 Anderson, 'Smyrna Fleet', pp. 108–10.
Villette-Mursay, *Mes Campagnes de mer*,
p. 222. Symcox, *French Sea Power*,
pp. 126–38. *House of Lords MSS* I,
200–203 and 215–27. *LMF* VI, 139–46.
NZW III, 349–62. Aubrey, *James Stuart's
Armada*, pp. 156–60. Bruijn, *Varend
Verleden*, p. 124. Johnston, 'Protection of
Trade', pp. 408–9. Burchett, *Complete
History*, pp. 481–8. Villiers, 'Marine de
Colbert', p. 195.
6 Quoted in Francis, *The Methuens and
Portugal*, pp. 52–3; cf. Krämer, *Maison
d'Orange-Nassau* I, 324.
7 Grey, *Debates* X, 318.
8 Lawson, 'Public Opinion', pp. 138–43.
Johnston, 'Protection of Trade',
pp. 408–9. Baxter, *William III*, pp. 306–9
and 315–16. James, 'Lords
Commissioners', pp. 121–4. Hattendorf,
'Rooke and Shovell', pp. 57–8. *HP
1690–1715* III, 869; IV, 554 and V, 298–303.
9 Lawson, 'Public Opinion', pp. 131–7,
145–57 and 173–4. Ehrman, *Navy*,
pp. 502–16. Corbett, *Mediterranean* II,
429. HMC *Buccleugh* II, 61–9. *LMF* VI,
187–92. Clark, *Wharton*, pp. 290–92.
Laughton, 'Commissioner's Note Book',

pp. 202–5. Burchett, *Complete History*, pp. 490–500. Aylmer, 'Navy, State, Trade, and Empire', p. 471.

10 Ehrman, *Navy*, pp. 517–26. Lawson, 'Public Opinion', pp. 157–70. HMC *Buccleugh* II, 140. Corbett, *Mediterranean* II, 431–46. Burchett, *Complete History*, pp. 504–23. Krämer, *Maison d'Orange-Nassau* I, 363–5. Symcox, *French Sea Power*, pp. 155–9.

11 Ehrman, *Navy*, pp. 526–53. Lawson, 'Public Opinion', pp. 171–99. HMC *Buccleugh* II, 171 and 175. *KMN* II, 180. Corbett, *Mediterranean* II, 450–54. *BND* No. 123, pp. 203–4. Stephen P. Payne, 'The Setting up of the English Dockyard at Cadiz, 1694–5', *Friends of the Royal Naval Museum . . . Yearbook* (1992), pp. 6–16.

12 Jean Boudriot and Hubert Berti, *The Bomb Ketch Salamandre, 1752*, trans. David H. Roberts (Paris, 1991), pp. 8–20.

13 *CSPD* 1694–5 p. 218, 10 Jul 1694.

14 Evelyn, *Diary* V, 218, 15 Sep 1695; cf. V, 186 and 216.

15 *LMF* VI, 169–73, 197–201 and 206–10. Johnston, 'Parliament and the Navy', pp. 18–19. Burchett, *Complete History*, pp. 500–504 and 526–31. Lawson, 'Public Opinion', pp. 204–8. HMC *Buccleugh* II, 213 and 219. Lespagnol, *Messieurs de Saint-Malo* I, 207. Benbow, *Brave Benbow*, pp. 24–6. Martin-Leake, *Leake* I, 66. Taillemite and Guillaume, *Tourville et Bévéziers*, p. 36. *BND* No. 134, pp. 228–30.

16 *CSPD* 1696 p. 223.

17 Lawson, 'Public Opinion', pp. 210–25. *LMF* VI, 214–18. Ehrman, *Navy*, pp. 572–4 and 602–3. Symcox, *French Sea Power*, pp. 164–8. Irrmann, 'Gallia Frustra'. Masson, *Histoire de la Marine* I, 159–62. Krämer, *Maison d'Orange-Nassau* I, 419 and 422. HMC *Portland* VIII, 47–8 and X, 8–11.

18 Bromley, 'French Privateering War'; 'A New Vocation'; and 'Jacobite Privateers'. Meyer, 'English Privateering 1688–1697'. Marsden, *Law and Custom* II, 123. J. Le Pelley, 'The Jacobite Privateers of James II', *MM* XXX (1944), pp. 185–93. Lespagnol, *La course malouine*; and *Messieurs de Saint-Malo* I, 307–402.

Crowhurst, *Defence of British Trade*. Malo, *Les Corsaires dunkerquois*. Clark, 'English and Dutch Privateers'. Starkey, *British Privateering*, pp. 19–78. Johan Francke, *Utiliteyt voor de gemeene saake: De Zeeuwse commissievaart en haar achterban tijdens de Negenjarige Oorlog, 1688–1697* (Middelburg, 2001). López Nadal, *El Corsarisme mallorquí*. Otero Lana, *Los corsarios españoles*.

19 Ehrman, *Navy*, pp. 54–8. Lespagnol, 'Guerre et commerce maritime', pp. 87–88. HMC *Finch* II, 411. Bromley, 'The North Sea in Wartime'. Meyer, 'English Privateering 1688–1697', p. 269. G. N. Clark, 'Trading with the Enemy and the Corunna Packets, 1689–97', *EHR* XXXVI (1921), pp. 521–39.

20 R. C. Anderson and F. E. Dyer, 'An Anglo-Danish Incident in 1694', *MM* XIV (1928), pp. 175–6 and 278–81. Marsden, *Law and Custom* II, 165–8.

21 HMC *Buccleugh* II, 119, to W. Blathwayt, 17 Aug 1694.

22 Symcox, *French Sea Power*, pp. 143–53 and 174–206. Bromley, 'French Privateering War'. *LMF* VI, 165–9. Masson, *Histoire de la Marine* I, 147–56. J. S. Bromley, 'The Loan of French naval vessels to privateering enterprises (1688–1713)', in Acerra, Merino and Meyer, *Les marines de guerre*, pp. 65–90; and *Corsairs and Navies*, pp. 187–212. Villiers, *Marine Royale* I, 153–66.

23 Known to French history as Jean Bart, but as he was a Flemish-speaker it seems proper to give him his Christian name in his own language.

24 HMC *Buccleugh* II, 86–90. Symcox, *French Sea Power*, pp. 140–42, 209–210 and 213–16. Masson, *Histoire de la Marine*, I, 150–52. Malo, *Les Corsaires dunkerquois*. Duguay-Trouin, *Vie*, p. 85. Bromley, 'Duguay Trouin', pp. 259–67. *LMF* VI, 218–222. Lawson, 'Public Opinion', pp. 237–40. Villiers, *Les Corsaires du Littoral*, pp. 242–59. *House of Lords MSS* II, 75–6.

25 Lespagnol, 'Guerre et commerce maritime', pp. 95–7. Symcox, *French Sea Power*, pp. 177–210 and 222–32. Jones, 'Limitations of British Sea Power',

pp. 38–9. Meyer, 'La Guerre de course', pp. 8–13. Bromley, 'The North Sea in Wartime', pp. 64–8; 'French Privateering War', pp. 240–41; and 'Duguay-Trouin', pp. 269–71. Johnston, 'Parliament and the Navy', pp. 236–8. Masson, *Histoire de la Marine* I, 147–56. Bruijn, *Varend verleden*, pp. 125–6. Villiers, *Marine Royale* I, 137–42.

26 Lawson, 'Public Opinion', pp. 317–18. Johnston, 'Protection of Trade', pp. 410–13; and 'Parliament and the Navy', pp. 34–42. Denman, 'Political Debate', p. 95.

27 Crowhurst, *Defence of British Trade*, pp. 46–8. Middleton, 'Chesapeake Convoy System'. Lawson, 'Public Opinion', pp. 317–22 and 326–7. Johnston, 'Protection of Trade', pp. 399–409 and 517–18; and 'Parliament and the Navy', pp. 215–24. Pearsall, 'Trade Protection 1688–1714', p. 117. James, 'Lords Commissioners', p. 277. Marsden, *Law and Custom* II, 220–22.

28 McNeill, 'Ecological Basis of Warfare.' Rodger, 'Weather', pp. 184–5. Christian Buchet, 'Des Routes maritimes Europe-Antilles et de leurs incidences sur la rivalité franco-britannique', *HES* XIII (1994), pp. 563–82.

29 Moses, 'British Navy and the Caribbean', pp. 28–30. Morgan, 'British West Indies', pp. 395–6. Buchet, *L'espace Caraïbe* I, 168–72. Lawson, 'Public Opinion', pp. 276–9. *LMF* VI, 248–50. *KMN* II, 182–3. Bassett, 'Caribbean', pp. 375–6.

30 Moses, 'British Navy and the Caribbean', pp. 30–36. Hrodej, *Du Casse* I, 163–85. Lawson, 'Public Opinion', pp. 285–6. *LMF* VI, 250–54. Buchet, *L'espace Caraïbe* I, 172–6; and 'Royal Navy and the Caribbean', pp. 30–35. Burchett, *Complete History*, pp. 15–18 and 531–7. Morgan, 'British West Indies', pp. 400–401.

31 Morgan, 'Baron de Pointis'. Hrodej, *Du Casse* I, 205–22. Bassett, 'Caribbean', pp. 382–92 and 416–17. *LMF* VI, 275–90. Ehrman, *Navy*, pp. 609–12. Symcox, *French Sea Power*, pp. 218–19. Merriman, *Sergison Papers*, pp. 299–311. Moses, 'British Navy and the Caribbean', pp. 38–9. Burchett, *Complete History*,

pp. 551–64. *KMN* II, 186–8. Buchet, *L'espace Caraïbe* I, 177–81, 195–203 and 476–88; and 'Convoyage', pp. 220–26. Masson, *Histoire de la Marine* I, 162–4.

32 Davies, *North Atlantic World*, p. 294. *LMF* VI, 293–5. Murray, 'Naval Skirmishing'. G. S. Graham, 'Britain's Defence of Newfoundland', *CHR* XXIII (1942), pp. 260–79. Innis, *Cod Fisheries*, pp. 97–109. D. J. Starkey, 'Devonians and the Newfoundland Trade', in *MHD* I, 163–71. Lounsbury, *British Fishery at Newfoundland*, pp. 126–81. Lenman, 'Colonial Wars', p. 153.

33 Chaudhuri and Israel, 'English and Dutch East India Companies'. Chapin, *Privateer Ships and Sailors*, pp. 8–10, 64–79 and 96–100. Ritchie, *Captain Kidd*. Joel H. Baer, ' "Captain John Avery" and the Anatomy of a Mutiny', *Eighteenth-Century Life* N.S. XVIII (1994), No. 1, pp. 1–26. Earle, *Pirate Wars*, pp. 111–23.

34 Denman, 'Political Debate', pp. 25 and 138. Kamen, *War of Succession*, pp. 1–5.

35 'Alle de menschen sijn hier seer gerust, ende bekommeren haer gedaghten weinigh op dit groote verandering van 's werels saecken. Het schijnt ofte het een straf van de Hemel is dat men hier soo weinigh gevoeligh is van hetgeene buyten dit eylandt passeert, alhoewel zij deselfde interesse ende bekommering behoorde te hebben als die aen het vaste landt leggen.' Krämer, *Maison d'Orange-Nassau* III, 249–50, to Antonie Heinsius, *Raadpensionaris* of Holland.

36 Anderson, *Naval Wars in the Baltic*, pp. 133–6. *NZW* III, 553–6. Burchett, *Complete History*, pp. 575–85. Hattendorf, 'Rooke and Shovell', p. 62. Svensson, *Svenska Flottans Historia* II, 121–5. Van Schelven, *Almonde*, pp. 137–48.

37 Denman, 'Political Debate', pp. 17–19.

11 An Additional Empire

1 Kamen, *War of Succession*, pp. 1–5. Greenhaw 'Policy for the Mediterranean', pp. 4–8. Francis, *First Peninsular War*, pp. 17–18. Rose, *England in the 1690s*, pp. 145–50. Lespagnol, 'Guerre et commerce maritime', pp. 85–6.

2 Walker, *Spanish Politics*, pp. 19–30. Francis, *First Peninsular War*, pp. 17–22. Kamen, *War of Succession*, pp. 143–74. Buchet, 'Convoyage'; also 'Les Liaisons atlantiques et de la nécessaire révision du concept de maîtrise des mers (1701–1763)', *CHM* 35 (1997), pp. 9–23. Perez-Mallaina Bueno, *Política Naval Española*, pp. 63–76 and 126–41.

3 Buchet, *L'espace Caraïbe* I, 209–16. Hattendorf, 'Benbow's Last Fight', *LMF* VI, 474–8. Hrodej, *Du Casse* I, 306–7 and II, 463–72. Burchett, *Complete History*, pp. 590–98. Benbow, *Brave Benbow*, pp. 39–58.

4 *CSPD* 1702–3 p. 303, Edward Harding to G. and T. Finch, 2 Oct 1702.

5 Owen, *War at Sea*, pp. 71–81. Burchett, *Complete History*, pp. 619–25. *LMF* VI, 316–19. Corbett, *Mediterranean* II, 478–83. Denman, 'Political Debate', pp. 155–7. Francis, *First Peninsular War*, pp. 45–51. Hattendorf, 'Rooke and Shovell', p. 63. Van Schelven, *Almonde*, pp. 161–5.

6 Calmon-Maison, *Château-Renault*, pp. 250–80. *LMF* VI, 320–31. *NZW* III, 587–96. *AE* VI, 23–42. Corbett, *Mediterranean* II, 488–91. Browning, *Rooke Journal*, pp. 227–34. Burchett, *Complete History*, p. 627. Owen, *War at Sea*, pp. 82–6. *BND* No. 124, pp. 204–8. Uring, *Voyages and Travels*, pp. 53–6. Martin-Leake, *Martin*, pp. 57–63. Van Schelven, *Almonde*, pp. 168–71.

7 Kamen, 'Spanish Silver Fleet'; and *War of Succession*, pp. 11 and 179–80. Masson, *Histoire de la Marine* I, 167.

8 Francis, 'Portugal and the Grand Alliance', p. 93, to Diogo de Mendonça Cortes Real, 12 Aug 1710.

9 Francis, 'Portugal and the Grand Alliance'. H. E. S. Fisher, 'Anglo-Portuguese Trade, 1700–1770', *EcHR* 2nd S. XVI (1964), pp. 219–33. Braudel, *Civilization* III, 361.

10 Boxer, *Dutch Seaborne Empire*, p. 118. Francis, *First Peninsular War*, pp. 21–2.

11 Corbett, *Mediterranean* II, 493–502. Laughton, *Torrington Memoirs*, pp. 110–19. Watson, 'Victualling', pp. 19–21 and 210. Coombs, *Conduct of the Dutch*, pp. 52–3 and 314–17. Owen, *War at Sea*, pp. 82–6. Hubert Lamb and Knud Frydendahl, *Historic Storms of the North Sea, British Isles and Northwest Europe* (Cambridge, 1991), pp. 59–69. Burchett, *Complete History*, pp. 646–60. Hughes, 'Encouragement of Seamen', p. 33. Hepper, *Warship Losses*, p. 23.

12 Bourne, *Queen Anne's Navy*, pp. 58–66, 74–85, 90–92, 124–5, 161 and 196–9. Burchett, *Complete History*, pp. 599–607. *LMF* VI, 487–90. Buchet, *L'espace Caraïbe* I, 206–8 and 216–20.

13 Gregg, *Queen Anne*, pp. 7–12 and 134–8. Hattendorf, 'Governmental Machinery', pp. 1–5 and 17–19. Denman, 'Political Debate', pp. 19–22. Johnston, 'Parliament and the Navy', pp. 48–50.

14 The well-known Admiral George Churchill is mentioned below. On his brothers Winston and Jasper, who died young, see notes by Frances Harris and Peter Le Fevre in *MM* LXVI (1980), pp. 357–8 and LXXVI (1990), pp. 67–9.

15 Hattendorf, 'Blenheim Campaign'; and 'Rooke and Shovell', p. 67–8. Francis, *The Methuens and Portugal*, pp. 269–76; and *First Peninsular War*, pp. 106–15. Ware, 'Torrington', pp. 88. *LMF* VI, 345–8. Corbett, *Mediterranean* II, 505–22. *NZW* III, 638–42. Laughton, *Torrington Memoirs*, pp. 138–46 and 191–5. Tunstall, *Byng Papers* I, 35–8. Martin-Leake, *Leake* I, 149–56. Burchett, *Complete History*, pp. 662–81. Owen, *War at Sea*, pp. 87–91.

16 'Ce que nous fimes hier suffit pour la réputation des armes du roi et de la Marine': P. Ausseur, 'Le Mentor du Comte de Toulouse', *Neptunia* 91 (1968), pp. 2–8, at p. 7, quoting (from MSS) the comte de Villette-Mursay – who later claimed to have opposed the decision: Villette-Mursay, *Mes Campagnes de mer*, pp. 62–3.

17 Corbett, *Fighting Instructions*, pp. 195–9. Tunstall, *Naval Warfare*, pp. 64–8. Laughton, 'Velez Malaga'. Van der Meij, ' "Een furieus gevegt" '. HMC *Portland* VIII, 143–7. *MF* VI, 349–68. *NZW* III, 649–51. Corbett, *Mediterranean* II, 524–35. Laughton, *Torrington Memoirs* pp. 150–63 and 196–7. Martin-Leake,

Leake I, 158–79. Owen, *War at Sea*, pp. 92–6.

18 It is sometimes said that the two battles were fought on the same day, but this arises from a confusion of calendars: Blenheim was on 13 August NS, Malaga on 13 August OS.

19 Hattendorf, 'Rooke and Shovell', pp. 69–70.

20 Martin-Leake, *Leake* I, 200–268. Francis, *First Peninsular War*, pp. 128–45. *LMF* VI, 368–75. Corbett, *Mediterranean* II, 536–43. Meyer, 'La Marine française de 1545 à 1715', p. 524. *NZW* III, 662–71.

21 Hattendorf, 'Rooke and Shovell', p. 71. Martin-Leake *Leake* I, 278–85. Francis, *First Peninsular War*, pp. 184–190. Owen, *War at Sea*, pp. 130–54.

22 James FitzJames, Marshal Duke of Berwick, was James II's bastard son and Marlborough's nephew. Henri de Massue, marquis de Ruvigny and Earl of Galway, was a Huguenot exile. It was typical of the period that the Spanish army was commanded by an Englishman, and the English army by a Frenchman.

23 Martin-Leake, *Leake* II, 22–7. Kamen, *War of Succession*, pp. 16–17. Tunstall, *Byng Papers*, I, 99–101. Burchett, *Complete History*, pp. 689–97. *NZW* III, 686–94. Owen, *War at Sea*, pp. 155–6.

24 Owen, *War at Sea*, p. 189; cf. Tunstall, *Byng Papers* I, 230.

25 Owen, *War at Sea*, pp. 158–91. *LMF* VI, 389–95. Tunstall, *Byng Papers* I, 195–6 and 216–35. Francis, *First Peninsular War*, pp. 250–56. Masson, *Histoire de la Marine* I, 170. Villiers, *Marine Royale* I, 167–74. Brun, *Port de Toulon* I, 124–6.

26 *Sailing Directions for the West Coasts of France, Spain and Portugal*, ed. James Penn (Hydrographic Office, London, 1867), p. 5.

27 The Bishop Rock is in 49°52' N, the Casquets in 49°43' N.

28 Rodger, 'Weather', pp. 187–9 and 193–5. Owen, *War at Sea*, pp. 118–19. W. E. May, 'The Last Voyage of Sir Clowdisley Shovel', *Journal of the Institute of Navigation* XIII (1960), pp. 324–32. G. J. Marcus, 'Sir Clowdisley Shovel's Last Passage', *JRUSI* CII (1957), pp. 540–48.

Hattendorf, 'Rooke and Shovell', pp. 73–4.

29 This is the Castilian form of the town's name, familiar to English readers: in the Minorquin dialect of Catalan, it is Maó. Puerto Mahón is the harbour.

30 Kamen, *War of Succession*, pp. 18–19. Martin-Leake, *Leake* II, 169–285. Dickinson, 'Capture of Minorca'. Burchett, *Complete History*, pp. 749–56. Snyder, *Marlborough–Godolphin* II, 980, 994 and 1,013. Hattendorf, 'Machinery for Planning', pp. 89–91. Owen, *War at Sea*, pp. 98–100. Tunstall, *Byng Papers* II, 295–303. R. G. Thurburn, 'The Capture of Minorca, 1708', *JSAHR* LV (1977), pp. 65–72.

31 Tunstall, *Byng Papers* II, 264–6, 327 and 330–31. Burchett, *Complete History*, pp. 768–75. Kepler, 'Jennings'. Max Guérout, 'Opérations de l'amiral de Norris sur les côtes de France en 1710', in *Guerres et Paix*, pp. 163–70.

32 Gibson, *Playing the Scottish Card*, pp. 41 and 93–105. Grant, *Scots Navy*, pp. 255, 316–17 and 346–7. Lenman, *Jacobite Risings*, pp. 80–89.

33 Tunstall, *Byng Papers* II, 4–37. Gibson, *Playing the Scottish Card*, pp. 118–59. Burchett, *Complete History*, pp. 740–48. Owen, *War at Sea*, pp. 238–268. Coquelle, 'Les Projets de descente' XV, 444–51. Villiers, *Les Corsaires du Littoral*, pp. 295–305. *LMF* VI, 459–64. Malo, *La Grande Guerre des corsaires*, pp. 84–97.

34 Buchet, *L'espace Caraïbe* I, 221–6. Burchett, *Complete History*, pp. 697–703. Bourne, *Queen Anne's Navy*, pp. 93–5 and 131–3. Owen, *War at Sea*, pp. 111–15.

35 Burchett, *Complete History*, pp. 705–16. Buchet, *L'espace Caraïbe*, I, 227–32. Kamen, *War of Succession*, pp. 183–6. *LMF* VI, 507–8. Bourne, *Queen Anne's Navy*, pp. 170–72. Baugh, 'Wager', pp. 109–11.

36 Hughson, 'Carolina Pirates', p. 287, quoting Governor Spotswood.

37 Bromley, 'Colonies at War', pp. 22–6. Graham, *Walker Expedition*, pp. 5–11. Morgan, 'Imperial Co-operation', pp. 178–93 (quoted p. 192). *LMF* VI, 521–5. Alsop, 'Age of the Projectors'.

38 Stewart P. Oakley, 'Trade, Peace and the Balance of Power: Britain and the Baltic, 1603–1802', in *In Quest of Trade and Security: The Baltic in Power Politics 1500–1900*, ed. Göran Rystad, Klaus-Richard Böhme and Wilhelm M. Carlgren (Stockholm, 1994–5, 2 vols.) I, 221–56.

39 HMC *Portland* VIII, 131–5. Anderson, *Naval Wars in the Baltic*, p. 141. Svensson, *Svenska Flottans Historia* II, 156–7.

40 Burchett, *Complete History*, pp. 726–7. Mediger, *Mecklenburg, Russland und England-Hannover* I, 225–6. Aldridge, 'Russell', pp. 166–7.

41 Granier, 'Coëtlogon', pp. 125–7. *LMF* VI, 334–6. *NZW* III, 617–24.

42 'Il seroit à souhaiter que M. de Saint-Pol ne trouvast pas tant de navires de guerre, et plus d'indiens ou de riches interlopes. Cela accomoderait bien mieux ses pauvres armateurs': Malo, *La Grande Guerre des corsaires*, p. 35, quoting Louis le Bigot de Gastines, *Intendant* of Brest.

43 Villiers, *Les Corsaires du Littoral*, pp. 286–94. Malo, *La Grande Guerre des corsaires*, pp. 15–16, 34–8 and 44–6. *LMF* VI, 413–18 and 428–35. *NZW* III, 613–14 and 710–12. Owen, *War at Sea*, pp. 111–16. Pearsall, 'Trade Protection', p. 120.

44 Malo, *La Grande Guerre des corsaires*, pp. 51, 55–6, 64–83. Bromley, 'Duguay Trouin', pp. 272–3. *LMF* VI, 436–56. Duguay-Trouin, *Vie*, pp. 18–29 and 160–70. Owen, *War at Sea*, pp. 195–205 and 220–35. Tunstall, *Naval Warfare*, pp. 73–8.

45 Owen, *War at Sea*, pp. 108–9. Pearsall, 'Trade Protection', p. 119.

46 Francis, *First Peninsular War*, p. 223.

47 Bromley, 'Duguay Trouin'.

48 Bromley, 'Saint-Malo'. Lespagnol, *Messieurs de Saint-Malo* II, 541–646. Crowhurst, *Defence of British Trade*, pp. 16–19.

49 Spate, *Pacific* II, 189–92.

50 Bromley, 'French Privateering War'; and 'Dunkirk Reconsidered'. Masson, *Histoire de la Marine* I, 171–2. Baetens, 'Flemish Privateering'. Lespagnol, 'Guerre et commerce maritime', pp. 89–98. Jones,

War and Economy, pp. 161–6. Villiers, *Marine Royale* I, 137–42. Christian Pfister-Langanay, 'Dunkerque, capitale de la course, croissance factice ou réelle sous Louis XIV?', in *Guerres maritimes*, pp. 139–54. S. de La Nicollière-Teijeiro, *La Course et les corsaires du Port de Nantes* (Paris and Nantes, 1896).

51 Armet, 'Convoys', pp. 80–96.

52 Verhees-van Meer, *De Zeeuwse Kaapvaart*. Meyer, 'English Privateering 1702–1713'; and 'Mascall's Privateers', *Archæologia Cantiana* XCV (1979), pp. 213–21. Bromley, 'Les Corsaires zélandais'; and 'A New Vocation'. Starkey, *British Privateering*, pp. 99–107; and 'Privateering Enterprise in Devon'.

53 Haversham, *Memoirs*, p. 28.

54 Bromley, 'The North Sea in Wartime', pp. 61–2. Johnston, 'Parliament and the Navy', pp. 288–304. Owen, *War at Sea*, pp. 56–60 and 284–5. Bourne, *Queen Anne's Navy*, pp. 135–8. Merriman, *Queen Anne's Navy*, pp. 344–50.

55 Holmes, *British Politics*, pp. xxvii, xliii–xliv and xlix–li. Gregg, *Queen Anne*, pp. 285–98. Rodger, 'Anglo-Dutch Alliance', pp. 14–18. Denman, 'Political Debate', pp. 35–6, 225–32, 291–4 and 302–4. François Crouzet, 'The Huguenots and the English Financial Revolution', in *Favorites of Fortune: Technology, Growth and Economic Development since the Industrial Revolution*, ed. P. Higonnet, D. S. Landes and H. Rosovsky (Cambridge, Mass., 1991), pp. 221–66.

56 Hattendorf, *Spanish Succession*, pp. 6, 62–3, 68 and 72. Holmes, *British Politics*, pp. 71–3. Denman, 'Political Debate', pp. 19–36 and 302–4. Rodger, 'Myth of Seapower' and 'Seekriegsstrategie'.

57 Watson, 'Victualling', p. 55, quoting PRO: SP 44/213, St John to Brig. Gen J. Hill, 1 May 1711.

58 Graham, *Walker Expedition, passim*. Martin-Leake, *Leake* II, 365–6. Denman, 'Political Debate', pp. 235 and 247–9. Burchett, *Complete History*, pp. 775–81. W. T. Morgan, 'The South Sea Company and the Canadian Expedition in the Reign of Queen Anne', *HAHR* VIII (1928), pp. 143–66.

59 Quoted by Coombs, *Conduct of the Dutch*, p. 280.
60 Coombs, *Conduct of the Dutch*, p. 292.
61 Gregg, *Queen Anne*, pp. 358–88. A. D. MacLachlan, 'The Road to Peace 1710–13', in *Britain after the Glorious Revolution, 1689–1714*, ed. Geoffrey Holmes (London, 1969), pp. 196–215.
62 Baugh, ' "A Grand Marine Empire" '. Davis, *Commercial Revolution*. Jones, *War and Economy*, pp. 161–9 and 194–208.
63 HMC *Buccleugh* II, 119, Shrewsbury to W. Blaythwayt, 17 Aug 1694: cf. p. 157 above.
64 Armitage, *Ideological Origins*, pp. 8–40, 105 and 143–4. Rodger, 'Sea-Power and Empire'.
65 Schulin, *Handelsstaat England*, p. 305, quoting the *Spectator* of 19 May 1711.
66 Haversham, *Memoirs*, p. 28.

12 Strife and Envy

1 Lawson, 'Public Opinion', p. 3. Ehrman, *Navy*, pp. 269–77, 298–304, 347–9 and 605–8. Baxter, *William III*, pp. 279, 306–9 and 315–16. HMC *Finch* IV, v–vii. Rose, *England in the 1690s*, pp. 46–7, 71–5 and 81–7. Watson, 'Victualling', p. 40.
2 Snyder, *Marlborough–Godolphin* I, xv–xvi. Hattendorf, 'Machinery for Planning'; and 'Governmental Machinery'.
3 He was a rear-admiral of 1672, and had previously served both on the Navy Board (Extra Commissioner 1675–80) and the Admiralty (1682–4).
4 Ehrman, *Navy*, pp. 279–99 and 359–64. Lawson, 'Public Opinion', pp. 106–10, 141–3 and 317–18. Johnston, 'Protection of Trade', pp. 408–13; and 'Parliament and the Navy', pp. 34–42. Denman, 'Political Debate', pp. 75–9. James, 'Lords Commissioners', pp. 102–15 and 187–95.
5 Henry Horwitz, *Parliament, Policy and Politics in the Reign of William III* (Manchester, 1977), pp. 62–3, quoting a letter of Gilbert Burnet. I owe this reference to the kindness of Professor Daniel A. Baugh.
6 Grey, *Debates* X, 168.
7 'De passie en de violentie van de menchen gaen verder als ick oyt hadt kunnen dencken; het scheynt ofte het een straf is van den Hemel op dese natie . . .' Krämer, *Maison d'Orange-Nassau* III, 509, to A. Heinsius, 22 Apr 1701.
8 Lawson, 'Public Opinion', pp. 4, 7. HMC *Portland* VIII, 57–61. Johnston, 'Parliament and the Navy', pp. 435 and 480–83. Denman, 'Political Debate', pp. 116–17.
9 *CSPD* 1702–3, p. 190, 18 Jul 1702.
10 Tanner, *Pepys's Naval Minutes*, pp. 319–20.
11 HMC *Buccleugh* II, 74.
12 Ehrman, *Navy*, pp. 298–9, 311–13, 405–7. Johnston, 'Parliament and the Navy', pp. 469–71, 480–83. HMC *Buccleugh* II, 324. Rodger, *Admiralty*, pp. 37–9.
13 Ehrman, *Navy*, pp. 570–72. James, 'Lords Commissioners', pp. 127–8. Rose, *England in the 1690s*, pp. 128–9. Johnston, 'Parliament and the Navy', p. 269.
14 Lower, 'Sergison', p. 67.
15 James, 'Lords Commissioners', pp. 187–95. Merriman, 'Gilbert Wardlaw's Allegations'. Aldridge, 'Russell', pp. 163–4.
16 Franklin, *Ship Models*, p. 5.
17 Hattendorf, 'Governmental Machinery', pp. 9–12. James, 'Lords Commissioners', pp. 200–202 and 228; and 'Lord High Admiral's Council'. Gregg, *Queen Anne*, pp. 266–7. Watson, 'Victualling', pp. 35–9. Synder, *Marlborough–Godolphin* II, 895, 1,028 and 1,035. Owen, *War at Sea*, pp. 3 and 6–7. Tunstall, *Byng Papers* I, lxv–lxix; II, 156–7, 182–4 and 188. *BND* No. 148, pp. 249–50. Rodger, *Admiralty*, pp. 43–6. Holmes, *British Politics*, pp. 111 and 370. Corbett, *Mediterranean* II, 504. *HP 1690–1715* III, 545–50.
18 Bolingbroke, *Letters and Correspondence . . .*, ed. Gilbert Parke (London, 1798, 4 vols.) III, 27, Bolingbroke to Strafford, 27 Aug 1712.
19 James, 'Lords Commissioners', pp. 246–57. Gregg, *Queen Anne*, p. 284. Snyder, *Marlborough–Godolphin* III, 1,207, 1,264, 1,273, 1,278 n.2, 1,383 and 1,404. Kepler, 'Jennings', pp. 14–17. Martin-Leake, *Leake* II, 344–5 and 365.
20 Martin-Leake, *Leake* II, 155–9. Pearsall,

'Trade Protection', p. 120. Johnston, 'Parliament and the Navy', pp. 288–300, 435, 444–5 and 466.

21 Hattendorf, 'Governmental Machinery', p. 14. Perhaps Harley was half-remembering Virgil's *Aeneid* I, 52–6: 'hic vasto rex Aeolus antro/ luctantis ventos tempestatesque sonoras/ imperio premit ac vinclis et carcere frenat./ Illi indignantes magno cum murmure montis/ circum claustra fremunt . . .'; 'Here King Aeolus in his vast cave controls the struggling winds and noisy tempests, and binds them with chains and prison. They protest with much murmuring and rage around the mountain barriers'. (I owe this suggestion to the kindness of Dr Roger Tomlin.)

22 *CJ* XVII, 278.

23 Watson, 'Victualling', pp. 56–65. Johnston, 'Parliament and the Navy', pp. 57–69 and 474–95.

24 James, 'Burchett', p. 488, quoting the anonoymous *Remarks on the Present Condition of the Navy . . .* (1700).

25 Ehrman, *Navy*, pp. 290–94, 558–67 and 651–63. James, 'Lords Commissioners', pp. 157–74; 'Admiralty Administration', pp. 17–19; and 'Admiralty Buildings'. Clark, *Wharton*, p. 308. Rodger, *Admiralty*, pp. 35–49. James and Shaw, 'Admiralty Administration', pp. 170–71. Burchett, *Complete History*, pp. 10–14. *HP 1690–1715* III, 408–10.

26 Merriman, *Sergison Papers*, p. 9.

27 Ehrman, *Navy*, p. 366.

28 Ehrman, *Navy*, p. 495 n.2.

29 Merriman, *Sergison Papers*, pp. 340–41; and *Queen Anne's Navy*, pp. 10–15, 83–4 and 90. James, 'Lords Commissioners', pp. 176–84. Lower, 'Sergison', pp. 64–5.

30 Merriman, *Sergison Papers*, pp. 154–5; also *House of Lords MSS* I, 125, Commanders-in-chief to Admiralty, 29 Apr 1694.

31 Glete, *Navies and Nations* I, 225 and II, 562–3. These are the most accurate figures. Contemporary lists, compiled on a different basis and not directly comparable, are in Ehrman, *Navy*, p. 625; Merriman, *Sergison Papers*, p. 365; and *Queen Anne's Navy*, p. 363.

32 Le Fevre, 'Seventeenth-Century Sea Officer', p. 8. Ehrman, *Navy*, p. 632. Merriman, *Sergison Papers*, pp. 104–6 and 125; and *Queen Anne's Navy*, pp. 62 and 365–72. Pool, *Navy Board Contracts*, pp. 50–60. Holland, *Ships of British Oak*, pp. 89–90. Mrs Wyatt was the widow of William Wyatt, who had already built a number of ships for the Navy, but she received the contract for the *Cumberland* in her own right.

33 HMC *Portland* VIII, 36, to R. Harley, 10 Aug 1693.

34 Duffy, 'Creation of Plymouth Dockyard'; 'Devon and Naval Strategy', pp. 182–4; and 'Western Squadron', pp. 6–63. Dummer, 'New Dock and Yard'. Ehrman, *Navy*, pp. 86–7 and 413–29. Coad, 'Plymouth Dockyard'; and *Royal Dockyards*, pp. 7–10 and 92–7. Kitson, 'Portsmouth Dockyard' XXXIII, 260–62 and XXXIV, 4–6.

35 Ehrman, *Navy*, pp. 98–108. Merriman, *Sergison Papers*, pp. 121, 136 and 272–4; and *Queen Anne's Navy*, pp. 105–6.

36 Marsh, 'Local Community' I, 206.

37 Saville, 'Industrial Development', pp. 519, 547–50 and 568–71. Merriman, *Queen Anne's Navy*, p. 46.

38 Merriman, *Queen Anne's Navy*, pp. 105 and 120–22. R. D. Merriman, 'Captain George St Lo, R.N., 1658–1718', *MM* XXXI (1945), pp. 13–22.

39 Trenail mooters mooted trenails (i.e. cut them with a circular gauge or 'moot'), but most were supplied by contractors or made by shipwright apprentices.

40 This famous yard specialized in East Indiamen. See Banbury, *Shipbuilders*, pp. 114–25.

41 Saville, 'Industrial Development', pp. 625–6 and 696–7. Ehrman, *Navy*, pp. 74–6 and 86–7. Merriman, *Queen Anne's Navy*, pp. 70, 132 and 373–4. Coad, *Royal Dockyards*, p. 3. Dummer, 'New Dock and Yard', pp. 100–103. Ann Veronica Coats, 'A Radically Different Bureaucracy: Dockyard Administration in the Late Seventeenth Century', in Cogar, *New Interpretations . . . Twelfth*, pp. 65–78.

42 Ehrman, *Navy*, pp. 67–9. Saville,

'Industrial Development', pp. 589 and 623–4. Pool, *Navy Board Contracts*, pp. 32–3 and 101–2.

43 Broadley, 'Rooke Correspondence', p. 64, to R. Harley, 25 May 1704.

44 Saville, 'Industrial Development', pp. 413–36. Merriman, *Sergison Papers*, pp. 145–6 and 155–8; and *Queen Anne's Navy*, pp. 140–41. Johnston, 'Parliament and the Navy', pp. 208–12.

45 PRO: E 134/1 Geo I/Hil/27; Deposition of William Franklin, 10 Jan 1714/5.

46 PRO: E 134/2 Geo I/Mich/27; Deposition of Nathaniel Cutler, 23 Nov 1715.

47 Merriman, *Queen Anne's Navy*, pp. 191–2. Ehrman, *Navy*, pp. 121–4. Manwaring, 'Dress of the British Seaman'. PRO: E 134/13 Anne/Trin/10, 1 Geo I/Hil/27 and 2 Geo I/Mich/27, depositions in suit Braddyll, Gough and Dawsonne con Franklyn.

48 Saville, 'Industrial Development', pp. 341 and 346–7. Johnston, 'Parliament and the Navy', pp. 182–3.

49 The western part of modern Latvia, then a duchy within the Commonwealth of Poland-Lithuania.

50 Malone, 'Baltic Naval Stores Trade'. Kirby, 'Pitch and Tar'. Merriman, *Queen Anne's Navy*, pp. 140, 142–3 and 158–67. Johnston, 'Parliament and the Navy', pp. 189–207. Pool, *Navy Board Contracts*, pp. 68–71. John J. Murray, 'Robert Jackson's "Memoir on the Swedish Tar Company", December 29 1709', *Huntington Library Bulletin* X (1946–7), pp. 419–28.

51 Malone, 'Baltic Naval Stores Trade', pp. 383–4 and 389–90. Ehrman, *Navy*, pp. 41–2. Merriman, *Queen Anne's Navy*, pp. 152–3.

52 The load was 50 cu. ft rough or 40 cu. ft sided; it was reckoned equal to the product of an average tree, or about a ton in weight.

53 Ehrman, *Navy*, pp. 36–54. Johnston, 'Parliament and the Navy', pp. 188–9. Rackham, *History of the Countryside*, pp. 87–93 and 221–3. G. Hammersley, 'The Crown Woods and their Exploitation in the Sixteenth and Seventeenth Centuries', *BIHR* XXX

(1957), pp. 136–61. Blake Tyson, 'Oak for the Navy: A Case Study', *Transactions of the Cumberland and Westmorland Antiquarian & Archæological Society* LXXXVII (1987), pp. 117–26.

54 HMC *Finch* II, 241, E. Russell to Nottingham, 4 Sep 1689.

55 Merriman, *Queen Anne's Navy*, p. 267, Victualling Board to Secretary of the Treasury, 30 Oct 1703.

56 Ehrman, *Navy*, pp. 145–64, 314–16, 324–7, 479–82 and 583–90. Merriman, *Sergison Papers*, pp. 235 and 339–40; and *Queen Anne's Navy*, p. 308. James, 'Lords Commissioners', pp. 68–9. Johnston 'Parliament and the Navy', pp. 152, 439–41, 500 and 502. *House of Lords MSS* I, v–xiii, 157–60, 172 and 277. Beveridge, *Prices and Wages*, pp. 520–31 and 565–82. Watson, 'Victualling', p. 330.

57 Watson, 'Victualling', p. 350, quoting PRO: ADM 110/5 p. 63, Victualling Board to Admiralty, 7 Sep 1710.

58 Watson, 'Victualling', *passim*, especially pp. 86–96, 112–21, 148–51 and 346–54. Merriman, *Queen Anne's Navy*, pp. 48–9, 58–9, 248–60, 340–42 and 359. Buchet, *Marine, économie et société*, pp. 31–2. J. D. Alsop and K. R. Dick, 'The Origin of Public Tendering for Royal Navy Provisions, 1699–1720', *MM LXXX* (1994), pp. 395–402.

59 Watson, 'Victualling', pp. 11–28, 152–61, 297–300, 313, 369–70 and 378–9. Buchet, *Marine, économie et société*, pp. 31–2 and 176–84. Kepler, 'Jennings', pp. 18–20.

60 Merriman, *Sergison Papers*, p. 222.

61 *KMN* II, 189–91. Ehrman, *Navy*, pp. 124–8, 176–7, 289 and 445–6. Merriman, *Sergison Papers*, pp. 208–11, 216–17 and 221–2. James, 'Lords Commissioners', p. 46. Watson, 'Victualling', pp. 184–94. *House of Lords MSS* V, 439. Johnston, 'Parliament and the Navy', pp. 461–3.

62 Tunstall, *Byng Papers* I, 79–80, to G. Byng, 14 Jun 1705.

63 Merriman, *Queen Anne's Navy*, pp. 30 and 224–37. *KMN* II, 192–255. Watson, 'Victualling', pp. 184–257, 314–17, 338, 356–9, 381–4 and 398. Kepler, 'Jennings', p. 27.

64 Merriman, *Queen Anne's Navy*,
pp. 241–57. Watson, 'Victualling',
pp. 226–35. Anderson, 'Prisoners of War',
pp. 77–85. Martel, *Le recrutement des
matelots*, pp. 287–98.

65 Cook, 'Practical Medicine'. Rodger,
'Medicine and Science'. *KMN* II, 202,
265–76. Holmes, *Augustan England*,
pp. 193, 197 and 203.

66 Watson, 'Victualling', pp. 30, 45–7,
260–95, 322–5, 339, 347, 386–9 and 399.
Greenhaw, 'Policy for the Mediterranean',
pp. 20–21.

67 Bromley, 'Prize Office'; and 'Profits of
Naval Command'. *House of Lords MSS* V,
438–45.

68 Tomlinson, 'Ordnance Office'; and *Guns
and Government*, pp. 159–71. Saville,
'Industrial Development', pp. 641–75.
Buchet, 'L'"Ordnance Board"', pp. 74–8.
Merriman, *Queen Anne's Navy*, pp. 66–7.
Caruana, *Sea Ordnance* I, 150–61.

69 Johnston, 'Parliament and the Navy',
pp. 73–124 and 500–512. Ehrman, *Navy*,
pp. 158–70, 324–38, 464–78. Merriman,
Sergison Papers, pp. 58 and 68. Watson,
'Victualling', p. 335. Lavery, 'Rebuilding',
pp. 114–15.

70 Ehrman, *Navy*, pp. 540–43 and 575–94.
Jones, *War and Economy*, pp. 11–38,
120–30, 228 and 240–50. Roseveare,
Financial Revolution, p. 38. Braudel,
Civilization III, 359–60.

71 Slightly higher than the figure in
Appendix VII, which is for the end of the
year.

72 Brewer, *Sinews of Power*, pp. 95–126.
Hughes, *Administration and Finance*,
pp. 160–62. Jones, *War and Economy*,
pp. 44–52, 65–7, 126, 131, 166–9 and
194–208. Watson, 'Victualling', pp. 343
and 359–65. Williams, 'Fountain of Gold',
pp. 36–9. Johnston, 'Parliament and the
Navy', pp. 141–62.

73 James, 'Lords Commissioners', p. 257.
Burchett, *Complete History*, p. 33.

13 Our Mob

1 Davies, *Gentlemen and Tarpaulins*,
pp. 222–4; and 'James II, William of
Orange', p. 92. Glass, 'The Profession
of Sea-Officer', pp. 141–4. D. B. Ellis,
'Admiral Sir James Wishart (1659–1723)',
*Leatherhead and District Local History
Society Proceedings* V, 4 (1991), pp. 106–11.

2 Ehrman, *Navy*, pp. 373 and 384–91. HMC
Finch IV, 192–3, 235–6 and 256. Glass,
'The Profession of Sea-Officer', pp. 161
and 197. Johnston, 'Parliament and the
Navy', pp. 53–4 and 428–34. Denman,
'Political Debate', p. 296.

3 Laughton, *Torrington Memoirs*, pp. 81–6.
Tunstall, *Byng Papers* I, 249–50. Snyder,
Marlborough–Godolphin II, 1,028.
Aldridge, 'Norris', pp. 132–5. Harding,
'Vernon', p. 157.

4 *HP 1690–1715* V, 472.

5 HMC *Finch* III, 153, to Nottingham, 13 Jul
1691.

6 Johnston, 'Parliament and the Navy',
pp. 433–4. Broadley, 'Rooke
Correspondence', p. 70.

7 *Letters Illustrative of the Reign of William
III . . . by J. Vernon*, ed. G. P. R. James
(London, 1841, 3 vols.) I, 405, to
Shrewsbury, 25 Sep 1697. Cf. Ritchie,
Captain Kidd, p. 192.

8 Lawson, 'Public Opinion', pp. 138–43.
Johnston, 'Parliament and the Navy',
pp. 55–6. and 435. Martin-Leake, *Leake* II,
155–9. Browning, *Rooke Journal*,
pp. 242–52. Hattendorf, 'Governmental
Machinery', p. 14. James, 'Lords
Commissioners', pp. 102–10 and 121–3.
Pearsall, 'Trade Protection', p. 120.

9 E.g. Pepys's friend the purser William
Gibson (Tanner, *Pepys Private
Correspondence* I, 118–24) and Sir Richard
Haddock (Laughton, 'Commissioner's
Note Book', pp. 157–68). Cf. Evelyn,
Diary V, 10.

10 HMC *Finch* IV, 290, to Nottingham, 4 Jul
1692.

11 *House of Lords MSS* II, vii–viii.

12 HMC *Finch* IV, 256. HMC *House of
Lords* IV, 235.

13 Hepper, *Warship Losses*, pp. 14–28.
Pearsall, 'Trade Protection', p. 120. Owen,
War at Sea, pp. 104–5, 111–15 and 231–4.

14 PRO: ADM 8/2 and 8/9, 1 Aug in each
case.

15 Merriman, *Queen Anne's Navy*, pp. 315
and 335. Rodger, 'Officers' Careers'.

BAW, pp. 102–4. For pay-scales see Appendix IV.

16 Ehrman, *Navy*, pp. 452–61. Merriman, *Sergison Papers*, pp. 265–70. Merriman, *Queen Anne's Navy*, pp. 314–15. Anderson, 'English Flag Officers'. Martin-Leake, *Leake* I, 162–3. Browning, *Rooke Journal*, pp. 258–61.

17 HMC *House of Lords* IV, 240, 6 Aug 1692.

18 Merriman, *Sergison Papers*, pp. 348–50 and 358. HMC *Finch* IV, 305, C. Mason to Nottingham, 10 Jul 1692. HMC *Portland* X, 35, Order by Pr. George, 26 Jun 1703. Tunstall, *Byng Papers* I, 249. Ehrman, *Navy*, pp. 452–7. Owen, *War at Sea*, p. 5. Van 't Hoff, *Marlborough-Heinsius*, p. 351. *NZW* IV, 16–19.

19 Hattendorf, 'Benbow's Last Fight'; and 'Rooke and Shovell', pp. 53–4. Edye, *Royal Marines*, pp. 352, 378–9, 462 and 509–510. *ODNB sv* G. Forbes. *HP 1715–54* II, 44. Bérenger, 'Les Hapsbourgs et la mer', pp. 30–31.

20 Merriman, *Queen Anne's Navy*, pp. 310–19. Tunstall, *Byng Papers* II, 281. *BAW* p. 98.

21 Lloyd, *British Seaman*, p. 90.

22 Benbow, *Brave Benbow*, pp. 6–17. *ODNB*. Holmes, 'The Professions and Social Change', p. 348. *HP 1715–54* I, 429 and II, 177.

23 Vergé-Franceschi, 'Les Officiers généraux en 1715'. Marie-Christine Varachaud, Michel Vergé-Franceschi and André Zysberg, 'Qui étaient les capitaines de vaisseau du Roi-Soleil', *RH* CCLXXXVII (1992), pp. 311–38.

24 Hughes, 'Encouragement of Seamen', p. 25.

25 Ehrman, *Navy*, p. 110. Johnston, 'Parliament and the Navy', p. 502. Lloyd, *British Seaman*, pp. 286–7 gives slightly higher figures; cf. Appendix VI.

26 Johnston, 'Parliament and the Navy', pp. 311–13 and 319. Jones, *War and Economy*, pp. 155–7. Earle, *Sailors*, pp. 201–3.

27 Charnock, *Marine Architecture* II, 447–8.

28 Ehrman, *Navy*, pp. 446–51. HMC *Finch* IV, 490–93. Bromley, *Manning*, p. xxvii. James, 'Lords Commissioners', p. 143. Johnston, 'Parliament and the Navy',

pp. 344 and 457–60. Merriman, *Queen Anne's Navy*, pp. 165–6 and 170–72. HMC *House of Lords* IV, 225. Martin-Leake, *Leake* I, 119.

29 *House of Lords MSS* I, 150–51, 8 Feb 1694.

30 Jones, *War and Economy*, pp. 154–7. Ehrman, *Navy*, pp. 110–14. Middleton, 'Chesapeake Convoy System', pp. 186–7. Crowhurst, *Defence of British Trade*, pp. 140–41.

31 Robert Crosfeild, *England's Glory Revived*, in Bromley, *Manning*, pp. 4–5.

32 Innis, *Cod Fisheries*, pp. 105–9 and 500. Lounsbury, *British Fishery at Newfoundland*, pp. 126–81. D. J. Starkey, 'Devonians and the Newfoundland Trade', *MHD* I, 163–71, at pp. 169–70. Crowhurst, *Defence of British Trade*, p. 112.

33 HMC *Finch* III, 50, to Nottingham, 6 May 1691. Cf. Burchett, *Complete History*, p. 436.

34 Johnston, 'Parliament and the Navy', pp. 322 and 344. James, 'Lords Commissioners', pp. 238–9.

35 James, 'Lords Commissioners', p. 145. Rogers, 'Liberty Road', p. 55. HMC *Portland* VIII, 199 and 219–23. Rodger, 'Devon Men', pp. 211–12.

36 W. L. Clements Library, Ann Arbor, Michigan: Shelburne MSS Vol. 139, No. 56.

37 George St Lo [or St Loe], *England's Interest; or, a Discipline for Seamen* (1694), in Bromley, *Manning*, p. 36.

38 Ehrman, *Navy*, pp. 115–20. Owen, *War at Sea*, pp. 16–17. HMC *House of Lords* IV, 225. Kepler, 'Jennings', pp. 21–2. Bishop, *Life and Adventures*, pp. 55–77, recounts the stratagems of a petty officer leading a press-gang.

39 Ingram, *Three Sea Journals*, pp. 112 and 117.

40 Owen, *War at Sea*, pp. 20–22. Harding, 'Vernon', p. 157.

41 Kitson, 'Bringing Round the *Royal Charles*', p. 49.

42 Merriman, *Queen Anne's Navy*, p. 193.

43 Johnston, 'Parliament and the Navy', pp. 323–4 and 505. Earle, *A City Full of People*, p. 78. Kitson, 'Bringing Round the *Royal Charles*', p. 40. *BAW*, p. 164.

44 Earle, *Sailors*, pp. 196–200.

45 Rogers, *Cruising Voyage*, p. 8.

46 Johnston, 'Parliament and the Navy', p. 308. Earle, 'English Sailors', pp. 75–7. Bromley, *Manning*, pp. 1–70. The figures came from the Sixpenny Office, which inherited the residual functions of the Register Office set up under the 1696 Act (for which see below). The careful calculations of Starkey, 'Market for Seafarers', suggest a true total of about 50,000 in the 1730s, including 'seamen' employed in inland navigation.

47 Johnston, 'Parliament and the Navy', pp. 395–8, 404–414 and 442–4. Merriman, *Queen Anne's Navy*, pp. 170–72, 184–8, 194–200. Bourne, *Queen Anne's Navy*, pp. 90–92 and 96–7. Bromley, 'Profits of Naval Command', p. 451.

48 Hughes, 'Encouragement of Seamen'. Ehrman, *Navy*, pp. 598–602. James, 'Lords Commissioners', pp. 147–9. Johnston, 'Parliament and the Navy', pp. 355–6.

49 Johnston, 'Parliament and the Navy', pp. 401–6. Bromley, 'Away from Impressment', pp. 185–6. Tunstall, *Byng Papers* II, 289. Merriman, *Queen Anne's Navy*, pp. 170–72 and 194–200.

50 Edye, *Royal Marines*, pp. 304–589. Merriman, *Sergison Papers*, pp. 314–30; and *Queen Anne's Navy*, pp. 177–9 and 207–13. Burchett, *Complete History*, pp. 615–18. Corbett, *Mediterranean* II, 475–7.

51 HMC *Buccleugh* II, 223, to Shrewsbury, 6 Sep 1695; cf. II, 218 and 301.

52 HMC *House of Lords* IV, 226. HMC *Finch* IV, 46. Martin-Leake, *Leake* II, 176.

53 Hattendorf, 'Rooke and Shovell', p. 60.

54 Merriman, *Queen Anne's Navy*, pp. 201–2. Hinchliffe, 'Impressment of Seamen'.

55 Historians often use the term *inscription maritime* with which it was rebaptized by the French revolutionaries.

56 E.g. by George St Lo, *England's Interest* (in Bromley, *Manning*, pp. 16–41). As a prisoner of war St Lo had observed the French system himself.

57 *Ex inf.* Professor André Zysberg.

58 Symcox, *French Sea Power*, pp. 13–22. Pilgrim, 'Colbert-Seignelay Naval Reforms', pp. 247–8 and 257–9; and 'French Naval Power', pp. 103–5, 109, 139–42 and 159. Perrichet, 'L'Administration des classes'. R. Mémain, *Matelots et soldats des vaisseaux du Roi* (Paris, 1936) *passim*, especially pp. 185–205. Martel, *Le recrutement des matelots*, pp. 176–205. J. S. Bromley, 'Quelques reflections sur le fonctionnement des Classes Maritimes en France, 1689–1713', *Les Cahiers de Montpellier* VI (1982), pp. 11–27 (also *Corsairs and Navies*, pp. 121–37). Masson, *Histoire de la Marine* I, 101–3. RAdm Ducasse, 'Les Marins protestants de Louis XIV et la révocation de l'Edit de Nantes', *RHA* 167 (1987), pp. 77–92. Alain Cabantous, *Dix mille marins face à l'océan* (Paris, 1991), pp. 186–7.

59 Earle, *Sailors*, pp. 11–25 and 42–9; and *A City Full of People*, pp. 75–7 and 81. Bishop, *Life and Adventures* p. 2. Barlow, *Journal* I, 163.

60 HMC *Buccleuch and Queensberry* II, 64, to Shrewsbury, 3 May 1694.

61 Merriman, *Sergison Papers*, p. 298.

62 Tunstall, *Byng Papers* I, 17. Merriman, *Queen Anne's Navy*, p. 213. Edye, *Royal Marines*, pp. 418 and 479.

63 Cockburn, *Seafaring People*, pp. 5–6.

64 Barlow, *Journal* II, 425–6.

65 Martin-Leake, *Leake* II, 222, 269 and 361. Owen, *War at Sea*, pp. 23–4. Phillips, 'Journal', p. 187. Maydman, *Naval Speculations*, p. 109. The monkeys were to keep or sell as pets, not to eat.

66 Rogers, *Cruising Voyage*, pp. xi–xii, 132 and 135.

67 *A Proposal to Man the Navy Royal of Great Britain* (1709), in Bromley, *Manning*, p. 48.

68 Earle, *Sailors*, pp. 130–31.

69 HMC *Finch* II, 238, to Nottingham, 4 Sep 1689.

70 *KMN* II, 180–88 and 241–6. Shaw, 'Hospital Ship'. Watson, 'Victualling', p. 210. Merriman, *Queen Anne's Navy*, pp. 223–6, 234–5 and 241.

71 Shaw, 'Hospital Ship', p. 426.

72 Alsop, 'The *Tiger*'s Journal'. It is

impossible to verify Leake's claim as no musters of the *Prince George* survive from this period.

73 Earle, *Sailors*, pp. 93–100.

74 Cooke, *Voyage to the South Sea*, pp. 23 and 26. 'Hautboy' = oboe.

75 Martin-Leake, *Martin*, p. 41. This is a life of Martin by his son, based on his journals, and I take this to be the father's voice.

76 Phillips, 'Journal', pp. 174–5. The author was a former naval lieutenant, but at the time of which he writes was commanding a merchantman of the Royal African Company.

77 E.g. 'Slush', *Navy Royal*, pp. 1–2. Laughton, 'Commissioner's Note Book', p. 150.

78 Earle, *Sailors*, pp. 152–8. Kemp, *British Sailor*, pp. 59, 82 and 88. Owen, *War at Sea*, p. 25. Lloyd, *British Seaman*, p. 240. Rogers, *Cruising Voyage*, pp. 12–14, 34 and 288. J. M. Beattie, *Crime and the Courts in England 1660–1800* (Oxford, 1986), pp. 461–4.

79 Browning, *Rooke Journal*, pp. 124–6 and 155. Merriman, *Queen Anne's Navy*, p. 335. Tunstall, *Byng Papers* II, 237–40, 310–21.

80 Tunstall, *Byng Papers* II, 147, to G. Byng, 6 Jan 1708.

81 Maydman, *Naval Speculations*, p. 147.

82 Scott, 'Naval Chaplain', pp. 88–90.

14 Great Frigates

1 Tanner, *Pepys's Naval Minutes*, p. 15.

2 *FDW* II, 283, quoting an anonymous account of the battle of the Kentish Knock by an English officer.

3 'En général les Anglois frégatent beaucoup davantage leurs vaisseaux qu'en Hollande, ni en France.' Clément, *Lettres de Colbert* III, ii, 326; cf. *GNZ* II, 52–5.

4 Pfister-Langanay, 'Charpentiers à Dunkerque'. *BND* No. 150 pp. 254–5. Tanner, *Pepys's Naval Minutes*, pp. 17–18 and 241. Johns, '*Constant Warwick*'. L. G. C. Laughton, 'The Cutting Down of the *Sovereign* in 1651', *MM* XIV (1928), pp. 62–3. Lavery, *Ship of the Line* I, 18–21. Hammond, 'Administration', p. 132. *ARN*, pp. 330–37.

5 Lavery, *Ship of the Line* I, 22–30. Fox, *Great Ships*, pp. 51–60. Penn, *Memorials* II, 144–5. Laughton, 'Gunnery, Frigates and the Line of Battle'. *FDW* IV, 255 and VI, 212. Glete, *Navies and Nations* I, 181 and 184. Rodger, 'Broadside Gunnery'.

6 Fox, 'Shipbuilding Programme of 1664'. Lavery, *Ship of the Line* I, 32–4; and *Deane's Doctrine*, pp. 11–12. *CPM* I, 221–6. Tanner, *Pepys's Naval Minutes*, pp. 200–201 and 243.

7 Hemingway, 'Surveyors of the Navy', pp. 43 and 50–54. Lavery, *Ship of the Line* I, 42–8. Lavery, *Deane's Doctrine*, pp. 42–8. Fox, *Great Ships*, pp. 156–8. Tanner, *Pepys's Naval Minutes*, pp. 243–4. *CPM* IV, 406 and 415.

8 Anderson, *Allin Journals* I, 147.

9 Anderson, *Third Dutch War*, pp. 188–9.

10 Anderson, *Third Dutch War*, p. 71, J. Narbrough's journal, 5 Apr 1672. 'Standing at her bearing' means standing up to her canvas, stiff.

11 Morrah, *Prince Rupert*, p. 365 (but I cannot trace his reference). Thompson, 'Haddock Correspondence', p. 21, Captain R. Haddock to his wife, 31 May 1673.

12 'Il a sa batterie noyée et il n'a pas deux pouces franc du dalot.' Delarbre, *Tourville*, p. 286, to Colbert, 13 Apr 1680.

13 Anderson, 'Comparative Naval Architecture', pp. 42–3 and 172–180. Lemineur, *Les Vaisseaux du Roi Soleil*, pp. 40–42. Dessert, *La Royale*, pp. 136–7. Mémain, *Rochefort*, p. 645. Villiers, 'Marine de Colbert', pp. 179–81. *GNZ* II, 12–13. *NZW* III, 154–5.

14 Lavery, *Ship of the Line* I, 54–68. Ehrman, *Navy*, pp. 625–32. *BND* Nos. 153–6 pp. 259–64. Merriman, *Sergison Papers*, pp. 80–84. Hemingway, 'Surveyors of the Navy', pp. 82–90.

15 Tanner, *Pepys's Naval Minutes*, p. 394.

16 Lavery, *Deane's Doctrine*, pp. 25–6. Charnock, *Marine Architecture* II, 483. *BND* No. 160 pp. 266–9. Mémain, *Rochefort*, p. 731. Delarbre, *Tourville*, p. 315. Beauchesne, *La construction navale*, p. 67. *NZW* III, 147–53. Hoving and Lemmers, *In Tekening gebracht*, pp. 13–20.

17 Appendices II and III.
18 Lavery, *Arming and Fitting*, pp. 115–16. Fox, *Great Ships*, pp. 186–90. *CPM* I, 233–40 and IV, 527–8. Tanner, 'Administration' XII, 703–7. Caruana, *Sea Ordnance* I, 86–92.
19 *CPM* IV, 549.
20 Owen, *War at Sea*, p. 30. Merriman, *Queen Anne's Navy*, pp. 66–7. Caruana, *Sea Ordnance*, I, 150–61.
21 Merriman, *Queen Anne's Navy*, pp. 360–61. *BND* Nos. 157–9 pp. 264–5. Lavery, *Ship of the Line* I, 68–71. Hemingway, 'Surveyors of the Navy', pp. 125–6. Anderson, 'Comparative Naval Architecture', pp. 309–11, whose figures for broadsides are all converted to lbs avoirdupois.
22 Dyer, 'Journal of Grenvill Collins', p. 210. 'Pinckle' = pintle.
23 Saville, 'Industrial Development', pp. 614–17. Knight, 'Lead and Copper Sheathing', p. 293. Lavery, *Arming and Fitting*, p. 61. Tanner, *Pepys's Naval Minutes*, pp. 115–16. *CPM* III, 66.
24 Waters, 'Rudder, Tiller and Whipstaff'. Franklin, *Ship Models*, pp. 181–4. Lavery, *Arming and Fitting*, pp. 13–19. Goodwin, *Construction and Fitting*, pp. 132–4. David H. Roberts, 'The Origin of the Steering Wheel', *MM* LXXV (1989), pp. 272–3. John Franklin, 'A Further Note on the Introduction of the Steering Wheel', *MM* LXXVI (1990), pp. 171–3. Llinares, *Marine, propulsion et technique* I, 99–100.
25 Moore, 'Rigging in the Seventeenth Century' II, 271 and III, 7–11. Lavery, *Ship of the Line* II, 71–106; and *Deane's Doctrine*, pp. 126–8. Howard, *Ships of War*, pp. 195–207. Fox, *Great Ships*, pp. 198–200. Anderson, *Allin Journals* I, 36 and 82; II, 71 and 109. Lees, *Masting and Rigging*.
26 Llinares, *Marine, propulsion et technique*, I, 53–6 and 99–102. *GNZ* II, 11, 17 and 25. Mémain, *Rochefort*, pp. 665–7. Lemineur, *Les Vaisseaux du Roi Soleil*, pp. 43–4. Dessert, *La Royale*, pp. 129–30 and 134–35. Rodger, 'Enlightenment'.
27 Fox, *Great Ships*, pp. 75–8. Powell and Timings, *Rupert and Monck*, p. 65. Winfield, *50-Gun Ship*, pp. 7–35. Baugh,
'National Institution', p. 123. Hemingway, 'Surveyors of the Navy', pp. 63–4 and 103–9.
28 Howard, *Ships of War*, pp. 156–8. Lavery, *Deane's Doctrine*, p. 16. Fox, *Great Ships*, p. 20. Tanner, *Pepys's Naval Minutes*, p. 241. Bellabarba and Osculati, *Royal Caroline*, pp. 7–11. Hemingway, 'Surveyors of the Navy', p. 123.
29 Boudriot and Berti, *L'Artillerie de mer*, pp. 144–54. Ware, *Bomb Vessel*, pp. 8–28. Caruana, *Sea Ordnance* I, 208–24. Goodwin, *Bomb Vessel Granado*, pp. 7–8 and 21. See also p. 155 above.
30 Wilson, 'Commonwealth Gun', p. 94.
31 Wilson, 'Commonwealth Gun'. Brown, 'Office of the Ordnance'. Smith, 'Iron Cannon of 7', pp. 14–16. Rodger, *Safeguard*, p. 389. Lavery, *Arming and Fitting*, pp. 85–6. Caruana, *Sea Ordnance* I, 66. Bull, 'Ordnance', pp. 482–7, quotes prices from 1657 as low as £16 1s and £13 19s a ton, which perhaps represents peacetime levels.
32 Smith, 'Iron Cannon of 7'. Fox, *Distant Storm*, pp. 67–71. Lavery, *Arming and Fitting*, p. 87. S. B. Bailey, 'John Browne and Prince Rupert's guns', in Smith, *British Naval Armaments*, pp. 9–10. Caruana, *Sea Ordnance* I, 77–106 and 148; II, 30.
33 Caruana, *Sea Ordnance* I, 190–92. Anderson, *Third Dutch War*, p. 215. Powell and Timings, *Rupert and Monck*, p. 99. Fox, *Distant Storm*, pp. 238–41.
34 Tomlinson, *Guns and Government*, pp. 107–17. Saville, 'Industrial Development', pp. 641–75. A. R. Hall, *Ballistics in the Seventeenth Century* (Cambridge, 1952), pp. 26–7. Aylmer, *State's Servants*, pp. 39–41. Hammond, 'Administration', pp. 276–7.

15 Pride and Prejudice

1 Elector of Brunswick-Lüneburg, strictly speaking, but the English always called the electorate after its capital.
2 Holmes, *British Politics*, pp. xii–xxxvi. Gregg, *Queen Anne*, pp. 131–4, 335–7. Goldie, 'Divergence and Union'.
3 Gregg, *Queen Anne*, pp. 380–88. Rodger,

'Sea-Power and Empire', pp. 169–70. Black, 'Britain's Foreign Alliances', pp. 574–6.

4 Black, *Britain as a Military Power*, pp. 21–4. Lenman, *Britain's Colonial Wars*, pp. 47–52; and *Jacobite Risings*, pp. 107–54. Tunstall, *Byng Papers* III, xxxiv–xxxv and 87–96.

5 Black, *Natural and Necessary Enemies*, pp. 7–11.

6 Black, 'Anglo-Spanish Naval Relations', pp. 236–8. Merino Navarro, 'La Armada en el siglo XVIII' II, 99. Hattendorf, 'Byng and Cape Passaro', pp. 19–23. Bruijn, *Dutch Navy*, pp. 150–52. Bérenger, 'Les Hapsbourgs et la mer', pp. 25–34.

7 Cranmer-Byng, *Pattee Byng's Journal*, p. 23.

8 *BND*, pp. 360–62. *AE* VI, 147–63. Hattendorf, 'Byng and Cape Passaro', pp. 24–35. Corbett, *Expedition to Sicily*, pp. 18–22. Cranmer-Byng, *Pattee Byng's Journal*, pp. 1–22. HMC *Polwarth* I, 587–9. Richmond, 'Expedition to Sicily'.

9 PRO: SP 42/74 f. 46; well known in the form quoted by Corbett, *Expedition to Sicily*, p. 20, as though this sentence were the whole letter.

10 Black, 'Anglo-Spanish Naval Relations', pp. 239–40. Cranmer-Byng, *Pattee Byng's Journal*, pp. 49–301. Hattendorf, 'Byng and Cape Passaro', pp. 37–8.

11 Starkey, *British Privateering*, pp. 111–15. Chapin, *Privateer Ships and Sailors*, pp. 209–16.

12 George Shelvocke, *A Voyage round the World by Way of the Great South Sea* (London, 1726). William Betagh, *A Voyage round the World* (London, 1728). Spate, *Pacific II*, pp. 210–13. Williams, *Great South Sea*, pp. 197–205.

13 *AE* VI, 165–71. HMC *Polwarth* II, 192.

14 Aldridge, 'Norris and the Baltic', pp. 15–89. Murray, *George I and the Baltic*, pp. 30–43, 102–15 and 161–215; and 'United Provinces'. Mediger, *Mecklenburg, Russland und England-Hannover* I, 225–47. HMC *Townshend*, pp. 91–102. HMC *Polwarth* I, 52. Hatton, *Diplomatic Relations*, pp. 74–83. Göran Behre, 'Gothenburg in French War Strategy 1649–1760', in *Scotland and*

Scandinavia 800–1800, ed. Grant G. Simpson (Edinburgh, 1990), pp. 107–18, at pp. 111–12.

15 Murray, *George I and the Baltic*, pp. 216–70. Mediger, *Mecklenburg, Russland und England-Hannover* I, 263. Anderson, *Naval Wars in the Baltic*, pp. 174–6. Hatton, *Diplomatic Relations*, pp. 103 and 121–2. M. S. Anderson, *Britain's Discovery of Russia, 1553–1815* (London, 1958), pp. 68–70. Barfod, *Niels Juels flåde*, pp. 210–24.

16 Murray, *George I and the Baltic*, pp. 285–317. Tunstall, *Byng Papers* III, 227–33. Anderson, *Naval Wars in the Baltic*, pp. 177–8. *BND* No. 179 pp. 322–3. HMC *Polwarth* I, 268, 277 and 314.

17 Hangö Udde, Hanko, Гангут, are the Swedish, Finnish and Russian forms.

18 P. A. Krotov, *Гангутская батапия 1714 года* (St Petersburg, 1996).

19 Mediger, *Mecklenburg, Russland und England-Hannover* I, 421–32. Anderson, *Naval Wars in the Baltic*, pp. 185–207. Aldridge, 'Norris', p. 142. Barfod, *Niels Juels flåde*, pp. 236–7. HMC *Polwarth* I, 512.

20 *BND* No. 181 pp. 323–4, to W. Stanhope, 11 Aug 1726.

21 Black, *Britain as a Military Power*, pp. 89–90. Baugh, 'Wager', pp. 105–6 and 113–18. HMC *Townshend*, pp. 116–17. *BND* Nos. 180 and 182, pp. 323–324. Rodger, 'Anglo-Dutch Alliance', p. 20.

22 *BNA*, p. 327. *KNM* III, 97–100. Other authors offer even higher figures, but there do not appear to be any trustworthy statistics of Hosier's losses.

23 *AE* VI, 188–9. Merino Navarro, 'La Armada en el siglo XVIII', II, 101. Baugh, 'Wager', pp. 114–15.

24 Ware, 'Royal Navy and the Plantations', p. 121.

25 Earle, *Pirate Wars*, pp. 157–208. Hughson, 'Carolina Pirates', pp. 287–369. John Atkins, *A Voyage to Guinea, Brazil & the West Indies, in His Majesty's Ships, the Swallow and Weymouth* (London, 1735), is an interesting narrative of an anti-pirate cruise on the West African coast in 1721.

26 Gwyn, *Warren Papers*, p. 5. May, 'Captain Frankland's *Rose*', p. 38.

27 Ware, 'Royal Navy and the Plantations',
pp. 122–3. W. E. May, 'The Surveying
Commission of *Alborough*, 1728–34', *AN*
XXI (1961), pp. 260–78.
28 Acerra and Zysberg, *L'Essor des marines*,
p. 65.
29 Perez-Mallaina Bueno, *Politica Naval
Española*, pp. 397–407 and 442–3.
Béthencourt Massieu, *Patiño*, pp. 21–4.
AE VI, 376–7. Black, 'Anglo-Spanish
Naval Relations'. Merino Navarro, 'La
Armada en el siglo XVIII', II, 97–101.
McNeill, *Atlantic Empires*, pp. 52–57.
Manera Regueyra, 'La epoca de Felipe V y
Fernando VI', pp. 171–86. Walker,
Spanish Politics, pp. 94–113. José Cervera
Pery, *La Marina de la Ilustración
(Resurgimiento y crisis del poder naval)*
(Madrid, 1986), pp. 57–70. Jean
McLachlan, 'The Seven Years' Peace and
the West India Policy of Carvajal and
Wall', *EHR* LIII (1938), pp. 457–77.
Federico F. de Bordejé y Morencos, 'El
inmovilismo táctico en el siglo XVIII',
RHN XIV (1996), 52, pp. 45–66. Rodger,
'Form and Function', p. 93.
30 'Le Commerce fait de la richesse et
conséquemment la puissance des Etats;
les forces navales sont absolument
nécessaires pour le soutien du commerce
maritime': Filion, *Maurepas*, pp. 49–50.
This was written in 1745, but he had said
similar things before.
31 Meyer and Acerra, 'La Marine française
vue par elle-même', pp. 231–5. Filion, 'La
Crise de la marine française'; and
Maurepas, pp. 49–58, 101–48 and 157–72.
Pritchard, *Naval Disaster*, pp. 21–2.
Meyer, 'La Marine française au XVIIIe
siècle', p. 155. Acerra and Zysberg, *L'Essor
des marines*, pp. 66–85. *MMF*, pp. 35–98.
J. Bertin, R. Lamontagne and F.
Vergneault, 'Traitement graphique d'une
information: les marines royales de
France et de Grande-Bretagne
(1697–1747)', *Annales* XXII (1967),
pp. 991–1,004, at pp. 992–3 and 1,000.
32 'De bon esprit, qui a des très bonnes
intentions, mais qui ne sait pas de quelle
couleur est la mer'; Taillemite, *L'histoire
ignorée*, p. 152, quoting Henri du
Trousset, sieur de Valincour.

33 Jeremy Black, 'British Neutrality in the
War of the Polish Succession, 1733–1735',
IHR VIII (1986), pp. 345–66 (quoted
p. 356 n.34). Black, 'Anglo-Spanish Naval
Relations', p. 239. Merino Navarro, 'La
Armada en el siglo XVIII', II, 102–3.
MMF II, 114–20.
34 Grahn, 'Guarding the New Granadan
Coasts'. Marsden, *Law and Custom* II,
270–71 and 277–9. Pares, *War and Trade*,
pp. 115–27. George H. Nelson,
'Contraband Trade under the Asiento,
1730–1739', *AHR* LI (1945–6), pp. 55–67.
Ogelsby, 'War at Sea in the West Indies',
pp. 6–10. Woodfine, 'Anglo-Spanish
War', pp. 193–4. Earle, *Pirate Wars*,
p. 188.
35 J. K. Laughton, 'Jenkin's Ear', *EHR* IV
(1889), pp. 741–9, at p. 742, to Newcastle,
12 Oct 1731.
36 Woodfine, *Britannia's Glories*, pp. 1–2. 15,
84–5, 130–31 and 171–80; 'Anglo-Spanish
War', pp. 187–96; and 'Ideas of Naval
Power', pp. 72–4. Temperley, 'War of
Jenkins Ear'. Ogelsby, 'War at Sea in the
West Indies', pp. 6–10. Harding,
Amphibious Warfare, pp. 19–23.
37 Woodfine, 'Anglo-Spanish War',
pp. 185–6, quoting the ministerial
pamphleteer Henry Etough.
38 Woodfine, *Britannia's Glories*, pp. 146–8.
It is to be feared that modern audiences,
unversed in history and grammar, read
Thomson's couplet as a statement of fact
rather than an exhortation.
39 Woodfine, *Britannia's Glories*, p. 235,
quoting the diplomat Sir Everard
Fawkener.
40 Harding, *Amphibious Warfare*, pp. 22–42.
Woodfine, 'Ideas of Naval Power',
pp. 72–3; and *Britannia's Glories*,
pp. 223–4. Baugh, 'Wager', pp. 121–2.
41 *BNA*, p. 15, to Newcastle, [7?] Dec 1738.
42 *VP*, pp. 6–46. Richmond, *War of 1739–48*
I, 45–9. *AE* VI, 254–7. Harding,
Amphibious Warfare, pp. 86–8; and
'Vernon', pp. 160–70. Spate, *Pacific II*,
p. 217. Buchet, *L'espace Caraïbe* I, 515–21.
J. F. King, 'Admiral Vernon at Portobello,
1739', *HAHR* XXIII (1943), pp. 258–82.
43 Stanley Ayling, *The Elder Pitt, Earl of
Chatham* (London, 1976), p. 66.

44 Woodfine, 'Ideas of Naval Power'; and *Britannia's Glories*, pp. 171–80 and 214. Wilson, 'Empire, Trade and Popular Politics'. Jordan and Rogers, 'Admirals as Heroes', pp. 203–10.

45 *VP*, p. 133. Ogelsby, 'War at Sea in the West Indies', pp. 80–81; and 'Spain's Havana Squadron and the Preservation of the Balance of Power in the Caribbean, 1740–1748', *HAHR* XLIX (1969), pp. 473–88, at pp. 475–9. Harding, *Amphibious Warfare*, p. 88. Pares, *War and Trade*, pp. 163–8. Buchet, *L'espace Caraïbe* I, 282–5.

46 Harding, *Amphibious Warfare*, pp. 89–122. *VP*, pp. 177–236. Woodfine, 'War of Jenkin's Ear'; and 'A Friend to the General'. Ogelsby, 'War at Sea in the West Indies', pp. 91–123. Julian de Zulueta, 'Health and Military Factors in Vernon's Failure at Cartagena', *MM* LXXVIII (1992), pp. 127–41. Zapatero, *La Guerra del Caribe*, pp. 32–62.

47 Harding, *Amphibious Warfare*, pp. 123–37. Ogelsby, 'War at Sea in the West Indies', pp. 124–37.

48 J. C. M. Oglesby, 'The British Attacks on the Caracas Coast, 1743', *MM* LVIII (1972), pp. 27–40. Buchet, *L'espace Caraïbe* I, 287–9. Richmond, *War of 1739–48* I, 241–57.

49 Williams, *Documents of Anson's Voyage*, p. 77.

50 Williams, *Prize of All the Oceans*, is much the best of many accounts of Anson's voyage; see also his editions of *Documents of Anson's Voyage*, and Walter and Robins, *Anson's Voyage*. Two versions of the journal of Lt Philip Saumarez are printed in Ross, *Saumarez* II, 348–368, and *Log of the Centurion*, ed. Leo Heaps (London, 1973).

51 Leach, *Arms for Empire*, pp. 213–15 and 220–23. Gwyn, 'Royal Navy in North America', pp. 133–134. May, 'Captain Frankland's *Rose*', pp. 45–6.

52 Ogelsby, 'War at Sea in the West Indies', pp. 232–63. *Privateering and Piracy in the Colonial Period: Illustrative Documents* ed. J. F. Jameson (New York, 1923), pp. 359–411. Starkey, *British Privateering*, pp. 117–20. *BND* Nos. 212–13 pp. 65–6.

53 Richmond, *War of 1739–48* I, 171–6. *HP 1715–54* II, 93–4. Black, 'Anglo-Spanish Naval Relations', p. 251.

54 Richmond, *War of 1739–48* I, 204–40, quoted I, 212. Baudi de Vesme, 'Il potere marittimo'.

55 Black, *Natural and Necessary Enemies*, pp. 41–3. Dann, *Hannover und England*, pp. 45–53.

16 A Strong Squadron in Soundings

1 Black, *Natural and Necessary Enemies*, pp. 41–6. Lodge, *Eighteenth-Century Diplomacy*, pp. 123–4.

2 Richmond, *War of 1739–48*, I, xvi (but I cannot trace his reference). Cf. *HP 1715–54* I, 451–2.

3 'Je suis étonné de la politique anglaise; ils n'envisagent toute l'Europe que comme une grande république faite pour les servir: ils n'entrent jamais dans les intérêts des autres et ne servent d'autre arguments persuasifs que de leurs guinées'. *Politische Correspondenz Friederich's des Grossen*, ed. J. G. Droysen et al. (Berlin, 1879–1920, 47 vols.), V, 314, to Heinrich Graf Podewils, 7 Feb 1747.

4 Baugh, ' "Blue-Water" Policy', pp. 42–50. Black, 'Britain's Foreign Alliances', pp. 590–94. Mimler, *Der Einfluss kolonialer Interessen*, pp. 40–42. Lodge, *Eighteenth-Century Diplomacy*, p. 127. Niedhart, *Handel und Krieg*, p. 66. Massie, 'Defence of the Low Countries', pp. 1–24. P. Geyl, *Willem IV en Engeland tot 1748* (The Hague, 1924), pp. 79–81. Pares, 'American versus Continental Warfare', pp. 429–35 and 447–8.

5 *PH* XII, 1077.

6 *BAW*, pp. 19 and 66–9. Richmond, *War of 1739–48* I, 182–90. Aldridge, 'Norris', p. 147.

7 *BAW*, pp. 68–70. Clowes, *Royal Navy* III, 81–2. Baugh, ' "Too Much Mixed in this Affair" ', pp. 25–9. *ODNB sv* Mathews and Lestock. *BND* No. 215, pp. 370–74.

8 Technically Lestock commanded the British Van Squadron and Rowley the Rear, but the fleet was in reverse order.

9 Tunstall, *Naval Warfare*, pp. 83–90. Creswell, *British Admirals*, pp. 63–79. *AE*

VI, 300–314. Mackay, 'Hawke', pp. 203–4. Carter, 'Journal of M. de Lage', pp. 227–51. *MMF* II, 141–6. Richmond, *War of 1739–48* II, 1–57. Martinez-Valverde, 'La campaña de Navarro'. [Cosme Álvarez] 'Una relación inédita sobre el combate de Tolón (1744)', *RHN* X (1992), 37, pp. 121–36. Rohan Butler, *Choiseul: Vol. I, Father and Son 1719–1754* (Oxford, 1980), pp. 495–6.

10 PRO: SP 42/28 f. 70, Admiralty to Newcastle, 2 Mar 1744.

11 Respectively Captain Hon. Fitzroy Henry Lee of the *Princess Royal*, and Captain Christopher O'Brien formerly of the *Royal Sovereign*, who died in February 1743. Lee was unpopular and accused of many vices; if there had been any suspicion of Jacobitism it would surely have been brought up against him. O'Brien (on whom see Cross, *Banks of the Neva*, p. 18) was a follower of Wager, who is unlikely to have sponsored anyone not loyal to the Hanoverians.

12 Richmond, *War of 1739–48* II, 63–93. Colin, *Louis XV et les Jacobites*, pp. 42–187. *BAW*, p. 71. Monod, *Jacobitism*, p. 283. *MMF* II, 154–6. Aldridge, 'Norris', p. 147. McLynn, *France and the Jacobite Rising*, pp. 19–25.

13 Luff, 'Mathews v. Lestock', pp. 46–9.

14 Haas, 'Rise of the Bedfords', pp. 4–11 and 35–8. *BAW*, pp. 72–81. *The Correspondence of the Dukes of Richmond and Newcastle, 1724–1750*, ed. T. J. McCann (Sussex Record Society Vol. 73, 1984) No. 238 p. 160. John B. Owen, *The Rise of the Pelhams* (London, 1957), p. 245.

15 Luff, 'Mathews v. Lestock', pp. 49–61. Richmond, *War of 1739–48* II, 55–7 and 254–71. Baugh, ' "Too Much Mixed in this Affair" '. *ODNB sv* Mathews and Lestock.

16 S. de La Nicollière-Teijeiro, *La Course et les corsaires du Port de Nantes* (Paris, 1896), pp. 164–202. Gibson, *Ships of the '45*, pp. 8–15. Mimler, *Der Einfluss kolonialer Interessen*, p. 46. Brindley, 'The Lyon and the *Elisabeth*'. Malo, *Les Derniers Corsaires*, pp. 6–16.

17 McLynn, *France and the Jacobite Rising*, pp. 132–66.

18 *VP*, p. 443.

19 *VP*, pp. 437–44, 537–87. Richmond, *War of 1739–48* II, 182–6. Harding, 'Vernon', pp. 173–4. Smith, *Grenville Papers* I, 48. Russell, *Bedford Correspondence* I, 55–8.

20 McLynn, 'Sea Power and the Jacobite Rising'. Gibson, *Ships of the '45*, pp. 1–41. Malo, *Les Derniers Corsaires*, pp. 22–33.

21 BL: Add. MSS 15956, f. 69, A. Keppel to G. Anson, 23 May 1747.

22 Meaning 'metropolitans'; Warren himself was Irish.

23 McNeill, *Atlantic Empires*, pp. 7–15 and 93–5. Leach, *Arms for Empire*, pp. 229–41. Gwyn, *Warren Papers*, pp. 81–115. Dull, *Loss of Canada*, Ch. 1.3. Richmond, *War of 1739–48* II, 205–18. Graham, *North Atlantic*, pp. 116–28. Mimler, *Der Einfluss kolonialer Interessen*, pp. 48–90. *BND* No. 216, pp. 374–8.

24 Where the British settlement of Halifax was founded soon afterwards, as a result of this expedition.

25 Pritchard, *Naval Disaster*, is the only complete and accurate account of this little-known catastrophe.

26 Diverrès, *L'Attaque de Lorient*. Harding, 'Expedition to Lorient'. Buffinton, 'Canada Expedition'. *MMF* II, 163. Richmond, *War of 1739–48* III, 3–6 and 25–35. Molyneux, *Conjunct Expeditions* I, 189–98.

27 The French western half of Hispaniola, the modern Haiti, not to be confused with the Spanish eastern half of the island, the modern Dominican Republic.

28 Taillemite, 'Une bataille de l'Atlantique', p. 132. Paul Butel, 'L'Essor de l'économie de la plantation a Saint-Domingue dans la deuxième moitié du XVIIIe siècle', in Acerra et al., *Etat, marine et société*, pp. 89–100.

29 Buchet, *L'espace Caraïbe* I, 291–9. Pares, *War and Trade*, pp. 273–7 and 297. Simpson, 'Pocock', pp. 21–3 and 26–8. Richmond, *War of 1739–48* II, 226–8 and III, 66–7. Villiers, *Marine Royale* I, 417–19 and 426–31.

30 Buchet, *L'espace Caraïbe* I, 299–311. Richmond, *War of 1739–48* II, 232–3 and III, 53–67. Taillemite, 'Une bataille de l'Atlantique', pp. 134–45.

31 Richmond, *War of 1739–48* II, 147–64; III, 6–7 and 38–9. Russell, *Bedford Correspondence* I, 70–71 and 77.

32 WA: Vol. XV f. 83.

33 WA: Vol. X f. 35, to Bedford, n.d. [1745].

34 WA: Vol. XVII f. 65, to Bedford, 2 Aug [1747].

35 Richmond, *War of 1739–48* III, 22, to Anson, 20 Jul 1746.

36 Duffy, 'Western Squadron'. Ryan, 'Blockade of Brest', pp. 176–82. Masson, *Histoire de la Marine* I, 190–93. Harding, 'Vernon', pp. 173–4. Rodger, 'Sea-Power and Empire', pp. 174–9.

37 PRO: SP 42/69, G. Anson to Newcastle, 11 May 1747.

38 Russell, *Bedford Correspondence* I, 214–19. Richmond, *War of 1739–48* III, 81–93. *MMF* II, 167–72. Lavery, *First Invincible*, pp. 16–24. Troude, *Batailles navales* I, 312–15. BL: Add. MSS 33009, ff. 229–31 is a narrative of the action, evidently by the Chevalier de Saint-Georges, Captain of the *Invincible*. Long, *Naval Yarns*, pp. 23–4 has a lower-deck account.

39 Richmond, *War of 1739–48* III, 95–8. Buchet, *L'espace Caraïbe* I, 314–15.

40 BL: Add. MSS 15957, f. 210. SzP: Box 74, T. Brett to P. Saumarez, 15 Aug 1747.

41 Buchet, *L'espace Caraïbe* I, 315–17. Mackay, *Hawke*, pp. 69–88; *Hawke Papers*, pp. 25–55; and 'Hawke', p. 206. *MMF* II, 172–6. Richmond, *War of 1739–48* III, 101–11. Troude, *Batailles navales* I, 316–18. Simpson, 'Pocock', pp. 39–40.

42 BL: Add. MSS 32810, f. 211, to Sandwich, 27 Oct 1747.

43 Richmond, *War of 1739–48* III, 68–72 and 124–47. Buchet, *L'espace Caraïbe* I, 317–19. *AE* VI, 342–5 and 350–53. Ogelsby, 'War at Sea in the West Indies', pp. 222–31. Long, *Naval Yarns*, pp. 30–33.

44 Richmond, *War of 1739–48* III, 178–225. Lenman, *Britain's Colonial Wars*, pp. 92–5.

45 Tunstall, *Naval Warfare*, pp. 50–54. Weber, *Seinboeken*, pp. 124–55.

46 Rodger, 'Tactics'.

47 BL: Add. MSS 15957, f. 195, 31 May 1747.

48 BL: Add. MSS 15957, f. 188, P. Warren to G. Anson, 20 May 1747.

49 *VP*, pp. 290–302. Corbett, *Fighting Instructions*, pp. 205–18. Tunstall, *Naval Warfare*, pp. 79–82 and 92–100. Richmond, *War of 1739–48* III, 253–67. Creswell, *British Admirals*, pp. 81–90. Mackay, *Hawke Papers*, pp. 42 and 183; and *Hawke*, pp. 56–7 and 180–83. Erskine, *Hervey's Journal*, p. 220.

50 Russell, *Bedford Correspondence* I, 367. Smith, *Grenville Papers* I, 74. Jack M. Sosin, 'Louisbourg and the Peace of Aix-la-Chapelle, 1748', *WMQ* 3rd S. XIV (1957), pp. 516–35. Mimler, *Der Einfluss kolonialer Interessen*, pp. 178–204. Rodger, *Insatiable Earl*, pp. 49–54.

17 A Scandal to the Navy

1 Baxter 'Seven Years War', p. 327.

2 *A Selection of the Papers of the Earl of Marchmont*, ed. Sir George Rose (London, 1831, 3 vols.) I, 219.

3 E. N. Williams, *The Eighteenth-Century Constitution 1688–1815: Documents and Commentary* (Cambridge, 1960), pp. 125–32.

4 Mark A. Thomson, *The Secretaries of State, 1681–1782* (Oxford, 1932), p. 65, quoting William Knox, Under-Secretary of the Colonial Department during the American War of Independence.

5 It is remarkable how many historians have complained that the orders and despatches for one or other expedition are missing, having looked only in military or naval records, instead of the State Papers where they belong.

6 *BND* No. 189, pp. 326–7; cf. Yorke, *Hardwicke* II, 23.

7 Speck, *Stability and Strife*, p. 254. Colley, *In Defiance of Oligarchy*, pp. 256–60. A. N. Newman, 'Leicester House Politics, 1748–1751', *EHR* LXXVI (1961), pp. 577–89. Langford, *A Polite and Commercial People*, p. 223. Black, *Natural and Necessary Enemies*, p. 46. Pares, 'American versus Continental Warfare', pp. 433–5.

8 The first citation in the *Oxford English Dictionary* (2nd edn) is 1810.

9 Rodger, 'La Mobilisation navale'.

10 Adams and Waters, *English Maritime Books*.

11 Hoste, *L'Art des armées navales*. Sebastien François Bigot de Morogues, *Naval Tactics, or a treatise of evolutions and signals* (London, 1767), trans. from *Tactique navale* . . . (Paris, 1763). Jacques Bourdé de Villehuet, *The Manoeuverer, or skilful seaman* . . . (London, 1788), trans. from *Le Manoeuvrier* . . . (Paris, 1765). Jacques Raymond, vicomte de Grenier, *The Art of War at Sea* . . . (London, 1788), trans. from *L'Art de la guerre sur mer* . . . (Paris, 1787). On these writers see Depeyre, *Tactiques et stratégies navales*, and Hubert Granier, 'La Pensée navale française au XVIIIe siècle', in Coutau-Bégarie, *La pensée navale* III, 33–56.

12 NMM: SAN/V/50 p. 32, to Sandwich, 16 Feb 1748.

13 Marshall, *Eighteenth Century England*, pp. 224–6 and 233–7. Haas, 'Pursuit of Political Success', p. 69. Lawson, *Grenville*, pp. 62–6.

14 Mimler, *Der Einfluss kolonialer Interessen*, pp. 197–204. Baugh, 'Withdrawing from Europe', pp. 1–5. Bob Harris, 'Patriotic Commerce and National Revival: The Free British Fishery Society and British Politics, c.1749–58', *EHR* CXIV (1999), pp. 285–313. Black, 'Naval Power and International Commitments', pp. 46–9.

15 'Les meilleures têtes et les plus riches bourgs d'Angleterre': *Journal et Mémoires du Marquis d'Argenson*, ed. E. J. B. Rathery (Paris, 1859–67, 9 vols.), VI, 103.

16 'Dans la recherche que j'ai faite des motifs qui avaient pu engager à prendre le parti extrême de reduire ainsi la marine sur un plus bas pied qu'elle n'avait encore été, j'ai reconnu que les raisons d'épargne et d'économie y avaient beaucoup moins déterminé que le système politique que l'on s'était formé dans la Régence . . . Les raisons que l'on pouvait avoir de réduire la marine pendant la Régence, n'ayant pas toujours subsisté depuis, il semble qu'on aurait dû la rétablir ensuite sur l'ancien pied': Vergé-Franceschi, *Les Officiers généraux en 1715* VI, 2,508. The regency had ended in 1723, the same year that Maurepas took office.

17 *NDAR* IV, 1,084, Vergennes to Caron de Beaumarchais, 2 May 1776.

18 Meyer, 'La Marine française au XVIIIe siècle', pp. 151–5 and 180. Crouzet, 'Second Hundred Years' War', pp. 434–8; and 'The Sources of England's Wealth: Some French Views in the Eighteenth Century', in *Shipping, Trade and Commerce: Essays in Memory of Ralph Davis*, ed. P. L. Cottrell and D. H. Aldcroft (Leicester, 1981), pp. 61–79. Pritchard, *Louis XV's Navy*, pp. 71–3 and 190–91. Dull, *Loss of Canada*, Ch. I.2. Harding, *Seapower and Naval Warfare*, pp. 204–5. Masson, *Histoire de la Marine* I, 182–3.

19 Horn, *Great Britain and Europe*, pp. 94–103. Carter, *Neutrality or Commitment*, pp. 72–3. Pares, *Colonial Blockade*, pp. 231–7. Rodger, 'Anglo-Dutch Alliance', pp. 20–23. Kent, *War and Trade*, pp. 48 and 138–9. PRO: SP 42/29 f. 404; SP 42/31 f. 141. NMM: SAN/F/24/38. Marsden, *Law and Custom* II, 321–2 and 326–7. Pritchard, 'Fir Trees, Financiers', pp. 346–7. Hugh Dunthorne, *The Maritime Powers, 1721–1740: A Study of Anglo-Dutch Relations in the Age of Walpole* (London, 1986).

20 Marshall, *Eighteenth Century England*, pp. 251–5. Langford, *A Polite and Commercial People*, p. 227. Speck, *Stability and Strife*, pp. 259–60.

21 Dull, *Loss of Canada*, Ch. II.1. Black, *Natural and Necessary Enemies*, pp. 56–9; and 'Anglo-French Relations in the Mid-Eighteenth Century'. Clayton, 'Newcastle, Halifax, and the Seven Years' War', pp. 571–90.

22 BL: Add. MSS 15956, f. 23, to Anson, 14 Jul 1755.

23 Corbett, *Seven Years' War* I, 36–58. Dull, *Loss of Canada*, Ch. II. Clayton, 'Newcastle, Halifax, and the Seven Years' War', pp. 591–601.

24 Corbett, *Seven Years' War* I, 50–73. Aman, *Une Campagne méconnue*. Mackay, *Hawke Papers*, pp. 123–8. Dull, *Loss of Canada*, Ch. II.4–6. Black, 'Anglo-French Relations in the Mid-Eighteenth Century', pp. 71–8. Le Goff, 'Naval Recruitment', p. 29 suggests a figure of 6–7,000 prisoners, including 3,800 able seamen.

25 Tunstall, *Byng and Minorca*, pp. 91–5. Gregory, *Minorca*, pp. 35 and 158. Anderson, 'Great Britain and the Barbary States', p. 95.

26 Richmond, *Loss of Minorca*, pp. 17–210, sets out the intelligence in detail.

27 *BND* No. 190, p. 327, 6 Dec 1755.

28 Corbett, *Seven Years' War* I, 88–103. Dull, *Loss of Canada*, Ch. III.1. Kemp, 'Boscawen's Letters to his Wife', p. 209.

29 Aman, *Une Campagne méconnue*, pp. 156–60. Villiers, *Marine Royale* I, 242–3. *MMF* II, 253–72. Cisternes, *La Campagne de Minorque*, pp. 195–6. Gregory, *Minorca*, pp. 172–3.

30 'Messieurs, il se joue là un jeu bien intéressant. Si M. de La Galissonière bat l'ennemi, nous continuerons notre siège en pantoufles; mais s'il est battu, il faudra avoir recours à l'escalade, aux derniers expédients . . .': *MMF* II, 271.

31 Corbett, *Seven Years' War* I, 106–13 and 129–30. Tunstall, *Byng and Minorca*, p. 153. PRO: ADM 1/383 f. 388, J. Byng to Admiralty, 4 May 1756. BL: Add. MSS 32865 f. 159, Anson to Newcastle, 31 May [1756]. Mackay, *Hawke Papers*, pp. 138–40. Richmond, *Loss of Minorca*, pp. 213–17.

32 Kemp, 'Boscawen's Letters to his Wife', p. 227: to his wife, 20 Jun 1756.

33 Tunstall, *Naval Warfare*, pp. 107–10; and *Byng and Minorca*, pp. 117–35. Creswell, *British Admirals*, pp. 94–103. *BND* No. 220 pp. 380–81. Corbett, *Seven Years' War* I, 113–28. Richmond, *Loss of Minorca*, pp. 211–12. Cisternes, *La Campagne de Minorque*, pp. 177–89. Erskine, *Hervey's Journal*, pp. 203–18.

34 Locker, *Celebrated Commanders sv* Hawke, p. 5. Locker's father was then one of Hawke's lieutenants. Cf. PRO: ADM 1/383 f. 445, J. Byng to Admiralty, 4 Jul 1756.

35 StRO: D1798/HM Drakeford/22, to Richard Drakeford, 31 Aug 1756.

36 Kemp, 'Boscawen's Letters to his Wife', p. 228: to his wife, 23 Jun 1756.

37 Rogers, *Crowds, Culture and Politics*, pp. 61–3. Tunstall, *Byng and Minorca*, pp. 171–7. Robert Phillimore, *Memoirs and Correspondence of George, Lord Lyttelton* (London, 1845, 2 vols.) II, 504

and 519. Ilchester, *Letters to Lord Holland*, p. 83. Baugh, ' "Too Much Mixed in this Affair" ', pp. 35–6.

38 Black, *Pitt*, p. 119.

39 The king had displayed considerable gallantry in action at Oudenarde in 1708, and at Dettingen in 1744, when he was the last British monarch to command his troops in battle.

40 Not least Corbett, *Seven Years' War* I, 133–4.

41 Tunstall, *Byng and Minorca*, pp. 204–62. Pope, *At 12 Mr Byng was Shot*, pp. 246–9 and 263–83. Erskine, *Hervey's Journal*, pp. 230–43. BL: Add. MS 35359 ff. 387–8. Russell, *Bedford Correspondence* II, 224 and 239. Walpole, *Memoirs of George II* II, 212. Langford, 'Pitt and Public Opinion', p. 72. Peters, *The Elder Pitt*, p. 69. Black, *Pitt*, pp. 136–7.

42 Langford, 'Pitt and Public Opinion', pp. 74–6. Ilchester, *Letters to Lord Holland*, p. 105. Middleton, 'A Reinforcement for North America'; and *Bells of Victory*, pp. 35–7.

43 Corbett, *Seven Years' War* I, 167–78. Graham, *North Atlantic*, pp. 163–7. Masson, *Histoire de la Marine* I, 199–203. *MMF* II, 359–60. Gwyn, 'Royal Navy in North America', p. 139. Middleton, 'Western Squadron', pp. 354–6.

44 Smith, *Grenville Papers* I, 208: to G. Grenville, 23 Sep 1757.

45 Mackay, *Hawke Papers*, pp. 152–79. *BND* No. 223 pp. 384–90. Hackmann, 'Military Expeditions', pp. 49–59. Corbett, *Seven Years' War* I, 197–222. Harding, *Amphibious Warfare*, pp. 181–4. Middleton, 'Coastal Expeditions', pp. 76–81. Molyneux, *Conjunct Expeditions* I, 200–211. Beatson, *Memoirs*, II, 64–75. Langford, 'Pitt and Public Opinion', p. 78.

46 Buchet, *L'espace Caraïbe* II, 1,078–9 and 1,258–62.

47 Baudi di Vesme, *La Politica Mediterranea Inglese*, p. 96. French, *British Way in Warfare*, pp. 49–50. Panzac, *Les Corsaires barbaresques*, pp. 35–7.

48 Middleton, *Bells of Victory*, pp. 23–29 and 35–8. P. F. Doran, *Andrew Mitchell and Anglo-Prussian Diplomatic Relations*

during the Seven Years War (New York, 1986), pp. 144–7. *BND* Nos. 192–4, pp. 329–31. Kent, *War and Trade*, pp. 134 and 170–72. Dull, *Loss of Canada*, Ch. III.5 and IV.5. Dann, *Hannover und England*, p. 140.

49 BL: Add. MSS 32881, f. 111, Anson to Newcastle, 29 June 1758, and ff. 189–90, Newcastle's reply, 7 July 1758.

50 Langford, 'Pitt and Public Opinion', pp. 77–9. Middleton, 'Coastal Expeditions', p. 75.

51 Hackmann, 'Military Expeditions', pp. 91–149. Corbett, *Seven Years' War* I, 275–301. Harding, *Amphibious Warfare*, pp. 181–4. Middleton, 'Coastal Expeditions', pp. 84–90. Lespagnol, *Messieurs de Saint-Malo* I, 208. Cormack and Jones, *Corporal Todd*, pp. 48–9 and 98–100. Pearsall, 'Landings on the French Coast', pp. 239–40.

52 The phrase coined by the military writer Basil Liddell Hart, whose ideas are analysed by Baugh, ' "Blue-Water" Policy'.

53 French, *British Way in Warfare*, pp. xiv–xvii. Niedhart, *Handel und Krieg*, pp. 64–5. Black, 'Naval Power and British Foreign Policy', pp. 97–102.

54 Masson, *Histoire de la Marine* I, 206–7.

18 Myths Made Real

1 'Dans ce pays-ci il est bon de tuer de temps en temps un amiral pour encourager les autres': *Candide*, Ch. 23. Translating 'encourager' as 'encourage' rather weakens the sense of the original.

2 *BAW*, p. 146.

3 'Savez-vous, Monsieur, ce que c'est un combat navale? . . . deux escadres sortent de deux ports opposés; on manœuvre, on se raconte, on tire des coups de canon, on abat quelques mâts, on déchire quelques voiles, on tue quelques hommes; on use beaucoup de poudre et de boulets . . . et la mer n'en reste pas moins salée!': [Louis Philippe] comte de Ségur, *Mémoires, ou souvenirs et anecdotes* (Brussels, 1825–7, 3 vols.) I, 213. I am greatly indebted to M. Etienne Taillemite for unearthing this reference.

4 'Beaucoup plus de bruit que de besogne n'est que trop souvent le produit net des combats navaux': *MMF* III, 213, to Vergennes, 21 Aug 1779.

5 'Il est de principe de guerre qu'on doit risquer beaucoup pour défendre ses propres positions, et très peu pour attaquer celles des enemis': Castex, *Les Idées militaires*, p. 43, to the marquis de Castries, 16 Mar 1781.

6 'La marine française a toujours préféré la gloire d'assurer et de protéger une conquête à celle, plus brillante peut-être, mais moins réelle, de prende quelques vaisseaux. Par là, elle a serré de plus près le but de la guerre': Castex, *Les Idées militaires*, p. 30.

7 Castex, *Les Idées militaires*, pp. 30–39. Masson and Muracciole, *Napoléon et la Marine*, pp. 18–20. Gonzalez-Aller and O'Donnell, 'Spanish Navy', pp. 70–71. Rodríguez Casado, 'La politia del reformismo', p. 611. François Caron, 'La Stratégie navale au temps de la marine à voile', in *La Lutte pour l'empire de la mer: histoire et géostratégie maritimes*, ed. Hervé Coutau-Bégarie (Paris, 1995), pp. 163–95, is an interesting example of a French admiral of today still arguing that battles were a distraction from war.

8 Buchet, *L'espace Caraïbe* I, 370–79. Corbett, *Seven Years' War* I, 365–7. PRO: ADM 1/235, T. Cotes to Admiralty, 9 Nov 1757 (quoted).

9 Lyon, *Sailing Navy List*, pp. 41–2. Demerliac, *Nomenclature* I, 36 (converting the *livre de Paris* to avoirdupois). These figures are better than those in *WW*, p. 58.

10 *MMF* II, 281–3. Le Goff, 'Naval Recruitment', pp. 10–15. Erskine, *Hervey's Journal*, pp. 271–4. PRO: ADM 1/384, H. Osborn to Admiralty, 12 Mar 1758; ADM 36/6098, slain list. John Entick, *The General History of the Late War* (London, 1763–4, 5 vols.) III, 58–9. Corbett, *Seven Years' War* I, 255–60.

11 Low, *Indian Navy* I, 125–36. Lenman, *Britain's Colonial Wars*, pp. 101–9. Richard Owen Cambridge, *An Account of the War in India . . . From the Year 1750 to the Year 1761 . . .* (London, 2nd edn 1762), pp. 120–29.

12 Corbett, *Seven Years' War* I, 324–50. Tunstall, *Naval Warfare*, pp. 112–13. Simpson, 'Pocock', pp. 84–9. *MMF* II, 376–9. J. H. McCall, 'A Kempenfelt Letter', *NR* XXVII (1939), pp. 294–300. PRO: ADM 1/161 ff. 262–4 and 275. Henry E. Huntington Library, San Marino, California: HM1000, G. Pocock to Admiralty, 15 May 1761.

13 Corbett, *Seven Years' War* II, 120–40. *MMF* II, 379–83. Tunstall, *Naval Warfare*, p. 113. PRO: ADM 1/161, f. 351; ADM 1/162, f. 53.

14 Corbett, *Seven Years' War* I, 317–32. Graham, *North Atlantic*, pp. 169–74. Wood, *Conquest of Canada*, pp. 167–202. J. Mackay Hitsman and C. C. J. Bond, 'The Assault Landing at Louisbourg, 1758', *CHR* XXXV (1954), pp. 314–30. François Caron, *La Guerre incomprise ou les raisons d'un échec (Capitulation de Louisbourg – 1758)* (Vincennes, 1983) prints documents but develops a somewhat eccentric interpretation.

15 Le Goff, 'Naval Recruitment', pp. 31 and 42. Masson, *Histoire de la Marine* I, 203. *MMF* II, 360. Antoine Poissonnier des Perrières, *Traité sur les maladies des gens de mer* (Paris, 1767), pp. 426–9, who was there, puts the losses at over 10,000.

16 Smelser, *Sugar Islands*, p. 15. Middleton, 'Chesapeake Convoy System', pp. 196–8. Villiers, *Marine Royale* II, 474–6.

17 Smelser, *Sugar Islands*. Gardiner, *Expedition to the West Indies*. Beatson, *Memoirs* II, 228–62. Corbett, *Seven Years' War* I, 375–95. Buchet, *L'espace Caraïbe* I, 385–97. Guy, 'Durant's Journal', pp. 34–8. Villiers, *Marine Royale* II, 479–81.

18 Corbett, *Seven Years' War* II, 33–40. Buchet, *L'espace Caraïbe* I, 397–8. *MMF* II, 285–90. Villiers, *Marine Royale* I, 252–3.

19 Stacey, *Quebec*; and 'Quebec, 1759: Some New Documents', *CHR* XLVII (1966), pp. 344–55. Dull, *Loss of Canada*, Ch. VI.3. Graham, *North Atlantic*, pp. 174–89. Wood, *Conquest of Canada*, pp. 93–139 and 203–322. *BND* No. 225 pp. 391–3. Masson, *Histoire de la Marine* I, 212–14. Lenman, *Britain's Colonial Wars*,

pp. 150–51. Corbett, *Seven Years' War* I, 396–476.

20 Middleton, 'Western Squadron', pp. 357–9. Masson, *Histoire de la Marine* I, 204–9. Dull, *Loss of Canada*, Ch. VI.1. Corbett, *Seven Years' War* II, 17–20. *MMF* II, 319–26. Villiers, *Marine Royale* I, 292–8. Bosher, 'Financing the French Navy'. Nordmann, 'Choiseul and the Last Jacobite Attempt'. Bamford, *Forests and French Sea Power*, p. 65.

21 The best analysis of the navigational hazards of Brest is by the cavalryman Desbrière, *Le Blocus de Brest*, especially pp. 7–14. Cf. *The Channel Pilot Pt. II, Coast of France*, ed. J. W. King (Hydrographic Office, London, 1859), pp. 417–20; and *Sailing Directions for the West Coasts of France, Spain and Portugal*, ed. James Penn (Hydrographic Office, 1867), pp. 1–30.

22 Rodger, 'Weather', pp. 184–5. Peter Allington et al., 'Shiphandling and Hazards on the Devon Coast', *MHD* II, 14–24, at p. 14. Meyer and Acerra, *La Marine Française*, p. 11.

23 C. J. Sölver and G. J. Marcus, 'Dead Reckoning and the Ocean Voyages of the Past', *MM* XLIV (1958), pp. 18–34. Chapuis, *Beautemps-Beaupré*, p. 107. Desbrière, *Le Blocus de Brest*, pp. 7–16.

24 Middleton, 'Western Squadron', pp. 360–64. Marcus, *Quiberon Bay*, pp. 89–104. Mackay, *Hawke Papers*, pp. 205–320; and *Hawke*, pp. 200–238. *BND* No. 224, pp. 390–91 and Nos. 250–52, pp. 442–4. Rodger, 'Victualling', pp. 45–8.

25 James Lind, *An Essay on the most Effectual Means of Preserving the Health of Seamen* (3rd edn 1779), in Lloyd, *Health of Seamen*, p. 121.

26 Mackay, *Hawke Papers*, p. 318, to the Admiralty. 'Keeping in' means keeping close in with Brest.

27 Le Goff, 'Naval Recruitment', pp. 49–50. *MMF* II, 329.

28 Mackay, *Hawke*, pp. 239–54; and *Hawke Papers*, pp. 344–8. Corbett, *Seven Years' War* II, 45–70. *MMF* II, 326–42. Marcus, *Quiberon Bay*, pp. 149–60. Troude, *Batailles navales* I, 381–95 and 401–3.

Tunstall, *Naval Warfare*, pp. 115–17. Creswell, *British Admirals*, pp. 109–19. Guy Le Moing, *La bataille navale des 'Cardinaux' (20 novembre 1759)* (Paris, 2003), is a good general account from printed sources.

29 Mackay, *Hawke Papers*, p. 347; to the Admiralty, 24 Nov 1759.

30 'Je ne sais pas tout, mais j'en sais beaucoup trop. Le combat du 20 de ce mois est l'anéantissement de la Marine et le terme des projets': Depeyre, *Tactiques et stratégies navales*, p. 103. Note that Bigot de Morogues was a bitter rival of Conflans.

31 'Voici une suite de ce que nous voyons depuis longtemps: des bévues, des preuves d'ignorance et enfin des sottises, beaucoup de bonne volonté, point de capacité, beaucoup de bravoure, point de tête, et la présomption sans méfiance. Voilà un raccourci de ce qui vient de se passer': *MMF* II, 340, anonymous writer from Rochefort, 25 Nov 1759.

32 Dull, *Loss of Canada*, Ch. VII.1–2. Dann, *Hannover und England*, p. 140. Brun, *Port de Toulon* I, 438–9. Corbett, *Seven Years' War* II, 93. Smith, *Grenville Papers* I, 350–51. Le Pourhiet-Salat, *La Défense des îles*, p. 164. Linÿer de la Barbée, *Ternay* I, 109–49. Jeremy Black, 'Fresh Fruit and Cricket: On Blockade in 1762', *MM* LXXIV (1988), p. 416.

33 Malo, *Les Derniers Corsaires*, pp. 61–99; and *Les Corsaires*, pp. 37–51. Beresford, 'François Thurot'. *MMF* II, 350. NMM: ELL/400/29–30.

34 Dull, *Loss of Canada*, Ch. VII.3.

35 Dull, *Loss of Canada*, Ch. VIII.2 and 5. Hackmann, 'Military Expeditions', pp. 167–91. Bonner-Smith, *Barrington Papers* I, 298–303. Corbett, *Seven Years' War* II, 160–70. Hebbert, 'Belle-Ile Expedition'. B. Holbrooke, 'The Siege and Capture of Belle Isle, 1761', *JRUSI* XLIII (1899), pp. 160–83 and 520–33.

36 StRO: D615/P(S)/1/10, to Anson, 28 Feb 1762.

37 Buchet, *L'espace Caraïbe* I, 401–10. Corbett, *Seven Years' War* II, 217–26. Spinney, *Rodney*, pp. 176–90. Rodger, 'Douglas Papers', pp. 244–70.

38 Marley, 'A Fearful Gift', pp. 403–7. Jean O. McLachlan, 'The Uneasy Neutrality: A Study of Anglo-Spanish Disputes over Spanish Ships Prized, 1756–1759', *CHJ* VI (1938–40), pp. 55–77. *AE* VII, 7. Mario Hernández Sánchez-Barba, 'Reformismo y modernizacion: El ejercito y la armada en el siglo XVIII', in Hernández Sánchez-Barba et al., *Las Fuerzas Armadas Españolas* I, 175–98, at I, 191. Dull, *Loss of Canada*, Ch. VII.4.

39 Syrett, *Havana*, pp. xiii–xx and 1–147.

40 Rear-Admiral Don Gutierre de Hevia, marqués del Real Transporte. He owed both his command and his improbable title to having been flag-captain of the ship which conveyed the new king from Naples to Spain in 1759.

41 *AE* VII, 41–9. Perez de la Riva, *La toma de la Habana*, pp. 24–7 and 225. David F. Marley, 'Havana Surprised: Prelude to the British Invasion, 1762', *MM* LXXVIII (1992), pp. 293–305. Castillo Manrubia, 'Perdida de la Habana', p. 67. Simpson, 'Pocock', pp. 168–93. Llaverías, *Papeles*, pp. 155–6.

42 'como de Ymbernada desaparejada': Marley, 'A Fearful Gift', p. 414.

43 Syrett, *Havana*, pp. 151–326. *AE* VII, 53–70. Buchet, *L'espace Caraïbe* I, 411–12 and 536–66. Llaverías, *Papeles*; and *Nuevos Papeles*. Corbett, *Seven Years' War* II, 246–84. Zapatero, *La Guerra del Caribe*, pp. 264–75. Perez de la Riva, *La toma de la Habana*.

44 Charnock, *Biographia Navalis* V, 139. *WW*, p. 268. *HC 1754–90* II, 254. I have seen indirect evidence, however, suggesting that he was the son of a prosperous shipmaster in the West India trade; if so, he could have started a naval career with some advantages.

45 Cushner, *Conquest of Manila*, p. 34, to the Secretary at War, 27 Jul 1762.

46 Cushner, *Conquest of Manila*, p. 30, to the Admiralty, 23 Jul 1762.

47 Cushner, *Conquest of Manila*, p. 35, to the Secretary at War, 27 Jul 1762.

48 By British reckoning; the Spaniards in the Philippines dated westabout, without the modern International Date Line, and so were one day behind.

49 Tracy, *Manila Ransomed*. Cushner, *Conquest of Manila. AE* VII, 85–90.
50 *BND* No. 196 p. 333, to Bute, 9 Jul 1761.
51 Crouzet, 'Second Hundred Years War', pp. 441–2. Innis, *Cod Fisheries*, p. 119.
52 For the British conquests of Goree and Senegal see A. J. Marsh, 'The Taking of Goree, 1758', *MM* LI (1965), pp. 117–30; and James L. A. Webb, 'The Mid-Eighteenth Century Gum Arabic Trade and the British Conquest of Saint-Louis de Sénégal, 1758', *JICH* XXV (1997), pp. 37–58.
53 Pearsall, 'Landings on the French Coast'. Harding, *Seapower and Naval Warfare*, p. 213. Syrett, *Havana*, p. 165; and 'British Amphibious Operations'.
54 *BND* No. 225, p. 393.
55 Syrett, *Havana*, p. 294.
56 Hackmann, 'Military Expeditions', pp. 183–91. Buchet, *L'espace Caraïbe* I, 565.
57 Crowhurst, 'The Admiralty and the Convoy System', pp. 163–72; and *Defence of British Trade*, pp. 58–63 and 191–2. Middleton, 'Chesapeake Convoy System', pp. 200–202. Mountaine, *Seaman's Vade-Mecum*, pp. 162–75. Buchet, 'La logistique anglaise', pp. 578–83; and *L'espace Caraïbe* I, 393. Starkey, *British Privateering*, pp. 161–80.
58 Middleton, 'Chesapeake Convoy System', pp. 194–7. Sheila L. Skemp, 'A World Uncertain and Strongly Checker'd', in Ultee, *Adapting to Conditions*, pp. 84–103. P. C. F. Smith, '*King George*, the Massachusetts Province Ship, 1757–1763: A Survey', in *Seafaring in Colonial Massachusetts*, ed. P. C. F. Smith (CSM Vol. 52, 1980), pp. 175–98.
59 Frank Spencer, 'Lord Sandwich, Russian Masts, and American Independence', *MM* XLIV (1958), pp. 116–27, at p. 123.
60 Pares, *Colonial Blockade*, pp. 152–224 and 241–300. Kent, *War and Trade*, pp. 86, 134–7 and 170–72. Carter, *Neutrality or Commitment*, pp. 88–9; and 'How to Revise Treaties without Negotiating: Commonsense, Mutual Fears and the Anglo-Dutch Trade Disputes of 1759', in *Studies in Diplomatic History: Essays in Memory of David Bayne Horn*, ed. Ragnhild Hatton and M. S. Anderson (London, 1970), pp. 214–35. PRO: SP 44/228 pp. 41 and 43. Kulsrud, *Maritime Neutrality*, pp. 79–106, 193–202 and 244–94.
61 Starkey, *British Privateering*, pp. 161–3 and 178–80. Kent, *War and Trade*, p. 148. Powell, *Bristol Privateers*, pp. 186, 207–13 and 231–2. Pares, *Colonial Blockade*, pp. 42–76. PRO: SP 44/228 pp. 54 and 66.
62 Peters, *The Elder Pitt*, pp. 106–7 and 236–47 (quoted p. 107). Baxter, 'Seven Years War'. Middleton, *Bells of Victory*, pp. 170–232; and 'Pitt, Anson and the Admiralty'.

19 The Great Wheels of Commerce and War

1 Julian Hoppit, 'The Myths of the South Sea Bubble', *TRHS* 6th S. XII (2002), pp. 141–65. Roseveare, *Financial Revolution*, pp. 45–58. Dickson, *Financial Revolution*, pp. 80–157. Carswell, *South Sea Bubble. BAW*, pp. 473–81. Binney, *Public Finance*, pp. 91–2.
2 *BNA* pp. 8–9 and 456–7. *BAW*, pp. 454–81, 495–6 and 508–14. Dickson, *Financial Revolution*, pp. 208–9 and 399–406. Roseveare, *Financial Revolution*, pp. 62–4. Wilkinson, 'Politics, Government and the Navy', pp. 103–4, 117, 126–44, 158–9. Coad, *Royal Dockyards*, pp. 41–2. Lavery, *Ship of the Line* I, 70–71. Buchet, *Marine, économie et société*, pp. 55–9. Beveridge, *Prices and Wages*, pp. 520–27. Hughes, *Administration and Finance*, pp. 290–91. J. D. Joslin, 'London Bankers in Wartime, 1739–84', in *Studies in the Industrial Revolution Presented to T. S. Ashton*, ed. L. S. Pressnell (London, 1960), pp. 156–77.
3 Mathias and O'Brien, 'Taxation', pp. 625–36. Velde and Weir, 'Financial Market'. Pritchard, *Louis XV's Navy*, pp. 178–201. Meyer, *Le Poids de l'état*, pp. 49–59. Legohérel, *Les Trésoriers généraux*, pp. 177–252. Riley, 'French Finances'; and *Government Finance*, pp. 107–12. Guéry, 'Les Finances de la monarchie française'. Weir, 'Tontines'. Bosher, *French Finances*, pp. 13, 23–4 and 303–4.

4 *BAW*, pp. 65–81. *BNA* pp. 6–7. Russell, *Bedford Correspondence* I, 36, 227 and 235. Nottingham University Library: NeC 649, H. Pelham to Newcastle, 18 Jul 1748. PRO: ADM 3/49–51.

5 HMC *Various* VI, 38–9, to G. B. Doddington, 16 Mar 1757.

6 *BAW*, pp. 72–81. PRO: ADM 3/49, 28 Dec 1744–28 Jan 1745.

7 R. A. Blackey, 'The Political Career of George Montagu Dunk, 2nd Earl of Halifax, 1748–1771: A Study of an Eighteenth-Century English Minister' (New York Ph.D. thesis, 1978), p. 128, quoting BL: Add. MSS 32939 ff. 408–9, to Hardwicke, 19 Jun 1762.

8 Rodger, *Admiralty*, pp. 64–7. *HP 1754–90* II, 220–21 and III, 475–6 (mistaken in suggesting Stephens had worked in the Victualling Office). *HP 1790–1820* V, 265–6. James, 'Burchett'; and 'Admiralty Establishment', pp. 24–5. Tunstall, *Byng Papers* III, 43–4. Sainty, *Admiralty Officials*, pp. 113, 116, 118 and 152. Collinge, *Navy Board Officials*, pp. 92 and 141. Namier, *Structure of Politics*, pp. 41–2. *BAW*, pp. 81–3. Wickwire, 'Admiralty Secretaries'; and 'King's Friends, Civil Servants, or Politicians', *AHR* LXXI (1965–6), pp. 18–42.

9 Morgan, 'Impact of War', pp. 33–52, 99, 105–8 and 288–90. Marini, 'Corps of Marines', pp. 164–77 and 187–206; and 'Parliament and the Marine Regiments, 1739', *MM* LXII (1976), pp. 55–65. Harding, *Amphibious Warfare*, pp. 66–70. Lowe, *Portsmouth Division*, pp. xiv–xv. *BNA* pp. 144–5. PRO: SP 42/33 ff. 35–59.

10 WA: Butcher MSS II/4/218 to Robert Butcher, 21 Dec 1748. The 'invalids' were claimants on the Chatham Chest. 'Calls' were to pay ships.

11 WA: Butcher MSS II/4/42, to Robert Butcher, 24 Oct 1748. On the Morris brothers, who are of some importance for Welsh literature, see *The Letters of Lewis, Richard, William and John Morris, of Anglesey (Morrisiaid Mon) 1728–1765*, ed. J. H. Davies (Aberystwyth, 1907–9, 2 vols.); and 'Additional Letters of the Morrises of Anglesey, 1735–86', ed. Hugh Owen, *Y Cymmrodor* XLIX, 1 (1947), pp.

i–xxx and 1–392; XLIX, 2 (1949), pp. xxxi–lii and 393–981.

12 Holmes, *Augustan England*, pp. 247–8. *BAW*, pp. 43–8. NMM: CLU/4 ff. 1–3. PRO: ADM 1/90 f. 589. Morgan, 'Impact of War', p. 184.

13 PRO: ADM 95/17, p. 332.

14 Coad, *Royal Dockyards*, pp. 3–15. *BAW*, pp. 262–308. *BNA* pp. 274–318. *BND* No. 242 pp. 436–7. *WW*, pp. 141–2.

15 *BNA* p. 309, to Navy Board, 18 Oct 1744.

16 Knight, 'Impressment to Task Work', p. 10.

17 Haas, 'Work and Authority'; and *Management Odyssey*, pp. 8–16 and 37. Knight, 'Impressment to Task Work', pp. 1–11. *BNA* pp. 266–7, 279–85 and 296–318. *BAW*, pp. 309–39. Ranft, 'Labour Relations'. Peter Linebaugh, *The London Hanged: Crime and Civil Society in the Eighteenth Century* (London, 1991), pp. 378–88. Ann Coats, 'Efficiency in Dockyard Administration 1660–1800: A Reassessment', *Age of Sail* I (2002), pp. 116–32, defends the yards.

18 *BAW*, pp. 83–92. Pool, *Navy Board Contracts*, pp. 79 and 105–8. *BNA*, pp. 21–32. Rodger, *Insatiable Earl*, pp. 23–9.

19 PRO: ADM 3/61.

20 PRO: ADM 7/658, p. 6.

21 Rodger, *Insatiable Earl*, pp. 64–6. Haas, 'Visitations and Reform', pp. 193–208; and 'Task Work', pp. 46–9. Middleton, 'Visitation of the Royal Dockyards'.

22 *BAW*, pp. 255–61. Pool, *Navy Board Contracts*, pp. 79–89. Wilkinson, 'Politics, Government and the Navy', pp. 267–9.

23 The original stone dock at Rochefort was abandoned as too small. The double dock, finished in 1728 after nearly forty years' effort, was inaccessible to ships bigger than Fourth Rates because of the shoal water of the Charente. The Fosse de Troulan at Brest was impossible to drain completely because a stream fell into it and its sill was below low-water level.

24 Mémain, *Rochefort*, 112–51. Ollivier, *Remarks*, pp. 21–3 and 112–18. Acerra, *Rochefort*, I, 51–70 and 81–90; III, 552–5 and 567–73. Bernard Cros, 'Les Formes de Pontaniou dans l'arsenal de Brest,

1683–1818', *Neptunia* 162 (1986), pp. 33–44 and 163 (1986), pp. 24–33.

25 Hamilton, *Martin Papers* I, 55. Merriman, *Queen Anne's Navy*, p. 102. HL 1805 II (19) No. 12, pp. 40–41. In both cases I have counted double docks as two.

26 Pool, *Navy Board Contracts*, pp. 98–104.

27 PRO: ADM 95/17, pp. 58, 68, 91, 216 and 234–5.

28 Pannell, 'The Taylors of Southampton', pp. 924–8. Llinares, *Marine, propulsion et technique* I, 103–4 and 135–42; and 'L'Introduction de la mécanisation dans la fabrication des poulies au XVIIIe siècle: Essai d'identification d'un modèle', *CHM* 31 (1995), pp. 95–104. Harris, *Industrial Espionage*, pp. 439–48, rates the French success with the Taylor system rather higher.

29 Kent, *War and Trade*, pp. 12–14, 36–44, 80–82 and 181. *BAW*, pp. 276–83. *BNA* pp. 238–9. Pool, *Navy Board Contracts*, pp. 68–71. Åström, 'English Timber Imports'. Malone, 'Baltic Naval Stores Trade'. PRO: ADM 49/32; SP 42/33, ff. 86–91. Kustaa Hautala, *European and American Tar in the English Market during the Eighteenth and Early Nineteenth Centuries* (Helsinki, 1963), pp. 17, 35, 67, 105–6, 164 and 186. Knight, 'New England Forests', pp. 222–4.

30 Kent, *War and Trade*, pp. 14, 18, 59–76 and 184. Fernández de Pinedo, 'Bloomery to Blast-furnace', pp. 21–6. PRO: ADM 49/32, pp. 65 and 156; ADM 49/146, p. 5. P. W. King, 'Iron Ballast for the Georgian Navy and Its Producers', *MM* LXXXI (1995), pp. 15–20.

31 Manwaring, 'Dress of the British Seaman', pp. 37–46. HMC *Du Cane*, pp. 10, 22–4 and 28–9.

32 There is something wrong with the table in Coad, *Royal Dockyards*, p. 3, showing a large naval establishment at Halifax in 1730, nearly twenty years before the settlement was founded.

33 *BNA* p. 391, to Navy Board, 8 May 1748.

34 Merriman, *Queen Anne's Navy*, p. 374. *BNA* pp. 325–65. *BAW*, pp. 343–64. *BND* No. 243 pp. 437–8. Buchet, 'Les arsenaux anglais', pp. 129–132 and 140–41.

35 *BAW*, pp. 365–72. Buchet, 'La logistique

anglaise'. Rodger, 'Douglas Papers', p. 246. PRO: ADM 1/307, Sir J. Douglas to Admiralty, 23 and 25 July 1760.

36 PRO: ADM 1/235, to Admiralty, 12 Dec 1756.

37 NMM: SAN/F/3/44, Memorandum of 29 Nov 1772.

38 Buchet, 'Les arsenaux anglais', pp. 125–8. PRO: ADM 1/234 f. 595, Rear-Admiral George Townshend to Admiralty, 24 Jul 1756; ADM 1/235, T. Cotes to Admiralty, 30 Aug 1757. Pawson and Buisseret, *Port Royal*, pp. 130–36. Wadia, *Bombay Dockyard*, pp. 39–48. Low, *Indian Navy* I, 174. Crewe, *Yellow Jack*, pp. 218 and 274.

39 Crewe, *Yellow Jack*, p. 274, E. Vernon to Admiralty, 10 Feb 1742 (quotation completed from Crewe, 'Naval Administration', p. 344).

40 Buchet, 'La logistique anglaise'. Syrett, 'The Navy Board and Transports for Cartagena'. Crewe, *Yellow Jack*, pp. 6–8, 218 and 263–84.

41 BL: Stowe MSS 152 f. 130; but Buchet, *Marine, économie et société*, p. 72 quotes the same table from PRO: ADM 110/19 with the figure for oil as 822 gals (1.15 per cent) instead of 322 gals.

42 *BAW*, pp. 52–61, 373–90 and 422–31. *BNA* pp. 401, 413–14, 432, 435 and 445–7. Baugh, 'National Institution', pp. 143–4. Watson, 'Victualling', pp. 369–70 and 378–9. Buchet, *Marine, économie et société*, pp. 35–73 and 216–20. *WW*, pp. 82–7.

43 *R&I* (1747), pp. 68 and 203. *BNA*, pp. 449–50. Carpenter, *Scurvy*, pp. 75–97. Rodger, 'Le Scorbut'; and 'Medicine, Administration and Society'.

44 *BNA*, pp. 402–3, 422, 426–8 and 439–44. *BAW*, pp. 431–9. Buchet, *Marine, économie et société*, pp. 90–98 and 292–300. Harding, *Amphibious Warfare*, pp. 52–6.

45 Aldridge, 'Victualling'. Tunstall, *Byng Papers* III, 287. Buchet, *Marine, économie et société*, pp. 158–203; and *L'espace Caraïbe* II, 868–918. Crewe, *Yellow Jack*, pp. 145–206. Harding, *Amphibious Warfare*, pp. 52–60. Syrett, 'The Victualling Board Charters Shipping, 1739–1748'.

46 Kemp, 'Boscawen's Letters to his Wife', p. 248.

47 Earle, *Sailors*, pp. 87–8. Cormack and Jones, *Corporal Todd*, p. 26.

48 Buchet, *Marine, économie et société*, p. 330.

49 Buchet, *L'espace Caraïbe* II, 925–91 and 1,067–1,083. Pritchard, *Louis XV's Navy*, pp. 178–83. Pares, *War and Trade*, pp. 421–68. Léon Vignols, 'L'Importation en France au XVIIIe siècle du bœuf salé d'Irelande', *RH* 159 (1928), pp. 79–95. R. C. Nash, 'Irish Atlantic Trade in the Seventeenth and Eighteenth Centuries', *WMQ* 3rd S. XLII (1985), pp. 329–56. Rodger, 'Victualling', p. 43.

50 Buchet, *Marine, économie et société*, especially pp. 337–8. Contrast this pioneering work with the complete silence of *The Agrarian History of England and Wales* V Pt. II, ed. Joan Thirsk (Cambridge, 1985).

51 *KMN* III, 3–4. Crimmin, 'Sick and Hurt Board'.

52 *KMN* II, 164–5; III, 39–43. Rodger, 'Le Scorbut' and 'Medicine, Administration and Society'. Carpenter, *Scurvy*, pp. 40–88; and 'James Lind's Revised Views of Scurvy', in Schadewaldt and Leven, *IX Deutsch-Französisches Symposium*, pp. 108–10. McBride, ' "Normal" Medical Science'. Lawrence, 'Disciplining Disease', pp. 81–9. Bartholomew, 'James Lind and Scurvy'. R. E. Hughes, 'James Lind and the Cure of Scurvy: An Experimental Approach', *MH* XIX (1975), pp. 342–51. Sir James Watt, 'Nutrition in Adverse Environments, 1: Forgotten Lessons of Maritime Nutrition', *Human Nutrition: Applied Nutrition* 36A (1982), pp. 35–45. Christopher Lloyd, 'Cook and Scurvy', *MM* LXV (1979), pp. 23–8.

53 Francis E. Cuppage, *James Cook and the Conquest of Scurvy* (Wesport, Conn., 1994), p. 31.

54 *WW*, pp. 100–103.

55 R. Elwyn Hughes, 'The Rise and Fall of the "Antiscorbutics": Some Notes on the Traditional Cures for "Land Scurvy" ', *MH* XXXIV (1990), pp. 52–64, quoted p. 57. Cf. Roy Porter, *Health for Sale:*

Quackery in England 1660–1850 (Manchester, 1989), pp. 136–7.

56 *KMN* III, 76, quoting T. Trotter.

57 *BAW*, pp. 179–86 and 202–6. *WW*, pp. 105–9. *SL*, pp. 45–51.

58 Coad, *Royal Dockyards*, pp. 293–301. *WW*, pp. 109–12. *BAW*, pp. 48–52. *BNA*, pp. 123–5, 137, 145–7 and 152–6.

59 John Howard, *An Account of the Principal Lazarettos in Europe* (Warrington, 2nd edn 1791), p. 180. Jacques Tenon, *Journal d'observations sur les principaux hôpitaux et sur quelques prisons d'Angleterre (1787)*, ed. Jacques Carré (Clermont-Ferrand, 1992), pp. 152–87. Axel Hinrich Murken, 'Zur Geschichte der europäischen Marinelazarette – Ihr Einfluss auf das Krankenhauswesen des 19. Jahrhunderts', in *Geschichte der Schiffahrtsmedezin: Verhandlung des Symposiums aus Anlass des 60. Geburtstages von Flottenarzt d. R. Professor Dr. med. Hans Schadewaldt*, ed. Heinz Goerke (Coblenz, 1985), pp. 93–117.

60 *VP*, p. 338, to Navy Board, 8 Oct 1740.

61 *BNA* p. 391, to Navy Board, 8 May 1748. Cf. *BAW*, pp. 216–18. Crewe, *Yellow Jack*, pp. 30–48. Buchet, 'Santé et expéditions géo-stratégiques', pp. 147–56.

62 Tomlinson, 'Wealden Gunfounding'. Williams, 'Carmarthenshire Ironmaster'. Caruana, *Sea Ordnance* II, 9–10, 17–21, 30–50, 76–89, 126 and 137.

63 West, *Gunpowder*, pp. 11–176. Caruana, *Sea Ordnance* II, 7. Morgan, 'Impact of War', p. 36. Lenman, *Britain's Colonial Wars*, p. 83.

64 Buchet, 'L'"Ordnance Board" '. Crewe, *Yellow Jack*, pp. 285–9. Harding, *Amphibious Warfare*, pp. 61–6. Syrett, 'The Ordnance Board Charters Shipping'.

65 Acerra, *Rochefort* III, 537–9. Pritchard, *Louis XV's Navy*, pp. 143–58.

66 Evans, 'Gift of the Sea'. Eames, 'Sea Power and Welsh History', p. 16. Harding, *Seapower and Naval Warfare*, p. 15.

67 Francis J. Murphy, 'Lyme Regis: Trade and Population 1575–1725. A Period of Decline?', *Proceedings of the Dorset Natural History & Archaeological Society* CXX (1998), pp. 1–17. I am grateful to Dr

Henry French for drawing my attention to this reference.

20 Disagreeable Necessities

1 *VP*, pp. 486 and 488, E. Vernon to Admiralty, 10 Oct 1745, and reply, 11 Oct.

2 *PH* XI, 422.

3 William Coxe, *Memoirs of the Administration of the Right Honourable Henry Pelham* (London, 1829, 2 vols.) II, 67.

4 Bromley, *Manning*, pp. xxxiv–xl and 82–121; and 'Away from Impressment', pp. 178–86. *BAW*, pp. 224–40. *BNA*, pp. 98–106. Lloyd, *British Seaman*, pp. 181–2.

5 Bromley, 'Navy and its Seamen', p. 150. *WW*, pp. 187. Gradish, *Manning*, pp. 107–10. Reed Browning, *The Duke of Newcastle* (New Haven and London, 1975), p. 264.

6 Pietsch, 'Urchins', and 'Ships' Boys and Charity', supersedes all previous work on the Marine Society. Note in particular his conclusion that 10,625 was the number of persons it clothed, not recruited.

7 Earle, *Sailors*, pp. 190–95. *BAW*, pp. 150–55. Lloyd, *British Seaman*, pp. 149–55. PRO: PC 1/6/39. Richmond, *War of 1739–48* I, 268. Starkey, 'Market for Seafarers', pp. 29 and 40. Bromley, 'Navy and its Seamen', pp. 157–8. Gradish, *Manning*, pp. 57–8 and 66–7. Rogers, 'Liberty Road', pp. 55–6.

8 Baugh, 'National Institution', p. 140. *BNA* pp. 120–22 and 152–6. *BAW*, pp. 171–93. Crewe, *Yellow Jack*, pp. 68–81. *KMN* III, 107–9. PRO: SP 42/29 f. 55.

9 Lloyd, *British Seaman*, p. 154. NMM: HAR/5, Notes by Sir George Lee on Broadfoot's Case. *WW*, p. 170, is misleading on this point.

10 *WW*, pp. 168–70. Lloyd, *British Seaman*, pp. 162–3. PRO: ADM 3/50, ff. 85 and 116. Powell, *Bristol Privateers*, p. 158. Rogers, *Crowds, Culture and Politics*, p. 59.

11 Firth, *Naval Songs and Ballads*, p. 226; cf. Powell, *Bristol Privateers*, p. 140.

12 *WW*, pp. 164, 168–9 and 175–6. Lloyd, *British Seaman*, pp. 159–60. Williams, 'Naval Administration', p. 486. Rogers, 'Liberty Road', pp. 67–70 and 75. Patrick McGrath, *The Merchant Venturers of Bristol* (Bristol, 1975), pp. 171–2. Edward Gillett and Kenneth A. MacMahon, *A History of Hull* (Hull, 1980), p. 235. PRO: ADM 7/298 No. 102. R. B. Rose, 'A Liverpool Sailor's Strike in the Eighteenth Century', *Transactions of the Lancashire and Cheshire Antiquarian Society* LXVIII (1958), pp. 85–92. Conway, *British Isles*, pp. 151–3, 273 and 279–80. John Bohstedt, *Riots and Community Politics in England and Wales 1790–1810* (Cambridge, Mass., 1983), pp. 22–3. W. Senior, 'The Battle of New Brighton', *MM* I (1911), pp. 148–51.

13 Senior, *Law Courts*, pp. 27–32. *BAW*, pp. 155–8. *BNA*, pp. 127–9. *WW* pp. 180–182. Powell, *Bristol Privateers*, pp. 231–2. Hutchinson, *Press-Gang*, pp. 224–31.

14 *VP*, p. 324; to Admiralty, 5 Sep 1742.

15 Lloyd, *British Seaman*, pp. 164–6. Pares, 'Manning of the Navy'. *BAW*, pp. 216–23. *BNA*, pp. 129–37. Crewe, *Yellow Jack*, pp. 63–143. Gwyn, *Warren Papers*, p. 185. *BND* No. 308, pp. 524–6. *The Journals of Ashley Bowen (1728–1813) of Marblehead*, ed. P. C. F. Smith (CSM Vols. 44 and 45, 1973) I, 9–13. Clark, 'Impressment of Seamen'. Lemisch, *Jack Tar vs John Bull*, pp. 18–36; and 'Jack Tar in the Streets'. Haffenden, 'Community and Conflict'. Lax and Pencak, 'Knowles Riot'. Linebaugh and Rediker, 'The Many Headed Hydra', pp. 16–23. Stout, 'Manning'. Lemisch, Linebaugh and Rediker cite press riots to support a Marxist interpretation of the American War of Independence in which the seamen are cast as the revolutionary proletariat; other historians remain sceptical.

16 Earle, *Sailors*, pp. 31–4. Rediker, *The Devil and the Deep Blue Sea*, pp. 121–46 and 304–6. Lawson, *Grenville*, pp. 105–8. Gradish, 'Navy Act'; and *Manning*, pp. 89–106. Press, *Merchant Seamen of Bristol*, pp. 5–9. *WW*, pp. 124–35 and 188–204. *BAW*, pp. 198–200. *BNA*, pp. 160–65.

17 *BAW*, p. 194, to Admiralty, 4 Jun 1741.

18 Hinchliffe, 'Norris Letters', p. 80. *WW*, pp. 119–24. NMM: TID/14, G. Pocock to R. Tiddeman, 16 Feb 1759. *R&I* (1747), p. 41 and Add. Art. 1.

19 Hinchliffe, 'Norris Letters', p. 82.

20 *VP*, pp. 408–9; to Captain G. Berkeley, Feb 1740.

21 *BAW*, pp. 206–15. *BNA*, pp. 126–7, 178–9 and 188–9. *VP*, p. 561. *WW*, pp. 137–44. Hinchliffe, 'Norris Letters', pp. 80–82. PRO: ADM 3/50 f. 21. Baugh, 'National Institution', pp. 144–8. Delafons, *Naval Courts Martial*, p. 197. Crewe, *Yellow Jack*, pp. 68–75 and 94–5.

22 Abell, *Prisoners of War*, pp. 1–9. Anderson, 'Exchange of Prisoners'. Le Goff, 'L'Impact des prises'; and 'Naval Recruitment', pp. 8–9, 20–31 and 47. Pares, 'Manning of the Navy', pp. 58–9.

23 Starkey, 'Market for Seafarers', pp. 40–41. Lloyd, *British Seaman*, pp. 286–8. Palmer and Williams, 'British Sailors', pp. 100–101. Appendix VI. These are numbers borne on ships' books; numbers mustered (i.e. actually present) were always lower.

24 Gilbert, 'Buggery', p. 87; cf. his 'Crime as Disorder'. Such language derives from French Marxist theorists of the 1960s, and is still popular with American Marxists like Rediker and Linebaugh.

25 *WW*, pp. 205–10.

26 Mountaine, *Seaman's Vade-Mecum*, pp. 193–245. NMM: DUF/6; TID/35. *R&I* (1731) and Add. Instructions (1756) *passim*. *SL*, pp. 4–51. *BNA*, pp. 6, 10–13 and 62–3.

27 *WW*, pp. 216–17. *SL*, pp. 62–89. Smith's original scheme is in BL: Add. MSS 35193, ff. 9–11; Howe's *Magnanime* order book is NMM: OBK/9.

28 *Instructions by way of Advice on Sea-Discipline &c from a Father to his Son*, printed in S. F. Bigot de Morogues, *Naval Tactics: or, A Treatise of Evolutions and Signals*, trans. 'a Sea-Officer' (London, 1767), pp. 73–112, quoted at p. 77. The 'Sea-Officer' was Lieutenant Christopher O'Brien, and the Advice is by his father.

29 *VP*, p. 429; E. Vernon to W. Hervey, 6 May 1741.

30 *BNA* p. 71, to Admiralty, 7 Oct 1740.

31 *WW*, pp. 205–16 and 226–37.

32 Earle, *Sailors*, pp. 175–82. Rediker, *The Devil and the Deep Blue Sea*, pp. 227–8. Powell, *Bristol Privateers*, pp. 219–20. *BP* I, xii–xiv. Beatson, *Memoirs* III, 89–90. Mackay, *Hawke Papers*, pp. 98–101. W. E. May, 'The Mutiny of the *Chesterfield*', *MM* XLVII (1961), pp. 178–87.

33 *BNA*, p. 74.

34 *WW*, pp. 237–44. Tucker, *St Vincent* I, 20–21. Gilbert, 'Nature of Mutiny', is based on courts martial records, and for this period is therefore a study of atypical mutinies which broke the rules and failed.

35 Woodfine, 'A Friend to the General', p. 41, quoting Lestanquet's diary.

36 WA: Vol. X f. 112, to Bedford, 22 Oct 1745.

37 PRO: SP 42/30 f. 366, Secretary of Admiralty to the Advocate General and Admiralty Solicitor, 16 May 1746.

38 Russell, *Bedford Correspondence* I, 105–12. Delafons, *Naval Courts Martial*, pp. 25–8 and 59–69. McArthur, *Courts Martial* I, 436–9. Glass, 'Naval Courts Martial'. *BAW*, pp. 7–8. PRO: SP 42/30 ff. 361–2; SP 42/31 f. 26.

39 Clowes, *Royal Navy* III, 274–5, 278–9 and 285–6. Laughton, *Studies*, pp. 261–2. Powell, *Bristol Privateers*, pp. 136–9. BL: Add. MSS 15955 f. 157 and 15956 f. 191. Russell, *Bedford Correspondence* I, 270–71. E. G. Thomas, 'Captain Buckle and the Capture of the *Glorioso*', *MM* LXVIII (1982), pp. 49–56 (quoted p. 51). Vaughan, *Commodore Walker*, pp. 170–81. Hepper, *Warship Losses*, pp. 34–8.

40 *BNA*, pp. 41–2, 63 and 81–4, quoted p. 82. PRO: ADM 7/678 No. 8.

41 Barrow, *Anson*, pp. 150–51. Jarrett, *Naval Dress*, pp. 26–40. Barker, 'Naval Uniform Dress'. Sausmarez, *Saumarez*, pp. 12–14. PRO: SP 42/32 ff. 306–9. SzP: Box 75, T. Brett to P. Saumarez, 1 Sep 1747. BL: Add. MSS 15956 f. 88 and 15957 f. 208. Rodger, 'Honour and Duty', p. 433.

42 PRO: ADM 3/61, 11 Aug 1749.

43 *SL*, p. 51, quoting the Additional *R&I* (1756).

44 PRO: ADM 3/61, 4 Aug 1749 and ADM 7/658 p. 55.

45 *BAW*, pp. 136–7. *BNA*, pp. 75–81. Barrow, *Anson*, pp. 145–50. SzP: Box 74,

T. Brett to P. Saumarez, 15 Aug 1747.
PRO: SP 42/60 f. 112. *PH* XXVII, 18,
quoting Lord Sandwich (in 1788) on the
origin of the scheme.

46 Keppel, *Keppel* I, 328. *HP 1754–90* III, 7.
WW, pp. 299–301.

47 Rodger, *Insatiable Earl*, pp. 61–2; and
'Honour and Duty', pp. 437 and 442–7.
BNA, pp. 86–7. Erskine, *Hervey's Journal*,
pp. 78–84. Gwyn, *Enterprising Admiral*,
p. 23. Baugh, ' "Too Much Mixed in this
Affair" ', pp. 33–4. Yorke, *Hardwicke* II,
84–5.

21 The Battle of the Legislature

1 Greene, 'Causal Relationship', p. 86. *BND*
No. 312, pp. 530–31. In 1778 Lord
Sandwich estimated the number of
American seamen lost to the Navy at
18,000: *PH* XIX, 963.

2 Morrison, *Hamilton and Nelson Papers* I,
57, to Sir William Hamilton, 20 Sep 1778.
'Château d'Espagne' = 'castle in Spain'.

3 Greene, 'Causal Relationship'. Baugh, ' "A
Grand Marine Empire" '.

4 Spate, *Pacific* III, 63–100. Baugh,
'Seapower and Science'. Cock, 'Precursors
of Cook'. Savours, 'Phipps Expedition'.
C. J. Phipps, *A Voyage towards the North
Pole Undertaken by His Majesty's
Command 1773* (London, 1774). Mackay,
Hawke Papers, pp. 424–8, prints both the
public and secret instructions issued to
Cook in 1768. I make no attempt to
summarize the literature on Cook and
exploration in a note. Glyn Williams,
' "To Make Discoveries of Countries
Hitherto Unknown". The Admiralty and
Pacific Exploration in the Eighteenth
Century', *MM* LXXXII (1996), pp. 14–27
is an admirable introduction.

5 Baugh, 'Withdrawing from Europe',
pp. 20–29. Spencer, *Sandwich Diplomatic
Correspondence*, pp. 8–17 and 60–66.
Michael Roberts, *Splendid Isolation,
1763–1780* (Reading, 1970), pp. 31–40.
Scott, *British Foreign Policy*, pp. 29–203.
M. S. Anderson, 'Great Britain and the
Russian Fleet, 1769–70', *Slavonic and East
European Review* XXXI (1952–3),
pp. 148–63.

6 Tracy, *Navies, Deterrence*, pp. 42–55; and
'Gunboat Diplomacy'. Lawson, *Grenville*,
pp. 207–10.

7 Langford, *First Rockingham
Administration*, p. 15, quoting the
pamphleteer 'Anti-Sejanus'.

8 Langford, *First Rockingham
Administration*. Brooke, *Chatham
Administration*. Peters, *The Elder Pitt*,
pp. 237–47. Tracy, *Navies, Deterrence*,
pp. 60–63. Rice, 'Manila Ransom'. Scott,
British Foreign Policy, pp. 90–124
(quoting, p. 100, a report by the diplomat
Sir Andrew Mitchell).

9 Etienne-François, comte de Stainville,
later duc de Choiseul. When he moved to
the foreign ministry in 1766, he was
succeeded by his cousin César-Gabriel de
Choiseul, duc de Praslin, with whom he
should not be confused.

10 Scott, 'Bourbon Naval Reconstruction'.
Chapuis, *Beautemps-Beaupré*, pp. 244–5.
*Correspondance secrète du comte de Broglie
avec Louis XV (1756–1774)*, ed. Didier
Ozanam and Michel Antoine (Paris,
1956–61, 2 vols.) I, 196 and 317–19. M. C.
Morison, 'The Duc de Choiseul and the
Invasion of England, 1768–1770', *TRHS*
3rd S. IV (1910), pp. 83–115.

11 Tracy, 'Falklands Islands Crisis'; and
Navies, Deterrence, pp. 78–96. Scott,
British Foreign Policy, pp. 143–53.

12 Mackay, *Hawke*, pp. 301–31. Tracy,
'Falklands Islands Crisis', pp. 60–68.
Rodger, *Insatiable Earl*, pp. 129–31. Philip
Lawson, 'Parliament and the First East
India Inquiry, 1767', *Parliamentary
History* I (1982), pp. 99–114, at p. 106,
gives an example of Hawke's damaging
political innocence.

13 North passed all his political career in the
Commons, and did not succeed as Earl
of Guildford until shortly before his
death.

14 Thomas, *Lord North*, pp. 39–55. *HP
1754–90* III, 204–12. Scott, *British Foreign
Policy*, pp. 155–69. *SaP* I, 19–29. Langford,
A Polite and Commercial People,
pp. 521–2. Nicholas Tracy, 'Parry of a
Threat to India, 1768–1774', *MM* LIX
(1973), pp. 35–48. Spinney, *Rodney*,
pp. 252–5.

15 Fortescue, *George the Third* III, 256, to North, 10 Sep 1775.

16 Paul Langford, 'Old Whigs, Old Tories, and the American Revolution', *JICH* VIII (1979–80), No. 2, pp. 106–30; and 'The Rockingham Whigs and America, 1767–1773', in *Statesmen, Scholars and Merchants: Essays in Eighteenth-Century History presented to Dame Lucy Sutherland*, ed. Anne Whiteman, J. S. Bromley and P. G. M. Dickson (Oxford, 1973), pp. 135–52. J. G. A. Pocock, '1776: The Revolution against Parliament', in *Three British Revolutions: 1641, 1688, 1776* (Princeton, 1980), pp. 265–88. P. D. G. Thomas, 'George III and the American Revolution', *History* N.S. LXX (1985), pp. 16–31. Van Alstyne, 'Parliamentary Supremacy', pp. 203–11. John Sainsbury, *Disaffected Patriots: London Supporters of Revolutionary America 1769–1782* (Gloucester, 1987). Ian R. Christie, 'Myth and Reality in Late-Eighteenth Century British Politics', in *Myth and Reality in Late-Eighteenth Century British Politics and Other Papers* (London, 1970), pp. 27–54; and 'British Politics and the American Revolution', *Albion* IX (1977), pp. 205–26. Rodger, *Insatiable Earl*, pp. 214–16.

17 Henry E. Huntington Library, San Marino, California: LO 6498, to Lord Loudon, 10 Oct 1775.

18 Baugh, 'Politics of British Naval Failure', pp. 222–6. Syrett, *American Waters*, pp. 30–31 and 56–60. Rodger, *Insatiable Earl*, pp. 213–14 and 225–6. Orlando W. Stephenson, 'The Supply of Gunpowder in 1776', *AHR* XXX (1925), pp. 271–81.

19 Carrington, *British West Indies*, pp. 68–85. Jamieson, 'War in the Leeward Islands', pp. 13–21 and 107–8. Syrett, *American Waters*, pp. 20–23. J. Franklin Jameson, 'St Eustatius in the American Revolution', *AHR* VIII (1903), pp. 683–708.

20 Piers Mackesy, *The Coward of Minden: The Affair of Lord George Sackville* (London, 1979), pp. 253–7. Valentine, *Germain*, pp. 116, 129–30, 147, 372, 377, 396, 474 and 494. Margaret M. Spector, *The American Department of the British*

Government, *1768–1782* (New York, 1940), pp. 27–30 and 79–88.

21 Rodger, *Insatiable Earl*, pp. 212–300; and 'Anson'. Haas, 'Pursuit of Political Success'. Broomfield, 'Sandwich at the Admiralty', pp. 7–10.

22 Fortescue, *George the Third* IV, 215–16 No. 2,446, North to George III, 10 Nov 1778 (writing in the third person).

23 *Memorials and Correspondence of Charles James Fox*, ed. Lord John Russell (London, 1853–7, 4 vols.) II, 38.

24 *PH* XXII, 827, quoting Henry Dundas in the Commons, 12 Dec 1781.

25 Thomas, *Lord North*, especially pp. 80–132.

26 Gruber, *Howe Brothers*; and 'Admiral as Peacemaker'. Baugh, 'Politics of British Naval Failure', pp. 27–33. Mackesy, *War for America*, pp. 61–102. Syrett, *American Waters*, pp. 48–51 and 69. *SaP* I, 80–97 and 163–5. Mahan, *War of American Independence*, p. 11. Whiteley, 'Siege of Quebec'. Laughton, 'Duncan Journals', pp. 121–38. Richard J. Koke, 'Forcing the Hudson River Passage', *New York Historical Society Quarterly* XXXVI (1952), pp. 459–66.

27 Willcox, 'Too Many Cooks'. Mackesy, *War for America*, pp. 103–44. Syrett, 'British Effort in America', pp. 177–80. H. W. Moomaw, 'The Denouement of General Howe's Campaign of 1777', *EHR* LXXIX (1964), pp. 498–512. Laughton, 'Duncan Journals', pp. 148–55.

28 Syrett, *Shipping and the American War*, especially pp. 156–60 and 198–9; and 'Navy Board and Merchant Shipowners'. Usher, 'Civil Administration', pp. 263–301; *SaP* I, 88 and 209–11. *BND* Nos. 256–60, pp. 448–54. NMM: SAN/V/10a/15. Talbott, *Pen and Ink Sailor*, pp. 36–9. David Syrett, 'Lord George Germain and the Navy Board in Conflict: the *Adamant* and *Arwin Galley* Dispute, 1777', *BIHR* XXXVIII (1965), pp. 163–71; 'Lord George Germain and the Protection of Military Storeships 1775–1778', *MM* LX (1974), pp. 395–405; 'The Procurement of Shipping by the Board of Ordnance during the American War, 1775–1782', *MM* LXXXI (1995), pp. 409–16; 'The

Victualling Board Charters Shipping, 1775–82', *HR* LXVIII (1995), pp. 212–24; and 'The West India Merchants and the Conveyance of the King's Troops to the Caribbean, 1779–1782', *JSAHR* XLV (1967), pp. 169–76.

29 P. C. F. Smith, *Fired by Manley Zeal: A Naval Fiasco of the American Revolution* (Salem, Mass., 1977). Syrett, *American Waters*, pp. 71–2.

30 Syrett, *American Waters*, pp. 63–9; and 'British Effort in America', pp. 172–3 and 185. Baugh, 'Politics of British Naval Failure', pp. 234–5. William J. Morgan, 'American Privateering in America's War for Independence, 1775–1783', *AN* XXXVI (1976), pp. 79–87.

31 Scott, *British Foreign Policy*, pp. 234–55. Baugh, 'Politics of British Naval Failure', pp. 239–44; and 'Why Did Britain Lose Command of the Sea?', pp. 153–6. *SaP* I, 202–4, 212–18, 235–8, 242–5, 249, 342–3 and 349–52. Tracy, *Navies, Deterrence*, pp. 129–53. Syrett, *European Waters*, pp. 9–16. Dull, *American Independence*, pp. 33–62 and 84–99.

32 By Osinga, *Frankrijk, Vergennes*.

33 Pritchard, 'French Strategy'. Dull, *American Independence*, pp. 37–48. Murphy, *Vergennes*, pp. 256–67. E. S. Corwin, 'The French Objective in the American Revolution', *AHR* XXI (1915–16), pp. 33–61.

34 PRO: ADM 2/1334 f. 62, orders to Lord Howe, 22 Mar 1778.

35 *SaP* I, 327–39 and 359–70. Mackesy, *War for America*, pp. 182–5. Syrett, *American Waters*, pp. 90–95; and *European Waters*, pp. 17–22. Charles R. Ritcheson, *British Politics and the American Revolution* (Norman, Okla., 1954), pp. 233–57. Duffy, 'Western Squadron', p. 76. Caron, *Chesapeake*, pp. 144–5.

36 Syrett, 'Home Waters or America?'; and *European Waters*, pp. 22–35. Dull, *American Independence*, pp. 110–15. Brown, 'Anglo-French Naval Crisis'; and *American Secretary*, pp. 149–72. Willcox, *Portrait of a General*, pp. 214–18. Fortescue, *George the Third* IV, 97–8 No. 2,275, Memo for Cabinet by Sandwich, 6 Apr 1778. *SaP* II, 374–6.

37 *SaP* I, 240, J. Robinson to Sandwich, 18 Aug 1777 (printing BL: Add. MSS 70990, ff. 88–90).

38 Keppel, *Keppel* II, 3–4. *SaP* II, 110–11. Rodger, *Insatiable Earl*, pp. 240–42 and 282–3. Broomfield, 'Keppel–Palliser Affair', pp. 196–7.

39 Hatch, 'Jervis–Clinton Letters', p. 95, to Sir H. Clinton, 15 Apr 1778.

40 NMM: SAN/F/15/7, to Sandwich, 4 Jul 1778.

41 *SaP* II, 15–38, 46–8, 54–6, 63–115 and 369–73. Mackesy, *War for America*, pp. 202–8. Broomfield, 'Keppel–Palliser Affair', pp. 197–8.

42 Black, *Britain as a Military Power*, p. 179.

43 BL: Add. MSS 9344 f. 36, to G. Jackson, 31 Jul 1778.

44 *SaP* II, 127–57. Creswell, *British Admirals*, pp. 120–31. Tunstall, *Naval Warfare*, pp. 137–41. Syrett, *European Waters*, pp. 36–47. Dull, *American Independence*, pp. 121–2. *MMF* III, 128–35. Vergé-Franceschi, *Marine et éducation*, pp. 353–4. Castex, *Les Idées militaires*, pp. 121–34. Mackay, *Hawke*, p. 345. Rodger, *Insatiable Earl*, pp. 244–5.

45 Rodger, *Insatiable Earl*, pp. 245–51; and 'Honour and Duty'. *SaP* II, 191–252 and 274–6. Davies, 'Faction', pp. 69–97. Broomfield, 'Keppel–Palliser Affair'. Beatson, *Memoirs* VI, 136–41. O'Gorman, *Rise of Party*, pp. 382–5. Syrett, *European Waters*, pp. 48–59. De Toy, 'Wellington's Admiral', pp. 29–31.

46 NMM: SAN/F/18/97, Walsingham to Sandwich, n.d. [Apr–May 1779]. BL: Add. MSS 61863 f. 82, Sandwich to North, 21 May 1779.

47 Fortescue, *George the Third* IV, 225–7 No. 2,460, anon. list of Keppel's officers, Nov 1778.

48 Kathleen Wilson, *The Sense of the People: Politics, Culture and Imperialism in England, 1715–1785* (Cambridge, 1995), pp. 256–8. George, *English Political Caricature*, pp. 161–2. Tucker, *St Vincent* II, 43–4. Hamilton, *Martin Papers* III, 291 n.1.

49 Owen, 'Howe and d'Estaing'. Syrett, *American Waters*, pp. 96–115. Mahan, *War of American Independence*, pp. 65–8.

MMF III, 156–62. Gruber, Howe Brothers, pp. 308–20. Ernest M. Eller, 'Washington's Maritime Strategy and the Campaign that Assured Independence', in Chesapeake Bay in the American Revolution (Centreville, Md., 1981), pp. 475–523, at p. 479. Laughton, 'Duncan Journals', pp. 159–62.

50 Jamieson, 'War in the Leeward Islands', pp. 131–57. David Syrett, 'D'Estaing's Decision to Steer for Antigua, 28th November 1778', MM LXI (1975), pp. 155–62. Stirling, Pages and Portraits I, 29–31. SaP II, 333–54. Bonner-Smith, Barrington Papers II, 120–28 and 160–65. Barrington, 'Letters', pp. 382–91. MMF III, 185–9. Conway, War of American Independence, p. 136.

51 Jamieson, 'Battle of Grenada'; and 'War in the Leeward Islands', pp. 187–98. Tunstall, Naval Warfare, pp. 162–3. Creswell, British Admirals, pp. 132–40. Mahan, War of American Independence, pp. 109–12. Owen, 'Battle of Grenada'. Bonner-Smith, Barrington Papers II, 308–10; and 'Byron in the Leeward Islands'. Villiers, Marine Royale II, 575–7. La Monneraye, Souvenirs, pp. 130–31. MMF III, 201–13. René Marie, 'D'Estaing aux Antilles', Revue Maritime N.S. 24 (1921), pp. 735–58. Syrett, American Waters, pp. 131–2.

52 Fortescue, George the Third, IV, 269, George III to North, 9 Feb 1779.

53 Fortescue, George the Third IV, 293 No. 2,565, to North, 1 Mar 1779.

54 BL: Add. MSS 70990 f. 32, 14 Sep 1779.

55 SaP II, 255–81 and III, 313–19. Rodger, Insatiable Earl, pp. 256–7. O'Gorman, Rise of Party, pp. 385–6 and 394. Davies, 'Faction', pp. 17–62. Gruber, Howe Brothers, pp. 212–13, 274, 295 and 328–36. HMC Abergavenny, pp. 24 and 26. NMM: SAN/F/41/124. Fabel, Bombast and Broadsides, pp. 130–32.

56 Dull, American Independence, pp. 97–105 and 126–52; and Diplomatic History, p. 109. Scott, British Foreign Policy, pp. 262–3 and 273. Patterson, The Other Armada, pp. 1–20. Pritchard, 'French Strategy', pp. 92–4. Voltes Bou, 'El intento hispanofrances', pp. 528–9.

Coquelle, 'Les Projets de descente', XVI, 145–8.

57 SaP III, 3–106. Patterson, The Other Armada, pp. 169–215. Syrett, European Waters, pp. 61–79. Phillips, 'Evangelical Administrator', pp. 126–31. AE VII, 233–9. BP I, 292–9. Fortescue, George the Third IV, 422–4 No. 2,763. Corbett, Maritime Strategy, pp. 257–8.

58 Lacour-Gayet, 'La Campagne navale de la Manche'. Taylor, 'French Fleet in the Channel'. Voltes Bou, 'El intento hispanofrances'. MMF III, 50–51 and 267–80. Dull, American Independence, pp. 152–8. Patterson, The Other Armada, pp. 59–70 and 160–68. Villiers, Marine Royale II, 580. Murphy, Vergennes, pp. 277–8. Caron, Chesapeake, pp. 291 and 521–36. Masson, Histoire de la Marine I, 263–66. Chapuis, Beautemps-Beaupré, p. 246. Loir, La Marine royale, pp. 125–9.

22 Distant Waters

1 Norris, Shelburne and Reform, pp. 117–39. Davies, 'Faction', pp. 128–9. George, English Political Caricature, p. 163. Christie, The End of North's Ministry, p. 268.

2 Dull, American Independence, pp. 170–74. Jamieson, 'War in the Leeward Islands', p. 194.

3 HP 1754–90 III, 368–70. WW, pp. 323–7. Spinney, Rodney, is the best biography, but generous to his hero's faults.

4 Syrett, European Waters, pp. 85–90. Spinney, Rodney, pp. 296–316. BP I, 65–7. AE VII, 249–68.

5 HMC Stopford-Sackville II, 153, to Ld. G. Germain, 27 Jan 1780.

6 [Les Anglais] 'marchaient beaucoup mieux que nous, d'autant qu'ils étaient tous doublés en cuivre et nous d'huîtres': Depeyre, Tactiques et stratégies navales, p. 50.

7 Knight, 'Lead and Copper Sheathing', pp. 299–302. BP III, 16. BND No. 286, p. 491. Goodwin, Construction and Fitting, pp. 225–7. Lavery, Arming and Fitting, pp. 62–5. Bingeman et al., 'Copper and Other Sheathing'. Cock, ' "The Finest

Invention in the World" '. Talbott, *Pen and Ink Sailor*, pp. 45–60.

8 *SaP* III, 158–60. Tunstall, *Naval Warfare* pp. 165–7. Jamieson, 'War in the Leeward Islands', pp. 207–17. Corbett, *Signals and Instructions*, p. 230. Creswell, *British Admirals*, pp. 143–51. Spinney, *Rodney*, pp. 320–32. Rodger, 'Tactics', pp. 292–3. Owen, 'Rodney and de Guichen', pp. 209–10. *MMF* III, 337–41. *BP* I, 52–62, 100–105 and 371–98.

9 Syrett, *American Waters*, pp. 134–40. Willcox, *Portrait of a General*, pp. 302–9. *KP* I, 135–76.

10 Rodger, *Insatiable Earl*, pp. 284–8. Syrett, *American Waters*, pp. 154–6. Willcox, 'Rhode Island', pp. 306–16. Davies, 'Faction', pp. 212–21. *SaP* IV, 164–5. Rodney, *Letter-Books* I, 10–71. Fraser, 'Green Memoranda', pp. 93–7. HMC *Stopford-Sackville* II, 191. Linÿer de la Barbée, *Ternay* II, 585–630. Spinney, *Rodney*, pp. 346–53.

11 Jamieson, 'War in the Leeward Islands', pp. 221–9. *BP* II, 104–6. W. R. Rowbotham, 'The West Indies Hurricanes of October 1780', *JRUSI* CVI (1961), pp. 573–84. J. W. Caughey, *Bernardo de Gálvez in Louisiana, 1776–1783* (Berkeley, Calif., 1934), p. 193. Zapatero, *La Guerra del Caribe*, p. 232. Carmen de Reparaz, *Yo Solo: Bernardo de Gálvez y la toma de Panzacola en 1781* (Barcelona, 1986), p. 46.

12 Mackay, *Hawke*, p. 228.

13 Rodger, *Insatiable Earl*, pp. 280–82. Bonner-Smith, *Barrington Papers* II, 338–41. Stirling, *Pages and Portraits* II, 222–3.

14 Callender, 'With the Grand Fleet'.

15 Jamieson, 'War in the Leeward Islands', p. 225. *AE* VII, 275–7. Crowhurst, *Defence of British Trade*, p. 91. 'Presa de un convoy británico de 55 velas por Don Luis de Córdoba (1780)', *RHN* XII (1994), 44, pp. 75–9.

16 *SaP* IV, 65, Sandwich, 11 Sep 1781.

17 Syrett, *European Waters*, pp. 133–9. *BP* I, 366–9. Bonner-Smith, *Barrington Papers* II, 350–53. *SaP* IV, 31 and 65. Rodger, *Insatiable Earl*, pp. 281–2.

18 Kaplan, *Russian Overseas Commerce*, pp. 52–67, 106–9 and 116–31. Madariaga, *Armed Neutrality*, pp. 283–300 and 442–5. Feldbæk, 'Denmark and the Baltic', I, 264. Kulsrud, *Maritime Neutrality*, pp. 325–33. Pearsall, 'Convoys in the North Sea', p. 106.

19 Syrett, *European Waters*, pp. 95–132 (essentially reprinting *Neutral Rights*). Miller, *Yorke*, pp. 69–100. *BND* Nos. 261 and 264–6, pp. 454–60. *NZW* IV, 406–15. Van Eyck van Heslinga, 'De vlag dekt de lading', pp. 102–4. H. M. Scott, 'Sir Joseph Yorke, Dutch Politics and the Origins of the Fourth Anglo-Dutch War', *HJ* XXXI (1988), pp. 571–89. Rodger, 'Anglo-Dutch Alliance', pp. 25–6.

20 Dull, *Diplomatic History*, pp. 124–6 and 208. Syrett, *Neutral Rights*, p. 35. Feldbæk, *Storhandelens Tid*, p. 88. Van Eyck van Heslinga, 'De vlag dekt de lading', pp. 153–4 and 181–3. David Starkey, 'British Privateering against the Dutch in the American Revolutionary War, 1780–1783', in *Studies in British Privateering, Trading Enterprise and Seamen's Welfare, 1775–1900*, ed. Stephen Fisher (Exeter, 1987), pp. 1–17.

21 Jameson, 'St Eustatius'. Jamieson, 'War in the Leeward Islands', pp. 229–45. *BP* II, 109–26. Breen, 'Rodney and St Eustatius'; and 'Yorktown Campaign', pp. 141–7. Hannay, *Hood Letters*, pp. 12–24. Kemp, 'Letters from the Leeward Islands', p. 136. O'Shaughnessy, *An Empire Divided*, pp. 217–31. Carrington, *British West Indies*, pp. 79–81. *NZW* IV, 458–69. *MMF* III, 372. Spinney, *Rodney*, pp. 359–77, 382–3 and 419–21.

22 Tornquist, *Count de Grasse*, pp. 35–42 and 47–8. Caron, *Chesapeake*, pp. 383–88. Shea, *French Fleet*, pp. 42–4, 114–16 and 175–7. Duffy, 'Hood', pp. 257–8. Baugh, 'Hood', pp. 302–4. Kemp, 'Letters from the Leeward Islands', p. 132. *SaP* IV, 133. Jamieson, 'War in the Leeward Islands', pp. 252–5.

23 Butterfield, 'Johnstone', pp. 30–36, 50–72 and 82. Willcox, 'Battle of Porto Praya'. Fabel, *Bombast and Broadsides*, pp. 144–61. HMC *Rutland* III, 41–6. Pasley, *Sea Journals*, pp. 136–74. Pernoud,

La Campagne des Indes, pp. 37–40. Chatterton, *Gambier* I, 117.

24 Zapatero, *La Guerra del Caribe*, pp. 233–6. *AE* VII, 288–91.

25 José Gella Iturriaga, 'El convoy y el desembarco español de 1781 en Menorca', *RHN* I (1983) 1, 9–30. Amador Marí Puig, 'Cors i comerç a Menorca: La comercialització de les preses (1778–1781)', in López Nadal, *El comerç alternatiu*, pp. 201–16. Though the island was captured at once, the garrison of Fort St Philip held out until February 1782.

26 Ross, *Saumarez* II, 371–6. *NZW* IV, 511–44. Clerk of Eldin, *Naval Tactics*, pp. 118–22. *SaP* IV, 19–21 and 83–121.

27 Syrett, *European Waters*, pp. 139–48. *MMF* III, 375–6. *SaP* IV, 4–14 and 32–66. Dull, *American Independence*, pp. 224–9. Breen, 'Yorktown Campaign', pp. 63–72.

28 *SaP* IV, 80–82. *BP* I, 134 and 361–2; II, 38–9.

29 Syrett, *European Waters*, pp. 148–50; and 'Count-down to the Saints', pp. 157–60. *BP* I, 356–7. *MMF* III, 377. Owen, 'Western Squadron, 1781–82', pp. 37–44. *SaP* IV, 14–17 and 76–8. Åke Lindwall, 'The Encounter between Kempenfelt and De Guichen, December 1781', *MM* LXXXVII (2001), pp. 163–79.

30 Willcox, 'Rhode Island', pp. 317–23. Fraser, 'Green Memoranda', pp. 128–31. *MMF* III, 360–62. Syrett, *American Waters*, pp. 167–70 and 175. Tunstall, *Naval Warfare*, p. 169.

31 Breen, 'Yorktown Campaign', pp. 158–61 and 258–302. Willcox, 'Road to Yorktown'; and *Portrait of a General*, pp. 409–31. Breen, 'Graves and Hood'. Sulivan, 'Graves and Hood'. Owen, 'Surrender at Yorktown'. Syrett, *American Waters*, pp. 180–219. *SaP* IV, 141–3 and 181–94. *BND* No. 231, pp. 403–5. *BP* I, 124–7. Tornquist, *Count de Grasse*, pp. 59–62 and 175. Shea, *French Fleet*, pp. 69–74 and 155–8. Hannay, *Hood Letters*, pp. 28–44. Chadwick, *Graves Papers*, pp. 59–60. Tunstall, *Naval Warfare*, pp. 172–6. Hale, 'Naval Side of Yorktown'. Creswell, *British Admirals*, pp. 153–62. Masson, *Histoire de la Marine* I, 271–2.

32 Rodger, *Insatiable Earl*, pp. 289–91. Mackesy, *War for America*, pp. 424 and 434–5. Hannay, *Hood Letters*, pp. 45–6.

33 Jamieson, 'War in the Leeward Islands', pp. 267–81. Hannay, *Hood Letters*, pp. 86–93. Tornquist, *Count de Grasse*, pp. 82–86 and 177. Caron, *Chesapeake*, pp. 446–51 and 466–9. Villiers, *Marine Royale* II, 598–9. Shea, *French Fleet*, pp. 97–104 and 167–72. Kerguelen-Trémarec, *Relation*, pp. 259–60. HMC *Rutland* III, 48–9. Duffy, 'Hood', pp. 260–61. Troude, *Batailles navales* II, 214–18. Owen, 'Hood at Saint Christopher's'. *MMF* III, 420–24. *BP* I, 144. Mahan, *War of American Independence*, pp. 198–202. Clerk of Eldin, *Naval Tactics*, pp. 229–38. Tunstall, *Naval Warfare*, pp. 177–8.

34 Jamieson, 'War in the Leeward Islands', pp. 282–301. Hannay, *Hood Letters*, pp. 101–29. Owen, 'Rodney and Grasse'. Spinney, 'Rodney and the Saints'; and *Rodney*, pp. 390–407. Mundy, *Rodney* II, 225–38 (cf. Blane, *Select Dissertations*, pp. 74–7). *BP* I, 151–80 and 263–83. Tunstall, *Naval Warfare*, pp. 179–84. Creswell, *British Admirals*, pp. 163–77. Laughton, 'Hood Papers', pp. 229–35. *MMF* III, 426–34. *BND* No. 232, pp. 406–11. Cornwallis-West, *Cornwallis*, pp. 118–29. HMC *Rutland* III, 53. Clerk of Eldin, *Naval Tactics*, pp. 239–62. Brenton, *Naval History* I, 126. Ross, *Saumarez* I, 75–8 and II, 390–96. Shea, *French Fleet*, pp. 120–26. Villiers, *Marine Royale* II, 601–3. Tornquist, *Count de Grasse*, pp. 91–103 and 181–7.

35 Wraxall, *Memoirs* II, 320–21. Stephen Conway, ' "A Joy Unknown for Years Past": The American War, Britishness and the Celebration of Rodney's Victory at the Saints', *History* LXXXVI (2001), pp. 180–99. Villiers, *Marine Royale* II, 732–8. Gérard de la Mardière, 'Le Conseil de guerre de Lorient (1783–1784)', *CHM* 19 (1989), pp. 16–36.

36 Davies, 'Faction', p. 281. George, *English Political Caricature*, pp. 165–6. Pasley, *Sea Journals*, p. 242. Wraxall, *Memoirs* II, 328–30. SuRO: Grafton MSS HA 513/4/3,

Grafton's Diary, 18 May 1782. Tucker, *St Vincent* I, 90.

37 Mackesy, *War for America*, pp. 472–86 and 509. Jamieson, 'War in the Leeward Islands', pp. 72 and 303–22. Norris, *Shelburne and Reform*, p. 243. Syrett, *Shipping and the American War*, pp. 234–6.

38 Davies, 'Faction', pp. 270–75 and 293. Buckingham, *Memoirs* I, 136. Knight, ' "Some Further Degree of Merit" ', p. 9. Mackesy, *War for America*, pp. 472–3. Keppel, *Keppel* II, 391–2. Rodger, *Insatiable Earl*, pp. 172–92; and 'Officers' Careers', p. 6.

39 Scott, *British Foreign Policy*, p. 325. *BP* II, 56 and 66–7. Phillips, 'Evangelical Administrator', pp. 299–301. Cannon, *Fox–North Coalition*, pp. 1–43.

40 Howe was already an Irish viscount, but an English title carried greater standing and a seat in the Lords.

41 Davies, 'Faction', p. 278. Owen, 'Western Squadron, 1781–82', pp. 47–9. Syrett, *European Waters*, pp. 153–9. Dull, *American Independence*, pp. 278 and 291. *MMF* III, 378–88. Corbett, *Maritime Strategy*, pp. 145–50. SuRO: HA 513/4/4, Grafton's Diary, 14 [or 15–16?] Jul 1782. Pearsall, 'Convoys in the North Sea', pp. 107–8.

42 Syrett, *European Waters*, pp. 159–63. *AE* VII, 308–44. Laughton, 'Duncan Journals', pp. 211–19. Gardner, *Recollections*, pp. 29–31. *MMF* III, 447–8. Barrow, *Howe*, pp. 152–4. Keith P. Hertzog, 'The Battle of Cape Spartel, 1782', *MM* LXXIII (1987), p. 148. 'Combate de Espartel (20 de octubre de 1782)', *RHN* XI (1993), 40, pp. 95–104.

43 Low, *Indian Navy* I, 178. Richmond, *Navy in India*, pp. 107–11 and 171–2.

44 Taillemite, *L'Histoire ignorée*, pp. 210–33. Loir, *La Marine royale*, pp. 241–3. Caron, *Suffren*, pp. 143–73, 214–24, 355 and 409–10. Cavaliero, *Admiral Satan*, p. 258. Masson, 'Suffren', pp. 181–4; and *Histoire de la Marine* I, 283–4. Vergé-Franceschi, *Marine et éducation*, p. 362. Pernoud, *La Campagne des Indes*, pp. 18–33. Richmond, *Navy in India*, pp. 88–90.

45 Richmond, *Navy in India*, Pernoud, *La Campagne des Indes*, Cunat, *Bailli de Suffren*, and Caron, *Suffren*, all give detailed narratives of the campaigns. See also *MMF* III, 495–552; *Relation détaillée*, pp. 3–22; Tunstall, *Naval Warfare*, pp. 185–6; Clerk of Eldin, *Naval Tactics*, pp. 263–87.

23 The British Lion Has Claws

1 Scott, *British Foreign Policy*, pp. 339–40. Ehrman, *Younger Pitt* I, 160. Black, *Foreign Policy in an Age of Revolutions*, pp. 16–17. Jones, *Britain and the World*, p. 249.

2 Cannon, *Fox–North Coalition. HP 1754–90* I, 87–96.

3 Pasley, *Sea Journals*, pp. 38–9.

4 *BND* Nos. 229–30, 233, 253 and 255; pp. 401–3, 412–20 and 444–8. Syrett, 'British Trade Convoys'. Pearsall, 'Convoys in the North Sea'; and 'Protection of Trade in the Eighteenth Century'. *SpP* IV, 295. Carrington, *British West Indies*, pp. 59–60 and 104–14. Clowes, *Royal Navy* III, 396.

5 Villiers, *Marine Royale* II, 641–71. Masson, *Histoire de la Marine* I, 287–8. Vergé-Franceschi, *Chronique*, pp. 669–70. Butel, 'France, the Antilles, and Europe'.

6 Carrington, *British West Indies*, pp. 128–30 and 141–65. Ehrman, *Younger Pitt* I, 333–36.

7 Rawson, *Nelson's Letters*. Oman, *Nelson*, pp. 69–71. *DLN* I, 171–86 and 226–30. *HCC*, pp. 16–17. Warner, *Collingwood*, pp. 18–21. Kirby, 'Nelson and American Merchantmen'.

8 Gascoigne, *Science*, pp. 94–102. Ehrman, *Younger Pitt* I, 337–41. Baugh, 'Withdrawing from Europe', p. 28.

9 Mackay, *In the Wake of Cook*, pp. 123–40.

10 Crowhurst, *Defence of British Trade*, p. 200. *BND* No. 270 p. 463. O'Shaughnessy, *An Empire Divided*, pp. 239–45.

11 Syrett, 'British Amphibious Operations'. Tunstall, *Naval Warfare*, pp. 119–56 and 192–200. Perrin, *British Flags*, pp. 166–8. *BP* I, 69, 72, 295–6 and 309–11. Corbett, *Fighting Instructions*, pp. 225–51; and *Signals and Instructions*. Depeyre,

Tactiques et stratégies navales, pp. 126–64.
Barrow, *Howe*, pp. 118–19, 129 and 142–3.
Creswell, *British Admirals*, pp. 178–85.
Rodger, 'Tactics'.

12 Villiers, *Marine Royale* II, 509–14. Loir, *La Marine royale*, pp. 33–47, 103–44 and 284–6. Taillemite, *L'Histoire ignorée*, pp. 178–82 and 191–8. Jurien de la Gravière, *Souvenirs*, I, 15–20 and 29–30. *MMF* III, 593–602. Masson, *Histoire de la Marine* I, 235–9. La Monneraye, *Souvenirs*, pp. 50–70. Vergé-Franceschi, *La Marine française*, pp. 146–159.

13 Rodríguez Casado, 'La politia del reformismo'.

14 Glete, *Navies and Nations* I, 274–84; II, 553, 579, 630 and 641; cf. Appendix II. Formicola and Romano, 'La Marina Napoletana'; and 'Vescelli Napoletani'. Radogna, *Storia della marina militare*, pp. 27–41.

15 Ehrman, *Younger Pitt* I, 239–40, 258–60, 312–14 and 517. Webb, 'Rebuilding and Repair', pp. 195–7. Binney, *Public Finance*, pp. 16–17. Morriss, *Royal Dockyards*, pp. 77–8. Aspinall, *George III* I, 202–6, No. 271. Robertson, 'Mobilisation', p. 15, quoting NMM: MID/2/13/6 (quoted).

16 Riley, *Seven Years War*; and *Government Finance*. Bosher, *French Finances*,
, pp. 23–4. Bonney, 'Eighteenth Century', pp. 343–7. Harris, 'French Finances', revises previous figures.

17 Jacques A. Barbier, 'Indies Revenue and Naval Spending: The Cost of Colonialism for the Spanish Bourbons, 1763–1805', *Jahrbuch für Geschichte von Staat, Wirtschaft und Gesellschaft Lateinamerikas* XXI (1984), pp. 171–88. Gervasio de Artíñano y de Galdácano, *La Arquitectura Naval Española (en madera)* (Madrid, 1920), pp. 182–3.

18 'Nauticus Junior' [Joseph Harris], *The Naval Atlantis; or, a Display of the Characters of such Flag Officers as were distinguished during the last War* (London, 1788–9, 2 vols. in 1) I, 4.

19 Knight, 'Howe', p. 285. Ehrman, *Younger Pitt* I, 315 and 517–19. Barrow, *Howe*, p. 178. *BP* II, x–xi, 138–47 and 258–9. Hamilton, *Martin Papers* I, 95–7. Schomberg, *Chronology* II, 169–82. HMC

Fortescue I, 326. Buckingham, *Memoirs* I, 368–9. Aspinall, *George III* I, 364–5, No. 435. Stirling, *Pages and Portraits* I, 219–20.

20 HMC *Fortescue* I, 324, to W. W. Grenville, 25 Apr 1788.

21 Buckingham, *Memoirs* I, 385, to Buckingham, 16 May 1788.

22 Crimmin, 'Admiralty Administration', p. 21, quoting the *Annual Register*.

23 Marsden, *Memoir*, p. 115.

24 Ehrman, *Younger Pitt* I, 315–17. *SpP* I, 8–10. Phillips, 'Evangelical Administrator', pp. 87–92. Glover, *Britain at Bay*, p. 35.

25 Webb, 'Nootka Sound Crisis', pp. 141–6. Aspinall, *Prince of Wales* II, 104–6 No. 535.

26 Aspinall, *Prince of Wales* II, 76–7, No. 513, 12 Jul [1790].

27 Ehrman, *Younger Pitt* I, 520–37. Jeremy Black, 'Anglo-French Relations in the Age of the French Revolution 1787–1793', *Francia* XV (1987), pp. 407–33, at pp. 411–15. Harlow, *Second British Empire* I, 130 and 143–4; II, 365. Jaap R. Bruijn, 'The Dutch Navy goes Overseas (c.1780–c.1860)', *TvZ* XX (2001), pp. 163–74, at pp. 163–6.

28 Evans, 'Nootka Sound Controversy', p. 621, to Auckland, 6 Aug 1790.

29 Ehrman, *Younger Pitt* I, 554–70. Evans, 'Nootka Sound Controversy'. Norris, 'Nootka Crisis'. Black, *Foreign Policy in an Age of Revolutions*, pp. 236–55; and 'Naval Power, Strategy and Foreign Policy', pp. 108–12. Gough, *Distant Dominion*, pp. 79–115; and *Northwest Coast*, pp. 116–45. Spate, *Pacific* III, 309–21. *AE* VIII, 5–24.

30 Webb, 'Ochakov Affair', p. 14.

31 Webb, 'Ochakov Affair'. Ehrman, *Younger Pitt* II, 18–27. Alan Cunningham, 'The Ochakov Debate', in *Anglo-Ottoman Encounters in the Age of Revolution*, ed. Edward Ingram (London, 1993), pp. 1–31. Black, *Foreign Policy in an Age of Revolutions*, pp. 297–9 and 494; and 'Naval Power, Strategy and Foreign Policy', pp. 113–15.

32 Mackay, 'Banks, Cook, and Empire'; and *In the Wake of Cook*, pp. 23–78 and

123–64. Gascoigne, *Science*, pp. 24–33. Gough, *Northwest Coast*, pp. 146–70. Frest, *Convicts and Empire*, pp. 144–8 and 154–7. King, ' "Ports of Shelter and Refreshment" ', pp. 201–3 and 208–9. Parkinson, *Eastern Seas*, p. 12. Glyndwr Williams, 'The Pacific: Exploration and Exploitation', in Marshall, *Eighteenth Century*, pp. 552–75.

33 Hay, 'Property, Authority', pp. 18–53. A. Roger Ekirch, *Bound for America: The Transportation of British Convicts to the Colonies, 1718–1775* (Oxford, 1987).

34 Alan Frost argues for strategic motives; David Mackay, Mollie Gillen and others are in varying degrees sceptical.

35 Alan Frost, 'The Choice of Botany Bay: The Scheme to Supply the East Indies with Naval Stores', *Australian Economic History Review* XV (1975), pp. 1–20, at p. 9.

36 Frost, *Convicts and Empire*; *Phillip*, pp. 137–53; and 'Botany Bay: An Imperial Venture of the 1780s', *EHR* C (1985), pp. 309–30. Mackay, 'Direction and Purpose'; and 'Far-Flung Empire: A Neglected Imperial Outpost at Botany Bay 1788–1801', *JICH* IX (1981), pp. 125–45. King, ' "Ports of Shelter and Refreshment" '. Mollie Gillen, 'The Botany Bay Decision, 1786: Convicts, not Empire', *EHR* XCVII (1982), pp. 740–66.

37 O'Brien and Engerman, 'Exports', pp. 185–6. Deane and Cole, *British Economic Growth*, p. 34. Butel, 'La Dynamique des marchés coloniaux', p. 102. Crouzet, 'Impact of the French Wars', pp. 189–91.

38 Harvey Mitchell, *The Underground War against Revolutionary France: The Missions of William Wickham 1794–1800* (Oxford, 1965), p. 18, J. B. Burges to Auckland, 28 Dec 1790.

39 Ehrman, *Younger Pitt* II, 52.

24 Plans of Improvement

1 Baugh, 'National Institution', p. 125. Mackesy, *War for America*, pp. 166–7. Rosier, 'Cost and Durability', pp. 20–27, showing 103 ships, First to Sixth Rate, laid down 1756–63.

2 Rodger, *Insatiable Earl*, pp. 96–7. Glete, *Navies and Nations* II, 551–2 and Appendix II, giving figures for ships of at least 300 metric tons displacement. Ehrman, *Navy*, p. 636. Middleton, 'Visitation of the Royal Dockyards', p. 29. Haas, *Management Odyssey*, p. 3.

3 Knight, 'Building and Maintenance', pp. 36–41. Rosier, 'Cost and Durability', pp. 40–41.

4 Wilkinson, 'Egmont'. Coad, *Royal Dockyards*, p. 12. Haas, *Management Odyssey*, pp. 42–3; and 'Visitations and Reform', pp. 193 and 200. Knight, 'Royal Dockyards', p. 45.

5 Mackay, *Hawke*, pp. 303–11; and *Hawke Papers*, pp. 393–477. Appendix VII. Haas, 'Visitations and Reform', pp. 202–3. Wilkinson, 'Politics, Government and the Navy', pp. 221–43.

6 Wilkinson, 'Politics, Government and the Navy', pp. 22–9, 44–8 and 101–44. Appendix VII. Webb, 'Navy and British Diplomacy', pp. 151–2. Williams, 'Naval Administration', pp. 43–8. Binney, *Public Finance*, pp. 140–46. Crimmin, 'Admiralty Relations with the Treasury', pp. 63–9. Mackay, *Hawke*, pp. 303–7. *SaP* I, 275–6. *PH* XIX, 986. Knight, 'Royal Dockyards', pp. 66–8.

7 *BND* No. 262, pp. 456–7.

8 PRO: ADM 7/661 f. 74, Minutes of Dockyard Visitation 1774.

9 Wilkinson, 'Politics, Government and the Navy', pp. 30, 34, 50–52 and 252–305. *SaP* IV, 301–14. Rosier, 'Cost and Durability'. Rodger, *Insatiable Earl*, pp. 131–41.

10 Rodger, *Insatiable Earl*, pp. 141–9. Knight, 'Royal Dockyards', pp. 210–20. Knight, *Portsmouth Dockyard Papers*, p. 141. *BP* II, 32–4. *SaP* IV, 278–9. *PH* XIX, 828. Williams, 'Naval Administration', pp. 284–99.

11 PRO: ADM 7/661 ff. 3–4.

12 PRO: ADM 7/661 f. 73.

13 Rodger, *Insatiable Earl*, pp. 155–9. Haas, 'Visitations and Reform', pp. 193–5. Knight, *Portsmouth Dockyard Papers*, pp. 136–40.

14 Rodger, *Insatiable Earl*, pp. 150–54. Knight, 'Royal Dockyards', pp. 116–34 and 157–76; and *Portsmouth Dockyard*

Papers, pp. xxxix–xlvii. *BND* No. 315 pp. 533–35. Haas, 'Task Work'; 'Wage Payment', pp. 99–112; and *Management Odyssey*, pp. 25–37. Williams, 'Naval Administration', pp. 402–17. Roger Morriss, 'Industrial Relations at Plymouth Dockyard, 1770–1820,' *MHD* I, 216–23, at 217–19.

15 Rodger, *Insatiable Earl*, pp. 160–62. Usher, 'Civil Administration', p. 72. Haas, *Management Odyssey*, pp. 17–21. Michael E. Moody, 'Religion in the Life of Charles Middleton, First Baron Barham', in *The Dissenting Tradition: Essays for Leland H. Carlson*, ed. C. Robert Cole and M. E. Moody (Athens, Ohio, 1975), pp. 140–63.

16 Phillips, 'Evangelical Administrator', p. 70, quoting BL: Add. MSS 24135.

17 *BND* No. 268 p. 460.

18 Rodger, *Insatiable Earl*, pp. 162–71. Phillips, 'Evangelical Administrator', pp. 66–9 and 121. Talbott, *Pen and Ink Sailor*, pp. 117–18. *BP* II, 3–47. *SaP* IV, 369–86. Knight, 'Royal Dockyards', pp. 20–34 and 175–91.

19 Morrison, *Hamilton and Nelson Papers* I, 74, C. Greville to W. Hamilton, 17 Sep 1781.

20 Rosier, 'Cost and Durability', pp. 49–53. Knight, 'Royal Dockyards', pp. 246–63 and 334–66; and 'New England Forests'. *SaP* IV, 284–5 and 362. Haas, *Management Odyssey*, pp. 38–42. Åström, 'English Timber Imports', pp. 16–19. Williams, 'Naval Administration', pp. 303–28.

21 Talbott, *Pen and Ink Sailor*, pp. 45–60. Deane and Cole, *British Economic Growth*, p. 57. R. O. Roberts, 'Copper and Economic Growth in Britain, 1729–1784', *National Library of Wales Journal* X (1957), pp. 65–74. Lavery, *Ship of the Line* I, 207. Roger Burt, 'The Transformation of the Non-ferrous Metals Industries in the Seventeenth and Eighteenth Centuries', *EcHR* 2nd S. XLVIII (1995), pp. 23–45.

22 HMC *Rutland* III, 38, to Rutland, 27 Sep 1781.

23 Cock, ' "The Finest Invention in the World" '. Gallagher, *Byron's Journal*, p. 140. Fortescue, *George the Third* III, 509

No. 2,100. PRO: ADM 7/662 f. 21. Bingeman et al., 'Copper and Other Sheathing', pp. 221–2. Knight, 'Copper Sheathing'. J. R. Harris, *The Copper King: A Biography of Thomas Williams of Llanidan* (Liverpool, 1964), pp. 47–9; and 'Copper and Shipping', pp. 552–9. Talbott, *Pen and Ink Sailor*, pp. 104–9. Williams, 'Naval Administration', p. 442. Lavery, *Arming and Fitting*, pp. 62–5.

24 Talbott, *Pen and Ink Sailor*, pp. 99–103, 119–21. *BP* II, 56, 66–7, 71–2, 172–3, 178–94, 208–17 and 302–3. Knight, 'Royal Dockyards', pp. 49, 70 and 148. NMM: MID/2/37/16. Phillips, 'Evangelical Administrator', pp. 76–83.

25 Alan Birch, *The Economic History of the British Iron and Steel Industry 1784–1879* (London, 1967), pp. 34–5. H. J. Schubert, *History of the British Iron and Steel Industry* (London, 1957), p. 313. Deane and Cole, *British Economic Growth*, p. 221. Goodwin, 'Iron in Ship Construction', pp. 29–30. Harris, 'Copper and Shipping', p. 557. Curryer, *Anchors*, pp. 65–71. Ehrman, *Younger Pitt* III, 755 n.4. Eric Alexander, 'Adam Jellicoe: A Flawed Investment', *MM* LXXXIX (2003), pp. 340–42.

26 Coad, *Royal Dockyards*, pp. 44–5. Knight, 'Royal Dockyards', pp. 37–44. *BP* II, 198–208, 235–49 and 298–315. Phillips, 'Evangelical Administrator', p. 228. Talbott, *Pen and Ink Sailor*, pp. 115–29.

27 Talbott, *Pen and Ink Sailor*, pp. 122–9 and 132–5. *BP* II, 232–33, 287 and 342–5. Phillips, 'Evangelical Administrator', pp. 76–99. *HP 1754–90* II, 47–8 and 136.

28 Norman Baker, *Government and Contractors: The British Treasury and War Supplies, 1775–1783* (London, 1971), pp. 241 and 247–8. Syrett, 'Atkinson'. *BND* No. 271, pp. 463–6. Usher, 'Civil Administration', pp. 141–4.

29 Baker, *Naval Ordnance*, pp. 1–7. Caruana, *Sea Ordnance* II, 11–17 and 257–79. Edwards, 'Wilkinson', pp. 526–35. Tomlinson, 'Wealden Gunfounding', pp. 388 and 396.

30 West, *Gunpowder*, pp. 177–84. Caruana, *Sea Ordnance* II, 252–6. Wilkinson-Latham, *British Artillery*, pp. 21–3.

31 Bamford, *Forests and French Sea Power*, pp. 113–29 and 141–72. Crook, *Toulon*, pp. 17–18. Villiers, *Marine Royale* II, 519–20 and 525–8. Acerra, *Rochefort* III, 565–7. Llinares, *Marine, propulsion et technique* I, 114–20.

32 Acerra, *Rochefort* III, 537–9. Villiers, *Marine Royale* II, 521–3. Gay, 'Le Fer'; and *Histoire des ancres*, pp. 137–54. Edwards, 'Wilkinson', pp. 535–43. Llinares, *Marine, propulsion et technique* I, 127–34. Harris, *Industrial Espionage*, pp. 248–83.

33 Merino Navarro, *La Armada Española*, pp. 49–53, 66–70, 100–102, 182, 194–7, 220–223, 257, 277–8, 294–303 and 354–6; 'La Armada en el siglo XVIII' II, 115–16, 124 and 135. Mühlmann, *Die Reorganisation der Spanischen Kriegsmarine*, pp. 68–70. Antonio Lafuente and José Luis Peset, 'Politica cientifica y espionaje industrial en los viajes de Jorge Juan y Antonio de Uluoa (1748–1751)', *Mélanges de la Casa de Velázquez* XVII (1981), pp. 233–62. Fernández de Pinedo, 'Bloomery to Blast-furnace', pp. 21–8. *Las Reales Fábricas de Sargadelos, el Ejército y la Armada*, ed. Pedro López Gómez (Museo do Pobo Galego, Santiago de Compostela, 1994).

25 A Golden Chain or a Wooden Leg

1 Mackay, *Hawke Papers*, p. 228; to Admiralty, 8 Jun 1759.

2 Rodger, 'Officers' Careers', pp. 5–9; Graphs 1.2 and 9.3. PRO: ADM 118/84, note s.d. 22 Nov 1790. HC 1822 (37) XIX, 229. Wareham, *Star Captains*, pp. 74–8.

3 Vernon, *Voyages and Travels*, p. 293. Firth, *Naval Songs and Ballads*, p. 229

4 Frank R. Lewis, 'John Morris and the Cartagena Expedition, 1739–1740', *MM* XXVI (1940), pp. 257–69, at p. 261.

5 NMM: SAN/F/4/66–7. Rodger, 'Officers' Careers', pp. 6–7. Bracknall, 'Lieutenants of 1793', pp. 30–31 and 56–7. *DLN* V, 51. *WW*, p. 270.

6 Spavens, *Narrative*, p. 113.

7 Rodger, 'Lieutenants' Sea-Time'; and *WW*, p. 326. *BP* I, 285–6.

8 Raikes, *Brenton*, pp. 34–8. Brenton, *Brenton*, pp. 2–3.

9 Vernon, *Voyages and Travels*, p. 293. Rodger, 'Lieutenants' Sea-Time'. *WW*, pp. 297–8. Taylor, *Mathematical Practitioners*, pp. 14–15 and 36. Dillon, *Narrative* I, 24–6. Raigersfeld, *Life*, pp. 37–8. *NCCC* p. 88. Crawford, *Reminiscences*, p. 17. Gordon, *Gordon*, p. 7.

10 Howse, *Greenwich Time*, pp. 61–78; and 'Lunar Distance Method'. Ashley, 'Longitude'. W. E. May, 'How the Chronometer Went to Sea', *Antiquarian Horology* IX (1976), 6, pp. 638–63 (a reference I owe to Dr Andrew Cook and Mr Jonathan Betts). Avery, 'Maritime Trade', pp. 270 and 291. Laughton, 'Duncan Journals', p. 117. Tatum, *Serle Journal*, pp. 26–7. Penrose, *Trevenen*, pp. 53–4. Huskisson, *Eyewitness to Trafalgar*, pp. 60–61. Mascart, *Chevalier de Borda*, pp. 211–365. Hamilton, *Martin Papers* I, 123–4.

11 *WW*, pp. 263–72. Conway, *British Isles*, pp. 36–7 and 99. Bracknall, 'Lieutenants of 1793', p. 44.

12 Cross, *Banks of the Neva*, pp. 166–202. A. W. Brian Simpson, *Cannibalism and the Common Law* (London, 1986), pp. 114–16. Richard H. Warner, 'Captain John Deane: Mercenary, Diplomat and Spy', in *People of the Northern Seas*, ed. Lewis R. Fischer and Walter Minchinton (St John's, Newfoundland, 1992), pp. 157–73.

13 Neeser, *Shuldham Despatches*, p. 262. NMM: SAN/F/18/12 and F/25/4.

14 Gwyn, *Enterprising Admiral, passim.*

15 *VP*, pp. 81, 100–101 and 147. PRO: ADM 1/235, T. Cotes to Admiralty, 9 Nov 1757; ADM 1/236 f. 60; ADM 1/1787, A. Forrest to Anson, 5 Oct 1760; CO 142/31 f. 15; PROB 11/959 f. 301. NMM: DOU/4 pp. 210 and 220; UPC/2/118–19; UPC/3/3, 12, 14–15 and 29. *The Diaries of Sylvester Douglas (Lord Glenbervie)*, ed. Francis Bickley (London, 1928, 2 vols.) I, 11–12 (quoted).

16 Moore, *Memoirs*, pp. 2–73; cf. PRO: ADM 36/5009 and ADM 33/548, ML 102 and SB 469 for details tending to confirm the anecdote on p. 18.

17 *HP 1754–90* II, 400 (quoted). Farrington,

Biographical Index, p. 251. *KP* I, vii–ix. *ODNB*. Aspinall, *Prince of Wales* II, 354–5. Lavery, 'Keith'.

18 Laughton and Sulivan, *James Journal*.

19 *ODNB*. Leyland, *Blockade of Brest* I, 25 n.1. Gardner, *Recollections*, p. 113. *SpP* II, 91.

20 Parkinson, *Pellew*, pp. 3–11 and 48–9. Rodger, 'Boscawen', pp. 88–9. *ODNB*. Stirling, *Pages and Portraits* II, 256–8.

21 *WW*, pp. 263–72. Conway, *British Isles*, p. 37. NMM: ADM/B/129, Navy Board to Admiralty, 1 May 1745. Krajeski, *Cotton*, pp. 2–14. *HP 1754–90* II, 259–60. NMM: SAN/V/13 p. 154 and SAN/F/19/60.

22 Bourchier, *Codrington* I, 1.

23 Aspinall, *George III* I, xvii.

24 *WW*, pp. 260–63. Lincoln, *Representing the Royal Navy*, pp. 22–3.

25 *NCCC* p. 15, to [O.M.?] Lane, 17 Nov. 1787. His reference is to William Falconer, *An Universal Dictionary of the Marine . . .* (London, 1780).

26 *BNA* pp. 57–67. Thomas, 'Portsmouth Naval Academy'. Dickinson, 'Portsmouth Naval Academy'. Sullivan, 'Royal Academy'. Mackay, *Hawke Papers*, p. 403. Hamilton, *Martin Papers* I, 23. NMM: SAN/F/4/86. *WW*, p. 265.

27 *BND* No. 328 p. 546, E. Barker to S. Homfray, 18 Jul 1800.

28 HMC *Rutland* III, 60.

29 Rodger, 'Honour and Duty', pp. 433–35.

30 Laughton, 'Hood Papers', p. 227, to Sir S. Hood, 11 Jun 1779.

31 Philip Ziegler, *King William IV* (London, 1971), p. 73.

32 Edgar K. Thompson, 'The Outfit of a Naval Cadet in the Reign of George II', *MM* LXI (1975), pp. 181–2. Brenton, *St Vincent* I, 19–20 (cf. BL: Add. MSS 29914, f. 134). *KP* II, x. H. T. Dickinson, 'The Rodneys and the Bridges', *MM* LIX (1973), pp. 313–16. *DLN* I, 52–3, V, 310–11 and VI, 42–3. PRO: PRO 30/8/44 f. 46. Dillon, *Narrative* I, 20. Jennings, *Croker Papers* I, 48. Lewis, *Social History*, p. 38. Mark, *At Sea with Nelson*, pp. 98–9. Morrison, *Hamilton and Nelson Papers* II, 239. *SVL* II, 259 and 288. *The Rutherfurds of that Ilk and their Cadets*, ed. J. H. Rutherford (Edinburgh, 1884), no

continuous pagination; Capt. W. G. Rutherford to J. C. Beresford, 4 Aug 1805. Phillimore, *Parker* I, 5. Crawford, *Reminiscences* I, 17. Clarke and McArthur, *Nelson* II, 368. Laughton, 'Cathcart Letters', p. 287.

33 *WW*, pp. 273–302. Rodger, 'Officers' Careers'. Vergé-Franceschi, *La Marine française*, pp. 291–8. Taillemite, 'Le Recrutement des officiers', pp. 40–41. Michel Vergé-Franceschi, 'Les Gérontes à la mer', in Buchet, *L'Homme, la santé et la mer*, pp. 253–69.

34 *WW*, pp. 328–43. Dandeker, 'Patronage'. Baugh, 'Wager'.

35 WA: Vol. XIV f. 36. Russell, *Bedford Correspondence* I, 150–51 and 161. Bonner-Smith, *Barrington Papers* I, 3–8. *WW*, pp. 315–16.

36 NMM: SAN/V/13 pp. 244–5; cf. De Toy, 'Wellington's Admiral', pp. 44–5.

37 HMC *Rutland* III, 22, to Rutland, 15 Nov 1779. For Leinster see Rodger, *Insatiable Earl*, pp. 176–7.

38 *SaP* IV, 298.

39 Buckingham, *Memoirs* I, 369, to Buckingham, 1 Apr 1788.

40 Rodger, *Insatiable Earl*, pp. 172–92.

41 *WW*, pp. 252–8.

42 Edward Thompson, *A Sailor's Letters* (London, 1767, 2nd edn, 2 vols.) I, 141.

43 *DLN* I, 3. Gardner, *Recollections*, p. 34. Dillon, *Narrative* I, 44. Vernon, *Voyages and Travels*, p. 18. Hamilton, *Martin Papers* I, 25–6. Scarfe, *Innocent Espionage*, p. 172 n.20. Clarke and McArthur, *Nelson* I, 65. Raigersfeld, *Life*, p. 36. Boteler, *Recollections*, p. 6.

44 Lavery, *Nelson's Navy*, pp. 104–8. Jarrett, *Naval Dress*, pp. 31–69.

45 NMM: JOD/23.

46 *SL*, pp. 94 and 117. Cf. Hamilton, *Martin Papers* I, 119–21 and 341.

47 Thursfield, 'Cumby', p. 331; and 'Cullen', p. 57. Dillon, *Narrative* I, 346. Parkinson, *Eastern Seas*, pp. 351–2 and 439. *KP* II, 24–5 and III, 319–20. Duff, 'Trafalgar Order Book', p. 88. *SL*, p. 184. Tucker, *St Vincent* I, 132 and 410. Phillimore, *Parker* I, 123. Gardner, *Recollections*, pp. 107–8. Mark, *At Sea with Nelson*, pp. 82–3.

48 Lee, *Memoirs*, p. 47. Boteler, *Recollections*, p. 55.

49 George Landmann, *Adventures and Recollections of Colonel Landmann* (London, 1852, 2 vols.) II, 270.

50 Fraser, 'Green Memoranda', p. 91.

51 *The Private Correspondence of David Garrick* (London, 1831, 2 vols.) II, 186.

52 Mackay, *Hawke Papers*, p. 15. Hawke had been a lieutenant in the *Scarborough* in 1732.

53 NMM: SAN/F/24/47, to Sandwich, 14 Aug 1780.

54 *WW*, pp. 19–24. *SL*, pp. 129–32. Jarrett, *Naval Dress*, p. 53. *BND* No. 318, pp. 537–8. *KMN* III, 10–12. Dillon, *Narrative* I, 247. Rodger, 'Naval Chaplain'. Taylor, *Sea Chaplains*, pp. 150–70. *DLN* I, 150, 197 and 204.

55 Gardner, *Recollections, passim*.

56 Boog Watson, 'Two Naval Surgeons', pp. 218–19.

57 Coleridge, *Devonshire House*, p. 93, B. F. Coleridge to his father, [1804?].

58 Stirling, *Pages and Portraits* I, 24.

26 Dividing and Quartering

1 *BP* I, 308, to C. Middleton, 28 Dec [1779?]. Kempenfelt was perhaps optimistic in expecting landmen to be competent to hand and reef (i.e. aloft) in only three months.

2 Starkey, 'Market for Seafarers'. Usher, 'Impressment', p. 682. Robinson, 'Coasting Fleet'. Palmer and Williams, 'British Sailors,' pp. 100–2.

3 Rogers, 'Liberty Road'. Wood, 'London and Impressment'. Conway, 'Politics of Mobilization', pp. 1,182, 1,191–2 and 1,199. Rodger, 'Myth of Seapower'. *SaP* III, 26–9. Barrow, 'Noble Ann Affair'. Nagle, *Journal*, pp. 183–4.

4 Figures from Usher, 'Impressment', with detailed figures for the Impress Service from the Shelburne MSS in the W. L. Clements Library; but he is too schematic in assuming only two methods of recruitment (Impress Service and sea) and only two categories of recruit (volunteers and pressed); cf. *WW*, pp. 145–82 for recruitment during the Seven Years' War.

5 Conway, *British Isles*, pp. 38 and 151–2. Charnock, *Biographia Navalis* VI, 546–7 (preferred to *NC* II, 549).

6 *WW*, pp. 164–82. Hoffman, *Sailor*, p. 60. Nagle, *Journal*, pp. 184–90. Rogers, 'Liberty Road', pp. 70–71. Usher, 'Civil Administration', pp. 245–6 stresses the corrupt practices of press gangs, but seems to be generalizing from one or two cases.

7 NMM: ROD/1, to Capt. R. Roddam, 8 Jul 1777.

8 Richardson, *Mariner of England*, p. 67. Cf. for other examples Boteler, *Recollections*, p. 44; Crawford, *Reminiscences*, pp. 74–5; Nicol, *Life and Adventures*, p. 158.

9 D. B. Ellison, 'Letters from a Pressed Man', *NR* LXXXII (1994), pp. 65, 134, 281 and 424–5, at p. 281, G. Price to his brother, 8 May 1805.

10 Rogers, *Crowds, Culture and Politics*, p. 88, quoting a 1751 pamphlet by 'Philonauta' (Sir Charles Knowles). Cf. Russell, *Theatres of War*, p. 8.

11 Rogers, 'Vagrancy, Impressment'. Cf. Lemisch, 'Jack Tar in the Streets', p. 383: 'the Navy pressed because to be in the navy was in some sense to be a slave'.

12 Rodger, *Insatiable Earl*, pp. 202–3. Bromley, 'Navy and its Seamen', p. 153. Lloyd, *British Seaman*, pp. 136–7. *PH* XVIII, 1,259. BL: Add. MSS 9,344, f. 100. Conway, 'British Mobilization', pp. 69 and 72. Beattie, *Crime and the Courts*, pp. 532–3, has lists of men pardoned on condition of serving in army or Navy, but no indication if they were accepted.

13 PRO: SP 42/51 f. 235, to Weymouth, 3 Oct 1777.

14 Notably Nagle, *Journal*; see the editor's comments at p. xxi. Cf. Spavens, *Narrative*, pp. 113–14; Nicol, *Life and Adventures*.

15 Nagle, *Journal*, p. 77.

16 Mackay, *Hawke Papers*, p. 466; cf. Rodger, 'Boscawen', pp. 87–8.

17 *PH* XVIII, 1,261.

18 Mulgrave Castle MSS: VI, 11/12, to Mulgrave, 24 Dec 1776.

19 *DLN* I, 76, H. Nelson to E. Locker, 12 Jul 1783.

20 *HCC* p. 27. Rodger, *Insatiable Earl*, p. 182. *SaP* III, 32–3 and IV, 73.

21 Usher, 'Impressment', pp. 682–5. PRO: ADM 49/3, musters of transports in N. America, 1776–9, contain many examples of desertion from transports to the Navy.

22 Blane, *Diseases of Seamen*, p. 229.

23 One in 862 in the month of April 1782, which I have expressed as an annual rate, but this was an especially healthy month: Blane, *Diseases of Seamen*, in Lloyd, *Health of Seamen*, p. 146.

24 Blane, *Diseases of Seamen*, p. 172.

25 Blane, *Diseases of Seamen* and *Select Dissertations, passim* (and extracts in Lloyd, *Health of Seamen*); cf. his correspondence in Rodney, *Letter-Books*. Jamieson, 'War in the Leeward Islands', pp. 80–94. Haycock, 'Dysentery'. Rodger, 'Medicine and Science', pp. 340–41. Cook, 'Practical Medicine', p. 25.

26 Blane, *Diseases of Seamen*, pp. 87–8. Pasley, *Sea Journals*, p. 150. Cf. Laurent Sueur, 'Les Maladies des marins français de la Compagnie des Indes et de la Marine Royale durant la 2e moitié du XVIIIe siècle', *RH* 589 (1994), pp. 121–30, at pp. 121–2.

27 Scarfe, *Innocent Espionage*, p. 172; this was the *Diadem*, Captain Thomas Symonds.

28 Le Goff, 'L'Impact des prises', pp. 110–17. Anderson, 'Prisoners of War'. Dull, *American Independence*, pp. 144–5. Alain Cabantous, *Dix mille marins face à l'océan* (Paris, 1991), pp. 191–2. Angel O'Dogherty, 'La Matrícula de Mar en el reinado de Carlos III', *AEA* IX (1952), pp. 347–70.

29 Lavery, *Arming and Fitting*, pp. 178–84. *SL*, pp. 241–5 and 257–62.

30 *SL*, p. 622, quoting Patton, *Strictures on Naval Discipline*.

31 Liardet, *Professional Recollections*, p. 133.

32 Nagle, *Journal*, p. 143. William Bradley was first lieutenant of the chartered transport *Waaksamheyd* bringing the crew of the wrecked *Sirius* home from New South Wales.

33 Vernon, *Voyages and Travels*, pp. 65–7. Thursfield, 'Cullen', pp. 69–70. Hoffman, *Sailor*, pp. 14–16. Dillon, *Narrative* I, 229–30. Spavens, *Narrative*, p. 71. *SL*,
p. 474. Earle, *Sailors*, pp. 96–7. *The Endeavour Journal of Joseph Banks 1768–1771*, ed. J. C. Beaglehole (Sydney, 1962, 2 vols.) I, 176–7. Huskisson, *Eyewitness to Trafalgar*, p. 19. [Janet Schaw], *Journal of a Lady of Quality*, ed. E. W. Andrews (New Haven, 1921), p. 70. Michael Durey, 'Crossing the Line in 1799: Plebeian Moral Economy on the High Seas', *MM* LXXX (1994), pp. 209–14. Moody, 'Irish Countryman' IV, 234–5 and V, 149. Barker, *Greenwich Hospital*, pp. 175–80. Richardson, *Mariner of England*, p. 171. These examples are drawn from the period roughly 1700 to 1815, but the ceremony was already ancient, and has not greatly changed today, apart from a reduction in the quantities of alcohol.

34 Pasley, *Sea Journals*, p. 74; cf. pp. 133 and 247. 'Summum bonum' = supreme good.

35 Gardner, *Recollections*, p. 60. Spavens, *Narrative*, p. 67. Cormack and Jones, *Corporal Todd*, pp. 24–5. Thursfield, 'Letters from the Lower Deck', p. 368.

36 *BNA* p. 303, quoting Commissioner Richard Hughes of Portsmouth in 1742. Thomas Trotter, *An Essay, Medical, Philosophical, and Chemical, on Drunkenness, and its Effects on the Human Body* (London, 2nd edn 1804), p. 49; the 'late war' is the American War.

37 Gardner, *Recollections*, pp. 50–52; cf. Nicol, *Life and Adventures*, p. 52.

38 Inglefield, *Naval Actions*, p. 129.

39 Brock, 'Letter Book', p. 682.

40 Inglefield, *Naval Actions*, pp. 130–31. *BP* I, 42. Laughton, 'Duncan Journals', p. 109.

41 Earle, *Sailors*, pp. 89–92. Blane, *Diseases of Seamen*, p. 288. Raigersfeld, *Life*, p. 43.

42 Spavens, *Narrative*, pp. 165–6.

43 Pasley, *Sea Journals*, p. 67; cf. p. 135.

44 Spavens, *Narrative*, p. 71.

45 Davis, *Narrative*, p. 36.

46 Thomas Swaine, *The Universal Directory for taking alive or destroying Rats and Mice* (London, 1783), pp. 75–9. *WW*, pp. 69–70 and 92–3. Steer, 'Blockade of Brest', p. 237. Kelly, *Eighteenth Century Seaman*, p. 26. Gordon, *Gordon*, p. 7. Morriss and Saxby, *Channel Fleet*, p. 421. Raigersfeld, *Life*, pp. 20–21 (quoted).

47 Some order books for this period are printed in Clarke and McArthur, *Nelson* I, 366–7 (Suckling's suggestions to his nephew), *BP* I, 39–45 (Middleton, *Ardent*, 1775); *KP* I, 29–42 and *NDAR* IX, 55–73 (Howe, 1776–7); Brock, 'Letter Book' (Duckworth, various ships 1776–82); *SL*, pp. 92–118 (Pr. William Henry, *Pegasus*, 1786–8); Hamilton, *Martin Papers* I, 341–8 (Pr William Henry, *Andromeda*, 1788).

48 Inglefield, *Naval Actions*, pp. 126–7. I am grateful to Mr Sam Willis for drawing my attention to this passage.

49 Nagle, *Journal*, p. 58.

50 Hoffman, *Sailor*, p. 60. 'Entered' here means volunteered.

51 Nagle, *Journal*, pp. 66, 86 and 107. Lincoln, *Representing the Royal Navy*, p. 26. Richardson, *Mariner of England*, p. 68. Davis, *Narrative*, pp. 70–72. Gardner, *Recollections*, p. 37. *SL*, pp. 380–82.

52 Davis, *Narrative*, pp. 13, 23 and 64 (quoted). Davis was taken in the rebel privateer *Jason* in 1779 and pressed into the *Surprise*, Capt. Samuel Reeve, who treated him with humanity.

53 Brock, 'Letter Book', p. 691.

54 Murray, *Durham*, pp. 4–6. *SL*, p. 613. Gardner, *Recollections*, p. 139. Jamieson, 'Tyranny of the Lash', pp. 60–62.

55 *SaP* III, 130 and 246–7. BL: Add. MSS 35193, ff. 197–8. Gilbert, 'Nature of Mutiny', p. 114 (quoted). For Jacobs see *WW*, p. 232. He was a Swede (PRO: ADM 106/2972); Green, *Anglo-Jewry*, p. 26, seems to be mistaken in claiming him as a Jew.

56 Barrow, *Howe*, pp. 165–8. Geddes, *Portsmouth*, pp. 5–6. Beatson, *Memoirs* VI, 416–18. *WW*, pp. 240–41 deals with demobilization mutinies in 1763.

57 There is a vast literature on this affair, much of it well worth avoiding, and scarcely any of it written by anyone who knows about the Navy. Gavin Kennedy, *Bligh* (London, 1978), is a serviceable life; Neil Rennie, *Far-Fetched Facts: The Literature of Travel and the Idea of the South Seas* (Oxford, 1995), pp. 141–59 gives a good summary of the mutiny and its reception; Greg Dening, *Mr Bligh's Bad Language: Passion, Power and Theatre on the Bounty* (Cambridge, 1992), pp. 57–63, and K. A. Reimann, ' "Great as he is in his own good opinion": The *Bounty* Mutiny and Lieutenant Bligh's Construction of Self ', in *Tradition in Transition: Women Writers, Marginal Texts, and the Eighteenth-Century Canon*, ed. Alvaro Ribeiro and James G. Basker (Oxford, 1996), pp. 198–218, offer interesting ideas.

58 *KP* I, 32. *SL*, pp. 95 (quoted), 151 and 183. Parkinson, *Pellew*, p. 67; and *Eastern Seas*, p. 439. Dillon, *Narrative* II, 302. Jackson, *Perilous Adventures*, p. 122. Phillimore, *Parker* I, 197 and 206. Duff, 'Trafalgar Order Book', p. 93.

59 Kemp, 'Boscawen's Letters to his Wife', pp. 181 and 198. *SL*, pp. 151 and 462. Perrin, 'Copenhagen', p. 448.

60 Boog Watson, 'Two Naval Surgeons', p. 215.

61 Hinchliffe, 'Norris Letters', p. 78. *NDAR* IX, 60. *KP* I, 36 and 40. Kemp, 'Boscawen's Letters to his Wife', p. 229. *WW*, pp. 55–9.

62 Tatum, *Serle Journal*, p. 11. Cf. Rodger, 'Naval Chaplain', p. 35.

63 Spavens, *Narrative*, pp. 108–9. Cormack and Jones, *Corporal Todd*, p. 27. Dillon, *Narrative* I, 30. *SL*, p. 105. Naish, *Nelson's Letters to his Wife*, pp. 56–7. Kemp, 'Boscawen's Letters to his Wife', p. 178. Earle, *Sailors*, pp. 91–5.

64 Lowe, *Portsmouth Division*, p. lv.

65 Lowe, *Portsmouth Division*, Introduction (an excellent brief survey). Marini, 'Corps of Marines', pp. 187–206. Inglefield, *Naval Actions*, pp. 139–40. *KP* I, 25.

66 Cormack and Jones, *Corporal Todd*, p. 26.

67 Lowe, *Portsmouth Division*, Introduction. *SL*, pp. 207–8 and 223–33. Cormack and Jones, *Corporal Todd*, pp. 23–31. *KP* I, 31. *BNA* pp. 144–5. W. B. Rowbotham, 'The 97th Regiment at the Action on the Dogger Bank, 1781', *JSAHR* XIX (1940), pp. 16–18.

68 Stark, *Female Tars*, p. 78.

69 Nicol, *Life and Adventures*, p. 43.

70 Stark, *Female Tars*, passim. *BP* I, 45. Gardner, *Recollections*, pp. 9, 57 and 212.

Dillon, *Narrative* I, 43. Nagle, *Journal*, pp. 62, 85 and 119. Scarfe, *Innocent Espionage*, p. 172 n.20. *DLN* I, 108. Raikes, *Brenton*, pp. 56–7. Earle, *Sailors*, pp. 101–3. *WW*, pp. 75–81. Gilbert, 'Buggery'.

71 Earle, *A City Full of People*, pp. 76–81 is almost the only approach to this subject in English, though analogous studies of merchant seamen and fishing communities have been written in French, German and Danish.

27 Science versus Technology

1 Rodger, 'Form and Function', pp. 85–6; and 'Enlightenment'.

2 Acerra, *Rochefort* III, 589 and 598. Acerra and Meyer, *Marines et Révolution*, p. 99.

3 Bromley, 'Second Hundred Years War'. Rodger, 'Form and Function', pp. 86–7.

4 Acerra and Zysberg, *L'Essor des marines*, pp. 121–30. Acerra, *Rochefort* II, 433–70; and 'Les Constructeurs'. Boudriot and Berti, *French Frigate*, pp. 36–7. Pritchard, 'Shipwright to Naval Constructor'. Antoine Picon, 'Technique', in *Dictionnaire européen des Lumières*, ed. Michel Delon (Paris, 1997), pp. 1,025–30. Lavery, *Ship of the Line* II, 17–25. Ollivier, *Remarks*, pp. 139–44. Hemingway, 'Surveyors of the Navy', pp. 17–21. PRO: ADM 7/662, ff. 9–10.

5 Hankins, *Science*, pp. 9–12, 20–21 and 28–9, 171–3. Keith Thomas, 'Numeracy in Early Modern England', *TRHS* 5th S. XXXVII (1987), pp. 103–32. Brewer, *Sinews of Power*, pp. 228–30. Patricia Fara, *Sympathetic Attractions: Magnetic Practices, Beliefs, and Symbolism in Eighteenth-Century England* (Princeton, 1996), pp. 21, 123–4 and 145. Mémain, *Rochefort*, pp. 697–9. A. R. Hall, *Ballistics in the Seventeenth Century* (Cambridge, 1952), pp. 163–4. Azar Gat, *The Origins of Military Thought, from the Enlightenment to Clausewitz* (Oxford, 1989), pp. 26–7. Harris, *Industrial Espionage*, pp. 561–2. Robin Briggs, 'The Académie Royale des Sciences and the Pursuit of Utility', *P&P* 131 (1991), pp. 38–88. Rodger, 'Enlightenment'.

6 Fincham, *Naval Architecture*, pp. xiii and xlvi–xlix. Boudriot and Berti, *Les Vaisseaux de 50 et 64 canons*, pp. 11–13 and 23–7. Mascart, *Chevalier de Borda*, pp. 83–90. C. Truesdell, 'Euler's Contribution to the Theory of Ships and Mechanics', *Centaurus* XXVI (1983), pp. 323–35. Timmerman, *Das Eindringen der Naturwissenschaft*, pp. 15 and 22–8. Harris, *Chapman*, pp. 74–83. Lavery, *Ship of the Line* II, 23. Llinares, *Marine, propulsion et technique* I, 148–58. Boudriot, *Seventy-Four Gun Ship*, I, 30–33. Pritchard, 'Shipwright to Naval Constructor', pp. 16–17. Meyer, 'L'Evolution de la guerre marine', pp. 129–36. Brown, 'Form and Speed', pp. 298–307. Villiers, *Marine Royale* II, 695–6. Rodger, 'Enlightenment'. Demerliac, *Nomenclature* III, 46.

7 '. . . muy útil nos será su viaje, porque en punto de mecánica somos ignorantísimos sin conocerlo, que es lo peor'. *AE* VI, 377–8, to Spanish ambassador in France, 24 Mar 1749.

8 Ollivier, *Remarks*. Bruijn, *Admiraliteit van Amsterdam*, pp. 9–12; and 'Engelse scheepsbouwers op de Amsterdamse Admiraliteitswerf in de achttiende eeuw: enige aspecten', *Medelingen van de Nederlandse Vereniging voor Zeegeschiedenis* 25 (1972), pp. 18–24. Hoving and Lemmers, *In Tekening gebracht*, pp. 13–32 and 142–3. *BNA* pp. 278–9. Antonio Lafuente and José Luis Peset, 'Politica cientifica y espionaje industrial en los viajes de Jorge Juan y Antonio de Uluoa (1748–1751)', *Mélanges de la Casa de Velázquez* XVII (1981), pp. 233–62. Merino Navarro, *La Armada Española*, pp. 49–53 and 100–102. Mühlmann, *Die Reorganisation der Spanischen Kriegsmarine*, pp. 68–74. PRO: SP 42/35, ff. 48–9. Bjerg and Erichsen, *Danske orlogsskibe* I, 33–45. Rodger, 'Form and Function', pp. 88–9.

9 *BND* No. 287, pp. 491–3. Lavery, *Ship of the Line*, I, 206. Rodger, 'Form and Function'.

10 Lavery, *Ship of the Line* I, 70–85; *Arming and Fitting*, pp. 117–19; and 'Rebuilding'. Ollivier, *Remarks*, pp. 35–40. *BNA*

pp. 208–9. Goodwin, *Construction and Fitting*, pp. 241–61. *BND* Nos. 279–80, pp. 481–3. Caruana, *Sea Ordnance* II, 43–62. *VP*, pp. 348–52. Winfield, *50-Gun Ship*, pp. 46–62.

11 Pool, *Navy Board Contracts*, p. 79.

12 *BNA* p. 224, to Admiralty, 18 Jun 1744.

13 Hemingway, 'Surveyors of the Navy', pp. 138–52, 172 and 195–6. *BNA* p. 199. *BND* No. 282 p. 484.

14 *BNA* pp. 200 and 225–32. *BAW*, pp. 251–3. Lavery, *Ship of the Line* I, 90–95 and 202–5. *BND* Nos. 281–4, pp. 483–90. PRO: ADM 3/49 ff. 104 and 244; ADM 3/51, 7 and 20 Jun 1745.

15 1,793 tons burthen by English measure, against 1,130 to 1,230 tons; 838 lb broadside (*livre de Paris*, equivalent to 905 lbs avoirdupois) against 522 lbs. Lavery, *First Invincible*, pp. 31–4.

16 Gardiner, *Frigates of the Napoleonic Wars*, pp. 139–41. Rodger, 'Form and Function', pp. 93–4.

17 *BND* No. 285, pp. 490–91. PRO: ADM 106/2116, 22 Sep 1749, 24 Apr and 28 May 1750. Lavery, *Ship of the Line* I, 96. Glete, *Navies and Nations* I, 267. Hemingway, 'Surveyors of the Navy', pp. 168–9.

18 Gardiner, *First Frigates*, pp. 93–117; *Frigates of the Napoleonic Wars*, pp. 87–98 and 131–41; and 'Frigate Design', pp. 83–92. Boudriot, *Seventy-Four Gun Ship*, and Goodwin, *Construction and Fitting* give exhaustive detail on French and British framing and fastening practices. *BNA*, pp. 234–5. Llinares, *Marine, propulsion et technique* I, 99–142, 156–68 and 177–201; II, 351–2. Acerra, *Rochefort* II, 388–9 and III, 552–85. Acerra and Meyer, *Marines et Révolution*, pp. 74–5. Boudriot and Berti, *French Frigate*, pp. 130–37. Acerra and Zysberg, *L'Essor des marines*, pp. 79–85. Beauchesne, *La construction navale*, pp. 137–8. Ollivier, *Remarks*, pp. 113, 136 and 161. Glete, *Navies and Nations* I, 247 makes the apt analogy with the battle-cruiser.

19 Bourdé de Villehuet, *Le Manœuvrier*, pp. 190–92.

20 '. . . doit être supérieure pour la marche et ordinairement on lui sacrifie tout pour cet avantage; on le fait plus léger de bois pour le rendre plus flottant et lui conserver une belle batterie; on s'applique moins à y appliquer les liaisons fortes, solides et multipliées, parce que le jeu de toutes les parties facilite la marche . . . En partant de ce principe, on doute que les constructeurs du roi s'exposent à entreprendre de bâtir des vaisseaux qui n'auraient pas toutes les qualités qui demande un vaisseau de guerre: ils craindraient de perdre leur réputation, car, pour eux, c'est le comble de la gloire que de faire des vaisseaux qui aient une belle batterie et qui marchent supérieurement.' Beauchesne, *La construction navale*, pp. 137–8, quoting an anonymous constructor about 1763.

21 'Les constructeurs des ports subalternes font tous des ouvrages de charlatan; ils font des bâtiments fort légers, fort longs et fort mal liés parce qu'ils sacrifient tout à la marche, et qu'ils sont bien certains de l'obtenir par là. C'est la première campagne qui donne la réputation aux bâtiments et aux constructeurs . . . nous avons été obligé de relier, tout de nouveau icy, à grand frais, pour les mettre en état de faire de secondes campagnes où ces bâtiments perdent leur marche précédemment vantée.' Mascart, *Chevalier de Borda*, pp. 390–91.

22 Brown, 'Form and Speed'; and 'The Speed of Sailing Warships, 1793–1840; an Examination of the Evidence', in Freeman, *Les Empires*, pp. 155–94. Gardiner, *Heavy Frigate*, pp. 108–11. Lavery, *Arming and Fitting*, passim.

23 Acerra, *Rochefort* II, 305–7, 341–3 and 380–81. Villiers, *Marine Royale* I, 216–21. *MMF* II, 93–8. Pritchard, *Louis XV's Navy*, pp. 129–30. Meyer and Acerra, 'La Marine française vue par elle-même', pp. 231–5. Boudriot and Berti, *French Frigate*, pp. 12–35 and 68–88. Acerra and Zysberg, *L'Essor des marines*, pp. 67–9.

24 Hemingway, 'Surveyors of the Navy', p. 103, quoting PRO: ADM 1/3588 f. 669, Navy Board to Admiralty, 27 June 1689.

25 Gardiner, *First Frigates*, pp. 7–9. Hemingway, 'Surveyors of the Navy', pp. 103–4, 123 and 144.

26 WA: Vol. XVI f. 73. Cf. *BNA*, p. 232 for the resulting order. 'Mr Slade the Builder' is Benjamin Slade, Master Shipwright of Plymouth and Anson's then favourite constructor; not to be confused with his younger kinsman Thomas. 'The body' means the underwater lines.

27 *BND* No. 283, pp. 485–6. Hemingway, 'Surveyors of the Navy', p. 165. Vaughan, *Commodore Walker*, pp. 40 and 80–90. It is fair to add that the *Médée*'s new owners had considerably increased her armament.

28 Bellabarba and Osculati, *Royal Caroline*, pp. 10–13 and 17–21. Gardiner, 'Frigate Design', pp. 4–12 and 80–92; and *First Frigates*, pp. 10–19 and 90–117. Bonner-Smith, *Barrington Papers* I, 12–15. Besides what is printed in these sources, some of the more interesting correspondence on early British frigate design is: StRO: D 615/P(S)/1/9/21–2, B. Slade to Anson, 31 May and 21 Jul 1747; D 615/P(S)/1/9/34, J. Goodwin to Anson, 16 Mar 1748. NMM: UPC/3/8, E. Wheeler to Anson, 2 Oct 1757. PRO: ADM 7/658 p. 55. BL: Add. MSS 15955 f. 119, W. Bately to Anson, 5 Jun 1747; f. 402, R. Gwynn to Anson, 27 Sep 1747.

29 Gardiner, *First Frigates*, pp. 22–8 and 42–6; *Heavy Frigate*, pp. 14–16. Boudriot and Berti, *French Frigate*, pp. 174–92.

30 Goodwin, *20-Gun Ship Blandford*, pp. 7–8. *BP* I, 18–19. NMM: MID/8/1/11; and DOU/4 p. 6. Lyon, *Sailing Navy List*, *passim*, for the various classes. Gardiner, *Fleet Battle and Blockade*, pp. 113–15; and *Campaign of Trafalgar*, pp. 105–7. Lavery, *Nelson's Navy*, pp. 52–7. Llinares, *Marine, propulsion et technique* I, 38–46. *DLN* III, 256.

31 *BND* Nos. 289 and 295, pp. 493–5 and 504–5. A. G. E. Jones, 'Sir Thomas Slade 1703/4–1771', *MM* LXIII (1977), pp. 224–6. Gardiner, *First Frigates*, pp. 22–37. Lavery, *Ship of the Line* I, 96–102. *ODNB*.

32 Baugh, 'National Institution', p. 125. Glete, *Navies and Nations* II, 383–6.

33 *Invincible, Vigilant, Superb*. On these names see Martine Acerra, 'La Symbolique des noms de navires de guerre dans la marine française, 1661–1815', *HES* XVI (1997), pp. 45–61.

34 Moya Blanco, 'La arquitectura naval', pp. 235–42. Manera Regueyra, 'El apogeo de la Marina Española', pp. 204–22. Gonzalez-Aller Hierro, 'El navio de tres puentes', pp. 56–60. Harbron, *Trafalgar*, pp. 40–46.

35 Acerra and Meyer, *Marines et Révolution*, pp. 66–72, 91 and 190. Meyer, 'L'Evolution de la guerre marine', pp. 123–8. Llinares, *Marine, propulsion et technique* I, 171–81. Acerra, *Rochefort* II, 361–6. Mascart, *Chevalier de Borda*, pp. 482–3. Taillemite, *L'Histoire ignorée*, pp. 287–8. Masson, *Histoire de la Marine* I, 392–3.

36 'Imitons le fini de leur main d'œuvre dans la charpente qui contribue à la durée par las justesse des assemblages, imitons les proportions vraiment maritimes de leur mâture, la coupe de leurs voiles triangulaires, la solidité de leur gréement, la perfection de leur poulies, celles de leurs cordages, ayons leur cabestan, leur câbles et surtout leurs ancres qui ont plus de tenue que les nôtres, étudions leur pratique dans la manœuvre, leur distribution pour la faciliter, tachons de nous approprier leur discipline et tenue intérieure d'où résultent tous les avantages qui tiennent à l'ésprit d'ordre et de subordination sans lesquelles il n'y a point d'armée ni sur mer ni sur terre . . .' Llinares, *Marine, propulsion et technique* II, 352.

37 'Plus savant que les nôtres': Harris, *Industrial Espionage*, p. 529.

38 Llinares, *Marine, propulsion et technique* I, 53–69, 105–27 and 177–81.

39 *KP* II, 376, to Keith, 26 Jul 1801.

40 Pearsall, 'Landings on the French Coast', pp. 213–23. Boscawen, 'Landing Craft'.

41 Bingeman, 'Gunlocks'. Caruana, *Sea Ordnance* II, 389–95. Lavery, *First Invincible*, p. 54. Bonner-Smith, *Barrington Papers* I, 16–17. Pope, *At 12 Mr Byng was Shot*, p. 321. Douglas, *Naval Gunnery*, pp. 397–400. Boudriot and Berti, *L'Artillerie de mer*, pp. 80–81.

42 Talbott, *Pen and Ink Sailor*, pp. 61–72. Lavery, *Ship of the Line* I, 116 and II, 151;

and 'Carronades and Blomefield Guns', pp. 15–19. *BND* Nos. 291–2 pp. 496–9. Gardiner, *Heavy Frigate*, pp. 97–104. Caruana, *Sea Ordnance* II, 161–86 and 195–211. Boudriot and Berti, *L'Artillerie de mer*, p. 99.

43 Lavery, 'Carronades and Blomefield Guns', pp. 22–6. Gardiner, *Frigates of the Napoleonic Wars*, pp. 114–20 and 128–30. Caruana, *Sea Ordnance* II, 284–354. Wilkinson-Latham, *British Artillery*, pp. 26–33.

44 Lloyd and Craig, 'Congreve's Rockets'. Wilkinson-Latham, *British Artillery*, pp. 34–7. This Congreve is not to be confused with his father Major-General Sir William, whom he succeeded in 1814 as Comptroller of the Royal Laboratory at Woolwich.

45 Lavery, *Ship of the Line* I, 129–40; and *Nelson's Navy*, pp. 35–48. Gardiner, *Heavy Frigate*, pp. 26–94; and *Frigates of the Napoleonic Wars*, pp. 9–30, 87–8 and 131–51. Steer, 'Blockade of Brest', pp. 114–15. *BND* Nos. 295 and 297, pp. 504–7. Morriss and Saxby, *Channel Fleet*, pp. 94, 296 and 309. Dillon, *Narrative* II, 283–4.

46 Gardiner, *Frigates of the Napoleonic Wars*, pp. 25–7, 34–9 and 56–74. Lambert, 'Empire and Seapower'. Wadia, *Bombay Dockyard*, pp. 194–201. Mann, *Flottenbau und Forstbetrieb*, pp. 21–53.

47 Morriss, *Royal Dockyards*, pp. 36–8; and 'The Admiralty and the East India Company (1770–1820)', in Haudrère, *Les Flottes des Compagnies des Indes*, pp. 255–63, at p. 262. Fincham, *Naval Architecture*, pp. 197–207. Lavery, *Ship of the Line* I, 140–50. Goodwin, *Construction and Fitting*, pp. 101–5. Gardiner, *Frigates of the Napoleonic Wars*, pp. 74–86 and 98–112. *BND* No. 299, pp. 509–11. *BP* III, 273.

48 Gardiner, *Heavy Frigate*, pp. 45–9; and *Nelson against Napoleon*, pp. 102–4.

49 Alex Roland, *Underwater Warfare in the Age of Sail* (Bloomington, Indiana, 1978), pp. 91–113. Wallace Hutcheon Jr, *Robert Fulton, Pioneer of Undersea Warfare* (Annapolis, Md., 1981), pp. 31–92.

50 Hall, *British Strategy*, pp. 45–6. *BP* II,

260–61. Gardiner, *Nelson against Napoleon*, pp. 85–7. Winfield, *50-Gun Ship*, p. 121.

51 Chapelle, *American Sailing Navy*, pp. 98–9, 127–34 and 237–8. Canney, *Sailing Warships*, pp. 23–43. Hagan, *This People's Navy*, pp. 32–7. Gardiner, *Naval War of 1812*, p. 31; and *Frigates of the Napoleonic Wars*, pp. 96–7. Robert W. Love Jr, *History of the U.S. Navy. I: 1775–1941* (Harrisburg, Pa., 1992), p. 53.

52 Gardiner, *Frigates of the Napoleonic Wars*, pp. 48–51. N. H. G. Hurst, ' "Magnificent" Hayes', *MM* LXVIII (1982), pp. 28–30. Hayes owed his nickname to having saved the *Magnificent* from shipwreck by a dramatic feat of seamanship. He was the great-nephew and heir of Adam Hayes, master shipwright of Deptford.

53 Smith, '*For the Purposes of Defense*', p. 3; and 'A Means to an End', p. 111.

54 Smith, '*For the Purposes of Defense*'; 'Jefferson's Naval Militia'; and 'A Means to an End'. Tucker, *Gunboat Navy*; and 'Jeffersonian Gunboats'.

28 Order and Anarchy

1 Minto, *Minto* II, 121, Sir G. Elliot to Lady Elliot, 7 Mar 1793.

2 Ehrman, *The Younger Pitt* II, 206–58. Philip Schofield, 'British Politicians and French Arms: The Ideological War of 1793–1795', *History* LXXVII (1992), pp. 183–201. Duffy, ' "Particular Service" '; and 'British Diplomacy', pp. 128–31.

3 Mackesy, 'Strategic Problems', p. 150.

4 Duffy, *Soldiers, Sugar and Seapower*, pp. 3–25.

5 Crook, *Toulon*, pp. 126–59; and 'Federalism and the French Revolution: The Revolt of Toulon in 1793', *History* LXV (1980), pp. 383–97. Cormack, *Revolution*, pp. 151–62 and 173–214. Henwood and Monage, *Brest*, pp. 53–234. Jennifer Mori, 'The British Government and the Bourbon Restoration: The Occupation of Toulon, 1793', *HJ* XL (1997), pp. 699–719. Ehrman, *Younger Pitt* II, 303–18. Ware, 'Toulon, 1793'. Rose,

Hood. Allardyce, *Keith*, pp. 64–82. Acerra and Meyer, *Marines et Révolution*, pp. 86–7. *AE* VIII, 33–9. *MF* III, 58–93. Brun, *Port de Toulon* II, 251–3.

6 Barrow, *Smith* I, 97–8, 128–35 and 151–6. Morrison, *Hamilton and Nelson Papers* I, 183–7 and 211. Brenton, *Naval History* I, 113. Buckland, *Miller Papers*, pp. 1–7, quoting (p. 6) Miller to his father, 13 Jan 1794.

7 Muir and Esdaile, 'Strategic Planning'. Duffy, *Soldiers, Sugar and Seapower*, p. 41 (quoted) and 52–6. Ehrman, *Younger Pitt* II, 261–326. *SpP* I, xix and 51–2.

8 Meaning the French part of what the British called the Windward Islands. There is a linguistic trap here, for the French 'Iles du Vent' are the English Windward and Leeward Islands together – the whole Lesser Antilles – and the 'Iles sous le Vent' are the Greater Antilles.

9 Duffy, *Soldiers, Sugar and Seapower*, pp. 113–14.

10 Duffy, *Soldiers, Sugar and Seapower*, pp. 42–134; and 'War, Revolution', pp. 118–19. Geggus, *Slavery, War, and Revolution*, pp. 100–124. Fewster, 'Prize-money'; and 'Jay Treaty'. Willyams, *West Indies*, is a defence of Grey and Jervis by Jervis's chaplain.

11 Aspinall, *George III* II, 290. Morriss and Saxby, *Channel Fleet*, pp. 1–4. Cooper, 'Methods of Blockade', pp. 524–8. Henwood and Monange, *Brest*, pp. 31–234. Hampson, *La Marine de l'An II*, pp. 71–159. Cormack, *Revolution*, pp. 215–74. *MF* III, 312–14.

12 The best modern accounts of this campaign are Duffy and Morriss, *Glorious First of June*; Masson, *Histoire de la Marine* I, 302–7; Cormack, *Revolution*, pp. 277–85; Creswell, *British Admirals*, pp. 186–9 and 198–213; Tunstall, *Naval Warfare*, pp. 205–10; Warner, *Glorious First of June*. Older treatments of varying politics are Lévy-Schneider, *Jeanbon Saint-André* I, 795–872; Havard, *Les ports de guerre* II, 366–89; Brenton, *Naval History* I, 129–51; *MF* III, 129–64. Some documents and narratives are: NMM: ELL/400/72; Jackson, *Great Sea Fights* I, 4–193 and 309–42; Morriss and Saxby,

Channel Fleet, pp. 34–41; Perrin, 'Brunswick–Vengeur Engagement'; *HCC*, pp. 44–6 (quoted p. 44); *NCCC*, pp. 19–24; Owen, 'Collingwood Letters', pp. 156–60; and 'Glorious First of June'; Dillon, *Narrative* I, 119–39; Long, *Naval Yarns*, pp. 164–71; Hamilton, *Martin Papers* I, 193; Bourchier, *Codrington* I, 13–29; Mrs Aubrey Le Blond, *Charlotte Sophie, Countess Bentinck: Her Life and Times, 1715–1800* (London, 1912, 2 vols.) II, 284–8.

13 Warner, *Glorious First of June*, pp. 94–100. Hamilton, *Martin Papers* III, 137. *BND* No. 325, p. 543. Ehrman, *Younger Pitt* II, 349. *HCC*, pp. 48–50.

14 McErlean, 'Corsica 1794'. Godfrey, 'Corsica, 1794'. Ehrman, *Younger Pitt* II, 345–7. Naish, *Nelson's Letters to his Wife*, pp. 151–69. Warner, *Portrait of Lord Nelson*, pp. 85–6. *DLN* I, 362–478. Oman, *Nelson*, pp. 141–51.

15 Minto, *Minto* II, 235, to Lady Elliot, 28 Mar 1794.

16 The new Secretary of State for War should not be confused with the existing Secretary at War, a minister of lower rank.

17 *SpP* I, 6–10. Ehrman, *The Younger Pitt* II, 403–18. Crimmin, 'Admiralty Administration', pp. 22–5. Morriss and Saxby, *Channel Fleet*, pp. 48–9.

18 Knight, 'Howe', p. 297. *HCC*, p. 66. *SpP* I, 26–7. Morriss and Saxby, *Channel Fleet*, pp. 16–18 and 26–8. Aspinall, *George III* II, 289–90. Duffy, 'Devon and Naval Strategy' I, 185–8. Avery, 'Maritime Trade', pp. 105–6. Cooper, 'Methods of Blockade', pp. 527–8.

19 Saxby, 'Blockade of Brest', pp. 27–8. Cornwallis-West, *Cornwallis*, pp. 267–72. *SpP* I, 67–8 and 74–5. Brenton, *Naval History* I, 229–30. Lambert, 'Cornwallis', pp. 360–61. Tunstall, *Naval Warfare*, pp. 211–12. *MF* III, 203–15. *NC* I, 278–82; III, 344–5; VII, 20–25; XXV, 363–70. Dillon, *Narrative* I, 192–4. Desbrière, *Le Blocus de Brest*, pp. 23–4. Gardiner, *Fleet Battle and Blockade*, pp. 48–9. Masson, *Histoire de la Marine* I, 310–11. Bourchier, *Codrington* I, 36–7.

20 Gardiner, *Fleet Battle and Blockade*, pp. 20

and 50–57. Desbrière, *Le Blocus de Brest*, p. 22. Barrow, *Smith* I, 165–8. William P. Avery, 'Thrust and Counter', *MM* LXXV (1989), pp. 333–48, at pp. 337 and 346.

21 Duffy, 'Hood', p. 271. *SpP* I, 31–2. Laughton, 'Hood Papers', pp. 243–6.

22 Benjamin, *Windham Papers* I, 294–5, to W. Windham, 2 Apr 1795.

23 Naish, *Nelson's Letters to his Wife*, p. 200, to Mrs Nelson, 14 Mar 1795.

24 *MF* III, 177–81 and 194–8. Benjamin, *Windham Papers* I, 301. Masson, *Histoire de la Marine* I, 308. Tunstall, *Naval Warfare*, pp. 212–13. Naish, *Nelson's Letters to his Wife*, pp. 181–3 and 204. *DLN* II, 10–17. Tracy, *Nelson's Battles*, pp. 21–2. Wyndham-Quin, *Tyler*, pp. 67–8. *HCC*, pp. 70–71. *NC* V, 302–6; IX, 351–7; XXVI, 184–5; XIX, 368–9.

25 Minto, *Minto* II, 407 n.1, Sir G. to Lady Elliot, 28 Jul 1795.

26 Naish, *Nelson's Letters to his Wife*, p. 216, to Mrs Nelson, 14 Jul 1795.

27 Duffy, *Soldiers, Sugar and Seapower*, pp. 136–61; and 'War, Revolution', pp. 125–34. *SpP* I, 160.

28 Duffy, *Soldiers, Sugar and Seapower*, pp. 163–70. *BP* II, 418–429 and III, 1–9. *SpP* I, 133–6, 166–72 and 179–83. Morriss and Saxby, *Channel Fleet*, pp. 48–9. Crimmin, 'Admiralty Administration', pp. 314–16. Talbott, *Pen and Ink Sailor*, pp. 136–43. Stewart, 'Leeward Isles Command', pp. 270–75.

29 Duffy, *Soldiers, Sugar and Seapower*, pp. 186–7. *SpP* I, 136 and 191–219. Crimmin, 'Admiralty Administration', pp. 162–4. Cornwallis-West, *Cornwallis*, pp. 291–304. Stewart, 'Leeward Isles Command', pp. 272–7. Byrn, *Crime and Punishment*, pp. 16–18. Tucker, *St Vincent* I, 145–8. De Toy, 'Wellington's Admiral', pp. 166–9.

30 Duffy, *Soldiers, Sugar and Seapower*, pp. 199–215. *SpP* I, 220–29. Cornwallis-West, *Cornwallis*, pp. 305–41. Schaber, 'Cornwallis', pp. 30–40. Dillon, *Narrative* I, 209–17. Edwina Boult, 'The Destruction of Admiral Christian's Fleet, 1795', *Age of Sail* I (2002), pp. 11–24. Lambert, 'Cornwallis', pp. 362–3. Stewart, 'Leeward

Isles Command', pp. 278–80. Richardson, *Mariner of England*, pp. 124–7.

31 *KP* I, 214.

32 Ehrman, *Younger Pitt* II, 562. Parkinson, *Eastern Seas*, pp. 78–81, 85–7 and 94–5. *NC* XXI, 358–64. *KP* I, 205–474. *NZW* V, 246–68.

33 Duffy, *Soldiers, Sugar and Seapower*, pp. 216–63 and 326–34. Geggus, *Slavery, War, and Revolution*.

34 *SpP* I, 313–37 and II, 3–91. Ehrman, *Younger Pitt* II, 631–6 and 643–4. Cooper, 'Methods of Blockade', pp. 542–5. Brenton, *St Vincent* I, 124–295. Tucker, *St Vincent* I, 140–248. Crimmin, 'St Vincent', pp. 328–33. *AE* VIII, 56–81. White, *1797*, pp. 8–23. Naish, *Nelson's Letters to his Wife*, pp. 283–313 and 334–44. *DLN* II, 234–316. Oman, *Nelson*, pp. 182–202. Morriss, *Cockburn*, pp. 28–31. Barrionuevo Cañas and Blas y Osorio, 'La Armada y Godoy'.

35 Desbrière, *Projets et tentatives* I, 71–232. *SpP* I, 264–5. Saxby, 'Blockade of Brest', pp. 29–30. Elliott, 'Ireland in French War Strategy', pp. 202–7.

36 'Notre détestable Marine ne peut et ne veut rien faire . . . quel composé bizarre: un grand corps dont les parties sont désunies et incohérentes; l'indiscipline organisée dans un corps militaire . . . l'orgueilleuse ignorance et la sotte vanité . . .': Masson and Muracciole, *Napoléon et la Marine*, p. 80.

37 Masson, 'La Marine sous la Révolution', pp. 378–9; and *Histoire de la Marine* I, 314–15. Lloyd, *St Vincent and Camperdown*, pp. 18–19.

38 *MF* III, 263–316. Elliott, *Partners in Revolution*, pp. 109–15. G. E. Cooper, 'Pellew and the Departure of the Bantry Expedition, December 1796', *MM* VI (1920), pp. 178–83; and 'Methods of Blockade', pp. 531–5. *SpP* I, 368–86. Steer, 'Blockade of Brest', p. 74. E. H. Stuart Jones, *An Invasion that Failed. The French Expedition to Ireland 1796* (Oxford, 1950). Desbrière, *Projets et tentatives* I, 171–81. *NC* VIII, 465–9. There were 960 survivors out of 1,280 men aboard the *Droits de l'Homme* (Troude, *Batailles*

navales III, 59); British sources tend to exaggerate the casualties.

39 Desbrière, *Projets et tentatives* I, 235–47. E. H. Stuart Jones, *The Last Invasion of Britain* (Cardiff, 1950). Ehrman, *Younger Pitt* III, 5–13. Sherwig, *Guineas and Gunpowder*, pp. 87–8. Bordo and White, 'A Tale of Two Currencies'. Cooper, 'Pitt, Taxation and War', pp. 94–9.

40 *SpP* III, 365–9. Lloyd, *St Vincent and Camperdown*, pp. 29–38. White, *1797*, pp. 42–44. Laughton and Sulivan, *James Journal*, p. 325. *AE* VIII, 83. Tucker, *St Vincent* I, 255 (quoted).

41 Parsons, *Nelsonian Reminiscences*, p. 323.

42 Elliot, *Memoir*, p. 8. This was the *Pelayo*, Captain Cayetano Valdés, which had been detached earlier in the day and had just rejoined the fleet.

43 Jackson, *Great Sea Fights* I, 197–254. Palmer, 'Sir John's Victory'. Gonzalez-Aller and O'Donnell, 'Spanish Navy', pp. 73–6. White, *1797*, pp. 45–63 and 152–4. Creswell, *British Admirals*, pp. 215–28. [B. Wyke], 'The Battle of Cape St Vincent', *JRUSI* LIX (1914), pp. 321–41. Tracy, *Nelson's Battles*, pp. 93–100. Ross, *Saumarez* II, 402–8. *SpP* I, 339–54. *AE* VIII, 92–101. Tucker, *St Vincent* I, 253–62. Lloyd, *St Vincent and Camperdown*, pp. 63–79. *NCCC*, pp. 35–42. Owen, 'Collingwood Letters', pp. 162–3.

44 *HCC* p. 82, to A. Carlyle, 22 Feb 1797.

45 White, *1797*, pp. 65–85. Drinkwater Bethune, *St Vincent*, pp. 1 and 83–5. *AE* VIII, 103–32. Lloyd, *St Vincent and Camperdown*, pp. 80–92. *DLN* II, 333–47 and 365–8. *NC* XXI, 300–306. Marianne Czisnick, 'Nelson and the Nile: The Creation of Admiral Nelson's Public Image', *MM* LXXXVIII (2002), pp. 41–60, at pp. 41–2.

46 Ehrman, *Younger Pitt* III, 3–66. Duffy, 'Pitt, Grenville', pp. 163–4. Mackesy, *Statesmen at War*, pp. 2–6. Meyer, Corvisier and Poussou, *La Révolution Française* I, 647–50. Battesti, *La Bataille d'Aboukir*, pp. x–xi. Sparrow, *Secret Service*, pp. 22–4. Balleine, *D'Auvergne*, pp. 55–94.

47 Sparrow, *Secret Service*, pp. 84–95, 124–5 and 132–6. Elliott, 'Ireland in French War Strategy', pp. 209–10.

48 Benjamin, *Windham Papers* II, 51, to W. Windham, 26 Apr 1797.

29 Infinite Honour

1 Robertson, 'Mobilisation', p. 67. Oprey, 'Naval Recruitment', pp. 31 (where he has forgotten that there were 16,000 men already in service in January 1793) and 60. *BND* No. 326 p. 544. HL 1794–5 X, 191.

2 Oprey, 'Naval Recruitment', p. 52. 'Ancient Britons' at this date often means Welsh-speakers.

3 Lloyd, *British Seaman*, p. 203. Oprey, 'Naval Recruitment', pp. 20, 32 and 47. *KP* III, 157–63. Geddes, *Portsmouth*, pp. 11–15.

4 Oprey, 'Naval Recruitment', pp. 38–60. Davids, 'Seamen's Organizations', pp. 161–7. McCord and Brewster, 'Labour Troubles'. Emsley, *British Society*, pp. 34–6.

5 The Quota Acts were: 35 Geo. III c. 5, which levied all English and Welsh counties for the Navy (9,420 men in total); 35 Geo. III c. 9, which levied English, Welsh and Scottish seaports for the Navy (19,866 men in total, each able seaman to count as two); 35 Geo. III c. 29, which levied Scottish counties, cities and burghs for the Navy (total 1,814 men); 37 Geo. III c. 4, which levied English and Welsh counties, some for the army and some for the Navy (naval total 6,146 men); and 37 Geo. III c. 5, which levied Scottish counties, cities and burghs for either service at the volunteers' choice (total 2,219 men). In addition there were several amending and explaining acts.

6 35° Geo. III c. 28.

7 Emsley, *British Society*, p. 55. Kemp, *British Sailor*, p. 180. *NC* VI, 301–6.

8 Oprey, 'Naval Recruitment' – the most extensive study of these acts – is cautious about committing himself to figures, but implies (p. 127) that the 1795 quotas (total 31,100) were more or less achieved, at least in England.

9 Emsley et al., *North Riding Naval Recruits*,

pp. 7–20. Oprey, 'Naval Recruitment', pp. 127–263. Brooks, 'Naval Recruiting in Lindsey'. *Sussex Enrolments under the Navy Acts 1795 and 1797* (Eastbourne, 1992).

10 E.g. by Kemp, *British Sailor*, p. 164; Lloyd, *British Seaman*, pp. 195–200; Gill, *Naval Mutinies*, pp. 315–16; Manwaring and Dobrée, *Floating Republic*, p. 16; Lewis, *Social History*, pp. 117–18; Wells, *Insurrection*, pp. 81 and 84–5. The brief passage in Emsley, *British Society*, p. 53, is almost the only sober and accurate account of the Quota Acts in print, but cf. Coats, '1797 Mutinies'; and Rodger, 'Mutiny', pp. 559–61.

11 Kennedy, 'United Irishmen', p. 16 (the only exact figure quoting documentary evidence which I have seen); cf. Emsley, 'Petty Offenders', p. 205. Contrast Wells, *Insurrection*, pp. 82–5 and Elliott, *Partners in Revolution*, p. 138.

12 Emsley, 'Petty Offenders'. Woodfine, ' "Proper Objects of the Press" '. Oprey, 'Naval Recruitment', pp. 39–40.

13 Phillimore, *Parker* I, 57, G. Parker, 17 Jun 1794.

14 *HCC*, p. 54, to Dr A. Carlyle, 3 Aug 1794.

15 Richardson, *Mariner of England*, pp. 105–6.

16 Gardner, *Recollections*, p. 139.

17 Naish, *Nelson's Letters to his Wife*, p. 187, H. Nelson to Mrs F. Nelson, 12 Nov 1794. Cf. Morrison, *Hamilton and Nelson Papers* I, 196 and Neale, *Cutlass and Lash*, pp. 87–91. The captain was William Shield, the admiral Hotham.

18 Nagle, *Journal*, p. 209. This is the nephew of the admiral.

19 Nicol, *Life and Adventures*, p. 159 (quoted). Neale, *Cutlass and Lash*, pp. 132–62. Gavin Kennedy, 'Bligh and the *Defiance* Mutiny', *MM* LXV (1979), pp. 65–8.

20 Neale, *Cutlass and Lash*, pp. 68–114.

21 Gill, *Naval Mutinies*, pp. 7–12. Bonner Smith, 'Naval Mutinies of 1797'. Aspinall, *George III* II, 572 n.3, No. 1,545.

22 Gill, *Naval Mutinies*, pp. 16–21. Saxby, 'Bridport and the Spithead Mutiny', pp. 171–3. Morriss and Saxby, *Channel Fleet*, pp. 191–216. *SpP* II, 101–74.

23 Manwaring and Dobrée, *Floating Republic*, p. 54.

24 Dillon, *Narrative* I, 189. Lavery, *Nelson and the Nile*, p. 54. Gill, *Naval Mutinies*, p. 264. Lewis, *Social History*, p. 122.

25 Gill, *Naval Mutinies*, pp. 360–76 prints the main documents bearing on these negotiations.

26 Gill, *Naval Mutinies*, pp. 55–82 and 94–7. Manwaring and Dobrée, *Floating Republic*, pp. 80–118. Morriss and Saxby, *Channel Fleet*, pp. 217–37. Henderson, 'Bridport Papers', pp. 750–51. Sharp, *Symonds*, pp. 8–16. Naish, *Nelson's Letters to his Wife*, pp. 346 and 67.

27 The mutineers do not seem to have known that their demand to be paid up to six months in arrears on sailing was already law under the 1758 Navy Act; cf. Gradish, *Manning*, pp. 88–96.

28 Gill, *Naval Mutinies*, pp. 43 and 278–81.

29 Gill, *Naval Mutinies*, pp. 107–141. Bonner-Smith, 'Mutiny at the Nore, 1797'. Lloyd, *St Vincent and Camperdown*, pp. 99–105. Manwaring and Dobrée, *Floating Republic*, pp. 121–69. Cunningham, *Narrative*.

30 Gill, *Naval Mutinies*, pp. 151–240. Camperdown, *Duncan*, pp. 107–65. *KP* II, 12–23. *SpP* II, 130–60. Manwaring and Dobrée, *Floating Republic*, pp. 170–231. Laughton, 'Nore Mutiny'. Lloyd, 'Mutiny at the Nore'. Brenton, *Naval History* I, 283–98. Stirling, *Pages and Portraits* I, 94–117. *SL*, pp. 426–7. Thursfield, 'Cullen', pp. 84–9.

31 Benjamin, *Windham Papers* II, 48, Countess Spencer to W. Windham, 20 Apr 1797. *SpP* II, 126, Arden to Spencer, 10 May 1797.

32 *SpP* II, 399, to Sir J. Jervis, 4 May 1797.

33 *SpP* II, 112, 114 and 399. Morriss and Saxby, *Channel Fleet*, pp. 219, 231. *HCC*, p. 85. Minto, *Minto* II, 393. *KP* II, 17. Willyams, *Mediterranean*, pp. 68–9. Stirling, *Pages and Portraits* II, 188.

34 Rodger, 'Mutiny', p. 554, surveying the views of Wells, *Insurrection*, Manwaring and Dobrée, *Floating Republic*, Gill, *Naval Mutinies*, Lewis, *Social History*, E. P. Thompson *The Making of the English Working Class* (London, 1978), Elliott,

Partners in Revolution, Moore, 'Direct Democracy' and others.

35 Manwaring and Dobrée, *Floating Republic*, implicitly commenting on the 1931 Invergordon Mutiny.

36 See the Bibliography under Brown, Coats, Doorne, MacDougall and Neale.

37 Gill, *Naval Mutinies*, pp. 361–2. Manwaring and Dobrée, *Floating Republic*, pp. 262–3. Coats, 'Delegates'.

38 Elliott, *Partners in Revolution*, p. 143. James Dugan, *The Great Mutiny* (London, 1966), pp. 63–4. Neale, 'Forecastle and Quarterdeck', p. 317.

39 Coats, 'Delegates', pp. 18–19.

40 Lewis, *Social History*, pp. 124–5.

41 Manwaring and Dobrée, *Floating Republic*, pp. 16–17.

42 Gill, *Naval Mutinies*, pp. 124–8. Brown, 'Sedition or Ships' Biscuits?', p. 19. Laughton, 'Mutiny at the Nore', pp. 295–6. Brenton, *Naval History* I, 297. Parker's own account of his life is printed in *SpP* II, 160–73.

43 Doorne, 'Floating Republic'. Brown, 'Sedition or Ships' Biscuits?'. Richardson, *Mariner of England*, pp. 138–9. Cunningham, *Narrative*.

44 Stirling, *Pages and Portraits* I, 101. Camperdown, *Duncan*, p. 162.

45 Brenton, *Naval History* I, 298.

46 Brown, 'Sedition or Ships' Biscuits?'. Mackaness, *Bligh* II, 41. Camperdown, *Duncan*, pp. 107–64. Laughton, 'Nore Mutiny', pp. 294–6. Lloyd, 'Mutiny at the Nore'. *KP* II, 12–23. Thursfield, 'Cullen', pp. 84–9. Brenton, *Naval History* I, 283–98. Stirling, *Pages and Portraits* I, 95–122. MacDougall, 'East Coast Mutinies'; and 'North Sea Squadron'.

47 Manwaring and Dobrée, *The Floating Republic*, pp. 250–51. Gill, *Naval Mutinies*, pp. 324–51. Doorne, 'Conspiracy Theory', pp. 3–6. Brown, 'Sedition or Ships' Biscuits?', p. 9. Ehrman, *Younger Pitt* III, 17–30. Wells, *Insurrection*, pp. 92–9. Royle, *Revolutionary Britannia?*, pp. 26–33. Emsley, *British Society*, pp. 62–3. Elliott, *Partners in Revolution*, pp. 136–44. Sparrow, *Secret Service*, pp. 17–19 and 118–19.

48 Laughton, 'Miscellaneous Letters', pp. 410 and 413, to Mrs C. Gillies, 19 and 20 Apr 1797.

49 To Clarence, 26 May 1797: note by Colin White in *Age of Sail* I (2002), p. 167.

50 Sermoneta, *Locks of Norbury*, pp. 237–8, to W. Lock, 10 May and 20 Jun 1797.

51 Brenton, *St Vincent* I, 364.

52 Nagle, *Journal*, p. 211.

53 *SpP* II, 410–11. Laughton, 'Jervis Orders', pp. 327–8. *DLN* II, 408–10 and VII Add. ccxxiv. *HCC*, p. 84.

54 Tucker, *St Vincent* I, 303 and 334–5. Laughton, 'Cathcart Letters', pp. 268–70.

55 Jones, 'Mutiny in Bantry Bay' (quoted pp. 206 and 207). Parkinson, *Pellew*, pp. 219–22. Tucker, *St Vincent* I, 313–16. *KP* II, 40. De Toy, 'Wellington's Admiral', pp. 235–6.

56 Jackson, 'Thompson Letter-Books', p. 317.

57 Morriss and Saxby, *Channel Fleet*, pp. 302–3 and 327–9. Stirling, *Pages and Portraits* I, 152–7. Brenton, *St Vincent* I, 376–7. Jackson, 'Thompson Letter-Books', pp. 314–21. *NCCC*, p. 70. Wells, *Insurrection*, pp. 145–50. Doorne, 'Floating Republic'. Elliott, 'French Subversion', pp. 46–8. Rodger, 'Mutiny', p. 562.

58 Pope, *Black Ship* (quoted p. 142). J. D. Spinney, 'The *Hermione* Mutiny', *MM* XLI (1955), pp. 123–36.

59 Pope, *Black Ship*, p. 290.

60 Barker, *Greenwich Hospital*, p. 148.

61 Stirling, *Pages and Portraits* I, 152–7 (quoted p. 155). *SL*, pp. 428–30 corrects some details of Hotham's memory.

62 Brenton, *St Vincent* II, 102.

63 *SL*, pp. 633–4, quoting two 1797 pamphlets by Patton, *Observations on the State of Discipline in the Navy . . .* and *Account of the Mutinies at Spithead and St Helens . . .*

64 *SVL* II, 147 and 157. Tucker, *St Vincent* I, 297 and 329; II, 137–8. *SpP* II, 119.

30 The Second Coalition

1 Markham, *Naval Career*, p. 140. Cf. Thursfield, 'Wilson', p. 143; *NCCC*, p. 49; *HCC*, p. 82; and Hoste, *Hoste* I, 91.

2 *SpP* II, 365–9. *AE* VIII, 139–46. Augusto

Conte y Lacave, *El ataque de Nelson a Cádiz* (Madrid, 1976). Buckland, *Miller Papers*, pp. 8–15. White, *1797*, pp. 91–8. Oman, *Nelson*, pp. 225–7. Pocock, *Horatio Nelson*, pp. 135–8. Brenton, *St Vincent* I, 362–74; and *Naval History* I, 381–3. Ross, *Saumarez* I, 186. Tucker, *St Vincent* I, 299.

3 White, *1797*, pp. 100–129; and 'Nelson Ashore, 1780–1797', in Hore, *Seapower Ashore*, pp. 53–78, at pp. 64–76. Lanuza Cano, *Ataque y derrota de Nelson*. Ontoria Oquillas, *Fuentes Documentales*. Buckland, *Miller Papers*, pp. 15–31. Naish, *Nelson's Letters to his Wife*, pp. 371–4.

4 Duffy, *Soldiers, Sugar and Seapower*, pp. 267–318. *AE* VIII, 133–7. Zapatero, *La Guerra del Caribe*, pp. 410–85.

5 Jackson, *Great Sea Fights* I, 257–342. Camperdown, *Duncan*, pp. 193–237 and 269–97. *NZW* V, 296–422. Crimmin, 'Canning and Camperdown'. De Groot, 'Bloys van Treslong'. *SpP* II, 197. Franks, 'Onslow', pp. 333–6. Roodhuyzen, *In Woelig Vaarwater*, pp. 149–54. Lloyd, *St Vincent and Camperdown*, pp. 120–72. Tunstall, *Naval Warfare*, pp. 219–24.

6 Linda Colley, 'The Apotheosis of George III: Loyalty, Royalty and the British Nation 1760–1820', *P&P* No. 102 (1984), pp. 94–129, at p. 110. Cookson, *Armed Nation*, p. 215. Russell, *Theatres of War*, p. 88. Ehrman, *Younger Pitt* III, 99. Camperdown, *Duncan*, pp. 250–55. Marsden, *Memoir*, pp. 91–2.

7 Mackesy, *Statesmen at War*, pp. 9–11. Gough, 'Europe and the Atlantic', pp. 543–7. *SpP* II, 239–318.

8 *SpP* II, 319, to H. Dundas, 25 Apr 1798.

9 *SpP* II, 313–51. James, *Naval History* II, 131–3. Popham, *Damned Cunning Fellow*, pp. 58–63. *NC* XVI, 273–6.

10 Duffy, 'War, Revolution', pp. 138–41. Elliott, 'Ireland in French War Strategy', pp. 211–15. Desbrière, *Projets et tentatives* II, 83 and 159–71. [J. H. Heath], 'The French Landing in Ireland, August 1798', *NR* XVI (1928), pp. 58–76. James A. MacCauley, 'The Battle of Lough Swilly, 1798', *IS* IV (1959–60), pp. 166–70.

11 'Tout s'use ici, je n'ai pas assez de gloire. Cette petite Europe n'en fournit pas assez.' Battesti, *La Bataille d'Aboukir*, p. xxx.

12 'Ce que ce petit bougre-là avait dans le ventre.' Rodger, *Second Coalition*, p. 37.

13 La Jonquière, *L'Expédition d'Egypte* I, 152, 169 and 197–528. Battesti, *La Bataille d'Aboukir*, pp. 1–31. Rodger, *Second Coalition*, pp. 15–45. Douin, *La Flotte de Bonaparte*, pp. 1–25. Acerra and Meyer, *Marines et Révolution*, p. 219.

14 Ehrman, *Younger Pitt* III, 148.

15 Ehrman, *Younger Pitt* II, 138–46. Duffy, 'British Naval Intelligence', pp. 278–85. Mackesy, *Statesmen at War*, pp. 16–24. Tucker, *St Vincent* I, 347. Lavery, *Nelson and the Nile*, pp. 91–103.

16 For Berry see *ODNB*; *DLN* VII, 24; Parsons, *Nelsonian Reminiscences*, pp. 24–32 and 41–3; Ludovic Kennedy, *Nelson and his Captains* (London, 2nd edn 1975), pp. 196–9; Howarth, *Trafalgar*, pp. 115–17; Duffy, 'La artillería en Trafalgar'.

17 Lavery, *Nelson and the Nile*, pp. 65–75. Barritt, 'Nelson's Frigates'. *DLN* III, 17–27 and VII, Add. cli.

18 Lavery, *Nelson and the Nile*, pp. 122–67. *DLN* III, 17–48 and VII, Add. cli–cliii. Duffy, 'British Naval Intelligence', pp. 286–8.

19 Jackson, *Great Sea Fights* II, 1–79. Lavery, *Nelson and the Nile*, pp. 150–212. Warner, *Nile*, pp. 75–121; and *Nelson's Battles*, pp. 48–77. Battesti, *La Bataille d'Aboukir*, pp. 74–218. Masson and Muracciole, *Napoléon et la Marine*, p. 108. La Jonquière, *L'Expédition d'Egypte* II, 392–430. *MF* III, 360–81. Herold, *Bonaparte in Egypt*, pp. 109–12. *DLN* III, 48–71 and VII Add., cliv–clx. Tracy, *Nelson's Battles*, pp. 105–21. Tunstall, *Naval Warfare*, pp. 224–7. Elliot, *Memoir*, pp. 9–20. Nicol, *Life and Adventures*, pp. 170–71. *BND* No. 234, pp. 421–2. *NC* I, 43–60 and VIII, 226–38.

20 Naish, *Nelson's Letters to his Wife*, p. 399.

21 Parkinson, *Eastern Seas*, pp. 114–39 and 182. *SpP* IV, 155–250. P. A. Ward, 'The Response of the Royal Navy's East India Command to the Invasion of Egypt in 1799, up to the Peace of Amiens' (Exeter MA dissertation, 2003).

22 *SpP* II, 454–82; III, xi–xii and IV, 186–7. Ehrman, *Younger Pitt* III, 149–50. HMC *Fortescue* IV, 328. Lavery, *Nelson and the Nile*, pp. 243–54. Oman, *Nelson*, p. 303.

23 Mackesy, *Statesmen at War*, p. 42. Rodger, *Second Coalition*, pp. 87–92. Saul, *Russia and the Mediterranean*, pp. 65–91. Sokol, 'Nelson and the Russian Navy', pp. 129–30.

24 *DLN* III, 138, to St Vincent, 30 Sep 1798.

25 Warner, *Nile*, pp. 142–3. *BND* No. 204, pp. 342–4. Radogna, *Storia della marina militare*, pp. 25–7. Fraser, *Beloved Emma*, pp. 204–5. Fothergill, *Hamilton*, pp. 282–3. Mackesy, *Statesmen at War*, p. 56. Gutteridge, *Nelson and the Neapolitan Jacobins*, pp. xii–xxv. John Robertson, 'Enlightenment and Revolution: Naples 1799', *TRHS* 6th S. X (2000), pp. 17–44.

26 *SpP* III, 12, to W. Pitt, 5 Aug 1799.

27 *SpP* III, 43–50 and 75–85. Douin, *La Campagne de Bruix*, pp. 67–97. Morriss and Saxby, *Channel Fleet*, pp. 243, 300, 322, 346–8, 368–9 and 376–82. Steer, 'Blockade of Brest', pp. 79–82. Rae, 'Blockade of Brest', pp. 53 and 90–91. Mackesy, *Statesmen at War*, pp. 97–101. Ryan, 'In Search of Bruix', pp. 82–5. De Toy, 'Wellington's Admiral', pp. 227–32. R. C. Saxby, 'The Escape of Admiral Bruix from Brest', *MM* XLVI (1960), pp. 113–19. Battesti, *La Bataille d'Aboukir*, pp. 143–7. La Jonquière, *L'Expédition d'Egypte* V, 136–48.

28 *SpP* III, 51–4 and 81–100. Douin, *La Campagne de Bruix*, pp. 98–228. Ryan, 'In Search of Bruix', pp. 86–9. Battesti, *La Bataille d'Aboukir*, pp. 143–50. La Jonquière, *L'Expédition d'Egypte* V, 162–4. *KP* II, 31–9. Mackesy, *Statesmen at War*, p. 168. Lavery, 'Keith', pp. 386–8. *AE* VIII, 176–7. Carlan, *Navios en secuestro*, pp. 31–40. Owen, 'Collingwood Letters', pp. 168–9.

29 *KP* II, 37. *SpP* III, 99–100. *DLN* III, 298–523 and VII Add., clxxx–viii. Lavery, *Nelson and the Nile*, pp. 282–3. Gutteridge, *Nelson and the Neapolitan Jacobins*. Giglioli, *Naples in 1799*. Warner, *Portrait of Lord Nelson*, pp. 183–95. Oman, *Nelson*, pp. 349–78.

30 *SpP* III, 133–212. Williams, 'Helder Campaign'. HMC *Fortescue* V, 338–41. *NZW* V, 449–79. Rodger, *Second Coalition*, pp. 176–94. Roodhuyzen, *In Woelig Vaarwater*, pp. 164–7. Pim Waldeck, 'De Vlieter: dieptepunt in de geschiedenis van de Nederlandse zeemacht. Relaas van een persoonlijke belevnis', *TvZ* XVIII (1999), pp. 29–46. Popham, *Damned Cunning Fellow*, pp. 66–78. Carden, *Memoir*, pp. 114–16. '1799 – De Brits-Russische invasie in Noord-Holland', ed. M. A. van Alphen et al, *Mars et Historia* XXXIII (1999), No. 4, thematic issue.

31 Barrow, *Smith* I, 290, to St Vincent, 9 May 1799.

32 Herold, *Bonaparte in Egypt*, pp. 289–308. La Jonquière, *L'Expédition d'Egypte* IV, 289–54, 439–506 and 574–83. Barrow, *Smith* I, 264–319. *NC* II, 159–60, 246–7, 437–9, 620–25 and XXII, 33–4. Battesti, *La Bataille d'Aboukir*, pp. 138–41. J. Miot, *Mémoires pour servir à l'histoire des expéditions en Egypte et en Syrie* (Paris, 2nd edn 1814), pp. 145–8 and 205–6. Sparrow, *Secret Service*, pp. 188–203.

33 Parkinson, *Pellew*, p. 228; to A. Broughton 1 Dec 1799.

34 *HCC*, p. 108, C. Collingwood to Dr A. Carlyle, 5 Dec 1799.

35 Morriss and Saxby, *Channel Fleet*, p. 619, to Sir Francis Baring, 8 Feb 1801.

36 *SpP* III, 295–384 and IV, 3–24. Morriss and Saxby, *Channel Fleet*, pp. 454–584 and 617–18. Steer, 'Blockade and Victualling'; and 'Blockade of Brest', pp. 88–95, 115, 118–21 and 197. Saxby, 'Blockade of Brest', pp. 31–2. De Toy, 'Wellington's Admiral', pp. 282–3. Ross, *Saumarez* I, 300. Thursfield, 'Cullen', p. 104. *NC* XIX, 290–91. Tucker, *St Vincent* I, 369; II, 9–15, 20–23 and 34–5. Warner, *Collingwood*, p. 107. Rae, 'Blockade of Brest', pp. 57, 69 and 81. Laird, 'Victualling', pp. 21 and 51.

37 Horsfield, *Leadership in War*, p. 58, to Sir J. Orde, 30 Nov 1798.

38 Brenton, *St Vincent* I, 339.

39 Steer, 'Blockade of Brest', pp. 97 and 179. De Toy, 'Wellington's Admiral', p. 282. Ross, *Saumarez* I, 304–5 and 322–3.

40 *SpP* III, 368–9. Parkinson, *Pellew*, pp. 252–68. Mackesy, *War without Victory*, pp. 125–32 and 148.

41 'Ce bougre-là nous a laissé ici ses culottes pleines de merde . . . nous allons retourner en Europe, et les lui appliquer sur la figure.' Rodger, *Second Coalition*, p. 132.

42 *SpP* IV, 31–3, 57–60 and 90–96. *DLN* III, 282–6. Herold, *Bonaparte in Egypt*, pp. 341 and 351. HMC *Fortescue* VI, 267. Ehrman, *Younger Pitt* III, 401–5. *SVL* I, 154–9. Sparrow, *Secret Service*, pp. 194–5. *KP* II, 199–202.

43 Morriss and Saxby, *Channel Fleet*, pp. 573–619. *SVL* I, 162–75. Masson and Muracciole, *Napoléon et la Marine*, pp. 130–31. Battesti, *La Bataille d'Aboukir*, pp. 165–67. *MF*, IV, 38–47. *KP* II, 234 and 368–70. Morriss, *Cockburn*, pp. 50–51.

44 Mackesy, 'Cadiz Expedition', quoting (p. 41) Lord Cornwallis. *SpP* IV, 136–47.

45 Mackesy, *War without Victory*, pp. 125–84. Ingram, 'Mediterranean Campaign'. *KP* II, 228–359. Rodger, *Second Coalition*, pp. 249–74. Battesti, *La Bataille d'Aboukir*, pp. 169–70. Gardiner, *Nelson against Napoleon*, pp. 78–81. John Nicol (*Life and Adventures*, p. 173) was in Cochrane's boat's crew and calls him 'beachmaster'.

46 Parkinson, *Eastern Seas*, pp. 166–80. Popham, *Damned Cunning Fellow*, pp. 83–100. Turner, 'Cape of Good Hope'.

47 Ehrman, *Younger Pitt* III, 495–533. Peter Jupp, 'Britain and the Union, 1797–1801', and Patrick Geoghegan, 'The Catholics and the Union', *TRHS* 6th S. X (2000), pp. 197–220 and 243–58. Mackesy, *War without Victory*, pp. 170–82.

48 Aspinall, *George III* III, 491–2 and IV, 11 n.4. Breihan, 'Addington Party', pp. 163–5. Mackesy, *War without Victory*, pp. 186–93. Crimmin, 'Admiralty Administration', p. 25. *SVL* I, 12–21. Cf. Ch. XXXI for St Vincent and Addington in politics.

49 Feldbæk, *Denmark and the Armed Neutrality*, pp. 13–66; and 'Anglo-Danish Convoy Conflict'. Harvey, *Collision of Empires*, pp. 90–97. Olson, *Wartime Shortage*, pp. 51–5.

50 *SVL* I, 319. Parker had been Hood's First Captain at the time of the 1791 mobilization.

51 Laughton, 'Miscellaneous Letters', pp. 415–24. Pope, *Great Gamble*, pp. 6–298. *SVL* I, 59–66 and 86. Warner, *Nelson's Battles*, pp. 108–9. *DLN* IV, 290–91. Oman, *Nelson*, pp. 419–35. Sparrow, *Secret Service*, pp. 223 and 237–9.

52 Feldbæk, *Slaget på Reden*, pp. 9–148; and *Denmark and the Armed Neutrality*, pp. 141–52. Pope, *Great Gamble*, pp. 309–66. Maria Ekberger, 'Københavns søefension i foråret 1801', *Marinehistorisk Tidsskrift* XVII (1984), pp. 3–25.

53 *DLN* IV, 299–309. Feldbæk, *Slaget på Reden*, pp. 148–235. Pope, *Great Gamble*, pp. 370–417. Jackson, *Great Sea Fights* II, 81–135. Tracy, *Nelson's Battles*, pp. 127–54. *NC* V, 334–43. Millard, 'Battle of Copenhagen'. Fremantle, *Wynne Diaries* III, 41–4. Buckingham, *Memoirs* III, 151–3. Elliot, *Memoir*, pp. 27–30. J. Neumann, 'Meteorological and Hydrographical Aspects of the Battle of Copenhagen, 2 April 1801', *Meteorological Magazine* CXXI (1992), pp. 100–107. Not all historians believe the story of the telescope, but there is no doubt about the signal.

54 Feldbæk, *Denmark and the Armed Neutrality*, pp. 156–205; and 'Humanity or Ruse de Guerre? Nelson's Letter to the Danes', *MM* LXXIII (1987), pp. 339–49. Pope, *Great Gamble*, pp. 418–506. Warner, *Nelson's Battles*, pp. 133–40. Aspinall, *George III* III, 517–18 and 542–5. *SVL* I, 67–79 and 90–99. *DLN* IV, 310–61. Morrison, *Hamilton and Nelson Papers* II, 133–53. *KP* II, 373. Susan Harmon, 'The Serpent and the Dove: Studying Nelson's Character', *MM* LXXV (1989), pp. 43–51.

55 Desbrière, *Projets et tentatives* II, 273–393. Aspinall, *George III* III, 582. *SVL* I, 133. *DLN* IV, 425–84. Oman, *Nelson*, pp. 467–76. Monaque, *Latouche-Tréville*, pp. 416–55; and 'Latouche-Tréville: The Admiral who Defied Nelson', *MM* LXXXVI (2000), pp. 272–84. 'The Public

Order Book of Vice Admiral Lord Nelson
. . . July–October 1801', ed. Colin White,
in Duffy, *Naval Miscellany VI*, pp. 221–55.
Dupont, *L'Amiral Decrès*, pp. 78–80.
Margaret Bradley, 'Bonaparte's Plans to
Invade England in 1801: the Fortunes of
Pierre Forfait', *Annals of Science* LI
(1994), pp. 453–75.

56 *SVL* I, 186–98. *KP* II, 379–81. Ross,
Saumarez, I, 342–8 and 403–13. *MF* IV,
50–64. Battesti, *La Bataille d'Aboukir*,
pp. 167–8. Masson and Muracciole,
Napoléon et la Marine, pp. 134–5.

57 Mackesy, *War without Victory*,
pp. 206–29. Rodger, *Second Coalition*,
pp. 279–87. *SVL* I, 112–23.

31 A Great and Virtuous Character

1 O'Brien, 'Political Economy of British
Taxation'; and 'Inseparable Connections',
pp. 66–8. Cooper, 'Pitt, Taxation and
War'.

2 Ellis, 'War and the French Economy'.
Florin Athalion, 'Le Financement des
guerres de la Révolution et de l'Empire',
in Aerts and Crouzet, *Economic Effects*,
pp. 22–9. Bonney, 'Eighteenth Century',
pp. 347–57. Harvey, *Collision of Empires*,
pp. 66–71. Kennedy, *Great Powers*,
pp. 170–75. David Kaiser, *Politics and
War: European Conflict from Philip II to
Hitler* (London, 1990), pp. 246–9 and
255–61.

3 Crimmin, 'Admiralty Relations with the
Treasury'. Morriss, *Royal Dockyards*,
pp. 77–8. *BND* Nos. 272 and 277, pp. 467
and 476. *SVL* II, 3–6.

4 Condon, 'Transport Board'. Crimmin,
'Admiralty Administration', pp. 164–5.
Phillips, 'Evangelical Administrator',
pp. 223–6. *BP* III, 121. *BND* No. 273,
p. 468.

5 Ian R. Christie, *The Benthams in Russia,
1780–1791* (Oxford, 1993). NMM: SAN/F/
26/103, Sir J. Harris to Sandwich, 13/24
Mar 1781, enc S. Bentham to Sandwich, 4/
15 Feb 1781. Coad, *Royal Dockyards*,
pp. 29–33 and 225–42. Morriss, *Royal
Dockyards*, pp. 46–54 and 210–13. Cooper,
'Portsmouth System'. A. Barlow, 'The
Blockmills at Portsmouth Dockyard in

the Eighteenth to Twentieth Century',
MM LXXXVIII (2002), pp. 81–9.

6 Marsden, *Memoir*, pp. 97–8, to A.
Marsden, 2 Jun 1800; cf. p. 109.

7 *SpP* II, 210–12. Tucker, *St Vincent* I,
416–18.

8 Tucker, *St Vincent* I, 423, to Spencer, 24
Aug 1797.

9 St Vincent, *Memoirs*, in *SVL* II, 439–41.

10 St Vincent, *Memoirs* in *SVL* II, 429, 434
and 437.

11 'Cases of alleged fraud in the
management of the Royal Navy,
1772–1821': unpublished note by Dr Roger
Morriss, to whom I am grateful for
permission to cite it.

12 Morriss, 'Labour Relations'; and
'St Vincent and Reform', pp. 269–77. *SVL*
II, 167–72. St Vincent, *Memoirs* in *SVL* II,
438–51. Tucker, *St Vincent* II, 133–6. Haas,
Management Odyssey, pp. 58–60.

13 Marsden, *Memoir*, p. 103.

14 Markham, *Naval Career*, p. 198; cf. p. 216.

15 *SVL* II, 167–203 and 211. Morriss, *Royal
Dockyards*, pp. 172–80. Ashworth,
' "System of Terror" '. Craig, 'St Vincent
Letters', pp. 472–3 and 477–8. Tucker,
St Vincent II, 207. Haas, *Management
Odyssey*, p. 60. James E. Candow, 'Sir
Isaac Coffin and the Halifax Dockyard
"Scandal" ', *Nova Scotia Historical Review*
I (1981), pp. 50–63.

16 *BP* III, 19–21 and 49. Ham, 'Coalition and
Isolation', pp. 10–11. Morriss, *Royal
Dockyards*, pp. 76–83; and 'St Vincent and
Reform', pp. 279–83.

17 Marsden, *Memoir*, p. 104, to A. Marsden,
26 Dec 1802.

18 *SVL* II, 17–25 and 201. Morriss, *Royal
Dockyards*, pp. 115 and 193–6; and
'St Vincent and Reform', pp. 270–73.

19 Parkinson, *Pellew*, p. 301, to A.
Broughton, 5 Mar 1804.

20 Breihan, 'Addington Party', pp. 163–74.
Morriss, *Royal Dockyards*, pp. 193–7. *SVL*
II, 19–20 and 480. Parkinson, *Pellew*,
pp. 284–7 and 312–13. *HP 1790–1820* IV,
755–6 and 868. Lloyd, *St Vincent and
Camperdown*, pp. 31–2. Popham, *Damned
Cunning Fellow*, pp. 103–10. Dixon,
'Bartholomew'.

21 Crimmin, 'Admiralty Administration',

pp. 279 and 287–8. Mike Baker, 'The English Timber Cartel in the Napoleonic Wars', *MM* LXXXVIII (2002), pp. 79–81. Pool, *Navy Board Contracts*, pp. 124–5. Haas, *Management Odyssey*, pp. 48–9. PRO: E 134/57 Geo III/Mich/4 and E 133/150/56–9, depositions in suit Attorney General vs Arthur Lindgren.

22 Breihan, 'Addington Party', p. 175. Aspinall, *George III* IV, 183–4 and 233. Morriss, *Royal Dockyards*, pp. 198–201. HC 1806 V. Ehrman, *Younger Pitt* III, 626–30. Barrow, *Autobiographical Memoir*, pp. 254–61. *BP* III, viii–xii.

23 Breihan, 'Addington Party', pp. 175–9. Ehrman, *Younger Pitt* III, 752–63. Murray, 'Admiralty' VI, 342–5. Cyril Matheson, *The Life of Henry Dundas, First Viscount Melville 1741–1811* (London, 1933), pp. 344–72.

24 Breihan, 'Addington Party', pp. 178–80. Ehrman, *Younger Pitt* III, 765–6. Corbett, *Trafalgar* I, 79–80 and 94–7. *SVL* II, 75–6. *BP* III, 73–8. HMC *Fortescue* VII, 257. Aspinall, *George III* IV, 315–16. Phillips, 'Barham' (quoted pp. 222 and 223). Lloyd, *Mr Barrow*, pp. 80–84. Talbott, *Pen and Ink Sailor*, pp. 149–52. Crimmin, 'Admiralty Administration', pp. 129–30.

25 Buckingham, *Memoirs* IV, 96, to Buckingham, 17 Nov 1806. His correspondence in this volume is much in this tone.

26 Breihan, 'Addington Party', pp. 180–83. Ham, 'Coalition and Isolation', pp. 66–8. *SVL* II, 77–9. Murray, 'Admiralty' VI, 349. Harvey, 'Ministry of All the Talents'. Emsley, *British Society*, p. 129.

27 Morriss, *Royal Dockyards*, pp. 53–61 and 202–14. *BND* No. 276, pp. 473–5. Coad, *Royal Dockyards*, pp. 107–17 and 138; and 'Two Early Attempts at Fire-Proofing in Royal Dockyards', *Post-Medieval Archaeology* VII (1973), pp. 88–90. Trevor M. Harris, 'Government and Urban Development in Kent: the Case of the Royal Naval Dockyard Town of Sheerness', *Archaeologia Cantiana* CI (1985), pp. 245–76 (quoted p. 265).

28 Marden, *Memoir*, p. 111, to A. Marsden, 24 Jan 1805.

29 Webb, 'Frigate Situation'. Morriss and Saxby, *Channel Fleet*, pp. 3–5. Morriss, *Royal Dockyards*, pp. 13–38; and 'Problems Affecting the Maintenance of the British Fleet in the Mediterranean, 1793–1815', in *Français et Anglais en Méditerranée*, pp. 171–80. *BP* III, 40–48, 104–8 and 273. Glete, *Navies and Nations* II, 375–86.

30 Crimmin, 'Establishment of the Admiralty Office', pp. 304–5.

31 Crimmin, 'Establishment of the Admiralty Office'; and 'Admiralty Administration', pp. 212–15. Sainty, *Admiralty Officials*, pp. 34–7.

32 Marsden, *Memoir*, p. 126, to A. Marsden, 4 Mar 1806. The Hon. Charles Grey was First Lord.

33 Barrow, *Autobiographical Memoir*, pp. 254, 291–2 and 299. Lloyd, *Mr Barrow*, pp. 75–7. Marsden, *Memoir*, pp. 105–10 and 128–30. Jennings, *Croker Papers* I, 19–23 (quoted p. 20).

34 Laird, 'Victualling', pp. 9–29.

35 Trotter, *Medicina Nautica* I, 128.

36 *BP* III, 2–4. *SpP* I, 103–5. *KMN* III, 159. De Toy, 'Wellington's Admiral', pp. 162–3. Trotter, *Medicina Nautica* I, 115–52. Steer, 'Blockade of Brest', p. 230. Morriss and Saxby, *Channel Fleet*, pp. 64–77, 111–25 and 154.

37 PRO: ADM 98/17, pp. 137–8 and 142, to Admiralty, 27 May 1795.

38 Craig, 'St Vincent Letters', p. 478, to T. Grenville, 28 Oct 1806.

39 Blane, *Diseases of Seamen*, p. 490. Laird, 'Victualling', pp. 47–65. Morriss and Saxby, *Channel Fleet*, pp. 111–25, 133, 142–5, 151–9, 522–3 and 544–5. Tucker, *St Vincent* II, 27–31. Risse, 'Health of Seamen', pp. 430–31 and 441.

40 PRO: ADM 98/24 p. 93 and ADM 98/99 p. 63. *HCC*, p. 228. Laird, 'Victualling', p. 79.

41 *DLN* V, 438, to Dr B. Moseley, 11 Mar 1804.

42 *DLN* V, 437; VI, 19, 25, 70, 141–2 and 335. Crimmin, 'Service of Nelson's Ships'. *KNM* III, 149–53. Lee, *Memoirs*, p. 179. Draper, 'Gillespie', p. 230. J. H. Rose, 'The State of Nelson's Fleet before Trafalgar', *MM* VIII (1922), pp. 75–81.

43 *DLN* VII, 8, to Admiralty, 18 Aug 1805.
44 Steer, 'Blockade of Brest', pp. 239–40.
Mark, *At Sea with Nelson*, pp. 68–71. Hay,
Landsman Hay, p. 41. Turner, 'Naval
Medical Service', pp. 126–7. Morriss and
Saxby, *Channel Fleet*, pp. 522, 546–7 and
559–61. De Toy, 'Wellington's Admiral',
pp. 192–7. Trotter, *Medicina Nautica* I,
138. R. Williamson Jones, 'The Royal
Navy and the Spread of Vaccination',
Journal of the Royal Naval Medical Service
LXXIII (1987), pp. 204–6.
45 Boog Watson, 'Two Naval Surgeons',
p. 221. Parkinson, *Eastern Seas*,
pp. 353–63. SL, pp. 520–23.
46 Sir James Watt, 'Naval Surgery in the
Time of Nelson', *Age of Sail* I (2002),
pp. 25–33. Janice Wallace, 'Bodies and
Battles: The Treatment of Casualties in
the British Navy during the 1790s' (Exeter
MA dissertation, 1996). Fraser, *Sailors
Whom Nelson Led*, p. 315. Robinson,
Nautical Economy, p. 50.
47 *KMN* III, 232–90. *SVL* II, 211. *BP* III,
122–31. Aspinall, *George III* IV, 362–3.
PRO: ADM 99/51, pp. 94–6, 98 and
135–42. Turner, 'Naval Medical Service'.
R. S. Allison, *Sea Diseases: The Story of a
Great Natural Experiment in Preventative
Medicine in the Royal Navy* (London,
1943), pp. 159–65.

32 A Thinking Set of People

1 Patton, *Strictures on Naval Discipline*, in
SL, p. 627. Cf. 'A.F.Y.' [Captain C. V.
Penrose] in *NC* XIX, 383–4.
2 *SL*, p. 436.
3 *SL*, p. 434.
4 Neale, 'Forecastle and Quarterdeck',
p. 450.
5 Richardson, *Mariner of England*, p. 220.
6 *HCC*, pp. 82–3, C. Collingwood to Dr A.
Carlyle, 3 Jun 1797.
7 *HCC*, pp. 86 and 123. Morriss and Saxby,
Channel Fleet, pp. 565 and 628. Stirling,
Pages and Portraits I, 119.
8 *NCCC*, p. 66, to J. E. Blackett, 1 May
1798.
9 Liddell Hart, *Private Wheeler*, p. 46.
10 Warner, *Collingwood*, pp. 110–11. *NCCC*,
pp. 51–4.

11 Hay, *Landsman Hay*, p. 66.
12 Lincoln and McEwen, *Lord Eldon's
Anecdote Book*, p. 14.
13 For Collingwood's humanity see, e.g.,
Raikes, *Brenton*, p. 314; *NCCC*, p. 312;
Hay, *Landsman Hay*, pp. 62–78.
14 Griffiths, *Points of Seamanship*, in *SL*,
p. 355.
15 *NC* XIX, 383–4, 'A.F.Y.'.
16 Coleridge, *The Friend* I, 540. Cf. Brenton,
St Vincent II, 346–7.
17 Stirling, *Pages and Portraits* I, 42–3.
Pemberton, *Pel. Verjuice*, p. 225.
18 Griffiths, *Points of Seamanship*, in *SL*,
p. 366 (quoted). Parkinson, *Eastern Seas*,
pp. 433–4. Pemberton, *Pel. Verjuice*,
pp. 222–5. Phillimore, *Parker* I, 206.
Crawford, *Reminiscences*, p. 67. Horsfield,
Leadership in War, p. 55. Cf. Firth, *Naval
Songs and Ballads*, pp. 317–20 for
seamen's songs complaining about useless
spit and polish.
19 Hoste, *Hoste* I, 216, to Revd D. Hoste,
12 Feb 1805. Cf. Thursfield, 'Wilson',
p. 243.
20 Hodgskin, *Naval Discipline*, p. 35.
Crawford, *Reminiscences*, pp. 32 and 197.
Moody, 'Irish Countryman' V, 51.
Griffiths, *Points of Seamanship*, in *SL*,
pp. 362–3. *SVL* I, 324. *SpP* II, 158. Byrn,
Crime and Punishment, pp. 92–3.
21 The best-known examples are
Pemberton, *Pel. Verjuice*; and Robinson,
Nautical Economy, on whom see Henry
Baynham, 'William Robinson, alias Jack
Nastyface', *MM* LXXXVII (2001),
pp. 77–80.
22 E.g. Leech, *Thirty Years from Home*;
Kelly, *Eighteenth Century Seaman*; Samuel
Stokes in Baynham, *Lower Deck*,
pp. 119–43.
23 *NC* XXIV, 289–90 – and this was Michael
Pakenham, who was by no means
insensitive. Readers of British humorous
magazines like *Punch* may observe a
similar transition in the 1970s as corporal
punishment in schools, hitherto a
reliable comic staple, became a sensitive
issue.
24 Richardson, *Mariner of England*, p. 106.
Cf. Boteler, *Recollections*, p. 11; Wareham,
Star Captains, p. 215; Thursfield, 'Letters

from the Lower Deck', p. 357; *NC* XIX, 382–4.

25 Hodgskin, *Naval Discipline*, p. ix, though even this angry and incoherent book insists on the necessity of severe punishments at sea. Cf. David Stack, *Nature and Artifice: The Life and Thought of Thomas Hodgskin (1787–1869)* (Woodbridge, 1998), pp. 34–55.

26 Hannay, *Naval Courts Martial*, p. 66.

27 Thursfield, 'Cumby', p. 333. Cf. *SL*, pp. 188 and 228–9.

28 Moody, 'Irish Countryman' IV, 232.

29 Byrn, *Crime and Punishment*, pp. 19 and 77–9.

30 Thursfield, 'Letters from the Lower Deck', p. 368, to his parents, 12 Oct 1809. Cf. *BND* No. 330 pp. 547–51 for a similar example from 1805.

31 Byrn, *Crime and Punishment*, pp. 108–9. McKee, *A Gentlemanly and Honorable Profession*, pp. 233–354. Harold D. Langley, *Social Reform in the United States Navy, 1798–1862* (Urbana, Ill. 1967), pp. 133–45. Cf. Brooks, *James Durand*, pp. 18 and 23–4; Leech, *Thirty Years from Home*, pp. 234–7.

32 Sproule, 'Burney's Opinions', p. 62.

33 For Burney's career see G. E. Manwaring, *My Friend the Admiral: The Life, Letters and Journals of Rear-Admiral James Burney* (London, 1931). Most of his time as a junior officer was spent under Captain James Cook, who is hardly likely to have been engaging in competitive sail drill; perhaps this was really hearsay rather than eye-witness. However as late as 1813 such a practice was referred to by Hodgskin as an evil 'now growing into disuse', which if he is to be believed suggests that it was not imaginary: *NC* XXX, 339.

34 Jamieson, 'Tyranny of the Lash'. Byrn, *Crime and Punishment*, pp. 74 and 108. Morriss, *Cockburn*, pp. 38–9. Wareham, *Star Captains*, pp. 219–24. *SL*, p. 463.

35 *DLN* VI, 211, to Lt H. Shaw, 4 Oct 1804.

36 Byrn, *Crime and Punishment*, pp. 19–20.

37 Bourchier, *Codrington* I, 132. Ross, *Saumarez* II, 95. Chamier, *Life of a Sailor*, p. 24. Fremantle, *Wynne Diaries* II, 164.

38 *NCCC*, pp. 51–2.

39 Thursfield, 'Wilson', pp. 145 and 179. Wareham, *Star Captains*, pp. 208–14. *KP* III, 324.

40 Griffiths, *Points of Seamanship*, in *SL* p. 360.

41 David Philips, 'A New Engine of Power and Authority: The Institutionalization of Law-Enforcement in England, 1730–1830', in *Crime and the Law: The Social History of Crime in Western Europe since 1500*, ed. V. A. C. Gattrell, Bruce Lenman and Geoffrey Parker (London, 1980), pp. 155–89. J. M. Beattie, 'The Pattern of Crime in England, 1660–1800', *P&P* 62 (1974), pp. 47–95, at p. 48. Byrn, *Crime and Punishment*, pp. 32–70. Neale, 'Forecastle and Quarterdeck', p. 351.

42 Derriman, *Marooned*.

43 Neale, 'Forecastle and Quarterdeck', pp. 377–402. *SL*, pp. 401–8.

44 Neale, 'Forecastle and Quarterdeck', p. 444, quoting PRO: ADM 1/5241.

45 Moody, 'Irish Countryman' V, 53.

46 From the official correspondence in PRO: ADM 1/1204, A1691 and A1718, it is clear that what Horton read out was the original complaint, not an official reprimand. He admitted the charge by throwing all the blame on his former 1st lieutenant. The Admiralty did not choose to take the matter further, and we cannot tell how far his reputation was damaged.

47 *KP* III, 320, to Admiralty, 1 Sep 1812.

48 Pack, *Nelson's Blood*, pp. 71–3. Lavery, *Arming and Fitting*, p. 293. Knight, *Portsmouth Dockyard Papers*, p. 116.

49 Pemberton, *Pel. Verjuice*, p. 217. Cf. Leech, *Thirty Years from Home*, p. 65.

50 Thursfield, 'Wilson', p. 153.

51 *SL*, pp. 152, 191, 358, 387–390, 497, 501–3 and 530–31. Hay, *Landsman Hay*, p. 42. Duff, 'Trafalgar Order Book', p. 92. *KP* III, 320–25. Thursfield, 'Letters from the Lower Deck', p. 368; 'Cumby', p. 333; and 'Wilson', p. 141. Robinson, *Nautical Economy*, p. 37. Liardet, *Professional Recollections*, pp. 37 and 284. Morriss, *Cockburn*, pp. 41–3. Dillon, *Narrative* I, 101–2, 109 and 290–291. Camperdown, *Duncan*, p. 167. Laughton, 'Cathcart Letters', p. 313. Byrn, *Crime and*

Punishment, pp. 125–33. Dillon, *Narrative* I, 101–2 and 290–91.

52 Ehrman, *Younger Pitt* III, 126.

53 *KP* III, 165. Wareham, *Star Captains*, pp. 50–52. *SpP* I, 74–5, 246 and II, 193. Oprey, 'Naval Recruitment', pp. 43–4. Parkinson, *Pellew*, pp. 82–3, 96 and 208–13. Morriss and Saxby, *Channel Fleet*, p. 270. *SVL* II, 303. Nagle, *Journal*, p. 173. Phillimore, *Parker* I, 147. Robertson, 'Mobilisation', p. 46. *DLN* I, 43 and 298. Ross, *Saumarez* I, 149–50 and 299. Maxwell, *Creevy Papers* I, 17. *HCC*, p. 37. Morriss, *Cockburn*, p. 37. Dillon, *Narrative* I, 109 and 361–2. Markham, *Naval Career*, pp. 110–11. P. S. Græme, *Orkney and the Last Great War, being Excerpts from the Correspondence of Admiral Alexander Græme of Græmeshall, 1788–1815* (Kirkwall, 1915), pp. 19–26. R. P. Fereday, *The Orkney Balfours, 1747–99: Trenaby and Elwick* (Oxford, 1990), p. 158. N. A. M. Rodger, 'The Inner Life of the Navy, 1750–1800: Change or Decay?', in *Guerres et Paix*, pp. 171–80, at pp. 177–8.

54 *BP* III, 59–66 and 80.

55 Markham, *Markham Correspondence*, p. 197, to J. Markham, 13 May [1806].

56 McCord, 'Impress Service'. Emsley, *British Society*, p. 100; and 'Social Impact', p. 217. Markham, *Markham Correspondence*, p. 198.

57 Sutton, *Lords of the East*, pp. 94–5. Laughton, 'Addison Journals', p. 372.

58 *SL*, pp. 632–3, quoting Captain Philip Patton's *Observations on Naval Mutiny* (1795). Lloyd, *British Seaman*, pp. 202–5. Jackson, *Perilous Adventures*, pp. 26–9. Hay, *Landsman Hay*, pp. 216–19. Crawford, *Reminiscences*, pp. 74–5. Parkinson, *Pellew*, p. 84. Lewis, *Social History*, pp. 44–50. Gardner, *Recollections*, p. 149.

59 Parkinson, *Pellew*, p. 84. Leech, *Thirty Years from Home*, p. 99.

60 Laughton, 'Cathcart Letters', pp. 310–11.

61 *SVL* I, 240–41 and II, 301. Laughton, 'St Vincent Letters', p. 331. Leyland, *Blockade of Brest* I, 9. Crawford, *Reminiscences*, p. 198. Marryat, *Abolition of Impressment*, pp. 23–34.

62 Rodger, 'Devon Men' I, 213–14.

63 Statistics drawn from 'The Ayshford Complete Trafalgar Roll', compiled and shortly to be published on CD-ROM by Pam and Derek Ayshford, to whom I am most grateful for permission to cite it.

64 Marryat, *Abolition of Impressment*, pp. 37–42; cf. Bromley, *Manning*, pp. 352–53.

65 *SL*, pp. 449–51. Some similar but less complete analyses are Hamilton, *Martin Papers* II, 10; Fraser, *Sailors Whom Nelson Led*, pp. 267–8; *KP* III, 321–3.

66 *SL*, p. 266. Crawford, *Reminiscences*, p. 199. Hay, *Landsman Hay*, pp. 67 and 70–74. *NCCC*, pp. 353 and 535. *NC* XXX, 313–14. Liardet, *Professional Recollections*, pp. 42–3.

67 Byrn, *Crime and Punishment*, pp. 160–61. Gill, *Naval Mutinies*, pp. 283–5. Other examples, besides those noted below, are Morriss, *Cockburn*, pp. 38–9 [George Cockburn, 1798]; *SL*, p. 153 [Edward Riou, 1799]; Nagle, *Journal*, p. 237 [F. G. Bond, 1800]; Thursfield, 'Wilson', p. 214 [Patrick Campbell, 1808]; Bourchier, *Codrington* I, 184 [Edward Codrington, 1810]; Thursfield, 'Cumby', p. 333 [W. P. Cumby, 1811]; Brooks, *James Durand*, pp. 61–2 [F. W. Aylmer, 1812]; Broadley and Bartelot, *Nelson's Hardy*, p. 221 [T. M. Hardy].

68 Griffiths, *Points of Seamanship* in *SL*, p. 365. Crawford, *Reminiscences*, pp. 149–50 and 175. Cf. Wareham, *Star Captains*, p. 194, for a similar case.

69 Phillimore, *Parker* I, 194–5 (based on the ship's musters).

70 Patton, *Strictures on Naval Discipline*, in *SL*, p. 627. Cf. Camperdown, *Duncan*, p. 167, for another admiral with similar views.

71 Liardet, *Professional Recollections*, pp. 131–2.

72 Richardson, *Mariner of England*, pp. 117–20 (quoted p. 119).

73 *NC* XIX, 289.

74 Tucker, *St Vincent* I, 231. *SVL* II, 301. *NC* XXI, 115–16. Hay, *Landsman Hay*, p. 173. Dillon, *Narrative* II, 125.

75 Patton, *Strictures on Naval Discipline*, in *SL*, p. 628.

76 Laughton, 'Addison Journals', pp. 346–53 and 372.

77 Brenton, *St Vincent* II, 82.

78 Hall, *British Strategy*, pp. 1–6. Emsley, 'Social Impact', p. 214. O'Brien, 'Impact of the Wars', p. 336. Cookson, *Armed Nation*, pp. 2–7.

79 Havard, *Les ports de guerre* II, 363–6. Masson and Muracciole, *Napoléon et la Marine*, pp. 253–5. Crowhurst, *French War on Trade*, pp. 207–12. Crimmin, 'Prisoners of War and Port Communities'; and 'The Prisoner of War Registers, 1793–1815: A Possible Archival Source for Maritime History', *MM* LXXX (1994), pp. 469–72. Masson, *Les Sépulcres flottants*, and Abell, *Prisoners of War*, are the best general studies.

80 Wilson, *Telegraphs*, pp. 11–16 and 24–7. Hilary P. Mead, 'The Admiralty Telegraphs and Semaphores', *MM* XXIV (1938), pp. 184–203. Lavery, *Nelson's Navy*, pp. 261–4.

81 Lloyd, *British Seaman*, p. 202. *HL* 1794–5 X, 187–9. *SVL* I, 133 and II, 413. *KP* III, 133–53. Popham, *Damned Cunning Fellow*, pp. 55–7. *NC* I, 480–87 and II, 52–5. Frost, *Phillip*, pp. 238–47. Nagle, *Journal*, p. 217. Brenton, *St Vincent* II, 107–8 and 116.

82 *DLN* VI, 22–8 and 33–5. Cyril Field, *Britain's Sea-Soldiers: A History of the Royal Marines* (Liverpool, 1924, 2 vols.) I, 262–3. McArthur, *Courts Martial* I, 206–10.

83 Mark, *At Sea with Nelson*, p. 105. Leech, *Thirty Years from Home*, p. 55.

84 *SL*, pp. 528 and 533–4 (quoted).

85 Petrides and Downs, *Sea Soldier*, p. 73.

86 Bourchier, *Codrington* I, 51. Richardson, *Mariner of England*, p. 209.

87 PRO: E 134/49 Geo III/East/5: deposition of J. Champion.

88 Ross, *Saumarez* I, 301. Steer, 'Blockade and Victualling', pp. 312–13.

89 Liardet, *Professional Recollections*, p. 306. Tucker, *St Vincent* II, 28. Brenton, *St Vincent* I, 440. Dillon, *Narrative* I, 397.

90 Bourchier, *Codrington* I, 299–300, to Mrs Jane Codrington, 23 Dec 1812.

91 Leech, *Thirty Years from Home*, p. 115, is another example.

92 Phillimore, *Parker* I, 198–202. C. E. Maude, 'The Capture of *La Topaze*, 1809', *NR* X (1922), pp. 346–51. Parkinson, *Eastern Seas*, pp. 437–40. *SL*, pp. 159–61, 183–4, 192–4, 234–7, 246–52, 268–9, 276–353, 419–20 and 526–7. Duff, 'Trafalgar Order Book', pp. 91 and 97. *KP* II, 413. HMC *Milne Home*, p. 159.

93 *SL*, p. 165.

94 Pemberton, *Pel. Verjuice*, p. 156.

95 H. B. Louis, *One of Nelson's 'Band of Brothers': Admiral Sir Thomas Louis, Bt* (Malta, [1951]), p. 63, quoting his order book of the *Minotaur*, 1800.

96 *SL*, pp. 134–43, 183–4 and 461. Gardner, *Recollections*, p. 108. Thursfield, 'Wilson', pp. 130 and 255 (quoted); and 'Cumby', p. 344. C. F. Jepson, 'A Sea Career in Nelson's Day – A Memoir', *Fighting Forces* VI (1930), pp. 68–77 and 222–33, at p. 224.

97 *BND* No. 330, p. 549, J. Powell, able seaman of the *Revenge*, to his mother, 12 Jun 1805.

98 Thursfield, 'Wilson', p. 257.

99 Brenton, *St Vincent* I, 439–40. Cf. Liardet, *Professional Recollections*, pp. 81–2.

100 Mark, *At Sea with Nelson*, p. 102. Hay, *Landsman Hay*, p. 102. Raigersfeld, *Life*, p. 45. Brenton, *Naval History* I, 168.

101 Hay, *Landsman Hay*, p. 94. Griffiths, *Points of Seamanship*, in *SL*, p. 362. Liardet, *Professional Recollections*, p. 304.

102 *NCCC*, p. 64, to J. E. Blackett, 26 Jan 1798.

103 Liddell Hart, *Private Wheeler*, p. 47.

104 Parkinson, *Pellew*, p. 415. Hoffman, *Sailor*, pp. 199–200. Brooks, *James Durand*, p. 59. *DLN* IV, 288 and VII, 44. Fremantle, *Wynne Diaries* II, 114 and III, 185. Thursfield, 'Wilson', pp. 164 and 197. Liardet, *Professional Recollections*, p. 302.

105 Richardson, *Mariner of England*, p. 113.

106 Mark, *At Sea with Nelson*, p. 84. I take these to have been *uillean* pipes, the Irish keyed bagpipe.

107 Rawson, *Nelson's Letters*, p. 54. Clarke and M'Arthur, *Nelson* II, 435. *KLM* III, 153. *NC* XV, 281. Hamilton, *Martin*

Papers II, 188. Richardson, *Mariner of England*, p. 255. Liddell Hart, *Private Wheeler*, p. 48. Coleridge, *Devonshire House*, p. 99. Fremantle, *Wynne Diaries* III, 211. Russell, *Theatres of War*, pp. 146–51.
108 Hoffman, *Sailor*, p. 229.
109 Crawford, *Reminiscences*, p. 142.
110 *NCCC*, p. 269, to his wife, 22 Jan 1807.
111 Barnby, 'Noah at Sea', p. 445.
112 Bourchier, *Codrington* I, 147. Fraser, *Sailors Whom Nelson Led*, p. 323. Raikes, *Brenton*, pp. 56–7 and 307–10. *SL*, p. 188 (quoted). *NC* I, 21 and XVII, 320–21. Hoffman, *Sailor*, p. 65. Richardson, *Mariner of England*, pp. 168–74. Camperdown, *Duncan*, p. 167. Gardner, *Recollections*, p. 212. Lloyd, *St Vincent and Camperdown*, pp. 144–5.
113 Thomas, *Newfoundland Journal*, p. 205. Stark, *Female Tar*, goes almost as far.
114 W. B. Rowbotham, 'Soldiers' and Seamen's Wives and Children in H.M. Ships', *MM* XLVII (1961), pp. 42–8.
115 Tucker, *St Vincent*, I, 193 and 414. *SL*, p. 211. Morriss and Saxby, *Channel Fleet*, p. 549.
116 Nicol, *Life and Adventures*, pp. 170–71. Lavery, *Nelson and the Nile*, pp. 116 and 218.
117 Crimmin, 'Service of Nelson's Ships', p. 54.
118 *NC* XIV, 478–9. Cf. A. D. Ridge, 'All at Sea: Observations on the Stepney Baptism Registers', *Archives* VI (1964), pp. 229–34, at p. 234.
119 *NC* XXVIII, 196–7.
120 The medal is in the Douglas-Morris Collection in the Royal Naval Museum, Portsmouth.
121 *NC* XVII, 309 and XX, 293.
122 *NC* XVIII, 342–3.
123 Lewis, *Social History*, p. 286.

33 Honour and Salt Beef

1 Morrison, *Hamilton and Nelson Papers* II, 209, R. Bulkeley to Nelson, 23 Mar 1803.
2 Jennings, *Croker Papers* I, 48. Cf. *NCCC*, p. 287.
3 Bracknall, 'Lieutenants of 1793', p. 25.
4 Huskisson, *Eyewitness to Trafalgar*, p. 10.

5 Phillimore, *Parker* I, 49.
6 *KP* III, 156 and 163–4. Lewis, *Social History*, pp. 89 and 152–3.
7 Lewis, *Social History*, pp. 44–56. Just over 1 per cent of his sample admitted to having been pressed, but for the reasons he gives, the true figure is likely to have been considerably higher.
8 Lewis, *Social History*, pp. 48 and 55–6. *WW*, pp. 267 and 272. Hamilton, *Martin Papers* I, 28. *HP 1790–1820* V, 416–17. Parkinson, *Pellew*, p. 367. Ross, *Saumarez* II, 72; it is difficult to verify that Sir William Mitchell had been court-martialled and flogged for desertion, as he had probably changed his name, but Ross is a sober witness who had served with him. Dillon, *Narrative* II, 158 mentions another mulatto officer.
9 N. A. M. Rodger, 'Officers, Gentlemen and their Education, 1793–1860', in Freeman, *Les Empires*, pp. 139–51.
10 Elliot, *Memoir*, p. 5. Dillon, *Narrative*, I, 84. Coleridge, *Devonshire House*, pp. 94 and 96. Crawford, *Reminiscences*, p. 105.
11 Chamier, *Life of a Sailor*, p. 19.
12 Chamier, *Life of a Sailor*, p. 10. This was the *Salsette* in 1809.
13 Hoste, *Hoste* I, 202. Crawford, *Reminiscences*, pp. 2–7.
14 Phillimore, *Parker* I, 138.
15 *NCCC*, p. 78, to J. E. Blackett, Nov 1799; cf. pp. 88 and 466; also Owen, 'Collingwood Letters', pp. 210–11.
16 Warner, *Collingwood*, pp. 236–7.
17 *SVL* II, 261, to Mrs Crespigny, 5 Sep 1802; cf. II, 341–2.
18 Bowers, *Naval Adventures* I, 175.
19 Brenton, *Brenton*, p. 227. Mark, *At Sea with Nelson*, p. 82. Hodgskin, *Naval Discipline*, p. 69 (quoted). Hoffman, *Sailor*, p. 116.
20 Phillimore, *Parker* I, 6, J. Jervis to Mrs M. Parker, 22 Feb 1793.
21 Thursfield, 'Cumby', p. 349.
22 Crawford, *Reminiscences*, p. 15. Gordon, *Gordon*, p. 10. Cf. Dillon, *Narrative* I, 44.
23 Phillimore, *Parker* I, 188 and 205.
24 Elliot, *Memoir*, pp. 2–3 and 5.
25 Phillimore, *Parker* I, 72.
26 Hoste, *Hoste* I, 314, to his mother, 29 May 1808.

27 Sullivan, 'Naval Schoolmaster', pp. 321–2. Lewis, *Social History*, p. 145.

28 *NCCC*, p. 417, to his wife, 28 Jul 1808.

29 *HCC*, pp. 261–2, to his sister Mary, 17 Dec 1808.

30 Wareham, *Star Captains*, p. 75. Rodger, 'Officers' Careers'.

31 Rodger, 'Officers' Careers', p. 7 and Graph 2.9. Morriss, *Cockburn*, pp. 7–17.

32 Lovell, *Personal Narrative*, p. 41.

33 Rodger, 'Lieutenants' Sea-Time'. Crawford, *Reminiscences*, p. 97. BP III, 389–91. Dillon, *Narrative* I, 290–91. Hoffman, *Sailor*, p. 124. PRO: ADM 107/ 24 ff. 548–50.

34 Elliot, *Memoir*, p. 5.

35 Elliot, *Memoir*, pp. 1, 25, 33 and 37. PRO: ADM 107/24 f. 627 and ADM 107/66 p. 26. *SVL* I, 209. *DLN* V, 199 and 365. *SpP* III, 339.

36 *DLN* V, 364, to St Vincent, 11 Jan 1804 (about Lord Duncan's son); cf. III, 5; V, 59 and 171; VI, 174 and 405.

37 *SVL* II, 323, to Nelson, 20 Nov 1803; cf. II, 356. *SpP* II, 54 and 393–4.

38 Dallas, *Parker*, pp. 12–18. Warner, *Portrait of Lord Nelson*, p. 299. *SVL* II, 323. Lewis, *Social History*, p. 225. Owen, 'Collingwood Letters', p. 184 (quoted), to Sir P. Parker, 1 Nov 1805.

39 William McAteer, 'Admiral Sir Charles Adam', *MM* LXIII (1977), pp. 264–72. *KP* I, 432.

40 Parkinson, *Pellew*, pp. 154–5, 190, 314–15 and 318. Hamilton, *Martin Papers* I, 298.

41 Markham, *Markham Correspondence*, p. 375, to J. Markham, 15 Aug [1806].

42 Michael W. McCahill, 'Peerage Creations and the Changing Character of the British Nobility, 1750–1850', *EHR* XCVI (1981), pp. 259–84. Rodger, 'Honour and Duty'.

43 Tucker, *St Vincent* II, 270; to Benjamin Tucker, 27 Mar 1806.

44 Tucker, *St Vincent* II, 267.

45 Tucker, *St Vincent* I, 414; to Sir J. Jervis, 21 Jun 1797; cf. *DLN* II, 398.

46 *NCCC*, p. 58.

47 *HCC*, p. 112; to Sir E. Blackett, 8 Apr 1800.

48 Markham, *Markham Correspondence*, p. 104, to J. Markham, 26 Jun [1803].

49 Markham, *Markham Correspondence*, p. 27, to J. Markham, 26 Aug 1803.

50 Wareham, *Star Captains*, p. 58. James, *Naval History* IV, 56–64. Carden, *Memoir*, p. 251. Richardson, *Mariner of England*, p. 300. Leech, *Thirty Years from Home*, pp. 31–70. Grafton got his son reinstated, but he was never employed again.

51 HMC *Various* VI, 418, to W. Cornwallis, 23 Jan 1806.

52 Hoste, *Hoste* I, 207, to his mother, 25 Nov 1804. Cf. Christopher Lloyd, *Captain Marryat and the Old Navy* (London, 1939), pp. 140–41 for more praise.

53 *SpP* II, 452, to Spencer, 12 Aug 1798. Cf. Bourchier, *Codrington* I, 149.

54 *SpP* II, 473.

55 *SpP* II, 377, to Spencer, 23 Mar 1797; cf. Maxwell, *Creevy Papers* I, 18.

56 Wareham, *Star Captains*, p. 123.

57 *SpP* II, 200, to Spencer, 15 Oct 1797; cf. Phillimore, *Parker* I, 152.

58 Aspinall, *George III* II, 328 n.1.

59 Lewis, *Social History*, pp. 45 and 202–27. Wareham, *Star Captains*, pp. 93–124.

60 *NCCC*, p. 260, 29 Dec 1806.

61 Lord Radstock's case was unusual; he received his peerage for naval services (as Jervis's third in command at the battle of St Vincent) which would have earned a baronetcy had he not already been of superior rank as a peer's son.

62 *SVL* I, 378–9 and 302, to Duncan, 28 Feb, and Dr Fidge, 4 Mar 1801.

63 *SpP* I, 189–90, Spencer to H. C. Christian, 28 Oct 1795.

64 *SpP* II, 73, to Spencer, 2 Dec 1796.

65 *SpP* II, 390–91, 13 Apr 1797.

66 Benjamin, *Windham Papers*, p. 313, Spencer to W. Windham, 10 Nov 1795.

67 Morriss and Saxby, *Channel Fleet*, p. 599.

68 A forthcoming Exeter University Ph.D. thesis by Miss Moira Bracknall should advance our knowledge a good deal.

69 *SVL* I, 313.

70 *SVL* I, 222.

71 *SVL* I, 331, to Sir J. Carter, 17 Feb 1801.

72 Brenton, *St Vincent* II, 62; to Mrs Montagu, 6 Apr 1801.

73 Phillimore, *Parker* I, 146. *SVL* I, 270.

74 Phillimore, *Parker* I, 165, to G. Parker, 14 Oct 1801.

75 Brenton, *St Vincent* II, 86; to Sir P. Stephens, 5 Oct 1801.

76 *SVL* II, 337.

77 *SVL* II, 329. Commanders were styled 'Captain'.

78 *SpP* II, 390, to Sir J. Jervis, 13 Apr 1797.

79 Rodger, 'Officers' Careers', pp. 7–10 and Table 3. Bracknall, 'Lieutenants of 1793', pp. 45–8. Clowes, *Royal Navy* V, 9–10. Unless otherwise noted, the argument of the following paragraphs is condensed from 'Officers' Careers'.

80 Delafons, *Naval Courts Martial*, pp. 76–7. A commander took rank with a lieutenant-colonel. Wareham, *Star Captains*, p. 117. Rodger, 'Officers' Careers'.

81 *DLN* V, 384, to St Vincent, 20 Jan 1804; cf. VI, 15.

82 Huskisson, *Eyewitness to Trafalgar*, p. 99. Brodie was a commander of February 1801.

83 PRO: ADM 1/5119/3 contains working papers from this exercise.

84 Warner, *Glorious First of June*, pp. 157–64. *DLN* II, 467–70 and III, 473. *SVL* I, 104 and 227–8. Tucker, *St Vincent* II, 105. Walker, *Nelson Portraits*, pp. 69–70 and 166–70. *SpP* II, 205–7. *BP* III, 351–2. Markham, *Naval Career*, p. 179.

85 Oman, *Nelson*, p. 126.

86 Brenton, *St Vincent* II, 52–62. *SVL* I, 222 and 271.

87 Tucker, *St Vincent* II, 175; to Sir W. Dickson, 1 Mar 1801.

88 *BP* III, 241. *KP* III, 177–8. Lewis, *Social History*, p. 198. Markham, *Markham Correspondence*, p. 57. Brenton, *St Vincent* II, 78–9 and 291. There is no connection with the modern rank of sub-lieutenant, created in 1860.

89 *DLN* II, 406–7, 5 Jul 1797.

90 Calculated from HC 1805 VIII p. 203.

91 Cornwallis-West, *Cornwallis*, p. 494, to W. Cornwallis, 1805.

92 *Rectius* who.

93 *BP* III, 84. 8 May 1805. Cf. *HP 1790–1820* III, 201–3.

94 *NCCC* pp. 549–50, to J. Clavell, 20 Oct 1809.

95 Hill, *Prizes of War*, p. 142. Gutridge, 'Naval Prize Agency', pp. 50–51. *WW*, pp. 128–30, 135–7 and 256–8.

96 Fraser, *Enemy at Trafalgar*, p. 234 n.1.

97 Bowers, *Naval Adventures* I, 246–7.

98 Lee, *Memoirs*, p. 50. Thursfield, 'Wilson', p. 218. Hill, *Prizes of War*, pp. 97–9.

99 Wareham, *Star Captains*, pp. 136–7. Hill, *Prizes of War*, pp. 176–7. Phillimore, *Parker* I, 224 and 283. Appendix IV.

100 Paget, *Paget Papers* II, 162.

101 *HP 1790–1820* IV, 707–8.

102 Parkinson, *Eastern Seas*, pp. 344–5 and 349. *KP* III, 218–19.

103 Mrs Arthur Traherne, *Romantic Annals of a Naval Family* (London, 1873), p. 207, H. C. Christian to his wife, 17 Feb 1798.

104 Hill, *Prizes of War*, pp. 20–23. Morriss, *Cockburn*, pp. 20–24.

105 *KP* I, 415, J. Blankett to J. Jackson, [c. Jun 1796].

106 Matthew Sheldon, 'How to Re-fit an Old Admiral for Sea', *MM* LXXXVII (2001), pp. 479–82. Parkinson, *Eastern Seas*, p. 349. *KP* III, 218–19.

107 Draper, 'Gillespie', p. 231.

108 Clarke and McArthur, *Nelson* II, 329, to A. Davison, 1803. Christopher Lloyd, 'Nelson's Prize Money', *MM* LXVI (1980), p. 224.

109 Gutridge, 'Prize Agency', p. 13. Hill, *Prizes of War*, pp. 201–9. Dillon, *Narrative* II, 111 and 119.

110 Gutridge, 'Prize Agency', pp. 152–3. *DLN* II, 390 and 459–60; IV, 181 and 233–6; V, 370; VII Add. cc. Tucker, *St Vincent* II, 68. *SVL* II, 335. *KP* II, 395–7. *NC* X, 432. Dillon, *Narrative* II, 270–72.

111 Gillespie, 'Dance's Battle', p. 164. Brenton, *St Vincent* I, 71.

112 Gutridge, 'Prize Agency'; and 'Naval Prize Agency', pp. 48–51. Hill, *Prizes of War*, pp. 101–4, 139–72 and 212–16.

113 Sugden, 'Cochrane', pp. 194–205 and 217–45. HC 1790–1820 III, 461–8. Hill, *Prizes of War*, pp. 106–16. Johnson, 'Civilizing Mammon'.

114 *NCCC*, p. 315. Chamier, *Life of a Sailor*, pp. 127 and 131.

115 *NC* XIX, 288, 'A.F.Y.' [C. V. Penrose].

116 Phillimore, *Parker* I, 148. Markham,

Markham Correspondence, p. 420.
Markham, *Naval Career*, pp. 141–3.
Brenton, *St Vincent* I, 380–83, 386–7 and
399. Tucker, *St Vincent* I, 206, 305–8 and
448. *HCC*, p. 89. *NC* XIX, 291, 'A.F.Y.'
[C. V. Penrose]. Owen, 'Collingwood
Letters', pp. 166–7.

117 Elliot, *Memoir*, p. 37.
118 *DLN* VII, 303, quoting Lord
Malmesbury.
119 Bourchier, *Codrington* I, 125.
120 *DLN* VII, 71, Captain G. Duff.
121 Fremantle, *Wynne Diaries* III, 199.
Bourchier, *Codrington* I, 46 and 49.
Petrides and Downs, *Sea Soldier*,
pp. 127–9. Elliot, *Memoir*, pp. 59–60.
122 Whitehill, *New England Blockaded*, p. 7.
123 Morrison, *Hamilton and Nelson Papers*
II, 205, to Nelson, 16 Jan 1803.
124 Bourchier, *Codrington* I, 53, E.
Codrington to his wife, 4 Oct [1805].
125 Hamilton, *Martin Papers* III, 398.
126 *NCCC*, p. 235, to his wife, 16 Jun 1806.
127 Bourchier, *Codrington* I, 202.
128 Bourchier, *Codrington* I, 300.
129 Fremantle, *Wynne Diaries*, II, 118.
130 *SVL* II, 359. Tucker, *St Vincent* I, 107.
White, *1797*, p. 112. Buckland, *Miller
Papers*, pp. 15–17. Fremantle, *Wynne
Diaries*, passim.
131 Reynold Ramseyer, *Montagu, Capitaine
de vaisseau, Philanthrope et bourgeois
d'honneur de La Neuveville en Suisse*
(Yens sur Morges, 1992), p. 67. Cf.
Stirling, *Pages and Portraits* I, 53, for
another case.
132 Morriss and Saxby, *Channel Fleet*, p. 386.
133 Thursfield, 'Cullen', p. 90. *KP* II, 16.
Dillon, *Narrative* I, 43 and II, 281. Gore,
Nelson's Hardy, pp. 40–41. Clowes,
Royal Navy V, 27.
134 J. H. Hubback and Edith C. Hubback,
Jane Austen's Sailor Brothers (London,
1906), p. 250. Popham, *Damned Cunning
Fellow*, p. 210. Gordon, *Gordon*, p. 104
(quoted).
135 *KP* III, 157, 164–5 and 179–81. *KMN* III,
31–5. Turner, 'Naval Medical Service',
pp. 123–4. Jarrett, *Naval Dress*, pp. 62–5.
136 J. G. Brighton, *Admiral Sir P. B. V. Broke
. . . A Memoir* (London, 1886), p. 188.
Raikes, *Brenton*, p. 392. Morriss and

Saxby, *Channel Fleet*, p. 323. Hamilton,
Martin Papers I, 264. [Richard
Seymour], *Memoir of Rear-Admiral Sir
Michael Seymour . . .* (London,
p.p. 1878), p. 55.

34 Gain and Loss

1 *SVL* II, 320, 21 Aug 1803.
2 *DLN* V, 396, to Sir J. Acton, 30 Jan 1804.
3 Hall, *British Strategy*, pp. 77–9, 86–7 and
106–11. Mackesy, *Mediterranean*,
pp. 3–30. *DLN* V, 36–7, 107, 247, 341–2,
366. Muir, *Defeat of Napoleon*, p. 166.
Oman, *Nelson*, pp. 518–57. Coleridge, *The
Friend* I, 577–8. Richard Holmes,
Coleridge: Darker Reflections (London,
1998), p. 18. John B. Hattendorf, 'Sea
Power as Control: Britain's Defensive
Naval Strategy in the Mediterranean,
1793–1815', in *Français et Anglais en
Méditerranée*, pp. 203–20, at p. 214. C.
Marchese, 'L'ammiraglio Nelson alla
Maddalena e la Marina Sarda di quei
tempi', *RiM* XXXV (1902), 4, 5–39.
4 Glover, *Britain at Bay*. *KP* III, 2–120.
Leyland, *Blockade of Brest* I, 169–74. Ham,
'Coalition and Isolation', pp. 11–18.
Barrow, *Smith* II, 127–53. Popham,
Damned Cunning Fellow, pp. 112–24. *BP*
III, 155–78. Crawford, *Reminiscences*,
pp. 55–66. McGuffie, 'Stone Ships
Expedition'. Lloyd and Craig, 'Congreve's
Rockets'.
5 'Que nous soyons maîtres du détroit six
heures, et nous serons maîtres du
monde!': to Latouche-Tréville, 2 Jul 1804,
in *Correspondance de Napoléon Premier*
(Paris, 1858–69, 32 vols.) IX, 514.
6 'Un rêve romanesque et épique': to the
Empress Josephine, 21 Jul 1804, in
Desbrière, *Projets et tentatives* IV, 113.
7 'La bizarrerie des projets de l'Empereur,
de leur mobilité, de leur contradiction.'
Dupont, *L'Amiral Decrès*, p. 275.
8 Desbrière, *Projets et tentatives* III, 79–170
and 289–305; IV, 3–146 and 177–466. *MF*
IV, 86–110. Masson and Muracciole,
Napoléon et la Marine, pp. 138–57. Glover,
Britain at Bay, pp. 77–102. Schom,
Trafalgar, pp. 75–115. *KP* III, 47–53.
Dupont, *L'Amiral Decrès*, pp. 111–21 and

138. *KP* III, 87–8. Dupont and Taillemite, *Guerres navales*, pp. 180–86.

9 Charles Ekins, *Naval Battles, from 1744 to the Peace in 1814, Critically Reviewed and Illustrated* (London, 2nd edn 1828), p. 233. Brenton, *Naval History* I, 204.

10 *HCC*, p. 149, to J. E. Blackett, 10 Oct 1803.

11 *DLN* VI, 100, to H. Elliot, 8 Jul 1804.

12 Leyland, *Blockade of Brest, passim,* especially I, 45–6, 175–9, 249–51, 366–8; II, 95–7, 117–24 and 176. Cornwallis-West, *Cornwallis*, pp. 398–458. Cooper, 'Methods of Blockade', pp. 545–9. Steer, 'Blockade of Brest', pp. 127–52. *Kent and the Napoleonic Wars*, ed. Peter Bloomfield (Gloucester 1987), pp. 101–7. Corbett, *Trafalgar* I, 15. *BP* III, 232–9.

13 Cornwallis-West, *Cornwallis*, p. 454.

14 Hall, *British Strategy*, p. 112. Leyland, *Blockade of Brest* I, 263–4 and 315; II, 64–5, 87–90 and 99–100. Cornwallis-West, *Cornwallis*, pp. 408–9. Ehrman, *Younger Pitt*, III, 703–6. Manera Regueyra, 'La Armada en el siglo XIX', pp. 24–5. *AE* VIII, 265–9 and 280–83.

15 Zulueta, 'Trafalgar'. Hermenegildo Franco Castañón, 'Trafalgar, génesis de una selección', *RHN* III (1985) 8, 55–80. Masson, *Histoire de la Marine* I, 348–9 and 395–6. Schom, *Trafalgar*, pp. 64–8. Masson and Muracciole, *Napoléon et la Marine*, pp. 125–6, 138–9, 163–4 and 221–4. Jurien de la Gravière, *Souvenirs* II, 47–8. Taillemite, *L'Histoire ignorée*, pp. 305–6. Battesti, *La Bataille d'Aboukir*, pp. 195–9.

16 Desbrière, *Trafalgar* I, 108 and 111. Corbett, *Trafalgar* I, 140–58. Masson and Muracciole, *Napoléon et la Marine*, pp. 163–4 and 170. Masson, *Histoire de la Marine* I, 348–53. Dupont, *L'Amiral Decrès*, p. 9. Acerra and Meyer, *Marines et Révolution*, p. 254. Desbrière, in *Projets et tentatives* and *Trafalgar*, gives the most detailed account of these schemes. Dupont and Taillemite, *Guerres navales*, pp. 186–95 provide a convenient summary, and Schom, *Trafalgar*, pp. 371–7, has a detailed chronology of them.

17 *DLN* VI, 338–45. Oman, *Nelson*, pp. 561–3. Corbett, *Trafalgar* I, 30–2 and 35–7.

18 Schom, *Trafalgar*, p. 198.

19 Schom, *Trafalgar*, p. 199. Dupont, *L'Amiral Decrès*, p. 147.

20 '. . . redonner constamment de l'énergie et de la décision à nos amiraux pour aller droit au but sans se laisser intimider aussi facilement qu'ils ont l'habitude de le faire.' Desbrière, *Trafalgar* I, 2 n.1.

21 Corbett, *Trafalgar* I, 71, to Admiralty, 12 Apr 1805.

22 Corbett, *Trafalgar* I, 58–75, 98–104 and 114–20. Schom, *Trafalgar*, pp. 202–3. Leyland, *Blockade of Brest* II, 225–7. Denis A. Orde, *Nelson's Mediterranean Command: Concerning Pride, Preferment and Prize Money* (Edinburgh, 1997), pp. 165–72.

23 Hall, *British Strategy*, pp. 114–16. Mackesy, *Mediterranean*, pp. 45–66. Corbett, *Trafalgar* I, 24–8, 54–7, 80–93 and 110–32. Leyland, *Blockade of Brest* II, 296–7.

24 Corbett, *Trafalgar* I, 137–40 and 172–7. Dowling, 'Convoy System', pp. 179, 184, 191, 197–8 and 210–14. Gardiner, *Campaign of Trafalgar*, pp. 36–9 and 121. Rowbotham, 'Diamond Rock'. Vivian Stuart and George T. Eggleston, *His Majesty's Sloop-of-War Diamond Rock* (London, 1978).

25 Oman, *Nelson*, pp. 574–8. Corbett, *Trafalgar* I, 178–85.

26 Leyland, *Blockade of Brest* II, 311–26 and 372–8. Tracy, 'Calder's Action'. Walters, *Memoirs*, pp. 32–4. *BP* III, 258–75. Desbrière, *Trafalgar* I, 73–89. Corbett, *Trafalgar* I, 200–230 and 274–82. *AE* VIII, 290–93 and 300–303. Oliver Warner, 'The Court-Martial of Sir Robert Calder, 1805', *HT* XIX (1969), pp. 863–8. S. Eardley-Wilmot, 'Sir Robert Calder's Action, July 22 1805', *United Service Magazine* CXLIV (1901), pp. 335–42.

27 Corbett, *Trafalgar* I, 209–13, 243–5; II, 266 and 285–301. Desbrière, *Trafalgar* I, 125–33. Masson and Muracciole, *Napoléon et la Marine*, pp. 170–79. Masson, *Histoire de la Marine* I, 356–8.

28 Mackesy, *Mediterranean*, pp. 72–3. Desbrière, *Trafalgar* I, 156–67. Elliott,

Partners in Revolution, pp. 339–40. Masson and Muracciole, *Napoléon et la Marine*, pp. 188–90. Masson, *Histoire de la Marine* I, 358–62.

29 Corbett, *Trafalgar* II, 367–70. Desbrière, *Trafalgar* I, 180–83, 197 and 206–14; II, 105–7. Zulueta, 'Trafalgar', pp. 308–10. Fraser, *Enemy at Trafalgar*, p. 66. *DLN* VII, 130–31.

30 Warner, *Portrait of Lord Nelson*, p. 336. Tracy, *Nelson's Battles*, p. 168. Taylor, 'Trafalgar', p. 283.

31 Bourchier, *Codrington* I, 51, to Mrs Jane Codrington.

32 *The Rutherfurds of that Ilk and their Cadets*, ed. J. H. Rutherford (Edinburgh, 1884), no continuous pagination.

33 Jackson, *Great Sea Fights* II, 322, to his mother, 22 Nov 1805.

34 *HCC*, p. 168, to Sir T. Pasley, 16 Dec 1805.

35 *HCC*, p. 130, to Dr A. Carlyle, 24 Aug 1801.

36 *DLN* VII, 241 n.9.

37 *DLN* VI, 443–5; VII, 89–92 and 149–50. Jackson, *Great Sea Fights* II, 160–82. Desbrière, *Trafalgar* I, 222–5, 256–65 and II, 131–2. Corbett, *Trafalgar* II, 380–91 and 400–426; *Fighting Instructions*, pp. 280–320 and 349–58. Creswell, *British Admirals*, pp. 230–56. Tunstall, *Naval Warfare*, pp. 247–59. Senhouse, 'Trafalgar', pp. 422–25. Hilary P. Mead, *Trafalgar Signals* (London, 1936). Perrin, *British Flags*, pp. 177–9. R. C. Anderson, 'The Lee Line at Trafalgar', *MM* LVII (1971), pp. 157–61. *Trafalgar Committee*.

38 There is a whole library about Trafalgar. The best modern studies are Corbett, *Trafalgar*; Gardiner, *Campaign of Trafalgar*; Warner, *Trafalgar* and *Nelson's Battles*; Taylor, 'Trafalgar'; Howarth, *Trafalgar*; Schom, *Trafalgar*; Terraine, *Trafalgar*; Tracy, *Nelson's Battles*, pp. 157–210; Masson, *Histoire de la Marine* I, 360–76; Manera Regueyra, 'La Armada en el siglo XIX', pp. 26–37. All biographies of Nelson describe it at length. The most valuable collections of documents and correspondence are *DLN* VII; Desbrière, *Trafalgar* II; Jackson, *Great Sea Fights* II, 137–327; *Trafalgar Committee*; *AE* VIII, 329–46; *NCCC*, pp. 119–41; *Nelson's Last Diary*, ed. Oliver Warner (London, 1971); Morrison, *Hamilton and Nelson Papers*. Other interesting narratives are Dillon, *Narrative* II, 51–2 and 57–60; Hoffman, *Sailor*, pp. 211–19; Allen, *Hargood*, pp. 149–53 and 278–92; Baird Smith, 'Defiance at Trafalgar'; Lovell, *Personal Narrative*, pp. 45–50; Fraser, *Enemy at Trafalgar*; Robinson, *Nautical Economy*, pp. 39–65.

39 *DLN* VII, 91.

40 Ogelsby, 'War at Sea in the West Indies', p. 31.

41 *NCCC*, pp. 124–5.

42 Bourchier, *Codrington* I, 31; the pithy expression seems to be the voice of Codrington rather than Howe.

43 Fraser, *Sailors Whom Nelson Led*, p. 157.

44 *SL*, pp. 168–70; *Nelson and the Nile*, pp. 188–9; and *Nelson's Navy*, pp. 172–8. *KP* I, 40. Acerra and Meyer, *Marines et Révolution*, pp. 251–2. Warner, *Nelson's Battles*, p. 205. Tracy, *Nelson's Battles*, pp. 43–5. Caruana, *Sea Ordnance* II, 352–4. *WW*, pp. 57–9.

45 Cisternes, *La Campagne de Minorque*, pp. 192–194. Tornquist, *Count de Grasse*, p. 101.

46 Douglas, *Naval Gunnery*, pp. 410–20. Padfield, *Broke*, pp. 47–8.

47 Roll, pitch, heave, surge, sway and yaw; they all affect gunlaying.

48 Penrose, *Trevenen*, p. 51.

49 Clowes, *Royal Navy* IV, 75. Tunstall, *Naval Warfare*, pp. 185–6. Sermoneta, *Locks of Norbury*, p. 240. Villiers, *Marine Royale* II, 619–20. *WW*, pp. 56–7.

50 *DLN* II, 13–14 and VII Add. clv. Jackson, *Great Sea Fights* I, 145. Tunstall, *Naval Warfare*, pp. 3–4. Clowes, *Royal Navy* III, 533. Richardson, *Mariner of England*, p. 217. Lévy-Schneider, *Jeanbon Saint-André* II, 860 n.4. Masson and Muracciole, *Napoléon et la Marine*, p. 284. Parkinson, *Eastern Seas*, p. 129. Letuaire, *Commandant Lucas*, p. 16.

51 'Qu'au boulet anglais qui nous tuait une vingtaine d'hommes, le boulet français répondait en coupant un mince cordage ou en faisant un trou à la voilure.'

Masson, *Histoire de la Marine* I, 401, quoting the Prince de Joinville.

52 Baird Smith, *'Defiance* at Trafalgar', p. 118.

53 Caruana, *Sea Ordnance* II, 359 quotes the maximum elevation of British guns; Spanish gun carriages were of similar design.

54 Warner, *Nelson's Battles*, p. 208.

55 Duffy, 'La artillería en Trafalgar'.

56 Bourchier, *Codrington* I, 63, to Mrs J. Codrington, 30 Oct [1805].

57 Taylor, 'Trafalgar', p. 313. Jackson, *Great Sea Fights* II, 215–17. Gardiner, *Campaign of Trafalgar*, pp. 134–5. *BP* III, 327.

58 *DLN* VII, 224, to Mrs Blackwood, 22 Oct 1805.

59 *NCCC*, p. 164, to Radstock, 12 Dec 1805.

60 *DLN* VII, 224–303. Fraser, *Enemy at Trafalgar*, pp. 350–64. Howarth, *Trafalgar*, pp. 221–2. Coleridge, *The Friend* I, 574. Pocock, *Horatio Nelson*, pp. 332–40. Jenks, 'Contesting the Hero'.

61 Corbett, *Trafalgar* II, 335–51 and 445–51. Cornwallis-West, *Cornwallis*, pp. 487–9. Desbrière, *Trafalgar* II, 334–97. Laughton, 'Strachan's Action'. Warner, *Nelson's Battles*, pp. 232–5. Gardiner, *Campaign of Trafalgar*, pp. 171–3. Dupont and Taillemite, *Guerres navales*, pp. 201–7. Tunstall, *Naval Warfare*, p. 259.

62 Ingram, 'Failure of British Sea Power' and 'Illusions of Victory', is the extreme exponent of this view, for whom all British naval victories were in fact strategic defeats, and the history of the nineteenth century is a myth designed to console the British for having lost the Napoleonic War.

63 Mackesy, *Mediterranean*, pp. 84–93.

35 A Continental System

1 Markham, *Markham Correspondence*, p. 44, to J. Markham, 29 Mar 1806.

2 Markham, *Markham Correspondence*, p. 45, J. Markham, 9 Apr 1806.

3 Ham, 'Coalition and Isolation', p. 66. Muir, *Defeat of Napoleon*, pp. 7–8. Buckingham, *Memoirs* IV, 83–103. Craig, 'St Vincent Letters', pp. 474 and 480–82.

4 Masson, *Histoire de la Marine* I, 398–400.

Tunstall, *Naval Warfare*, pp. 259–60. Dowling, 'Convoy System', pp. 225–7 and 241–53. Dupont and Taillemite, *Guerres navales*, pp. 211–16.

5 Parkinson, *Eastern Seas*, pp. 105–6 and 156–8. Allen, *Hargood*, pp. 77–97.

6 Parkinson, *Eastern Seas*, pp. 210–35. J. M. Wraight, 'Nathaniel Dance and the Battle of Pulo Auro, 1804', in Haudrère, *Les Flottes des Compagnies des Indes*, pp. 265–81. Gillespie, 'Dance's Battle'. *MF* IV, 296–300. Roger Lepelley, *Marins de l'Isle de France, 1802–1810* (p.p., 1995), pp. 40–45.

7 Parkinson, *Eastern Seas*, pp. 252, 265, 278–84, 291–2 and 298–9; and *Pellew*, pp. 321–6 and 342–72. *HC 1790–1820* IV, 356, and V, 417.

8 W. G. Perrin, 'The Second Capture of the Cape of Good Hope, 1806', in *Naval Miscellany III*, pp. 191–285. Turner, 'Cape of Good Hope'. Hall, *British Strategy*, pp. 144–8. Grainger, *Royal Navy in the River Plate*; and 'River Plate'. Popham, *Damned Cunning Fellow*, pp. 134–65. Harvey, 'Ministry of All the Talents', pp. 634–6. Charles F. Mullet, 'British Schemes against Spanish America in 1806', *HAHR* XXVII (1947), pp. 269–78. King, ' "Ports of Shelter, and Refreshment" ', pp. 208–211. Walters, *Memoirs*, pp. 41–63. Markham, *Markham Correspondence*, pp. 280–98. Mokyr and Savin, 'Stagflation', pp. 227–8.

9 There is some uncertainty over these 'secret clauses', which may not have existed in the form the British government believed, but something of the sort was clearly implied by the strategic situation and the general tenor of the Tilsit agreement.

10 Paget, *Paget Papers* II, 314, to Sir A. Paget, 31 Jul 1807.

11 Feldbæk, 'Denmark in the Napoleonic Wars', pp. 89–92; and 'Denmark and the Baltic' I, 278–9. Ryan, 'Causes of the British Attack'; and 'Copenhagen Operation'. Søby Andersen, 'Denmark between the Wars', pp. 231–8. Hall, *British Strategy*, pp. 155–62. Harvey, *Collision of Empires*, pp. 98–102. Chatterton, *Gambier* II, 13–54. Ham,

'Coalition and Isolation', pp. 131–58. Sparrow, *Secret Service*, pp. 343–6. Frantzen, *Truslen fra Øst*, pp. 113–34. Carr, 'Gustavus IV', pp. 52–6. Hilary Barnes, 'Canning and the Danes, 1807', *HT* XV (1965), pp. 530–38. Sven G. Trulsson, *British and Swedish Policies and Strategies in the Baltic after the Peace of Tilsit in 1807: A Study of Decision-Making* (Lund, 1976), pp. 19–70. Popham, *Damned Cunning Fellow*, pp. 177–9.

12 *HCC*, p. 180.

13 Owen, 'Collingwood Letters', p. 215, to W. Spencer-Stanhope, 7 Oct 1809.

14 *NCCC*, pp. 165–6 and 177–8. Owen, 'Collingwood Letters', pp. 151–2. Mackesy, *Mediterranean*, pp. 103–57. Saul, *Russia and the Mediterranean*, pp. 187–216. Daly, 'Russian Navy', pp. 169–70. Barrow, *Smith* II, 157–207.

15 Rose, 'Duckworth's Expedition'. Mackesy, *Mediterranean*, pp. 157–94. Paget, *Paget Papers* II, 299 and 309. *NCCC*, pp. 183–7. Hall, *British Strategy*, pp. 141–3. Barrow, *Smith* II, 208–58. *NC* XVII, 463–7 and XXVI, 363–84. Crawford, *Reminiscences*, pp. 130–38.

16 *NCCC*, p. 276, to Capt J. Clavell, 23 Mar 1807.

17 Saul, *Russia and the Mediterranean*, pp. 217–22. Daly, 'Russian Navy', pp. 176–9. Mackesy, *Mediterranean*, pp. 226–30. Horward, 'Portugal and the Anglo-Russian Naval Crisis', pp. 48–52. Barrow, *Smith* II, 259–80. Krajeski, *Cotton*, pp. 53–66.

18 Marzagalli, *Les Boulevards de la fraude*, pp. 68–106. Crouzet, 'Blocus mercantile', pp. 163–6. Harvey, *Collision of Empires*, pp. 103–9. Tracy, *Attack on Maritime Trade*, pp. 76–7. *BND* No. 207 pp. 351–4. *KP* II, 185–6 and 202–9. Bonney, 'Eighteenth Century', p. 378. Bonnel, *La France, les Etats-Unis*, pp. 228–30. Perkins, *Prologue to War*, pp. 149–83.

19 Gregory, 'Madeira'. Carr, *Gustavus IV*, pp. 58–63. Hall, *British Strategy*, pp. 163–5. Ryan, 'Ambassador Afloat', pp. 240–41; and *Saumarez Papers*, pp. 15–20 and 46–7. Ham, 'Coalition and Isolation', pp. 166, 196–7, 210–11, 215–22 and 243. Hamilton, *Martin Papers* II, 1–6

and 31–9. Daly, 'Russian Navy', pp. 179–81.

20 Sparrow, *Secret Service*, pp. 362–8. Ryan, *Saumarez Papers*, pp. 30–31 and 36–40. Ross, *Saumarez* II, 110–13.

21 Krajeski, *Cotton*, p. 79. The latin root of the word 'expedition' implies speed.

22 Horward, 'Portugal and the Anglo-Russian Naval Crisis', pp. 57–70. Krajeski, *Cotton*, pp. 84–127. Hall, *British Strategy*, pp. 169–72.

23 Muir, *Defeat of Napoleon*, pp. 65–78. Carden, *Memoir*, pp. 221–31. Hall, *British Strategy*, p. 173; and 'Peninsular War', pp. 409–10. Hamilton, *Martin Papers* II, 65.

24 *HCC*, pp. 215–64. Mackesy, *Mediterranean*, pp. 231–99. *NCCC*, pp. 331–482. Owen, 'Collingwood Letters', pp. 153–4 and 204–9. Cochrane, *Autobiography*, pp. 146–211. Sugden, 'Cochrane', pp. 106–9. Thomas, 'Operations on the Coast of Catalonia', pp. 49–50. Marryat, *Marryat* I, 19–20. Warner, *Collingwood*, pp. 196–211. Aspinall, *Prince of Wales* VI, 335–6.

25 *HCC*, p. 269.

26 *NCCC*, pp. 532–3.

27 *HCC*, pp. 301–3. Mackesy, *Mediterranean*, pp. 311–61. Crawford, *Reminiscences*, pp. 185–91. Thomas, 'Operations on the Coast of Catalonia', p. 51. Hall, 'Peninsular War', pp. 406–8.

28 Sugden, 'Cochrane', pp. 112–44. Cochrane, *Autobiography*, pp. 211–51. Chatterton, *Gambier* II, 192–295. Silvestre, *Les Brûlots anglais. MF* IV, 323–44. Jurien de la Gravière, *Souvenirs* II, 151. *NC* XXII, 104–6. Richardson, *Mariner of England*, pp. 242–53. Steele, *Marine Officer* II, 158–9.

29 Hall, *British Strategy*, pp. 65–7 and 174–9. Muir, *Defeat of Napoleon*, pp. 89–104. De Toy, 'Wellington's Admiral', pp. 405–91. Glover, *Britain at Bay*, p. 24. Bond, *Grand Expedition*. Carl Christie, 'The Royal Navy and the Walcheren Expedition of 1809', in *New Aspects of Naval History*, ed. Craig L. Symonds (Annapolis, Md., 1981), pp. 190–200. McGuffie, 'Walcheren Expedition'. Ham, 'Coalition and Isolation', pp. 267–89.

30 Hall, *British Strategy*, pp. 184–6. Morriss, *Cockburn*, pp. 61–3.

31 Hall, *British Strategy*, pp. 186–8. Parkinson, *Eastern Seas*, pp. 364–408. Duffy, 'World-Wide War', pp. 197–202. H. C. M. Austen, *Sea Fights and Corsairs of the Indian Ocean* (Port Louis, 1934), pp. 139–65. Dupont and Taillemite, *Guerres navales*, pp. 176–9. Walters, *Memoirs*, pp. 73–100. Michael Mason, *Willoughby the Immortal* (p.p., Oxford, 1969) adds some details from the MSS of a leading participant.

32 Parkinson, *Eastern Seas*, pp. 378 and 412–16. Hall, *British Strategy*, p. 189. De Moor, 'Unpleasant Relationship', pp. 55–6.

33 Ryan, *Saumarez Papers*, pp. 58–76 and 208–11; 'Defence of British Trade'; and 'The Melancholy Fate of the Baltic Ships in 1811', *MM* L (1964), pp. 123–34. Ross, *Saumarez* II, 252–67. Feldbæk, *Storhandelens Tid*, pp. 201–6; and 'Denmark and the Baltic', I, 279–81. F. Beutlich, *Norges Sjøvæbning, 1750–1809* (Oslo, 1935). Woodman, *Victory of Seapower*, pp. 129–35.

34 Olson, *Wartime Shortage*, pp. 60–71.

35 Masson, *Histoire de la Marine* I, 416.

36 Ryan, 'Trade between Enemies', p. 190.

37 Marzagalli, *Les Boulevards de la fraude*, pp. 108–278. Masson, *Histoire de la Marine* I, 410–15. Gregory, *Malta*, pp. 212–25. Crouzet, 'Wars, Blockade and Economic Change', p. 571.

38 Mokyr and Savin, 'Stagflation', pp. 225–7. M. S. Anderson, 'The Continental System and Russo-British Relations during the Napoleonic Wars', in *Studies in International History: Essays presented to W. Norton Medlicott*, ed. K. Bourne and D. C. Watt (London, 1967), pp. 68–80.

39 Hill, *Prizes of War*, pp. 45–57.

40 Ryan, 'Defence of British Trade', p. 464.

41 Ryan, 'Trade with the Enemy'; 'Defence of British Trade', pp. 463–6. Crouzet, *L'Economie britannique*, pp. 203–5 and 853–9; and 'Blocus mercantile'. Marzagalli, *Les Boulevards de la fraude*, pp. 108–9. Hamilton, *Martin Papers* II, 248–50. Tracy, *Attack on Maritime Trade*, pp. 79–80.

42 Dowling, 'Convoy System', p. 1, quoting PRO: ADM 1/3994, to Admiralty, 19 Sep 1814.

43 Avery, 'Maritime Trade'. Dowling, 'Convoy System'. Crowhurst, *Defence of British Trade*, pp. 41–74. Hill, *Prizes of War*, p. 62.

44 Masson, *Historie de la Marine* I, 316–17 and 404–9; and 'La Marine sous la Révolution', p. 380. Crowhurst, *French War on Trade*; *Defence of British Trade*, pp. 23–4; and 'Profitability in French Privateering, 1793–1815', *BH* XXIV (1982), pp. 48–60. Malo, *Les Corsaires*, pp. 107–11; and *Les Derniers Corsaires*, pp. 180–259. Acerra and Meyer, *Marines et Révolution*, p. 212.

45 HMC *Milne Home*, p. 146, to G. Home of Wedderburn, 4 Sep 1811.

46 Ryan, *Saumarez Papers*; and 'Ambassador Afloat'. Carr, 'Gustavus IV', pp. 64–5. Ross, *Saumarez* II, 169–251. Ham, 'Coalition and Isolation', pp. 181 and 192.

47 Donald B. Horward, 'Admiral Berkeley and the Duke of Wellington: The Winning Combination in the Peninsula', in Cogar, *New Interpretations . . . Eighth*, pp. 105–20. De Toy, 'Wellington's Admiral', pp. 466–576; and 'Wellington's Lifeline', pp. 362–3. Glover, *Britain at Bay*, pp. 24–5. Watson, 'The United States and the Peninsular War', pp. 861–9. Morriss, *Cockburn*, pp. 78–9. Godfrey Davies, 'The Whigs and the Peninsular War, 1808–1814', *TRHS* 4th S. II (1919), pp. 113–31.

48 Harvey, *Collision of Empires*, pp. 143–8 and 158–62. Muir, *Defeat of Napoleon*, pp. 141–62 and 213–15. Figures vary from time to time and source to source, but the proportions are always at least four to one.

49 Krajeski, *Cotton*, pp. 160–67. Mackesy, *Mediterranean*, pp. 363–76. Thomas, 'Operations on the Coast of Catalonia', pp. 52–5. Clowes, *Royal Navy* V, 478–81. Sondhaus, 'Napoleon's Shipbuilding Program', pp. 357–8. James, *Naval History* V, 233–42. Edouard Even, 'Le Capitaine de Vaisseau Edouard Dubordieu – vaillant marin bayonnais de la

République et de l'Empire', *Marins et Océans* III (1992), pp. 103–117.

50 Notably Glover, 'The French Fleet'.

51 Sondhaus, 'Napoleon's Shipbuilding Program'. Masson and Muracciole, *Napoléon et la Marine*, pp. 224–314. Masson, *Histoire de la Marine* I, 382–402 and 419–21; and 'La Marine sous la Révolution', pp. 386–7. Acerra, *Rochefort* II, 273–85. Dupont, *L'Amiral Decrès*, pp. 188–91 and 195. Jurien de la Gravière, *Souvenirs* I, 340–41 and II, 15 and 158–60. Christian Epin, *Les Ouvriers des arsenaux de la marine sous Napoléon* (Montreuillon, 1990).

36 No Greater Obligations

1 Ryan, 'Trade between Enemies', p. 191. Muir, *Defeat of Napoleon*, pp. 220–31. Daly, 'Russian Navy', pp. 181–2. Bonnel, *La France, les Etats-Unis*, pp. 289–93.

2 Hamilton, *Martin Papers* II, 409, T. B. Martin to Keith, 21 Sep 1813.

3 Hall, 'Peninsular War'; and *British Strategy*, p. 193. Muir, *Defeat of Napoleon*, pp. 207 and 277–8. Popham, *Damned Cunning Fellow*, pp. 197–209. Hamilton, *Martin Papers* II, 346–71. *KP* III, 261–3 and 307.

4 De Toy, 'Wellington's Lifeline', pp. 363–4. Sherwig, *Guineas and Gunpowder*, p. 255. Muir, *Defeat of Napoleon*, p. 206. Watson, 'The United States and the Peninsular War', pp. 865–72.

5 Perkins, *Prologue to War*, pp. 197–209, 245–60, 305, 315–19 and 336–41. Bonnel, *La France, les Etats-Unis*, pp. 34–6 and 290–303. Hickey, *War of 1812*, pp. 22 and 42–3. Crouzet, 'Blocus mercantile'. Emsley, 'Social Impact', p. 221.

6 Smith, 'For the Purposes of Defense', p. 6.

7 Perkins, *Prologue to War*, pp. 8–10, 23, 54–66, 347 and 360–63. Stagg, 'Madison and the Coercion of Great Britain'; and *Mr Madison's War*, pp. 39–47. Bonnel, *La France, les Etats-Unis*, pp. 303–4. Kastor, 'Naval Mobilization', pp. 460–63.

8 Perkins, *Prologue to War*, pp. 89–139. Steel, 'Anthony Merry'; and 'Impressment'. Ritcheson, 'Pinckney's London Mission', pp. 531–5. Selement, 'Impressment'.

9 Perkins, *Prologue to War*, pp. 90–92. Older sources like J. F. Zimmerman, *Impressment of American Seamen* (New York, 1925), pp. 255–75, offer higher figures.

10 Ritcheson, 'Pinckney's London Mission', pp. 536–8. Glover, *Britain at Bay*, pp. 200–204. De Toy, 'Wellington's Admiral', pp. 576–88.

11 *NCCC*, p. 316, to Vice-Adm. E. Thornborough, 18 Oct 1807.

12 Tucker and Reuter, *Injured Honor*, is a thorough account of the affair. Cf. C. E. S. Dudley, 'The *Leopard* Incident, 1807', *HT* XIX (1969), pp. 468–74; and Perkins, *Prologue to War*, pp. 190–97. For Berkeley's political career see *HC 1790–1820* III, 191–3; and De Toy, 'Wellington's Admiral', pp. 45–7, 108–9, 116 and 171.

13 Bartlett, 'Gentlemen Versus Democrats', p. 147. Perkins, *Prologue to War*, pp. 373–4, 400–401 and 418–19.

14 Dudley, *Wooden Wall*, pp. 69–82. Goldenberg, 'Blockade', pp. 424–7. Morriss, *Cockburn*, pp. 87–9. Hickey, *War of 1812*, pp. 167–71. Kert, 'Fortunes of War', pp. 5–6. Dudley and Crawford, *Naval War of 1812* I, 202–3. Donald R. Hickey, 'American Trade Restrictions during the War of 1812', *Journal of American History* LXVIII (1981), pp. 517–38. Faye Kert, 'Taking Care of Business: Privateering and the Licensed War of 1812', in Starkey et al., *Pirates and Privateers*, pp. 135–43.

15 Smith, 'For the Purposes of Defense', p. 3.

16 Stagg, *Mr Madison's War*, pp. 195–207.

17 Bourchier, *Codrington* I, 310.

18 *KP* III, 323.

19 Dudley and Crawford, *Naval War of 1812* II, 59.

20 Dudley and Crawford, *Naval War of 1812* I, 237–47, 548–53 and 639–49; II, 69–75, 213–24, 232–7 and 631–2. Canney, *Sailing Warships*, pp. 122–3. Pullen, *Shannon and Chesapeake*, pp. 36–8. Carden, *Memoir*, pp. 260–65. Gardiner, *Naval War of 1812*, pp. 40–53. Hepper, *Warship Losses*, pp. 141–7.

21 Tyrone G. Martin, 'Isaac Hull's Victory Revisited', *AN* XLVII (1987), pp. 14–21. Leech, *Thirty Years from Home*, pp. 143 and 149. Gardiner, *Frigates of the Napoleonic Wars*, pp. 129–30.

22 Graham and Humphreys, *Navy and South America*, pp. 141–2. Dudley and Crawford, *Naval War of 1812* III, 724–44.

23 Padfield, *Broke*, pp. 27–30 and 144–82. Pullen, *Shannon and Chesapeake*. Dudley and Crawford, *Naval War of 1812* II, 126–34. D. L. Dennis, 'The Action between the *Shannon* and the *Chesapeake*', *MM* XLV (1959), pp. 36–45.

24 Dudley, 'Chauncy'. Dudley and Crawford, *Naval War of 1812* I, 267–374; II, 403–628; and III, 371–706. Drake, 'Yeo and Prevost'. Skaggs, 'Joint Operations'. Maloney, 'War of 1812', pp. 57–9. Stagg, *Mr Madison's War*, pp. 329–35 and 401–4. Hagan, *This People's Navy*, pp. 83–6. E. A. Cruikshank, 'The Contest for the Command of Lake Ontario in 1812 and 1813', *Transactions of the Royal Society of Canada* 3rd S. X (1916), pp. 161–223.

25 Dowling, 'Convoy System', pp. 83–94 and 162–6. Muir, *Defeat of Napoleon*, p. 237. Barry J. Lohnes, 'British Naval Problems at Halifax during the War of 1812', *MM* LIX (1973), pp. 317–33. Kert, 'Fortunes of War', p. 2; and 'Cruising in Colonial Waters: The Organization of North American Privateering in the War of 1812', in Starkey et al., *Pirates and Privateers*, pp. 141–54. I have not adopted the figures cited by Dudley, *Wooden Wall*, pp. 138–42, from old and unreliable sources.

26 Whitehill, *New England Blockaded*, p. 4.

27 Broadley and Bartelot, *Nelson's Hardy*, p. 162, to his brother Joseph, 1 May 1813.

28 Whitehill, *New England Blockaded*, p. 41.

29 Dudley and Crawford, *Naval War of 1812* II, 134–9, 160–64, 183–4 and 272–3. Goldenberg, 'Blockade', pp. 429–36; and 'Blue Lights', pp. 386–93. Jennings, *Croker Papers* I, 44–5. Kert, *Prize and Prejudice*, pp. 151–2.

30 Hagan, *This People's Navy*, p. 89. Goldenberg, 'Blue Lights', pp. 394–5. Kert, 'Fortunes of War', p. 11.

31 Muir, *Defeat of Napoleon*, pp. 243–324.

Sherwig, *Guineas and Gunpowder*, p. 4.

32 Hall, *British Strategy*, pp. 198–200. Watson, 'The United States and the Peninsular War', pp. 870–75. Hickey, *War of 1812*, pp. 172–4. Dudley, *Wooden Wall*, pp. 105 and 112. Muir, *Defeat of Napoleon*, p. 237. Kert, 'Fortunes of War', pp. 4 and 10.

33 Morriss, *Cockburn*, pp. 89–96. Dudley and Crawford, *Naval War of 1812* II, 344–6 and III, 1–172. Bartlett, 'Gentlemen Versus Democrats', pp. 149–54. Hickey, *War of 1812*, pp. 153–4. Petrides and Downs, *Sea Soldier*, pp. 182–94. Chamier, *Life of a Sailor*, p. 177.

34 Morriss, *Cockburn*, pp. 96–110. Stagg, *Mr Madison's War*, pp. 408–18. Dudley and Crawford, *Naval War of 1812* III, 189–271. Elers Napier, *The Life and Correspondence of Admiral Sir Charles Napier* (London, 1862, 2 vols.) I, 76–88. Gordon, *Gordon*, pp. 179–81. 'Narrative of the Naval Operations in the Potomac . . .', *United Service Journal* 53 (1833), pp. 469–81.

35 Harrison Bird, *Navies in the Mountains: The Battles on the Waters of Lake Champlain and Lake George, 1609–1814* (New York, 1962), pp. 262 and 312–30. Bartlett, 'Gentlemen Versus Democrats', pp. 156–8. Wilburt S. Brown, *The Amphibious Campaign for West Florida and Louisiana, 1814–1815: A Critical Review of Strategy and Tactics at New Orleans* (Alabama, 1969). Stagg, *Mr Madison's War*, pp. 383–5. Hickey, *War of 1812*, p. 309. Dudley and Crawford, *Naval War of 1812* III, 596–8 and 607–17.

36 'L'établissment d'un juste équilibre en Europe exigeant que la Hollande soit constituée dans les proportions qui la mettent à même de sountenir son indépendence par ses propres moyens . . .' Lutun, 'Les Clauses navales', p. 51, quoting Secret Art. 3.

37 De Moor, 'Unpleasant Relationship', p. 59.

38 Lutun, 'Les Clauses navales', p. 54.

39 Lutun, 'Les Clauses navales'. Duffy, 'British Diplomacy', pp. 143–4; and 'World-Wide War', pp. 203–6. P. J. Marshall, 'Britain without America – A

Second Empire?', in Marshall, *Eighteenth Century*, pp. 576–95, at pp. 582–3.

40 *KP* III, 328–409. Hall, *British Strategy*, pp. 202–4. Morriss, *Cockburn*, pp. 121–31. Stirling, *Pages and Portraits* II, 2–11.

41 Samuel E. Finer, 'State and Nation-Building in Europe: The Role of the Military', in *The Formation of National States in Western Europe*, ed. Charles Tilly (Princeton, 1975), pp. 84–163, at p. 152.

42 Duffy, 'British Diplomacy', p. 142; and 'World-Wide War', p. 205. Kennedy, *Great Powers*, pp. 174–80.

43 'Grossbrittanien hat keinem Sterblichen mehr Verbindlichkeiten, als gerade diesem Bösewicht, denn durch die Begebenheiten, die er herbeigeführt hat, ist England's Größe, Wohlstand und Reichthum so sehr hoch gesteigert worden. Sie sind die Herren des Meeres und haben weder in dieser Herrschaft, noch im Welthandel eine Nebenbuhlerschaft mehr zu fürchten.' F. C. F. von Müffling, *Aus meinem Leben* (Berlin, 1851), p. 275, to Gen. Frhr. von Müffling, 29 Jun 1815.

Conclusion

1 Ingram, 'Illusions of Victory'.

2 Black, *Britain as a Military Power*, pp. 87–103; and 'Naval Power and British Foreign Policy', pp. 97–9. G. S. Graham, *The Politics of Naval Supremacy* (Cambridge, 1965), pp. 1–30. Robin Ranger, 'The Anglo-French Wars: 1689–1815', in *Seapower and Strategy*, ed. Colin S. Gray and Roger W. Barnett (Annapolis, Md., 1989), pp. 159–85. Jones, 'Limitations of British Sea Power'. Mackesy, 'Strategic Problems'. Kennedy, *British Naval Mastery*, pp. 135–6; *Great Powers*, p. 126; and 'The Influence and the Limitations of Sea Power', *IHR* X (1988), pp. 2–17. French, *British Way in Warfare*, pp. xiv–xvii. Michael Howard, *The Continental Commitment* (London, 1972) is the *locus classicus* of the argument, but deals only with the twentieth century.

3 Sir Michael Howard and Piers Mackesy.

4 Gray, *Leverage of Sea Power*.

5 Kennedy, *British Naval Mastery*.

6 Baugh, 'Why did Britain Lose Command of the Sea'. Rodger, 'Continental Commitment'.

7 Rodger, 'Myth of Seapower'.

8 *Naval Speculations*, Preface (unpaginated).

9 *Politics* VI.6 §2.

10 O'Brien, 'Fiscal Exceptionalism', pp. 3–5. Wheeler, *World Power*, pp. 1–18, 45–6, 94–5 and 195–213.

11 Acerra and Zysberg, *L'Essor des marines*, p. 53. Vergé-Franceschi, *La Marine française*, pp. 49, 110 and 124–6. Dessert, *La Royale*, pp. 74–6, 101–10, 170–74, 238–61 and 284–6.

12 *Thoughts on the Naval Strength of the British Empire* (London, 2nd edn 1795), p. 13.

13 Brewer, *Sinews of Power, passim*; and 'The Eighteenth-century British State: Contexts and Issues', in Stone, *Imperial State*, pp. 52–71.

14 Stone, introduction to *Imperial State*, pp. 14–17. Meyer, *Le Poids de l'état*, pp. 128–9.

15 Harling and Mandler, 'From "Fiscal-Military" State to Laissez-Faire State'. Samuel E. Finer, 'State and Nation-Building in Europe: The Role of the Military', in *The Formation of National States in Western Europe*, ed. Charles Tilly (Princeton, 1975) pp. 84–163.

16 Charles Tilly, *Coercion, Capital and European States, AD 990–1990* (Oxford, 1990), pp. 56–61.

17 Aristide R. Zolberg, 'Strategic Interactions and the Formation of Modern States: France and England', in *The State in Global Perspective*, ed. Ali Kazancigil (Paris and Aldershot, 1986), pp. 72–106, at pp. 94–5.

18 This seems to sum up the argument of Ertman, *Birth of the Leviathan*.

19 Cookson, *Armed Nation*, pp. 2–7. Childs, '1688', p. 420. Brewer, *Sinews of Power*, pp. 64–79. Rodger, 'Myth of Seapower'. Armitage, *Ideological Origins*, pp. 143–4, 173 and 185.

20 Mathias and O'Brien, 'Taxation'. O'Brien, *Power with Profit*; 'Political Economy of British Taxation'; and 'Fiscal Exceptionalism'. Mokyr and Savin,

'Stagflation', p. 208. Ertman, *Birth of the Leviathan*, p. 220.

21 Crouzet, *L'Economie britannique*, pp. 856–72; and 'Wars, Blockade and Economic Change'. Harvey, *Collision of Empires*, pp. 30–39. H. V. Bowen, *War and British Society 1688–1815* (Cambridge, 1988), pp. 56–80. Deane and Cole, *British Economic Growth*, pp. 28–31, 185 and 281.

22 Kennedy, *Great Powers*, p. 100.

23 O'Brien, 'Impact of the Wars'. Thomas and McCloskey, 'Overseas Trade and Empire'. Wrigley, 'Divergence'. Crouzet, 'Second Hundred Years War', pp. 448–50. Bonney, 'Eighteenth Century', pp. 319–21. Davis, *Commercial Revolution*, pp. 10–23.

24 Baugh, ' "A Grand Marine Empire" '; and 'Withdrawing from Europe'. Jacob M. Price, 'The Imperial Economy 1770–1776', in Marshall, *Eighteenth Century England*, pp. 78–104. O'Brien, 'Inseparable Connections'. O'Brien and Engerman, 'Exports'. Thomas and McCloskey, 'Overseas Trade and Empire', pp. 92–3. Kenneth Morgan, 'Mercantilism and the British Empire, 1688–1815', in Winch and O'Brien, *Political Economy*, pp. 165–91. Brewer, *Sinews of Power*, pp. 183–210. Cain and Hopkins, *British Imperialism*, pp. 19–36, 64 and 87–9. John J. McCusker and Russell R. Menard, *The Economy of British America, 1607–1789* (Chapel Hill, 1985), pp. 39–45. Peggy K. Liss, *Atlantic Empires: The Network of Trade and Revolution, 1713–1826* (Baltimore, 1983), pp. 3–5.

25 P. K. O'Brien, 'Path Dependency, or Why Britain Became an Industrialized and Urbanized Economy Long Before France', *EcHR* XLIX (1996), pp. 213–49. Wrigley, 'Society and Economy'; and 'Divergence', pp. 118–25. Crafts, *Economic Growth*, pp. 48–69, 115 and 121–9. Olson, *Wartime Shortage*, pp. 49–71. Buchet, *Marine,*

économie et société, pp. 335–8. Evans, 'Gift of the Sea'. David S. Landes, *The Unbound Prometheus: Technological Change and Industrial Development in Western Europe from 1750 to the Present* (Cambridge, 1969), pp. 47–8 and 77–8. Mokyr, 'Industrial Revolution', pp. 18–24. Jeffrey G. Williamson, 'The Impact of the French Wars on Accumulation in Britain: Another Look', in Aerts and Crouzet, *Economic Effects*, pp. 30–37.

26 Wrigley, 'Society and Economy', p. 81; and 'Divergence', pp. 140–41.

27 Padfield, *Maritime Supremacy*, Introduction. Glete, *Navies and Nations* I, 13. André Corvisier, 'Armées, état et administration dans les temps modernes', *Francia* IX (1980), pp. 509–519, at p. 509. Jaime Vicens Vives, 'Estructura administrativa estatal en los siglos XVI y XVII', in *Obra Dispersa*, ed. M. Batllori and E. Giralt (Barcelona, 1967, 2 vols.) II, 359–77, at pp. 361–2. Rodger, 'Military Revolution at Sea'.

28 Langford, *A Polite and Commercial People*, p. 697.

29 Roughly the argument of Otto Hintze, for whom see Perry Anderson, *Lineages of the Absolutist State* (London, 1974), pp. 134–5; and Thomas Ertman, 'The Sinews of Power and European State-Building Theory', in Stone, *Imperial State*, pp. 33–51, at pp. 34–5.

30 P. K. O'Brien is the outstanding exception among economic historians.

31 Clive Trebilcock, ' "Spin-off" in British Economic History: Armaments and Industry, 1760–1914', *EcHR* 2nd S. XXII (1969), pp. 474–90, at pp. 475–8.

32 Mokyr, 'Industrial Revolution', pp. 7–9.

33 W. G. Perrin, 'The Salute in the Narrow Seas and the Vienna Conference of 1815', in *Naval Miscellany III*, pp. 287–329. Rodger, *Safeguard*, pp. 78–9, 99, 114 and 380–83.

ENGLISH GLOSSARY

This covers historical and nautical terms only in the senses in which they occur in this book; it is not meant to be in any way exhaustive. Those familiar with modern nautical vocabulary will note that seventeenth- and eighteenth-century usage was in some cases different. For currencies, weights and measures see also the Note on Conventions.

aback, adj. 1. (Of a sail) filled by the wind the wrong way, propelling the ship astern rather than ahead. 2. **taken** — (of a ship whose sails are aback) stopped suddenly.

abaft, see **aft**.

abeam, adj. In the direction at right angles to the ship's centreline.

able, adj. (Of a seaman) skilful.

aboard, 1. adj. On board. 2. adv. Of motion towards a ship.

admiral, sb. 1. The officer commanding a squadron of ships. 2. The Lord (High) Admiral, an officer of the crown with jurisdiction over Admiralty and naval affairs. 3. A flag-officer of the rank of Admiral of the White or Blue (eighteenth century). 4. — **General** (sometimes **General** —), commander-in-chief (seventeenth century). 5. — **of the Fleet**, a) commander-in-chief (seventeenth century); b) most senior flag rank (eighteenth century). 6. **port** —, flag-officer commanding ships in and around a naval port. 7. **rear** —, **vice** —, see **rear-admiral**, **vice-admiral**. 8. **yellow** —, captain retired with the rank of rear-admiral.

afore, see **fore**.

aft, abaft, adj. Towards the stern or after part of the ship.

agent, sb. 1. — -**Victualler**, sb. senior official of the Victualling Board in charge of victualling in an outport or squadron abroad. 2. **Navy** —, banker or man of business taking care of a sea officer's financial affairs in his absence. 3. **prize** —, man of business taking charge of the captors' interest in a prize.

ahead, adj., adv. Relating to the ship's head or direction of forward movement.

aloft, adj., adv. 1. Relating to the masts and rigging, upwards. 2. On deck.

alongside, adj. Side by side.

amidship(s), adj. Along or relating to the middle or centreline of the ship.

anneal, vb. To glaze or fuse, to heat in a furnace to make a hard coating.

artificer, sb. A craftsman, a skilled man.

ashore, adj., adv. Towards or on the shore.

astern, adj. Behind a ship, in the direction from which she is moving.

athwart, athwartships, adj. Across, at right angles to the ship's centreline.

back, vb. 1. To trim sails so that they catch the wind on the wrong side and check the ship's way. 2. (Of the wind) to change in an anti-clockwise direction.

ballast, sb. Stones, gravel or other weight stowed low in a ship to improve her stability.

bar, sb. A shoal across the mouth of a tidal estuary.

barge, sb. 1. A small coastal or riverine cargo vessel. 2. A type of ship's boat.

barrel, sb. 1. A cask of specified capacity, usually 30–36 gallons. 2. The tube forming the principal part of a gun.

basin, sb. An body of water enclosed by quays, especially one impounded so that ships may lie afloat regardless of the state of tide.

battery, sb. 1. The broadside guns mounted on one deck, or one side, of the ship. 2. A group of guns mounted ashore. 3. **floating** —, a stationary raft or hulk mounting heavy guns.

beach, vb., To run a ship aground or ashore.

beachmaster, sb. Sea officer responsible for organizing the disembarkation in an amphibious assault.

beam, sb. 1. The width of the ship. 2. The direction at right angles to the centreline. 3. A timber running from side to side of a ship to support a deck.

bear, vb. 1. To enter names in the ship's books as part of the ship's complement. 2. To lie or point in a particular direction. 3. — **away**, to bear up, to turn downwind. 4. — **down**, to bear up. 5. — **up**, to turn downwind.

bearing, sb. A direction.

beat, beat up, vb. (Of a ship) to work to windward by successive tacks, to proceed obliquely to windward with the wind first on one side and then the other.

before, adj. 1. In front of, ahead of. 2. — **the mast, foremast**, relating to common seamen, those who (in a merchant ship) berth in the forecastle.

below, adj. Within the body of a ship.

bend, vb. To make a sail fast to its yard, mast or stay.

berth, sb. 1. A place for a ship to lie at anchor or alongside a quay. 2. A place for a man to sleep. 3. **sick** —, a flat or space in a ship set apart to accommodate the sick.

berth, vb. To find or allocate space for men to sleep or ships to anchor.

bewpers, sb. Bunting, a light woollen cloth for flags.

bilge, sb. 1. The angle of the ship's hull between side and bottom. 2. — **and bilge**, adj. close alongside, touching.

bill, bill of exchange, sb. 1. A payment order, usually drawn on a named person and payable within a specified period. 2. **Navy** —, **Victualling** —, negotiable bills issued by the Navy and Victualling Boards in payment for goods or services.

binnacle, sb. A locker containing the steering compasses, standing immediately before the wheel.

block, sb. 1. A pulley. 2. A solid model of the ship's hull, designed to show her underwater lines. 3. **double** —, a pulley with two sheaves. 4. **single** —, a pulley with one sheave.

blockship, sb. A ship deliberately sunk to block a channel.

board, vb., To go aboard a ship.

boarder, sb. A member of the ship's company told off to attack the enemy by boarding.

boatswain, sb. 1. A ship's officer responsible for sails, rigging and ground tackle. 2. — 's **call**, a whistle used to convey orders. 3. —'s **mate**, a petty officer assisting the boatswain.

boltsprit, see **bowsprit**.

bomb, bomb vessel, sb. 1. A warship designed to carry one or two heavy mortars for shore bombardment. 2. — **ketch**, a ketch-rigged bomb.

bonnet, sb. A strip of canvas laced to the foot of a sail to increase its area.

boom, sb. 1. A light running spar, particularly one extending the foot of a sail. 2. A spare spar. 3. A floating barrier protecting a harbour.

bound, adj. Intended for a specified destination.

bounty, sb. A sum of money payable as an inducement, reward or compensation.

bow, sb. Either side of the foremost part of the ship's hull, as it widens from the stem. **on the** —, adj. said of a ship or object on a bearing somewhere between right ahead and abeam.

bowman, sb. A member of a boat's crew rowing the foremost oar.

bowsprit, boltsprit, sb. A spar projecting over the bows, spreading various items of rigging and one or more sails.

brail, sb. A line or tackle which hauls a sail against its yard or spar to allow it to be secured.

break, vb. 1. To dismiss an officer from his service. 2. To disband a regiment or military organization. 2. — **her sheer** (of a ship's hull), to lose longitudinal rigidity, to deform.

bream, vb. To burn off weed from the bottom of a ship in dock.

breech, sb. The rear end of a gun.

brig, sb. 1. A vessel square-rigged on two masts. 2. — **-sloop**, a brig-rigged sloop.

bring to, vb. (Of a ship) to heave to or stop, usually by backing one or more sails.

bring up, vb. 1. To lift, hoist. 2. To stop, to arrest.

broad, broad on, adj. Making a large angle with.

broadside, sb. 1. The side of the ship. 2. The number of guns mounted or bearing on one side. 3. The simultaneous fire of these guns. 4. The total weight of shot fired by all the guns of the ship. 5. — **on**, adj. of a ship showing her broadside at right angles to the observer's line of sight, or to a named point of reference.

buccaneer, sb. A Caribbean outlaw living by raiding and looting.

bulkhead, sb. A vertical partition within a ship.

bulwark, sb. A barrier around the side of a deck.

bumboat, sb. A shore boat selling goods alongside a ship at anchor.

buoy, sb. A float, anchored as a navigational marker or as a means of mooring ships.

burthen, **burden**, sb. The internal volume or cargo capacity of a ship.

cable, sb. 1. A large rope or hawser, particularly the anchor cable. 2. The standard length of an anchor cable, 120 fathoms.

caisson, sb. A watertight chest or float, used to seal the mouth of a dry dock.

calibre, sb. The bore or internal diameter of a gun.

canister, **canister shot**, sb. Anti-personnel shot made up of musket balls enclosed in a tin canister.

cannon, **full cannon**, **cannon of 7**, sb. A heavy gun of 7-inch calibre, firing shot of 42 lbs weight.

cant, vb. To turn (a ship, gun etc.), to change the heading or direction.

capstan, sb. A mechanical device for hauling in cables, consisting of a vertical revolving drum turned by bars inserted in its rim.

captain, sb. 1. A post-captain. 2. A master and commander, later commander. 3. The form of address of the commanding officer of any armed ship or vessel. 4. — **of the fleet**, a captain or rear-admiral assisting the commander-in-chief. 5. — **of the forecastle**, a petty officer in charge of the forecastle men, handling headsails and ground tackle. 6. — **of the foretop** (**maintop**, **mizzentop**), a petty officer in charge of the topmen of the foremast (mainmast, mizzenmast). 7. **First** —, the captain of the fleet. 8. **gun-**—, a rating commanding a gun's crew. 9. **post-**—, an officer of the rank of captain. 10. **Regulating** —, captain or commander in charge of a district of the Impress Service.

careen, vb. To heel a ship over to expose one side of her underwater hull for cleaning or repairs.

carronade, sb. A type of short gun, of heavy calibre but small charge and short range.

cartridge, sb. A cloth or paper bag containing the propellant charge of a gun.

cat, **cat-of-nine-tails**, sb. A nine-tailed whip.

catamaran, sb. 1. A type of raft, used as a surf-boat on the Coromandel Coast of India. 2. Any raft or float.

caulk, vb. To make seams watertight.

caulking, sb. Material for caulking, usually oakum and pitch.

chase, sb. 1. The pursuit of one ship or squadron by another. 2. The ship pursued. 3. The outer portion of the barrel of a gun. 4. — **gun**, a gun mounted to fire ahead or astern. 5. **general** —, order to a squadron to pursue a beaten enemy without regard to order. 6. **stern** —, pursuit in which the pursued lies dead ahead of the pursuer.

chaser, see **chase gun**.

cheer ship, vb. To cause the ship's company to salute by cheering together.

chips, sb. Offcuts of wood, supposedly waste, taken as a perquisite by dockyard shipwrights.

chock, sb. A block of wood.

clean, sb. To clean weed and barnacles from a ship's bottom.

clear, vb. 1. To leave a port, to get a safe distance from some danger. 2. — **away**, to disengage, disentangle, unfasten, remove or prepare to remove. 3. — **for action**, to prepare the ship for action by removing and stowing away loose fittings and gear.

clerk of the cheque, sb. The senior financial official of a dockyard.

clew, sb. One of the lower corners of a sail.

close-hauled, adj., adv. Steering as nearly towards the wind as possible.

colours, sb. Flags, especially the national ensign.

commander, sb. 1. The commanding officer of any armed ship or vessel, the captain. 2. An officer of the rank of master and commander (1674–1794). 3. An officer of the rank of commander (from 1794). 4. The senior officer commanding a squadron of warships.

commander-in-chief, sb. A senior officer appointed to command a squadron or station.

commanding officer, see **officer**.

commission, vb. To establish a warship as an active unit for command, administrative and financial purposes.

commissioner, sb. 1. A member of the Navy Board not being one of the Principal Officers, especially one on detached service in charge of a naval establishment. 2. A member of the Victualling, Sick and Hurt or Transport Boards.

commodore, sb. 1. The senior captain for the time being of a group of warships in company (seventeenth century). 2. A post-captain appointed commander-in-chief of a squadron or station, having the temporary rank of a rear-admiral. 3. A senior post-captain ordered by the commander-in-chief to take command of a squadron or division. 4. The senior master commanding a convoy of merchant ships, particularly East Indiamen.

compass, sb. A instrument indicating the bearing of the magnetic poles.

compass, adj. Curved.

complement, sb. The total ship's company authorized for her size or Rate.

con, vb. To steer or pilot a ship in confined waters.

conduct money, sb. Travelling expenses.

constable, sb. A parish official responsible for law and order.

convoy, sb. 1. A body of merchant ships under escort. 2. The warships providing the escort.

convoy, vb. To protect a body of merchant ships.

cooper, sb. 1. An artificer skilled in making and repairing casks. 2. A rating employed to assist the purser to dispense beer and other liquids.

cordage, sb. Rope or rigging.

corvette, sb. French term for a brig-sloop.

course, sb. 1. The direction of a ship's movement. 2. The foresail or mainsail, the lowest square sails. 3. The variable time elapsing between the issue of a Navy Bill and its payment. 4. **In** —, adj. payable in numbered sequence of issue.

court martial, sb. A court held under naval or military law.

coxswain, sb. A petty officer in charge of a boat's crew.

crank, adj. Unstable, excessively tender.

crew, sb. The group of men required to man a ship, boat, gun etc.

crimp, sb. A seller of seamen's labour, often obtained by force or fraud.

cringle, sb. An eye sewn into a sail.

cruiser, sb. A warship, of any size or type, sent on detached operations, especially against enemy merchantmen.

culverin, sb. A long gun firing a shot of about 18 lbs (seventeenth century).

cutlass, sb. A type of short heavy single-bladed sword.

cutt, sb. A type of short gun (seventeenth century).

cutter, sb. A small vessel fore and aft rigged on a single mast.

davit, sb. A light spar used as a crane, particularly to lower ship's boats into the water.

dead, adj. Directly, straight.

deals, sb. Softwood planks.

deck, sb. 1. A floor or platform within a ship. 2. — **head**, the underside of the deck overhead. 3. **gun** —, the deck carrying the main battery (seventeenth–nineteenth century). 4. **half** —, the after end of the main deck, below the quarterdeck. 5. **lower** —, a) the gun deck or (in a two- or three-decker) lowest gun deck; b) the ratings of the ship's company as a whole, those who berth on the lower deck. 6. **main** —, the highest deck running the whole length of the ship. 7. **quarter** —, a deck above the main deck over the after part of the ship. 8. **spar** —, a light deck connecting quarter deck to forecastle. 9. **upper** —, a continuous weather deck incorporating quarterdeck and forecastle. 10. **weather** —, a deck exposed to the sky.

demi-culverin, sb. A long gun firing a shot of about 9 lbs (seventeenth century).

dismantle, vb. To remove masts and spars.

disrate, vb. To reduce a man to a lower rate.

Dissenter, sb. A member of a Protestant church or sect dissenting from the Church of England.

division, sb. One of the parts of a squadron of warships, or of a ship's company.

dock, sb. 1. An excavation or basin for ships. 2. — **yard**, see **yard**. 3. **double** —, a dry dock long enough to take two ships at once. 4. **dry** —, a dock with gates, capable of being drained of water to expose the underwater hull of ships within it. 5. **graving** —, a dry dock. 6. **mast** —, a basin for keeping masts and spars under water. 7. **wet** —, a basin impounding the water so that ships may lie afloat at all states of the tide.

double, double on, vb. To attack a ship or squadron from both sides.

double-ended, adj. (Of a ship) having bow and stern of similar design.

drake, sb. A type of short gun (seventeenth century).

draught, sb. 1. The depth of water required to float a ship. 2. A plan or chart. 3. The drawings showing the design of a ship.

draught, vb. To design a ship on paper.

draw, vb. 1. To haul. 2. (Of a sail) to be filled with wind, to pull. 3. (Of a ship) to require a specified depth of water to float her.

drive, vb. To drift.

driver, sb. A gaff sail set on the mizzenmast of a ship, or the mainmast of a brig.

ducking, sb. The dropping a man into the water from a height, as a punishment.

East Indiaman, sb. A merchant ship belonging to one of the East India companies.

easting, sb. Distance run or made good to the eastward.

ebb, sb. The falling tide.

embargo, sb. An order forbidding merchant ships to sail.

embark, vb. To board or be loaded on board a ship.

ensign, sb. A flag flown aft by warships and merchantmen to indicate nationality.

enter, vb. To become a member of a ship's crew.

entrepôt, sb. A port or dock dealing in imported cargoes transshipped for export.

Episcopalian, sb. A Protestant belonging to a church with bishops, especially the Church of England or one of its affiliates.

establishment, sb. A scheme fixing the number of guns, dimensions etc. of the ships of a Navy.

excise, sb. An internal production or consumption tax.

extra, sb. Overtime.

eye, sb. A circular or tear-shaped metal fitting let into a sail or splice.

factory, sb. A trading establishment overseas.

fair, adj. 1. Smooth. 2. Favourable.

falls, sb. The hauling part of a purchase, part of the running rigging led down to the deck.

fast, adj. 1. Secure. 2. **make** —, vb., to tie up.

fasten, vb. To fix together the timbers of a ship.

fastening, sb. A joint, bolt or knee fixing a ship's timbers together.

fetch, sb. The weight or magnitude of a wave.

fetch, vb. To catch, reach, attain.

firemaster, sb. Ordnance Board official in charge of powder and pyrotechnics.

fireship, sb. A small warship fitted with combustibles in order to destroy enemy ships by setting herself on fire and running alongside them.

fireshot, see **shot**.

five-water, adj. Diluted with five parts of water to one of spirits.

flag, sb. 1. An admiral's distinguishing flag. 2. — -**captain**, the captain of a flagship. 3. — **rank**, admiral's rank. 4. — **ship**, the admiral's ship.

flat, sb. An internal space in a ship, especially one off which other compartments open.

flatboat, flat-bottom boat, sb. A landing craft.

fleet, sb. A body of merchantmen, or of warships and merchantmen in company.

flip, sb. A sort of hot punch, made with beer, spirits and sugar.

flood, sb. The rising tide.

floor, sb. The bottom of the hold, the ship's bottom.

flotilla, sb. 1. A group of small warships. 2. Coastal warships considered as a whole.

following, sb. A group of junior officers or men attaching their careers to a particular senior officer.

foot, sb. The lower edge of a sail.

fore, afore, adj. Towards the bow of the ship.

fore-and-aft, adj. Of a type of rig in which sails of various shapes are bent to masts or stays and move about positions parallel to the ship's centreline.

forecastle, sb. A deck built over the forward end of the main deck.

foremast, see **before** and **mast**.

foresail, see **sail**.

form, hull —, sb. The shape of the underwater hull.

forward, adj., adv. Relating to the fore part of ship, or motion towards the bow.

foul, adj. 1. (Of rope etc.) obstructed, tangled. 2. (Of the weather) stormy. 3. (Of a ship's hull) weed-grown, in need of cleaning.

foul, vb. 1. To obstruct, tangle or dirty. 2. — **the range**, to cross another ship's line of fire.

fouling, sb. 1. The process whereby a ship's underwater hull becomes foul. 2. The weed, barnacles etc. responsible.

founder, vb. To sink.

frame, sb. 1. A pair of timbers erected on the keel to support the ship's sides, in the manner of a pair of ribs. 2. The assembly of keel and frames, the ship's skeleton. 3. **in** —, adj. (of a ship under construction) with frames erected but still unplanked.

freeboard, sb. The minimum height of the ship's side above the waterline.

freight, sb. 1. A consignment of precious metals or jewels carried by a warship. 2. The commission earned by the captain for safe conveyance of such a consignment. 3. — **rate**, the prevailing cost of chartering a merchant ship.

frigate, sb. 1. A small sailing warship of fine form and high speed (seventeenth century). 2. A cruising warship with an unarmed lower deck, mounting her battery on the main deck.

full, adj. (Of a ship's hull form) voluminous or capacious in proportion to length and beam.

furl, vb. To bundle up a sail to its yard, mast or stay.

futtock, sb. One of the constituent timbers making up a frame in way of the bilge and side.

gaff, sb. 1. A short spar hinged at the masthead, supporting the peak of a fore-and-aft foresail, mainsail or driver. 2. —**-rig**, a form of fore-and-aft rig in which the principal sails are quadrangular, their peaks supported by gaffs. 3. — **sail**, one whose peak is supported by a gaff.

gage, see **weather gage**.

gall, sb. A sore.

galleon, sb. A type of armed merchantman used by Spain for long-distance trade.

galley, sb. 1. A type of small boat. 2. A small sailing warship or merchantman fitted to row with sweeps. 3. A type of inshore warship propelled primarily by oars. 4. The kitchen or cook-room of a ship.

galliot, sb. A small vessel, usually sprit-rigged.

gangsman, sb. A member of a press-gang.

gangway, sb. 1. A light bridge connecting forecastle and quarterdeck. 2. **at the —**, adj. relating to that part of the quarterdeck where the gangways began, and where men were flogged.

gauge, sb. The capacity of a container.

gauntlet, see **run the gauntlet**.

gear, sb. Rigging or equipment.

general, sb. A commander-in-chief (seventeenth century).

get the wind, vb. To gain the weather gage.

gibe, vb. To shift a fore and aft sail to the other tack, as in wearing ship, hence to wear or turn abruptly.

girdle, vb. To add planking along the ship's waterline to improve stability and buoyancy.

glass, sb. 1. A half-hour glass, used to tell time aboard ship. 2. A measure of time, half an hour.

grain, sb. The line of the ship's course prolonged ahead.

grape, **grapeshot**, sb. Anti-personnel shot made up of small shot secured together in such a way as to fly apart on firing.

grog, sb. Diluted spirits.

ground, sb. 1. The beach or seabed. 2. — **tackle**, see **tackle**.

ground, vb. 1. To run aground. 2. To beach a ship in order to work on her underwater hull at low tide.

guardship, see **ship**.

gun, sb. 1. A piece of artillery. 2. — **deck**, see **deck**. 3. — **lock**, a flintlock firing mechanism for a great gun. 4. — **port**, a port cut to allow guns mounted below decks to fire out. 5. — **room**, a space at the after end of the main or lower deck. 6. — **shot**, the range of a gun. 7. — **tackle**, tackle rigged to run out the gun after firing. 8. **chase** —, see **chase**. 9. **great** —, a heavy gun, a carriage gun.

gunboat, sb. A small armed vessel mounting one or two carriage guns.

gunbrig, sb. A small brig-rigged war vessel.

gunner, sb. An officer responsible for the ship's heavy guns.

gunwharf, sb. An Ordnance establishment supplying the Navy with ship's guns, carriages and related stores.

half-deck, see **deck**.

halyard, sb. A rope or tackle used to hoist a yard or sail.

hammock, sb. A hanging canvas bed.

hand, sb. A member of a ship's company, a sailor.

hand, vb. To reef or furl a sail.

handspike, sb. A wooden bar or lever.

handy, adj. Handling easily, manoeuvrable.

hanging, sb. The position or angle of a deck in relation to the ship's structure.

hatch, hatchway, sb. An opening in a deck.

haul, vb. 1. To pull on a rope. 2. — **up,** to alter course into the wind, to be close-hauled.

head, sb. 1. The foremost part of the ship's hull, projecting outwards and forward of the stem and partly supporting the bowsprit. 2. The ship's heading, the direction in which she points. 3. — **sail,** see **sail.** 4. — **sea,** see **sea.** 5. — **wind,** see **wind.**

head, vb. (Of the wind) to blow from ahead, to stop the progress of a ship.

heave, vb. 1. To haul a rope. 2. (Of a ship) to rise and fall in a swell. 3. — **down,** to careen. 4. — **to,** (of a ship) to stop or lie to by backing some of the sails.

heavy, adj. (Of the weather) stormy.

heel, vb. (Of a ship) to incline or be inclined to one side or the other.

heel, sb. The foot or bottom of mast, rudder etc.

helm, sb. 1. The tiller. 2. The means of steering a ship.

hog, vb. (Of a ship's hull) to lose structural rigidity, to deform, so that bow and stern drop relative the middle of the hull.

hogshead, sb. A cask of specified size, varying with different liquids.

hoist, vb. To lift or raise with a purchase.

hold, sb. The lowest internal space of a ship, below all the decks.

holdfast, sb. An anchorage point to which to make fast a purchase to lift heavy weights.

hoy, sb. 1. A type of sailing barge, square rigged on a single mast. 2. — **man,** the master of a hoy.

hulk, sb. The hull of an old ship moored for various purposes in harbour.

hull, sb. The body or main structure of a ship or vessel.

hydrodynamics, sb. The study of the forces acting in or through liquids in motion, or on bodies in motion in liquid.

hydrostatics, sb. The study of the forces acting in or through liquids at rest, or on bodies at rest in liquid.

idler, sb. A dayman, a non-seaman member of a ship's company not obliged to stand watches.

impress, press, vb. 1. To recruit men, often by force. 2. To imprest.

impress, adj. 1. Relating to recruitment or impressment. 2. — **Service,** the naval recruitment organization.

impressment, sb. The recruitment of men by force.

imprest, sb. An advance payment.

imprest, prest, vb. 1. To issue an advance against future expenses. 2. To make a first payment of wages by way of establishing a contract of employment.

inboard, adj., adv. In, into the ship.

Indiaman, see **East Indiaman.**

inshore, adj., adv. Near, towards the shore.

instrument, sb. An agent, subordinate, employee (seventeenth century).

interloper, sb. A ship trading in defiance of the monopoly of a chartered company.

irons, sb. 1. Ironwork in general. 2. **in** —, adj. said of a ship pointing into the wind and unable to pay off on either tack. 3. **rudder** —, the fittings by which the rudder is hinged.

jack, sb. A type of national flag flown forward, particularly by warships.

jib, sb. A triangular headsail hoisted on a stay set between the foretopmast and the bowsprit.

jibboom, sb. An extension to the bowsprit.

judge-advocate, sb. An official acting as the clerk of the court to a court martial.

keel, sb. 1. The timber lying centrally along the length of the bottom of the ship, forming a spine upon which other parts of her frame are erected. 2. A type of square-rigged barge native to the River Tyne. 3. — **man**, one of the crew of a keel. 4. **sliding** —, a centre-board.

kersey, sb. A type of coarse woollen cloth.

ketch, sb. A small vessel square or fore-and-aft rigged with a main mast and a smaller mizzen aft.

knee, sb. A timber angle-bracket connecting two or more ship's timbers.

lading, loading, sb. The ship's cargo.

landfall, sb. The point at which the deep-sea navigator meets or intends to meet the coast.

landman, landsman, sb. An unskilled member of a ship's company.

landward, adj., adv. Towards the land.

lanyard, sb. A piece of light line connecting or securing something.

larboard, adj. Relating to the port or left-hand side of the ship.

large, adj. Relating to a course with the wind abaft the beam.

Lascar, sb. An Indian seaman.

lask, lask away, vb. To sail large, but not right before the wind (seventeenth century).

lateen, adj. Of a type of fore-and-aft rig in which large triangular sails are bent to yards which are set so that the foot is made fast on deck and the middle hoisted to the masthead.

latitude, sb. A position lying on a line around the earth parallel to the Equator, hence fixed in a north–south direction.

lay, vb. 1. (Of a gun) to aim or point. 2. — **up** (of a ship) to place out of service, in reserve.

lead, sb. A weight on a marked line, used for sounding.

leads, sb. Inshore channels amongst the coastal islands of Norway, Sweden etc.

league, sb. A measure of distance, three miles.

lee, sb. 1. The direction towards which the wind is blowing. 2. The water sheltered from the wind by the land or by a ship. 3. — **shore**, a coastline towards which the wind is blowing.

leeward, adj. Relating to the direction towards which the wind is blowing.

leewardly, adj. (Of a ship) tending to drift rapidly to leeward when trying to sail close-hauled.

leeway, sb. The extent to which the wind blows a ship to leeward of her apparent course.

let go, vb. To cast off, to free, to loose, to drop anchor.

letter of marque, sb. 1. A licence permitting a privately owned warship to attack the shipping of a named enemy in wartime. 2. A merchantman trading in wartime, provided with such a licence in order to be able to take advantage of chance captures.

lieutenant, sb. 1. A commissioned sea officer immediately junior to the captain. 2. — **commander**, — **in command**, a lieutenant commanding a small warship. 3. **first (second, third** etc.) —, lieutenant ranking first (second, third etc.) in seniority after the captain.

line, sb. 1. — **abreast**, A formation in which the ships of a squadron sail on the same course abeam of one another. 2. — **ahead**, a formation in which one or more ships follow a leader, imitating his movements. 3. — **of battle**, a fighting formation in which the ships of a fleet form a straight line in a predetermined order. 4. — **of bearing**, a formation in which a squadron of ships lie in a straight line diagonal to their course. 5. **centre** —, a line down the middle of the ship from bow to stern. 6. **water** —, see **waterline**.

lines, sb. Lines on a plan describing the underwater shape of a ship's hull.

linstock, sb. A short staff with a grip for holding slowmatch, used to fire a gun.

lock, see **gunlock**.

longboat, sb. The largest of the ship's boats.

longitude, sb. A position lying on a straight line drawn around the earth's surface from one pole to the other, hence fixed in an east–west direction.

loose, vb. To hoist or let drop sail, to make sail.

lower-deck, adj. Relating to the ratings of the ship's company as a whole.

lubber, sb. An incompetent seaman.

luff, sb. The windward edge of a sail.

luff, luff up, vb. To turn into the wind.

lugger, sb. A small fore-and-aft rigged vessel with quadrangular sails bent to running yards.

lunar, sb. An observation of the motions of the moon relative to certain stars, permitting a calculation of the ship's longitude.

magazine, sb. 1. A storehouse. 2. A storehouse for explosives. 3. A compartment in the ship for storing powder.

mainmast, see **mast**.

mainsail, see **sail**.

maintop, see **top**.

mainyard, see **yard.**

make and mend, sb. An occasion for the ship's company to mend clothes, a half-holiday.

make sail, vb. To set sail.

man the side, vb. To honour a senior officer coming aboard by assembling a guard of honour.

mast, sb. 1. A vertical spar or spars supporting sails, rigging and other spars. 2. **fore** —, the foremost mast. 3. **lower** —, the lowest and principal element of fore, main or mizzen mast, on which the topmast is stepped. 4. **made** —, a mast made up of more than one tree assembled together. 5. **main** —, the tallest (usually second) mast. 6. **mizzen** —, see **mizzen**. 7. **topgallant** —, **top** —, see **topgallantmast**, **topmast**. 8. — **dock**, see **dock**. 9. — **head**, the top of a lower, top or topgallantmast.

master, sb. 1. The commanding officer of a merchant ship. 2. A warrant sea officer responsible for the navigation and pilotage of a warship. 3. — **and commander**, a quasi-rank intermediate between lieutenant and post-captain (1674–1794). 4. — **attendant**, a yard officer responsible for pilotage, moorings and yardcraft. 5. — **'s mate**, a petty officer assisting the master. 6. **quarter** —, see **quartermaster**. 7. — **shipwright**, see **shipwright**.

match, sb. 1. A type of small rope treated with an inflammable composition. 2. **quick** —, fast-burning match, used to ignite explosives etc. 3. **slow** —, slow-burning match, used to fire guns and as a delayed-action detonator of explosives.

mate, sb. 1. A deck officer of a merchant ship. 2. A petty officer assisting a warrant officer or more senior petty officer; usually used in compound form, e.g. **boatswain's** —, **master's** —, **quartermaster's** — etc.

Mercator's projection, sb. A method of laying down the earth's surface on a map in which the parallels of latitude and longitude cut at right angles, thus allowing a straight course to be represented as a straight line in spite of the curvature of the earth's surface, but at the cost of gross distortion of the polar regions.

meridian, sb. A line connecting positions on the same latitude or longitude.

mess, sb. A unit of some number of men, a division of the ship's company for the distribution of victuals.

metacentre, sb. The point of intersection of two or more perpendicular lines, passing through the ship's centre of buoyancy, drawn when she is upright and heeled. To ensure stability the metacentre must lie a sufficient distance above the centre of gravity.

midshipman, sb. 1. An inferior or petty officer. 2. A boy or young man hoping to become a commissioned officer. 3. — **extraordinary**, an unemployed officer, borne as a midshipman additional to the ship's authorized complement (seventeenth century). 4. — **ordinary**, a former volunteer per order or volunteer of the Royal Naval Academy, borne as a midshipman additional to complement.

mizzen, sb. 1. The aftermost mast of a ship or ketch. 2. — **peak**, the upper end of the mizzen yard or gaff. 3. **mizzentop**, see **top**. 4. — **yard**, the yard of the lateen mizzen sail (seventeenth to mid-eighteenth century).

mole, sb. A breakwater, a barrier protecting a harbour from the force of the seas.

moor, vb. To secure a ship by two anchors, or by making fast to a buoy.

mooring, moorings, sb. 1. The ground tackle by which a ship or buoy rides. 2. A mooring buoy and its ground tackle considered as a whole.

mould loft, sb. A building or storey of a building having a large unobstructed floor on which a ship's lines could be laid out at full scale in order to cut moulds or templates to guide the shipwrights in building the ship.

muster, sb. 1. A record of the names of the ship's company or dockyard workforce. 2. An assembly held to compile or check the muster. 3. — -**master**, an official responsible for mustering ships' companies and recruits. 4. **false** —, a fraudulent entry in a muster.

muster, vb. To assemble people in order to take a muster.

Navy Agent, see **agent**.

Navy Bill, see **bill**.

neap, see **tide**.

night, sb. (In a dockyard) a period of five hours' overtime.

Nonconformist, sb. A member of a Protestant church or sect refusing to conform to the Church of England.

observation, sb. A measurement of the position of sun, moon or star for the purpose of calculating latitude or longitude.

officer, sb. 1. A person having rank and authority in a disciplined service. 2. **commanding** —, a) the senior officer of a squadron of warships; b) the officer commanding a ship in the absence of her captain. 3. **commissioned**—, a sea officer appointed by Admiralty commission: a captain, commander or lieutenant. 4. **naval** —, an official of the Navy Board (seventeenth–eighteenth century); an officer of the Navy (nineteenth–twentieth century). 5. **petty** —, a senior rating. 6. **sea** —, a commissioned or warrant officer of the Navy (seventeenth–eighteenth century). 7. **standing** —, one of the four warrant officers (purser, boatswain, gunner and carpenter) appointed permanently to a ship whether in or out of commission. 8. **warrant** —, a sea or subordinate officer appointed by warrant from one of the naval boards.

offing, sb. The open sea, as viewed from on shore or inshore.

onshore, adj., adv. Towards or on the shore.

Ordinary, sb. 1. A part of the Navy Estimates, in theory to support routine activities. 2. Ships in reserve, and the staff to maintain them.

ordnance, sb. 1. Heavy guns. 2. adj. Relating to the Ordnance Board.

outboard, adj., adv. Relating to, towards, the outside of the ship.

packet, sb. A vessel employed under Post Office contract to carry mails.

parallel, sb. A meridian of latitude or longitude.

pay, vb. 1. To coat with pitch. 2. — **off**, a) to discharge a ship's company with their whole wages, to place a ship out of commission; b) (of a ship in stays) to fall off on to one or other tack.

peak, sb. 1. The after topmost corner of a gaff or sprit-rigged sail. 2. **mizzen** —, see **mizzen**.

pendant, pennant, sb. 1. A narrow flag or streamer, distinguishing a warship from a merchantman. 2. A rope securing the running block of a purchase to the object being hauled. 3. **broad** —, a swallow-tailed short pendant flown by a commodore.

petticoat breeches, sb. An article of seaman's clothes, a sort of divided skirt of canvas.

pig, sb. An ingot of iron or other metal.

pinch-gut money, sb. Short-allowance money, a payment in compensation for short rations.

pintle, pinckle, sb. A vertical pin fixed to the stern post, part of the arrangement hinging the rudder.

pipe, sb. An order conveyed by the boatswain's call.

pipe, vb. To give an order by the boatswain's call.

pitch, vb. To dip head and stern alternately into the waves.

plane, adj. 1. Of a chart representing the earth's surface as flat. 2. — **sailing**, navigation on a plane chart, hence crude or elementary.

plot, vb. To mark a ship's position on a chart.

point, sb. 1. A point of the compass, one of the thirty-two divisions of the compass card. 2. The interval between two points, an arc of 11¼°. 3. A point of sailing, one of the directions relative to the wind in which a vessel may sail.

point, vb. 1. (Of a ship) to head in a particular direction relative to the wind. 2. To lay a gun on some particular target. 3. — **high** (of a ship) to lie particularly close to the wind when close-hauled.

poop, sb. A short deck built over the after end of the quarterdeck.

port, sb. 1. An opening cut in a ship's side. 2. **gun** —, a port out of which a gun is fired.

post-captain, see **captain**.

powder, sb. 1. Gunpowder. 2. **cylinder** —, a type of powder made with charcoal formed in cylinders.

press, prest, sb. 1. See **impress, imprest**. 2. — **gang**, a party of men employed on impressment. 3. **press-master**, an official employed in recruiting men. 4. — **warrant**, an order empowering a named officer to impress seamen. 5. **hot** —, a campaign of impressment not respecting protections.

prime, vb. To prepare, especially to prepare a gun for firing.

priming, priming powder, sb. Fine gunpowder used to detonate the main propellant charge of a gun.

privateer, sb. A privately owned warship licensed by letter of marque to capture enemy shipping for profit.

prize, sb. 1. A captured enemy ship. 2. — **agent**, see **agent**. 3. — -**money**, the proceeds of selling a prize.

proof, prove, vb. To make trial of a gun by firing it.

protection, sb. A certificate of exemption from impressment.

pull, vb. To row.

purchase, sb. An arrangement of rope led through pulleys in order to haul at a mechanical advantage.

purser, sb. An officer responsible for victuals.

pursery, sb. The purser's business.

quadrant, sb. A navigational instrument capable of taking sights or angles up to 90°.

quarter, sb. 1. The sides of the ship's stern. 2. (pl.) a) Each man's post or station in action; b) accommodation ashore. 3. The outer part of a yard. 4. Mercy, safety on surrender. 5. — **bill**, a list allocating each man his station in action. 6. — **deck**, see **deck**. 7. — **master**, a petty officer assisting the master to handle the ship. 8. **on the** —, in a direction between abeam and right aft, diagonal to the ship's course. 9. **sick** — **s**, accommodation ashore for sick and wounded men.

quarter, vb. To appoint men to their action stations.

quoin, sb. A wedge inserted between the breech of the gun and the bed of the gun-carriage, to adjust the elevation of the gun.

race, tiderace, sb. A channel through which the tide floods or ebbs at speed.

rack, vb. (Of a ship's hull) to distort by twisting.

rake, sb. An angle from the vertical.

rake, vb. To fire down the length of an enemy ship from ahead or astern.

rank, sb. A permanent status conferred by a sea officer's commission or warrant.

rate, sb. 1. One of the six classes into which the larger warships were divided. 2. One of the titles of the ratings or common men of the ship, being both a job description and an impermanent, local status analogous to rank.

rate, vb. 1. To assign men to their ratings. 2. To judge the quality of something, to ascertain the accuracy of a watch.

rating, sb. 1. A man's rate. 2. A man so rated, one of the 'common men' of a ship's company having no rank.

razee, sb. A ship modified by being 'cut down' by one deck.

reach, sb. A stretch of river.

reach, vb. To sail with the wind abeam.

rear-admiral, sb. 1. An admiral third in command of a fleet (seventeenth century). 2. The flag-officer commanding the rear division of a fleet (seventeenth century). 3. A rear-admiral's flagship (seventeenth century). 4. A flag-officer of the rank of Rear-Admiral of the Red, White or Blue (eighteenth century).

rebuild, great rebuild, sb. A partial or complete reconstruction of a ship.

reckoning, sb. 1. A calculation of the ship's position. 2. **dead** —, an estimate of the ship's position without benefit of observations, by calculating course, speed and drift from a known point of departure.

reef, sb. 1. A tuck taken in a sail to reduce its area. 2. A line of submerged rocks. 3. — **earring**, a long reef-point rove through a cringle at each end of a row of reef-points, to make fast the reefed sail to the yard-arms. 4. — **point**, a short length of line secured through a sail in order to be made fast around the yard or boom to take in a reef.

reef, vb. To shorten sail by bundling part of the sail against yard or boom.

reeve, vb. To run or lead a piece of running rigging through a block, eye etc.

refit, sb. The process of repairing a ship and putting her in good condition for service.

reformado, sb. A former soldier of a disbanded regiment, hence by extension a person of long experience.

relief, sb. A ship or person ordered to take the place of another.

rhino, sb. (Slang) ready money, cash.

ride, vb. To lie at anchor

rider, sb. An additional timber laid (usually athwartships) over the internal planking of the hold.

rig, sb. 1. The style or arrangement of a ship's masts and sails. 2. **ship** —, see **ship** 2.

rig, vb. To prepare or set up something, particularly a ship's masts and rigging.

rigger, sb. One who rigs ships, a seaman employed in a dockyard.

rigging, sb. 1. The ropes supporting and controlling the masts and spars. 2. **running** —, rigging controlling the movement of sails and movable spars. 3. **standing** —, rigging supporting the masts.

road, **roadstead**, sb. An open anchorage.

roll, vb. (Of a ship) to heel from one side to the other under the pressure of the waves.

ropeyard, sb. A naval rope factory.

rudder, **ruther**, sb. 1. A paddle or blade turned to steer the ship. 2. — **irons**, see **irons**.

rummage, vb. To search thoroughly, especially to search the cargo of a ship.

run, vb. 1. To sail downwind, in the direction towards which the wind is blowing. 2. To desert from a ship or convoy. 3. — **out**, to haul out a gun to its firing position. 4. — **the gauntlet**, to undergo a punishment of walking between two lines of sailors being struck by each with a rope's end.

running, adj. Hoisting, moving.

sag, vb. (Of a ship's hull) to lose structural rigidity, to deform, so that the middle of the hull drops relative to bow and stern.

sail, sb. 1. A piece of cloth spread aloft by masts and rigging to catch the wind and propel a ship. 2. Some number of ships. 3. — **cloth**, heavy canvas for sails. 4. — **plan**, an arrangement of sails. 5. **easy** —, a reduced sail plan, for slow speed. 6. **fore** —, the fore course, the lowest square sail set on the foremast. 7. **head** —, a sail set forward of the foremast. 8. **main** —, the main course, the lowest square sail set on the mainmast. 9. **stay** —, a trangular sail set on one of the stays supporting a mast from ahead. 10. **studding** —, a light sail temporarily spread outboard of a square sail in light airs. 11. **top** —, a square sail hoisted on the topmast, above the course.

sail, vb. 1. (Of any sort of ship) to move, to proceed. 2. **make** —, to hoist, spread sail. 3. **shorten** —, to reduce, take in sail.

scantlings, sb. The structure of the ship's hull.

schooner, sb. A small sailing vessel fore-and-aft rigged on two masts.

scupper, sb. A port or channel to carry water off a deck and over the ship's side.

scuttle, vb. 1. To cut a hole in the ship's deck or side. 2. To sink a ship deliberately.

sea, sb. 1. A wave or waves. 2. — **board**, the coast. 3. — **boat**, a) a ship considered as behaving well or badly in heavy seas; b) a ship's boat kept prepared for immediate lowering at sea. 4. — **Fencible**, member of a sort of coastal militia (1793–1810). 5. — **keeping**, the ability of a ship to remain at sea in all weathers. 6. — **legs**. The ability to stand or walk steadily on a moving deck. 7. — **mark**, a beacon, tower or other prominent object serving to assist the navigator to fix his position in relation to the coast. 8. — **officer**, see **officer**. 9. — **way**, the open sea with a swell running. 10. **head** —, a wave or waves coming at the ship from ahead.

seaward, to seaward, adj., adv. In the direction of the open sea.

sectary, sb. A member of a religious sect.

section, sb. A cross-section of a ship's hull.

secure, vb. To make fast, fix, restrain, set in order.

serve, vb. (Of the wind) to be fair, to blow in a convenient direction for sailing.

set, sb. The direction of flow of a current.

sextant, sb. A navigational instrument capable of taking sights or angles up to 120°.

shag, sb. A type of cloth having a pronounced nap.

shallop, sb. 1. A small cruising warship. 2. A type of ship's boat (seventeenth century).

shanty, sb. A seaman's working song.

sharp, adj. (Of a ship's hull) with fine bows, narrow forward.

sheathe, vb. To cover the ship's underwater hull with planks or plates to protect against the shipworm.

sheer, sb. 1. The curve of the ship's hull along her length, as bow and stern rise from the horizontal. 2. The longitudinal rigidity of the ship's hull. 3. — **plan**, a draught of the ship seen from the side.

sheer, sheer up, vb. 1. To alter course sharply. 2. — **off**, to alter course away from something.

sheet, sb. A rope or tackle controlling the clew of a sail.

shell, sb. A hollow shot containing an explosive or incendiary charge.

shift, vb. 1. To exchange, replace or move. 2. — **flag**, (of an admiral) to change flagship.

ship, sb. 1. A seagoing vessel. 2. A vessel square-rigged on three masts (seventeenth–nineteenth century). 3. — **handling**, the skill of manoeuvring a vessel. 4. — **master**, the master of a merchant ship. 5. — **mate**, a fellow-member of a ship's company. 6. — **of the line**, a warship large enough to form part of the line of battle. 7. — **sloop**, a ship-rigged sloop. 8. **armed** —, an armed merchant ship on charter to the Navy, usually as a convoy escort. 9. **battle** —, a ship of the line. 10. **flag** —, an admiral's ship. 11. **great** —, one of the largest class of ship of the line (seventeenth century). 12. **guard** —, a warship kept in commission in port in peacetime. 13. **private** —, a warship not carrying an admiral. 14. **register** —, a Spanish merchantman officially registered to trade with the Americas.

ship, vb. 1. To bring inboard, to stow. 2. — **water**, to take in water through stress of weather.

shipworm, sb. The *teredo navalis*, a marine borer native to the Caribbean which infests timber.

shipwright, sb. 1. A carpenter skilled in shipbuilding. 2. **master** —, the yard officer responsible for all building and repairs.

shoal, adj. Shallow.

shoal, sb. A sandbank, reef or area of shallow water.

shoal, vb. To apportion shipwrights or other artificers equally among gangs by allowing the foremen to pick in turn.

short-allowance money, **shorto**, sb. A payment in compensation for short rations.

shorten sail, vb. To reduce the number or area of sails set.

shot, sb. 1. A bullet or (non-explosive) projectile fired from a great gun. 2. **canister** —, see **canister**. 3. **chain** —, hollow shot formed in two halves containing and linked by a length of chain, designed to damage rigging. 4. **dismantling** —, one of a number of types of shot designed to damage masts and spars. 5. **grape** —, see **grape**. 6. **fire** —, hollow shot filled with an incendiary compound.

shroud, sb. A stay supporting a mast from the side.

sight, sb. A navigational observation of some heavenly body.

silt, vb. To become more shallow through the accumulation of mud, sand etc.

skylark, vb. To play in the rigging.

sling, sb. 1. A bight or loop of rope used to lift heavy articles. 2. (pl.) Chains temporarily securing a running yard in the hoisted position, close up to the masthead.

sling, vb. 1. To lift or hoist something. 2. To secure a yard with slings.

slip, sb. An inclined plane running into the water, on which a ship is built, or one up which vessels may be hauled for repairs.

slip, vb. 1. To haul a small vessel up a slip for repairs. 2. To cast off a rope, especially to cast off (and buoy) the cable, in order to sail without waiting to weigh anchor.

sloop, sb. 1. A small cruising warship, having only one internal deck, and mounting her main battery on the upper deck. 2. A commander's command. 3. A cutter-rigged coasting vessel (West Indies).

slops, sb. Naval-issue clothes.

slopship, sb. A hulk in which new recruits are washed and issued with clean clothes.

slowmatch, see **match**.

smack, sb. A cutter-rigged fishing vessel.

smart, adj. Quick.

sound, vb. To take a sounding, to measure the depth of water beneath a ship.

sounding, sb. 1. A measurement of the depth of water. 2. **soundings**, the sea area within the 100-fathom line, capable of being sounded; the Western Approaches to the British Isles.

spar, sb. 1. A mast, pole or boom. 2. — **deck**, see **deck**.

speaking trumpet, sb. A megaphone.

spin a yarn, vb. To tell a story.

splice, sb. The union of two or more ropes or parts of ropes spliced together.

splice, vb. To marry two rope's ends, or two parts of the same rope, by parting the strands and weaving them into one another.

spread, sb. The breadth of a sail or length of a yard.

spread, vb. To stretch, extend, keep apart.

spring, sb. A hawser led from the capstan, out of the ship aft and made fast some way along the anchor cable, hauling on which will cant an anchored ship to bring her broadside to bear as desired.

spring, vb. (Of a mast or spar) to split along the grain.

spring tide, see **tide**.

sprit-rig, sb. A form of fore-and-aft rig in which the peak of the principal sail is supported by a running spar hinged at the base of the mast.

spritsail, sb. 1. A sail set on a yard below the bowsprit. 2. — **topsail**, a sail set on a small mast stepped on the end of the bowsprit.

square, adj. 1. (Of sails) broad in proportion to height. 2. (Of the cross-section of a ship's hull) having vertical sides and a flat floor. 3. At right angles. 4. — **rig**, sb. a rig in which quadrangular sails are bent to yards lying horizontal to the masts on which they are set, and move about positions at right angles to the ship's centreline.

square, vb. To set at right angles, to put in order, to tidy.

stand off, vb. To sail away from, to keep a distance from.

standard, sb. 1. A tall straight tree, grown amongst underwood. 2. A standing knee, one joining the upper side of a deck beam to the ship's side.

standing, adj. Fixed.

starboard, adj. Relating to the right-hand side of the ship.

start, vb. To punish informally with a stick or rope's end.

station, sb. 1. A geographical area assigned to a particular ship or squadron. 2. — **bill**, a list assigning each member of a ship's company his duties. 3. — **ship**, a warship assigned to a particular overseas station.

stave, sb. A plank tapered at each end, forming part of the shell of a cask.

stay, vb. 1. To tack. 2. **in stays**, adj. of a ship pointing into the wind while in the process of going about. 3. **miss stays**, vb. in tacking, to fail to turn into the wind and to fall back on to the original tack.

staysail, see **sail**.

stem, stempost, sb. 1. A timber rising in a curve from the keel and forming the centrepiece of the bows. 2. **stem for stem**, adv. head on.

stern, sb. 1. The after end of the ship. 2. — **post**, a straight timber erected on the after end of the keel, supporting both the rudder and the structure of the stern. 3. — **chaser**, a chase gun pointing aft.

steward, sb. A rating responsible for serving or managing victuals.

stick, sb. A spar.

stiff, adj. Having large reserves of stability, heeling little to the pressure of the wind.

stockfish, sb. Dried cod.

stocks, sb. Heavy timbers laid on the slip to support the ship's structure as she is built.

stop the tide, vb. To make progress in a calm by drifting with the favourable tide and anchoring with the unfavourable.

stow, vb. To put away.

stowage, sb. The ship's capacity to stow stores.

straggle, vb. To wander ashore, to be absent from duty.

stream, sb. The tide or current.

stretch, vb. To sail towards, to set a course for.

strike, vb. 1. To lower a mast, spar, sail etc. 2. To strike colours, to surrender. 3. To run aground.

studding-sail, see **sail**.

sub-lieutenant, sb. Position of a midshipman or master's mate, passed for lieutenant but not commissioned, acting as watchkeeping officer of a small warship (1802–14).

suit, sb. A complete set of sails.

supernumerary, sb. A member of a ship's crew additional to her established complement.

surge, sb. Bodily movement of the ship ahead or astern.

swallow the anchor, vb. To give up a seagoing career.

sway, sb. Bodily movement of a ship from side to side.

sweep, sb. 1. A large oar. 2. The movement of something (e.g. the tiller) revolving about a fixed point. 3. A wooden or metal slide forming part of the arc of a circle, designed to guide the sweep of a tiller etc.

table money, sb. An entertainment allowance.

tack, sb. 1. A rope or tackle serving to haul down the clew of a square sail. 2. The course held by a ship beating to windward. 3. **larboard** —, **port** —, the tack on which the wind blows from the left-hand side of the ship. 4. **starboard** —, the tack on which the wind blows from the right-hand side of the ship.

tack, vb. 1. To shift tacks, to go about, to turn into the wind and so onto the opposite tack. 2. To beat to windward by successive tacks.

tackle, sb. 1. A purchase formed of cordage rove through two or more blocks. 2. Rigging or gear in general. 3. **ground** —, anchors and their cables. 4. **gun** —, a purchase used to handle a carriage gun.

take aback, see **aback.**

tally, sb. A label or distinguishing mark.

tarpaulin, sb. 1. A waterproof canvas cloth used for hatch-covers, coats etc. 2. An officer brought up in merchant ships, a person of low birth (seventeenth century).

task work, sb. (In a dockyard) piece work.

taunt, adj. (Of a mast or rig) tall in proportion to the spread of the yards or the size of the ship.

telegraph, sb. 1. An overland visual signalling system. 2. A vocabulary for the composition of naval flag signals.

tender, sb. A vessel employed to assist or serve another, an auxiliary.

tender, tender-sided, adj. Having low reserves of stability, yielding easily to the pressure of the wind.

thick, adj. (Of the weather) misty, hazy.

three-decker, sb. One of the largest class of ship of the line, having three gun decks.

ticket, sb. 1. A document or certificate. 2. A financial obligation in lieu of cash.

tide, sb. 1. The diurnal rise and fall of sea-level. 2. (In the dockyards) a period of one and a half hours' overtime. 3. — **race**, see **race**. 3. **neap** —, one of the tides of least range, occurring twice a month. 4. **spring** —, one of the tides of greatest range, occurring twice a month.

tier, sb. 1. A layer, e.g. of casks stowed in the ship's hold. 2. **ground** —, the lowest tier of casks in the ship's hold.

tiller, sb. 1. A bar inserted in the head of the rudder by which the ship is steered. 2. — **flat**, a space in which the tiller moves.

top, sb. 1. A platform built at the head of the lower mast, serving to spread the shrouds of the topmast and provide a space for men working aloft. 2. — **gallant**, see **topgallant**. 3. — **hamper**, ship's structure or equipment carried high up, tending to increase windage or reduce stability. 4. — **man** (likewise **foretopman** etc.), a seaman skilled in working aloft. 5. — **mast**, a mast fitted to the top of the lower mast and extending it. 6. — **sail**, see **sail**. 7. — **sides**, the upper part of the ship's structure, clear of the water-line. 8. — **timber**, a structural timber forming the uppermost section of a frame on each side. 9. — **weight**, the weight of ship's structure or equipment carried high, hence tending to reduce stability. 10. **fore** —, **main** —, **mizzen** —, a) the platform built at the head of the foremast, mainmast, mizzenmast; b) the fore, main or mizzen topmast head, the head of the topmast or topgallantmast.

topgallant, topgallant sail, sb. 1. A square sail set on the topgallantmast, above the topsail. 2. — **mast**, a mast fitted to the top of the topmast and extending it. 3. — **yard**, the yard set on the topgallantmast, spreading the topgallant.

touch-hole, sb. A hole bored into the bore of the gun at its inner end for the insertion of priming to fire the gun.

treenail, trenail, sb. 1. A wooden peg or pin used to fasten together the parts of the hull of a wooden ship. 2. — **mooter**, an artificer who cuts trenails.

triage, sb. Medical term for the sorting of emergency cases by degree of urgency.

trice, trice up, vb. To secure an article to something overhead.

trim, vb. To adjust the set of the sails, or the angle at which the ship floats.

truck, sb. 1. The solid wheel of a naval gun carriage. 2. A disc of wood protecting the top of a mast.

truck, vb. To swap.

truss, sb. A diagonal bracing timber.

tumblehome, sb. The inward slope of the ship's side above the waterline.

turn-over, sb. 1. The process of transferring men from one ship to another. 2. A man so transferred.

turn over, vb. To transfer a man from one ship to another.

two-decker, sb. A ship of the line having two complete gundecks.

tye, sb. The pendant of the topsail halyard purchase, rove through a block or blocks at the masthead and so to the yard.

unhandy, adj. Unmanoeuvrable, clumsy.

unmoor, vb. To weigh anchor, to cast off a mooring.

upperworks, sb. The upper portion of the ship's structure.

van, sb. The leading one of three divisions of a fleet.

variation, magnetic variation, sb. The movement of the magnetic poles, hence the varying difference of bearing between true and magnetic north.

veer, vb. 1. To pay out a cable. 2. To alter course sharply. 3. To wear. 4. (Of wind) to change in a clockwise direction.

vice-admiral, sb. 1. An officer second in command of a squadron (seventeenth century). 2. The flag-officer commanding the van division of a fleet. 3. The deputy of the Lord Admiral in one of the maritime counties or colonies. 4. A vice-admiral's flagship (seventeenth century). 5. An flag-officer of the rank of Vice-Admiral of the Red, White or Blue (eighteenth century).

victual, vb. To supply victuals.

victualler, sb. 1. A victualling contractor or agent. 2. A ship transporting victuals.

victuals, sb. Foodstuffs.

volunteer, sb. 1. A person volunteering to serve. 2. An unemployed officer serving unofficially in the hope of filling a vacancy. 3. A 'Boy 1st Class', an officer cadet (from 1794). 4. A pupil of the Royal Naval Academy, Portsmouth (1731–1812). 5. — **per order**, a young man training to be an officer under royal patronage (1661–1731).

voucher, sb. A receipt or other document authenticating a payment.

wake, sb. The track of the ship's passage through the water astern.

wall-sided, adj. Of a ship having no tumblehome, with vertical topsides.

wardroom, sb. 1. A space in which the commissioned officers, and some warrant officers, berthed and messed. 2. — **rank**, the status of officers permitted to use the wardroom.

watch, sb. 1. One of the seven divisions of the nautical day. 2. One of the two or three divisions of the ship's company, taking turns to be on duty. 3. The length of one watch, a spell of duty on deck. 4. — **bill**, a list of the ship's company divided into watches.

water, sb. 1. **high** —, **low** —, the tide standing at either end of its range. 2. — **line**, sb. The line of the water surface against the ship's hull. 3. — **man**, a river boatman, especially one plying for hire on the Thames.

water, vb. To supply a ship with fresh water.

way, sb. 1. The movement of a ship though the water. 2. **in** — **of**, adj. in a line with, adjacent to. 3. **steerage** —, sb., movement at a speed sufficient to allow the ship to be controlled by the helm. 4. (pl.) Pairs of heavy timbers laid as rails on a launching slip down which the ship slides into the water. 5. **under** —, adj. moving through the water.

wear, vb. 1. To alter course from one tack to the other by turning before the wind. 2. To fly a particular flag or carry some distinguishing mark.

weather, adj. 1. Relating to the direction from which the wind is blowing. 2. — **gage**, sb. the windward position in relation to another ship or fleet.

weather, vb. To get to windward of something.

weatherliness, sb. The quality of being weatherly.

weatherly, adv. (Of a ship) tending to drift little to leeward when close-hauled.

weigh, vb. To raise something (most often an anchor) from the seabed.

westing, sb. Distance run or made good to the westward.

wet, adj. (Of a ship) tending to ship seas easily.

wharf, sb. A quay, a harbour wall at which ships may lie.

whip, sb. A purchase made up of two single blocks.

whipstaff, sb. A vertical lever fixed to the inboard end of the tiller by which to steer the ship (seventeenth century).

wind, sb. 1. The direction from which the wind blows. 2. The windward position, the weather gage. 3. **head** —, a wind coming from ahead, one making progress on that course impossible. 4. **off the** —, adv. sailing with the wind abaft the beam. 5. **on the** —, adv. sailing close-hauled.

wind and water, between, adj. on the waterline.

windage, sb. The ship's susceptibility to the lateral pressure of the wind, hence the extent to which she makes leeway.

windward, adj. Relating to the direction from which the wind is blowing.

work, vb. 1. To beat to windward. 2. (Of a ship's hull) to flex or move under the strain of the waves. 3. To handle a ship, especially to tack or wear.

works, sb. 1. Parts of the ship's structure. 2. **upper** —, parts of the ship's structure above the main deck, not part of the hull structure.

yacht, sb. A small naval vessel used for communication, to convey important passengers etc.

yard, sb. 1. A spar hung horizontally from a mast to spread the head or foot of a square sail. 2. An establishment to build, repair and supply warships. 3. — -**arm**, the extreme ends of a yard. 4. — **craft**, boats and other craft employed in a naval yard. 5. — **man**, an employee of a naval yard. 6. **dock** —, a naval yard with one or more dry docks. 7. **main** —, the yard spreading the mainsail.

yaw, sb. Deviations from side to side of the ship's course under pressure of wind and sea.

yawl, sb. A type of ship's boat.

FOREIGN GLOSSARY

For ranks and currencies see also the Note on Conventions.

armé en flûte, adj. (French) Of a warship 'fitted as a transport' by dismounting her main battery.

bailli, sb. (French) A rank in the Knights of Malta, to which a number of French sea officers belonged.

Baron, sb. (French, Dutch etc.) A title of nobility.

Bey, sb. (Turkish) The governor of a province.

chevalier, sb. (French) A title of nobility, an hereditary knighthood.

Contrôleur-Général des Finances, sb. (French) A ministerial office, a sort of auditor-general or chief book-keeper.

Compagnie des Indes, sb. (French) The East India Company.

comte, sb. (French) A title of nobility, count.

corso, sb. (Italian) A system of state-sponsored privateering local to the Mediterranean, waged by Muslim states against Christian and vice versa.

Dey, sb. (Turkish) The title of the ruling princes of Algiers.

directieschepen, sb. (Dutch) Municipal warships, provided as convoy escorts by the authorities of a seaport.

duc, sb. (French) A title of nobility, duke.

Graaf, sb. (Dutch) A title of nobility, count.

Graf, sb. (German) A title of nobility, count.

guarda-costa, sb. (Spanish) A 'coast guard', a private warship licensed to cruise for profit against smugglers.

Heer [van], sb. (Dutch) Lord [of], title indicating landed proprietorship and hence noble status.

ingénieur-constructeur, sb. (French) The title of senior naval constructors, equivalent to the English 'Master Shipwright'.

intendant, sb. The civil official responsible for a French dockyard or naval establishment.

jacht, sb. (Dutch) A type of small fast vessel used for transporting passengers on inshore and inland waters.

Jernkontoret, sb. (Swedish) The state monopoly iron-exporting organization.

kommandeur, sb. (Dutch) Senior officer, commodore.

last- en veilgelden, sb. Tonnage dues levied by the Dutch admiralties.

maître charpentier, sb. (French) 'Master Carpenter': the older form of the professional title of French master shipwrights.

maître constructeur, sb. (French) 'Master Constructor': a later form of the professional title of French master shipwrights.

marqués, sb. (Spanish) A title of nobility, marquis.

marquis, sb. (French) A title of nobility, marquis.

Munitionnaire-Général, sb. The victualling contractor or firm responsible both for financing and supplying the victuals of the French navy.

Nabob, sb. 1. Title of various Indian princes. 2. A dismissive term for an Englishman trying to buy his way into national politics with a fortune made in India.

Nawab, sb. The title of various Indian princes.

Raadpensionaris, sb. (Dutch) Permanent secretary of one of the Dutch provincial or local assemblies. The *Raadpensionaris* of Holland was in practice the most important salaried official in the Dutch government.

ria, sb. (Spanish) A deep inlet, a fjord.

skärgårdsflottan, sb. (Swedish) The inshore fleet, the 'island guard'.

Statholder, sb. (Dutch) An elective or hereditary provincial, and by extension national, office of military and naval commander-in-chief.

système des classes, sb. (French) The naval conscription system.

Trésoriers-Généraux de la Marine, sb. (French) The two central bankers or financiers of the French navy.

vaquero, sb. (Spanish) Cowboy.

ABBREVIATIONS

AE	Fernández Duro, *Armada Española*
AEA	*Anuario de Estudios Americanos*
AHN	*Acta Historiae Neerlandicae*
AHR	*American Historical Review*
AN	*American Neptune*
ARN	Oppenheim, *Administration of the Royal Navy*
BAW	Baugh, *British Naval Administration in the Age of Walpole*
BH	*Business History*
BIHR	*Bulletin of the Institute of Historical Research*
BL	British Library
BLO	Bodleian Library, Oxford
BMGN	*Bijdragen en Mededeelingen betreffende de Geschiedenis der Nederlanden*
BMHG	*Bijdragen en Mededeelingen van het Historisch Genootschap*
BNA	Baugh, *Naval Administration 1715–1750*
BND	Hattendorf et al., *British Naval Documents*
BP	Laughton, *Barham Papers*
CCSP	Macray, *Calendar of Clarendon State Papers*
CHJ	*Cambridge Historical Journal*
CHM	*Chronique d'Histoire Maritime*
CHR	*Canadian Historical Review*
CJ	*Journals of the House of Commons*
CPM	Tanner, *Calendar of Pepysian Manuscripts*
CRE	*[Papers of the] Consortium on Revolutionary Europe*
CS	Camden Society
CSM	Colonial Society of Massachusetts
CSPC	*Calendar of State Papers Colonial, America and West Indies*
CSPD	*Calendar of State Papers Domestic*
DLN	Nicolas, *Despatches and Letters of Lord Nelson*
DNB	*Dictionary of National Biography*
DSP	Pepys, *Diary of Samuel Pepys*
EcHR	*Economic History Review*
EHR	*English Historical Review*
FDW	Gardiner and Atkinson, *First Dutch War*
FHS	*French Historical Studies*
GC	*Great Circle*

GNZ	Colenbrander, *De Groote Nederlansche Zeeoorlogen*
HAHR	*Hispanic American Historical Review*
HC	House of Commons Sessional Papers
HCC	Hughes, *Collingwood Correspondence*
HES	*Histoire Economie et Société*
HG	Historisch Genootschap (te Utrecht)
HJ	*Historical Journal*
HL	House of Lords Sessional Papers
HLQ	*Huntington Library Quarterly*
HMC	Historical Manuscripts Commission
HP	*History of Parliament, Commons*
HR	*Historical Research*
HS	Hakluyt Society
HT	*History Today*
IHR	*International History Review*
IJMH	*International Journal of Maritime History*
IJNA	*International Journal of Nautical Archaeology*
IS	*Irish Sword*
JBS	*Journal of British Studies*
JEcH	*Journal of Economic History*
JEEH	*Journal of European Economic History*
JICH	*Journal of Imperial and Commonwealth History*
JMH	*Journal of Modern History*
JMR	*Journal for Maritime Research* [www.jmr.nmm.ac.uk/]
JRUSI	*Journal of the Royal United Service Institution* [later *Royal United Services Institute*]
JSAHR	*Journal of the Society for Army Historical Research*
KMN	Keevil, Lloyd and Coulter, *Medicine and the Navy*
KP	Perrin and Lloyd, *Keith Papers*
LMF	La Roncière, *La Marine française*
LRB	Powell, *Letters of Robert Blake*
MAff	*Military Affairs*
MCC	Magdalene College, Cambridge
MF	Chevalier, *La Marine française*
MH	*Medical History*
MHD	Duffy et al., *The New Maritime History of Devon*
MM	*Mariner's Mirror*
MMF	Lacour-Gayet, *La Marine militaire de la France*
NC	*Naval Chronicle*
NCCC	Newnham Collingwood, *Collingwood Correspondence*
NDAR	Clark, Morgan and Crawford, *Naval Documents of the American Revolution*
NM	*Northern Mariner*
NMM	National Maritime Museum

NR	*Naval Review*
NRS	Navy Records Society
NS	New Series, New Style
NWCR	*Naval War College Review*
NZW	De Jonge, *Geschiedenis van het Nederlandsche Zeewesen*
ODNB	*Oxford Dictionary of National Biography*
OS	Old Style
P&P	*Past and Present*
PH	Cobbett, *Parliamentary History*
PRO	Public Record Office
R&I	*Regulations and Instructions relating to His Majesty's Service at Sea*
RGPks	Rijks Geschiedkunige Publicatiën, kleine serie.
RH	*Revue Historique*
RHA	*Revue Historique des Armées*
RHD	*Revue d'Histoire Diplomatique*
RHN	*Revista de Historia Naval*
RiM	*Rivista Marittima*
SaP	Barnes and Owen, *Sandwich Papers*
SEHR	*Scandinavian Economic History Review*
SHR	*Scottish Historical Review*
SJH	*Scandinavian Journal of History*
SL	Lavery, *Shipboard Life*
SpP	Corbett and Richmond, *Spencer Papers*
StRO	Staffordshire Record Office
SuRO	Suffolk Record Office
SVL	Bonner-Smith, *St Vincent Letters*
SzP	Sausmarez Papers, Sausmarez Manor, Guernsey
T&C	*Technology and Culture*
TRHS	*Transactions of the Royal Historical Society*
TSG	*Transactions of the Société Guernsiaise*
TSP	Thurloe, *State Papers of John Thurloe*
TvG	*Tijdschrift voor Geschiedenis*
TvZ	*Tijdschrift voor Zeegeschiedenis*
VOC	Vereinigde Oostindische Compagnie (the Dutch 'United East India Company')
VP	Ranft, *Vernon Papers*
WA	Woburn Abbey, Bedfordshire (Bound MSS of the 4th Duke of Bedford unless otherwise indicated)
W&S	*War and Society*
WiH	*War in History*
WMQ	*William and Mary Quarterly*
WW	Rodger, *Wooden World*

BIBLIOGRAPHY

This is a selective list of the works which I found most useful in writing this volume, including all those which are cited twice or more in the notes. It does not pretend to be a comprehensive bibliography of British naval history for this period (for which see the forthcoming work by Eugene Rasor). Annual volumes of journals are given in roman numerals, and individual numbers or issues in arabic.

Abell, Francis, *Prisoners of War in Britain, 1756 to 1815* (London, 1914). A careful work, quoting documents but without references.

Acerra, Martine, *Rochefort et la construction navale française, 1661–1815* (Paris, 1993, 1 vol. in 4). Of wider importance than the title indicates.

— ed., *L'Invention du vaisseau de ligne (1450–1700)* (Paris, 1997).

— 'Les Constructeurs de la marine (xviie–xviiie siècle)', *RH* CCLXXIII (1985), pp. 283–304.

— 'Les Forces navales françaises au début de la Ligue d'Augsbourg', in *Guerres maritimes*, pp. 15–24.

Acerra, Martine, José Merino and Jean Meyer, eds., *Les Marines de guerre européennes, XVII–XVIIIe siècles* (Paris, 1985). An important collection.

Acerra, Martine and Jean Meyer, *Marines et Révolution* (Rennes, 1988). A stimulating general history, incorporating much new evidence, unfortunately without references.

Acerra, Martine, Jean-Pierre Poussou, Michel Vergé-Franceschi and André Zysberg, eds., *Etat, marine et société: Hommage à Jean Meyer* (Paris, 1995).

Acerra, Martine and André Zysberg, *L'Essor des marines de guerres européennes (vers 1680–vers 1790)* (Paris, 1997). A good introduction, with many ideas but few references.

Adams, Thomas R. and David W. Waters, *English Maritime Books printed before 1801* (J. C. Brown Library, Providence, R. I., and National Maritime Museum, Greenwich, 1995). An essential work of reference.

[Admiralty], *Ocean Passages for the World: Winds and Currents*, ed. Boyle T. Somerville (Admiralty, 1923 edn). Sailing directions for ocean passages: this is the last edition to be primarily intended for voyages under sail.

Aerts, Erik and François Crouzet, eds., *Economic Effects of the French Revolutionary and Napoleonic Wars* (Louvain, 1990). An important collection of papers.

Aitzema, Lieuwe van, *Saken van Staet en Oorlogh* (The Hague, 1st S. 1669–72,

6 vols.). An important contemporary chronicle, printing many public documents.

Albion, R. G., *Forests and Sea Power. The Timber Problem of the Royal Navy, 1652–1862* (Cambridge, Mass., 1926). A pioneering work, one of the first to take the administrative history of the Navy seriously. Many of its arguments have been undermined by later research.

Aldridge, David, 'Sir John Norris and the British Naval Expeditions in the Baltic Sea 1715–1727' (London Ph.D. thesis, 1971).

— 'The Navy as Handmaid for Commerce and High Policy 1680–1720', in Black and Woodfine, *British Navy*, pp. 51–69.

— 'Admiral Edward Russell, Pre- and Post-Barfleur', in *Guerres maritimes*, pp. 155–72.

— 'Sir John Norris, 1660?–1749', in Le Fevre and Harding, eds., *Precursors of Nelson*, pp. 128–49.

Allardyce, Alexander, *Memoir of George Keith Elphinstone, Viscount Keith* (Edinburgh, 1882). A pallid Victorian biography.

Allen, Joseph, *Memoir of the Life and Services of Admiral Sir William Hargood* (p.p. Greenwich, 1841). Prints a few documents not otherwise available.

Allyn, Richard, *A Narrative of the Victory obtained by the English and Dutch Fleets . . . near La Hogue in the Year 1692* (London, 1744). The author, chaplain of the *Centurion*, was sick ashore at the time of the battle, but copied the captain's and lieutenant's journals of his ship.

Alsop, J. D., 'The Age of the Projectors: British Imperial Strategy in the North Atlantic in the War of the Spanish Succession', *Acadiensis* XXI (1991–2), pp. 30–53.

— 'Sickness in the British Mediterranean Fleet: The *Tiger*'s Journal of 1706', *W&S* XI, 2 (1993), pp. 57–76.

Aman, Jacques, *Une Campagne navale méconnue à la veille de la guerre de Sept Ans: L'escadre de Brest en 1755* (Vincennes, 1986).

Anderson, J. L., 'Climatic Change, Sea-Power and Historical Discontinuity: the Spanish Armada and the Glorious Revolution of 1688', *GC* V (1983), pp. 13–23.

— 'Combined Operations and the Protestant Wind: Some Maritime Aspects of the Glorious Revolution of 1688', *GC* IX (1987), pp. 96–107.

— 'Prince William's Descent upon Devon, 1688: the Environmental Constraints', in *Lisbon as a Port Town, the British Seaman and other Maritime Themes*, ed. Stephen Fisher (Exeter, 1988), pp. 37–55.

Anderson, M. S., 'Great Britain and the Barbary States in the 18th Century', *BIHR* XXIX (1956), pp. 87–107.

Anderson, Olive, 'The Treatment of Prisoners of War in Britain during the American War of Independence', *BIHR* XXVIII (1955), pp. 63–83.

— 'The Establishment of British Supremacy at Sea and the Exchange of Naval Prisoners of War, 1689–1783', *EHR* LXXV (1960), pp. 77–89.

Anderson, R. C., *Naval Wars in the Baltic during the Sailing Ship Epoch, 1522–1850*

(London, 1910). One of the early works of a great scholar of enormous breadth and learning; precise, polyglot and wilfully boring.

— ed., *The Journal of Edward Mountagu, First Earl of Sandwich . . . 1659–1665* (NRS Vol. 64, 1929).

— ed., *The Journals of Sir Thomas Allin, 1660–1678* (NRS Vols. 79 and 80, 1939–40).

— ed., *Journals and Narratives of the Third Dutch War* (NRS Vol. 86, 1946).

— et al., *Lists of Men-of-War 1650–1700* (Society for Nautical Research Occasional Publication No. 5, Pts I–V, 1935–9)

— 'The Operations of the English Fleet, 1648–52', *EHR* XXXI (1916), pp. 406–28.

— 'Comparative Naval Architecture, 1670–1720', *MM* VII (1921), pp. 38–45, 172–81, 308–14.

— 'The Royalists at Sea in 1649', *MM* XIV (1928), pp. 320–38.

— 'The Royalists at Sea in 1650', *MM* XVII (1931), pp. 135–68.

— 'Naval Operations in the Latter Part of the Year 1666', in Perrin, *Naval Miscellany III*, pp. 3–47.

— 'The Royalists at Sea, 1651–1653', *MM* XXI (1935), pp. 61–90.

— 'English Flag Officers, 1688–1713', *MM* XXXV (1949), pp. 333–41.

— 'The First Dutch War in the Mediterranean', *MM* XLIX (1963), pp. 241–65.

Anderson, Sonia P., 'The Anglo-Dutch "Smyrna Fleet" of 1693', in *Friends and Rivals in the East: Studies in Anglo-Dutch Relations in the Levant from the Seventeenth to the Early Nineteenth Century*, ed. Alistair Hamilton, Alexander H. De Groot and Maurits H. van den Bogert (Leiden, 2000), pp. 95–116.

Andrewes, William J. H., ed., *The Quest for Longitude* (Cambridge, Mass., 1996). Proceedings of a symposium covering most aspects of the subject.

Andrews, Kenneth R., *Ships, Money and Politics: Seafaring and Naval Enterprise in the Reign of Charles I* (Cambridge, 1991).

Armet, Helen, 'Convoys to the Trade on the East Coast of Scotland', *Book of the Old Edinburgh Club* XXVIII (1953), pp. 76–111.

Armitage, David, *The Ideological Origins of the British Empire* (Cambridge, 2000).

Asaert, G., Ph. M. Bosscher, J. R. Bruijn and W. J. van Hoboken, eds., *Maritieme Geschiedenis der Nederlanden* (Bussum, 1974–8, 4 vols.).

Ashley, Raymond E., 'The Search for Longitude', *AN* LI (1991), pp. 252–66. A practical navigator's history.

Ashworth, William J., ' "System of Terror": Samuel Bentham, Accountability and Dockyard Reform during the Napoleonic Wars', *Social History* XXIII (1998), pp. 63–79. Attempts to link Bentham and St Vincent.

Aspinall, A., ed., *The Later Correspondence of George III* (Cambridge, 1962–70, 5 vols.).

— ed., *The Correspondence of George Prince of Wales, 1770–1812* (London, 1963–71, 8 vols.).

Åström, Sven-Erik, 'English Timber Imports from Northern Europe in the Eighteenth Century', *SEHR* XVIII (1970), pp. 12–32. See also his articles

'Nordeuropeisk trävaruexport till Storbritannien 1760–1810', *Historiallinen Arkisto* LXIII (1968), pp. 133–51; and 'Britain's Timber Imports from the Baltic, 1775–1830: Some New Figures and Viewpoints', *SEHR* XXXVII (1984), pp. 57–71.

Aubrey, Philip, *The Defeat of James Stuart's Armada 1692* (Leicester, 1969).

Avery, R. W., 'The Naval Protection of Britain's Maritime Trade, 1793–1802' (Oxford D.Phil. thesis, 1983). Clear and complete treatment of the subject.

Aylmer, G. E., *The State's Servants: The Civil Service of the English Republic, 1649–1660* (London, 1973).

— *The Crown's Servants: Government and Civil Service under Charles II, 1660–1685* (Oxford, 2002). The last two of a trilogy, essential for the understanding of English government in the seventeenth century.

— 'Navy, State, Trade, and Empire', in Canny, *Origins of Empire*, pp. 467–81.

Baetens, R., 'The Organization and Effects of Flemish Privateering in the Seventeenth Century', *AHN* IX (The Hague, 1976), pp. 48–75 [originally 'Organisatie en resultaten van de Vlaamse Kaapvaart in de 17e eeuw', *Mededelingen Academie voor Marine van België* XXI (1969–70, pub. Antwerp 1973), pp. 89–125].

Baird Smith, David, 'The *Defiance* at Trafalgar', *SHR* XX (1923), pp. 116–21. Letters of a midshipman.

Baker, Emerson W. and John G. Reid, *The New England Knight: Sir William Phips, 1651–1695* (Toronto, 1998).

Baker, H. A., *The Crisis in Naval Ordnance* (National Maritime Museum, 1983). The introduction of Blomefield-pattern guns.

Balleine, G. R., *The Tragedy of Philippe d'Auvergne* (Chichester, 1973).

— *All for the King: The Life Story of Sir George Carteret* (St Helier, 1976).

Baltharpe, John, *The Straights Voyage or St Davids Poem*, ed. J. S. Bromley (Luttrell Society, Oxford, 1959). A petty officer's narrative, in doggerel verse, of a Mediterranean voyage in 1670.

Bamford, P. W., *Forests and French Sea Power 1660–1789* (Toronto, 1956).

Banbury, Philip, *Shipbuilders of the Thames and Medway* (Newton Abbot, 1971). Private shipyards rather than the royal dockyards.

Barfod, Jørgen H., *Niels Juels flåde* (Copenhagen, 1997). The fourth and latest volume (covering 1660–1720) of a detailed history of the Danish navy.

Barker, Derek, 'The Naval Uniform Dress of 1748', *MM* LXV (1979), pp. 243–54. Diagrams of the first officers' uniforms.

[Barker, M. H.] 'An Old Sailor', *Greenwich Hospital, A Series of Naval Sketches descriptive of the Life of a Man-of-War's Man* (London, 1826). Naval anecdotes based on identifiable incidents. His *Tough Yarns: A Series of Naval Tales and Sketches to please all hands* (London, 1835) prints more sentimental stories, not so clearly based on real characters.

Barlow, Edward, *Barlow's Journal of his Life at Sea in King's Ships, East and West Indiamen and other Merchantmen from 1659 to 1703*, ed. Basil Lubbock (London, 1934, 2 vols.). Eloquent and lugubrious journal of an eternal pessimist. It requires a careful reading to discover that Barlow's career was actually quite successful.

Barnes, G. R. and J. H. Owen, eds., *The Private Papers of John, Earl of Sandwich* (NRS Vols. 69, 71, 75 and 78, 1932–8). An essential documentary collection, whose publication changed scholarly understanding of the American War of Independence.

[Barrett, R. J.], 'Naval Recollections of the Late American War', *United Service Journal* 149–50 (1841), pp. 455–7 and 13–23. A midshipman of the *Hebrus* on the American coast, 1814–15.

[Barrington, Samuel], 'Some Letters of Admiral the Hon. Samuel Barrington', *MM* XIX (1933), pp. 279–91 and 381–403. Some of these are not printed elsewhere.

Barrionuevo Cañas, Margarita and Juan Manuel de Blas y Osorio, 'La Armada y Godoy', *RHN* VII (1989), 24, pp. 147–63.

Barritt, M. K., 'Nelson's Frigates, May to August 1798', *MM* LVIII (1972), pp. 281–95.

Barrow, Sir John, *The Life of Richard Earl Howe, K.G.* (London, 1838).

— *The Life of George Lord Anson* (London, 1839).

— *An Autobiographical Memoir . . .* (London, 1847).

— *The Life and Correspondence of Admiral Sir William Sidney Smith* (London, 1848, 2 vols.).

Barrow was a great civil servant but not a great biographer. He did, however, print documents, and his official position gave him some unique information.

Barrow, Tony, 'The *Noble Ann* Affair 1779: A Case Study of Impressment during the American Revolutionary War', in *Pressgangs and Privateers: Aspects of the Maritime History of N.E. England 1760–1815*, ed. Barrow (Whitley Bay, 1993), pp. 13–22.

Bartholomew, Michael, 'James Lind and Scurvy: A Revaluation', *JMR* (Jan 2002).

Bartlett, C. J., 'Gentlemen Versus Democrats: Cultural Prejudice and Military Strategy in Britain in the War of 1812', *WiH* I (1994), pp. 140–59.

Bartlett, Thomas, David Dickson, Dáire Keogh and Kevin Whelan, eds., *1798: A Bicentenary Perspective* (Dublin, 2003).

Bassett, W. G., 'The Caribbean in International Politics (1670–1707)' (London Ph.D. thesis, 1934).

Battesti, Michèle, *La Bataille d'Aboukir 1798: Nelson contrarie la stratégie de Bonaparte* (Paris, 1998). Important scholarly account of the battle of the Nile from French sources.

Battick, J. F., 'Cromwell's Navy and the Foreign Policy of the Protectorate, 1653–1658' (Boston Ph.D. thesis, 1967). A valuable study of grand strategy.

— ed., 'Richard Rooth's Sea Journal of the Western Design, 1654–55', *Jamaica Journal* V (1971), No. 4, pp. 3–22.

— 'A New Interpretation of Cromwell's Western Design', *Journal of the Barbados Museum and Historical Society* XXXIV (1972), pp. 76–84.

— 'Cromwell's Diplomatic Blunder: The Relationship between the Western

Design of 1654–55 and the French Alliance of 1657', *Albion* V (1973), pp. 279–98.

Baudi di Vesme, Carlo, *La Politica Mediterranea Inglese . . . 1741–1748* (Turin, 1952).

— 'Il potere marittimo e la guerra di successione d'Austria', *Nuova Rivista Storica* XXXVII (1953), pp. 19–43.

Baugh, Daniel A., *British Naval Administration in the Age of Walpole* (Princeton, 1965). An indispensable book by the leading authority; much wider in scope than its title indicates.

— ed., *Naval Administration, 1715–1750* (NRS Vol. 120, 1977).

— 'Sir Samuel Hood: Superior Subordinate', in Bilias, *George Washington's Opponents*, pp. 291–326.

— 'Maritime Strength and Atlantic Commerce: the Uses of "A Grand Marine Empire"', in Stone, *Imperial State*, pp. 185–223.

— 'Great Britain's "Blue-Water" Policy, 1689–1815', *IHR* X (1988), pp. 33–58.

— 'Why Did Britain Lose Command of the Sea During the War for America?' in Black and Woodfine, *British Navy*, pp. 149–69.

— 'The Eighteenth-Century Navy as a National Institution', in Hill, *Royal Navy*, pp. 120–60. A masterly survey.

— 'Seapower and Science: The Motives for Pacific Exploration', in *Background to Discovery: Pacific Exploration from Dampier to Cook*, ed. Derek Howse (Berkeley, Calif., 1990), pp. 1–55.

— 'The Politics of British Naval Failure, 1775–1778', *AN* LII (1992), pp. 221–46. Essential to understanding the American War.

— 'Sir Charles Wager, 1666–1743', in Le Fevre and Harding, *Precursors of Nelson*, pp. 100–126. The only biography of this important figure.

— 'Withdrawing from Europe: Anglo-French Maritime Geopolitics, 1750–1800', *IHR* XX (1998), pp. 1–32.

— '"Too Much Mixed in this Affair": The Impact of Ministerial Politics in the Eighteenth-Century Royal Navy', in *New Interpretations in Naval History*, ed. R. C. Balano and C. L. Symonds (Annapolis, 2001), pp. 21–43.

Baumber, Michael, *General-at-Sea: Robert Blake and the Seventeenth-Century Revolution in Naval Warfare* (London, 1989).

— 'The Navy during the Civil Wars and the Commonwealth, 1642–1651' (Manchester MA thesis, 1967).

— 'Parliamentary Naval Politics 1641–49', *MM* LXXXII (1996), pp. 398–408.

Baxter, Stephen B., *William III* (London, 1966).

— 'The Conduct of the Seven Years War', in *England's Rise to Greatness, 1660–1763*, ed. Stephen B. Baxter (Berkeley, 1983), pp. 323–48.

Baynham, Henry, *From the Lower Deck: The Old Navy 1780–1840* (London, 1969). An anthology of memoirs, some from manuscripts but mainly taken from rare printed works.

Beatson, Robert, *Naval and Military Memoirs of Great Britain from 1727 to 1783* (London, 1804, 6 vols.). A careful near-contemporary historian. By 'Naval and Military' he meant naval and combined operations.

Beattie, J. M., *Crime and the Courts in England 1660–1800* (Oxford, 1986).

Beauchesne, Geneviève, *Historique de la construction navale à Lorient de 1666 à 1770* (Vincennes, 1979).

Beckett, J. V. and Michael Turner, 'Taxation and Economic Growth in Eighteenth-century England', *EcHR* 2nd S. XLIII (1990), pp. 377–403. Important for the economic consequences of war.

Beddard, Robert, ed., *The Revolutions of 1688* (Oxford, 1991).

— 'The Protestant Succession', in *The Revolutions of 1688*, pp. 1–10.

— 'The Unexpected Whig Revolution of 1688', in *The Revolutions of 1688*, pp. 11–101.

Bellabarba, Sergio and Giorgio Osculati, *The Royal Yacht Caroline 1749*, trans. Anne J. Stone (London, 1989) [originally *Royal Caroline (1749)* (Milan, 1986)].

Benbow, William A., *Brave Benbow* (p.p. Victoria, BC, 1987).

Benjamin, L. S., ed., *The Windham Papers* (London, 1913, 2 vols.). William Windham, Secretary at War 1794–1801 and Secretary for War 1806–7.

Bennett, Geoffrey, 'Admiral Ushakov: Nelson's Russian Ally', *HT* XXI (1971), pp. 724–31. A careless dash through Mordvinov's edition of his correspondence.

Bent, J. T., ed., 'Extracts from the Diaries of Dr John Covel, 1670–1679', in *Early Voyages and Travels in the Levant*, ed. J. T. Bent (Hakluyt Soc. Vol. 87, 1893). A voyage to Constantinople in 1670.

Bérenger, Jean, 'Les Hapsbourgs et la mer au XVIIIe siècle', in Acerra et al., *Etat, marine et société*, pp. 25–34.

Beresford, Marcus, 'François Thurot and the French Attack at Carrickfergus, 1759–60', *IS* X (1971–2), pp. 255–74.

Béthencourt Massieu, Antonio, *Patiño en la política internacional de Felipe V* (Valladolid, 1954). Spanish naval minister from 1720 to 1726.

Beveridge, Sir William, *Prices and Wages in England from the Twelfth to the Nineteenth Century. Vol. I Price Tables: Mercantile Era* (London, 1939, all published). A massive collection of statistical information, intended as the basis for an economic history which was overtaken by the war. Indispensable, though not without some weaknesses.

Bilias, George A., ed., *George Washington's Opponents: British Generals and Admirals in the American Revolution* (New York, 1969). An uneven collection of short biographies.

Bingeman, J. M., 'Gunlocks: Their Introduction into the Navy', in Smith, *British Naval Armaments*, pp. 41–4.

Bingeman, J. M., J. P. Bethell, P. Goodwin and A. T. Mack, 'Copper and Other Sheathing in the Royal Navy', *IJNA* XXIX (2000), pp. 218–29.

Binney, J. E. D., *British Public Finance and Administration, 1774–92* (Oxford, 1958).

Binns, J., 'Sir John Lawson: Scarborough's Admiral of the Red', *Northern History* XXXII (1996), pp. 90–110.

Bishop, Matthew, *The Life and Adventures of Matthew Bishop of Deddington in Oxfordshire* (London, 1744). A petty officer's memoirs.

Bjerg, Hans Christian and John Erichsen, *Danske orlogsskibe 1690–1860* (Copenhagen, 1980, 2 vols.). Technical history of Danish warship designs.

Black, Jeremy, *Natural and Necessary Enemies; Anglo-French Relations in the Eighteenth Century* (London, 1986).

— ed., *The Origins of War in Early Modern Europe* (Edinburgh, 1987).

— ed., *Knights Errant and True Englishmen: British Foreign Policy, 1660–1800* (Edinburgh, 1989).

— *The Rise of the European Powers 1679–1793* (London, 1990).

— *Pitt the Elder* (Cambridge, 1992).

— *British Foreign Policy in an Age of Revolutions 1783–1793* (Cambridge, 1994).

— *Britain as a Military Power, 1688–1815* (London, 1999).

— 'British Intelligence and the Mid-Eighteenth Century Crisis', *Intelligence and National Security* II (1987), pp. 209–29.

— 'Naval Power and British Foreign Policy in the Age of Pitt the Elder', in Black and Woodfine, *British Navy*, pp. 91–107.

— 'Anglo-Baltic Relations 1714–1748', in Minchinton, *Britain and the Northern Seas*, pp. 67–74.

— 'Britain's Foreign Alliances in the Eighteenth Century', *Albion* XX (1988), pp. 573–602.

— 'Anglo-French Relations in the Mid-Eighteenth Century', *Francia* XVII (1990), pp. 45–79.

— 'Anglo-Spanish Naval Relations in the Eighteenth Century', *MM* LXXVII (1991), pp. 235–58.

— 'British Naval Power and International Commitments: Political and Strategic Problems, 1688–1770', in Duffy, *Parameters*, pp. 39–59.

— 'Naval Power, Strategy and Foreign Policy, 1775–1791', in Duffy, *Parameters*, pp. 93–120.

Black, Jeremy and Philip Woodfine, eds., *The British Navy and the Use of Naval Power in the Eighteenth Century* (Leicester, 1988). An important collection of essays.

Blake, Richard C., 'Transmission of the Faith and Transformation of the Fleet: the Religious Education of the Royal Navy 1770–1870', in *Foi chrétienne et milieux maritimes (XVe–XXe siècle)*, ed. Alain Cabantous and Françoise Hildesheimer (Paris, 1987), pp. 50–67. The Evangelical Revival at sea.

Blane, Sir Gilbert, *Observations on the Diseases of Seamen* (London, 3rd edn 1799).

— *Select Dissertations on Several Subjects of Medical Science* (London, 1822). One of the foundation texts of epidemiology and medical statistics. Extracts are printed by Lloyd, *Health of Seamen*.

Blok, P., *The Life of Admiral De Ruyter*, trans. G. J. Renier (London, 1933) [originally *Michiel Adriaansz. de Ruyter* (The Hague, 1928)]. An abridged translation of an old-fashioned literary biography, weak on his naval career, but the only reasonably full life in English.

Bond, Gordon C., *The Grand Expedition: The British Invasion of Holland in 1809* (Athens, Georgia, 1979). The Scheldt Expedition (which in fact invaded Zealand, and never came near Holland).

Bonnel, Ulane, *La France, les Etats-Unis et la guerre de course (1797–1815)* (Paris, 1961).

Bonner-Smith, David, ed., *The Barrington Papers* (NRS Vols. 77 and 81, 1937–41).

— ed., *Letters of Admiral of the Fleet the Earl of St Vincent whilst First Lord of the Admiralty, 1801–1804* (NRS Vols. 55 and 61, 1922–7). Essential documents, indifferently edited.

— 'The Naval Mutinies of 1797', *MM* XXI (1935), pp. 428–49 and XXII (1936), pp. 65–86. Deals only with the first Spithead mutiny; prints many documents.

— 'Byron in the Leeward Islands, 1779', *MM* XXX (1944), pp. 38–48 and 81–92. Documents not printed in NRS volumes.

— 'The Mutiny at the Nore, 1797', *MM* XXXIII (1947), pp. 199–203. An army officer's diary.

Bonney, Richard, ed., *Economic Systems and State Finance* (Oxford, 1995). An important collection studying the relation of tax systems and state formation.

— 'The Eighteenth Century. II. The Struggle for Great Power Status and the End of the Old Fiscal Regime', in Bonney, *Economic Systems*, pp. 315–90.

Boog Watson, William N., 'Two British Naval Surgeons of the French Wars', *MH* XIII (1969), pp. 213–25.

Bordo, Michael D. and Eugene N. White, 'A Tale of Two Currencies: British and French Finance During the Napoleonic Wars', *JEcH* LI (1991), pp. 303–16.

Boscawen, Hugh, 'The Origins of the Flat-Bottomed Landing Craft 1757–58', *Army Museum* (1984), pp. 23–30.

Bosher, J. F., *French Finances 1770–1795: From Business to Bureaucracy* (Cambridge, 1970).

— 'Financing the French Navy in the Seven Years' War: Beaujon, Goossens et Compagnie in 1759', *BH* XXVIII (1986), pp. 115–33.

Boteler, John Harvey, *Recollections of my Sea Life from 1808 to 1830*, ed. David Bonner-Smith (NRS Vol. 82, 1942) [originally p.p. 1883]. Picaresque memoir of the Napoleonic War.

Boudriot, Jean, *The Seventy-Four Gun Ship: A Practical Treatise on the Art of Naval Architecture*, trans. David H. Roberts (Rotherfield, Sussex, 1986–8, 4 vols.) [originally *Le vaisseau de 74 canons* (Grenoble, 1973–7, 4 vols.)]. A classic work of antiquarian scholarship (and the English version is a masterpiece of technical translation). Alone or in collaboration the author has since issued a series of similar works on other types of French warship, some of which are listed below.

— *Historique de la corvette, 1650–1850: Monographie La Créole, 1827* (p.p. Paris, 1990).

— *L'Artillerie de mer: Marine française 1650–1850* (Paris, 1992).

Boudriot, Jean and Hubert Berti, *L'Artillerie de mer: Marine française 1650–1850* (Paris, 1992).

— *The History of the French Frigate 1650–1850*, trans. David H. Roberts (Rotherfield, East Sussex, 1993) [originally *La Frégate: Marine de France*

1650–1850 (1992), with additional material from *La Frégate de 8 la Renommée (1744)* (1993), *La Frégate de 12 la Belle-Poule (1765)* (1985), and *La Frégate de 18 la Vénus (1782)* (1979)].

— *Les Vaisseaux de 50 et 64 canons: Etude historique 1650–1780* (Paris, 1994).

Bourchier, [Jane] Lady, *Memoir of the Late Admiral Sir Edward Codrington* (London, 1873, 2 vols.). Extensive and revealing correspondence between Codrington and his wife.

Bourdé de Villehuet, J., *Le Manœuvrier, ou Essai sur la théorie et la pratique des mouvements du navire et des évolutions navales* (Paris, 1765). A geometrical exercise in tactics and ship-handling, intended for young officers. There was a very incompetent English translation: *The Manoeuverer, or Skilful Seaman: being an Essay on the Theory and Practice of the Various Movements of a Ship at Sea*, trans. J. N. Jouin de Sauseuil (London, 1788).

Bourne, Ruth, *Queen Anne's Navy in the West Indies* (New Haven, 1939).

Bowers, William, *Naval Adventures during Thirty-Five Years' Service* (London, 1833, 2 vols.). Evocative memoirs, better for atmosphere than detail.

Boxer, C. R., *The Dutch Seaborne Empire 1600–1800* (London, 1965). A classic history.

— 'The Third Dutch War in the East (1672–4)', *MM* XVI (1930), pp. 343–86.

— 'M. A. De Ruyter, 1607–1676', *MM* XLIV (1958), pp. 3–17.

— 'Some Second Thoughts on the Third Anglo-Dutch War, 1672–1674', *TRHS* 5th S. XIX (1969), pp. 67–94.

— 'Admiral De Ruyter through English Eyes, 1607–1676', *HT* XXVI (1976), pp. 232–40.

Bracknall, Moira, 'One Hundred Naval Lieutenants of 1793: a Survey of their Careers' (Exeter MA dissertation, 2000).

Braddick, Michael J., *The Nerves of State: Taxation and the Financing of the English State, 1558–1714* (Manchester, 1996).

Bradley, Peter T., *The Lure of Peru: Maritime Intrusion into the South Sea, 1598–1701* (London, 1989). European buccaneers.

Bradshaw, Brendan and John Morrill, eds., *The British Problem, c.1534–1707: State Formation in the Atlantic Archipelago* (London, 1996). 'The Atlantic Archipelago' here means the British Isles, rather than the Azores as one might naturally suppose.

Brandt, Gerard, *Het Leven en Bedryf van den Heere Michiel de Ruiter* (Amsterdam, 1687). The classic life of the great Dutch admiral by his son-in-law; still the fullest and in many respects the best.

Braudel, Fernand, *Civilization and Capitalism, 15th–18th Century* (London, 1981–4, 3 vols.).

Breen, Kenneth, 'The Navy in the Yorktown Campaign: The Battle of the Chesapeake 1781' (London M.Phil. thesis, 1971).

— 'Graves and Hood at the Chesapeake', *MM* LXVI (1980), pp. 53–65.

— 'Divided Command: the West Indies and North America, 1780–1781', in Black and Woodfine, *British Navy*, pp. 191–206.

— 'Sir George Rodney and St Eustatius in the American War: A Commercial and Naval Distraction, 1775–1781', *MM* LXXXIV (1998), pp. 193–203.

Breihan, John R., 'The Addington Party and the Navy in British Politics, 1801–1806', in *New Aspects of Naval History*, ed. Craig L. Symonds (Annapolis, Md., 1981), pp. 163–89.

Brenner, Robert, *Merchants and Revolution: Commercial Change, Political Conflict, and London's Overseas Traders, 1550–1653* (Cambridge, 1993).

— 'The Civil War Politics of London's Merchant Community', *P&P* 58 (1973), pp. 53–107.

Brenton, Edward Pelham, *The Naval History of Great Britain* (London, 2nd edn 1837, 2 vols.). Brenton was not a great analytical historian, but an honest man who used documents and who knew many of the people and incidents of the Great Wars in which he had served.

— *Life and Correspondence of John, Earl of St Vincent* (London, 1838, 2 vols.). A friendly but not uncritical life, making much use of the admiral's papers.

Brenton, Sir Jahleel, *Memoir of Captain Edward Pelham Brenton* (London, 1842). By his brother.

Brewer, John, *The Sinews of Power: War, Money and the English State, 1688–1783* (London, 1989). An important book which awoke many historians to the subject.

Bridenbaugh, Carl and Roberta, *No Peace beyond the Line: The English in the Caribbean, 1624–1690* (New York, 1972).

Brindley, H. H., 'The Action between H.M.S. *Lyon* and the *Elisabeth*, July 1745', in Perrin, *Naval Miscellany III*, pp. 83–119.

Broadley, A. M., ed., 'The Unpublished Correspondence of Admiral Sir George Rooke . . . 1703–05', *History*, 1st S. II (1913), pp. 57–70.

Broadley, A. M. and R. G. Bartelot, *Nelson's Hardy: His Life, Letters and Friends* (London, 1909).

[Brock, P. W.] 'Beaver', 'An Order and Letter Book of the American Revolutionary War', *NR* XXVII (1939), pp. 679–93. Kept by Lieutenant, later Captain, J. T. Duckworth, 1776–82.

Bromley, J. S., ed., *The Manning of the Royal Navy: Selected Public Pamphlets 1693–1873* (NRS Vol. 119, 1974). Typical of Bromley's fastidious scholarship and instinct for the questions other historians had not thought to ask.

— *Corsairs and Navies 1660–1760* (London, 1987). A collection of his articles, many of which are otherwise extremely difficult to find.

— 'Away from Impressment: The Idea of a Royal Naval Reserve, 1696–1859', in *Britain and the Netherlands VI: War and Society*, ed. A. C. Duke and C. A. Tamse (The Hague, 1977), pp. 168–88.

— 'The British Navy and its Seamen after 1688: Notes for an Unwritten History', in *Charted and Uncharted Waters*, ed. Sarah Palmer and Glyndwr Williams (National Maritime Museum, n.d. [1982]), pp. 148–63.

— 'Duguay Trouin: The Financial Background', *MM* LXXI (1985), pp. 259–85.

— 'A New Vocation: Privateering in the Wars of 1689–97 and 1702–13', in

A People of the Sea: The Maritime History of the Channel Islands, ed. A. G. Jamieson (London, 1986), pp. 109–147. [In part a revision of 'The Channel Island Privateers in the War of the Spanish Succession', *TSG* XIV (1950), pp. 444–78; and *Corsairs and Navies 1660–1760* (London, 1987), pp. 339–73; a fuller version of the last section is printed in *Corsairs and Navies*, pp. 374–87].

— 'Colonies at War', in *Corsairs and Navies*, pp. 21–8. [originally in *History of the English Speaking Peoples* LX (1970), pp. 1,921–7].

— 'The North Sea in Wartime, 1688–1713', in *Corsairs and Navies*, pp. 43–72 [originally in *BMGN* XCII (1977), pp. 270–99].

— 'The Importance of Dunkirk Reconsidered, 1688–1713', in *Corsairs and Navies*, pp. 73–102.

— 'The French Privateering War, 1702–13', in *Corsairs and Navies*, pp. 213–41 [originally in *Historical Essays Presented to David Ogg*, ed. H. F. Bell and R. L. Ollard (London, 1963), pp. 203–31].

— 'The Jacobite Privateers in the Nine Years War', in *Corsairs and Navies*, pp. 139–66 [originally in *Statesmen, Scholars and Merchants: Essays in Eighteenth-Century History Presented to Dame Lucy Sutherland*, ed. J. S. Bromley, A. Whiteman and P. G. M. Dickson (Oxford, 1973), pp. 17–43].

— 'Les Corsaires zélandais et la navigation scandinave pendant la Guerre de Succession d'Espagne', in *Corsairs and Navies*, pp. 435–48 [originally in *Le Navire et l'économie maritime du Nord de l'Europe*, ed. M. Mollat (Paris, 1961), pp. 93–109].

— 'Prize Office and Prize Agency at Portsmouth, 1689–1748', in *Corsairs and Navies*, pp. 463–94 [originally in Webb et al., *Hampshire Studies*, pp. 169–99].

— 'The Profits of Naval Command: Captain Joseph Taylor and his Prizes', in *Corsairs and Navies*, pp. 449–62 [originally in *Wirtschafskräfte und Wirtschaftswege II: Wirtschaftskräfte in der Europäiaschen Expansion. Festschrift für Hermann Kellenbenz*, ed. J. Schneider (Stuttgart, 1978), pp. 529–44].

— 'The Second Hundred Years War', in *Corsairs and Navies*, pp. 495–503 [originally in *Britain and France: Ten Centuries*, ed. D. Johnson, F. Crouzet and H. Bédarida (London, 1980), pp. 164–72 and 374].

— 'The Trade and Privateering of Saint-Malo during the War of the Spanish Succession', in *Corsairs and Navies*, pp. 279–98 [originally in *TSG* XVII (1964), pp. 631–47].

Brooke, John, *The Chatham Administration 1766–1768* (London, 1956).

Brooks, F. W., 'Naval Recruiting in Lindsey, 1795–7', *EHR* XLIII (1928), pp. 230–40. The Quota Acts in Lincolnshire.

Brooks, George S., ed., *James Durand: An Able Seaman of 1812* (New Haven, 1926). An American seaman's memoir.

Broomfield, J. H., 'The Keppel–Palliser Affair, 1778–1779', *MM* XLVII (1961), pp. 195–207.

— 'Lord Sandwich at the Admiralty Board: Politics and the British Navy, 1771–1778', *MM* LI (1965), pp. 7–25.

Brown, A. G., 'Sedition or Ships' Biscuits? A Study of the Nore Mutiny of 1797' (Exeter MA dissertation, 2002).

Brown, David K., 'The Form and Speed of Sailing Warships', *MM* LXXXIV (1998), pp. 298–307. Important technical analysis by a naval architect. See also his 'The Speed of Sailing Warships, 1793–1840; an Examination of the Evidence', in Freeman, *Les Empires*, pp. 155–94.

Brown, Gerald S., *The American Secretary: The Colonial Policy of Lord George Germain, 1775–1778* (Ann Arbor, 1963).

— 'The Anglo-French Naval Crisis, 1778: A Study of Conflict in the North Cabinet', *WMQ* 3rd S. XIII (1956), pp. 3–25.

Brown, Ruth Rhynas, 'Notes from the Office of the Ordnance: the 1650s', *Wealden Iron Research Group Bulletin* 2nd S. XX (2000), pp. 39–55.

Browning, Oscar, ed., *The Journal of Sir George Rooke . . . 1700–1702* (NRS Vol. 9, 1897). The diary of Rooke's secretary, in a very untrustworthy edition. Professor John B. Hattendorf is preparing a new edition of this important manuscript.

Bruijn, Jaap R., ed., *De Oorlogvoering ter Zee in 1673 in Journalen en Andere Stukken* (HG 3rd S. 84, 1966). Journals of De Ruyter and other Dutch admirals during the Third Dutch War.

— *De Admiraliteit van Amsterdam in rustige jaren 1713–1751* (Amsterdam, 1970). An important study of Dutch naval administration.

— *The Dutch Navy of the Seventeenth and Eighteenth Centuries* (Columbia, S.C., 1993).

— *Varend Verleden: De Nederlandse Oorlogsvloot in de 17de en 18de eeuw* (Amsterdam, 1998). Excellent short history of the Dutch navy in its great age. It is a revised and extended version of his earlier work in English, above.

— 'Dutch Privateering during the Second and Third Anglo-Dutch Wars', *AHN* XI (1978), pp. 79–93.

— 'Cornelis Tromp (1629–1691): een niet-gewaardeerd dienaar van de heren', *TvG* XCVI (1983), pp. 179–92.

— 'Mercurius en Mars uiteen. De uitrusting van de oorlogsvloot in de zeventiende eeuw', in *Bestuurders en Geleerden*, ed. S. Groenveld, M. E. H. N. Mout and I. Schöffer (Amsterdam, 1985), pp. 97–106.

— 'The Dutch Navy in Its Political and Social Economic Setting of the Seventeenth Century', in Wilson and Proctor, *1688*, pp. 45–58.

— 'William III and his Two Navies', *Notes and Records of the Royal Society of London* XLIII (1989), pp. 117–32.

Brun, V, *Guerres maritimes de la France: Port de Toulon, ses armaments, son administration, depuis son origine jusqu'à nos jours* (Paris, 1861, 2 vols.).

Bryant, Arthur, *Samuel Pepys* (Cambridge, 1933–8, 3 vols.). Full-dress literary biography; but Bryant's genius did not run to administrative history.

Buchet, Christian, *La Lutte pour l'espace Caraïbe et la façade atlantique de l'Amérique centrale et du sud (1672–1763)* (Paris, 1991, 2 vols.). An important comparative study of British and French naval logistics in the West Indies.

— ed., *L'Homme, la santé et la mer* (Paris, 1997). Proceedings of a conference on medicine at sea.

— *Marine, économie et société: un exemple d'interaction: l'avitaillement de la Royal Navy durant la guerre de sept ans* (Paris, 1999). A very important analysis of British naval victualling, with implications for agricultural as well as naval history.

— 'Convoyage et opérations combinées aux Amériques: les leçons et les retombées sur la guerre en Europe', in *Guerres maritimes*, pp. 213–26.

— 'L'"Ordnance Board" et la logistique en armes pour les flottes anglaises aux Antilles (1689–1763)', in Acerra et al., *Etat, marine et société*, pp. 73–87.

— 'Santé et expéditions géo-stratégiques au temps de la marine à voile', in *Marine et technique au XIXe siècle* (Vincennes, 1988), pp. 141–62.

— 'Les Modalités évolutives de la logistique anglaise en matériel naval dans l'espace Caraïbe (1689–1763)', *HES* XI (1992), pp. 571–96.

— 'The Royal Navy and the Caribbean, 1689–1763', *MM* LXXX (1994), pp. 30–44.

— 'Révélateurs d'une détermination coloniale: les arsenaux anglais de l'espace caraïbe au XVIIIe siècle', *HES* XVI (1997), pp. 125–49.

— 'Les Liaisons atlantiques et de la nécessaire révision du concept de maîtrise des mers (1701–1763)', *CHM* 35 (1997), pp. 9–23. See also his 'Des routes maritimes Europe-Antilles et de leurs incidences sur la rivalité franco-britannique', *HES* XIII (1994), pp. 563–82.

Buckingham and Chandos, [Richard Grenville] Duke of, *Memoirs of the Court and Cabinets of George the Third* (London, 2nd edn 1853–5, 4 vols.). Correspondence of one branch of the Grenville clan.

Buckland, Kirstie, ed., *The Miller Papers* (Shelton, Notts., 1999). Letters and diary of Captain R. W. Miller, one of Nelson's favourites.

Buffinton, Arthur H., 'The Canada Expedition of 1746: Its Relation to British Politics', *AHR* XLV (1940), pp. 552–80.

Bull, S. B., 'The Furie of the Ordnance: England's Guns and Gunners by Land 1600–1650' (Wales Ph.D. thesis, 1988).

Burchett, Josiah, *A Complete History of the Most Remarkable Transactions at Sea* (London, 1720). An attempt at a universal naval history: important for the period 1689–1712, when he was Secretary of the Admiralty and could draw on official documents and inside knowledge.

Burney, James, *History of the Buccaneers of America* (London, 1816); otherwise Vol. IV of *A Chronological History of the Voyages and Discoveries in the South Sea or Pacific Ocean* (London, 5 vols., 1803–17). A serviceable general history collecting many rare printed narratives.

Butel, Paul, 'France, the Antilles, and Europe in the Seventeenth and Eighteenth Centuries: Renewals of Foreign Trade', in Tracy, *Rise of Merchant Empires*, pp. 153–73.

— 'La Dynamique des marchés coloniaux au XVIIIe siècle, l'exemple britannique', in *Les Européens et les espaces océaniques au XVIIIe siècle* (Association des historiens modernistes des universités, Bulletin No. 22, Paris, 1998), pp. 99–108.

Butterfield, C. A., 'Commodore George Johnstone: A Study in Eighteenth-Century Naval Command' (Exeter MA dissertation, 1997).

Byrn, John D., *Crime and Punishment in the Royal Navy: Discipline on the Leeward Islands Station 1784–1812* (Aldershot, 1989). A sober contribution to the subject.

Cain, P. J. and A. G. Hopkins, *British Imperialism: Innovation and Expansion 1688–1914* (London, 1993).

Calendar of State Papers Colonial, America and West Indies (London, 1860–1969, 44 vols. covering 1574–1738). Papers of the Secretaries of State dealing with colonial (including much military and naval) business.

Calendar of State Papers Domestic (London, 1875–1947, 54 vols. covering 1649–1704). Calendars of varying completeness of the domestic (including military and naval) papers of the Secretaries of State.

Callender, Sir Geoffrey, 'With the Grand Fleet in 1780', *MM* IX (1923), pp. 258–70 and 290–304.

— 'Sir John Mennes', *MM* XXVI (1940), pp. 276–85.

Calmon-Maison, J. J. R., *Le Maréchal de Château-Renault (1637–1716)* (Paris, 1903).

Camperdown, [R. A. P. Haldane-Duncan] 3rd Earl of, *Admiral Duncan* (London, 1898). Biography of the author's ancestor, printing correspondence and papers.

Canney, Donald L., *Sailing Warships of the US Navy* (London, 2001).

Cannon, John, *The Fox–North Coalition: Crisis of the Constitution, 1782–4* (Cambridge, 1969).

Canny, Nicholas, ed., *The Oxford History of the British Empire Vol. 1: The Origins of Empire, British Overseas Enterprise to the Close of the Seventeenth Century* (Oxford, 1998).

Capp, Bernard, *Cromwell's Navy: The Fleet and the English Revolution, 1648–1660* (Oxford, 1989). Essential study of politics and religion in the English Republican Navy.

Carden, J. S., *A Curtail'd Memoir of Incidents and Occurrences in the Life of John Surman Carden*, ed. C. T. Atkinson (Oxford, 1912). Memoir of a captain during the Napoleonic War; written in old age, to defend a chequered record, but nevertheless full and interesting.

Carlan, J. M., *Navios en secuestro: La Escuadra española del Oceano en Brest (1799–1802)* (Madrid, 1951).

Caron, François, *La Guerre incomprise ou la victoire volée (Bataille de la Chesapeake – 1781)* (Vincennes, 1989).

— *La Guerre incomprise ou le mythe de Suffren* (Vincennes, 1996).
Useful studies printing many documents, in support of eccentric interpretations which seem to refer as much to modern French politics as to the events of the eighteenth century.

Carpenter, Kenneth J., *The History of Scurvy and Vitamin C* (Cambridge, 1986). Essential to dispel the many errors which hang about this subject.

Carr, Raymond, 'Gustavus IV and the British Government, 1804–9', *EHR* LX (1945), pp. 36–66.

Carrington, Selwyn H. H., *The British West Indies during the American Revolution* (Dordrecht, 1988).

Carswell, John, *The South Sea Bubble* (London, 1960).

— *The Descent on England: A Study of the English Revolution of 1688 and its European Background* (London, 1969).

Carter, A. C., *Neutrality or Commitment: The Evolution of Dutch Foreign Policy, 1667–1795* (London, 1975).

Carter, T. G., ed. and trans., 'The Journal of M. de Lage de Cueilly, Captain in the Spanish Navy, during the Campaign of 1744', in Laughton, *Naval Miscellany II*, pp. 207–88. Narrative by a French officer aboard a Spanish ship at the battle of Toulon. The editor naively accepts his claim to have been in command.

Caruana, Adrian B., *The History of English Sea Ordnance 1523–1875. I: The Age of Evolution, 1523–1715; II: The Age of the System, 1715–1815* (Rotherfield, East Sussex, 1994–7). An important work of great antiquarian erudition and practical knowledge, but unreliable in detail and largely devoid of historical analysis.

Castex, R. V. P., *Les Idées militaries de la Marine du XVIIIme siècle: De Ruyter à Suffren* (Paris, 1911). A learned and hard-hitting Mahanite polemic.

Castillo Manrubia, Pilar, 'Perdida de la Habana, 1763', *RHN* VIII (1990), 28, pp. 61–77.

Cavaliero, Roderick, *Admiral Satan: The Life and Campaigns of Suffren* (London, 1994). A good, balanced popular history, using documents and sources in Provençal.

Chadwick, French Ensor, ed., *The Graves Papers and other Documents* (Naval History Society, New York, 1916). Official correspondence of Rear-Admiral Thomas Graves, 1780–81, and other documents relating to the battle of the Chesapeake.

Chamier, Frederick, *The Life of a Sailor* (London, 1850). Autobiographical novel of the Napoleonic War.

Chandaman, C. D., *The English Public Revenue, 1660–1688* (Oxford, 1975).

Chapelle, Howard I., *The History of the American Sailing Navy: The Ships and their Development* (New York, 1949). A classic study, but Canney's *Sailing Warships* revises it on many points.

Chapin, Howard M., *Privateer Ships and Sailors: The First Century of American Colonial Privateering, 1625–1725* (Toulon, 1926).

Chaplin, W. R., 'Nehemiah Bourne', *CSM* XLII (1952–6), pp. 28–155.

Chappell, Edwin, ed., *The Tangier Papers of Samuel Pepys* (NRS Vol. 73, 1935).

— *Shorthand Letters of Samuel Pepys* (Cambridge, 1933).

Chapuis, Olivier, *A la mer comme au ciel: Beautemps-Beaupré et la naissance de l'hydrographie moderne (1700–1850)* (Paris, 1999).

Charnock, John, *Biographia Navalis* (London, 1794–8, 6 vols.). A collective biography of post-captains with seniority from 1660 to 1766. It was compiled with the help of Admiralty records and shares many of their deficiencies, notably a tendency to confuse officers with the same or similar surnames.

— *History of Marine Architecture* (London, 1801, 3 vols.). Another example of Charnock's undiscriminating zeal.

Chatterton, Georgiana Lady, *Memorials, Personal and Historical, of Admiral Lord Gambier* (London, 1861, 2 vols.). Uncritical, but prints many documents.

Chaudhuri, K. N. and Jonathan I. Israel, 'The English and Dutch East India Companies and the Glorious Revolution of 1688–9', in Israel, *Anglo-Dutch Moment*, pp. 407–438.

Chevalier, E., *Histoire de la marine française depuis les débuts de la monarchie jusqu'au traité de paix de 1763* (Paris, 1902).

— *Histoire de la marine française pendant la guerre de l'independence americaine* (Paris, 1877).

— *Histoire de la marine française sous la première République* (Paris, 1886).

— *Histoire de la marine française sous le Consulat et l'Empire* (Paris, 1886). A solid history in the old style. For convenience I have cited these books as four volumes of a single work, though they were not issued as such.

Childs, John, '1688', *History* LXXIII (1988), pp. 398–424.

Christie, Ian R., *The End of North's Ministry 1780–1782* (London, 1958).

Cisternes, Raoul de, *La Campagne de Minorque, d'après le journal du Commandeur de Glandevez* (Paris, 1899). A participant's narrative of the 1756 Minorca expedition.

Clarendon, Edward Hyde, Earl of, *The History of the Rebellion and Civil Wars in England*, ed. W. D. Macray (Oxford, 1888, 6 vols.).

Clark, Dora Mae, 'The Impressment of Seamen in the American Colonies', in *Essays in Colonial History presented to Charles McLean Andrews by his Students* (New Haven, 1931), pp. 198–224.

Clark, G. N., *The Dutch Alliance and the War against French Trade, 1688–1697* (Manchester, 1923).

— 'English and Dutch Privateers under William III', *MM* VII (1921), pp. 162–7 and 209–17.

Clark, J. C. D., ed., *The Memoirs and Speeches of James, 2nd Earl Waldegrave, 1742–1763* (Cambridge, 1988).

Clark, J. Kent, *Goodwin Wharton* (Oxford, 1984). Politics and the fairies in the age of William III.

Clark, W. B., W. J. Morgan and Michael J. Crawford, eds., *Naval Documents of the American Revolution* (Washington, 1964ff., 10 vols. to date). A massive collection, now advanced as far as 1777 and much improved in its editorial standards. Some important naval documents are embedded among the trivia, but others which should be there are not.

Clarke, James Stanier and John McArthur, *The Life of Admiral Lord Nelson, K. B., from his Lordship's Manuscripts* (London, 1809, 2 vols.). The official life; miserably inadequate to the authors' opportunities.

Clayton, T. R., 'The Duke of Newcastle, the Earl of Halifax, and the American Origins of the Seven Years' War', *HJ* XXIV (1981), pp. 571–603.

Clément, Pierre, ed., *Lettres, instructions et mémoires de Colbert* (Paris, 1861–82, 8 vols. in 10).

Clerk of Eldin, John, *An Essay on Naval Tactics, Systematical and Historical* (Edinburgh, 2nd edn 1804). A celebrated work of theory, and, in some people's opinion, of influence.

Clowes, William Laird, *The Royal Navy: A History from the Earliest Times to the Present* (London, 1897–1903, 7 vols.). The first and so far only attempt to write a complete history of the Royal Navy, most of it by a single hand (though failing health obliged Clowes to recruit collaborators for his later volumes). Thorough, scholarly and remarkably comprehensive, but now very largely outdated.

Coad, Jonathan G., *The Royal Dockyards 1690–1850: Architecture and Engineering Works of the Sailing Navy* (Aldershot, 1989). The docks and buildings of the naval yards at home and abroad: elegant, complete and scholarly. His *Historic Architecture of the Royal Navy: An Introduction* (London, 1983) is exactly that.

— 'The Development and Organisation of Plymouth Dockyard, 1689–1815', in *MHD* I, 92–200.

Coats, Ann, 'The 1797 Mutinies in the Channel Fleet: A Native, or Foreign-inspired, Revolutionary Movement?', in Coats and MacDougall, *1797 Mutinies*.

— 'The Delegates: A Radical Tradition', in Coats and MacDougall, *1797 Mutinies*.

— 'Spithead Introduction', in Coats and MacDougall, *1797 Mutinies*.

Coats, Ann and Philip MacDougall, eds., *The 1797 Mutinies – Papers of the Spithead and Nore Bicentenary Conferences, 1997* (forthcoming; I am grateful to authors and editors of this collection for the opportunity to read and cite it in advance of publication).

Cobbett, William, ed., *The Parliamentary History of England* (London, 1806–20, 36 vols.). The most important of the early collections of Parliamentary debates, later taken over by T. C. Hansard.

Cochrane, Thomas, Earl of Dundonald, *The Autobiography of a Seaman* (London, 2nd edn 1861). A mendacious work of self-justification, to be used with extreme caution. Unfortunately almost all his biographers (to say nothing of Marryat, Forester and O'Brian) have adopted it uncritically.

Cock, Randolph, 'Precursors of Cook: The Voyages of the *Dolphin*, 1764–8', *MM* LXXXV (1999), pp. 30–52.

— '"The Finest Invention in the World": The Royal Navy's Early Trials of Copper Sheathing, 1708–1770', *MM* LXXXVII (2001), pp. 446–59.

Cockburn, William, *An Account of the Nature, Causes, Symptoms and Cure of the Distempers that are incident to Seafaring People* . . . (London, 1696–7, 3 parts in 2). Case-book of a naval physician.

Cogar, W. B., 'The Politics of Naval Administration, 1649–1660' (Oxford D.Phil. thesis, 1983).

— ed., *New Interpretations in Naval History: Selected Papers from the Eighth Naval History Symposium* (Annapolis, 1989).

— ed., *New Interpretations in Naval History: Selected Papers from the Twelfth Naval History Symposium* (Annapolis, 1997).

Coleman, D. C., 'Naval Dockyards under the Later Stuarts', *EcHR* 2nd S. VI (1953–4), pp. 134–55.

Colenbrander, H. T., ed., *Beschieden uit Vreemde Archieven omtrent de Groote Nederlandsche Zeeoorlogen 1652–1676* (RGPks Vols. 18–19, The Hague, 1919). Documents on the seventeenth-century naval wars from non-Dutch archives.

Coleridge, [Bernard] Lord, *The Story of a Devonshire House* (London, 1905). Family correspondence.

Coleridge, Samuel Taylor, *The Friend*, ed. Barbara E. Rooke (London, 1969, 2 vols.). Includes a good deal of naval interest from his time as secretary to Sir Alexander Ball at Malta.

Colin, J., *Louis XV et les Jacobites: le projet de débarquement en Angleterre de 1743–1744* (Paris, 1901). One of a series of meticulous studies prepared by the Historical Section of the French General Staff.

Colledge, J. J., *Ships of the Royal Navy* (Newton Abbot, 1969–70, 2 vols.; there are 2nd and 3rd edns of Vol. I, London, 1987 and 2003). An 'historical index' of British warships giving essential basic information.

Colley, Linda, *In Defiance of Oligarchy: The Tory Party 1714–60* (Cambridge, 1982)

— 'The Reach of the State, the Appeal of the Nation: Mass Arming and Political Culture in the Napoleonic Wars', in Stone, *Imperial State*, pp. 165–84.

Collinge, J. M., *Office-Holders in Modern Britain VII: Navy Board Officials 1660–1832* (London, 1978). Indispensable groundwork for administrative history. Unfortunately it only covers the Navy Board and Navy Office, not the financial departments and the dockyards which also came under the Navy Board.

Condon, M. E., 'The Establishment of the Transport Board – A Subdivision of the Admiralty – 4 July 1794', *MM* LVIII (1972), pp. 69–84.

Conn, Stetson, *Gibraltar in British Diplomacy in the Eighteenth Century* (New Haven, 1942).

Contamine, Philippe, ed., *War and Competition between States* (Oxford, 2000).

Conway, Stephen, *The War of American Independence 1775–1783* (London, 1995).

— *The British Isles and the War of American Independence* (Oxford, 2000).

— 'The Politics of British Military and Naval Mobilization, 1775–83', *EHR* CXII (1997), pp. 1179–1201.

— 'British Mobilization in the War of American Independence', *HR* LXXII (1999), pp. 58–76.

Cook, Alan, *Edmond Halley: Charting the Heavens and the Seas* (Oxford, 1998).

— 'An English Astronomer on the Adriatic: Edmond Halley's Surveys of 1703 and the Imperial Administration', *Mitteilungen des Österreichischen Staatsarchivs* XXXVIII (1985), pp. 123–62.

Cook, Harold J., 'Practical Medicine and the British Armed Forces after the "Glorious Revolution"', *MH* XXXIV (1990), pp. 1–26.

Cooke, Edward, *A Voyage to the South Sea, and Round the World, perform'd in the years 1708, 1709, 1710 and 1711* . . . (London, 1712). Woodes Rogers' privateering expedition to the Pacific.

Cookson, J. E., *The British Armed Nation, 1793–1815* (Oxford, 1997).

Coombs, Douglas, *The Conduct of the Dutch: British Opinion and the Dutch Alliance during the War of the Spanish Succession* (The Hague, 1958).

Cooper, Carolyn C., 'The Portsmouth System of Manufacture', *T&C* XXV (1984), pp. 182–225. The Brunel-Maudslay block mills.

Cooper, Guy E., 'The Methods of Blockade and Observation Employed during the Revolutionary and Napoleonic Wars', *JRUSI* LXI (1916), pp. 523–50.

Cooper, Richard, 'William Pitt, Taxation and the Needs of War', *JBS* XXII (1982), pp. 94–103.

Coquelle, P., 'Les Projets de descente en Angleterre', *RHD* XV (1901), pp. 433–52 and 591–624; XVI (1902), pp. 134–57. A survey from Foreign Ministry archives of all plans, 1666–1782.

Corbett, Julian S., ed., *Fighting Instructions 1530–1816* (NRS Vol. 29, 1905). Important documents, though the interpretation of them was later revised by Corbett himself and others.

— ed., *Signals and Instructions, 1776–1794* (NRS Vol. 35, 1909). Further documents, filling gaps in and revising the conclusions of his earlier volume.

— *Some Principle of Maritime Strategy* (London, 1911). A fundamental work, still widely studied.

— *England in the Mediterranean: A Study of the Rise and Influence of British Power within the Straits 1603–1713* (London, 2nd edn 1917, 2 vols.).

— *England in the Seven Years' War: A Study in Combined Strategy* (London, 2nd edn 1918, 2 vols.).

— *The Campaign of Trafalgar* (London, 2nd edn 1919, 2 vols.). The most important, and least outdated, of Corbett's strictly historical (as opposed to editorial or analytical) works.

Corbett, Julian S. and H. W. Richmond, eds., *Private Papers of George, Second Earl Spencer* (NRS Vols. 46, 48, 58 and 59, 1913–24). First Lord of the Admiralty 1794–1801.

[Corbett, Thomas], *An Account of the Expedition of the British Fleet to Sicily in the Years 1718, 1719 and 1720* (Dublin, 5th edn 1739).

Cormack, Alan and Alan Jones, eds., *The Journal of Corporal William Todd 1745–1762* (Army Records Society Vol. 18, Stroud, 2001). An intelligent NCO who served some time afloat as a Marine.

Cormack, William S., *Revolution and Political Conflict in the French Navy, 1789–1794* (Cambridge, 1995).

Cornwallis-West, G., *The Life and Letters of Admiral Cornwallis* (London, 1927).

Coutau-Bégarie, Hervé, ed., *L'Evolution de la pensée navale* (Paris, 1990–99, 7 vols.). A valuable collection of studies on naval thinkers of all nations and periods.

Coxere, Edward, *Adventures by Sea* . . . , ed. E. H. W. Mayerstein (London, 1945). A late-seventeenth-century seaman's memoir.

Crabtree, Roger, 'The Idea of a Protestant Foreign Policy', in *Cromwell, A Profile*, ed. Ivan Roots (London, 1973), pp. 160–89.

Crafts, N. F. R., *British Economic Growth during the Industrial Revolution* (Oxford, 1985).

Craig, Hardin, ed., 'Letters of Lord St Vincent to Thomas Grenville, 1806–1807', in Lloyd, *Naval Miscellany IV*, pp. 469–93.

Cranmer-Byng, J. L., ed., *Pattee Byng's Journal, 1718–1720* (NRS Vol. 88, 1950). Sir George's son and diplomatic agent.

Crawford, Abraham, *Reminiscences of a Naval Officer* (London, 1999) [originally 1851]. Entertaining memoir of the Great Wars.

Creswell, John, *British Admirals of the Eighteenth Century: Tactics in Battle* (London, 1972). An important study of the development of tactical ideas.

Crewe, Duncan, *Yellow Jack and the Worm: British Naval Administration in the West Indies, 1739–1748* (Liverpool, 1993). Not a children's book, as the title might suggest, but a sober study of naval logistics.

— 'British Naval Administration in the West Indies 1739–48' (Liverpool Ph.D. thesis, 1978). His book is a revised version of this thesis, which however contains some information not in the published version.

Crimmin, Patricia K., 'Admiralty Administration, 1783–1806' (London M.Phil. thesis, 1967).

— 'Admiralty Relations with the Treasury, 1783–1806: The Preparation of Navy Estimates and the Beginnings of Treasury Control', *MM* LIII (1967), pp. 63–72.

— 'The Financial and Clerical Establishment of the Admiralty Office, 1783–1806', *MM* LV (1969), pp. 299–309.

— 'George Canning and the Battle of Camperdown', *MM* LXVII (1981), pp. 319–26.

— 'Prisoners of War and British Port Communities, 1793–1815', *NM* VI (1996), 4, 17–27.

— 'John Jervis, Earl of St Vincent, 1735–1823', in Le Fevre and Harding, *Precursors of Nelson*, pp. 324–50.

— 'Letters and Documents relating to the Service of Nelson's Ships, 1780–1805: A Critical Report', *HR* LXX (1997), pp. 52–69.

— 'The Sick and Hurt Board and the Health of Seamen, c. 1700–1806', *JMR* (Dec 1999). Essential contributions to administrative history. Other articles by Miss Crimmin are cited in the notes.

Crook, Malcolm, *Toulon in War and Revolution: From the Ancien Régime to the Restoration, 1750–1820* (Manchester, 1991).

Cross, Anthony, *By the Banks of the Neva: Chapters from the Lives and Careers of the British in Eighteenth-Century Russia* (Cambridge, 1997). Including many naval men.

Crouse, Nellis M., *The French Struggle for the West Indies, 1665–1713* (New York, 1943). A competent, discursive operational history from printed sources.

Crouzet, François, *L'Economie britannique et le blocus continentale (1806–1813)* (Paris, 1958, 2 vols.). The fundamental study of this essential subject.

— 'Wars, Blockade and Economic Change in Europe, 1792–1815', *JEcH* XXIV (1964), pp. 567–88.

— 'The Impact of the French Wars on the British Economy', in Dickinson, *Britain and the French Revolution*, pp. 189–209.

— 'The Second Hundred Years War: Some Reflections', *French History* X (1996), pp. 432–50.

— 'Blocus mercantile et blocus offensif: L'Orde en Conseil du 26 avril 1809', in Acerra et al., *Etat, marine et société*, pp. 163–76.

Crowhurst, Patrick, *The Defence of British Trade 1689 to 1815* (Folkestone, 1977).

— *The French War on Trade: Privateering 1793–1815* (Aldershot, 1989).
  Two inaccessible but learned and important studies.

— 'The Admiralty and the Convoy System in the Seven Years War', *MM* LVII (1971), pp. 163–73.

Cunat, Charles, *Histoire du Bailli de Suffren* (Rennes, 1852). A solid operational history of old school, partisan but using and printing documents.

[Cunningham, Sir Charles], *A Narrative of Occurrences that took place during the Mutiny at the Nore* . . . (Chatham, 1829). Captain of the frigate *Clyde*.

Curry, J., 'English Sea-Chaplains in the Royal Navy (1577–1684)' (Bristol MA dissertation, 1956). Unreliable.

Curryer, Betty Nelson, *Anchors: An Illustrated History* (London, 1999). English-speaking anchors, in this case: it should be read in conjunction with Gay.

Cushner, Nicholas P., ed., *Documents Illustrating the British Conquest of Manila, 1762–1763* (CS 4th S. VIII, 1971). Excellent collection from British, Spanish and Jesuit archives.

[Dallas, Sir George], *A Biographical Memoir of the late Sir Peter Parker* (London, 1815). The short life of a successful frigate captain, by his father-in-law.

Daly, Robert W., 'Operations of the Russian Navy during the Reign of Napoleon I, 1801–1815', *MM* XXXIV (1948), pp. 169–83. Based mainly on western sources, but uses a few Russian books.

Dampier, William, *A Voyage to New Holland*, ed. James A. Williamson (London, 1939).

— *A New Voyage Round the World*, ed. N. M. Penzer and Sir Albert Gray (London, 1927, from 7th edn of 1729).
  The most scholarly and ineffectual of the buccaneers.

Dandeker, Christopher, 'Patronage and Bureaucratic Control: The Case of the Naval Officer in English Society 1780–1850', *British Journal of Sociology* XXIX (1978), pp. 300–320. Elementary analysis.

Dann, Uriel, *Hannover und England 1740–1760: Diplomatie und Selbsterhaltung* (Hildesheim, 1986). Since translated as *Hanover and Great Britain 1740–1760: Diplomacy and Survival* (Leicester, 1991).

Davids, Karel, 'Seamen's Organizations and Social Protest in Europe, c. 1300–1850', *International Review of Social History* XXXIX (1994), Supp., pp. 145–70.

Davies, John A., 'An Enquiry into Faction among British Naval Officers during the War of the American Revolution' (Liverpool MA dissertation, 1964).

Davies, J. D., *Gentlemen and Tarpaulins: The Officers and Men of the Restoration Navy* (Oxford, 1991). Essential for the social and political history of the period.

— 'Devon and the Navy in the Civil and Dutch Wars, 1642–88', in *MHD* I, 173–8.

— 'The Birth of the Imperial Navy? Aspects of Maritime Strategy, c.1650–90', in Duffy, *Parameters*, pp. 14–38.

— 'James II, William of Orange, and the Admirals', in *By Force or by Default? The Revolution of 1688–1689*, ed. Eveline Cruikshanks (Edinburgh, 1989), pp. 82–108.

— 'The English Navy on the Eve of War, 1689', in *Guerres maritimes*, pp. 1–14.

— 'Pepys and the Admiralty Commission of 1679–84', *HR* LXII (1989), pp. 34–53.

— 'The Navy, Parliament and Political Crisis in the Reign of Charles II', *HJ* XXXVI (1993), pp. 271–88.

— 'Wales and Mr Pepys's Navy', *Maritime Wales* XI (1987), pp. 101–11.

Davies, K. G., *The Royal African Company* (London, 1957).

— *The North Atlantic World in the Seventeenth Century* (Minneapolis, 1974).

Davis, Joshua, *A Narrative of Joshua Davis* . . . (Boston, 1811). An American seaman's memoir covering the 1770s and 1780s; published with additions, evidently by another hand, intended to dress it for the 1811 market.

Davis, Ralph, *A Commercial Revolution: English Overseas Trade in the Seventeenth and Eighteenth Centuries* (Historical Association, London, 1967).

— *The Rise of the English Shipping Industry in the Seventeenth and Eighteenth Centuries* (Newton Abbot, 2nd edn 1971).
Important studies by a great economic historian.

Deane, John Bathurst, *The Life of Richard Deane* . . . (London, 1870). Prints many letters of the Commonwealth 'General at Sea'.

Deane, Phyllis and W. A. Cole, *British Economic Growth 1688–1959: Trends and Structure* (Cambridge, 2nd edn 1967).

De Groot, S. J., 'Schout-bij-nacht J. A. Bloys van Treslong (1757–1824). Terecht een zondebok of niet?' *TvZ* XIII (1994), pp. 131–47. Discusses who was to blame for the Dutch defeat at Camperdown.

De Jonge, J. C., *Geschiedenis van het Nederlandsche Zeewesen* (Haarlem, 2nd edn 1858–62, 5 vols.). An irreplaceable standard naval history, written from documents since lost.

Delafons, John, *A Treatise on Naval Courts Martial* (London, 1805).

Delaporte, André, 'The Prairial Battles: The French Viewpoint', in Duffy and Morriss, *Glorious First of June*, pp. 12–24.

Delarbre, J., *Tourville et la marine de son temps* (Paris, 1889). Still valuable for the documents it prints.

Delmas, Jean, ed., *Histoire militaire de la France II* (Paris, 1992).

Demerliac, Cdt Alain, *La Marine de Louis XIV: Nomenclature des vaisseaux du Roi-Soleil de 1661 à 1715* (Nice, 1995).

— *La Marine de Louis XV: nomenclature des navires français de 1715 à 1774* (Nice, 1995).

— *La Marine de Louis XVI: nomenclature des navires français de 1774 à 1792* (Nice, 1996).

— *La Marine de la Révolution: nomenclature des navires française de 1792 à 1799* (Nice, 1999).

— *La Marine du Consulat et du Premier Empire: nomenclature des navires français de 1800 à 1815* (Nice, 2003).

    Essential reference books, giving basic information about French warships and other armed vessels (Indiamen, privateers, convoy escorts etc.). I have cited them as five volumes of a single work.

De Moor, J. A., '"A Very Unpleasant Relationship". Trade and Strategy in the Eastern Seas: Anglo-Dutch Relations in the Nineteenth Century from a Colonial Perspective', in Raven and Rodger, *The Anglo-Dutch Relationship*, pp. 49–69.

Denman, T. J., 'The Political Debate over War Strategy, 1689–1712' (Cambridge Ph.D. thesis, 1985).

Depeyre, Michel, *Tactiques et stratégies navales de la France et du Royaume-Uni de 1690 à 1815* (Paris, 1998). A study of writers about tactics rather than tactics itself.

Derrick, Charles, *Memoirs of the Rise and Progress of the Royal Navy* (London, 1806). A collection of lists and statistics relating to the ships of the Navy, compiled by a Navy Office clerk.

Derriman, James, *Marooned: The Story of a Cornish Seaman* (Emsworth, 1991). The Jeffery case.

Desbrière, Édouard, *The Naval Campaign of 1805: Trafalgar*, trans. and ed. Constance Eastwick (Oxford, 1933, 2 vols.) [originally *La Campagne maritime de 1805: Trafalgar* (Paris, 1907, 2 vols.)]. Essential for the Trafalgar campaign; prints most of the French and many Spanish documents. The English translation is much better than the original, Miss Eastwick having painstakingly corrected the very numerous errors of transcription, translation and referencing made by Col. Desbrière's copyists.

— *Le Blocus de Brest de 1793 à 1805* (Paris, 1902).

— *1793–1805: Projets et tentatives de débarquement aux Iles Britanniques* (Paris, 1900–1902, 4 vols.).

    Further important contributions by the Historical Section of the French General Staff, which was anxious to avoid the mistakes of the past next time it tried to invade. The French navy, by contrast, has never cared to investigate these campaigns too closely.

Dessert, Daniel, *La Royale: vaisseaux et marins du Roi-Soleil* (Paris, 1996). A refreshingly iconoclastic approach to the traditional pieties of French naval history.

— *Tourville* (Paris, 2002).

— 'La Marine royale, une filiale Colbert', in *Patronages et clientèlismes 1550–1750*

(France, Angleterre, Espagne, Italie), ed. Charles Giry Deloison and Roger Mettam (Lille and London, n.d.), pp. 69–83.

De Toy, Brian M., 'Wellington's Admiral: The Life and Career of George Berkeley, 1753–1818' (Florida State University Ph.D. thesis, 1997).

— 'Wellington's Lifeline: Naval Logistics in the Peninsula', *CRE* VII (1995), pp. 359–68.

De Waard, C., ed., *De Zeeuwsche Expeditie naar de West onder Cornelis Evertsen de Jonge, 1672–1674* (Linschoten Ver. Vol. 30, 1928).

Dewar, Alfred, 'Blake's Last Campaign', *United Service Magazine* NS XLIII (1911), pp. 117–28.

Dickinson, H. T., *Liberty and Property: Political Ideology in Eighteenth-century Britain* (London, 1977).

— ed., *Britain and the French Revolution* (Basingstoke, 1989).

— 'The Capture of Minorca in 1708', *MM* LI (1965), pp. 195–204.

Dickinson, H. W., 'The Portsmouth Naval Academy, 1733–1806', *MM* LXXXIX (2003), pp. 17–30.

Dickson, P. G. M., *The Financial Revolution in England: A Study of the Development of Public Credit, 1688–1756* (London, 1967).

Dictionary of National Biography, ed. Leslie Stephen and Sidney Lee (London, 1885–1901, 63 vols. + later supps.). Aged but irreplaceable, until 2004 when the *Oxford Dictionary of National Biography* replaced it. Unless otherwise indicated, references are to the article on the person under discussion.

Dietz, Brian, 'Dikes, Dockheads and Gates: English Docks and Sea Power in the Sixteenth and Seventeenth Centuries', *MM* LXXXVIII (2002), pp. 144–54.

Dillon, Sir William Henry, *A Narrative of my Professional Adventures (1790–1839)*, ed. Michael A. Lewis (NRS Vols. 93 and 97, 1953–6). A pompous and humourless memoir, but detailed and accurate.

Diverrès, P., *L'Attaque de Lorient par les anglais (1746)* (Rennes, 1931). A scholarly study using French and British manuscripts.

Dixon, Conrad, 'To Walk the Quarterdeck: The Naval Career of David Ewan Bartholomew', *MM* LXXIX (1993), pp. 58–63.

Doorne, Christopher, 'A Floating Republic? Conspiracy Theory and the Nore Mutiny of 1797', in Coats and MacDougall, *1797 Mutinies*.

Douglas, General Sir Howard, *A Treatise on Naval Gunnery* (London, 4th edn 1855). Sums up the accumulated experience of centuries of experience with smooth-bore naval guns. The author, an artilleryman, was the son of the naval gunnery innovator Sir Charles Douglas.

Douin, Georges, *La Flotte de Bonaparte sur les côtes d'Egypte: les prodromes d'Aboukir* (Cairo, 1922).

— *La Campagne de Bruix en Méditerranée, mars–août 1799* (Paris, 1923). Careful and precise studies by a writer not blind to Napoleon's mistakes.

Dowling, C., 'The Convoy System and the West Indian Trade 1803–1815' (Oxford D.Phil. thesis, 1965).

Drake, Frederick C., 'Commodore Sir James Lucas Yeo and Governor General

George Prevost: A Study in Command Relations 1813–14', in Cogar, *New Interpretations . . . Eighth*, pp. 156–71.

Draper, J. N., 'With Nelson in the Mediterranean: Private Papers of Dr Leonard Gillespie', *Chambers Journal* 8th S. XIV (1945), pp. 229–33 and 317–19.

Drinkwater Bethune, John, *A Narrative of the Battle of St Vincent . . .* (London, 2nd edn 1840) [originally Anon., *A Narrative of the Proceedings of the British Fleet . . . on 14th February 1797* (1797)]. An eye-witness narrative from Nelson's point of view.

Dudley, Wade G., *Splintering the Wooden Wall: The British Blockade of the United States, 1812–1815* (Annapolis, 2003).

Dudley, William S., 'Commodore Isaac Chauncy and U.S. Joint Operations on Lake Ontario, 1813–14', in Cogar, *New Interpretations . . . Eighth*, pp. 139–55.

Dudley, William S. and Michael J. Crawford, eds., *The Naval War of 1812: A Documentary History* (Washington, 1985–2002, 3 vols. to date). An excellent documentary collection.

[Duff, Captain George], 'The Trafalgar General Order Book of H.M.S. *Mars*', *MM* XXII (1936), pp. 87–104.

Duffy, Michael, *Soldiers, Sugar and Seapower: The British Expeditions to the West Indies and the War against Revolutionary France* (Oxford, 1987). An admirable monograph on strategy and operations.

— ed., *Parameters of British Naval Power, 1650–1850* (Exeter, 1992).

— ed., *The Naval Miscellany Vol. VI* (NRS Vol. 146, 2003).

— ' "A Particular Service": the British Government and the Dunkirk Expedition of 1793', *EHR* XCI (1976), pp. 529–54.

— 'British Policy in the War against Revolutionary France', in Jones, *Britain and Revolutionary France*, pp. 11–26.

— 'British Diplomacy and the French Wars, 1789–1815', in Dickinson, *Britain and the French Revolution*, pp. 127–45.

— 'Pitt, Grenville and the Control of British Foreign Policy in the 1790s', in Black, *Knights Errant*, pp. 151–77.

— 'War, Revolution and the Crisis of the British Empire', in *The French Revolution and British Popular Politics*, ed. Mark Philp (Cambridge, 1991), pp. 118–45.

— 'Devon and the Naval Strategy of the French Wars 1689–1815', in *MHD* I, 182–91.

— 'The Establishment of the Western Squadron as the Linchpin of British Naval Strategy', in Duffy, *Parameters*, pp. 60–81.

— 'The Creation of Plymouth Dockyard and its Impact on Naval Strategy', in *Guerres maritimes*, pp. 245–74.

— 'British Naval Intelligence and Bonaparte's Egyptian Expedition of 1798', *MM* LXXXIV (1998), pp. 278–90.

— 'World-Wide War and British Expansion, 1793–1815', in Marshall, *Eighteenth Century*, pp. 184–207.

— 'Samuel Hood, First Viscount Hood 1724–1816', in Le Fevre and Harding, *Precursors of Nelson*, pp. 248–77.

— 'The Man who Missed the Grain Convoy: Rear Admiral George Montagu and the Arrival of Vanstabel's Convoy from America in 1794', in Duffy and Morriss, *The Glorious First of June*, pp. 101–19.

— '"Science and Labour": The Naval Contribution to Operations Ashore in the Great Wars with France', in *Seapower Ashore: 200 Years of Royal Navy Operations on Land*, ed. Peter Hore (London, 2001), pp. 39–52.

— 'La artillería en Trafalgar: adiestramiento, táctica y moral de combate', in *Trafalgar y el mundo atlántico*, ed. Agustín Guimerá, Alberto Ramos and Gonzalo Butrón (Madrid, 2004). An important paper, which is to be published in English.

Duffy, Michael, Stephen Fisher, Basil Greenhill, David J. Starkey and Joyce Youings, eds., *The New Maritime History of Devon* (London, 1992–4, 2 vols.).

Duffy, Michael and Roger Morriss, eds., *The Glorious First of June: A Naval Battle and its Aftermath* (Exeter, 2001).

Duguay-Trouin, René, *Vie de Monsieur Du Guay-Trouin, écrite de sa main*, ed. Henri Malo (Paris, 1922). Modest and reliable memoirs of the great Malouin privateer who rose to be an admiral.

Duhamel du Monceau, Henri Louis, *Elémens de l'architecture navale, ou traité pratique de la construction des vaisseaux* (Paris, 2nd edn 1758).

Dull, Jonathan R., *The French Navy and American Independence: A Study of Arms and Diplomacy, 1774–1787* (Princeton, 1975).

— *A Diplomatic History of the American Revolution* (New Haven and London, 1985).

— *The French Navy and the Loss of Canada: A Study of Arms and Diplomacy, 1748–1763* (Lincoln, Nebraska, forthcoming; I am grateful to Dr Dull for allowing me to read this book in manuscript).

— 'Mahan, Sea Power, and the War for American Independence', *IHR* X (1988), pp. 59–67.

— 'Why Did the French Revolutionary Navy Fail?', *CRE* XVIII (1989), Pt 2, pp. 121–37.

Dummer, Edmund, 'Account of the General Progress and Advancement of His Majesty's New Dock and Yard at Plymouth', ed. Michael Duffy, in Duffy, *Naval Miscellany VI*, pp. 93–147.

Dupont, Maurice, *L'Amiral Decrès et Napoléon* (Paris, 1991).

Dupont, Maurice and Etienne Taillemite, *Les Guerres navales françaises du Moyen Age à la Guerre du Golfe* (Paris, 1995). Compressed history, very useful for reference.

Dyer, Florence E., *The Life of Admiral Sir John Narbrough* (London, 1931).

— 'The Journal of Grenvill Collins', *MM* XIV (1928), pp. 197–219.

— 'Captain John Narborough and the Battle of Solebay', *MM*, XV (1929), pp. 222–32.

— 'Captain Christopher Myngs in the West Indies', *MM* XVIII (1932), pp. 168–87.

Eames, Aled, 'Sea Power and Welsh History, 1625–1660' (Wales MA dissertation, 1954).

— 'Sea Power and Caernarvonshire, 1642–1660', *Transactions of the Caernarvonshire Historical Society* XVI (1955), pp. 29–51.

Earle, Peter, *The Wreck of the Almiranta: Sir William Phips and the Hispaniola Treasure* (London, 1979).

— *The Sack of Panamá* (London, 1981).

— *A City Full of People: Men and Women of London 1650–1750* (London, 1994).

— *Sailors: English Merchant Seamen 1650–1775* (London, 1998). The best general study of eighteenth-century seamen.

— *The Pirate Wars* (London, 2003).

— 'English Sailors, 1570–1775', in van Royen et al., *'Those Emblems of Hell'?*, pp. 73–92.

Edwards, Ifor, 'John Wilkinson and the Development of Gunfounding in the Late Eighteenth Century', *Welsh History Review* XV (1990–91), pp. 524–44.

Edye, L., ed., *The Historical Records of the Royal Marines: Vol. I 1664–1701* [all published] (London, 1893).

Ehrman, John, *The Navy in the War of William III, 1689–1697: Its State and Direction* (Cambridge, 1953). Indispensable study of organization, administration and politics.

— *The Younger Pitt* (London, 1969–96, 3 vols.). A massive and definitive work.

— 'Pepys's Organization and the Naval Mobilization of 1688', *MM* XXXV (1949), pp. 203–39.

Ekberg, Carl J., *The Failure of Louis XIV's Dutch War* (Chapel Hill, N.C., 1979).

Elias, Johan E., *Schetsen uit de Geschiedenis van ons Zeewezen* (The Hague, 1916–30, 6 vols.). Highly detailed studies of the First Dutch War, inspired in part by the need to correct the errors of Gardiner and Atkinson.

— *De Vlootbouw in Nederland in de eerste Helft der 17e Eeuw, 1596–1655* (Amsterdam, 1933). Dutch warship design.

Elliot, Sir George, *Memoir of Admiral the Hon. Sir George Elliot, written for his Children* (p.p. London, 1863). Genial reminiscences, many of them more or less true.

Elliott, Marianne, *Partners in Revolution: The United Irishmen and France* (New Haven, 1982).

— 'French Subversion in Britain in the French Revolution', in Jones, *Britain and Revolutionary France*, pp. 40–52.

— 'The Role of Ireland in French War Strategy, 1796–1798', in *Ireland and the French Revolution*, ed. Hugh Gough and D. J. Dickson (Dublin, 1990), pp. 202–19.

Ellis, Geoffrey, 'War and the French Economy (1792–1815)', in Aerts and Crouzet, *Economic Effects*, pp. 6–13.

Emsley, Clive, *British Society and the French Wars, 1793–1815* (London, 1979).

— 'The Recruitment of Petty Offenders during the French Wars 1793–1815', *MM* LXVI (1980), pp. 199–208.

— 'The Impact of War and Military Participation on Britain and France, 1792–1815', in *Artisans, Peasants and Proletarians, 1760–1860: Essays Presented to Gwyn A. Williams*, ed. Emsley and James Walvin (London, 1985), pp. 57–80.

— 'The Social Impact of the French Wars', in Dickinson, *Britain and the French Revolution*, pp. 211–27.

Emsley, Clive, A. M. Hill and M. Y. Ashcroft, eds., *North Riding Naval Recruits: The Quota Acts and the Quota Men 1795–1797* (Northallerton, 1978). Lists of the men recruited for the North Riding of Yorkshire (by Hill and Ashcroft), combined with an analysis (by Emsley) of the equivalent returns for Kent, Leicestershire, Lincolnshire, Northumberland, Nottinghamshire and Sussex.

Erskine, David, ed., *Augustus Hervey's Journal* (London, 2nd edn 1954). Remarkable and revealing private journal of a very untypical sea officer.

Ertman, Thomas, *Birth of the Leviathan: Building States and Regimes in Medieval and Early Modern Europe* (Cambridge, 1997).

Esquemeling, John, *The Buccaneers of America*, ed. W. S. Stallybrass (London, [1923]). A famous account by a participant. This hugely popular book has a very complex bibliography in many languages: this is a modern-spelling version of the 1684–5 London edition.

Evans, F. T., 'Wood since the Industrial Revolution: A Strategic Retreat?', *History of Technology* VII (1982), ed. A. R. Hall and Norman Smith, pp. 37–55.

Evans, Howard V., 'The Nootka Sound Controversy in Anglo-French Diplomacy – 1790', *JMH* XLVI (1974), pp. 609–40.

Evans, Laurence, 'The Gift of the Sea: Civil Logistics and the Industrial Revolution', *Historical Reflections/Réflections Historiques* XV (1988), pp. 361–415.

Evelyn, John, *The Diary of John Evelyn*, ed. E. S. De Beer (Oxford, 1955, 6 vols.). Pepys's friend and contemporary, who shared many of his scholarly and naval interests.

Fabel, Robin F. A., *Bombast and Broadsides, The Lives of George Johnstone* (Tuscaloosa, 1987). Not chiefly concerned with his naval life.

Farrington, Anthony, *A Biographical Index of East India Company Maritime Service Officers 1600–1834* (British Library, 1999). Many East India officers also served in the Navy.

Feldbæk, Ole, *Denmark and the Armed Neutrality 1800–1801: Small Power Policy in a World War* (Copenhagen, 1980).

— *Slaget på Reden* (Copenhagen, 1985). The best general study of the battle; it has now appeared in English as *The Battle of Copenhagen 1801*, trans. Tony Wedgwood (London, 2002).

— *Dansk Søfarts Historie 3, 1720–1814: Storhandelens Tid* (Copenhagen, 1997). One of the seven volumes of the excellent 'Maritime History of Denmark'.

— 'The Anglo-Danish Convoy Conflict of 1800', *SJH* II (1977), pp. 161–82.

— 'Denmark and the Baltic, 1720–1864', in *In Quest of Trade and Security: The Baltic in Power Politics 1500–1990*, ed. Göran Rystad, Klaus-Richard Böhme and Wilhelm M. Carlgren (Stockholm, 1994–5, 2 vols.) I, 257–95.

— 'Denmark in the Napoleonic Wars: A Foreign Policy Survey', *SJH* XXVI (2001), pp. 89–101.

Fernández Duro, Cesáreo, *Armada Española desde la unión de los Reinos de Castilla y de Aragón* (Madrid, 1895–1903, 9 vols.). Aged but unreplaced standard history, printing many documents from unreliable transcripts.

Fernández de Pinedo, Emilano, 'From the Bloomery to the Blast-furnace: Technical Change in Spanish Iron-making (1650–1822)', *JEEH* XVII (1988), pp. 7–31.

Fewster, Joseph M., 'Prize-money and the British Expedition to the West Indies of 1793–4', *JICH* XII (1983–84), pp. 1–28.

— 'The Jay Treaty and British Ship Seizures: The Martinique Cases', *WMQ* XLV (1988), pp. 426–52.

Filion, Maurice, *Maurepas: ministre de Louis XV (1715–1749)* (Montreal, 1967).

— 'La Crise de la marine française, d'après le mémoire de Maurepas de 1745 sur la marine et le commerce', *Revue d'Histoire de l'Amérique Française* XXI (1967), pp. 230–42.

Fincham, John, *A History of Naval Architecture* (London, 1851). Aged work still of some value for the period of the author's lifetime.

Firth, C. H., ed., *The Narrative of General Venables* (CS N.S. Vol. 60, 1900).

— 'Blake and the Battle of Santa Cruz', *EHR* XX (1905), pp. 228–50.

— ed., *Naval Songs and Ballads* (NRS Vol. 33, 1908).

— ed., 'The Battle of Santa Cruz: Sir Richard Stayner's Narrative', in Laughton, *Naval Miscellany II*, pp. 127–36.

Firth, C. H. and R. S. Rait, eds., *Acts and Ordinances of the Interregnum, 1642–1660* (London, 1911, 3 vols.).

Fisher, Sir Godfrey, *Barbary Legend: War, Trade and Piracy in North Africa 1415–1830* (Oxford, 1957). A vigorous case for the defence.

Forbes, Eric G., *Greenwich Observatory: Vol. I, Origins and Early History (1675–1835)* (London, 1975).

Forester, C. S., ed., *The Adventures of John Wetherell* (London, 1954). A lower-deck memoir.

Formicola, Antonio and Claudio Romano, 'La Marina Napoletana nel contesto Mediterraneo alla fine del XVIII secolo', *RiM* CXIX (Nov 1986), pp. 61–72.

— 'Vescelli Napoletani: Breve storia degli esemplari realizzati dall'avento dei Borbone alla conquista Garibaldina (1734–1860)', *RiM* CXX (Mar 1987), pp. 57–74.

Fortescue, Sir John, ed., *The Correspondence of King George the Third, from 1760 to December 1783* (London, 1927–28, 6 vols.). An essential source, but also a byword among historians for editorial blunders. L. B. Namier's *Additions and Corrections to Sir John Fortescue's Edition of the Correspondence of King George III (Vol. I)* (Manchester, 1937) unfortunately covers only the first volume.

Fothergill, Brian, *Sir William Hamilton: Envoy Extraordinary* (London, 1969).

Fox, Frank L., *Great Ships: The Battlefleet of King Charles II* (London, 1980). Pepys's documents and the Van de Veldes' drawings permit a remarkably detailed survey.

— *A Distant Storm: The Four Days' Battle of 1666* (Rotherfield, Sussex, 1996). Learned and thorough.

— 'The English Naval Shipbuilding Programme of 1664', *MM* LXXVIII (1992), pp. 277–92.

— 'Hired Men-of-War, 1664–67', *MM* LXXXIV (1998), pp. 13–25 and 152–72.

Français et Anglais en Méditerranée de la Révolution française à l'indépendence de la Grèce (1789–1830) (Vincennes, 1992). Proceedings of a conference, issued with no editor named.

Francis, A. D., *The Methuens and Portugal, 1691–1708* (Cambridge, 1966).

— *The First Peninsular War, 1702–1713* (London, 1975).

— 'Portugal and the Grand Alliance', *BIHR* XXXVIII (1965), pp. 71–93.

Franklin, John, *Navy Board Ship Models 1650–1750* (London, 1989).

Franks, R. D., 'Admiral Sir Richard Onslow', *MM* LXVII (1981), pp. 327–37.

Frantzen, Ole Louis, *Truslen fra Øst: Dansk-norsk flådepolitik 1769–1807* (Copenhagen, 1980).

Fraser, Edward, *The Enemy at Trafalgar* (London, 1906).

— *The Sailors Whom Nelson Led* (London, 1913). Good collections of narratives.

Fraser, Flora, *Beloved Emma: The Life of Emma Lady Hamilton* (London, 1986).

Fraser, Henry S., 'The Memoranda of William Green, Secretary to Vice-Admiral Marriott Arbuthnot in the American Revolution', *Rhode Island Historical Society Collections* XVII (1924), pp. 54–64, 90–104, 126–40; and XVIII (1925), pp. 112–28 and 154–60.

Freeman, Edward, ed., *Les Empires en guerre et paix, 1793–1860: journées franco-anglaises d'histoire de la Marine, Portsmouth, 23–26 mars 1988* (Vincennes, 1990).

Fremantle, Anne, ed., *The Wynne Diaries* (Oxford, 1935–40, 3 vols.). Three teenage girls at sea with the Mediterranean Squadron in the 1790s.

French, David, *The British Way in Warfare 1688–2000* (London, 1990).

Frost, Alan, *Convicts and Empire: A Naval Question 1776–1811* (Melbourne, 1980).

— *Arthur Phillip 1738–1814, His Voyaging* (Melbourne, 1987). Sea officer, spy and first Governor of New South Wales.

Fulton, T. W., *The Sovereignty of the Sea* (Edinburgh, 1911).

Gallagher, Robert E., ed., *Byron's Journal of his Circumnavigation, 1764–1766* (HS 2nd S. CXXII, 1964).

Gardiner, R., *An Account of the Expedition to the West Indies . . .* (Birmingham, 3rd edn 1762). A good plain narrative of the operations of 1758–9 by a captain of Marines.

Gardiner, Robert, *The First Frigates: Nine-Pounder and Twelve-Pounder Frigates, 1748–1815* (London, 1992).

— *The Heavy Frigate. Eighteen-Pounder Frigates: Vol. I, 1778–1800* (London, 1994). The intended second vol. was absorbed into:

— *Frigates of the Napoleonic Wars* (London, 2000).

— 'Frigate Design in the Eighteenth Century', *Warship* Nos. 9–12 (1979), pp. 3–12, 80–92 and 269–77.
  Essential studies of the evolution of warship designs.
— ed., *Navies and the American Revolution, 1775–1783* (London, 1996).
— ed., *Fleet Battle and Blockade: The French Revolutionary War 1793–1797* (London, 1996).
— ed., *Nelson against Napoleon: From the Nile to Copenhagen, 1798–1801* (London, 1997).
— ed., *The Campaign of Trafalgar 1803–1805* (London, 1997).
— ed., *The Naval War of 1812* (London, 1998). Five volumes in a series of introductory histories, extra-illustrated but by no means elementary. A sixth is edited by R. Woodman.
Gardiner, S. R., *History of the Commonwealth and Protectorate, 1649–1656* (London, 2nd edn 1903, 4 vols.).
Gardiner, S. R. and C. T. Atkinson, eds., *Letters and Papers Relating to the First Dutch War, 1652–1654* (NRS Vols. 13, 17, 30, 37, 41 and 66, 1899–1930); incorporating the *Corrigenda*, ed. A. C. Dewar (NRS 1932), which corrects many readings of the Dutch MSS after Elias, *Schetsen*. Full printing of English and (translated) Dutch documents.
Gardner, J. A., *Recollections of James Anthony Gardner*, ed. Sir Vesey Hamilton and J. K. Laughton (NRS Vol. 31, 1906). Entertaining and libellous memoirs of a junior officer. There is also a slightly abridged edition under the author's original title: *Above and Under Hatches . . .*, ed. Christopher Lloyd (London, 1955).
Gascoigne, John, *Science in the Service of Empire: Joseph Banks, the British State and the Uses of Science in the Age of Revolution* (Cambridge, 1998).
[Gatty, Alfred and Margaret], *Recollections of the Life of the Rev. A. J. Scott . . .* (London, 1842). Naval chaplain, linguist, diplomat and intelligence officer, present at Copenhagen and Trafalgar.
Gay, Jacques, *Six millénaires d'histoire des ancres* (Paris, 1997).
— 'Le Fer dans la marine en bois: l'exemple de la flotte de guerre française (1665–1815)', *Histoire et Mesure* III (1988), pp. 53–86.
Geddes, Alistair, *Portsmouth during the Great French Wars 1770–1800* (Portsmouth, 1970).
Geggus, David Patrick, *Slavery, War, and Revolution: The British Occupation of Saint Domingue 1793–1798* (Oxford, 1982).
George, M. D., *English Political Caricature to 1792; A Study of Opinion and Propaganda* (Oxford, 1959).
Geyl, P., 'Stukken betrekking hebbende op den Tocht naar Chatham en berustende op het Record Office te London', *BMHG* XXXVIII (1917), pp. 358–435.
Gibson, John S., *Ships of the '45: The Rescue of the Young Pretender* (London, 1967).
— *Playing the Scottish Card: The Franco-Jacobite Invasion of 1708* (Edinburgh, 1988).
Giglioli, Constance H. D., *Naples in 1799: An Account of the Revolution of 1799 and of the Rise and Fall of the Parthenopean Republic* (London, 1903).

Gilbert, Arthur N., 'Buggery and the British Navy, 1700–1861', *Journal of Social History* X (1976), pp. 72–98.

— 'Crime as Disorder: Criminality and the Symbolic Universe of the 18th Century British Naval Officer', in Love, *Changing Interpretations*, pp. 110–122.

— 'The Changing Face of British Military Justice, 1757–1783', *MAff* XLIX ['XLVIV'] (1985), pp. 80–84.

— 'The Nature of Mutiny in the British Navy in the Eighteenth Century', in *Naval History: The Sixth Symposium of the U.S. Naval Academy*, ed. Daniel M. Masterson (Wilmington, Del., 1987), pp. 111–20.

Gill, Conrad, *The Naval Mutinies of 1797* (Manchester, 1913). Partial and unsatisfactory, but still the only more or less scholarly treatment in print.

Gillespie, R. St J., 'Sir Nathaniel Dance's Battle off Pulo Auro', *MM* XXI (1935), pp. 163–86.

Gilpin, William, *Memoirs of Josias Rogers, esq., Commander of His Majesty's Ship Quebec* (London, 1808).

Glass, R. E., 'The Profession of Sea-Officer in Late Seventeenth-Century England' (California, Berkeley Ph.D. thesis, 1990).

— 'The Image of the Sea Officer in English Literature, 1660–1710', *Albion* XXVI (1994), pp. 583–99.

— 'Naval Courts-Martial in Seventeenth-Century England', in Cogar, *New Interpretations . . . Twelfth*, pp. 53–64.

Glete, Jan, *Navies and Nations: Warships, Navies and State Building in Europe and America, 1500–1860* (Stockholm, 1993, 2 vols.). Essential reading for any serious naval historian.

Glover, Richard, *Britain at Bay: Defence against Bonaparte, 1803–14* (London, 1973).

— 'The French Fleet, 1807–14: Britain's Problem, and Madison's Opportunity', *JMH* XXXIX (1967), pp. 233–52.

Godfrey, J. H., ed., 'Corsica, 1794', in Lloyd, *Naval Miscellany IV*, pp. 359–422.

Goldenberg, Joseph A., 'Blue Lights and Infernal Machines: The British Blockade of New London', *MM* LXI (1975), pp. 385–97.

— 'The Royal Navy's Blockade in New England Waters, 1812–1815', *IHR* VI (1984), pp. 424–39.

Goldie, Mark, 'Divergence and Union: Scotland and England, 1660–1707', in Bradshaw and Morrill, *The British Problem*, pp. 220–45.

Gonzalez-Aller Hierro, José Ignacio, 'El navio de tres puentes en la Armada Española', *RHN* III (1985), 9, 45–77.

Gonzalez-Aller, José Ignacio and Hugo O'Donnell, 'The Spanish Navy in the 18th Century', in Howarth, *Battle of St Vincent*, pp. 67–83.

Gooch, L., 'Catholic Officers in the Navy of James II', *Recusant History* XIV (1978), pp. 276–80.

Goodwin, Peter, *The Construction and Fitting of the Sailing Man of War, 1650–1850* (London, 1987).

— *The 20-Gun Ship Blandford* (London, 1988).

— *The Bomb Vessel Granado 1742* (London, 1989).

— 'The Influence of Iron in Ship Construction: 1660 to 1830', *MM* LXXXIV (1998), pp. 26–40.
Important contributions on the technology of the wooden warship.

Gordon, Elizabeth, Adelaide and Sophia, eds., *Letters and Records of Admiral Sir J. A. Gordon G.C.B., 1782–1869* (p.p. London, 1890).

Gore, John, *Nelson's Hardy and His Wife* (London, 1935). Essentially a life of Lady Hardy based on her diaries etc.

Gough, Barry M., *Distant Dominion: Britain and the Northwest Coast of North America 1579–1809* (Vancouver, 1980).

— *The Northwest Coast: British Navigation, Trade and Discoveries to 1812* (Vancouver, 1992).
Substantial parts are common to these two books.

Gough, Hugh, 'The Crisis Year: 'Europe and the Atlantic in 1798', in Bartlett et al., *1798*, pp. 538–48.

Gradish, Stephen F., *The Manning of the British Navy during the Seven Years' War* (London, 1980). A promising study published in a very imperfect condition after the author's early death.

— 'Wages and Manning: The Navy Act of 1758', *EHR* XCIII (1978), pp. 46–67.

Graham, Gerald S., ed., *The Walker Expedition to Quebec, 1711* (NRS Vol. 94, 1953).

— *Empire of the North Atlantic: The Maritime Struggle for North America* (Toronto and London, 2nd edn 1958).

— 'Considerations on the War of American Independence', *BIHR* XXII (1949), pp. 22–34.

Graham, Gerald S. and R. A. Humphreys, eds., *The Navy and South America 1807–1823* (NRS Vol. 104, 1962).

Grahn, Lance, 'Guarding the New Granadan Coasts: Dilemmas of the Spanish Coast Guard in the Early Bourbon Period', *AN* LVI (1996), pp. 19–28.

Grainger, John D., ed., *The Royal Navy in the River Plate, 1806–1807* (NRS Vol. 135, 1996).

— 'The Navy in the River Plate, 1806–1808', *MM* LXXXI (1995), pp. 287–99.

Granier, Hubert, 'Le Maréchal de Coëtlogon', *Marins et Océans* II (1993), pp. 107–41.

Grant, James, ed., *The Old Scots Navy, from 1689 to 1710* (NRS Vol. 44, 1914).

Gray, Colin S., *The Leverage of Sea Power: The Strategic Advantage of Navies in War* (New York, 1992).

Green, Geoffrey L., *The Royal Navy and Anglo-Jewry 1740–1820* (p.p. Ealing, 1989).

Greene, Jack P., 'The Seven Years' War and the American Revolution: The Causal Relationship Reconsidered', *JICH* VIII (1979–80), No. 2, pp. 85–105.

Greenhaw, Thomas D., 'Factors Influencing Royal Naval Policy for the Mediterranean, 1702–1705' (Auburn Ph.D. thesis, 1978).

Gregg, Edward, *Queen Anne* (London, 1980).

Gregory, Desmond, *Minorca, the Illusory Prize: A History of the British Occupations of Minorca between 1708 and 1802* (London, 1990).

— *Malta, Britain, and the European Powers, 1793–1815* (Madison, Wis., 1996).

— 'British Occupations of Madeira during the Wars against Napoleon', *JSAHR* LXVI (1988), pp. 80–96.

Grey, Anchitel, ed., *Debates of the House of Commons from the year 1667 to the year 1694* (London, 1763, 10 vols.).

Griffiths, Anselm John, *Observations on some Points of Seamanship with Practical Hints on Naval Economy* (Cheltenham, 1824). Thoughtful comments on naval discipline; extracts are printed by Lavery, *Shipboard Life*.

Groenveld, Simon, 'The English Civil Wars as a Cause of the First Anglo-Dutch War, 1640–1652', *HJ* XXX (1987), pp. 541–66.

— ' "J'equippe une flotte très considerable": The Dutch Side of the Glorious Revolution', in Beddard, *The Revolutions of 1688*, pp. 213–45.

Grove, Gerhard L., ed., *Til Orlogs under de Ruyter: Dagbogsoptegnelser af Hans Svendsen, en Dansk Sømand i Hollandsk Tjeneste fra 1665 til 1667* (Copenhagen, 1909). Highly coloured reminiscences of a Dane serving in the Dutch Marines during the Second Dutch War.

Gruber, Ira D., *The Howe Brothers and the American Revolution* (Chapel Hill, N.C., 1972).

— 'Richard Lord Howe: Admiral as Peacemaker', in Bilias, *George Washington's Opponents*, pp. 233–59.

Guerres et paix 1660–1815: journées franco-anglaises d'histoire de la marine . . . (Vincennes, 1987).

Guerres maritimes (1688–1713): IVes Journées franco-britanniques d'histoire de la marine (Vincennes, 1996).

Guéry, Alain, 'Les Finances de la monarchie française sous l'ancien régime', *Annales: Economies, Sociétés, Civilisations* XXXIII (1978), pp. 216–39.

Gutridge, A. C., 'Prize Agency 1800–1815, with Special Reference to the Career and Work of George Redmond Hulbert' (Portsmouth Polytechnic M.Phil. thesis, 1988).

— 'Aspects of Naval Prize Agency 1793–1815', *MM* LXXX (1994), pp. 45–53.

Gutteridge, H. C., ed., *Nelson and the Neapolitan Jacobins: Documents Relating to the Suppression of the Jacobin Revolution at Naples, June 1799* (NRS Vol. 25, 1903).

Guttridge, G. H., *The Colonial Policy of William III in America and the West Indies* (Cambridge, 1922).

Guy, Alan J., ed., 'George Durant's Journal of the Expedition to Martinique and Guadaloupe, October 1758–1759', in *Military Miscellany I*, ed. Alan J. Guy, R. N. W. Thomas and Gerard J. De Groot (Army Records Society Vol. 12, 1996), pp. 1–68.

Gwyn, Julian, *The Enterprising Admiral: The Personal Fortune of Admiral Sir Peter Warren* (Montreal, 1974). Especially valuable for its coverage of an admiral's business and financial affairs.

— ed., *The Royal Navy and North America: The Warren Papers, 1736–1752* (NRS Vol. 118, 1973).

— 'Shipbuilding for the Royal Navy in Colonial New England', *AN* XLVIII (1988), pp. 22–30.

— 'The Royal Navy in North America, 1712–1776', in Black and Woodfine, *British Navy*, pp. 129–47.

Haas, J. M., *A Management Odyssey: The Royal Dockyards, 1714–1914* (Lanham, Md., 1994). Modern management theory as a key to administrative history.

— 'The Rise of the Bedfords, 1741–1757: A Study in the Politics of the Reign of George II' (Illinois Ph.D. thesis, 1960).

— 'The Introduction of Task Work into the Royal Dockyards, 1775', *JBS* VIII (1969), No. 2, pp. 44–68.

— 'The Pursuit of Political Success in Eighteenth-Century England: Sandwich, 1740–71', *BIHR* XLIII (1970), pp. 56–77.

— 'The Royal Dockyards: The Earliest Visitations and Reform 1749–1778', *HJ* XIII (1970), pp. 191–215.

— 'Methods of Wage Payment in the Royal Dockyards, 1775–1865', *Maritime History* V (1977), pp. 99–115.

— 'Work and Authority in the Royal Dockyards from the Seventeenth Century to 1870', *Proceedings of the American Philosophical Society* CXXIV (1980), pp. 423–8.

Hackmann, William K., 'British Military Expeditions to the Coast of France, 1757–1761' (Michigan Ph.D. thesis, 1969).

Haffenden, P. S., 'Community and Conflict: New England and the Royal Navy, 1689–1775', in *The American Revolution and the Sea; Proceedings of the 14th Conference of the International Commission for Maritime History* (National Maritime Museum, 1974), pp. 84–94.

Hagan, Kenneth J., *This People's Navy: The Making of American Seapower* (New York, 1991).

Hale, Richard W., 'New Light on the Naval Side of Yorktown', *Proceedings of the Massachusetts Historical Society* LXXI (1959), pp. 124–32. A suggestive sketch with no proper references.

Haley, K. H. D., *An English Diplomat in the Low Countries: Sir William Temple and John De Witt, 1665–1672* (Oxford, 1986).

— *The British and the Dutch: Political and Cultural Relations through the Ages* (London, 1988).

Hall, Christopher D., *British Strategy in the Napoleonic War, 1803–15* (Manchester, 1992).

— 'Addington at War: Unspectacular but not Unsuccessful', *HR* LXI (1988), pp. 306–15.

— 'The Royal Navy and the Peninsular War', *MM* LXXIX (1993), pp. 403–18.

Ham, V. R., 'Strategies of Coalition and Isolation: British War Policy and North-West Europe, 1803–1810' (Oxford D.Phil. thesis, 1977).

Hamilton, Sir Richard Vesey, ed., *Letters and Papers of Admiral of the Fleet Sir Thomas Byam Martin* (NRS Vols. 12, 19 and 24, 1898–1903). Informative correspondence and memoirs.

Hammond, Wayne N., 'The Administration of the English Navy, 1649–1660' (British Columbia Ph.D. thesis, 1974).

Hampson, Norman, *La Marine de l'An II: Mobilisation de la flotte d'océan 1793–1794* (Paris, 1959).

— 'The "Comité de Marine" of the Constituent Assembly', *HJ* II (1959), pp. 130–48.

Hankins, Thomas L., *Science and the Enlightenment* (Cambridge, 1985).

Hannay, David, ed., *Letters written by Sir Samuel Hood . . . 1781–3* (NRS Vol. 3, 1895).

— *Naval Courts Martial* (Cambridge, 1914). An historical survey of court-martial records.

Harbron, John D., *Trafalgar and the Spanish Navy* (London, 1988). Uncritical, but one of the few works in English on the eighteenth-century Spanish navy.

Harding, Richard, *Amphibious Warfare in the Eighteenth Century: The British Expedition to the West Indies, 1740–1742* (Woodbridge, 1991).

— *The Evolution of the Sailing Navy, 1509–1815* (Basingstoke, 1995).

— *Seapower and Naval Warfare 1650–1830* (London, 1999).
The last two are excellent textbooks.

— 'Sailors and Gentlemen of Parade: Some Professional and Technical Problems Concerning the Conduct of Combined Operations in the Eighteenth Century', *HJ* XXXII (1989), pp. 35–55.

— 'Edward Vernon, 1684–1757', in Le Fevre and Harding, *Precursors of Nelson*, pp. 150–75.

— 'The Expedition to Lorient, 1746', *Age of Sail* I (2002), pp. 34–54. The most detailed account in English.

Haring, C. H., *The Buccaneers in the West Indies in the XVII Century* (London, 1910).

Harland, John, *Seamanship in the Age of Sail* (London, 1984). Fundamental to the understanding of naval warfare.

Harlow, Vincent Y., *The Founding of the Second British Empire, 1763–1793* (London, 1952–64, 2 vols.).

Harris, Daniel G., *F. H. Chapman: The First Naval Architect and his Work* (London, 1989). Enthusiastic but uncritical.

Harris, F. R., *The Life of Edward Mountagu, K.G., First Earl of Sandwich* (London, 1912, 2 vols.).

Harris, J. R., *Industrial Espionage and Technology Transfer: Britain and France in the Eighteenth Century* (Aldershot, 1998).

— 'Copper and Shipping in the Eighteenth Century', *EcHR* 2nd S. XIX (1966), pp. 550–68.

Harris, Robert D., 'French Finances and the American War, 1777–1783', *JMH* XLVIII (1976), pp. 233–58.

Harris, Simon, *Sir Cloudesley Shovell: Stuart Admiral* (Staplehurst, Kent, 2001). Illustrates how hard it is to write a good life without knowing much about the times.

Harvey, A. D., *Collision of Empires: Britain in Three World Wars, 1793–1945* (London, 1992).

— 'The Ministry of All the Talents: the Whigs in Office, February 1806 to March 1807', *HJ* XV (1972), pp. 619–48.

Hatch, Marie Martel, ed., 'Letters of Captain Sir John Jervis to Sir Henry Clinton, 1774–1782', *AN* VII (1947), pp. 87–106.

Hattendorf, John B., *England in the War of the Spanish Succession: A Study of the English View and Conduct of Grand Strategy, 1702–1712* (New York, 1987).

— 'The Machinery for the Planning and Execution of English Grand Strategy in the War of the Spanish Succession, 1702–1713', in Love, *Changing Interpretations*, pp. 80–95.

— 'English Grand Strategy and the Blenheim Campaign of 1704', *IHR* V (1983), pp. 3–19.

— ed., 'Benbow's Last Fight', in Rodger, *Naval Miscellany V*, pp. 143–206.

— 'English Governmental Machinery and the Conduct of War, 1702–1713', *W&S* III, 2 (1985), pp. 1–22.

— 'Admiral Sir George Byng and the Cape Passaro Incident, 1718: A Case Study of the Use of the Royal Navy as a Deterrent', in *Guerres et paix*, pp. 19–38.

— 'Sir George Rooke and Sir Cloudesley Shovell c1650–1709 and 1650–1707', in Le Fevre and Harding, *Precursors of Nelson*, pp. 42–77.

Hattendorf, John B., R. J. B. Knight, A. W. H. Pearsall, N. A. M. Rodger and Geoffrey Till, eds., *British Naval Documents 1204–1960* (NRS Vol. 131, 1993). An introductory collection of 'essential' documents for British naval history.

Hatton, Ragnhild, *Diplomatic Relations between Great Britain and the Dutch Republic, 1714–1721* (London, 1950).

Haudrère, Philippe, ed., *Les Flottes des Compagnies des Indes, 1600–1857* (Vincennes, 1996).

Havard, Oscar, *Histoire de la Révolution dans les ports de guerre* (Paris, 1912–13, 2 vols.). The French Revolution as a plot by British freemasonry to destroy the French navy.

Haversham, John Lord, *Memoirs of . . . John Lord Haversham, from the year 1640 to 1710* (London, 1711).

Hay, Douglas, 'Property, Authority and the Criminal Law', in *Albion's Fatal Tree, Crime and Society in Eighteenth-Century England*, ed. Hay et al. (London, 1975), pp. 17–64.

Hay, M. D., ed., *Landsman Hay: Memoirs of Robert Hay 1789–1847* (London, 1953).

Haycock, David Boyd, '"Exterminated by the Bloody Flux": Dysentery in Eighteenth-Century Naval and Military Medical Accounts', *JMR* (Jan 2002).

Heath, Helen Truesdell, ed., *The Letters of Samuel Pepys and his Family Circle* (Oxford, 1955).

[Heath, J. H.], 'The French Landing in Ireland, August 1798', *NR* XVI (1928), pp. 58–76. Extracts from the journal of Captain Graham Moore of the *Melampus*.

Hebbert, F. J., 'The Belle-Ile Expedition of 1761', *JSAHR* LXIV (1986), pp. 81–93.

Hemingway, J. P., 'The Work of the Surveyors of the Navy during the Period of the Establishments: A Comparative Study of Naval Architecture between 1672 and 1755' (Bristol Ph.D. thesis, 2002).

[Henderson, C. F.], 'Bridport Papers, 1797', *NR* XXI (1933), pp. 749–52.

Hendra, Peter, '"He that is soon angry, dealeth foolishly": Thomas Penrose (1627–1669) and the Stresses of Command', *Cornwall Family History Society Journal* 62 (Dec 1991), pp. 18–20.

Henwood, Philippe and Edmond Monange, *Brest: un port en révolution, 1789–1799* ([Rennes], 1989).

Hepper, David J., *British Warship Losses in the Age of Sail, 1650–1859* (Rotherfield, Sussex, 1994). An excellent reference book, giving information on the cause of each loss abstracted from courts martial and other records.

Hernández Sánchez-Barba, Mario, ed., *Las Fuerzas Armadas Españolas: Historia institucional y social* (Madrid, 1986, 8 vols.).

Herold, J. Christopher, *Bonaparte in Egypt* (London, 1963).

Hickey, Donald R., *The War of 1812: A Forgotten Conflict* (Urbana, Ill., 1989).

Hill, J. R., ed., *The Oxford Illustrated History of the Royal Navy* (Oxford, 1995). Some important contributions, but also some considerable gaps.

— *The Prizes of War: The Naval Prize System in the Napoleonic Wars, 1793–1815* (Stroud, 1998). Primarily its legal aspects.

Hinchliffe, G., 'Impressment of Seamen during the War of the Spanish Succession', *MM* LIII (1967), pp. 137–42.

— 'Some Letters of Sir John Norris', *MM* LVI (1970), pp. 77–84.

Historical Manuscripts Commission:

No. 15 *The Manuscripts of the Marquess of Abergavenny* . . . (1887).

No. 45 *Report on the Manuscripts of His Grace the Duke of Buccleuch and Queensberry . . . preserved at Montagu House* (1899–1926, 4 vols.).

No. 20 *The Manuscripts of the Earl of Dartmouth* (1887–96, 3 vols.).

No. 61 *Report on the Manuscripts of Lady Du Cane* (1905).

No. 71 *Report on the Manuscripts of Allan George Finch, esq.* . . . (1913–, 5 vols.).

No. 30 *The Manuscripts of J. B. Fortescue, esq.* . . . *at Dropmore* (1892–1927, 10 vols.).

No. 39 *The Manuscripts of J. Eliot Hodgkin, esq.* . . . (1897).

No. 17 *The Manuscripts of the House of Lords* (1887–94, 4 vols.). Covers 1678–93; continued by the NS below.

No. 51 *Report on the Manuscripts of F. W. Leyborne-Popham, esq.* . . . (1899).

No. 57 *Report on the Manuscripts of Colonel David Milne Home* . . . (1902).

No. 67 *Report on the Manuscripts of Lord Polwarth* . . . (1911–40, 4 vols.).

No. 29 *The Manuscripts of His Grace the Duke of Portland* . . . (1891–1931, 10 vols.).

No. 24 *The Manuscripts of His Grace the Duke of Rutland* . . . (1888–1905, 4 vols.).

No. 49 *Report on the Manuscripts of Mrs Stopford-Sackville* . . . (1904–10, 2 vols.).

No. 18 *The Manuscripts of the Marquess Townshend* (1887).

No. 55 *Report on Manuscripts in Various Collections* (1901–14, 8 vols.).

History of Parliament:

The House of Commons 1690–1715, ed. Eveline Cruikshanks, Stuart Handley and D. W. Hayton (Cambridge, 2002, 5 vols.).

The House of Commons 1715–1754, ed. Romney Sedgwick (London, 1970, 2 vols.).

The House of Commons 1754–1790, ed. Sir Lewis Namier and John Brooke (London, 1964, 3 vols.).

The House of Commons 1790–1820, ed. R. G. Thorne (London, 1986, 5 vols.). Indispensable sources for Parliamentary business and biographies.

Hoak, Dale, 'The Anglo-Dutch Revolution of 1688–89', in *The World of William and Mary: Anglo-Dutch Perspectives on the Revolution of 1688–89*, ed. Hoak and Mordechai Feingold (Stanford, 1996), pp. 1–26.

Hodgskin, Thomas, *An Essay on Naval Discipline* (London, 1813).

Hoffman, Frederick, *A Sailor of King George: The Journals of Captain Frederick Hoffman, R.N., 1793–1814*, ed. A. Beckford Bevan and H. B. Wolryche-Whitmore (London, 1901). A cheerful memoir written in old age, evidently somewhat improved.

Holland, A. J., *Ships of British Oak: The Rise and Decline of Wooden Shipbuilding in Hampshire* (Newton Abbot, 1971).

Hollond, John, *Two Discourses of the Navy, 1638 and 1659*, ed. J. R. Tanner (NRS Vol. 7, 1896). A naval administrator enlarges on the malpractices of his colleagues and superiors.

Holmes, Geoffrey, *Augustan England: Professions, State and Society, 1680–1730* (London, 1982).

— *British Politics in the Reign of Anne* (2nd edn, London, 1987).

— *The Making of a Great Power: Late Stuart and Early Georgian Britain 1660–1722* (London, 1993).

— 'The Professions and Social Change in England, 1680–1730', in *Politics, Religion and Society in England, 1679–1742* (London, 1986), pp. 309–50 [originally *Proceedings of the British Academy*, LXV (1979), pp. 313–54].

Hope, Ronald, *A New History of British Shipping* (London, 1990).

Hore, Peter, ed., *Seapower Ashore: 200 Years of Royal Navy Operations on Land* (London, 2001).

Horn, D. B., *Great Britain and Europe in the Eighteenth Century* (Oxford, 1967).

Hornstein, Sari R., *The Restoration Navy and English Foreign Trade 1674–1688* (Aldershot, 1991).

— 'Tangier, English Naval Power, and Exclusion', in *Restoration, Ideology and Revolution*, ed. Gordon J. Schochet (Washington, D.C., 1990), pp. 327–384.

Horsfield, John, *The Art of Leadership in War: The Royal Navy from the Age of Nelson to the End of World War II* (Westport, Conn., 1980).

Horward, Donald D., 'Portugal and the Anglo-Russian Naval Crisis (1808)', *NWCR* XXXIV (1981), pp. 48–74.

[Hoste, Harriet Lady], *Memoirs and Letters of Capt. Sir William Hoste* (London, 1833, 2 vols.).

Hoste, Paul, *L'Art des armées navales ou traité des evolutions navales* (Lyon, 1697).

Influential work by a Jesuit naval chaplain, representing the ideas of his patron Tourville. There is an abridged translation by Christopher O'Bryen, *Naval Evolutions: or a System of Sea-Discipline . . .* (London, 1762).

House of Lords, *The Manuscripts of the House of Lords*, NS (London, 1900–78, 12 vols.). Continues the series published by the Historical Manuscripts Commission.

Hoving, A. J. and A. A. Lemmers, *In Tekening gebracht: De achttiende-eeuwse scheepsbouwers en hun ontwerpmethoden* (Amsterdam, 2001). Eighteenth-century Dutch naval architecture.

Howard, Frank, *Sailing Ships of War 1400–1860* (London, 1979). A pioneering study.

Howarth, David, *Trafalgar: The Nelson Touch* (London, 1969). One of the better general accounts of the battle.

Howarth, R. G., ed., *The Letters and Second Diary of Samuel Pepys* (London, 1932). The 'second diary' is the Tangier diary, better read in the reliable edition by Chappell.

Howarth, Stephen, ed., *Battle of St Vincent 200 Years* (Shelton, Notts., 1998).

Howell, Colin and Richard J. Twomey, eds., *Jack Tar in History: Essays in the History of Maritime Life and Labour* (Fredericton, N.B., 1991).

Howse, Derek, *Greenwich Time and the Longitude* (London, 1997) [This is a 2nd edn of *Greenwich Time and the Discovery of the Longitude* (Oxford 1980)].

— 'The Lunar-Distance Method of Measuring Longitude', in Andrewes, *Longitude*, pp. 149–61.

Hrodej, Philippe, *L'Amiral du Casse: l'élévation d'un Gascon sous Louis XIV* (Paris, 1999, 2 vols.).

Hughes, Edward, *Studies in Administration and Finance 1558–1825* (Manchester, 1934).

— ed., *The Private Correspondence of Admiral Lord Collingwood* (NRS Vol. 98, 1957).

Hughes, Gillian, 'The Act for the Increase and Encouragement of Seamen, 1696–1710. Could It Have Solved the Royal Navy's Manning Problem?', in *Guerres maritimes*, pp. 25–34.

Hughson, S. C., 'The Carolina Pirates and Colonial Commerce (1670–1740)', in *Johns Hopkins University Studies in Historical and Political Science* XII (1894), pp. 241–370.

Huskisson, Thomas, *Eyewitness to Trafalgar: Thomas Huskisson RN, 1800–1808*, ed. D. B. Ellison (Royston, 1985).

Hussey, Frank, *Suffolk Invasion: The Dutch Attack on Landguard Fort, 1667* (Lavenham, 1983).

Hutchinson, J. R., *The Press-Gang Ashore and Afloat* (London, 1913). Serious research and fanciful conclusions, largely disconnected from one another.

Hutton, Ronald, *The Restoration: A Political and Religious History of England and Wales, 1658–1667* (Oxford, 1985).

— *Charles the Second, King of England, Scotland and Ireland* (Oxford, 1989).

— *The British Republic 1649–1660* (London, 1990).

Ilchester, [Giles Fox-Strangeways] Earl of, ed., *Letters to Henry Fox, Lord Holland* (Roxburghe Club, London, 1915).

Incháustegui Cabral, J. Marino, *La gran expedición ingles contra las Antillas Mayores. I: El Plan Antillano de Cromwell (1651–1655)* (Mexico City, 1958). A derivative work, mainly from printed sources but including some Spanish documents not printed elsewhere. The later volumes proposed were never published.

[Inglefield, Captain John] 'An Officer', *A Short Account of the Naval Actions of the Last War . . .* (London, 1788).

Ingram, Bruce S., ed., *Three Sea Journals of Stuart Times* (London, 1936).

Ingram, Edward, 'A Scare of Seaborne Invasion: The Royal Navy at the Strait of Hormuz, 1807–1808', *MAff* XLVI (1982), pp. 64–8.

— 'The Failure of British Sea Power in the War of the Second Coalition, 1798–1801', in *In Defence of British India: Great Britain in the Middle East, 1775–1842* (London, 1984), pp. 67–77.

— 'Illusions of Victory: The Nile, Copenhagen and Trafalgar Revisited', *MAff* XLVIII (1984), pp. 140–43.

— 'The Geopolitics of the First British Expedition to Egypt. II: The Mediterranean Campaign, 1800–1', *Middle Eastern Studies* XXX (1994), pp. 699–723.

Innes, Mary C., *A Memoir of William Wolseley, Admiral of the Red Squadron* (London, 1895). A slight memoir with a few letters.

Innis, Harold, *The Cod Fisheries: The History of an International Economy* (Toronto, 2nd edn [1954]).

Irrmann, Robert H., 'Gallia Frustra: Edward Russell and the Attempted Jacobite Invasion of 1696', in *Essays in Modern European History by Students of the Late Professor William Thomas Morgan*, ed. John J. Murray (Bloomington, Indiana, 1951), pp. 49–70.

Israel, Jonathan, ed., *The Anglo-Dutch Moment: Essays on the Glorious Revolution and Its World Impact* (Cambridge, 1991).

— *The Dutch Republic: Its Rise, Greatness and Fall, 1477–1806* (Oxford, 1995).

— 'The Dutch Republic and the "Glorious Revolution" of 1688/9 in England', in Wilson and Proctor, *1688*, pp. 31–44.

— 'Spain, the Spanish Embargoes, and the Struggle for the Mastery of World Trade, 1585–1660', in *Empires and Entrepots: the Dutch, the Spanish Monarchy and the Jews, 1585–1713* (London, 1990), pp. 189–212.

— 'England's Mercantilist Response to Dutch World Trade Primacy, 1647–1674', in *Britain and the Netherlands X: State and Trade. Government and the Economy in Britain and the Netherlands since the Middle Ages*, ed. Simon Groenveld and Michael Wintle (Zutphen, 1992), pp. 50–61.

— 'The Emerging Empire: The Continental Perspective, 1650–1713', in Canny, *Origins of Empire*, pp. 423–44.

Israel, Jonathan I. and Geoffrey Parker, 'Of Providence and Protestant Winds: the Spanish Armada of 1588 and the Dutch Armada of 1688', in Israel, *Anglo-Dutch Moment*, pp. 335–63.

Jackson, George Vernon, *The Perilous Adventures and Vicissitudes of a Naval Officer 1801–1812*, ed. Harold Burrows (Edinburgh, 1927).

Jackson, T. Sturges, ed., *Logs of the Gre Sea Fights, 1794–1805* (NRS Vols. 16 and 18, 1899–1900). Also letters and ot r documents.

— ed., 'From the Letter-Books of Sir Charles Thompson, Bart., Vice-Admiral', in Laughton, *Naval Miscellany II*, pp. 297–322.

James, Duke of York, *Memoirs of the English Affairs, chiefly Naval . . . 1660 to 1673, Written by His Royal Highness James Duke of York . . .* (London, 1729). Actually the Duke's naval out-letter book.

James, G. F., 'The Lord High Admiral's Council', *MM* XXII (1936), pp. 427–9. Prints Prince George's 1702 instructions.

— 'Josiah Burchett, Secretary to the Lords Commissioners of the Admiralty, 1695–1742', *MM* XXIII (1937), pp. 477–98.

— 'The Admiralty Establishment, 1759', *BIHR* XVI (1938), pp. 24–7.

— 'Some Further Aspects of Admiralty Administration, 1689–1714', *BIHR* XVII (1939), pp. 13–27.

— 'The Admiralty Buildings, 1695–1723', *MM* XXVI (1940), pp. 356–74.

James, G. F. and J. J. S. Shaw, 'Admiralty Administration and Personnel, 1619–1714', *BIHR* XIV (1936), pp. 10–24 and XVI (1937), pp. 166–83.

James, William, *The Naval History of Great Britain . . .* (London, 7th edn 1886, 6 vols.). A highly detailed and generally accurate history of operations from 1793 to 1837, particularly useful for minor actions, though narrow, partisan and devoid of any general historical awareness. There is an index to this edition compiled by C. G. Toogood (NRS Vol. 4, 1895).

Jameson, J. Franklin, 'St Eustatius in the American Revolution', *AHR* VIII (1903), pp. 683–708.

Jamieson, Alan G., 'The Occupation of Tangier and its Relation to English Naval Policy in the Mediterranean, 1661–1684' (Durham MA dissertation, 1960).

— 'War in the Leeward Islands: 1775–1783' (Oxford D.Phil. thesis, 1981). Much the best treatment of this war in the West Indies.

— 'The Battle of Grenada and Caribbean Strategy, 1779', in *Naval History: The Seventh Symposium of the U.S. Naval Academy*, ed. William B. Cogar (Wilmington, Del., 1988), pp. 55–62.

— 'Tyranny of the Lash? Punishment in the Royal Navy during the American War, 1776–1783', *NM* IX (1999), 1, 53–66.

Japiske, N., ed., *Correspondentie van Willem III en van Hans Willem Bentinck, eersten Graaf van Portland* (RGPks Vols. 23, 24, 26–8; The Hague, 1923–37).

Jarrett, Dudley, *British Naval Dress* (London, 1960).

Jenks, Timothy, 'Contesting the Hero: The Funeral of Admiral Lord Nelson', *JBS* XXXIX (2000), pp. 422–53.

Jennings, Louis J., ed., *The Correspondence and Diaries of the late Right Honourable John Wilson Croker . . .* (London, 1884, 3 vols.). The combative Irish politician, man of letters and First Secretary of the Admiralty 1809–30.

Johns, A. W., 'An Account of the Society for the Improvement of Naval

Architecture', *Transactions of the Institution of Naval Architects* LII (1910), pp. 28–40.

— 'The Stability of Sailing Warships', *The Engineer* CXXXIV (July–August 1922).

— 'The *Constant Warwick*', *MM* XVIII (1932), pp. 254–66.

Johnson, Paul, 'Civilizing Mammon: Laws, Morals, and the City in Nineteenth-Century England', in *Civil Histories: Essays Presented to Sir Keith Thomas*, ed. Peter Burke, Brian Harrison and Paul Slack (Oxford, 2000), pp. 301–19. Deals with the Cochrane Stock-Exchange fraud, among other things.

Johnston, J. A., 'Parliament and the Navy, 1688–1714' (Sheffield Ph.D. thesis, 1968).

— 'Parliament and the Protection of Trade 1689–1694', *MM* LVII (1971), pp. 399–413.

Jones, Clyve, 'The Protestant Wind of 1688: Myth and Reality', *European Studies Review* III (1973), pp. 201–21.

Jones, Colin, ed., *Britain and Revolutionary France: Conflict, Subversion and Propaganda* (Exeter, 1983).

Jones, D. W., *War and Economy in the Age of William III and Marlborough* (Oxford, 1988).

— 'Sequel to Revolution: The Economics of England's Emergence as a Great Power, 1688–1712', in Israel, *The Anglo-Dutch Moment*, pp. 389–406.

Jones, E. H. Stuart, 'Mutiny in Bantry Bay, 1799', *IS* I (1949–53), pp. 202–9.

Jones, J. R., *Britain and Europe in the Seventeenth Century* (London, 1966).

— *Britain and the World 1649–1815* (Brighton, 1980).

— *Charles II, Royal Politician* (London, 1987).

— *The Anglo-Dutch Wars of the Seventeenth Century* (London, 1996). The best overall treatment of these wars.

— 'The Dutch Navy and National Survival in the Seventeenth Century', *IHR* X (1988), pp. 18–32.

— 'Limitations of British Sea Power in the French Wars, 1689–1815', in Black and Woodfine, *British Navy*, pp. 33–49.

— 'French Intervention in English and Dutch Politics, 1677–88', in Black, *Knights Errant*, pp. 1–23.

— 'William III and the English', in Wilson and Proctor, *1688*, pp. 13–30.

Jordan, Gerald and Nicholas Rogers, 'Admirals as Heroes: Patriotism and Liberty in Hanoverian England', *JBS* XXVIII (1989), pp. 201–24. Compares Vernon and Nelson.

Journals of the House of Commons 1547–[1815] (London, 1742–1815, 70 vols.). A record of proceedings, not debates.

Junge, Hans-Christoph, *Flottenpolitik und Revolution: Die Enstehung der englischen Seemacht während der Herrschaft Cromwells* (Stuttgart, 1980).

Jurien de la Gravière, Pierre Roch, *Souvenirs d'un amiral* (Paris, 1860, 2 vols.). Memoirs of Napoleon's navy.

Kamen, Henry, *The War of Succession in Spain 1700–15* (London, 1969).

— 'The Destruction of the Spanish Silver Fleet at Vigo in 1702', *BIHR* XXIX (1966), pp. 165–73.

Kaplan, Herbert H., *Russian Overseas Commerce with Great Britain during the Reign of Catherine II* (Philadelphia, 1995).

Kastor, Peter J., 'Toward "the Maritime War Only": The Question of Naval Mobilization, 1811–1812', *Journal of Military History* LXI (1997), pp. 455–80.

Keevil, J. J., C. C. Lloyd and J. L. S. Coulter, *Medicine and the Navy, 1200–1900* (Edinburgh, 1957–63, 4 vols.). A massive but unsystematic and uncritical collection of material. Vols. II (ed. Keevil) and III (ed. Lloyd and Coulter) cover this period.

Kelly, Samuel, *An Eighteenth Century Seaman*, ed. Crosbie Garstin (New York, 1925). A lower-deck memoir, covering the years 1778 to 1795.

Kemp, N. M., 'Letters from the Leeward Islands, 1781', *NR* XXIII (1935), pp. 127–37. From Samuel to Alexander Hood.

Kemp, Peter, *The British Sailor, A Social History of the Lower Deck* (London, 1970). Lightweight, and now substantially outdated.

— ed., 'Boscawen's Letters to his Wife, 1755–1756', in Lloyd, *Naval Miscellany* IV, pp. 163–256. Charming and valuable letters, indifferently edited.

Kempthorne, G. A., 'Sir John Kempthorne and His Sons', *MM* XII (1926), pp. 289–317.

Kennedy, Paul M., *The Rise and Fall of British Naval Mastery* (London, 2nd edn 1983). A now classic history, stressing the economic underpinnings of sea power.

— *The Rise and Fall of the Great Powers: Economic Change and Military Conflict from 1500 to 2000* (London, 1988).

Kennedy, W. Benjamin, 'The United Irishmen and the Great Naval Mutiny of 1797', *Eire-Ireland* XXV (1990), 3, pp. 7–18.

Kent, H. S. K., *War and Trade in Northern Seas: Anglo-Scandinavian Economic Relations in the Mid-Eighteenth Century* (Cambridge, 1973).

Kepler, J. S., 'Sir John Jennings and the Preparations for the Naval Expedition to the Mediterranean of 1711–1713', *MM* LIX (1973), pp. 13–33.

Keppel, Thomas, *The Life of Augustus Viscount Keppel* (London, 1842, 2 vols.).

Kerguelen-Trémarec, Y. J. de, *Relation des combats et des évènements de la guerre maritime de 1778 entre la France et l'Angleterre* (Paris, 1796).

Kerrigan, Paul M., 'Ireland in Naval Strategy 1641–1691', in *Conquest and Resistance: War in Seventeenth-Century Ireland*, ed. Pádraig Lenihan (Leiden, 2001), pp. 151–76.

Kert, Faye Margaret, *Prize and Prejudice: Privateering and Naval Prize in Atlantic Canada in the War of 1812* (St John's, Newfoundland, 1997).

— 'The Fortunes of War: Commercial Warfare and Maritime Risk in the War of 1812', *NM* VIII (1998) 4, 1–16.

King, Robert J., '"Ports of Shelter, and Refreshment . . ." Botany Bay and Norfolk Island in British Naval Strategy, 1786–1808', *Historical Studies* XXII (1986), pp. 199–213.

Kirby, Brian S., 'Nelson and American Merchantmen in the West Indies, 1784–1787', *MM* LXXV (1989), pp. 137–47.

Kirby, David, 'The Royal Navy's Quest for Pitch and Tar during the Reign of Queen Anne', *SEHR* XXII (1974), pp. 97–116.

Kitson, Frank, *Prince Rupert: Admiral and General-at-Sea* (London, 1998).

Kitson, Vice-Admiral Sir Henry, 'Bringing Round the *Royal Charles*', *MM* XXIII (1937), pp. 36–52.

— 'The Early History of Portsmouth Dockyard, 1496–1800', *MM* XXXIII (1947), pp. 256–65, XXXIV (1948), pp. 3–11, 87–97 and 271–9.
Two articles written from records of the dockyard.

Knight, R. J. B., ed., *Portsmouth Dockyard Papers 1774–1783: The American War* (Portsmouth Record Series Vol. 6, 1987). The realities of naval administration.

— ed., *Shipbuilding Timber for the British Navy: Parliamentary Papers, 1729–1792* (Delmar, N.Y., 1993).

— 'The Royal Dockyards in England at the Time of the War of American Independence' (London Ph.D. thesis, 1972).

— 'Sandwich, Middleton and Dockyard Appointments', *MM* LVII (1971), pp. 175–92.

— 'The Introduction of Copper Sheathing into the Royal Navy, 1779–1786', *MM* LIX (1973), pp. 299–309.

— 'The Performance of the Royal Dockyards in England during the American War of Independence', in *The American Revolution and the Sea; Proceedings of the 14th Conference of the International Commission for Maritime History* (National Maritime Museum, Greenwich, 1974), pp. 139–43.

— 'Early Attempts at Lead and Copper Sheathing', *MM* LXII (1976), pp. 292–4.

— 'The Building and Maintenance of the British Fleet during the Anglo-French Wars 1688–1815', in Acerra et al., *Les Marines de guerre*, pp. 35–50.

— 'New England Forests and British Seapower: Albion Revisited', *AN* XLVI (1986), pp. 221–9

— 'From Impressment to Task Work: Strikes and Disruption in the Royal Dockyards, 1688–1788', in Lunn and Day, *Work and Labour Relations*, pp. 1–20.

— 'Richard, Earl Howe, 1726–1799', in Le Fevre and Harding, *Precursors of Nelson*, pp. 278–99.

— '"Some Further Degree of Merit": the Fall and Rise of the Reputation of Lord Sandwich' (unpublished paper; I am grateful to Professor Knight for permission to cite it).

Knighton, C. S., *Pepys and the Navy* (Stroud, 2003). Now the best introduction to the subject.

Korr, Charles P., *Cromwell and the New Model Foreign Policy: England's Policy towards France, 1649–1658* (Berkeley, Calif., 1975).

Krajeski, Paul Christopher, *In the Shadow of Nelson: The Naval Leadership of Admiral Sir Charles Cotton, 1753–1812* (Westport, Conn., 2000).

Krämer, F. J. L., ed., *Archives ou correspondance inédite de la Maison d'Orange-*

Nassau, 4th S. (Leiden, 1907–9, 3 vols.). This series covers the reign of William III in England.

Kulsrud, Carl J., *Maritime Neutrality to 1780: A History of the Main Principles Governing Neutrality and Belligerency to 1780* (Boston, 1936).

La Bédoyère, Guy de, ed., *Particular Friends: The Correspondence of Samuel Pepys and John Evelyn* (Woodbridge, 1997).

Lacour-Gayet, G., *La Marine militaire de la France sous les règnes de Louis XIII et de Louis XIV: I, Richelieu, Mazarin 1624–1661* (Paris, 1911).

— *La Marine militaire de la France sous le règne de Louis XV* (Paris, 1902).

— *La Marine militaire de la France sous le règne de Louis XVI* (Paris, 1905). Scholarly and still useful; Vol. II of *Louis XIII et XIV* never appeared. For convenience of citation I have treated these as three volumes of a single work.

— 'La Campagne navale de la Manche en 1779', *Revue Maritime* CL (1901), pp. 1,629–73.

Laird, Emma, 'The Victualling of the Channel Fleet in 1800' (Greenwich MA dissertation, 2001).

La Jonquière, C. de, *L'Expédition d'Egypte 1798–1801* (Paris, 1899–1907, 5 vols.). Another of the massive and scholarly productions of the Historical Section of the French General Staff. The strain of maintaining their official belief in Bonaparte's infallibility is visible.

Lambert, Andrew, 'Empire and Seapower: Shipbuilding by the East India Company at Bombay for the Royal Navy, 1805–1850', in Haudrère, *Les Flottes des Compagnies des Indes*, pp. 149–71.

— 'Sir William Cornwallis, 1744–1819', in Le Fevre and Harding, *Precursors of Nelson*, pp. 352–75.

La Monneraye, Pierre-Bruno-Jean de, *Souvenirs de 1760 à 1791*, ed. Philippe Bonnichon (Société de l'Histoire de France, Paris, 1998).

Langford, Paul, *The First Rockingham Administration 1765–1766* (London, 1973).

— *The Eighteenth Century, 1688–1815* (London, 1976).

— *A Polite and Commercial People: England 1727–1783* (Oxford, 1989).

— 'William Pitt and Public Opinion, 1757', *EHR* LXXXVIII (1973), pp. 54–80.

Lanuza Cano, Francisco, *Ataque y derrota de Nelson en Santa Cruz de Tenerife* (Madrid, 1955). A detailed, sober account with numerous documents printed in full.

La Roncière, Charles de, *Histoire de la marine française* (Paris, 1899–1932, 6 vols.). A monument to nineteenth-century scholarship, taking the history only to 1714.

Latham, Robert, William Matthews and Charles Knighton, eds., *Samuel Pepys and the Second Dutch War: Pepys's Navy White Book and Brooke House Papers* (NRS Vol. 133, 1995).

Laughton, J. K., ed., *Memoirs Relating to the Lord Torrington* (CS NS Vol. 46, 1889). The career of George Byng, by someone close to him.

— *Studies in Naval History: Biographies* (London, 1887).

— ed., *The Naval Miscellany Vol. I* (NRS Vol. 20, 1902).

— ed., *Letters and Papers of Charles, Lord Barham, Admiral of the Red Squadron, 1758–1813* (NRS Vols. 32, 38 and 39, 1906–10).
— ed., *The Naval Miscellany Vol. II* (NRS Vol. 40, 1912).
— 'Jenkin's Ear', *English Historical Review* IV (1889), pp. 741–9.
— 'Journals of Henry Duncan, Captain Royal Navy 1776–1782', in *Naval Miscellany I*, pp. 105–219.
— 'Extracts from the Papers of Samuel, First Viscount Hood', in *Naval Miscellany I*, pp. 221–58.
— 'Letters of the Hon. William Cathcart', in *Naval Miscellany I*, pp. 259–332.
— 'Extracts from the Journals of Thomas Addison of the East India Company's Service 1801–1829', in *Naval Miscellany I*, pp. 333–74.
— 'Miscellaneous Letters', in *Naval Miscellany I*, pp. 387–444.
— 'Extracts from a Commissioner's Note Book, Annis 1691–1694', in *Naval Miscellany II*, pp. 137–205. Sir Richard Haddock, Controller of the Navy.
— 'The Mutiny at the Nore', in *Naval Miscellany* II, pp. 293–6.
— 'Orders by Sir John Jervis', in *Naval Miscellany II*, pp. 323–8.
— 'Some Letters of Lord St Vincent', in *Naval Miscellany II*, pp. 329–32.
— 'Operations on the Coast of Egypt, 1801', in *Naval Miscellany* II, pp. 333–49.
Laughton, J. K. and J. Y. F. Sulivan, eds., *Journal of Rear-Admiral Bartholomew James, 1752–1828* (NRS Vol. 6, 1906).
Laughton, L. G. Carr, 'Sir Richard Strachan's Action', *United Service Magazine* CXLV (1902), pp. 459–63.
— 'The Battle of Velez Malaga, 1704', *JRUSI* LXVIII (1923), pp. 367–90.
— 'Gunnery, Frigates and the Line of Battle', *MM* XIV (1928), pp. 339–63.
Lavery, Brian, ed., *Deane's Doctrine of Naval Architecture, 1670* (London, 1981).
— *The Ship of the Line* (London, 1983–4, 2 vols.). An essential study of the evolution of warship design.
— *The Arming and Fitting of English Ships of War 1600–1815* (London, 1987).
— *The Royal Navy's First Invincible* (Portsmouth, 1988). The prize of 1747, whose wreck has been excavated.
— *Nelson's Navy: The Ships, Men and Organisation 1793–1815* (London, 1989). A sort of naval encyclopedia.
— ed., *The Line of Battle: The Sailing Warship 1650–1840* (London, 1992). The relevant volume in the excellent series *Conway's History of the Ship*, ed. Robert Gardiner.
— *Nelson and the Nile: The Naval War against Bonaparte 1798* (London, 1998).
— ed., *Shipboard Life and Organisation, 1731–1815* (NRS Vol. 138, 1998). Important for social history.
— 'The Rebuilding of British Warships 1690–1740', *MM* LXVI (1980), pp. 5–14 and 113–27.
— 'The Revolution in Naval Tactics (1588–1653)', in Acerra et al., *Les Marines de guerre*, pp. 167–74.
— 'Carronades and Blomefield Guns: Developments in Naval Ordnance, 1778–1805', in Smith, *British Naval Armaments*, pp. 15–27.

— 'George Keith Elphinstone, Lord Keith, 1746–1823', in Le Fevre and Harding, *Precursors of Nelson*, pp. 376–99.

Lawrence, Christopher, 'Disciplining Disease: Scurvy, the Navy, and Imperial Expansion 1750–1825', in *Visions of Empire: Voyages, Botany, and Representations of Nature*, ed. D. P. Miller and P. H. Reill (Cambridge, 1996), pp. 80–106.

Lawson, J. A., 'Naval Policy and Public Opinion in the War of the League of Augsburg, 1689–1697' (Leeds MA thesis, 1952).

Lawson, Philip, *George Grenville, A Political Life* (Oxford, 1984).

Lax, John and William Pencak, 'The Knowles Riot and the Crisis of the 1740s', *Perspectives in American History* X (1976), pp. 163–214.

Leach, D. E., *Arms for Empire: A Military History of the British Colonies in North America, 1607–1763* (London, 1973).

Lediard, Thomas, *The Naval History of England . . . 1066 to . . . 1734* (London, 1735, 2 vols.). Arguably the first scholarly British naval history; dry and plain but still of some value for the seventeenth and eighteenth centuries.

Lee, J. T., *Memoirs of the Life and Services of Sir J. Theophilus Lee* (p.p. London, 1836). Service at sea as a boy between 1795 and 1805.

Leech, Samuel, *Thirty Years from Home, or a Voice from the Main Deck* (Boston, 1844). Evocative lower-deck memoir by a man taken in the *Macedonian* in 1812, presented (if not rewritten) for the US market of the 1840s.

Lees, James, *The Masting and Rigging of English Ships of War, 1625–1860* (London, 1979). Essential technical reference.

Le Fevre, Peter, 'Sir George Ayscue, Commonwealth and Restoration Admiral', *MM* LXVIII (1982), pp. 189–202.

— 'John Tyrrell (1649–1692): A Restoration Naval Captain', *MM* LXX (1984), pp. 149–60.

— 'Tangier, the Navy, and its Connection with the Glorious Revolution of 1688', *MM* LXXIII (1987), pp. 187–90.

— '"A Sacrifice to the Allies"? The Earl of Torrington and the Battle of Beachy Head, 30 June 1690', in *Guerres maritimes*, pp. 53–92.

— 'Arthur Herbert, Earl of Torrington, 1648–1716', in Le Fevre and Harding, *Precursors of Nelson*, pp. 19–41.

— 'Re-creating a Seventeenth-Century Sea Officer', *JMR* (May 2001).

Le Fevre, Peter and Richard Harding, eds., *Precursors of Nelson: British Admirals of the Eighteenth Century* (London, 2000).

Le Goff, T. J. A., 'L'Impact des prises effectuées par les Anglais sur la capacité en hommes de la marine française au XVIIIe siècle', in Acerra et al., *Les Marines de guerre*, pp. 103–22.

— 'Naval Recruitment and Labour Supply in the French War Effort, 1755–59', in *New Aspects of Naval History: Selected Papers from the 5th Naval History Symposium* (Baltimore, 1985).

— 'Les Gens de mer devant le système des classes (1755–1763): résistance ou passivité?', in Lottin et al., *Les Hommes et la mer*, pp. 463–80.

— 'Problèmes de recrutement de la marine française pendant la Guerre de Sept Ans', *RH* CCLXXXIII (1990), pp. 205–33.

Legohérel, Henri, *Les Trésoriers généraux de la Marine (1517–1788)* (Paris, 1965).

Lemineur, Jean-Claude, *Les Vaisseaux du Roi Soleil* (Nice, 1996). French warship design of the later seventeenth century.

— 'La Marine de Louis XIV: une marine nouvelle de conception française', in Acerra, *L'Invention du vaisseau de ligne*, pp. 29–37.

Lemisch, Jesse, *Jack Tar vs John Bull: The Role of New York's Seamen in Precipitating the Revolution* (New York, 1997). Originally a 1962 Yale Ph.D. thesis, advancing a sentimental Marxist interpetation.

— 'Jack Tar in the Streets: Merchant Seamen in the Politics of Revolutionary America', *WMQ* 3rd S. XXV (1968), pp. 371–407.

Lenman, Bruce, *The Jacobite Risings in Britain 1689–1746* (London, 1980).

— *Britain's Colonial Wars 1688–1783* (Harlow, 2001).

— 'Colonial Wars and Imperial Instability, 1688–1793', in Marshall, *Eighteenth Century*, pp. 151–68.

Le Pourhiet-Salat, Nicole, *La Défense des îles bretonnes de l'Atlantique des origines à 1860* (Vincennes, 1983).

Lespagnol, André, *Entre l'argent et la gloire: la course Malouine au temps de Louis XIV* (Rennes, 1995).

— *Messieurs de Saint-Malo: une élite négociante au temps de Louis XIV* (Rennes, 1997, 2 vols.) [originally St Malo, 1990].

— 'Guerre et commerce maritime durant la phase initiale de la "Seconde Guerre de Cent Ans" 1688–1713', in *Les Européens et les espaces océaniques au XVIIIe siècle*, ed. Yves-Marie Bercé (Association des historiens modernistes des universités, Bulletin No. 22, Paris, 1997), pp. 83–98.

Letuaire, Henri, ed., *La Bataille de Trafalgar racontée par le Commandant Lucas . . .* (2nd edn, Toulon, 1914). Captain of the *Redoutable*.

Lévy-Schneider, Léon, *Le Conventionnel Jeanbon Saint-André* (Paris, 1901, 2 vols.). Warmly Republican in tone.

Lewis, A. F. P., *Captain of the Fleet: The Career of Admiral Sir William Domett, GCB, 1751–1828* (p.p. London, 1967).

Lewis, Michael, *England's Sea-Officers: The Story of the Naval Profession* (London, 1939). A classic of its day, parts of it still usable with caution.

— *A Social History of the Navy 1793–1815* (London, 1960). Lewis was a pioneer of naval social history: this is his best book, based on solid research in printed sources (though he hardly ever looked at manuscripts).

— *Spithead: An Informal History* (London, 1972).

Leyland, John, ed., *Despatches and Letters Relating to the Blockade of Brest, 1803–1805* (NRS Vols. 14 and 21, 1899–1902).

Liardet, Captain Francis, *Professional Recollections on Points of Seamanship, Discipline &c* (Portsea, 1849). They reflect wartime experience but post-war attitudes.

Liddell Hart, B. H., ed., *The Letters of Private Wheeler, 1809–1828* (London, 1951).

Lincoln, A. L. J. and R. L. McEwen, eds., *Lord Eldon's Anecdote Book* (London, 1960).

Lincoln, Margarette, *Representing the Royal Navy: British Sea Power, 1750–1815* (Aldershot, 2002). The public image of the Navy.

Lind, H. D., *Kong Frederik den Tredjes Sømagt: Det Dansk-Norske søværns historie 1648–1670* (Odense, 1896).

Linebaugh, Peter and Marcus Rediker, 'The Many Headed Hydra: Sailors, Slaves and the Atlantic Working Class in the Eighteenth Century', in Howell and Twomey, *Jack Tar in History*, pp. 11–36. A Marxist interpretation, based on generous enthusiasm rather than dialectical rigour.

Linÿer de la Barbée, Maurice, *Le Chevalier de Ternay* (Grenoble, 1972, 2 vols.).

Llaverías, Joaquín, ed., *Papeles sobre la toma de la Habana por los Ingleses en 1762* (Havana, 1948).

— *Nuevos Papeles sobre la toma de la Habana por los Ingleses en 1762* (Havana, 1951). Documents from the Archivo Nacional of Cuba, with an introduction by Llaverías, its director; the actual editor's name does not appear.

Llinares, Sylviane, *Marine, propulsion et technique: l'évolution du système technologique du navire de guerre français au XVIIIe siècle* (Paris, 1994, 1 vol. in 2). Rigging as the key to naval history; it is indeed an informative and revealing approach to it.

Lloyd, Christopher, ed., *The Naval Miscellany Vol. IV* (NRS Vol. 92, 1952).

— *St Vincent and Camperdown* (London, 1963).

— ed., *The Health of Seamen* (NRS Vol. 107, 1965). Extracts from the writings of the naval physicians James Lind, Thomas Trotter and Sir Gilbert Blane.

— *The British Seaman 1200–1860: A Social Survey* (London, 1968). Based on a valuable study of the Impress Service.

— *Mr Barrow of the Admiralty: A Life of Sir John Barrow 1764–1848* (London, 1970). Second Secretary of the Admiralty for almost forty years.

— 'New Light on the Mutiny at the Nore', *MM* XLVI (1960), pp. 286–95. Letters of a midshipman of the *Nassau*.

Lloyd, Christopher and Hardin Craig, Jnr, eds., 'Congreve's Rockets 1805–1806', in Lloyd, *Naval Miscellany IV*, pp. 423–68.

Loades, David, *England's Maritime Empire: Seapower, Commerce and Policy, 1490–1690* (London, 2000).

Locker, Edward H., *Memoirs of Celebrated Commanders* (London, 1832). Eccentric production by a retired admiral's secretary, based on his extensive collection of manuscripts and the recollections of his father, follower of Hawke and mentor of Nelson.

Lodge, Sir Richard, *Studies in Eighteenth-Century Diplomacy, 1740–1748* (London, 1930). The negotiation of the peace of Aix-la-Chapelle, 1748.

Loir, Maurice, *La Marine royale en 1789* (Paris, 1892).

Long, W. H., ed., *Naval Yarns* (London, 1899). An odd collection of authentic historical narratives.

López Nadal, Gonçal, *El Corsarisme mallorquí a la Mediterrània occidental 1652–1698: un comerç forçat* (Palma de Mallorca, 1986).

— ed., *El comerç alternatiu: corsarisme i contraban (xx. XV–XVIII)* (Palma de Mallorca, 1990). Mediterranean privateering.

Lottin, Alain, Jean-Claude Hocquet and Stéphane Lebecq, eds., *Les Hommes et la mer dans l'Europe du Nord-Ouest de l'antiquité à nos jours* (*Revue du Nord* extra number, 1986).

Lounsbury, R. G., *The British Fishery at Newfoundland, 1634–1763* (New Haven, 1934).

Love, Robert W., Jr, ed., *Changing Interpretations and New Sources in Naval History: Papers from the Third United States Naval Academy History Symposium* (New York, 1980).

— *History of the U.S. Navy. I: 1775–1941* (Harrisburg, Pa., 1992).

Lovell, William Stanhope, *Personal Narrative of Events from 1799 to 1815* (London, 2nd edn 1879). A midshipman's memories.

Low, C. R., *History of the Indian Navy (1613–1863)* (London, 1877, 2 vols.). The Bombay Marine and its successors.

Lowe, J. A., ed., *Records of the Portsmouth Division of Marines, 1764–1800* (Portsmouth Record Series Vol. 7, 1990). One of the few good sources on the eighteenth-century Marines.

Lower, Arthur R. M., *Great Britain's Woodyard: British America and the Timber Trade, 1763–1867* (Montreal, 1973).

Lower, M. A., 'Some Notices of Charles Sergison . . .', *Sussex Archaeological Collections* XXV (1873), pp. 62–84.

Luff, P. A., 'Mathews *v.* Lestock: Parliament, Politics and the Navy in Mid-Eighteenth England', *Parliamentary History* X (1991), pp. 45–62.

Lunn, Kenneth and Ann Day, eds., *History of Work and Labour Relations in the Royal Dockyards* (London, 1999).

Lutun, Bernard, 'Les Clauses navales des traités de 1814 à 1815 et l'équilibre européen', in *Aspects du désarmement naval*, ed. Hervé Coutau-Bégarie (Paris, 1994), pp. 29–83.

Lyon, David, *The Sailing Navy List: All the Ships of the Royal Navy – Built, Purchased and Captured – 1688–1860* (London, 1993). An essential reference work and tool of technical history.

MacDougall, Philip, 'The East Coast Mutinies, May–June 1797', in Coats and MacDougall, *1797 Mutinies*.

— '"We Went Out with Admiral Duncan, We Came Back without Him": Mutiny and the North Sea Squadron', in Coats and MacDougall, *1797 Mutinies*.

Mackaness, George, *The Life of Vice-Admiral William Bligh* (New York, 1931, 2 vols.).

Mackay, David, *In the Wake of Cook: Exploration, Science and Empire, 1780–1801* (London, 1985).

— 'Direction and Purpose in British Imperial Policy, 1783–1801', *HJ* XVII (1974), pp. 487–501.

— 'A Presiding Genius of Exploration: Banks, Cook, and Empire, 1767–1805', in *Captain James Cook and his Times*, ed. Robin Fisher and Hugh Johnston (Seattle, 1979), pp. 21–39.

Mackay, Ruddock F., *Admiral Hawke* (Oxford, 1965).

— ed., *The Hawke Papers. A Selection, 1743–1771* (NRS Vol. 129, 1990).

— 'Lord St Vincent's Early Years (1735–55)', *MM* LXXVI (1990), pp. 51–65.

— 'Edward, Lord Hawke, 1705–1781', in Le Fevre and Harding, eds., *Precursors of Nelson*, pp. 200–223.

Mackesy, Piers, *The War in the Mediterranean, 1803–1810* (London, 1957).

— *The War for America, 1775–1783* (London, 1964).

— *Statesmen at War: The Strategy of Overthrow 1798–1799* (London, 1974).

— *War without Victory: The Downfall of Pitt 1799–1802* (Oxford, 1984). Important scholarly studies of the grand strategy and operations of these wars. Both services are fully covered, but the author's sympathies are perhaps more military than naval.

— 'Problems of an Amphibious Power: Britain against France, 1793–1815', in *Assault from the Sea: Essays on the History of Amphibious Warfare*, ed. Merrill L. Bartlett (Annapolis, Md., 1983), pp. 60–68. [Originally *NWCR* XXX (1978), pp. 16–25].

— 'Strategic Problems of the British War Effort', in Dickinson, *Britain and the French Revolution*, pp. 147–64.

— ' "Most Sadly Bitched": The British Cadiz Expedition of 1800', in Freeman, *Les Empires*, pp. 41–57.

Macleod, Emma Vincent, *A War of Ideas: British Attitudes to the Wars against Revolutionary France 1792–1802* (Aldershot, 1998).

Macray, W. D., et al., eds., *Calendar of the Clarendon State Papers Preserved in the Bodleian Library* (Oxford, 1869–1970, 5 vols.). Papers of Charles II's chief minister in exile and in the early years of his reign.

Madariaga, Isabel de, *Britain, Russia and the Armed Neutrality of 1780: Sir James Harris's Mission to St Petersburg during the American Revolution* (London, 1962).

Mahan, A. T., *The Major Operations of the Navies in the War of American Independence* (London, 1913). Written towards the end of Mahan's life, when he had begun to base his books on historical research.

Malo, Henri, *Les Corsaires: mémoires et documents inédits* (Paris, 1908).

— *Les Corsaires dunkerquois et Jean Bart* (Paris, 1913–14, 2 vols.).

— *La Grande Guerre des corsaires: Dunkerque (1702–1715)* (Paris, 1925).

— *Les Derniers Corsaires: Dunkerque (1715–1815)* (Paris, 1925). Scholarly studies of privateering from Dunkirk and neighbouring ports.

Malone, Joseph J., 'England and the Baltic Naval Stores Trade in the Seventeenth and Eighteenth Centuries', *MM* LVIII (1972), pp. 375–95.

Maloney, Linda, 'The War of 1812: What Role for Sea Power?', in *In Peace and War: Interpretations of American Naval History, 1775–1978*, ed. Kenneth J. Hagan (Westport, Connecticut, 1978), pp. 46–62.

Manera Regueyra, Enrique, ed., *El buque en la Armada Española* (Madrid, 1981). Lavishly illustrated survey, with contributions by several leading scholars.

— 'La epoca de Felipe V y Fernando VI', in ibid., pp. 169–200.

— 'El apogeo de la Marina Española (Carlos III y Carlos IV)', in ibid., pp. 201–32.

— 'La Armada en el siglo XIX', in Hernández Sánchez-Barba, *Las Fuerzas Armadas Españolas*, IV, 11–140.

Mann, Michael, *Flottenbau und Forstbetrieb in Indien 1794–1823* (Stuttgart, 1996). An 'environmental history' of the Malabar teak forests and Dundas's ship-building programme.

Manwaring, G. E., 'The Dress of the British Seaman from the Revolution to the Peace of 1748', *MM* X (1924), pp. 31–48.

— ed., 'Two Letters from Blake to Montagu, 1656–7', in Perrin, *Naval Miscellany III*, pp. 331–8.

Manwaring, G. E. and Bonamy Dobrée, *The Floating Republic: An Account of the Mutinies at Spithead and the Nore in 1797* (London, 1935). A political interpretation, implicitly commenting on the 1931 Invergordon 'mutiny'.

Marcus, Geoffrey, *Quiberon Bay: The Campaign in Home Waters, 1759* (London, 1960). Thorough, but old-fashioned even in its day.

Marini, Alfred J., 'The British Corps of Marines, 1746–1771, and the United States Marine Corps, 1798–1818: A Comparative Study . . .' (Maine Ph.D. thesis, 1979).

Mark, William, *At Sea with Nelson: Being the Life of William Mark, a Purser who served under Admiral Lord Nelson*, ed. W. P. Mark-Wardlaw (London, 1929) [originally written 1846].

[Markham, Sir Clements], *A Naval Career during the Old War . . .* (London, 1883). The author's ancestor John Markham.

— ed., *Selections from the Correspondence of Admiral John Markham . . . 1801–4 and 1806–7* (NRS Vol. 28, 1904).

Marley, David F., 'A Fearful Gift: The Spanish Naval Build-up in the West Indies, 1759–1762', *MM* LXXX (1994), pp. 403–17.

Marryat, Florence, *Life and Letters of Captain Frederick Marryat* (London, 1872, 2 vols.).

Marryat, Captain Frederick, *Suggestions for the Abolition of the Present System of Impressment in the Naval Service* (London, 1822). Extracts are also printed by Bromley, *Manning*, pp. 347–55.

Marsden, R. G., ed., *Documents relating to Law and Custom of the Sea* (NRS Vols. 49 and 50, 1915–16).

— 'Early Prize Jurisdiction and Prize Law in England', *EHR* XXIV (1909), pp. 675–97.

Marsden, William, *A Brief Memoir of the Life and Writings . . .* (p.p. London, 1838). Secretary of the Admiralty 1794–1807.

Marsh, A. J., 'The Navy and Portsmouth under the Commonwealth', in Webb et al., *Hampshire Studies*, pp. 115–40.

— 'The Local Community and the Operation of Plymouth Dockyard, 1689–1763', *MHD* I, 201–8.

Marshall, Dorothy, *Eighteenth Century England* (London, 2nd edn 1973).

Marshall, P. J., ed., *The Oxford History of the British Empire Vol. II: The Eighteenth Century* (Oxford, 1998).

Martel, Marie-Thérèse de, *Etude sur le recrutement des matelots et soldats des vaisseaux du Roi dans le ressort de l'intendance du port de Rochefort (1691–1697): aspects de la vie des gens de mer* (Vincennes, 1982).

Martin-Leake, Stephen, *Life of Captain Stephen Martin, 1666–1740*, ed. Clements R. Markham (NRS Vol. 5, 1895). The author's father, Leake's follower and brother-in-law.

— *The Life of Sir John Leake*, ed. Geoffrey Callender (NRS Vols. 52–3, 1920). A tedious work of family piety by the admiral's nephew the herald, but closely based on letters and journals. Callender's editing is pompous and ignorant.

Martínez-Valverde, Carlos, 'La campaña de Don Juan José Navarro en el Mediterraneo y la batalla de Cabo Sicié (1742–1744)', *RHN* I (1983), 2, 5–28.

Marzagalli, Silva, *Les Boulevards de la fraude: Le négoce maritime et le Blocus continental, 1806–1813* (Lille, 1999).

Mascart, Jean, *La Vie et les travaux du Chevalier Jean-Charles de Borda (1733–1799): Episodes de la vie scientifique au XVIIIe siècle* (Lyon, 1919).

Massie, Alistair W., 'Great Britain and the Defence of the Low Countries, 1744–1748' (Oxford D.Phil. thesis, 1987).

Masson, Philippe, *Histoire de la Marine* (Paris, 2nd edn 1992, 2 vols.). A stimulating, not to say iconoclastic, popular history, based on much research but without references.

— *Les Sépulcres flottants: prisonniers français en Angleterre sous l'Empire* (Rennes, 1987). A sober analysis (the title aside) of a subject which in France tends to stir up more passion than scholarship.

— 'La Marine sous la Révolution et l'Empire', in Delmas, *Histoire militaire de la France II*, pp. 371–90.

— 'Pierre-André de Suffren de Saint-Tropez: Admiral Satan (1729–1788)', in Sweetman, *Great Admirals*, pp. 172–91.

Masson, Philippe and José Muracciole, *Napoléon et la Marine* (Paris, 1968).

Matcham, M. E. *A Forgotten John Russell, Being Letters to a Man of Business, 1724–1751* (London, 1905). A dockyard clerk and Navy Agent.

Mathias, Peter, 'Swords and Ploughshares: The Armed Forces, Medicine and Public Health in the Eighteenth Century', in *The Transformation of England* (London, 1979), pp. 268–78 [originally in *War and Economic Development: Essays in Memory of David Joslin* (Cambridge, 1975), pp. 73–90].

Mathias, Peter and Patrick O'Brien, 'Taxation in Britain and France, 1715–1810. A Comparison of the Social and Economic Incidence of Taxes Collected for the Central Governments', *JEEH* V (1976), pp. 601–50. A very important article, which continues to stimulate debate and reinterpretation.

Maxwell, Sir Herbert, ed., *The Creevy Papers* (London, 1903, 2 vols.). Including correspondence with Creevy's friend Captain Graham Moore.

May, W. E., 'Captain Frankland's *Rose*', *AN* XXII (1962), pp. 37–62. Stationed at the Carolinas in the 1740s.

— 'Midshipmen Ordinary and Extraordinary', *MM* LIX (1973), pp. 187–92.

Maydman, Henry, *Naval Speculations and Maritime Politicks: Being a Modest and Brief Discourse of the Royal Navy of England, of its Oeconomy and Government* (London, 1691). A retired purser's obscure and prolix denunciation of novelty and tyranny, carefully avoiding anything too specific.

McArthur, John, *Principles and Practice of Naval and Military Courts Martial* (London, 4th edn 1813, 2 vols.).

McBride, William M., ' "Normal" Medical Science and British Treatment of the Sea Scurvy, 1753–75', *Journal of the History of Medicine and Allied Sciences* XLVI (1991), pp. 157–77.

McCord, Norman, 'The Impress Service in North-East England During the Napoleonic War', *MM* LIV (1968), pp. 163–80.

McCord, Norman and David E. Brewster, 'Some Labour Troubles of the 1790s in North East England', *International Review of Social History* XIII (1968), pp. 366–83.

McDonnell, Hector, 'Irishmen in the Stuart Navy, 1660–90', *IS* XVI (1984–6), pp. 87–104. Cf. the corrections supplied by J. D. Davies, 'More Light on Irishmen in the Stuart Navy, 1660–90', ibid., pp. 325–7.

McErlean, John M. P., 'Corsica 1794: Combined Operations', in *New Interpretations in Naval History*, ed. Jack Sweetman (Annapolis, Md., 1993), pp. 105–28.

McGuffie, T. H., 'The Walcheren Expedition and the Walcheren Fever', *EHR* LXII (1947), pp. 191–202.

— 'The Stone Ships Expedition against Boulogne, 1804', *EHR* LXIV (1949), pp. 488–503.

McKee, Christopher, *A Gentlemanly and Honorable Profession: The Creation of the U.S. Naval Officer Corps, 1794–1815* (Annapolis, 1991).

McLynn, F. J., *France and the Jacobite Rising of 1745* (Edinburgh, 1981).

— *Crime and Punishment in Eighteenth-Century England* (London, 1989).

— 'Sea Power and the Jacobite Rising of 1745', *MM* LXVII (1981), pp. 163–72.

McNeill, J. R., *Atlantic Empires of France and Spain: Louisbourg and Havana, 1700–1763* (Chapel Hill, N.C., 1985).

— 'The Ecological Basis of Warfare in the Caribbean, 1700–1804', in Ultee, *Adapting to Conditions*, pp. 26–42.

McNeill, William H., *The Pursuit of Power: Technology, Armed Force and Society since A.D. 1000* (Oxford, 1983).

Mediger, Walter, *Mecklenburg, Russland und England-Hannover 1706–1721: Ein Beitrag zur Geschichte des Nordischen Krieges* (Hildesheim, 1967, 2 vols.).

Mémain, René, *La Marine de guerre sous Louis XIV: le matériel, Rochefort, arsenal modèle de Colbert* (Paris, 1937).

Merino Navarro, José Patricio, *La Armada Española en el Siglo XVIII* (Madrid, 1981). An important study of naval policy and administration.

— 'La Armada en el siglo XVIII', in Hernández Sánchez-Barba, *Las Fuerzas Armadas Españolas*, II, 85–147.

Merriman, R. D., ed., *The Sergison Papers* (NRS Vol. 89, 1950). Sergison was Secretary of the Navy Board, 1690–1719.

— ed., *Queen Anne's Navy: Documents concerning the Administration of the Navy of Queen Anne, 1702–1714* (NRS Vol. 103, 1961).

— 'Gilbert Wardlaw's Allegations', *MM* XXXVIII (1952), pp. 106–31. An investigation into alleged corruption in the Navy Office, 1699.

Meyer, Jean, *Le Poids de l'état* (Paris, 1983). The rise of the centralized state.

— *Béveziers (1690): La France prend la maîtrise de la Manche* (Paris, 1993). The battle of Beachy Head.

— 'La Course: romantisme, exutoire sociale, réalité économique', *Annales de Bretagne* LXXVIII (1971), pp. 307–44.

— 'L'Evolution de la guerre marine et de son matériel (1650–1815)', in Acerra et al., *Les Marines de guerre*, pp. 123–46.

— 'La Marine française de 1545 à 1715', in *Histoire militaire de la France I: Des origines à 1715*, ed. Philippe Contamine (Paris, 1992), pp. 485–525.

— 'La Marine française au XVIIIe siècle', in Delmas, *Histoire militaire de la France II, 1715–1871*, pp. 151–94.

— 'Le Face-à-face des systèmes logistiques français et anglais en Méditerranée pendant les guerres de la Révolution et de l'Empire', in *Français et Anglais en Méditerranée*, pp. 181–202.

— 'La Guerre de course de l'Ancien Régime au XXe siècle: essai sur la guerre industrielle', *HES* XVI (1997), pp. 7–43.

Meyer, Jean and Martine Acerra, *Histoire de la Marine Française des origines à nos jours* (Rennes, 1994). Stimulating popular history, full of new ideas and new research, but without references.

— 'La Marine française vue par elle-même (XVIIe–XVIIIe siècles)', in *Guerres et paix*, pp. 231–43.

Meyer, Jean, André Corvisier and Jean-Pierre Poussou, *La Révolution Française* (Paris, 1991, 2 vols.).

Meyer, W. R., 'English Privateering in the War of 1688 to 1697', *MM* LXVII (1981), pp. 259–72.

— 'English Privateering in the War of the Spanish Succession 1702–1713', *MM* LXIX (1983), pp. 435–46.

Middleton, A. P., 'The Chesapeake Convoy System, 1662–1763', *WMQ* 3rd, S. III (1946), pp. 182–207.

Middleton, Richard, *The Bells of Victory: The Pitt-Newcastle Ministry and the Conduct of the Seven Years' War, 1757–1762* (Cambridge, 1985).

— 'A Reinforcement for North America, 1757', *BIHR* XLI (1968), pp. 58–72.

— 'Pitt, Anson and the Admiralty, 1756–1761', *History* NS LV (1970), pp. 189–98.

— 'Naval Administration in the Age of Pitt and Anson, 1755–1763', in Black and Woodfine, *British Navy*, pp. 109–27.

— 'British Naval Strategy 1755–62: The Western Squadron', *MM* LXXV (1989), pp. 349–67.

— 'The Visitation of the Royal Dockyards, 1749', *MM* LXXVII (1991), pp. 21–30.

— 'The British Coastal Expeditions to France, 1757–1758', *JSAHR* LXXI (1993), pp. 74–92.

Millard, F. M., 'The Battle of Copenhagen', *Macmillan's Magazine* LXXII (1895), pp. 81–93. Notes of the contributor's father Midshipman W. S. Millard of the *Monarch*.

Miller, Daniel A., *Sir Joseph Yorke and Anglo-Dutch Relations, 1774–1780* (The Hague, 1970).

Mimler, Manfred, *Der Einfluss kolonialer Interessen in Nordamerika auf die Strategie und Diplomatie Grossbritanniens während des Österreichischen Erbfolgekrieges, 1744–1748* (Hildesheim, 1983).

Minchinton, Walter, ed., *Britain and the Northern Seas* (Pontefract, 1988).

Minto, Nina [Kynynmound] Countess of, *Life and Letters of Sir Gilbert Elliot, First Earl of Minto* (London, 1874, 3 vols.).

Mokyr, Joel, 'The Industrial Revolution and the New Economic History', in *The Economics of the Industrial Revolution*, ed. Mokyr (London, 1985), pp. 1–51.

Mokyr, Joel and N. Eugene Savin, 'Stagflation in Economic Perspective: The Napoleonic Wars Revisited', in *Research in Economic History* I, ed. Paul Uselding (Greenwich, Conn., 1976), pp. 198–259.

Molyneux, Thomas More, *Conjunct Expeditions: or Expeditions that have been carried on jointly by the Fleet and Army, with a Commentary on a Litoral War* (London, 1759, 2 vols.). A careful history of amphibious operations, introducing a text-book on how to conduct them.

Monaque, Rémi, *Latouche-Tréville: l'amiral qui défiait Nelson* (Paris, 2000).

Monod, Paul K., *Jacobitism and the English People, 1688–1788* (Cambridge, 1989).

Moody, T. W., 'An Irish Countryman in the British Navy, 1809–1815', *IS* IV (1960), pp. 149–56 and 228–45; V (1961), pp. 41–55, 107–16, 146–54 and 236–50. Trustworthy memoir of a farmer's son from Antrim.

Moore, Alan, 'Rigging in the Seventeenth Century', *MM* II (1912), pp. 267–74, III (1913), pp. 7–13 and IV (1914), pp. 260–65.

Moore, Joseph Price, III, ' "The Greatest Enormity that Prevails": Direct Democracy and Workers' Self-Management in the British Naval Mutinies of 1797', in Howell and Twomey, *Jack Tar in History*, pp. 76–104. Some interesting Marxist ideas, which might have been applied to effect by someone who knew anything about the subject.

'Moore, Mark', *Memoirs and Adventures of Mark Moore* (London, 1795). Picaresque adventures of a New Englander during the Seven Years' War. The incidents seem to be authentic, but his name is probably not.

Mordvinov, R. N., ed., *Адмирап Ушаков* (Moscow, 1951–55, 3 vols.). Correspondence and papers of Admiral F. F. Ushakov, commanding the Russian Mediterranean Fleet 1798–1800. There is some correspondence with Nelson (all printed in Russian).

Morgan, G. W., 'The Impact of War on the Administration of the Army, Navy and Ordnance in Britain, 1739–1754' (Leicester Ph.D. thesis, 1977).

Morgan, William T., 'Some Attempts at Imperial Co-operation during the Reign of Queen Anne', *TRHS* 4th S. X (1927), pp. 171–94.

— 'The British West Indies during King William's War (1689–97)', *JMH* II (1930), pp. 378–409.

— 'The Expedition of the Baron de Pointis against Cartagena', *AHR* XXXVII (1931–2), pp. 237–58.

Morrah, Patrick, *Prince Rupert of the Rhine* (London, 1976).

Morrill, John, 'The Sensible Revolution', in Israel, *The Anglo-Dutch Moment*, pp. 73–104.

— 'The British Problem, *c.* 1534–1707', in Bradshaw and Morrill, *The British Problem*, pp. 1–38.

Morrison, Alfred, ed., *The Collection of Autograph Letters . . . The Hamilton and Nelson Papers* (p.p. 1893–4, 2 vols.). An important collection of Nelson's private letters.

Morriss, Roger, *The Royal Dockyards during the Revolutionary and Napoleonic Wars* (Leicester, 1983).

— *Cockburn and the British Navy in Transition: Admiral Sir George Cockburn 1772–1853* (Exeter, 1997).

— 'Labour Relations in the Royal Dockyards, 1801–1805', *MM* LXII (1976), pp. 337–46.

— 'St Vincent and Reform, 1801–04', *MM* LXIX (1983), pp. 269–90.

— 'Government and Community: The Changing Context of Labour Relations, 1770–1830', in Lunn and Day, *Work and Labour Relations*, pp. 21–40.

— 'Charles Middleton, Lord Barham, 1726–1813', in Le Fevre and Harding, *Precursors of Nelson*, pp. 300–323.

— 'The Glorious First of June: The British View of the Actions of 28, 29 May and 1 June 1794', in Duffy and Morriss, *Glorious First of June*, pp. 46–100.

Morriss, Roger and Richard Saxby, eds., *The Channel Fleet and the Blockade of Brest, 1793–1801* (NRS Vol. 141, 2001).

Moses, Norton H., 'The British Navy and the Caribbean, 1689–1697', *MM* LII (1966), pp. 13–40.

Mountaine, William, *The Seaman's Vade-Mecum and Defensive War by Sea* (London, 1756). A handbook for the shipmaster and purser.

Mountfield, Stuart, 'Captain Greenvile Collins and Mr Pepys', *MM* LVI (1970), pp. 85–96. A pioneer English hydrographer.

Moya Blanco, Carlos, 'La arquitectura naval en el siglo XVIII', in Manera Regueyra, *El buque en la Armada Española*, pp. 233–55.

Mühlmann, Rolf, *Die Reorganisation der Spanischen Kriegsmarine im 18. Jahrhundert* (Cologne and Vienna, 1975).

Muir, Rory, *Britain and the Defeat of Napoleon 1807–1815* (New Haven and London, 1996). Excellent survey of British strategy, primarily from the military point of view.

Muir, R. J. B. and C. J. Esdaile, 'Strategic Planning in a Time of Small Government: The Wars against Revolutionary and Napoleonic France, 1793–1815', in *Wellington Studies I*, ed. C. M. Woolgar (Southampton, 1996), pp. 1–90.

Mulloy, Sheila, 'The French Navy and the Jacobite War in Ireland, 1689–91', *IS* XVIII (1990), pp. 17–31.

Mundy, Major-General [G. B.], *The Life and Correspondence of the late Admiral Lord Rodney* (London, 1830, 2 vols.). Mundy selected and rewrote the correspondence in an heroic attempt to rescue his father-in-law's reputation.

Murphy, Orville T., *Charles Gravier, Comte de Vergennes: French Diplomacy in the Age of Revolution, 1719–1787* (Albany, 1982).

Murray, A., *Memoir of the Naval Life and Services of Admiral Sir Philip C. H. C. Durham* (London, 1846).

Murray, John J., *George I, the Baltic and the Whig Split of 1717: A Study in Diplomacy and Propaganda* (London, 1969).

— 'Anglo-French Naval Skirmishing off Newfoundland, 1697', in *Essays in Modern European History by Students of the Late Professor William Thomas Morgan*, ed. Murray (Bloomington, Indiana, 1951), pp. 71–84.

— 'The United Provinces and the Anglo-Dutch Baltic Squadron of 1715', *Bijdragen voor de Geschiedenis der Nederlanden* VIII (1953), pp. 20–45.

Murray, Sir Oswyn A. R., 'The Admiralty', *MM* XXIII (1937), pp. 13–35, 129–47 and 316–31; XXIV (1938), pp. 101–4, 204–25 and 329–52, 458–78; XXV (1939) pp. 89–111 and 216–28. An unfinished history of the Admiralty by one of its greatest Secretaries.

Nagle, Jacob, *The Nagle Journal: A Diary of the Life of Jacob Nagle, Sailor, from the Year 1775 to 1841*, ed. John C. Dann (New York, 1988). Nagle preserved into old age an innocent eye and a retentive memory of an extraordinary career.

Naish, G. B. P., ed., *Nelson's Letters to his Wife and other Documents, 1785–1831* (NRS Vol. 100, 1958). An important collection, excellently edited, not by Naish, who took the credit, but by Katherine Lindsay-MacDougall.

Namier, L. B., *The Structure of Politics at the Accession of George III* (London, 2nd edn 1957).

Naval Chronicle, The (London, 1799–1818, 40 vols.). A periodical for officers, full of all sorts of official and unofficial information on naval operations and affairs. There is a useful 'Consolidated edition' (i.e. of extracts rearranged in chronological order) by Nicholas Tracy (London, 1998–9, 5 vols.), and an *Index to Births Marriages and Deaths* compiled by Norman Hurst (p.p. 1989).

Neale, Jonathan, *The Cutlass and the Lash: Mutiny and Discipline in Nelson's Navy* (London, 1985).

— 'Forecastle and Quarterdeck: Protest, Discipline and Mutiny in the Royal Navy, 1793–1814' (Warwick Ph.D. thesis, 1990). Naval history from a Trotskyite perspective; something of a contrast to the Michael Lewis approach, and full of valuable insights, especially for those who do not share the author's politics. Reversing the usual order, Dr Neale wrote his book first and followed it with the Ph.D. thesis, which incorporates and greatly expands it.

Neeser, Robert W., ed., *The Despatches of Molyneux Shuldham . . . January–July 1776* (New York, 1913, Naval History Society Vol. III).

Newnham Collingwood, G. L., *A Selection from the Public and Private Correspon-*

dence of Vice-Admiral Lord Collingwood: Interspersed with Memoirs of his Life (London, 4th edn 1829). No British admiral ever wrote better than Collingwood, but unhappily his son-in-law could not resist the temptation to tamper with his prose.

Nicol, John, *The Life and Adventures of John Nicol, Mariner* (New York, 1936; originally Edinburgh, 1822). A career on the lower deck during the American and French Revolutionary Wars.

Nicolas, Sir N. H., ed., *The Despatches and Letters of Vice Admiral Lord Viscount Nelson* (London, 1844–5, 7 vols.; Vol. 1 only 2nd edn 1845). Fundamental for the life of Nelson. Nicolas was a careful and honest editor, but he was forced to copy some letters from untrustworthy sources like Clarke and McArthur, and the total of Nelson letters now known is almost double what he printed.

Niedhart, Gottfried, *Handel und Krieg in der Britischen Weltpolitik, 1738–1763* (Munich, 1979).

Nordmann, Claude, 'Choiseul and the Last Jacobite Attempt of 1759', in *Ideology and Conspiracy: Aspects of Jacobitism, 1689–1759*, ed. Eveline Cruickshanks (Edinburgh, 1982), pp. 201–17 [originally 'Choiseul et la dernière tentative jacobite de 1759', *RHD* XCIII (1979), pp. 223–46].

Norris, John, *Shelburne and Reform* (London, 1963).

— 'The Policy of the British Cabinet in the Nootka Crisis', *EHR* LXX (1955), pp. 562–80.

[O'Beirne, Thomas Lewis], *A Candid and Impartial Narrative of the Transactions of the Fleet under the Command of Lord Howe* (London, 1779). Howe's chaplain anonymously defends his conduct. The pretence of candour and impartiality is more than usually flimsy; the tone of violent invective presumably expresses Howe's feelings, which he was not capable of doing for himself.

O'Brien, Patrick K., *Power with Profit: The State and the Economy, 1688–1815* (London, 1991).

— 'The Political Economy of British Taxation, 1660–1815', *EcHR* 2nd S. XLI (1988), pp. 1–32.

— 'The Impact of the Revolutionary and Napoleonic Wars, 1793–1815, on the Long-Run Growth of the British Economy', *Review of the Fernand Braudel Center* XII (1989), pp. 335–95.

— 'Inseparable Connections: Trade, Economy, Fiscal State, and the Expansion of Empire, 1688–1815', in Marshall, *Eighteenth Century*, pp. 53–77.

— 'Fiscal Exceptionalism: Great Britain and Its European Rivals. From Civil War to Triumph at Trafalgar and Waterloo', in Winch and O'Brien, *Political Economy 1688–1914*, pp. 245–65.

O'Brien, P. K. and S. L. Engerman, 'Exports and the Growth of the British Economy from the Glorious Revolution to the Peace of Amiens', in *Slavery and the Rise of the Atlantic System*, ed. Barbara L. Solow (Cambridge, 1991), pp. 177–209.

O'Brien, P. K. and P. A. Hunt, 'The Rise of a Fiscal State in Britain, 1485–1815', *HR* LXVI (1993), pp. 129–76. A series of articles of fundamental importance.

O'Byrne, W. R., *A Naval Biographical Dictionary* (London, 1849). Information (mostly supplied by themselves) about all commissioned officers then alive, including many survivors of the French Wars.

Ogelsby, J. C. M., 'War at Sea in the West Indies 1739–1748' (Washington Ph.D. thesis, 1963).

— 'Spain's Havana Squadron and the Preservation of the Balance of Power in the Caribbean, 1740–1748', *HAHR* XLIX (1969), pp. 473–88.

O'Gorman, Frank, *The Rise of Party in England: The Rockingham Whigs 1760–82* (London, 1975).

Ollard, Richard, *Man of War: Sir Robert Holmes and the Restoration Navy* (London, 1969).

— *Pepys: A Biography* (London, 2nd edn 1991).

— *Cromwell's Earl: A Life of Edward Mountagu 1st Earl of Sandwich* (London, 1995).

Ollivier, Blaise, *18th Century Shipbuilding: Remarks on the Navies of the English and the Dutch* . . . trans. and ed. David H. Roberts (Rotherfield, East Sussex, 1992). The report (printed in the original and in translation) of a 1739 espionage trip to England and the Netherlands by the chief constructor of Brest dockyard.

Olson, Mancur, *The Economics of the Wartime Shortage: A History of British Food Supplies in the Napoleonic Wars and in World Wars I and II* (Durham, N.C., 1963).

O'Malley, Leslie Chree, 'The Whig Prince: Prince Rupert and the Court vs Country Factions during the Reign of Charles II', *Albion* VIII (1976), pp. 333–50.

Oman, Carola, *Nelson* (London, 1947). Outdated, but still the last full and scholarly life. The forthcoming biography by R. J. B. Knight will replace it.

Ontoria Oquillas, Pedro, Luis Cola Benítez and Daniel García Pulido, eds., *Fuentes Documentales del 25 de Julio de 1797* (Santa Cruz de Tenerife, 1997). Prints or reprints all known Spanish, French and British sources on Nelson's attack on Tenerife, with translations into Spanish as necessary.

Oppenheim, M., *A History of the Administration of the Royal Navy and of Merchant Shipping in relation to the Navy* . . . *1509 to 1660* . . . (London, 1896). A work of fundamental importance. It is still used so heavily that it is worth pointing out its two chief defects: Oppenheim was extremely prejudiced against royal government and all its works; and his references, quotations and figures are very untrustworthy.

— 'The Navy of the Commonwealth', *EHR* XI (1896), pp. 20–81.

Oprey, Christopher, 'Schemes for the Reform of Naval Recruitment, 1793–1815' (Liverpool MA dissertation, 1961). One of the few studies of the Quota Acts.

O'Shaughnessy, Andrew Jackson, *An Empire Divided: The American Revolution and the British Caribbean* (Philadelphia, 2000). Economic consequences of American independence.

Osinga, Jacob, *Frankrijk, Vergennes en de Amerikanse Onafhankelijkheid, 1776–1783* (Amsterdam, [1982]). Presents an interesting (and strangely neglected) argument about French policy towards the American rebellion.

Otero Lana, Enrique, *Los corsarios españoles durante la decadencia de los Austrias: El corso español del Atlántico peninsular en el siglo XVII (1621–1697)* (Madrid, 1992).

Oudendijk, Johanna K., *Johan De Witt en de Zeemacht* (Amsterdam, 1954).

Owen, Captain C. H. H., 'An Eyewitness Account of the Glorious First of June 1794', *MM* LXXX (1994), pp. 335–8.

— 'Letters from Vice-Admiral Lord Collingwood, 1794–1809', in Duffy, *Naval Miscellany VI*, pp. 149–220.

Owen, J. H., *War at Sea under Queen Anne, 1702–1708* (Cambridge, 1938).

— 'Rodney and de Guichen, 1780', *NR* XIII (1925), pp. 195–212 and 433–46.

— 'The Navy and the Surrender at Yorktown, 1781', *NR* XIV (1926), pp. 18–33 and 223–48.

— 'The Battle of Grenada, 6th July 1779', *NR* XIV (1926), pp. 458–75.

— 'Operations of the Western Squadron, 1781–82', *NR* XV (1927), pp. 33–53.

— 'Howe and d'Estaing in North America, 1778', *NR* XV (1927), pp. 257–83.

— 'Hood at Saint Christopher's, 1782', *NR* XV (1927), pp. 496–518. Though printed anonymously, this is another of Commander Owen's careful analyses of naval operations during the American War.

— 'Rodney and Grasse, 1782', *NR* XVI (1928), pp. 148–59, 213–38 and 436–46.

— 'Letters from Sir Samuel Hood, 1780–1782', *MM* XIX (1933), pp. 75–87.

Oxford Dictionary of National Biography, ed. Colin Matthew and Brian Harrison (Oxford, 2004, 60 vols.). The successor of the DNB, which it incorporates in enormously revised, expanded and improved form.

Pack, A. J., *Nelson's Blood: The Story of Naval Rum* (Emsworth, 1982).

Padfield, Peter, *Broke and the Shannon* (London, 1968). Sir Philip Broke, the gunnery expert and victor of the *Shannon–Chesapeake* action.

— *Tide of Empires: Decisive Naval Campaigns in the Rise of the West* (London, 1979–82, 2 vols.).

— *Maritime Supremacy and the Opening of the Western Mind: Naval Campaigns that Shaped the Modern World, 1588–1782* (London, 1999). 'Maritime supremacy is the key which unlocks most, if not all, large questions of modern history . . .'

Pagano de Divitiis, Gigliola, ed., *Il commercio inglese nel Mediterraneo dal '500 al '700: Corrispondenza consolare e documentazione britannica tra Napoli e Londra* (Naples, 1984). A calendar with selected transcripts.

Paget, Sir A. B., ed., *The Paget Papers* (London, 1896, 2 vols.).

Paget, Edward Clarence, *Memoir of the Hon. Sir Charles Paget . . .* (London, 1913).

Palmer, M. A. J., 'Sir John's Victory: The Battle of Cape St Vincent reconsidered', *MM* LXXVII (1991), pp. 31–46.

— 'The "Military Revolution" Afloat: The Era of the Anglo-Dutch Wars and the Transition to Modern Warfare at Sea', *WiH* IV (1997), pp. 123–49.

Palmer, Sarah and David M. Williams, 'British Sailors, 1775–1870', in van Royen et al., *'Those Emblems of Hell'?*, pp. 93–118.

Pannell, J. P. M., 'The Taylors of Southampton: Pioneers in Mechanical Engineering', *Proceedings of the Institution of Mechanical Engineers* CLIX (1955), 46, pp. 924–31.

Panzac, Daniel, *Les Corsaires barbaresques: La fin d'une épopée 1800–1820* (Paris, 1999).

Pares, Richard, *War and Trade in the West Indies, 1739–1763* (Oxford, 1936).

— *Colonial Blockade and Neutral Rights, 1739–1763* (Oxford, 1938).

— 'American versus Continental Warfare, 1739–1763', *EHR* LI (1936), pp. 429–65.

— 'The Manning of the Navy in the West Indies 1702–63', *TRHS* 4th S. XX (1937), pp. 31–60.

Parker, Geoffrey, 'Europe and the Wider World, 1500–1750: The Military Balance', in Tracy, *Political Economy of Merchant Empires*, pp. 161–95.

Parkinson, C. Northcote, *Edward Pellew, Viscount Exmouth, Admiral of the Red* (London, 1934).

— *War in the Eastern Seas, 1793–1815* (London, 1954).

Parsons, G. S., *Nelsonian Reminiscences: Leaves from Memory's Log* (London, 1843). Literary recollections, not highly trustworthy.

Pasley, Thomas, *Private Sea Journals 1778–1782*, ed. R. M. S. Pasley (London, 1931). Revealing private thoughts of a frigate captain.

Patterson, A. Temple, *The Other Armada: The Franco-Spanish Attempt to Invade Britain in 1779* (Manchester, 1960).

— *Portsmouth: A History* (Bradford-on-Avon, 1976).

Patton, Philip, *Strictures on Naval Discipline, and the Conduct of a Ship of War . . .* (Edinburgh, 1799). Extracts are printed in Lavery, *Shipboard Life*, pp. 622–31.

Pawson, Michael and David Buisseret, *Port Royal, Jamaica* (Oxford, 1975).

[Pearsall, A. W. H.], *The Second Dutch War 1665–1667* (National Maritime Museum, Greenwich, 1967).

— ed., 'Naval Aspects of the Landings on the French Coast, 1758', in Rodger, *Naval Miscellany V*, pp. 207–43.

— 'The Royal Navy and Trade Protection 1688–1714', *Renaissance and Modern Studies* XXX (1986), pp. 109–23.

— 'The Royal Navy and the Protection of Trade in the Eighteenth Century', in *Guerres et paix*, pp. 149–62.

— 'British Convoys in the North Sea 1781–1782', in Minchinton, *Britain and the Northern Seas*, pp. 105–12.

— 'The Invasion Voyage: Some Nautical Thoughts', in Wilson and Proctor, *1688*, pp. 165–74.

— 'The War at Sea', in *Kings in Conflict: The Revolutionary War in Ireland and Its Aftermath, 1689–1750*, ed. W. A. Maguire (Belfast, 1990), pp. 92–105.

— 'Escorts and Convoys and the English East India Company', in Haudrère, *Les Flottes des Compagnies des Indes*, pp. 213–21.

Pemberton, Charles Reece, *The Autobiography of Pel. Verjuice*, ed. Eric Partridge (London, 1929). Radical pamphlets loosely cast in the form of naval autobiography.

Pemsel, Helmut, *Seeherrschaft: eine maritime Weltgeschichte* (Koblenz, 1995,

2 vols.). A combined atlas and chronology of world naval history. An earlier version, entitled *Von Salamis bis Okinawa* (Munich, 1975), appeared in English as *Atlas of Naval Warfare: An Atlas and Chronology of Conflict at Sea from Earliest Times to the Present Day* (London, 1977, trans. D. G. Smith), but the translation was indifferent and the expanded version is much superior.

Penn, Granville, *Memorials of the Professional Life and Times of Sir William Penn* . . . (London, 1833, 2 vols.). Prints Penn's papers.

[Penrose, C. V.], *A Memoir of James Trevenen*, ed. Christopher Lloyd and R. C. Anderson (NRS Vol. 101, 1959).

Pepys, Samuel, *The Diary of Samuel Pepys*, ed. Robert Latham and William Matthews (London, 1970–83, 11 vols.).

— *Pepys' Memoires of the Royal Navy 1679–1688*, ed. J. R. Tanner (Oxford, 1906) [originally London, 1690]. Pepys's defence of his naval administration.

Pérez de la Riva, Juan, ed., *Documentos ineditos sobre la toma de la Habana por les Ingleses en 1762* (Havana, 1963). Documents from British and French archives.

Perez-Mallaina Bueno, Pablo Emilio, *Política Naval Española en el Atlántico 1700–1715* (Seville, 1982).

Perkins, Bradford, *Prologue to War: England and the United States 1805–1812* (Berkeley, Calif., 1961).

Pernoud, Régine, *La Campagne des Indes: lettres inedites du Bailli de Suffren* (Mantes, 1941).

Perrichet, Marc, 'L'Administration des classes de la Marine et ses archives dans les ports bretons', *Revue d'Histoire Economique et Sociale* XXXVII (1959), pp. 89–112.

Perrin, W. G., *British Flags* (Cambridge, 1922).

— ed., *The Naval Miscellany Vol. III* (NRS Vol. 63, 1928).

— ed., 'The Engagement between H.M.S. *Brunswick* and *Le Vengeur* on 1st June 1794', in *Naval Miscellany III*, pp. 155–69.

— ed., 'Letters of Lord Nelson, 1804–5', in *Naval Miscellany III*, pp. 173–90.

— ed., 'The Bombardment of Copenhagen, 1807 – Journal of Surgeon Charles Chambers of H.M. Fireship *Prometheus*', in *Naval Miscellany III*, pp. 365–466.

Perrin, W. G. and Christopher Lloyd, eds., *The Keith Papers* (NRS Vols. 62, 90 and 96, 1927–55).

Peter, Jean, *L'Artillerie et les fonderies de la marine sous Louis XIV* (Paris, 1995).

Peters, Marie, *The Elder Pitt* (London, 1998).

Petrides, Anne and Jonathan Downs, eds., *Sea Soldier: An Officer of Marines with Duncan, Nelson, Collingwood and Cockburn. The Letters and Journals of Major T. Marmaduke Wybourn RM, 1797–1813* (Tunbridge Wells, 2000).

Pfister-Langanay, Christian, 'Stratégie, construction navale et charpentiers à Dunkerque sous Louis XIV', in Acerra, *L'Invention du vaisseau de ligne*, pp. 47–60.

Phillimore, Augustus, *The Life of Admiral of the Fleet Sir William Parker* . . . (London, 1876–80, 3 vols.). Prints extensive and interesting correspondence.

Phillips, I. Lloyd, 'The Evangelical Administrator: Sir Charles Middleton at the Navy Board 1778–1790' (Oxford D.Phil. thesis, 1974).

— 'Lord Barham at the Admiralty, 1805–6', *MM* LCIV (1978), pp. 217–33.

Phillips, Captain Thomas, 'Journal of a Voyage made in the *Hannibal* of London, Ann. 1693, 1694 . . .', in *A Collection of Voyages and Travels*, ed. A. Churchill, Vol. VI (London, 1732), pp. 171–239.

Pietsch, Roland W. W., 'Ships' Boys and Charity in the Mid-Eighteenth Century: The London Marine Society (1756–1772)' (London Ph.D. thesis, 2003).

— 'Urchins for the Sea: The Story of the Marine Society in the Seven Years War', *JMR* (Nov 2000).

Pilgrim, Donald G., 'The Uses and Limitations of French Naval Power in the Reign of Louis XIV: The Administration of the Marquis de Seignelay, 1683–1690' (Brown Ph.D. thesis, 1969).

— 'The Colbert-Seignelay Naval Reforms and the Beginning of the War of the League of Augsburg', *FHS* IX (1975), pp. 235–62.

Pincus, Steven C. A., *Protestantism and Patriotism: Ideologies and the Making of English Foreign Policy, 1650–1668* (Cambridge, 1996).

— 'Popery, Trade and Universal Monarchy: The Ideological Context of the Outbreak of the Second Anglo-Dutch War', *EHR* CVII (1992), pp. 1–29.

Pocock, Tom, *The Young Nelson in the Americas* (London, 1980).

— *Horatio Nelson* (London, 1987).

— *A Thirst for Glory: The Life of Admiral Sir Sidney Smith* (London, 2nd edn 1998).

Pool, Bernard, *Navy Board Contracts 1660–1832: Contract Administration under the Navy Board* (London, 1966).

— 'Some Notes on the Building of Warships by Contract in the late 17th Century', *MM* XLVIII (1962), pp. 89–111.

Pope, Dudley, *At 12 Mr Byng was Shot . . .* (London, 1962). Pope wrote lively narratives, often based on new evidence, which work well in detail, but his combative ignorance of the wider historical context let him down.

— *The Black Ship* (London, 1963) The *Hermione* mutiny.

— *The Great Gamble* (London, 1972). His best book, and the most detailed account of the battle of Copenhagen – but Feldbæk explains the politics, diplomacy and strategy which were out of Pope's reach.

Popham, Hugh, *A Damned Cunning Fellow: The Eventful Life of Rear-Admiral Sir Home Popham . . . 1762–1820* (Tywardreath, Cornwall, 1991).

Powell, J. R., ed., *The Letters of Robert Blake, Together with Supplementary Documents* (NRS Vol. 76, 1937). Important documents, but many of them were copied from other NRS volumes or Thurloe's *State Papers*, and the transcriptions of the rest are untrustworthy.

— *The Navy in the English Civil War* (London, 1962). The only proper book on the subject.

— *Robert Blake, General-at-Sea* (London, 1972).

— ed., 'The Journal of John Weale, 1654–1656', in Lloyd, *Naval Miscellany IV*, pp. 85–162.

— 'The Expedition of Blake and Mountagu in 1655', *MM* LII (1966), pp. 341–69.

— 'John Bourne, Sometime Vice-Admiral', *MM* LXII (1976), pp. 109–17.

Powell, J. R. and E. K. Timings, eds., *The Rupert and Monck Letter Book, 1666* (NRS Vol. 112, 1969). Printed from poor transcripts.

Powell, J. W. D., *Bristol Privateers and Ships of War* (Bristol, 1930).

Powley, Edward B., *The English Navy in the Revolution of 1688* (Cambridge, 1928).

— *The Naval Side of King William's War* (London, 1972).

Poynter, F. N. L., ed., *The Journal of James Yonge (1647–1721) Plymouth Surgeon* (London, 1963). A naval surgeon of the 1650s and 60s.

Press, Jonathan, *The Merchant Seamen of Bristol, 1747–1789* (Bristol, Historical Association, 1976).

Pritchard, James, *Louis XV's Navy, 1748–1762: A Study of Organization and Administration* (Montreal, 1987).

— *Anatomy of a Naval Disaster: The 1746 French Expedition to North America* (Montreal and Kingston, 1995).

— 'From Shipwright to Naval Constructor: The Professionalization of 18th-Century French Naval Shipbuilders', *T&C* XXVIII (1987), pp. 1–25.

— 'Fir Trees, Financiers, and the French Navy during the 1750s', *Canadian Journal of History* XXIII (1988), pp. 337–54.

— 'French Strategy and the American Revolution: A Reappraisal', *NWCR* XLVII (1994), pp. 83–108.

Prud'homme van Reine, Ronald, *Rechterhand van Nederland: Biographie van Michiel Adrianszoon de Ruyter* (Amsterdam, 1996).

— *Schittering en schandaal: Biografie van Maerten en Cornelis Tromp* (Amsterdam, 2001).

Pullen, H. F., *The Shannon and the Chesapeake* (Toronto, 1970).

Raban, Peter, 'Channel Island Privateering, 1739–1763', *IJMH* I, 2 (1989), pp. 287–99.

Rackham, Oliver, *The History of the Countryside* (London, 1986). Important for forestry and timber supplies.

Radogna, Lamberto, *Storia della marina militare delle Due Sicilie (1734–1860)* (Milan, 1978).

Rae, M. A., 'The Blockade of Brest and the French Atlantic Ports, including Ferrol, in the Revolutionary and Napoleonic Wars, 1796–1806, Together with the Use of Torbay as a Port of Refuge' (Exeter MA dissertation, 2000).

Raigersfeld, Jeffrey Baron de, *The Life of a Sea Officer*, ed. L. G. Carr Laughton (London, 1929) [originally p.p. c. 1830]. A colourful memoir of service during the French Wars.

Raikes, Henry, *Memoir of the Life and Services of Vice-Admiral Sir Jahleel Brenton* (London, 1846). Based on a manuscript autobiography, more concerned with the life of the soul than the career of the officer.

Ranft, B. McL., ed., *The Vernon Papers* (NRS Vol. 99, 1978).

— 'The Significance of the Political Career of Samuel Pepys', *JMH* XXIV (1952), pp. 368–75.

— ed., 'Prince William and Lieutenant Schomberg, 1787–1788', in Lloyd, *Naval Miscellany IV*, pp. 267–93.

— 'Labour Relations in the Royal Dockyards in 1739', *MM* XLVII (1961), pp. 281–91.

Raven, G. J. A. and N. A. M. Rodger, eds., *The Anglo-Dutch Relationship in War and Peace, 1688–1988* (Edinburgh, 1990).

Rawson, Geoffrey, ed., *Nelson's Letters from the Leeward Islands . . .* (London, 1953).

Rediker, Marcus, *Between the Devil and the Deep Blue Sea: Merchant Seamen, Pirates and the Anglo-American Maritime World 1700–1750* (Cambridge, 1987). A survey of printed sources, interpreted in the light of French Marxist thinkers of the 1960s; plus a short study of mutiny and piracy from colonial Vice-Admiralty court records. An interesting project, but it called for serious research, and the author's knowledge of the maritime world was too slender to support his theoretical ambitions.

Rees, Thomas, *A Journal of Voyages and Travels by the late Thomas Rees, Serjeant of Marines* (London, 1822). A slight memoir.

Regulations and Instructions Relating to His Majesty's Service at Sea (Admiralty, 1st edn 1731; Additional Articles added 1756; completely revised 1806).

Relation détaillée de la campagne de M. le Commandeur de Suffren (Port Louis, 1783). Anonymous account by a Mauricien, well informed but hostile to the sea officers.

Reynolds, Clark G., ed., *Global Crossroads and the American Seas* (Missoula, Mont. 1988).

Rice, Geoffrey W., 'Great Britain, the Manila Ransom, and the First Falkland Islands Dispute with Spain, 1766', *IHR* II (1980), pp. 386–409.

Richardson, William, *A Mariner of England: An Account of the Career of William Richardson . . . As Told by Himself*, ed. Spencer Childers (London, 1908). A warrant officer's memoirs.

Richmond, Sir H. W., ed., *Papers Relating to the Loss of Minorca in 1756* (NRS Vol. 42, 1913).

— *The Navy in the War of 1739–48* (Cambridge, 1920, 3 vols.).

— *The Navy in India 1763–1783* (London, 1931).

— *Statemen and Sea Power* (Oxford, 1946).

— *The Navy as an Instrument of Policy 1558–1727* (Cambridge, 1953).

— 'The Expedition to Sicily, 1718, under Sir George Byng', *JRUSI* LIII (1909), pp. 1,135–52.
Richmond was both the most intellectual of admirals and the most seamanlike of historians.

Riley, James C., *International Government Finance and the Amsterdam Capital Market, 1740–1815* (Cambridge, 1980).

— *The Seven Years War and the Old Regime in France: The Economic and Financial Toll* (Princeton, 1986).

— 'French Finances, 1727–1768', *JMH* LIX (1987), pp. 209–43.

Risse, Guenther B., 'Britannia Rules the Seas: the Health of Seamen, Edinburgh, 1791–1800', *Journal of the History of Medicine* XLIII (1988), pp. 426–46.

Ritcheson, Charles R., *British Politics and the American Revolution* (Norman, Okla., 1954).

— 'Thomas Pinckney's London Mission, 1792–1796, and the Impressment Issue', *IHR* II (1980), pp. 523–41.

Ritchie, Robert C., *Captain Kidd and the War against the Pirates* (Cambridge, Mass., 1986).

Roberts, Michael, 'Cromwell and the Baltic', *EHR* LXXVI (1961), pp. 402–46.

Robertson, Stuart. 'The Mobilisation of the British Navy at the Start of the French Revolutionary War 1793/4' (Exeter MA dissertation, 2000).

Robinson, Dwight E., 'Secret of British Power in the Age of Sail: Admiralty Records of the Coasting Fleet', *AN* XLVIII (1988), pp. 5–21.

Robinson, Gregory, 'Admiralty and Naval Affairs, May 1660 to March 1674', *MM* XXXVI (1950), pp. 12–40.

Robinson, M. S., *The Paintings of the Willem van de Veldes* (National Maritime Museum, Greenwich, 1990, 2 vols.).

[Robinson, Sir T., ed.], 'Sir John Narbrough's Voyage to the South Sea', in *An Account of Several Late Voyages and Discoveries* (London, 2nd edn 1711), pp. 1–128.

[Robinson, William] 'Jack Nastyface', *Nautical Economy, or Forecastle Reflections of Events during the Last War* [originally 1836]. I have cited the edition entitled *Memoirs of a Seaman*, ed. Oliver Warner (London, 1973).

Rodger, A. B., *The War of the Second Coalition, 1789 to 1801: A Strategic Commentary* (Oxford, 1964).

Rodger, N. A. M., *The Admiralty* (Lavenham, Suffolk, 1979). Sketchy and unreliable.

— *Articles of War* (Havant, 1982). Those of 1661, 1749 and 1866; a convenient source of reference for those who do not have a set of the Statutes to hand.

— ed., *The Naval Miscellany, Vol. V* (NRS Vol. 125, 1985).

— *The Wooden World; An Anatomy of the Georgian Navy* (London, 1986).

— *The Insatiable Earl: A Life of John Montagu, Fourth Earl of Sandwich, 1718–1792* (London, 1993).

— *The Safeguard of the Sea. A Naval History of Britain, Vol. 1, 660–1649* (London, 1997). The preceding volume of this work.

— 'Stragglers and Deserters from the Royal Navy during the Seven Years' War', *BIHR* LVII (1984), pp. 56–79.

— 'The Victualling of the British Navy during the Seven Years' War', *Bulletin du Centre d'Histoire des Espaces Atlantiques* No. 2 (Bordeaux, 1985), pp. 37–53.

— 'The Douglas Papers, 1760–1762', in *Naval Miscellany V*, pp. 244–283. Sir James Douglas as commander-in-chief Leeward Islands.

— 'Le Scorbut dans la Royal Navy pendant la Guerre de Sept Ans', in Lottin et al., *Les Hommes et la mer*, pp. 455–62.

— 'Medicine, Administration and Society in the Eighteenth-Century Royal Navy', in Schadewaldt and Leven, *IX Deutsch-Französisches Symposium*, pp. 126–32.

846 · BIBLIOGRAPHY

— 'Lieutenants' Sea-Time and Age', *MM* LXXV (1989), pp. 269–72.
— 'The British View of the Functioning of the Anglo-Dutch Alliance, 1688–1795', in Raven and Rodger, *The Anglo-Dutch Relationship*, pp. 12–32.
— 'Devon Men and the Navy, 1688–1815', *MHD* I, 209–15.
— 'The Continental Commitment in the Eighteenth Century', in *War, Strategy and International Politics: Essays in Honour of Sir Michael Howard*, ed. Lawrence Freedman, Paul Hayes and Robert O'Neill (Oxford, 1992), pp. 39–55.
— ' "A Little Navy of your Own Making". Admiral Boscawen and the Cornish Connection in the Royal Navy', in Duffy, *Parameters*, pp. 82–92.
— 'La Mobilisation navale au XVIIIème siècle', in Acerra et al., *Etat, marine et société*, pp. 365–74.
— 'The Naval Chaplain in the Eighteenth Century', *British Journal for Eighteenth-Century Studies* XVIII (1995), pp. 33–45.
— 'The Development of Broadside Gunnery, 1450–1650', *MM* LXXXII (1996), pp. 301–24.
— 'Medicine and Science in the British Navy of the Eighteenth Century', in *L'Homme, la santé et la mer*, ed. Christian Buchet (Paris, 1997), pp. 333–44.
— 'Sea-Power and Empire, 1688–1793', in Marshall, *Eighteenth Century*, pp. 169–83.
— 'Die Entwicklung der Vorstellung von Seekriegsstrategie in Grossbritannien im 18 und 19 Jahrhundert', in *Seemacht und Seestrategie im 19. und 20. Jahrhundert*, ed. Jörg Duppler (Hamburg, 1999), pp. 83–103.
— 'Weather, Geography and Naval Power in the Age of Sail', *Journal of Strategic Studies* XXII (1999), No. 2/3, pp. 178–200 [also in *Geopolitics, Geography and Strategy*, ed. Colin S. Gray and Geoffrey Sloan (Ilford, 1999).
— 'George, Lord Anson (1697–1762)', in Le Fevre and Harding, *Precursors of Nelson*, pp. 177–99.
— 'Commissioned Officers' Careers in the Royal Navy, 1690–1815', *JMR* (July 2001).
— 'Honour and Duty at Sea, 1660–1815', *HR* LXXV (2002), pp. 425–47.
— 'Form and Function in European Navies, 1660–1815', in *In het kielzog. Maritiemhistorische studies aangeboden aan Jaap R. Bruijn bij zijn vertrek als hoogleraar zeegeschiedenis aan de Universiteit Leiden*, ed. Leo Akveld et al. (Amsterdam, 2003), pp. 85–97.
— 'Image and Reality in Eighteenth-century Naval Tactics', *MM* LXXXIX (2003), pp. 280–96.
— 'Mutiny or Subversion? Spithead and the Nore', in Bartlett et al., *1798*, pp. 549–64.
— 'Navies and the Enlightenment', in *Science and the French and British Navies 1750–1850*, ed. Pieter van der Merwe (National Maritime Museum, 2003), pp. 5–23.
— 'The Military Revolution at Sea' (to appear).
— 'Queen Elizabeth and the Myth of Seapower in English Politics, 1568–1815', to appear in *TRHS* 6th. S. XIV (2004).
Rodney, G. B., *Letter-Books and Order-Book of George, Lord Rodney . . . 1780–82*

[ed. Dorothy C. Barck] (New York Historical Society, 1932, 2 vols.). Official correspondence. Rodney's more revealing private correspondence is being edited by Professor David Syrett for the Navy Records Society.

Rodríguez Casado, Vicente, 'La politia del reformismo de los primeros Borbones en la marina de guerra española', *AEA* XXV (1968), pp. 601–18.

Rodríguez Demorizi, Emilio, 'Invasión inglesa de 1655', *Boletin del Archivo General de la Nacion* [i.e. of the Dominican Republic] XIX (1956), pp. 6–161 and XX (1957), pp. 6–70. Prints important documents from Spanish archives on the 'Western Design'.

Rogers, Nicholas, *Crowds, Culture and Politics in Georgian Britain* (Oxford, 1998).

— 'Liberty Road: Opposition to Impressment in Britain during the American War of Independence', in Howell and Twomey, *Jack Tar in History*, pp. 53–75.

— 'Vagrancy, Impressment and the Regulation of Labour in Eighteenth-Century Britain', in *Unfree Labour in the Development of the Atlantic World*, ed. Paul E. Lovejoy and N. Rogers (Newbury Park, 1994), pp. 102–13.

Rogers, P. G., *The Dutch in the Medway* (London, 1970).

Rogers, Woodes, *A Cruising Voyage round the World* (London, 1712). 'Cruising' here means privateering.

Rommelse, Gijs, 'English Privateering against the Dutch Republic during the Second Anglo-Dutch War (1664–1667)', *TvZ* XXII (2003), pp. 17–31.

Roodhuyzen, Thea, *In Woelig Vaarwater: Marineofficieren in de jaren 1779–1802* (Amsterdam, 1998).

Roos, Doeke, 'Johan Evertsen: Admiraal van Zeeland, 1637–1666; Een vereerd en verguisd zeeheld', *TvZ* XXI (2002), pp. 123–35. I was not able to see his *Twee eeuwen varen en vechten; het admiralengeslacht Evertsen (1550–1750)* (Flushing, 2003) before this work went to press.

Rose, Craig, *England in the 1690s: Revolution, Religion and War* (Oxford, 1999).

Rose, J. Holland, *Lord Hood and the Defence of Toulon* (Cambridge, 1922).

— 'Sir John Duckworth's Expedition to Constantinople', *NR* VII (1920), pp. 485–501.

Roseveare, Henry, *The Financial Revolution 1660–1760* (London, 1991).

Rosier, B. A. R., 'A Comparative Study of the Cost and Durability of Ships of the Line Built for the Royal Navy during the Seven Years War and the American War of Independence' (Exeter MA dissertation, 1997).

Ross, Sir John, *Memoirs and Correspondence of Admiral Lord de Saumarez* (London, 1838, 2 vols.). A serviceable life, and a primary authority for Saumarez's Baltic command, when the then Lieutenant Ross was his Swedish interpreter and confidential diplomatic agent.

Routh, E. M. G., *Tangier: England's Lost Atlantic Outpost, 1661–1684* (London, 1912).

— 'The English Occupation of Tangier', *TRHS* NS XIX (1905), pp. 61–78.

Rowbotham, W. B., 'The Diamond Rock', *NR* XXXVII (1949), pp. 385–95 and XXXVIII (1950), pp. 53–64.

— 'Soldiers in Lieu of Marines', *JSAHR* XXXIII (1955), pp. 26–34.

Rowe, Violet A., *Sir Henry Vane the Younger: A Study in Political and Administrative*

History (London, 1970). A dominant figure in the naval administration of the English Republic.

Rowen, Herbert H., *John de Witt, Grand Pensionary of Holland, 1625–1672* (Princeton, 1978).

— *John De Witt: Statesman of the True Freedom* (Cambridge, 1986).
Two different biographies of the same man. The handling of naval affairs is uncertain.

Royle, Edward, *Revolutionary Britannia? Reflections on the Threat of Revolution in Britain 1789–1848* (Manchester, 2000).

Russell, Gillian, *The Theatres of War: Performance, Politics and Society, 1793–1815* (Oxford, 1995).

Russell, Lord John, ed., *Correspondence of John, Fourth Duke of Bedford* (London, 1842–6, 3 vols.). Many of these letters are silently abbreviated, but what is printed is reasonably trustworthy.

Ryan, A. N., ed., *The Saumarez Papers: Selections from the Baltic Correspondence of Vice-Admiral Sir James Saumarez, 1808–1812* (NRS Vol. 110, 1968).

— 'The Causes of the British Attack upon Copenhagen, 1807', *EHR* LXVIII (1953), pp. 37–55.

— 'The Defence of British Trade in the Baltic, 1807–13', *EHR* LXXIV (1959), pp. 443–6.

— 'Trade with the Enemy in Scandinavian and Baltic Ports during the Napoleonic Wars: For and Against', *TRHS* 5th S. XII (1962), pp. 123–40.

— 'William III and the Brest Fleet in the Nine Years War', in *William III and Louis XIV: Essays 1680–1720 by and for Mark A. Thomson*, ed. Ragnhild Hatton and J. S. Bromley (Liverpool, 1968), pp. 49–67.

— ed., 'Documents Relating to the Copenhagen Operation, 1807', in Rodger, *Naval Miscellany V*, pp. 297–329.

— 'The Royal Navy and the Blockade of Brest, 1689–1805: Theory and Practice', in Acerra et al., *Les Marines de guerre*, pp. 175–94.

— 'Trade between Enemies; Maritime Resistance to the Continental System in the Northern Seas (1808–1812)', in *The North Sea, Highway of Commerce and Culture*, ed. Arne Bang-Andersen, Basil Greenhill and Egil Harald Grude (Stavanger, 1985), pp. 181–94.

— 'An Ambassador Afloat: Vice-Admiral Sir James Saumarez and the Swedish Court, 1808–1812', in Black and Woodfine, *British Navy*, pp. 237–58.

— 'In Search of Bruix, 1799', in *Français et Anglais en Méditerranée*, pp. 81–90.

Sainsbury, Anthony B., 'Commodore Duckworth and the Capture of Minorca, 1798', in *Français et Anglais en Méditerranée*, pp. 221–8.

[St Vincent], *Memoirs of the Administration of the Board of Admiralty under the Presidency of the Earl of St Vincent* (London, [1805] never issued). A defence of St Vincent's administration, written in his name, probably by his secretary Benjamin Tucker, but suppressed before publication. Only three copies are known to have survived, but it is conveniently reprinted as an appendix to Bonner-Smith, *St Vincent Letters*.

Sainty, J. C., *Office-Holders in Modern Britain IV: Admiralty Officials 1660–1870* (London, 1975).

Saul, Norman E., *Russia and the Mediterranean 1797–1807* (Chicago, 1970).

Sausmarez, Sir Havilland de, *Captain Philip Saumarez, 1710–1747, and his Contemporaries* (Guernsey, 1936).

Saville, R. V., 'Some Aspects of the Role of Government in the Industrial Development of England, 1686 to 1720' (Sheffield Ph.D. thesis, 1978).

— ed., 'The Management of the Royal Dockyards, 1672–1678', in Rodger, *Naval Miscellany V*, pp. 94–142.

Savours, Ann, '"A Very Interesting Point in Geography," The 1773 Phipps Expedition towards the Pole', *Arctic* XXXVII (1984), pp. 402–28.

Saxby, Richard, 'The Blockade of Brest in the French Revolutionary War', *MM* LXXVIII (1992), pp. 25–35.

— 'Lord Bridport and the Spithead Mutiny', *MM* LXXIX (1993), pp. 170–78.

Scarfe, Norman, ed., *Innocent Espionage: The La Rochefoucauld Brothers' Tour of England in 1785* (Woodbridge, 1995).

Schaber, James R., 'Admiral Sir William Cornwallis and the Blockade of Brest, 1801–1806' (Oxford D.Phil. thesis, 1977).

Schadewaldt, Hans and Karl-Heinz Leven, eds., *IX Deutsch-Französisches Symposium zur Geschichte der Schiffahrts- und Marinemedizin* (Düsseldorf, 1988).

Schoenfeld, Maxwell P., 'The Restoration Seaman and His Wages', *AN* XXV (1965), pp. 278–87.

Schom, Alan, *Trafalgar: Countdown to Battle 1803–1805* (London, 1990). A popular account, ignorant of the sea and full of careless errors, but making good use of French sources.

Schomberg, Isaac, *Naval Chronology, or an Historical Summary of Naval and Maritime Events* (London, 1802, 5 vols.). A chronological history and reference book of British naval history with extensive appendices.

Schulin, Ernst, *Handelsstaat England: Das politische Interesse der Nation am Aussenhandel vom 16. bis ins frühe 18 Jahrhundert* (Wiesbaden, 1969). Mainly a survey of contemporary publications.

Scott, H. M., *British Foreign Policy in the Age of the American Revolution* (Oxford, 1990).

— 'The Importance of Bourbon Naval Reconstruction to the Strategy of Choiseul after the Seven Years' War', *IHR* I (1979), pp. 20–35.

Scott, Walter F., 'The Naval Chaplain in Stuart Times' (Oxford D.Phil. thesis, 1935).

Selement, George, 'Impressment and the American Merchant Marine 1782–1812', *MM* LIX (1973), pp. 409–18.

[Senhouse, Humphrey], 'The Battle of Trafalgar', *Macmillan's Magazine* LXXXI (1900), pp. 415–25. A letter of Lieutenant Senhouse of the *Conqueror* to his mother, 27 Oct 1805.

Senior, William, *Naval History in the Law Courts* (London, 1927).

Sermoneta, [Vittoria Caetani] Duchess of, *The Locks of Norbury: The Story of a Remarkable Family in the XVIIIth and XIXth Centuries* (London, 1940).

Sharp, James A., *Memoirs of the Life and Services of Rear-Admiral Sir William Symonds . . .* (London, 1858). Early service in the French Wars, before he became a controversial naval architect.

Shaw, J. J. Sutherland, 'The Hospital Ship, 1608–1740', *MM* XXII (1936), pp. 422–9.

— 'The Commission of Sick and Wounded and Prisoners, 1664–1667', *MM* XXV (1939), pp. 306–27.

Shea, J. D. G., ed., *The Operations of the French Fleet under the Count de Grasse in 1781–2* (New York, 1864). Three anonymous French journals in a poor English translation.

Sherwig, John M., *Guineas and Gunpowder: British Foreign Aid in the Wars with France, 1793–1815* (Cambridge, Mass., 1969).

Shomette, Donald G. and Robert D. Haslach, *Raid on America: The Dutch Naval Campaign of 1672–1674* (Columbia, S.C., 1988). Based on De Waard, q.v.

Silvestre, J., *Les Brûlots anglais en Rade de l'île d'Aix (1809)* (Paris, 1912). Scholarly study of the action known in English as 'Basque Roads', printing many documents.

Simpson, Richard Fulton, 'The Naval Career of Admiral Sir George Pocock, K.B., 1743–1763' (Indiana Ph.D. thesis, 1950).

Skaggs, David Curtis, 'Joint Operations during the Detroit-Lake Erie Campaign, 1813', in Cogar, *New Interpretations . . . Eighth*, pp. 121–38.

Smelser, Marshall, *The Campaign for the Sugar Islands. 1759: A Study of Amphibious Warfare* (Chapel Hill, N.C., 1955).

Smith, David Bonner, *see* Bonner Smith.

Smith, Gene A., *'For the Purposes of Defense': The Politics of the Jeffersonian Gunboat Program* (London, 1995).

— '"For the Purposes of Defense": Thomas Jefferson's Naval Militia', *AN* LIII (1993), pp. 30–38.

— 'A Means to an End: Gunboats and Jefferson's Theory of Defense', *AN* LV (1995), pp. 111–21.

Smith, Robert D., ed., *British Naval Armaments* (Royal Armouries, London, 1989).

— 'Iron Cannon of 7', *Journal of the Ordnance Society* IV (1992), pp. 9–20.

Smith, Waldo E. L., *The Navy and its Chaplains in the Days of Sail* (Toronto, 1961).

Smith, W. J., ed., *The Grenville Papers: Being the Correspondence of Richard Grenville Earl Temple, K.G., and the Right Hon: George Grenville, Their Friends and Contemporaries* (London, 1852–3, 4 vols.).

Smyth, W. H., *The Sailor's Word-Book: An Alphabetical Digest of Nautical Terms* (London, 1867). An extensive but haphazard, unscientific and often ambiguous posthumous work, heavily used by the editors of the *Oxford English Dictionary* for their forays into nautical vocabulary, in many cases with unfortunate consequences.

'Slush, Barnaby', *The Navy Royal: or a Sea-Cook turn'd Projector* (London, 1709).

Anonymous social commentary, evidently written by a gentleman officer in defence of the privileges of his rank.

Snyder, Henry L., ed., *The Marlborough Godolphin Correspondence* (Oxford, 1975, 3 vols., paginated as one).

Søby Andersen, Henning, 'Denmark between the Wars with Britain, 1801–7', *SJH* XIV (1989), pp. 231–8.

Sokol, A. E., 'Nelson and the Russian Navy', *MAff* XIII (1950), pp. 129–37.

Sondhaus, Lawrence, 'Napoleon's Shipbuilding Program at Venice and the Struggle for Naval Mastery in the Adriatic 1806–1814', *JMH* LIII (1989), pp. 349–62.

Sonnino, Paul, 'The Origins of Louis XIV's Wars', in Black, *Origins of War*, pp. 112–31.

Spalding, Thomas Alfred, *A Life of Richard Badiley, Vice-Admiral of the Fleet* (London, 1899). English commander-in-chief in the Mediterranean during the First Dutch War.

Sparrow, Elizabeth, *Secret Service: British Agents in France 1792–1815* (Woodbridge, 1999).

Spate, O. H. K., *The Pacific since Magellan, II: Monopolists and Freebooters* (London, 1983).

— *The Pacific since Magellan, III: Paradise Found and Lost* (London, 1988).

Spavens, William, *The Narrative of William Spavens, a Chatham Pensioner*, ed. N. A. M. Rodger (Folio Society, London, 2000) [originally Louth, 1796]. An original and valuable lower-deck memoir of the Seven Years' War. There is another modern printing (Chatham Press, London, 1998, with an introduction by NAMR), but this is the better edition.

Speck, W. A., *Stability and Strife: England 1714–1760* (London, 1977).

— *Reluctant Revolutionaries: England and the Revolution of 1688* (Oxford, 1988).

— 'The Orangist Conspiracy against James II', *HJ* XXX (1987), pp. 453–62.

Spencer, Frank, ed., *The Fourth Earl of Sandwich: Diplomatic Correspondence 1763–1765* (Manchester, 1961).

Spinney, David, *Rodney* (London, 1969). A complete and accurate biography by an uncritical enthusiast.

— 'Rodney and the Saints: A Reassessment', *MM* LXVIII (1982), pp. 377–89.

Sproule, H. D., 'James Burney's Opinions on the Naval Mutinies of 1797', *MM* XLVI (1960), pp. 61–2.

Stacey, C. P., *Quebec, 1759: The Siege and the Battle* (Toronto, 1959).

Stagg, J. C. A., *Mr Madison's War: Politics, Diplomacy and Warfare in the Early American Republic, 1783–1830* (Princeton, 1983).

— 'James Madison and the Coercion of Great Britain: Canada, the West Indies and the War of 1812', in *Canada and the Commonwealth Caribbean*, ed. B. D. Tennyson (London, 1988), pp. 51–103.

Stark, Suzanne J., *Female Tars: Women Aboard Ship in the Age of Sail* (London, 1996).

Starkey, David, *British Privateering Enterprise in the Eighteenth Century* (Exeter, 1990).

— 'War and the Market for Seafarers in Britain, 1736–1792', in *Shipping and Trade, 1750–1950: Essays in International Maritime Economic History*, ed. Lewis R. Fischer and Helge W. Nordvik (Pontefract, 1990), pp. 25–42.

— 'Privateering Enterprise in Devon, 1689–1815', *MHD* I, 224–31.

Starkey, David J., E. S. van Eyck van Heslinga and J. A. de Moor, eds., *Pirates and Privateers: New Perspectives on the War on Trade in the Eighteenth and Nineteenth Centuries* (Exeter, 1997).

Steckley, George F., 'Litigious Mariners: Wage Cases in the Seventeenth-Century Admiralty Court', *HJ* XLII (1999), pp. 315–45.

Steel, Anthony, 'Anthony Merry and the Anglo-American Dispute about Impressment, 1803–6', *CHJ* IX (1949), pp. 331–58.

— 'Impressment in the Monroe-Pinckney Negotiations, 1806–7', *AHR* LVII (1952), pp. 352–69.

Steele, Sir Robert, *The Marine Officer, or Sketches of Service* (London, 1840, 2 vols.).

Steer, D. M., 'The Blockade of Brest by the Royal Navy, 1793–1805' (Liverpool MA dissertation, 1971).

— 'The Blockade of Brest and the Victualling of the Western Squadron, 1793–1805', *MM* LXXVI (1990), pp. 307–16.

Stewart, James, 'The Leeward Isles Command, 1795–1796', *MM* XLVII (1961), pp. 270–80.

Stirling, Mrs A. M. W., *Pages and Portraits from the Past, being the Private Papers of Admiral Sir William Hotham, G.C.B. Admiral of the Red* (London, 1919, 2 vols.). Diaries, characters and reminiscences of the Navy during the French Wars.

Stone, Lawrence, ed., *An Imperial State at War: Britain from 1689 to 1815* (London, 1994).

Stout, Neil R., *The Royal Navy in America, 1760–1775: A Study in the Enforcement of British Colonial Policy in the Era of the American Revolution* (Annapolis, Md., 1973).

— 'Manning the Royal Navy in North America, 1763–1775', *AN* XXIII (1963), pp. 174–85.

Sue, Eugène, *Histoire de la Marine Française: XVIIe siècle, Jean Bart* (Paris, 1835–6, 5 vols.). Actually a life of Bart; almost valueless as such, with a strong Republican animus, but prints useful documents.

Sugden, John, 'Lord Cochrane, Naval Commander, Radical, Inventor (1775–1860): A Study of his Earlier Career, 1775–1818' (Sheffield Ph.D. thesis, 1981). A sober and critical life of Cochrane: a marvel indeed, but unfortunately unpublished.

Sulivan, J. A., 'Graves and Hood', *MM* LXIX (1983), pp. 175–94.

Sullivan, F. B., 'The Naval Schoolmaster during the Eighteenth Century and the Early Nineteenth Century', *MM* LXII (1976), pp. 311–26.

— 'The Royal Academy at Portsmouth, 1729–1806', *MM* LXIII (1977), pp. 311–26.

Sutton, Jean, *Lords of the East: The East India Company and its Ships* (London, 1981).

Svensson, S. Artur, ed., *Svenska Flottans Historia* (Malmö, 1942–5, 3 vols.). A standard history of the Swedish navy.

Sweetman, Jack, ed., *The Great Admirals: Command at Sea 1587–1945* (Annapolis, 1997).

Symcox, Geoffrey, *The Crisis of French Sea Power 1688–1697: From the Guerre d'Escadre to the Guerre de Course* (The Hague, 1974).

Syrett, David, *Shipping and the American War, 1775–83* (London, 1970). The logistics of supporting British armies across the Atlantic.

— ed., *The Siege and Capture of Havana 1762* (NRS Vol. 114, 1970).

— *Neutral Rights and the War in the Narrow Seas, 1778–1782* (Fort Leavenworth, Kans., [1985]).

— *The Royal Navy in American Waters 1775–1783* (Aldershot, 1989).

— *The Royal Navy in European Waters during the American Revolutionary War* (Columbia, S.C., 1998).

Professor Syrett is now preparing a complete naval history of this war which will incorporate the above two volumes.

— 'The Methodology of British Amphibious Operations during the Seven Years' and American Wars', *MM* LVIII (1972), pp. 269–80.

— 'The Organization of British Trade Convoys during the American War, 1775–83', *MM* LXII (1976), pp. 169–81.

— 'The Navy Board and Merchant Shipowners during the American War, 1776–1783', *AN* XLVII (1987), pp. 5–13.

— 'The Failure of the British Effort in America, 1777', in Black and Woodfine, *British Navy*, pp. 171–90.

— 'Home Waters or America? The Dilemma of British Naval Strategy in 1778', *MM* LXXVII (1991), pp. 365–77.

— 'Christopher Atkinson and the Victualling Board, 1775–82', *HR* LXIX (1996), pp. 129–42.

— 'The Victualling Board Charters Shipping, 1739–1748', *IJMH* IX, 1 (1997), pp. 57–67.

— 'Admiral Rodney, Patronage and the Leeward Islands Squadron, 1780–2', *MM* LXXXV (1999), pp. 411–20.

— 'The Ordnance Board Charters Shipping, 1755–62', *JAHR* LXXVII (1999), pp. 9–18.

— 'Count-down to the Saints: A Strategy of Detachments and the Quest for Naval Superiority in the West Indies, 1780–2', *MM* LXXXVII (2001), pp. 150–62.

— ' "This Penurious Old Reptile": Rear-Admiral James Gambier and the American War', *HR* LXXIV (2001), pp. 63–76.

— 'The Navy Board and Transports for Cartagena, 1740', *WiH* IX (2002), pp. 127–41.

More of Professor Syrett's numerous articles are mentioned in the notes.

Syrett, David and R. L. DiNardo, eds., *The Commissioned Sea Officers of the Royal Navy 1660–1815* (NRS Occasional Publications Vol. 1, 1994). An alphabetical list with dates of promotion: an essential means of reference, but it derives from Admiralty records and is consequently not altogether complete or accurate.

Taillemite, Etienne, *L'Histoire ignorée de la Marine Française* (Paris, 1988). Episodes of French naval history, written from an unrivalled knowledge of the archives.

— *Dictionnaire des marins français* (Paris, 2nd edn 2002). An admirable biographical dictionary.

— 'Le Recrutement des officiers de vaisseau au XVIIIe siècle: une politique incohérente', *Neptunia* 161 (1986), pp. 38–47.

— 'Une bataille de l'Atlantique au XVIIIe siècle: la guerre de Succession d'Autriche', in *Guerres et paix*, pp. 131–48.

— 'Une marine pour quoi faire? La stratégie navale de Louis XIV', in *Guerres maritimes*, pp. 93–101.

— 'Une amitié évolutive: Tourville et Seignelay', in Acerra, *L'Invention du vaisseau de ligne*, pp. 241–6.

Taillemite, Étienne and Pierre Guillaume, *Tourville et Béveziers* (Paris, 1991).

Talbott, John E., *The Pen and Ink Sailor: Charles Middleton and the King's Navy, 1778–1813* (London, 1998). Mainly his administrative career as Controller of the Navy.

Tanner, J. R., ed., *A Descriptive Catalogue of the Naval Manuscrits in the Pepysian Library*, ed. J. R. Tanner (NRS Vols. 27, 36 and 57, 1903–23). A calendar of important sections of Pepys's official papers.

— *Samuel Pepys and the Royal Navy* (Cambridge, 1920). An admirable summary of the then state of knowledge, most of it the fruit of Tanner's own work.

— ed., *Samuel Pepys's Naval Minutes* (NRS Vol. 60, 1926). Notes collected for Pepys's projected history of the Navy.

— ed., *Private Correspondence and Miscellaneous Papers of Samuel Pepys, 1679–1703* (London, 1926, 2 vols.).

— ed., *Further Correspondence of Samuel Pepys, 1662–1679* (London, 1929).

— 'Pepys and the Popish Plot', *EHR* VII (1892), pp. 281–90.

— 'Naval Preparations of James II in 1688', *EHR* VIII (1893), pp. 272–83.

— 'The Administration of the Navy from the Restoration to the Revolution', *EHR* XII (1897), pp. 17–66 and 679–710; XIII (1898), pp. 26–54; XIV (1899), pp. 47–70 and 261–89.

— 'Samuel Pepys as a Naval Official', in *Naval and Military Essays*, ed. Julian S. Corbett and H. J. Edwards (Cambridge, 1914), pp. 55–82.

Tatum, Edward H., Jr, ed., *The American Journal of Ambrose Serle, Secretary to Lord Howe 1776–1778* (San Marino, Calif., 1940).

Taylor, A. H., 'The French Fleet in the Channel, 1778 and 1779', *MM* XXIV (1938), pp. 275–88.

— 'The Battle of Trafalgar', *MM* XXXVI (1950), pp. 281–321.

— 'The Four Days Fight and St James's Day Fights', *NR* XLI (1953), pp. 287–302.

— 'Sandwich and the Ship of the Line', *NR* XLI (1953), pp. 134–43.

— 'Galleon into Ship of the Line', *MM* XLIV (1958), pp. 267–85 and XLV (1959), pp. 14–24 and 100–114.

Taylor, E. G. R., *The Mathematical Practitioners of Hanoverian England, 1714–1840* (Cambridge, 1966).

Taylor, Gordon, *The Sea Chaplains: A History of the Chaplains of the Royal Navy* (Oxford, 1978).

Taylor, S. A. G., *The Western Design: An Account of Cromwell's Expedition to the Caribbean* (Kingston, Jamaica, 1965).

Tedder, Arthur W., *The Navy of the Restoration* (Cambridge, 1916). Possibly the best book of naval history ever written by a future Marshal of the Royal Air Force.

Temperley, Harold V., 'The Causes of the War of Jenkins Ear', *TRHS* 3rd S. III (1909), pp. 197–236.

Teonge, Henry, *The Diary of Henry Teonge, Chaplain on board H.M.'s Ships Assistance, Bristol and Royal Oak, 1675–1679*, ed. G. E. Manwaring (London, 1927). Cheerful diary of a Warwickshire clergyman forced to sea to escape his creditors.

Terraine, John, *Trafalgar* (London, 1976).

Thomas, Aaron, *The Newfoundland Journal of Aaron Thomas, Able Seaman in H.M.S. Boston*, ed. Jean M. Murray (London, 1968). A voyage to Newfoundland, 1794–5, narrated with a fantastic and whimsical sense of humour which makes it difficult to know what to believe.

Thomas, J. H., 'Portsmouth Naval Academy: An Educational Experiment Examined', *Portsmouth Archives Review* III (1978), pp. 11–39.

Thomas, Peter D. G., *Lord North* (London, 1976).

Thomas, Robin N. W., 'British Operations on the Coast of Catalonia 1808–1811', in *New Lights on the Peninsular War*, ed. Alice D. Berkeley (Lisbon, 1991), pp. 47–56.

Thomas, R. P. and D. N. McCloskey, 'Overseas Trade and Empire 1700–1860', in *The Economic History of Britain since 1700. Vol. 1, 1700–1800*, ed. R. Floud and D. N. McCloskey (Cambridge, 1981), pp. 87–102.

Thompson, Edward Maunde, ed., 'Correspondence of the Family of Haddock, 1657–1719', in *Camden Miscellany VIII* (CS N.S. Vol. 31, 1883).

— ed., 'Correspondence of Admiral Herbert during the Revolution', *EHR* I (1886), pp. 522–36.

Thornton, A. P., *West-India Policy under the Restoration* (Oxford, 1956).

Thurloe, John, *A Collection of State Papers of John Thurloe . . .* , ed. T. Birch (London, 1742, 7 vols.). Secretary of State under the Commonwealth and Protectorate.

Thursfield, H. G., ed., *Five Naval Journals 1789–1817* (NRS Vol. 91, 1951).

— ed., 'The Rev. E. Mangin, 1812', in *Five Naval Journals*, pp. 1–39. A discontented chaplain.

— ed., 'Peter Cullen, esq., 1789–1802', in *Five Naval Journals*, pp. 41–119. A naval surgeon, involved in the Nore mutiny among other episodes.

— ed., 'Robert Mercer Wilson, 1805–1809', in *Five Naval Journals*, pp. 121–276. A pressed able seaman; lucid and intelligent.

— ed., 'Captain William Pryce Cumby, 1811–1815', in *Five Naval Journals*, pp. 327–49.

— ed., 'Letters from the Lower Deck', in *Five Naval Journals*, pp. 351–76.

Timmerman, Gerhard, *Das Eindringen der Naturwissenschaft in das Schiffbauhandwerk* (Munich, 1962). A conventional whiggish account in the style of the period.

Tomlinson, H. C., *Guns and Government: The Ordnance Office under the Later Stuarts* (London, 1979).

— 'The Ordnance Office and the Navy, 1660–1714', *EHR* XC (1975), pp. 19–39.

— 'Wealden Gunfounding: An Analysis of Its Demise in the Eighteenth Century', *EcHR* XXIX (1976), pp. 383–400.

Tornquist, Karl Gustav, *The Naval Campaigns of Count de Grasse during the American Revolution 1781–1783*, trans. Amandus Johnson (Philadelphia, 1942) [originally *Greve Grasses Siö-Batailler och Krigs-Operationerne uti Vest-Indien* (Stockholm, 1787)]. Memoir of a Swedish officer in the French fleet.

Toudouze, Georges, *La Bataille de la Hougue* (Paris, 1899).

— 'La Hougue: de la victoire mutilée à la légende mensongère', *Neptunia* 46 (1957), pp. 8–15. Based on his 1896 Sorbonne thèse de licence, originally published in the *Revue Maritime*.

Tracy, James D., ed., *The Rise of Merchant Empires: Long-Distance Trade in the Early Modern World, 1350–1750* (Cambridge, 1990).

— ed., *The Political Economy of Merchant Empires* (Cambridge, 1991).

Tracy, Nicholas, *Navies, Deterrence and American Independence: Britain and Seapower in the 1760s and 1770s* (Vancouver, 1988).

— *Attack on Maritime Trade* (London, 1991).

— *Manila Ransomed: The British Assault on Manila in the Seven Years War* (Exeter, 1995).

— *Nelson's Battles: The Art of Victory in the Age of Sail* (London, 1996).

— 'The Gunboat Diplomacy of the Government of George Grenville, 1764–1765: The Honduran, Turks Island and Gambian Incidents', *HJ* XVII (1974), pp. 711–31.

— 'The Falklands Islands Crisis of 1770; Use of Naval Force', *EHR* XC (1975), pp. 40–75.

— 'Sir Robert Calder's Action', *MM* LXXVII (1991), pp. 259–70.

Trafalgar Committee, i.e. *Report of a Committee Appointed by the Admiralty to Examine . . . the Tactics Employed by Nelson at the Battle of Trafalgar* [Cd. 7120, 1913].

Trotter, Thomas, *Medicina Nautica: An Essay on the Diseases of Seamen* (London, 1797, 2 vols.). Extracts are also printed in Lloyd, *Health of Seamen*.

Troude, O., *Batailles navales de la France* (Paris, 1867–8, 4 vols.).

Tucker, Jedediah Stevens, *Memoirs of Admiral the Right Hon. the Earl of St Vincent* (London, 1844, 2 vols.). The official life, originally commissioned from Tucker's father, St Vincent's secretary. The son was just as partisan but knew much less about the Navy; he does, however, print documents.

Tucker, Spencer C., *The Jeffersonian Gunboat Navy* (Columbia, S.C., 1993). Construction and operations of the gunboats, rather than the policy behind them.

— 'The Jeffersonian Gunboats in Service, 1804–25', *AN* LV (1995), pp. 97–110.

Tucker, Spencer C. and Frank R. Reuter, *Injured Honor: The Chesapeake–Leopard Affair June 22, 1807* (Annapolis, 1996).

Tunstall, Brian, *Admiral Byng and the Loss of Minorca* (London, 1928).

— ed., *The Byng Papers* . . . (NRS Vols. 67, 68 and 70, 1930–32). Mainly Sir George Byng, Lord Torrington.

— *Naval Warfare in the Age of Sail: The Evolution of Fighting Tactics 1650–1815*, ed. Nicholas Tracy (London, 1990). Edited version of a massive posthumous manuscript, largely written in the 1930s, deriving a history of tactics from a minute analysis of signal book and fighting instructions.

Turnbull, A., 'The Administration of the Royal Navy from 1660 to 1673' (Hull Ph.D. thesis, 1974).

Turner, Eunice H., 'Naval Medical Service 1793–1815', *MM* XLVI (1960), pp. 119–33.

Turner, L. C. F., 'The Cape of Good Hope and Anglo-French Conflict, 1797–1806', *Historical Studies: Australia and New Zealand* IX (1961), pp. 368–78.

Ultee, Maarten, ed., *Adapting to Conditions: War and Society in the Eighteenth Century* (Tuscaloosa, Alabama, 1986).

Uring, Nathaniel, *The Voyages and Travels of Captain Nathaniel Uring*, ed. Alfred Dewar (London, 1928) [originally 1726].

Usher, Roland G., 'The Civil Administration of the British Navy during the American Revolution' (Michigan Ph.D. thesis, 1943).

— 'Royal Navy Impressment during the American Revolution', *Mississippi Valley Historical Review* XXXVII (1950), pp. 673–88. An important study, based on the Shelburne Manuscripts.

Vale, V., 'Clarendon, Coventry and the Sale of Naval Offices, 1660–8', *CHJ* XII (1956), pp. 107–25.

Valentine, Alan, *Lord George Germain* (Oxford, 1962).

Van Alstyne, Richard W., 'Parliamentary Supremacy versus Independence: Notes and Documents', *HLQ* XXVI (1963), pp. 201–33.

Van der Kuijl, Arjen, *De glorieuze overtocht: De expeditie van Willem III naar Engeland in 1688* (Amsterdam, 1988). A good general account of the 1688 invasion.

Van der Meij, C. O., ' "Een furieus gevegt": De zeeslag bij Malaga, 1704, De Engels–Nederlandse betrekkingen in de beginjaren van de Spaanse Successieoorlog' (Leiden doctoral thesis, 1995).

Van Eyck van Heslinga, E. S., 'De vlag dekt de lading. De Nederlandse koopvaardij in de Vierde Engelse oorlog', *TvZ* I (1982), pp. 102–13.

Van Foreest, H. A. and R. E. J. Weber, *De Vierdaagse Zeeslag 11–14 Juni 1666* (Amsterdam, 1984). Notes and documents bearing on the Four Days' Battle.

Van Royen, Paul C., Jaap R. Bruijn and Jan Lucassen, eds., *'Those Emblems of*

Hell'? European Sailors and the Maritime Labour Market, 1570–1870 (St John's, Newfoundland, 1997).

Van Schelven, A. L., Philips van Almonde: Admiraal in de gecombineerde vloot 1644–1711 (Assen, 1947).

Van 't Hoff, B., ed., The Correspondence, 1701–1711, of John Churchill, first Duke of Marlborough, and Anthonie Heinsius, Grand Pensionary of Holland (HG 4th S. Vol. 1, 1951).

Van Waning, C. J. W. and A. Van der Moer, Dese Aengenaeme Tocht: Chatham 1667, herbezien door zeemansogen (Zutphen 1981). A 'seaman's view' of the Medway Raid.

Vaughan, H. S., ed., The Voyages and Cruises of Commodore Walker (London, 1928). A noted privateer of the 1740s.

Velde, François R. and David R. Weir, 'The Financial Market and Government Debt Policy in France, 1746–1793', JEcH LII (1992), pp. 1–39.

Venning, Timothy, Cromwellian Foreign Policy (London, 1995).

Vergé-Franceschi, Michel, Les Officiers généraux de la marine royale, 1715–1774 (Paris, 1990, 7 vols.). Flag-officers' careers and connections reconstructed in minute detail.

— Marine et éducation sous l'Ancien Régime (Paris, 1991).

— Abraham Duquesne: Huguenot et marin du Roi-Soleil (Paris, 1992). See also his 'Un tricentenaire: 1688–1988 Abraham Duquesne (1610–1688) et la marine de son temps', HES VII (1988), pp. 325–45.

— La Marine française au XVIIIe siècle: guerres, administration, exploration (Paris, 1996).

— Chronique maritime de la France de l'Ancien Régime, 1492–1792 (Paris, 1998).

— 'Les Officiers généreaux de la marine royale en 1715', RH CCLXXIII (1985), pp. 131–57.

— 'Duguay-Trouin (1673–1736): un corsaire, un officier général, un mythe', RH CCXCV (1995), pp. 333–52.

— 'Duquesne et Tourville, deux officiers généraux de la Marine Royale au XVIIe siècle', in Guerres maritimes, pp. 35–50.

Verhees-van Meer, J. Th. H., De Zeeuwse Kaapvaart tijdens de Spaanse Successie-oorlog 1702–1713 (Middelburg, 1986).

Vernon, Francis, Voyages and Travels of a Sea Officer (p.p. London, 1792).

Vigié, Marc, 'Galères et "Sea-power" en France au XVIIe siècle', RHA 182 (1991), pp. 45–56.

Villette-Mursay, Philippe [Le Vallois], Marquis de, Mes campagnes de mer sous Louis XIV, ed. Michel Vergé-Franceschi (Paris, 1991).

Villiers, Patrick, Marine Royale, corsaires et trafic dans l'Atlantique de Louis XIV à Louis XVI, (Dunkirk, 1991, 2 vols.). Stimulating but not completely reliable.

— Les Corsaires du Littoral: Dunkerque, Calais, Boulogne, de Philippe II à Louis XIV (1568–1713) (Villeneuve d'Ascq, 2000).

— 'Marine de Colbert ou Marine de Seignelay. Victoire de Barfleur et progrès technique', in Guerres maritimes, pp. 173–96.

Voltes Bou, Pedro, 'El intento hispanofrances de desembarco en Inglaterra del año 1779', *Hispania* XXVII (1967), pp. 528–607.

Wadia, R. A., *The Bombay Dockyard and the Wadia Master Builders* (p.p. Bombay, 2nd edn 1957).

Walker, Geoffrey J., *Spanish Politics and Imperial Trade, 1700–1789* (London, 1979).

Walker, Richard, *The Nelson Portraits* (Royal Naval Museum, Portsmouth, 1998).

Walpole, Horace, *Memoirs of King George II*, ed. John Brooke (New Haven and London, 1985, 3 vols.). Spiteful gossip.

Walter, Richard and Benjamin Robins, *A Voyage around the World by George Anson*, ed. Glyndŵr Williams (London, 1974). The authorized account of Anson's famous voyage; a publishing sensation in its day, and one of the classics of the literature of the sea.

Walters, Samuel, *Samuel Walters, Lieutenant R.N.: His Memoirs*, ed. C. Northcote Parkinson (Liverpool, 1949). The obscure career of a boatbuilder's son during the Napoleonic War.

Warburton, Eliot, *Memoirs of Prince Rupert and the Cavaliers* (London, 1849, 3 vols.).

Ware, Christopher, *The Bomb Vessel: Shore Bombardment Ships in the Age of Sail* (London, 1994).

— 'The Royal Navy and the Plantations 1720–1730', in Reynolds, *Global Crossroads*, pp. 121–6.

— 'Toulon, 1793', in *Français et Anglais en Méditerranée*, pp. 23–37.

— 'George Byng, Viscount Torrington, 1663–1733', in Le Fevre and Harding, *Precursors of Nelson*, pp. 78–99.

— 'The Glorious First of June: The British Strategic Perspective', in Duffy and Morriss, *Glorious First of June*, pp. 25–45.

Wareham, Tom, *The Star Captains: Frigate Command in the Napoleonic Wars* (London, 2001).

Warner, Oliver, *A Portrait of Lord Nelson* (London, 1958). One of the best lives, sensitive and perceptive.

— *Trafalgar* (London, 1959).

— *The Battle of the Nile* (London, 1960).

— *The Glorious First of June* (London, 1961).

— *Nelson's Battles* (London, 1965). Revises his earlier *Nile* and *Trafalgar*, adding Copenhagen.

— *The Life and Letters of Vice-Admiral Lord Collingwood* (London, 1968). Another admirable biography.

Warnsinck, J. C. M., *De Retourvloot van Pieter de Bitter (Kerstmis 1664–Najaar 1665)* (The Hague, 1929). A detailed narrative of the battle of Bergen in its context, printing the principal Dutch, English and Danish documents.

— *Admiral De Ruyter: De Zeeslag op Schooneveld Juni 1673* (The Hague, 1930).

— *De Vloot van de Koning-Stadhouder, 1689–1690* (Amsterdam, 1934).

— *Abraham Crijnssen: De verovering van Suriname en zijn aanslag op Virginië in 1667* (Amsterdam, 1936).

— *Drie zeventiende-eeuwsche admiraals* (Amsterdam, 1938). Piet Heyn, Witte de With and Jan Evertsen.

— *Van Vlootvoogden en Zeeslagen* (Amsterdam, 2nd edn 1941). Collected articles by the great Dutch naval historian, mostly from *Marineblad*.

— 'Een Nederlandsch Eskader in de Middellandsche Zee 1651–1653', in *Van Vlootvoogden en Zeeslagen*, pp. 167–40.

— 'De laatste Tocht van van Wassanaer van Obdam, Voorjaar 1665', in *Van Vlootvoogden en Zeeslagen*, pp. 270–328. The battle of Lowestoft.

Waters, David W., 'The Rudder, Tiller and Whipstaff', in *Vice-Almirante A. Teixeira da Mota, In Memoriam* (Lisbon, 1987–9, 2 vols.) I, 353–78.

Watson, G. E., 'The United States and the Peninsular War, 1808–1812', *HJ* XIX (1976), pp. 859–76.

Watson, P. K., 'The Commission for Victualling the Navy, the Commission for Sick and Wounded Seamen and Prisoners of War and the Commission for Transport, 1702–1714' (London Ph.D. thesis, 1965).

Webb, John, Nigel Yates and Sarah Peacock, eds., *Hampshire Studies presented to Dorothy Dymond* . . . (Portsmouth, 1981).

Webb, Paul, 'The Navy and British Diplomacy, 1783–1793' (Cambridge Ph.D. thesis, 1971).

— 'The Naval Aspects of the Nootka Sound Crisis', *MM* LXI (1975), pp. 133–54.

— 'The Rebuilding and Repair of the Fleet, 1783–93', *BIHR* L (1977), pp. 194–209.

— 'Sea Power in the Ochakov Affair of 1791', *IHR* II (1980), pp. 13–33.

— 'The Frigate Situation of the Royal Navy 1793–1815', *MM* LXXXII (1996), pp. 28–40.

Weber, R. E. J., *De Seinboeken voor Nederlandse Oorlogsvloten en Konvoien tot 1690* (Amsterdam, 1982). Dutch signal books.

— 'The Introduction of the Single Line Ahead as a Battle Formation by the Dutch 1665–1666', *MM* LXXIII (1987), pp. 5–19 [originally in Dutch in *Marineblad* 90 (1980), pp. 331–42].

Weir, David R., 'Tontines, Public Finance, and Revolution in France and England, 1688–1789', *JEcH* XLIX (1989), pp. 95–124.

Wells, Roger, *Insurrection: The British Experience 1795–1803* (Gloucester, 1983).

West, Jenny, *Gunpowder, Government and War in the Mid-eighteenth Century* (Woodbridge, 1991).

Wheeler, James Scott, *The Making of a World Power: War and the Military Revolution in Seventeenth-Century England* (Stroud, 1999).

— 'English Financial Operations during the First Dutch War, 1652–54', *JEEH* XXIII (1994), pp. 329–43.

— 'Prelude to Power: The Crisis of 1649 and the Foundation of English Naval Power', *MM* LXXXI (1995), pp. 148–55.

— 'Navy Finance, 1649–1660', *HJ* XXXIX (1996), pp. 457–66.

White, Colin, *1797 Nelson's Year of Destiny: Cape St Vincent and Santa Cruz de Tenerife* (Stroud, 1998).

Whitehill, W. M., ed., *New England Blockaded in 1814: The Journal of Henry*

Edward Napier, Lieutenant in H.M.S. Nymphe (Peabody Museum, Salem, 1939).

Whiteley, W. H., 'The British Navy and the Siege of Quebec, 1775–6', *CHR* LXI (1980), pp. 3–27.

Wickwire, Franklin B., 'Admiralty Secretaries and the British Civil Service', *HLQ* XXVIII (1965), pp. 235–54.

Wickwire, Mary B., 'Naval Warfare and the American Victory', in *The World Turned Upside Down: The American Victory in the War of Independence*, ed. John Ferling (New York, 1988), pp. 185–98.

Wilkinson, Clive, 'British Politics, Government and the Navy before American Independence 1763–1778' (East Anglia Ph.D. thesis, 1997).

— 'The Earl of Egmont and the Navy, 1763–6', *MM* LXXXIV (1998), pp. 418–33.

Wilkinson-Latham, Robert, *British Artillery on Land and Sea 1790–1820* (Newton Abbot, 1973).

Willcox, William B., *Portrait of a General: Sir Henry Clinton in the War of Independence* (New York, 1964).

— 'The Battle of Porto Praya, 1781', *AN* V (1945), pp. 64–79.

— 'Rhode Island in British Strategy, 1780–1781', *JMH* XVII (1945), pp. 304–331.

— 'The British Road to Yorktown: A Study in Divided Command', *AHR* LII (1946), pp. 1–35.

— 'British Strategy in America, 1778', *JMH* XIX (1947), pp. 97–121.

— 'Too Many Cooks: British Planning before Saratoga', *JBS* II (1962), No. 1, pp. 56–90.

Williams, Coleman O., 'The Royal Navy and the Helder Campaign, 1799', *CRE* XVI (1986), pp. 235–47.

Williams, Glyndŵr, ed., *Documents relating to Anson's Voyage round the World, 1740–1744* (NRS Vol. 109, 1967).

— *The Great South Sea: English Voyages and Encounters, 1570–1750* (London, 1997).

— *The Prize of All the Oceans: The Triumph and Tragedy of Anson's Voyage Round the World* (London, 1999).

— ' "The Inexhaustible Fountain of Gold": English Projects and Ventures in the South Seas, 1670–1750', in *Perspectives of Empire: Essays presented to Gerald S. Graham*, ed. John E. Flint and Glyndŵr Williams (London, 1973), pp. 27–53.

Williams, L. J., 'A Carmarthenshire Ironmaster and the Seven Years' War', *BH* II (1959), pp. 32–43.

Williams, M. J., 'The Naval Administration of the Fourth Earl of Sandwich' (Oxford D.Phil. thesis, 1962).

Willyams, Cooper, *An Account of the Campaign in the West Indies in the Year 1794* (London, 1796). A 'short account of their brilliant exertions in their country's cause', dedicated to Sir Charles Grey and Sir John Jervis, and published at lavish expense in an attempt to retrieve their reputations.

— *A Voyage up the Mediterranean in his Majesty's Ship the Swiftsure* (London, 1802). Including the battle of the Nile.

Wilson, Charles, *Profit and Power: A Study of England and the Dutch Wars* (London, 1957).

Wilson, Charles and David Proctor, eds., *1688: The Seaborne Alliance and Diplomatic Revolution* (National Maritime Museum, 1989).

Wilson, Geoffrey, *The Old Telegraphs* (Chichester, 1976).

Wilson, G. M., 'The Commonwealth Gun', *IJNA* XVII (1988), pp. 87–99.

Wilson, Kathleen, 'Empire, Trade and Popular Politics in Mid-Hanoverian Britain: The Case of Admiral Vernon', *P&P* 121 (1988), pp. 74–109.

Winch, Donald and P. K. O'Brien, eds., *The Political Economy of British Historical Experience, 1688–1914* (Oxford, 2002).

Winfield, Rif, *The 50-Gun Ship* (London, 1997).

Wood, John A., 'The City of London and Impressment 1776–1777', *Proceedings of the Leeds Philosophical and Literary Society* VIII (1956–9), pp. 111–27.

Wood, William, ed., *The Logs of the Conquest of Canada* (Champlain Society Vol. 4, 1909). The logs of H.M. ships in the 1758–60 campaigns.

Woodfine, Philip, *Britannia's Glories: The Walpole Ministry and the 1739 War with Spain* (Woodbridge, 1998).

— 'The War of Jenkin's Ear: A New Voice in the Wentworth–Vernon Debate', *JSAHR* LXV (1987), pp. 67–91.

— 'The Anglo-Spanish War of 1739', in Black, *Origins of War*, pp. 185–209.

— 'Ideas of Naval Power and the Conflict with Spain, 1737–1742', in Black and Woodfine, *British Navy*, pp. 71–90.

— ed., 'A Friend to the General: Extracts from the Journal of Major George Lestanquet, September 14th 1741 to April 14th 1742', *JSAHR* LXXI (1993), pp. 26–41, 127–32 and 253–65.

— ' "Proper Objects of the Press": Naval Impressment and Habeas Corpus in the French Revolutionary Wars', in *The Representation and Reality of War: The British Experience. Essays in Honour of David Wright*, ed. Keith Dockray and Keith Laybourn (Stroud, 1999), pp. 39–60.

Woodman, Richard, *The Victory of Seapower: Winning the Napoleonic Wars 1806–1814* (London, 1998).

Worden, Blair, *The Rump Parliament 1648–1653* (Cambridge, 1974).

— 'Oliver Cromwell and the Sin of Achan', in *History, Society and the Churches: Essays in Honour of Owen Chadwick*, ed. Derek Beales and Geoffrey Best (Cambridge, 1985), pp. 125–45.

Wraxall, Sir N. W., *The Historical and Posthumous Memoirs of Sir Nathaniel William Wraxall*, ed. Henry B. Wheatley (London, 1884, 5 vols.). An eighteenth-century back-bencher.

Wright, I. A., ed., 'Spanish Narratives of the English Attack on Santo Domingo, 1655', *Camden Miscellany XIV* (CS 3rd S. Vol. 37, 1926).

Wrigley, E. A., 'Society and Economy in the Eighteenth Century', in Stone, *Imperial State*, pp. 72–95.

— 'The Divergence of England: The Growth of the English Economy in the Seventeenth and Eighteenth Centuries', *TRHS* 6th S. X (2000), pp. 117–41.

Wyndham-Quin, W. H., *Sir Charles Tyler, G.C.B., Admiral of the White* (London, 1912).

Yerxa, Donald A., 'Vice-Admiral Samuel Graves and the North American Squadron, 1774–1776', *MM* LXII (1976), pp. 371–85.

Yorke, Philip C., *The Life and Correspondence of Philip Yorke, Earl of Hardwicke, Lord High Chancellor of Great Britain* (Cambridge, 1913, 3 vols.).

Zahedieh, Nuala, ' "A Frugal, Prudential and Hopeful Trade": Privateering in Jamaica, 1655–89', *JICH* XVIII (1990), pp. 145–68.

Zapatero, Juan Manuel, *La Guerra del Caribe en el siglo XVIII* (San Juan, P.R., 1964). Mainly about Spanish fortifications, especially those of San Juan, and their defence against British attacks.

Zulueta, Julian de, 'Trafalgar – The Spanish View', *MM* LXVI (1980), pp. 293–318.

INDEX

Many entries have dates added in order to differentiate between similar-appearing incidents occurring over the span of this history. Abbreviations used to show nationalities of foreign warships are: (D) Dutch, (Dk) Danish, (Fr) French, (Rus) Russian, (Sp) Spanish. The abbreviation 'Br' has only been used for British warships for those that were originally French; thus: (Fr, later Br).